Clipper Studies in the Theatre
ISSN 0748-237X
Number Eighteen

OLYMPIANS
OF THE
SAWDUST CIRCLE

A Biographical Dictionary

of the

Nineteenth Century American Circus

by

William L. Slout

R. REGINALD
The Borgo Press
San Bernardino, California ▫ MCMXCVIII

THE BORGO PRESS

Publishers of Fine Books Since 1975
Post Office Box 2845
San Bernardino, CA 92406
United States of America

✱ ✱ ✱ ✱ ✱ ✱ ✱

Library of Congress Cataloging-in-Publication Data

Slout, William L. (William Lawrence)
    Olympians of the sawdust circle : a biographical dictionary of the
nineteenth century American circus / by William L. Slout.
    p. cm. — (Clipper studies in the theatre, ISSN 0748-237X ; no. 18)
    Includes bibliographical references and index.
    ISBN 0-8095-0310-7 (cloth). — ISBN 0-8095-1310-2 (pbk.)
    1. Circus performers—United States—History—19th century—Biography—
Dictionaries. I. Title. II. Series.
GV1811.A1S56 1998   97-36043
791.3'092'273—dc21   CIP
[B]

FIRST EDITION

INTRODUCTION

Some time around 1970 I began to edit a serialized piece from the New York *Clipper*, written by Charles Durang and adapted from memoirs, under the title *The Theatrical Rambles of Mr. and Mrs. John Greene*, the content of which presented an enchanting history of American theatre during the first half of the nineteenth century. After being put into manuscript form, it became the first book of mine accepted by The Borgo Press. While cruising through the reels of microfilm that have made the New York *Clipper* accessible to a host of researchers of early popular amusements, my interest was arrested by the numerous brief biographies and obituaries that appeared almost weekly, particularly those connected with the people of the circus. One must admire such professionals who, through courage and stamina and a love for the little world under their canvas pavilions, withstood the travails of travel and the uncertainties of a nomadic existence. My attachment led to a gradual accumulation of such biographical material from the pages of the *Clipper*, and then from any and all other sources I came across. This volume contains nearly thirty years of such collecting and compiling.

I do not claim this work to be a complete listing of people involved in the circuses of the nineteenth century. It is far from complete. There is no single life long enough to collect the facts and figures of such an extensive and elusive group of professionals. This being so, it is difficult to close a research half-finished; but, at seventy-five years of age, prudence dictates. It is time to halt my inquiry and publish, so that others can make use of it. I leave it to the next generation of circus historians to correct and complete what I have started.

There are problems one encounters when dealing with people and events of an earlier century. Accounts within memoirs are often apocryphal. Autobiographers sometimes romanticize or misstate. Unrefined newspaper typesetting causes misinformation. Surnames and dates, for example, frequently vary from one source to another. I have tried diligently to be factual within the biographical entries and to warn the reader when a question of accuracy occurs. I hope I have succeeded.

This is merely a reference book. Consequently, the narrative style is compacted and circus titles are generally abbreviated, particularly the ones that have a life of several years. This has been done, of course, to save space and avoid lengthy repetition.

I am indebted to Fred Dahlinger, Jr., and his staff at the Robert L. Parkinson Library and Research Center, Circus World Museum, Baraboo, Wisconsin, for much of the content. I am also grateful to the numerous individuals who have shared their notes with me and the several circus historians who have deposited their papers and collected items at the library for others to use. I hope this book can provide similar value to present and future circus researchers.

William L. Slout

William Cameron Coup

A

AARON, AL. Minstrel performer, P. T. Barnum's, 1873.

ABAR, ALEX. Alex Abar's Pavilion Show, 1889.

ABAR, WILLIE. Alex Abar's Pavilion Show, 1889.

ABBEY, JEROME E. AND CORINNE. Jugglers, tumblers. Yankee Robinson's, 1883; Ringling Bros.', 1887; F. J. Taylor's, 1891.

ABBOTT, CHARLES. Old fashioned clown, Dr. James L. Thayer's, 1869. Left the ring to perform on the comic stage and in pantomimes.

ABBOTT, J. N. Frank H. Rich Circus (**Frank H. Rich, Col. Charles Whitney, J. N. Abbott,** proprietors), 1886.

ABDELL, JAMES. Leaper, John Robinson's, 1869-73.

ABEE, MONS. Gymnast, with Thompson, Smith & Hawes, 1866; Whitmore & Co.'s Hippocomique, 1868.

ABEL, PROF. HENRY. Band leader. Orton's, 1857; Orton & Older, 1858-60; John Wilson's, Australia, 1866-67; remained behind when Wilson took his troupe to India.

ACKERMAN, ELLA. James R. Cooke's, winter 1864-65.

ADALINE, MLLE. Circassian woman, Cooper, Bailey & Co., 1879.

ADAMS, CHARLES H. (1828-May 4, 1891) English clown and Pantaloon. Born in Bristol. Married **Mary Ann Cooke,** daughter of circus proprietor **Thomas E. Cooke;** father of clowns **James R.,** and **George H. Adams.** With Ryan's, Madame Ducrow's, Powell's, Hengler's, Batty's and Cooke's circuses, 1840s, 1850s. Was written that he "draws wonderful music from a penny whistle." 1865, at Hengler's, was described as, "the celebrated horseman from the *Cirque Napoleon,* Paris." Performed as "the mighty Jehu of the 19th century" and as a French a clog dance on the tight rope, 1866. Newsome's, 1860s, horseman, trainer, and eccentric clown. Came to America, 1867, and joined L. B. Lent's; Cooke's, Tenth and Callowhill Streets, Philadelphia, January, 1868; J. M. French's later that year; Cole's, 1872. In partnership with equestrian manager, **A. Henry,** around 1868; in own management, 1869. Last season out, with James R. Adams' "A Crazy Lot" Co. Died at the home of his father-in-law, Paterson, NJ.

ADAMS, CORA. Juggler, J. M. Barry's Great American, 1894.

ADAMS, FRANK. Managed car #2, John Robinson's, 1889; car #1, 1890-93.

ADAMS, GEORGE. Nixon's Amphitheatre, Broadway opposite Waverly Place, NYC, winter 1871-72.

ADAMS, GEORGE ERNEST. (August 24, 1876-January 29, 1898) German comedian and noted violinist. Son of **George H. Adams** and **Rose Adams;** brother of **James R. Adams.** Born in Montreal, Canada, and received education at a boarding school. Made stage debut at a very young age with his father and continued performing until about 1892, when ill health compelled retirement. Died of consumption at the home of his parents, Paterson, NJ.

ADAMS, GEORGE H. "GRIMALDI". (May 16, 1853-May 26, 1935) Clown, pantomimist, general performer. Born in London, the son of **Charles H. Adams,** a famous Pantaloon. Career began as an infant with his uncle, **James E. Cooke.** Struck out on his own and went to Spain, 1860, to perform with Ciniselli's as well as Price's Circus. After returning to England, joined Hengler's in Liverpool, 1862. Following year, went to Paris and performed with a circus on the *Champs Elysees.* Became associated with the **Nicolo Family** and worked in the Risley business as an apprentice. Shortly, Nicolo left for America (doomed to drown with the sinking of the *Evening Star);* after which, Adams traveled through Scotland with a circus, 1864, and the following year went to Dublin to join his father who was with Newsome's as clown. There, apprenticed to **Hubert Mears,** the circus manager, and continued with him until 1870, during which time he became an expert gymnast, a contortionist (called the "Alpine Wonder"), and a first-class rider. [M. B. Leavitt: "George Adams' great specialty was a clown act on stilts."] Sailed for America that year to join his parents and engaged with Stone & Murray in the fall season, remaining as a tumbling clown and general performer until the spring of 1874. With W. W. Cole's, 1874-76, assumed the title of "Grimaldi" Adams. Married Miss **Rosina Cooke,** daughter of **Henry Cooke,** October 19, 1874, Galveston, TX. During the winter seasons, performed in variety theatres, much of the time at the Theatre Comique, NYC. Later, organized "Grimaldi" Adams' Royal "Humpty Dumpty" Troupe, closing the season at the Olympic Theatre, NYC., April, 1877. John H. Murray's tenting season, 1877. 1877-78, featured with Nick Roberts' "Humpty Dumpty" Co. touring California, and later Tony Denier's "Humpty Dumpty" Troupe for 3 seasons, dropping the title of "Grimaldi" in the final year. Went into partnership with **Adam Forepaugh** in producing a "Humpty Dumpty" company. [Charles H. Day: "He was ambitious and persevering as a boy and deserving and meritorious as a man. As a boy with the old Murray circus, he could do almost anything in the ring and do it well—leap, tumble, ride and play clown, a good all-around performer, as the Cooke blood in his veins entitles him to be."] Died age 82.

ADAMS, HARRY. (d. 1859) Lee & Bennett, San Francisco, 1856-57; Rowe & Marshall, 1857-58. Died in Australia.

ADAMS, JAMES CAPEN "GRIZZLY BEAR". (October 22, 1812-October 25, 1860) California hunter and trapper and exhibitor of wild beasts. Born in Medway, MA. When gold rush fever struck, 1849, migrated to California, ultimately moving into the mountains to live. At some point, killed a female bear, then captured and trained her two cubs; acquired other native animals of the region and began a menagerie collection. The bears were trained to walk on their hind legs, talk on cue, wrestle, etc. A nasty encounter with one in the Sierra Nevadas, 1855, resulted in his sustaining severe wounds to his head and neck, leaving an indentation in his skull the size of a silver dollar. Shortly after that incident, moved out of the mountains and began exhibiting his collection, first in San Jose and then in San Francisco. Entered the circus business, 1856, with West Coast circus man **Joseph Rowe**, until Rowe left with a circus for Hawaii. Moved his California menagerie East, 1860, and went into business with **P. T. Barnum** and **James M. Nixon**. Before leaving, again had an encounter with one of his bears, which opened the injury on his skull, exposing a portion of his brain. Adams' California Menagerie opened at Broadway and 13th St., NYC., April 30, 1860, and continued until July 7th. After a doctor's suggestion that injuries would soon cause his death, and wishing to leave his wife with financial security, sold his half of the menagerie to Barnum. That fall Nixon took Cooke's Royal Circus with Old Grizzly Adams Bear Menagerie on a tour of the New England states. Adams struck a deal to go along for 10 weeks at a total salary of $500. After fulfilling most of the contract, left the show, retired to his daughter's home in Neponset, MA, where he died.

ADAMS, JAMES ROBERT "PICO". (January 28, 1856-August 30, 1915) Clown. Born in Kent, England, the son of **Charles H. Adams** and **Mary Ann Cooke**, and brother of the pantomimist and clown, **George H. Adams**. Served a 7 year apprenticeship to **Ethardo**, the English circus manager, before coming to America, 1870, at which time he first engaged with James M. Nixon's. Around 1875, joined W. W. Cole's; followed by a sojourn in Havana with Orrin Bros., winter 1879-80; W. W. Cole's, 1880, and Australian tour (left San Francisco, October 23, 1880). George H. Adams' "Humpty Dumpty" Co., 1881, under the management of **Adam Forepaugh**; William O. Dale Stevens', 1883; John B. Doris', 1885 (known as "Pico" Adams); Dockrill's, South America, winter 1885-86. Starred in his own production of "A Crazy Lot"; also connected with Thompson and Lundy, Luna Park, Coney Island, and with the same management at Colonial Theatre, NYC., as assistant stage manager. Member of the NYC Hippodrome company from its opening, April 12, 1905, until it abandoned its spectacle productions. Married English actress, **Becky Taylor**, December 1891. Died in NYC.

ADAMS, J. M. Business manager, Dan Rice's, 1891.

ADAMS, JOHN C. Band leader. R. Sands & Co., 1851-52; Pennsylvania Circus Troupe, 1860.

ADAMS, JOHN G. Tumbler. S. O. Wheeler's, 1865; Mag-

inley, Carroll & Co., 1868; James M. Nixon's Southern, 1870.

ADAMS, JOHNNY. Cosmopolitan Circus, Museum and Menagerie, December 1871.

ADAMS, MRS. CHARLES H. See Mary Ann Cooke.

ADAMS, MRS. GEORGE H. See Rosina Cooke.

ADAMS, P. Acrobat and leaper, Haight's Great Southern, 1874.

ADAMS, THOMAS "LITTLE TOMMY". (1837-April 21, 1895) Clown. Made his debut in Detroit, MI. For 2 years was principal clown with Sells Bros.' Worked in many variety houses throughout the country. Was at one time the partner of **Harry Watson**. Died in Kansas City, MO, of consumption.

ADAMS, W. S. Agent. Spalding & Rogers' *Floating Palace*, 1853; Rufus Welch's, 1855; James M. Nixon's, 1859; Dan Rice's, 1859-60; Robinson & Lake, 1860.

ADELAIDE, MLLE. Principal equestrienne from Batty's Royal Circus, London. Henler's circus, 1870s; first time in America, John H. Murray's, 1875. [John Turner: "Daring rider performing a series of poses and leaps on horseback."]

ADELE, MLLE. European equestrienne secured by John Wilson for 1868 circus season in California.

ADMIRAL DOT [r. n. Leopold Kahn]. (1858-October 26, 1918) "The California Dwarf," born in San Franciso. When exhibited, advertised as 25" high and weighing 15 pounds. P. T. Barnum's, 1871-73, 1876, 1884; Springer's, 1875; Barnum & Bailey, 1889. Appeared in British naval uniform, sang, danced and played musical instruments. Married another midget, **Dottie Swartwood**, and fathered 2 children. After spending some 20 years in show business, retired to inn keeping at Admiral Dot's Hotel at White Plains, NY. The place comprised 48 rooms, a bowling alley, a ballroom, banquet hall and restaurant. As one of the largest holders of property in that city, owner of a solid business block and several dwellings, accumulated around a quarter of a million dollars in assets. Died a few hours after his daughter had been buried at White Plains, NY.

ADOLPHE, MISS. Rider. James West's company, NYC, 1820, newly arrived from Paris. Married **William Blanchard**, 1822.

ADRIEN. French juggler. Price & Simpson, 1825. This may be the same Adrien, the magician, showing his "curious and recreative experiments, Washington Hall, NYC, 1822, which included such titles as "The Flower Garden," "The Sociable Box," "The Enchanted Lyre," "The Ladies' Jewel," "The Pyramids of Egypt," "The Dutch Coffee House," "Automaton's Visible Buffooneries," "The Hen Which Is No Egg," etc. Resurfaced, March 1835, at the City Saloon, NYC, where, as advertised, made Madam Adrien "appear and disappear in a wonderful manner never before attempted in New York." What was announced as a farewell season in America began in July, 1836, at the American Museum and supposedly terminated at Vauxhall Garden in August, 1838. This was just another of the illusionist's tricks, his presence continued for at least 10 years.

AGAZZI, LIZZIE [Mrs. Elizabeth Clarisse]. (d. 1938) English equestrienne. W. W. Cole's and Adam Forepaugh's (1883-84); Barnum & Bailey, for the show's first appearance in England. Appeared with principal circuses of Europe—2 seasons Carl Hagenbeck's, Germany, and Circo Price, Madrid; also, George Sanger and Hengler shows. 3 years a member of circus, Covent Garden, London, under Holland management, taking part in a command performance at Sandringham Park, 1885. 2 sons, **Erno** and **Will**, wire walkers, appeared in English vaudeville for years. Died London hospital, age 82, after 45 years of retirement.

AGER, HARRY. Lion tamer, Chiarini's, India, 1881-82.

AGLER, J. D. See Anthony Parker.

AGRA, ZULUMA. Circassian lady, P. T. Barnum's, 1873-74.

AGRATI, SIGNOR G. Contracting agent, Cooper, Bailey & Co. Australian tour, 1877.

AHEARN. Gymnast, John Robinson's, 1892.

AIKEN, GEORGE. Agent, John Robinson's, 1879; assistant treasurer, 1880; agent, 1881; manager car #1, 1882-87; railroad agent, 1888-93. Contractor, Sells Bros.', 1890; general agent and railroad contractor, Walter L. Main, 1891-94; railroad contractor, Barnum & Bailey, 1895-97, 1900; railroad agent, Forepaugh-Sells, 1898; traffic manager, Pawnee Bill's, 1899; traffic manager and contracting agent, John Robinson's, 1901-02, 1909; railroad contractor, Miller's 101 Ranch, 1911; general agent, Robinson's Famous Circus, 1911; railroad contractor, Buffalo Bill's Wild West, 1913; general agent, Howes' Great London, 1915.

AINSLEY, NED. Clown, Lake's, 1869-71.

AINSWORTH, JOSEPH. G. G. Grady's, 1868.

AJAX [Frank Maguire]. Contortionist. Shelby, Pullman & Hamilton, 1881; "The Human Corkscrew and Boneless Wonder, the Perplexity of the Medical Profession," George S. Cole's, 1895.

ALANTREE, MLLE. Leaper and tumbler, Washington Bros.', 1887.

ALBEE, E. F. Vaudeville impresario. Joined the Barnum show around 1876. Spent 12 years with such circuses as P. T. Barnum's, Barnum, Bailey & Hutchinson's, Adam Forepaugh's, Sells Bros.', Burr Robbins', VanAmburgh's, Norris', and Great London.

ALBERTI, SIGNOR. Bareback and somersault rider, Anderson & Co., 1878.

ALBERTINE, MISS. Aerialist, G. M. Eldred & Co., 1859.

ALBINO BROTHERS. See Three Albinos.

ALBINO FAMILY. Gardner & Hemmings (under the Barnum name), Washington, DC, fall 1862; Mabie's, 1863. Under Barnum's management several years.

ALBION BROTHERS [William, Frank, Charles "Mike"].

Gymnasts and acrobats, brother and ladder acts. Burr Robbins', 1886. **William** left the group in August of that year and was replaced by **William Wertz** of **Wertz Brothers**. King & Franklin, 1887; Shield's, 1888; Charles Andress', 1889; LaPearl's, 1892. **William** (William A. Bannerman), head of the 3 original **Albion Brothers**, died Philadelphia, November 15, 1911. Was in the profession for 35 years with several partners including **Abe Arenson, Adolph Mayer**, and his brother **Charles**.

ALBION FAMILY. Gymnasts and acrobats. Shields', fall 1886; Irwin Bros., 1887; E. H. Howes', 1888; Miller & Runnells, 1888; Edward Shipp's, winter 1889-90; W. H. Harris' Nickel-Plate, 1890.

ALDABO, EUSEBIO. Contortionist, Barnum, Bailey & Hutchinson, 1881.

ALDABRO. Gymnast, John Robinson's, 1876. May be the same as above.

ALDEN, D. A. Sideshow talker, W. W. Cole's, 1880.

ALDERMAN, WILLIAM. Treasurer, George W. DeHaven's, 1869.

ALDINE, LIZZI. Sells Bros.', Pacific coast, fall 1886.

ALDRICH, A. Scenic rider, Bowery Amphitheatre, 1841.

ALDRIDGE, M. A. Press agent, Robbins & Colvin, 1881.

ALEDA, MASTER. General performer, Stone & Rosston, 1864.

ALEE, SIGNOR. Contortionist. Joseph Cushing's, 1867; S. O. Wheeler's, 1868.

ALEE, WILLIE. Contortionist. Son of **Signor Alee**. Joseph Cushing's, 1867; S. O. Wheeler's, 1868. Advertised as "Famous Whalebone Boy, who will dislocate his joints and compress himself into the smallest compass of any living boy." Could fit himself into a box 15" x 18".

ALEXANDER, C. A. Agent. W. W. Cole's, 1875; contracting agent, P. A. Older's, 1871.

ALEXANDER, ELIZA. English giantess, Adam Forepaugh's, 1882-83.

ALEXANDER FAMILY. Levi J. North's, 1859.

ALEXANDER, G. W. Band leader, G. G. Grady's, 1874.

ALEXANDER, HENRY COOPER. English giant, Adam Forepaugh's, 1882-83.

ALEXANDER, J. Agent. H. M. Bennett's, 1856; Rowe's, 1857; Hinkley & Kimbal, 1858; Mitchell's, 1858; Olympic Circus, 1859; Lathrop, Peoples & Franklin, 1860; Lee & Ryland's Cosmopolitan Circus, San Francisco, 1866; Lee & Ryland's Hippodrome, San Francisco, 1866.

ALEXANDER, LILLIAN. With her *manège* horse Abdullah in an act entitled "Central Park Pastimes," George S. Cole's, 1895.

ALEXANDER, MASTER. (b. 1817) Purportedly Russian. Debut, Newbury, MA, July 1, Lafayette Circus, 1827-28; Providence Circus; Sweet & Hough, 1835; Eagle Circus, 1836; Miller, Yale, Sands, 1837; A. Hunt & Co., 1838.

4

ALEXANDER, SPENCER. (d. October 29, 1911) Better known as "Delavan." Boss hosler, John O'Brien's, Ringling Bros.' for many years.

ALFREDO, ALF. Gymnast, Valkinburg's, 1881.

ALFREDO FAMILY [William, Lewis, Emma]. Trapeze artists, featuring an act which involved the use of a bicycle on a line stretched from pole to pole. **William** rode the bike back and forth while **Lewis** and **Emma** performed on 2 trapeze bars suspended from it. Sells Bros., 1879; John Robinson's, 1881. While performing with the latter circus, June 12, 1882, Pueblo, CO, a stake that supported the ropes, made soft by an afternoon storm, pulled out of the ground and the rigging collapsed. **Emma** caught herself from falling but her husband plunged to the ground, landing on his head. **Lewis** died a few hours later, 28 years of age.

ANGELIQUE, MLLE. Hippotheatron, NYC, winter 1864-65.

ALI. Arabian attendant of Bucheet, the 2-year old, 1,000 pound hippopotamus that arrived in the USA aboard the steamer *City of Manchester*, October 19, 1860, accompanied by **Frank J. Howes**. The first hippo to make port on this continent. It was loaded onto the *DeSoto*, October 22, bound for New Orleans and exhibition at the Spalding & Rogers museum. Then, in early January, was shipped to Havana where it was placed before the public under a canvas pavilion opposite the Tacon Theatre for a period of 8 weeks. G. F. Bailey & Co., 1863.

ALLEE, BILLY. First collector of circus ephemera of note. St. Joseph, MO.

ALLEN, A. E. A. E. Allen's Great Eastern, 1879-80.

ALLEN, JOHN F. Clown. Dan Rice's, 1856-57; Slaymaker & Nichols, 1864.

ALLEN JOSEPH. Clown, Holland & McMahon, Chicago, fall 1885; King & Franklin, 1887.

ALLEN, TOM. Maginley & Bell, 1864.

ALLEN, WASHINGTON. (b. September 10, 1831) Side show curiosity, armless man. Born in Perry County, OH. Antonio & Wilder, 1859; Antonio Bros.', 1860; Antonio Bros. & Melville, 1861; Mabie's, 1862.

ALLEN, WHITING. (June 9, 1856-July 27, 1911) Agent. Born in Delaware, OH. Began as a professional by writing for the *Herald* in his home town. Later, moved to Chicago and continued journalistic pursuits until 1879, at which time became press representative for W. C. Coup's circus; followed by engagement with Adam Forepaugh's, where he wrote couriers and did other special work, 1882; John B. Doris', 1883; agent, W. T. Carleton Opera Co., winter 1884; Barnum & Bailey, traveling with the show in both the United States and Europe (Bailey is said to have stated that Allen made the show thousands of dollars at the turn of a single word); left the show, 1905, to become associated with Bailey's brother-in-law, J. T. McCaddon, in taking a circus to France, a venture that was doomed to failure. Moved into the theatrical field as business manager and press representative for dramatic shows; for one season, in charge of publicity department, Metropolitan Opera House, NYC., 1911 [M. B. Leavitt: "Mr. Oscar Hammerstein admits that it is largely due to Whiting Allen that the Philadelphia Opera House came into existence."]. Rejoined Barnum & Bailey, but was forced to give up the engagement because of ill health. Assisted Leavitt in editing his book, *Fifty Years in Theatrical Management*, published in 1912. Final employment, the Kinemacolor Moving Picture Co., Chicago. As a press agent, was considered to be inventive, with infinite resource. [Louis E. Cooke: "He had the faculty of covering almost any subject in a clear and comprehensive manner. He was equally at home on musical, operatic, dramatic and circus subjects, and once within his room and left to himself would turn out as good copy as one ever read."] Had a keen perception of story possibilities and was a superb courier writer. Married the former **Nellie Gibbons**, sister of Captain Edward Gibbons of the National Steamship Lines, December 20, 1882, in Philadelphia. Died at Sherman House, Chicago, of heart failure. Wife's death followed, April 16, 1914.

ALLENSHAW, PROF. [or Allreinshaw]. Band leader, P. T. Barnum's, 1871.

ALLISON, C. W. Press agent. Welch & Sands, 1880; New Great Pacific, 1881.

ALMONTE, EDWARD MIDDLETON ["Ted"]. (1842-April 10, 1878) Clown, leaper. Born in England. Began career about 1863 for circus manager **Edward Ginnett**. Then **Benjamin Bonn** and his Russian Circus; Sanger's for 3 seasons; came to America, 1871, with Howes' Great European as an Italian trick clown, remaining with the firm for 2 years; L. B. Lent's; Imperial Brazilian Hippodrome, Philadelphia, winter 1872-73; returned to Hengler's, England; reappeared in America with John Murray's, 1874-75, advertised as "From Hengler's Grand Cirque, London. The Children's Clown will amuse the little folks." Springer's, 1875; Chiarini's, 1875; Parisian Circus, Operti's Tropical Garden, Philadelphia, fall 1876; winter circus, New National Theatre, Philadelphia, 1876-77; P. T. Barnum's, 1876-78. Died while performing with the latter show, NYC.

ALPINE, CHARLES H. and **PEARL.** Triple bar, revolving trapeze, and high-wire, Goodrich's, 1897.

ALWARD, GUS. Alward & Co.'s Allied Shows, 1883; Alward & Way's Allied shows, 1883.

ALWARD, JENNIE. Hurdle rider, dancing rope artist. Married **John W. Cleveland** [r. n. John Roberts], Holton, KS, May 27, 1893, when both were with the Wallace Show. W. B. Reynolds, 1895; Winter Circus, Chicago, 1895; Robert Huning's, 1896; LaPearl's Danville, IL, winter 1896-97; hurdle and 4-horse act, Wood & Ewers, 1897. See John W. Cleveland.

AMBROSE, CAPT. Chief billposter, G. F. Bailey & Co., 1874.

AMBROSE, TOM. Ringmaster, F. J. Taylor's, 1891.

AMENT, CAPT. W. D. (d. May 26, 1943) Trick skater and expert rifle shot. Harris' Nickel-Plate, 1890; Ament's Big Ten Cent Show, 1895; Ament's Combined Shows, 1896; Ament's Big City Show, 1898-1902; carnival, 1903; Ament & Meehan, 1907. Retired, 1911.

AMES, CLARK T. (d. November 2, 1870) Ames' Southern Menagerie, 1866; Ames' Crescent City Museum and Zoological Institute, New Orleans, October, 1867; supplied menagerie, Haight, Chambers and Ames', 1867; C. T. Ames', 1868-70. Ames' estate sold an elephant and performing den of lions to **Andrew Haight**, 1871. His wife, known professionally as **Ella Eugenia**, was a lion tamer. Shot in the groin and killed in Dawson, GA, by drunken rowdies trying to force their way into a matinee.

AMES, MRS. CLARK T. "ELLA EUGENIA." See Eugenie DeLorme.

AMHERST, JOHN H. (1776-August 12, 1851) Equestrian. Born in London. First appeared on stage, "The Blue Devils," July 14, 1817, at Haymarket Theatre. As secretary and agent for **Thomas Cooke**, came with Cooke to USA, 1836, where he was considered to be the first literary bill-puffer in this country. A classic scholar and member of the English Dramatic Authors' Society of London. Creator of many plays, including the equestrian drama, "The Battle of Waterloo," next to "Mazeppa," most frequently performed piece at Astley's Royal Amphitheatre, London. Large, portly man of polished manners and imposing appearance, gifted with an amusing literary style. Later, became well known for his connection with Welch's Philadelphia circus. Died at Blockley Hospital, Philadelphia, in abject poverty and was buried by the Actors' Order of Friendship.

AMICK, ROSE [professionally Rose LeClaire]. (d. May 20, 1882) Midget. Height, less than 3'; weight 45 pounds. The daughter of **Mr.** and **Mrs. Joel Amick**, both of whom were portly. P. T. Barnum discovery, she traveled with his show both in the United States and abroad for 15 years. Several years exhibited with an 800 pound woman as sisters. Died at Newmarket, Clark County, IN, age 28, leaving a sizable sum of money in the bank.

AMOUR, JULIE. Equestrienne, Howes' Great European, 1864.

AMOUR, THERESA. Principal equestrienne, James Robinson's, 1872.

ANDAREAU, ROSE. *Manège*, Wallace & Anderson, 1890.

ANDERSON, JAMES. Boss hostler, John Robinson's, 1867.

ANDERSON, JAMES T. (1837-April 23, 1911) Proprietor, Dr. James L. Thayer's, 1870; manager, Anderson & Co. (owned by Sells Bros.), 1878-80; assistant manager, Sells Bros.', 1883. Bought the Nathans show at auction which fur-

nished the nucleus for Wallace & Co., for which he was managing partner, 1884. Treasurer, Wallace & Co., 1885; advance agent, Dockrill's, South America, 1885; manager, Wallace & Co., 1889; manager, Wallace & Anderson, 1890-91; assistant manager, Adam Forepaugh's, 1893-94; manager, Walter L. Main's, 1903. Died at his home in Cleveland, OH, age 74.

ANDERSON, JAMES, JR. Press agent, Albert M. Wetter's New Model Shows, 1893, but left the show early.

ANDERSON, JOSEPH. Elephant handler, Great Wallace, 1898. A professional for 20 years, was killed by the elephant Nero, June 3, 1898, at Racine, WI. The elephants had been unloaded from the railroad cars and driven to a water trough by Anderson. A bicyclist road up and leaned in front of where the elephants were drinking. Suddenly, Nero took hold of the rear wheel of the bicycle, throwing the rider off, and tossed the wheel 25' in the air. Anderson jabbed Nero behind the ear. The gesture infuriated the animal. Nero turned on Anderson, grabbed him with his trunk and, "lifting him as though he were a peanut," dashed him 3 or 4 times against the ground, hammered him against the water trough, threw him on the ground, stood over him, buried his tusks in him and disemboweled him. Then trampled him "into a jelly," picked up the remains and threw it against a fence on the roadside.

ANDERSON, MILES. Treasurer, Hendry's New London Shows, 1892.

ANDERSON, W. C. Contracting agent, James Robinson's, 1870; general business agent, James Robinson's, 1871.

ANDREAS, JOHN. Slack-rope performer. Pupil of Ben Stoker. Harrington & Buckley, 1830; Fogg & Stickney, November 1830; William Harrington's, 1832-33; Nathan A. Howes', winter 1833; Palmer & Harrison, 1834; slack-rope, posturing, Bancker & Harrington, 1835; J. W. Bancker's, 1836; Luddington's, 1837; Brown & Co., 1837; Noel E. Waring's, 1838.

ANDRES, W. S. See Doc "Rev." Wadell.

ANDRESS, CHARLES. (January 15, 1852-August 26, 1933) Showman, legal adjuster. Born in Canada. Began career at the age of 10 as a child ventriloquist, imitator, and fiddler, 1865, which attracted the attention of a magician named **Captain Thomas** (one account gives the name as **Prof. Hertz**), who took him on as an apprentice. After 2 years, the magician returned to England because of ailing health; Andress soon developed his own act of magic, bird calls and ventriloquism, augmented by some trained animals. By 1872, was operating the Andress' Carnival of Novelties. Claimed to be the first to use the word "carnival" in describing a show. Charles Andress' Carnival of Curiosities, Trained Animal Exposition and Congress of Living Wonders, 1888; Charles Andress' Big Circus, 1889; took **Willie Sells** as a partner, 1890. "I began to find out when too late, that my troubles had only begun," Andress wrote to the *New York Clipper*. "The show for some unknown reason was very badly handled. No salaries were

6

paid, and in less then five weeks it was in the hands of a receiver." The show was attached for performers' salaries totaling $6,000. From a total investment of $25,000, the outfit was sold at auction for a mere $2,964 (Andress wasn't the first to be "burned" by Willie Sells). W. H. Harris' Nickel-Plate, 1892; Andress & Showers', 1896; annex manager, W. H. Harris' Nickel-Plate, 1892-93, 1897; E. Davis', 1894; G. W. Hall's, 1894; Ringling Bros.', 1895, as legal adjuster for 10 years; Barnum & Bailey, 5 years, going to Europe with the show. Invented a mechanical stake driver run by a gasoline engine that was in general use by 1912. Announced his retirement, 1907, after 45 years in show business. Had investments in real estate in Great Bend, KS, a place that eventually became his home. Married there at age 80 to 27 year old **Virginia Prichard**, November 9, 1930. A son was born the following year. Died of influenza in Great Bend.

ANDREWS, A. B. Boneless boy, G. G. Grady's, 1869.

ANDREWS, BILLY. (1840?-Dec. 9, 1895) Clown. Orton Bros.', 1865-68; John W. Robinson's (not "Old John"), 1870; Wootten & Haight, 1871; Great Eastern, 1872; North American Circus (**Asa B. Stow**, manager), 1873; partner with Wootten for a circus troupe, 1873; Basye's, 1879; returned from retirement to fill engagement with the St. Louis Circus, winter 1879-80; press agent and clown, Thornton's, 1880; clown, Shelby, Pullman & Hamilton, 1881. Wife was **Lotino Andrews**. Died in Kankakee, IL, at the insane asylum.

ANDREWS, GEORGE. Contortionist and acrobat, G. G. Grady's, 1871.

ANDREWS, J. H. Leaper and tumbler, W. H. Stone's, 1881.

ANGELA, MLLE. Female Sampson, John Robinson's, 1872.

ANGELO. Aerialist, Robinson & Howes, 1863.

ANGELS, LOUIS. Equestrian director, with Montgomery Queen's, 1887.

ANGEVINE, CALEB SUTTON. (April 4, 1798-July 19, 1859) Menagerie and circus proprietor. 1821, set up exhibition rooms, 37 Bowery, NYC; operated circus with **Samuel Clift**, **Hart B. Doolittle, Ichabod Doolittle**, 1824; partner, June, Titus, Angevine & Co., 1827, 1834; Unit #1, Zoological Institute, 1835-36; New York Unit, Zoological Institute, 1837; June, Titus, Angevine & Co., menagerie, 1838-39; June, Titus, Angevine & Co., circus, 1838-39; June, Titus, Angevine & Co., circus and menagerie, 1840; June, Titus, Angevine & Co., 3 units, 1841; VanAmburgh & Co. (**Lewis B. Titus, John June**, Caleb S. Angevine and **Gerard Crane**, proprietors), Europe, 1842-45; partner, VanAmburgh & Co., 1846-47. Retired, 1848. Buried in June Cemetery, North Salem.

ANNEREAU, JEANNETTE. Rider. Lee & Marshall, 1855; Lee & Bennett, 1857; H. C. Lee's, 1859; Lee, Worrell & Sebastian, 1863. Had 2 children from marriage to **Annereau**, a son, **Jeannot**, and a daughter, **Charlotte**. Married **H. C. Lee**, March 19, 1856.

ANSON, BILLY. Superintendent of menagerie, Gollmar Bros.', 1897.

ANTONIO, ANTOINE. Vaulter. Great Western, 1855; Levi J. North's, 1856; John Robinson's, 1857; tented variety, William Davison & Co., 1858; Spalding & Rogers, winter 1858; Spalding & Rogers, 1859-60; Spalding & Rogers, South America, 1862

ANTONIO BROTHERS [Guglielmo, Philip Augustus, Lorenzo, Alphonso]. Acrobats. Edward Eldred's, 1834; Hubbell's, 1849; Mann, Moore & Co., 1853; L. G. Butler & Co., 1854-56; Antonio, Carroll & Co. (with **W. B. Carroll**), 1857; Antonio & Wilder, 1858-59; Wood's Theatre, St. Louis, winter 1859-60; Antonio Bros.', 1860-61; circus sold to a Mr. **Norton** of Chicago (probably **Horace Norton**), April 1863. **Guglielmo** (1820-1902) was the oldest of the 3 brothers. Spalding & Rogers, 1859; Stowe & Norton, 1869; James Robinson, 1870. Then came **Philip Augustus** (d. 1895), the acting manager for Antonio & Wilder's, 1859. In retirement from the circus profession, 1862, he and Alphonso, kept a saloon under the Everett House, St. Louis. **Lorenzo** (1826-1828) the youngest of the brothers. 4th member of the troupe was **Alphonso "Fons" Antonio**, real name **McGlassy** (1835?-August 19, 1895). Retired from show business and became part owner of a cafe under the Olympic Theatre, St. Louis, MO. Once considered wealthy, was in poor circumstances at time of death at Carondelet, MO, age about 60. Assumed a suicide, since his body was found floating in a pond.

ANTONIO CHARLES "DEAF CHARLEY" [r. n. Charles Wright]. (1841-1875) Clown, horizontal bar and cannon ball performer. A native of Providence, RI. Traveled with various circuses for some 15 years. Acrobat, Dan Rice's Paris Pavilion, 1871, and July 27 of that year married **Miss Lottie Harris** of Fox's American Theatre, Philadelphia; A. W. Davis', 1874. Died in Toledo, OH, of pneumonia.

ANTONIO, DIAVOLO [r. n. Antonio Migasi]. Acrobatic father of the **Antonio Brothers**. Performed at the old Park Theatre and at Niblo's Garden, NYC, 1835, and with his 3 sons introduced a manner of the Risley business. Retired from performing around 1851 and became the troupe manager. See Antonio Brothers.

ANTONIO, MAY. Juggling and slack-wire, and ascensionist, Barnum, Bailey & Hutchinson, 1881.

ANTONIO, TILLIE. Stowe's, 1868.

ANTONIO, WASHINGTON "WASH". Acrobat. P. T. Barnum's, 1872-73; trick clown, North American, 1875; Dockrill's, South America, winter 1885-86; Frank Brown's, South America, 1889.

ANTONY, CARL. (1824-1904) Equestrian, horse trainer. Performed in Europe and America and at one time was owner of a Swiss circus. Trained and exhibited the dozen black stallions for P. T. Barnum's, 1878-79; W. C. Coup's, 1880. Married **Kate Stokes**, daughter of **Spencer Q. Stokes**, Pittsburgh, PA, September 10, 1878. Later divorced. Died in

Greenwich, CT.

ANZO. Contortionist, John Robinson's, 1888.

ARABIAN BROTHERS [G. W. King, C. R. Teese]. Gymnasts. George Bailey & Co., 1869, 1871; John Stowe & Sons, 1871.

ARBUCKLE, JOHN. Clown, Springer's, 1875.

ARBUCKLE, O. S. (November 22, 1845-December, 1882) Clown. Born in Ohio. James T. Johnson's, 1872; H. Harlan's, 1875; Joel E. Warner's, 1876; Great Oriental Pavilion Show, 1877; Ed G. Basye's, 1878; cannoneer for concert, Cooper, Bailey & Co., 1879; California Circus, 1880. Died in San Juan, Puerto Rico, while working for the Ohio Telephone Company, which was establishing phone service there.

ARCHER, EMMA. Gymnast, W. W. Cole's, 1886.

ARCHER, GEORGE W. (d. February 7, 1865) Globe performer. Banks, Archer & Rockwell, 1849; Levi J. North's, 1853-55; H. M. Smith's, 1856-57; Spalding & Rogers, 1858; Satterlee & Bell, 1858; Hyatt & Co., 1859. Drafted into the Union Army, January 1864. Died in Baltimore.

ARCHER, WILLIAM. (d. May 24, 1850) Palmer & Harrington's, 1834; Palmer's Circus and Gymnastic Arena, 1835; J. W. Bancker's National Gymnasium and American Arena Co., 1836; C. H. Bacon's, 1837; H. H. Fuller's Olympic Circus, 1838; June, Titus, Angevine & Co., Bowery Amphitheatre, NYC, 1839; Howes & Mabie's Olympic, 1841; S. H. Nichols', 1842; Banks, Archer & Rockwell, 1846-50. Died in Cuba of yellow fever.

ARDELL, MLLE. Aerialist who slid from the top of the tent to the ground with her hair suspended on a wire. With Miles Orton's, 1885.

ARGANDI, SIGNOR. Rider, VanAmburgh & Co., 1881.

ARIZONA, CHARLES. Great New York (**E. Hamilton**, **F. W. Sergeant**, proprietors), 1877.

ARLENE BROTHERS. Gymnasts, New York Central Park Circus, 1877.

ARLINGTON, BILLY. Concert, Montgomery Queen's, 1876.

ARLINGTON, ED. (1874-October 23, 1947) Secretary, Walter L. Main's, 1893-94; excursion agent, Ringling Bros.', 1897; railroad agent, Barnum & Bailey, 1901-06; manager, Pawnee Bill's, 1907; proprietor, 101 Ranch, 1908-15.

ARLINGTON, FREDDIE. Female trapezist, St. Germain's Imperial Circus, 1889.

ARLINGTON, GEORGE. (d. December 1, 1923) Sideshow manager of **Lalloo** (or Laloo), the double-bodied boy, and the original **Aztecs**. VanAmburgh's, 1885; Barnum & Bailey, 1888; proprietor and general agent, Washburn & Arlington, 1890-91; superintendent of concert, Barnum & Bailey, 1899.

ARLINGTON, W. C. Gymnast, J. W. Wilder's, 1872.

ARMOUR, AL. Clown, Richards' (George W. Richards, proprietor), 1887; W. H. Harris' Nickel-Plate, 1891.

ARMSTRONG, CHARLES. Press agent, James T. Johnson's, 1885.

ARMSTRONG, F. Levi J. North's National Amphitheatre, 1857-60.

ARMSTRONG, GARDNER J. Tumbler. Davis & Crosby's, 1859; Thayer & Noyes, 1877.

ARMSTRONG, H. D. Business manager, Col. Spicer's, 1886.

ARMSTRONG, J. (d. 1857) Lee & Bennett's, 1856-57. Died in San Diego, California.

ARMSTRONG, J. A. Dog circus, Miller & Runnells, 1888.

ARMSTRONG, JAMES A. Band leader, G. G. Grady's, 1872.

ARMSTRONG, JEANNETTE. Equestrienne. Stone, Rosston & Murray's, Front Street Theatre, Baltimore, winter 1866-67; Stone, Rosston and Murray's, 1867; Cuba, 1868; double equestrian act with **Tom Armstrong** for G. A. Huff & Co., 1870; James Robinson's, 1871; principal act, Adam Forepaugh's, 1872; Haight's Great Southern, 1874; Adam Forepaugh's, 1876; Thayer & Noyes, 1877; New York Central Park, 1877; equitation, Adam Forepaugh, 1878-79; Batcheller & Doris, 1880; VanAmburgh's, 1883; principal equestrienne, Pullman, Mack & Co., 1884. Married **Henry Burdeau**, gymnast, Philadelphia, October 31, 1872.

ARMSTRONG, JOHN. Lee & Marshall, 1853; J. L. & N. M. Hinkley, 1857; Rowe & Marshall, 1857-58, and with the show in Australia, 1858; Pennsylvania Circus Troupe, 1860.

ARMSTRONG, THOMAS. Equestrian. With Spalding & Rogers, 1855-56; clown, Levi J. North's, 1857-60; VanAmburgh's, 1859; Levi J. North's, Chicago, 1859; Mabie's & Nathans, 1861; Nixon's Cremorne Garden Circus, Washington, DC, October-December 1862; double equestrian act with **Jeannette Armstrong**, G. A. Huff & Co., 1870; vaulter, G. G. Grady's, 1870.

ARMSTRONG, WILLIAM. See William Nixon.

ARMSTRONG, WILLIS. Rider, vaulter. Star State Circus, 1852; Mabie & Crosby, 1858; Levi J. North's, 1859; VanAmburgh's, 1860; Madigan & Gardner, winter 1860-61; Madigan's, 1861; Madigan & Carroll, 1862.

ARNAL. Dancer, Pepin & Breschard, 1813.

ARNOLD, RICHARD A. Superintendent, picture gallery and statuary, museum, P. T. Barnum's, 1873.

ARRILLA, MLLE. EMMA [or Arilla]. Equestrienne. VanAmburgh's, 1871; VanAmburgh & Co.'s Menagerie, Siegrist's French and Frost's American Circus Combined, 1871; J. W. Wilder's, 1872.

ARSTINGSTALL, GEORGE. (d. February 11, 1904) One of the top elephant trainers and performers. Born in Marietta, VA, where he received a common school education. Spoke six languages but still maintained the accent from his native state. In appearance, had brown, piercing eyes, and jet black hair and mustache. Just before the Civil War, although inexperienced, joined Dan Rice's as an animal tamer and worked with a troupe of Grizzly Adam's bears that Rice had purchased. After leaving Rice, exhibited Lipman's sacred bull, 1866. Began making hot air balloon ascensions, but after falling 68' in one at Portsmouth, OH, decided animal training was a bit safer. Buckley's, 1868. Went to Europe and worked with a variety of animals including lions, tigers, and hyenas. Howes' Great London, 1876-78; during the latter year the elephants Mandarin and Hebe were bred, resulting in the first baby of the breed to be born in America and live, Columbia, March 10, 1880. Cooper, Bailey & Co., 1879-80; Barnum's Great London, 1881-85. Bred Chief and Queen, resulting in a second birth, Baby Bridgeport, February 2, 1882. Found by a Bridgeport, CT, policeman on a night in mid-February, 1887, on the tracks of a railroad in an apparent suicide attempt. Said to have been still greatly effected by the death of Jumbo, as well as being in a state of depression growing out of "an affair of the heart." Later denied the story. Retired to go into business in Bridgeport and perhaps to get married. April 2, 1887, sailed for Germany to train elephants for Hagenbeck; returned to USA, February 7, 1892. Joined Adam Forepaugh's to oversee 14 elephants. Shortly, developed an act consisting of 2 American panthers, 2 Asiatic leopards, 2 lions, 2 dogs—great Dane and mastiff, a black bear, all going through a drill in the same ring. Retired after 1894 season. Imported animals for DeSilva & Gaylord, 1895. Was exhibiting the dwarf elephant, Kedah, 1896; ran the maze ride, Sea beach, Coney Island, 1899. Died at Leachdale, PA.

ARTHUR, BOB. General performer, John H. Murray's, 1877.

ASH, WILLIAM. Clown, John Robinson's, 1875-83.

ASHBURN, A. W. Manager, Washington Bros.', 1887.

ASHBY, CLARENCE and **EVA.** Equestrian director, etc., LaPearl's, 1893.

ASHBY, JOSEPH. (1847-September 17, 1926) Trick, scene act, and 4-horse rider. Son of **Joe Ashby**, Punch and Judy showman; brother of **Happy Ashby** and half-brother of **Alf Burgess.** Began with the Sangers at age 9 turning somersaults on horseback and remained with them 16 years as a rider. Sangers', Agricultural Hall, London, performing St. George in *St. George and the Dragon*; Bell and Myers', traveling on the continent. Married equestrienne **Marie Charlton,** 1871, at Marseilles. Performed together, Franconi's, Renz', Salamonsky's, Pinder's, Cinisclli's, Rancy's, Carre's, Corty-Althoff's, etc. In England with Powell and Clarke's, Belfast, 1875; Hengler's, London and the provinces, 1878-81. USA joined Adam Forepaugh's as principal bareback rider, 1881; Great Australian Circus, winter 1881-82; then returned to England. With wife and son **George,** Circus Zaeo, Italy, 1887; later, started a circus in Italy with **Archie Pearson,** but it failed. Hengler's, Covent Garden, 1889-90; Arundel's, Birmingham, 1897; Crouestes's, 1891-92. Died, age 79, at his home, 47 St. George Street, Birmingham, where he had lived in retirement.

ASHBY, Marie [nee Charlton]. Equestrienne. Once said to be one of the best horsewomen in Europe. Daughter of **William Charlton,** musician. Apprenticed to **Frederick John Ginnett.** Married **Joseph Ashby,** 1871, Marseilles, when touring with Bell and Myers. Hengler's, Hull, 1874, and provinces, 1878-80; Whitmee's, Oxford, 1893. Had 3 sons, including rider **George Ashby,** who died in Barcelona. See Joseph Ashby.

ASHE, FRANCES L. (d. November 10, 1907) Mother of **Ashton Troupe** of acrobats; wife of **William R. Ashe.** Died at Toledo, OH.

ASHE, WILLIAM R. ["Billy"]. Clown. G. G. Grady's, 1868, 1873; Warner & Henderson, 1874; Springer's, 1875; Joel E. Warner's, 1876; Hamilton & Sergeant, 1878; Dr. A. W. Hager's, 1878; John Robinson's, 1879-86; Holland & McMahon, 1886; Holland & Gormley, 1888-89; John F. Wood's, fall 1889. Married **Frances L. Ashe.**

ASHLEY, FRED. (d. March 1, 1865) Gymnast and fancy dancer. Died of injuries while performing, age 29.

ASHLEY, H. Co-proprietor, Great Orion Circus at Old Bowery Theatre, NYC, fall 1861.

ASHLEY, MARY. Bareback rider, Adam Forepaugh's, 1881.

ASHTON, ALBERT G. Gymnast, Montgomery Queen's, 1875.

ASHTON BROTHERS [Harry, Willian]. Gymnasts. L. B. Lent's, 1874; John Robinson's, 1881; Nathans & Co., 1882-83; W. W. Cole's, 1883; Burr Robbins', 1884; Shields', 1887; Ringling Bros.', 1890-92; bars and brother act, L. W. Washburn's, 1895; L. B. Lent & Co., 1896.

ASHTON, FRANK. Gymnast, contortionist. Son of gymnast **William H. Ashton** and brother of **William Ashton, Jr.** Thayer & Noyes, 1864; O. S. Wheeler's, 1865; New York Champs Elysees, 1866; Wootten & Haight, 1871; Smith & Baird, 1872; Great Eastern, 1874; L. B. Lent's, 1876; posturing, leaper, Barnum, Bailey & Hutchinson, 1881-82; S. H. Barrett's, 1885; P. T. Barnum's, 1886; Gardner & Donovan, 1886; Sells Bros.', 1887; James Donovan's, winter 1891-92; Adam Forepaugh's, 1892.

ASHTON, HARRY. Ringling Bros., 1891.

ASHTON, JOSIE [Mrs. Josephine Gagnon]. (1870-April 28, 1912) Equestrienne. Burr Robbins', 1880, when she bought the retired James Robinson's ring horse for $1,200, said to be the most perfectly gaited horse that ever went into the ring, and kept him for many years. P. T. Barnum's, 1886; Gardner & Donovan, South America, 1886; Sells Bros.', 1887, 1889; principal act and flying rings, Adam Forepaugh's, 1893; Ringling Bros.', 1894; Barnum & Bailey, 1895; flying rings, Barnum & Bailey, London, winter 1898; Hippodrome, Luna Park, Coney Island, 1905; Al F. Wheeler's, 1910. Died of cancer in Orange, NJ.

ASHTON, LAURA. Gymnast, John Robinson's, 1883-85.

ASHTON, LILLIAN. Adam Forepaugh's, 1892.

ASHTON, MAMIE. Gymnast, John Robinson's, 1884-87; Ringling Bros.', 1891.

ASHTON, M. E. Agent, Tribbey & Co.'s Mastadon Dime Circus, 1887.

ASHTON, SAM. Acrobat. Horizontal bar act with **Frank Clifton** and **Albert Gaston**, Montgomery Queen's, 1875.

ASHTON, TONY. Piloted a variety show in Indiana, 1879; equestrian manager, Hall's, 1886; singing clown and troupe of dogs, Stevens & Smith, 1898.

ASHTON, WILLIAM H. Gymnast, globe on horse-back. Sands, Nathans & Co., 1859; Niblo & Sloat, 1860; R. Sands', 1861; Rogers & Ashton's troupe of acrobats, 1861; Spalding & Rogers, 1862; Miles' Circus Royale, 1863; teamed with **H. W. Penny**, Thayer & Noyes, 1864; clown, O. S. Wheeler's, 1865; New York Champs Elysees, 1866; John Robinson's, 1867-68; performing posturing, acrobatic and contortion acts with his 2 boys, **Frank** and **William, Jr.**, Chestnut Street Theatre, Philadelphia, winter 1868.

ASHTON, WILLIAM, JR. Gymnast. Son of gymnast **William H. Ashton** and brother of **Frank Ashton**. Thayer & Noyes, 1864; contortionist, O. S. Wheeler's, 1865; New York Champs Elysees, 1866; Springer's, 1875; W. W. Cole's, 1876; Burr Robbins', 1877, 1779, 1885; Ringling Bros.', 1891; clown, Welsh Bros.', 1895. A daughter, **Etta May Ashton**, was a vaudeville performer. Wife died, June 12, 1907, Cincinnati, OH.

ASHTON, ZOE. S. H. Barrett's, 1885.

ASPINALL, MISS [also Aspinwall]. Dancer. Married a **Mr. Moreland**, 1826. West & Blanchard, 1824; Price & Simpson, 1825-26; Mount Pitt Circus, 1827; Blanchard's Amphitheatre, NYC, 1830.

ASTEN, ISAAC. Equestrian. One of the earliest native riders in America. First known as a trampoline artist, throwing somersaults, making leaps into lighted galleries, over 10 horses, or over a phalanx of men holding muskets with fixed bayonets. Became a rider in horse dramas and later an equestrian director. First appears on record at the Broadway Circus, NYC, Price & Simpson's company, 1823-25; ringmaster, Olympic Circus, Philadelphia, 1823; West & Blanchard, from August 1825; Lafayette Circus, 1826, 1828; Fogg & Stickney, 1828; Mount Pitt Circus, NYC, 1826-28; Washington Circus, Martinique, 1830; Palmer & Fogg, winter 1831; riding master, Washington Circus, 1832; riding master, Fogg & Stickney, 1833; Buckley & Weeks, 1834-35; ringmaster, Palmer's, March 1836; Green & Waring, April, 1836; J. J. Hall's, winter 1837.

ASTON BROTHERS. Nathans & Co.'s, 1882.

ASTON, CHARLES. Clown. Howes & Sands, 1834-35; Boston Amphitheatre (managed by **H. H. Fuller**), 1837; Welch, Bartlett & Co., 1840. Wife was a competent equestrienne, listed as a member of the Grecian Arena and Classic Circus (**P. H. Nichols**, proprietor), 1841.

ATHERTON, CARRIE. Vocalist and dancer, Bunnell sideshow, P. T. Barnum's, 1879

ATHLEAU, ROSA. Pullman, Mack & Co., 1884.

ATKINS, PROF. Aeronaut from Toledo, OH. Lost his life while with Mike Lipman's circus at Decatur, AL, May 27, 1872, age 20. Was about to ascend in his balloon, when he remarked apprehensively, "This is the last ascension I'll ever make." And it was. The balloon plummeted into the Tennessee River from a height of about a half-mile and the young man drowned.

ATKINSON, A. Detective, Cooper, Bailey & Co., 1876-79.

ATTERBURY, ROBERT LEE. (b. February 10, 1866) Born at Paris, MO. Entered amusement business, 1883, with Burr Robbins'. Dr. James L. Thayer's, 1884; G. W. Donaldson's, 1885; F. H. Rich's, 1886; Burr Robbins, 1887; Grenier Bros.', 1888; French & Co., 1889; Adam Forepaugh's, 1890-91; McMahon's, 1892; Miles Orton's, 1893; Sells & Rentfrow, 1894; W. D. Reynolds', 1895-96; Dan Shelby's, 1897; Wintermute Bros.', 1898-99; Hutchinson & Co., 1900; Cullen Bros.', 1901; Walter McDonald's, 1902; Younger & James Wild West, 1903; Kirkhart & Reichold, 1904; Hutchinson & Co., 1905; W. P. Hall's, 1906; Barnum & Bailey, Buffalo Bill, 1907; Rice Bros.', 1908; LaMont Bros.', 1909-10. Organized Atterbury Bros.' Wagon Shows, 1910, which he managed until the fall of 1924; bought Col. Hoogawonnie Circus, 1925, and continued same until 1927, when changed the title to Cook Bros.' and continued until 1930. Joined Harrington's, 1931, and furnished 5 acts put on by the Atterbury Troupe of aerialists. Owned and managed the Atterbury Trained Animal Circus. Married **Miss Grace Smith**, 1900, who died 3 years later; then married second wife, **Rose**, 1908.

ATWOOD, A. D. Band leader, G. F. Bailey & Co., 1860-63.

ATWOOD, J. B. Press agent, W. W. Cole's, 1874.

AUBREY, CHARLOTTE. Adam Forepaugh's, 1875.

AUGUSTA, MLLE. First appearance in America, James M. Nixon's Cremorne Garden Circus, Washington, DC, October-December 1862.

AUGUSTE, HENRI. Spalding & Rogers, winter 1864-65.

AURITA, MLLE. Tight-rope, with Howes' New London, 1887.

AUSTIN, BILLY. Band leader, Hamilton & Sargeant, 1877.

AUSTIN BROTHERS [Richard, Michael]. Trapeze and horizontal bars. O'Conner & Co., 1869-70; Alexander Robinson's, 1871; P. A. Older's, 1872; P. T. Barnum's, 1872-73.

AUSTIN, CARRIE. See Charles Austin.

AUSTIN, CHARLES. General performer and clown. Montgomery Queen's, 1874; challenge musket drill, Palace of Wonders, P. T. Barnum's, 1876; tumbler, Thayer & Noyes, 1877; Coup's Equescurriculum, 1878; knockabout clown, Reese, Levis & Dolphin, 1885; Orrin Bros.', winter 1889-90. Equestrienne wife, **Carrie**, worked with him, performing a "lightning drill and bayonet combat," as well as handling their troupe of performing dogs.

AUSTIN, EDWARD. (d. December 3, 1915) Boss hostler.

Native of Norway. Started with Mabie's shortly after coming to his country. After the death of Mabie, traveled for several years with VanAmburgh, Howes' London, and Barnum & Bailey. Died at the age of 83 in Delavan, WI, where he had lived for more than 60 years. [D. W. Watt: "He was a man of excellent habits, always attending strictly to business and was considered by all the big shows in the country to be the best man in the business up to the time that he had to retire on account of old age."]

AUSTIN FAMILY [R. G., Rose, Aimee, George E.]. General performers. Orrin Bros.', winter 1883-84; W. W. Cole's, 1885; Coney Island, 1892; Bentley's, 1895. **Aimee Austin** or **Mrs. Phil D. Green**, (February 22, 1870-January 11, 1907) aerialist, sometimes called the "Human Fly," born in London and began performing with **Rose Austin** at age 9 as part of the **Austin Sisters** aerial act at the Circus Rentz, Berlin, under the management of her brother-in-law, **R. G. Austin**. Performed with various circuses throughout Europe before coming to America. In the winter, 1882, the family was engaged by **Ernest Cooke**, agent for W. W. Cole; at the close of the season, Orrin Bros., Mexico; re-engaged with Cole for 1884. In the fall of that year, **R. G. Austin** formed the R. G. Austin Australian Novelty Co. W. W. Cole again, 1885; 1886, went to England. Australian Variety Co. on the road as late as 1891. **Aimee** died of cancer in Pittsburgh, PA. **George E. Austin**, rider and leaper, was connected with Cooper & Bailey's, 1879-80; Adam Forepaugh's, 1884-85; also John O'Brien's, 1885; White & Markowit, 1889. **Addie Austin**, or **Mrs. Frank Brown**, (December 23, 1853-June 8, 1889) equestrienne, sister of **George E. Austin**; born in Mexico, MO; member of the D'Atalie family of acrobats who made their debut, 1870. Bareback rider, P. T. Barnum's, 1872-75; Montgomery Queen's, 1876; Cooper, Bailey & Co., tour of Australia and South America, 1876-78; W. W. Cole's (which left San Francisco for Australia and New Zealand, October 23, 1880), 1880-83; Cantelli & Leon, Cuba, winter 1882-83; Carlo Bros.', South America, 1884. Married **Frank Brown**, fall 1883, a union which produced 3 children. Brown managed his own circus from about 1886 to 1889. Addie died in South America.

AUSTIN, LULU. Outside ascension and revolving globe, Hurlburt & Hunting, 1885.

AUSTIN, MIKE. Horizontal bar act, Dan Rice's Paris Pavilion Circus, 1871

AUSTIN, NATHAN W. "NAT". (1834-June 1, 1892) Gentlemanly English clown and excellent general performer—equestrian, a good leaper and still vaulter, a superior juggler on horseback and globe ascensionist (rolling a globe up an inclined to the top of the tent and back, after which the globe opened and out popped his trick dog). John A. Dingess called his appearance in the ring "majestic and refined." With A. V. Cadwell's, 1853; Lee & Marshall, 1855-56; James A. Rowe's, 1857; Hinkley & Kimball, 1857; Rowe & Marshall, Australia,

1858; Lent's National Circus, Philadelphia, 1859; Nixon & Co., 1859; VanAmburgh's, 1859-60; Antonio Bros.', 1861; Howard's Athenaeum, Boston, Goodwin & Wilder, winter 1861-62; Goodwin & Wilder, 1862; National Circus, Philadelphia, winter 1863-64; National Circus, Cincinnati, 1864; Hippotheatron, NYC, late winter 1864; Melville's Australian, 1864; James M. Nixon's, 1864; Hippotheatron, NYC, February, October 1864; co-proprietor (with **Richard Platt**), Hippotheatron, NYC, September 1865; S. O. Wheeler's, 1865; John Robinson's, 1866; Stone, Rosston & Co., 1867; Stone, Rosston & Murray, 1868; Dr. James L. Thayer's, 1869; Stone & Murray, 1870; Nixon's Amphitheatre, Broadway opposite Waverly Place, NYC, winter 1871-72; Adam Forepaugh's, 1872; Montgomery Queen's, 1873-75; John Wilson's, San Francisco, 1875; left with Cooper, Bailey & Co. for Australia, November 8, 1880. First wife was wire ascensionist and rope dancer **Jeanette Ellsler**. Divorced in 1876. Married **Madame D'Atalie**, May 11, 1876, both being on Montgomery Queen's. Cooper, Bailey & Co.'s Australian tour, 1877-80. Wife died, 1891. Austin died at the State Lunatic Hospital, Worcester, MA, age 58, after about a 12 year retirement from the circus profession.

AUSTIN, PERCY W. (d. 1875) Youthful prodigy. Pupil of Nathan Austin. S. O. Wheeler's, 1863. Left the circus business and settled in Durham, NC, employed with Lawrence & Johnson, painters. Died from the wounds of the premature discharge of a cannon being fired in honor of a local political victory.

AUSTIN, PROF. Dogs and ponies, Hunting's, 1889.

AUSTIN, W. Band leader, Great Western, 1876.

AUSTIN, W. H. Manager, George F. Bailey & Co., 1857, 1859, 1861-62.

AUSTIN, WILLIAM. Gymnast, son of Nathan Austin, with Goodwin & Wilder, 1862; manager, George F. Bailey's, 1870.

AUSTIN, W. W. With newly invented family steam carriage, Spalding & Rogers, 1864.

AUSTRALIAN FOUR [Dan Kennedy, Bert Richardson, John Casselli, Charles Reuch]. W. W. Cole's, 1881. **Richardson** was clown, Frank Robbins', 1888.

AVELO, F. Clown, Gregory Bros.', 1884-85.

AVELOS, GEORGE. See William H. Franklin.

AVERY, FRANK. Double Horizontal bars (with Hugo Moulton), Barnum & London, 1885.

AVERY, LIZZIE. Aerialist, Howes' London, 1897.

AVERY, WILLIAM. Barnum, VanAmburgh and Castello's, 1867; Jesse W. Foster's, South America, 1894.

AVOLLO, JOE. (d. July 19, 1889) Lemen Bros.'

AXTELL, W. Acrobat, John Robinson's, 1892-93.

AYERS, ANDREW JACKSON. See Gus Brooks Clarke.

AYMAR, ALBERT F. Equestrian. Brother of **John P., Lewis D., Walter B.**, and **William T. Aymar**. Winter circus, Niblo's Garden, NYC, 1843-44; John Tryon's, Bowery Amphitheatre,

NYC, 1844; Sands, Lent & Co., 1848-49; Den Stone's, 1854; Washburn's, 1855, 1857; Flagg & Aymar, 1856; Antonio & Wilder, 1858; Robinson & Lake, Cincinnati, 1859; Antonio Bros.', 1860; Goodwin & Wilder, Boston, 1861; Robinson & Lake, 1861-62; Thayer & Noyes, 1862-63; Robinson & Howes, which became Howes & Norton, 1864; DeHaven & Haight, 1865; New American Theatre, Philadelphia, winter 1865-66; Franklin J. Howes', 1865; Caldwell's, 1867; Lake's, 1868; Dan Rice's, 1868; Stowe & Norton, 1869; equestrian director, clown and rider, John Stowe & Sons, 1871; C. W. Noyes', 1872; James W. Wilder & Co., 1873; Warner & Henderson, 1874; clown, Howes & Cushing, 1875. Had a farm near Berrien Springs, MI, in the 1870s, where he fitted up a practice ring. By 1878 was keeping a bowling alley and restaurant there.

AYMAR, CHARLES. Performed as an equestrian chiefly in California with such as Orrin Bros.', San Francisco, 1863.

AYMAR, EDWARD. Cooper, Bailey & Co., 1876.

AYMAR, ELIZABETH. Equestrienne. At Niblo's Garden, NYC, 1843-44; John Tryon's, Bowery Amphitheatre, NYC, 1844; Washburn's, 1855; Robinson & Lake, Wood's Theatre, Cincinnati, 1859; Antonio Bros.', 1860; Goodwin & Wilder, Boston, 1861; Robinson & Lake, 1861-62; Thayer & Noyes, 1862-63; Howes & Norton, 1864; New American Theatre, Philadelphia, winter 1865-66; Franklin J. Howes', 1865; Caldwell's, 1867; Lake's, 1868; Dan Rice's, 1868; Stowe & Norton, 1869; John Stowe & Sons, 1871; C. W. Noyes', 1872; Warner & Henderson, 1874.

AYMAR, EMMA. Equestrienne, Great European, 1865.

AYMAR, FRANK. Clown, Charles Noyes', winter 1871-72.

AYMAR, JAMES. Clown. Parisian Circus, Philadelphia, fall 1876; Basye's, 1879.

AYMAR, JENNIE. Allen's Great Eastern, 1879.

AYMAR, JOHN. (1826-1843) Acrobat and rider, brother of **Walter B.** and **William T. Aymar.** From Patterson, NJ. Apprenticed to Aaron Turner from 1833 to perhaps 1838, when he stopped being listed as Master Aymar. Rode with the winter circus at Richmond Hill, NYC, 1837; Thomas Taplin Cooke's, 1838; S. H. Nichols', 1838-39; Welch, Bartlett & Co., 1839; Grecian Arena and Classic Circus, 1841; Howes & Mabie, 1843. There was a **John Aymar** recorded as an equestrian with the winter circus at Niblo's Garden, 1843-44, and with Welch & Mann, 1845. The latter engagements are questionable for he may have been dead. A **John Aymar** was killed in England attempting to do a triple somersault. Was one of 4 Aymars to enter the circus business. Is remembered as an intelligent young man and an entertaining conversationalist, a performer of some ability and daring. Was said to be the first on record to do a double-somersault over 4 horses. Is also recorded as having completed a triple somersault with Batty's Circus, London. Legend has it that he met a performer who had seen some Arabs in Paris accomplish the triple in

practice. Aymar then became determined to perfect the feat, apparently using no springboard, relying entirely on extraordinary strength. Performed the triple at the benefit of **Tom Barry**, the clown. Was killed some time later when he tried to repeat the feat, landing on his forehead and braking his neck, age 25 or 33, depending on which source one uses. There is disagreement as to when and where this occurred. One source gives Manchester, England, as the place; another states that he was killed at Batty's Circus, St. Hilliers, Isle of Jersey, England, August 17, 1843; but he probably died in 1859. Wife was an equestrienne with John Tryon's circus at the Bowery Amphitheatre, NYC, 1843.

AYMAR, LOTTIE. Bareback equestrienne and trapeze performer. Daughter of **Walter B. Aymar.** Records show her performing as early as 1861 with Bassett & Aymar, South America; later, Sells Bros.', 1882; Adam Forepaugh's, 1883; New York and New England (**O. J. Ferguson's**), 1884; Dockrill's, winter 1885-86; Miller, Okey & Freeman, 1886; Barnum & Bailey, 1889; Orrin Bros.', winter 1889-90; Ringling Bros.', 1891-94; McDonald & Reichhold, 1896; Sig. Sautelle's, 1897. First husband **Harry Wambold**. Later married **Doc Miller**, high pedestal equilibrist, 1891.

AYMAR, PAULINE. Equestrienne, Warner & Henderson's, 1874.

AYMAR, W. FREDERICK. (d. December 22, 1897) Formerly known as **William F. Aymar**; son of **William T. Aymar**, the proprietor of Flagg & Aymar. Franconi brought his mother to America as a special feature for the Franconi Royal Hippodrome, NYC. At 7, Frederick was doing a posturing act. Principal rider, Metcalf's, 1868; Adam Forepaugh's, 1869; Centennial Circus, 1870; Walter B. Aymar's, South America, early 1870s; troupe returned to the United States, 1875, and performed at Bidwell's Academy of Music, New Orleans; ringmaster, Lowande's Great Brazilian, 1877; ringmaster and clown, P. T. Barnum's, 1878-79; Allen's Great Eastern, 1879-80; Sell Bros.', 1880-81; agent, Burr Robbins', 1885; Jane Coombs Dramatic Co., winter 1886-87; equestrian director, King & Franklin, 1888-90; returned to Sells management with S. H. Barrett's New United Monster Shows; Charles Bartine's, 1890; equestrian director and clown, Walter L. Main's, 1892; press agent, Walter L. Main's, 1893; and equestrian director, Walter L. Main's, 1894-97. Died at his home in Dayton, Ohio.

AYMAR, WALTER B. (1832-June 9, 1891) Equestrian. Brother of **John P., Lewis D., Albert F.,** and **William T. Aymar.** Juvenile rider, Nathan Howes', 1845, at age 15. With William, took a circus company overland to California, said to be the first troupe to do so. The brothers then visited Peru and other South American countries. Western unit, June, Titus, Angevine & Co., 1842; John Tryon's, 1845; Sands, Lent & Co., 1846-48; Alvah Mann's, 1849; advertised by Spalding & Rogers, 1850-52, as "the modern centaur and great bareback trick rider"; Green B. Johnson's, 1851; Sands, Nathans & Co., 1854; Spalding & Rogers, 1851-54; bareback rider, Washburn's, 1855; Flagg & Aymar, 1856; John Robinson's, 1856; Sands & Nathans, 1857; Nixon & Kemp, 1857. Advertised as: "He performs with astonishing rapidity, The Erratic Spheres, or Revolving Orbs while lying on his back, on the back of his horse." Nixon & Kemp, 1857; Burt & (Yankee) Robinson's, 1858; co-proprietor (with **George J. Arnold**), Louisa Wells Equestrian Troupe, winter 1858-59; Wilson's "Dan Rice", California, 1860; Bassett's, South America, 1861. Following year, company encountered financial trouble; Bassett was taken ill and unable to continue; Aymar and wife took over. Robinson & Howes, 1864; equestrian director, Burr Robbins', 1879-80; Allen's Great Eastern, 1880; Cooper & Jackson, 1881; Sells Bros.', 1882; scenic rider, William O. Dale Stevens', Boston, 1883; equestrian director, Cooper, Jackson & Co., 1884; O. J. Ferguson's, 1884; Dockrill's, South America, winter 1885-86. Wife, **Maggie** (nee **Manley**), died, NYC, June 8, 1909, leaving a daughter, **Lottie**, and a son, **William**.

AYMAR, WILLIAM F. See W. Frederick Aymar.

AYMAR, WILLIAM T. (June 23, 1830-March 16, 1883) Clown and general performer. Born in Brooklyn, NY. Brother of **Walter B., Lewis D., Albert F.,** and **John P.** Entered circus business, 1841, after being trained by John. Took what was said to be the first circus to go overland to California with brother Walter; then visited Peru and other South American countries. After 6 months, returned to San Francisco where he opened a livery stable. Subsequently, returned to the circus business: Sands & Lent, 1848-50; Spalding & Rogers, 1851-52; Den Stone's, 1854. Reported to have somersaulted over 10 horses, Washburn's, 1855. Co-proprietor, Flagg & Aymar, 1856; Joe Pentland's, 1857-58; Louisa Wells' Equestrian Troupe, 1859; Wilson's "Dan Rice," 1860; Bassett & Aymar, South America, 1861; Robinson & Lake, 1862; Orrin Bros.', San Francisco, 1863; Frank J. Howes', 1865; clown and leaper, New York Champs Elysees, 1866; Adam Forepaugh's, Philadelphia, winter 1866-67, where he finished his leaps by throwing himself over the elephant Hannibal; Barnum, VanAmburgh & Castello, 1867; clown, Dan Castello's, 1867-68; Adam Forepaugh's, 1869; European and American, winter 1869-70; Newton's, 1872; clown, leaper, tumbler, P. T. Barnum's, 1873; general director, Allen's Great Eastern, 1879-80; Beckett's, 1881. A good general performer who somersaulted over horses and elephants, did a Pete Jenkins act, and was among the first to do the perch in America. During performance with a circus at Coney Island, injured himself, causing lung hemorrhaging, which led to his death.

AYMAR, WILLIAM, JR. (d. December 29, 1888) Son of equestrian family of **Walter** and **Maggie Aymar** (nee **Margaret Manley**). Acrobat, P. T. Barnum's, 1877; John H. Murray's, West Indies, winter 1878-79; Allen's Great Eastern, 1879; Sells Bros.', 1882; Hilliard & Main, 1883; bareback somersault rider, New York and New England (O. J. Ferguson, proprietor), 1884; Walter L. Main's, 1888; Frank A. Gardner's, West Indies, winter 1888-89. Died in Kingston, Jamaica.

AYRES, DAVID. Gymnast. Fell from a trapeze bar, Truxillo, Peru, December 18, 1864.

AYRES, PROF. G. G. Grady's, 1869.

B

BABCOCK, ANSON. See A. D. VanZandt.

BABCOCK, PROF. Troupe of 12 performing horses, Albert Hose's, 1893.

BABCOCK, STEPHEN SLY. (1824-1894) Moved to Delavan, WI, 1846, and engaged in farming and the grocery business. Formed a partnership with H. Buckley & Co., 1857, and traveled throughout the southwest, Gulf States, Cuba and other West Indies. Experienced 2 years of countless setbacks, ranging from attacks by Indians and bandits to a shipwreck in the Carribbean. General agent, Dan Castello & William C. Coup's, 1870. After retiring from the circus business, was elected county sheriff and also town president of Delavan.

BACKENSTOE, ED. 40-horse and chariot driver, James M. Nixon's, 1859; Backenstoe's Cosmopolitan Circus (boat and wagon), 1868; controlled outside and inside privileges, James Robinson's, 1869, exhibiting the **Albino Children** and the bearded child, **Martini**, and his trained mice, plus monkeys, bears and birds; managing director, Backenstoe's Cosmopolitan Circus, 1871-72; had a circus sold at sheriff's auction in Memphis, October 17, 1872. Was located in Eureka, CA, 1905, where he was a meat and milk inspector.

BACKUS, CHARLES. (1831-June 21, 1883) Ethiopian entertainer. Born in Rochester, NY. Was known primarily as a negro minstrel. Married 3 times—the first wife, **Leo Hudson**, from whom he was separated, died in 1873; married actress **Kate Newton**, 1868, who died shortly after the first wife; 1876, married **Tizzie Mason**. Was financially engaged with his brother in a grocery store in Rochester and in a jewelry store on Broadway, NYC. Died of Bright's desease in the latter city, age 52. Early professional employment with Hubble & Co., 1842; 1852, moved to California and 2 years later formed the Backus Minstrels in San Francisco Hall; took a company to Australia, 1855, returning to San Francisco Hall the following year; made a tour of the California interior, 1859, as Horn & Backus Minstrels; went back to Australia with the San Francisco Minstrels. While there, abandoned minstrelsy for the circus, joining as clown with Burton's for some 8 months; in England, appeared as a clown, Astley's Amphitheatre; returned to California, 1861, and organized a company for a tour; revisited England, 1882, where he was a member of the Moore & Burgess' Minstrels.

BACON, CHARLES H. Rider. As an 8 year old apprentice, made debut at the Lafayette Amphitheatre, NYC, in its initial season, August 1825; Washington Gardens, Boston, October 1825; Price & Simpson, Washington Amphitheatre, Boston, 1826; William Harrington's, 1829; clown, William Blanchard's, 1830; Aaron Turner's, 1830; rider, Fogg & Stickney, 1830; William Harrington's, 1831-32; Palmer & Harrington, 1834; rider, Bancker & Harrington, 1835; J. W. Bancker's, 1836; Nathan A. Howes', 1836; Charles H. Bacon's, 1837-38; rider and proprietor, Bacon & Derious, 1838; rider, Welch & Mann, 1841; Welch & Delavan, Baltimore, 1841; riding master, Howes & Mabie, 1841; clown, Rockwell & Stone, 1846; scenic rider, Victory Circus, 1847; clown, June & Titus, 1848; Levi J. North's New York Amphitheatre, 1851; R. Sands, G. C. Quick & Co., 1853.

BACON, JOSEPH. Rider. Nathan A. Howes', 1836; Bacon & Derious, 1838; Welch, Bartlett & Co., 1839.

BACON, MRS. C. H. Bancker & Harrington's National Gymnasium and American Arena Co., 1835.

BACON, OLIVER ["Master"]. Rider, Frost, Husted & Co., 1836.

BADER, EUGENE. Acrobat, VanAmburgh's, 1881.

BALIET, I. S. Treasurer, LaPearl's, 1897.

BAILEY, CHARLES. Boss canvasman. James T. Johnson's, 1884; Forepaugh & Samwells (**W. R. Forepaugh, Thomas Samwells**, proprietors), 1886; cookhouse and candy stand privileges, Gollmar Bros.', 1897.

BAILEY, CURT L. Co-proprietor, Bailey & Winan, 1889-90; proprietor, Bailey's, 1891.

BAILEY, EDDIE. Morosco's Royal Russian Circus, 1885.

BAILEY, FREDERICK HARRISON. (1814-1881) Agent, business manager. Nephew to **Hachaliah Bailey**. Was known as Col. Bailey, discoverer of the young **James A. Bailey** and the source of his name. First mentioned as agent with Banigan & Kelly, 1847; later that year, Raymond & Waring; agent, Welch, Delavan & Nathans, 1850; manager, Welch's National Circus, Raymond & Co.'s and Driesbach & Co.'s Menageries United, 1852; agent, Ballard & Bailey, 1855; Welch & Lent, 1856; associated for many years with old John Robinson and Robinson & Lake, 1859-63, 1865-68, 1871-78; business manager, Lake & Co., 1864; manager, National Circus, Cincinnati, 1865; agent, Great Union Combination (Robinson's), 1865; advertiser, Haight & Chambers, 1867; advertiser, Hemmings, Cooper & Whitby, 1869; agent, John Robinson's, 1871; Charles Noyes', 1871; general agent, Ed G. Basye's, 1878; railroad contractor, Sells Bros.', 1878. Was divorced from his wife, **Kate Bailey**, Cincinnati, May 17, 1879, after about 16 years of marriage. His step-daughter, **Frankie Bailey**, married **Charles Robinson**, son of old John.

BAILEY, GEORGE FOX. (October 29, 1818-February 20, 1903) Born in North Salem, NY, the nephew of old **Hachaliah Bailey** and son-in-law of **Aaron Turner**. One of **P. T. Barnum's** silent partners, 1876-80. One of the greatest showmen of his generation. Started in the circus field with Aaron Turner's, where he learned the business; married

14

Turner's daughter and later became his partner at a time when P. T. Barnum was Turner's treasurer. When Turner retired, Bailey took control of the show; was out with the title of Ballard & Bailey, 1855, and by 1860 was advertising the show under his own name, G. F. Bailey & Co. Acquiring a hippopotamus years before Barnum, he toured the midwest, 1857, under the title of The Grand Metropolitan Quadruple Combination Consisting of George F. Bailey & Co.'s Circus, Herr Driesbach's Menagerie, G. C. Quick's Colossal Hippopotamus, and Sands, Nathans & Co.'s Performing Elephants. After several years of solo operation, became a partner, 1858, with Avery Smith, John Nathans and Lewis June, second generation "Flatfoots." They took out the Barnum show, 1876-80. Retired after being in the business for 40 years. Died in NYC, age 85, leaving an estate of over a half-million dollars.

BAILEY, HACHALIAH. (1775-September 2, 1845) Native of Stephentown (later named Somers), Westchester County, NY. A shrewd businessman, bought an elephant, "Old Bet," for $1,000 around 1808. With other animals added, monkeys and a bear or two, the Bailey caravan toured the nearby centers of population with what was said to be the second elephant to be exhibited in America. Erected an inn, 1823, in North Salem which was named the Elephant Hotel. A wooden replica of "Old Bet" was placed on a stone foundation in front of it and dedicated in 1827. Was the father of **James P.**, **Joseph T.** and **Lewis** and uncle of **George F. Bailey.** Died at age 70.

BAILEY, IDA. Trained dogs, with Charles Bartine's, 1892.

BAILEY, KATE. Equilibrist and ascensionist, George W. DeHaven's, 1865.

BAILEY, LEWIS. Partner with **J. Purdy Brown**, 1825, in a circus venture, Brown's first season under canvas, which marked the beginning of the use of tents for traveling circuses. Listed as riding master, J. Purdy Brown's troupe in the South, 1828.

BAILEY, JAMES ANTHONY [r. n. James Anthony McGinness]. (July 4, 1847-April 11, 1906) Born in Detroit, MI. Father died, 1852, his mother a few years later. At age 11 was working on a farm for $3.50 a month and board. Age 13 joined Robinson & Lake, June 17, 1860, in Pontiac, MI, and came under the tutelage of advance agent **Frederick H. Bailey**, from whom he took the name. Remained with this show through 1862, working in the off season as a bill poster in Cincinnati. Winter, 1863, employed at the Nashville (TN) Theatre, bill posting, selling tickets and ushering. Became a sutler's clerk that year, selling provisions to the soldiers until the end of the Civil War. When only 18, re-entered circus business as assistant agent and boss billposter, Lake's Olympiad, 1866-67; general agent, Lake's, 1868-69; half owner concert privileges, Hemmings, Cooper & Whitby, 1870; general agent, Hemmings & Cooper, 1871; all privileges (with George Middleton), Hemmings & Cooper, 1872; bought Hemming's quar-

ter-interest, 1873; after Whitby was killed the following year, Bailey acquired his holdings. Circus went to Australia, 1876, and met with considerable success, being the first in the antipodes; then toured New Zealand and South America. Following South American tour, the only unsuccessful one Bailey experienced, the show returned to the United States, December, 1878. Illuminated the performances by electricity, the first time for a tented exhibition, 1879. Winter quarters, Philadelphia, 1880, the first baby elephant in captivity was born, creating a publicity sensation. Cooper & Bailey joined with the Barnum show, 1881. There followed a succession of circus phenomena: the famous Jumbo acquisition; the instigation of 3 rings under a single canvas and a hippodrome track; Bailey's purchasing the interests of J. L. Hutchinson, W. W. Cole and J. E. Cooper in the Barnum & London Shows, October 27, 1887, at Madison Square Garden, the show henceforth being known as Barnum & Bailey; Barnum & Bailey's London engagement, 1890; acquiring of the Adam Forepaugh circus, 1891, following the death of Forepaugh; the Barnum & Bailey Circus European tour, 1898; and Bailey's purchase of the Sells Bros. circus and Buffalo Bill's Wild West show. Married **Miss Ruth Louisa McCaddon**, who was born in Zanesville, OH, 1868. Died at his home, "The Knolls," Mt. Vernon, NY, leaving an estate worth 5 to 8 million dollars and a legacy as the greatest showman of his day. His wife died March 11, 1912, at Hobe Island, FL

BAILEY, JAMES PURDY. (1812-1853) Agent. Son of **Hackaliah** and brother of **Lewis** and **Joseph T. Bailey.** Brown's, 1832-33; co-proprietor, Joseph T. and James P. Bailey's, 1834-35; manager, Ludlow & Smith, 1841; agent, Robinson & Foster, 1843.

BAILEY, JOSEPH TODD. (b. 1807) Son of **Hackaliah** and brother of **Lewis** and **James P. Bailey.** Co-proprietor, J. T. and J. P. Bailey's Menagerie and Circus, 1834-35.

BAILEY, LEWIS. Son of **Hackaliah** and brother of **James P.** and **Joseph T. Bailey.** Believed to have been in partnership with **J. Purdy Brown** when the concern was the first to use a canvas tent, 1825; co-proprietor, Purdy, Carley & Bailey's meneagerie, 1831.

BAILEY, MOLLIE KIRKLAND [Mrs. A. H. Hardesty]. (November 2, 1844-October 2, 1918) One of the few successful female circus managers. After starting in show business at age 16, took over circus management when husband, **Gus Bailey**, died, June, 1896, continuing a show that had been operated since 1870. That year the show was reported having an outfit of 20 wagons, 60 head of horses and 35 people in the company. Children and other family members were involved in the troupe's activity, which created a "folksy" atmosphere. The show toured Texas and surrounding states as Mollie Bailey's Great Southern Show, abandoning wagons for rail in 1907. Died at Houston, TX, age 82.

BAILEY, MONT. Boss canvasman, Wintermute Bros.',

1897.

BAILEY, SOLOMON. (1788-1859) Animal keeper. Probably connected with Bailey, Brown & Co., 1832; J. T. and J. P. Bailey's, 1834; Menagerie and Aviary from the Zoological Institute, Philadelphia, 1835; the Zoological Exhibition from Baltimore, 1836.

BAILS, TONY. Manager of the variety troupe with Haight & Chambers' Circus, 1867.

BAIRD, BANCK. Band leader, Cooper & Co.'s, 1897.

BAIRD, ED. Advance agent, Wintermute Bros.', 1897.

BAIRD, J. W. (1848-January 12, 1908) Showman. Born in Salem, OH. Began professional career, 1866, as a trick bicycle rider; joined Johnson's the following year; then organized Smith & Baird's Circus, 1872, but closed early when a large section of the seats fell and fatally injured members of the audience. Privileges, Great Eastern, 1874; organized Baird & Howell, 1875, which was short-lived; following the season, organized Baird's Minstrels which functioned until 1889. Retired from the road because of illness and settled in Portland, OR, to engage in a real estate business. Died there, age 60.

BAKER, A. W. Contracting agent, G. G. Grady's, 1871.

BAKER BROTHERS. Acrobats and hat spinners, Albert M. Wetter's New Model Shows, 1893.

BAKER, C. A. Calliope player, Barnum & London, 1884-85.

BAKER, CHARLES H. ["Pop"]. (December 9, 1836-April 28, 1915) Born in Buffalo, NY, the son of a museum manager, which influenced him to organize his own sideshows. Got credit for bringing negro minstrel **George Primrose** into the circus. Curiosities "discovered" include **Dr. DeGrandell Danis,** "human skeleton;" **Mme. Squires,** bearded lady; **Fannie Wallace,** fat lady; **Jim Dukes,** whose strength was all in his shoulders; as well as, a duck with 6 feet, an elephant with but 3 feet, and a monkey who was friendly with an untamed kangaroo. Amazed the public in the 1860s when he brought out an educated pig. Later years, conducted a glass blowing stand in Cleveland and other cities until failing health forced retirement. All in all, was in the entertainment business 59 years. Died in Toledo, OH, age 79.

BAKER, D. L. Buckley & Co.'s Circus, 1857-58.

BAKER, J. J. Band leader, Dan Ducello's United Exhibitions, 1879.

BAKER, JOE. See Joseph Hampshire.

BAKER, JOSEPH. Boss canvasman, P. T. Barnum's, 1871-72.

BAKER, MAUDE. Gardner & Donovan, South America, 1886.

BAKER, RICHARD. Detective, P. T. Barnum's, 1873.

BAKER, TOM. Ethiopian performer. Orton & Older, 1859; clown, Mabie's, 1860; R. Sands & Co., 1861.

BAKER, THOMAS. Leader of promenade orchestra, James M. Nixon's Cremorne Gardens, NYC, 1862.

BALDOCK, JAMES E. Charles Bartine's, 1888.

BALDWIN, PROF. CHET. Aeronaut, George W. Hall's, 1897.

BALDWIN, DAN. Principal leaper and tumbler, Bruce L. Baldwin's, 1894.

BALDWIN, E. Acrobat, G. A. Courtney's, West Indies, 1880-81.

BALDWIN, BRUCE L. Showman. Went to California with Yankee Robinson, 1877; when the show collapsed, went with a dime museum up the Columbia River country; co-owner, Young Bros. & Baldwin, 1892; proprietor, Baldwin's Railroad Shows, 1893-94.

BALDWIN, CHARLES M. Boss hostler, F. J. Taylor's, 1891.

BALDWIN, C. S. Assistant manager, Ed G. Basye's Cosmopolitan Circus, 1878.

BALDWIN, EDWARD. Gymnast, Hamilton & Sergeant, 1877-78; balancer, Barnum, Bailey & Hutchinson, 1881; London Sensation Show, 1879; Orrin Bros.', 1883; Daniel Shelby's, 1888.

BALDWIN, EDWARD O. Boxer (with **James O. Conner**), Howes Trans-Atlantic Circus and Risbeck's Menagerie (**Frank Howes,** proprietor), 1868.

BALDWIN, GEORGE. Bill poster, P. T. Barnum's, 1873.

BALDWIN, HENRY. Boss hostler, Gardner & Hemmings, 1863.

BALDWIN, LOTTIE. Single trapeze, Barnum, Bailey & Hutchinson, 1881.

BALDWIN, O. F. Proprietor, Baldwin, Wall & Co.'s Great Eastern, 1880.

BALDWIN, PLATT. Juggler. Howes & Mabie, 1841; Dr. Gilbert R. Spalding's, 1844.

BALDWIN, SAM. Robinson & Howes, 1864.

BALDWIN, SILAS D. (March 4, 1825-June 3, 1867) Juggler. Born in New Jersey. Entered show business at 13 years of age, beginning as a contortionist in hall shows; later played bones in minstrel band at the Coliseum on Broadway. Joined the circus as a contortionist but later became one of the most popular jugglers in the business. An imposing figure with his height of 6' 4". Dr. Gilbert R. Spalding's, 1842, 1844-45, 1847; S. P. Stickney's, 1846, 1848-49; Robinson & Eldred, 1850; World Circus, 1851; Spalding & Rogers, 1853-54; Flagg & Aymar, 1856; John Robinson's, 1857; Robinson & Lake, Wood's Theatre, Cincinnati, 1859; Robinson & Lake, 1860; G. K. Goodwin, 1860; Tom King's, 1862; Antonio Bros.', billed as the "Hindu Juggler," 1862; Lake & Co., 1864; Howe & Norton, 1864; National Circus, Cincinnati, 1865; Lake's, 1865; Dan Castello's, 1866; Dan Rice's, managed by **Adam Forepaugh,** 1866. Died of typhoid fever at Harrisburg, PA, while with O'Brien & Whitby's Circus.

BALE, HARDY. See H. Hardella.

BALIZE, SIGNOR. Lion king. Campbell's Zoological and Equestrian Institute, 1870; Sheldenburger's & Co., 1871.

BALL, J. A. Proprietor, Ball's Great Coliseum, 1864; partner, Ball & Fitzpatrick's, 1865; Thompson, Smith & Hawes, 1866; Caldwell's Occidental Circus, 1867.

BALL, RICHARD GUY. (January 1, 1844-August 10, 1905) Contracting agent. Born in Philadelphia. Had only 3 months formal schooling but became a well informed man. Career began as a candy butcher for **Jake Jakeway** of L. B. Lent's, 1859; following year, at age 16, joined the advance of Gardner & Hemmings, 1860, under general agent W. H. Gardner, and continued under Gardner's supervision until 1863, when, in mid-season, acquired the candy stands with the show. When war broke out, joined the army and saw service with Company D, First Michigan Cavalry until 1865. After leaving the service, managed the advance with Dr. James L. Thayer's, 1866; but was back with Gardner, who was an agent for John O'Brien's, 1867-72; following year, became general agent for the show; rejoined Gardner as contracting agent, Cooper & Bailey, 1874-78, visiting Australia and South America; contracting agent, Adam Forepaugh's, 1879; Cooper & Bailey, 1880; P. T. Barnum's, 1880; Barnum, Bailey & Hutchinson, 1881-84 until illness was followed by death. Died at Home of Incurables. After starting in the business for $10 a month and board, he ended as one of the highest salaried contracting agents. In his prime, was considered superior at contracting bill posters, hotel proprietors, liverymen and city and state officials. Due to a generous nature, his financial condition left him helpless as an invalid.

BALL, T. T. Agent, Hobson Bros., 1893.

BALLARD, ED M. (1873-November 6, 1936) Proprietor, Hagenbeck & Wallace, 1917; American Circus Corp., 1921-29.

BALLARD, OSMOND. Sideshowman. Connected in the 1850s with Bailey & Co. Exhibited the "What Is It?" under the name of the **Wild African Boy**, "the connecting link between man and monkey," before the oddity came into the possession of **P. T. Barnum.** Broadway Menagerie, 1853; proprietor, Ballard, Bailey & Co., 1855-56; early 1860s, set up a concert saloon, the "What Is It?" at 600 Broadway, NYC.

BALLON, MRS. Fat woman, Sheldenburger & Co., 1871.

BALNAN, JAMES [r. n. James Murphy]. (d. May 24, 1908) Clown, Adam Forepaugh's, 1892. Died in NYC.

BANCKER, ED H. (December 23, 1836-October 3, 1902) Ethiopian performer. Born in New Orleans. Played the drum in the band of Sam Stickney's circus at age 10 alongside the celebrated **Ned Kendall.** With Dan Rice's following year as Ethiopian performer. First appeared NYC, 1853, Old Broadway Theatre, doing bones solo for T. D. Rice's benefit; followed by engagements with various minstrel troupes. In New Orleans at outbreak of Civil War, where he enlisted in the Fifth Louisiana Regiment and served in the post band at Richmond, VA; later, went to the front and was taken prisoner and sent to Washington, DC, before being pardoned by President Lincoln. At Old Bowery Theatre, NYC, George Christy's Minstrels, July, 1865; member of the variety troupe, Haight & Chambers' circus, 1867; author of several Ethiopian sketches, among them "The Wig Maker," "Too Hot For Comfort," "The Colored Policeman," etc. Also said to be the originator of the "change act" in which he changed from black to white and black again within a few seconds. Died in Minneapolis, MN, with suspicion that he was murdered for the $100 he had in his posession; connected at the time with the "A Night Before Christmas" Co. as the blind fidler.

BANCKER, JAMES W. (d. February 22, 1866) Rider, general performer. Native of New York and a true descendant of the early Knickerbockers; name can be traced to Dedrick Bancker, the Verryvongers, Von der Schiders, and the Von Spiglers. An uncle, **Abraham Bancker,** was a celebrated spy for General Washington. As a youth was fond of the drum and became a masterful performer of it at the age of 8. Began his profession at the old Richmond Hill Circus, NYC, as a "cross vaulter," which consisted of varied and difficult leaps. James West's, 1825, performing feats of balancing and still-vaulting; J. Purdy Brown's company, 1825; Lafayette Amphitheatre, NYC, its initial season, 1825-26; Samuel McCracken's company, 1825-26; Parson's (**Samuel McCracken,** manager), Albany, 1826; Tivoli Gardens, Philadelphia, 1826; J. Purdy Brown's, 1827; Samuel Parsons', Troy, NY, 1828; rider, Bernard & Page, 1829; clown, Fogg & Stickney, 1830-31; scenic rider, John Lamb's, 1831. His own equestrian company appeared at the Richmond Hill Circus, NYC, 1832, and toured the New England states that year. Formed a partnership with **William Harrington,** another expert rider, 1835, and toured the South with Bancker & Harrington's National Gymnasium and American Arena Co. Harrington died within a year and Bancker took **George Sweet** as partner but refused to do business with the monopolistic Zoological Institute, which sent an opposition circus to break them, giving away tickets, performing for no admission, and using every means, fair and unfair, to destroy them. After being hounded through Pennsylvania, New York, and Canada, Sweet gave in and Bancker, discouraged, sold out to the Institute. Manager, James Raymond's Olympic, 1843-44; agent, Mann, Welch & Delavan, 1844-45; Welch's National Circus, Philadelphia, 1845; Welch & Delavan, 1847; agent, Welch, Delavan & Nathans, 1848-49; agent, Welch & Lent's, 1855-56; agent, L. B. Lent's, 1859. For many years was associated with **L. B. Lent** as partner and other business capacities. After retirement from the circus, kept a saloon in Philadelphia on Walnut Street near Eighth. All in all, was considered a dashing rider, a clown of the "old school," one of the early practitioners of scenic riding, and one of the best cross vaulters ever seen in America, as well as a first class advertiser. At one time threw 30 successive forward somersaults (or jerk forwards). The first American showman to use the word "circus" to describe a company rather than a building when, in 1824, he advertised Bancker's New York Circus. He may have been the first American-born circus proprietor. On the afternoon of February 21, 1866, a benefit was given for him at Fox's American Theatre, Philadelphia, to lend comfort to his declining years. At the close of the performance he accompanied **Frank Brower** and **Sam Sanford** to the nearby saloon, formerly kept by him. At about 4:00 p.m., was taken seriously ill, necessitating his two companions to convey him to his residence. There he fell into an insensible state until 1:00 a.m. of the 22nd, when he quietly passed away, terminating what had been a lengthy professional career of over 40 years.

BANCKER, S. W. Agent. Married **Miss E. J. Dickinson**, 1859.

BANCROFT, ALF T. Clown, Prof. E. Hamilton's Great New York Circus, 1877.

BANIGAN, PETER. Turner's, 1841; treasurer, Rockwell & Stone, 1843, 1846; manager, Raymond & Waring, 1846-47; co-proprietor, Banigan & Kelly (Raymond & Co.) menagerie, 1847.

BANKS, C. R. Manager, N. B. and T. V. Turner's, 1841; treasurer, Rockwell & Stone, 1843; treasurer, Rockwell & Stone (Stone's unit), 1846; Banks & Archer, Central America, winter 1846; manager, Rockwell & Stone (Banks unit), 1847; Banks & Archer, Central America, 1847; Banks & Archer, Central America, 1848; Banks, Archer & Rockwell, South America, 1849-50.

BANKS, LOUISA. See Louisa Brower.

BANKS, WILLIAM. Clown. Died May 27, 1873, Chicago.

BANNERMAN, WILLIAM A. See Albion Brothers.

BAUSCHER, A. C. Annex manager, Gollmar Bros.', 1897.

BENNETT, H. M. (March 2, 1831-April 11, 1902) California banker. Co-proprietor, Lee & Bennett's California Circus, San Francisco, 1856-57.

BENNETT, SAM. 4-horse rider, Holland, Bowman & McLaughlin, 1890; jockey hurdle rider, F. J. Taylor's, 1891.

BAPTISTE, MONS. Man monkey, at Hippotheatron, 14th Street, NYC, 1864.

BARBER, ORRIN. Menches & Barber, 1887; proprietor, Orrin Barber's, 1888.

BARCLAY, ESTELLE. Juvenile equestrienne. Dan Rice's, 1857-60. Was variously billed as "Mlle. Estella," "Mlle. Estrella," and "Mad'lle Estrello." Playing off the **Ella Zoyara** rage at Niblo's Garden, NYC, 1860, Rice billed her as Ella Zoyara that season. Probably the sister of **Fred Barclay**. Married comedian **Frank Drew**, 1860, and disappeared from the ring.

BARCLAY, FRED. (August 3, 1850-July 22, 1907) Rider, general performer. Native of Washington, DC. Adopted by **Dan Rice** and trained for the ring. First performed, 1857. Advertised as "A precocious youth in a dashing act of Retro Equitation, introducing Bounds, Leaps, Pirouettes and Som-

ersaults on his Golden Cream." Dan Rice's, 1857-60; Cooke's Royal Circus, Niblo's Garden, NYC, January 1860. Probably the brother of **Estelle Barclay**. Volunteered for the Spanish-American War with the First Florida Infantry, Co. E. While encamped in Cuba, contracted malaria and never really recovered. Cooke's Royal Amphitheatre, Niblo's Garden, NYC, January, 1860; Goodwin & Wilder, Howard Athenaeum, Boston, 1861; Dan Rice's, 1860-62, 1866-68; United States Circus (**Frank Howes, Joseph Cushing**, proprietors), 1867; Charles Noyes' (former Paris Pavilion, set up in New Orleans under the proprietorship of Spalding and Bidwell), April, 1870, Texas, 1870; equestrian and somersault performer, Philadelphia Circus, corner of Tenth and Callowhill Streets, winter 1870-71; Dan Rice's Paris Pavilion Circus, 1871-72, in an enactment of the sports and pastimes of the Comanche tribe, including a buffalo hunt, called "Life Pictures on the Prairies." [St. Louis *Missouri Democrat*, 1871: "He is, moreover, an actor of no mean ability, as was manifested by his impersonation of a Comanche warrior."] James E. Cooper's, 1873; rider, Maginley & Co., 1874; Cooper and Bailey, 1875; Cooper, Bailey & Co., Australian tour, 1876-78; bareback, somersault and principal rider, Robinson's, winter 1877-78; W. W. Cole's, California, 1880, and for Australian tour; principal rider, Sells Bros.', 1878; gymnast and rider, John Robinson's, 1878-79; principal rider, W. W. Cole's, 1881; bareback, somersault, hurdle, bounding jockey rider, Nathans & Co.'s, 1882; Orrin Bros.', Mexico, March 1883; Nathans & Co.'s, 1883; principal bareback rider, Pullman, Mack & Co., 1884; Orrin Bros.', Mexico, February 1884; bareback rider, French & Monroe, 1885; Pubillones' Circus, Cuba, 1886-87; hurdle and Indian rider, Howes' New London, 1887. Died in San Francisco.

BARCLAY, MRS. ANNIE. Cooper, Bailey & Co. Australian tour, 1877. Probably the wife of **Fred Barclay**.

BARETTA THEODORE. Acrobat. Baretta-LaRosa Circus, 1886; Ringling Bros.', 1887; hurdle rider, Doris & Colvin, 1887; Ferguson's, 1888; gymnast and clown, Walt McCafferty's Great Golden Shows, 1894.

BARGETT, JAMES. Sideshow privilege, Maginley, Carroll & Co., 1867.

BARGUS. General performer, H. P. Madigan's, 1856.

BARKER, ACE. Gymnast. John Robinson's, 1868; Cole & Orton, 1871; D. S. Swadley's, 1872.

BARKLEY, JOHN C. Contortionist. Orton's, 1855, October 1856, February 1857; Mabie's, October 1856, 1857-60.

BARLOW, BILLY. (1849?-October 10, 1914) Clown, with trained dogs and monkeys, 1868. Died at Argenta, AR, age 65.

BARLOW, FRED. Bounding jockey, Gollmar Bros.', 1893.

BARLOW, PETER. Rider, Barnum & Bailey, 1892.

BARMORE, WESLEY. Actor and theatrical manager. Under the name of **S. E. Harris**, stage manager, Welch's National, Philadelphia, 1853; took out a circus in Ohio and Indiana,

1854, moving partly by canal boat; show was auctioned off at Hamilton, OH, May 1855. [Stuart Thayer: "Barmore's company would have been a completely unimportant part of circus history, but for one feature. His troupe hosted the first double perch act in America.... The first understander was **William Libby**; **George Dunbar** and **Frank Donaldson** were the climbers."] Stage manager, Welch & Lent, Philadelphia, 1855.

BARNABO, A. Spanish somersault rider, VanAmburgh's, 1874.

BARNELL, MONS. George W. DeHaven's, 1865.

BARNES, ALPHEUS GEORGE. (1862-1931) Native of Lobo, Ontario, Canada. Started a wagon show, 1895, with the proceeds from the sale of his farm, specializing in exhibiting wild animals at fairs and carnivals for a number of years before organizing a full blown circus.

BARNES, DWIGHT BENNETT. (1846-1935) Attorney. Settled in Delavan, WI, 1855. Played a major role in obtaining finances for various circuses quartered there, and was occasionally the receiver in cases when shows failed. When the Centennial Circus folded, 1876, became the possessor of several small tents, one of which was sold to **Al Ringling**, 1879.

BARNES, WILLIAM. Buckley & Co.'s Circus, 1857-58.

BARNET. Clown. Cayetano's, New Orleans, summer 1817; Pepin & Barnet, Natchez, MS, June 1823.

BARNUM, CHARLES. Boss canvasman, Great Chicago, 1879.

BARNUM, ED D. Boss sideshow canvasman, King & Franklin, 1889.

BARNUM, GEORGE H. Sideshow owner, Dan Rice's, 1881.

BARNUM, HENRY. (1827-July 22, 1902) Born in Bridgeport, CT, a distant relative of **P. T. Barnum**. Entered show business, 1856. Assistant to **Hyatt Frost**, VanAmburgh's, 1866; manager, Barnum and VanAmburgh's, 1867; manager and proprietor (with **O. J. Ferguson, John Lyke**, and **James E. Kelley**) VanAmburgh & Co.'s Golden Menagerie, 1869-71; owned a 10th interest in James E. Kelley's Howes' Great London Circus, 1873-76. Poor economic conditions in the country forced the latter show into sale, January 29, 1877, the new owners being **John Parks** and **Richard Dockrill**. Manager, Cooper & Bailey, 1879-80; superintendent and parade router, Barnum & London, 1884; special agent, Adam Forepaugh's, 1892-93; assistant contractor, Sells & Rentfrow, 1894; Barnum & Bailey, 1895; purchasing agent, Buffalo Bill Wild West Show, 1902. Married **Elizabeth Wilson** of Connersville, IN. Died in a West Superior, WI, Hotel of heart failure, age 75.

BARNUM, PHINEAS TAYLOR. (July 5, 1810-April 7, 1891) Started in business on his own, 1828, opening a fruit and confectionery store. 1831, opened a store of general merchandise. Same year, started a weekly paper, the *Herald of Freedom*, shortly finding himself in jail for libel. Moved to NYC, winter 1834-35, securing a job as a "drummer" for several Chatham Street establishments. Next, opened a boarding house and purchased an interest in a grocery store. Not content with this, purchased the celebrated **"Joice Heth"** for $1,000 and started in show business, opening adjacent to Niblo's Garden with receipts averaging $1,000 a week. This success led to engaging **Sig. Vivalia**, who performed remarkable feats of balancing, plate spinning, etc. Became a ticket seller and secretary and treasurer of Aaron Turner's Circus, 1836. Followed by purchasing a steamboat and with an acting company visited the principal cities on the Mississippi River. Spring 1840, staged variety performances at Vauxhall Garden, NYC, which did not prove profitable. It was there that the celebrated jig dancer, **John Diamond**, was first introduced. With this failure, spring 1841, settled in NYC as an agent for "Sears' Pictorial Illustration of the Bible." September 1841, became a "puff writer" for the Bowery Amphitheatre. By December, had secured Scudder's Museum. For this, purchased the **Fejee Mermaid** from **Moses Kimball** of the Boston Museum, 1842. Introduced **Tom Thumb** to the public the same year. Brought the **Swiss Bell Ringers** to America, 1844. Sailed for Europe with Tom Thumb in January, 1844, remaining abroad until 1847. Toured the USA with the midget that same year. Promoted the sensational **Jenny Lind**, 1850. Traveled as a temperance lecturer, 1851-52. Started a weekly pictorial, *The Illustrated News*, fall 1852. Entered the circus business with **W. C. Coup** and **Dave Castello**, 1871, when more than 60 years old, supplying the cash and reputation for what was perhaps the greatest wagon show of all time. Went on rails the second year, making it possible to play primarily in the larger cities. Remodeled the Hippotheatron, 14th Street, NYC, and opened it on November 18, 1872, but it was destroyed by fire on December 24 of that year. Opened P. T. Barnum's Roman Hippodrome (not a circus) at 26th Street, between Madison and Fourth Avenues, April 1874. That summer took out both his World's Fair and Circus and Barnum's Hippodrome, the former being leased to the management of **John O'Brien**. By the end of 1875, Coup was out of the picture, so Barnum turned to the last of the "Flatfoots"—**George F. Bailey, Lewis June, John J. Nathans**, and **Avery Smith**—to oversee his interests. These men managed Barnum's circus property from 1876 through 1880. Replaced by **James A. Bailey**, who combined his show with Barnum's for the Barnum & London Combined Shows, which had a profitable life from 1881 through 1885, until Bailey left the partnership. Barnum then induced **W. W. Cole** and **J. E. Cooper** to handle the circus operation for 1886, 1887. Bailey returned for the season of 1888 with full control of management for Barnum & Bailey's Greatest Show on Earth. Winter 1889-90, circus was taken to London's Olympic Coliseum. It has been said the no show had its equal for sheer spectacle, size and equipment. Barnum died in Bridgeport, CT. His widow, Mrs. **Nancy Barnum**, was remarried to Demitri Callias Bey, August 7, 1895, NYC. Two rites were performed, one of them in the Greek church. See various biographies for fuller detail.

BARNUS, C. C. Agent, Washburn's, 1855.

BAROTI. Italian ascenionist. With partner, **Signor Volante**, a duel act to the top of the tent and passing each other on the return, Joe Pentland's, 1859.

BARRACLOUGH, JAMES ["Master"]. Driver of 18 Shetland ponies, pulling the Fairy Phaeton wagon, John H. Murray's, 1874.

BARRELLI BROTHERS. Gymnasts, Sheldenburger's European, 1871.

BARRES, JOSEPH. (d. March 11, 1908) Agent, S. H. Barrett's, 1885. Died in Indianapolis, IN.

BARRETT, JENNIE. Great Wallace Show, 1893.

BARRETT, LEWIS. (d. October 15, 1923) Son of **S. H. Barrett**. Was with his father's show for a number of years. Later, became secretary to **Louis E. Cooke** of the Buffalo Bill show. Connected with the 101 Ranch show and then secretary of the Johnny J. Jones Exposition; also general agent of the Greater Southern Shows. Brother was **Sheldon H. Barrett**, known as a Pacific coast showman. After retirement, became associated with J. B. Morton of the Morton Sign Co., Knoxville, TN. Died at his home in that city.

BARRETT, SHELDON HOPKINS. (November 9, 1845-May 16, 1900) Born in Albion, NY, but moved to Cleveland with his family, 1865. Becoming neighbors of the Sells family; attended public school with young **Allen, Lewis** and **Peter Sells** and, ultimately, married their sister, **Rebecca F. Sells**, around 1869. When the Woodward Ave. Street Railway was established as the first streetcar line in Cleveland, Barrett and Lewis and Peter Sells were employed as conductors. After about 3 years, Barrett was taken into the office of the company and became the cashier, holding that position until 1880 when induced by the Sells to take over the management of their No. 2 outfit, James A. Anderson's Circus. The show changed from wagon to rail and was called the S. H. Barrett Circus. Barrett assumed the advance as well as the management when agent **Charles Castle** was taken ill. Remained in advance for the 6 years the show was under his name. Merged with Sells Bros.', 1888, and Barrett became general agent. Sells Bros.' combined with Adam Forepaugh's, 1896. Died while agenting Sells-Forepaugh's, at the United States Hotel, Boston, from pneumonia, age 55.

BARRETTA, THEODORE. Equestrian director, Mayo's Model Show, 1884.

BARRIERE, HOPPOLITIE. Erected a canvas pavilion at Chatham Gardens, 1823, which may have been the first time in America for amusements to be performed under canvas. Shortly, through the efforts of rival theatre manager, **Stephen Price**, the place was closed by the enforcement of fire laws. Barriere then built the Chatham Theatre, which was occa-sionally used for circus performances.

BARRIS, IKE. (d. September, 1885) Equestrian and clown. Sherman's for 4 seasons. Last appearance, Morosco's, San Francisco, 1885. While practicing the horizontal bars, fell and died the same day.

BARRY, FRANCES. Wire ascensionist, Cooper & Jackson, 1880.

BARRY, FRANK. Bareback rider. Above average height, and very massively built. Entered the ring at 10 years of age. 1856-61, served apprenticeship to Spalding & Rogers. Went to Europe at the outbreak of the Civil War and had engagements in almost every European capital. 1868, when performing in Russia, fell in attempting to reach his horse's back after a long leap and broke his leg. Was laid up for 7 months. Spalding & Rogers, 1857, 1860; Sanger's, England, 1862; P. T. Barnum's, 1873; Montgomery Queen's, 1874.

BARRY, FRANKIE [Mrs. Kirkpatrick]. (d. May 30, 1903) Daughter of showman **J. M. Barry** and owner and trainer of the Challenge Troupe of French poodles. Col. Spicer's, 1886; outside wire-walker, Sieber & Howe's, 1887; treasurer, Great American Shows (J. M. Barry, manager), 1894-95; Walter J. McDonald's, 1900. Died, Carbondale, KS, from typhoid fever after having been in the business for about 25 years.

BARRY, J. M. Showman father of **Frankie Barry**. VanAmburgh's, 1881; manager, Col. Spicer's Circus, 1886; manager, George Sieber & Co., 1887; manager, but may have been a partner, George Sieber, Cole's Ten Cent Show, also called Cole & Sieber's Ten Cent Show, 1890-91 (the two had operated together for several years); Great American Shows (J. M. Barry, manager), 1893-97.

BARRY, JOHN [or Berry]. Rider and leaper. Spalding & Rogers, 1857-61; Goodwin & Wilder, Howard Athenaeum, Boston, 1861; Goodwin & Wilder, summer 1862; Robinson & Howes, winter 1863; Thayer & Noyes, 1863; John Wilson's, Southwest Pacific, 1865-67; Stone & Murray, 1869; Dr. James L. Thayer's, 1870; Siegrist & Frost, 1871; principal somersault rider, J. W. Wilder's, 1872; Stevens & Begun, 1874; Burr Robbins', 1875; bareback rider, Great Universal Fair, 1877; Great Roman Hippodrome, 1877; tumbler and leaper, P. T. Barnum's, 1879; John H. Murray's, West Indies, winter 1878-79; principal somersault rider, Stickney's, 1880; Dan Rice's, 1881; John Robinson's, 1882; somersault act, W. H. Harris' Nickel-Plate, 1884.

BARRY, LEWIS. (d. December 31, 1891) Cole Bros.'

BARRY, THOMAS. (1839-January 16, 1909) Clown. Born in Manchester, England; professional debut, Pablo Fanque's, Free Trade Hall, Manchester, in pony race, 1847. Apprenticed to **Ned Briarly** to learn clowning. Performed alternately with Bell's, Fanque's, Hengler's, and Newcomb's circuses. Took out his own show for a short time, 1865; but inevitably went back with his former managers. Came to USA and engaged with Stone & Murray, 1869; L. B. Lent's, NYC, 1870; Thayer

& Noyes, 1870, switching to Murray & Stone in August. Returned to England to work for Hengler, 1871, but was back with Murray for summer season, remaining until 1877. Adam Forepaugh's, 1878; W. C. Coup's, 1879; in England after the summer season, for Tom Batty's; returned to USA and joined W. C. Coup, 1880. With **H. R. Jacobs**, ran a sideshow at Coney Island, 1881; but joined Murray & Stone late in the season, playing Long Island towns; went South during the winter with W. C Coup's; Adam Forepaugh's, 1882; W. O. Dale Steven's Great Australian, winter 1882-83; took the "Sea on Land" exhibit to Coney Island with **C. Sylvan**, 1883; took out an Indian Medicine Show that winter for **Healy & Bigelow**; joined VanAmburgh's, 1885; returned to England during the winter and was with Rolland's, London, 1885-86; back with Frank A. Robbins', 1886. Fall of that year, bought an interest in an "Uncle Tom's Cabin" company with **George Peck**. Later, joined forces with **George O. Starr**, of the Barnum & Bailey show, and took out the Starr Opera Co. Managed Lewis Phillips' Pavillion at Dutchtown, NY, and later took out a production of "Putnam, the Iron Son of '76". Following this, assumed the management of the Grand Street Museum, NYC, and continued managing theatrical enterprises for several years. Was the second to sail the Thames, from Vauxhall to Westminster, in a wash tub drawn by 4 geese, 1884. The tub was actually motivated by a row boat some distance ahead. Rival of the English Shakespearean clown, **William Wallett**. At various times he unsuccessfully embarked into the restaurant business. [Day: "For Tom has much of the English professionals desire to run 'a public' and surround himself with friends to whom he can recall the past as he serves a glass.... Mr. Barry has always been both a jester and gentleman and one of the emigrants from abroad who has never boasted of his intimacy with the Queen and the royal family at 'ome' or made himself odious in the dressing room by relating how much better everything is done 'over there.'"] Died suddenly in Albany, NY.

BARTELS, WILLIAM. (d. July 12, 1907) Animal dealer. Supplied animals for all kinds of circuses and menageries from a firm located at 160 Greenwich St., NYC. Died while dining in a restaurant.

BARTHOLOMEW, DAN. Bartholomew's Circus, 1891, opened in Salt Lake City and toured the mountain region.

BARTHOLOMEW, GEORGE. (May 13, 1833-March 5, 1911). Son of Noah W. Bartholomew, a farmer in Erie County, NY, with a reputation for being able to subdue and handle the most fractious and vicious horses. Inherited his father's fame and talent. Family moved to Jackson, MI, 1836; another move took the family to Missouri. George left for Southern California, 1848, arriving in San Jose. Trained and exhibited a horse named Young America, of which he refused an offer of $10,000. Opened a pleasure garden, Denver, CO, 1871. During this time, broke and trained Bravo and Beneto

and the famous leaper, Nettle; introduced the School of Educated Horses and toured through Colorado. After exhibiting for 5 weeks in St. Louis, through some unfortunate deal, lost his entire troupe of horses and found himself penniless. Returned to California and accumulated more stock and, July 4, 1879, performed at a public garden in Oakland to an audience of 10,000, the beginning of the Equine Paradox and a turning point of furtune. Brought his show east, 1880, and with 17 performing horses exhibited in the Exposition Building, Chicago, and other principal cities, and, finally, 5 months in New York City. The tour continued into 1881—Philadelphia, Baltimore, Washington, Harrisburg, Reading, etc. Secured John Mishler, Reading theatre manager, to undertake the management of Bartholomew's Equine Paradox; the show was booked throughout the USA to enormous success. Bartholomew & Co.'s Pacific Circus, 1856; proprietor, Rocky Mountain Circus, 1860; Bartholomew's Circus Co., West Coast, 1861-62; Bartholomew's Great Western, 1867-69; opened a summer garden, Denver, 1871; Bartholomew's Equine Paradox, 1881-93.

BARTINE, CHARLES F. [r. n. Charles F. Basore]. (September 19, 1844-July 2, 1920) Ethiopian entertainer and proprietor. Born in Germantown, OH. Served in the Civil War. Entered show business, 1865, with Hooley's Minstrels as a black face comedian. VanAmburgh's; Lake's; Rice & Manning Minstrels; United States Minstrels; Dodge & Bartine's Great World Varieties, 1868; end man, William Henry Rice's Minstrels, 1872; Charley Bartine & Co., 1872; Great Minstrels of the United States (the title of an organization formed in Cincinnati, OH), 1873-74, also called Bartine Bros. & Barlow Bros.' Novelty Troupe. Had a circus on the road featuring the gymnastics of the **Bartine Family**, 6 in number, as early as 1872 and continued with circuses under his name until he retired around 1912. In 1880, was in partnership with **Sid C. France** for the Bartine Five-Clown Circus and Electric Light Pavilion. Purchased the Seamon House, Montpelier, IN, 1889, with the intention of establishing winter quarters there. Out with Charles Bartine's Circus, 1890; Bartine's Consolidated Shows (Charles Bartine, **L. C. Miller**, proprietors), 1892. That fall, purchased all the rights and interest in the Bartine Circus from his partner. Listed as general manager with the New Bartine Consolidated Shows (**Col. James S. Totten** & Co., proprietors), 1896. Children, **John, Billie** and **Elva May** were in the dramatic business. Died at his home in Connersville, IN, age 75, where he and wife were running a boarding house.

BARTINE, HARRY. (b. 1839) General performer. Good looking and well formed and possessed remarkable elasticity. [John A. Dingess: Bartine was "extremely smart in his exercises on the slack rope" and "endowed with an ambition only equalled by his courage."] Welch & Lent, 1855-56; Welch's, Philadelphia, 1857-58, 1860; slack rope, L. B. Lent's, 1856-60. October 14, 1859, quarreled with circus performer William **Kincade** in a Reading, PA, gambling saloon. Enraged, Kincade drew a revolver and shot Bartine in the shoulder, seriously wounding him. Enlisted in the 25th New York Regiment for 2 months, 1861. In Australia, 1864-1871.

BARTINE, MAUD. Bartine Five-Clown Circus and Electric Light Pavilion (Charles Bartine, **Sid C. France**, proprietors), 1880. Married **George Minnviller**, musician, June 7, 1888, in Payne, OH.

BARTINE, NELLIE [or Nettie?]. Bartine Five-Clown Circus and Electric Light Pavilion (Charles Bartine, **Sid C. France**, proprietors), 1880; Bartine's Circus (Charles Bartine, **L. C. Miller**, proprietors), 1892; Charles Bartine's Consolidated Shows, 1893.

BARTINE, TED. Charles Bartine's Consolidated Shows, 1893.

BARTLEMES, LEWIS. Dancing barrel, screen and Maltese cross performer, Lowande & Hoffman, 1887.

BARTLETT, F. A. Superintendent of excursions, P. T. Barnum's Roman Hippodrome, 1875; P. T. Barnum's, 1876.

BARTLETT, JONAS "PONY". Co-proprietor, Welch & Bartlett, 1838-40; bought Welch's interest, January 1841, when **William Delavan** became his partner, changing the title to Bartlett & Delavan; Clayton & Bartlett (**John Clayton** and Jonas Bartlett, proprietors), 1844. For a time, proprietor of the famous Branch Hotel, NYC; later, disposed of it to **Tom Hyer** to become landlord of the Washington Hotel at the Battery.

BARTLETT, WALTER. Zoological director, with VanAmburgh's, 1874.

BARTLOW, CHARLES. Elephant keeper, Yankee Robinson's for 5 years before he was killed in a battle with the elephant "Big Tom," April 9, 1909. The bull stood 9' 2" high and weighed 7,200 pounds. Bartlow was the 6th victim in the animal's 19 years in captivity.

BARTON, THADDIUS. Manager, Nixon's Royal Amphitheatre, 1860-61. It was announced in May, 1863, that **James M. Nixon** and Thaddeus Barton had leased the circus lot in Baltimore on Calvert Street, known as the "City Spring" lot, for the purpose of erecting a summer garden, similar to what Nixon had done in New York. Within short order the report came out that the Baltimore city council had rejected the plan, explaining that the lot was to be closed and fixed up for what it was intended—a city spring. May have been involved with Nixon in a Washington venture that followed. Business manager, Nixon's Cremorne Garden Circus, 1863. Could he be the Barton who was a general performer for H. P. Madigan, 1856?

BASINGER, H. 10-horse bandwagon driver, Rockwell & Stone, 1846.

BASNADO. Head balancing trapeze artist, Walt McCafferty's Great Golden Shows, 1894.

BASORE, CHARLES F. See Charles F. Bartine.

BASSETT, CHARLES H. ["Doc"]. (1828-October 1862) Showman and ringmaster. Started in the circus business at age

16, driving 4 ponies for a small chariot of Sands & Nathans; remained with the show until 1858. Following year, sailed for California with the elephants Victoria and Albert, which were sold on his arrival to circus manager **John Wilson**. Equestrian manager for Wilson at the American Theatre, San Francisco, which had been fashioned into an amphitheatre, spring 1860; following spring, combined with **William** and **Walter Aymar** and **William Painter** for a tour of California; the next year the group established a circus in Peru, South America, which proved to be an unsuccessful venture. Was taken ill with a fever and died in Equador.

BASSETT, D. Rider, Quick, Sands & Co., Baltimore, 1833.

BASSLER, EUGENE. Detective, Howes' Great London, 1876.

BASTIAN, MLLE [Mrs. Harry Gurr]. (1850-June 26, 1875), Gymnast and trapeze performer. Native of Philadelphia. J. E. Warner & Co., 1871-73; W. W. Cole's, 1874. Husband, **Harry Gurr**, performed as a "man-fish" and gymnast. She died in Battle Creek, MI, age around 25.

BASYE, ED G. Proprietor, Ed G. Basye's Cosmopolitan Circus and Equestrian Exposition, 1878-79.

BATCHELLER, FRANK. Gymnast, Melville, Maginley & Cooke, 1875.

BATCHELLER, GEORGE H. (1827-1913) Leaper and showman. Joined a minstrel show at age 14. Began in the circus business as a tumbler with Isaac Burtis', 1843, and added leaping later. Clayton & Bartlett, 1844; Howes & Mabie, 1845-48; Stone & McCollum, 1849; R. Sands', 1850; champion vaulter, Joe Pentland's, 1851; June, Angevine & Titus, 1852-53; Joe Pentland's, 1854-55; H. P. Madigan's, 1856; Howes & Cushing, England, 1857-58; Miles & Toole, 1863; Thayer & Noyes, where he was leaping over 10 horses and an elephant; Mrs. Charles H. Warner's, Philadelphia, winter 1864-65; James M. Nixon's, Washington, DC, 1865; George W. DeHaven's, 1865-66; Gardner & Hemmings, Baltimore, winter 1865-66; Mike Lipman's, winter 1866-67; Philadelphia Circus, winter 1867-68; Cooke's Circus, Philadelphia, winter 1868; privileges (with **Ham Norman**), John O'Brien's, 1871; Great Eastern, 1874. Had several apprentices who took his name including **William** and **John Batcheller**. Was one of the best leapers of his day, at home and abroad. Several years associated with **John B. Doris** in the management of privileges for various firms and, ultimately, placed their own circus on the road. Became a partner with **B. F. Keith** in a dime museum, Boston, which ultimately led to the creation of vaudeville in the United States.

BATCHELLER, JOHN F. Tumbler, gymnast, "champion" leaper. Chiarini's, Cuba, 1866; Forepaugh's, 1867; Brien's (**John V. O'Brien**, proprietor), 1868; Stone & Murray, 1871; L. B. Lent's, 1872; leaper, tumbler, P. T. Barnum's, 1873; Haight's Great Eastern, 1874; Howes' Great London, 1876; P. T. Barnum's, 1878; Cooper, Bailey & Co., 1879-80; Orrin

Bros.', Havana, winter 1879-80; Barnum, Bailey & Hutchinson, 1881-82; VanAmburgh & Co., 1883; F. J. Taylor's, 1892.

BATCHELLER, MRS. WILLIAM H. High-wire ascension, Barnum, Bailey & Hutchinson, 1881.

BATCHELLER, PAULINE [nee Pauline V. Jankins]. Wife of **William H. Batcheller.** Concert singer, Cooper, Bailey & Co., Australian tour, 1877-78, 1880. See William H. Batcheller.

BATCHELLER, WILLIAM H. [r. n. Patrick Quirk]. Outstanding leaper. Entered circus business as an apprentice to **George F. Batcheller,** 1867, with a circus operated by **Mike Lipman.** Engaged the same season with a circus at Tenth and Callowhill Streets, Philadelphia. Adam Forepaugh's, 1868, but left in mid-season to join Col. C. F. Ames', 1868-69; C. W. Noyes', 1870, but the show failed in Texas; at which time joined the John W. Robinson's; C. W. Noyes', 1871, winter 1871-72; W. W. Cole's, remaining until January, 1873; L. B. Lent's until the end of 1873 summer season; W. W. Cole's, 1874, 1877-78; Howes' Great London, 1875-77; Orrin Bros.', Havana, winter 1878-79; Cooper & Bailey, 1879-80, where he was advertised as performing a double somersault over 15 elephants. Stayed on when Cooper & Bailey was united with Barnum's, forming Barnum, Bailey & Hutchinson. Stevens' Australian Circus, performing on variety stages prior to the summer season, 1882; Lockwood & Flynn, 1887; John E. Heffron's, 1889-90. Achievements as a performer included a single somersault over 31 horses and a double somersault over 29 horses, both at Glen's Falls, NY, while with W. W. Cole's, August 6, 1875; a double somersault over 8 elephants side by side, St. Louis, MO, while with Howes' Great London, April 23, 1876; double somersault over one elephant placed on pedestals 4¼ feet high, Chicago, September 5, 1876; double somersault over 11 elephants placed side by side, except the last 2 which were head to head, the third elephant, the largest of the herd, being placed on two 4' pedestals, while with Cooper & Bailey, June 21, 1880, Haverhill, MA. Feats were all witnessed by reputable circus people. Married **Pauline V. Jenkins** (professionally known as **La Belle Pauline**), Pensacola, Florida, January 3, 1876.

BATES, ANNA. See Anna Hannon Swan.

BATES, GEORGE M. (1851-August 18, 1926) Elephant keeper. Born in Natick, MA. Joined Barnum and London, 1882, by 1885 was an elephant keeper; was present at the killing of Jumbo. Retired, 1908, after 25 years with Barnum & Bailey. Sideshow ticket taker, Miller Bros.' 101 Ranch, 1909-13. Died at Warwick, RI.

BATES, JACOB. Equestrian. Performed in Centre Square, Philadelphia, 1772; the Bull's Head in Bowery Lane, NYC, 1773; 1787, took over a Philadelphia circus structure that had been erected by a **Mr. Poole** for a riding school. Repertory included riding up to 4 horses at one time and the comic sketch of "The Tailor's Ride to Brentford." Credited with introducing the riding sketch of "Billy Buttons" to USA.

BATES, J. G. Band leader, VanAmburgh's, 1881.

BATES, MARTIN VAN BUREN ["Capt."]. (November 9, 1845-1919) Giant. Native of Whitesburg, KY. Billed as the "Kentucky Giant." One of the largest and tallest men in the world, but one of intelligence and kindness. Grew normally until passing the 7th grade, then began to shoot up at a rapid rate; age 13, weighed 300 pounds. During those early years, was obese, but when height reached 7' 2½", the fat was replaced by 470 pounds of power and muscle. Acquired the best education the mountains afforded and then taught in the mountain schools prior to Civil War. At the advent of war, volunteered as a Confederate soldier and served under **Captain E. A. Webb,** of Whitesburg. Performed duties with distinction and was eventually commissioned a captain. Instrumental in breaking up the lawless guerrilla bands that were a menace to the mountain regions. At war's end and at age 28, moved to Cincinnati, where he joined the Wiggins & Benoit circus at a wage of $100 a month and expenses. Soon moved up to employment with John Robinson's at $400 a month. Married the "Nova Scotia Giantess," a woman an inch or two taller than himself, in London, England, June 17, 1871, when both were booked on a European tour by **Judge Ingalls.** Was with W. W. Cole's, 1878-1880. The pair was on the road for 7 years, during which time they received enormous salaries, most of which went into savings. At the end of that time they retired to Seville, OH, where Bates had built a home proportionately large. After the death of Anna, Bates married **Anne LaVonne** of Cincinnati, a woman of normal stature.

BATES, ROBERT. Agent, Stowe's, 1870.

BATES, WALTER. Tumbler, Dan Rice's, 1878.

BATTERSBY, HANNAH. (1842-April 15, 1889) Giantess. Exhibited by **Jake Reed** with Adam Forepaugh's, 1869; P. T. Barnum's, 1877; Adam Forepaugh's, 1880. Married **John Battersby,** the human skeleton.

BATTERSBY, JOHN. Skeleton man, exhibited by **Jake Reed,** Adam Forepaugh's, 1869.

BAUER, P. Calliope player, Sells Bros.', 1877.

BAUM, DAN. (d. August 22, 1890) Elephant trainer, P. T. Barnum's.

BAYET, THOMAS. Alex Robinson's, 1870.

BEAL. Clerk, Pepin's, West Indies, 1819-20.

BEAN, U. Buckley & Co.'s, 1857.

BEASLEY, BOB. Double trapeze, break-away ladder, and iron jaw (with **Laura Gaulf**), Goodrich's, 1897.

BEASLEY, GEORGE. Keeper of menagerie, June & Titus, 1849; (under the name **Hideralso**) Raymond's, 1850-53; Mabie Bros.', 1857-59.

BEATTY, ALEX. Concert minstrel performer, P. T. Barnum's, 1873.

BEATTY, GEORGE [at various times, Bentie, Batty, Baity]. (1835-June 1, 1858) Bareback rider. Born in St. Louis, MO.

Dan Rice's, 1852; New Orleans Hippoferean, winter 1854; Crescent City Circus, 1855; H. M. Smith's, May-July 1856; Orton's, September 1856, February 1857; Washburn's, 1857; E. Ganung & Co., 1858.

BEATY, JOHN. American Hippocolosiculum, 1866.

BEAUMONT. Actor, Pepin & Breschard, Baltimore Olympic Circus, combining stage and ring performances, opened November 6, 1811. An editor of a local paper was prompted to remark that "this project of uniting theatrical and equestrian performances may lead to the most dangerous perversion of an amusement, which in its proper form is both dignified and instructive." Arrangement was short lived.

BECK, FRANK M. Proprietor, Irwin Bros.', 1887.

BECK, G. H. Maginley & VanVleck, 1863.

BECK, TILLIE. See Charles W. Lingard.

BECKER, FRED. Program agent, Adam Forepaugh's, 1875.

BECKETT, ADAM A. Assistant manager, Great Australian, 1877; proprietor, Beckett's Great Exposition Circus, 1881, a consolidation of the Great Australian and the Great Exposition, which toured the Great Lakes in the steamer *Granite State*; took to wagons in July. Continued as a circus proprietor at least through 1887.

BECKLEY, ED. (1836-1892) Assistant manager, P. T. Barnum's, 1871.

BEDOUIN ARABS. Earliest troupe in the country probably occurred in 1838-39. August 6, 1838, three of the genuine articles were at the Park Theatre, NYC. That year an Arab company was advertised at the New Theatre in Charleston, SC. What may have been the same act was mentioned by **Sol Smith** performing at the Government Street Theatre, Mobile, 1839; Broadway Circus, 49 Broadway, NYC, the same year; troupe of 11, Nixon's Alhambra, NYC, 1863; L. B. Lent's, old Wallack's Theatre, NYC, December 1863; L. B. Lent's Broadway Amphitheatre, NYC, 1864; troupe of 14, Howes Great European, 1865; J. M. French's, 1869, advertised "Terrific exploits of physical vigor. during their exhibitions of intrepidity, these Desert Sons discharge muskets while revolving in mid-air, turn Somersaults over a bridge of bayonets, and erect lofty pyramids of living men."

BEGGS, G. W. Said to be proprietor of a small circus in 1852, with no wagons, no seats, probably no tent. The company transported their equipment on the backs of mules.

BEHRENS, NATHANIEL. (1848?-May 30, 1913) Was employed by Barnum & Bailey for many years, during which time he traveled throughout the world in search of novelties for the circus. Was in some way responsible for importing the "white elephant," as well as Jumbo and the Zulus. At one time traveled Europe with his own circus. Died of pneumonia, NYC, age 65.

BELCHER, J. E. Privileges, Sautelle Pavilion Shows, 1885.

BELDING, J. Leader of female band, John Robinson's, 1884.

BELFORD, GEORGE W. (d. May 10, 1937) Acrobat, aerialist and circus proprietor. Part of a team billed as "**The Three Belfords**" (**George, Charles, Harry**), featuring their ladder act, 1882; Gregory Bros.', 1885; equestrian director, James T. Johnson's, 1888; Gregory & Belford (**C. J. Gregory**, George Belford, proprietors), 1892; M. K. Houlton's, 1893; proprietor, Burton & Belford's New Consolidated 25 Cent Shows, 1894; Belford & Howard's New Big Wagon Show, 1895; proprietor, manager, Belford Carnival of Novelties, 1896. At one time, performed with his wife, **Mollie**, in an aerial act. By 1910 there were 7 Belfords billed as a Risley act. That year George Belford purchased 126 acres of land at Kendallville, IN. Died of a stroke there, age 71.

BELFORD, MOLLIE. See George Belford.

BELL. Irishman clown, rope-dancer, leaper and otherwise general performer. Thomas Steward's troupe, 1808; slack rope, Boston Circus, managed by Bates & Davis, 1810; Robert Davis', Salem, MA, February 1810; trampoline, Pepin & Breschard, fall 1810; Philadelphia, where he turned a somersault over 4 horses; clown, Pepin & Breschard, spring 1811, Lancaster, PA.; Pepin & Breschard, Philadelphia, winter 1811-12; Langley & Co., Charleston, winter/spring 1813-14. Performed a feat of vaulting a horse and then somersaulting to the ground; also leaped over 4 horses and burst through a balloon at the full height of his leap.

BELL, CHARLES. Rider. Dan Rice's, 1878; clown, Thornton's, 1880; Rice-Stowe-Oates, 1881; hurdle and jockey rider, Valkingburg's, 1881; W. H. Stowe's, winter 1881-82; Robinson & Myers, 1883; clown, Pullman's, 1885. While master of transportation, the Robert Hunting Circus, 1896, died from an freak accident. As the circus train was pulling out of Danielsonville, CT, August 8, the engineer was handling the cars roughly. Bell alit from the train and ran ahead to reprimand him. In so doing, he fell in the darkness to the street some 25 feet below.

BELL, DON. Rider, Barnum & London, 1886.

BELL FAMILY. Consisting of **Eliza Mazzotti**, trick and principal equestrienne; **James, William, John** and **Richard**, bareback and principal riders, posturers, the Olympians, and aerial performers. With Great European (**Avery Smith, G. C. Quick, John Nathans** & Co., proprietors), 1868; Courtney & Sanford, Lima, Peru, fall 1870.

BELL, JAMES G. (d. August 31, 1895) Hurdle and jockey rider. Sells Bros.', 1881, 1886; Wallace & Co., 1889; Irwin Bros.', 1893; John W. Robinson's, 1895. Died in Cincinnati.

BELL, JERONIMO "JERRY" [r. n. Lee]. Rider, Spanish speaking clown. Englishman by birth, brother of **Richard** and **Charles Bell**. During career in the United States, Cooper & Bailey, 1879-80; Barnum, Bailey & Hutchinson, 1881; Orrin Bros.', Havana and Mexico, winter 1881-82; Sells Bros.', 1882; Adam Forepaugh's, 1883; Orrin Bros.', Mexico, winter 1883-1884; Sells Bros.', 1884-85; Orrin Bros.', Mexico, winter, 1885-86; Barnum & London, 1886; Barnum-Forepaugh,

1887; Sells Bros.', California, 1889. Latter engagement ended his performing in America before returning to England.

BELL, OLIVER. (d. August 19, 1867) General performer. Frost & Co., 1836; C. H. Bacon, 1837; Bacon & Derious, 1838-39; Welch & Bartlett, 1840; Broadway Circus, NYC, 1840; contortionist, Ludlow & Smith, 1841; principal rider, Major Brown's Mammoth Coloseum, 1857; equestrian and gymnast, Hyatt & Co., 1859; management, Satterlee & Bell's, 1860; bareback rider, George W. DeHaven's, 1861-62; trained horses for the new Maginley's Cosmopolitan Circus and equestrian director during the 1863-64 seasons; co-proprietor, Horner & Bell, 1865; scenic rider, Palmer's Great Western, 1865; principal rider, Caldwell's, 1867; same year, equestrian director, George W. DeHaven's. Drowned while the company was crossing Three Rivers, Canada, apparently walking off the boat in the dark. Body was found 5 days later about 3 miles from the spot of the crossing.

BELL, RICARDO. (1858-March 12, 1911) Clown. Father of the **Bell Family** of performers. Born in London. Came to USA and joined Cooper & Bailey, 1868; went to South America and Mexico for 10 years; G. A. Courtney's, West Indies, 1880-81; clown and hurdle act, Barnum, Bailey & Hutchinson, 1881; joined Orrin Bros.', 1882, with whom he remained as principal clown until 1906, a period of 24 years. Conducted his own circus in Mexico for 4 years; the family (**Ricardo Bell, Sr., Ricardo, Jr., Celia, Alberto, Eddie, Carlos, Nellie**) with Walter L. Main's, 1887. Died of Bright's desease, age 53.

BELL, WILLIAM. (d. 1908.) Animal trainer.

BELLFONTAINE, FRANK. (d. October 1913) Barnum's original tattooed man. Became chef at Hotel Brewster, NYC.

BELLMONT BROTHERS. G. G. Grady's, 1871.

BELMONT BROTHERS. 4 gymnasts and acrobats, dancing globe, posturing. Seth B. Howe's, 1866; Dr. James L. Thayer's, 1869; G. G. Grady's, 1870, 1873; J. E. Warner's, 1871; Montgomery Queen's, 1874; W. C. Coup's, 1879; Sautelle Pavilion Shows, 1885; Wheeler Bros.' (**Alson Wheeler, D. Wheeler,** proprietors), 1894.

BELMONT, CHARLES. Gymnast. Brother of **Lottie** and **Daisy Belmont;** performed with Lottie, on the trapeze. Wootten & Andrews', 1874; Cooper, Bailey & Co., 1876; Montgomery Queen's, 1877; equestrian director and principal clown, W. H. Harris' Nickel-Plate, 1884; VanAmburgh & Reiche Bros., 1885; Adam Forepaugh's, 1886; Phillips-Scott, 1888; manager, Belmont Elite Circus, 1889; amusement director, Rice's, 1896.

BELMONT, DAISY [Mrs. William Showles]. (1871?-January 22, 1896) Bareback rider. Made circus debut with Courtney & Sandford, Chile, 1873, carried on by **Micanor,** the Italian equestrian, before she was 3 years old; performed in songs and dances, Theatre Comique, St. Louis, 1875; with sister and brother, **Lottie** and **Charles,** Cooper & Bailey, California trip, 1876, singing and dancing in the concert; Mont-

gomery Queen's, 1877; Cooper & Bailey, that same year, trip to Asia, Australia and South America; concert feature, W. C. Coup, 1879-81; first appearance on revolving globe, Maybury, Pullman & Hamilton, 1882; W. H. Harris' Nickel-Plate, 1883, in "Circus-ring Exposed," which showed how rider training was taught by the use of the Stokes' "mechanic"; remained with the show until August, 1884, performing in the concert, doing a globe act and learning to ride; pad rider and developing bareback techniques, S. H. Barrett & Co.; VanAmburgh's, 1885, emerging as a skillful bareback hurdle rider; principal act, Adam Forepaugh's, 1886-87; feature performer, Belmont Elite Show, 1888-89. October 8, 1889, married **William Showles.** Olympia, London, Barnum & Bailey, winter 1889-90; Sells Bros.', 1890-91, accompanying the show to Australia, 1891-92. Returned to America ill and never recovered, dying in Chicago from Bright's desease, age 25. Appearance in the ring, with blonde hair and a plump and petite figure, was said to be the embodiment of grace and feminine loveliness.

BELMONT, EDDIE. Leaper and acrobat. Barnum & London, 1884; VanAmburgh's, August 4, 1885, attempted a double somersault from a springboard over elephants and horses at Medina, NY, but slipped as he made the run, missed the mattress and fell into the ring on his head and shoulders. Died August 6 from the injuries sustained.

BELMONT, JAMES. Clown. One of the early 19th century circus performers, called by Charles Durang "a very curious and racy clown." First appeared in America as an acrobat with Davis & Co., Boston, 1815-16; James West's company as vaulter and clown, 1821; while in Baltimore, performed the first sword swollowing act seen in this country; clown, Simpson & Price (formerly **James West's**), 1822, Philadelphia, Baltimore; William Blanchard's, 1823; John Rogers', NYC, 1823-24.

BELMONT, JOE. Leaper, Richards' Circus (**George W. Richards,** proprietor), 1887-88.

BELMONT, LOTTIE. Gymnast. Sister of **Charles** and **Daisy Belmont.** Sometimes billed as **Lotino.** Worked with her brother on the trapeze. Described as a performer of beauty and grace. Wootten & Andrews, 1874; Cooper, Bailey & Co., 1876; Montgomery Queen's, 1877; W. C. Coup's, 1880; W. H. Harris' Nickel-Plate, 1884; VanAmburgh & Reiche Bros., 1885; Phillips-Scott Union Pacific, 1888; Belmont Elite, 1889.

BELMONT, MAMIE. Adam Forepaugh's, 1886. That year, married **George W. Kline,** Boston, April 19.

BEMER, O. F. General agent, New York Champs Elysees, 1866.

BEN ALI, SI HASSAN. Manager, troupe of Arabs bearing his name, Ringling Bros.', 1893.

BENARDE, H. Haight & Chambers, 1867.

BENCH, MONS. Trick rider, Ballard & Bailey, 1855.

BENCHLEY, JOHN. Proprietor, Benchley & Stone's Lafayette Circus, 1837-38.

BENEDICT, MATTIE. Tandem *manège* act, Barnum, Bailey & Hutchinson, 1881.

BENJAMIN, ASHBURY. Spotted boy, Cooper, Bailey & Co., 1879.

BENNER BROTHERS. North American Circus (**Asa B. Stow,** manager), 1873.

BENNETT, GEORGE. General performer, with Howes & Sanger, 1872.

BENNETT, H. M. (March 2, 1831-April 11, 1902) Born at Burlington, VT. Lee & Bennett's Great North American Circus, San Francisco, 1856-59. Returned East to NYC, 1860. Interested in various show ventures during Civil War; subsequently engaged in theatrical business. Died at his stock farm, Farmingdale, NJ, age 71, leaving a fortune estimated at 2 million dollars.

BENNETT, MAJOR. Dwarf, Dan Castello's, 1876.

BENNETT, SAM [r. n. Rooney]. 4-horse rider and bounding jockey act. W. H. Harris' Nickel-Plate, 1888; Holland & Gormley, 1889; J. F. Wood's, winter 1889-90; Holland, Bowman & McLaughlin, 1890.

BENOIT, MONS. See Benoit Tourniaire.

BENOIT, SAMUEL. Billed as an Equestrian Prodigy, New York Champs Elysees, 1865.

BENSAID, TILLIE. Algerian female Hercules, with Carlo Bros.', South America, 1876.

BENSELL, MRS. ROBERT. Equestrienne, Frost, Husted & Co., 1836.

BENSELL, ROBERT. Band leader, Frost, Husted & Co., 1836.

BENSHAW, J. L. B. Lent's, 1862.

BENSLEY, EUGENE W. (February 10, 1870-March 2, 1915) Gymnast, equilibrist, general performer. Born in West Farms, NY. Featured at 9 years of age with the Barnum show at Madison Square Garden, performing a high wire act with his father, **James Bensley,** who was known as "The Great Bensley," and at the Harry Enoch's Varieties, Philadelphia, in a crystal pyramid novelty act. After father's death, 1903, took up football juggling and traveled with Adam Forepaugh's, Barnum & Bailey, Ringling Bros.', Gollmar Bros.', Andrew Downie's, Sig. Sautelle's, Sells & Downs, Frank E. Robbins', Guy Bros.', and Al G. Field's Minstrels. Also performed in major parks, fairs and expositions and was with Tony Pastor's Road Show, as well as playing the standard variety circuit in the winter season. Worked until only a few weeks before his death in Philadelphia from Bright's desease, age 45.

BENSLEY, JAMES. (1840?-August 7, 1904) Gymnast. Began performing, 1865, as one of the **Bensley Brothers,** trapeze and horizontal bar artists; toured that year with L. B. Lent's; 1877, introduced his son in a novel act for vaudeville. Horizontal bar, barrel, and crystal pyramid performer, Great American Circus, 1878; Great Transatlantic Allied Shows, 1879; Adam Forepaugh's, 1880; Huffman's Dime Circus,

winter 1885-86; Howes New Colossal Shows, 1888; Bartine's, 1889, as well as Barnum & Bailey, Roberts & Gardner, Howes London, Rogers', Gollmar Bros.', and Downie's. Died in Belleville, Ontario, Canada, age 64.

BENSLEY, WILLIAM. Equilibrist. Howe's New Colossal Shows, 1888; Bartine's, 1889.

BENSON, GEORGE W. Supt. of candy privilege, Cooper, Bailey & Co., 1876.

BENT, A. K. Band leader, Wintermute Bros.', 1897.

BENTLEY, GEORGE H. Treasurer. Ben Maginley's, 1863; ringmaster, Howes' European, 1865.

BENTLEY, J. B. Proprietor, Bentley's Old Fashioned Circus, 1895.

BENTLEY, T. A. Manager, A. A. Beckett's Great Exposition Circus, 1881.

BENTON, TONY. Comedian and comic singer. New York Champs Elysees, 1866; Dan Rice's Paris Pavilion, 1873.

BERDEAUX, JOSEPH. Acrobat, G. G. Grady's, 1868-74.

BERGER, E. S. Band leader, Thayer & Noyes, 1862.

BERLETTE. General performer. Stone & Rosston, 1865; Stone, Rosston & Murray, 1867.

BERNARD, BURT. Rider, Johnson & Co., 1881.

BERNARD, CHARLES. (August 20, 1861-January 27, 1938) Born in Beechvale (or Benton), OH. Started in show business, 1876, Croker Magic Lantern Show; later, with small traveling companies and on concessions in summer until 1880; Shelby, Pullman & Hamilton, 1881. Until 1900, theatrical agent, winters—John Griffith's *Faust* (Leslie Davis management), Carl Brehm's *Ten Nights in a Barroom*; Burt Imson's *Uncle Tom's Cabin.* Circuses, summers—John B. Doris', Adam Forepaugh's, W. E. Wallace's, J. H. LaPearl's, Walter L. Main's. Outdoor advertising plant owner, 1900-12; proprietor, Dixie Zoo (traveling), 1912-17; press agent with Sparks', 1918-19; treasurer, Rhoda Royal's, 1920; contracting agent, Andrew Downie's Walter L. Main's, 1921-24. Retired to Savannah. Wrote *As Told on a Sunday Run, Red Wagon Stories,* and *Half-Century Circus Reviews,* as well as articles for *Bandwagon, Hobbies, Billboard.* Died there at his home, age 77.

BERNARD, CHARLES. Greco-Roman wrestler, Barnum, Bailey & Hutchinson, 1881.

BERNARD, G. A. Stereopticon manager, Cooper, Bailey & Co., 1880; Barnum, Bailey & Hutchinson, 1881-82.

BERNARD, HARRY. Rider. Joe Pentland's Circus, 1855; Hippotheatron, NYC, September 1865. Left New York on October 19 with James M. Nixon's troupe aboard the *Catherine Whiting,* headed for Galveston; but after leaving New York, the ocean became so rough that the ship had to lay overnight at Sandy Hook. On the 23rd a heavy gale set in and the following day one of the ring horses went overboard. By nightfall, all of the horses had been washed into the sea. At height of the storm the ship's engine gave out, exposing the boat and passengers to the mercy of the angry elements for a period of 32 hours. Finally, the steamer went ashore 5 miles south of Carysfort Reef, FL, October 28. Member of the Donaldson Troupe (**Frank Donaldson, Miaco Brothers**, Harry Bernard and **Petite Angelo**), performing gymnastics with Thayer & Noyes, winter 1865-66; Tom King's, 1861, Washington, DC; Lake's, 1866; Haight & Chambers, 1867; John Robinson's, 1867.

BERNARD, HIRAM G. One of the early circus promoters. 1827, Bernard and Black conducted circus performances in the barn of Dr. Forest's Hotel, York, Ontario. In the circus business with **Captain Page** from 1828 through 1831. Byram G. Bernard's circus, 1830; September 29, 1830, granted a license to perform in Detroit, perhaps bringing the first such exhibition to that city; appeared in Albany and Toronto the same year. It is supposed that he retired as a wealthy man in Toronto.

BERRY, ASA. (d. July 8, 1880) Cayetano's Co., Charleston, SC, 1812-13, where he did ground and lofty tumbling; clown, Langley & Co., Charleston, winter and spring, 1813-14; Breschard's troupe, Savannah, latter part of 1814. Wife died in April of that year. J. W. Myers', 1856; boss hostler, Sloat & Shepard, 1857, ringmaster, Niblo & Sloat, Cooke's Amphitheatre, London, 1860; veterinarian, P. T. Barnum's, 1871-74; master of horse, Adam Forepaugh's, 1875; P. T. Barnum's, 1877. Died in Brewster Station, NY.

BERRY, GREEN. (d. August 29, 1877) General agent, with Howes' Great London, 1871, contracting agent, 1872; excursion agent, P. T. Barnum's, 1877. Was killed when the show lost an advertising car which was attached to a train that broke through an overpass on Four Mile Creek, three miles west of Altoona, Iowa, and seven miles east of Des Moines. The creek was swollen from heavy rainfall and the pressure of the water had weakened the bridge supports, causing the bridge to collapse and the train to go with it. Six of the billing crew were were also killed instantly and four others injured.

BERRY, JACK. Acrobatic clown. Buckley & Co., 1857-58; Robinson & Lake, 1859-60; John Robinson's, 1863-64, 1881-82.

BERRY, JOE. Principal tumbler, Dan Rice's, 1877.

BERRY, MILES. General manager, New York and Philadelphia Consolidated Circus, fall 1888.

BERTINE, MLLE. General performer, Welch & Lent, 1855.

BERTRAM SISTERS [Minnie, Stella]. W. H. Stowe's, winter 1881-82; Burr Robbins', 1885.

BEST, SAMUEL. Advance agent, P. T. Barnum's, 1875.

BESTWICK, R. W. Leaper, tumbler, vaulter. M. O'Conner & Co., 1870; L. B. Lent's; 1871; W. W. Cole's, 1876.

BETTS, CHARLES. Calliope player, advance car #1, Barnum, Bailey & Hutchinson, 1881.

BETTS, S. O. Manager, Den Stone's, 1854; agent, Great Western, 1855; agent, Joe Pentland's, 1858.

BIATT, WILLIAM [Master Tommy]. Acrobat, Alexander Robinson's, 1870-77.

BIBB, W. S. Treasurer, Bruce L. Baldwin's, 1894.

BIBBY, EDWIN. Greco-Roman wrestler (with **William Hoefler**), Barnum, Bailey & Hutchinson, 1881.

BICKLE, GEORGE. Clown, Walter L. Main's, 1885.

BIDWELL, DAVID. (June, 1821-December 18, 1889) Born in Stuyvesant, NY. Educated at a "seminary" in Kinderhook. Began as a boy working on a Hudson River steamboat, of which his father, **Alex Bidwell**, was master. 8 years working the boats in the summer and at the New York theatres in the winter. Became proprietor of a New York restaurant, which he ran successfully for some 18 years. One of the founders of a hotel, the Empire House, on Barclay Street, NYC, 1843. Joined brother, **Henry**, in a ship chandlery business, New Orleans, 1846. Bought the Phoenix House, 1850; built the Academy of Music, New Orleans, 1853, then called Amphitheatre; fitted it as the Pelican Theatre, 1854. Went into partnership with Spalding & Rogers, 1856, when the men took a 10 year lease on the Pelican Theatre—the Spalding & Rogers Amphitheatre, later renamed the Academy of Music. Became exclusive owner, 1870; Spalding, Rogers & Bidwell dissolved, 1866, with Rogers' retirement; continued association with Spalding until around 1875, with the two acquiring theatres in St. Louis, Mobile, Memphis, and the Tacon Theatre, Havana. 1873, bought the St. Charles Theatre, New Orleans; 1880, became lessee of the Grand Opera House (formerly the Varieties Theatre). With these acquisitions, controlled the amusement business in that city until his death. [M. B. Leavitt: "Bidwell was gruff and blunt in manner, and always wanted his pound of flesh.... It was David Bidwell who advanced the money that enabled Klaw and Erlanger to buy out the booking agency of H. S. Taylor and enter upon a business career that included the formation of the managerial body known as the 'theatrical Syndicate.'"] With **Spalding** and **Avery Smith**, built a circus for the Paris World Exposition of 1867. A self-made man, Bidwell was physically large, hearty in manner, goodhearted and generous.

BIGELOW. Rider, Howes & Mabie, 1841.

BILLINGS, JOSEPH. Leaper, John Robinson's, 1877-78.

BINGHAM, J. W. Ventriloquist, Bunnell sideshow, P. T. Barnum's, 1879.

BINGLEY, C. H. Bingley & Stevens Bros., 1886, sold at sheriff's sale in the fall; Hall & Bingley, 1888; Bingley & Stevens in receivership, 1890.

BIRCH, CHARLIE. Whittemore, Thompson & Co., 1865.

BIRDSALL, MASTER. (b. 1815) Rider. A pupil of Benjamin Brown. Debut, Fredericksburg, VA, January 4, 1826. Brown & Bailey, 1826-28; J. P. Brown's, 1829-31; Fogg & Stickney, winter 1829.

BISHOP BROTHERS. Aerialists, acrobats, leapers. Began, 1886, F. J. Taylor's Creston Railroad Show. Later in the season, leased to Stevens & Bingley; closed it 2 weeks later. Trapeze and brother act, F. J. Taylor's, 1887-91; Walter Mc-Caferty's, 1891; Fred Buchanan's, 1892-97; fair dates fall of 1897 and all of 1898; F. J. Taylor's, 1899; Forepaugh-Sells, 1901-04; Campbell Bros.', 1905-07; and Yankee Robinson's, 1909.

BISHOP, W. General performer, with Howes & Sanger, 1872.

BISSELL, P. Advertising agent, North American Circus and Balloon Show, 1875.

BLACK, HARRY. Equestrian director, C. W. Kidder & Co.'s, 1893.

BLACK, PROF. Performing ponies, John Robinson's, 1889-91.

BLACK, ROBERT G. Ass't sup't, museum, P. T. Barnum's, 1873; museum sup't, Adam Forepaugh's, 1875.

BLACK, W. B. and **HARRY.** Proprietors, Black Bros.', 1887.

BLACKBURN, JOSEPH. (d. February 26, 1841) Clown and juggler on horseback. Became, as Charles Durang expressed it, one of the "most celebrated of racy and droll" native born clowns of his day. The combination of "uncommon humor and visual activity" led to his being dubbed "the American Grimaldi." Multi-talented, he was one of a few early circus people to keep a diary. His letters from Europe, 1838, were published in several of the American newspapers. Composed at least one song, "Sich a Gettin' Up Stairs," which he probably used in the ring. Friend and sidekick to the great rider and somersaulter **Levi J. North**, with whom he went on a tour of England. [George Stone: Considered him "a man of extraordinary ability" and one who "possessed a good education and figured as a poet of no ordinary pretensions."] William Harrington's, 1825, 1832; William Blanchard's, 1828; Harrington & Buckley, 1830; Page's, 1830; J. W. Bancker's, 1832; Brown's, 1835; Brown & Co., 1836; Eagle Circus, 1837; Frost & Co., 1837; Noel E. Waring's, winter 1837-38; Charles H. Bacon's, 1837-38; Raymond & Waring, 1839; Philadelphia Circus, 1840; western unit of June, Titus, Angevine & Co., 1841. Died on board the steamer *Express Mail* near Horse Shoe Bend and was buried in Memphis, TN.

BLACKFORD, J. H. Contractor, Great Western, 1876.

BLACKMORE, J. Rider, slack-rope performer. Appeared at the Royal Circus, London, as early as 1803. American activity included appearances with James West's, Philadelphia, 1816; Pepin & West, Philadelphia, 1817; West's, 1818. One of his feats was to stand on his head on a quart bottle placed on the saddle of a moving horse. Remained in America until 1818.

BLACKWELL, WILLIAM. Lake's Hippo-Olympiad, 1866.

BLACKWOOD, JAMES. (b. 1832) Rider. Apprenticed to **S. B. Howes**; used the name **James Howes** until apprenticeship ended, 1842. Cole & Co., 1837; Cole, Miller, Yale, winter 1837; Miller, Yale, Howes, 1838; Titus, Angevine, winter 1838; June, Titus & Angevine, 1839; Yale & Co., 1840; June,

Titus & Angevine, winter 1840; Howes & Mabie, winter 1841; 1842, 1845; Dr. Gilbert R. Spalding's, 1846-48; Stone & McCollum, 1848; Stickney's New Orleans Circus (**S. P. Stickney, North & Jones,** proprietors), 1849; J. M. June's, winter 1850; Spalding & Rogers, 1852.

BLAISDELL, S. J. W. Bancker's, New York State, 1832.

BLAISDELL, W. B. (d. October 18, 1888) Proprietor, Golden State Circus, Sacramento, CA, 1868. 85' round top, 5 baggage vans, passenger coach holding 12, 8 ring horses. After the engagement there, the company toured the state. Married **Julia Peak** of the **Peak Family** of glass blowers. Died age 55.

BLAKE, WILLIAM. (d. May 24, 1866) Gymnast and acrobat. *L'échelle*, Slaymaker & Nichols, 1863; Robinson & Howes, 1864; Great European, 1865; Frank J. Howes', 1865; John Robinson's, 1865-66. Died Louisville, KY.

BLAKELY, T. H. Slack-wire performer, vaulter. Price & Simpson, 1824-27; accompanied the troupe to the Broadway Circus, NYC, in May of the latter year, which became his final engagement with circuses. Turned to the dramatic stage and performed as an actor until at least mid-century. There was a Blakely, a contortionist, with Mabie Bros., 1859.

BLANCHARD, CECELIA. See Blanchard Family.

BLANCHARD, ELIZABETH. See Blanchard Family.

BLANCHARD FAMILY [Mr. and Mrs. William Blanchard, sons George and William, daughter Cecelia]. **William Blanchard**, English circus proprietor, opened a new amphitheatre, Baltimore, 1820, and realized a fortune, but subsequently lost it all. Opened at the old Chatham Garden, NYC, and failed. Performed in Albany, 1826, after a Canadian tour. Died in Louisville, KY, 1837, and buried by the Masonic fraternity. All family members performed. **Cecelia** broke her leg while riding, Utica, NY, 1828, which was later amputated. Son **William**, a bareback rider, died in Martinique, West Indies, 1831.

BLANCHARD, MISS C. G. G. Grady's, 1869.

BLANCHARD, GEORGE. See Blanchard Family.

BLANCHARD, G. E. Balloon ascensionist, 1826-30. May have been the George Blanchard above.

BLANCHARD, H. L. Gymnast, Hippocomique, 1865.

BLANCHARD, JEAN PIERRE. Balloon ascensionist. One of the earliest of American aeronauts. A native of France, he had, even at a young age, an inventor's curiosity. 1781 constructed a flying machine fashioned after the manner of birds in flight, having four huge wings operated by hand and foot levers. The contraption was, of course, a failure, but once the **Montgolfier brothers** had proven the principle of lighter than air flight, Blanchard wasted no time in accepting the balloon as a legitimate device for exhibition and experimentation and in the ensuing years made 44 flights throughout the European continent. Greatest triumph, however, 8 years before coming to USA, occurred when he crossed the English Channel with **Dr. John Jeffries** of Boston (this was the first air voyage between nations, hailed "the eighth wonder of the world"), January 7, 1785. At 8:00 a.m. the balloon ascended over the white cliffs of Dover, a tribute to Blanchard's imagination—the gondola, shaped like a bathtub, had a rear fin and four wing-like rudders, attachments intended to steer and propel the balloon. The flight, which was fraught with hair raising events, terminated shortly after 3 o'clock in the afternoon in a wooded area not far from Calais. Shortly after arriving in America, Blanchard ascended from the yard of the Walnut Street prison, Philadelphia, January 9, 1793. President George Washington and an assemblage of dignitaries watched the hydrogen-filled balloon rise to over 5,000 feet and disappear in its travel of 15 miles before alighting into a patch of woods near Woodbury, NJ. The craft carried Blanchard, his black dog, and a letter of introduction from the President—it being the first piece of air mail on the America continent (this was Blanchard's 45th ascension but his first on our side of the Atlantic Ocean). Short time after the first American voyage, he was given permission to construct a rotunda on the Governor's lot on Chestnut Street, where he exhibited the balloon being prepared for his 46th flight. At John Bill Ricketts circus, corner of Twelfth and Market Streets, 1793, sent up a balloon with a parachute attached containing a cat and a monkey; some form of slow ignition was rigged to release the parachute at a certain altitude, which allowed the quadrupeds a safe floatation earthward. The ascension at Ricketts' amphitheatre marked the first balloon act with an American circus.

BLANCHARD, WILLIAM. See Blanchard Family.

BLANCHE, MLLE. General performer, with Driesbach & Howes, 1868.

BLANCHETTE, C. E. Business manager with the Parisian Circus at Operti's Tropical Garden, Philadelphia, fall 1876.

BLANCHETTE, EXZAVIOR. Thompson, Smith & Hawes, 1866.

BLANCHETTE, FRANK. Gymnast, contortionist, with Den Stone's, 1873.

BLANFORD, CHRISTINE. John Robinson's, 1868.

BLEECKER, FRED. Program agent, Adam Forepaugh's, 1875.

BLISS, ALBERT G. See Bliss Family.

BLISS, ALEXANDER. Rider, P. T. Barnum's, 1871.

BLISS BROTHERS. See Bliss Family.

BLISS, CATHERINE. See Bliss Family.

BLISS, CHARLES. See Bliss Family.

BLISS FAMILY [Charles Sr.; wife Catherine; sons Charles Jr., Albert, Joseph, and George; and daughters Mrs. V. E. Wilham, Mrs. Louise Murphy and Mrs. Frank A. Robbins]. **Charles Bliss Sr.** (1826?-July 21, 1906) "Signor Bliss," ceiling walker, clown, called the "Human Fly." Born in Bavaria. After coming to America, traveled for years with Dan Rice's; also connected with Crane & Co., 1849; Rufus Welch's, 1852; Sands, Nathans & Co., 1857; VanAmburgh's, winter 1857-58; Nixon & Kemp, 1858-59; Old Cary's, 1864; George W. De-

Haven's, 1865; Haight & Chambers, 1866; J. M. French's, 1869. Died in Madison, WI, age 80. **Louise Bliss**, an aerialist, slack wire ascensionist, dancer. **Charles Bliss Jr.**, Dutch clown, died in Madison, WI, 1926, age 77. Began at the age of 6 and when a young man he went to Spain and gained fame as a tumbler. When 25, set a record by turning 75 flips around the arena without stopping. Clown, tumbler, barrel-dancer, perhaps working as an individual act, connected with Stone & Murray, 1869; Great Roman Hippodrome and Congress of Novelties (**William D. Curtis**, proprietor), 1877; Cooper & Bailey, 1880; Orrin Bros.', Mexico, winter 1880-81; Sells Bros.', 1883; Holland & McMahon (**George Holland, John McMahon**, proprietors), Chicago, fall 1885; P. T. Barnum's, 1886; Adam Forepaugh's, 1893; Orrin Bros.', Mexico, 1894. **George Bliss** (d. December, 1909), acrobat, but specialized in long distance leaping; Haight & Chambers, 1866; J. M. French's, 1867; Cooper & Bailey, 1880; P. T. Barnum's, 1886; *Gran Circo Pubillones*, Cuba, winter 1888-89; Orrin Bros.', Mexico, winter 1889-90; somersault artist and high leaper, New York Circus, 1893, which sailed up the Hudson on a chartered steamer, stopping at various cities. Claimed to be one of the original **Leotard Brothers** with **George Lair** and **Lewis Mette**. In 1880, was working as the **Leotards** with **George Schrode** and **Ed Snow**. **Albert G.** (d. November 17, 1932), at age 8, performing with his family in a small traveling circus, 1857, as one of a group of tumblers. Was a trouper for 75 years. Died in Madison, WI, age 83. **Albert, Charles** and **George** were together as the **Bliss Brothers**, leapers and tumblers, P. T. Barnum's, 1872-73, 1877; Frank Stowe's, 1874; Cooper, Bailey & Co., 1879-80; Barnum, Bailey & Hutchinson, 1881-85.

BLISS, GEORGE. See Bliss Family.

BLITZ, EUGENE. Facial artist and Punch and Judy, John H. Murray's, 1877.

BLITZ, FRANÇOIS R. (d. November 22, 1910) Son of Signor Blitz, the magician and ventriloquist. Sideshow privilege, Col. Hayward's Circus and Roman Hippodrome, which had an early demise; solicitor and Punch and Judy operator, sideshow, Adam Forepaugh's, 1879; sideshow privilege, Stickney's Imperial Parisian Circus, 1880; Blitz's Mammoth Dime Show, 1881; privileges, A. A. Beckett's, 1884; manager, Millie Christine Co., 1891. Died age 57.

BLOCK, ROBERT. Museum director, Adam Forepaugh's, 1875.

BLODGETT, WASH. Agent, Sprague's Colossal Circus, 1880.

BLONDIN [r. n. Jean Francois Gravelet]. (1822?-February 22, 1897) Wire-walker and acrobat. Born in Hesdin, Pas de Calais (another source gives Saint-Omer), France. Adopted the name of the artist with whom he had been apprenticed. Fair-haired with light eyes, below average height and weight, wore a mustache and a chin piece, and was noted for his ease, precision, and amazing grace. Visited NYC, **Ravel Troupe**, 1850s; later, performed with the **Martinetti Troupe**, 1857. Proprietor of a circus company for 2 years. Made his real mark in America by crossing Niagara River on a rope, June 30, 1859. The rope, 1,100 feet in the air, was 3¼" in diameter and 1,300' long. At times performed a drum feat on the wire that consisted of a backward somersault while beating a drum in correct time with an accompanying orchestra. Also did the same type of feat while playing a violin. With Madigan & Gardner, Front Street Theatre, Baltimore, winter 1860-61. After a year of continued success, returned to Europe, where he astounded the public with more high wire performances. It is said that one of his great feats occurred in London when he turned a somersault on stilts while 170' in the air. [George Middleton: "I have seen nearly all the tight rope walkers, but there was only one great artist—he was Blondin."] The last public appearance was in Belfast, Ireland, 1896, at 72 years of age. Died in London from diabetes the following year.

BLOOD, HARRY. Member of the variety troupe, John Robinson's, 1861; Robinson & Lake, 1862; Robinson & Bros.', 1863; Haight & Chambers, 1867; Lake's, fall 1867.

BLUM, PAUL C. Contracting agent, Washburn & Arlington, 1891.

BLYTHE, GEORGE. (d. 1836) Equestrian director. Englishman, formerly a director of Astley's Amphitheatre, London. Recruited and enticed to America by **Steven Price** as director of the Walnut Street Theatre, Philadelphia, making his first appearance in this country on May 1, 1823. Brought with him many circus novelties from London, which served him well as a 2-horse rider and equestrian director with Simpson & Price's circus from 1823-27. Opened a circus, Savannah, GA, January 13, 1827. Later, with Aaron Turner's, Philadelphia, for a winter engagement, 1833-34. Understood horses and was an excellent groom, horseman and horse breaker and occupied himself in teaching ladies and gentlemen the art of riding with ease and safety. Stood 5' 11" in height and possessed a muscular build—broad of shoulders and deep of chest; a skilled boxer but was civil and well-behave. Called a fine, jolly fellow, a stalwart, robust, florid-faced Britisher from the horse guards. [Charles Durang: "What George had learned in the hippodrome art he exercised with a true Briton's usual industry and honesty. Genius he had not; education was not his portion; but we can aver that he had a good heart. He kept the circus boys and grooms to their duties, and, we believe, they all liked him."] Died in poverty on Staten Island, where he kept a porter house.

BOCCACIO, BRONCHO. Lion tamer. Born on Cape Cod from a Spanish mother and a Cuban planter father. Became a sailor, also spent many years as a hunter. While in South Africa, joined Fellis' Circus and turned his attention to training animals. Later went to Europe and performed at the *Menagerie Alexiano*, Marseilles. An engagement with Sir Charles

Wombwell in England followed, where he worked with the famous lion, Wallace. Later came to America to exhibit Wallace.

BODKIN, MIKE S. Associate. Joined Adam Forepaugh's, 1880, and for 20 years was connected with the privileges. [D. W. Watt: He "was a man of unquestioned integrity and always held a responsible position in different departments, and many times was called in consultation with Mr. Forepaugh as to what was best to do in this or that department."]

BODISCO, SIGNOR. Monkey man, H. Buckley & Co., 1857-58, his first season in America.

BOGARDUS. Apprentice rider and pupil of Pepin. Pepin, Breschard & Cayetano, NYC and Baltimore, 1813-14. Continued with Cayetano & Co. in a tour of the the West and accompanied the company when it moved to New Orleans, 1816-17, performing a 2-horse riding act with his apprenticeship apparently finished. Was at Roulestone's Amphitheatre, Boston, summer 1818; with Villalave's company, late summer and fall of the same year. Returned to Pepin's troupe, 1819-21; Lafayette Amphitheatre, NYC, in its initial season, 1825. As a mature rider, performed exhibition riding with and without reins and rode standing on his toes as the horse circled the ring.

BOGARDUS, CAPT. A. H. (September 17, 1833-March 23, 1913) Sharpshooting act. Born in Albany County, NY. Shot 100 birds with 100 shots, Dexter Park, Chicago, July 1869. Won American wing shot championship, 1871. Went to England, 1875; defended his title there until 1878 when he returned to the USA. W. W. Cole's, 1882; one-third owner Buffalo Bill's, 1883-84; Adam Forepaugh's, 1884-87, 1889-91; Sells Bros.', 1888. Worked with sons **Eugene**, **Edward**, **Peter**, and **Henry**. [D. W. Watt: "When Capt. Bogardus and his four sons would step into the hippodrome track to commence their shooting the glass ball in the air, the ovation that they would always receive was certainly a high compliment. The Bogardus family were not only fine in their business, but all high class gentlemen and the kind you would always be glad to introduce as your friends."] He was a man of giant strength, standing 6' and weighing 220 pounds. Published a book, *Field, Cover and Trap Shooting*, 1874. Died at his home in Lincoln, IL.

BOGARTY, GEORGE. Levi J. North's Circus, 1859.

BOISSET BROTHERS [4, including Fred, Hugo]. Horizontal bar and Brother Act, Barnum, Bailey & Hutchinson, 1881.

BOGLE, JOSEPH W. Advance courier agent, P. T. Barnum's, 1875.

BOLINO, TOM. Clown, Rivers & Derious, 1857-59.

BOLLER, WILL F. Proprietor, Allen's, 1882-86; William Sells, 1891; Rippal & Boller, 1897; Boller Bros.', 1898.

BOLUS, CHARLES. Boss canvasman, Adam Forepaugh's, 1872.

BONFANTE, SIGNORITA. Haight & Chambers, 1867.

BONNEY, C. A. Musical albino, Robert Hunting's, 1894.

BOOKER, JOHNNY. Ethiopian performer, buffo singer and clown. Yankee Robinson's, 1857-58; George F. Bailey & Co., 1859-60, 1864; as Booker & Howard's Minstrels, L. B. Lent's, 1865; ringmaster and manager of concert, Great Commonwealth Circus, 1879. Was dangerously wounded by a ball from a pistol entering the left breast, just below the collar bone, passing through the lung and lodging somewhere in that locality, Dayton, OH, October 1864, while traveling with Bailey's Circus.

BOONE, DANIEL E. ["Col."]. (1841?-October 12, 1903) Showman and animal trainer, born in Kentucky. Adam Forepaugh's, 1891. Died in San Francisco, age 62.

BOOTH, J. General performer, Spalding & Rogers, 1850.

BOOTH, JONAS. Printer, living in NYC. Made the first poster from pine block for a circus.

BOOTH, SAMUEL. Ran one of the largest show printing houses in the country (as did his father before him), Centre Street, NYC.

BOSHELL, DAN. Died in Bedford, Va., December 21, 1918.

BOSHELL FAMILY [Alfred A., Val, Ada, Louise, Carrie, Amy]. **Alfred A.** (1874?-August 27, 1909) was a various times advertising agent for Klaw & Erlanger, Jacob Litt and others. Died of tuberculosis at the home of his brother, **Val**, in St. Paul, MN, age 35. **Louise**, equestrienne and wire-walker. Appears to have been the most talented of the group and to have had the longest career. Connected with C. T. Ames', 1870; John Robinson's 1872; Adam Forepaugh's, 1878, 1880; Cooper, Bailey & Co., 1879; "Queen of the Floating Wire," Barnum, Bailey & Hutchinson, 1881. Married principal rider, **Frank Melville**, Ishpening, MI, August 3, 1878. Died at her home in Jacksonville, FL, October 15, 1934, age 78.

BOSWICK, DICK. Ben Maginley's, 1863.

BOSWOLD, CHARLES ["Prof."]. Band leader, with L. B. Lent's New York Circus, 1862-72.

BOULEN. Clown and rider. Pepin, Breschard & Cayetano, Baltimore, winter 1813-14; Pepin & Breschard, Charleston, fall 1814. It is believed he accompanied Pepin to Europe sometime after the beginning of January, 1815. Was back with Pepin in Philadelphia and Lancaster, PA, summer 1817, and continued with him for a tour of the West Indies, 1819-20.

BOURDON, H. Gymnast, Rivers & Derious, 1859.

BOWEN, ELI. (b. October 14, 1844) "The Legless Wonder" or "The Legless Acrobat"; two feet of different sizes growing directly from the hip joints. Born in Richland County, OH, one of 10 children, the other 9 being completely normal. Age 13, 1857, started traveling with Major Brown's Colosseum. Adam Forepaugh's (Pullman Bros.' sideshow), 1876; Cooper, Bailey & Co., 1879; Barnum & Bailey, England, 1897. For his sideshow performance, did tumbling tricks and acrobatic work on a pole. Married an attractive young lady of 16, **Mattie Haight**, and fathered a large and healthy family.

BOWENS. General performer, R. Sands', 1849.

BOWERS, COONEY. Agent, W. H. Harris' Nickel-Plate, 1891.

BOWERS, DAVID P. Virginia Serenader, Raymond & Waring, 1844.

BOWERS, CHARLES. Ringmaster, S. O. Wheeler's, 1865.

BOWMAN, B. L. Ringmaster, Holland, Bowman & McLaughlin, 1890; manager and sideshow orator, Rentz', 1891; sideshow proprietor, World's Fair Aggregation, 1892. Wife handled a troupe of educated dogs.

BOYD, ORLANDO J. (d. February 18, 1893) Great Transatlantic Allied Shows (Orlando J. Boyd, **S. C. Peters**, proprietors), 1879; manager car #1, John Robinson's, 1880-81; advance manager, O'Brien, Handenberger, Astley & Lowanda, 1884; Frank A. Robbins', 1888-89. Died in Philadelphia.

BOYD, W. C. (b. July 4, 1850) Agent. Born in Amenia, Duchess County, NY, the home of Hyatt Frost. Being in the general provision business there, his first contact with the circus was selling meat to Frost's VanAmburgh & Co. in winter quarters. Engaged by that organization, 1879; general agent, Cooper & Jackson, 1880, 1882; press agent, W. W. Cole's, 1883, 1886; general agent, Doris & Colvin, 1887; Adam Forepaugh's, 1888-92. Also connected with Cooper & Bailey, P. T. Barnum's, Forepaugh-Sells Bros.', Beveridge Wild West, Walter L. Main's, LaPearl's, Burbridge & Boyd. Connected with the theatrical units of *Shennandoah*, *Held by the Enemy*, *Jim the Penman*, *Rudolph and Adolph*, Matthews & Bulger, *The Man from Mexico*, *The Young Mrs. Winthrop*, *Foxy Grandpa*, *On the Mississippi*, *The Bowery*, *The Private Secretary*, Al G. Field's Minstrels, *The Passing Show*, *The Irish Alderman*, *Down in Dixie*, Princess Chick Opera Co.; manager of the Park Theatre, Indianapolis, and the Wonderland Theatre, Detroit.

BOYD, WILLIAM. Advertiser. Association's Celebrated Menagerie and Aviary, Baltimore, 1837; VanAmburgh & Co.'s, 1859.

BOYLAN, F. O. Contracting agent, Great Chicago, 1879.

BOYLE, JOHN E. Press agent, John B. Doris', 1884-85; general contracting agent, E. H. Howes & Co., 1888; Adam Forepaugh's, 1889. Following 1889, was working for the *Daily Times*, Buffalo, NY.

BOYLE, M. F. Whittemore, Thompson & Co.'s Equescurriculum, 1865

BOYTON, PAUL ["Capt."]. (1847?-April 19, 1924) Born in Pennsylvania. Famous for the journeys taken and exploits performed on water throughout the world. First known for his ability as a diver, "The American Pearl Diver." Exhibited and demonstrated a patented life-saving suit (see illustration). Once, to show its usefulness, he disembarked from a steamer some miles from the Irish coast and made his way through a heavy sea to land. He next crossed the English Channel in it, spring 1875, leaving the French shore on May 27 and arriving in England the following day, covering about 34 miles en route. March 20, 1878, he crossed the Straits of Gibraltar. After a stay on the Continent for several years, returned to the USA, where he accomplished lengthy journeys on Western rivers. With Barnum & Bailey, 1888, performed in an artificial lake constructed within the circus tent. The tank eventually became a swimming pool at Barnum & Bailey's Bridgeport winter quarters. Had water show adjacent to Pawnee Bill show, Antwerp Exposition, 1894; Boyton's Sea Lion Park, Coney Island, 1895-1901. Son **Joseph** was treasurer Ringling-Barnum, 1891. Died age 77.

BRACKEN, WILLIAM. See William Painter.

BRADBURY, ROBERT. (1774?-July 21, 1831) Originally a cabinet maker in Liverpool, made his debut as a clown at the Liverpool Theatre. A man of great strength. As a tumbler specialised in making amazing leaps and taking dangerous falls, for which he was well padded. Appeared at Sadler's Wells, 1803, said to be of the Royal Circus. A rival to Grimaldi, of whom he was a friend. Came from England with the James West company, 1816; Pepin's, Baltimore, 1817.

BRADLEY, J. W. Treasurer, Castello & VanVleck, 1863.

BRADO, ROBERT. Treasurer, John H. Murray's, 1881.

BRADY, G. F. Boss canvasman, F. J. Taylor's, 1891.

BRADY, SAM. Concert manager, VanAmburgh's, 1876.

BRAINARD, ALBERT. Treasurer, Great New York Circus (**E. Hamilton, F. W. Sergeant,** proprietors), 1877.

BRANDEN, HARRY. Contortionist. Cross & LeRoy, 1884; Lemen Bros.', 1887; Shields', 1887-88; W. H. Harris' Nickel-Plate, 1889; aerialist, Gollmar Bros.', 1898; wire-walker, Gollmar Bros., 1900.

BRANDON, HARRY. "Spanish king," W. H. Harris' Nickel-Plate, 1891; stilt wire walker, Gollmar Bros.', 1897.

BRANDON, WILLIAM H. (1819?-March 12, 1871) Keeper of elephant Hannibal, VanAmburgh's. Died in Athens, NY, age 52.

BRANDT, JOHN. Gymnast and modern Hercules, Alexander Robinson's, 1876.

BRANNAN, EDWARD L. (b. July 3, 1859) Candy privilege (with **Billy Watson**), Lively's Great Allied Shows, 1878; advance agent, Fulford & Co., 1890. Also Cooper & Hemmings; Sam McFlinn's; G. W. Hall's; Cooper, Jackson & Co.; Sells Bros.'; Forepaugh-Sells; William Sells'; etc.

BRATTON, CHARLES. Orchestra leader, Robert Hunting's, 1894.

BREEN, WILLIAM L. Candy privilege manager, Barnum, Bailey & Hutchinson, 1882.

BREMMER, L. C. Banjoist, W. N. Smith's Ethiopians, with VanAmburgh & Co., 1860.

BRENNER, HERR. Strongman, Howes & Mabie, 1845-46.

BRENT, TOMMY. Bareback rider, tumbler, George F. Bailey & Co., 1860.

BRESCHARD, JEAN BAPTISTE CASMIERE. Eques-

trian. Frenchman of "excellent address and personal appearance." Was a partner of the Pepin & Breschard circus, who brought their horses and company from Spain in the winter of 1807 and performed in Boston until they opened in NYC, June 2, 1808, in the circus, corner of Broadway and Anthony Street. May have run continuously until the end of December. The company opened in Philadelphia at Ninth and Walnut Streets, February 2, 1809; returned to NYC, opening July 1, 1809, and continuing until August 26; were back in June of the following year, until they closed the season on September 29; organized the Olympic Circus, Baltimore, 1811; moved it to Philadelphia, opening the season on June 18, which lasted until September 28. Breschard was connected with **William Twaits** in managing the Olympic Circus in Philadelphia, 1812, for the production of horse dramas. There again, this time with **Pepin**, opening August 30, 1813. Stud of horses, though roughly broken, were excellent animals; the company was numerous and well appointed; costumes were the best thing of that kind that had been seen in America. The company seems to have alternated seasonally between New York and Philadelphia, offering both circus performances and horse dramas. Last connection with management was in Boston, January 14, 1815, with only he and his wife mentioned in the advertisement. It is supposed that he went to Europe for a time, but, 1817, was performing as an acrobat in a hall show, being the last word on both Breschard and his wife. He rode with extreme elegance and modesty; was a model performer, executing everything with elegance, while in full military habit; a man of excellent dress and manner. Charles Durang described his riding as "a genteel comedian attired for the polished drawing room."

BRESCHARD, MRS. JEAN. Received praise as a horsewoman, as she leaped her horse through 2 barrels. See above.

BRESLAW, C. James West's company, 1819-20.

BREWER, JAMES W. (1822?-April 23, 1860) Gymnast known for his work on the horizontal bars and bottle acts. Native of Boston. Strongman, John Tryon's, Bowery Amphitheatre, NYC, 1845; Rockwell & Stone, 1846; Col. Mann's, 1849; went to California, 1849, with several performers; A. W. Tell's, 1851; Col. Mann's, 1852; Australia, 1853-54; Lee & Marshall, 1855. November 27, 1858, he shot **Benjamin F. Moulton**, for which he was tried and acquitted on grounds of self-defense. Died at St. Helena, CA, age about 38.

BREWER, LON. Boss canvasman, Sig Montanio's, 1881.

BRIAN, F. Mrs. Charles Warner's winter circus, Philadelphia, corner of Tenth and Callowhill Streets, December 1868.

BRICKWOOD, CHARLES. Banjoist and comedian, Ducello's United Exhibitions, 1879.

BRIDGES, AMELIA. (d. September 7, 1885) Equestrienne, commonly referred to as "Madame Bridges." Worked her trick pony, Dove, and, as an equestrienne, made changes of clothing while riding. First husband was **John B. Bridges**, with whom she had a son, **John, Jr.** After Bridges died, 1879, she married circus proprietor **Andrew Gulig** of *Circo Americano*, Brazil. New York Champs Elysees, 1866; Mike Lipman's, 1867; G. G. Grady's, 1868, 1872; George W. DeHaven's, 1869; John W. Robinson's (not "Old John"), 1870; tight-rope act, Chiarini's, 1872; G. G. Grady's, 1874; John Wilson's, San Francisco, 1874; H. Harlan's, 1875; Carlo Bros., South America, 1876-77; American Circus, South America, 1879.

BRIDGES, JOHN B. (1816?-December 13, 1879) Equestrian, clown. Husband of **Amelia Bridges** and father of **John, Jr.** and **Amelia Carlo**, wife of **George Carlo** of the **Carlo Brothers**. New York Champs Elysees, 1866; Dan Castello's, winter 1866-67; G. G. Grady's, 1874; H. Harlan's, 1875; Joel E. Warner's, 1876; Carlo Bros.', South America, 1876-77; American Circus, South America, 1879. Had property in St. Charles, IL, where he was made a Freemason in Lodge No. 48. Died in South America, age 53.

BRIDGES, JOHN, JR. Son of **Amelia** and **John B. Bridges**. Equestrian with the American Circus (**A. Guilig, G. Ravell, W. H. Franklin**, proprietors), South America, 1879.

BRIGGS, ADA. Fat lady, Barnum, Bailey & Hutchinson, 1882.

BRISTOL, CHARLES. Agent. Responsible for bringing **Frank Howes** into the business, 1851.

BRISTOL, CLIFFORD. Son of **D. M. Bristol**. Agent, VanAmburgh's, 1847.

BRISTOL, DE LOSS M. (d. May 11, 1926) Father of **Clifford Bristol**. Prof. Bristol's Equescurriculum (horses and mules), 1885-91; Prescott's Great Eastern, 1896. Died at home of his son, Exeter, age 78.

BRITTNER, W. P. Musical director, Mrs. Charles H. Warner's, 1863-64.

BRITTON, A. T. String band leader, George W. DeHaven's, 1865.

BROCK, FRED. Contortionist, E. O. Rogers', 1891.

BROCK, HARRY. Clown, A. B. Rothcilds & Co., 1875.

BROCKWAY, LEVI J. Equestrian director, Beckett's Great Exposition Circus, 1881.

BROKER, JOHNNY "MASTER". Boy gymnast, Dr. James L. Thayer's, 1870.

BRONSON, GEORGE R. Agent. Sands & Howes, 1840; June, Titus, Angevine & Co., 1841; VanAmburgh & Co., southern tour, winter 1859-60, summer 1860; Mabie's Menagerie, 1862, 1864; manager, Stone & Rosston, 1865; advertiser, Stone, Rosston & Murray, 1868; railroad agent, Haight's Great Eastern, 1874; Howes's Great London, 1875; railroad contractor and general director, Adam Forepaugh's, 1877; advance director, D. W. Stone's, 1878; railroad contractor, Sells Bros.', 1880. [Peter Sells: "George Bronson was another great agent. He was a splendid type of a man. Of extraordinary habits and great knowledge of the country, he commanded a large salary as a railroad contractor."]

BROOKS, CHARLES H. Contracting agent, W. H. Harris' Nickel-Plate, 1884.

BROOKS, GEORGE. Minstrel, Alexander Robinson's, 1875-76.

BROOKS, RICHARD ["Sailor Dick"]. Boss animal man, Burr Robbins', 1879.

BROOKS, SILAS M. (d. April 7, 1906) Balloonist. Entered the entertainment business, 1848, when engaged by Barnum to form a Druid band; manufactured crude horn instruments and grotesque costumes and created a successful feature until over-shadowed by the Jenny Lind craze. Organized a circus featuring a balloon ascension. When **Paulin**, his aeronaut, was taken ill, Brooks donned his garb and made the ascension himself. Finding it to his liking, continued in that capacity, making himself a fortune. Died, however, in the poor house in Collinsville, CT.

BROOKS, T. Animal tamer. Quick, Sands & Co., Baltimore, 1833; VanAmburgh's, 1847-49; G. C. Quick, 1850-51; Sands & Quick, 1852-53.

BROTHERTON, FRANÇOIS. Wire-walker, juggler, balancer, tight-rope ascensionist and troupe of trained dogs, Cooper & Chapin, 1874.

BROTHERTON, CHARLES ["Master"]. Son of **François Brotherton**. Aerial suspensionist, Cooper & Chapin's Circus and Menagerie, 1874.

BROWER, FRANCIS MARION ["Frank"]. (November 30, 1823-June 4, 1874) Clown, minstrel performer, actor. Born in Baltimore and grew to become a leading performer in negro minstrelsy, possessing a store of anecdotes, which he related in his own unique style. [John A. Dingess: "In private life, he was a genial companion, engaging in his manners, and his conversation bristled with distinctive intellect."] Spent much of his formative career in the circus business, including such engagements as juggler, Cincinnati Circus, 1841; eastern unit, June, Titus, Angevine & Co., 1842; Nathan A. Howes, winter 1842-43; Ogden & Hobby, 1842; Welch & Mann, 1845-46; Welch, Delavan & Nathans, 1847-48; R. Sands & Co., 1849; Robinson & Eldred, 1850; Johnson & Co., 1852; Wesley Barmore's, 1854; Sands, Nathans & Co., 1854; Welch & Lent, 1856; Welch's National Circus, winter 1856; Sands & Nathans, 1857. Married equestrienne **Louisa Banks Brower**. [T. Allston Brown: "The appearance of Frank in the ring is the cue for mirth; and his jests, always chaste and original, are such as would make a stoic hold his sides. I have spent many an hour listening to the laughter-provoking jests of Uncle Frank and must confess that, as a clown, I think he has but few equals."] Brower died in Philadelphia.

BROWER, LOUISA [formerly Louisa Howard, *nee* Banks]. Equestrienne wife of **Frank Brower**. Born in Baltimore, MD. Act consisted of leaping over high objects and darting through balloons and, it is said, with style and finish. Buckley & Weeks, 1834-35; Boston Lion's, 1836; J. J. Hall's, 1837; Raymond & Waring, 1840; Welch & Mann, 1842-46; Welch's,

1847-49; Risley & McCullum, England, 1851; Barmore's, 1854; Sands, Nathans & Co., 1854; Welch & Lent, 1855-56; Welch's National Circus, winter 1856; Sands & Nathans, 1857. Advertised as an "elegant equestrienne in her graceful horseback performance known as 'The Venetian Carnival'." [T. Allston Brown: "This celebrated and wonderful equestrienne received a greater amount of sincere, unbought and enthusiastic applause than was ever awarded to any person who has attempted the daring and heroic art which she practiced. Her unrivaled grace and astounding daring have been themes of eulogium, astonishment and admiration in all of the more populous cities of Europe. She is the only equestrienne, who ever graced this country, who rides with the daring and elegance taught only by the Parisian schools; and she is acknowledged to have no superior in any part of the world."]

BROWN, BANDANA. Ethiopian entertainer. Great Western, 1846; Dr. Gilbert R. Spalding's, 1847; Stone & McCollum, 1848.

BROWN, BENJAMIN. (1798-1842) Cousin of **J. Purdy Brown.** Born in Croton Falls, Westchester County, NY. In charge of caring for an elephent exhibited by **Hackaliah Bailey** and **Edward Finch**, 1820, a job he retained until at least 1823. Riding master, J. Purdy Brown's, 1826, where he performed the horse Conqueror as well; managed a circus and menagerie, 1828; co-proprietor with brother, **Herschel J. Brown**, Royal Pavilion Circus/Olympic Circus, West Indies, 1829-30 (menagerie is said to have consisted of "a few old, worn out animals").

BROWN, C. F. Gymnast, tumbler, Joel E. Warner & Co., 1871.

BROWN, CHARLES. (d. February 7, 1865) Clown. As an apprentice, appeared as Charles Mateer, after his master, John Mateer. Performed under own name with Spalding's North American, February 1846. New Orleans Circus, December 1850; Dan Rice's, 1851; Spalding & Rogers, 1852-57; Burt & Robinson, 1858; Great Railroad Circus, 1859; George W. DeHaven's, 1860. Died in Cincinnati.

BROWN, CHRISTOPHER C. Brother of showman **Ben Brown.** Brown Bros.', 1826-29. Drove the first elephant exhibited in the United States. Moved her from place to place at night and exhibited during the day in barns and outhouses at a shilling a head, children half price. [Ben Brown: "My brother Christopher was the first man to put up a canvas...."]

BROWN, FANNY. Daughter of **Thomas McFarland** (r. n. William Brown). Acrobat, Ross & Carlo, 1865; left with John Wilson's for the Southwest Pacific, September 1865. Married **William Carlo**, San Francisco, 1866. Chiarini's, South and Central America, 1869; *manège* and pantomimist, Carlo Bros.', South America, 1876.

BROWN, FRANK. English clown, equestrian. The son of **Henry Brown**, clown and circus proprietor. Orrin Bros.', Mexico, winter 1880-81; Shelby, Pullman & Hamilton, 1881;

Cantelli & Leons, Havana, Cuba, winter 1882-83.

BROWN, GEORGE W. (July 10, 1844-December 20, 1918) Gymnast, equestrian. Born in Reading, PA. Gardner & Hemmings, 1863-64; Robinson & Deery, 1864; Gardner & Hemmings, Philadelphia, winter 1865-66, and summer 1866; Dan Rice's, 1867; Adam Forepaugh's, 1869; Philadelphia Circus, winter 1867-68; Mrs. Charles Warner's, Philadelphia, fall 1869; Great Combination, 1871; J. W. Wilder's, 1872; Warner & Henderson, 1874; Springer's, 1875; Cooper, Bailey & Co., 1876; Orrin Bros.', Mexico, winter 1882-83, 1884-85; Dockrill's, South America, winter 1885-86; Tony Lowande's, Havana, Cuba, fall 1893. Highly rated forward tumbler, doing 8 or 10 in a swing. Between about 1867 and 1871, worked with **Joseph Sanford** as a gymnastic partner. Died at his home in Kansas City, MO.

BROWN, HERSCHEL J. (1803-1864) The brother of **Ben Brown.** Brown Bros.', 1826-29; B. F. Brown & Co., 1830-32.

BROWN, JEFF. Minstrel performer, P. T. Barnum's, 1873.

BROWN, JESS. Leaper, King & Franklin, 1887; proprietor, Brown's, 1895.

BROWN, J. M. Agent. Committed suicide December 2, 1909, Columbus, OH, by drinking carbolic acid. Was about 55 years of age.

BROWN, JOSHUAH PURDY. (1802?-June 6, 1834) A native of Somers, Westchester County, NY. In 1825, was a partner with **Lewis Bailey** in a circus venture, his first season under canvas and one which marked the beginning of the use of tents for traveling circuses. Stuart Thayer credits him with "Americanizing" the circus, initializing the wagon traveling show with its own portable theatre, making one-day stands. Moved his companies great distances and explored new territories; was the first to take a circus to Virginia, 1826; as early as 1828, moved up and down the Mississippi Valley to be the first circus to enter the then western area, where he set up companies in Natchez and New Orleans; continued the practice of the permanent circuses by featuring hippodramas under canvas; 1832, toured with a combined circus and menagerie (under the title of Brown's Circus and Menagerie), one of the first to do so. Thayer correctly suggests that since Brown had his show on the road as early as 1825, the year the canvas tent was introduced as a circus covering, and survived the vicissitudes of travel and competition, he must have been a practitioner of good management and of astute business choices.

BROWN, KATIE. Child equestrienne. 10 year old apprentice traveling on O'Brien's circus when she was taken from the train at Frankford, PA, by the Society to Protect Children from Cruelty and returned to her mother, a **Mrs. Coles**, and sent back to school because she came under a new law that prevented the training of children under 16 years of age for public performances. In all probability she had been under the tutelage of **Madame Louise Tourniaire**.

BROWN, LOUISE. See Louise Tourniaire.

BROWN, MINNIE. Equestrienne and vocalist, Dan Rice's, 1878.

BROWN, MOLLY ["Little Mollie"]. (May 17, 1860-January 9, 1924) Equestrienne. Born in Somerset County, NJ, the daughter of the famous equestrienne **Mme. Louise Tournaire**. Began a professional career at age 6, and as a child performer had remarkable strength and endurance and was an outstanding pad and bareback rider. Credited with being the first woman to turn a somersault on a bare-backed horse from a standing position, 1873. Earliest reference was as **Marie**, L. B. Lent's Equescurriculum, 1865; George W. DeHaven's, 1866; S. O. Wheeler's, 1867-68; S. P. Stickney's, 1869; Campbell's, 1870; Batcheller & Doris, 1870; Sheldenburger's, 1871; John O'Brien's, 1873; P. T. Barnum's, 1873; Montgomery Queen's, 1874; New National Theatre, Philadelphia, winter 1876-77; Adam Forepaugh's, 1877; D. W. Stone's, 1878; P. T. Barnum's, 1878; Batcheller & Doris, 1879-1880; Circus Royal, 1881; John V. O'Brien's, 1883; O'Brien, Handenberger, Astley & Lowanda, 1884. [Elmira, NY, *Gazette*, July 2, 1873: "Old and experienced circus riders consider it quite a feat to turn somersaults on a horse going at full speed but here is a young girl twelve years old, the only female who has the bravery and skill to accomplish it, performing the feat with an ease and grace that call forth the most enthusiastic applause."] Was married clandestinely to **Clarence W. Farrell**, February, 1878, who was for many years treasurer of Frank A. Robbins' Shows. Second husband was **James J. Files**, nonprofessional. Died in Philadelphia, survived by 2 daughters, **Louise** and **Viola**.

BROWN, MRS. FRANK. See Addie Austin.

BROWN, OSCAR. (d. 1842) Brother of **J. Purdy Brown**. Took over the circus after J. Purdy died, 1834, and ran it from 1834 to 1837. Previously, had operated Brown & Green's Menagerie and Circus, 1832, in Ohio with partner **J. B. Green**; had the circus out, 1835, under the title Brown's Mammoth Arena Circus Co.; which was sold to Fogg & Stickney at end of the 1837 season, terminating a 13 year career in management, which generally established a pattern of opening in New Orleans, moving north in the spring and south in the fall.

BROWN, S. Adam Forepaugh's, 1871.

BROWN, S. E. Proprietor, Major Brown's Mammoth Coloseum, 1856-57.

BROWN, T. ALLSTON ["Col."]. (January 16, 1836-April 2, 1918) Known as the antiquarian of the theatrical world, few men in America had a broader or more comprehensive knowledge of American amusements and their representatives. Perhaps the most underrated amusement historian of the 19th century, although his interest in factual material nullified an eloquence of style. Where others were primarily interested in the "higher drama," Brown concerned himself with a broader stage; and where others identified themselves with their immediate theatrical provinces, Brown kept no provincial borders.

Varied experiences in the theatrical profession as literary correspondent, publisher, editor, business agent, advance man, circus treasurer, theatre manager, and talent agent supplied him with an intimate understanding of the business and its people, and the mobility required by the nature of his various employments allowed him to collect material from the innumerable cities he visited. [M. B. Leavitt: "Col. T. Allston Brown was the first agent of his time and the recognized historian of the American stage. A resumé of stage history and life of its people would not be complete without due reference to Col. Brown, for no man in all America has a broader or more comprehensive knowledge of the American stage and its representatives."] Born in Newburyport, MA. Grandfather was the **Rev. Charles William Milton**, who was the minister in one church in that town 42 years. 1852, removed to Philadelphia and in September, 1855, became the Philadelphia correspondent of the New York *Clipper*, being known as "Young Rapid." April, 1858, founded a dramatic paper, *The Tattler*, which later changed its name to *The Philadelphian*. Shortly after, was connected with the dramatic department of Col. Fitzgerald's *City Item*. May, 1860, began the publication of a series of dramatic articles for *The New York Programme*. His "A Complete History of the Amphitheatre and Circus" was first serialized in the theatrical columns of the New York *Clipper* in eight installments, running from December 22, 1860, through February 9, 1861. Contributed three other historical series to the pages of the *Clipper*—A "History of the American Stage," ran in seventeen installments from July 28 through November 17, 1860; another and far more lengthy theatrical record began in March of 1888 as "The Theatre in America," described as "Its Rise and Its Progress During a Period of 156 Years, A Succinct History of Our First and Famous Plays and Playhouses, Opening Bills, Casts of Characters, Distinguished Actors and Actresses, Notable Debuts, Deaths, Fires, Etc., Etc", which served as the foundation for a work that was published in 1903, a detailed, three volume *A History of the New York Stage from the First Performance in 1732 to 1901*, reissued in 1964; the "Early History of Negro Minstrelsy," a painstaking documentation of "it's rise and progress in the United States," was carried by the *Clipper* in 59 installments, beginning in the anniversary issue of February 17, 1912, and ending on March 8, 1914, being the most complete record of minstrelsy yet assembled. A book, also called *History of the American Stage*, was first published in 1870 and was reissued in 1969, containing biographical sketches of members of the profession that appeared on the American stage from 1733 to 1870. The totality of these works, added to his years of contributions to the pages of the New York *Clipper*, establishes him as a leading historian of American amusements. In January, 1860, first entered the theatrical business, going in advance of the Cooper English Opera Co.; December of that year, treasurer, Gardner & Madigan's Circus; treasurer,

H. P. Madigan's, summer 1861. While at the Front Street Theatre, Baltimore, **M. Blondin**, the rope walker, was one of the
attractions, whose main act was to ascend on a rope with a
man on his back, from the stage to the upper gallery, one hundred feet above the parquet seats. At one performance the man
to go on Blondin's back failed to materialize at the critical
moment, and to save the act Brown volunteered and made the
ascension, for which act of bravery the entire press of Baltimore announced him as "Colonel" T. Allston Brown, a title
that has clung to him ever since. Was business manager for
Isabella Cubas, Spanish *danseuse* and pantomimist, winter
1862; Dan Rice's, 1862, afterwards with Tom King's, Baltimore and Washington. When James M. Nixon opened the
Cremorne Gardens on Fourteenth Street that year, Col. Brown
was engaged as business manager; after the Garden closing,
October 9, the circus part of the show went to Washington for
the winter and Col. Brown accompanied it. February, 1863,
agent, Hart & Simmons' Minstrels; writer, Thayer & Noyes,
summer 1863; fall 1863, became dramatic editor of the New
York *Clipper* and published a showman's guide the same year;
April, 1870, resigned from the *Clipper* to establish a dramatic
agency; manager of Theatre Comique (Broadway near Spring
Street) after retiring temporarily from the agency business in
March, 1877, and transferring his interest to his brother, **J.
Alexander Brown**; went on the road with Dion Boucicault's
Shaugbraun, returning to the agency business in January,
1878; September 1882, manager, **Hanion Brothers** in *Le
Voyage En Suisse*, he having engaged them in Europe for an
American tour of three years; manager, **Marie Aimee**; then a
tour with **Mrs. Gen. Tom Thumb**; next with **Charles Arnold**
in *Hans the Boatman*. Died in Philadelphia, age 82.
BROWN, TOM. Master of transportation, Cook & Whitby's,
1892.
BROWN, W. C. Leader of string band, G. F. Bailey & Co.,
1861.
BRUNSTADT. Great Norwegian Giant. Bunnell's Museum,
1881; Barnum, Bailey & Hutchinson, 1882.
BRYAN, W. T. Proprietor, Bryan & Williams, 1894.
BRYANT, JAMES. Acrobat, Buckley, Weeks & Co., 1835;
Boston Lion Circus, 1836; New Jersey Circus, 1845; Great
Empire Circus, 1846; Robinson & Eldred, 1847.
BRYANT, RUFUS. Trapeze performer, Great London Pavil-
ion Show, 1876.
BRYANT, WILLIAM T. Performer, Pinafore Concert Co.,
Adam Forepaugh's, 1879.
BUCHANAN, ROBERT. Boss canvasman, John Robinson's,
1869-70.
BUCHANAN, CHARLES. Spalding & Rogers, November
1863.
BUCKLEY, DANIEL. Thayer & Noyes, 1865. Was thrown
out of a bill wagon going down a steep hill in Maryland and
suffered a broken leg. Presumably it was amputated.

BUCKLEY, EDWARD G. (September 16, 1836-March 30,
1892) Rider. Son of **Matthew** and **Marianne Buckley**, brother of **Henry, Page** and **Laura**. Started as rider with Mabie
Bros.' at 15 and after 14 years with them, traveled with Harry
Buckley's, Buckley-Babcock's, Coup-Castello's, Buckley's
Roman Hippodrome, Buckley-Colvin and Castello's Centennial Circus; also Stickney & Buckley, 1844; S. P. Stickney's,
1845; Howes & Mabie, 1846; E. F. Mabie's, 1847-48; ringmaster, Buckley & Co., 1857; assistant manager, P. T. Barnum's, 1871; concert privilege, P. T. Barnum's, 1872; concert,
candy stand and reserve seat privileges, Burr Robbins', 1877;
press agent, Burr Robbins', 1885; William C. Coup's Equescurriculum and Indian Exhibition. Married **Helen Gaskell**; 3
children from the union—**Matthew, James, Harriet.** Active
in circus business for 50 years. Died of pneumonia in Chicago.
BUCKLEY, GEORGE. (d. 1865) Acrobat. Was a pupil of
William Harrington. Palmer & Harrington, 1834; Bancker &
Harrington, 1835; J. W. Bancker's, 1836; Brown & Co., 1837;
A. Hunt & Co., 1838; Raymond's menagerie and circus, 1839;
Raymond & Waring, Philadelphia, 1840; eastern unit of June,
Titus, Angevine & Co., 1841; Welch & Mann's, winter 1841;
then R. Sands, United Kingdom, 1842, 1845; VanAmburgh's,
1844; United Kingdon to South Africa, with Franklin, 1860.
Died in Lucknow, India, 1865.
BUCKLEY, HARRY. (March 1, 1829-September 8, 1884)
Son of **Matthew** and **Marianne Buckley** and the brother of
Edward and **Page.** Became an accomplished violinist. Over
six-feet tall, weighing over 200 pounds, was large for a principal rider. 4-horse rider, Mabie Bros.', at age of 12; Boston
Lion Circus (Raymond & Weeks, proprietors), 1836-37; S. H.
Nichols', 1839, 1842; S. P. Stickney's, 1845; Howes & Mabie,
1846; E. F. Mabie's, 1847-51; manager, H. Buckley & Co.'s
National Circus, organized in Delavan, WI, 1857; 1858, took
out the Buckley-Babcock North American Circus, which was
on the road for 2 years without a break, ending up in the Carribbean aboard a sailing vessel; Mabie's Menagerie and Nathans' Circus, 1861; sideshow privilege (with **W. C. Coup**)
Mabie's, 1863; sideshow privilege (with **Billy Cook**), Yankee
Robinson's, 1867; P. T. Barnum's, 1871-72; concert privileges, P. T. Barnum's, 1872-73; returned to Delavan, WI, and
organized the Roman Hippodrome which had a $3000 daily
expense and 1000 on the payroll—playing without a big top,
only at fairgrounds, at first, but later acquired a tent; menag-
erie manager, Dan Rice's, 1877, manager, 1878. Later in life
owned a hardware store in Delavan, WI, and, with **W. C.
Coup**, built the first cheese factory in that state. Moved to
Chicago, 1882, and died there 2 years later.
BUCKLEY, JAMES. (?-1849) Rider. Harrington's, 1832;
Palmer & Harrington, 1834; Bancker & Harrington, 1835-36;
Brown & Co., 1836; June, Titus, Angevine & Co., Bowery
Amphitheatre, 1840; A. Hunt & Co., 1838; eastern unit of
June, Titus, Angevine & Co., 1841; VanAmburgh's, England,

1844; Richard Sands', England, 1845; Robinson & Eldred, 1847; Stickney's Grand National, 1848. Died in New Albany, IN, of cholera.

BUCKLEY, JAMES PAGE. (October 3, 1848-February 11, 1918) Born in Missouri, youngest son of **Matthew and Marianne Buckley** and brother of **Edward and Harry**. Cookhouse manager for P. T. Barnum's, 1872; manager, W. C. Coup's, 1893; equestrian director, Coup & Dice, 1894; co-proprietor, W. C. Coup's Educated Horses, 1896; F. J. Gentry's, 1896; proprietor, Page Buckley's Dog, Horse and Pony Show, 1898. Died at New Lisbon, WI.

BUCKLEY, LAURA. (November 23, 1833-October 1917) Born in Philadelphia. Daughter of **Matthew and Marianne Buckley** and sister of **Harry, Ed, and Page**. Debut, Buckley, Hopkins, 1838; Buckley, Hopkins, Tufts, 1839; Buckley & Stickney's, 1844; S. P. Stickney's, 1845; Howes & Mabie, 1846; E. F. Mabie's, 1847-48. Retirement came, 1850, with marriage to **Edmund Foster Mabie**. Married **Orlando Crosby**, December 5, 1870, at Delavan, WI. Died in Elroy, WI.

BUCKLEY, MARIANNE. (1802-1877) The wife of **Matthew Buckley** and mother of **Edward, Henry, Page** and **Laura**; a performer until 1839. Boston Lion Circus (Raymond & Weeks, proprietors), 1836.

BUCKLEY, MATTHEW B. (June 15, 1800-February 28, 1897) Rider, general performer, showman, the "grandfather" of the Delavan, WI, circus colony. The father of **Harry, Edward** and **Page Buckley**. Born in London, England, came to USA, 1826; had a long and distinguished career, performing as a rider, slack-rope performer, pantomimist, dancer, musician and still vaulter. A quiet, genteel man, as effective on the stage as in the arena; began as a youthful clown and rider at English fairs; at a still early age, apprenticed as a rider to manager Astley of Astley's Amphitheatre, London, 1811. Price & Simpson brought him to America, where he made his debut at the Lafayette Amphitheatre, NYC, June 27. Headed his own company, 1828, which he continued intermittantly. Harrington & Buckley, 1830; John Lamb's, 1831; Fogg & Stickney, 1832. Purchased a small show from **John Lindsey** and **Nathan Miller**, 1833, calling it Buckley & Co.; following year, was out under the name of Buckley & Weeks, lasting 3 seasons. Boston Lion Circus (Raymond & Weeks, proprietors), 1836-37; co-proprietor with **Henry Rockwell** and **H. Hopkins** in a circus enterprise, Buckley, Rockwell, Hopkins & Co., 1838; S. H. Nichols', 1839; Raymond & Waring, 1839; S. P. Stickney's partner in a venture, 1840; joined S. P. Stickney's New Orleans Circus, 1844, and by August of that year was a partner in the company; equestrian manager, S. P. Stickney's, 1845; clown and rider, Howes & Mabie, 1846; ringmaster, E. F. Mabie's, 1847-48. Retired from circus life to Delavan, WI, 1854; co-owner H. Buckley & Co., 1857. On 90th birthday amazed Delavanites by doing a backsomersault in the business district. Died at his home, age 97.

BUCKLEY, SOPHIA. Equestrienne, singer, Palmer's Circus and Gymnastic Arena, 1835; Palmer's Pavilion Circus, 1836.

BUELL, ASA. Elephant trainer, John Robinson's, 1868; boss animal man, John Robinson's, 1874-75.

BUGBEE, D. Agent, Spalding & Rogers, 1851.

BUISLAY FAMILY [Henri Agoust, Adolphe, Martha, Julio, Etienne, Rosita, Augustine, Greuet, Justin, Master Joaquin, Mlle. Luisa]. French athletes, gymnasts and trapeze performers. Came to California from France and started a small, one-ring circus. As gymnasts and antipodean artists, featured feats of the "Spiral Mountain" and the "Niagara Leap." **August** (1847?-November 19, 1911), acrobat, parachutist, was the most prominent. When the first gas filled balloons came into vogue, the intrepid trapeze performer, began making ascensions, parachuting from the floating balloon. Was a partner with **David R. Hawley** of the gymnastic team of Buislay & Hawley in the early 1880s. August died in San Francisco, age 64. **Mme. Martha** (Mrs. August Buislay) *manège* performer, was described as "the most remarkable leaper over high gates under saddle in America." Arrived from Mexico, 1865. John Wilson's, San Francisco, 1865; Lee & Ryland, California, 1866; Great European, 1868. **Julio** listed with Courtney & Sanford's, Lima, Peru, fall 1870. **August** (with **Hawley**), Barnum, Bailey & Hutchinson, 1881-82; Leon & Dockrill, Iron Amphitheatre, Havana, winter 1881-82; gymnast and trapeze performer, Orrin Bros.', 1882-83; trapeze artist, Burr Robbins', 1884; Barnum & London, 1885; bar performer, Robinson's, California (**Frank Frost**, manager), 1886. **Hortense** Buislay married **Eduardo Codona**; marriage produced a daughter, **Victoria**, and sons **Alfredo** and **Lalo**, aerialists.

BUNGAREE. Fire eater, first time in America, Melville, Maginley & Cooke's Circus, 1875.

BUNNELL, GEORGE B. (d. May 3, 1911) Museum and sideshow proprietor. Born in Southport, CT. Brothers **John** and **Samuel** were also in the sideshow business. Sideshow, P. T. Barnum's, 1871-72; ass't manager, 1873; asst't manager, P. T. Barnum's Roman Hippodrome, 1875; Palace of Wonders privilege, P. T. Barnum, 1876; sideshow proprietor, P. T. Barnum's, 1879. Proprietor, New American Museum during the late 1870s and 1880s; proprietor, Bunnell's Museum, Broadway and Ninth Street, NYC. Died age 57.

BURDEAU, HENRY. Gymnast, clown, and stilt performer. Various times a partner of **Charles S. Burrows** and **W. F. Hogle**. Rivers & Derious, 1856-59; Bowery Amphitheatre, 1857-58; R. Sands', 1860-62; Spalding & Rogers, South America, 1862; Robinson & Howes, 1863; Robinson & Howes, 1864; George W. DeHaven's, 1865; Haight & Chambers, 1866-67; (with **Charles S. Burrows**) Cooke's, Philadelphia, January 1868; (with **Burrows**) Bryan's, 1869; (with **Hogle**) comic stilt act, Dr. James L. Thayer's, 1870; (with **Burrows**) James Robinson's, 1870. Formed a partnership with **W. F.**

Hogle and **Dr. James L. Thayer** for the tenting season of 1870. (with **Hogle**) Mrs. Charles Warner's, Philadelphia, winter 1870-71; G. G. Grady's, 1871; (with **Burrows**) Adam Forepaugh's, 1872; John H. Murray, 1873; Haight's Great Eastern, 1874; Adam Forepaugh's, 1876; New York Central Park Circus, 1877; Adam Forepaugh's, 1879; Batcheller & Doris, 1880; Welsh & Sands, post-season 1880; VanAmburg & Co., 1883. Married **Jeanette Armstrong**, equestrienne, Philadelphia, October 31, 1872. Both had been members of Adam Forepaugh's the prior season.

BURDEAU, JEANETTE. See Jeanette Armstrong.

BURDETT, CHARLES ["Major"]. (1850?-May 25, 1882) Dwarf. Born in Cumberland, MD. Twin brother of **Fannie Burdett**, also a dwarf. First exhibited, 1872; P. T. Barnum's, 1874; W. W. Cole's, 1878-79; Adam Forepaugh's, 1880-82. Died in Pontiac, MI, age 32.

BURDETT, FANNIE. Dwarf, sister of **Major Burdett**. P. T. Barnum's, 1874.

BURDICK, A. D. For some years private groom of **Mme. Dockrill** after she first came over to this country from Europe.

BURDICK, EPHRAIM H. Proprietor, Burdick & Main, 1879. Don Allen purchased William Main's interest, 1880, making it Burdick & Allen.

BURGESS, JOSHUAH. Proprietor, Burgess' Menagerie, 1832; sideshow manager, Zoological Institute, Boston, 1836; collection of birds and reptiles, Macomber, Welch & Co.'s touring the Maritimes, 1836. Went down with the sinking of the *Royal Tar* that year.

BURGESS, SAM. Proprietor, Sam Burgess' American Circus, 1850.

BURGESS, TOM. Clown and comic singer. Dan Rice's, 1851-52; Levi J. North's, 1859; George W. DeHaven's, 1860; Castello & VanVleck, 1863-64; DeHaven & Co., 1865; Palmer's Great Western, 1865; Dan Castello & Co., 1866; Perry Powers', 1867; Haight & Chambers, 1867.

BURK, NETTIE. (d. July 2, 1932) Feature equestrienne attraction. The daughter of a horse breeder; learned to ride on her father's farm in Stony Fort, NJ. Entered the ring around 1860 with a small circus traveling out of NYC. From this, attracted the attention of **Adam Forepaugh**, who signed her for a season. **Barnum** then took her away from Forepaugh. She toured Europe and all the foreign capitals. Later, organized her own act which included horses, trained dogs and a clown. Fell in love with a bartender by the name of **Jackson**, married him and dropped out of show business. After Jackson's death, worked at various jobs until she was 68, hiding her identity. When friends found her destitute, they enlisted the aid of the Actors Fund to care for her. Died in NYC, age 90.

BURK, SEARGENT. Champion lightning drill of the world, P. T. Barnum's, 1873.

BURK, T. K. (1853-August 24, 1893) Treasurer, King, Burk & Co. New Railroad Shows, 1883-87; T. K. Burk's Equine

College, 1889; T. K. Burk's Railroad Circus, 1890-92. Died, age 40, at the home of his sister (Mrs. John Miller), Peru, IN. Buried Paw Paw, MI.

BURK, TOM. Candy privilege (with Frank Ketchum), Great Western, 1876.

BURKE, ED. Equestrian director, Bruce L. Baldwin's, 1894.

BURKE, ELLA. L. B. Lent's, 1859-60.

BURKE, HARRY. Treasurer, George W. Richard's, 1887.

BURKE, L. NICHOLAS. Clown, L. B. Lent's, 1862.

BURKE, SERGEANT. Zouave drillist. Sideshow, P. T. Barnum's, 1875.

BURKE, THOMAS EWING. (d. March 22, 1926) Brother of **Billy Burke** and an uncle of **Billie Burke**, the actress. Died of a stroke in Fredericktown, OH.

BURKE, TONY. Orator, Robert Hunting's, 1894.

BURKE, WILLIAM ETHELBERT ["Billy"]. (October 23, 1845-October 5, 1906) Clown, who sang comic songs and tumbled. Father of **Billie Burke**, the actress. Agent Charles Day described him as a happy-go-lucky, genial individual. Born at Waterford, Knox County, Ohio. His father arranged for him to become druggist apprentice to S. S. Tuttle of Frederickton, Ohio. Next became a drygoods clerk in Pittsburgh. But soon abandoned that for performing as end man with Tumble's Varieties. This was cut short when at only 16 he joined the Union army, with which he was involved in 6 major battles before being seriously wounded in the Battle of Arkansas Post and given an honorable discharge. However, during his Army days he was extremely popular because of his comical songs and jokes about the daily life of a Civil War soldier. After the war, engaged for a short stint with a minstrel troupe, 1865, which did not last long. Joined James M. Nixon's circus company, which, after a brief southern tour, set sail for Galveston, TX. The ship encountered a severe storm and was all but destroyed. Burke was picked up by the United States steamship, *South Carolina* and landed at New Orleans. There, joined Thayer and Noyes playing up the Red River on the steamer *Ida May*. Unluckily, a storm wrecked this vessel, although Burke escaped with only the loss of his wardrobe. Thayer & Noyes' Circus, 1866; Mike Lipman's, winter 1866-67; Mrs. Charles Warner's, Philadelphia, fall 1869; Adam Forepaugh's, 1870, 1877, 1879-81, 1887, 1893; James Robinson's, 1870-72; DeHaven & Stokes, 1873; Montgomery Queen's, 1874-75; Adam Forepaugh's, 1876; Den W. Stone's, 1878; Barnum, Bailey & Hutchinson, 1881-82; with clown elephant "Sidney," Sells Bros.', 1885-86 [Salina, KA, *Republican*: "Billy Burke, of the Sells Brothers' Shows, is an old soldier, but none of his jokes are. That accounts for his successful drilling of 'Sid.'"]. Great Eastern, 1889; Barnum & Bailey, 1895; Rice's, 1896. [D. W. Watt: "His assumed air of deference to the ringmaster and his slyness in 'taking a rise' out of him, his injured innocence when caught with the penny whistle concealed in his capacious pockets, his gusto in singing the regulation 'clown song,' which constitutes one of the performance, his condescension in holding up the paper hoops and banners while assisting at the graceful equestrienne acts of **Mme. Dockrill** and **Miss Daisy Belmont**, his undisguised admiration for those charming ladies, expressed in eloquent pantomime that which had to be seen to be appreciated."] One of the greatest vocal jesters of the tented world died in England.

BURKE, W. S. Proprietor, Burke's, 1895.

BURKO, BILLY. Pantomime clown, Dan Rice's Paris Pavilion, 1871-72.

BURNELL, GEORGE. Sideshow operator. Sands' & Co., 1863; Seth B. Howe's European, 1867.

BURNES, EDWARD ["Chip"]. (1850?-October 13, 1883) Lecturer. Began his career, 1866, L. B. Lent's, P. T. Barnum's, Adam Forepaugh's and other circus enterprises. Last engagement, Windsor Museum, Bowery, NYC. Died in that city, age 33.

BURNISH, BENJAMIN. Acrobat, rider. Lamb & Co.'s American Amphitheatre, winter 1839; Welch, Bartlett & Co., 1840; rider, June, Titus, Angevine & Co., western unit, 1841; rider, Dan Rice's, 1848-49; Stoke's, 1850-51; Washburn's, 1855-56; Nixon & Sloat, 1860.

BURNISH, W. E. Scenic rider, Dan Rice's, 1849.

BURNS. Lion tamer, DeMott & Ward's, 1868.

BURNS, BARNEY. Rider and clown, Joseph D. Palmer's, 1835-36.

BURNS, ORNEY. Broke his neck in Cincinnati, OH, from a vaulting board, 1838, and died 4 days later.

BURNS, THOMAS. Robinson & Howes, 1863.

BURR, WILLIAM. Bonist, minstrel troupe, Gardner & Hemmings, 1863.

BURRELL, W. Mabie's, 1860.

BURROUGHS, DR. Imported a 3 year old rhinoceros into Philadelphia, fall 1830, the second of its kind to appear in this country. The animal was exhibited at that time with Raymond & Ogden's menagerie.

BURROUGHS, WATKINS. Equestrian. Born in England. Made his stage debut at the Surrey Theatre, London. First appearance in America, 1825, Park Theatre, NYC, as Harry Dornton in *The Road To Ruin*. Stage manager, Lafayette Amphitheatre, NYC, where circus performances and horse dramas were given. Price & Simpson's, Washington Amphitheatre, Boston, 1826; rider, Yeaman's, 1831; J. T. and J. B. Bailey's, 1834. Eventually returned to England.

BURROWS, CHARLES S. [or Burroughs]. (d. April 17, 1901) Gymnast, acrobat and stilt performer. Worked with various partners—**Whitney, Burdeau, Keefe, Kelley**. At one time, trapeze act consisted of balancing on ladders, chairs, etc., while the trapeze was swinging. Levi J North's (with **Whitney**), 1860; Castello & VanVleck (with **Kelley**), 1863-64; Howes & Norton (formerly Robinson & Howes), 1864;

James R. Cooke's (with **Keefe**), winter 1864-65; split troupe from the Thayer & Noyes organization, under the management of Dr. Thayer, that moved by steamboat along the tributaries of the Mississippi (with **Kelley**), 1865; Thayer & Noyes (with **Kelley**), 1866; Haight & Chambers (with **Burdeau**), 1867; Cooke's (with **Burdeau**), Philadelphia, 1868; Bryan's (with **Burdeau**), 1869; Dr. James L. Thayer's (with **Burdeau**), 1869; James Robinson's (with **Burdeau**), winter 1869-70; Campbell's (with **Burdeau**), 1870; Rosston, Springer & Henderson (with **Burdeau**), 1871; Adam Forepaugh's (with **Burdeau**), 1872; Montgomery Queen's, (with **Burdeau**), 1873-74; ladder of glass, Montgomery Queen's, 1875; Adam Forepaugh's, 1876; Great International Circus, Philadelphia, winter 1876-77; D. W. Stone's, 1878. Kept a tavern on Ninth & Arch Streets, Philadelphia, beginning around 1879. [Charles H. Day: "Burrows always was a conniver, as long ago as he was committee on hay and oats with Forepaugh. He managed to save some money and after the Den Stone show ceased traveling at Chicago, while George Bronson went home to Kansas to see the hogs and other members of his family, Burrows concluded to get out of the sawdust and make dust. Since then he has, as they say in the Quaker City, been 'keeping tavern.' Right well has the tavern kept Burrows.... There is one peculiarity at Burrows—he has no slate. Trust died before C. S. opened shop.... But when it comes to a bit of sensible charity, 'Cucumber,' as the boys call him, will put his hand in his pocket and produce his full share."] Died in Philadelphia after ten years of retirement.

BURROWS, WILLIAM P. Treasurer, Clayton & Bartlett's New York Pavilion Circus, 1844. Show lasted only a season.

BURSLEM. Clown, West's circus, 1821. Sang such songs as "London Sights," "Barney, Leave the Girls Alone" and "The Dandies of 1821."

BURT, A. S. Agent. Yankee Robinson's, 1853-59; Great European, 1865; Lake's, 1867; advertising agent, Yankee Robinson's, 1868; contracting agent, Ben Maginley's, 1874; Thayer & Noyes, 1877; general agent, VanAmburgh & Co., winter 1877-78.

BURT, F. Light and heavy balancing, Albert Hose's, 1893.

BURT, JAMES. Acrobat and clown. J. B. Green & Co., 1833; Green & Brown, 1834; Bacon & Derious, 1838; trick clown, Spalding & Rogers, 1856; Slaymaker & Nichols, 1864. Retired to keeping a cigar store in Philadelphia.

BURT, SAM ["Le Jeune"]. Vaulting rider, Stone & McCollum, 1849-50; hurdle racer, Spalding & Rogers, 1851-52; Crystal Amphitheatre, 1853, 1856; Nathans & Co., 1857; George F. Bailey & Co., 1859, 1862; First National Union Circus (combination of Nixon's Royal Circus and Sloat's New York Circus), 1861; L. B. Lent's, 1861; Chiarini's, 1861; G. F. Bailey & Co., 1860, 1862-64; bareback rider, G. F. Bailey & Co., New Orleans, winter 1863-64 (this being the first equestrian exhibition in that city in 3 years); Slaymaker & Nichols,

1864; bareback rider, Stone & Rosston, 1865; George W. De-Haven's, 1866; Stone, Rosston & Murray, Baltimore, winter 1866-67, 1867; bareback rider, Cooke's Circus, Philadelphia, winter 1867-68; Stone & Murray, 1868-69; Great European, 1870; bareback, hurdle and somersault rider, Adam Forepaugh's, 1872; James W. Wilder & Co., 1873; Pete Conklin's, 1873; John Robinson's, 1876.

BURT, NELLIE. James W. Wilder & Co., 1873. May be the wife of **Le Jeune Burt.**

BURT, WILLIAM: *Corde volante.* Stone, Rosston & Co., 1866; Den Stone's, 1873; Great International, Offenbach Garden, Philadelphia, winter 1876-77.

BURT, W. J. General agent, John Robinson's circus, 1882.

BURTAH, ANDY. Contortionist, Main & Sargeant, 1891.

BURTIS, ISAAC. Proprietor, Military Garden, Brooklyn, 1843. Interest in Clayton & Bartlett's Circus, 1844; interest in Howes & Mabie, 1845-48.

BURTON BROTHERS [Clarence, Tony]. Acrobats and trapeze performers, Alexander Robinson's, 1875. Clarence was with Robinson, 1870-77. **The Three Burton's,** ladder act, brother act, Main & Sargeant, 1891.

BURTON, JACOB. Equestrian. Bancker's New York Circus, 1824; West's, 1825; McCracken's, 1825-26; Parson's (**Samuel McCracken,** manager), Albany, NY, 1826; Samuel Parsons' Albany Circus (**Simon V. Wemple,** manager), Troy, NY, 1828. Was a native of Albany. Joined the army and died in Florida.

BUSBY, MEROE. Female race rider, P. T. Barnum's Roman Hippodrome, 1875.

BUSHNELL, DAN. Slack-wire, Burr Robbins', 1876.

BUSHNELL, G. W. Proprietor, Bushnell & Costello, 1876. May have been the Bushnell below.

BUSHNELL, PROF. Rider and general performer. Entered the ring, 1853. 1857, met with an accident, a horse throwing up his head as he was vaulting over it and striking him a hard blow, from the effects of which was 18 months in recovering. With his wife, revived the celebrated feat of William Tell, as he was able to throw a knife with such accuracy as to cleave an apple in two upon her head. Dan Rice's, 1862; slack-wire and impalement, P. T. Barnum's, 1873.

BUTLER. Keeper, Purdy, Welch, Macomber & Co.'s menagerie, 1834.

BUTLER, AMELIA. Female clown, Nixon & Kemp, 1858.

BUTLER, FRANK [r. n. Frank Bean]. (d. December 18, 1882) Barnum, Bailey & Hutchinson, 1882. At the end of the season, while performing in Little Rock, AR, stricken with malaria. Died at his home, Georgetown, MA.

BUTLER, FRANK E. (d. November 22, 1922) Marksman. Husband of **Annie Oakley.** Married her when she was 16 after having lost to her in a shooting competition. James T. Johnson's, 1883; Sells Bros.', 1884; Buffalo Bill's Wild West Show, 1885. At times worked as a team: Butler & Baughman; Butler, Graham and Butler; Butler and Oakley. Died, age 76, in Ferndale, MI.

BUTLER, JOHN. Strong man, Flagg & Aymar's, 1856.

BUTLER, L. G. Proprietor, L. G. Butler's, 1853-55; Butler's Great Western, 1856.

BUTLER, ROBERT. Singing and pantomime clown. Nixon & Kemp, 1858; New American Theatre, Philadelphia, December 1865; E. G. Smith's National Pantomime Troupe, NYC, in a comic pantomime of the "Black Crook," 1867; J. W. Wilder's, 1872; concert director, Cooper, Bailey & Co., 1879; Circus Royal, 1882.

BUTLER, STEPHEN. Showman. Born around 1801. Native of Onondago, NY. Leased the Raymond & Weeks menagerie, 1834. This included the great war elephant Hannibal. By January of the following year the show was operating with the title of Butler, Bancker & Co. Retired from the menagerie business that year.

BUTLER, W. D. Director of aquarium, W. C. Coup' New United Monster Show, 1879.

BUTTERS, ARTHUR. Band leader, Bruce L. Baldwin's, 1894.

BYETTE, THOMAS. Monkey rider and gymnast, Alexander Robinson's, 1875.

BYRNES, BARNEY. Known from Quebec to New Orleans as a job actor. First sang "Long-Tail Blue" and "Sich a Getting Up Stair," written and composed by **Joe Blackburn.** Very eccentric and talented. Originated many of the best "gags" still popular with his successors. With Bancker's, 1824; William Harrington's, 1831-32; Howes & Sands, 1834; vaulter, Palmer & Harrington, 1834; Palmer's, 1835; Bancker & Harrington, 1835; Brown & Co., 1836; winter circus at Richmond Hill, NYC, 1837; negro minstrel, E. C. Yale & Co., 1840; assistant ringmaster, Welch & Mann, 1841; Bartlett & Delavan, 1841.

BYRNES, MASSA. Negro ditties, Howes & Mabie, 1841.

BYRON BROTHERS. Double trapeze, Howes & Sanger, 1872.

T. Allston Brown

C

CADWALLADER, GEORGE J. 4, 6-horse rider, equestrian director. Was an ex-jockey apprenticed to **William Blanchard**. Later, took **John Glenroy** as apprentice. William Blanchard's, 1829-30; Royal Circus, 1831; Fogg & Stickney, 1832; Joseph D. Palmer's, 1833; Palmer & Harrington, 1834; Palmer's, 1835-36; Sweet & Hough, 1835; Bacon & Derious, 1838; Welch, Bartlett & Co., 1839-40; equestrian director, Broadway Circus, NYC, 1840; Bartlett & Delavan, 1841; Welch & Delavan, Baltimore, 1841; Welch & Mann, 1841, 1843; Robinson & Foster, 1843; connected with one of Welch & Mann's troupes (Mann's unit to Surina, etc.), 1843-44; Mann, Welch & Delavan, 1844-45; Welch & Mann, 1846-47; Welch's, 1850-55; Welch & Lent, 1856.

CADWELL, A. V. Proprietor and scenic rider, New York Circus, September 1852; Mann's, August 1852; proprietor, New York Circus, 1853; proprietor, Olympian Arena, 1854; rider, Pacific, 1855; Risley's, October 1855; Bartholomew's, 1856.

CADWELL, MME. Wire ascensionist, Wheeler & Goodwin, 1867.

CAHOON, PROF. J. B. Hurlburt & Leftwich (J. B. Cahoon, R. R. Leftwich, proprietors), 1894; horse trainer, Milwaukee Mid-Winter Circus, Exposition Music Hall, Milwaukee (**L. J. Rodriguez**, manager), winter 1894-95.

CAICEDO, JUAN A. Tight-wire, Barnum & London, 1884.

CAIN, JOHN. General performer, Aaron Turner's, 1842.

CALDWELL, F. B. Treasurer, Caldwell's Occidental, 1867; railroad contractor, Great Chicago, 1879.

CALDWELL, J. H. ["Dr."]. Horse trainer and proprietor, Caldwell's Occidental Circus, 1867. Robbed and murdered by two traveling companions near Henderson, TX, summer of 1868.

CALENDAR. Contortionist, Frost, Husted & Co., 1836.

CALLAHAN, C. D. Equestrian, clown. Native of NYC. One of the early scenic riders. Although he had a long history of performing in Albany, most of his professional life occurred in Mexico and South America. William Harrington's, 1825; Parson's, 1826; William Blanchard's, 1830; Fogg & Stickney, 1830-31; Front Street Theatre, Baltimore, 1831; J. W. Bancker's, 1832; clown, S. H. Nichols', Albany Amphitheatre, winter 1843; T. L. Vermule's, 1845; Old Dominion, 1845; Rockwell & Co., 1847.

CALLAHAN, E. Gymnast, Alex Robinson's, 1874.

CALLAHAN, GEORGE. Sideshow ventriloquist, Barnum, Bailey & Hutchinson, 1882.

CALLAN, JOHN. Strong man. Dan Rice's, 1870; Rice's Paris Pavilion Circus, 1871.

CALLIN, GEORGE. Acrobat and tumbler, P. T. Barnum's, 1872.

CAMBRIDGE, A. G. Business manager, S. P. Stickney & Son's, 1874.

CAMEO & TIPP. Double trapeze, Hart, France & Co.'s, 1888.

CAMERON, D. A. Herculean performer, Dan Rice's, 1855.

CAMERON, JAMES VON. Equestrian director, G. K. Goodwin's, 1860; equestrian director, ringmaster, and 4-horse rider, Hippotheatron, NYC, winter 1864-65; Melville's, 1864; S. O. Wheeler's, 1867-68; co-proprietor, Metchear & Cameron, 1870; Great Australian, 1870; ringmaster and 40-horse driver, Ben Maginley's, 1874; proprietor, Cameron's Great Oriental, 1875.

CAMERON, T. F. Museum manager, Barnum & London, 1884.

CAMMEA, LEON. New York Champs Elysees, 1866.

CAMP, E. N. Camp's Grand Southern Circus, 1880.

CAMPBELL. Englishman and the most famous of the early clowns. Came to America, 1816, with the James West circus troupe as star performer. Acted as "clown to the rope," and, among his other laughable feats, would ascend a pole 18 feet high, put his breast upon it, and in that state would turn around like the "fly of a jack," with his hands and feet extended in the air. The troupe introduced the practice of still vaulting from a springboard, of which Cambell excelled, executing "many novel and amusing feats," such as leaping over 3 horses with a pony standing on the backs of 2 of them. Was with West during his NYC turn at the Park Theatre for Price & Simpson and into the engagements at Boston and Providence that followed; also with Pepin & West, Olympic, Philadelphia, fall, 1817; Pepin's, Olympic, Philadelphia, for hippodramas, 1818; Pepin's, NYC, spring, 1819; Pepin's, West Indies, 1819-20. Shows up again as singing clown with J. Purdy Brown's, 1825-27. According to Stuart Thayer, the latter was Campbell's first engagement in the United States since 1820.

CAMPBELL, AL G. (1858-March 4, 1937) General agent and proprietor, Campbell Bros.', 1894-95, 1897-1912. See Campbell Brothers.

CAMPBELL, ARCHIBALD "ARCHIE." (November 16, 1830-July 31, 1882) Clown. Born at Ireland. Moved to Bethany, VA, at age 6. Was nephew of a famous divine and founder of the Campbellite Church. Possibly graduated from William and Mary's College, 1853, with high honors; but, because of records lost during the Civil War, this cannot be confirmed. McFarland's, 1852; Reynolds', 1854; Robinson & Eldred, 1856; Robinson & Lake, 1860. Remained with Rob-

42

inson, primarily as clown, off and on until his death, with the exception of his years of service with the Union Army during the war. After being captured by the Confederates at the Stoneman raid, 1864, spent some time in Andersonville prison. Following release, was connected with Nixon's Amphitheatre, Washington, 1865; Thayer & Noyes, 1865-66; December, 1865, part of a split troupe from the Thayer & Noyes organization, under the management of Dr. Thayer, which moved by steamboat along the tributaries of the Mississippi River. Albisu's, Havana, 1866; John Robinson's, 1867-68; with Cooke's, Philadelphia, 1868; 1875 to 1882, cook house manager and steward for Robinson. Died of consumption in Redding, California.

CAMPBELL BROTHERS [Al, Edward, Lee, Fred, John, Charles]. Tumblers and leapers. Lemen Bros.', 1891; Denver Dick's Wild West and Sioux Indian Medicine Company, 1894. Included was **Charles Campbell**, slack wire performer—"Introducing his wonderful waltzing wire."). Proprietors, Campbell Bros. Great Railroad Show, 1894-95, 1897-1912. **John** was the advertiser; **Edward** (1861-April 8, 1950) was treasurer.

CAMPBELL, G. H. Vocalist, Rockwell & Stone, 1846; general agent, Rockwell & Co., 1847.

CAMPBELL, JAMES R. Leaper, tumbler. P. T. Barnum's, 1873; John Robinson's, 1874-75; Cooper, Bailey & Co., 1879-80; D. W. Stone's, 1878; Sells Bros.', 1879; W. W. Cole's, 1880-81; Cantelli & Leon, Havana, Cuba, winter 1882-83; Wallace & Co., 1885; Miller, Okey & Freeman, 1886.

CAMPBELL, J. F. Proprietor, Campbell's New York and Philadelphia Zoological and Equestrian Institute, 1878.

CAMPBELL, J. K. Courtney & Sanford's Minstrels, a party made up in New York to travel with Courtney & Sanford's Circus, South America, which sailed from New York, July 23, 1873.

CAMPBELL ["Master"]. Monkey performer, with L. B. Lent's, 1860.

CAMPBELL, T. W. Treasurer, H. W. Smith's 1869.

CAMPBELL, R. C. Agent. Started in business as a bill poster. Contracting agent, W. W. Cole's, 1881-1883; Callender's Minstrels, winter, 1882-83; with Adam Forepaugh's, 1888-1892. Settled in Chicago and organized the American Bill Posting Company with **Burr Robbins**. Remained in this business for some years; then sold his share to Robbins for $150,000. Settled in London where he organized a company along the same lines, which was also a money-maker. Returned to USA and built a home overlooking the Hudson River, NYC. Developed business interests in NYC. May, 1913, his body was found floating in the Hudson River, age 62. He had on his person a watch studded with diamonds and rubies said to be worth $1,000, quite a sum of money and some valuable papers, all of which were missing, which led to the belief that he had been murdered. [D. W. Watt: "He was a

high class gentleman and was honest in all his dealings. Any lot owner who had done business with Bob Campbell was always glad to see him come their way again."] Considered one of the brightest agents of his time, aggressive, loyal and a man of great energy.

CAMPBELL, W. T. Privileges, Barnum & London, 1884.

CANE, MONS. General performer. Sands & Lent, 1848-49; Col. Mann's, 1849; Rivers & Derious, 1855; Flagg & Aymar, 1856; John Robinson's, 1857; Spalding & Rogers' *Floating Palace*, 1858-59.

CANFIELD. Strong man. John Tryon's, Bowery Amphitheatre, NYC, 1843; Welch's, 1849-50; Spalding & Rogers, 1851; Mann & Moore, 1853; Spalding & Rogers, 1856.

CANHAM, TOM. Band leader and keyed bugle player. Spalding & Rogers, 1850; Dan Rice's, 1857-59; Thayer & Noyes, 1863; John Robinson's, 1866-70.

CANHAM, MME. Equestrienne, Dan Rice's, 1859. Most probably the wife of **Tom Canham**.

CANNEA, LEON. Bareback on 4 ponies, with New York Champs Elysees, 1866.

CANTONE FAMILY. Statuary posing, Gollmar Bros.', 1896.

CAPP, DWIGHT. Contracting agent, Hilliard & Hunting, 1878.

CAPPALINO, SIGNOR. (d. January 14, 1891) Animal act, Russian bears. Levi J. North's, 1854; Rivers & Derious, 1855-57.

CAPPOLO, SIGNOR. (d. January 14, 1891) Clown, trapeze performer, contortionist. Consolidation Circus (**W. B. Hough**, manager), 1866; Sells Bros.', 1874; Sadler's, 1875. Died at Port townsend, WA, where he had been performing at the Standard Theatre. Age, about 45.

CAPULO, PROF. Punch and Judy performer, L. B. Lent's, 1876.

CARBREY, A. Whittemore, Thompson & Co., 1865.

CARDELIA, F. C. Organist and harmonic bell ringer, Spalding & Rogers' *Floating Palace*, 1859.

CARDELLO, CHARLES W. Gymnast. Teamed with **Walter Victorelli**, 1875, as **Cardello & Victorelli**, horizontal bar performers. Hilliard & Hunting, 1875-77; Campbell's (John V. O'Brien's), 1878; left in May to join Cooper & Bailey, South America; Batcheller & Doris, 1879-80; American Four Combination, 1881; Sells Bros.', 1884; Miles Orton's, 1885; James Donovan's, Bermuda, winter 1891-92.

CAREY, HENRY. (1861-August 16, 1891) Rider and general performer. Born in Utica, NY. Much of his career spent in Mexico, Cuba and Central America. 4 and 6-horse rider, Alex Robinson's, 1873-76; leaper, Cooper & Bailey, 1880; Orrin Bros.', Mexico, winter 1880-81; Barnum, Bailey & Hutchinson, 1882; catapult act, Cantellis & Leon, Havana, winter 1882-83; Orrin Bros.', Mexico, 1886; director, Howes', 1888; Frank A. Gardner's, South America, 1889. Died in Port Limon, Costa Rica, of heart trouble.

CARIETOR, CHARLES. G. G. Grady's, 1869.

CARL, C. General performer, Horner & Bell, 1865.

CARLE, J. H. Gymnast, J. Hudson's, 1872-73; dog act, Col. Spicer's, 1886.

CARLEY. Co-proprietor, Carley, Purdy & Wright's menagerie, 1830; Purdy, Carley & Bailey's menagerie, 1831.

CARLISLE, JAMES. (1837?-February 16, 1864) Gymnast, general performer, Welch's, Philadelphia, 1856. Died in Chicago of dropsy, age 27.

CARLISLE, RICHARD RISLEY. See Richard Risley.

CARLO FAMILY [Felix, George, William, Frederick, Leo, Harry, Amelia, Fanny, Hattie]. Gymnasts and clowns. **Felix** (r. n. William Lawrence, 1810?-March 28, 1884) was born in London of French-English descent. Joined an English circus as a gymnast at an early age and for a number years performed on the British Isles. Principal member of a French circus troupe in Paris, 1844 to 1846. Latter year, came to the USA and made a debut at the Bowery Amphitheatre, NYC, October 19. Two of his specialties were dancing on his head and the ladder flight. Henry Rockwell's, 1847; Spalding & Rogers, 1849-51; Robinson & Eldred, 1852; Castle Garden, NYC, October 23, 1854; S. B. Howes', 1855; H. P. Madigan's, 1856; John Tryon's, Bowery Circus, around 1857; Whitby's, 1859. Last connection with circus performing, Niblo's Garden, spring 1861, under the management of James M. Nixon. Remainder of his career was devoted to theatrical appearances. Died in NYC, age 74. **William** (d. September 14, 1879), an acrobat, managed the Carlo Brothers' Circus for many years with his brothers, touring Australia and California. Married actress **Fanny Brown** in San Francisco, 1866. Bailey & Co., Spalding & Rogers' Academy of Music, New Orleans, winter 1863-64, this being the first equestrian exhibition in that city in 3 years; Wilson, Zoyara & Carlo, California, 1864; John Wilson's, Australia (and remained behind when Wilson took his troupe to India), 1866-67; Chiarini's, South America, winter 1869-70; Olympic Theatre, NYC, with his brothers, 1874-75; P. T. Barnum's, 1876. Organized a circus with his brothers to tour South America. Much time in later years devoted to training horses. Died at Kingston, Jamaica, of Bright's disease. The **Carlo Brothers** (William, Frederick, George) continued to be favorites in South America. Chiarini's, Hippotheatron, NYC, 1872; organized a tour for South America, 1876, and sailed from New York in January, 1877. [M. B. Leavitt: "It was the strongest array of circus talent ever united for such a tour. It embraced many of the principal performers of Barnum's, Castello's, Coup's, and various other shows. Every member was capable of presenting 3 or more acts, as it was necessary to change the program nightly in the Spanish speaking countries, and the performers had to be generally versatile."] The **Carlo Family (George, Fred, Harry, Amelia, Hattie)**, equestrians and gymnasts, Orrin Bros.',

Mexico, winter 1880-81; Shelby, Pullman & Hamilton, 1881. **Carlo children** were Leo, Hattie, Harry.

CARLO, FANNY. See Fanny Brown.

CARLO, LEO. Rider. Apprentice of George Carlo. See Carlo Family.

CARLO, NICOLO. Juggler, with Rosston, Springer & Henderson, 1871.

CARLOSS, CLARENCE. Gymnast, with Howes & Cushing, 1875.

CARLTON, GEORGE. Gymnast, clown, first time in USA, Gardner & Hemmings', Philadelphia, 1865.

CARNALLA BROTHERS [3 in number]. Barrett's, 1887; Adam Forepaugh's, 1889.

CARNES, MISS. Equestrienne. *Allemande* on horseback, Pepin, Breschard & Cayetano, Philadelphia, fall 1813; Pepin, Breschard & Cayetano, Baltimore, winter 1813; West's, 1820.

CARNES. Apprentice through 1821. Debut, April 17, 1818. James West's, 1818-21; Simpson & Price, Philadelphia, Baltimore, 1822; Simpson & Price, "C" Street Circus, Washington, DC, winter 1822-23; with his trained dogs, Richmond Hill Amphitheatre, summer 1823; John Rogers', Brooklyn, NY, fall 1823; William Blanchard & William West's, Canada, 1825.

CAROLE, MME. GULIEME. Equestrienne, Spalding & Rogers, 1850.

CARON FAMILY [or Carron, Mlle. Angelique, Mons. L. Caron, Masters Alphonse and George]. Equestrians and acrobats, J. M. French's, 1870. **AL**, knock-about clown, Barnum & London, 1885.

CARPENTER, DAN. Great Eastern Menagerie, Museum, Aviary, Circus and Balloon Show (Dan Carpenter and **R. E. J. Miles** & Co., proprietors), 1872.

CARPENTER, EDWARD. Shetland pony driver, John H. Murray's, 1875.

CARPENTER, FRANK. Equestrian. VanAmburgh's, 1856; Hyatt Frost's, 1857; Sands, Nathans & Co., Broadway Theatre, NYC, 1858; VanAmburgh's southern, winter 1859-60; Howes', 199 Bowery, NYC, winter 1863-64; Stone & Rosston, 1864; Gardner & Hemmings, 1864, 1866; Hippotheatron, 14th Street, NYC, November 1864; New York Champs Elysees, 1865; Nixon's Amphitheatre, Washington, 1865.

CARPENTER, J. Sands, Nathans & Co., Broadway Circus, 1857-58; VanAmburgh's, 1859.

CARR, ED. Equestrian director, Downie & Gallagher, 1892.

CARR, LOUIS B. As Carr Brothers with **Henry Burdeau**, trapeze and brother act, Robinson & Howes, 1864; George W. DeHaven & Co. (operated by **Andrew Haight**), 1865-66; Yankee Robinson's, Chicago, 1866; C. T. Ames', 1868. **Louis** was connected with George W. DeHaven's, 1867; (with **Winnie**) C. T. Ames', 1868. Married **Kate Phillips** of Louisville, KY, January 20, 1867, while with DeHaven's at St. Paul, MN.

CARR, THOMAS. Rider. Robinson & Howes, 1863; rode a

44

buffalo as part of his act, American Circus for the Paris Exposition, 1867; contracting agent, Harper Bros.' European, 1893.

CARRE, PAULINE. Jesse W. Foster's, 1894; Bentley's, 1895.

CARRIER, J. T. Whitney Family's, 1887; Orrin Barber's, 1888.

CARRINGTON, J. M. ["Col."]. Proprietor, J. M. Carrington's Great Southern Circus, 1874-75.

CARRINGTON, SAMUEL. Proprietor for the Crystal Palace Show, 1872.

CARRISKIE, WILLIAM. Slack-rope, Welch & Delavan, 1841.

CARROLL, ANNIE. Equestrienne. Bound servant of **W. B.** and **Mary Ann Carroll** and mother of **Edna Snow**. Married gymnast **Eddie Snow**, 1887; but sued for divorce April, 1892. Spalding, Rogers & Van Orden, 1851; Great Eastern, 1872-73; Maginley & Co., 1874; Cameron's, 1875; John H. Murray's, 1877; Adam Forepaugh's, 1879-80, 1886; VanAmburgh's, 1882; Wallace & Co., 1885; Great European, Cosmopolitan Rink, Broadway & 41st Street, NYC, winter 1885-86; Doris & Colvin, 1887; Dan Rice's, 1891; W. B. Reynolds' Consolidated Shows, 1892; Charles McMahon's, 1893. It was announced, October 5, 1918, that she had ruined her own health by nursing her daughter, Edna, a well known soubrette, who had been sick for 3 years of cancer of the stomach.

CARROLL BROTHERS. P. T. Barnum's, 1877-80; W. C. Coup's, 1881.

CARROLL, CORNELIA. (1843?-1917) Dancer, actress, and equestrienne. Daughter of **Horace W. Smith**; wife of **William Carroll**. A native of New Orleans and a theatrical protégé of **Ben DeBar**, actor-manager of the St. Charles Theatre in that city. Died in Washington, DC, in her 74th year.

CARROLL, DOLLY VARDEN. Male rider. Probably an apprentice to **W. B. Carroll**. May have dressed as a little girl in a carrying act with **Barney Carroll**, hence the name of Dolly. Haight's Great Eastern, 1874; Cameron's Great Oriental, 1875.

CARROLL, EDWARD. Tumbler, gymnast. Alexander Robinson's, 1871; W. H. Harris' Nickel-Plate, 1894.

CARROLL, ELIZA. Maginley, Carroll & Co., 1868.

CARROLL, JAMES. Hurdle and pad rider, Robinson's, California (**Frank Frost**, manager), 1886.

CARROLL, JOHN. (d. July 26, 1912) Equestrian, Shakespearean clown and jester. Cole & Orton, 1871; W. W. Cole's, 1873. At one time, manager Grand Central Varieties, Galveston, TX. Identified with the Sells-Floto Circus for a number of years and was considered an experience horse trainer and handler. Wife, **Nellie Page**, was in the profession also. Divorced **Felicita**, another wife, May 6, 1876, Galveston. Died from tuberculosis.

CARROLL, MARIE ["Marie Elise"]. (November 12, 1844-August 18, 1874) Equestrienne. Adopted daughter of **W. B.**

and **Mary Ann Carroll**. Eloped with John J. Brand, August 1859; her father offered $50 reward for her return and the arrest of Brand. Married clown and circus manager **Ben Maginley**. Had classical dance training and was said to be the only female "trick rider" in the country in 1871. Featured for leaping over 16' banners and jumping through 22" balloons. Olympic Theatre, New Orleans, summer 1848; Spalding & Rogers, 1850 (at that time was advertised as a lion tamer who, with her "faithful dog, Fidele," entered the den "of an infuriated leopard."). Spalding, Rogers & Van Orden's People's, 1851; H. Buckley & Co., 1857-58; Davis & Crosby, 1859; Maginley & VanVleck,, 1863; James M. Nixon's Alhambra, NYC, fall 1863; Old Cary's, 1864; principal rider, Ben Maginley's, 1864; Haight & Chambers, 1866; Maginley, Carroll & Co., 1867-68; Bailey & Co., 1870; Joel E. Warner's, 1872. Died of consumption at her residence in Westchester, NY, age 29.

CARROLL, MARY ANN. [Mrs. W. B. Carroll, nee Mary Ann Sprague]. (d. May 18, 1900) Equestrienne. James Raymond's, 1843-44; Dr. Gilbert R. Spalding's, 1845; Davis & Crosby, 1859; Old Cary's, traveling up and down the Mississippi River area by boat and railroad, 1864; Maginley, Carroll & Co., 1867. During the latter year, was thrown from her horse and injured to the extent that her career was considered finished. The accident was said to have been caused by the ringmaster lowering his whip in front of the horse too soon, allowing the animal to enter the ring unexpectedly, throwing Mrs. Carroll and stepping on her chest. Died at her home in Westchester, NY.

CARROLL, PRIMROSE. Clown, with Adam Forepaugh's, 1893.

CARROLL, W. B. ["Barney"]. (March 13, 1816-July 14, 1889) Rider and vaulter. Born in Knoxville, TN. Joined a small show at age 12, apprenticing to **George Sweet**, 1830, and learning to become a leading 1 and 2-horse rider, leaper and acrobat. 1844, created a sensation by riding bareback and carrying a boy on his head, supposedly the first time the feat had been done. Other feats included leaping over 8 or 9 horses and a 2-horse act with his 5 year old "daughter." [John A. Dingess: "His 2-horse carrying act, with the little waif Dolly Verden, was one of the most beautiful feats performed in the arena."] Had few equals as an equestrian manager and was known as a prompt and diligent worker. Yeaman's, 1831; French, Hobby & Co., 1835; Palmer's, 1836; Waring and Raymond, New Orleans, winter 1837-38; Ludlow & Smith, American Theatre, New Orleans, 1840; N. A. Howes', 1842; James Raymond's, 1842-44; equestrian manager, Rockwell & Stone, 1843; also, rider, John Tryon's, Bowery Amphitheatre, NYC, 1843, 1846; Dr. Gilbert R. Spalding's, 1844-46; Sands, Lent & Co., 1846; Howes & Co., 1847; Sands, Lent & Co., Chatham Theatre, 1847, and also at the Bowery Amphitheatre that winter season; Dan Rice's, 1850; Spalding & Rogers,

American Theatre, New Orleans, winter 1850-51; Davis & Crosby, 1859; Nixon's, Washington, DC, fall 1862; James M. Nixon's Alhambra, NYC, fall 1863; Madame Macarte's European Circus (**James M. Nixon**, proprietor), 1863; equestrian director, Maginley & VanVleck, 1863; Old Cary's, traveling up and down the Mississippi River area by boat and railroad, 1864; Maginley & Bell, 1864; Thayer & Noyes, winter 1865-66; George W. DeHaven's, operated by **Andrew Haight**, 1865-66; Haight & Chambers, 1866. Teamed with Ben Maginley in a circus venture, Maginley, Carroll & Co., 1867-68. Went as far as Omaha, NE. Carroll wanted to continue further west but Maginley was fearful of the Indians. Equestrian director, George W. DeHaven's, 1869; Mike Lipman's, fall 1869; H. W. Smith's, winter 1869-70; equestrian director, James W. Robinson's, 1870; Haight & Co., winter 1871-72; rider, Haight's Great Eastern, 1873-74. Established a performing school, 1874, enrolling pupils during the winter seasons, specializing in training bareback riders. Equestrian director, Cameron's, 1875; VanAmburgh's, 1876, 1882; Nathans & Co.'s, 1883; John H. Murray's, 1877; Adam Forepaugh's, 1879; equestrian director, Frank A. Robbins', 1888. Last appearance, ringmaster, circus on Fourth Avenue and 14th Street, NYC, 1889. Died at his home near Van Ness, Westchester County, NY, age 74.

CARROLL, WILLIAM ["Willie"]. Rider and leaper. Adopted son of **W. B. Carroll**. Antonio & Carroll, 1857; Davis & Crosby, 1859; Maginley & Carroll, 1868; John Robinson's, 1869-72; leaper and vaulter, H. M. Smith's, 1870; gymnast, John Robinson's, 1872; clown, Goldenburg's, 1874; rider, Great Eastern, 1872; rider, Cameron's Great Oriental Circus, 1875. May the same man that was acrobat and sideshow song and dance man, P. T. Barnum's, 1877; tumbler and leaper, P. T. Barnum's, 1879-80.

CARROLL, WILLIAM. See William Miaco.

CARSON, KIT. Acrobat, leaper and tumbler, with John H. Murray's, 1874.

CARTER, EDWARD ["Ned"]. Gymnast, vaulter, slack rope. Parson's circus, Albany, before connecting with Bancker's, 1824; Samuel McCracken's, 1825-26; rider, Parson's Amphitheatre, Albany, 1826; Tivoli Gardens, Philadelphia, July 1826; J. Purdy Brown's, 1828.

CARTER, JAMES. Banjoist, Welch & Mann, 1846. May be the J. B. Carter listed below.

CARTER, JAMES. (1813?-May 11, 1847) Wild beast tamer with conflicting origins. One version states he was brought to England from America by **VanAmburgh** and introduced by **Andrew Ducrow** at Astley's, 1839. Another has it **George Wombwell**, having seen **Henri Martin** at Drury Lane, 1831, hired Carter, a handsome young farm boy who had run away from home with a traveling freak show, and trained him to become a rival to Martin. In any event, Carter's stay in the United States was comparatively brief. In England, Ducrow

engaged him at Astley's, 1839, for a spectacle, *Afghan*, in which he performed with a whole menagerie on stage behind a network of strong wire. Critics claimed his lions and tigers were too docile. Next drama at Astley's, *The Lion of the Desert; or, The French in Algiers*, he descended from the grid with one of his leopards in a balloon. **VanAmburgh** leased the Royal Lyceum Theatre and English Opera House for Carter and himself to perform as "lion brothers" in *Aslar And Ozines! or, the Lion Hunters Of The Burning Zaara*. They also appeared in *Mungo Park; or The Arabs Of the Niger*. In this piece Carter was drawn across the stage in a chariot by a team of lions. The play also included a tiger fight. Died in England, age 34.

CARTER, J. B. Dan Rice's, 1858; Courtney & Sanford's Minstrels, a party made up in New York to travel with Courtney & Sanford's Circus in South America, which sailed from New York, July 23, 1873.

CARTER, JOHN. Acrobat and elephant performer. A. Hunt & Co., 1838; Dan Rice's, 1855-56, where he was trainer for the famed elephant Lalla Rookh.

CARTER, NED. Lion tamer, William West's, 1825.

CARVELLO, FRANK. Contracting agent, Gillmeyer, Bryson & Co., 1888.

CARVER, WILLIAM F. ["Dr."]. (d. August 31, 1927) Wild West performer, "Champion shot of the World." Dr. Carver Co., 1883; Dr. Carver's Wild West, 1884; partner with William Cody, original Buffalo Bill Wild West Show, 1884; arrested for libeling Cody, 1885, W. W. Cole's, 1886; Adam Forepaugh's, 1888-89; Dr. Carver's Wild America, 1892. Died at Sacramento, CA.

CARVER, WILLIAM. Cousin of **Hyatt Frost**. Formerly interested in VanAmburgh's. Retired to a farm in Madison County, IN, 1882.

CARY, CARRIE. Probably the daughter of **V. Cary**. Old Cary's Great World Circus, 1864.

CARY, H. leaper, Barnum, Bailey & Hutchinson, 1881.

CARY, O. S. Advance manager, Hurlburt & Hunting, 1885; advance manager, C. W. Kidder & Co.'s, 1893.

CARY, WILLIAM. Cooper, Bailey & Co., 1880.

CARY, V. ["Old Cary"]. Clown and proprietor. Said to have managed every kind of outfit "from the five-legged dog show to a menagerie." Haight & Chambers', 1866. Proprietor and clown of Old Cary's Great World Circus, which started in Little Rock, AR, and toured through Illinois, Indiana, Ohio, Michigan, and Wisconsin by rail and boat, 1864.

CASE, A. O. 2nd car manager, John Robinson's, 1882.

CASEY, CHARLES. Knockabout clown, Harry Thayer & Co.'s, 1890.

CASH, CHARLES. Scenic rider, John Forepaugh's, California, 1888.

CASH, GEORGE. Snake and alligator exhibit, Van Amburgh & Co., 1880; manager, Great Pacific Consolidated Show,

1894.

CASINO, ANDREW and **ALICE.** Gymnasts and double trapeze, Howes & Cushing, 1875.

CASS, A. O. Car manager, John Robinson's, car #2, 1882-87; car #1, 1888-89; car #2, 1892.

CASSELLI, JOHN. See Australian Four.

CASSIDY, C. W. (d. June 6, 1887) Agent, Howes & Cushing, 1857, on their trip to England; in Liverpool, organized the first band of "Female Christy Minstrels."

CASSIM, JAMES. (1851?-May 13, 1879) Acrobat. Born in England of a Scotch mother and an East Indian father. Both died when he was a young boy. Around 1870, formed a partnership with **Edwin Fritz** and performed under the name of **Cassim & Fritz**, traveling through France and Spain, then to India and South America. Following this, engaged for a year at the Bella Union Theatre, San Francisco; later, at the Theatre Comique, St. Louis and at the Metropolitan Theatre, NYC, the latter under the management of **R. W. Butler**. Traveled with L. B. Lent's for 2 seasons, performing in variety theatres in the winter. Howes & Cushing, 1875; Cooper & Bailey, 1876, and went with the show to Australia and South America. Returning, opened at Niblo's Garden, NYC, December 23, 1878. Cassim then joined Cooper & Bailey, 1879 season, during which was crushed by a train while walking on the railroad tracks near his sleeping car at Johnstown, PA., age 28.

CASSIMER, MONS. Performing drummer. Claimed to have been chief drum-major for the French army. Feats included the beating of 12 drums at once; with a single drum, dramatizing the "Battle of Waterloo," imitating the morning call, assembly of troops, volleys of musketry, cannonading, the charge, retreat, rally, etc. Rockwell & Stone, 1845.

CASSUS, JOHN. Bird act, sideshow, Cooper, Bailey & Co., 1880.

CASTELLANO, ISIDRO. Tumbler, leaper, jockey racer, Barnum, Bailey & Hutchinson, 1882.

CASTELLO, ARTIE [or Costello]. Swinging *perche*, Van-Amburgh's, 1896. Brother of **Dave Castello** (or Costello).

CASTELLO BROTHERS. See Costello Brothers.

CASTELLO, DAN. (1832 or 1834-July 27, 1909) Showman, clown, leaper and vaulter. Exact date of birth has never been established. The death certificate gave it as 1832; an 1873 Barnum show press release said it was 1827; Sturtevant's files list 1834; and Chindahl's notes give a choice of 1827 or 1834; Gordon Yadon's biography in *Banner Line* (March 15, 1968) includes an inclination to go with the 1832 date. Born in Kingston, Ontario, and raised near Syracuse, NY. Father was a quarryman who worked for a firm named Blood & Cady. Became acrobat, leaper, clown, and animal trainer. Trained the bull named Don Juan. At his best, vaulted over 16 horses from the low *batteau*. [As described: "In leaving the batteau he would shoot into the air to a height of about 20 feet as straight as an arrow, then by a very quick turn of the neck and bending

of the knees he would turn a somersault in a twinkling and strike on his feet in an erect position."] Began circus career, 1849, but no reference to him occurs until 1854. That year, moved to Delavan, WI, and joined the Mabie Bros.' as an acrobat. May have served an apprenticeship in the previous 5 years with June & Turner. With Mabies', 1854-55. First announcement of his appearing as clown, 1856, John Robinson's. By 1857, was married to **Frances Castello**, who appeared with him as a rider on Harry Buckley's. This union was eventually blessed with a son and a daughter, neither of whom became performers. Mid-season, 1857, left the Buckley show to join Major Brown's. Spalding & Rogers, New Orleans, winter 1857-58; Satterlee & Bell, 1858; Nixon & Co, 1859 (advertised as **Pedro Gonzalez**). Went to England, October 1859; took the educated bull, Don Juan, and a trained buffalo with him. Connected with Hengler's, 1860. **Charles Dickens** saw him at the Alhambra, London, and wrote, "he did not jump, he flew." Latter part 1860, joined Howes & Cushing in Ireland. Injured in an attack by the buffalo, and later while performing a leap, returned to USA, October, 1860. Appeared with Spalding & Rogers, NYC, that winter, and aboard the *Floating Palace*, New Orleans, early 1861, but soon came north with Spalding & Rogers because of the peril of war. George W. DeHaven & Co., 1862; Castello & Van Vleck, 1863; Robinson & Howes, Chicago, winter 1863-64. Organized Dan Castello's Own Great Show, 1864, St. Paul, MN. Chartered the steamboat *Jeannette Roberts* and toured down the Mississippi and up and down the Ohio. In the fall, spent 2 weeks in Memphis, and then descended the Mississippi to take advantage of the presence of the Union Army on the lower river. The circus remained close to this audience until spring. 1865, the route was an up river journey to Nashville; there, combined with show owned by **Seth B. Howes**, and managed by Howes' son, **Egbert**. At the end of the Howes-Castello season, **James M. Nixon** became a partner, January 1866, buying the Howes' equipment and leasing some of its animals. When the circus emerged from Frederick, MD, April 1868, and opened its season in Wheeling, WV, it was called Castello, Howes & Nixon. The show went as far west as Kansas City, and ended the season in Mobile, Alabama, for the winter. 1869, season began with a route across the South to Savannah, then north to Virginia and west to Tennessee, and out to Kansas. Reached Omaha just as the Union Pacific Railroad was finishing its track to California. At Nixon's urging the show (10 cages, a bandwagon, 2 elephants and 2 camels) was loaded on the railroad to proceed across the plains, the first circus in history to go coast to coast in a single season. Castello later said they netted $1,000 a day for 31 straight days. Much of the circus was sold in California, with Castello's half of the profits amounting to $60,000. Joined W. C. Coup, 1870, in putting a company on a Great Lakes steamer, visiting towns where a circus was a great novelty. Castello, Coup and P. T. Barnum each put up $60,000 to take out the Barnum show, 1871-75. [P. T. Barnum: "Give me Dan Castello and money enough to reach the first stop and I'll come home with a fortune at the end of the season, I don't care if it rains every day."] Left circus business; went into a mining enterprise, putting up about $80,000, owning about all of Deadwood, ND, but went broke. Dan Castello's Centennial Circus, 1876; Hudson & Co.; 1881; 1883-90, Harris' Nickel- Plate; Castello title used by **J. E. Noble**, 1890. Died of Bright's disease, Rochester, NY.

CASTELLO, DAN. (1836?-April 23, 1901) Clown. Said to have been started in the ring by **P. T. Barnum**. As a clown, had a ready wit and a talent for extemporizing songs. After years with Barnum and Forepaugh, retired with a small fortune, married, and settled in New London, CT, in the hotel business. Was too much of a sport, however, and money simply slipped away. Upon losing the hotel, engaged as a steamboat hand but eventually landed in the Bowery, NYC, doing odd jobs. Died in the back room of Taylor's Hotel, destitute at age 65.

CASTELLO, DAN, JR. An apprentice of **Dan Castello's** who made his ring debut in 1870. It is not known if he was adopted by the Castellos. Died at Racine, WI, November 7, 1903, age 44.

CASTELLO, DAVE [r. n. Dave C. Laughlin]. (1860-October 16, 1922) Jockey and bareback rider, and 2-horse carrying act performer. Bareback somersault rider, P. T. Barnum's, 1871-74, 1877; boy bareback and hurdle rider, Howes & Cushing, 1875; Chiarini's, San Francisco, 1879; Hilliard & DeMott, 1881; Cole's; Cooper, Jackson & Co., 1882-83; W. H. Harris' Nickel-Plate, 1885-87, 1891; Albert Hose's, 1893; somersault riding act, Robert Hunting's, 1894-95; Stickney & Donovan, Central and South America, 1897; VanAmburgh & Co., 1896; Norris & Rowe's, 1908. Wife **Ada** was a principal equestrienne and *manège* performer. Died, in Henderson, NC, age about 60.

CASTELLO, ERNEST. John Robinson's, 1868.

CASTELLO FAMILY [George, Elmo, William, Minnie]. Great Wallace, 1891; Sells Bros.'s Australian tour, 1891-92.

CASTELLO, FRANCES [Mrs. Dan Castello]. Apparently a rider appearing in the grand entry only. Castello & VanVleck, 1863; Dan Castello's, 1866-70; P. T. Barnum's, 1871.

CASTELLO, GEORGE. (d. February 3, 1903) General agent, Walter B. Aymar's circus company, South America, early 1870s; outside privileges manager, P. T. Barnum's, 1872-73; contracting agent, Anderson & Co., 1879; general agent, Hilliard & Main, 1883; with Joseph McMahon, purchased equipment from Terrell Bros.', 1892; last engagement, Pawnee Bill's Wild West Show. Died in Cook County Hospital, Chicago.

CASTELLO, HARRY. Adolescent rider, P. T. Barnum's, 1871.

CASTELLO, HENRY. Clown, H. P. Madigan's, 1856.

CASTELLO, JOHNNY. Adolescent rider, P. T. Barnum's, 1871.

CASTELLO, WILLIAM. Robinson & Deery, 1864; ringmaster, Alexander Robinson's, 1875.

CASTILE, A. H. General performer, VanAmburgh's, 1874.

CASTILIAN BROTHERS. C. T. Ames', 1868.

CASTILLA, MISS. Wire-walker and rider. At one time was married to **James McFarland**. Levy J. North's National Amphitheatre, 1857-60; wire ascensionist, George W. DeHaven & Co.'s, 1865. Was the object of her former husband's jealousy, which brought about his death. See James McFarland.

CASTILLO. Ringmaster, John Robinson's, 1868.

CASTINELL, GEORGE. High-wire free act, Washington Bros.', 1887.

CASTINEYRA, ALICE. Race rider, P. T. Barnum's Roman Hippodrome, 1875.

CASTLE BROTHERS. M. O'Conner & Co., 1870.

CASTLE, CHARLES H. (September 6, 1816-September 25, 1884) Agent. Born in Waterbury, CT. First engaged with Dan Rice's, 1850-53. Entered into management with **Harry Whitbeck** and **Wash Kidwell**, 1853, to form Whitbeck & Co.'s One-Horse Show, an enterprise that lasted only one season. Spalding & Rogers' *Floating Palace*, 1853-54; Dan Rice's, 1855-60; Thayer & Noyes', 1862; Goodwin & Wilder, 1862; Bryan's, with Mrs. Dan Rice, 1863; Mrs. Charles Warner's, 1864; Dan Rice's, 1865; Adam Forepaugh's, 1867; John O'Brien's, 1868-73, 1878; general agent, John Robinson's, 1872; advance agent, Spalding & Ryan's, 1873; P. T. Barnum's, 1874-75; Batcheller & Doris, 1879; Sells Bros.'s, 1880. Married twice, the last time to **Mrs. S. Jones**. Lovingly called "Old Roughhead," was considered a companionable and able story teller, as well as a fair singer and jig dancer. [John A. Dingess: "The most eccentric of all circus agents with whom I have been acquainted and whose untiring energy was never for a moment allowed to flag."] One of the best known circus agents of his day died at his home in Syracuse, NY.

CASTLE, FRED R. (March 30, 1854-December 29, 1913) Leaper and tumbler. Born in Ogdensburg, NY. When one year old his parents moved to Galesburg., IL. Entered the circus profession, 1868, as an acrobat with M. O'Connor's Great Western, working in conjunction with **Harry Lamkin**, doing leaps and ground tumbling. Remained with that show through 1871 season. Dan Rice's, 1872; somersault rider, Smith & Baird, 1872; Transatlantic Shows, winter 1872-73; P. A. Older's, 1873; Transatlantic Shows, winter 1873-74; VanAmburgh's, 1874; Sells Bros.', 1875-78; Adam Forepaugh's, 1879-82 (on this show did a double somersault over 14 elephants). After which, left the show and moved to Clayton, KS, and tried farming and raising stock until 1897, when he joined Campbell Bros.' Following that, Buckskin Bill's for 2 seasons; Cosmopolitan Carnival; Snyder and Anderson several seasons furnishing calliope music; a year with Kennedy Carnival Co. Last traveling season, Herbert A. Kline's, 1911. Married **Mlle. Yerba** (a Miss Harris). In his late years, confined himself to buying, selling and leasing show property and traveling with his steam calliope. Contracted a cold, December 24, 1913, while visiting the Eschman shows; was rendered worse through a fire which destroyed his home on the 26th in Hot Springs, AR. Died at the Home Hotel of bronchial pneumonia.

CASTOR, GEORGE T. (d. January 20, 1891) Gymnast. Was before the public some 19 years, with Adam Forepaugh's, John V. O'Brien's, Batcheller & Dorris'; Walter L. Main's, 1885-90. With partner, **Correia**, known as the **American Japs.** [George S. Cole: "Castor and Correia did the best high perch act I ever saw. Mr. Correia held the thirty foot pole while Mr. Castor mounted it and went through a wonderful performance. They did a fine double trapeze, and Mr. Castor went in leaps and tumbling, besides at times playing ring master, and in case of sickness working performing dogs and trick horses. He was an all around performer...."] Died at his home in Frankfort, PA.

CASTRONI, MATTIE ROBINSON. Rider and mounted broadsword fencer. Barnum & Bailey, 1893, and then joined B. F. Wallace's to drive a tandem team and do her specialty of fencing on horseback with her husband, **Prof. G. M. Castroni.** Wore costumes of armor and velvet in the style of Italian 15th century.

CATHERS, JOHN (1853?-February 18, 1908) Started in the business, 1887, with the Lowande, Hoffman & Cathers'; Cathers & Shellcross', 1889; interest in Wyoming Wild West Show, 1895; last venture, Cathers, Downs & Bailey, stranded in Quebec, Canada. Died from intestinal trouble in Philadelphia, age 55.

CAUSSIN, MADAME. Wire-walker. From Franconi's in Paris, arrived USA with her husband in June, 1818. Joined Pepin's company, Olympic, Philadelphia, at that time and remained with him into the following year.

CAUSSIN, MONS. Strong man and general performer. Pepin's company, 1819. Act consisted of supporting 8 people while on his hands and knees. Arrived in America with his wife, a wire-walker, in June, 1818, coming from Franconi's circus in Paris.

CAVALLA, CHARLES [this may be Charles Covelli]. Clown. G. G. Grady's, 1870; Alexander Robinson's, 1872-73.

CAVANAUGH, W. B. Clown. Spalding & Rogers, 1859; G. F. Bailey & Co., 1861; sideshow performer, director and comic vocalist, Van Amburgh's, 1866.

CAYETANO, MRS. First mentioned, 1814, as a member of Cayetano's company performing in the West. Stuart Thayer believes that she could possibly be **Mrs. Redon,** who had been a member of Pepin, Breschard, Cayetano organization but whose name disappears after 1814.

CAYETANO. (d. 1817) Rider, acrobat and clown. Pepin &

Breschard, 1809. Took a circus group to Newburyport, MA, where he opened April 2, 1810; closed on May 17; then went to Exeter and Portsmouth, NH; the company returned to NYC in time to join Pepin & Breschard, and open with them on June 21. Had his own troupe which opened at Davis' Boston Circus, January 31, 1811; then went on to other nearby New England cities; was in Albany and NYC, spring 1812, and carried the distinction of being the first such to exhibit an elephant—"Old Bet," displayed, June 25, 1812. Company was in Charleston, SC, fall 1812, where sometime during the run Caytano's circus combined with Pepin & Breschard's; together they returned to NYC, July, 1813. Along with partners Pepin and Breschard, took the first organized circus company west of the Appalachians, spring 1814, when the troupe performed at Pittsburgh and at Cincinnati. It is not known how long the company stayed but Pepin & Breschard were back in Charleston that fall. Cayetano remained in the West where he performed with his troupe in such places as Cincinnati, Chillicothe, Lexington, Louisville, Natchez, New Orleans, etc. Epidemic of yellow fever hit the city of New Orleans, summer 1817, causing Cayetano's circus to be closed. A victim of the plague, by November 7, was dead. Performed a comic act on 2 horses, "Fish Woman, or The Metamorphasis," as an "immensely fat fish woman, in a huge bonnet and uncouth garments," and then divesting himself of various layers of clothing, made a final bow as an "elegant cavalier." Conducted feats of horsemanship with "hooks, hat and glove," ending with a leap of four ribbons. Did an act, "Madame Angold," when, dressed as a woman, he burlesqued a riding lesson. Performed the pyramid with a boy on his shoulders as "Flying Mercury." Enacted a comic fist fight with another clown. Rode seated in a chair placed atop his mount. Leaped over ribbons while his feet were tied together.

CEBALLOS, T. R. (1843?-March 20, 1906) Balloonist. Traveled through Australia and the Orient with Orrin Bros.'; Cuba and South America with Hadwin & Williams; West Indies with R. H. Dockrill's; and toured America and Europe with Barnum & Bailey. Also, managed his own show through South America. Died in Bridgeport, CT, age 63.

CELESTE, BELLE. (1849?-February 24, 1898) Gymnast. Sister of **Rose** and **Gene Celeste.** Considered to be one of the finest female gymnasts in America. At one time worked in partnership with **C. C. Matthews,** gymnast, and **George Austin,** wire walker. Married **William Ducrow** in Boston while both were with Lent's New York Circus, May 18, 1874. Some time later, married **George Wambold.** Connected with P. T. Barnum's, Adam Forepaugh's and others. Allen's Great Eastern, 1880; Holland & McMahon, 1887-88; high-wire, Albert Hose's, 1893. Forced to retired shortly following because of injuries incurred by a fall from a trapeze while with Markowitz' in Cleveland. Died at her home in Chicago from peritonitis, age 49.

CELESTE, ROSE [Mrs. G. DeYoung]. (b. February 4, 1848) Wire-walker. Sister of **Belle** and **Gene Celeste**. Born in Jacksonville, FL. Made first ascension at the Cliff House, San Francisco, 1864. Later, connected with Lee & Ryland, San Francisco, winter 1866-67; Allen's Great Eastern, 1880.

CERITO FAMILY [Leon, Blanche, Maude]. Trapeze performers. First appeared in America, VanAmburgh's, 1881.

CHABERT, DR. JULIEN XAVIER. (d. August 29, 1859) Fire eater, known as the "Fire King." Born in France. First appeared in NYC, Old Clinton Hall, Nassau St., 1832. In his act, remained in an immense body of fire until his entire apparel was consumed; swallowed large spoonfuls of pure Florence oil, heated to 340 degrees; swallowed 10 grains of phosphorous (4 grains being sufficient to kill another human). Died of consumption in NYC.

CHAGROIS, MASTER. Equestrian, Pepin's troupe in the Midwest, 1823.

CHALET, M. Concert ventriloquist, Cooper, Bailey & Co.'s Circus, Australian tour, 1877-78.

CHAMBERS, DR. C. S. T. Agent. George W. DeHaven's (operated by **Andrew Haight**), 1866; Haight & Chambers, 1867; C. T. Ames', 1868-69. Said to have left his position as business manager with Ames', November 1869, to retire from the profession and work for a wholesale house in Cincinnati. Later source stated he retired to keep a jewelry store in Charleston, WV, 1871.

CHAMBERS, SAM ["Silver Top"]. (about 1837-May 1, 1887) Clown. Born in Pennsylvania. Ran away from home as a boy, later joining a circus in a minor capacity. Ultimately, became proprietor and clown with Chambers Circus, where he was christened "Old Silver Top." During the Civil War, was in command of a Pennsylvania regiment. Following the fighting, became a temperence lecturer. Married a woman 25 years his junior, Corydon, IN, about 1877, with whom he reared 2 children. Died in Greensburg, IN, at which time he was traveling for a Madison cracker firm.

CHAMBERS, WASHINGTON. (d. 1861) Clown. Welch & Delavan, 1841; Welch & Mann troupe (with Mann's unit to Surina, etc.), 1843-44; Mann, Welch & Delavan, 1844, 1845; Welch & Mann, 1846; Welch, Delavan & Nathan, 1848-49; Buckley & Co., 1857-58; Orton & Older, 1858; Robinson & Lake, 1859. Fell from the flies in St. Louis Theatre and was killed.

CHAMBERS, WILLIAM. Equestrian, VanAmburgh & Co., 1881.

CHAMBERS, WILLIAM W. (June 11, 1863-February 9, 1935) Born at Frankford, PA. 1880, Batchellor & Doris as an apprentice. Because he was skillful handling long strings of ponies, was dubbed "The Star Kid Driver." Drove for Adam Forepaugh's, 1882-85, 1887-90; Frank A. Robbins, 1886; Sells Bros.' and Forepaugh-Sells', 1891-1906, elephant trainer and superintendant of animals. Later, with Ringling Bros.' and others until 1918. Died at Columbus, OH.

CHAMPION, CHARLES. Acrobat, leaper, Rockwell & Stone, 1845; Rockwell's Amphitheatre, Cincinnati, 1846.

CHAMPLIN, DANIEL. Tight-rope and general performer. American who performed balancing feats on the wire with James West's circus troupe, 1821-22. With West for the Englishman's last appearance in this country, 1822. With Joseph Cowell's, 1823; wire-walker, William Blanchard's, 1823; tight-rope performer, John Rogers', 1823-24; riding master and vaulter, J. Purdy Brown's, 1825-26, 1829; rider and wire-walker, Parson's Amphitheatre, Albany, 1826; balancing and juggling, Fogg & Co., 1828. A small but muscular man, agile on his feet and an excellent wrestler; few men, larger or smaller, could upend him. Died in Mobile, AL.

CHAMPLIN, WILLIAM. Master of Horse, Rice-Stowe-Oates, 1881.

CHANDLER, J. M. Assistant, Yankee Robinson's, 1868; general agent, Older's, 1871-72; general agent, Great Trans-Atlantic, 1873; Stevens & Begun, 1874.

CHANG YU SING. Chinese Giant, Barnum, Bailey & Hutchinson, 1881-84.

CHANNON, H. Ringmaster, Howes' Great London, 1872; L. B. Lent's, 1873.

CHAPIN, B. Manager and proprietor, B. Chapin & Co., 1874. Show closed after 5 weeks and re-organized, adding **Charles Cooper** to management as a half-interest and changing the title to Cooper & Chapin's.

CHAPMAN, PROF. Trained horses, Nixon's Amphitheatre, Chicago, 1872.

CHAPPELLE, W. J. Press agent, Shelby, Pullman & Hamilton, 1881.

CHARDILER, CHARLES. Lion performer, John Forepaugh's, California, 1888.

CHAREST FAMILY. Aerialists. Rode high-wheeled bikes across the wire, S. H. Barrett & Co., 1883. **Mons. George Charest**, high-wire and outside ascension, W. H. Harris' Nickel-Plate, 1884; Burr Robbins', 1885.

CHARLES, GEORGE. Booker & Howard's Minstrels, L. B. Lent's, 1865.

CHARLES, MASTER. 8 year old apprentice with Pepin & Breschard, 1811-12, this being his first season. Pepin, Breschard & Cayetano, 1813; moved over with Ceyatano when Pepin & Breschard disbanded, Cayetano probably taking over his apprenticeship. Continued with him, 1814-16.

CHARLTON, MARIE. See Marie Ashby.

CHARLTON, NATHANIEL DANIEL. (d. June 25, 1889) English equestrian clown, gymnast, stilt walker. Fanque's, Thomas Cooke's, and Newsome's in England; Cooke's Royal Amphitheatre (**James M. Nixon**, proprietor), Niblo's Garden, NYC, 1860; James M. Nixon's, 1860, billed as the "oldest of gymnasts." [New York *Clipper*: "The powers of equilibrium possessed by this artist, especially in the drunken scene, at once surprising and amusing to the extreme."]

CHARMON, C. H. Ringmaster, with Howe's Great London, 1871.

CHARRISKIE, WILLIAM. Slack-rope, Welch & Mann, 1841.

CHARVATT, FRANK P. Balancer, VanAmburgh & Co., 1876; crystal pyramids, Smith & Baird's, 1872; VanAmburgh & Co., 1880, 1882.

CHAUNCEY, CHARLEY. Fat boy, Dan Castello's, 1876.

CHEAKEY BROTHERS. Leapers, VanAmburgh's, 1874.

CHESEBROUGH. Rope-walker, Canadian Davis & Co., Boston, 1816. In June, left to do hall shows in New England.

CHESLEY, J. T. Agent, E. G. Smith's, 1867.

CHESTNUT, WILLIAM. Minstrel entertainer, Welch & Delavan, Baltimore, 1841.

CHEW, ROBERT. Proprietor, L. C. Palmer's, 1872.

CHIARINI, ANGELO. Rope-walker. Died November 28, 1861, of injuries from a fall in San Francisco.

CHIARINI, GUISEPPI. (1823-April 13, 1897) Equestrian, showman, called the "Franconi of America." Came to this country about 1852 with wife and their daughter, **Josephine**. At that time, was a horse trainer, performing with a stud of dancing and trick horses. Appeared at the Bowery Amphitheatre, NYC, November 7, 1853, while his daughter performed as Little Eva in *Uncle Tom's Cabin* at Barnum's Museum, Broadway and Ann Street. Manager, Franconi's Hippodrome, 1853; Sands & Chiarini, 1854. Mme. Chiarini made debut, Bowery Amphitheatre, April 3, 1854. Chiarini & Raymond, 1855; Chiarini's Royal Spanish Circus, Cuba, 1856-57. Brought his company to the Hippotheatron, 14th Street, NYC, June 25, 1866; later, played under canvas in a lot on Bleecker Street, between Charles and Perry. Took his circus all over the world—South and Central America, Mexico, Africa, East Indies, China and Japan. [Edward Orrin: "Chiarini's was the only circus to perform before the King of Siam and his wives. The king chartered a boat to bring the troupe from Singapore to Bangkok."] In 1858, Chiarini and Orrin combined their circuses for a tour of the West Indies, which lasted for 2 years. During later period of management, Chiarini confined circus operations to Cuba and South America. At one time owned considerable property in South America. Died at the Hotel Americano, Panama, age 82. [Charles H. Day: "Chiarini is one of the most venturesome and, at the same time, one of the greatest circus managers of the day."]

CHILDERS, JOSEPH H. Lecturer, Adam Forepaugh's, 1872.

CHILDERS, SAM. H. Buckley & Co., 1857-58.

CHILDS, JOE. Clog dancer, King's, 1862; concert manager, Dan Rice's, 1878.

CHIPPS, JOHN. Madigan & Gardner, Front Street Theatre, Baltimore, 1860-61.

CHIRISKI, MARTINI. Tight-rope. Thayer & Noyes, 1867;

John Robinson's, 1879.

CHRISTIE, FRANKIE. James M. Nixon's, 1863. Married clown **Jimmy Reynolds**, Allentown, PA, July 23 of that year.

CHRISTOPHER, CAPT. THOMAS. Treasurer, Howes' Great London, 1871-72.

CHURCH, JAMES [with Annie Church]. Slack-wire, Dan Rice's, 1852.

CHURCHILL. Rider, Boston Lion Circus (Raymond & Weeks, proprietors), 1836.

CLAIR, CARL. Band master. King & Franklin, 1891; Barnum & Bailey, 1893-1906; accompanied the show to England, 1898, where he was married to **Christina Matilda Weedon**, a non-professional, St. Anne's Church, London, December 5, 1899. Was with the show at least through the 1905 season and probably beyond. [C. G. Sturtevant: "Mr. Clair was a thorough musician and knew the circus program requirements. During the five year European tour his band was highly praised everywhere, and in Europe they know good music."]

CLAIRE SISTERS [Maggie, Minnie, Rose]. Trapeze performers. W. W. Cole's Circus, 1877-78; Metropolitan Circus, Havana, winter 1878-79; W. W. Cole's Australian tour (leaving San Francisco, October 23, 1880); Leon & Dockrill, Iron Amphitheatre, Havana, winter 1881-82; flying rings, Barnum, Bailey & Hutchinson, 1881-82; Sells Bros.', 1884; Rentz's, St. Petersburg, Russia, 1887; John Robinson's, 1892. **Maggie** married **Harry K. Long**, Carlisle, PA, September 6, 1879; bride and groom were members of W. W. Cole's at the time. **Rose** died in 1892. **Minnie** (Mrs. J. F. Sauers) died at her home in Detroit, MI, February 28, 1902, age 54.

CLAPP, DWIGHT. Agent. Hamilton & Sargeant, 1877-78; joined Hilliard & Hunting in Canada, August 1878; Hilliard & Main, 1883; Walter L. Main's, 1886-88.

CLARE, CARRIE. (d. June 28, 1898) Fat woman. Traveled with her midget sister, **Rose**, appearing in museums and circuses from 1883 to 1897. Connected with John Robinson's, Sells Bros.', and Walter L. Main's, 1893. After the death of her sister, exhibited as a fat lady bicycle rider. Last appearance was with another obese female cyclist on the Washburn circus, fall 1897. Died at Fort Scott, KS.

CLARE, ROSE. See Carrie Clare.

CLARISSE, MRS. ELIZABETH. See Lizzie Agazzi.

CLARK, BOBBY. Clown, with Alex Robinson's, 1874-75; Charles Lee's, 1889.

CLARK, BURT H. Animal keeper. Hunter, Brown & Bailey, 1827; Brown Bros.', 1828-31; elephant man, J. B. Green & Co., 1831; J. P. Brown & Green, 1832; J. B. Green's, 1833.

CLARK, DICK [or Dan]. (d. January 1, 1873) Rider, acrobat. Cousin of Dan Rice. Dan Rice's (managed by **Adam Forepaugh**), 1866; Dan Rice's, 1869-70; H. M. Smith's, 1870; Rice's Paris Pavilion Circus, 1871-72. Died of small pox in New Orleans.

CLARK, E. Dwarf, with a circus on Sansom Street, Philadelphia, 1833-34.

CLARK, G. BROOKS. Vocalist, concert, Adam Forepaugh's (Pullman Bros.' sideshow), 1876.

CLARK, GUS L. Clown, Herr Driesbach's Menagerie and Howe's Circus, 1868; ringmaster, Adam Forepaugh's. With the latter, rode at the head of the street procession in an open barouche impersonating Adam Forepaugh, while Forpaugh was back at the lot cutting up meat for the animals.

CLARK, HARRY. Trapeze performer. Cosmopolitan Circus, Museum and Menagerie, 1871; John Wilson's, California, 1873.

CLARK, J. A. ["Dr."]. Sideshow, L. B. Lent's, 1873.

CLARK, J. D. General agent, Great London Pavilion Show, 1876.

CLARK, JOHN. Thayer & Noyes, 1862; Howes & Norton (formerly Robinson & Howes), 1864. May be the man listed below.

CLARK, JOHN C. (1834?-September 19, 1916) Clown. Spalding & Rogers, 1852; Dan Rice's, 1855, 1858; S. Q. Stoke's, 1862; rope-walker, Palmer's Great Western, 1865. Died at Long Branch, NJ, age 82.

CLARK, M. L. (1857-October 4, 1923) Proprietor, M. L. Clark's, 1892-97, 1902-21, 1923-26. Headquartered, Alexandria, LA, for many years. Wife's name was **Fannie**.

CLARK, MME. Fat lady. North American, 1872; P. T. Barnum's, 1873.

CLARK, NELLIE. Acrobat, G. G. Grady's, 1873.

CLARK, THOMAS. Tumbler, gymnast, Alex Robinson's, 1871.

CLARK, W. Clown, vaulter. Pepin & West, Olympic, Philadelphia, fall 1817; West's, 1818.

CLARKE, BURKIT "KIT." (1845-July 4, 1918) Agent. Born in NYC. Advance agent, Satterlee & Bell at age 13; programmer, steamboat *Banjo*, 1859. Took up the study of photography in Chicago, 1861-63. Mabie's, 1863; VanAmburgh's, 1864-67; director of press work, Adam Forepaugh's, for 9 years during the 1870s, being one of the first agents to use illiterative advertising; treasurer, Sheldenburger & Co., 1871; business manager, the Imperial Brazilian Hippodrome, Philadelphia, winter 1872-73. Managed **Prof. Hartz** and **Zera**, magicians; business affairs, John A. Stevens, 1878-79; M. B. Leavitt's musical troupe, The Rentz Company, 1880; accompanied Haverly's Minstrels to London; and for a time managed Keller, the magician. Had the distinction of being a friend and fishing companion of Grover Cleveland and Joseph Jefferson. Devoted time in retirement to the writing of short stories and other items. Died at his home in Flatbush, NY, age 86.

CLARKE, DR. Descriptive lecturer, P. T. Barnum's, 1874.

CLARKE, GEORGE F. Aeronaut, C. W. Noyes'. Killed at Memphis, TN, May 31, 1872, when, in making his ascension, the conveyence struck a building and the ropes supporting his

trapeze gave way, causing him to fall about 50.

CLARKE, GEORGE M. Clown. The United States Circus (**Frank Howes, Joseph Cushing**, proprietors), 1867; Howes Trans-Atlantic Circus and Risbeck's Menagerie (**Frank Howes**, proprietor), 1868; J. M. French's, 1869-70; George W. Bailey & Co., 1871-74; clown, P. T. Barnum's, 1876; equestrian director, Glenan & Austin, 1892. Resident of Vermont, was a minstrel manager and ran a grist mill with equal success; also a song writer and composer. As a clown, was not possessed of any humor but sang with sentiment that caught on in the ring and made him a favorite in New England. For many years, traveled with the "Flatfoots."

CLARKE, GUS BROOKS [r. n. Andrew Jackson Ayers]. (d. November 1886) Connected with the minstrel and circus ring. At time of death was manager, Syracuse Museum. Died in that city.

CLARKE, HENRY. Gymnast, Melville, Maginley & Cooke, 1875.

CLARKE, JAMES. Negro minstrel, VanAmburgh's northern, 1859.

CLARKE, J. S. Agent, Collins' Oriental Combination, 1877.

CLARKE, ROBERT. Clown, Alexander Robinson's, 1871-77.

CLAVEAU, JOSEPH. Clown. Yeaman circus, 1833; Joseph D. Palmer's, 1833, 1835-36; Palmer & Harrington, 1834; a member of the Ravel Family, 1836-37; Cincinnati Circus, 1841; John Mateer's, 1843-44; Howes & Mabie, 1844-46; Great Western, 1846. [T. Allston Brown: "He was a good fellow. He had visited, professionally and often, most of the West Indies Islands, many portions of South America, Mexico, etc."] Committed suicide in Iowa City, IA.

CLAYTON, GRACE. Female clown, with Macarte Sisters', 1870.

CLAYTON, JOHN. Proprietor. Clayton, Bartlett & Welch, 1839-40; Clayton & Welch's giraffe exhibition, 1841; Clayton & Bartlett, 1844-45.

CLEARY, JOHN H. [Signor Martino]. (d. May 8, 1940) Horizontal bars and trapeze artist. First professional engagement, Hayward Minstrels. In 1887, combined with two other performers in act billed as **Three Milo Bros.**; later, appeared in vaudeville as single; was with New Orleans Minstrels in South and Southwest. Last circus, Washburn's. Retired 1914. Died at the Shetucket Club, Norwich, CT, age 78.

CLEMENTS, JOHN. Band leader, Alex Robinson's, 1875.

CLEMENTS, ROBERT (1860?-September 28, 1912) Born in Brookville, PA. Managed the American Hotel, Pittsburgh, for 18 years before going into the circus business, when he managed Walter L. Main's for 4 seasons. Held a similar position with Pawnee Bill's Wild West Show. Formed a partnership with **Samuel Scribner** and put out the Scribner & Clements Show. After withdrawing from the circus business, became treasurer for the Trocadero Theatre, Chicago. Died at

Punxsutawney, PA, age 52.

CLEVELAND, JENNIE. See Jennie Alward and John W. Cleveland.

CLEVELAND, JOHN W. [r. n. John Roberts]. (1871?-July 31, 1897) Equestrian. Entered the profession, 1885, with the Weldon Circus; followed by an engagement with Wallace & Anderson, where he remained for 10 years. Married **Jennie Alward**, hurdle rider and dancing rope artist, both with Wallace's, Holton, Kansas, May 27, 1893. Bareback riders, W. B. Reynolds', 1895; Winter Circus, Chicago, 1895; Robert Hunting's, 1896; LaPearl's Danville, IL., winter 1896-97; hurdle and 4-horse act, Wood & Ewers, 1897. Cleveland died of consumption, age 26.

CLEVELAND, P. H. Master of horse, James T. Johnson & Co. (**James T. Johnson, G. O. Smith**, P. H. Cleveland, proprietors), 1881.

CLIFFORD, JAMES. Contortionist. Tumbler, W. W. Cole's, 1878; Holland, Bowman & McLaughlin, 1890; Hurlburt & Leftwich, 1894.

CLIFFORD, MRS. THOMAS. Entry rider, P. T. Barnum, 1876.

CLIFFORD, THOMAS. (d. July 10, 1919) Tumbler and leaper. Native of Binghamton, NY. Began career, 1860, with Yankee Robinson's. Dan Rice's (rail and boat), 1870; Cosmopolitan Circus, winter 1871-72; James Robinson's, New Orleans, winter 1872-73; James W. Wilder & Co., 1873; Montgomery Queen's, 1874; leaper and tumbler, P. T. Barnum, 1876; W. W. Cole's, 1878; Adam Forepaugh's, 1879. Died in Chicago.

CLIFTON, CHARLES. Great International Circus, Offenbach Garden, Philadelphia, winter 1876-77.

CLIFTON, FRANK. Gymnast, acrobat. James T. Johnson's, fall 1872; Imperial Brazilian Hippodrome, Philadelphia, winter 1872-73; horizontal bar act with **Sam Ashton** and **Albert Gaston**, Montgomery Queen's, 1875; Maybury, Pullman & Hamilton, 1882; Orrin Bros.', winter 1882-83; clown, Burk & Co., 1884; equestrian director and talking clown, Cross & LeRoy, winter 1884.

CLIFTON, JOHN. Holland & Gormley, 1889.

CLIFTONS [Billy, Jessie]. Aerialists, Walter L. Main's, 1886; comic mule act, English knockabout clowns, Charles Lee's Great London Shows, 1895-96.

CLINE. Gymnast, Alex Robinson's, 1866; (with **Penny**) Dan Rice's, 1868.

CLINE, ANDRE [Herr Cline Seiltanzer]. (circa 1806-December 3, 1886) Rope-dancer. Although English born, preferred the German title of "Herr." Brother of **P. S. Cline**, the actor, and **Frank Cline**, the violinist. One of the great artists of his day. [Charles Durang: "He was highly polished in style and attitude. His pictorial display of the contending emotions ... was exceedingly well executed."] On the tight rope, performed with grace and eloquence, unique from other artists by his expressive pantomime and intelligence of character. One routine was to represent a sailor dancing the hornpipe on the wire, followed by depicting the tragic passion of the sailor as he experienced the horrors of a storm at sea. Would conclude the act by the ascension from the stage to the dome of the house "in a blazing revolving sun, surrounded by fireworks." Also made an ascension from the stage to the gallery pushing a wheelborrow. First appeared in America, May 12, 1828, coming under contract to **Charles Gilfert**, manager of the Bowery Theatre, NYC, the terms being £2,000 for one year with privilege of renewal. Performed for **James Caldwell** at the Camp Street Theatre, New Orleans, as well as in Philadelphia, and other major theatres. In New Orleans, was publicly dismissed by the manager over some dispute; whereupon, Cline appealed to the audience, explaining his side of the controversy; manager Caldwell followed with his version. The audience, disinterested, summarily hissed them both. An irate Caldwell then barred Cline from ever performing on the Camp Street stage. Nevertheless, Cline was back under Caldwell's management at the St. Charles Theatre, that city, during the 1841-42 season. Chestnut Street Theatre, Philadelphia, 1834; Welch & Mann, 1841; Stone & Rockwell, 1846; Rockwell's Amphitheatre, Cincinnati, 1846; Dan Rice's, 1852-53; Levi J North's, 1860; S. P. Stickney's, 1861; Gardner & Hemmings, 1862; Madame Macarte's European Circus (**James M. Nixon**, proprietor), 1863. [John A. Dingess: "He was a most daring and dexterous performer in the various feats of his profession, in which he was entirely unrivaled until the appearance of the Ravel Troupe."] Having accumulated quite a fortune in England, brought it with him and deposited it in an American bank; the bank failed and he lost some $40,000. Retired from performing and settled in NYC.

CLING, GEORGE W. Principal rider, Adam Forepaugh's, 1884.

CLINTON, HERR. Horizontal bars, Gardner & Hemmings, 1860.

CLINTON, JACK. Clown and equestrian manager, Goldenberg's Colossal Aggregation, 1874-75.

CLINTON BROTHERS. Acrobats, P. T. Barnum's, 1874.

CLOFULLIA, MME. FORTUNE [r. n. Josephine Boisdechene]. (b. March 25, 1831) Bearded lady. Born in Versoix, Switzerland. USA debut at Barnum's Museum, 1853, as "The Bearded Lady of Geneva."

CLONEY, C. Gymnast, Lake & Co.'s, 1863.

CLOWNEY, CHARLES. Horizontal bars, Levi J. North's, 1863.

CLUTTER, T. Maginley, Carroll & Co., 1867.

COAKLEY, JOHN. Holland & Gormley, 1888; W. H. Harris' Nickel-Plate, 1888.

COATE, ALEC. Acrobat, Welch, Bartlett & Co., 1839.

COBB, WILLIS. (1841?-November 19, 1913) As a boy, trained the family house dog to make change from a handful of dimes and nickels and to pick trumps out of a deck of cards. Got a job exhibiting with VanAmburgh's; later, and for many years, devoted his attention to lions and other ferocious animals. [D. W. Watt: "The management soon found a handy man in Willis Cobb. He was thoroughly reliable and could always be found at his post whether lecturing in the sideshow on freaks, driving a team over the road dark nights, or acting as manager of the show. Willis Cobb was always in the job.... They used to say that Willis Cobb could make a tame lion roar louder and open his mouth wider than any man who ever put a foot on sawdust."] Press agent in advance of circuses for some 40 years and the originator of many publicity stunts. Also developed and performed animal acts. Performing horse, Fred Hunt, and his dogs and goats, National Circus, Cincinnati, winter 1864-65; 4 trained dogs, George Metcalfe's, St. Louis, 1866; performing dogs and monkeys, New York Champs Elysees, 1866; ringmaster (presumably the animals were along as well) Perry Powers', 1867; trained dogs, Nixon, Howes & Castello, 1868; VanAmburgh's, 1870-71; Joel E. Warner & Co., 1872; John Robinson's, 1873. Joined Sells Bros.', 1874, as press agent, clown and with his troupe of performing dogs and remained with the show in that capacity for several years. By 1887, was listed as press agent with Wallace & Co. (Wallace & Anderson, 1890; Wallace & Co., 1891; Cook & Whitney, 1892-93). Retired about 1903 after marrying a sister of the Sells brothers. A first wife had died in Columbus, OH, August 25, 1881. Cobb died in Cleveland, OH, age 72.

COBELLO BROTHERS. Acrobats, Dan Rice's, 1891.

CODET. Pupil of **Rugieri**, European rope-walker. Pepin & Breschard, 1808-10; Cayetano & Co., 1810-12, specializing in feats of horsemanship (company performed in NYC, 1812, along with the Crowninshield elephant). Had his own company, Montreal, Canada, 1812. Pepin, Breschard & Cayetano, 1813; Pepin & Breschard, 1814. May have died in South Carolina or Georgia, late 1814.

CODONA, ADELAIDE [or Cordona]. Rider of single and 6-horse feats. Cooper & Bailey, 1879-80; bareback, principal, and flaming zone hurdle act, Barnum, Bailey & Hutchinson, 1881; Sells Bros.'; 1882; principal rider, Adam Forepaugh's, 1883; Orrin Bros.', Mexico, winter 1883-84; 4-horse rider, Sells Bros.', 1884-85; Orrin Bros.', Mexico, winter 1885-86; bareback rider, P. T. Barnum's, 1886.

CODONA, HARRY [or Cordona]. Rider. Orrin Bros.', San Francisco, 1863; equestrian director, Dan Rice's, 1864; New York Champs Elysees, 1866; Adam Forepaugh's, 1867; pad rider leaping through small balloons, Bryan's, 1868; Ames', 1869; equestrian director and rider, Sheldenburger's, 1871; Dan Rice's Paris Pavilion, 1873; equestrian director, Sadler's, 1875; Sells Bros.', 1877; equestrian manager, Ed G. Basye's, 1878-79; equestrian director, Anderson & Co., 1879; Cooper & Co., winter 1879-80; clown, Leon & Dockrill, Havana, winter 1881-82. His wife, **Amelia**, was an equestrienne and

tight-rope performer; son, **Dave**, was listed, 1868, as a pony rider and contortionist.

CODONA, HORTENSE BUISLAY. (September 21, 1869-September 21, 1931) Born in Mexico City. Married **Edward Codona** at age 14 in Panama while the Buislay and Codona families were performing there. They became the parents of **Rose, Victoria, Alfredo, Avelardo,** and **Edward, Jr.** See Buislay Family.

COFFIN, CAPT. Billed as the Nova Scotia Giant. Toured England with **Judge H. P. Ingalls** as manager. While there, married a giantess; the ceremony being conducted at Martin Church, Trafalgar Square, with the square so packed with bystanders waiting to get a glimpse of the tall bride and groon that omnibuses were unable to pass through.

COGSWELL, FRED. (d. August 22, 1872) Animal keeper. Died at Chandlersville, OH.

COHEN, GUS. Clown, Beckett's Railroad Circus, 1887.

COLE, ALBERT H. "BERT." (b. August 15, 1869) Son of **George S. Cole.** Born in Kenosha, WI. Filled a variety of positions over the years, including those of advertiser, treasurer and announcer. First connected with Nixon's Amphitheatre, Chicago, of which his father was half-owner, 1872; Montgomery Queen's, 1873-77; Great Anderson, 1878-79; Burr Robbins', 1880; Hilliard & DeMott, 1881; Cole's, 1882; Hilliard & Main, 1883; Frank A, Robbins, 1886; Walter L. Main's, 1888; George S. Cole's, 1895. 20 years with Hagenbeck & Wallace beginning around 1900, then with one show or another until retirement to Tottenville, Staten Island, 1929.

COLE, A. W. Sideshow lecturer, Barnum, Bailey & Hutchinson, 1881.

COLE, EDWARD C. Sideshow director, orator, Cooper, Bailey & Co., 1879.

COLE, GEORGE S. (1834-March 21, 1910) Father of **May** and **Bert Cole.** Born on the Madrid Road near Potsdam, NY. After leaving school at the age of 15, was clerk at the post office, Ogdensburg, NY. Three years later, 1852, left the job to join Mabie Bros.' as an assistant in the ticket wagon. Business-like, neat, and pleasant in dealing with the public, he soon rose to position of treasurer. Treasurer, H. Buckley & Co., 1857; treasurer, Yankee Robinson's, 1866; treasurer, James M. French's, 1868; privileges, Adam Forepaugh's, 1869; treasurer and half owner, James M. Nixon's Amphitheatre, Chicago, 1872; treasurer, James W. Wilder & Co., 1873; treasurer, Montgomery Queen's, 1874-77; treasurer and layer-out, Anderson & Co., 1878-79; concert privilege, Burr Robbins', 1880; concert privilege, Hilliard & DeMott, 1881-82; Cole's Circus (George S. Cole, **Bill Monroe,** and **Matt Leland,** proprietors), winter 1882-83, traveling by chartered steamer *Parol,* showing under canvas along the Mississippi between St. Louis and New Orleans; concert privilege, Hilliard & Main, 1883; Pullman, Mack & Co., 1884; press agent, Frank A. Robbins', 1885-87, compiled route book, 1886; press agent and concert privilege, Walter L. Main's, 1888-92; Cole's Colossal Circus (George S. Cole, **John Sparks**, proprietors), 1892-93; Cole & Lockwood's All New United Shows (George S. Cole, **A. L. Lockwood, Jr.**, proprietors), 1894; George S. Cole's, 1895, which collapsed September 4 of that year; advertising banner concession, Walter L. Main's, 1896; the same, Robinson & Franklin Bros.', 1897; elephant banners advertising privilege, John Robinson's, 1898-1909; and part of 1909 season, 101 Ranch show. [Sam A. Scribner, manager Columbia Amusement Co.: "Mr. Cole was one of the straightest, most honorable business men I ever met and at the same time one of the most delightful associates."] Went to Jacksonville, Florida, to open with Howes' Great London, 1910, but on March 21, died suddenly from a heart attack. An important member of the American circus for over 50 years, filling many job capacities and performing them with devotion and expertise. [Walter L. Main, in a letter to the New York *Clipper:* "I first met Cole in 1883 and traveled with him for two years with the Hilliard Circus, then one of the largest wagon shows on the road. I was agent and Cole had charge of the concert and was Mr. Hilliard's right-hand man. When I went into the business for myself, Cole was one of the first men I engaged and he worked for me five consecutive years and our business relations were always very pleasant. Cole was a very interesting conversationalist and very original. Those were happy years. Cole was with me about all the time I traveled by wagons and he always led the parade and was principal door-keeper. He was one man I could always depend upon and one of the few men who turned in all of the door money. George S. Cole was a true friend and a more loyal subject never worked for the Main show. I was prosperous all those years and I feel that the secret of my success was due to the honorable people I was surrounded with."]

COLE, IRA. Born in New York State. Manager and famous wrestler of his day. Connected with the Eagle Circus/ Cole & Co., 1837, exhibiting through West and Southwest; Ira Cole's Zoological Institute, 1838; Miller, Cole & Gale, St. Louis, 1838.

COLE, JOHNNY. Sideshow performer, Melville, Maginley & Co., 1863.

COLE, LEW. Museum manager, Great American Circus, Museum and Menagerie, 1893.

COLE, MARY ANN. See Mary Ann Cooke.

COLE, SAM. Proprietor, Cole & O'Neil, 1873; manager, North American Circus and Balloon Show, 1875.

COLE, WILLIAM. (d. 1858) Husband of the former **Mary Ann Cooke** and father of the great showman **W. W. Cole**. A posturer, contortionist and clown with the circus belonging to his father-in-law, **Thomas Taplin Cooke**, which newly arrived from England, 1836-38. The company first performed in a building erected on Walnut Street, Philadelphia. After the circus was left devastated from a theatre fire, Cooke and his family returned to England, but William and Mary Ann, remained in USA. Welch, Bartlett & Co., 1839; E. C. Yale & Co. 1840; June, Titus, Angevine & Co., Bowery Amphitheatre, 1840; Howes & Mabie, 1841-43; Rockwell & Stone, 1843; John Tryon's, Bowery Amphitheatre, NYC, 1845; Nathan A. Howes', 1845; Rockwell & Stone, 1845; dog act, Howes & Co., 1846; Victory Circus, 1847; J. M. June's, 1851; P. A. Older & Co.'s, 1852; "feats of dexterity," Driesbach & Mabie, 1853.

COLE, W. L. Proprietor, W. L. Cole's, 1889-90; Sieber & Cole, 1891.

COLE, WILLIAM W. (1847-March 10, 1915) Born in NYC, the son of contortionist **William H. Cole** and high school rider and wire walker **Mary Ann Cooke**. First year in the business, H. Buckley & Co., 1857. Four years after his father died his mother married **Miles Orton** of Orton Bros.' Young Cole learned the circus business growing up on the show, beginning as ticket seller and general helper and progressing to sideshow spieler, layer-out, ringmaster, bill-poster and advance agent. Became a sideshow proprietor, 1867. Ringmaster and sideshow privileges, Stowe & Orton, 1870. Following the divorce of Orton and his mother, he launched Cole & Orton, 1871, from Quincy, IL, as a 50-horse wagon show, a cage of performing lions and an elephant leased from J. M. French. Added 10 cages the following year. Again enlarged in 1874 (**Miles Orton** was said to have had an interest in the show), beginning in Galveston as W. W. Cole's New York and New Orleans Circus and Menagerie. That year the show went to California and back. Took the show to Australia and New Zealand, 1880, leaving San Francisco, October 23, and returning, 1881. Married a Quincy, IL, girl, **Margaret Kable**, 1885. Closed and sold the circus at auction on the Canal Street lot, New Orleans, 1886, to become part owner with Barnum & London and to look out for James A. Bailey's interest. After 2 years, sold his share to Bailey, October 27, 1887, and retired until 1898, when he purchased ¼ interest in Forepaugh-Sells Bros. Circus and the Buffalo Bill's Wild West Show, acting as executive head of those organizations while Barnum & Bailey was on tour in Great Britain and the Continent. With Bailey's death, the governing board of Barnum & Bailey elected him managing director for a one year term, replacing **George Starr**. At the expiration, Cole permanently retired. Accomplishments included a genius for routing a show into new territory; the first circus and menagerie to cross the continent entirely by rail and tour California, 1873; although not the largest of shows, he employed the better acts, used lavish advertising and issued large amounts of lithos, heralds, etc.; was one of the first to use lithograph posters extensively; said to have been the first person to earn a million dollars from circus operation; died leaving assets of around 5 million dollars and rated one of the richest men the circus ever produced.

COLEMAN. European Running globe performer, John Wilson's, 1868, California.

COLEMAN BROTHERS. Classical groupings, Holland & McMahon, 1885.

COLEMAN, FRANK ["Col."]. (1849?-1904) Announcer, called the "Silver Tongued Orator" because of his clear, deep voice. Began his career in San Francisco around 1875 by engineering the first outdoor sword contest attempted in America, a bout between **Duncan D. Ross** and **Capt. E. N. Jennings**. Going East, joined Barnum & Bailey as chief announcer; also connected with Adam Forepaugh's, W. W. Cole's, etc. Some time later, went abroad, assuming the name of "Sir Roger Moore," where he is said to have prospered and, according to his claim, met all the crowned heads of Europe. Always well dressed and a talented conversationalist. Died in NYC.

COLEMAN, HARRY "HANDSOME HARRY." (1876?-February 4, 1915) Fat man. A native of Shelbourne Falls, MA. Weighing some 750 pounds, was said to be the largest man in point of weight and stature on exhibit at the time. Connected with various circus sideshows; appearing at one in Washington, DC, when he died at age 39.

COLEMAN, THOMAS ["Picaninny"]. Negro minstrel with Welch, Bartlett & Co.; 1839; Welch & Delavan; 1841; Great Western Circus, 1846, 1847.

COLLETT. Band leader and violinist, Ricketts', Philadelphia, 1795. There was also a **Master Collett**, rider with Price & Simpson's circus troupe, 1826-27.

COLLINS, CHARLES H. Press agent, L. B. Lent's, 1876.

COLLINS, GREENLEAF W. (1837-1906) Hotel operator. Bought Mabie's winter quarters' hotel, Delavan, WI. Later had the Delavan House, an establishment patronized by circus people. When the Centennial Circus went bankrupt in mid-season, 1876, he made arrangements to lease the menagerie for the remainder of the year and took it out under G. W. Collins & Co.'s Museum and Circus, moving chiefly in Wisconsin, Illinois, and Indiana.

COLLINS, WILLIAM L. Proprietor, Collins' Oriental Combination, 1877; London Sensation Show (W. L. Collins & Co.), 1879.

COLSON, N. T. Band leader, Mabie's, 1859; Dan Rice's, 1865-66.

COLSTON GEORGE. Musical director, with Robinson & Howes, November 1863; orchestra leader, Nixon's Amphitheatre, Chicago, 1872.

COLTON, MISS. Race rider, P. T. Barnum's Roman Hippodrome, 1875.

COLUMBUS, GEORGE. Contortionist and general performer, first appearing in America, Stone & Murray, 1869-72.

COLVIN, ERASMUS DARWIN. (June 30, 1843-October 23, 1901) Born in Clyde, Wayne County, NY. Toured with circuses in the summer and worked as cashier for the St. Charles Hotel restaurant in the winter. Charles H. Day stated that Colvin knew everyone in the circus business. Frugal, care-

ful with money, and a shrewd investor. Assistant treasurer, Sands, Nathan & Co., 1862-64; treasurer, L. B. Lent's, 1864-68; protector of Adam Forepaugh's interest, Gardner & Kenyon, 1869; manager, Adam Forepaugh's, 1870-71, 1873; manager, George F. Bailey & Co., 1872; manager, Montgomery Queen's, 1874-77; manager, W. C. Coup's, 1877; privileges, John H. Murray's, 1878; general manager, W. C. Coup' New United Monster Show, 1879; bought an interest in Burr Robbins', January 1881, and went out with Robbins & Colvin's Great American and German Allied Shows; manager, Nathans & Co., 1882; manager, VanAmburgh, Charles Reich & Bros., 1885; assistant manager, W. W. Cole's, 1886; Doris & Colvin, 1887; manager of privileges, Frank A. Robbins', 1888; assistant manager, Walter L. Main's, 1893-94. Beginning 1890s, was a purchaser of horses and other animals for circus organizations and the representative for animal sales in the United States for the **Carl Hagenbeck** animal importing business. Also business partner of **E. H. McCoy** in managing the Bijou Theatre, Chicago; a stock holder and director of the National Printing Co., Chicago; and the owner of a pony stock farm at New Lennox, Ill. [Charles H. Day: "It was a sad day for W. C. Coup when he lost Colvin's counsel and services. Had he retained both, it is my opinion that he would not today be numbered with the great army of 'has beens.'"] After having come from his home in Chicago to supervise a shipment of animals to Barnum & Bailey in Europe, died at the Sturtevant House, NYC, from rheumatic fever that induced a heart disease.

COMOSH, JOHN. See John Worland.

COMPTON, F. Singing clown. Began with Dan Rice's, 1849. Spent the latter portion of his life knocking about the country in a covered wagon of his own construction, repairing guns and sewing machines.

CONANT, AUGUSTINE. (September 8, 1828-1915) Born in Acton, MA. Began as a roustabout and teamster, Spalding & Rogers, 1850-53. By 1865, was a financial backer of S. O. Wheeler's and remained as backer and treasurer through 1868. Leased out equipment to and boss of the ticket wagon for Metchear & Cameron, 1870; also supplied equipment to Nixon's New York and Nixon's Southern circuses, 1870. Died at the age of 86.

CONCK, J. H. (d. March 30, 1882) Sideshow manager, W. H. Stowe's, 1882. Died in the burning of the *Golden City* steamer at Memphis, TN.

CONDON, J.: Boss canvasman, John Robinson's, 1892.

CONE, TOM. Clown, Whitney Family's New Enterprise, 1887.

CONKLIN, GEORGE. (December 7, 1845-February 25, 1924) Lion tamer and elephant trainer. Learned much about elephants from Stewart Craven. Began as an advance courier for Haight & Chambers. Brother of **John** and **Pete Conklin**. Born in Cincinnati. Mabie Bros.', 1859; Great European, 1865; Haight & Chambers, 1866; O'Brien's, 1867-1871; zoological director, W. W. Cole's, 1875, including the Australian tour which left San Francisco, October 23, 1880, and continuing at least through the 1886 season. Head animal trainer for Barnum & Bailey for more than 20 years, including their London engagement. Was attacked many times by his animals and bore the scars to prove it. Loved the animals and the bustle of circus life. Wrote a series of circus articles for the *Saturday Evening Post*, which were later published in book form by Harper Bros. Retired in 1906, but as his savings diminished, went to work in the post office at Bridgeport, CT. Died in that city.

CONKLIN, H. Gymnast, VanAmburgh & Co., 1874.

CONKLIN, JOHN. (about 1838-September 15, 1885) Cannon ball performer. Brother of **George** and **Pete Conklin**. Born in NYC. Began as an entertainer, 1850's, Frank Western's Museum, Cincinnati, OH. Some claim he was the first performer to catch a cannon ball fired from a cannon, which perhaps inspired the designation of "The Modern Hercules." Married in San Francisco to Miss **Phoebe Frost (Madame Sanyeah)**, gymnast from Carlisle, England, November 4, 1872. Last engagement, Rentz's Circus, Germany, spring 1885. (Conklin Bros.) Brown's, 1855; cannon balls, Mabie's, 1857-60; Robinson & Lake, Wood's Theatre, Cincinnati, 1859; Robinson & Lake, 1860; Tom King's, Washington, DC, winter 1861-62; (Conklin Bros.) Maginley & VanVleck's, 1863; (Conklin Bros.) Howes' European, winter 1864; (Conklin Bros.) Maginley, Black & Co., 1864; New American Theatre, Philadelphia, winter 1865-66. Brothers performed in variety halls and theatres during the Civil War. **John** and **Pete** took over the old W. B. Reynolds & Co.'s Circus and Menagerie, calling it the Conklin Bros. Great American Circus and Menagerie, 1866; combined with **George M. Kelley** and **William LaRue** to form the Great Combination Circus, 1871-72. John was also with Bryan's, 1869; Campbell's, 1870; Bailey & Co., Central and South America and the West Indies, fall 1874. Died at the residence of his brother, Pete, in St. Louis, MO.

CONKLIN, JOHN. (d. 1838) Equestrian. Born in Cincinnati, OH. Vaulter, Page's, 1830; Stickles & Co., 1832; vaulter, Bancker & Harrington, 1835-36; vaulter, Frost, Husted & Co., 1836; J. J. Hall's, 1836; 2-horse rider, Frost & Co. 1837; 2-horse rider, W. Gates & Co., 1838; vaulter, A. Hunt & Co., 1838. Died in Cincinnati from the effects of a fall from two horses.

CONKLIN, PETER. (May 28, 1842-January 1, 1924) Brother of **John** and **George Conklin**. Born in NYC. Joined Clark's American Troupe of Ethiopian Minstrels, Cincinnati, age 12, but the show soon folded. Joined other entertainers, 1855, in organizing Jim's Great American Valise Troupe, but he soon left and the group disbanded. Connected with Major Brown's, 1856, with his brother, **John**. E. F. Mabie's, 1857, remaining until around 1861, during which time he became a

singing clown. At outbreak of the Civil War, returned to Cincinnati and with his brothers formed **Conklin Brother's Gymnasts** and performed in variety halls and theatres during the conflict. With Campbell's Minstrels briefly before going to England, 1863; returned to the United States, 1864, and joined Dan Castello's for a short time. Then, S. B. Howes', 1865, billed as "the great Western clown." Was with Howes, February, 1865, when the circus played New Orleans. [New Orleans *Times*: "Pete Conklin, the clown, during his brief stay amongst us has won the golden opinions from all men, and proved himself one of the mainstays of the great show. His odd jokes and joking oddities have nightly been received with delight, until at last his appearance in the ring was attended with a universal grin from the audience, on the *qui vive* as they were rich things to come. His local hits were to the point, but the point was tipped with gold, kindly but sarcastic. He always commanded the attention of his audience; is one of the most promising clowns we have ever seen, and we sincerely hope to see him soon again."] As a singing clown, had a deep voice that has been described as a "delicate avalanche of thunder." A badge of identity was a large diamond pin. At Vicksburg, was presented with a splendid horse and accoutrements by Gen. Morgan L. Smith. (Conklin Bros.) Maginley & VanVleck's, fall 1863; (Conklin Bros.) Maginley's, 1864; (Conklin Bros.) Maginley, Black & Co., 1864; (Conklin Bros.) Seth B. Howes' European, 1864-65; New American Theatre, Philadelphia, winter 1865-66; John Robinson's, 1868; director and clown, Imperial Brazilian Hippodrome, Philadelphia, winter 1872-73; John O'Brien's, 1873; A. B. Rothcilds & Co., 1875; Cooper, Bailey & Co., 1876; Great International, Philadelphia, winter 1876-77; Burr Robins', 1877-78 (was keeping a restaurant in Philadelphia at this time.); DeHaven & Dutton, 1879; Batcheller & Doris, 1879; Sells Bros.', 1881; Ryan & Robinson, 1882; John Robinson's, 1883; J. S. McCue's, California, 1883; W. W. Cole's, 1883; Martell's, 1884; equestrian director and sideshow manager, Bailey & Winans, 1890; formed Conklin & Gilchrist Boat Show, 1891; W. B. Reynold's, 1892; Winter Circus, Grand Opera House, Newark, NJ, 1894.

CONKLIN, W. A. Financial manager, Frank A. Robbins United Shows (**Frank A. Robbins, Gil Robinson, John W. Hamilton**, W. A. Conklin, proprietors), 1898.

CONKLIN, WILL E. Contortionist. With Charles Andress', 1889; Holland & Gormley, fall 1889.

CONLEY, HARRY. Elephant handler, John V. O'Brien's, 1871.

CONLEY, PATRICK. (d. June 30, 1888) With John V. O'Brien's. Killed at age 22 from a trapeze accident.

CONNELLY, FRANK. Bill writer, a former city editor of the Philadelphia *Times*, hired by Adam Forepaugh to assist **Fred Lawrence** in writing advertising. Together they were responsible for enveigling **Prof. Leidy**, a man from the University of

Pennsylvania, into certifying the authenticity of Forepaugh's "white elephant."

CONNER, CLAUDE. (1836?-November 8, 1894) Gymnast. One of **Goldie Brothers** acrobatic team along with **George Goldie** and **Henry P. O'Neil**. Their last season on the road, 1868, Stone & Murray. Following retirement from the entertainment business, was night watchman at the Union Square Theatre, NYC. Died of Brights disease there.

CONNER, GEORGE F. Agent. Welch & Delevan, 1849; Dr. Gilbert R. Spalding's, 1849-51; sideshow manager, Burr Robbins', 1886.

CONNER, JAMES. Acrobat, Palmer's, 1835.

CONNER, JAMES O. Boxer (with Edward O. Baldwin), Howes Trans-Atlantic Circus and Risbeck's Menagerie (Frank Howes, proprietor), 1868.

CONNER, MORRIS. Chief billposter, Great International, 1874.

CONNERS, ED. Manager of sideshow, Bruce L. Baldwin's, 1894.

CONNERS, JOHN. Clown. George W. Richard's, 1887; W. H. Harris' Nickel-Plate, 1888.

CONNERS, M. A. Program agent, John Robinson's, 1874.

CONOVER, DAN. Clown, Lee's, California, 1859.

CONOVER, H. E. Acrobat, contortionist, Indian rubber man. Eastern unit of June, Titus, Angevine & Co., 1841-42; posturer, Welch's, Philadelphia, 1843; Welch & Mann's 2nd unit, 1845; Sands, Lent & Co., 1846-47.

CONOVER, SOL. Variety performer, Haight & Chambers', 1867.

CONRAD BROTHERS [William, Richard, Charles]. **William** (r. n. William Conner, d. September 28, 1891), acrobatic and musical clown. Son of **Harry Connor**, the English somersault thrower, who died in 1887. As acrobatic violinists they were acknowledged the best; described as the most wonderful musical clowns in the world. **William** performed backwards somersaults on the tight rope and **Richard** performed on the flying trapeze without a net, doing acrobatic tricks between. These may be the same **Conrad Brothers** who were clowns and gymnasts with Sands, Nathans & Co., 1857-58; Spalding & Rogers *Floating Palace*, 1859; G. F. Bailey & Co., 1860-61; Chiarini's, winter 1861-62; Gardner & Hemmings, 1862; Nixon's Cremorne Gardens, NYC, spring 1862; Nixon's, Washington, DC, fall 1862; Bryan's, with Mrs. Dan Rice, 1863; tight-rope performers, Agricultural Hall, London, 1863-64; Melville's Australian, 1864; the National Circus, Cincinnati, winter 1864-65; Great Union, 1865; John Robinson's, 1866. **William** was also a champion leaper with the Parisian Circus, assembled for the Paris Exposition, 1867; gymnastics and comic scenes, L. B. Lent's, 1868-70; Great European, 1870; John Robinson's, 1871-72; clown, Howes' Great London, 1875-77; clown and his dogs, Den Stone's, 1878; the Metropolitan Circus, Havana, winter 1878-79; German clown

and performing dogs, John Robinson's, 1879; Conrad & Watson's Transatlantic Circus, South America, 1880; P. T. Barnum's, 1884-86.

CONROY, THOMAS. (1859?-January 3, 1918) Clown with John O'Brien's, Dan Rice's, Cather & Shallcross, Pullman & Hamilton, King & Franklin. Died at his home in Brooklyn, NY, age 59.

CONSTABLE, GEORGE. Clown and general performer. Orton & Older, 1856-60; Bassett's (leaving for South America, November 21, 1862); equestrian director and clown, Golden State Circus (**W. B. Blaisdell**, proprietor), California, 1868; Leihy, Lake & Co., 1870; Lee's, 1871; Atlantic and Pacific, 1871; Charles Noyes', winter 1871-72. Constable and wife were drowned from an explosion on the steamer *Oceanus* on the Mississippi River, spring 1872.

CONSTANTINE, CHARLES. Ballet master, John Robinson's, 1891-93.

CONTRABAND LEWIS. See Louis Willis.

CONTURIER, C. Agent, Haight's Great Eastern, 1874.

CONWAY, PAULINE. Rider, Montgomery Queen's, 1876.

CONWELL, WILLIAM D. Contortionist. Howes' Great London, 1876-77; Orrin Bros.', Havana, winters 1878-79, 1879-80; leaper, Cooper, Bailey & Co., 1880.

CONY, TOM. Clown and general performer. North's National Amphitheatre, 1857-60; Maginley's, Memphis, 1863; Maginley & VanVleck, 1863. Co-proprietor and stage manager, Olympic Amphitheatre, Memphis, 1864-65. Noted for his character of Jocko in *Jocko; or, The Brazilian Ape*.

COOK, BILLY. Sideshow privilege (with **Harry Buckley**), Yankee Robinson's, 1867.

COOK, ETTIE. Ames' New Orleans Circus and Menagerie, October 1869.

COOK, EUGENE. Acrobat, Alexander Robinson's, 1875.

COOK, FRANK. Athlete, John Robinson's, 1886-92. Feature act consisted of the use of a spring against a horse.

COOK, HARVET T. General agent, Bruce L. Baldwin's, 1894.

COOK, HELEN. Equestrienne. P. T. Barnum's, 1873; Burr Robbins', 1880.

COOK, JOHN. "Boy wonder and youthful clown" and 2-pony act. San Francisco Circus and Roman Hippodrome, 1872; John Wilson's Palace Amphitheatre, San Francisco, 1874-75. He may have been the son of **Wooda Cook**.

COOK, MOODY. Somersault rider, Lake's, 1871.

COOK, PROF. Magician, Great American Circus, Museum and Menagerie, 1893.

COOK, VINNIE. English equestrienne of great beauty. Brought to America by Barnum and arrived in New York just 26 days before his establishment on 14th Street was destroyed by fire. P. T. Barnum's, 1871-73; Adam Forepaugh's, 1874.

COOK, WOODA. Rider, leaper. Considered skillful and graceful. Was started in the circus business by **Charles W.**

Noyes for whom he worked several years (with Thayer & Noyes), around 1865. Began as a boy hurdler but developed into a somersault rider and leaper, turning 25 consecutive backward somersaults with the C. W. Noyes' Circus, 1869-71; C. W. Noyes' Crescent City Circus, spring 1870 (former Paris Pavilion, set up in New Orleans under the proprietorship of Spalding and Bidwell); Dan Rice's Paris Pavilion Circus, 1871. Married **Millie Turnour**, Shreveport, LA, March 1872, while with C. W. Noyes' Crescent City Circus. The marriage did not last. Spalding & Bidwell, New Orleans, 1870; John H. Murray's, 1873-75; John Wilson's, 1874; Hengler's, England, winter 1874-75; Montgomery Queen's, 1877; VanAmburgh's, winter 1877-78; John H. Murray's, 1878; Great American, 1878; Orrin Bros.', Havana, spring, 1878; Adam Forepaugh's, 1879-80; W. W. Cole's Australian tour (which left San Francisco, October 23, 1880); Orrin Bros.', Mexico, winter 1881-82; VanAmburgh's, fall 1882-83; William Hollands Covent Garden Circus, London, January 1885, billed the "Celebrated American Horseman," in a great hurricane hurdle act.

COOKE, ADELAIDE. Equestrienne, from Batty's Royal Circus, England. First time in America, John H. Murray's, 1875.

COOKE, ALFRED. Equestrian, slack-rope performer with Thomas Cooke's circus company arrived from England, 1837. The troupe performed in a building erected on Walnut Street, Philadelphia.

COOKE, CLARA. Pad rider, first appearance in America, Adam Forepaugh's, 1883.

COOKE, CORNELL. Stone & Orton, July 1870.

COOKE, ELLEN. Equestrienne. Wife of **James Cooke**. John Wilson's, San Francisco, 1874; Melville, Maginley & Cooke, 1875; principal equestrian, Montgomery Queen's, 1877; John H. Murray's, 1880; Robbins & Colvin, 1881; Maybury, Pullman & Hamilton, 1882; Orrin Bros.', winter 1882-83; John Robinson's, 1883; Ringling Bros.', 1892.

COOKE, EMILY HENRIETTA [Mrs. John Henry Cooke]. Equestrienne. Performed with her husband throughout his USA tour. [Alexander Dumas: "She is the paragon of grace and her superb equestrianism is realization of the ecstacy of delight. What she accomplishes, no mortal ever attempted; what she performs, no one can imitate. To see her is to be enchanted; not to see her is a regret. Her riding is intensely thrilling to witness, and indelible to the memory."] See John Henry Cooke.

COOKE, ERNEST. Principal clown, Cole's, 1882-84, 1886.

COOKE, GEORGE. Rider. Cooke's equestrian company, 1836; James R. Cooke's, winter 1864-65; Stone & Murray's, 1868-70.

COOKE, HENRY. Acrobat, tight-rope performer. Cooke's Circus, 1836, which had just arrived from England. The company performed in a building erected on Walnut Street, Philadelphia. Later, co-proprietor, Melville, Cooke & Sands, 1863;

trained dogs and monkeys, R. Sands' Circus, 1863; Maginley & VanVleck, winter 1863-64; Maginley's, Memphis, TN, 1864; Dan Rice's, 1864; performing dogs, Hippotheatron, NYC, late winter 1864; John Wilson's, 1865. Also connected with W. W. Cole's for several years.

COOKE, HENRY WELBY. (d. 1882) Equestrian. Englishman who came to USA with equestrienne wife, **Katherine**, and his children, **Clarence** and **Alice**. The Cookes lost their 3 year old son, **Harold Edwin Cooke**, 1871. Juggling and hurdle riding, John H. Murray's, 1871-72; bounding jockey, W. W. Cole's, 1873; equestrian director, W. W. Cole's, 1874; Springer's, 1875. Died in England.

COOKE, HUBERT. English jockey rider, from Batty's, England. First appearance in America, John H. Murray's, 1875.

COOKE, JAMES. (1845?-January 22, 1920) English clown and gymnast, came to America, 1871, Howes' Great London. Died in Blythe, England, age 75.

COOKE, JAMES EDWIN. (June 13, 1841-April 20, 1907) English champion leaper, 2-4-6-horse rider, "Pickwick Act" and an all around performer. Born in Glasgow, Scotland, with ancestry in the circus business which could be traced back 200 years to the beginning of the Cooke's Royal Circus on the Continent. Came to the United States from Paris, 1867, to join Howes' with his wife, **Carlotta DeBerg**, whom he had married on September 30, 1860. [M. B. Leavitt: "He was a fine equestrian and impersonated several Charles Dickens' characters as a scenic act."] Howes' European, 1864; Mrs. Charles Warner's, Philadelphia, winter 1864-65; equestrian sailor act, Spalding & Rogers, New Orleans, winter 1864-65; Dan Castello's, 1865; clown, John Wilson's, San Francisco, 1865; Thayer & Noyes, 1866; leaper and 4-horse rider, L. B. Lent's, 1867; proprietor, Cooke's Circus, 10th and Callowhill Streets, Philadelphia, winter 1867-68; pad act, James M. French's, 1868; Stone & Murray's, Boston, winter 1868-69; leaper, rider, European & American Circus, 1870; Rosston, Springer & Henderson, 1871-72; Den Stone's, 1873; 6-horse rider, John H. Murray's, 1874-75; Carlo Bros.', South America, 1877; clown and tight-rope performer, Montgomery Queen's, 1877; James E. Cooke's Royal Circus, 1880-82; Orrin Bros.', Mexico, winter 1880-81; equestrian director and clown, Frank A. Robbins', 1885. A series of unfortunate investments kept him from a life of wealth in his later years. Had interest in several circuses, including shows of his own, which resulted in financial disaster. Died in Jersey City, NJ.

COOKE, JAMES M. [r. n. Patrick Hoey]. (June 18, 1836-April 28, 1880) Clown and general performer. Born in Dublin. Began professionally as a youth, acting minor roles in Mrs. Ellen Burke's traveling theatre, which exhibited chiefly at fairs. Said to have "spouted Shakespeare in a dress suit." Conducted feats of acrobatics and contortion on his own until about age 16, then joined Bell's Circus. Later, worked for other circus organizations, visiting Europe with one of them as a vaulter. Taking the great **W. F. Wallett** as his model, turned to clowning and for some time was a jester at Astley's Amphitheatre, London. Came to America, May 11, 1863, and was engaged by **James M. Nixon**, making debut in Washington, DC, (one source gives Alexandria, VA) on May 26 of that year; NYC, opening August 31, with the tent being pitched on East 14ᵗʰ Street, opposite the Academy of Music, J. M. Nixon's Alhambra Pavilion, fall 1863; Hippotheatron, NYC, late winter 1864; clown for Barney Carroll's 2-horse act and his carrying act with William Odell, Slaymaker & Nichols, 1864. John Wilson's, California, 1865; while there, September 28, made a rope ascension from the Cliff House, San Francisco, to Seal Rock, a distance of 300 yards and a height of 90' above the sea, his first attempt at rope walking in public. Went to Australia with the company in October and remained there when they moved on to India, appearing with the World's Circus, managed by **Samuel O. Abell**. On return to San Francisco, appeared with Chiarini's, opening on May 26, 1868. In co-partnership with John Wilson, erected a hippodrome building in that city. Shortly, joined Lee & Ryland, traveling through the state. Returning in the fall, organized Cooke's Champion Circus, opening at the Metropolitan Theatre, San Francisco, a venture that lasted only a few weeks. On January 30, 1870, in the City Gardens, attempted a feat of carrying a bear upon his back while walking a tight rope. The bear, weighing about 100 pounds, was muzzled and tied in an open box and strapped to the walker's back. After about two-thirds of the journey, the bear began to wiggle, causing Cooke to lose his balance and begin to fall. He managed to cling to the tight rope and was helped to the ground. The act was tried again and this time succeeded. Returning to the East, performed with many of the principal circuses, notably Dan Rice's (rail and boat), 1870; Rice's Paris Pavilion, 1871-72; James W. Wilder & Co., 1873; Howes & Sanger, 1872-73; equestrian director, P. T. Barnum's, 1874; Great Eastern, 1874; Melville, Maginley & Cooke, 1875. Last appeared in public as a clown, equestrian director, P. T. Barnum's, 1879; Stickney's, NYC, winter 1879-80, and ringmaster, P. T. Barnum's, American Institute, spring 1880. Was engaged to perform with John H. Murray's for the summer season but died of pneumonia, NYC. Wife was equestrienne **Helen Cooke**.

COOKE, JOHN HENRY. (1838-1917) Equestrian, born in NYC, the son of **Henry Cooke** and grandson of old **Thomas Cooke**. Performed for all the equestrian establishments in England, France and Spain—Hengler's, Sanger's, Astley's, *Cirque Napoleon* and the *Cirque L'Imperatrice*. Came to USA again, 1867, and first appeared with his wife, **Emily Henrietta Cooke**, and son, **Master George**, with Lent's. Stone & Murray's, 1868-71; L. B. Lent's, 1872; John H. Murray's, 1873. After 1876, toured Scotland and England with his own show. Had a muscular, well formed figure. As a performer, was classed among the best in his profession, with specialties

of juggling on horseback and a spectacular 6-horse act. His stud of horses was the envy of showmen everywhere. Died in England, past his 80ᵗʰ year.

COOKE, LOUIS E. (May 17, 1850-March 18, 1923) Agent. Born in Tioga, PA; moved to Kalamazoo, MI, with his parents, 1861. Entered the profession in the late 1870s and became one of the most prominent in the business. Not only was he a writer of note but an authority on the history of the circus, being involved in the business for about 40 years. Wrote numerous articles for the *Billboard* special editions. Prior to his death was writing a book called *Circus Life and History* but never finished. Began his career with W. W. Cole's, with whom he accompanied on his famous trip to Australia as general agent. Later connected with Adam Forepaugh's and also served with James A. Bailey as confidential agent and manager for over 20 years. Was responsible for bringing about some of the most famous circus deals: made arrangemnts whereby Buffalo Bill's Wild West Show was organized under Bailey's management; arranged for the consolidation of the Forepaugh and Sells Brothers shows; brought about an amicable business relationship between the Ringling Brothers and the Barnum & Bailey shows; designed an advertising car for the 1896 Barnum & Bailey Circus, said at that time to be the "most perfect advertising car ever placed upon railway tracks"—60' in length and equipped with most every convenience and appliance known to car builders. Worked in various capacities of agentry—business agent, general agent, contracting agent, etc. W. W. Cole's around 1878-84; Adam Forepaugh's, 1885-87; Barnum & Bailey, 1889, 1894-1905; Two Bills Shows, 1912; United States Circus Corp., 1917. While with the Cole show, 1881, married **Kitty Bartlett**, daughter of O. H. Bartlett, Newark, NJ, lumber dealer. In 1896, was listed as owner of the Continental Hotel in Newark, NJ. Temporarily retired from show business, 1913 or 1914, to manage it. Closely identified with the Buffalo Bill Wild West Exhibition; and with the 101 Ranch Show when it toured Europe, 1914. When the Buffalo Bill and the Pawnee Bill Far East shows combined, 1909, joined them as general agent and railrad contractor and remained until they left the road for good after 5 seasons. Returned to the circus field around 1917 when on November 12 was appointed general manager of the advance force of the U.S. Motor Circus by **Frank P. Spellman**, president of the United States Circus Corp. Died in Newark, age 73.

COOKE, MARY ANNE. (1818?-November 23, 1897) **Thomas Cooke's** daughter. Came to America with his circus company, 1836. Married to contortionist **William H. Cole**, also in the troupe. Their son, born 1847, was **William Washington Cole**, renowned circus proprietor. After the circus was left devastated from a theatre fire, Cooke and his family returned to England, but Mary Ann remained with her husband. Following his death, she married **Miles Orton**, August 27, 1862.

They divorced May 20, 1878, Circuit Court, St. Louis, MO; after which, she and her son continued on with a small circus organized from her portion of the property settlement. Died at her home in Patterson, NJ, age 79. Early performing career was as a high school rider and wire-walker. Prior to the marriage to Orton, was connected with Howes & Mabie, 1841; John Tryon's, Bowery Amphitheatre, New York City, 1843-45; Nathan A. Howes', 1845; Rockwell & Stone, 1845; Victory Circus, 1847; John Tryon's, Bowery Amphitheatre, NYC, 1847; H. Buckley & Co., 1857; L. B. Lent's, 1858.

COOKE, MRS. JAMES EDWIN. See Carlotta DeBerg.

COOKE, ROSINA. (1846?-October 20, 1919) Equestrienne, *manège* act. Born in Manchester, England, the daughter of **Henry Cooke** and sister of **John Henry Cooke**. With W. W. Cole's, 1874-75, married **George H. "Grimaldi" Adams**, a clown with the show, in Galveston, TX, October 19, 1874, from whom she bore 2 children. Died at Manhattan Square Hotel, NYC, age 73, leaving an estate of about $100,000.

COOKE, SUSIE. James R. Cooke's, winter 1864-65.

COOKE, THOMAS EDWIN. (May 5, 1802-November 18, 1897) Clown, born at Beck's Hill, England, son of wealthy English circus proprietor **Thomas Cooke**. Began as an acrobat at age 17 with his father's circus, later becoming a tight-rope walker and clown. Married **Miss Diprose**, 1825. Come to USA with his brother, **Thomas Taplin Cooke**, who brought over a circus, 1836. Performed at Vauxhall Gardens in NYC; then went to Boston, Philadelphia and Baltimore. At the latter, the Front Street Theatre, 1838, the place caught on fire, destroying the horses and wardrobe. Returned to USA with his wife, 1867, and settled in Patterson, NJ, and remained there until he died of pneumonia.

COOKE, THOMAS EDWIN. (1835?-February 16, 1874) Equestrian, eldest son of **Thomas Taplin Cooke** and grandson of old **Thomas Cooke**. Made his debut as a rider at 18 months old, 1837. From a family of circus performers, his brothers were **James E.** and **William Cooke**, his sisters **Mary Ann Cole** and **Rosina Adams**, his son **James E. Cooke**, his cousin **John Henry Cooke**, and his nephew **W. W. Cole**. Was an expert rider, wrestler, jumper and acrobat. As a rider, was expected to rival his brothers but suffered injuries from being thrown out of a runaway carriage and never reached his potential. However, assumed proprietorship of **Thomas Taplin Cooke's** circus, 1838, when the Cooke clan returned to England, and became for a time "Barnum of England." Died in Liverpool, England.

COOKE, THOMAS TAPLIN. (1782-1866) Born at Warwick, England, the son of circus pioneer, **Sir Thomas Cooke** and father of **Mary Ann Cooke**. Succeeded his father as head of the Cooke circus and was the proprietor of Cooke's equestrian company that came to America, 1836, with 40 members of the family, including 7 sons and 5 daughters, 30 or 40 of the finest horses imported to that date, some full-blooded Arabians and a number of small Burmese ponies, which were ridden by the infant prodigies of the Cooke clan. Erected a building at the corner of Ninth & Chestnut, Philadelphia, an amphitheatre of stone and brick that seated 2,000, which the opening bill termed Cooke's Extensive Equestrian Establishment and New Arena. The ring was 43' in diameter, larger than was usually allowed for equestrian exhibitions. Performances began on August 28, 1837, doors opened at 7:00 and the program began at 7:30, boxes were 75¢, the pit 50¢, and children under ten were admitted for half price. Company roster included the **Polish Brothers**, gymnasts; **Mrs. Cole**, equestrienne; **Williams** and **Wells**, clowns; **Woolford**, ringmaster; **Sprake**, orchestra leader; **Whitby**, head groom. The season closed December 21. After 6 months the building was destroyed by fire. Cooke raised more money and moved his company to the Front Street Circus, Baltimore; but on the morning of February 3, 1838, that place was destroyed by fire and, having no insurance, lost everything. The entertainment world was shocked by the disaster. **Thomas Hamblin**, who had undergone a similar conflagration and had recovered handsomely, gave Cooke his theatrical spotted horse, Mazeppa. The managers of Fogg & Stickney's Amphitheatre in Cincinnati gave a free benefit. Cooke's Circus reopened at their establishment in Philadelphia, March 12, and closed on the 26th. Apparently, the amphitheatre was unsuitable for staging equestrian dramas; in any case, the company moved to the American Theatre (later called the Walnut Street) and opened there April 2, 1838, with a new stud of American horses and an added dramatic corps, where they produced Lord Byron's melodramatic story of "Mazeppa." The run came to an end on May 5. After an unfortunate year in America, Cooke left for England, where he produced such spectacles as *Mazeppa* and *Alexander The Great's Entry Into Babylon* and performed in them himself until his death, age 84. Throughout his life he sired between 13 and 19 children, most of whom became circus performers.

COOKE, VINNIE. Premier English rider. Brought to America by P. T. Barnum, 1873. Adam Forepaugh's, 1874.

COOKE, WILLIAM. (1808-May 7, 1886) Equestrian and circus proprietor. Second son of **Thomas Taplin** and **Mary Ann Cooke**. Rider, acrobatic clown, rope walker and strong man. In 1834 was touring with his own company. With Thomas Cooke's circus company, 1836, when they came to America from England. Described, 1842, performing on the slack rope as "standing erect on the cord and revolving one hundred times." Another feat was to hold up a board bearing 6 children while hanging head downward with his ankles strapped to a slack wire, yet, while in this position, he would hold the girth of a horse beneath him and lift the animal from the ground. Gave up acrobatics to direct equestrian dramas and train performing animals. Leased Astley's Amphitheatre, Westminster, 1853, from **William Batty**, and continued there until 1860. Said to have made a fortune with pantomime, *The Battle of Waterloo*, 1853; but, had it not been for the profits of his simultaneous tenting shows, would have been bankrupt. Possessing £50,000 when he took on the lease, when it ended he had but £10,000. Retired in 1860, although his company continued tenting for two years under the management of **William Cooke Jr.** Had a circus under his name, Cooke's Equestrian Troupe (James M. Nixon, proprietor), Niblo's Garden, NYC, 1860.

COOLEY, HARRY. Elephant man, John O'Brien's, 1882.

COOPER BROTHERS. Acrobats, Hudson & Castello (J. M. Hudson and Dan Castello, proprietors), 1881.

COOPER, CHARLES F. (1849-December 18, 1884) Born in Greenfield, MI. A butcher by trade, had interest in the sideshow of Yankee Robinson's when the company made its Kansas tour. Was with various shows, 1870-75. Trouped a river show down the Mississippi, 1876. Managed VanAmburgh's sideshow, 1878-80. Winter 1880, along with **Tom Haley**, had another river show. Following spring, organized Cooper & Jackson with **Lyman A. Jackson**, which they operated for 2 seasons. Took in **J. Ferguson** as a partner under the title Cooper, Jackson & Co., 1883, went into the Mexican interior that year, as far as Monterey and back. Went out, 1884, as New York and New England Circus, continued until sold at a sheriff's auction, December 1, 1884. Died of consumption in Memphis, TN.

COOPER, ED. Holland, Bowman & McLaughlin, 1890.

COOPER, FRANK C. (d. October 10, 1920) General agent, Gregory Bros.', 1884, treasurer, 1885; Gregory & D'Alma, 1889; business manager and press agent, Gregory & Belford, 1892; general agent, George S. Cole's, 1895. Died at Booneville, MS.

COOPER, GEORGE F. Cooper, Jackson & Co., 1883.

COOPER, GEORGE W. (d. May 4, 1920) Forepaugh's concert, 1891. Died in Soldiers home, Leavenworth, KS.

COOPER, H. Part interest in Major Brown's, 1857. Title was changed for the following year to Cooper & Myers' Circus of all Nations. Company disbanded before the season's end.

COOPER, HENRY. The English Giant. Brought to USA by **Adam Forepaugh** on a 3 year contract, 1882. Stood about 8' 4", and while he was not fleshy, weighed around 400 pounds.

COOPER, JAMES EBENEZER. (November 2, 1832-January 1, 1892) Showman. Born in London. Came to America with his parents when less than a year old and settled in Philadelphia. Father was **John Henry Cooper**, a blacksmith and wheelwright. After father's death, went into business for himself at the age of 15. Ran a line of omnibuses on the old Second Street Pike from Philadelphia to Fox Chase. After 3 years, sold the business and moved to Washington, DC, where he started another omnibus line. Within 3 months, controlled every line in the city. Remained there until 1863 when he returned to Philadelpia and entered the circus business with **Dan Gardner, Richard Hemmings** and **John O'Brien** at National Hall, corner of Twelfth and Market Streets. After 5 weeks on the road, bought out O'Brien and continued under the firm of Gardner, Hemmings & Cooper. The show was enlarged and a menagerie of VanAmburgh animals was added, 1865. **W. H. Gardner** puchased an interest in the fall of that year. Dan Rice was hired for the tenting season, 1867, at a salary of $1,000 a week and expenses, said to be the largest salary to date ever paid to a single performer. During the season Dan Gardner sold Cooper his interest in the show because of an altercation with Rice. In the fall W. H. Gardner sold his share to **Harry Whitby.** Seasons of 1868 through 1870, the show went out as Hemmings, Whitby & Cooper (**James A. Bailey** was the general agent during the latter 2 years, working for a salary of $100 a week, purported at the time to be the largest salary ever received by an agent). Whitby was shot and killed during the 1870 tour. Next year the show went out as Hemmings & Cooper. James A. Bailey purchased Hemmings' interest, 1872, which established the firm of Cooper & Bailey's International Ten Allied Shows, with the men remaining together until 1880. 1876, the show sailed for Australia, stopping at Hawaii and the Fiji Islands and touring Australia, New Zealand and the East Indies before sailing for South America. After visiting the principal cities of Peru, Chile, Argentina and Brazil, the company arrived back in the United States, landing in NYC, December 10, 1878. The show was enlarged even more with the addition of Howes' Great London Circus and Sanger's Royal British Menagerie for the seasons 1879-80. In the fall, 1880, Cooper sold his interest to **James L. Hutchinson** and retired from circus proprietorship. Re-entered the business, 1886, in partnership with **Hutchinson, W. W. Cole,** and **P. T. Barnum,** which operated for 2 years as P. T. Barnum's Greatest Show on Earth. Then, fall 1887, **James A. Bailey** acquired Cooper's interest and again Cooper went into retirement. With the death of **Adam Forepaugh,** 1890, Cooper purchased the show, winning out over a group of British investors. Spent over $100,000 in refitting the organization and met with the greatest financial success of his career in circus management. Took pleasure in owing fast horses, fine carriages, and the best harnesses money could buy. Owned an impressive private barn to house his equine hobby on Broad Street, Philadelphia. Said to have been a gentle mannered and generous person, who owned a vast amount of Philadelphia real estate at the time of his death, as well as property in nearly every state in the country. Died at his residence, 1826 North Broad Street, Philadelphia, leaving a wife, 2 sons, and a daughter.

COOPER, JOHN. Pinkerton detective, Barnum, Bailey & Hutchinson, 1882-84.

COOPER, REUBEN W. Supt. of cookhouse, Cooper, Bailey & Co., 1876; Barnum, Bailey & Hutchinson, 1882.

COPELAND, HORACE. Lemen Bros.', October 1891.

CORBETT, WILLIAM. Clown, Great Oriental Pavilion Show, 1877.

CORBYN, E. Long bearded man, Cooper, Bailey & Co., 1880.

CORBYN, MYRTLE. Four-legged female curiosity, Cooper & Bailey, 1879-80.

CORDELIA. See Cordelia Julick.

CORDELIA, CHARLES. Gymnast and leaper, Montgomery Queen's, 1874.

CORDELLA, MINNIE. Swinging rings, Cooper, Bailey & Co. Australian tour, 1877.

CORDELLA, ROSA. Equestrienne, with Cooper & Jackson, 1880.

CORDOVA, HARRY. Press agent, Batcheller & Doris, 1879; railroad contractor, John O'Brien's, 1881; advertising manager, Nathans & Co., 1882-83.

CORINTH, JOSEPH. Howes' European, winter 1864.

CORNWALL, ZACK. Agent, Ella Zoyara's, 1863.

CORNWELL, D. Proprietor (with **J. B. Townley**), Great Oriental Pavilion Show, 1877.

CORNWELL, SAMIVEL. Business agent, with Gardner & Hemmings, 1860.

CORNWELL, WILLIAM. Metropolitan Circus, Havana, winter 1878-79.

CORREIA, JOHN [or Juan] and **MARIETTA.** Aerialist and equestrienne. London Show, 1886; Mid-Winter Circus, Petersburg, IL, winter 1894-95; Walter L. Main's, 1896; Shipp's, Petersburg, IL, winter 1897-98, 1898-99; Buchanan Bros.' (from Sioux Falls, SD), 1898; Tony Lowande's, Cuba, winter 1901-02. **Marietta** was the daughter of **Martinho Lowande, Sr.,** and the sister of the Lowande boys, **Oscar, Tony, Alexander A.,** and **Martinho, Jr. John Corriea Jr.** was a beginning wire performer in the late 1890s.

CORRIGAN, M. Triangle player, W. N. Smith's Ethiopians with VanAmburgh's Menagerie, 1860.

CORSON, WILLIAM. Leaper and tumbler, Smith & Baird, 1872.

CORVELLA BROTHERS. Great New York Circus (**E. Hamilton, F. W. Sergeant**, proprietors), 1877-78. **Frank Corvella,** business manager and trapeze performer, Moore Bros.', 1887. **Robert Corvella** (r. n. **Robert Hoagland**), acrobat, a native of Bound Brook, NJ. While giving a trapeze performance during a balloon ascension at a fair in Phoenix, NY, September 14, 1878, was severely injured from a 50 foot fall and succumbed, May 5, 1879, at his home, Bound Brook, NJ.

COSTELLO, ARTIE. See Artie Castello.

COSTELLO, DAN. See Dan Castello.

COSTELLO, DAVE. See Dave Castello.

COSTELLO, FRED and MILLIE. With J. M. Carrington's Southern Show, 1874-75.

COSTELLO, GEORGE. See George Castello.

COSTELLO, JOHN. (d. April 22, 1901) Clown. One time a member of a group of **Costello Brothers.** Around 1880, met and married a **Mrs. Roberts** of New London, CT, opened a saloon there and operated it until his wife's death; at which time he sold out and moved to NYC. Death came in that city as he was planning to join Adam Forepaugh's.

COSTELLO, PROF. Sword swallower, Sheldenburger & Co., 1871.

COSTELLO, WILLIAM [often spelled Costillo]. (1815-February 17, 1890) Ringmaster and juggler. Born in Boston. Joined a circus at age 16 and worked in the business for half a century with the distinction of being one of the first to introduce globe spinning and tank balancing with the feet. An able horseman and ringmaster for the age's most notable riders. Connected with Spalding & Rogers' *Floating Palace* and VanAmburgh & Co.; as well as Robinson & Eldred, 1849-53; Major Brown's, 1857; Eldred's, 1857; Cooper & Myers, 1858; ringmaster, Robinson & Lake, 1859-62; Lake & Co., 1864-65; John Robinson's, 1867; ringmaster and plate spinner, Alexander Robinson's, 1874-77. Retired about 1880; died 10 years later, Utica, NY, age 75.

COSTELLO BROTHERS [William, Harry, George]. Aerialists, acrobats, horizontal bars performers. Wallace & Co., 1884; W. H. Harris' Nickel-Plate, 1885-86; Ringling Bros.', 1887; brothers act and bars, F. J. Taylor's, 1891; Sells Bros.' Australian tour, 1891-92, 1894-95; Adam Forepaugh's, 1893; Hurlburt & Leftwich, 1894. **George** died from the effects of a fall from a train, December 1, 1895, at Chattanooga, TN, age 30. **Harry** (r. n. John Henry Laughlin) lost his balance while practicing a return act and fell 20' to the ground; died from the injuries, Memphis, TN, October 6, 1894, age 24. **William** (r. n. William Thomas Laughlin), entered the profession as a pantomimist and acrobat. Performed on the revolving globe with Alex Robinson's, 1874; W. H. Harris' Nickel-Plate, 1888; horizontal bars, Charles Andress', 1889; (with wife, **Annie**) New Bartine Consolidated Shows, 1896. Died, Norfolk, VA, December 28, 1898, from ailments induced by a fall in August of the previous year while performing on aerial horizontal bars with the Forepaugh-Sells Show, age about 30.

COSTELLO, MINNIE. Aerialist, F. J. Taylor's, 1891.

COSTENTENUS, GEORGE. Tattooed from head to foot, P. T. Barnum's, 1876-80.

COTTRELL, JACK. Boss hostler, John Robinson's, 1879-81.

COTTRELL, JOHN. Clown, rolling globe, leaper, from Hengler's Circus, London. First appearance in America, John H. Murray's, 1874-75; revolving globe, Cooper, Bailey & Co.'s Australian tour, 1876-78.

COTTRELL, LOUISE. Bareback rider. John H. Murray's, 1875; Cooper & Bailey's Australian tour, 1876-78.

COTY, PETER ["Master"]. A new apprentice with Pepin & Breschard at Charleston, November, 1814, and remained with Pepin through 1829 when the troupe disbanded in Nashville,

TN. That year, married a **Miss Payne** at Charleston. Joseph D. Palmer's, 1833; Edward Eldred's, 1834; Aaron Turner's, 1835; rider, Benchley & Stone, 1837-38; John Mateer's, 1843-44; Welch & Mann, 1843-44. Credited with introducing foot juggling to America. One of his feats was balancing a 12 foot pole on his feet.

COUCH, J. W. Proprietor, J. W. Couch's Comic Circus and Brilliant Museum, 1880; sideshow manager, W. H. Stowe's, when he lost his life in the burning of the steamer *Golden City*, February 30, 1882.

COULDOCK, FRED L. Advertiser. Rivers & Derious, 1857; Mabie's, 1864; Thayer & Noyes, 1867; Hemmings, Cooper & Whitby, 1868; George F. Bailey's, 1870-73; contracting agent, P. T. Barnum's, 1876-80; Adam Forepaugh's, 1881.

COUP, GEORGE. Brother of W. C. Coup. Candy privilege, P. T. Barnum's, 1871-76.

COUP, W. B. Band leader, Hurlburt & Leftwich, 1894.

COUP, WILLIAM CAMERON. (August 4, 1836-March 4, 1895) Born in Mt. Pleasant, Indiana, 1837, one of 6 children of a tavern owner. Left a job in a printing office, 1852, to join P. T. Barnum's Caravan, a traveling museum and menagerie, 1851-54. First job was apparently as a roustabout. Tells in his autobiography, *Sawdust and Spangles*, of being with the L. G. Butler circus, 1850s. Conducted a wax figure show in the Caribbean, winter 1860. Joined Mabie's, sideshow manager (with **Harry Buckley**), 1861-65; Yankee Robinson's, 1866, managing the sideshow and serving as assistant manager of the circus. Mrs. Coup prevailed upon her husband to abandon show life after the 1869 season. Bought a farm in Delavan, built a cheese factory, and invested in a local bank. With **Dan Castello**, organized, 1870, on a Great Lakes steamer, Dan Castello's Great Circus & Egyptian Caravan. At the end of the season, talked **P. T. Barnum** into coming out of retirement and going into the circus business with them. Was general manager of the show, which netted a $400,000 profit, 1871. Following year, was instrumental in getting the show to travel by rail, devising loading and unloading methods and arranging special excursions from the outlying towns to the show site. Introduced a second ring, developed ingenious advertising and promotional stunts such as the Devil's Whistle, mass litho posting and small town excursions by bands, clowns, etc., to create interest in the show which was in the area. Continued with the Barnum organization, 1871-75. Built the New York Aquarium in partnership with **Charles Reiche**, which was an immediate success. Reiche wanted the aquarium to open on Sunday but Coup opposed it. Finally, after months of wrangling over the Sunday matter, Coup suggested that they flip a coin to see who would become sole owner. Reiche agreed and Coup lost the flip. Organized Equescurriculum, 1878, and later changed its name to the United Monster Shows. Railroad wreck near Cairo, IL, 1882, finished the show and also put Coup deep in debt from countless claims. Later, organized an Indian Exhibition show, started a museum in Chicago, and also had a traveling museum on rails known as Coup's Enchanted Rolling Palaces, which also was ruined by a railroad accident in Pennsylvania. Refused all financial assistance by his many friends and tried to pay of all debts. Formed another horse show and even a dog circus, both of which were successful on a small scale. Was forced to retire, 1894, and went to Jacksonville, FL, where he died a year later. [P. T. Barnum: "He was a capital showman and a man of good judgment, integrity, and excellent executive ability."]

COUP, ZACK. (1848?-January 12, 1895) Showman brother of **W. C. Coup**. Contracted by P. T. Barnum to secure the famous white whale, which he successfully accomplished. During the expedition, he and a companion were shipwrecked on the Shetland Islands. At one time, was connected with the Royal Aquarium, London. Later, was manager for **Zazel**, the human catapult. Various years with Sells Bros.'—one year had the candy franchise—accompanying them to Australia, 1893. Died in Columbus, OH, about 47 years old, after having been in show business for 21 years.

COURTNEY, F. E. Contracting agent, Hudson & Castello's (**J. M. Hudson** and **Dan Castello**, proprietors), 1881.

COURTNEY, G. A. (d. April 19, 1882) Proprietor, G. A. Courtney's Zoological Circus, West Indies, 1880; Mexico, 1881.

COURTNEY, HARRY. Director of amusements and trapeze performer, Moore Bros.', 1887.

COUSINS, J. Doris winter circus, Forty-Second Street, NYC, 1880 (**E. S. Doris**, proprietor; **John B. Doris**, manager).

COUTURIER, CARTER. Advance agent, P. T. Barnum's Roman Hippodrome, 1875; Pat Ryan's, 1882.

COVELL, ZILLAH. See Mrs. Edward Orrin.

COVELLI, CHARLES. (d. 1870) Ethiopian performer, with Blair's Band, a party that worked on a barge at the foot of Steamboat Wharf, Troy, NY, June, 1854. Opened a saloon with minstrel performer, **Thomas Pendergast**, Utica, NY, 1868. Partner dropped dead, March 6, 1869, in Utica in the arms of Covelli. Covelli died the following year.

COVELLI, CHARLES. (1829?-October 4, 1894) Rider, clown, and ringmaster. Born in NYC. Performed abroad with many of the foreign companies. Upon return to the USA, was connected with Robinson & Lake, 1863; Robinson & Deery, 1864; Alex Robinson's, 1865; principal rider, G. G. Grady's, 1869-71; equestrian director, Cosmopolitan, winter 1871-72; rider, Burr Robbins', 1874; clown, Great Roman Hippodrome, 1877; Basye's, 1879; clown, Thornton's, 1880; Ringling Bros.', 1886; around the latter year, was connected with the St. Louis Museum as manager and press agent; advance agent Sieber & Cole, 1891. Died in St. Louis, MO, age 65. Equestrienne wife, **Mary**, professionally known as **Mme. Lucille**, died in St. Louis shortly after, on October 20th.

COWELL, JOSEPH. (August 7, 1792-November 14, 1863)

Born in Kent, England. Made acting debut January 23, 1812, Davenport, England, as Belcour in the *West Indian*. First appeared in London at the Drury Lane Theatre, 1812, as Samson Rawbold in the *Iron Chest*. American stage debut, October, 1821, as L'Clair in *Foundling of the Forest* and Crack in *Turnpike Gate* at the Park Theatre, NYC. Manager of the Walnut Street Circus, Philadelphia, and of Price & Simpson's circus troupe, 1825-26, which he bought a half-interest in the following year. Granddaughters were the famous actresses, the **Bateman Sisters**. Died in London.

COWLES, M. B. Agent, W. W. Cole's, 1880-81.

COX, SAMUEL P. Contracting agent, John B. Doris', 1883-85; Adam Forepaugh's, 1878-87.

COX, W. O. Second brigade agent, Hunting's, 1896.

COXEY, W. D. Press agent, Adam Forepaugh's, 1889.

COYLE, HENRY. With Levi J. North's, 1859; trick clown, George W. DeHaven's, 1865. See Henry C. North.

COYLE, JAMES. Gymnast. Burr Robbins, 1879; Barnum & London, 1884-85.

COYLE, JOHN H. Burr Robbins', 1885; treasurer, Robert Hunting's, 1896-97.

COYLE, MIKE. (1838?-July 26, 1918) Born in Whitesboro, NY, and moved to Weedsport while still a child. Connected for many years as chief publicist for P. T. Barnum and was one of his closest friends. A picturesque and unique personality with a wide circle of friends and admirers, a typical showman, a large man with a pleasant face who performed at different times as business manager, transportation manager, and treasurer. James Melville's, 1864; Stone, Rosston & Murray, 1865-66; 1867, purchased interest in the latter and remained with the show through the season of 1877; winter 1870, connected with the management of the tour of the pugilists **John C. Heenan** and **James Mace**; Howes' Great London, 1878; Adam Forepaugh's, 1880-94. [D. W. Watt: "Mike stood six feet, one inch, was straight as an arrow and had a fine commanding appearance. He never did business ahead of the show with the different people he had to deal with but what they were always glad to see him come again."] Announced retirement from circus activity, January 1909, and purchased the farm on which the famous Arrowhead Mineral Springs were located, in the village of Weedsport. Entered into a partnership with a local gentleman, **C. S. Caywood**, to improve the springs and promote the sale of the water. Died at the Willard House, Weedsport, NY, age 80. Left an estate valued at $16,000.

COYLE, WALTER E. Press agent, L. B. Lent's, 1874.

CRAIG, J. D. Dan Castello's, 1866.

CRAIG, JOE. (d. March 12, 1905) Giant, standing 7' 8" and weighing over 400 pounds; traveled with Barnum & Bailey and others. Died in Mt. Sterling, KY.

CRAIG, PROF. Musical director, Collins' Oriental Combination, 1877.

CRAMER, GEORGE P. Equestrian manager, Johnson & Co., 1866; partner, Hampson & Cramer, 1867; proprietor, Cramer's Great Western, 1868-69.

CRANE, GEORGE J. Clown, Older, Carane & Co., 1884.

CRANE, GERARD. (January 3, 1791-February 11, 1872) One of the pioneers of American menageries. Began in the business by exhibiting an elephant through the countryside. Toured with a lion and lioness, 1818. Later exhibited birds and small animals in partnership with June, Angevine and Titus. With **Lewis B. Titus** exhibited an elephant, 1826. As proprietor, connected with Gregory, Crane & Co., 1833-34; Crane & Eldred with a combined circus and menagerie, 1834-35; later had an interest in the menagerie of Macomber, Welch & Co. Continued in management until at least 1836. Accumulated a sizeable fortune before retirement from the business, being president of one or more banks and insurance companies. Died in Westchester, NY, age 82.

CRANE, JEREMIAH. Showman brother of **Gerard** and **Thadeus Crane**. With them, was an early exhibitor of animals.

CRANE, JOHN PLATT. Proprietor, Crane & Co., 1849-50; manager, J. M. June's, 1851.

CRANE, MOSES CLARK. (d. December 23, 1893) Associate who had various circus jobs during his lifetime. With Van-Amburgh's for nearly 10 years as assistant manager, etc. At one time had interest with Hyatt Frost in the show. Connected with numerous circuses since 1870, his first being with the Great London, of which his brother-in-law, **J. J. Parks**, was part owner. Barnum, Bailey & Hutchinson's, 1881. Last show business job as manager for Kohl & Middleton's Museum circuit, Chicago. Retired around 1888 and died of blood poisoning at his home in Millerton, NY.

CRANE, S. E. Contracting and advertising agent. Dan Rice's, 1870; Rice's Paris Pavilion, 1871; manager, Paris Pavilion (not Rice's), 1873.

CRANE, THADDEUS. (December 31, 1779-October 16, 1849) Son of **Col. Thaddeus Crane**, brother of **Gerard** and **Jeremiah Crane** and an early exhibitor of animals. One of the founders of the Zoological Institute. Married **Martha Titus** (d. March 25, 1872).

CRAPO, CAPT. AND MRS. Featured exhibit, Howes' Great London, 1878. They had recently crossed the Atlantic in their little boat *New Bedford*, which could also be viewed. The engaging couple related the story of their rough experience.

CRAVEN, LILLIAN MARTIN [nee Lilly Mondena Martin, later Mrs. George M. Larwill]. (September 18, 1852-September 29, 1957) Born in Philadelphia. Married elephant trainer Stewart Craven, October 1868. There was a son born December 27, 1869, Charles Stewart Craven. Chariot rider and appeared in specs with Adam Forepaugh's, John V. O'Brien's, Cooper & Bailey, and P. T. Barnum's beinning in 1868. Learned the art of glass blowing which she practiced with various circuses with which her husband was associated.

CRAVEN, STEWART. (May 15, 1833-January 16, 1890) Elephant man. Native of Chester, Wayne Co., OH, and considered the greatest of all trainers and keepers. A large, powerful man, who had an amazing understanding of animals. Described in 1880 as rather tall and slightly built, with eyes quick and keen, black hair sprinkled with gray, and a full beard in which the gray was more prominent. First appeared with VanAmburgh's, 1853, where he trained the great elephant Tippo Saib to hold a perch while he climbed atop and performed gymnastic tricks. Also stood on the elephants tusk and performed a juggling act while the animal trotted around the ring at full speed. With Mabie's, 1859, conquered Canada, later known as Romeo, one of the fiercest of elephants; trained Empress for **John O'Brien**; Mabie & Nathans, 1860-61; worked gymnastic elephants with Mabie's, Winter Garden, Chicago, 1862; Dan Rice's (O'Brien and Forepaugh, proprietors), 1865-66; left for Europe, 1867, because of ill health; trained the 5 performing elephants of Howes' Great London, 1872; for a time worked for **Adam Forepaugh** as keeper of Romeo, also trained 7 elephants for him, 1876, but left the organization because of problems with the strong minded manager; Cooper & Bailey, 1880, where he trained 12 in military drill, the pyramid, a tight-rope walker, and a clown, called superior to anything done before. [George Conklin: "He was the only man I ever knew who could ride an elephant standing up."] Married to **Lillian Craven**, a chariot rider and spec performer. Died of consumption in Dallas, TX, age 56.

CRAWFORD, F. General performer. Rockwell & Stone, 1846; R. Sands', 1849.

CRAWFORD, OLIVE. Snake charmer, Walter L. Main's, 1893.

CRAYCROFT, B. R. Agent, J. H. LaPearl's, 1891-94.

CREIGHTEN, W. H. Clown. Fogg & Co., 1828; Asa T. Smith's, 1829; Yeaman's, 1831; Brown's, 1832-33; French, Hobby & Co., 1835; Drury, Van Tassle, Brown & Co., 1837; Waring & Raymond, New Orleans, winter 1837-38; Brown & Mills (later as Waterman & Co.), 1838; Waring & Raymond, 1842; James Raymond's, 1843-44; Old Dominion, 1845.

CROCKETT, JAMES. (1835?-1865) Lion tamer. Born in Preston, England, the son of a circus musician. Started career as a band member with Sanger's. Because of weakened lungs, was forced to seek another profession. When manager Sanger bought 5 lions but had no one to handle them, Crockett became their tamer, his sole asset being an imposing stature. However, proved to be a man of wonderous nerve and magnetism. On one occasion, 6 lions, 5 males and a female, came loose in Astley's Amphitheatre, London. By the time Crockett arrived, they had killed a groom and were roaming about the place, when single-handedly, without any weapon but a whip, he eventually caged them. Soon was performing the feats of VanAmburgh and Carter, traveling through Great Britain and Ireland, receiving plaudits for his courage. Filled an engagement at Astley's Amphitheatre, receiving a large salary, following with one at the *Cirque Napoleon* in Paris; then Berlin, Vienna, St. Petersburg and other European cities. Was engaged by Seth B. Howes in England and brought to America, 1864, appearing first in Detroit. The recipient of many gifts from royalty, exemplified by a diamond ring from Queen Victoria. On July 6, 1865 (or perhaps July 4), in Cincinnati, was effected by the intense heat. With a crowded house expectantly awaiting his act, he fell prostrate and soon died, age 30—it having been a very hot day, and having ridden in the procession all that morning with a tin helmet on his head and no protection from the sun.

CRONCK, J. H. (d. March 30, 1882) At one time, sideshow proprietor, W. H. Stowe's.

CROSBY, BENJAMIN. (1827-March 21, 1886) Agent. Born in Brewster, NY. Early employment was as a salesman for a patent pill concern before becoming associated with various circuses. Contracting agent, Dan Castello's, 1866; assistant manager, James M. French's, 1867; Maginley & Carroll, 1868; business agent, VanAmburgh's, 1871; general agent, Den Stone's, 1873; contracting agent, VanAmburgh's, 1874-76. For the last 8 years of his life, was active in the hotel business in New Canaan, CT, where he died.

CROSBY, CHARLES. Gymnast. E. F. & J. Mabie's, 1851; (billed as **Carlos Crosbiere**) Spalding & Roger, 1852-56; H. P. Madigan's, 1856;

CROSBY, DOLLY. Wallace & Co., 1886.

CROSBY, E. Rider, E. F. & J. Mabie's, 1849-50.

CROSBY, FRANK C. (d. May 25, 1917) Performed for 35 years with such circuses as Howes Great London, Wallace's, and Col. G. W. Hall's. Also proprietor of his own circus, Crosby's Mammoth Pavilion Shows, 1889. Died in Chicago.

CROSBY, GEORGE. VanAmburgh's, 1880.

CROSBY, HART. Cousin of **Nathan** and **Seth B. Howes**. With Nathan Howes & Co., 1826. Broke his neck attempting a gymnastic feat, March 9, 1827.

CROSBY, NELSON. (1814-1899) Said to be one of the first in this country to exhibit buffalos with a traveling circus. Was in charge of a small herd which went with Mabie Bros.'

CROSBY, SETH ORLANDO. (d. April 28, 1890) With Adam Forepaugh's, VanAmburgh's.

CROSBY, WILLIAM. 2-horse rider, with Mabie & Crosby, 1851; Major Brown's, 1856-57; Mabie & Crosby, 1858; Yankee Robinson's, 1859.

CROSS, DAN. Bareback and hurdle rider, M. O'Conner & Co., 1869-70.

CROSS, E. J. Proprietor, Cross & LeRoy's Trans-Atlantic Circus (E. J. Cross and **Walter LeRoy**, proprietors), winter 1884.

CROSS, WILLIAM. Importer of elephants, 1870s, 1880s.

CROSSETT, RALPH. Boss canvasman, Reichold Shows,

1897.

CROSSLEY, JOHN T. Scottish sports (performed with **William Elder**), W. C. Coup's, winter 1878-79; Cooper, Bailey & Co., 1879-80; Barnum, Bailey & Hutchinson, 1881-84-85.

CROSSMAN, EUGENE H. Boyd & Peters, 1880.

CROUESTE, EDWIN ["Ned"]. (b. 1841) Clown. Born in Bromley, England. Son of **Charles** and **Mary Crowhurst**, one of 4 brothers associated with the circus. First appeared before the public as a clown, 1857. Joined a circus run by his brother, Vauxhall Gardens, 1858. Subsequently, American clown, **James Myers**, engaged him for the Pavillion Theatre, London. After which, he stayed on for the traveling season. Then joined Howes & Cushings, 1860, and toured through Ireland before returning with Myers for a short time. Followed with an 18 month tour with the Italian *Cirque* through the British Isles. 1863, took part in a race on the Thames, with **Garratt** and **Ricoli**, in tubs drawn by geese, a stunt first attributed to **Dickie Usher**. Tenting season, 1863, again with Howes, with whom he accompanied to America, April 1864, for a tour of the United States; Hippotheatron, NYC, winter 1864-65; Lent's New York Circus, 1866. From there, was connected with Nixon's; Stone, Rosston & Co. and others. Formed Edwin Croueste's Grand Circus, late 1880s. At Dewsbury, England, opened an iron circus, 1891. Converted the place into the Empire Variety Theatre, February 1894. Died, 1914, in Bradford Workhouse Hospital, in poor circumstances, due to the decline in circus and poor health.

CROWE, MELL. Gymnast, acrobat, and tight-rope artist. Howes' European, winter 1864-65; Thompson, Smith & Hawes, 1866; Mike Lipman's, winter 1866-67; L. B. Lent's, 1867; clown and leaper, Adam Forepaugh's, 1867.

CROWLEY, WILLIAM G. (1850?-October 4, 1884) Press agent. Originally a journalist. Began in the circus business, 1874, and became known as an aggressive but charming professional. Sells Bros.', P. T. Barnum's, Burr Robbins', and Great London. Left with Cooper, Bailey & Co. for Australia, November 8, 1876, 1877-80. Composed the Australian route book. Adam Forepaugh's, 1881-82. Subsequently, returned to the profession of journalism. Died in Rochester, NY, age 34.

CROWN, THOMAS. Advertiser, P. T. Barnum's, 1875.

CROWNINSHIELD, JACOB. Sea captain credited with bringing the first elephant to America. Of Indian origin, the animal arrived, 1796, and was sold to a **Mr. Owen**, who exhibited in Philadelphia, Baltimore and along the eastern seaboard, possibly until 1822.

CRUM, WILLIAM C. (1831?-February 9, 1901) Agent. A native of New York. Cousin of **Dan Rice** (Rice's mother was Elizabeth Crum). Began career as editor and proprietor of the Rochester *Evening News*. With Dan Rice's at least 1852, 1859. From at least 1859-61, lived in Girard, PA, Rice's adopted home, and acted as Rice's agent. Through friendship with P. T. Barnum's son-in-law, **S. H. Hurd**, became inter-

ested in circus work, joining as director of publications, P. T. Barnum's, 1871, general agent, 1872, manager of publications, 1873. Director of pubications, Batcheller & Doris, 1880; Adam Forepaugh's, 1887; W. C. Coups'; John V. O'Brien's, as well as others. Considered by some to be the first to write in the familiar courier advertising style, which occurred while he was with the Barnum & Bailey. A fluent penman who prepared material in a dignified style, which ultimately became obsolete and which may have prompted a return to the newspaper business in Idlewild, Fla., with the *Farmer's Alliance Advocate* and later *Florida State Republican*. Also prominent in Republican politics in that state. While serving as postmaster at Peck, after appointing a Negro assistant, was waylaid by an angry mob and beaten severely, from which he never quite recovered. Died in Hyde Park, FL, in his 70th year. [Louis E. Cooke: "Being possessed of a brilliant education and a fluent writer, he could handle the classics to perfection.... He was one of the most skillful manipulators of circus adjectives I have ever met, and in my acquaintance with him I became greatly impressed with his ability and complete knowledge of everything pertaining to the circus world."]

CUBA, BELEN. Female bareback rider, Chiarini's, San Francisco, 1872.

CUBAN BROTHERS. Dan Castello's, 1868.

CUBAS, ISABEL. (1837-June 20, 1864) Beautiful Spanish pantomimist and *danseuse*. Born in Valencia del Cid. Came to USA, 1861. September of that year appeared at the Winter Garden, NYC, where she attracted public notice as a fascinating and voluptuous performer. Came under the management of James M. Nixon and, it was said, was married to him. This report was false, since he was still married to his wife, Caroline. Nixon's Cremorne Gardens, NYC, spring 1862; Nixon's, Washington, DC, fall 1862.

CULBERTSON, C. R. Treasurer, C. W. Kidder & Co.'s, 1893.

CULBERTSON, SAMUEL. Proprietor, Gilliam, Gifford & Culbertson's (**Franklin A. Gilliam**, **Lew Gifford**, Samuel Culbertson, proprietors), 1897.

CULLEN, ANDREW. Presented troupe of Iroquois Indians, Stone & Rosston, 1865; Driesbach & Howes, 1868; assistant manager and treasurer, Howes & Cushing, 1875.

CULLEN, ED C. General agent, Forepaugh & Samwells (**W. R. Forepaugh**, **Thomas Samwells**, proprietors), 1886; Irwin Bros., 1889.

CULLINS, J. M. General agent, John F. Stowe & Co., 1888-89.

CUMMINGS, FRANK. Clown, John B. Doris', 1886.

CUNNINGHAM, J. Contortionist, Wintermute Bros.', 1890.

CURLEY, J. Boss canvasman, New York and New England, 1884.

CURRY, G. W. Great Combination (**George M. Kelley**, **Pete** and **John Conklin**, **William LaRue**, proprietors), 1871.

CURTIS, GEORGE. Gymnast, Cole & Orton, 1871.

CURTIS, HARRY. Clown, P. T. Barnum's, 1877.

CURTIS, T. Manager, Welch, Bartlett & Co., 1840.

CURTIS, WILLIAM D. Proprietor, Great Roman Hippodrome and Congress of Novelties, 1877; proprietor, Great Eastern, 1878; manager, the London Sensation Show (**W. L. Collins & Co.**, proprietors), 1879.

CURTIS, T. Manager, Welch, Bartlett & Co., 1840.

CUSHING, JOSEPH ["Col."]. (November 14, 1818-March 3, 1884) Born at Dover, NH, the son of **Peter** and **Sally Austin Cushing**. Cared little for farming, so, while still in his teens, left Dover for Gloucester, MA, where he was employed in a fish market. Went with a small circus. Shortly, bought the lemonade and candy concessions on the show. Then bought the sideshow and before the end of the season owned the entire show. The firm grew to a 40 wagons and toured the eastern part of the country and Canada for several seasons with financial success. In partnership with **Seth B. Howes**, March 25, 1857, on the steamer *Southampton*, sailed from New York for Liverpool with the Great American Circus on board. Took along his 20 year old bride of a day, **Hamah Marie Lemmure**, the daughter of a Cambridge, MA, family, educated in France, spoke French well, played the harp and could ride horses. Wife rode the grand entry as well as performing high school exhibitions. January 24, 1860, sold out his half interest to **Seth Howes**. February 14, 1860, with **Mr. Fillingham**, a London Banker, and Seth Howes formed a new partnership to take a circus to Germany during the summer. March 23, 1860, bought a hippopotamus for $9,000 and sent it on exhibition with **Frank Howes** (no relation to Seth) to Liverpool. May 28, 1860, went into the fight game and presented a match between **Sayres** and **Heenan** at the Alhambra. June 3, 1860; took the fighters on a tour of Scotland. October 1, 1860, sent word to Frank Howes at Liverpool to take the hippo to America.

Formed a new circus and opened, November 26, 1860, and continued until September 11, 1862. Returned to the USA with $100,000 in cash. 1863, formed another circus and toured the eastern states and Canada. Took into partnership **Frank Howes**, and went to Manchester, England, Howes as acting manager. Formed a show titled Wheeler & Hitchcock, which he sent to Canada. Show went broke and was left there. Paid all bills, took over the show and toured the eastern states with it, returning to Dover, NH, at the end of the season with a nice profit. 1877, decided to take a circus to South America, sailing on the steamer, *North Star*. Returned to Dover, 1879, the project not a financial success. During the afternoon, March 1, 1884, while driving home behind a team of lively horses, they shied, which threw him out of the carriage striking his head hard when he hit the ground. Never regained consciousness and passed away 2 days later. Wife died January 6, 1894. [John Glenroy: "Cushing was a man greatly respected, and of all the managers whom I have served under I never thought so much of any one as I did of him.... If there was one other man among all the other circus proprietors, with whom I have been engaged, to whom I would compare Colonel Cushing it is to General Welch.... They were much alike, whole-souled, generous men, both of them, and their generosity proved the ruin of each of them."]

CUSHMAN, LOTTIE. Cooper, Jackson & Co., 1882.

CUTLER, GEORGE: (August 8, 1843-February 16, 1892) Born in Clover Hollow, NY. Died in Chenango Bridge, NY. Strong man, cannon ball juggler, gymnast. Robinson & Lake, 1863-66; Philadelphia Circus, winter 1867-68; slack wire and cannon ball performer, Gardner & Kenyon, 1868; James M. French's, 1869; Gardner & Forepaugh, 1870; "man of steel," Rosston, Springer & Henderson, 1871; James E. Cooper's, 1872; ringmaster and cannon ball performer, Adam Forepaugh's, 1875. Cutler's wife was a wire performer.

James E. Cooper

D

DABELLA, H. D. Contracting agent, H. C. Lee's Great Eastern, winter 1877-78.

D'ALMA FAMILY [Lottie, Bessie, Harry, Maude, John, Millie]. Acrobats. Composed of **Lottie** on the slack-wire, **Harry** doing outside ascensions, **Maude** equestrienne and rolling globes, and **John** exhibiting feats of strength. The family was with Pullman, Mack & Co., 1884; John Robinson's, 1884, 1887-91; King, Burk & Co., 1885; Walter L. Main's, 1886. **Madame D'Alma** was an aerialist with Doris & Colvin, 1887. **John, Harry, Bessie, Maude, Millie** and **Lottie** were with Gregory & D'Alma, 1889; **Millie** with L. J. Duchack's, 1889; **Maude**, bareback rider with Walter L. Main's, 1899; **Madame D'Alma**, trapeze performer with Frank A. Robbins', 1886, was married to the boss hostler, **John O'Griffin** on September 7, 1886. **Harry D'Alma**, born in Clearfield, PA, the son of **John** and **Lottie D'Alma**, and brought up in the circus profession, was at various times connected with Main & Sargeant, L. W. Washburn's, Walter L. Main's, John Robinson's, Gregory & D'Alma, Hall & McFlinn, Sells & Rentfrow, Great Syndicate Shows, and *Circo Chiarini*. At the time of death was performing with the *Circo Escoces*. Died in Guatemala City, Central America, from consumption, age 22. **John**, acrobat, died in Chicago, May 16, 1922, age 70. Had a successful dog and pony show on the road for 10 or more years. Became a competent animal trainer in later years.

D'ARLEY, G. W. Proprietor, D'Arley's, 1886.

DARLING, CHARLES. Advertising agent, Harper Bros.' European, 1893.

DARTELL BROTHERS. Aerialists, Gollmar Bros.', 1892.

D'ATALIE, ADELAID. Principal rider, W. W. Cole's, 1881.

D'ATALIE, ANGELA "MME. D'ATALIE". (d. May 23, 1891) Iron-jawed woman, billed as "the Female Sampson." First husband, **Mons. D'Atalie**, was a French athlete. Philadelphia Circus, corner of Tenth and Callowhill Streets, winter 1870-71; John V. O'Brien's, 1871; John Robinson's, 1872; Kleckner & Co., 1872; chariot driver and iron-jaw performer, P. T. Barnum's, 1873; P. T. Barnum's Roman Hippodrome, 1874-75. The D'Atalies performed with two children who, in 1872, were designated as **Young Zephyr**, who did an act called "The Enchanted Glasses" and, *Tout Petit*, a little clown. These boys had been taken from a poor house and trained. After the death of **Mons. D'Atalie** on the Barnum show, 1873, she married the clown, **Nat Austin**, May 11, 1876, both being on Mongomery Queen's, California. Was with Cooper, Bailey & Co. when they left for their tour of Australia on November 8, 1876 (assisted by pupils **Addie** and **Eugene**), and remained with the show into 1880s. Said to be a most amiable woman and well educated. See Mons. D'Atalie.

D'ATALIE, FRANCIS. Acrobat, with Montgomery Queen's, 1876. Most likely, the adopted son of **Mme.** and **Mons. D'Atalie**. See above.

D'ATALIE, JOE. Acrobat, Montgomery Queen's, 1876. Most likely, abopted the son of **Mme.** and **Mons. D'Atalie**. See above.

D'ATALIE, MONS. (1842-May 19, 1873) French athlete and iron-jawed man. Born in Paris. Until the age of 20 was engaged in "commercial pursuits," but during this time won celebrity as an amateur athlete. After losing a large sum of money in business, decided to become a professional performer. First engagement being for **M. Dejean**, director of the *Cirque Napoleon*. Followed with an appearance at the Paris Hippodrome, where he performed the feat of lifting a 178 pound weight with one hand from the ground to above his head, being 6 pounds greater than his own weight. Appeared at the Alhambra Palace, London, and then for the next 3 years toured throughout the British Isles. Came to the United States with the Lydia Thompson Burlesque Troupe, making a debut at Wood's Museum, July 4, 1870 (another source states that he came to USA with a troupe of French wrestlers). Nixon's, Niblo's Garden, NYC, 1870; John V. O'Brien's, 1871; P. T. Barnum's, 1873. Was assisted by wife **Mme. Angela** and 2 boys called "**Young Zephyr**" and "*Tout Petit*." The boys had been taken from a poor house and trained. Died while with the Barnum show, Fall River, MA. Buried in Brookline Catholic Cenetery, MA.

D'JALMA, MME. Flying rings, Beckett's, 1887.

D'JALMA, PRINCE SADI. Gymnast and tumbler. John Stowe & Sons, 1871; contortionist, John V. O'Brien's, 1871-72; the "man of mystery," Ben Maginley & Co., 1874; George F. Bailey & Co., Central and South America and West Indies, fall 1874.

D'OME, WILLIAM. Acrobat, Hudson & Castello's, 1881.

DA COMA, ARTHUR and ROSE. Orrin Bros.', Mexico, April 1893; Edward Shipp's Winter Circus, Petersburg, IL, 1893-94; Ringling Bros.', 1896.

DAILEY, THOMAS A. (d. November 16, 1935) Advertising car manager for many years. Started career, April 1875, as billposter in advance of A. B. Rothchild's (**J. V. O'Brien's**). Remained 2 seasons. Later, going over to the **Hyatt Frost** and **O. J. Ferguson** VanAmburg show, where he remained in the billposting brigade, 1877-81. J. H. Rice's (**John O'Brien's**), 1882; boss billposter on one of the advertising cars, Barnum, Bailey & Hutchinson, 1883 and 9 consecutive seasons; last 2 years, 1890-1891, car manager. Advertising car manager, Ringling Bros.', 1892 and remained with them for many years, retiring in 1935. Member of the Knights of Columbus Elks.

Struck and killed by an auto at Lancaster, PA, age 80.

DAIR, JESSIE. Gymnast and iron jaw lady, Belmont Elite Circus, 1889; flying trapeze and perch, Gollmar Bros.', 1892.

DALE, DAN. Assistant treasurer, John Robinson's, 1882; cook house manager, 1883-84; assistant treasurer, 1885-92; treasurer, 1893.

DALE, M. T. Assistant treasurer, VanAmburgh's, 1874.

DALE, WILLIAM O., JR. (1859?-April 14, 1932) Rider. Son of the accomplished bareback rider, **William O. Dale**. After his father's death, his mother married **P. Connolly**, an actor for many years engaged at the Bowery Theatre, NYC. Mrs. Dale was also in the theatre. At "not yet 12 years of age," was bareback rider. VanAmburg's, 1871; Central Park Menagerie and Den Stone's, 1872; bareback and trick rider, Baird, Howell & Co., 1874; W. W. Cole's, 1878, and again in New Orleans, California, and on the Australian tour (which left San Francisco, October 23, 1880), 1880-81; W. C. Coup's, 1879-80; 4-horse rider, Sherman & Hinman, San Francisco, 1883; Orrin Bros.', winter 1884-85; somersaulter and 4-horse rider, VanAmburgh & Reiche Bros.', 1885; Orrin Bros.', Mexico, 1886; bareback rider, Doris & Colvin, 1887; rider, Wallace & Co., 1888; Barnum & Bailey, 1892; jockey act, Adam Forepaugh's, 1893; somersault principal rider, Scribner & Smith, 1894; the Mid-Winter Circus, Petersburg, IL, winter 1894-95; principal bareback somersault rider, with George S. Cole's, 1895; Rice's Circus Carnival, 1896; equestrian director, Sun Bros.', 1907, 1910. Died in Bellevue Hospital, NYC, age 73. Featured an act of riding 4 horses and somersaulting from the back of one to another. Late in his career, left the big shows to ride in the smaller circuses. Rode bareback past the age of 60.

DALE, WILLIAM O., SR. Rider and vaulter. Native of Cincinnati. A performer of fine reputation. Frost, Husted & Co., 1836; Eagle Circus, 1836; Frost & Co., 1837; A. Hunt & Co., 1838; Raymond & Waring, 1839; Welch, Bartlett & Co., 1839-40; Bartlett & Delavan, 1841; Welch & Mann, 1841; VanAmburgh's, United Kingdom, 1843-?; Howes & Cushing, United Kingdom, 1846; John Tryon's, NYC (where he was in a vaulting match with James MacFarland, September 28), 1846; Howes & Co., 1847; Rockwell & Co., 1848; Welch's, Philadelphia, 1849-50; performed on "Floating Cord," Welch & Mann, Philadelphia, 1846; Johnson & Co., 1851-52; Spalding & Rogers, 1856; Harry Buckley's, 1857; Orton & Older, 1858; Spalding & Rogers' *Floating Palace*, 1859; Buckley's, 1860. Subsequently, went blind and became an inmate of a charitable institution in Cincinnati, 1865. A fund was raised through the efforts of the New York *Clipper*, with many circus people contributing what they could. Died penniless.

DALVIN, HELEN. W. W. Cole's, 1883.

DALY, POLLY. L. B. Lent's, 1872.

DAMAJANTE, NALA. Hindoo snake charmer, Barnum & London, 1885.

DAMON, W. A. Walter L. Main's, 1889.

DANFORTH, H. C. Railroad contractor, Nathans & Co., 1882.

DANZEFF, ULLRIG. Russian athlete. First season in America, Stone & Murray, 1869.

DARE, ANNIE. Contortionist, John F. Wood's, winter 1889-90.

DARE, LEONA. Trapezist, New York debut, Nixon's Amphitheatre, Broadway opposite Waverly Place, NYC, winter 1871-72; Joel E. Warner's, 1872. Married **George Hall**, one of the **Hall Brothers**, NYC, 1876; later separated in Europe.

DARIOUS, HERR ALEXANDER. Animal performer, Adam Forepaugh's, 1872; zoological director, 1875.

DARTELLE BROTHERS. Flying return act, with Gollmar Bros.', 1893.

DARWIN, JACK. Juvenile gymnast and acrobat, Joel E. Warner & Co., 1872.

DASHAWAY, CHARLES. (1856?-February 7, 1910) Gymnast. Married to equestrienne **Minnie Perry**. Circus Ciniselli, St. Petersburg, Russia, 1883; Sells Bros.', 1886; John B. Doris', 1888; James Donovan's, Bermuda, winter 1891-92. Died at his residence, Brooklyn, NY.

DASHWAY, WILLIAM. Gymnast. John H. Murray's, 1880; (with **Wilton**) Nathans & Co.'s, 1882; Sells Brothers, 1886.

DAVENE TROUPE [William, Lizzie, Lucy]. French gymnasts and aerialists. Came to America from England to join P. T. Barnum's, 1879-80; Barnum, Bailey & Hutchinson, 1881; Sells Bros.', 1882-83. In Wilkes-Barre, PA, May 3, 1881, **Lizzie Davene**, performing her catapult act, failed to properly time her somersault and fell to the ground, landing partly upon her head. Was carried to her dressing room in a paralysed state and never recovered, dieding a month later, June 3. **William M. Davene** (r. n. William Morris, 1844-November 20, 1908), born in London. Married **Vara Doborhova (Lucy Davene)**, trapeze performer, January 1, 1888; both were with Frank A. Robbins'. He died in Norfolk, VA.

DAVENPORT, ALBERT M. ["Stick"]. (December 2, 1871-September 10, 1932) Rider. Son of **John L. Davenport Sr.** and **Ella Hollis Davenport**, and the brother of **John Jr., May, Louise** and **Bertha** (the latter a non-professional), and the nephew of **Orrin M. Hollis**. Made debut at age 8 as 2-pony rider with Burr Robbins', 1879. By 1891, was a principal and somersault rider, tumbler and leaper. Divorced wife, **Isabel Cummings**, 1928. Beckett's Great Exposition, 1881; Burr Robbins', 1884-86; Ringling Bros.', 1889, 1902; F. J. Taylor's, 1891; John Robinson's, 1893, 1908; Walter L. Main's, 1894-1904; Forepaugh & Sells, 1896-99, 1901; Sells & Gray, 1900; New York Circus Co., winter 1900-01; Cole Bros.', 1906-07; Campbell Bros.', 1907, 1910; Rice Bros.', 1909; Norris & Rowe, 1909-10; Mackey's European, 1909; Robinson's Famous, 1911; Yankee Robinson's, 1913, 1915; Hagenbeck-Wallace, 1914; Coop & Lent, 1916-18; Marsh-Davenport, 1917; Santos & Artigas, 1919-20; Campbell, Bailey & Hutchinson; 1920-22; World Bros.', 1923; Robbins Bros.', 1924-26; Al G. Barnes', 1926-30; Forepaugh-Lind, 1926. [D. W. Watt: "Sticks first learned to ride in the old Burr Robbins ring barn when he was but 9 or 10 years old, and his first appearance before an audience was in Janesville, riding a hurdle on two Shetland ponies."] Died in Fort Worth, TX.

DAVENPORT, BILLY. Rider, S. H. Barrett's, 1887.

DAVENPORT BROS. [Louis, Charles, George]. Gymnasts and acrobats. George W. DeHaven's, 1870; James Robinson's, 1872; L. B. Lent's, 1874; Great Eastern, 1874; Cooper and Bailey, 1875; Great Chicago, 1879; Cooper & Jackson, 1880; Brother act and scientific sparring, Barnum, Bailey & Hutchinson, 1882; brother act by **Frederick** and **Louis**, Barnum & London, 1884; Burr Robbins', 1886; Dan Rice's, 1891. **Charles Davenport** (r. n. **Michael Levy**), with Adam Forepaugh's, 1879, was injured and forced to retire from performing. Died in Cincinnati, OH, September 11 (or 12), 1906. **George Davenport**, concert performer, Dutch comic, Cooper, Bailey & Co., 1876; Cooper, Bailey & Co. Australian tour, 1877. Died in Cincinnati, December 21, 1891, age 30. **Louis Davenport** (r. n. **Edward H. Trainer)**, acrobat, John Robinson's, 1869-71; Charley Bartine's, 1872; as one of the **Davenport Brothers**; Great Eastern, 1874; John Robinson's, 1881; clown, Beckett's, 1887.

DAVENPORT, CYRUS. Howes' European, winter 1864.

DAVENPORT, ELLA [nee Ella Hollis]. See John L. Davenport, Sr.

DAVENPORT, GEORGE. General agent, with Rockwell & Stone, 1843-44; Mann, Welch & Delavan, 1845; manager, Welch's National Circus, 1847. Can this be the same George Davenport who was a Dutch comic in concert with Cooper, Bailey & Co.'s Circus, Australian tour, 1877-78?

DAVENPORT, JOHN L., JR. (December 24, 1869-April 6, 1947) Principal somersault and bounding jockey rider. He learned the art of riding from his father; began professionally, 1878, Sells Bros.'. Did first twisting forward somersault from one horse to another runnning in tandem, 1902. Continued riding as late as 1929, at which time he was with Gentry Bros.' Earlier, with Sells Bros.', 1878; Beckett's Great Exposition Circus, 1881; Burr Robbins', 1884-86; Ringling Bros.', 1889, 1918; Adam Forepaugh's, 1891; John S. McMahon's, 1892; John Robinson's, 1893, 1921, 1923; Sanger & Lent, 1893; F. J. Taylor's, 1894; Walter L. Main's, 1895; Sig. Sautelle's, 1895; Forepaugh-Sells, 1897; Walter J. McDonald's, 1900-01; Sun Bros.', 1902; Yankee Robinson's, 1908; Robinson Famous, 1911; Hagenbeck & Wallace, 1920; Gollmar Bros.', 1922; Gentry Bros.', 1928-29; Cole Bros.', 1929.

DAVENPORT, JOHN L., SR. *(*March 22, 1836-February 3, 1916) Rider, clown, gymnast. Native of Savannah, GA. He started in the circus business at age 14. Sometimes called "the American clown," become one of the best of the old school

clowns. As a singing clown, often netted as much as $50 a week selling song books. Was proficient as ringmaster, principal equestrian, and clown. Robinson & Eldred, 1850; Spalding & Rogers, 1852-57; Antonio & Wilder, 1859; James M. Nixon's, 1860; Howes & Cushing, to Great Britain, 1860, where he remained until 1863. Returned to America that year and was associated with Thayer & Noyes, Chicago, fall 1863; Robinson & Howes, Chicago, winter 1863-64; Howes & Norton (formerly Robinson & Howes), fall 1864; National Circus, Cincinnati, winter 1864-65; Great Union Combination (John and Alex Robinson), 1865; Frank J. Howes', 1865; New American Theatre, Philadelphia, winter 1865-66, summer 1866; Yankee Robinson's, Chicago, winter 1866-67; Dodge & Bartine, 1868; Mike Lipman's, 1869; Levi J. North's, 1869; James Robinson's, 1871; Lake's Hippo-Olympiad, 1871; Kleckner & Conklin (**John O'Brien's**), 1872; Sells Bros.', 1873-74, 1876-79; D. F. Dunham's, 1875; Cooper & Jackson, 1880; Beckett's, 1881; Burr Robbins', 1884-88; Ringling Bros.', 1889; equestrian director, F. J. Taylor's, 1891; Criterion Theatre, Chicago (last appearance as clown), 1893; equestrian director, Howe's London, 1896; Lemon Bros.', 1905; Walter J. McDonald's, 1900, 1906; Yankee Robinson's, 1908. Married pad rider, **Ella Hollis**, 1869, and raised a family of riders—**John, Jr., Albert, May, Orrin**, and **Louise**. Built a ring barn in Newport, KY, by 1858, where he trained horses and circus riders in the off season. Died at his home in Chicago. [D. W. Watt: "Uncle John was always a good mixer, made friends with the landlord and other businessmen of the town that he might meet. No difference how poor the hotels, Uncle John never made a kick, but always said that these towns gave us the best they had and that was all we could expect."]

DAVENPORT, KATE. Dodge & Bartine, 1868.

DAVENPORT, LEW. Great Roman Hippodrome, 1877.

DAVENPORT, MAY. Equestrian daughter of John L. Davenport, Sr. Howes' London (**J. C. O'Brien**, manager), 1896; New York Circus Co., West Indies, winter 1900-01; jockey and carrying act, Walter L. Main's, 1901; Forepaugh-Sells, 1907; Barnum & Bailey, 1909-13.

DAVENPORT, WALTER. W. C. Coup's New United Monster Show, 1879.

DAVEY, T. Treasurer, James M. Nixon's, 1870.

DAVIDSON, JOEL S. Clown. Hemmings, Cooper & Whitby, 1870; Sells Bros.', 1874, 1877, 1880; Anderson & Co., 1879; S. H. Barrett & Co., 1883.

DAVIDSON, PROF. Stock director, Albert M. Wetter's New Model Shows, 1893.

DA VINCI, CARLOTTA. "Sprite of the elfin drama," P. T. Barnum's, 1871.

DAVIS, ANNIE. Equestrienne, Burr Robbins', 1875.

DAVIS, A. W. Had a menagerie out, 1874, traveling on the Great Lakes with the steamboat *Huron*. Proprietor and manager, Sadler's Great English, 1875; A. W. Davis' Great Moral Show, Monster Manegerie and Grand Olympian Exposition; general manager, Great Transatlantic Allied Shows, 1879. He jumped the show in June 1881, leaving the company stranded. The show collapsed.

DAVIS, BARNEY. See Plutano and Waino.

DAVIS, CHARLES [or Davies]. Clown, Dan Rice's Paris Pavilion, 1872; L. B. Lent's, 1874; leaper and tumbler, P. T. Barnum's, 1876.

DAVIS, CHARLES A. Agent. Brother of agents **James R.** and **Thomas Davis.** Particularly good at writing and working up interviews with his stars and proprietors. [D. W. Watt: "It was said of him in the business that he never was in his sleeper more than ten or fifteen minutes before the train pulled out, and yet Charlie Davis was never left. Much of his work for the day following he would do in the hotel in the evening after the night show and always stepped on the train about the time that it was ready to pull out for the next town."] Spalding & Rogers' *Floating Palace*, 1857-59; Thayer & Noyes, 1865; L. B. Lent's, 1868; Maginley, Carroll & Co., 1868; Batcheller & Doris, 1882; Callender's Minstrels, winter, 1882-83; joined Adam Forepaugh's, 1883 and remained for several years. [Roland Butler: "His various styles of publications advertising the Famous Original Wild West and Forepaugh Show Combined in 1890 were vividly written and were splendid specimens of the art of bill writing."]

DAVIS, CHARLES L. (b. October 21, 1852) Was born in Baltimore, MD, of a theatrical family. Faced the footlights for the first time at age 4. Clowned and worked the concert, Dan Rice's, Thayer & Noyes, W. W. Coles', etc. At 17, made business manager, Baltimore Museum. Later, associated with the Odeon Theatre, Baltimore; Theatre Comique, Providence, RI; Capital Theatre, Hartford, CT; Metropolitan Theatre, NYC. In addition to duties as stage manager, appeared in Dutch songs, banjo playing, sketches and afterpieces. Created a full length play from a sketch, *Alvin Joslin*, and toured in the lead role for several seasons, making a small fortune.

DAVIS, D. F. Treasurer, Dr. James L. Thayer's, 1880; general agent, Burk's, 1891.

DAVIS, E. Clown, Raymond & Co., 1852.

DAVIS, EDWARD F.

DAVIS, EDWARD F. (d. February 25, 1918) Davis' New Orleans Circus, 1879; excursion agent, John B. Doris', 1883, general agent, 1884-85; advertising car superintendent, Adam Forepaugh's, 1887; advance agent, Hunting's New York Cirque-Curriculum, 1888; general agent and railroad contractor, Andress', 1890; railroad contractor, W. H. Harris' Nickel-Plate, 1891; general contracting agent, B. E. Wallace's, 1892-93; proprietor, Empire Shows, 1893; Davis' New Orleans Circus, 1894; Davis' "Uncle Tom's Cabin" Co., 1901; contracting agent, B. E. Wallace's, 1906.

DAVIS, GEORGE. Downie & Gallagher, 1893.

DAVIS, HARRY. Press agent, Bailey & Winan, 1890.

DAVIS, HIRAM. See Plutano and Waino.

DAVIS, HOMER. Proprietor cook house, P. T. Barnum's, 1873; agent, Howes' Great London, 1878; proprietor, Homer Davis' New Show, 1879; advance agent, Cooper & Bailey, 1880.

DAVIS, JAMES C. Ringmaster, treasurer. Shot and killed **Mlle. LaRosa**, trapeze performer, Cincinnati, March 22, 1872. The two had recently left the Cosmopolitan Circus. **Mlle. LaRosa** was the wife of **J. W. Whettony**, also with the circus; but she and Davis had been living together for some months. There was some question as to whether or not the shooting had been accidental. Davis was found guiltless by the coroner's jury and discharged.

DAVIS, JAMES P. (1830?-April, 1902) Began with L. B. Lent's, 1851; also with Antonio & Wilder's, 1859. Died in Ypsilanti, MI, age 72.

DAVIS, JAMES R. ["Jumbo"]. (1852?-September 17, 1886] Press agent, Batcheller & Doris, 1880; P. T. Barnum's, 1882-83; railroad contractor, John B. Doris', 1885. Rose from a twenty-five-dollar-a-week job to a place with James A. Bailey, which paid him $5,000 a year. For some years was Barnum's purchasng agent abroad. Traveled extensively in Asia and Africa in search of animals for exhibition. The brother of agent **Charles A.** and showman **Thomas H. Davis.** Shortly before his death, was engaged as manager of Kohl & Middleton's Museum, Cincinnati. Died in that city of consumption, age 34.

DAVIS, J. CHARLES. Agent. Born in Montgomery County, NY, the eldest son of **Rev. A. S. Davis.** Educated at Little Falls Academy and Madison University. Began a professional career as agent for the Cosmopolitan Circus and Menagerie, under the tutelage of **Charles Stow.** Connected at various times with James Robinson's, Adam Forepaugh's, P. T. Barnum's, and John H. Murray's. Served as press agent for two international expositions; toured Australia, New Zealand and Tasmania as manager and part owner (with **Frank Frost**). With an English opera company, toured India, China, South Africa. Visited the Orient and eastern islands as correspondent for several publications and as foreign agent for Barnum, Bailey & Hutchinson. Returned to New York City, May 23, 1885, after an absence of 7 years. Directed several athletic events in Madison Square Garden that summer. Joined the Barnum show in the spring, 1885. Business manager, of People's Theatre, NYC, 1885-86 season. Promoted the presidential campaign of Gen. Butler for People's Party. Worked on behalf of the Actors Fund.

DAVIS, J. D. In charge of stock, Wheeler Bros.', 1894.

DAVIS, JIM. Contractor, John Robinson's, 1892.

DAVIS, J. L. Dog act, Dan Rice's Paris Pavilion, 1871-72.

DAVIS, J. O. Contracting agent, John Stowe & Sons, 1871.

DAVIS, JOE. Clown, Anderson & Co., 1879.

DAVIS, MARGARET. English equestrienne, Barnum &

Bailey, 1892.

DAVIS, M. H. Proprietor, Davis', 1890.

DAVIS, MONS. Wild beast tamer, VanAmburgh's, 1865-66, 1868. Advertised as feeding "four savage lions raw meat from his naked hands."

DAVIS, NATHAN. (d. January 5, 1917) Animal trainer. John O'Brien's, Cooper & Bailey, Buffalo Bill's; Astley & Lowanda, 1884.

DAVIS, PROF. Dog act, Gardner & Donovan, South America, 1886; Hobson Bros.', 1887. Could this be J. L. Davis?

DAVIS, RICHARD. Rider, Jim Myers', 1856.

DAVIS, ROBERT. Rider and vaulter. Bought Roulestone's Amphitheatre, Boston, with a **Mr. Bates** (an actor) and opened a circus there, 1810, which ran January 11-February 22. Took the company to Salem, MA, where he opened on February 27 in partnership with a **Mr. Leeds.** Had his circus, Davis & Co., Boston, 1815, where it ran October 19-March 4, 1816; re-opened May 21-June 17; moved to Portland, ME, for an August engagement. Listed as principal rider with a circus that opened in Portland, July 10, 1821. Riding included "the wonderful feat of the weather-cock," probably an act of standing on the saddle on one foot, body parallel to the ground, and forming the resemblance of a weathercock.

DAVIS, STEWART. Equestrian director and ringmaster. Husband of equestrienne **Annie Worland.** Great Pacific Circus, 1877-78; Cooper & Jackson, 1880.

DAVIS, THOMAS H. (1859?-June 8, 1911) Agent. Born in South Bend, IN. Brother of agents **James R.** and **Charles A. Davis.** Agent, with Adam Forepaugh's, 1875; excursion agent, Barnum & London, 1884; manager of excursions, Adam Forepaugh's, 1885. Later, went around the world buying freaks for Barnum & Bailey. On one such trip, bought the "sacred white elephant" for the show. Became manager of the museum in Milwaukee, WI, 1885-86, for **Jacob Litt.** Two years later, formed a theatrical partnership and produced *The Stowaway, In Old Kentucky, The Ensign,* Gus Heege in *Ole Olson* and *Jon Jonson,* and David Warfield in *The Nutmeg Match.* Partnership ended, 1894. Along with **William T. Keogh** and **J. J. Rosenthal,** was in charge of the tour of John Kernell in *The Hustler.* With Keogh, had other attractions on the road—*The White Rat, On The Bowery, McFadden's Elopement,* etc., in addition to managing the old Star Theatre, Broadway and Thirteenth Street, NYC. Partnership ended, 1899. In latter years, was publisher of the magazine *The Home Life* and a real estate operator. In 1892, married **Ida E. Roof** of Massilon, OH. Died from cancer at his home in White Plains, NY, age 52.

DAVIS, WILLIAM. Clown, Tivoli Gardens, Philadelphia, 1826; Bernard & Page, 1829; T. L. Stewart's Tremont Circus Co., 1831; Buckley, Weeks & Co., 1835; Grecian Arena, 1841; Mons. LeTort's, 1842; John Mateer's, 1843-44; 4-horse rider, Rockwell & Stone, 1845; Robinson & Eldred, 1847.

DAVIS, W. M., JR. (July 19, 1819-April 13, 1903) Born in Covington, NY. Began career as a musician with VanAmburgh's, 1839. After 7 years with that show and with Raymond & VanAmburgh as advance agent and manager, joined Mabie's in the same capacity for 9 years. Claimed that, while acting as manager, 1858, originated the practice of camping on the circus lot with sleeping, dining and horse tents. This was confirmed by both **James H. DeMott** and **George S. Cole.** The claim was also contested by **James Essler** who said he was with Mabies the year in question. Davis' last engagement, contracting agent, Cole & Orton, 1871; at the end of the season, after 18 years of trouping, retired. Died in Marble Rock, IA.

DAVY, GEORGE. Ringmaster, with Castello & VanVleck, 1863-64.

DAWES, SAMUEL. Gardner & Donovan, South America, 1886.

DAWLEY, DAVE. Carlo Bros.', South America, 1877.

DAWN, SIGNOR. Knockabout clown. Wallace & Co., 1884; Main & VanAmburgh, 1890.

DAY. Keeper, Mammoth Menagerie from Zoological Institute, New York, 1837.

DAY, CHARLES H. (1842?-October 3, 1907) One of the leading agents and bill writers of his day, being most active in the circus business from 1874 to 1885. Often worked under the title of "Director of Publications," which usually appeared along with his name on the various booklets and bills he created. Noted for his originality of thought and expression, for his ability to put on paper that "which oft was thought but ne'er so well expressed." His couriers (advertising booklets) were always original, "surpassing in range of thought and vividness any published by circuses at that time." In 1875, while with Adam Forepaugh's, was considered to be one of the best all-around publicity men in the business. With Forepaugh's advertisement budget, was able to create copy for heralds, magazines, newpapers and hand bills in abundance. Wrote every line for a 16 page newspaper, *The Adam Forepaugh Illustrated Feature Journal,* which included features of interest for every member of the household—helpful hints, poems, recipes, remedies for common ailments, a children's department. Credited with the idea for Forepaugh's $10,000 Beauty Contest and the pre-arranged selection of actress **Louise Montague** as the winner, first brought out for the season of 1881. Her appearance with the show was profitable for Forepaugh; with his street pageant, "Lalla Rookh's Departure from Delhi," with Miss Montague paraded atop the famous elephant, was a press agent's dream. Early in his career, was manager and agent for negro minstrel companies, such as William Arlington's, W. W. Newcomb's, Sam Sharpley's, and W. S. Cleveland's. Circus connections included John H. Murray's, 1873-75: L. B. Lent's, 1876; Coup's Equescurriculum, 1878; Den W. Stone's, 1878; Adam Forepaugh's, 1879-81, 1887;

Cooper, Jackson & Co., 1882; P. T. Barnum's, 1884; Sells Bros.', 1886. As a free lance writer, published more than one hundred pieces: series of circus stories for *The Home Magazine* beginning in the June issue of 1899 with "Tales of the Old Circus Man"; serialized story, "Van Amburgh, Elephant Performer and Lion Trainer," *Golden Hours*, 1900; authored the book, *The Adventures of Young Adam Forepaugh, the Elephant Trainer*; contributed articles to the New York *Clipper* over a 35 year period; served on the staff of *Music and Drama*. Was considered by his colleagues to be "a man of energy and resource." One called him "a spectacular figure in the amusement world." A gentleman of the old school, he was a congenial, convivial companion. After retirement, married **Gertrude H. Garvey** of NYC, November 29, 1901. Day was 59, his bride 23. Died in New Haven, CT, of erysipelas, age 65.

DAY, HIRAM T. (d. 1897) Clown and a valuable general performer, rider, tumbler, ringmaster. Acrobat, Welch & Mann, 1846; acrobat, Welch's, 1847; Dan Rice's, 1848-49; Spalding & Roger, American Theatre, New Orleans, fall 1851; G. C. Quick's, 1852; Sands, Quick & Co., Baltimore, 1853; Sands & Chiarini, 1854; John Robinson's, 1857-58, 1861-63; Robinson Bros.', 1863; Metropolitan Circus, 1864; Alex Robinson's, 1865; Deery & Robinson, 1865; International Comique and New York Circus, 1868; Alex Robinson's, 1869-75; Metchear & Cameron, 1870; Great Australian, 1870; rider, Collins' Oriental Combination, 1877.

DAY, JAMES. Clown and female impersonator, Haight & Chambers', 1867. Native of Canada. Committed suicide in Galveston, TX, January 21 1868, age 18, by taking morphine. At the time of death was employed by the Melodeon Concert Hall, Galveston.

DAY, JENNIE. Wire performer, ascensionist, and *danseuse*. Lipman's, 1866; member of variety troupe, Haight & Chambers, 1867.

DAY, NELLIE. Haight & Chambers, 1867. See above.

DAY, TOM. Leaper, Haight & Wootten, 1871.

DAY, WILLIAM. Contortionist. Robinson & Foster, 1843; Stickney & Buckley, 1844; S. P. Stickney's, 1845; Great Western, 1846; slack-rope, Welch & Mann, 1846.

DAYTON. Clown, Sells Bros.', 1884. While with the show in the spring of the year, fell dead performing in the ring.

DAYTON, GEORGE C. Manager of curiosities, Bunnell sideshow, P. T. Barnum's, 1879.

DAYTON, GRETA. High-wire, Lemen Bros.', 1892.

DAYTON, PETE. Walter L. Main's, 1887.

DEACON, LILLIE. *Manège* and trick horse performer. First appearance in America, Adam Forepaugh's, 1882-83; Barnum & Bailey, 1889. Married **Adam Forepaugh, Jr.,** 1882.

DEAN, A. J. Manager, Great National, 1874.

DEAN, C. L. Press agent, Adam Forepaugh's, 1893.

DEAN, EFFIE. Holland & Gormley, 1889.

DE AULEY, MLLE. Equestrienne, George W. DeHaven's, 1865.

DE BACH, MONS. F. and MME. Parisian equestrians. Appeared in Manchester, Liverpool, London, and many of the European capitols before coming to USA, early 1850s. One of the sensational acts was DeBach's globe ascension on the spiral column. Did juggling on horseback and was said to have introduced Americans to the antipodean globe exercises on horseback. **Mme. DeBach** was graced with a pleasing face and figure. Her act of equitation on 6 Arabian steeds was said to have been phenomenal in its artistry. Appearing in full Grecian costume, she bounded from one horse to the other. [John A. Dingess: "This lady presented one of the most beautiful scenes of female courage, skill and classic beauty ever witnessed."] Welch & Lent, Walnut Street Circus, Philadelphia, 1855; Nixon & Kemp, 1857; Sands, Nathans & Co., Broadway Theatre, NYC, 1857-58; L. B. Lent's, 1858; Joe Pentland's, 1859; Levi J. North's, 1859; globe act on horseback, Cooke's Royal Amphitheatre, Niblo's Garden, NYC, 1860 (April-June); James M. Nixon's, 1860; Levi J. North's, 1860; Gardner & Hemmings, 1861.

DE BAR, BOB. Clown, American Circus, fall 1878; Trans-Atlantic, 1879. Married Miss **Nellie Skidmore**, non-professional, July 2, 1879, Richmond, IN..

DE BAR BROTHERS. Gymnasts, Sadler's, 1875.

DE BAR, BEN AND NELLIE. Boyd & Peters, 1880.

DE BARRY, PAUL. New American Theatre, Philadelphia, December, 1865.

DE BERG, CARLOTTA [Mrs. James E. Cooke]. (1841?-November 24, 1915) Equestrienne. Born in England. Became one of the greatest female riders of her day. Made her debut in NYC, April 23, 1866. At the Hippotheatron, 1867, was billed as the "most dashing and daring equestrienne the world has ever known." L. B. Lent's, 1866-67, 1874: J. M. French's, 1870; European and American, winter 1870-71; Rosston, Springer & Henderson, 1871-72; Nixon's Amphitheatre, Broadway opposite Waverly Place, NYC, winter 1871-72; Den Stone's, 1873; Carlo Bros.', South America, 1877; James E. Cooke's, 1880-82. Died at her home in Jersey City, N. J., age 74.

DE BOISE, PAULINE. Female Samson, E. O. Rogers', 1891.

DE BONNAIRE, LEWIS. Trapeze performer, DeBonnaire's Great Parisian Exposition, 1880-85; clown and comic singer, Howes' New London, 1887.

DE BONNAIRE, MINNIE. DeBonnaire's Great Parisian Exposition, 1880-85; manageress, Great Parisian Shows, 1892.

DE BRENT, AMY. James Robinson's, 1870.

DE BUCH, MONS. HENRI. Whitby & Co., 1867 (J. V. O'Brien, proprietor).

DE BURDY, FRANK. Tattooed man. Sells Bros.', 1885; Burr Robbins', 1886. Married Miss Emma Kohl of Chicago,

Burlington, IA, July 25, 1885.

DE CAMP, CAPT. J. A. Acrobat and strong man. Howes & Sands, 1834; Palmer & Harrington, 1834; Bancker & Harrington, 1835; J. W. Bancker's, 1836; ringmaster, Palmer's, 1836; ringmaster, eastern unit of June, Titus, Angevine & Co., 1841; Sands', United Kingdom, 1842; VanAmburgh's, United Kingdon, 1843-44; John Tryon's, Bowery Amphitheatre, NYC, 1845; ringmaster, Welch & Mann, 1846; ringmaster, Sands, Lent & Co., 1847; R. Sands & Co., 1849; Welch's, 1850; Joe Pentland's, 1854.

DE CARMO, A. CARLOS. Spalding & Rogers, 1864.

DE CASTRO, LOUIS. George Sieber & Co., 1887.

DECKER, FRANK. Frank Rich's, 1886.

DECKER, J. H. Sells Bros.', 1886.

DECKER, MAJOR. (1849?-October 28, 1893) Midget. Engaged by VanAmburgh's when 20 years old. Connected with Barnum's, Coup's, Sells Bros.', Hyatt Frost's, Dan Rice's, and John O'Brien's. Worked in dime museums during the winter seasons. Regular height was 32"; weighed around 75 pounds. Although usually made large salaries, spent much of it for liquor. Chronic alcoholism caused his death at Mackinac House, Chicago, age 44.

DE CODONA, MME. FRANCES. Iron jaw woman, Cooper and Bailey, 1875-76.

DE COERT, EMILE. Juggler and general performer, Great Australian, 1870.

DE COMA FAMILY [Arthur, Rose]. Acrobats. With W. W. Cole's, California, 1880; Adam Forepaugh's, 1886; Frank A. Gardner's, South America, 1889; juggling and slack wire, Andy McDonald's, 1892; Orrin Bros.', Mexico, spring 1893; Edward Shipp's Winter Circus, 1893-94, Petersburg, IL. Performed an act that consisted of riding a bicycle on a wire over 50' above the arena; a trapeze was attached to it upon which two of the members performed feats of agility.

DE COMPAS FAMILY. Shelby's Golden Circus, 1888.

DE CORAL, MADAME. *Manège*, scene and principal rider and gymnast, Howes & Cushing, 1875.

DE COSTA, JUAN ANTONIA. Flying-ring gymnast, Lowande & Hoffman, 1887.

DE CROERT, EMILE. Juggler and general performer, Australian Circus, 1870.

DEER BROTHERS. Full-blooded Indians performers, with Walter L. Main's, 1893. Featured in a chase for a bride with **Jim Deer's** wife, **Georgia Deer**, who was an Anglo and an excellent rough rider.

DE FABIER, LOUIS. Ringmaster, John Robinson's (Great Union Combination), 1865.

DE FORREST, CLARA. Equestrienne, Mt. Pitt Circus, NYC, 1826.

DE FORREST, GUY. Acrobat, Burr Robbins', 1874.

DE GARMO, MAT. Parson's circus, Albany, 1820s.

DE GLORIAN BROTHERS. Aerialists, John Wilson's, Cal-

ifornia, 1865.

DE GRAFF, LEWIS. Rider, Leaman's Columbia Garden, Baltimore, summer, fall, 1805. Closed at Leaman's, August 8, and moved to the Pantheon of that city, performing until January 20, 1806.

DE GRANVILLE, MILLIE [r. n. Alma Hayes]. (May 31, 1852-February 2, 1902) Strong woman, "the lady with the jaws of iron." Born in Montreal, Canada. Came into the profession, 1867, Tony Pastor's Theatre, billed as the "female Hercules." Held a cannon on her shoulders while it was fired. With Great International, 1874; John Wilson's, San Francisco, 1874-75; VanAmburgh's, 1876; P. T. Barnum's, 1877; Cooper & Bailey, 2nd Australian tour, 1877-78; Orrin Bros.', Havana, spring 1879; John Robinson's, 1882-83; John B. Doris', 1884; Orrin Bros.', Mexico, winter 1885-86; Adam Forepaugh's, 1887-88. Married **Jack Walhalla** with Cooper & Bailey, Australia, March 10, 1878. Married second husband, **Dr. Louis G. Knox**, veterinary surgeon, Boston, 1889. Died at Danbury, CT.

DE GROOT, MAJOR. Oddity. William Blanchard & William West's, Canada, 1825-26; Quick & Mead, 1826; Handy & Welch, 1830.

DE HAVEN, CLAUDE. (November 3, 1839-June 3, 1888) Agent. Born in New Orleans. Press agent, George W. Bailey & Co., 1873; advertising agent, Maginley & Co., 1874; press agent, Howes & Cushing, 1875; Tony Pastor's, winter 1875-76; John H. Murray's, 1876; press agent, Great London, 1878; advertiser, Tony Pastor's New Theatre, NYC, 1879; special agent, Sells Bros.', 1880. Also Barnum's, John Robinson's, Stone & Murray, Batcheller & Doris, Adam Forepaugh's, and advance agent for the M. B. Levitt Specialty Co., this being his last engagement with an amusement organization. Died in Providence, RI, where he had resided since 1879 and where he was running a small newspaper, *The Indicator*. Was called by a colleague of the press, "a true Bohemian."

DE HAVEN, ED. Clown, George F. Bailey & Co., 1872-73.

DE HAVEN, GEORGE W. (March 22, 1837-August 27, 1902) Born in Jackson, IL. At age 12 his widowed father gave him $200 in gold and told him to shift for himself. Purchased a team of oxen and a plow and hired out for farm work. Through thrift and investment in labor, acquired a threshing machine to work the wheat fields. 1858, bought an interest in a circus, Satterlee, Bell & Co. In partnership with **Oliver Bell**, took out a railroad show, 1859. Proprietor, George W. DeHaven's, 1860-62. The latter year, took a showboat along the Mississippi River and its tributaries. Maginley & VanVleck, 1863. In partnership with **Andrew Haight**, 1865; 1866, with **Guerin** and **St. Germaine**, took out DeHaven's Imperial Circus; 1868, connected with **Ladd** and **Alderman** for a season. Balloon ascensions became a popular attraction with circuses in the years following the war, and DeHaven appears to be the first to use them as a free act outside the circus tent. The practice began in 1870 with no fanfare and seemingly no thought of it being innovative [New York *Clipper*, 1870: "One of the aeronauts connected with DeHaven's Circus was recently severely injured by falling from the balloon into a summer house at Davenport, Iowa, and his substitute was drowned at Dubuque by falling in the river, we are informed."]. DeHaven moved about in Iowa, Illinois, and Indiana; then, at the end of July, **R. E. J. Miles** purchase the circus, which continued to function under the DeHaven banner. The company traveled the Ohio River on their boat *Victor* until they reached Wheeling, WV, when they transferred to moving on the Baltimore and Ohio Railroad. At this time it was announced: "A balloon ascension is now made daily in connection with the circus." 1871, with **Jacob Haight**, he secured the privileges of the Empire City Circus. Following this, with Miles and the two Haights, became a partner in the Great Eastern Manegerie, Museum, Aviary, Circus and Balloon Show, 1872; privileges, L. B. Lent's, 1873; Great Chicago Show, with **S. Q. Stokes**, 1873; general manager, American Racing Association, 1875; general manager, Great Roman Hippodrome, 1877; manager, H. C. Lee's, winter 1877-78; manager, Great Chicago, 1879; manager, Silas Dutton's Southern, winter 1879-80; had a novelty company under canvas, 1881; proprietor, Great Eastern, 1883; manager, Col. G. W. Hall's, 1886; proprietor, George W. DeHaven's Show Company, Museum, Theatre, Triple Show and Free Menagerie, 1887. Organized and put on the road 33 different circuses during his career. Infirm for 11 years prior to his death because of a stroke. Died in Cedar Rapids, IA, age 65.

DE HAVEN, J. Clown, George F. Bailey & Co., 1871.

DE HAVEN, PROF. PAUL. Balloonist, North American, 1875.

DE JALMA, MME. Flying-rings, Beckett's Railroad Circus, 1887.

DE LACY, WILLIAM [r. n. William Merrill]. (d. June 16, 1889) Leaper. Suffered from a fall, June 15, 1889, Fairfield, IA, while attempting a double somersault over 5 horses and 3 men and died the next day. Had decided to give up doing this particular feat because of the danger involved. It was to be his last attempt. In reality, he had some hesitancy about it, for he said to a companion before executing it, "Jack, I am afraid of this." Previously, he had been engaged with Alfred Miaco's novelty company, 1888, and with Frank A. Gardner's, South America, that year.

DELANCEY, ROBERT. Gymnast, Alex Robinson's, 1866.

DELAND, SAMUEL B. Manegerie manager, E. F. & J. Mabie's, 1849-59; agent, Mabie's, winter season 1851-53, manager, 1854-58, 1860.

DELANE. See Thomas L. Huntley.

DE LANEY, FRANK. Assistant manager, L. B. Lent's, 1876; magician and solicitor, Miles Orton's, 1880.

DE LA RUE, ELISE. Gymnast, S. P. Stickney & Son's, 1874.

DELAVAN, GEORGE. Clown, G. G. Grady's, 1870.

DELAVAN, S. Veterinary surgeon, P. T. Barnum's, 1875.

DELAVAN, T. H. Delavan's Great Dime Show, 1884; Delavan, Adams & Palmer, 1884; Delavan & Grant, 1885; business manager, Delavan's Circus, 1886-87.

DELAVAN, WILLIAM A.: (1804-November 11, 1873) Born in Patterson, Putnam Co., NY. One of the earliest circus and manegerie proprietors. Co-owner with Miller, Mead & Delavan, 1834; director, Association's Celebrated Menagerie, Philadelphia, 1835; manager, Nathan A. Howes', 1836; bought into a partnership with **Jonas Bartlett**, 1841, the title becoming Bartlett & Delavan; proprietor, Welch & Delavan, Baltimore, 1841; manager, Welch, Mann & Delavan, 1844-45, 1849; Welch & Delavan, 1847. Subsequently, returned to NYC and kept the Monument House, Union Square. Died in Sharon, NY, age 69.

DE LAVE FAMILY. Welch & Sands (Sells Bros., proprietors), 1880.

DE LAVE, MONS. Wire-walker. Walked across the Genesee River, just in front of the falls, on a 900' rope stretched 100' to 140' above the water, 1859. Walked from the roof of the National Theatre, NYC, to the other side of the street, March 1860; and in June of that year walked a rope strung across the Passaic River at Patterson, NJ. S. P. Stickney's, 1861; Madigan's Great Show, 1861.

DE LEON, ALBERT. Gymnast, J. W. Wilder's, 1872.

DE LEON, LEON. Gymnast, J. W. Wilder's, 1872; Orrin Bros.', Havana, 1878.

DELEVANTI BROTHERS [Lewis Kline, H. W. Penny]. Gymnasts. Mabie's, 1862; Gardner & Hemmings, National Hall, Philadelphia, fall 1862; Rivers & Derious, 1864; Nixon's Amphitheatre, Washington, 1865; Alex Robinson's, 1866; Seth B. Howes', fall 1866; Chiarini's, Havana, winter 1866-67; S. O. Wheeler's, 1867; S. P. Stickney's, 1869; European and American Circus, winter 1869-70.

DELEVANTI, THOMAS. James T. Johnson's, 1888.

DEL FUEGO. Adam Forepaugh, 1888.

DEL FUEGO, LULU [Mrs. Frank Foignet]. (1867?-December 22, 1911) General performer. Entered the circus business in the early 1880s with the old John Robinson show. Was also connected with the Mighty Haag, 1911. Died in Chicago, age 44.

DELHAUER, WILLIAM. Contortionist and wire ascensionist, Sells Bros.', 1881-82.

DELIYEDE, PETE. Band leader, G. G. Grady's, 1871.

DELL, EDDIE. Contortionist, Gollmar Bros.', 1892.

DELMAINE, HARRY. Egyptian juggler, Lowande & Hoffman, 1887; Lowande's Winter Circus, 1889-90.

DELMAR, MLLE. JEANETTE. French equestrienne, W. W. Cole's, 1886.

DELMATO, NINA. *Manège* and trick horse performer, Holland, Bowman & McLaughlin, 1890.

DELMONT BROTHERS [Eddie, Frank]. Gymnasts. Great Commonwealth, transported by boat, *William Newman*, 1879; John H. Murray's, 1880; McDonald & Wells, 1892.

DE LONG, ED. Guilford & Cannon, winter 1889-90; stilts and knockabout clown, Cooper & Co. (J. R. W. Hennessey, proprietor and manager), 1897.

DE LONG, SAM. Frank Rich's, 1886.

DEL ORIENTE, MAGO. Magician, Great Southern Menagerie and Varieties, 1859.

DE LORME, EUGENIA [Mrs. Clark T, Ames]. Female lion tamer. G. N. Eldred's, 1858-59; Robinson & Lake, 1859-62; John Robinson's, 1864; Haight, Chambers and Ames', 1867; C. T. Ames', 1868-70. Attacked by a lion while performing, Sunbury, PA, August 20, 1869, and badly injured. Following the death of Ames, married **H. K. Robinson**, Memphis, TN, January 2, 1872, a non-professional.

DE LOUIS, GEORGE [r. n. Charles P. Raymond]. (October 24, 1822-June 26, 1875) Born in Rouen, France. Pad rider, leaper and trapeze performer. Gardner & Hemmings, 1863-64; along with his trained dogs Kate, Matt and Jennie, Thayer & Noyes, 1865-66; with his dogs, Chiarini's, Havana, fall 1866; James M. French's, 1867. While performing, New Orleans, fell from a trapeze, causing an injury that led to death.

DELSMORE, MISS. Rider, Dr. G. R. Spalding's, 1844-47.

DELVY, FRED and **BLANCHE.** Double trapeze, Albert M. Wetter's New Model Shows, 1893.

DEMAR, MOLLIE. Serio-comic, John H. Murray's, 1877.

DEMEREAN, HELENE. James Robinson's, 1870.

DE MONTAGUE, MME. Cooper, Jackson & Co., 1882.

DE MONTFORD, ETELKA. Gymnast, W. W. Cole's, 1886.

DE MORA, FRANK. Contortionist, Orrin Bros.', Mexico, winter 1889-90; Sells Bros.', 1894.

DEMOREST, JAMES. Equestrian and leaper. Bryan's, 1869; Campbell's, 1870; Rosston, Springer & Henderson, 1872.

DE MOTT, CHARLES. Adam Forepaugh's, 1867.

DE MOTT FAMILY [James, Josephine, Josie, Louise, William]. In the manner of such equestrian clans as the Stickneys and the Sherwoods, they worked together as a family until James DeMott's retirement. **James DeMott** (1838-October 5, 1902) Born in East Troy, NY, of French and German ancestry. Ran away from home at age 10 and joined S. B. Howes United States Circus, 1848. Apprenticed to **William Smith**, a 4- horse rider. The next year, was with John Platt Crain's Co.; 1850, visited the West Indies under the management of **Harry Whitby**. Sands & Lent, 1851; Nathans, Quick, 1852; Welch, Sands, Quick & Nathans, 1852; Washington Circus, Thirty-ninth and Sixth Ave., NYC, 1853; L. G. Butler's, 1854; Sands, Nathans, 1855; Mabie's, 1856-60; Niblo & Sloat, West Indies, fall 1860; Goodwin & Wilder, Howard's Athenaeum, Boston, 1861. While with the George F. Bailey show, 1861, married **Josephine Tourniaire**. The union produced 3 outstanding

equestrians, **Josie**, **William** and **Louise**, who were raised within the world of the circus and who were gradually schooled into becoming a performing part of it. There were also 5 other children. George F. Bailey & Co, 1862; S. O. Wheeler's, 1863; Robinson & Howes, winter 1863-64; Tom King's, 1864; Seth B. Howes', 1865-66; Thayer & Noyes, 1866; sideshow privilege (with **David Henderson**), principal bareback rider, Adam Forepaugh's, 1867; DeMott & Ward, 1868; John O'Brien's, 1869; managed Campbell's, 1870, and Sheldenberger's, 1871, both owned by **John V. O'Brien**; privileges, Springer, Rosston & Henderson, 1872; James E. Cooper's, winter 1872-73; privileges, Cooper & Bailey, 1873-74; managed and had interest in Rothschild's (another O'Brien show), 1875-76; Hamilton's New York Circus, 1877; ringmaster and equestrian director, Hamilton & Sargeant's, 1878; Hunting, Hilliard & DeMott, 1879; Hilliard & DeMott, 1880-81; John O'Brien's, 1882; Orrin Bros.', Mexico, fall, winter 1882-83; John Robinson's, 1884-89; Orrin Bros.', fall, winter 1888-89; Europe with Barnum & Bailey, fall 1889; John Robinson's, 1890-93. In mid-career, lost his savings in the English bank of Jay Cook & Co. [Josephine DeMott Robinson: "My father was a miserable business man, one who always refused to tie himself to contracts and whose honesty was proverbial in the show business."] Following the last season with Robinson, retired from the circus business and settled in Frankford, PA, where he resided for many years and where he eventually died after a 3-week illness. **Josephine "Josie"** (circa 1870-February 21, 1920), eldest daughter of **James** and **Josephine** and a graceful and daring equestrienne. [John A. Dingess: She "was the very perfection of art and the embodiment of one's wildest dreams."] At 19 years of age, married grifter **George H. Hines**, Selina, NC, September 30, 1889, under a veil of controversy, presumably having been duped into the union. Served papers for divorce in November of that same year, claiming coercion; then married **Charles M. Robinson**, son of old John. Died at home of her adopted daughter, Camille, in Frankford, PA. **Louise**, second daughter of **James** and **Josephine**, and sister of **Josie** and **William**, was an attractive rider of high school horses. Carried on the equestrian family tradition by marrying **Robert Stickney, Jr.** See Robert Stickney, Jr. Began on John Robinson's in both principal riding acts and *manège*. After marriage to Stickney, 1893, she and her husband usually appeared on the same program Later, concentrated on *manège*, both from the side saddle and from the 4-wheeled buggy or cart. By 1909, then on Hagenbeck-Wallace, she entered the arena dressed all in white, riding in a high seated 4-wheeled cart, drawn by a milk-white horse with a cake-walking white dog performing underneath. After leaving the circus, she and her husband appeared on the vaudeville circuit. 1923, retired to North Platte, NE, where Robert engaged in breaking high school and trick horses. **William** was within a year of the age of his sister, **Josie**. Married

78

in Philadelphia, December 5, 1892, to **Katie Smith**, a non-professional. At the time, was performing in theatres with "The Country Circus" Co. Later, Walter L. Main's, 1895; John Robinson's, 1902-08; principal rider, performing an Indian riding act, Two Bills' Show, 1912. As a principal, hurdle and somersault rider, career extended from 1874 until 1925. A second wife, **Eunice Stokes DeMott**, who survived him, was a principal rider performing with him as early as 1910-11, riding *manège* and doing a double carrying act. After their riding careers ended, they conducted a school of dance and acrobatics, Baltimore, MD.

DE MOTT, GARY. (December 10, 1830-March 27, 1863) Equestrian and clown. Den Stone's, 1854; VanAmburgh's, 1855; Mabie's, 1857-59; R. Sands', 1861; L. B. Lent's, 1862. Also performed as comedian in equestrian dramas, such as *Jack Sheppard* and *Dick Turpin*. Died in NYC.

DENIER, JOHN. Tight-rope ascensionist, Howes', 199 Bowery, NYC, winter 1863-64.

DENIER, TONY. (d. 1917) Clown and pantomimist. Adam Forepaugh's, 1867, for several years, perhaps until 1877. Became famous for his performances in *Humpty Dumpty*, touring both in the USA and abroad.

DENMAN, GEORGE ["Deafy"]. (b. 1872) Born in NYC. Cookhouse, Sells Bros.', 1890; elephants, Sells Bros.', 1891-95; Barnum & Bailey, Europe, 1896; Forepaugh-Sells, 1911; Ringling Bros.', 1919-1932.

DENZER BROTHERS [Valentine, Jacob, Charles, Randolph]. Gymnasts from the Rentz's German Amphitheatre, Hamburg. **Valentine** was an antipodean globe performer. For a time, part owner in the Denzer Circus. Left to go into the clothing business. At time of death, had been away from show business about 20 years. Died in West Hoboken, NJ, November 2, 1900, age 70. **Jacob** worked on stilts and the trapeze. Died of consumption in Lowell, OH, October 25, 1863. The brothers performed with Sands, Nathans & Co., Bowery Circus, 1858-59; Niblo & Sloat, 1860; G. F. Bailey & Co., 1862; S. O. Wheeler's, Boston, 1864; Mrs. Charles H. Warner's, Philadelphia, winter 1864-65; Stone & Rosston, 1865; Stone, Rosston & Murray, Front Street Theatre, Baltimore, winter 1866-67; Seth B. Howes', 1867; Great London, 1874.

DE ORMER BROTHERS [4]. Leapers and tumblers, Gollmar Bros.', 1892.

DE PAUL, EMMA. Lowande's Brazilian Circus, 1889.

DERIMS, E. Welch & Mann, Philadelphia, 1847.

DERIOUS, EDWIN ["Ned"]. (1808-July 19, 1888) Rider and vaulter. Born in Philadelphia; apprenticed with a showman by the name of **Hunt** at a very early age, becoming a fine athlete, a good rider, vaulter, and tight rope performer. J. Purdy Brown's, 1827, 1829; Benjamin Brown's, 1828; Palmer & Harrington's, 1834; vaulter and rider, Palmer's, 1835-37. Acquired half interest in Bacon's company, 1838, Bacon & Derious' Olympic Circus. Company broke up in Richmond, VA,

and equipment was purchased by Welch & Bartlett. Welch, Bartlett & Co., 1840; Broadway Circus, NYC, 1840; eastern unit of June, Titus, Angevine & Co., 1841; Bartlett & Delavan, 1841; Welch & Mann, 1841; VanAmburgh's Roman Amphitheatre, England, 1842-44; Welch's, 1847; Rivers & Derious' Grecian Arena, 1852; Rivers & Derious with Herr Driesbach's, 1853; Rivers & Derious, 1857-58; Sands, Nathans & Co., Broadway Theatre, NYC, 1858; Dan Rice's, 1858, where he appeared on the enchanted ladder, tossed the globe on horseback, rode bareback, etc.; monkey man, Rivers & Derious', 1859; Gardner & Hemmings, 1862; Gardner & Hemmings (under the Barnum name), Washington, DC, fall 1862; Slaymaker & Nichols, 1864; Mrs. Dan Rice's, 1864; Gardner & Hemmings, National Hall, Philadelphia, 1865; New American Theatre, Philadelphia, winter 1865-66; Dan Rice's, 1866; equestrian manager, Parisian Circus, 1867. In Paris at the opening of the Exposition of 1867, was gored by a buffalo, stricken with paralysis, and for 10 years prior to death was an invalid. Died in Philadelphia.

DERIOUS, GEORGE. Rider. Son of rider **Edwin Derious**. Welch's, 1849; Rivers & Derious, 1851-52; Driesbach, Rivers & Derious, 1853; Ballard's, winter 1853; Rivers & Derious, 1855-58; man monkey, Gardner & Hemmings, 1861-62; Bryan's, with Mrs. Dan Rice, 1863; Dan Castello's, 1866.

DEROCK, ELFIE. Wire ascensionist, Sherman & Hinman, 1883.

DE ROSA, GEORGE. Frank Rich's, 1886.

DERR, JOHN. General performer, Flagg & Aymar, 1856.

DERR WILLIAM R. (1810?-June 7, 1878) Equestrian. Varied career combining the ring and the stage. Around 1835, traveled with the Grand Combined Circus as the "Modern Hercules" and as part of a 4-brothers pyramid act, along with **D. Morgan, W. Smith,** and **L. Lipman**. Clown, James W. Bancker's, 1832; clown, Aaron Turner's, 1833, 1835; J. J. Hall's, West Indies, 1837; strong man, H. H. Fuller's, 1838; strong man, June, Titus, Angevine & Co., Bowery Amphitheatre, 1840; Henry Rockwell & Co., winter 1841; clown, Welch & Mann, 1841; clown, John Tryon's, Bowery Amphitheatre, NYC, 1843; horse-breaker, Rockwell & Stone, 1845; trainer and ringmaster, June & Co., 1851; ringmaster, Joe Pentland's, 1852. In 1853, developed a starring reputation as a "horse actor" or "horse charmer" in equestrian dramas by touring the country with his prize mount, Ingomar. For a period of time following the war, settled in St. Louis, MO, at the Varieties, with a repertory that included such horse spectacles as *Putnam, Mazeppa,* and *El Hyder*. Around 1868, traveled in support of the equestrian actress **Kate Fisher** and for whose productions he trained and furnished the horses. Died in Morrisiana, NY, age 68. Derr's wife was listed as "a great hurdle *act de manège*," with Washburn's Great Indian Amphitheatre and Circus, 1855.

DERRIOTT, JAMES. Mabie's, 1860.

DERTH, MAJOR F. [or H.]. Teamster. 40-horse hitch driver, with Spalding & Rogers, 1858-59; driver 40-horse bandwagon, Dan Rice's, 1873. 1859 ads stated Derth had been the teamster of the 40-horse hitch for 10 years, yet earlier ads show **J. W. Paul**. [Stuart Thayer: "It is possible that Derth drove the hitch over the road and Paul drove it in parade."]

DE VALLEROT, PROF. Press agent, G. F. Bailey & Co., 1874.

DEVAN, WILLIAM. McMahon's, 1888; F. J. Taylor's, 1892.

DEVANIER, JOSEPHINE [Josephine Webb]. Rope ascensionist. Madame Macarte's European Circus (**James M. Nixon**, proprietor), 1863; Mrs. Charles Warner's, Continental Theatre, Philadelphia, fall 1864; double equitation and grand *haut ecole* acts, Spalding & Rogers, New Orleans, winter 1864-65; Dan Castello's, 1865; Thayer & Noyes, winter 1865-66; outdoor wire ascension prior to each performance, New York Champs Elysees, 1865-66; Thayer & Noyes, 1866; L. B. Lent's, 1867; pad act, French's, 1868; Cooke's, Philadelphia, winter 1867-68; Academy of Music, New Orleans, winter 1868-69.

DEVEAU, WILLIAM F. P. Assistant ticket agent, P. T. Barnum's, 1873.

DE VEAUX, TOMMY. Clown, Great Western, 1876.

DEVERAUX, GEORGE. Acrobat, Alexander Robinson's, 1875.

DEVERE, ANN. James T. Johnson's, 1884.

DEVERE, CARRIE. Concert performer, John H. Murray's, 1875. May have been the wife of **William Devere**.

DEVERE, CHARLES [r. n. Charles Dingley]. (1823-July 7, 1868) General and versatile performer, capable of clowning, leaping and tumbling, but specialty was performing on the slack-rope. When a mere youth, ran away from home and found employment at a bowling alley in Albany, NY. Soon jobbed out as a cabin boy on a canal boat on the Ohio River. 1839, joined Turner's circus. Following year, went to the West Indies, remaining for 3 years. Rejoined Turner's, 1843, and remained in the circus business until 1849. Then went to work in a printing office. 1850, traveled with a panorama of *Napoleon* but returned to circus performing, 1851. Appeared with Great Orion Circus, Old Bowery, NYC, 1861; Nixon's Cremorne Garden Circus, Washington, DC, October-December 1862; James M. Nixon's, fall 1865. Went to California for three years, then to Australia and the Orient. 1867, advertised the feat of throwing a boomerang 300'. Became known as a "Jonah," one who brought bad luck to the circus troupe, a reputation impossible to live down. Died in San Francisco, CA.

DEVERE, DAN. Banjoist, J. Hudson's, West Indies, 1872-73.

DEVERE, EDA. Equestrienne, Cooper & Jackson, 1880.

DEVERE, FRANK. Charles Lee's, 1888; Downie & Gallagher, 1893.

DEVERE, GEORGE. Great Australian Circus Co., 1877.

DEVERE, HARRY. Clown, World's Fair Aggegation, 1892. Same year, with **Ed Keetch**, assumed ownership of the show and retitled it Devere & Keetch's Colossal Shows and Pyrotechnical Sensation.

DEVERE, HELENE. W. H. Harris' Nickel-Plate, 1886.

DEVERE, J. F. C. Bareback and hurdle rider, E. Stowe's, 1870.

DEVERE, MAY. Cooper & Jackson, 1880.

DEVERE, MME. (1855?-June 18, 1912) Bearded lady. Born in Kentucky. Began career at the age of 17. Connected for some 40 years with the principal circuses and museums in America. Married sideshow manager **J. W. Devere**. Died of a heart attack in Oelwein, IA, age 57, while with the Patterson Carnival Co.

DEVERE, WILLIAM [r. n. William Bell]. (d. December 14, 1882) Banjoist and singer. Served as a drummer during the Civil War. Subsequently, joined with **Tommy Brand** as the **Devere Brothers**. After Brand's death, teamed with **Robert Williams** as **Devere & Williams**. The two separated after 1880-81 season. Next joined **George Devere** and again performed as **Devere Brothers**, parting in 1882. Business manager, National Theatre, Hackensack, NJ; museum director, Alexander Robinson's, 1875.

DE VERNE, L. Ringmaster, Great Oriental Pavilion Show, 1877.

DE VERNE, SAM. Banjoist, Denver Dick's Wild West and Sioux Indian Medicine Company, 1894.

DE VILLANUEVA, JOSE. Equilibrist, calisthentist, Spalding & Rogers, 1857-59.

DEVINE, CAROLINE. Equestrienne. Boston Lion Circus, 1836; S. H. Nichols', 1838, 1840.

DEVINE, GEORGE. Minstrel performer, P. T. Barnum's, 1873.

DEVINO BROTHERS. Triple bar, Bailey & Winan, 1890.

DEWEY, H. J. Program agent, Burr Robbins', 1874.

DE WITT, HENRY. Acrobat, Melville, Maginley & Cooke, 1875.

DE YOUNG, MRS. G. See Rosa Celeste.

DIABOLA "DIB" [r. n. R. Moody]. Fire king and and a man of many faces. A hard, conscientious worker, was for some years with the Burr Robbins', where he did several turns in the sideshow, concert feature in the big show, and made all the announcements in the big show, as he had a loud, clear voice which could be heard in all parts of the canvas. Was the kind that got the most out of life. After putting in several years on a salary with the Burr Robbins', finally took an interest in the privileges, which was not a good investment. After closing the season, quit the business and settled in Chicago where he opened a buffet and restaurant at Sixty-First and State Streets. Also Cooper, Bailey & Co., 1879. Died in 1884 or 1885. [D. W. Watt: "He was a good storyteller, and the night was never too dark, nor the roads so heavy, when I would drive by Dib and his wife, but what he would always say 'Beautiful night, elegant roads,' or something of the kind."]

DIAMOND, BILLY. Clown, E. A. Griffith's, 1894.

DIAMOND BROTHERS. Sells Bros.', 1885.

DIAMOND, C. Clown, Hilliard & Hunting, 1877.

DIAMOND, FRANK. Howe's New Colossal Shows, Mexican and Wild West Expositions (E. H. Howes & Co., proprietors), 1888.

DIAMOND, HARRY. Assistant advance agent, Holland & Gormley, 1888-89.

DIAMOND, J. Concert, John Robinson's, 1871.

DIAMOND, JOHN. (1823?-October 29, 1857) Jig dancer. Performed at the Franklin Theatre, NYC, spring 1839. In the fall of that year, moved to the New Chatham Theatre, where in addition to dancing played the role of Black Ike in *Shabby Genteel*. Danced for **P. T. Barnum**, Vauxhall Garden, NYC. Barnum, after playing out the Diamond excitement and tiring of putting up with his revengeful disposition, dropped him. At one time, enlisted in the American army and nearly lost his life in Mexico. Was sentenced to be shot for attacking a superior officer. Fortunately, the peace treaty saved him the rifle squad. Danced for many years with **Jim Sanford**. Both men dressed "in the height of flashy extravagance." At one time was a rival of **Dick Pelham**. They had a match dance at the Chatham Theare for $500 a side, February 13, 1840. As a circus performer, Welch, Bartlett & Co., 1839; Ludlow & Smith, 1841; Henry Rockwell & Co., winter 1841; Rockwell & Stone, 1843; Mann, Welch & Delavan, 1845; G. N. Eldred, 1847; Dan Rice's, 1849. Died at Blockley Alms House, Philadelphia, age 34.

DICE, CARL. Business manager, W. C. Coup's, 1894.

DICKENSON, ENAM M. Singer. Palmer & Harrington, 1834; Buckley & Weeks, 1835; J. W. Bancker's, 1836; Bacon & Derious, 1838; Welch, Bartlett & Co., 1839; S. H. Nichols', 1839-42; Broadway Circus, NYC, 1840; Bartlett & Delavan, 1841; Welch & Mann, 1841; Mann, Welch & Delavan, 1844; Welch & Mann, 1845; clown, S. P. Stickney's, 1847; Dr. Gilbert R. Spalding's, 1847; Spalding & Rogers, 1850-51.

DICKERSON, CHARLES. Dan Castello's, winter 1867-68; James Robinson's, 1870.

DICKEY, SAM. (d. November 11, 1888) Clown. Started in circus business around 1860. Burr Robbins', 1874, 1879, 1883; Miles Orton's, 1880, 1885; Wallace & Co., 1886; John F. Stowe & Co., 1888; Weldon & Hummel. A powerful man who knew no fear. One account lists him as dying in Cincinnati, November 11, 1888; another states that he died in the poor house of Wayne County, Mich., September 7, 1889, after whitening his face for the ring with a secret preparation which eventually attracted blood poisoning and caused partial paralysis; still another, that he died of consumption in a hospital in Chicago.

DICKINSON, CHARLES. Treasurer, James Robinson's, 1870.

DICKSON, JOE. Clown, Hyatt & Co., 1859.

DICKSON, JOHN. Agent, New York Olympic, 1867.

DIEFENBACH, PHIL. (d. May 17, 1899) Clown and negro minstrel show manager, Haight & Chambers, winter 1866-67; Maginley & Carroll, 1868; clown, Ames', 1869; Lake's, 1869; ringmaster, James Robinson's, 1870-72, equestrian director, 1873; ringmaster, Pat Ryan & Co., 1873; Jackley's, 1874; ringmaster, P. T. Barnum's, 1874; equestrian director, Cooper, Bailey & Co., 1876; Great Eastern, 1878. Moved into circus management with Thayer, Diefenbach & Lewis' Great Show and London Sensation, 1878. Following year, took out Diefenbach's New Trans-Atlantic Shows. Continued as circus proprietor under such titles as Diefenbach's Transatlantic Circus, 1888; Phil Diefenbach's, 1892-97; Diefenbach & Hamilton's (Phil Diefenbach, **William Hamilton**, proprietors), 1899. **Mrs. Diefenbach** was wardrobe woman with the old Dan Rice and John Robinson circuses when she was known as **Maggie Roe**. Marriage to Diefenbach produced a daughter, **Katie**. Diefenbach died from lung cancer, Trenton, TN, after being sick for 2 years, which necessitated spending all of the income for medicine and doctors and left his widow destitute and appealing for support. She died at her home in Hamilton, OH, June 8, 1901, age 56.

DIEGO. Rider and general performer, probably apprenticed with Pepin & Breschard, 1809. Described by one source as being 11 years old at the time; however, another source stated he was 15 in 1812, when apprenticeship had recently ended. Remained with the company through 1814. Then went with Davis & Co., Boston, fall 1815; Pepin, Philadelphia and Lancaster, summer 1817; Olympic Circus, Philadelphia, summer 1817.

DIGNEY, LUKE. Boss canvasman, Cooper, Bailey & Co. Australian tour, 1877.

DILKS, JOHN M. See John M. LaThorne.

DIMPLE, DOTTIE. (1863?-May 7, 1912) Equestrienne. Began performing at 8 years of age as one of the Dimple Sisters, **Dottie** and **Dollie**, with Yankee Robinson's. For a number of years, Adam Forepaugh's as a trick and bareback rider. Also a song and dance soubrette in vaudeville and burlesque and, later, owned and managed several theatres in the West. Married to **Harry Rex Burton**. Died in Kalamazoo, MI, from chronic asthma, age 49.

DINEGAR, ROBERT C. General agent, with Montgomery Queen's, 1876.

DINGESS, JOHN A. (1829-April 15, 1901) Agent. Born in Charleston, WV. Brother of **Robert S. Dingess.** Worked for various circus and minstrel companies and at one time was representative for **Tony Pastor.** Dan Rice's, 1849; VanAmburgh's, 1855; Mabie's, 1856-57; Harry Buckley's, 1857; Spalding & Rogers *Floating Palace*, 1858-59; Dan Rice's,

1860-61; manager, Burgess, Prendergast, Hughes & Donniker's Minstrels, 1865, through the East; manager, Dingess & Green's Minstrels, an organization that opened in Champaign, IL, November 18, 1866; Lake's Hippo-Olympiad, 1868; Dan Rice's, 1869; John Robinson's, 1870-71; general business agent, John Stowe & Sons, 1871; Great Eastern, 1872; Great Chicago, 1873; Older's Great Trans-Atlantic, 1873; Adam Forepaugh's, 1874-75; Ryan & Robinson, 1882. Also with many theatrical companies, including Director & Ulman's Opera House Stock Co., Guiseppina Marlacchi Ballet Troupe (1870), Lisa Weber's British Blonds (1871), Arlington's Minstrels, Mrs. James A. Oates Burlesque and Opera Co., treasurer for Tony Pastor's Theatre, NYC, etc. After retirement, 1880s, devoted some time to writing a book on circus life. Although never published, the hand written manuscript is at the Harry Hertzberg Circus Collection and Museum, San Antonio, TX. A typewritten copy is at the Robert L. Parkinson Library and Research Center, Baraboo, WI. Died in NYC, age about 80.

DINGESS, ROBERT S. (March 15, 1826-March 15, 1894) Agent and advertiser. Brother of agent **John A. Dingess**. Entered the business with the American Circus; followed by an engagement with Spalding & Rogers *Floating Palace*, 1850-51, 1853, 1856-60; Dan Rice's, 1860-61; Antonio Bros.', 1862; Arlington & Donniker's Minstrels, winter 1862-63; Arlington, Kelly, Leon, Donniker & Jones' Minstrels, 1863; Melville's Australian Circus, 1864; Yankee Robinson & Dan Scott, 1866-67; William Lake's, winter 1866-67, 1868; Nixon, Castello & Howes, 1867; George F. Bailey's, 1868-69; John Robinson's, 1869-70, 1872; Adam Forepaugh's, 1870-75, 1880; Montgomery Queen's, 1876; general director, W. C. Coup' New United Monster Show, 1879; Pullman, Dingess & Co. (**Henry Pullman**, R. S. Dingess, proprietors), 1885; John T. Long's, 1890; W. B. Reynold's, 1892, (last engagement). At times cranky and not an easy man to get along with, was known among fellow professionals as "Black Hawk." In wagon show days, was considered to have superior knowledge of the West, which made him in great demand. [D. W. Watt: "While Bob Dingess was thorough in his work in the business, he was not what you might call a companionable man, for he wore a bad scowl on his face that must have been made of buckskin or corduroy as he wore it for at least twenty-five years that I know of, and the last time I saw him it was still in good condition. But Dingess was a tireless worker and could always be found at his post early and late and many a long trip would he make over the country during the show season, looking up the best possible country to take the show into.... Bob Dingess probably knew more about the country and the conditions from California to Maine than anyone in the business."]

DINNEFORD, WILLIAM. (d. December 8, 1852) Equestrian. According to T. Allston Brown, was a man of many oc-

cupations—actor, author, manager, auctioneer, broker and merchant. Born in London and came to American for the purpose of commerce. At one time was in the billiard table business. [Charles Durang: "Mr. William Dinneford was a dashing young Israelite from London, of fine personal appearance."] American acting debut, Philadelphia, Chestnut Street Theatre, 1823; New York debut, Lafayette Theatre, 1826; Mount Pitt Circus (Gen. Sanford, proprietor); Washington Gardens, Boston, 1827. Subsequently became manager of the Franklin Theatre, Chatham Square, Palmo's Opera House, Bowery Theatre, NYC. Traveled throughout the country with various theatrical groups until, in August 1845, opened The Byron, a lodging and eating establishment, 157 Broadway, NYC. Died in Panama.

DIVO, DON. Contortionist, F. J. Taylor's, 1891.

DIXON. Comic songs, Samuel Parsons' Albany Circus (under the management of **Simon V. Wemple**). Troy, NY, 1828; American Arena. Washington, DC, winter 1828-29.

DOBBINS, J. Excursion agent, John Robinson's, 1892.

DOBSON BROTHERS. Gymnasts and acrobats, James T. Johnson & Co., 1869.

DOCK, SAM. (December 24, 1863-July 3, 1953) Began trouping, 1883, and continued without a miss until at least 1951. Harris Nickel-Plate, 1885; Beckett's, 1886; Dock & Jordan, 1887; one-third interest, Welsh Bros.', 1890-01; Flying Jordans, 1892; half interest, Wheeler & Co., 1893; superintendent, Wheeler's, 1893; Welsh's Great Golden Shows, 1893; Dock Keystone Shows, 1895; Great Keystone Shows, 1914; manager, Brison Bros.', 1929. Last had a show of his own, 1942; but continued to work dogs, ponies and monkeys through 1951.

DOCKRILL, ELISE. (1852-1919) Daughter of **Rose Kennebel** and sister of **Francois** and **Eugene Kennebel**. French clowns. A one, 4 and 6-horse rider. Said to be the first woman to ride and drive 4 horses. Praised as an attractive rider "on a fine gray horse coursing around the ring at full speed," leaping over banners and jumping through "balloons." One of her most thrilling feats was grasping the girdle of the horse and supporting herself with only her hands while the steed leaped over fences. Named "The Empress of the Arena" by Barnum, who offered $10,000 to anyone to equal her 6-horse act. Commanded a weekly salary of $500 for full 12 months of the year while with Barnum between 1872-79, also had half use of Barnum's private railroad car. 1877, took over the Great London Circus with husband **Richard Dockrill**, **John J. Parks**, and **Homer Davis**. P. T. Barnum's, Hippotheatron, NYC, December 1872 (first appearance in USA on December 16); Great London, 1877-78; P. T. Barnum's, 1879-80; Barnum, Bailey & Hutchinson, 1881-82; Nathans & Co.'s, 1883. Injured in a fall at Cohoes, NY, and another at Portsmouth, VA, 1883. Walter L. Main's, 1899. Suffered dislocated knee while alighting from a horse in Caracas, Venezuela, and was unable to ride again. When the circus company became afflicted with yellow fever, the Dockrills returned to USA without a penny, having lost over $100,000 in 7 months. By 1912, they had a home at Delavan Lake, WI. Lost a daughter, **Eliza Hermina**, to diphtheria, September 10, 1881, age 7. Died in poverty in Delavan, WI, and is buried in an unmarked lot. See below.

DOCKRILL, RICHARD H. (August 9, 1843-December 28, 1922) Born in Cork, Ireland. Equestrian and equestrian director, who, with his wife, **Elise Kennebel**, were first noted as French riders with Howes' Great American Circus and Menagerie, London, England, 1870. Came to America the following year with the circus. Performed a *manège* act with his horse, Ellington, exhibiting "riding-school" techniques in galloping, waltzing, etc. Was also proficient as a scenic rider but had greatest ability as an equestrian director, for which he was considered one of the best of his day. With **John J. Parks** and **Homer Davis**, purchased the **Seth B. Howes** show, January, 1877, taking it on the road for 2 years, Dockrill's Parisian Circus and Grotesque Mardi Gras. Sold the show to **James A. Bailey** and **James E. Cooper**, 1879. First American engagement, P. T. Barnum's, winter, 1872, terminating with the burning of the Hippotheatron, NYC, December 24, where their horses were lost. Howes' Great London, 1873; John Wilson's, California, 1873-74; P. T. Barnum's, 1880; in partnership with Leon De Leon, Leon's Iron Amphitheatre, Havana, fall 1881; equestrian director, Barnum, Bailey & Hutchinson, 1881-82; Nathans & Co., 1883; Dockrill's, South America, 1885-86; Barnum & Bailey, 1892-93, 1905; Walter L. Main's, 1899, 1901, 1904; Norris & Rowe's, 1908. Daughter, **Rose**, married **George Holland**.

DOCKRILL, ROZELLE E. "ROSE". (d. March 7, 1920) Bareback and forward bareback and jockey rider. Daughter of **Elise** and **Richard Dockrill**. Made debut on bareback with Barnum & Bailey, 1893; famous for combining the somersault and toe dance on horseback. John G. Robinson & Franklin Bros.', 1896; Ringling Bros.', 1897; Walter L. Main's, 1899. Married **George E. Holland** in Savannah, GA, November 11, 1901. Died on March 7, 1920, at daughter's home in Delavan, WI.

DODDS, JOSEPH. Band leader, Shedman Bros.', 1894.

DODE, DAVID HENRY. (d. August, 1888) Giant, 7' 3", P. T. Barnum's.

DODGE, BEN. Sells Bros.', 1879.

DODGE, HARRY. Press agent, John Wilson's, 1875.

DODGE, J. Advertising agent, Cooper, Bailey & Co. Australian tour, 1877. May be the same as below.

DODGE, J. A. Director, Crystal Palace Circus, California, 1872.

DODGE, OLIVER. Rider, horse trainer. First started in the circus business, 1853. Wesley Barmore's, 1854; VanAmburgh's, 1855; Yankee Robinson's, 1856-57; L. B. Lent's, 1858; Alex Robinson's, 1862; Miles' Circus Royale, Canada,

1863; Metropolitan, 1864; ringmaster, Yankee Robinson's, Chicago, 1866; Smith & Baird, 1872.

DOER, MONS. J. W. Bancker's, New York State, 1832.

DOGGET, EDWARD. Sideshow manager, Gardner & Hemmings, 1863.

DOLPHIN, T. G. (d. July 29, 1890) Advance agent, Reese, Levis & Dolphin, 1885; P. T. Barnum's.

DOLSON, AL. General agent, Bailey & Winan, 1890.

D'OME, WILLIAM. Acrobat, Hudson & Castello (**J. M. Hudson** and **Dan Castello**, proprietors), 1881.

DOMINION BROTHERS [William, John, Clifford]. Alex Robinson's, 1870.

DONAHUE, JAMES. Concert clog dancer, leaper, Cooper, Bailey & Co., 1880; Barnum, Bailey & Hutchinson, 1881.

DONAHUE, VICTOR. Master of transportation, Bruce L. Baldwin's, 1894.

DONALD, GEORGE. Rider. L. B. Lent's, 1871; P. T. Barnum's, 1874; Melville, Maginley & Cooke, 1875; Great Australian, National Theatre, Philadelphia, winter 1881-82.

DONALDSON, FRANK. Gymnast. Began in the circus business, Aaron Turner's, 1842, as a posturer at $12 a week. Great Western, 1845; Spalding & Rogers, 1852-59; George F. Bailey & Co., 1860; Chiarini's, Havana, winter 1861-62; Dan Castello's, 1870; perch act (with **George Dunbar**) P. T. Barnum's, 1871; man monkey, J. W. Wilder's, 1872; John H. Murray's, 1873. By 1879, was devoting his days to patenting his inventions.

DONALDSON, GEORGE W. [r. n. George W. Blanchard]. (1853?-February 1914) Cannon ball performer and strong man. John Robinson's, 1879; DeHaven & Lee, around 1880; sold interest in Donaldson & Rich, 1885; World's Columbian Exposition, Chicago, 1893. At one time a partner of **Charley "Pop" Baker**, the glass blower. Died at his home in Detroit in his 62nd year.

DONALDSON, HOMER. Contortionists. Robinson & Lake, Wood's Theatre, Cincinnati, 1859; Sells Bros.', 1884-86; Roberts & Gardner, 1886.

DONALDSON, JAMES. Agent, Collins' Oriental Combination, 1877.

DONALDSON, VIRGINIA. Variety performer as comedienne and *danseuse*, J. W. Wilder's, 1872.

DONALDSON, W. H. (April 19, 1864-August 1, 1925) Founder and publisher of the Billboard Publishing Co. The son of William M. Donaldson from Dayton, KY. After completing his education, young Donaldson went to work for his father in an art store and picture frame establishment in Cincinnati. Shortly, his father opened a poster business, 127 East 8th St., which was the beginning of the Donaldson Lithographing Co. of Newport, KY. Continued to work for his father as a poster salesman. 1894, he and **James Hennegan** founded the *Billboard*. Starting as a monthly, the first issue contained 8 pages devoted solely to the billposting trade. A disagreement with the leaders of the billposting association led to the *Billboard's* divorce from participation in the field of outdoor publicity. An agricultural fair department and a circus department were added as features. When **James Hennegan** retired, Donaldson assumed entire control of the paper. Married **Jennie Hasson**, daughter of **William Hasson**, a prominent cordage manufacturor, 1885.

DONALDSON, WILLIAM B. (1823-April 16, 1873) Comic singer, John T. Potter's, 1845-46; singer, John Tryon's, Bowery Amphitheatre, NYC, 1847; clown, VanAmburgh's, 1857-58; Tom King's, 1858; Robinson & Lake, 1860; clown, Mike Lipman's, 1867; clown, Broadway Circus, NYC, February, 1858. May, 1871, leased Lockwood House, Poughkeepsie, NY, which was opened for minstrel performances. Astonished people by his remarkable left-hand playing on the banjo, not simply picking and fingering with the left hand, but entirely reversing the position in which the instrument is ordinarily held. Died in Poughkeepsie, NY.

DONALDSON, WASHINGTON HARRISON: (October 10, 1840-1875) Balloonist. Born in Philadelphia, the son of alderman **David L. Donaldson**. As a child was fond of sports and became proficient at balancing on a ladder, walking the tight-rope, etc.; also acquired the magician's and ventriloquist's art and performed as such for several years. Subsequently, became interested in aeronautics and performed on a trapeze suspended from a balloon. While in Philadelphia, Broad and Norris Streets, 1874, ascended in a small one-man balloon; the rig became unmanageable and descended near Atco, NJ;. Three telegrams were sent to Philadelphia, stating that Donaldson had fallen from a great height and been killed, which created quite a sensation. The wires were signed by "J. M. Spencer, M.D." Shortly, other telegrams announced that Donaldson was alive. It later came out that Donaldson had sent the telegrams himself and that losing the balloon was a pre-arranged publicity stunt. Made many ascensions for Barnum's Roman Hippodrome, 1874-75, until he disappeared, July 15, 1875, over Lake Michigan; after leaving the Chicago show lot in a tattered balloon for a free attraction that day. He was carried out over the lake where he encountered a storm; his body was never recovered.

DONALDSON BROTHERS. Contortionists, Sells Bros.', 1886.

DONAVAN, JOHN. Cooper, Bailey & Co., 1879.

DONAVAN, WILLIAM. (d. April 16, 1873) Leaper, acrobat. Great Railroad, 1859; Robinson & Lake, 1858-60; Antonio & Melville, 1861; Antonio Bros.', 1862; L. B. Lent's, 1863-64, 1866; Howe & Norton, fall 1864; J. M. French's, 1867. Died in Poughkeepsie, NY.

DONCASTER, MARIE. Rider, Palmer's, 1836.

DONEGANI. Brought a company of tumblers, wire dancers and posturers to Philadelphia, December 1790, and gave exhibitions in Oeller's Hotel, Chestnut Street.

DONETTI, CARLOS. Animal trainer. Performed the Great Parisian Troupe of Acting Monkeys, Dogs and Goats on the steamers *Banjo* and *James Raymond*. Spalding & Rogers, 1858; Donetti & Woods, 1859.

DONNELLY, CHARLES. Lion king. Pullman & Hamilton, 1878.

DONNELLY, JAMES. Museum director. Springer's, 1875.

DONNELLY, JOE. Lockwood & Flynn, 1887.

DONOVAN, ANNIE [nee Annie Pogue]. (d. October 21, 1902) Bearded lady. Born in Virginia. Lost her father at 8 month old. As a baby had hair longer than her body and developed facial hair early, eventually having a heavy black beard and mustache. Taken to NYC at 9 months of age and exhibited at Barnum's Museum. Entire life as an oddity was spent in Barnum's employ; except, in 1865, when Barnum's museum burned, a showman abducted her and exhibited her privately throughout Europe until 1867, when he was arrested in Canada and recovered by her mother. Married showman **Robert Elliot**, 1880, but was divorced in 1895. Then married **William Donovan**, wardrobe man. He died, 1900. She died of consumption, age 37, at her home, 187 Cornelia Street, Brooklyn, where she lived with her mother, **Mary Pogue**. In accordance with her wish, was buried with beard unshaven.

DONOVAN, JAMES. (December 5, 1853-June 28, 1902) Leaper. John O'Brien's, 1877-78; Great London, 1879-80; in Europe, 1880-83; Gardner & Donovan, South America, 1886-87; Sturges & Donovan, 1888; *Gran Circo Estrellas Del Nortis*, West Indies, fall 1888; Stickney & Donovan, 1889; James Donovan's New American Circus, Bermuda, winter 1891-92; Donovan's South American Circus, Cuba, winter 1894-95; (James Donovan, **Frank Long**, proprietors) Donovan & Long, Central America, winter 1896-97; Stirk & Donovan, 1897; Donovan & Stickney's New Combined North American Circus, West Indies, winter 1897-98; bought out partner **Robert Stickney**, spring 1898; manager with the New York Circus Co., West Indies, winter 1900-01.

DONOVAN, JERRY C. (1845?-May 28, 1898) Painter by trade, but gave it up to join the circus. Contracting agent, Sells Bros.' for 12 years until the close of the 1896 season; Great Wallace Shows, remaining until death. Died at his home in Columbus, OH, age 53.

DONOVAN, MRS. A. Costume mistress, P. T. Barnum's, 1873; P. T. Barnum's Roman Hippodrome, 1874-75.

DONOVAN, W. A. (d. December 26, 1869) John Robinson's, 1858; Great Railroad, 1859; Robinson & Lake, 1860; *l'echelle perileuse*, Antonio Bros.', 1861; L. B. Lent's, 1866. Died in NYC.

DOOLEY, E. H. (d. May 15, 1887) Lion tamer, Beckett's; Miles Orton's, 1880, 1885; Tribbey & Co.'s Mastadon Dime Circus, 1887.

DOOLEY, J. Boss animal man, John Robinson's, 1882.

DOOLITTLE. Rider and partner with **John B. Green** in

84

Green & Doolittle, 1825. Went into the menagerie business the following year.

DORIAN, ALFRED. Contortionists, glass eater, sword walker and "all-around circus freak." Cooper, Jackson & Co., 1883; Frank A. Gardner's, West Indies, 1884; Holland & McMahon, 1887; Dan Shelby's, fall 1888; Orrin Bros.', winter 1888-89; Frank A. Gardner's, Central and South America, 1888-89; F. J. Taylor's, 1892; John Robinson's, 1892-93; Pubillones', Havana, winter 1892-93; Sells Bros.', 1894; LaPearl's, 1894; W. H. Harris' Nickel-Plate, 1895; Sands & Ashley, 1895. Married **Bertha Harrod**, aerialist, Virginia, IL, May 9, 1894, but the marriage lasted only about 2 years. Connected with M. L. Clark's, 1896, until he left, June 27, and killed himself some days later by taking poison. Failed marriage had led to dissipation.

DORIN, W. F. Business manager, Shedman Bros.', 1894.

DORIS, ED F. Dr. James L. Thayer's, 1880.

DORIS, E. S. Doris' winter circus, Forty-second Street, NYC, 1830 (E. S. Doris, proprietor; John B. Doris, manager).

DORIS, JOHN B.: (January 14, 1848-February 6, 1912.) Native of Vermont. Ran away from home and joined Dan Rice's at the age 14. 1863, while still very young, purchased privileges with **George Batcheller** for the Dan Rice show. After accruing sufficient capital, Batcheller & Doris launched a circus, 1865, which continued successfully for 20 years. Bought out his partner, 1881, and went out as John B. Doris' until 1889, before disbanding and opening the Doris Museum, Eighth Ave., between 27th and 28th Streets, NYC. Ran the establishment for 12 years and then sold out to the proprietors of Huber's Museum on 14th Street. Obtained control of Princess Theatre, 29th and Broadway, where he produced *Orange Blossom* to no success. Subsequently, became manager to **May Robson, Wilton Lackaye** and other stars. Married to **Ella E. Stokes,** daughter of circus man **Spencer Q. Stokes,** 1887. They had no children. Died at his home, NYC.

DORIS, MARGARET. Equestrienne, Barnum & Bailey, 1892.

DORIS, WILLIAM J. (d. August 3, 1913) Privileges, Walter L. Main's, 1901; sideshow and privilege manager, Buckskin Bill's Wild West, 1902. Died age 57.

DORR, EMMA. Slack-wire, Ringling Bros.', 1891; ascensionist, Young Bros. & Baldwin, 1892.

DORR FAMILY [William, Josie, William, Jr.]. Robinson's Combined Shows, 1892; Great American Circus, 1893; Fulford & Co., 1890; Sieber & Cole, 1891; J. M. Barry's Great American Circus, 1894; W. F. Kirkhart's, 1895; Great Eastern, 1896. **William H. Dorr** (July 1862-November 18, 1896) aerialist and general performer, born in San Francisco, CA. Perch and brother act, Barnum & London, 1884-85. Died while performing with Frank A. Gardner's, St. Pierre, Martinique, West Indies, age 34. **Josie** had trained dogs, featuring her riding dog, Beauty, with J. M. Barry's Great American, 1894.

DORR, HENRY. Gymnast, treble horizontal bars, Cooper, Bailey & Co., 1876.

DORR, HOWARD. Gymnast and posturer. Batcheller & Doris, 1870; San Francisco Circus, 1872; Cooper, Bailey & Co., 1876; Great Roman Hippodrome, 1877; Anderson & Co., 1879; Batcheller & Doris, 1880.

DOTRELLA, SIGNOR. Iron jaw man, W. W. Cole's, 1886.

DOUGHERTY, HUGH. Double somersault leaper, Bailey & Winan, 1890.

DOUGLASS, PROF. Band leader, Gardner, Kenyon & Robinson, 1869.

DOUVILLIER. Cayetano's Co., in New Orleans, summer 1817. Had worked as an actor for Philip Lailson, NYC, 1797.

DOWD, CATHERINE. (1832-May 25, 1886) Fat woman. Born in Ireland. Exhibited with various circuses and museums. At one time weighed nearly 400 pounds. Died in NYC.

DOWD, PROF. Strong man, Robbins & Colvin, 1881.

DOWD, TOM. Member of variety troupe with Haight & Chambers, 1867.

DOWN, SIGNOR. Knockabout clown, Walter L. Main's, 1887-88.

DOWNIE, ALEXANDER. (April 9, 1806-March 29, 1843) Trampoline performer. Born in NYC. Joined Aaron Turner's as clown, 1820, and on horseback executed the feat of somersaulting from a mount at full speed. 1829, threw 21 "jerk forwards" off a vaulting board at the Washington Circus, Philadelphia. Also 7 forward off a swing at Blanchard's Amphitheatre, NYC, 1830, and gave "the clown's act on horseback, with the sailor's description of a fox-chase." A very popular entertainer who once threw 80 somersaults without stopping. Married a **Miss Montgomery**, an actress at the Bowery Theatre, NYC, 1838. Their daughter, **Louise**, born in 1841, was a drum performer. Price & Simpson, 1824-25; Washington Gardens, Boston, spring 1825; Lafayette Amphitheatre, NYC, 1825-26; William Harrington's, 1825; Parson's Amphitheatre, Albany, 1826; Parsons' Albany Circus, Troy, NY, 1828; William Harrington's, touring the West, summer 1829; William Blanchard's, 1830; clown, Fogg & Stickney, 1830-32; clown, Green & Brown, 1834; Bancker & Harrington, 1835; leaper, Brown's, 1835-36; clown, the winter circus, Richmond Hill, NYC, 1837; clown, Broadway Circus, NYC, 1840; Welch, Bartlett & Co., 1839-40; Henry Rockwell & Co., winter 1841. Died in Puerto Rico while with Welch's Circus.

DOWNIE, ANDREW [r. n. McPhee]. (August 13, 1863-December 17, 1930) Born in Stephens Township, near Exeter, Ontario, Canada. As a child, moved with his parents to Stratford, Ont. Learned to tumble in his father's barn. For years he did a "spade" dance and break-away ladder act in vaudeville. 1884, with **Clarence Austin,** launched Downie & Austin Parlor Circus, a one-ring affair. Ryan & Robinson, 1886; billed as the "human spider," Lowande & Hoffman, 1887; aerialist and clown, Irwin Bros.', 1887-88. Married **Christina**

Hewer in Guelph, Ontario, 1890, known as **Millie LaTena**. Had Diamond Minstrels on the road, 1891; following season, took out Andrew Downie's Dog and Pony Circus; Downie & Gallagher's Shows (Andrew Downie, **J. P. Gallagher**, proprietors), 1891-92; Downie's New United Shows, 1893; end of 1902 season, took a repertoire company through Canada and later a Tom show; fall 1910, shipped his show to Oxford, PA, where he combined with **Al F. Wheeler** for the Downie & Wheeler Shows, 1911-13. 1914, launched the LaTena Wild Animal Circus, a 10-car show; 1916, the show was enlarged to 15 cars. Winter 1917-18, leased the title of the Walter L. Main circus and in 3 years made a fortune. Use of the title expired at the end of the 1921 season, at which time retirement was planned by purchasing 2,200 acres of land in Northwestern Canada with the expectation of developing it for sale. Sold his circus equipment to the Miller brothers of the 101 Ranch fame, 1924. 1926, took out a railroad circus under his own name which he operated until 1930. One of the first circuses to adopt motorized travel, the Downie Bros. Motorized Circus. Died at his home in Medina, NY, age 67.

DOWNIE, BEN. Stow, Long & Gumble, 1889.

DOWNIE BROTHERS. Tight-wire act, Reese, Levis & Dolphin, 1885.

DOWNS, GEORGE. Acrobat. American Arena, Washington, DC, winter 1828-29; William Harrington's, touring the West, summer 1829; rider, Harrington & Buckley, 1830; rider, John Lamb's, 1831; Yeaman's, 1833; Joseph D. Palmer's, 1833, 1835-36; Palmer & Harrington, 1834.

DRAKE, B. M. Contracting agent, Ringling Bros.', 1891-92.

DRAKE, W. O. "MASTER". W. Gates & Co., 1838.

DRAPER FAMILY. Trick bicycle riders, Shedman Bros.', 1894.

DRAYTON, HERR CHARLES. General performer. Cannon ball act, John Wilson's, 1875; tumbler and leaper, Montgomery Queen's, 1877; Orrin Bros.', Havana, winter 1877-78; cannon ball, Adam Forepaugh's, 1879; animal tamer, W. C. Coup's, 1880-82; Orrin Bros.', Mexico, winter 1882-83; Sells Bros.', 1883; Pullman & Dingess, 1885; Frank H. Rich's, 1886; Oliver's, 1892; W. F. Kirkhart's, 1895; (with wife **Madeline**) Howes' London, 1896; Donovan & Long, Central America, winter 1896-97; Ringling Bros.', 1889; the Haag Circus, 1899; cannon ball performer and foot juggler, Gollmar Bros., 1900.

DREW, BILLY. One of Bunnell's Minstrels, R. Sands', 1863.

DREW, FRANK. Assistant to **James L. Hutchinson** with privileges, VanAmburgh's, 1876.

DREW, FRANK. Clown, Dan Rice's, 1860. Married **Estella Barclay**, an equestrienne with the show, that year. Was also an actor.

DREW, GEORGE E. Hebrew-dialect clown, with John B. Doris', 1883.

DREXEL, W. Strong man, Stone & Rosston, 1865; Stone, Rosston & Murray, 1867; Stone & Murray, 1869.

DRIESBACH, HERR JACOB. (November 2, 1807-December 5, 1877) Wild beast tamer of renown. Born in Sharon, NY. In youth was a "runner" for the Albany boats. Entered the circus business about 1842 with Raymond & Waring, and continued, as the show changed hands to Raymond & Weeks and on to VanAmburgh's and Herr Driesbach's Menagerie for some 20 years. Was said to be the first man to train a leopard. Walked the streets with one, which had "a string tied to it" in the shape of a chain. Taught the animal to attack him in the cage while he was working a lion. During the winter season, 1853-54, Driesbach was in NYC with Raymond & Weeks' menagerie on Broadway, south of Spring Street. Clarry & Reilly, printers, made their first bill in four colors for him. Married a non-professional from Wooster, OH, around 1856, and entered into the occupation of farming. Also kept a hotel nearby, which was always a refuge for itinerant showmen. Possibly the first wild beast tamer recorded by photography. By 1873, was living in retirement at Apple Creek Station, Wayne County, OH, where he died, age 70.

DRISCO, PROF. R. H. Zoological director, Howe's Great London, 1874.

DU BOIS, EMMA. Trapeze artist, Sells Bros.', 1885; S. H. Barrett's, 1887.

DU BOIS, FREDERICK A. Agent, Dr. James L. Thayer's, 1869.

DU BOIS, LOUISE. Equestrienne, George F. Bailey & Co., 1859.

DU BOIS, PAULINE. Female Hercules, with Main & VanAmburgh, 1890.

DU BOIS, PIERRE. Strong man, James M. Nixon's, 1870. Performed a feat of firing off a 700 pound cannon placed upon his shoulders.

DU BOIS, WILLIAM A. Keeper, Philadelphia Zoological Garden (for **James Raymond**), 1844; Raymond & Waring, 1845.

DUBSKY, ROSINA. Equestrienne and tight-rope performer. Principal pad rider, Adam Forepaugh's, 1881; Batcheller & Doris, 1882; Orrin Bros'., Mexico, winter 1883-84; Frank A. Robbins', 1885; T. Sidley's, 1885; Sparrow's, 1886; Frank A. Robbins', 1888. Husband died in Cuba, April 1880. Married **James Murray** a few years later.

DUCELLO, DAN. Proprietor, Dan Ducello's, 1876-79. Performed lions, etc.

DUCHACK, L. J. Proprietor and manager, L. J. Duchack's New London Railroad Shows, 1889.

DUCROW, BELLOTA. Frank A. Gardner's, South America, 1889.

DUCROW BROTHERS. John Wilson's Palace Amphitheatre, San Francisco, 1874.

DUCROW, CHARLES. Dr. James L. Theyer's, 1880.

DUCROW, CLARENCE. Somersault rider, San Francisco Circus, 1872.

DUCROW, DAN. (1855-August 11, 1930) Acrobat and clown. Born in California. Joined the Great World Circus as a trick mule rider when he was 9 years old. Toured the Orient and Australia with the Pioneer Circus. Acrobat, Montgomery Queen's; later, with McIntyre & Heath when the team was with Sells Bros.'; Orrin Bros.', Mexico; Pubillones', Havana, winter 1884-85; performing donkeys, Frank A. Gardner's, South America, 1889. Was also with Barnum & Bailey and Ringling Bros.' with his brother, **Toto**, as **Ducrow Brothers** clown act. The act broke up when Toto went into the movies. Died in Pittsburgh, PA, age 75.

DUCROW, EDGAR. Stickney's Grand National, 1848.

DUCROW FAMILY. Frank A. Gardner's, South American, 1888.

DUCROW, GEORGIE. Baby hurdle rider, L. B. Lent's New York Circus, 1867-68.

DUCROW, GUSTAVE. George F. Bailey & Co., 1863.

DUCROW, JAMES. Ed G. Basye's,1878.

DUCROW, LOUIS. Frank A. Gardner's, South America, 1889.

DUCROW, MASTER EDGAR. Lee & Bennett's, San Francisco, 1856-57.

DUCROW, MRS. WILLIAM. See Belle Celeste.

DUCROW, WILLIAM J. [r. n. William Johnson]. (1845?-September 25, 1909) After apprenticing to L. B. Lent, took the name of Ducrow. General performer, John Robinson's, 1857-62; L. B. Lent's, 1859-62, 1864, 1867-68, 1874, 1876; Goodwin & Wilder, Boston, 1861; L. B. Lent's Broadway Amphitheatre, NYC, 1862, winter, 1863-64; Spalding & Rogers, New Orleans, winter 1864-65; Stone & Murray, 1871; equestrian director, Burr Robbins', 1879-80; VanAmburgh's, 1881; W. C. Coup's, 1882; ringmaster, Barnum & London, 1884; Pubillones', Havana, winter 1885-86; equestrian director, Barnum & Bailey, 1887-88, where he presented a trained zebra act; equestrian director, Adam Forepaugh's, 1893; Donovan's, in Cuba, winter 1894-95; equestrian director, Barnum & Bailey, London, 1898; equestrian director, Barnum & Bailey, 1908. Married **Belle Celeste** while both were appearing with Lent's New York Circus, Boston, May 18, 1874. Died at the Elk's National Home, age 64.

DUFFEE. Black performer who displayed leaping agility, horsemanship, and vaulting, with feats such as leaping over a hoop and whip, dancing the hornpipe, and dashing around the ring on the tips of his toes. An apprentice with Pepin & Breschard, 1809; went with Cayetano Mariotini's group to Newburyport and Exeter, MA, and Portsmouth, NH, in the spring of 1810 and returned to NYC in time to rejoin Pepin & Breschard for the company's opening, June 21; with Cayetano & Co. in Canada, fall 1811-13, and Pepin, Breschard & Cayetano, NYC, summer 1813; then went with the company to Philadelphia for the fall season; with Pepin, Breschard & Cayetano, Baltimore, winter 1813-14; Pittsburgh and Cincinnati beginning in the spring, 1814. Turned up with a small troupe performing in Chillicothe, OH, August 1815, where he "rode on his head with his feet in the air" and executed the "Lion's Leap" through a hoop and over two swords. At New Orleans with Cayetano, 1816, performing his trick horse, Colin. By beginning of 1817, had left Cayetano's company.

DUFFY, COL. OWEN. Boss canvasman, Maginley & Co., 1874.

DUGANE, C. E. Program agent, S. P. Stickney & Son's, 1874.

DULHAUER, WILLIE. Contortionist, the Great New York, 1877.

DUMILIEU, VICTOR. Magician, J. Purdy Brown's, 1827.

DUMONT, PAULINE. *Manège*, S. H. Barrett's, 1887.

DUMONT, W. H. (1860?-January 2, 1900) Advertiser, Barnum & Bailey, 1895. Later, was superintendent of Keith's Union Square Theatre, NYC. Died of pneumonia at his home in NYC, age about 40.

DUNBAR, ALONZO. Property master, P. T. Barnum's, 1879.

DUNBAR, GEORGE [r. n. George A. Nice]. (January 26, 1830-September 27, 1884) Light balancer, acrobat, clown, and general performer. Born in Baltimore where his father was captain of a Chesapeake Bay schooner. Entered the profession at an young age and remained almost until his death. Juggler, Chinese equilibrist and posturer, Mann, Welch & Delavan, 1845-47; Spalding & Rogers, 1850, advertised as "the most expert equilibrist and necromancer of the age"; gymnast, (with **Magilton** and **Donaldson**) again with Spalding & Rogers, 1855; Dunbar and **Magilton** together, Sands, Nathans & Co., Bowery Circus, 1858; Dan Rice's, 1858. The two then made a successful European tour. In their *perche* act, Dunbar held the pole while Magilton performed at the top. Later, Magilton fell and was paralyzed. Member of the Donaldson Troupe, **Frank Donaldson**, **Miaco Brothers**, **Harry Bernard** and **Petite Angelo**, doing the Zampillaerostation. Also, Thayer & Noyes, winter 1865-66; [with **Rochford**] Whitby & Co., 1867; [with **Donaldson**] perch act, P. T. Barnum's, 1871; one of the original **Four Russian Athletes**, organized around 1872; perch, Barnum, Bailey & Hutchinson, 1882. Considered one of the finest light balancers of his time, he was tall and well formed and could twist himself into "fantastic" shapes. [John A. Dingess: The team of Dunbar and Henry Magilton were outstanding for "uniqueness, activity and originality of their movements.... As an equilibrist he had no equal in the world."] Died of consumption and in poverty at his residence, NYC.

DUNBAR, GEORGE W. [r. n. William Gerhardt]. (1844?-October 10, 1916) Aerialist. Native of Johnstown, PA. Barrett & Co., 1882; Cantellis & Leon, Havana, 1882; W. W. Cole's, 1883; Welsh Bros.', 1897; Barnum & Bailey, England, 1898;

Major Gordon's, 1910. Beginning around 1890, performed with his wife, **Della Dunbar**, known as the **Flying Dunbars**, double trapeze performers. Della died in Brooklyn, NY, May 24, 1898, age 33, having performed with her husband for about 8 years prior to her death. George died in NYC, age 72.

DUNBAR, JOHN. Purchased M. O'Connor & Co.'s Great Western Circus, September 1, 1871. Was a resident of Swan City, NE.

DUNBAR, R. Adam Forepaugh's, 1878.

DUNBAR, THEODORE. (d. May 25, 1881) Gymnast, acrobat and leaper. While traveling with a circus, 1879, was accused of robbery and sent to prison for a 12 year sentence. Died of consumption in the penitentary, Columbus, OH.

DUNBAR, WILLIAM. Property master, Barnum, Bailey & Hutchinson, 1882.

DUNGEE, MRS. ANTHONY. Strong woman. Appeared in NYC, August 1753, with her husband. Called "The Female Samson," her performance consisting of extending her body between 2 chairs and bearing the weight of 300 lbs. on her chest, which was struck with sledge hammers by 2 men. From the same position, she bore the weight of 6 men. She lifted an anvil by her hair and perform other feats of strength.

DUNGEE ANTHONY JOSEPH. Wire-walker. Performed in NYC, August 1753, in the new exhibition hall of Adam Van-Denberg. While on the slack-wire, balanced 7 pipes on his nose, balanced a straw on the head of a drinking glass, juggled balls, and danced the hornpipe.

DUNHAM, C. L. American Hippocolosiculum (Thompson, Smith & Hawes, proprietors), 1866.

DUNHAM, D. F. Proprietor and manager, D. F. Dunham's European Circus, 1875; privileges, Hilliard & Hunting, 1877.

DUNN. Rider, Frost & Co., 1837.

DUNN, IRA. Rider, Robert Davis' circus venture, Salem, MA, February. 1810; back with Davis & Co., Boston, October 1815, billed as a one-legged acrobat.

DUNN, MARTIN. (January 3, 1832-September 24, 1884) Native of Portland, ME. Was for several seasons manager for Yankee Robinson's and L. B. Lent's. After leaving the profession, went into the express business. Died in NYC.

DUNN, MICHAEL. Boss canvasman, Curtis' Great Roman Hippodrome, 1877.

DUNN, R. J.: H. Buckley & Co., 1857-58.

DUNNIVAN, J. Contracting agent, S. H. Barrett's, 1885.

DU NORD, MME. Female lion tamer, Hemmings, Cooper & Whitby, 1868.

DUNSWORTH, CHARLES M. Gardner & Donovan, South America, 1886; Roberts & Gardner, 1886; Frank A. Gardner's; Central and South America, winter 1887-88.

DUPE, RICHARD. Contortionist, Harry Thayer & Co.'s, 1890.

DUPONT BROTHERS [Thomas, William, Master Henry].

Triple brother act, Lowande's Brazilian Circus, South America, 1880.

DUPONT, LOUIS. Contortionist, Great American Circus, Museum and Menagerie, 1893.

DUPREE, CHARLOTTE. Slack-wire, Pepin & West at the Olympic Circus, Philadelphia, fall 1817, this being her American debut. Remained with James West's management 1818-22, the latter year being West's final appearance in America. The following year, Simpson & Price, Philadelphia and Baltimore.

DUPREE, EUGENE. Hurdle rider, H. M. Smith's, 1870.

DUPUE, BILLY. Clown, Collins' Oriental Combination, 1877.

DUPUE, GEORGE. Rider, Collins' Oriental Combination, 1877.

DUPUE, MILLIE. Equestrienne, Collins' Oriental Combination, 1877.

DURAND, ANNIE. Jockey and *manège* act, Gollmar Bros.', 1895.

DURAND, A. P. General performer, Howes & Mabie, 1845; Robinson & Eldred, 1847, 1849; Spalding & Rogers, 1852-54; Yankee Robinson's, 1857; Nixon & Kemp, 1858; Joe Pentland's, 1859 (had teamed with **Painter** since 1855). Following year, the two were with the Aymar brothers (**Walter** and **William**) when they went to California and were engaged with John Wilson's organization under the banner of Dan Rice's Circus, 1860-62; performed in South and Central America, Bassett & Aymar, 1861; Orrin Bros.', San Francisco, 1863; (with **Painter**) Bay View Park, San Francisco, 1866; Lee & Ryland's Hippodrome, San Francisco, 1866.

DURAND, J. H. Broadway Amphitheatre, 1857; Bowery Circus, NYC, January 1858.

DURAND, LOUIS. Morosco's Royal Russian Circus, 1885.

DURAND, MLLE. Buckley & Co., 1857.

DURAND SISTERS. Statuary posing, Gollmar Bros.', 1893.

DURAND, WILLIAM W. (1837-December 10, 1886) Press agent. Born in Indiana and educated at White River Academy. Printer and journalist under **George D. Prentice** at the Louisville *Journal* and a drug clerk there for a time during the Civil War. Later, was on the editorial staff of the Cincinnati *Press.* Entered the circus business as a press agent about 1867. Great Eastern, 1872-74; P. T. Barnum's Hippodrome, 1875; Adam Forepaugh's, 1876; Great London, 1878; Adam Forepaugh's, 1879, 1885-86; J. H. Haverly's minstrel company, winter 1879-80; then Cooper & Bailey, 1880; Barnum, Bailey & Hutchinson, 1881-84, 1886. In the 1880s was said to draw a larger salary than anyone connected with the show, at times $7,000 a year and expenses. [Louis E. Cooke: "Billy Durand, as he was usually called, was one of the most congenial fellows I have ever happened to meet, and I shall never forget the kindly manner in which I was greeted by him when I first entered the circus field and came in contact with him in op-

88

position work."] It was announced, 1877, that he was operating a grocery store in Bloomington, IN. Died at the railway station in Indianapolis while managing the Museum in that city. As an agent, was considered one of the best writers in the business; copy was always forceful and original. [Charles H. Day: "He smoked like a chimney and chewed plug tobacco.... He is a sledge-hammer writer and, in opposition, goes in for knock-down blows and has more force and ability to a square inch than half a dozen inflated, self-conceited windbags, who call themselves circus writers."]

DURANG, JOHN. Acrobat, clown and wire walker. Ricketts', Philadelphia, 1795-1800. With **Lewis DeGraff**, gave limited circus performances in Philadelphia, July 1800, and at Leaman's Columbia Garden, Baltimore, summer and fall 1805. The company closed at Leaman's October 8, and opened at the Pantheon in that city, giving performances until January 20, 1806. Left the first memoir of American circus life.

DURO, MME. Female Hercules, Irwin Bros.', 1887.

DUSCHACK, I. J. Proprietor, Duschack's, 1889.

DU SOLLE. Olympic Circus, Philadelphia, July 2, 1817 for a short engagement.

DUTCHER, CHARLEY. (d. June 1, 1889) P. T. Barnum's.

DUTTON, ARTHUR. Infant son of **William Dutton**, L. B. Lent's, 1868.

DUTTON, DOLLIE. (d. January 6, 1890) Midget. 29" high, weighed 15 pounds.

DUTTON, EFFIE. Equestrienne. Howes' Great London, 1897; John Robinson's, 1898; 1900, 1907.

DUTTON, JAMES. Somersault rider. Howe's Great London, 1897; John Robinson's, 1907.

DUTTON, SAWYER. W. W. Cole's, 1886.

DUTTON, SILAS. Co-proprietor (with **J. R. Smith**), Great Chicago, 1879; Silas Dutton's Southern Circus, winter 1879-80.

DUTTON SISTERS. Equestriennes, Sells & Rentfrow's, 1893. May have been **William Dutton's** daughters.

DUTTON, WILLIAM, JR. Rider. Son of the well known rider, equestrian director. Principal double somersault leaper, Cooper & Co.'s Great United Shows (**J. R. W. Hennessey**, proprietor and manager), 1897; leaper, Sells & Downs, 1905. Wife was Helene Smith. Son was born June 1, 1880.

DUTTON, WILLIAM, M. SR. (1843-December 24, 1906) Equestrian and general performer. Born in Toronto, Canada. Made circus debut, 1860, at the old Wood's Theatre, Cincinnati, for winter season of Lake & Robinson. John Robinson's, 1861-65; National Circus, Cincinnati, winter 1864-65; George W. DeHaven's, 1865; William Lake's, 1866; Yankee Robin

son's, Chicago, fall 1866; Hitchcock & Cushing, 1867; equestrian director, G. W. DeHaven's, 1866-67; somersault rider, L. B. Lent's, 1868, 1871-72; P. T. Barnum's, 1871; W. W. Cole's, 1874; rider, Adam Forepaugh's, 1875-78; Orrin Bros.', Havana, winter 1878-79; Cooper & Bailey, 1879-80; Barnum, Bailey & Hutchinson, 1881-82; William O. Dale Stevens', Park Square, Boston, spring 1883; Barnum & Bailey, 1885-86; W. W. Cole's, 1886; somersault bareback rider, Doris & Colvin, 1887; Sells & Rentfrow's, 1893 [Orin Copple King: Advertised as "performing at will forward and backward somersaults on the bare back of his swiftly running steed. One of the most dashing Equestrains (sic) of the age, engaged at an enormous salary to ride at each performance of this faultless exhibition."]. Equestrian director, Hummel & Hamilton, October 1896; equestrian director, Howes' Great London, 1897; the Haag Circus, 1899; equestrian director, John Robinson's, 1900. Claimed to have performed a triple somersault with William Lake's in rehearsal at Elkhorn, Illinois, 1860. Vaulted over 12 horses, John Robinson's, August 12, 1865. With Lake's, Lowell, IN, fall 1866, succeeded in turning a triple somersault from a spring board. Dutton's riding was described as elegant and graceful, and his somersaults accomplished with remarkable ease. Was married, 1865, in Chicago to **Iza Stowe**. She died of Bright's disease in NYC, February 1873. Sons **Arthur** and **William Dutton Jr.** survived that union. A second wife, **Helena Smith**, was the daughter of **William Smith, Sr.**, 4-horse circus rider. While with John Robinson's, was assulted on October 18, 1906, in Cincinnati, OH, and suffered from a fractured skull. Died at the Galt House, Cincinnati, a few months later, age 63, having never recovered from his accident.

DUVAL BROTHERS [Clifton, Livingston, Eugene]. Triple horizontal bars, Den W. Stone's, 1878.

DUVAL, MME. Iron jaw lady, S. H. Barrett's, 1887.

DUVAL, MONS. Contortionist, Antonio Bros.', 1660-61.

DUVERNEY, WILLIAM [or Duverna]. Contortionist. Was called "the greatest dislocationist in existance," while with Cooke's Royal Amphitheatre (James M. Nixon, proprietor), Niblo's Garden, NYC, 1860; James M. Nixon's, 1860; R. Sands, 1861; Goodwin & Wilder, Howard Athenaeum, Boston, 1861; Spalding & Rogers, West Indies, 1862-64; Hippotheatron, NYC, with Spalding & Rogers, spring 1864; Hippotheatron, NYC, fall 1864; Chiarini's, New Orleans and Havana, fall 1866, and Mexico City, fall 1867, San Francisco, 1868.

DWYER, W. H. Manager, G. G. Grady's, 1873; manager, Great Australian, 1877.

E

EAGAN, JOHN R.. (1853-1921) Was brought from Iowa to Delavan, WI, as a young boy where he was befriended by **Eugene B. Hollister**, who was traveling with Yankee Robinson's. Bought the ticket selling privilege, Buckley's, 1874; Buckley-Colvin's, 1875; Centennial Circus, 1876. Retired from the circus business and bought a store in LaCrosse, WI, known as Racketts, which was a forerunner of the five and ten variety store. Some time later, bought the bank in Darrien, WI, and became a highly respected civic leader.

EAGLE, HENRY A. (1850-1938) Partner, with **Theodore J. Sullivan,** of Sullivan & Eagle, makers of parade wagons for small to medium size traveling amusements. First organized in 1879, the firm operated from 1880 into the 1910s. Their output included at least 8 steam calliopes to various shows.

EAGLES J. Boss hostler, John Robinson's, 1882-93.

EARLE SISTERS [Hazel, Maude]. Trapeze and contortion act. Orrin Bros.', Mexico, 1889; Frank A. Gardner's, South America, 1896; Robinson-Franklin, 1897; Great Wallace, 1899; Sells & Gray, 1900-01. Their mother was **Lola**, a gymnast.

EARLO, FRANK. Singing clown, Gollmar Bros.', 1897.

EATON,, E. K. (d. March, 1898) Band leader, Sands, Lent & Co., 1846.

EATON, GEN. Agent, Handy & Welch, touring the West Indies and South America, 1829.

EATON, GILBERT "GIL". (d. October 16, 1866) Agent. Son of **Erasmus Eaton**, wealthy citizen of Troy, NY, and senior member of the great car building firm there. Stone & McCollum, 1847-50; Driesbach's, 1856; partner with **Levi J. North**, 1860; Zorara Equirotator Circus, 1863; Tom King's, 1864. While staying at the Lincoln Hotel, Lincoln, IL, suffered a knife wound and died within a half-hour's time, murdered by a man named Warwick who had been drinking.

EBERLE, SOPHIE, HARRY, and **DAVID.** Brothers and sister. Price & Simpson, Washington Amphitheatre, Boston, 1826; Washington Gardens, Boston, summer 1827; Sandford's Mount Pitt Circus, Spring 1828; William Blanchard's troupe, 1829. **Sophie** was the wife of **Charles LaForrest.**

s, 1864. While staying at the Lincoln Hotel, Lincoln, IL, suffered a knife wound and died within a half-hour's time, murdered by a man named Warwick who had been drinking.

EBERLE, SOPHIE, HARRY, and **DAVID.** Brothers and sister. Price & Simpson, Washington Amphitheatre, Boston, 1826; Washington Gardens, Boston, summer 1827; Sandford's Mount Pitt Circus, Spring 1828; William Blanchard's troupe, 1829. **Sophie** was the wife of **Charles LaForrest.**

ECKLES, FRANK. Program agent, W. W. Cole's, 1875.

ECTOR, LUCIAN. See Tremaine Brothers.

EDDY, J. Acrobat, John Robinson's, 1886-87.

EDGAR, J. Rider, Dan Rice's, 1851.

EDGERTON, GEORGE. Equestrian director, Harry Thayer & Co.'s, 1890.

EDSON, CALVIN. (1789-1833) Curiosity, billed as "The Living Skeleton." Born in Stafford, CT. Exhibition weight was 58 pounds to a standing height of 5 '3". Formerly weighting 135 pounds, Edson attributed his loss to sleeping on a damp ground following the battle of Plattsburgh. First stage appearance, old Chatham Theatre, NYC, as Jeremiah Thin in *Rochester*, May 1830. Performed the same role in Philadelphia, June 24, 1830.

EDWARDS, C. Horizontal bars, Harry Thayer & Co.'s, 1890.

EDWARDS, TOM. Business agent, with G. G. Grady's, 1871.

EDWARDS, BILLY and **BLANCHE.** Irwin Bros.', 1888.

EDWARDS, D. S. John Robinson's, 1871.

EDWARDS, FRANK [r. n. Edward Francis Maitland McQuad]. (April 22, 1834-October 1, 1893) Agent. Born in Scotland and came to America, 1846, with his parents. Entered into show business as manager for **Jennie Reynolds**, noted Scotch vocalist. Metchear & Cameron, 1870; also L. B. Lent's; Stone, Rosston & Murray; Howes & Cushing, Charles W. Noyes', Dan Castello's, Great American, and Great Australian. Married **Lizzie Coleman** of Syracuse, NY, 1886. Died of Bright's disease in Rochester, NY.

EDWARDS, GEORGE H. Sideshow performer, VanAmburgh's, 1866; pantomimist, Stone & Murray, 1870.

EDWARDS, HARRY. Yankee Robinson's, 1859.

EDWARDS, ROBERT. Singer, Welch & Mann, 1846.

EDWARDS, SAMUEL G. (d. August, 1914) Rider. P. T. Barnum's, Forepaugh-Sells', and Ringling Bros.'

EDWARDS, THOMAS A. ["Col."]. (July 21, 1832-December 23, 1904) Born in Ulster County, NY. Began his circus career as business manager for Spalding & Rogers, 1849, and remained with the firm until 1857. Left to join an expedition with Gen. Albert Sidney Johnson against the Mormons, as scout and dispatch bearer. Served in the Civil War and afterward as scout and Indian fighter. Contracting agent, G. G. Grady's, 1871; toured the country with **Donald McKay** and a band of Warm Spring Indians in the war drama, *Donald McKay, the Hero of the Lava Beds*, 1872. Took the show to Europe, 1874; with the company, 1876, at the opening of the Philadelphia Centennial Exhibition. Same year, organized a medicine show with **McKay** and **Kit Carson**, the Oregon Indian Medicine Co., which he managed until his death in Corry, PA.

EDWARDS, WILLIAM [r. n. William James Conley]. (d.

June 9, 1896) Gymnast and acrobat. Started as top mounter for the **Stirk Family**, bicyclists, and also as a 3 brother act. With the Minor & Rooney Co., 1881-82; following, joined Healy & Biglow, performing with their shows in Boston and NYC for 2 years; Adam Forepaugh's in a Japanese ladder act with a partner; later, associated with **Frank L. Long** doing a flying trapeze act and, as **Long & Edwards**, traveled in the United States and South America for 5 years. Also with such circuses as John V. O'Brien's, Irwin Bros.', Barnum & Bailey, Frank A. Gardner's, Nick Roberts', W. O'Dale Stevens', and Pubillone's. Later, Walter L. Main's, 1889; pyramid of tables and horizontal bars, Frank A. Gardner's, South America, winter 1892-93. Died in Boston after having been in the business for 16 years.

EGGLESTON [or Eagleston]. Vaulter, Price & Simpson's, 1827; strong man, Washington Circus, Philadelphia, 1828; Fogg & Stickney, Washington Amphitheatre, Philadelphia, 1830.

EGGLESTON, L. Charles Lee's, 1893.

ELBRECK, R. E. Assistant manager and treasurer, W. H. Stowe's, 1881.

ELEBRADO, DAN. Boss hostler, New York and New England, 1884.

EL NINO EDDIE. See Eddie Rivers.

ELCHERETHE, MLLE. Trained monkeys, W. C. Coup's Equescurriculum, 1887.

ELDER, WILLIAM. Scottish sports (with **Crossley**), W. C. Coup's, winter 1878-79; Cooper, Bailey & Co., 1879-80; (with **Crossley**), leaper, Barnum, Bailey & Hutchinson, 1881-84-85.

ELDRED, EDWARD SPENCER. (1811-1850) Brother of **Gilbert** and **Hiram Eldred**. Born in Pawnal, VT. Early on, operated boats on the Erie Canal and was also connected with the J. W. Butterfield stage coach line. Opened a circus, Crane & Eldred's, 1834; also that year, Edward Eldred's American Circus; as a member of the Zoological Institute, was out with the Zoological Exhibition and American Circus, 1835; proprietor, Hoadley, Latham, Eldred & Co., 1838. Had 8 children, none of whom were connected with the circus business. Died in Newport, NY.

ELDRED, GILBERT NAZIAH "GIL". (1813-September 7, 1885) General performer—rider, clown, acrobat and horse trainer. Brother of **Edward** and **Hiram Eldred**. Came into the circus business as clown, 1834, for his brother, **Edward**. Clown, Ludlow & Smith, 1841; Robinson & Foster, 1842-44. Partner of old **John Robinson**, beginning 1845. Partnership came to an end in Richmond, VA, June 28, 1856, after 11 years together. The ultimately split caused ill feelings. At parting, Eldred declared to Robinson that within 5 years he would be the "richest showman in the world." As it happened, Robinson went on to make a fortune, while Eldred lost his show. [Stuart Thayer: He "made up in willingness what he

lacked in talent."] Between 1853-57, engaged in ceiling walking. Took out G. N. Eldred's Great Rotunda Southern Circus and Menagerie, the proprietors or partial owners being Sands, Nathans & Co., 1858. This group foreclosed on Eldred because he was unable to continue payment on menagerie animals Robinson & Eldred had leased in 1852. That year the show became one of the first American circuses to visit Mexico. Went to Europe, 1861, where he stayed for the remainder of his life, exhibiting trained horses, both in England and on the Continent until at least 1867. Died in Sunderland, England, age 72, a poor man.

ELDRED, HIRAM. Brother of **Edward** and **Gilbert**. Agent for the Eldred circus.

ELDRIDGE, JEANETTE. *Manège*, Wallace & Anderson, 1890.

ELDRIDGE, W. S. 2-horse rider, P. T. Barnum's. Married **Lulu Lewis** in St. Louis, September 12, 1875.

ELLINGHAM, ROBERT [performed at times as Robert White]. (October 10, 1819-February 18, 1892) Negro minstrel, Aaron Turner's, 1836; Brown & Mills, 1838; June, Titus, & Angevine, 1841-42; Sands, Lent & Co., 1846; Welch-Delavan-Nathans, 1849-50; ringmaster, Spalding & Rogers', 1853-57; VanAmburgh's, Broadway Theatre, NYC, winter 1857-58; James M. Nixon's, 1860; George Bailey & Co., 1862-66; equestrian director, Barnum, VanAmburgh and Castello, 1867; Dan Castello's, winter 1867-68; lecturer on natural history, VanAmburgh's, 1870-71; P. T. Barnum's, 1873; Cooper & Bailey, 1879-80; ringmaster, Barnum, Bailey & Hutchinson, 1881; Orrin Bros.', Mexico, winter 1881-82; Batcheller & Doris, 1882; Adam Forepaugh's, 1883. Gifted with a powerful voice. Died at Clarksville, MA.

ELLIOTT BROTHERS. Horizontal bar act, LaPearl's, 1897.

ELLIOTT, E. E. Contracting agent, W. W. Cole's, 1880.

ELLIOTT FAMILY [Kate, Polly, Anne, Maggie, Thomas, James, Mattie]. Bicycle and unicycle artists, Barnum & Bailey, 1883; Barnum & London, 1884; W. C. Coup's, 1887.

ELLIOTT, JESSE C. (d. November 8, 1922) Co-partner and ticket agent, Fulford & Co.'s Great United London Shows (**A. K. Fulford**, **William McClintock**, **W. M. Lyttle**, Jesse C. Elliott, proprietors), 1890. Prior to this, had operated a sporting goods store in Topeka, KA. The show was on the road only one season, after which Elliott went back to dealing in sporting goods. In 1907, opened Topeka's second nickelodeon and later acquired the Crystal, Aurora, and Isis Theatres in that city.

ELLIS, CHARLES H. Acrobat, leaper and tumbler. Campbell's, 1869; John H. Murray's, 1873-74; leaper, Great London, 1880; general agent, Miles Orton, 1888.

ELLIS, CHARLES T. Dutch comedian, Palace of Wonders, P. T. Barnum, 1876; concert privilege, New York Central Park Circus, 1877; Cooper, Bailey & Co., 1880.

ELLIS, ROBERT. Elephant handler, Great Eastern, 1872.

ELLSBEY, MABLE. Performing ponies, dogs, goats, and monkeys, Washington Bros.', 1887.

ELLSLER, JAMES. Leaper. John W. Robinson's (not "Old John's"), 1870; Wootten & Haight, 1871.

ELLSLER, JEANETTE. Tight-rope walker. Feature attraction for Lee & Marshall, California, 1855-56; James A. Rowe's, California, 1857; Hinkley & Kimball, California, 1858; back East, Nixon & Co., winter, 1858-59; VanAmburgh's, winter 1859-60; Antonio Bros.', 1861; Goodwin & Wilder, Howard Athenaeum, Boston, winter, 1861-62; Goodwin & Wilder's North American, 1862; S. O. Wheeler's, 1863, 1865; Melville's Australian, 1864; Ben Maginley's, 1864; Stone, Rosston & Murray, 1868-71; J. W. Wilder's, 1873; North American Circus (**Asa B. Stow**, manager), 1873; rider, rope-walker, Montgomery Queen's, 1874. Married to clown **Nat Austin**. The two performed together for 20 years, but were divorced in the spring of 1876. See Nat Austin.

ELLSLER, LOUIS. Gymnast, John Tryon's, Bowery Amphitheatre, NYC, 1845.

ELLSLER, PROF. Aeronaut, Charles Noyes', winter 1871-72.

ELLSWORTH, GEORGE. Bayonet exercise or lightning drill, Cooper, Bailey & Co., 1880; Barnum, Bailey & Hutchinson, 1881; Leon & Dockrill, Iron Amphitheatre, Havana, winter 1881-82.

ELLWOOD, ROBERT. Lion performer, Sells Bros.', 1872.

ELMER, FRED. Triple bar performer, Lowande & Hoffman, 1887.

ELMORE, GEORGE. Boss canvasman, Alexander Robinson's, 1875.

ELMS, JAMES. Cannon ball performer, balancer, leaper and tumber, Cooper, Jackson, 1882.

ELTON BROTHERS [Sam, Albert, Frank]. Brother act, Barnum, Bailey & Hutchinson, 1882; aerialists, Adam Forepaugh's, 1884.

ELVIRA, MLLE. See Mrs. Richard Hemmings.

EMERSON, E. D. Boss canvasman, G. F. Bailey & Co., 1871-74.

EMERSON, WESLEY. Boss canvasman, Irwin Bros.', 1887; Robert Hunting's, 1894.

EMIDY, JOSEPH A. (1834?-December 26, 1905) Band leader. Born in Turo, Cornwall, England. As a young man traveled with the Sanger show. Was a master of the cornet but played the violin as well. Later, was leader of the band at the Crystal Palace, London, and at Agricultural Hall, Liverpool. Came to the USA, 1872, under contract to Montgomery Queen, and remained with the show until 1875. Became conductor with D. W. Stone's, 1878. Subsequently, retired from circus life to teach and compose music. For over 20 years was the leader of the Woonsocket, RI, cornet band. Died at his home there, age about 71.

EMIDY, RICHARD S. (June 16, 1837-November 13, 1885) Musician, brother of **Joseph A. Emidy**. Born in Turo, Cornwall, England. Howes' Great London, 1871-73; L. B. Lent's, 1874. Following this, traveled with several minstrel companies. Died in Chicago, .

EMILE, "MASTER." Rider, Pepin & Barnet, New Orleans, 1822-23.

EMMETT, DANIEL DECATUR. (October 26, 1815-June 28, 1904) Pioneer of negro minstrelsy and composer of the famous song, "Dixie." Born in Mt. Vernon, OH, where he was considered a boy prodigy with the fiddle. Ran away from home at the age of 14 to avoid learning the blacksmithing trade. About 4 years later made performing debut traveling with a circus—Cincinnati Circus of **Charles Rogers** as a member of the orchestra, 1840. During this period, learned to play the banjo from a man named **Ferguson**. Rejoined the Cincinnati Circus the following year, when he and **Frank Brower** were popular entertainers. This led to the organization of the famous Virginia Minstrels with Emmett, **Frank Brower**, **William Whitlock** and **Richard Pelham**. First public appearance was at the Chatham Theatre, NYC, for the benefit of Pelham, January 31, 1843. Performed dates in the United States before going to England to introduce negro minstrelsy there. The troupe soon split up. Emmett and Pelham went to Astley's Amphitheatre. Later, Emmett joined June & Sands' there for the remainder of the summer, 1843. Also had an engagement with Cooke's Circus. Sailed for NYC, September, 1844. Became a member of the Christy Minstrels for a time but beginning in 1858 was with Bryant's Minstrels for 7 years. Circus credits include Ethiopian performances with the eastern unit of June, Titus, Angevine & Co., 1842; banjoist, Nathan A. Howes' winter circus, 1842; banjoist, Ogden & Hobby, 1842; Dr. Gilbert R. Spalding's, 1842; banjoist, John Tryon's, Bowery Amphitheatre, NYC, 1845, 1846; Nathan A. Howes', Bowery Circus, 1845; Ethiopian performer, Nathan Howes', Bowery Circus, 1845-46; Howes & Co.'s, 1846; Dr. Gilbert R. Spalding's, 1847-48. In regard to the writing of "Dixie," Emmett is quoted as saying: "One Saturday night in 1859 while I was a member of Bryant's Minstrels at Mechanics' Hall, New York City, Dan Bryant came to me and asked 'Can't you get us up a walk-around for next week that we can do with one rehearsal, for we will have to put it in on Monday night.' Sunday I wrote 'Dixie' and called it 'I Wish I Was In Dixie' which was a Northern circus expression and not a Southern one as many have supposed." (the expression was used when cold weather set in on a season) Emmett, who made very little from the song, during the latter years of his life experienced poor circumstances. At this time he was a ward of **Al G. Field**. His farewell tour was with the Al G. Field's Minstrels. Field stated that Emmett would pore for hours over a book depicting historical military clashes, but rarely read a newspaper or magazine dealing with current events. Died at his home in Mt. Vernon, OH. His wife died in

Chicago, March 12, 1917, age 81.

EMMETT, HARRY. (d. January 4, 1872) Leaper and stilt performer, Backenstoe's. Died at Vicksburg, MS, of typhoid fever.

EMMETT, HARRY. Concert manager, Bailey & Winan, 1890.

EMMINGS, DOLLY. *Manège*, Gollmar Bros.', 1893.

EMMINGS, HARRY. Band leader, Gollmar Bros.', 1893.

ENGLEMAN, PAUL. Zoological director, Springer's, 1875.

ENOCHS, HARRY. Associate, Spalding & Rogers, 1858; VanAmburgh's, 1859; concert privilege, Adam Forepaugh's, 1868; inside and outside privileges, Hemmings, Cooper & Whitby, 1869; privileges, John V. O'Brien's, 1872; special agent, Adam Forepaugh's, 1888; Forepaugh's, 1894.

ENOCHS, JOE. Son of **Harry Enochs.** Horse dealer, Philadelphia, 1876; with his father on Adam Forepaugh's, 1894. 1881, started keeping a hotel, Atlantic City, known as "Enochs' Cottage."

ERWIN, BILLY. Maginley, Carroll & Co., 1867.

ERWIN, CHARLES L. Privileges, John Robinson's, 1889.

ERWIN, JAMES. (May 15, 1848-January 3, 1885) Sideshow manager. Born in Dublin, Ireland, but came to America as an infant. Entered the circus business as a sword swallower for a few years around 1865; then became an operator of his own sideshow. During the Civil War, was twice sentenced to be shot for dissertion; first time, as a mere boy, he was pardoned by President Lincoln; the second time, succeeded in escaping. Later years, was considered one of the best shots in Indiana. Was married once but the union was not a happy one. Died of pneumonia in Indianapolis.

ERWOOD, R. J. Conducted a one-ring circus on boat in the Ohio River, 1892.

ESAU. Bearded child, P. T. Barnum's, 1871.

ESSEN, JOHN. Cannon ball performer, John Robinson's, 1858.

ESSLER, JAMES. Ringmaster, Mabie's, 1857; Maginley & Bell, 1864; Maginley & Carroll, 1868; James Robinson's, 1874.

ETAW, CHINOWSKI. (1877?-October 24, 1893) Japanese juggler, Barnum & Bailey for 5 seasons, whose youthful feats attracted great attention. Died at age 16.

ETTA, MLLE. (May 8, 1857-June 1, 1883) Contortionist, vocalist, dancer and actress. Born in Syracuse, NY. Became a professional entertainer at the age of 8. United States Circus, 1867; hall shows until 1871 and variety theatres until 1876; J. E. Warner's, 1876; Pullman Bros.', 1877; Batcheller & Doris, 1879; Adam Forepaugh's, 1880; Denier's "Humpty Dumpty" troupe, 1881; John B. Doris', 1882; Barnum & Bailey, 1883. When with the latter, became ill and died, age 26. Was married to **Harry Blodgett.**

EUGENE BROTHERS [Emery, Tom]. Horizontal bar performers, Adam Forepaugh's, 1888-89.

EVANS, HARRY. Singing clown, Cooper & Co. (J. R. W. Hennessey, proprietor and manager), 1897.

EVANS, HAYSE. General contractor, Robert Hunting's, 1894.

EVANS, IRA. Treasurer, Stowe & Orton, 1870.

EVANS, ED. Clown, W. W. Cole's, 1885.

EVANS, JOHN D. (d. April 24, 1887) Contracting agent, America's Racing Association, 1875; candy stand privilege, W. W. Cole's, 1878, treasurer, 1881.

EVANS, MACK. Advance agent, Hunting's, 1889.

EVANS, THOMAS. (d. April 30, 1887) Evans' dog and Monkey Circus.

EVARTS, HARRY. (d. April 28, 1889) Press agent. Entered the show business as a performer with Dr. Gilbert R. Spalding's, 1847-48; Dan Rice's, 1849; George F. Bailey & Co., 1860. Booker & Evarts Minstrels organized, 1860, for a tour through New England; January, 1861, they were on a Mississippi River floating palace; February, Evarts left the company, having been stricken with paralysis and losing the use of his left arm. Ringmaster, W. C. Coup's, 1875-76; press agent, W. C. Coup's, 1879-81; VanAmburgh's, 1883; Sells Bros.', 1884-85, 1887; Adam Forepaugh's, 1886, 1888. Was an able writer and as a show "talker" earned the title of the "Little Giant Orator." While on his way to join Adam Forepaugh's, 1889, was judged to have been a fatality from the train wreck at Hamilton, Canada, April 28. Although the body could not be identified among the cremated victims of the disaster, his name did not appear on the list of survivors and papers pertaining to him were not found in the rubble Wife Florence lived in Corning, NY.

EVERETT, EDWARD. Press agent, Orrin Barber's, 1888.

EVERETT, H. Punch and Judy performer, magician, sideshow, Cooper, Bailey & Co., 1876.

EVERETT, H. B. Press agent, S. H. Barrett & Co., 1883.

EVERITT, L. H. Clown, Yankee Robinson's, 1866.

EVERS, JENNIE. (1860?-1884) Sells Bros.' some 5 years. Died in Bristol, TN, age 24.

EVERSELL, J. Rider, Mons. LeTort's, 1842; equestrian manager, John Mateer's, 1844; Cincinnati Circus, 1845.

EVERSELL, J. [also Ebersole]. Apprentice rider, Brown & Weeks, 1834; J. T. & J. P. Bailey, 1835; Ludington, Smith & Bailey, 1836; Brown, Mills (apprenticeship ended), 1837; Brown, Mills, Waterman, 1838; Ludlow & Smith, 1841; Fogg & Stickney, 1841; Mons. LeTort's, 1842; equestrian manager, Mateer's, 1843; Cincinnati Circus (Swiss Bros.'), 1845; Dr. Gilbert R. Spalding's, to March 1846.

EVERTS, P. Dr. Gilbert R. Spalding's, 1847.

EWERS, CHARLES. (d. February 16, 1909) Hurdle rider, Sells Bros.', 1877, equestrian director, 1879, 1882; hurdle and 4-horse bareback rider, Anderson & Co., 1878; Orrin Bros.', Havana, winter 1879-80, 1882-83; Adam Forepaugh's, 1880, equestrian director, 1881; 4 and 6-horse rider, S. H. Barrett &

Co., 1883; jockey rider, Wallace & Co., 1886-89; jockey rider, Wallace & Anderson, 1890; Cook & Whitby's, 1892; Ringling Bros.', 1893; 4-horse and bounding jockey, Sautelle's, 1895, 1898-99; general manager, Wood & Ewers' (Charles Ewers, **George Wood**, proprietors), 1897; Charles Lee's, 1901. Married to **Jennie Turnour,** who was killed while performing with Barrett's, April 26, 1884. Ewers died at age 54.

EWERS, JENNIE. See Jennie Turnour.

EWERS, THOMAS. Contracting agent, Wood & Ewers (Charles Ewers, **George Wood**, proprietors), 1897.

EWERS, W. E. Treasurer, Wood & Ewers' Golden Gate Wagon Shows (Charles Ewers, **George Wood**, proprietors), 1897.

EWING, ELLA. (March 9, 1872-January 10, 1912) Giantess. Born in Lewis County, MO. At age 25, was 7½' tall and weighed 250 pounds. As "The Saintly Giantess," traveled with Barnum & Bailey for several years; also Buffalo Bill's Wild West Show, where she was featured in a poster. Died of consumption.

EWING, H. J. Treasurer, Bailey & Winan, 1890.

Hyatt Frost

F

FAGAN, J. P. General agent, Cross & LeRoy, winter 1884.

FAIRCHILD, THOMAS R. (1862?-March 29, 1903) General performer. Began career with W. C. Coup's. Died in Chicago from pneumonia, age 41.

FAIRY QUEEN. Advertised sister of **Commodore Foot.** James M. Nixon's Amphitheatre, Chicago, 1872.

FANLON, LOUIS [r. n. Louis Neidrack]. Gymnast, clown. Born in Schorarie County, NY. About 18 years of age teamed with **Rudolph Mette,** famous clown and acrobat, performing as one of the **Mette Brothers,** P. T. Barnum's, John Murray's, Great Eastern. After marriage to a **Miss Marie Hass,** 1879, the team split up. Went to Cuba with the **Leotards,** an organization of acrobats, 1880. On return, joined Great London; later, Barnum, Bailey & Hutchinson and Sells Bros.' Toured South America with own show around 1890.

FANNING, F. F. Proprietor, Fanning's, 1891.

FARANTA, SIGNOR [or Faranti; P. W. Stemple]. (1846-January 10, 1924) Contortionist. Old time "bending act" performer. Great European, 1865; Frank J. Howes', 1865; Thayer & Noyes, winter 1865-66; Haight & Chambers, 1866; George F. Bailey & Co., 1867, 1869; Amphitheatre, Louisville, January 1868; Dan Rice's, 1870; Montgomery Queen's, 1874-75; John Wilson's Palace Amphitheatre, San Francisco, 1875; Pat Ryan's, 1882. Retired to New Orleans, constructed the Iron Building there, 1880s, seating some 5,000. [Charles H. Day: "When Faranta struck New Orleans he had just eight Mexican dollars in his pockets. And they were valued at just eighty-five cents each."] 1914, lived at Elks Club, New Orleans.

FARINI, GUILLERMO ANTONIO [r. n. William Leonard Hunt]. (June 10, 1838-January 17, 1929) "The Great Farini," born to **Hannah** and **Thomas Hunt** near Lockport, NY, the second oldest of 9 children. Thomas Hunt was at various times a school teacher, grocery store and general store proprietor and farmer. Farini first saw a circus during his formative years of the 1840s. Possessed of natural athletic ability, he studied and copied the circus performers who visited Bowmanville, Canada. Exhibited his first circus at age 12, only to be closed down by his irate parents. Continued to practice stunts on the wire. 1859, Blondin's expoits over Niagara Falls was an inspiration; so on October 1 of that year, as an attraction for the agricultural fair of Port Hope, Canada, Signor Farini made his first appearance on the high wire, crossing a stream in the center of town and performing a strong man act at Port Hope's town hall by having a rock broken on his chest, lifting heavy weights and conducting a rope-pull against a dozen or so men. This led to performances at small fairs in Canada and, shortly, with Dan Rice's floating circus. Offered a challenge to Blondin, 1860, and by July had promoted local sponsors and was making preparations for crossing at the Falls, a distance of 1,800', farther than Blondin had attempted. The time came, August 15, the same day scheduled for a Blondin crossing. The debut was respectable and was followed by more attempts during the summer season. Although less polished, the stunt proved he was able to match with Blondin's wire-walking feats. Married, 1861, and entered the Union army in a regiment of engineers, eventually rising to the rank of Captain. While performing in Havana, 1862, his wife, who was on the wire with him, fell and was mortally injured. Appeared at the Hippotheatron, NYC, summer 1864. August 9, 1864, while attempting to wade through the rapids near the edge of the falls on stilts, fell into the water and was swept toward the brink; at the last moment he caught hold of a tree branch which saved him from certain death. Said to have married a millionairess from Nova Scotia that year but nothing is known of the union. Around 1865, went to England, adopted an orphaned boy, whom he advertised as **El Nino,** and schooled him for his act. 1866, the "Flying Farinis" performed at Cremorne Gardens and the Alhambra Palace, London. 1870, Farini presented a **Mlle. Lulu** to the public, who became a sensational attraction on both continents. 1877, after Lulu suffered an inury while performing at Hengler's Circus, Dublin, Farini admitted that Lulu was none other than his adopted son **El Nino.** In 1871, married **Alice Carpenter,** an English woman, who bore him 2 sons; but the couple underwent a sensational divorce, 1880. Became an author around 1875 with his book *Ferns Which Grow In New Zealand.* Followed with 3 other books. 1877, developed what is said to be the first sucessful human cannon ball act, featuring his protégé, the original **Zazel.** Became an ingenious developer of spectacular acts and was noted as possibly being the model for George du Maurier's character of Svengali. Married a German aristocrat's daughter, **Anna Muller,** 1886. Retired from show business, 1890s, to devote himself to his inventions and to his interest in botany. Published a 4th book, 1897, *How to Grow Begonias.* 1899, moved to Toronto, Canada, and became involved in stock market speculation, vice-president of a gold-mining company, manager of a whip company. Studied art, somewhere around 1900, and became interested in promoting young artists. Died, age 91.

FARINI, PROF. Cannoneer, P. T. Barnum's, 1880.

FARNSWORTH, CARLOS H. (1821?-March 7, 1883) An agent in the circus business for 27 years. Mabie's, 1857; Davis & Crosby, 1859; George F. Bailey & Co., 1861-65; advertiser, G. F. Bailey & Co., 1867; VanAmburgh's, 1868; Campbell's, 1869; general business agent, VanAmburgh's, 1871; contracting agent, Adam Forepaugh's, 1875. For 6 years before death

96

was a deputy sheriff, Fairfax, Canada. Died in Fletcher, VT, age 62. While in the line of duty one night, was kicked and knocked senseless by one of his horses and found the next morning frozen to death.

FARNUM BROTHERS [Richard, James]. Pyramid chair performers. With Adam Forepaugh's, 1888-89; F. J. Taylor's, 1892.

FARRAN, RAY. Female fancy shooter, Gollmar Bros.', 1896.

FARRELL, FRANK. Equestrian director, Bailey & Winan, 1890.

FARRELL, JOE. H. Buckley & Co., 1857-58.

FARRELL, ROBERT. Clown, Brown's, 1832, 1833.

FARRELL, SAM. Holland & Gormley, 1888.

FARRER, HUGH. Program agent, Melville, Maginley & Cooke, 1875.

FARWELL, TOM. A printer who was co-proprietor (with Daniel McLaren, Dan Rice's father), Dan Rice's, 1858.

FAULKS. Equestrian. Performed as early as 1771 in Philadelphia at Centre Square with such feats as playing a French horn while standing on the saddle of a moving mount; riding 2 horses at full gallop, with one foot in the stirrup of each horse, then throwing himself upon his back and rising again; riding 3 horses at once at full speed and vaulting from one to the other; riding a galloping horse, mounting and dismounting many times. [T. Allston Brown: "These feats were much inferior to those we see in the circus at the present day but they must have excited a great stir among our ante-revolutionary inhabitants."]

FAUST & ECTOR [E. And T. Faust, W. Ector]. Gymnasts, Howes' Great London, 1871-72.

FAUST, A. J. Assistant agent, Gregory Bros.', 1884.

FAUST, LEW. Frank Rich's Great Eastern Railroad Alliance, 1886.

FAUST, PORT. Clown, G. G. Grady's, 1869

FAY, DILLY. See Henry W. Waugh.

FAY, MISS LEA. Beckett's, 1881.

FAY, THOMAS E. (March 27, 1852-March 13, 1907) Boss canvasman. Born in Portland, ME. Joined Great Eastern as canvasman, 1872; also connected with L. B. Lent's, 1876; W. W. Cole's, 1878; Adam Forepaugh's, 1879; become boss canvasman, Burr Robbins', 1880; Robbins & Colvin, 1881. Since then, was with various shows in that capacity. Last engagement, Campbell Bros.', 1905-06. Died in St. Charles, MN.

FAYLING. Double somersaulter, Warner, Henderson & Co., 1874.

FAYLOR, JOHN. Tumbler, W. R. Blaisdell's, California, 1868.

FELICIA, ARIANA [or Adriane, Arlene]. Special import from "*La Cirque Imperiale*, Paris, and the Royal Amphitheatre, London," appeared in an act called "*Les Reine Des Fees.*" It is unclear what this queen of the fairies did for such billing but the advertised credentials were sufficient to justify it; although elsewhere she was identified as a rival of Zoyara. L. B. Lent's, September 1861; L. B. Lent's, Hippozoonomadon, 1862.

FELIX. Apprentice rider, Pepin & Breschard, NYC, 1810-11.

FELLON ["Master"]. "The iron boy," feats of strength, Crystal Palace Circus, 1872.

FERGUSON, ED O. General agent. A. P. Collier's Shows, 1897; George W. Hall, Sr.'s, 1900.

FERGUSON, O. J. Driesbach's, 1857; VanAmburgh's for a number of years—advertiser, treasurer and co-proprietor from at least 1869-81. Sold interest in VanAmburgh's, circa 1882. After which, was manager, Nathans & Co., 1882; manager, Cooper, Jackson & Co., 1883; proprietor, O. J. Ferguson's New York and New England Circus, 1884; general agent, Frank A. Robbins', 1885; assistant manager, Adam Forepaugh's, 1887; proprietor, Ferguson's Coliseum Circus, 1888; general superintendant, Sig. Sautelle's, 1898.

FERGUSON, ROBERT D. (1842?-April 15, 1870) Rider. Born in England, brought to America by **Ben Jennings**, the clown. Traveled with Levi J. North and other circuses. Upon retiring from the ring, kept a hotel in Cairo, IL. For the 4 years prior to death, ran a saloon in Memphis, TN. Died of consumption, age 28.

FERNANDEZ, EUGENE. General performer. Flagg & Aymar, 1856; John Robinson, 1856.

FERRIS, JOE. (1872?-September 3, 1916) Sideshow ticket taker for many years with Ringling Bros.' Died at Cedar Rapids, IA, age 44.

FERRIS, THEODORE. Lion tamer. Cooper, Bailey & Co., 1879-80; Orrin Bros.', Mexico, winter 1883-84; Great Wallace, 1900-02; Orrin Bros.', Mexico, winter 1899-1900.

FERRIS, WALTER. Frank Rich's Great Eastern Railroad Alliance, 1886.

FERRIS, WYLIE. Equilibrist. King & Franklin, 1887; Charles Lee's London Circus, 1888.

FERRON, CHARLES H. ["Fanola"]. (1858?-July 6, 1896) Bareback rider. At one time had a small circus which traveled about the country selling patent medicines after the performances. His wife was also a rider. Left the circus business to become a vender of patent medicines and horse trainer. Committed suicide by taking morphine at the Ludlow Street Jail, NYC, age 38, after being sentenced the day of his death to 11 months in the peritentiary for counterfeiting trademarks. Some time before, in connection with a man named **Curtis**, formed a firm, the International Propaganda Co., and begun to flood the market with imitations of remedies produced by a patent medicine concern. The victimized company brought a civil action and obtained a judgment of $30,000 by default, and upon execution of the judgment, Ferron was to serve 6 months in jail. The term had not expired when he was sentenced to the penitentiary.

FETAUX, JOSEPH. Rider, Sadler's Great English Circus, 1875.

FIDLER, J. Agent for Barnum's autobiography, P. T. Barnum's, 1876.

FIELD, AL G. [r. n. Alfred Griffith Hatfield]. (November 7, 1848 or 1850-April 3, 1921) Negro minstrel, clown, equestrian director, proprietor. Born in Leesburg, VA. Equestrian director and clown, Collins' Oriental Combination, 1877; clown, Boyd & Peters, 1878; equestrian director and candy stand and reserved seat privileges, London Sensation Show, 1879; clown and manager of concert, Miles Orton's, 1880-82; John Robinson's, 1882; equestrian manager, Weldon & Co. winter 1884; equestrian manager and clown, Wallace & Co., 1884-86. Formed a minstrel troupe, 1886 (first advertisement appeared in the New York *Clipper*, July, 1886, for an October performance at Marion, OH). The company, that year numbering 27 people, continued successfully until Field's death. By 1898, the show was enlarged to 60 people traveling on 2 specially built railroad cars, the "Southland" and the "Dan Emmett." In 1895, organized the Al G. Field Real Negro Minstrels and a "Darkest America" Co., which were on the road for 2 years. 1898, sold the Real Negro Minstrels to **Oliver P. Scott** and leased the other show to **John W. Vogel**. Became known as the "Millionaire Minstrel" because of his successful managerial activities. Was also a good minstrel performer, remembered for his monologues. Training in management came from working with Sells Bros.' and with Duprez & Benedict's Minstrels, both outfits noted for their advertising practices. It is said that Field was the first minstrel manager to carry entire stage settings and scenery and the first to use a special train of cars for transporting his troupe. Was a devoted family man and fond of dogs and horses. Carried a fine pair of horses with the show to drive about in the cities visited. Permanent residence was in Columbus, OH, where he owned considerable real estate, including "Maple Villa" Farm in the Olentangy Valley near the city, where he bred blooded horses, pedigreed cattle, game fowl, and hogs. 1909, was listed as director of the Central National Bank of Columbus, the Columbus Casualty Co., and had an interest in the street railway system there. Is the author of the book *Watch Yourself Go By*. Died at his home in Columbus, OH, of Bright's desease.

FIELD, TILDA. Wallace & Co., 1885. Was probably Al G. Field's wife.

FIELDER, DICK. Agent for Barnum's autobiography, P. T. Barnum's, 1879.

FIELDING, MAGGIE. Equestrienne, E. Stowe's Northwestern Circus, 1871.

FIELDS, GEORGE. Advertising agent, with Haight's Great Southern, 1874.

FILKINS, ROBERT ["Col."]. Agent, Robbins & Colvin, 1881.

FILLIS, CHARLES. Rider, Wootten & Haight's, 1871.

FILLUP, ORLANDO. Cooper, Bailey & Co., 1879.

FILMORE, WILLIAM. Program agent, Alexander Robinson's, 1875.

FINCH, ED. Leased the elephant, Little Bet, 1823, from Hackaliah Bailey and had success in his exhibitions of her. 1826, in partnership with **Agrippa Martin**, toured the Tippo Sultan Menagerie; and in association with **Albert Miller**, as Finch, Miller & Co. Had the "Grand Caravan," some 10 animals, on the road in 1830-31. Co-proprietor with Purdy, Welch, Finch & Wright's menagerie, 1832.

FINCKUM, J. Orton Bros.', 1865.

FINN, JAMES LEON. (d. May 2, 1888) Bareback rider. W. W. Cole's; Barrett's, 1887.

FIRTH, WILLIAM. H. Buckley & Co., 1857-58.

FISH, BENJAMIN. (1833?-November 12, 1908) Born in Birmingham, England. Joined P. T. Barnum at the time Tom Thumb was being introduced to Great Britain, and for many years treasurer of the Barnum show and personal representative to Barnum. Was the last of 3 executors of the Barnum estate and, as such, had full charge of it. Died in Bridgeport, CT, of heart failure, age 75.

FISH, CHARLES W. (November 23, 1848-May 5, 1895) Rider. Born in Philadelphia. Mother died shortly after birth, which prompted a move to Cincinnati with his grandmother. At age 9 was placed under the care of **James Macfarland**, then traveling with Spalding & Rogers. Around 1857, McFarland was killed during a domestic quarrel. The following year Fish was indentured for 78 months to **Charles J. Rogers**. Traveled with Spalding & Rogers' company throughout the South and West and into Canada. Also accompanied them to the West Indies and South America. While returning from the latter, the ship was wrecked, April 2, 1864, near Long Beach Island, off the New Jersey shore. The company lost everything except 3 horses from a stud of 24. The apprenticeship being over, joined Frank J. Howes', 1865. Following this engagement, rejoined Spalding & Rogers in New Orleans. Mike Lipman's, 1866, 1869; Nixon, Costello & Howes, 1867-68; Dr. James L. Thayer's, 1869; James M. French's, 1869-70; George Ryland's, California, 1870; J. E. Warner & Co., 1871; L. B. Lent's, 1872. This was followed by a tour of the British Isles with the Hengler circus and then to Moscow at the *Cirque Hinne* with the Ciniselli Royal Italian Circus, where he was dubbed "the Patti of the *Cirque*" by Prince Kourakin, who presented him with an elegant cigar holder. In St. Petersburg was entertained by Prince Schamyl of Circassia, whose lady presented him with a laurel wreath on his benefit night, the highest honor bestowed on visiting artists. A tour of Europe for the Renz circus followed, throughout which he appeared before various royal families. On returning to USA, was connected with Montgomery Queen's, 1874-75; P. T. Barnum's, 1876-78; International Circus, Offenbach Garden, Philadelphia, winter 1876-77; Orrin Bros.', Havana, winters 1877-78,

98

1878-79, 1879-80, 1884-85; Cooper & Bailey, 1879-80; Burr Robbins', 1880; Robbins & Colvin, 1881; W. O'Dale Stevens' Australian Circus, performing in variety theatres prior to summer season, 1882; Sells Bros.', 1882; W. O'Dale Stevens' Australian Circus, Boston, spring 1883; Burr Robbins', 1884; Frank A. Robbins', 1885-88; the *Gran Circo Pubillones*, Cuba, winter 1888-89; Barnum & Bailey, 1889, 1891; Walter L. Main's, 1892; opened with the Winter Circus, Philadelphia, November 19, 1892, and remained through the run; Ringling Bros., 1893. [D. W. Watt: "He was what was known as a forward and back somerset rider and thousands of times when he would be turning a somerset on a horse he would slip and go off onto the ground on purpose just to show bandwagon the people how he could get back. He could leave the ring at almost any angle and leap onto the horse's back and stay there. To the average audience that was the best act that Charlie Fish did."] He was lithe and slight of frame and blessed with agility and grace. May have been the first to do a somersault on a horse and land on a single foot. Was before the public more than 30 years and was one of the best bareback riders of his time. "Robinson was declared the more dashing rider," Fish once remarked, "but I was declared the champion trick rider of the world, a title I am ready and willing to defend against all comers." [John A. Dingess: found his act "one of extreme mediocrity," and further, "self-esteem and egotism overbalanced all his artistic ability.... Fish's diminutive size and general appearance were greatly against him."] Retirement came in 1894 because of failing health. In addition to riding skills, Fish was interested in painting and writing. In 1888, authored Frank A. Robbins' route book and in 1894 contributed a series of drawings for Ringling Bros.' book. Died from blood poisoning at home in Chicago.

FISH, HAMILTON. Treasurer, P. T. Barnum's, 1877.

FISH, JOHN. Secretary, P. T. Barnum's, 1872.

FISHER BROTHERS. Gymnasts. Hilliard & Hunting, 1879; Walter L. Main's, 1882; John B. Doris', 1886; Adam Forepaugh's, 1887; human meteors, Wallace & Co., 1889; Walter L. Main's, 1892; flying trapeze, Adam Forepaugh's, 1893.

FISHER, FRANK. (1871?-April 9, 1899) Animal trainer. Formerly with the Barnum show, was employed by Lemen Bros.' for 7 years until he was killed by the elephant Rajah in Lemen Bros.' winter quarters in Argentine, KS, age about 28.

FISHER, FRED H. (July 2, 1855-November 7, 1914) Member of **The Flying Fishers**. Born in Rockford, IL. Connected with many of the leading shows, the last being John Robinson's Ten Big Shows. After retirement, moved from Cincinnati to LaCrosse, WI, where he conducted the Hotel LaCrosse Annex. Died at the LaCrosse Hospital of diabetes.

FISHER, GEORGE H. Press agent, Scribner & Smith, 1895.

FISHER, JOHN E. Indian rubber man. Rockwell & Co.'s, 1848; Stone & McCollum, 1850; Johnson & Co., 1852; Joe Pentland's, 1854; Sands, Nathans & Co., 1855; Lee & Marshall, 1856.

FISHER, PROF. Balloon ascensionist, G. G. Grady's, 1871.

FISHER, SILAS. "Great Canadian Giant." Stood 7' tall and at age 30 weighed 245 pounds. Traveled 6 years with the likes of P. T. Barnum's, Adam Forepaugh's, Burr Robbins', and others for a weekly salary of $25 to $50.

FISHER, WALTER. Contracting agent, Walter L. Main's, 1893.

FISTLER, H. A. Advertiser. Was keeping a saloon in Chicago, corner of Clark and Monroe Streets, 1867.

FITCH, MATILDA. Dancer, Great European, 1865

FITCH, TIMOTHY L. Ethiopian performer, Great European, 1865; Frank J. Howes', 1865; assistant manager, W. W. Coles, 1877-78.

FITZGERALD, DANIEL J. (1852-1904) Associate. Born in Massachusetts. Married to **Carrie Mueller**, professionally known as **Carrie Armstrong**, 1882. Museum, San Francisco, 1883; Denby's Trans-Continental, 1884; Barnum & Bailey, Royal Italian, W. W. Cole's, Sherman's, Sherman & Hinman, Denby's. At one time was a partner in Friar, Gaylord & Fitzgerald. General agent, Walter L. Main's, 1895; manager, 1899; assistant manager of the show, 1904.

FITZGERALD, F. Boss canvasman, Springer's Royal Cirq-Zoolodon, 1875.

FITZGERALD, JAMES. Equilibristic, juggler, baton drillist and club tosser. Howe's, 1888; Gollmar Bros.' for several years beginning 1892, listed as ringmaster, 1897.

FITZGERALD, JAMES MICHAEL. See James Robinson.

FITZGERALD, JOSEPH. Club juggler, Main & Sargeant, 1891.

FITZGERALD, RICHARD. (July 4, 1842-June 24, 1889) Amusement agent and manager. Born in Wheeling, WV, but reared in NYC. Professional career began, 1865, as proprietor of Parker's Opera House and Virginia Hall in Alexandria, VA. Later, manager of the Canterbury, Richmond. The same year was with Spalding & Bidwell at their Academy of Music, New Orleans. Summer 1866, business manager, New York Champs Elysees. Fall of that year became associated with **James Conner** in a dramatic agency. After Conner's death, returned to work for Spalding & Bidwell at their Olympic Theatre, St. Louis. Next, went back to the dramatic agency business at the corner of Houston and Broadway, NYC. Shortly, took actor **T. G. Riggs** as a partner and moved to 512 Broadway. 1871, managed the Charles M. Barras "Black Crook" Co. and later Kiralfy's "Humpty Dumpty" Co. Two seasons as agent with Cameron & Co.'s Oriental Circus (1875), and Tubbs & Co.'s New York Circus. After which, returned to the dramatic agency business, NYC. Was said to be a most companionable man with only 2 weaknesses—"his large-heartedness and his love of Masonry, Lodge No. 273."

FITZGERALD, S. A. Band leader, North American, 1877.

FITZGIBBON, JOHN. See Santiago Gibbonoise.

FITZPATRICK, JOHN L. (d. January 14, 1906) Acrobat. For 15 years a bar performer, 8 of which were spent with Robert Hunting's. Also connected with Gregory Bros.' Was a member of **Ricardo & Fitz**. Died in Ottawa, Canada.

FITZROY FAMILY. Orton Bros.', 1864.

FITZWILLIAMS, FRANK. Irish athlete and strongman. S. H. Barrett & Co., 1883; cannon balls, John Robinson's, 1885, 1889-92.

FLAKE, JAMES. Caldwell's Occidental Circus, 1867.

FLETCHER, JOHN. Boss canvasman, G. G. Grady's, 1871.

FLETCHER, R. Clown, Adam Forepaugh's, 1875.

FLETCHERS [Lily, Charles, William]. Artistic skaters. Orrin Bros.', Mexico, 1883; Barnum & London, 1884. **William**, listed as "W. Flatcher," leaper and tumbler, W. H. Stowe's, 1881.

FLINT. Animal trainer. John Sears' menagerie, 1833; Waring, Tufts & Co., 1834; Associations Celebrated Menagerie and Aviary from the Zoological Institute, NYC, 1835; the same, Baltimore, 1837.

FLOTOW, PRINCE. French grotesque, Wallace & Co., 1884.

FLYNN, ARTHUR. Treasurer, Holland & Gormley, 1889.

FLYNN, JOHN. Gregory, Merritt & Co., 1886.

FLYNN, MARK. Alex Abar's, 1889.

FLYNN, PATRICK ["Patsey"]. (d. May 9, 1890) P. T. Barnum's.

FLYNN, PETE. Agent, car #1, Metropolitan Circus, 1897.

FOGG, JEREMIAH P. Proprietor. Lived in Westchester County, NY. In charge of a menagerie featuring the elephant Columbus, 1819; with **Ebeneezer Howes** in running a small menagerie in the South, 1826, combined with Quick & Mead's (one of the earliest circuses using the canvas pavilion). The company traveled from South Carolina to Alabama. **S. P. Stickney** rode for this circus for 3 years before joining up with Fogg in their joint enterprise. Firm of Fogg & Stickney (Jeremiah Fogg, S. P. Stickney) was a nursery for some fine talent, **Levi J. North** and **Charles J. Rogers** among others. Fogg and Stickney remained partners for 12 years, 1828-42. At the end of the 1837 season, they bought Oscar Brown's circus, in which Fogg had previously had a minor interest. Retired after the 1842 season.

FOLEY, CHARLES. Clown, Great North American, 1873; concert performer, Irish comedian, Cooper, Bailey & Co., 1876.

FOLEY, G. J. Proprietor, Foley's, 1890.

FOLEY, TOM. Boss canvasman, Howes & Cushing, South America, 1876.

FOLEY, WILLIAM H. Clown, Joseph Rowe's, California, 1849; Foley's California Circus, 1850-51.

FONTAINBLEAU, MME. Gymnast, P. A. Older's, 1871.

FONTAINE, MLLE. Gardner & Hemmings, Front Street Theatre, Baltimore, January, 1866.

FOOTE, COMMODORE. Midget. James M. Nixon's Nixon's Cremorne Gardens (formerly Palace Gardens), NYC, spring 1862; October-December, Washington, DC; Nixon's Amphitheatre, Chicago, 1872. Exhibited in various other circuses and museums.

FORBES, CHARLES. General contracting agent, Bartine's, 1889. [Charles H. Day: "No one doubts that Mr. Forbes is a close, calculating businessman, just the one to make billboard contracts, hire lots and the like ahead of a show; but when it comes to writing anything except his name to a check and filling out a statement of local expenses, he is as much at a loss as **William W. Durand** would be in writing biblical poetry."]

FORBES, SPENCER. Chief bill poster, John Robinson's, 1874.

FORD, GEORGE. Gymnast, John Robinson's, 1881.

FORD, T. J. Railroad contractor, Miles Orton's, 1888.

FORD, WILLIAM A. (1840?-May 5, 1875) Treasurer, John H. Murray's, 1875. Died at Fall River, MA, of pneumonia, age 35. Home was in East Boston, MA.

FOREPAUGH, ADAM, JR. (1859-March 29, 1919) Son of old **Adam Forepaugh**. Devoted considerable time to training animals, being one of the leading elephant and horse trainers of his day. 1889, the Forepaugh show exhibited the trapeze horse Eclipse; a herd of dancing elephants; John L. Sullivan, the boxing elephant; and Blondin, the "tight-rope" walking pony. When the show was sold to Cooper, Bailey and Barnum, Forepaugh, Jr., was retained for a seasonal salary of $10,000. Also considered an outstanding equestrian director. [D. W. Watt: "He could certainly put in more acts and run a show faster than any equestrian director that his father ever had. Young Adam was the equestrian director of the Forepaugh show for several years before the death of his father. He, too, was a great rider and one of the greatest elephant trainers that the world ever knew. Yet he was a good handler of people and had the respect of all the people in the dressing rooms."] At one time, had his own circus out, the Adam Forepaugh, Jr., Show, but lacked the business sense of his father. Married to performer, **Lillie Deacon**. Retired because of ill health, 1893. Died at his home in Philadelphia.

FOREPAUGH, ADAM, SR. [r. n. Adam Forbach]. (February 28, 1831-January 22, 1890) Born in Philadelphia of German ancestry. Left school at age 9 to become a butcher, working for $4.00 a month and board. Eventually gravitated to buying and selling stock, primarily horses and cattle. Moved to NYC and soon became one of the city's largest dealers in horses, supplying several horse railroad companies with all their animals as well as stock used by the Brooklyn lines. Made a fortune selling horses to the government during the Civil War. It was through horse selling that Forepaugh got into the circus business, at which time he changed the family name. 1864, sold 44 horses to **John O'Brien** for $9,000 to form the Tom

King Excelsior Circus. When the money came due, was forced to take a share of the show as payment. April, 1865, with O'Brien, purchased the **Jerry Mabie** menagerie, consisting of 12 cages, two elephants and other animals, for $25,000. The show was divided into the Great National Circus, with Mrs. Charles Warner as the attraction, and the Dan Rice Circus, with which Rice was paid $1,000 per week and a guarantee of 26 weeks for his services and his name. Forepaugh took charge of the latter show himself. Same year, sold three-quarters interest in the Great National Circus to **Den Stone, Frank Rosston** and **George Bronson**, and later sold the remainder to **Samuel Booth**. Continued with the Dan Rice circus. Winter 1865-66, the Rice show performed in Philadelphia, at which time Forepaugh severed business relationship with O'Brien. Went out under his own name, 1866, traveling through the East with 22 cages of wild animals. Sent two one-ring shows out, 1868, but the following year was back to one show, a policy he maintained for the rest of his career. Louisville, June 10, 1869, used two round top pavilions, one for the menagerie and the other for performance. When Forepaugh started out with the Rice show, he had 110 horses, 14 cages, and one ticket wagon, with daily expenses of from $500 to $600. By 1877, when the show last traveled by wagons, it used 300 employees—35 to handle the tents and 65 to drive. By 1880, the outfit traveled on 3 trains of railroad cars, and had 60 cages, 290 horses, 400 employees, and a daily expense of $4,000. Was the first to incorporate the wild west spectacle into his ring performance and was the first manager to exhibit the menagerie under a separate tent in connection with a circus. The idea was contributed by **Joel E. Warner** and put into effect at St. Louis, 1868 (according to Warner); however, it may have been 1869 and the place Louisville (Forepaugh). The show carried more animals in the menagerie than any other circus and paid the highest prices for European talent. Was said to be "the master of his business as no man before him was and as no man probably will be in the future." 1870s, Forepaugh's and Barnum's were the two largest shows on the road, and were in constant competition, fighting for the same territory, until, in 1882, Barnum sued for peace. At that time, they made a 2-year agreement to divide the territory and alternate going over the circuits but, 1884, they were at it again, with the famed "white elephant" incident serving as the cause. Forepaugh once exclaimed, "I have a boy and Mr. Barnum has none. My show will outlast his." Was twice married. The first wife, **Mary Ann Blaker** (April 1, 1835-December 1, 1872), the daughter of Ulysses Blaker of Philadelphia, died of consumption in Philadelphia. The second, **Mary G. Tallman**, married, Philadelphia, October 7, 1884. He never smoked, chewed, or drank; in manner, had a rough exterior, loved a joke, was haughty to his minor employees, shrewd in business, and attentive to the small details of his organization. Always sat at the main entrance of the show, making his face familiar to everyone who went through the gate. Died at his residence, leaving a large estate.

FOREPAUGH, ANDREW JACKSON "JACK". (1835-November 8, 1896) Brother of **Adam Forepaugh, Sr.** Born in Philadelphia. Lion tamer with Forepaugh's, 1868, 1888. John O'Brien's, 1870; superintendant of menagerie and lion performer, J. E. Warner & Co., 1871; Springer, Rosston & Henderson, 1871-73; zoological director and lion tamer, Montgomery Queen's, 1873-76, accompanying the show to California and Australia. Son, **Harry**, at 5 years of age, was riding in a lion's cage on his father's knee while with Montgomery Queen's, 1874. Also connected with Maybury, Pullman & Hamilton for a time. Later, occupied himself with buying and selling horses. Started a carting business in Philadelphia, 1891, which was carried on until his death in that city, age 61.

FOREPAUGH, CHARLES. (d. July 17, 1929) Brother of **Adam Forepaugh, Sr.** In the horse trading business with his brother, Philadelphia, and in show business for more than 50 years. Claimed to be the first circus performer to thrust his head into the mouth of a lion. Died at West Berlin, NJ, age 92.

FOREPAUGH, GEORGE W. (1828-June 4, 1910) Attendant. Brother of **Adam Forepaugh, Sr.**, and father of **John A. Forepaugh**. Worked in various capacities on the Adam Forepaugh circus. Later years, was doorman for the Forepaugh Theatre, Philadelphia. Died there of apoplexy, age 82.

FOREPAUGH, IRVING. Superintendent of animals, Rosston, Springer & Henderson, 1871.

FOREPAUGH, JOHN A. (August 9, 1852-June 7, 1895) Born in Philadelphia, son of **George W.** and nephew of **Adam Forepaugh, Sr.** Began as a circus rider at age 6 but left to attend school. 1864, joined Mrs. Charles Warner's at the old Continental Theatre, Philadelphia, and resumed his riding. At age 16 was manager for his uncle and continued until 1881 when he became manager for the O'Brien show. Returned to Forepaugh's, however, and remained until 1885. Proprietor, John Forepaugh's, California, 1888. With Adam Forepaugh's death and the purchase of the show by Cooper & Bailey, remained on as manager for the new owners. Was one of the proprietors of the Broad Street Casino, Philadelphia, for 2 years. Managed the Forepaugh Theatre in that city, which was named by him, for 11 years; also managed the Masonic Temple Theatre, Baltimore. Died at his home in Philadelphia.

FOREPAUGH, JOHN A. (March 27, 1831-January 13, 1906) Born in Philadelphia, elder brother of **Adam Forepaugh, Sr.**, and father of **William R. "Bib" Forepaugh**. Began circus career, 1866, most of which was managerial with Adam Forepaugh, Dan Rice, Forepaugh & Gardner, Springer, Rosston & Henderson, Forepaugh's Winter Circus, Philadelphia, and Forepaugh's Theatre, Philadelphia. Was elected an honorary member of the Aristocratic Philadelphia Centennial Club, 1874. Went completely blind several years prior to death.

FOREPAUGH, JOSEPHINE F. [Mrs. Ludwig Simmeth]. (1850-September 6, 1907) Gymnast. Born in Lewisburg, PA. Married **William R. Forepaugh** in the early 1870s. Using the professional names of **Alice Napier** and **Alice Murdell**, was connected with Montgomery Queen's, Rosston, Springer & Henderson, Adam Forepaugh's, Ringling Bros.', Orrin Bros.', S. H. Barrett's, Walter L. Main's, Burr Robbins', Frank A. Robbins', John Shields', etc. Died in Philadelphia, age 57.

FOREPAUGH, MAMIE. Equestrienne. Sells Bros.', 1894; Sig. Sautelle's, 1897.

FOREPAUGH, PATSY [r. n. M. J. Meagher]. Clown, with Adam Forepaugh's, 1889, during which time he went into the ring with John L. Sullivan, the boxing elephant. Superintendent of animals, Great Wallace, 1893. Killed by the elephant, Sid, December 20, 1899, at the winter quarters of Forepaugh-Sells Bros.', Columbus, OH. Had been the keeper of Sid for many years and had had no trouble with the animal; but this particular time when the elephants were led into the training circle for their daily exercise, Sid became unruly. Forepaugh jabbed him with his stick, which infuriated the beast, who threw him to the ground and fell upon him, piercing him with one of his tusks on which was a brass ball 6 inches in diameter.

FOREPAUGH, WILLIAM M. Treasurer. Maginley & Co., 1874; A. B. Rothcilds & Co., 1875.

FOREPAUGH, WILLIAM R. "BIB". (January 29, 1854-May 11, 1897) Acrobat. **Adam Forepaugh, Sr.'s**, nephew. Born in Philadelphia. Appeared with Charles F. Warner's at age 12. Later, performed under the title of the **Forepaugh Brothers** with **C. C. Mathews** and **Nelson Curry**. Next with **Blanche Fontainbleu**, and then with **Alice Napier**, whom he married, 1873, and fathered 5 children. See Josephine Forepaugh. Was "The Man Fly" with Mrs. Charles Warner's, Philadelphia, winter 1870-71; Ralston, Springer & Henderson, 1872; Montgomery Queen's, 1873; Burr Robbins', 1874-75; Adam Forepaugh's, 1876, where, with **Frank R. Clifton**, introduced a 5-bar act. Remained with this show until joining John Robinson's, 1884-85. Took out Forepaugh & Samwells (W. R. Forepaugh, **Thomas Samwells**, proprietors), 1886; equestrian director, John Forepaugh's, California, 1888. Returned to John Robinson's, 1890-92; Adam Forepaugh, Jr.'s, 1893; Frank A. Robbins', playing fair dates, 1896. Died of injuries as a result of a railroad collision, Tampa, FL.

FOREPAUGH SISTERS. Aerialists, with John Robinson's, 1892.

FORESTER, BLANCHE. Equestrienne, Warner & Henderson, 1874.

FORESTER, JULIEN. Clown, P. T. Barnum's, 1871.

FORREST, CHARLES. Dodge & Bartine, 1868.

FORREST, FANNIE. James M. Nixon's, NYC, 1863-64.

FORREST, FRANK M. Contracting agent, Cooper & Co., 1874.

FORREST, HUBERT. General performer, L. B. Lent's, 1858-66.

FORTIER, A. *Perche equipoise*, Mabie's, 1859.

FOSHAY, J. W. Treasurer, Sands, Lent, 1848; proprietor, R. Sands Circus, 1949, 1860-61; treasurer, Howes' European, 1865-69.

FOSTER, ANSON B. Proprietor, Anson B. Foster & Co., 1836; manager, James Raymond's, 1840.

FOSTER, B. A. ["Col."]. Purchased James T. Johnson's, June 17, 1885, Downs, KS, and changed the title to Col. Foster's New York Circus and Museum.

FOSTER, CHARLES J. Rider. Benchley & Stone's Lafayette Circus, 1837-38; Philadelphia Circus (**James Raymond** and **Joel E. Waring**, proprietors), 1840; Welch & Mann, 1841; Bartlett & Delavan, 1841; Robinson & Foster, 1843; Welch's, 1847.

FOSTER, EMMA. Equestrienne. Hemmings, Cooper & Whitby, 1868; J. W. Wilder's, 1872.

FOSTER, F. E. VanAmburgh &Co., 1871.

FOSTER, GEORGE. Gardner & Hemmings, Continental Theatre, Philadelphia, February 1865.

FOSTER, HENRY. Albino, Cooper, Bailey & Co., 1876, Australian tour, 1877.

FOSTER, JACK. Clown. Rivers & Derious, 1857-59; George F. Bailey & Co., 1860-61; Gardner & Hemmings, 1862-63.

FOSTER, JESSE W. "COL." (d. June 5, 1909) Agent. Worked several years for circuses in the West Indies, Central and South America. Chiarini's, South America, 1875; Gardner & Donovan, South America, 1886; Frank A. Gardner's, South America, 1889-93; proprietor, Jesse W. Foster's New York Circus, South America, 1894; general representative and director, Donovan's South American, Cuba, winter 1894-95; representative and general agent, Frank A. Gardner's, South America, 1895-96; Stickney & Donovan, West Indies, 1897-98; Martinho Lowande's, winter 1899-1900. Died from spinal meningitis at his home, NYC.

FOSTER, JOB. Lost his life while traveling with Robinson & Lake's Circus, 1851.

FOSTER, JOHN J. (November 13, 1830-May 26, 1906) Clown. Born in Chambersburg, PA (Cumberland Valley, Franklin Co.). Entered the circus business, 1846, Robinson & Eldred's. Bowery Circus, NYC, January 1858; Rivers & Derious', 1859; Madigan & Gardner, Front Street Theatre, Baltimore, winter 1860-61; George F. Bailey & Co., 1860-61; Gardner & Hemmings, National Hall, Philadelphia, fall 1862; Goodwin & Wilder, 1862, 1872; Gardner & Hemmings, 1863; Rivers & Derious, 1864; James M. Nixon's, 1865; Thayer & Noyes, 1866; Barnum & VanAmburgh's, 1866; Lipman's, 1866; Central Park Circus, NYC, 1867; Dan Rice's, 1867; Hemmings, Cooper & Whitby, 1868; Lake's, 1869; G. A. Huff & Co., 1870; James M. Nixon's, 1870; VanAmburgh &

Co., 1872; Wilder's North American, 1872; Burr Robbins', 1874; concert performer, Ethiopian entertainer, Cooper, Bailey & Co., 1876; excursion agent, P. T. Barnum's, 1877; director of operations, Campbell's, 1878; press agent, Adam Forepaugh's, 1879-80; Barnum, Bailey & Hutchinson, 1881; press agent, John Robinson's, 1882; Frank A. Robbins', 1883, 1885; Sparrow's, 1886; Roberts & Gardner, 1886; C. W. Kidder & Co.'s, 1893; New York Circus, 1893, which sailed up the Hudson on a chartered steamer, stopping at various cities; George S. Cole's, 1895; VanAmburgh & Co., 1896. Was active in show business up until 3 years prior to death, which occurred at the Actor's Home on Staten Island, NY, age 76. Daughter, **Mary E.**, married **Silas H. Moore**, non-professional, June 5, 1879, NYC.

FOSTER, JOSEPH. Clown. Came to the United States with **Thomas Cooke**. Titus, Angevine, 1838; Fogg & Stickney, 1839; American Theatre troupe, Fogg & Stickney, 1840; Bartlett & Delavan, 1841; American Theatre, September 1841; partner, Robinson & Foster, 1842-44; equestrian director, Welch & Mann, winters 1846-47, 1847-48, 1848-49.

FOSTER, LUCIUS. Boss canvasman, P. T. Barnum's, 1877.

FOSTER, M. Principal rider, Rivers & Derious, 1857.

FOSTER, MAMIE. Hemmings, Cooper & Whitby, 1868.

FOSTER, MRS. JOHN. Hemmings, Cooper & Whitby, 1868.

FOSTER, NAPOLEON. (January 31, 1804-April 9, 1877) Director of spectacles and horse dramas. Born in Edinburgh, Scotland. Began as an actor and later assisted in the production of pantomimes at Astley's Amphitheatre and the Adelphi in London. Came to the United States with Cooke's company, 1836. Remained in the country when Cooke returned to England. Connected with the company at the Baltimore Amphitheatre, 1838. Staged spectacles for **William E. Burton**, 1840, Philadelphia. Stage manager for Philadelphia Amphitheatre and other theatrical enterprises in that city off and on for the next several years. In the interim, joined S. P. Stickney's, 1851, Amphitheatre, Baronne Street, New Orleans. Married 3 times and had numerous children.

FOSTER, NED. Privileges, Dan Castello's, 1880, acquired in June from E. W. Wiggins.

FOSTER, NICK G. Negro minstrel, Spalding & Rogers *Floating Palace*, 1859.

FOSTER, PEARL. Sideshow albino, Cooper, Bailey & Co., Australian tour, 1876-78.

FOSTER, R. Cannon balls, Robinson & Eldred, 1850.

FOSTER SISTERS. James M. Nixon's, fall 1870.

FOWLER, CHARLES LEE. Clown and comic vocalist. Maginley, Carroll & Co., 1867; M. O'Conner & Co., 1870; Haight & Co., winter 1871-72.

FOWLER, BERT. Agent, World's Fair Aggegation, 1892.

FOWLER, HARVEY N. Proprietor, hotel de Barnum, P. T. Barnum's, 1876.

FOWLER, JAMES. Leaper and tumbler, Hamilton & Sargeant, 1878.

FOWLER, O. B. Agent. Haight, Chambers & Ames', 1867; Driesbach & Howes, 1868.

FOWLER, WILLIAM. Aerial performer. Cooke's, 1882; Sig. Sautelle's, 1886. Married **Fannie Traver**, non-professional, 1886.

FOWLER, WILLIAM M. Asssistant treasurer, Maginley & Co., 1874.

FOWLER, WILLIAM W. Born in Brooklyn, NY. First entered the circus profession on the business staff of Robinson & Eldred. Later connected with Spalding & Rogers, Jerry Mabie's, Sands & Nathans, Harry Buckley's and others, as treasurer, layer-out agent, and in other capacities. For several years, business manager of the **Carter Zouave Troupe**. Season of 1867-68, agent, **Peak Family** of Swiss bell ringers. For 10 years, business manager, **Berger Family** and **Sol Smith Russell**. At the time of death, manager and part owner of the "Two Sisters" Co. Died of pneumonia in Toronto, Canada, age 63.

FOX, CHARLES. H. Buckley & Co., 1857-58.

FOX, EDWARD. Leaper, John Robinson's, 1874-75.

FOX, JOHN. Master of transportation, King & Franklin, 1889.

FRANCE, F. F. Hart, France & Co. (**H. H. Hart**, F. F. France, proprietors), 1889.

FRANCIS, GEORGE. Tumbler and leaper, P. T. Barnum's, 1879-80; advance agent, Hurlburt & Hunting, 1887.

FRANCIS, MILLIE. Consolidation Circus (managed by **W. B. Hough**), 1866.

FRANCIS, WILLIAM. (d. July 21, 1892) Aerialist.

FRANCOIS BROTHERS. Great International Circus, Offenbach Garden, Philadelphia, winter 1876-77.

FRANCONI, ANGELINE. Equestrienne daughter of **Henri Franconi**. Franconi's New York Hippodrome, 1853; Levi J. North's, Chicago, 1857-58.

FRANCONI, HENRI. (October 24, 1818-January 22, 1905) Equestrian and showman. Came to America from France, 1853, for Franconi's Hippodrome, NYC. Hippoferean, 1855; Franconi's, 1855; Robinson & Eldred, November, 1855-June, 1856; Eldred's, 1856-57; John Robinson's, 1868-70, where he performed the trained horses Grey Eagle and Stonewall; equestrian director, Adam Forepaugh's, 1871. Died in South Hatfield, PA.

FRANK, TONY [or Franks]. (1839?-May 5, 1878) Band leader, Adam Forepaugh's, beginning, 1869, and continuing until his death during his 10th year. A native of Buffalo, NY. Was considered a thorough musician and well respected person. Died at the American Exchange Hotel, Virginia City, NV, age 39. His brother Charles, also with the Forepaugh show, accompanied the body to Brunswick, ME, for interment.

FRANKIE, M. Master of horse, George W. DeHaven's,

1865.

FRANKLIN, B. Gymnast, John Robinson's, 1876.

FRANKLIN, E. A. Sideshow manager, Howes' New Colossal Shows, 1888.

FRANKLIN, HARRY. Lake's Hippo-Olympiad, 1869.

FRANKLIN, HIRAM W. Pad rider, slack-rope artist and vaulter. One of the first of American leapers to accomplish a double somersault from the *battoute* board, 1850s. Palmer's, 1835; Sweet & Hough, 1835; Nathan A. Howes', 1836; June, Titus, Angevine & Co., 1839-42; Howes & Mabie, 1841, 1843; Rockwell & Stone, 1838, 1842; tight-rope, Nathan A. Howes' winter 1842; trampoline, John Tryon's, Bowery Amphitheatre, NYC, 1843; tight-rope, Rockwell & Stone, 1843-46; Rockwell's Amphitheatre, Cincinnati, 1846; tight-rope, Robinson & Eldred, 1847; Rockwell & Co., 1847-48; equestrian director, National Circus, Philadelphia, 1852; Welch & Lent, 1854, 1856; L. B. Lent's, 1859. Considered a good pad rider and proficient as a vaulter and slack rope performer. Odell quotes from the New York *Herald* of January 31, 1844, which describes Franklin as "the beautiful, fearless rider and unsurpassed vaulter." It goes on to say that "his double somersault and his wild gallop on his bare-back steed are feats of the most extraordinary interest which can be conceived." By this time, the double-somersault must have been a regular part of Franklin's performance. His double leaps, double somersaults, performance on the slack-wire and accomplishments as an equestrian made him one of the most versatile and talented performers of his day. Ultimately, succeeded in turning a triple somersault. Said to have thrown 76 consecutive sommersaults during a single performance. Was in South America, April 1864, where it was rumored that his ship foundered and sank (another source places the ship lost in the Mauritius in the Indian Ocean; and still another, lost at sea off the Cape of Good Hope).

FRANKLIN, J. D. Tattooed man, Robert Hunting's, 1894.

FRANKLIN, JOHN. Clown. L. B. Lent's, 1855-60; Madigan & Gardner, Front Street Theatre, Baltimore, 1860-61; principal rider, S. P. Stickney's, 1869.

FRANKLIN, J. W. Rider, leaper, tumbler, gymnast, Carlo Bros.', South America, 1877.

FRANKLIN, THOMAS, JR. Rider. Was with his father, **Thomas Franklin**, at Ricketts' circus, NYC, 1797. Also, with his father, had a short-lived circus venture, 1799. Operated a circus company in conjunction with a **Mr. Lattin**, rider and clown, 42 South Fifth Street, Philadelphia, spring 1802. In July, was performing at Vauxhall Garden, NYC. Combined with a **Mr. Robertson** in a circus venture (who could have been the balloonist), February 1803, at Newport, RI. Thomas Stewart's, Boston, 1809, Cayetano & Co., Canada, fall 1811.

FRANKLIN, THOMAS, SR. Clown. Father of rider **Thomas Franklin, Jr.** Member of English troupe (Breuning), 1786; Benjamin Handy troupe (UK, Breuning), 1788; Handy &

Franklin, 1789; Handy & Franklin, 1792; Franklin's, 1792; Hughes' (UK), 1793. With Ricketts' circus, New York City, 1797, and a southern tour with **Francis Ricketts** that same year. Thayer credits him with taking out the fourth multi-act circus in America, in association with a **Mr. Johnson** (or **Johnston**), an actor. They exhibited their equestrian skills in a piece called *The Peasant of the Alps* at a location that had once been the site of Lailson's circus. Began in NYC, February 8, 1799, and continued until March 19. Also made other stops but apparently was soon disbanded. Lattin & Franklin, 1802; Langley & Co., 1802. One of Franklin's feats was that of balancing a horse on which his son was seated, perhaps by holding up a platform while on his hands and knees; however it was accomplished, must have been a man of great strength. Died in America.

FRANKLIN, W. E. (March 3, 1853-March 29, 1936) Agent. Born near Lexington, IL. In charge of reserve seat privilege for **Joel E. Warner**, 1874; show closed before the end of the season; Franklin went with Doc Hoffman's. Agent, Pullman & Hamilton, 1875; general agent, Shelby, Pullman & Hamilton, 1876-1881; agent, King, Burk & Co., 1883-1887; King & Franklin, 1888. Following King's death, Franklin operated the show alone. Railroad contractor and excursion agent, Barnum & Bailey, 3 years; general agent, Walter L. Main's, 1895; John Robinson's, 1896-97; 1897-98. Went out with Robinson & Franklin Shows; then joined Hagenbeck-Wallace as general agent, with which he remained 9 years. Followed with an engagement with Sells-Floto, 1909-10. Then retired from the business to Valparaiso, IN. Died at his home, St. Petersburg, FL, age 73.

FRANKLIN, WILLIAM H. [r. n. George Avelos]. (d. December 16, 1883) Rider. Welch's, 1849; Rivers & Runnell, 1850; Madison & Stone, 1852-53; Welch & Lent, 1854-55; Rowe & Co.'s Pioneer Circus, San Francisco, 1856; Lee & Bennett, San Francisco, 1857; Hinkley & Kimball, 1858; Kimball's, 1859; Lathrop, Peoples, Franklin, 1860; John Wilson's, California, 1862; Gardner & Hemmings (under the Barnum name), Washington, DC, fall 1862; Lee & Ryland, San Francisco, winter 1866-67; principal rider, Golden State Circus (**W. B. Blaisdell**, proprietor), California, 1868; Chestnut Street Theatre, Philadelphia, winter 1868-69; Stone & Murray, 1869; Rosston, Springer & Henderson, 1871; clown and pad act, Adam Forepaugh's, 1872-75; Imperial Brazilian Hippodrome, Philadelphia, winter 1872-73; Adam Forepaugh's, 1876; Carlo Bros.', South America, 1877; American Circus (**A. Guilig, G. Ravell**, W. H. Franklin, proprietors), South America, 1879. Married **Sallie Stickney**, 1872, while both were with Adam Forepaugh's. Died in Brazil.

FRANKS, TONY. See Tony Frank.

FRANZ, R. C. High stilt performer, Great Oriental Pavilion Show, 1877.

FRASER, WILLIAM H. (1819?-May 1893) Equestrian. Native of Scotland. Gained most prominence with Barnum, Bailey & Hutchinson. Died of injuries from a fall down a flight of stairs at his home, age 74.

FRASH, TAYLOR. Rider, Warner & Henderson, 1874.

FRAZER, DICK. Frank Rich's, 1886.

FRAZER, H. E. Treasurer, Homer Davis' New Show, 1879.

FRAZER, R. W. Caldwell's, 1867.

FREDERICKS, GEORGE. Trapeze performer. Parisian Circus, Operti's Tropical Garden, Philadelphia, fall 1876; single trapeze, Stickney's Imperial Parisian Circus, 1880; Adam Forepaugh's, 1881.

FREDERICKS, MLLE. VanAmburgh & Co., December 1859.

FREDERICKS, WILLIAM. British rider. Advertised as: "Bareback rider and Exponent of the 'Bounding Jockey' from Hengler's Grand *Cirque*, London. He also presents his Performing Goat 'Pete' in the amusing act of *The Crown and the Goat*." John H. Murray's, 1874, first appearance in America.

FREELY BROTHERS. Trapeze, P. T. Barnum's, 1871.

FREEMAN, CHARLES. Sideshow giant. Bowery Amphitheatre, 1841; L. B. Lent's, 1860. This must be the man who was a rider with a circus at Arcadian Gardens, NYC. With his 7' frame, rode 2 horses and could execute a double-somersault. February 5, 1842, sparred with **Ben Count** at the Bowery Theatre, NYC. Had previously been on exhibit at the American Museum. Afterwards, was a pugilistic hero who, under the title of Freeman, the American Giant, fought Perry, the Tipton Slasher, England. Died there of consumption.

FREEMAN, L. Contortionist, June & Turner's, 1845-46.

FREEMAN, WILLIAM H. Miller, Stowe & Freeman (**Charles A. Miller, James B. Stowe**, William H. Freeman, proprietors), 1887.

FREEMAN, W. W. Press agent. Sells Bros.', 1882; Miller, Stowe & Freeman (**Charles A. Miller, James B. Stowe**, William H. Freeman, proprietors), 1886-87.

FREES, J. Agent, John Robinson's, 1887.

FREMONT, W. H. Contracting agent, Bartine's, 1896.

FRENCH, CHARLES. 10-horse band chariot driver, Dan Rice's, 1870.

FRENCH, CHARLES and FAMILY [Lilly, Harry, Eric, George]. Bicyclists and skaters Clown, Delavan's, 1886.

FRENCH FAMILY [Laura, Lilly, Harry, Eric, George]. Bicyclists and skaters, Barnum & Bailey, 1889.

FRENCH, HARRY. Member of Holton & Gates' Harmoniums, a minstrel band organized for the the Simon Pure American Circus, New York, October 1, 1866.

FRENCH, JAMES M. (August 7, 1821-January 10, 1902) Born in Woodstock, CT. Became a nationally-known menagerie owner whose quarters were on Woodward Avenue, Highland Park, Michigan. Left his father's farm at 12 years of age and located in the South, where he ran a general store in the Tuckapaw Region of Louisiana. A good judge of horses and livestock, started a horse market in New Orleans and dealt in the finest animals for carriage and road purposes and supplied all the wealthy people in that city and throughout the Southwest. Went into the cotton business and many times ran blockades on the Mississippi. Joined the Confederate Army and served at the front. Had one-third interest in Thayer & Noyes, 1866. 23 days of rain made it necessary for his partners to borrow from him. Shortly, was forced to attach the show in Detroit, September 25, 4 weeks before scheduled closing. J. M. French's Great Oriental Circus and Egyptian Caravan opened April 20, 1867 in Detroit. The Egyptian Caravan part of the title represented the results of a good business deal. Before the war, 1856-57, the Army had imported a shipload of camels to establish a mail route from San Antonio, TX, to the Pacific Coast, the Jeff Davis camel experiment. They were sold when the project failed, the ones in California, 1864, and those in Texas, 1866. French bought 40 of the animals for a minimal price. Hitched a team of 12 of them to his big bandwagon for the street parade, allegedly the first ever broken to work in harness without the assistance of horses (both Sands and Howes had 10-camel hitches, 1848, being the first groups brought into this country). His elephant, Empress, imported in 1869, was said at that time to be the largest ever brought to America. After his circus was auctioned off at Trenton, NJ, November 3, 1870, he kept the animals and took them to Detroit where he built quarters on Woodward Avenue and leased them to traveling shows in the summer and housed them at the Michigan quarters in the winter. Intended to quit circus management for other pursuits; however, the J. M. French's Oriental Circus and Egyptian Caravan was reported on the road in 1871. The same year, leased animals to Cole & Orton. Had the concert privilege, G. G. Grady's, 1872; leased animals to J. E. Warner, 1873; leased animals to Warner, Springer & Henderson, 1874; exhibited animals on a lot on Woodward Avenue, 1875; leased to Excelsior Circus and Menagerie, 1875. At its early closure, he placed an ad in the August 21 New York *Clipper*: "The Excelsior Circus & Menagerie having closed at Prescott, Ontario, for want of money and brains is now at my place. Can be fitted out on short notice." 1876, organized a show with L. B. Lent for which he was general manager; left the firm mid-July that year. Leased to the Great Roman Hippodrome, 1877, which collapsed in Buffalo in July. Then leased to George W. DeHaven's Hippodrome, 1878. Announced plans to give Roman Hippodrome races at horse tracks and county fairs. Was to lease animals to Lincoln Park Zoo, Chicago, but lost them when on May 22, 1879, the animal building in Detroit and the entire menagerie were destroyed by fire before they could be shipped. Later, opened a variety theatre with clown **Jerry Hopper**, November 1884, Sheboygan, MI, and ran the Grand Central Hotel there until 1892, when he sold out and moved back to Detroit. Took great pleasure in owning race horses and, through this, was Director of the Gents Driving Club, which built a half-mile track in Highland Park. Died at his residence, 20 Lincoln Ave., Detroit, after succumbing to an attack of erysipelas, age 81.

FRENCH, L. H. [Leigh Hill]. French & Co., 1883; French & Monroe, boat show, 1885; Howes' New London (French and Monroe, proprietors), 1888; French's New Sensation, showboat, 1890.

FRENCH, REUBEN. Agent with a menagerie as early as 1830. Managed for the Zoological Institute, French, Hobby & Co., on the road as a menagerie, 1834; was possibly the French connected with Quick & Mead, 1826, who traveled on horseback and kept his advertising paper in two saddlebags, possibly making him the first to advance a tented circus.

FRESH, TAYLOR. Rider, with Warner & Henderson, 1874. Also had his own show.

FRIDAY, FRITZ. Band leader, John Robinson's, 1859-60; John Robinson's, 1864-65, 1869-72.

FRIERBERG, LEW. Orchestra leader, Wintermute Bros.', 1897.

FRIHE, JOHN. Orchestra leader, Castello & VanVleck, 1863.

FRISBIE, ALFRED. See Alfred Miaco.

FRITZ, EDWIN. Acrobat. Around 1870 formed a partnership with **James Cassim** and performed under the name of **Cassim & Fritz**, traveling through France and Spain, then to India and South America. Following, were engaged for a year at the Bella Union Theatre, San Francisco. Succeeding engagements were at the Theatre Comique, St. Louis and the Metropolitan Theatre, NYC, the latter under the management of **R. W. Butler**. Traveled with L. B. Lent's for 2 seasons, performing in variety theatres in the winter. Howes & Cushing (**F. B. Howes** and **Joseph Cushing**, proprietors), 1875; Cooper & Bailey, 1876, and accompanying the show to San Francisco, then to Australia and South America. Returned to NYC and opened at Niblo's Garden, December 23, 1878; knockabout clown, Great Commonwealth Circus, 1879; tumbler and leaper, P. T. Barnum's, 1879-80, 1885; Pat Ryan's, 1882. Married to performer **Kittie Sharpe**.

FRITZ, JOHN. Cole's Colossal Circus (**George S. Cole, John H. Sparks**, proprietors), 1893; Cole & Lockwood, 1894.

FROST, C. Contracting agent, VanAmburgh's, 1871.

FROST, CHARLES. (October 10, 1822-August 1905) Old time circus man and brother of **Hyatt Frost**.

FROST, FRANK. Nephew of **Hyatt Frost**; manager of Robinson's Circus, California, 1886. That same year, put out the show under the VanAmburgh name, which exasperated his uncle. [Hyatt Frost: "I have worked hard for forty years to become sole manager of the menagerie and circus and title of VanAmburgh & Frost Shows and I have no interest whatsoever in the so-called show now in California and never did have. I would not, under any circumstances, permit the public to be deceived under the name VanAmburgh & Frost by paying their money to see an imitation show, owned and run by men who have so grossly pilfered me of my good name and title. Many an old 'forty-niner' now in California is personally acquainted with me and is well aware that I never had anything to do with any show but the best."] General manager, John Forepaugh's, California, 1888.

FROST, H. C. Assistant treasurer, Alex Robinson's, 1870.

FROST, HYATT. (March 4, 1827-September 3, 1895) Born Southeast, Putnam County, NY. Joined Raymond & Waring at age 19, working for the candy privilege man. Subsequently, with VanAmburgh's, managed by **James Raymond**. At the outset, went ahead of the show doing the billing, but became manager when Raymond died. Purchased the show, 1857, with **Ira Gregory**. Married **Miss Sarah Halstead**, January 19, 1864. 1868, a partner in the Barnum, VanAmburgh & Co.'s Museum, NYC, when the establishment was destroyed by fire, sustaining a $200,000 loss (the men also owned VanAmburgh & Co.'s Great Golden Menagerie). Established the use of a cook tent, 1871. 1881, determining the need of a rest after over 35 years in the circus business, advertised VanAmburgh & Co. for auction. Last managerial venture was with the Reiche Brothers, animal importers, 1885. Shortly after that, Frost, a "black-bearded, piratical-looking" man, retired reasonably well off. Died at his home near Amenia, NY.

FROST, I. P. Proprietor (with **N. R. Husted**), Frost, Husted & Co., 1836; proprietor, Frost & Co., 1837.

FROST, PHOEBE. See Madame Sanyeah.

FRYER, ROBERT W. [or Freyer]. Horse trainer, bronco horses, dogs and goats, with Coup's Equescuricculum, 1878. At the close of the season, built an establishment for training horses and dogs in Independence, IA. One of the acts developed was a moving pyramid with 7 horses, culminating in a "statuesque tableau." Another was a performance on stilts by a pony, never before successfully accomplished. Exhibited a trick horse and performing mules, Caldwell's Occidental Circus, 1867; equestrian manager, P. A. Older's, 1872 (and married his daughter); equestrian director, Nathans & Co., 1882; W. C. Coup's, 1879-81; equestrian director, Barnum & London, 1884; proprietor, Fryer's New United Shows, East Indies, Australia and South America, 1886-87.

FUEGO, SIGNOR. "The Fire Fiend, revolving in the air amid a globe of fire," J. W. Wilder's, 1872.

FUHRMAN, KARL [or Carl]. Organist for the Spalding & Rogers' Appollonicon, 1849, band leader, 1850; organist, 1852-53.

FULFORD, ABEL H. ["Abe"]. (August 9, 1848-1913) Born in Belleville, Canada. Co-proprietor and business manager, Fulford & Co.'s Great United London Shows (A. K. Fulford, **William McClintock, W. M. Lyttle, Jesse C. Elliott**, proprietors), 1890. Had at one time been a partner with **W. M. Lyttle** in a stage coach line. Prior to his brief fling in show business, he and his brother had been partners in a construction business, chiefly doing excavations and road building. The circus was on the road only one season. Died in Topeka, KS, age 66.

FULLER, CHARLES W. (March 1, 1826-April 9, 1888) Agent. Franconi's, 1853; Rivers & Derious, 1854-55; J. W. Myers', 1856; Nixon & Kemp, 1857-58; James M. Nixon's, 1859-60; first managerial job was as proprietor, Monitor Show, 1865, which carried a wagon fashioned to represent the gunboat Monitor, containing a stereoptic and panoramic views of the Civil War; S. O. Wheeler's, 1863; contracting agent, L. B. Lent's, 1864, 1867-72; general manager, P. T. Barnum's Roman Hippodrome, 1874-75; general agent and railroad contractor, Cooper, Bailey & Co., 1876-77; general manager, Coup's Equescurricculum, 1878; Cooper & Bailey, 1879-82; railroad director, Adam Forepaugh's, 1884-85; railroad contractor, Barnum & Bailey, 1886-87. Was twice married. After some 30 years in the circus business, had an interest in the Fuller Detective Agency, managed by his step-son. Died at his home in NYC.

FULLER, EDWARD. G. G. Grady's, 1868.

FULLER, H. A. Candy stand privileges, New York Champs Elysees, 1866; Australian Circus, 1870.

FULLER, H. H. Proprietor (with **A. R. Fuller**), Olympic Circus, 1835; manager, Macomber, Welch & Co., 1836; manager, Boston Amphitheatre, 1837; proprietor, H. H. Fuller's Olympic Circus, 1838.

FULLER, W. E. Assistant manager, Cook & Whitby, 1892; assistant manager, Great Wallace (**B. E. Wallace**, proprietor), 1893, general agent, 1896.

FULTON, JOHN. (d. December 6, 1887) Joined Yankee Robinson's, 1855, in charge of the candy stand and remained 3 years. Went into the sideshow business, traveling with several circuses until the outbreak of Civil War. Enlisted but was sent home after an injury from falling off a horse. Started in the museum business, Indianapolis, IN. Joined Yankee Robinson's again, 1866; sideshow privilege, Lake's Hippo-Olympiad, 1867; sideshow privilege (with **George Middleton**), Hemmings, Cooper & Whitby, 1870; candy stand (with **George Coup**), P. T. Barnum's, 1871; sideshow, Sells Bros.', 1872; sideshow and candy stand, George F. Bailey & Co., 1873; sideshow, Warner, Henderson & Springer, 1874; Melville, Maginley & Cooke, 1875; candy stand (with **George Coup**), P. T. Barnum's, 1876; A. S. Burt's, 1883; sideshow manager, Frank A. Robbins', 1882, 1884-87. Died in NYC.

FULTON, M. Acrobat and leaper, Haight's Great Southern, 1874.

FUNK, AD. Agent, Walt McCafferty's Great Golden Shows, 1894.

FUQUA, JAMES. Boss hostler, Cooper, Bailey & Co., 1876-80; Barnum, Bailey & Hutchinson, 1881-82.

FUREY, ROBERT. General performer, Howes & Sanger, 1872.

FURSMAN, GEORGE W. (1847-April 27, 1903) Born in Nassau, NY. John H. Murray's; Burr Robbins'; privileges, Sells Bros.', 1878; treasurer, Campbell's, 1878; VanAmburgh's, 1879; Robbins & Colvin, 1881; Buffalo Bill's Wild West Show, 1895-1897. Formed a partnership with **George Peck**, Peck & Fursman, and put out several companies. Married **Georgia Millson** around 1881. A daughter, **Eugenie**, was married in 1902 to **William Sweeney**, bandmaster of the Buffalo Bill Wild West Show.

FUSNER, JESSE L. Talking and singing clown. Walter L. Main's, 1887, 1892; Sam MacFlinn's, 1888; Lee's Great London, 1893, where he worked the parade as a rube, stopping to make inquiries, etc.

G

GAFFNEY, ANDREW [or Gafney]. (March 25, 1826-August 11, 1892) Strong man performer, billed as the "Irish Giant." Born in Ontario, Canada. Started in the circus business by driving a wagon, which he did for several years before he became a performer. Being a man with a powerful physique, eventually, as one source indicates, pursuaded his employer, **W. W. Cole,** to get **Isaac VanAmburgh** to watch him toss cannon balls, which landed him his first job as a performer and began a career that continued until his death. Another source reveals the beginning of his strong man act was with Raymond & VanAmburgh, 1852. Was one of the first men to toss cannon balls in America and perhaps the first to introduce the feature of pulling against horses. One time, in competition with **John Jennings,** he tossed the 4 pound weight 115'. As a cannon ball performer, juggled 25 to 50 pound cannon balls, threw them in the air, and caught them on his neck and shoulders. Also was the understander in a perch-pole act. Orton Bros.', 1856-1867; Stowe & Orton, 1869-70; John Stowe & Sons, 1871; VanAmburgh & Co., 1874, 1879-81; Carlo Bros.', South America, 1877; Frank Robbins', 1883-88; Ringling Bros.', 1891. By 1860, was living in McGregor, IA, and tending bar in the off-season. Was married twice and had 2 children by the first wife. Died at his home in NYC.

GAGE, CHARLES. Animal trainer, Hilliard & DeMott, 1880.

GAGENBACHS. Frank Rich's Great Eastern Railroad Alliance, 1886.

GAGLIANI, MLLE. Parisian equestrienne, Front Street Theartre, Baltimore, early winter 1860.

GAGNON, MRS. JOSEPHINE. See Josie Ashton.

GALE, GEORGE. Stage manager, William Blanchard & William West's, Canada, 1825.

GALE, M. F. Gas engineer, P. T. Barnum's, 1873.

GALLAGHER, JAMES. Gymnast. Older's, 1871; Cosmopolitan Circus, winter 1871-72; Haight's Great Eastern, 1874; Cooper, Bailey & Co., 1876; VanAmburgh's, 1883.

GALLAGHER, J. P. Downie & Gallagher (**Andrew Downie,** J. P. Gallagher, proprietors), 1891-92; J. P. Gallagher's New Columbian Shows, 1893-94; VanAmburgh & Gallagher's New Railroad Shows, 1900-01.

GALLAGHER, MARQUESE. VanAmburgh's, 1882.

GALLAGHER, THOMAS A. Pinkerton detective, Barnum, Bailey & Hutchinson, 1881-82.

GANUNG, EDWARD. (b. 1799) Treasurer, Joseph D. Palmer's, 1834-36; manager, June, Titus, Angevine & Co., 1839; director, Aaron Turner's, 1849; Mabie & Ganung, 1954; E. Ganung & Co., 1858.

GANWEILER, GEORGE. Band leader, with Adam Fore-paugh's, 1889 and into the 1890s; also with Ringling Bros.' [C. G. Sturtevant: "The outstanding characteristic of Ganweiler was his tremendous zeal and efficiency. A master musician himself, he was a terror to incompetents and shirkers.... Yet men knew if they had a season under Ganweiler that was the only recommendation needed, and to good competent men he was most considerate and paid top money."]

GARBUTT, J. Clown, H. C. Lee & Co., California, 1870.

GARCIA. Acrobat, Pepin's company, Philadelphia, 1816, and Lancaster for summer 1817; Pepin & West, Olympic, Philadelphia, fall 1817; Pepin's company, NYC, spring 1819; Pepin, West Indies, 1819-20; Pepin's, 1821-22; vaulter and clown, Pepin & Barnet, 1822-26.

GARDNER, CAMILLA [sometimes advertised as "Madame Camille"]. (September 20, 1821-October 21, 1869) Equestrienne wife of Dan Gardner. Born in Bedford, PA. Began professional career, 1835, Old Bowery Amphitheatre, NYC, under the management of Henry Rockwell. An early rival with Marie Macarte for riding honors, she gave birth to 9 children, 5 of whom were living when she died—**William H., Eliza** (Mrs. Charles Kenyon), **Maggie, Camilla** ("La Petite Camille," Mrs. Sam Holdsworth), and **Eddie.** Thomas Taplin Cooke's, 1838; Howes & Mabie, 1841; performed act of "Lady Sylphide," Welch's, Philadelphia, 1843; Nathan A. Howes', winter 1843-44; Howes & Gardner (**Nathan A. Howes** and **Dan Gardner,** proprietors), 1844; Rockwell & Stone, 1843-44; Crane & Co., circa 1847; Crane & Co., 1849; Welch's National Circus, 1850, 1858; Rivers & Derious, 1857; L. B. Lent's, 1858; Madigan & Gardner, Front Street Theatre, Baltimore, 1860-61; Gardner & Hemmings, 1861-68. Died in Philadelphia.

GARDNER, DAN. (October 25, 1816-October 7, 1880) Showman, general performer, clown, juggler, etc. Born in NYC. Patriarch of the performing Gardner family. Father was in the printing trade, wanted his son to follow him. Worked in the print shop for a time but, not enjoying the profession, ran off some time around 1826 and became an assistant property man for the Mount Pitt Circus, NYC. Performed for the first time there, 1828, singing "Push Along, Keep Moving" and playing clown for **Archie Madden** during an equestrian act. Performed on the slack-rope, Palmer & Harrington, 1834; juggler, Bancker & Harrington, 1835; juggler, Charles H. Bacon's, 1837-38; rider, Thomas Taplin Cooke's, 1838; tumbler, June, Titus, Angevine & Co., 1840-41; clown, Howes & Mabie, 1841; clown, Nathan A. Howes', winter 1942; Nathan A. Howes', winter 1843-44; Howes & Gardner (**Nathan A. Howes** and Dan Gardner, proprietors), 1844; John Tryon's, Bowery Amphitheatre, NYC, 1845; Rockwell & Stone, 1846;

Rockwell & Co., 1847; Crane & Co., 1849; Welch's, 1850; Rivers & Derious, 1857; L. B. Lent's, 1858. Organize a show with **Richard Hemmings** and **James Madigan** at Philadelphia, 1860, Gardner, Hemmings and Madigan. Began at Camac's Woods, then moved the show to dates in Pennsylvania before returning to Philadelphia's Continental Theatre and a short winter engagement. Now called Madigan & Gardner's, the company transported to the Front Street Theatre, Baltimore, for a December 3 opening. Tom King's, Washington, DC, winter 1861-62. Gardner and Hemmings took **John O'Brien** as a partners 1862; **James E. Cooper** bought up O'Brien's interest, 1863, and the show was billed as Gardner, Hemmings and Cooper. 1866, the firm engaged **Dan Rice** at $1,000 per week. 1867, Gardner sold his share of the show to James Cooper because of an altercation with Rice. Went in with **John O'Brien** in the Gardner & Kenyon Show, 1868. Manager, James Robinson's, 1869; clown, P. T. Barnum's, 1871; Cooper, Hemmings & Whitby, 1871; and James E. Cooper's, 1872. In retirement, resided in Philadelphia and spent summers in Atlantic City, where he was the proprietor of the Columbia House. First wife was **Camilla** (see above). Second wife, **Mary J.**, formerly **Mrs. Samuel Cornwell**, who, between 1860 and 1870, was employed as wardrobe mistress in theatres throughout the country. She died July 25, 1905, in Philadelphia.

GARDNER, EDWARD. Son of **Dan** and **Camilla Gardner**. Gardner & Hemmings, 1859-63; James Robinson's, 1869; agent, James E. Cooper's, 1872; treasurer, Adam Forepaugh's, 1873.

GARDNER, ELIZA [Mrs. Charles Kenyon]. Equestrienne, serio-comic singer, skipping rope dancer. Daughter of **Dan** and **Camilla Gardner**. As a single or with her faanily, Rivers & Derious, 1857-58; Madigan & Gardner, Front Street Theatre, Baltimore, 1860-61; Tom King's, 1862; Gardner & Hemmings, 1862; principal rider, National Circus, Philadelphia, winter 1863-64; Gardner & Hemmings, 1860-66; Lipman & Stokes', 1866; Philadelphia Circus (managed by **Dan Gardner**), winter 1867-68; James Robinson's, 1869; Handenburger & Co. (**John O'Brien**, proprietor), 1871; Backenstoe's, 1872; Adam Forepaugh's, 1873. Married December 3, 1865, to a circus non-performer and later to circus manager **Charles Kenyon**. Last husband died in Peoria, IL, July 20, 1892, age 47. Their 2 daughters, **Ella** and **Minnie**, were stage performers.

GARDNER, FRANK A. (March 30, 1855-October 9, 1905) Bareback hurdle rider, leaper, tumbler, equestrian director, proprietor. Once considered the world champion double somersault leaper. Born in Oswego, NY. After his family moved to Macomb, IL, where **James T. Johnson's** circus wintered, young Frank became enchanted with circus life and joined as an apprentice, 1865. Was hired away from Johnson, 1870, by the **Michael O'Conner** show but, before the season ended,

was back with Johnson. VanAmburgh's, 1871, where, in White Cloud, KS, he and **John Barry** both turned double somersaults over 10 and 12 horses; Dan Rice's, 1872, when he is reported to have executed a "double somersault over 10 horses placed side by side and a pyramid 3 high covering a distance of 25'." That year the New York *Clipper* announced that he was the second man ever to turn a double somersault over 13 horses abreast. Rider, leaper, and gymnast, Dan Rice's Paris Pavilion, 1871-72; Noyes' Crescent City, winter 1872-73; Great Eastern, 1873; Great New York and New Orleans, 1873; VanAmburgh's, 1874; Springer's Royal Cirqzoolodon, 1875; Burr Robbins', 1875; W. W. Cole's, 1877, 1879-80, 1883. While with Cole's, 1880, the press described his performance as one of vaulting over camels and elephants for a distance of 50' and a height of 15' as he turned a double somersault along the way. Orrin Bros.', Havana, winter 187778, 1879; leaper, Cooper, Bailey & Co., 1878; Barnum, Bailey & Hutchinson, 1881; Dockrill & Leon, Havana, winter 1881-82; Sells Bros.', 1884-87; Barrett's, 1887; equestrian director, Howes Great London, 1903. Toured South America for several years with his own company. Frank A. Gardner's Circus, West Indies, 1884; Roberts & Gardner (**Nick Roberts**, F. A. Gardner, proprietors), 1886; Gardner & Donovan, South America, 1886; Frank A. Gardner's, Central and South America, winter 1887-88; Frank A. Gardner's *Circo Americano*, Panama, Central and South America, 1888; Frank A. Gardner's, West Indies and South America, 1891-96. For 5 years prior to his death was equestrian director for VanAmburgh's. Wife, **Mildred**, was a *manège* performer; daughter, **Lulu**, worked the rings, did loop walking and the trapeze. Small in stature, but strong and well-proportioned, Gardner was one of the greatest leapers of all times, ranking at the very least on a par with **Fred O'Brien** and **William H. Batcheller**.

GARDNER, HENRY A. Rider and acrobat. Welch, Bartlett & Co., 1840; June, Titus, Angevine & Co., 1841-42; Rockwell & Stone, 1843; Howes & Mabie, 1843; winter circus, Niblo's Garden, 1843-44; Dr. Gilbert R. Spalding's, 1844-46; S. P. Stickney's, 1846-48; Aaron Turner's, 1849; Crane & Co., 1850; Dan Rice's, 1851; Major Brown's Mammoth Coloseum, 1857; Cooper & Myers' Circus of All Nations, 1858; Davis & Crosby, 1859; Robinson & Lake, 1865; Orton Bros.', 1867-69.

GARDNER, MARIA CELESTE. Equestrienne, P. T. Barnum's, 1871.

GARDNER, MILDRED. *Manège*. "Empress of the SideSaddle," Sells Bros.', 1885.

GARDNER, WILLIAM F. ["Doc"]. Agent. Raised in West Union, IA. Commenced in the business with W. W. Cole's, where he remained about 3 years. After that show closed, went to Barnum & Bailey for some years, not only in this country but in Europe. After the return to USA, and the show fell into the hands of the Ringlings, Gardner also followed to the Ringlings, where he was connected with the advance for 7 years.

Later, was in advance of the motion picture, *The Birth of a Nation.*

GARDNER, WILLIAM HENRY. (July 19, 1842-April 19, 1906) Eldest child of **Dan** and **Camilla Gardner.** Born in NYC. Recognizable by his red moustache and small stature. Welch's National Circus, Philadelphia, 1857-58; began as an advertiser for Gardner & Hemmings, 1861; Chestnut Street Theatre, Philadelphia, 1865; part owner, Gardner & Hemmings, 1866; sold interest to Harry Whitby, 1867; manager, Gardner & Kenyon's, 1868, agent, 1869; advertiser, James Robinson's, 1869; agent, John O'Brien's, 1870-71; general director, James E. Cooper's, 1872; general agent, Cooper & Bailey, 1873-74, privileges for the latter, 1875-76; accompanied them to Australia and South America as assistant manager, 1877-78; general agent, Anderson & Co. (Sells Bros.), 1879; general agent, Adam Forepaugh's, 1880; Barnum, Bailey & Hutchinson, 1881, serving as general agent continuously until 1892. Announced retirement in November of that year but, shortly, acquired part interest in the Pawnee Bill Show, 1893-94. Railroad contractor, Walter L. Main's, 1894; general agent, Buffalo Bill's Wild West Show, 1895-97; went to Europe as general agent for Barnum & Bailey, 1897, remaining until 1901; Forepaugh-Sells, 1902-03. After retiring again, 1904, soon bought into the Hagenbeck show and became its general agent. Died of pneumonia, NYC, an illness he contracted while attending the funeral of the great **James A. Bailey.** [Charles H. Day: "W. H. G. is a fine advertiser and a fair writer and, what is quite as good, a judge of good writing. The bill posters in the country ought to get him up a gold medal for getting them good salaries. He has done more to raise their wages than any other man in the business."]

GARHOLT, G. Beckett's Great Exposition, 1881.

GARRETT, CHARLES. (d. March 19, 1889) Sears & Garrett Menagerie (Rivers & Derious), 1857; manager, George K. Goodwin's, 1860; Wambold & Whitby, 1861; Goodwin, Wilder & Rice, 1862; Garrett's Union Museum (sideshow of O'Toole & Miles, Canada), 1863; also sideshow, Thayer & Noyes, 1864; went into hall shows, 1865. Died in Worcester, MA.

GARSON, FRED. Vaulter. Price & Simpson, 1827; Palmer & Harrington, 1834; ringmaster, Joseph D. Palmer's, 1835, Frost, Hosted & Co, 1836; clown, Frost & Co., 1837; W. Gates & Co., 1838; Philadelphia Circus, 1840; Bowery Amphitheatre, 1841; ringmaster, Bartlett & Delavan, 1841, ringmaster, Welch & Mann, 1841; Stickney & Buckley, 1844. clown, S. P. Stickney's, 1845-47.

GAROUX, EMILE. Dancing barrel, magic cross. Dr. James L. Thayer's; Lowande's Great Brazilian, 1877.

GARVEY, H. J. Lion king, VanAmburgh's, 1881.

GARVEY, JOHN. Strong man and juggler, Olympic Circus, 1935; Nathan A. Howes', 1836; Richmond Hill, winter circus, NYC, 1837; tranca act, J. W. Stocking's, 1839; flying cord, S.

H. Nichols & Co., winter 1843; acrobat, T. L. Vermule's, 1945; Welch & Mann, 1846.

GARWOOD, E. B. Advance agent, Hawkins & Loomis Dog and Pony Show, 1997.

GASSETT, CHARLES. See Charles Garrett.

GASTON, ALBERT. (October 20, 1851-June 20, 1931) Gymnast and leaper, Montgomery Queen's, 1874; triple horizontal bar act with **Sam Ashton** and **Frank Clifton,** Montgomery Queen's, 1875; **Gaston, Levantine & Leopold,** vaulters and tumblers, Montgomery Queen's, 1876; Robinson & Colvin, 1881; "English Knockabout Pantomimist," S. H. Barrett & Co., 1882-84; retired, 1885, to clerk at Nutt Hotel, Crawfordsville, IN; clown, John Robinson's, 1891-92; M. L. Clark & Sons, 1912; Howes', 1921. Died at Percy Williams Home, East Islip, LI.

GASTON, JEANETTE. Equestrienne, Joel E. Warner's, 1876.

GATES, CHARLES A. Holton & Gates' Harmoniums, a minstrel band organized for the the Simon Pure American Circus, New York, October 1, 1866.

GATES, WILLIAM. (d. September 17, 1843) Clown. Bancker's, 1824; William West's, 1825; Samuel McCracken's, 1825-26; manager, Parson's, 1826; (presumably) proprietor, W. Gates & Co., 1838; Welch, Bartlett & Co., 1840. Also a low comedian, one of the most popular ever to play the Bowery Theatre, NYC. [Noah Ludlow: He was "a quiet, unpretending man, of sound mind and manly nature, genial and well disposed to all mankind."]

GAUL, HENRY K. Band leader, Aaron Turner's, 1841; Howes & Mabie, 1844-45; Stone & McCollum, 1846-50; G. B. Johnson's, 1851-52; Franconi's Hippodrome, 1953; Flagg & Aymar, 1856; John Robinson's, 1856-57.

GAULF, LAURA. Double trapeze, break-away ladder, and iron jaw (with **Bob Beasley**), Goodrich's, 1897.

GARVIE, EDWARD. Press agent, Harper Bros.' European, 1893.

GAYLER, CHARLES [or Gaylor]. (April 10, 1820-May 29, 1892) Press agent. Born on Oliver Street, NYC, but went to Ohio, 1836. Began a career as a school teacher, then became a lawyer and journalist and, for a brief time, an actor, making his debut as Hamlet, 1849, at the National Theatre, Cincinnati. Shortly thereafter, his first play, *The Gold Hunters,* was produced there. As a lawyer, practiced on the same circuit as Abraham Lincoln. Moved to NYC, 1850, and was active as a theatrical manager, theatrical reviewer and playwright. Said to have written some 300 plays. Along with Bronson Howard, was responsibile for initiating the American Dramatists Club. As a circus agent, was with Seth B. Howes', 1864; VanAmburgh's, 1869; P. T. Barnum's, 1878-80. Married **Grace Christian,** 1846. Died of Bright's disease at his residence, Brooklyn, NY, age 72. [Charles H. Day: "Gayler made a dollar for the 'Flatfoots' with his pen and had the good sense to know how to charge for it."]

GAYLER, FRANK C. Press agent, Frank A. Robbins', 1887-89.

GAYLER SISTERS. Queen's Circus and Menagerie (**Polly** and **Austin,** proprietors), 1887.

GAYLORD, EDWARD. Excursion agent, Cooper, Bailey & Co., 1876.

GAYLORD, J. B. (October 2, 1941-June 7, 1900) Agent. Born in Geneva, OH, but moved to Iowa with his parents at age 11 and settled on a farm near Independence. Enlisted in the Union Army, 1961, and served throughout the war. Entry into the circus business came, 1868, as agent for Orton Bros.' Miles Orton, 1869; W. W. Cole's, 1871-75; general advance manager, Cooper & Bailey, 1876-78, playing in Australia, Java, and South America; W. W. Cole's, 1878-81, some of that time in Australia; Cooper, Jackson & Co., 1882. Went abroad with Barnum & Bailey; in advance of Fryer's New United Shows, a trained animal outfit, East Indies, Australia and South America, 1886-87; Sells Bros.', Australia, 1888; Sturtevant & Holland, 1891. Went to Singapore, 1892-93, returning with a cargo of wild animals; another trip the following year resulted in his bringing back a number of natives of Malaya and other East Indian countries; another trip for animals occurred, 1895. Married **Olive I. Brooks,** 1871, a union that produced 2 daughters. Died at his home in Independence, MO.

GAYLORD, LEE. Signor Montanio's Great New York, 1881.

GAYLORD, LOWRENZO ["Low"]. (January 19, 1836-April 7, 1878) Born in Westfield, MA. At the early age of 12 left home and launched into show business, singing ballads with John Green's Circus. Clown, Spalding & Rogers, but left the circus and settled down in Philadelphia, where he began a career as a negro minstrel by leasing old Southwark Hall in Second Street, which was opened as Gaylord & Dupont's Opera House. 1877, was taken sick and confined to his bed until he died in poverty from consumption.

GAYLORD, WILLIAM. Contortionist, Sells Bros.', 1877; Cantellis & Leon, winter circus, Havana, 1882; Frank Robbins', 1883; Gregory Bros.', 1984; Orrin Bros.', Mexico, fall 1885.

GAVAZZENI, SIG. HENRICO. With Haight, Chambers & Ames', 1867.

GEASLEY, ADOLPH. Sells Bros.', a first year organization, 1872.

GEBEST, CHARLES. Band leader, John Robinson's, 1880--93.

GEBLER, MATTHEW. (1938?-July 5, 1899) Ringmaster, clown and lecturer. Born and raised in Philadelphia. As a youth, hung about theatres and then went on the stage, a singer of comic songs. As circus performer, was with Rosston, Springer & Henderson, 1871; Barnum's, O'Brien's, Rivers',

Forepaugh's and others. Was a somewhat magician and Punch and Judy manipulator, and lecturer. Announcer for Pawnee Bill's Wild West Show around 1894, and for a time a lecturer at Bradenburgh's Museum, Nineth and Arch Streets, Philadelphia, and Huber's Museun, NYC. Also traveled with medicine shows as lecturer and doctor. Died in the county hospital, Lancaster, PA, age nearly 62.

GEE, JOHN. Boss canvasman, Donaldson & Rich, 1885.

GEIGER, OTTO. Privileges, Hobson Bros.', 1893.

GENIMAL PEANUTS. (1864?-December 17, 1902) Midget clown of Japanese descent. 2' 1" in height. With Barnum's and Forepaugh-Sells circuses for a number of years. Died in NYC, age 38.

GENIN, J. N., JR. Treasurer, P. T. Barnum's, 1871-73; P. T. Barnum's Roman Hippodrome, 1874-75.

GENTRY, J. W. ["Will"]. (d. December 8, 1938) Proprietor, Prof. Gentry's Great Dog and Pony Show, 1894. Died in Miami, FL, age 70.

GEORGE, F. W. Agent. Formerly a member of Dan Rice's company; World's Fair Aggegation, 1892.

GEORGE, HUGH. W. H. Harris' Nickel-Plate, 1889.

GEORGINE BROTHERS. Stowe & Norton's, 1869.

GERARD, FRANCISCO. See Francisco Girard.

GERARD, JAMES. Clown, L. B. Lent's, 1876.

GERETTA, MLLE. Equestrieime and globe performer, Ryland's, Califoniia, 1872.

GERMAN BROTHERS. Gymnasts, Sands, Nathans & Co., 1857.

GERMANI, SIGNOR LUIGI. (1820-December 5, 1902) Italian rider and juggler, and capable general performer. Born in Milan, Italy. A member of the Royal Italian Circus at age 18. Came to America, 1846, and joined Welch's, Philadelphia, as a riding juggler. Mann, Welch & Delavan, 1846; Welch's, 1847; Welch, Delavan & Nathans, 1848; Dan Rice's, New Orleans, winter 1848. November 29, 1948, on a wager, performed the unprecedented feat of juggling 5 balls with one hand. Although he repeated it on other occasions, never performed it in public. Great Western (Stone & McCollum, proprietors), 1849; P. A. Older & Co.'s, 1852. Left the circus business and became active and wealthy in St. Louis, MO, real estate. Also trained horses for a pastime, one of which was Black Eagle, sold to Howes & Cushing for their trip to England. Returned to Europe, 1868. However, died at his home, Philadelphia, age 83, after having appeared before most of the crowned heads of Europe and having received a decoration from Queen Victoria.

GERMON, TONY. Ethiopian entertainer, Welch, Delavan & Nathans, 1949.

GERRISH, J. A. Proprietor and manager, J. A. Gerfish's American Museum and Zoological Exposition, 1874.

GESSLEY, RUDOLPH. Treasurer, John Robinson's, 1899.

GEYER, ALBERT. Leaper, posturer (with **Ashton),** Barnum,

Bailey & Hutchinson, 1881.

GIAVELLI, MONS. LEON. Trained dogs, Dr. James L. Thayer's, 1870.

GIBBONOISE, DON SANTIAGO [r.n. John Fitzgibbon]. (July 1, 1836-February 26, 1923) Contortionist. Born in Louisville, KY. Moved with his parents to Indiana and located on the O'Conner farm west of Cannelburg. Married **Mary McDonald,** a union that produced 8 children. She died around 1919. Tom King's, Washington, DC, winter 1861-62; L. B. Lent's, Broadway Amphitheatre, NYC, winter 1963-64; Yankee Robinson's, 1864, 1866; National Theatre, Cincinnati, fall 1864; Perry Powers', 1867; Great European, 1868; Campbell's, 1869; Hemmings, Cooper & Whitby, 1870; Sells Bros.', 1872-73; Dan Rice's, 1873; Great International, 1874-75. His challenge of $1,000 in the New York *Clipper* to anyone capable of reproducing his feats stood unaccepted for 30 years. Died in Evansville, IN.

GIBBONS, HARRY. Clown, John W. Robinson's, 1870; Smith & Baird's, 1972.

GIBBONS, PHILLIP. Concert performer, song and dance man, Cooper, Bailey & Co., 1976; horizontal bars, Adam Forepaugh's, 1889.

GIBBS, CLARK. Clown. Lake's Hippo-Olympiad, 1865-66; director of minstrel concert, Thayer & Noyes, 1868; clown and snare drummer, Charles Noyes', 1970; Vanburgh & Co., 1870-71.

GIBLER, PROF. Band leader, Robbins & Colvin, 1881.

GIBSON, BILLY. Concert manager, C. W. Kidder & Co.'s, 1893.

GIBSON, HOWARD. Proprietor, Gibson's, 1890.

GIBSON, WALTER. Clown, Charles Lee's, 1887; talking and singing clown, Moore Bros.', 1887.

GIFFORD, LEW. Gilliam, Gifford & Culbertson (**Franklin A. Gilliam,** Lew Gifford, **Samuel Culbertson,** proprietors), 1897.

GILBERT, G. H. Proprietor (with **G. G. Grady**) and treasurer, G. G. Grady's, 1867.

GILBERT, HARRY. Broadway Amphitheatre, NYC, 1857-58.

GILBERT, JOHN. H. C. Lee's, fall 1870.

GILFORT BROTHERS [2 in number]. Roman gladiators and feats of strength, Barnum, Bailey & Hutchinson, 1882-85.

GILKINSON, DR. JAMES A. Strong man and clown. Frost & Co., 1836-37; Eagle Circus, 1838; W. Gates & Co., 1838; clown, Portage City Circus (**Hiram Orton's**), 1854; clown, Orton's, 1855; proprietor, J. A. Gilkinson's, 1856; clown, George W. DeHaven's, 1862; Orton Bros.', 1864-67. Retired from the profession in the fall of the latter year.

GILLAM, R. Smith & Baird's, 1872.

GILLESPIE, FRANK. Clown. Diefenbach's, 1889; Charles Bartine's, 1891.

GILLETTE BROTHERS [Alf, Frank]. Acrobats, Great Eastern, 1883; (Alf, Agnes, Frank) Frank H. Rich's (**Frank H. Rich, Col. Charles Whitney, J. N. Abbott,** proprietors), 1886.

GILLETTE, L. C. General agent, Whitney's New Imperial, 1894.

GILLETTE, M. General agent, Whitney Family New Enterprise, 1887; Whitney's Imperial Shows, 1892.

GILLIAM FAMILY [Franklin A., Mabel, Lydia, Maude, Primrose, Charles, Frank]. Acrobats, aerialists, clowns, posturers, bounding rope, flying trapeze, slack-wire, contortion and juggling, Gollmar Bros.', 1892-96; Gilliam, Gifford & Culbertson's One-Ring Circus (Franklin A. Gilliam, **Lew Gifford, Samuel Culbertson,** proprietors), 1897.

GILLIAM, M. 3-horse rider, Leihy, Lake & Co., California, 1870.

GILLIAN BROTHERS. Flying trapeze, James P. Johnson's, 1870.

GILLMEYER, W. H. General manager, Gillmeyer, Bryson & Co.'s Great Eastern, 1888.

GILMORE, WILLIAM. Clown, Forepaugh & Samwells, 1886.

GINE, PROF. ALEJO. Juggler and general performer. Native of Chile, S.A. Performed in circuses and theaters since 7 years of age, when he was sold by his father to an actor doing tumbling stints on the South American stage. Traveled with the Chilean tumbler until about 15 years old, when he came to New York. Got a position as tumbler with P. T. Barnum's. From tumbling, went to juggling and then to bareback riding. Drifted into the sideshow business as a contortionist. Cut away from the circus after a time and entered into small time vaudeville doing a juggling act.

GINGER, LEW. Clown and minstrel show manager. G. G. Grady's, 1870; Macarte Sisters', fall 1870; Lake's Hippo-Olympiad, 1871.

GINTY, H. Gymnast and trick clown, Spalding & Rogers, 1854-1855.

GIRARD, FRANCISCO [or Gerard]. Clown. L. B. Lent's, 1874; P. T. Barnum's, 1874.

GIRARDEAU, MARIA CELESTE. Bareback rider, P. T, Barnum's, 1871.

GISE, HARRY. Boss canvasman, Cooper, Bailey & Co., 1876.

GIVEN, JAMES. Contortionist, Yankee Robinson's, 1860.

GLADSTONE, SAM. Agent, Dr. James L. Thayer's, 1884.

GLENROY, JOHN R. (March 21, 1828-June 15, 1902) Rider. Born in Washington, DC. When 2 years of age, was orphaned. Moved to Baltimore and was adopted by **Hannah Murdock,** an aunt of the actor, **James E. Murdock.** Early playmate was equestrian **William Kincade.** Joseph D. Palmer's, 1835, Baltimore, where he became apprenticed under **George J. Cadwallader,** principal rider for the show. First ring appearance riding alone, after 12 months with the company, 1836. Bacon & Derious, 1838; Welch, Bartlett & Co., 1839-40; Bartlett & Delavan, 1841; Welch's, Philadelphia, 1841; Welch & Mann, 1841-47; as "the Equestrian Hero," John Tryon's, Bowery Amphitheatre, NYC, 1843; advertised as "Glenn Roi" as well as "Glenroy" with Dan Rice's, 1848-52; left Rice's over some disagreement; joined the Star State Circus, Mobile, AL; Harry Whitbeck's, 1853, for a tour of Cuba; returned to the States, 1857, and joined Dr. Gilbert R. Spalding's; in the fall, connected with Pancho Lopas' for a trip through Central America; L. B. Lent's, 1959; George W. De-Haven's, 1960-61; Thayer & Noyes, 1962; Castello & VanVleck, 1863-64; Robinson & Howes, fall 1863; Howes & Norton, fall 1864; Franklin J. Howes', 1865; New American Theatre, Philadelphia, winter 1865-66; Consolidation Circus, 1866; S. O. Wheeler's, 1867; Alex Robinson's, 1869-76; W. H. Stowe's, winter 1881-82. Professional life in the circus lasted until October 1877, or a period of 42 years. Said to be the first to accomplish a somersault on the back of a horse without the benefit of a pad, 1849. Author of the book, *The Ins and Outs of Circus Life*, written when he was clerk at the Merrimac House, Boston.

GLENWOOD, ROSA. Equestrienne, Baird, Howell & Co., 1874.

GLICK H. E. Advertiser, Dr. James L. Thayer's, 1884.

GLUE BROTHERS. Acrobatic song and dance, concert, Cooper, Bailey & Co., 1879.

GOBAY, JOSEPH A. Advertising agent, John B. Doris', 1883.

GOBER, M. Buckley & Co., 1857.

GODEAU. Tight-rope performer, James West's, NYC, 1820, newly arrived from Paris; with a circus in Portland, ME, summer 1821; James West's company, NYC, 1822, this being West's last appearance in America.

GOETZE, WILLIAM F. Musical director, Cook & Whitby's, 1892-93.

GOFFE, MONS [r. n. Vale]. Discovered by English showman, **John Richardson**, working as a pot boy in a public house, where he was entertaining the patrons by walking on his hands, holding pewter mugs, etc. Traveled with the Richardson show, performed as a monkey man in London theatres; Ryans' Circus, Cheltenham, 1941. In America, strong man, Brown's, 1834; monkey man, Palmer's, 1935; monkey man, Sweet & Hough's, 1835; Vauxhall Gardens, London, 1858. [John Turner: "Possessed considerable pantomimic powers, although he was of squalid appearance, could scarcely speak intelligently and appeared to be of weak intellect. Incredibly agile and possessed of great strength."]

GOLIATH, MONS. French giant, P. T. Barnum's, 1871.

GOINE, HARRY. Boss canvasman, A. A. Beckett's, 1881.

GOLDENBURG, J. A. Manager and one of the proprietor brothers, Goldenburg's, 1874.

GOLDENBURG, W. S. Proprietor and treasurer, Goldenburg's, 1874.

GOLDIE, FRANK. Adam Forepaugh's, 1899.

GOLDIE, GEORGE. Gymnast, trapeze performer. Active in 1860s with a troupe consisting of Goldie, **Henry P. O'Neil, H. W. Penny** and **Claude Conner.** (With **Penny**) S. O. Wheeler's new amphitheatre, site of the old National Theatre, Boston, winter 1864-65; S. O. Wheeler's, summer 1865; Stone, Rosston & Co., 1865-66; Stone, Rosston & Murray, Front Street Theatre, Baltimore, winter 1866-67; Stone, Rosston & Murray, summer 1867.

GOLLMAR BROTHERS [Walter, Claude, Fred, Charles, Ben, Jacob]. Cousins of the Ringling brothers. Founded their circus, Baraboo, WI, 1891. **Ben F.** (1865-March 15, 1947) served as secretary and treasurer; **Charles A.** (d. February 18, 1929), manager; **Walter** (April 3, 1869-June 4, 1933), equestrian director; **Fred C.**, general agent; **Jacob C.** (d. May 24, 1896), manager of the concert and handled the front door; **Claude C.**, chief of the bill brigade; **E. T.**, manager of annex. Jacob left the organization early. By 1903, the show had grown to a large railroad organization traveling mostly in the central plain states. The final season under the original brothers was 1916. Jacob, oldest of the brothers, died in Baraboo, WI, age 45. He had 3 sons and a daughter. **Maude** (1875-1956), daughter of **Jacob**, began her career as a bareback rider with the brothers' circus. Was married to **Elbridge Hocum**, circus bareback rider. **Charles** died at Baraboo. **Walter**, who retired around 1913 and lived in Evansville, WI, died in Madison, WI. He was prominent in community affairs, particularly in the Rock County Fair of Evansville. Served as president of the fair board for 3 years, also as vice-president and director. 1906, he married **Miss Jessie Hall**, daughter of **Col. George W. Hall.**

GOLSON, FRED. Clown and pantomimist. Died in New Orleans.

GONZALES, ADOLPH ["Chili"]. (1850-September 22, 1901) Leaper and somersaulter, billed as the "Chilian Sprite." Born at Santiago, Chili, and brought to the United States when but 4 years of age. Apprenticed to **L. B. Lent**, 1859-63; Robinson & Howes, 1864; John Wilson's, 1865; "Chilian Wonder and Champion of the Double Somersault," American Theatre, Philadelphia, mid-February, 1866; Frank Howes', 1866; Lake's, 1869; principal leaper, M. O'Conner & Co., 1869-70; Charles Noyes', Texas, 1870; Spalding & Bidwell, New Orleans, 1870; C. T. Ames', 1870; VanAmburgh's, 1871; Dan Rice's Paris Pavilion Circus, 1871; Australia with Chiarini's, 1871; gymnast, Great Eastern, 1872; tumbler, Cooper, Bailey & Co., Australian tour, 1877. Later, returned to Australia, married, and remained there for 10 years. Died in Melbourne, Australia, age 60. Said to have performed a triple somersault, Sparta, WI, Howes' European, June 10, 1866.

GONZALO, SIGNOR. Tight-rope performer, John Rogers', NYC, 1823-24.

GOOD, AL. Bandmaster, W. W. Cole's, 1886.

GOODHART, GEORGE W. Advertiser, VanAmburgh's, 1879; Cooper & Bailey, 1880-81; John B. Doris', 1885; Barnum & Bailey, 1888; Adam Forepaugh's, 1889. Retired to home in Grand Rapids, MI, after 50 years in the business.

GOODING, E. D. Ringmaster, Ames' New Orleans Menagerie and Circus, 1868, 1870.

GOODISON, WILLIAM. Orrin Bros.', Mexico, February 1884.

GOODLEY, JAMES. H. Buckley & Co., 1857-58.

GOODMAN, JAMES. Gymnast, G. G. Grady's, 1871.

GOODRICH, JAMES W. (d, September 12, 1903) Entered the circus business around 1888, performing a trapeze and high-wire act with his wife. Was with Ringling Bros.', Sell Bros.', and other shows of note. Eventually, organized his own wagon show, Great Goodrich Shows, which became a railroad circus after 3 seasons, performing in the South and Southwest. Took out a large wagon show, 1901, consisting of 32 wagons and cages, moving through the eastern part of the country, Goodrich, Hoffman & Southy's. Following year, with **Downing** as a partner, organized Goodrich & Downing's "Uncle Tom's Cabin" Co. and engaged the ex-boxer, **John L Sullivan**, to star as Simon Legree. 1903, director of the Hargreaves Railroad Circus and Menagerie. Later that year, **W. C. Quintard** of Stamford, CT, and Goodrich started a dog and pony show organized in Bridgeport, CT, opening July 20 at Port Jefferson, LI. At Far Rockaway, August 19, Tony Lowande arranged with Goodrich to add his trained elephant, lions, goats and dogs to the show, which changed the show title to Goodrich & Quintard's Great Trained Animal Exposition. September 7, at Little Coney Island, Goodrich received a fatal injury inflicted by the elephant and died in Union Hill, NJ.

GOODSPEED, JOHN W. Waterman & Co.'s, 1938; dog act, E., F. & J, Mabie's, 1848-50; Dan Rice's, 1849.

GOODWIN, CHARLES. General performer, with Howes' Great London, 1972.

GOODWIN, GEORGE K. (September 30, 1830-August 1, 1882) Born in Dover, NH. May have been a dancing master at one time. Had a pawn shop in Salem Street, Boston, managed Artemus Ward, the American humorist; directed a pedestrian tour of Edward Payson Weston from Boston to Chicago. October, 1859, purchased the equipment of **James M. Nixon's** overland circus, and, at the same time, **John Sears'** menagerie. With stilt-walker, juggler, trick drummer and a minstrel troupe, went on tour as George K. Goodwin's Royal Menagerie and Great Moral Exhibition, 1960. In partnership with S. O. Wheeler at Howard's Athenaeum, Boston, 1861. After having the menagerie in Boston burn, the company moved to Howard's Athenaeum for duration of the season. Manager, Slaymaker & Nichols, 1864. Announced an agreement with S. O. Wheeler, September 10, 1866, for a 2-year partnership of Wheeler & Goodwin's International Circus and Model Arena,

a partnership that was not carried forward. Ran the first dollar store in Philadelphia, 1866. Took out a panorama of the Civil War, 1861. Operated 2 theatres in Philadelphia, 1979. Died in that city.

GOODWIN, WILLIAM. Howes' European, winter 1864.

GORE, WILLIAM. Assistant manager, L. J. Duchack's, 1989.

GORMAN BROTHERS. Character delineators, S. P. Stickney & Sons, 1874.

GORMAN, EUGENE. Minstrel performer, with Haight & Chamber's, winter 1866-67. May have been one of the above.

GORMAN, HUGH. Band leader, Wheeler Bros.', 1894.

GORMAN, MILES O. Lightning Zouave drill and Irish specialties, Ducello's United Exhibitions, 1879.

GORMAN, PAULINE. See Pauline Lee.

GORMAN, WILLIAM E. ["BUD"]. (1852-1940) Rider. Once a pupil of **James Robinson**; sister, **Laura**, was Robinson's wife. Married equestrienne **Pauline Lee**, September 26, 1883, San Francisco. That year was with Sherman's Educated Horses, California, performing his hurricane hurdle and bounding jockey act; later, as manager, rider and equestrian director; James Robinson's, 1870-72; Haight's Great Eastern, 1874; John Wilson's, San Francisco, 1875; bareback rider, Montgomery Queen's, 1875; bounding jockey, Cooper, Bailey & Co., 1876-78, and left with them for Australia, November 8, 1876; Adam Forepaugh's, 1879; Welch & Sands, 1880; Sells Bros.', 1880-81, 1885-86; Great Australian Circus, National Theatre, Philadelphia, winter 1881-82; hurdle rider, Sherman & Hinman, Califonia, 1883; 4-horse rider, Sells Bros.', 1886; Walter L. Main's, 1887; hurdle and jockey rider, Great Wallace, 1889-90; hurdle rider, Sells Bros.', 1893-94; equestrian director and 35-horse act, Forepaugh-Sells Bros.', 1899-1905; equestrian director, Hagenbeck & Wallace, 1918. After the death of his first wife, married equestrienne **Gladys Lanigan**.

GORMLEY, PATRICK M. (1829-1879) Sideshow privilege with early Delavan, WI, circuses; operated a talking machine, P. T. Barnum's sideshow, early 1870s.

GORMLEY, EVERETT M. (1862-1948) Brother of **Frank Gormley**. Native of Delavan, WI. 24 hour man, Burr Robbins', 1880s; also connected with French & Monroe; Rentz & Ashley; Holland-Gormley, 1888; Edward G. Holland's, 1892. Building contractor in Delavan upon retirement.

GORMLEY, FRANK D. (May 19, 1858-September 26, 1916) Long time resident of Delavan, WI. Son of Mr. and Mrs. Patrick Gormley. Married **Nettie Smith**, 1893. 8 years treasurer, Burr Robbin's, 1880s; manager, French & Monroe and Rentz & Ashley; Holland & Gormley's New Allied Railroad Shows **(George Holland**, F. D. Gormley, proprietors), 1888-89; show was taken over by **John F. Woods** for John F. Woods Allied Shows, November 1989. Was a tobacco salesman upon retirement. Died of a chronic spinal condition.

GOROUX, EMILE and **MONA.** Gymnasts, oriental juggling, and dancing barrel. Adam Forepaugh's, 1874; Howes & Cushing, 1875.

GORTON, JOE. Band leader, John Stowe & Şons, 1871.

GOSHEN, COL RUTH [r. n. Routh Goshan]. (May 5, 1837-February 12, 1889) Sideshow giant, known as "The Palestine Giant." Of Arabic parents, the youngest of 14 or 15 children, all remarkable for their size and strength. Served with distinction in the Crimean War and later in the Mexican army. P. T. Barnum is said to have met him on the street and hired him at once, showing him with the circus in the summer and exhibiting him in the NYC museum in the winter. It is said he received a salary of $40 a week and expenses. Was the largest giant Barnum produced, being advertised at 7' 6", shoulders 2' 6", and waist 77". Actual height measurement for his coffin was 7' 2". Height was accentuated by comparison with the dwarfs, **Major Atom** and **Brig. Gen. Spec**, who ran around his legs as he walked. In his prime, weighed 560 pounds. P. T. Barnum's, 1879-80; Nathans & Co.'s, 1882. Died of Bright's disease and dropsy in Clyde, NJ.

GOSNEY, E. J. Advance agent, Lemen Bros.', 1893.

GOSSETT, CHARLES. (d. March 19, 1889) Entered the circus business, 1857, with **John Sears** in the management of a small menagerie, traveling through the eastern states as a sideshow to Rivers & Derious. Managed George K. Goodwin's, 1860; Wambold & Co., 1861; Goodwin & Wilder, 1862; managed, Gossett's Union Museum, a sideshow to O'Toole & Miles, Canada, 1863; sideshow, Thayer & Noyes, 1864. Since that time, connected with hall shows, managing the **Siamese Twins**, the **Hanoverian Family**, the **Noss Family** and others. Died of "melancholy insanity" in Worcester, MA.

GOSSIN, JOHN. Clown, rider, tumbler and still vaulter. Born in Pittsburgh, PA. Surnamed the "Grimaldi of America," was an immense favorite of audiences in the United States, with wit said to be original, spontaneous and timely. As a young man, was polite and handsome, wore long black hair in ringlets, about 5' 10" in height, with a splendid physique and lack of "personal vanity." A favorite in NYC, played for several seasons at 37 Bowery, opposite the Old Bowery Theatre. [John A. Dingess: Gossin was "one of the very best clowns that ever entered the equestrian arena ... and one of the few clowns who was an extraordinary general performer."] He married a beautiful equestrienne from Lexington, KY, but lived life fully and was fond of the bottle; so, subsequently, his wife divorced him. Became dissipated and broken in spirit, an instability that led him to killing a man in the South. Acquitted of the murder, he soon died of yellow fever in Natchez, MS. Stickles & Co., 1832; Fogg & Stickney, 1933; Green & Brown, 1834; Aaron Turner's, 1936; J. W. Bancker's, 1836; Welch, Bartlett & Co., 1839; June, Titus, Angevine & Co., 1839-40, Bowery Amphitheatre; S. H. Nichols', 1841; Aaron Turner & Sons, 1842; Welch & Mann, 1843, 1848; John

Tryon's, Bowery Amphitheatre, NYC, 1843-44; Rockwell & Stone, 1845; Rockwell's Amphitheatre, Cincinnati, 1846; Howes & Co. 1846; Victory Circus (Sackett & Covell), 1847; Welch, Delavan & Nathans, 1849; Bowery Amphitheatre, 1851; J. M. June's, 1851; Spalding & Rogers' *Floating Palace,* 1852.

GOSSIN, LUCINDA. Equestrienne. Wife of **John Gossin.** See above. June, Titus, Angevine & Co., 1939-40, Bowery Amphitheatre; S. H. Nichols', 1841; Aaron Turner & Sons, 1842; Welch & Mann, 1843, 1848; John Tryon's, Bowery Amphitheatre, NYC, 1843-44; Rockwell & Stone, 1845; Rockwell's Amphitheatre, Cincinnati, 1846. Divorced Gossin and married a rich Spaniard in Havana.

GOUCHE, MONS. Clown, James T. Johnson's & Co., 1869.

GOUFFE, MONS. Strong man, Brown's, 1834; monkeyman, J. D. Palmer's, 1835; monkey-man, Sweet & Hough's, 1835.

GOULD, A. F. Treasurer, W. H. Harris' Nickel-Plate, 1891.

GOULD, JAY. Clown, Fulford & Co., 1890.

GRACE, VICTORIA. (d. August 4, 1880) Aerialist, "Little Vic, Queen of the Air." Native of Philadelphia. Connected with Barnum's, Forepaugh's, Howes', Orrin Bros.', Leon Dolores Troupe in Cuba, and Clifton & McMann in Central America. Made good money but spent all, being addicted to opium, and drifted into debt and poverty. Died at age 36, unknown, in a New Orleans charity hospital.

GRACI, HERR. Juggler and cquilibrist, with W. C. Coup's Equescurriculum, 1887.

GRADY, CHARLES. Clown, G. G. Grady's, 1870-74.

GRADY, G. G. (1831-July 11, 1895) Clown, proprietor and manager of G. G. Grady's Old Fashioned Circus from 1866 to 1879, based at Kenton, OH. One of Grady's acts was riding a horse bareback while playing a violin. The show was one of the earliest to travel with a balloon ascensionist as a free act. In mid-July, 1874, it was attached by the sheriff in Shelbyville, IL, and the property advertised for sale. Was out with Grady & Beatty's Circus, 1879; following year, was giving sideshow performances at political meetings in Indiana. Died at his home in Indianapolis, IN, age 64, after having retired from business about 3 years before.

GRADY, HELEN OGDEN [or Ella, sometimes professionally known as **Maude Sheppard**, serio-comic]. Wife of G. G. Grady. Born in Findlay, OH. After her marriage to Grady, performed for several years. The couple had a son but the marriage ended in a separation. Subsequently, as Ella Grady, with her trick horse "G. G.", P. T. Barnum's (P. A. Older, proprietor), 1872-73; Barnum's Roman Hippodrome, 1875, where she drove a 4-horse chariot in the hippodrome races; 4-horse charioteer, Coney Island Roman Races, Brighton Beach Fairgrounds, 1879. Upon retiring, married **George A. Barringer**, officer of a ship of the White Star Line which sailed between New York and England.

GRADY, JOHN H. Clown, G. G. Grady's, 1869.

GRADY, WILLIAM. "Antipodean gymnastics and muscular evolutions," Rockwell & Co.'s, 1838.

GRAHAM, A. H. General advance agent, Albert M. Wetter's New Model Shows, 1893.

GRAHAM, CHARLES [r. n. Charles Taylor]. (June 1839-September 3, 1873) Clown and ringmaster. Born in Sussex, England, and apprenticed to a Mr. Cooke at an early age. Came to USA via an engagement in Australia. Connected with the principal circuses on the West Coast; but most recently before his death, with James Robinson's. Died in St. Joseph, MO.

GRAHAM, JOHN. (d. 1886) Marksman partner of Frank Butler, Sells Bros.', 1881; Graham & Butler in variety theatres, 1882. That year, illness caused retirement, replaced by Annie Oakley.

GRAHAM, LEW. (d. September 19, 1935) Sideshow manager and announcer. Came up from the ranks, starting as a ticket seller. Barnum & Bailey, 1889-99; Ringling Bros.', 1911. Life member of the Crawfordsville, IN, Elks. Died in a sanitarium, Middletown, NY, age 73.

GRAHAM, SAM. James W. Wilder & Co., 1873.

GRAHAM, WILLIAM J. General contracting agent, Moore Bros.', 1887.

GRANVILLE, CAPT. Giant, Sheidenburger & Co., 1871.

GRANVILLE, D. F. Living skeleton, Central Park Menagerie, 1872.

GRANVILLE, LOTTIE. Slack-wire, with George S. Cole's, 1895.

GRAPERIAN FAMILY. Trick roller skaters, Irwin Bros.', 1887.

GRAPEWINE, ELSIE. Flying rings, Albert M. Wetter's New Model Shows, 1893.

GRAPEWINE, G. E. Musical director, Albert M. Wetter's New Model Shows, 1893.

GRAVE, A. E. Advertising agent, Perry Powers' Combination Circus, 1867.

GRAVELET, JEAN FRANCOIS. See M. Blondin.

GRAVEN, THOMAS. Tumbler. French, Hobby, 1835; J. D. Palmer's, 1836; H. A. Woodward & Co., 1938; Cincinnati Circus, 1841; Howes & Mabie, 1845-46; Great Western, 1846-47; Stickney's New Orleans Circus, 1849; Spalding, Rogers & Van Orden, 1851; Spalding & Rogers, 1855; equestrian director, Cooper & Myers, 1858; Davis & Crosby, 1859.

GRAVES, L A. H. Buckley & Co., 1857-58.

GRAY. Animal keeper, Raymond & Ogden's menagerie, 1833. Stuart Thayer reported that Gray was the first to be documented with the feat of putting his head in a lion's mouth, 1834.

GRAY, EDWARD. Keeper of cages and vans, Howes' Great London, 1871.

GRAY, HARRY. General agent, L. J. Duchack's, 1889.

GRAY, JAMES HUDSON. Contracting agent, Lee & Scribner, 1884-85; Lee's London Circus, 1886; J. H. Gray's Great Oriental Dime Show, 1887-88; manager, Loomer Opera House, Willimantic, CT, 1893; Great Eastern 25 Cent Show (J. H. Gray, H. C. Wheeler, managers), 1899; Sells & Gray's United Shows, 1900.

GRAY, NEIL. Clown and comic vocalist, Thompson, Smith & Hawes, 1866.

GRAY, NELLIE. Adam Forepaugh's, 1886.

GRAY, O. R. Cooper, Jackson & Co., 1882.

GRAY, OLLIE. Aerialist, Frank A. Gardner's, 1891.

GRAY, WILLIAM. Rider, Adam Forepaugh's, 1871; clown, Andress' New Colossal Shows, 1889.

GRECIAN BROTHERS [Alfred, Charles, George, Frank]. Acrobats, H. M. Smith's, 1870.

GREEN, BILL. Driver 24-hitch bandwagon, Robinson & Eldred, 1852.

GREEN, DAN. Boss canvasman, Perry Powers' Combination Circus, 1867.

GREEN, HENRY. Builder of Spalding & Rogers' Apollicon, constructed of 1,000 instruments and introduced for the 1849 season.

GREEN, HOWARD. See LaVan Brothers.

GREEN, JAMES B. (1804-1882) Proprietor, J. B. Green's menagerie, 1831. Acquired an elephant, making Green's circus the first in the country to travel with one. Oscar Brown, Brown & Green's in Ohio, 1832; James B. Green & Co., 1833; Green & Brown (probably Oscar W. Brown) and later as Green & Bailey (probably Lewis Bailey), 1834; show property was liquidated, 1835; manager, Mammoth Eagle Circus, 1836.

GREEN, JOHN B. Rider, strong man. Rider, James W. Bancker's, Albany, 1824-25; took on a partner named Doolittle for a traveling venture, 1825, performing the flying horseman and acting as riding master; Parson's, 1826; a circus at Tivoli Gardens, Philadelphia, summer 1826; Asa Smith's, 1928; strong man, J. D. Palmer's, 1836; strong man, Cincinnati Circus, 1841; strong man, Aaron Turner's, 1842.

GREEN, JOHN P. Manager, Sands, Nathans & Co., 1857.

GREEN, MAJOR. Sideshow dwarf, John V. O'Brien's, 1871.

GREEN, MRS. PHIL. See Aimee Austin.

GREEN, SAMUEL S. Horse trainer, J. B. Green & Co., 1933; Green & Brown's, 1834.

GREEN, WILLIAM H. (1813?-1871) Driver, 24-hitch that pulled a bandwagon, Robinson & Eldred, 1852; Dan Rice's, 1857-58; Tom King's, 1864; horse trainer, Palmer's Great Western, 1865; boss hostler, John Robinson's, 1868; 6-horse rider, Dan Rice's for many years. This may be the same William Green who was a 2-horse rider at Tivoli Garden Pavilion Circus, Philadelphia, 1926. Died in Baltimore, age 58.

GREENE, ENOCH W. C. (d. December 27, 1877) Agent, Levi J. North's and others. For many years thereafter, was publisher and editor of *The Sunday Transcript,* Philadelphia. Died in Philadelphia.

GREENE, MRS. PHILLIP D. See Aimee Austin.

GREENE, P. B. Agent, Sears & Forbes, 1858.

GREENWOOD, ALEX. One-legged hurdle rider, the Great Pacific Circus and Congress of Educated Horses (**M. M. Hilliard, R. Hunting,** proprietors), 1878.

GREER, LEO. Head balancing trapeze performer and cannon ball juggler, Denver Dick's Wild West and Sioux Indian Medicine Company, 1894.

GREGOIRE, MONS. German Hercules, Nixon & Kemp, 1858; Nixon & Co., 1859.

GREGORY, BESSIE. General performer, Herr Driesbach & Howes, 1868.

GREGORY BROTHERS [John, Thomas, Arthur, Joseph]. Howes Trans-Atlantic Circus and Risbeck's Menagerie (Frank Howes, proprietor), 1868.

GREGORY, BESSIE. Singer, Howes Trans-Atlantic Circus and Risbeck's Menagerie (Frank Howes, proprietor), 1868.

GREGORY, C. W. [or J. W.]. Managing director, VanAmburgh's southern, 1860.

GREGORY FAMILY [Jean, Victor, Albert, Arthur]. 4 boy gymnasts, trapeze, horizontal bars and revolving globes; **Gertrude,** with her troupe of performing dogs, goats and ponies; **Mlle. Gerhnell,** with her trained poodles. Driesbach & Howes, 1868. **Arthur** was a gymnast and bar performer, P. T. Barnum's, 1873.

GREGORY FAMILY (Charles J., George, James, Delia, Bessie]. Gymnasts. **Gregory Brothers** were originally coniposed of **James, George,** and **Charles J.** The latter was proprietor of the Gregory Brothers' Circus, which traveled throughout the world. **Charles** (r. n. C. J. Skelton, d. June 25, 1911), was born at St. Andrews, Canada, July 4, 1854. At one time was a partner with **John Winfield** in the circus business; also proprietor and manager, Gregory Bros.' Metropolitan Circus, 1885; Gregory & Belford's Circus (C. J. Gregory, **George Belford,** proprietors), 1892. Wife's name was **Delia M.** With daughter, **Bessie,** performed a foot balancing act, Robert Hunting's, 1897; and who, as the last of the Gregory Family, died in Ottawa, Canada, after having been in show business for more than 40 years. **George** (r. n. Skelton), bar performer; born in Ottawa, Canada, and entered the circus profession, 1880, when his brother **Charles** took him on as one of the Gregory Brothers. **John Winfield** was the other member of the troupe. They opened that year with Gillmore & Benton for the winter; was joined by brother **James,** making the act the **Three Gregory Brothers.** When James died, around 1890, **John L Fritz** replaced him. **Charles, George,** and **John Fritz,** triple bars, balancing trapeze, dancing barrel, table and cross, reapers and tumblers, Cole's Colossal Circus, 1893; Cole & Lockwood, 1894. Later, **George** was a member of several acrobatic teams. Last partner was **Bob Starkey.** These

two were with Orrin Bros.', Mexico, 1897. **George** died in NYC, November 30, 1897, age 12. **Gregory Family** were with James Robinson's, 1872; Boyd & Peters, 1880; John Robinson's, 1881; Frank Robbins', 1882; joined George W. Maxwell's "Black Crook" Co., September, 1882; Gregory Brothers' Circus (Charles J. Gregory, proprietor), 1883-85; Gregory, Merritt, 1886; W. H. Harris' Nickel-Plate, 1886; Walter L. Main's, 1887-88; Gregory & D'Alma, 1899; riders, aerialists, acrobats and gymnasts, George S. Cole's, 1895. **William Gregory** (1855-March 24, 1884), son of **Charles J.,** left Ottawa at age 13, 1868, joining in the family act and accompanying them on a world tour. Later, organized his own company and visited Tunis and Algiers and then France, where he remained until a time shortly before his death in Geneva, Switzerland, age 29. There was also a **James Gregory** listed as program agent, G. G. Grady's, 1874; Gregory Brothers' Circus, 1885.

GREGORY, GERTRUDE. Troupe of trained dogs, Howes Trans-Atlantic Circus and Risbeck's Menagerie (**Frank Howes,** proprietor), 1868.

GREGORY, IRA W. Managing director, VanAmburgh's southern, 1856-61.

GREGORY, JOHN. Bill poster, P. T. Barnum's, 1873.

GREGORY, SPENCER. Menagerie operator in the 1830s and stockholder in the Zoological Institute. Co-proprietor, with **Gerard Crane,** Gregory, Crane & Co., 1833-34; proprietor, Gregory, Washburn & Co.'s menagerie, 1835.

GREGORY, THOMAS. Program agent, Sells Bros.', 1874.

GRENIER, THOMAS L. Grenier's Circus and Menagerie, Chicago, 1884. Took over operation of the former Burr Robbins' circus, 1888; advertised it for sale at season's end.

GRESSLEY, PROF. S. "The man without arms," 1874.

GREY, BILLY. Sideshow performer, VanAmburgh's, 1866.

GREY, HENRY. Howes' European, winter 1864.

GRIFFIN, CHARLES E. Magician and ventriloquist, sideshow manager. Robert Hunting's, 1885-92; New York Museum, February 1887; Charles E. Griffin's Bohemian Glass Blowers and Wizard's Annex, winter 1889. Wrote *Four Years in Europe with Buffalo Bill.* Wife professionally known as **Olivia.**

GRIFFIN, J. Manager, Howe's New Colossal Shows, 1888.

GRIFFIN, JAMES. Clown, Hilliard & Hamilton, 1875.

GRIFFIN, W. H. H. Leaper, Wootten & Haight, 1871.

GRIFFITH, E. A. E. A. Griffith's Circus, 1894.

GRIGGS, JOHN. H. Buckley & Co., 1857-58.

GRIGGS, MISS. Slack-rope, with circus in Portland, Maine, summer 1821.

GRIM, GEORGE. Clown, Robert Hunting's, 1891.

GRISWOLD, C. [or Griswald]. Agent, S. H. Nichols', 1838-42; Dr. Gilbert R. Spalding's, 1844; Welch & Delavan, 1847; advertiser, J. O. Howes', 1848.

GROSÈ. English clown, Howes' Great European, 1864.

GROSVENOR, NATALIE. Barnum, VanAmburgh & Castello, 1867.

GROVER, B. H. Agent, J. S. McCue's National Circus, 1883.

GRUPE, CHARLEY H. German clown and sideshow minstrel, Mabie's, 1859-60.

GUERIN. Rider, Pepin's equestrian troupe, St. Louis, 1823; tight-rope, Pepin & Barnet, Natchez, MS, June, 1823; rider, Pepin's, 1826; vaulter, Asa T. Smith's, 1829.

GUERIN, DAVID. Proprietor, George W. DeHaven's, 1867. Is this the same man as above?

GUICE, LIZZIE. Equestrienne, LaPearl's, 1897.

GUILFORDS. Roman staturary, Sells Bros.', 1887.

GUILFORD, D. C. Guilford & Cannon's, winter 1889-90.

GUILFORD, GEORGE J. (d. February 21, 1900) Agent. Outstanding for his bill writing and ability to handle the press. [Charles H. Day: "George is a particularly gifted man but he lacks industry; so less deserving men have come more prominently to the front."] Campbell's, 1869; James Robinson's, 1870; G. F. Bailey & Co., 1871; Dan Rice's, 1872; Springer's Royal Cirq-Zoolodon, 1875; W. W. Cole's, 1875; director of publications, W. C. Coup' New United Monster Show, 1879-80; Barnum, Bailey & Hutchinson, 1881; Sells Bros.', 1882; Wallace & Co., 1886. Settled in Cincinnati and in later years didn't travel but wrote for many shows from his home. Died in that city.

GUILOT, MONS. Strong man, Nathan A. Howes' winter circus, 1842; S. H. Nichols & Co., 1843. Pulled against 2 horses, fired a 600 pound cannon from his body, and held a plank in his teeth upon which 3 men stood.

GUITIERREZ, R. R. Adam Forepaugh's, 1888.

GULIG, ANDREW [or Guilig]. Rider. G. G. Grady's, 1868-74; H. Harlan's, 1875; J. E. Warner's, 1876; Carlo Bros.', South America, 1877; American Circus (A. Gulig, **G. Ravell, W. H. Franklin,** proprietors), South America, 1879. Married **Amelia Bridges** after her husband died.

GULLEN, GIL. Clown, vaulter and general performer, Price & Simpson, 1827; sack wire performer, Washington Circus, Philadelphia, 1828; Mammoth Eagle Circus, 1836; Aaron Turner's, 1837; Richmond Hill, NYC, winter 1837; Charles H. Bacon's, 1837-38.

GULLEN, MRS. GIL. Equestrienne. Aaron Turner's, 1836--37; Mammoth Eagle Circus, 1836; June, Titus, Angevine & Co., 1839, Bowery Amphitheatre; H. H. Fuller's Olympic Circus, 1838; Welch, Bartlett & Co., 1839; Henry Rockwell & Co., winter 1841; Grecian Arena and Classic Circus, 1841; S. H. Nichols', 1842; John Tryon's, Bowery Amphitheatre, NYC, 1844, 1846; John T, Potter's, 1846.

GUNN, JAMES. Jockey racer, Barnum, Bailey & Hutchinson, 1882.

GURR, HARRY. Double trapeze, Joel E. Warner's Great Pacific Menagerie and Circus, 1871-73; W. W. Cole's, 1874. Also performed as a "man-fish" and gymnast.

GURR, MRS. HARRY. See Mlle. Bastian.

GUTHEREG & BROWN. Head balancing, Cooper, Jackson & Co., 1884.

GUTTING, ED. Trapeze, O. J. Ferguson's, 1884.

Andrew Haight

H

HAAG, ERNEST. Built a flatboat about 1894, Shreveport, LA, and floated down the Red River with a 5 people show. By 1899, had a sizeable Southern wagon show circus on the road.

HABENO, SAM. Gymnast, John Robinson's, 1883-84.

HACUM, JAMES E. Hurdle jockey and 4-horse rider, Gollmar Bros.', 1897.

HACUM, E. V. Somersault rider, Gollmar Bros.', 1897.

HAFEY, C. M. General agent, Williams & Co., 1892.

HADLEY, JOHN. Lion tamer. Alex Robinson's, 1870; Hilliard & DeMott, 1880.

HADLEY, MLLE. Tight-rope, John Robinson's, 1868.

HAGAR, WILLIAM D. (1847?-December 28, 1897) Born near Amsterdam, NY. Clerked in a dry goods store in Chicago, 1874, when he met and married **Jennie Morgan**, called "The American Nightingale." Shortly, became agent for hall shows and continued until 1877, when (with **H. S. Sanderson**) he secured the privileges for John H. Murray's. Following year, in partnership with **Kohl** and **Middleton**, privileges, W. C. Coup's, which lasted 2 seasons; 1882-84, privileges, Barnum, Bailey & Hutchinson; fall 1882, Hagar, Campbell & Co., proprietors of the museum on Nineth and Arch Streets, Philadelphia; continued privileges for P. T. Barnum's for several years. Died of cancer of the stomach in Wauseon, OH, age about 50. Previous to death, had made arrangements to control the privileges with Buffalo Bill's Wild West Show and to represent Bailey's and Cole's interest in the company.

HAGARMAN, ADAM. Leon W. Washburn's, 1896.

HAGENBECK CARL. (1844-April 14, 1913) Rare animal collector. Son of a fish monger, Hamburg, Germany. Soon after birth, father received a polar bear as payment of a debt, and later acquired 2 trained seals and a monkey; thus, the animal collection was started. Menagerie exhibited at local fairs and soon the elder Hagenbeck was the proprietor of a traveling caravan. In no time zoological societies around the world learned of the Hagenbeck collection and began placing orders for exotic animals. First exhibition in USA, World's Columbian Exposition, Chicago, 1893. Also exhibited at the world's fairs at Denver and St. Louis. Partner in Hagenbeck & Wallace circus. Sons, **Lorenz** and **Henry**, were killed in battle during the European war, 1914.

HAGER, DR. A. W. Proprietor, Hager's Paris Circus, 1878.

HAIGHT, ANDREW. (December 25, 1831-February 8, 1886) Born in Dresden, NY, son of **Daniel Haight**, merchant and drover. After father's death, embarked in the mercantile business there, successfully operating 2 stores. Moved to Beaver Dam, WI, and again became active in business, owning 2 large stores, speculating in real estate, and building and managing a hotel, Clark House, complete with a pool room and gambling parlor. Had a third store and hotel, New London, WI, managed by his brothers. Joined forces with **George W. DeHaven** in a circus enterprise. Show started from Beaver Dam, April 1865; bought out DeHaven's interest in October of that year (one source says at Natchez, another at New Orleans); show spent the winter months traveling in the South; then Haight became the first manager to take a circus to Texas after the war. The following year, organized Haight & Chambers' Palace Show and Menagerie with his agent, **Doc C. S. T. Chambers**, a wagon show that used rail for long jumps. 1867, had a river show that folded in Houston, TX, January, 19, 1868; starting at New Orleans on the river steamer, *Coosa;* soon met with misfortunes, flood interfering with the planned itinerary and forcing the show to miss many of the stands; at Henderson, KY, the boat's engineers allowed the boilers to burn out, requiring the *Coosa* to be towed by 2 boats; at St. Louis, a cholera epidemic forced the company into quarantine; at Pittsburgh the *Coosa* was run into by a tow boat and sunk; the season's disasters resulted in a $75,000 loss, and the Haight & Chambers show dissolved; Chambers went on the Colonel Ames show as general agent, taking the animals with him; the outfit, which was quite a large one for the time, having been built up from a 115' round top to a 180', with good stock and equipment, was sold and Haight went to Memphis, TN, where he opened a hotel for the balance of the year. Went out as agent for Stone & Murray, 1869-70, and established a reputation for ability in the advance, second to none. Bought an elephant and performing den of lions from the C. T. Ames estate, 1871, and organized the Empire City Circus with **P. Bowles Wootten** (also referred to as Wootten and Haight's New York Circus and Menagerie), a mule dealer from Atlanta, GA, and had a successful season (DeHaven had the privileges and made $30,000); the proprietors did not agree and the show, by common consent, was auctioned off, Haight buying most of the property, DeHaven the rest. Organized the Great Eastern Menagerie, Museum, Aviary, Circus and Balloon Show with **R. E. J. Miles** and **George W. DeHaven**, 1872, a grift show that started with little or no capital, bringing in $100,000 the first year; 1873, the show was one of the most extensively advertised on the road at that time, 3 bands featured in the parade and performances in 2 rings simultaneously; meeting with enormous competition from other circuses, Haight and agent, **W. W. Durand**, erected large stands of lithos and bought whole broadsides of newspaper space; show ran continuously over 2 years. 1874, controlled an interest in Great Southern Show. With **DeHaven** and **Miles**, put out a huge hippodrome show, American Racing Association, 1875, in opposition to Barnum's Hippodrome, ending in failure. Retired, 1876, to keep the City Hotel, at corner of State and Sixteenth Streets, Chicago. Returned to the circus business, 1879, as railroad contractor for Adam Forepaugh's; W. C. Coup's, 1880-82; Barnum, Bailey, & Hutchinson, 1883-84, and until his death. Was a tireless worker and loyal to his employees, a persuasive talker which acquire for him the nickname of "Slippery Elm." Neither drank nor smoked; wore clothes cut after the fashion of a cleric, which gave rise to the story that he was once a preacher. [W. W. Durand: "He was esteemed and popular everywhere and received large salaries—$5,000 and $6,000 the last few years, most of which he gave away. I know that he was suberbly generous, and he heaped benefits on others which he ought to have kept for his own.... He bore no malice, and loved all mankind with a heart as tender as a woman's. His room in hotels was the home of crowds of show people everywhere, and all were made welcome alike, whether manager or canvasman."] Left no children, only his wife, **Margaret**, said to have been cheerful and angelic, always at his side.

HAIGHT, JACOB. Brother of **Andrew Haight**. Treasurer, Haight, Chambers & Ames, 1867; treasurer, Great Eastern, 1872; second in command, Great Eastern, 1873-74.

HAILEY, EDWARD. Clown, Dan Rice's, 1870; Rice's Paris Pavilion Circus, 1871.

HAINES, CHARLES R. Proprietor, with **David Guerin**, DeHaven's Imperial Circus, 1867.

HAINES, FRANK. Child prodigy 4-pony act, W. H. Harris' Nickel-Plate, 1891.

HALE, WILLIAM. General performer, with Aaron Turner's, 1842.

HALEY, E. C. Boss canvasman, with Melville, Maginley & Cooke, 1875.

HALEY, THOMAS. (d. February 26, 1882) Sideshow privilege, with G. G. Grady's, 1874. Died at Orwell, OH.

HALL & WILLIAMS. Clog dancers, concert, with Cooper, Bailey & Co., 1879.

HALL, G. A. Contractor, Great Western, 1876.

HALL, BOB. Minstrel band organized to travel with Raymond & Waring, 1847; sideshow performer, VanAmburgh's, 1866.

HALL, CHARLES S. (1864?-February 11, 1896) Son of **George W. Hall, Sr.** Sideshow manager, King & Franklin, 1889. Had a circus under his management, 1891-95, the latter year as Hall & Showers'. **Showers** had performing dogs, ponies and monkeys.

HALL, CHARLES T. (d. April 22, 1889) General contracting agent, Great Western, 1876; also Adam Forepaugh's, P. T. Barnum's, W. C. Coup's. Wife was **Fanny Tyson**.

HALL, FRANK. Troupe of educated dogs, pigs, geese and mules, George W. Hall, Jr.'s, 1896.

HALL FRANK W. Cosmopolitan Circus, Museum and Menagerie, winter 1871-72.

HALL FRED C. Contortionist, Cooper, Jackson & Co., 1882; Indian-rubber man, Pullman, Mack & Co., 1884; Ringling Bros.', 1885; W. H. Harris' Nickel-Plate, 1886.

HALL, GEORGE WASHINGTON, JR. (1856-1930) Son of circus manager **George W. Hall**. Sideshow operator, with Priest's Great Western, 1886; Charles Bartine's, 1888; sideshow manager, Gollmar Bros.', 1893. Took out a circus, 1894-1903, G. W. Hall, Jr.'s Circus and Trained Animal Shows; during 1896, the show was said to carry 30 head of stock, 4 cages of animals, 3 camels, and an elephant. Subsequently, with Myers & Eller's Carnival; VanAmburgh's (managed by **Mugiven** and **Bowers**). Went out with own show again, 1905-1912. Family residence in Evansville, WI. Hall's wife died there February 19, 1917, age 53.

HALL, GEORGE WASHINGTON, SR. ["Popcorn"]. (December 5, 1837-May 21, 1918) Born in Lowell, MA. When 7 years old, moved with his parents to Manchester, NH. Did not take to books or school, left home at the age of 10, went to Lawrence, where he found employment as an errand boy with a man by the name of **Adset**, at $1 per week. Sold popcorn for the Boston centennial, which led to selling peanuts with Howes & Cushing. Gradually rose through the ranks, filling various positions with many of the big shows of his day. Went to Wisconsin, 1860, and ran a sideshow with R. Sands' one season; then a season with Mabie's and a one with VanAmburgh's. Was probably the George W. Hall who was elephant handler with Madigan's, 1861; L. B. Lent's, 1861-62; lion tamer and elephant handler, Gardner & Hemmings, 1866; Barnum, VanAmburgh and Castello, 1867-68; Dan Castello's, winter 1867-68; J. M. French's, 1869; Rosston, Springer & Henderson, 1871. Ran a museum in Memphis, TN, 1870s and 1880s. Fitted up a steamboat in Little Rock, AR, 1879, *Floating American Museum*, and exibited in the river towns between Little Rock and New Orleans. Proprietor of his own circus for many years, beginning in 1881, which became Col. G. W. Hall's Big United States and Great Eastern Circus. 1984, **George W. DeHaven** was associated with the show; following year, **DeHaven** and **Silas Dutton**, a Chicago livery operator, bought out Hall's interest with Hall remaining to handle the sideshow. In connection with a man named **Bingley**, returned to management, 1886, by traveling through Mexico. Chartered a schooner, *Emma Fox*, January 1, 1887, which carried his show to the West Indies and South America, stopping at all the Windward Islands, the Bahamas, Trinidad and then to the mainland. August 1889, joined forces with **Sam McFlinn**, a partnership that lasted through the season of 1891. Was showing at Vera Cruz, Mexico, 1898, when the Spanish war broke out. All in all, was on the road continuously for 21 years, operating everything from 2 to 15 car shows, the last season being 1902. Saw many ups and downs, but was always equal to the emergencies. Considered one of the leading sideshow orators of his day. **George W. DeHaven**, when manager of the Great Eastern, paid the him $250 per week one entire season for talking at the door. Two sons, **George, Jr.,** and **Charles,** were also circus proprietors, beginning in the 1890s. Spent the latter years of his life on his farm near Evansville, WI, taming beasts considered hopeless. Died there, age 83. Had property in Memphis and by 1913 extensive real estate holdings throughout the country; owned 17 residential buildings in Evansville, 600 acres of land in Rock County, WI, $20,000 worth of real estate in Tampa, FL, 22 lots on West 38th Street, Denver, CO.

HALT, JAMES H. H. Buckley & Co., 1857-58.

HALL J. J. Proprietor, J. J. Hall's Mammoth Eagle Circus/Boston Arena Co., 1836; advertiser, Associations Celebrated Menagerie and Aviary, Zoological Institute, Baltimore, 1837; proprietor, J. J. Hall's, West Indies, 1837; Hall's Circus and Menagerie, 1837-38; Hall, Nathans & Tufts New York Circus and Arena Co., 1839-40.

HALL, ORRIN F. General agent, Cooper & Co., 1874.

HALL, R. G. Contracting agent, Barnum & Bailey, 1889.

HALL TOM. Trapeze performer, Joel E. Warner's, 1872; equestrian director, Crosby's Mammoth Pavilion, 1889.

HALLAM. Clown, Price & Simpson, 1826.

HALLDEAN, MME. Sideshow bearded lady, with John V. O'Brien's, 1871; L. B. Lent's, 1873; P. T. Barnum's, 1874.

HALLECK T. E. Assistant agent, Stevens & Begun, 1874.

HALLETT, ALTA. Female gymnast. Batcheller & Doris, 1870; flying rings, Campbell's, 1878; flying rings, VanAmburgh's, 1879; John H. Murray's, 1880. While performing her trapeze act, Murray's Pony Circus, Cambridge, MA, July 5, 1880, fell and sustained an injury that may have disabled her for life.

HALLIDAY, CLARENCE. (d. October 22, 1890) Wallace & Co.

HALPINE, CHARLES GRAHAM. (November 20, 1829--August 3, 1868) Journalist, poet. Born in Ireland. Came to America, 1851. For a short period of time, P. T. Barnum's private secretary. By 1852, co-editor of a Boston humor weekly, *The Carpet-Bag.*

HALSTED, E. O. ["Charlie"]. (April 2, 1817-April 18, 1892) Born in Ulysses Tompkins County, NY. Began in show business, P. T. Barnum's, NYC, 1842, and was connected with him in one way or another for over a quarter of a century. Also with Spalding & Rogers, Nathans & Sands, Dan Rice's, L. B. Lent's, and others. Said to have possessed a fortune 2 or 3 times but either gave it away or lost it through imprudent investments. Died in comparative poverty, Quincy, MI, age 75.

HALSTEAD, PETER S. Transportation master, P. T. Barnum's, 1872-80.

HAMBHICHI. Bamboo pole performer, with Barnum & Bailey, 1892.

HAMILTON, ELWOOD. For 10 years ran a "one-horse" show featuring the trick horse Sir Henry. For 8 years exhibited

Indians and ran a variety show. In the circus business, Hilliard & Hamilton, 1875; manager and co-proprietor, Hilliard, Hamilton & Hunting, 1876; Hamilton & Sargeant (Prof. E. Hamilton, **F. W. Sargeant,** proprietors), 1877-79; purchased Sargeant's interest, 1880; Hamilton & Knowlton, collapsed Cortland, OH, September 6, 1881; trained dogs, A. F. Tuttle's Olympic Show, 1892.

HAMILTON, FRANK. Trainer, Dan Rice's, 1853.

HAMILTON, FRED. Master of properties, P. T. Barnum's, 1872-73.

HAMILTON, HELENA. *Manège,* Leon W. Washburn's, 1896.

HAMILTON, JAMES MADISON. (November 20, 1847-February 21, 1901) Agent, privilege man. Born in Connersville, IN. Candy butcher at age 10 or 12. Eventually became agent and railroad contractor. Thayer & Noyes, 1867; press agent, P. T. Barnum's, 1877; special advance representative, Cooper & Bailey, 1880; Barnum, Bailey & Hutchinson, 1881; treasurer, Shelby, Pullman & Hamilton, 1881; general railroad contractor, Great Wallace, 1893; invested in Hummel & Hamilton's Great Syndicate Shows, 1896; this was J. N. Rentfrow's New Great Syndicate Shows which had collapsed August 8 and was purchased by James M. Hamilton and **John F. Hummel** of Cincinnati; sunk his savings in this venture and lost it. General advance manager, Frank A. Robbins' **(Frank A. Robbins, Gil Robinson, John W. Hamilton, W. A. Conklin,** proprietors), 1898; assistant manager, LaPearl's, 1899. Career covered more than 40 years.

HAMILTON, JOHN. Privilege manager, King & Franklin, 1889; transportation manager, Wallace& Co., 1891.

HAMILTON, JOHN W. (d. December 24, 1922) Agent. Brother of agent **Tody Hamilton.** L. B. Lent's, 1864; one-third owner Mayberry, Pullman & Hamilton, which lost him $20,000; also connected with W. W. Cole's, Great Wallace, Sells-Floto, Walter L. Main's, Hagenbeck-Wallace. November 1877, sailed for Bermuda as press agent for Howes & Cushing, in which **Jacob Lorillard** was a partner. After reaching his destination and contracting debts, the proprietors cancelled the stand because of opposition from John H. Murray's. When money was not forthcoming for salary and debts, Hamilton sued Lorillard for $350. Press agent, Cooper, Bailey & Co., 1879-80; Barnum, Bailey & Hutchinson, 1881. Left the Barnum & Bailey organization to manage Mt. Morris Theatre. [Charles H. Day: "Jack is fiery and pugnacious and never so happy when engaged in a newspaper broil."] Died in Zanesville, OH.

HAMILTON, MORG. Layer-out, Great Western, 1876.

HAMILTON, RICHARD F. ["Tody"]. (1846?-August 16, 1916) Agent. Brother of **John W. Hamilton.** Born in NYC. A newspaper man by instinct and training. Father, **William C. Hamilton,** was managing editor of a New York paper when Tody was born. Began career in a newspaper office at the early age of 12. Belonged to the school of robust and vigorous young men always in places where there was the most danger of personal conflict or something exciting to make a live story with big headlines. It was said that whenever there was a dearth of real news Tody could, and often did, start out with a few of his friends and in the course of an evening create enough thrilling items to fill the columns of all the New York newspapers. Of great physical energy and winning personality, he made friends everywhere and retained them because of his purely democratic character and merry demeanor. Always open-handed and liberal to a fault, prolific in ideas and writing, he piled up alliterations and adjectives and found unlimited pleasure in coining new words or reconstructing old ones into telling phrases. When about 18 years old, worked a year for the New York *Herald*. Later, was a Wall Street speculator and became a rich man at 21 years of age, only to lose it again "on the Street." Returned to journalism for a time. 1875, manager of the Aquarium, NYC; 1880, press agent for the newly built Iron Pier, Long Branch, NJ; during that year, published the *Evening Journal*, which lasted but 9 weeks; engaged by Barnum, Bailey & Hutchinson, 1881, as press agent, a position that lasted until 1907, when he retired. A life member of the New York Press Club; the newspapermen of America gave him a testimonial at the Waldorf-Astoria when he retired from the Barnum & Bailey show. [Louis E. Cooke: "There is no question in my mind but that he has turned out more good copy and invented more schemes to feed the press and attracted attention to the shows that he has represented than any other living man."] Was with Barnum & Bailey in Europe for 5 years, returning to the United States on October 28, 1902. Connection with the "big show" made him one of the most famous press agents of his era. [Doc Waddell: "If we wished to know who was 'The Greatest of All Circus Press Agents,' we would say 'Tody' Hamilton. I would not take a single laurel from his brow, my hat is off to him, and always will be. His power was along the line of creative news. His heart was with the newspapers. He loved the boys of the press and they loved him."] Died of heart disease in Baltimore, MD, age 70.

HAMILTON, TONY. (March 29, 1867-October 13, 1896) Hurdle rider and horse trainer. Born in Radner, IL. Became a rider, 1892, and by 1895 was a principal somersault and hurdle rider with Leon W. Washburn's. Wife, **Millie**, was an equestrienne as well. Died at his home at Lewistown, IL.

HAMILTON, WILLIAM. Diefenbach & Hamilton's **(Phil Diefenbach**, William Hamilton, proprietors), 1899.

HAMLIN, DAVID. S. H. Nichols', 1842-43.

HAMMOND, C. E. Bandmaster, Wallace & Co., 1884.

HAMMOND, C. D. Manager advertising car #5, Barnum, Bailey & Hutchinson, 1882.

HAMO HASH. Gymnast, Sells Bros.', 1872, Arab act, Adam Forepaugh's, 1874.

HAMPSHIRE, JOSEPH [Joe Baker]. (1827-June 22, 1898) One of the early boss canvasmen. Born in Yorkshire, England. Beginning around 1847, connected with James Robinson's, VanAmburgh's, Dan Rice's, P. T. Barnum's, Adam Forepaugh's, W. C. Coup's, and others. For the last 15 years, with Miner's New York theatres.

HANDENBURGER, JOHN. Director of publications, Handenburger & Co. **(John V. O'Brien**, proprietor), 1871.

HANDLEY, J. T. Troupe of glassblowers, Walter L. Main's, 1893.

HANDY, EMAN. Handy & Welch, 1830; Welch, Macomber & Purdy's menagerie (Boston Zoological Association), 1832. Made an excursion to Africa, 1833, to secure animals for the exhibition.

HANKEN, GEORGE. Gymnast, G. G. Grady's, 1874.

HANLEY, J. Minstrel performer, Spalding & Rogers' *Floating Palace*, 1859.

HANKINS, JAMES R. Somersault rider, French, Hobby & Co., 1835; Welch, Delavan & Nathans, 1848; rider, Welch, Delavan & Nathans, 1849; Sands & Quick, 1852; Mann & Moore, 1853; Welch & Lent, 1854-55; Rivers & Derious, 1856-57; Sands, Nathans & Co., Broadway Circus, NYC, 1858; Levi J. North's, 1859; L. B. Lent's, 1860; Niblo & Sloat **(L B. Lent**, manager), West Indies, 1860-61; Antonio Bros.', 1862; S. Q. Stokes', 1863; scenic rider, Mrs. Dan Rice's, 1864; J. F. Orrin's, South America, 1865-66; S. O. Wheeler's, 1867; acrobat, P. T. Barnum's, 1877.

HANLON BROTHERS [Alfred, George, Frederick, William, Edward, Thomas]. Acrobats, gymnasts, and pantomimists. Noted English performers of both stage and ring. **Thomas** was born in Manchester, 1836; **George**, Ashtonunder-Lyne, Lancashire, 1840; **William**, Manchester, 1842; **Alfred**, Manchester, 1844; **Edward**, Liverpool, 1846; **Frederick**, Liverpool, 1848. The brothers performed many dangerous feats. **Alfred** showed special skill in balancing a ladder upright, ascending and descending it, all on a swinging trapeze. They all somersaulted from the shoulders of one gymnast to another. **Thomas** and **Alfred** were the powerfully built men of the group and served as carriers in the pyramid. **George, William** and **Alfred** left England at an early age and traveled extensively, touring the world with their tutor, **Prof. John Lees**. At the death of Lees, after being away 14 years, they returned to Europe. With **Thomas, Edward** and **Frederick**, they organized the gymnastic and acrobatic troupe famous throughout Europe and America. Made their USA debut, Niblo's Garden, NYC, 1858, under **James M. Nixon's** management. **George** and **Thomas** returned to Niblo's for Nixon's proprietorship of Cooke's Royal Circus, January 1860, where the *l'echelle perileuse* performed by **Thomas** was found to be stimulating and unique: after going through a sequence of gyrations on a swing attached to the ceiling at one end of the proscenium, the gymnast suddenly released himself from it and, flying some 20' or 30' through the air, grabbed onto a rope on the other side. And the double act *par terre* by **Thomas** and **George** was considered a beautiful and astonishing performance and something never before witnessed in America. Great muscular strength and their lithe and agile movements, together with the grace and ease with which they performed each exercise, marked the whole exhibition one of unequaled excellence and merit and made them the "trump cards" of the Nixon troupe. **William** did not join at this time due to an injury but may have been added some months later. They continued with Nixon's summer and fall tour, 1860. In NYC, December 12, 1861, **William** unveiled his Zampillaerostation, performed in the manner of the acrobat, **Leotard**, but observed to be more difficult and more finished than the Frenchman's. The modest and unassuming brothers practiced for months before attempting a public exhibition of this act. The Academy of Music, NYC, was the venue selected for the debut. From the first tier of boxes a standing place had been erected with an iron ladder attached for mounting the perch. About 20' from this, in the parquet, an iron framework stood from which the first trapeze hung. Some 50' beyond was a second iron framework with its hanging trapeze. Another 30' further was a third such swing suspended from the proscenium. 18' beyond that was a platform to serve as a landing place for the acrobat. All of the preceding were secured by iron wires of a half inch thickness to the boxes on either side. As the act began, **William** positioned himself on the platform some 25' above ground level. Two other Hanlons were stationed at the center trapeze swings to assist him in his flight to the stage. At a given signal the gymnast swung on the first trapeze, leaped to the second, sent up to meet him by a brother, and then the third, sent up by the other brother, and finally landed on the stage platform—all this with somersaults as he passed from one trapeze to the next. A New York *Clipper* observer assessed it to be "the most surprising, graceful, and perfect acrobatic feat ever attempted," adding, "we have no doubt but that it will be the sensation of the season." The Hanlons visited California, 1862; following that, toured South America, returning in January, 1865. They had a short circus venture as management under the title of Hanlon, Spalding & Rogers Show, 1865; George Metcalfe's Hippotheatron, St. Louis, spring 1866. In Chicago, 1865, they were persuaded by the acrobatic clown, **Agoust** (William Bridges), to perform a pantomime act. 1867, the troupe went to the *Folies Bergeres,* Paris, where they established a reputation as pantomimic artists, later performing in such pieces as *The Village Barber, Do, Mi, Sol, Do, The Journey in Switzerland, Une Soiree en Habit Noir, Les Cascades du Diable, Le Boulanger,* and *Le Gymnase Paz.* **William** died February 8, 1923, age 79. He had retired from the stage in 1915. **Thomas** died in Harrisburg, PA, April 5, 1868, in a state of insanity induced by a fall during a performance in Cincinnati and injuring his head. His suffering led to suicide. Wife, **Jane,** died October 24, 1894. **Alfred,** fourth in age of

the 6 brothers, died of consumption, June 21, 1886, Pasadena, CA. **Frederick,** born in Everton, near Liverpool, 1848; died at Nice, France, April 26, 1886. He was apprenticed to the Hanlons' father at an early age. Was one of the troupe that came to Niblo's Garden, 1860. **Robert,** who was at one time a member of the Hanlon Brothers act but not an original Hanlon, appearing as "Little Bob," and startling audience with his dive from the dome of a build into a net below, died in London, June 30, 1907.

HANLON, JAMES. Came to America, 1890, with the Hanlon-Volters troupe. Academy of Music, NYC, August 1890; Adam Forepaugh's, 1891.

HANLON, ROBERT. One of the original Hanlon "Midgets," came to America, 1890, with the Hanlon-Volters troupe. Academy of Music, NYC, August 1890; Adam Forepaugh's, 1891.

HANLON, WILLIAM [r. n. O'Mara]. (d. July 13, 1891) Acrobat. Born in London, England. 25 years with the Hanlon-Volters act. Came to America August 1890. Fell from the dome of the Academy of Music, NYC, at the opening of the Hanlon-Volter and Martinetti Pantomime and Novelty Co. there. Recovered rapidly from the accident. (with Robert and James Hanlon) Adam Forepaugh's, 1891. [John Ringling: "Billy Hanlon was as accomplished an aerialist as there ever was living."] Died in Clinton, IA, by the breaking of a trapeze, age 31.

HANNER, WILLIAM H. and sister **LOUISE.** Balloon ascensionists, Cook & Whitby, 1893.

HANNON, MARIE. Dan Rice's (**Adam Forepaugh,** proprietor), 1866.

HANNON, RICHARD H. Gymnast. Castello & VanVleck, 1863, Maginley & Bell, 1964; trapeze artist (with **Price**) S. B. Howes' European, 1865; New American Theatre, Philadelphia, winter 1865-66; Dan Castello's, 1866, winter 1867-68; J. M. French's, 1869; Mike Lipman's, 1869; G. A. Huff & Co., 1870.

HANNOR & POWERS. Dan Castello & Co., 1866.

HANNUM, ZURUBY. Circassian lady, P. T. Barnum's, 1876.

HANSON, JOSEPH H. Railroad contractor, W. H. Harris' Nickel-Plate, 1884.

HAPGOOD, HARRY. Agent, with Noyes' Crescent City, 1872; press agent, Frank A. Robbins', 1885.

HARDELLA, H. [r. n. Hardy Bale]. Contortionist. Ran away from his home in Petersburg, IL, at the age of 13 and joined M. O'Conner's. Some time later joined Charles Hunter's, Pittsburg, KS, where he took the name of "Hardella the wonderful contortionist." Performed as **Hardelia Brothers** (with **William Lucifer** and **William McCall**), DeBonnaire's Great Persian Exposition, 1883, 1885; Mayo's Model Show, 1884; Walter L. Main's, 1886.

HARDESTY, MRS. A. H. See Molly Bailey.

124

HARDING, CHARLES. Acrobat and clown, Beckett's, 1881; W. H. Harris' Nickel-Plate, 1884; clown and principal leaper, John Robinson's, 1886.

HARDING, GEORGE. General agent, Cooper & Co., 1874.

HARDY, SYLVIA. (d. August 25, 1888) Giantess, 7' tall. P. T. Barnum's.

HARE, CHARLES W. Rider, S. H. Nichols & Co., winter 1843; T. L. Vermule's, 1845; manager and rider, Old Dominion Circus, 1845; Dr. Gilbert R. Spalding's, 1846; Victory Circus, 1847.

HARLAN, ED. Bounding rope act, W. F. Kirkhart's Great American, 1894.

HARLAN, H. Proprietor, H. Harlan's Great Inter-Ocean Circus, 1875.

HARPER, D. J. Harper Bros.' European (P. N. and D. J. Harper, proprietors), 1892.

HARPER, EDWARD. Ethiopian performer, Boston Lion Circus (Raymond & Weeks, proprietors), 1836.

HARPER, L. J. [or J. L.]. Program agent, P. T. Barnum's, 1874.

HARPER, P. N. Harper Bros.' European (P. N. and D. J. Harper, proprietors), 1892.

HARPIER, JOHN. Clown. As **Mons. Harpier Rochford,** S. P. Stickney's, 1848; Dan Rice's, 1849, 1851; S. Q. Stokes', 1850; Levi J. North's, 1851; Sam Lathrop's, winter 1851; Lathrop-Maltby, spring 1852; Star State, fall 1852; Whitbeck's, Cuba, winter 1853; as **Roch Harpier,** Whitbeck's, 1953-54; L. G. Butler's, 1855; Antonio & Co., St. Louis Varieties, 1855; Harper & Antonio, Victoria, TX, 1856.

HARRINGTON, ANNIE. (d. August 21, 1904) Came to the USA with Barnum & Bailey when they returned from England. With the company for 2 seasons, then joined the Hanlon Brothers' troupe for 3 years.

HARRINGTON, LOUIS. Acrobat, Palmer's, 1835; rider, Welch & Delavan, 1841.

HARRINGTON, WILLLIAM. (b. 1804) Native of Boston, MA. One of the early riders in America and considered above average in ability. First appeared at Lafayette Circus, NYC; formed his own company, 1826; 2-horse rider, American Arena, Washington, DC, winter 1828-29; own show out, 1829. While performing at Sunbury, PA, August 19, 1829, the entire company was arrested and charged with witchcraft. Rider and co-proprietor, Harrington & Buckley, 1830, William Harrington's, 1831-32; Palmer & Harrington's, 1834; Bancker & Harrington's, 1835; Sweet & Hough's, 1835; Welch & Delavan, 1841; Mons. LeTort's, 1842; Ogden & Hobby, 1842; Risley act with his son, Rockwell & Stone, 1846-47. While with Rockwell's, St. Louis, fell from a horse and injured his head. Thereafter showed signs of being deranged, making several attempts at suicide, and on the last try shooting himself in the head. When friends attempted to intercede, discharged the revolver at them but missed the mark, then, inviting them to watch him kill himself, sat on a pile of wood, lodged a bullet into his brain, and died on the spot.

HARRIS, CALLIE. Bareback rider, W. H. Harris' Nickel--Plate, 1889-94.

HARRIS, D. H. (October 7, 1849-April 6, 1914) Husband of **MMe. Marantette,** equestrienne, and manager of the Marantette high school horses which appeared at circuses and fairs. Born in Frankfort, KY. After growing into manhood, became a master horseman and for years was connected with the leading showmen of the world—Barnum's, Forepaugh's, Ringling's, etc., in the purchase of horses. Began work with **MMe. Marantette** in May, 1882, in the management of her business. October, 1895, they were married. Died at his home at Mendon, MI, age 64.

HARRIS, DOT L. Slack-wire, World's Fair Aggegation, 1892. Had formerly performed with theatrical companies as an actress.

HARRIS, FRANKIE. Rider, W. H. Harris' Nickel-Plate, 1884-90; jockey and hurdle rider, Great Exposition Circus, 1895.

HARRIS, HENRY. "Aerial flights," Flagg & Aymar, 1856.

HARRIS, S. E. See Wesley Barmore.

HARRIS, SIGNOR. Horizontal bars, World's Fair Aggregation, 1892.

HARRIS, WILLIAM H. (February 23, 1841-February 10, 1901) Born in Cookville, Ontario, Canada. Father kept a hotel in Trafalgar. Began as a clerk in a store. Father set him up with his own store, which he later sold at auction and moved to Chicago with $3,000, 1861. Intended to go into the hotel business, but, not finding a suitable property, lost most of his money in speculation. With $200 bought into a touring theatrical enterprise with Prof. W. J. McAllister. Bought into another show with Wash Blodgett, Prof. Vandamein's Gift Show, which failed to make money. Left for Chicago and got employment at $7 a week as a glassware packer. Next, became clerk in the bank of C. C. Parks & Co. With backing from Richard T. Spikings, opened Northwest Bill Posting Co. A consolidation with Bradway & Callahan soon followed. Harris sold out, 1870, and started in a men's furnishing business but was burned out by the fire of 1871. Re-established in a new location, took in W. R. Cobb as partner. Sold out to Cobb, 1879. Shortly bought an egg case company. Later, dealt with stocks and bankrupt sales. Fall 1882, entered the circus business as proprietor of Harris' Nichel-Plate Shows, opening May 5, 1883, which he conducted up to the time of death. Married Miss Clara Sargent, 1867. Their daughter was married to C. E. Wilson. Died in Chicago.

HARRISON, HARRY. Contortionist. Holland & McMahon, Chicago, fall 1885; Forepaugh & Samwells, 1886; King & Franklin, 1887.

HARRISON, HUGH. Sideshow manager, Walter L. Main's, 1892; manager, 1893.

HARRISON, J. D. Sideshow manager, Walter L. Main's, 1893.

HARRISON, MME. Mind reader, Walter L. Main's, 1892. Possibly the wife of **Hugh Harrison**.

HARRISON, ROBERT. Tambourinist, minstrel troupe, with Gardner & Hemmings, 1863.

HARRISON, W. B. Supt. museum department, P. T. Barnum's, 1871.

HART, BILLY. Bunnell's minstrel troupe, R. Sands', 1863; Irish comedian, concert, Adam Forepaugh's (Pullman Bros.' sideshow), 1876.

HART, HARRY. Clown and general performer. S. O. Wheeler's, 1868; Orton & Co., 1869.

HART, H. H. Hart, France & Co. (H. H. Hart, **F. F. France**, proprietors), 1889.

HART, JOHN. Adam Forepaugh's, 1878.

HART, ORLANDO PORTER ["Port"]. (d. October 24, 1992) Hostler in the days of wagon shows. Connected with P. T. Barnum's, Dan Rice's, and Adam Forepaugh's. Drove the large chariots with 24 horses at the head. Had a show of his own for some years. Last job before retirement from show business was as boss canvasman and master of transportation, Booth & Collier's "Uncle Tom's Cabin" Co. (another source gives McFadden's "Uncle Tom's Cabin" Co.) Later, drove a coach running between Wilkesbarre and Danville and between Wilkesbarre and Easton, PA. Died at Wilkesbarre after having been ill for over a year with peritonitis and dropsy.

HART, O. W. Assistant manager, W. W. Cole's, 1874.

HART THOMAS. Assistant doorkeeper, P. T. Barnum's, 1873.

HARTER, MARY A. See Cleo Hernandez.

HARTLEY, H. W. Whitmore, Thompson & Co., 1865.

HARTMAN, FRITZ. Band leader. Madigan's, 1861; Gardner & Hemmings, 1863; P. T. Barnum's, 1872-73; P. T. Barnum's Roman Hippodrome, 1874-75.

HARTZELL, GEORGE. Principal clown, Scribner & Smith, 1894.

HARVEY, JULKIAN ["Jule"]. Clown, Mabie's, 1859; agent, Orton Bros.', 1868.

HARVEY, MARIE. Pantomime actress, Joseph D. Palmer's, 1835.

HARVEY, NAPOLEON. Animal trainer, G. K. Goodwin's, 1860.

HARVEY, ROBERT MITCHELL. (b. June 2, 1869) Born in Sidney, IA. Rider, Adam Forepaugh's, 1884; W. F. Kirkhart's Great American Railroad Circus **(W. F. Kirkhart, R. M. Harvey, proprietors)**, 1895-1900; manager, Coop & Lent, 1918.

HASKINS, CHARLES H. Advertiser. At one time part of the bill posting firm of Cornell & Haskins. [M. B. Leavitt: He "knew every billboard in the United States, and for many seasons went ahead of the Barnum show, also the Hippodrome, as chief advertising agent."] S. O. Wheeler's, 1865, 1867; chief bill poster, L. B. Lent's, 1874; Barnum's Roman Hippodrome, 1875.

HASKINS, CHARLES P. (d. November 5, 1880) Punch and Judy in sideshow and in charge of Wild Men of Borneo, W. C. Coup's, 1880. Died in Dawson, GA. Had worked for Dr. Hanford Warner, proprietor of the Wild Men, for 11 years.

HASKINS, GEORGE. Yankee Robinson's, Chicago, 1866.

HASLETT, JOSEPH. Gymnast, (with **Ashton**) Sands & Nathans , 1859.

HASSABOURA, SAM. Japanese equilibrist, S. H. Barrett, 1882.

HASSAN, ALI. Arabian gymnast, Gardner & Hemmings, National Hall, Philadelphia, 1865.

HASSEN, ALI [Sie Hassen Ben Ali]. (d. July, 1914) Came to USA with Arab troupe, 1886. Died in Morocco.

HASWELL, JAMES. Flying-man, Robinson's Circus, California **(Frank Frost,** manager), 1886.

HAT, DOLLY. Acrobat, John Robinson's, 1889.

HATCH GUS. Advertiser, Spalding & Rogers, 1847-1864. Kept a tavern in Kansas, 1885. [Charles H. Day: "There's Gus Hatch, prospering in Kansas City and standing in with the real estate ring that are coining cash."]

HATCH, JAMES A. Hitchcock, Hatch & Co. Was keeping a hotel in suburban New Haven, CT, 1877.

HATCHER, JOSEPH T. Exhibitor of curiosities, P. T. Barnum's, 1872-73, sideshow manager, 1874.

HATFIELD, ALFRED GRIFFITH. See Al G. Field.

HATFIELD, FRED. Clown, Denver Dick's Wild West and Sioux Indian Medicine Company, 1894.

HAVEN, S. B. Cole & Co., 1837.

HAVILAND D. Riding master, Dr. Gilbert R. Spalding's, 1845-46.

HAVILAND, GEORGE R. Treasurer, James M. French's, 1867; Romelli & Co., 1872; G. F. Bailey & Co., 1874.

HAWES. Co-proprietor, Thompson, Smith & Hawes, 1866.

HAWKINS, DOC. Ben Maginley's, 1863.

HAWKINS, JAMES. Rider, winter circus, Chestnut Street Theatre, Philadelphia, December 1868; Wootten & Haight, 1871.

HAWKINS, JOHN H. Co-proprietor, Hawkins & Loomis Dog and Pony Show, 1997.

HAWLEY, DAVID R. (June 6, 1849-June 10, 1886) Gymnast and flying trapeze. Was throughout his 20 years in the business considered "a daring, almost reckless, performer." Performed a double somersault from a trapeze to a diagonal rope, 1872, Middlesex Hall, England. Was the earliest recorded aerialist using steel trapeze cables. Partner of **August Buislay,** early 1880s; for a time, teamed with **T. E. Miaco** as well as **Harry Moulton.** Thompson, Smith & Hawes, 1866; P. T. Barnum's, 1871; Adam Forepaugh's, 1874-78; L. B. Lent's, 1876; Adam Forepaugh's, 1878; Woodward's Garden,

San Francisco, CA, late fall 1878; (with **Buislay**) Barnum, Bailey & Hutchinson, 1881-82; (with **Buislay**) Leon & Dockrill, Iron Amphitheatre, Havana, winter 1881-82; (with **Buislay**) Orrin Bros.', Mexico, winter 1882-83; Cantelli & Leon, Havana, winter 1882-83; Pubillones', Havana, winter 1884-85; Sparrow's, 1886. On June 5, 1986, while practicing a triple somersault, landed on his shoulder in the net which caused concussion of the spine. June 9, 1886, married **Maude Oswald**, equestrienne, from his hospital bed, General Hospital, Montreal, Canada. Died the following day.

HAWLEY, E. Concert privilege, G. G. Grady's, 1874.

HAYDEN, PROF. J. W. Balloonist. Lake's Hippo-Olympiad, winter 1870-71; billed as a "French aeronaut," Stone & Murray, 1871.

HAYDEN, W. R. Transportation agent, W. W. Cole's, 1874; general manager, 1877; general agent, 1878; railroad contractor, 1879-81.

HAYDEN, WILLIAM. Cooper, Bailey & Co., 1880.

HAYES, GEORGE. Knife thrower, Robert Hunting's, 1894.

HAYES, ISAAC. Howes' European, winter 1864.

HAYES, LIZZIE. Trapeze performer, Boyd & Peters, 1879.

HAYS, TIM. Concert performer, Dan Castello & Co., 1866.

HAZELETT, JOSEPH. Gymnast and monkey man. Dr. Gilbert R. Spalding's, 1848; Sands', 1850-52; Joe Pentland's, 1854; Washburn's, 1855; Spalding & Rogers, 1856; G. F. Bailey & Co., 1857-58; Sands, Nathans & Co., 1859; James Robinson's, 1870.

HAZEN, B. Band leader, George W. DeHaven's, 1865.

HEATH, TOM. (1853-August 18, 1938) Of the famous comedy duo of **McIntyre and Heath,** teamed in 1874. Believed to have been born in or near Philadelphia, 1853. 1884 was married to **Grayce Margaret Speurl**. Son born, 1902, but died 1919. Before joining with McIntyre, each had played with different partners in singing, dancing and comedy turns in the hinterlands. Formation was intended to be only temporary; merger worked so well that partnership was retained. Early on, billed as **Alexander & Hennery**, playing noted *Ham Tree* skit. Among the first teams to dance the buck and wing, occasion being at Tony Pastor's Theater, NYC, 1879. Also claimed to have originated Negro ragtime, 1874. Tunes introduced by them included such classics as "Dem Golden Slippers," "Old Black Joe" and "My Old Kentucky Home." Great Universal Fair and World's Wonder Exposition (**William O. Monroe**, proprietor), 1877; Anderson & Co., 1879. Last show in which the team appeared was *America Sings*, a musical produced in Boston, 1934. Both men were in excellent financial circumstances. McIntyre died, 1937, age 80. Mrs. Heath died, 1929. Heath died of a heart attack at his home in Setauket, LI, age 85. See James McIntyre.

HECK, LOUIS. Concert minstrel violinist, George F. Bailey & Co., 1860; band leader, Sells Bros.', 1874-81. [Peter Sells: "Louis Heck was a most precise man in everything and prided himself on speaking English correctly, although he was a German."] Left the show, 1880s, and settled in Topeka, KS, where he gave music lessons and catered orchestras for social events.

HECTOR & FANE. Gymnasts, from Theatre Royal, Drury Lane, London, first time in America, John H. Murray's Railroad Circus., 1875.

HEDDEN, BILLY. Concert minstrel, Spalding & Rogers' *Floating Palace*, 1859.

HEDGES, HENRY. Program agent, Howes' Great London, 1875; contractor, Cooper, Bailey & Co,, 1879; mail agent, Cooper, Bailey & Co., 1880; manager, advance car #1, Barnum, Bailey & Hutchinson, 1881-82.

HEDGES, LOUIS M. Program agent and assistant manager, Howes' Great London, 1874; assistant manager, Cooper, Bailey & Co., 1879-80; superintendent, Barnum, Bailey & Hutchinson, 1881-82.

HEELEY BROTHERS. Contortionists, with W. H. Harris' Nickel-Plate, 1884.

HEEN, LIZZIE. Gymnast, John Robinson's, 1883.

HEFFRON, JOHN E. General agent, with Shield's, 1987-88; manager, Great Eastern, 1899, winter 1989-90.

HEFFRON, WILLIAM. Robinson & Howes, 1864.

HEIDLER, J. W. Agent at large, Cooper, Bailey & Co., 1876.

HEIGHT, GEORGE. Horizontal bars, Harry Thayer & Co.'s, 1890.

HELENE SISTERS. Riders, Melville, Maginley & Cooke, 1875.

HELLSTROM, ALEXANDER. Gymnastic clown, Barnum & Bailey, 1892.

HELM PROF. Band leader, Levi J. North's, 1857.

HELMREICH, FREDERICK W. (1848?-July 13, 1910) Athlete. Born in Germany and came to America as a child, settling in Michigan. Particularly skilled in leaping, boxing and fencing. Joined John Robinson's, where he remained for several years; later, P. T. Barnum's. After leaving the circus business, became the first athletic instructor at the Denver Athletic Club and one of the top physical trainers in the country. Died in Denver, age 62.

HELOISE, MLLE. See Sallie Stickney.

HEMMICK, F. Acrobat, John Robinson's, 1874-75.

HEMMINGS, ELVIRA ["Mlle. Elvira," Mrs. Richard Hemmings]. See Elvira Whitby and Richard Hemmings.

HEMMINGS, JAMES. Equestrian, running globe, juggler. Hemmings, Cooper & Whitby, 1868; Mrs. Charles Warner's, Philadelphia, winter 1868-69; Bryan's, 1869.

HEMMINGS, RICHARD. (January 4, 1834-February 19, 1919) Gymnast. Born in Birmingham, England, the son of an actor who performed for a number of years with Edmund Kean. First appeared in public, Queen's Theatre, Manchester, 1839, as a baby monkey in a monkey ballet with **Mons.**

Goffe. Continued to perform in pantomimes and horse dramas, training himself in the art of riding, tumbling and tightrope work through the instruction of **Mons. Caldi**, the great dancing master, and **Signor Chiarini**. Joined his uncle and the famous Hemmings troupe of acrobats who traveled as **Professor Hemmings and His Wonderful Infants** until 1849. Apprenticed to **William Batty**, London. During the World's Exhibition, 1851, performed as a riding act. Following this, was with the Mlle. Macarte Co., and Pablo Fanque's. Last engagement in England, Vauxhall Gardens Winter Circus, London, 1855. October 9 of that year, left Southhampton on the side-wheeler, *Erickson*, for NYC and was engaged by Chiarini for his Cuban circus. Afterwards, VanAmburgh & Co., 1857-58; New National Circus (John Tryon, proprietor), winter 1957-58; Sloat & Shephard, 1858; Sloat & Shepherd's "Joe Pentland", 1859. Went into partnership with Dan Gardner, Gardner & Hemmings, starting with 3 ring horses for their first stand, Comac's Woods, Philadelphia. Then, Front Street Theartre, Baltimore, early winter, 1860. Winter 1861, the company was under the Gardner, Hemmings & Madigan title. 1863, Gardner & Hemmings joined with the VanAmburgh menagerie, 12 cages of animals, plus elephants and camels. James Cooper bought an interest, 1865, making it Gardner Hemmings & Cooper. Dan Rice was engaged as a special feature, 1867, for $1,000 per week. Show changed hands again, 1868, making it Hemmings, Cooper & Whitby, which continued through 1870. After Whitby was shot and killed during a riot in Vicksburg, MS, the show went out as Hemmings & Cooper for 2 seasons with James A. Bailey as advertising manager. Hemmings sold out to Cooper at the end of 1872 season and the show went out the following year as Cooper & Bailey. Also connected with Hippotheatron, NYC, winter 1863-64; S. O. Wheeler's, Boston, winter 1864-65; Adam Forepaugh's, 1875-80; John O'Brien's, 1883. Retired from the business, 1883, and settled in Philadelphia. His wife, Elvira, was an equestrienne. See Elvira Whitby.

HENDERSON, ABE. (September 10, 1836-October 14, 1876) Born at Port Hope, Ontario. Came to USA at age 16. Manager, James Robinson's, 1870-71; Rosston, Springer and Henderson, **(Frank H. Rosston, Andrew Springer**, Abe Henderson, **Adam Forepaugh**, proprietors), 1871. Forepaugh bought out his partners, October 1872. Henderson bought half interest in Joel E. Warner's, January 1874, Warner & Henderson's Great Pacific Combination (Henderson, manager; Warner, general agent); manager, Springer's Royal Cirq-Zoo-lodon, 1875. Died of an ulcerated liver at his home in Gerard, PA, where he had lived since 1864, age 40.

HENDERSON, ALEX. Co-proprietor, James Robinson's Circus and Animal Show, 1870.

HENDERSON, DAVID. Associate, Howes & Norton (formerly Robinson & Howes), 1864; Nixon's Amphitheatre, Washington, DC, 1865; Dan Rice's (managed by **Adam Fore-**paugh), 1866; sideshow privilege (with **James DeMott**), Adam Forepaugh's, 1867; chief bill poster, Howes' Great London, 1874.

HENDERSON, JOHN W. Agent, Katie Putnam company, early 1870s; Adam Forepaugh's, 1874.

HENDLEY, PAULINE. Equestrienne, with Lake's Hippo-Olympiad, 1869. Husband **Sam** was also with the company.

HENDRICKS, SAMUEL J. Ludlow & Smith, 1841; Dr. Gilbert R. Spalding's, 1845; S. P. Stickney's, 1846-47; Great Western **(Dennison Stone, Thomas McCollum**, proprietors), 1846.

HENDRICKS, W. QUINNETT. (May 28, 1850-February 28, 1932) Miles Orton's, 1865; Yankee Robinson's, 1866; North American (George W. DeHaven, manager), 1868; Backenstoe's, 1869; Great Western, 1870; Great Eastern, 1871; Great American Racing Association, 1875; Charles Bartine's, 1878; John Robinson's, 1881; Sam Stickney's, 1883; Cooper & Jackson, 1883;; clown, New York and New England (**O. J. Ferguson, proprietor**), 1884; W. H. Harris' Nickel-Plate, 1884-85; bought half interest in Priest show, 1886; Ringling Bros.', 1886; Miller Bros.', 1889; Gollmar Bros.', 1890; LaPearl's, 1892, 1897; co-proprietor, Mullen's Big Railroad Show, 1893; advance car manager, Campbell Bros.', 1899-1906; Fred Buchanan's Yankee Robinson's, 1907-08; Reaver & Kelly's Uncle Tom's Cabin Co., 1920. See Quinnett Family.

HENDRICKSON, WILLIAM. Partner of John Wilson, California. John Wilson filed suit against him for dissolution of their partnership, 1864. Trouble between the two first occurred, 1859, when Wilson had a unit of their circus in South America and Hendrickson was managing another on the West Coast. After a successful season the previous year, money was laid aside for real estate investment. When Wilson returned he was informed that Hendrickson's company had a losing season and the reserve funds were used up in an attempt to keep the show running; but this could not be verified because "the books had been lost." Later, Wilson learned that certain real estate had indeed been purchased by Hendrickson using partnership money. Finding this to be irregular, Wilson sued for a deed to one-half of the property so purchased, as well as for the dissolution of the partnership.

HENDRY, W. W. Proprietor, Hendry's new London Shows, 1892.

HENGLER, JENNIE LOUISE. Double riding and driving *manège* act, P. T. Barnum's, 1877. Daughter of English manager **Charles Hengler**.

HENNESSEY, JAMES. Cornetist in Sunshine Pop Gibler's band, Burr Robbins', 1881. [D. W. Watt: "He was one of the finest in the business in his day and on account of his youth, when young Hennessey would step out in front and play a solo, he was always greeted by thousands who would cheer him to the echo and they would not be satisfied until the young man would respond to a second number."] Only other year with a circus, Ringling Bros.', 1892.

HENNESSEY, J. R. W. Manager, Valkingburg & Co., 1881-82; manager, Siegrist, Howe & Co., winter 1984; name changed to Atlantic and Pacific Shows, 1885, collapsed in Georgetown, TX; manager, Senor Cortina's Spanish, Mexican and Wild West Show, 1885; Cooper & Co. (J. R. W. Hennessey, proprietor and manager), 1896-1901.

HENRI, PROF. G. [and children]. Gymnasts, Dan Rice's Paris Pavilion, 1873.

HENRICO, SIGNOR [r. n. Thomas H. Williams]. Clown. Boston Lion Circus, 1936; Whittinore, Thompson & Co., 1865.

HENRICOS [3]. Trapeze and horizontal bar, Great Oriental Pavilion Show, 1877.

HENRIQUE, JUAN. Spanish bareback rider, Herr Driesbach & Howes, 1868.

HENRIQUE, CARLOTTA. Rider, L. B. Lent's, 1874; Shelby, Pullman & Hamilton, 1881.

HENRY, C. Concert minstrel, Orton & Older, 1859.

HENRY, JOHN. Rider, Stone & Murray, 1868.

HENRY, M. Rider. Aaron Turner's, 1837; Robinson & Foster, 1843.

HENRY, WILLIAM. Treasurer, John B. Doris', 1883.

HENRY, WILLY. General performer, Thompson, Smith & Hawes, 1866.

HENSHAW, WILLIAM. Sideshow lecturer, with Barnum, Bailey & Hutchinson, 1882.

HEPP, JOE [r. n. Warren A. Patrick]. Ringling Bros.' prior to 1895. In the circus business around a dozen years before becoming western manager for New York *Clipper* and writer of the column under the *nom de plume* of "Joe Hepp." One of the founders of the Showmen's League of America, for which he was the secretary for some years.

HERBERT, COCO. Clown, Barnum & Bailey, 1893.

HERBERT BROTHERS [Edward, Fred, Charles; also Fred, John, Frank]. Acrobats, high stilts, and Roman ladders. Natives of Muncie, IN. Joel E. Warner's, 1876, collapsed early; John Robinson's, 1877-78; W. W. Cole's, 1878; Orrin Bros.', Havana, winter 1878-79; P. T. Barnum's, 1879; Adam Forepaugh's, 1880-83; Leon & Dockrill, Iron Amphitheatre, Havana, winter 1881-82; Orrin Bros.', Mexico, winter 1885-86; Irwin Bros.', 1889. **Fred Herbert**, tumbler and trapeze artist, Hemmings, Cooper & Whitby, 1869-70; James E. Cooper's, 1872; Sells Bros.', 1872-73; bicycle riders, Adam Forepaugh's, 1883. While with Sells, married **Miss Lida Jones** of Muncie, IN, July 27, 1872, at Dwight, IL.

HERBERT, PROF. Trained geese, Dan Rice's, 1891.

HERMAN. Equestrian, with Lailson's, Philadelphia, 1797, 1798. Stood on his moving mount and placed one of his feet in his mouth and leaped his horse through a 6' hogshead.

HERMAN, G. Concert minstrel, Albizu's, Havana, fall 1866.

HERMAN, J. A. [r. n. Simonson]. (January 1, 1823-January 23, 1901) Born in Brooklyn, NY. First appeared in public with a concert company in white face, 1840, Croton Hall, located at the junction of Bowery and Division Street, NYC. First appeared in black face with a small minstrel band, consisting of **Duke Morgan, Alfred Delapere, William Harrington**, and **Raymond**, with Mabie's, appearing in the sideshow. 1848, Kimberly's Campbell Minstrels at Society Library Rooms, NYC; Holton & Gates' Harmoniums, Simon Pure American Circus, NYC, October 1, 1866; took his leave of the stage at Hooley's Opera House, Brooklyn, about 1871; then reappeared at Hooley's Opera House, Brooklyn, 1874, remaining about 2 weeks; after which, retired from the profession. November 1874, was proprietor of a hotel on the site of the old Union Racetrack, LI.

HERMAN, R. Barnum, VanAmburgh and Castello, 1867.

HERN, EVAN EVANS. See Eph Horn.

HERNANDEZ, A. M. Yankee Robinson's, 1868.

HERNANDEZ, CLIO [r. n. Mary A. Harter]. (d. December 31, 1898) Equestrienne, principal and 4-horse rider, Wallace & Co., 1886-87. Was apparently married to **J. C. Harrington** at one time; by 1890, was married to **P. W. Donovan**. Donovan died in Oswego, NY, March 12, 1896. Cleo died from acute pneumonia.

HERNANDEZ, JAMES [Sometimes Juan, but r. n. Mickey Kelly]. (1832-July 19, 1861) Native of Albany, NY. Excellent pad rider, a rival of **James Robinson**, and celebrated in the capitols of Europe. After serving an apprenticeship with old **John Robinson**, performed with Charles Bacon's (billed as Master Robinson), winter 1837; Bacon & Derious, 1838; took the name of **Hernandez** while with Ludlow & Smith's American Theatre Troupe, New Orleans, winter season 1840-41. Probably a member of the troupe **Sol Smith** took to Havana, winter 1841-42. 1843, as an 11 year old, was advertised as "the pet, the pride, the champion of the arena." Robinson & Foster, 1842-44; Sands, Lent & Co., 1846-47; went to, 1849, recruited by **William Batty**, Astley's Royal England Amphitheatre. [George Speaight: "There was nothing very sensational about the feats he achieved; he sprang from the horse's back while standing and kneeling; he skipped with a small hoop or riding whip, passing it three or four times round his body in one leap; he leaped over flags spread three abreast, nearly nine foot in breadth, facing both front and back; he stood on one foot, with the other in his hand and on his head. But it was the manner in which he presented it that made his performance so remarkable. Every feat was cleanly and successfully accomplished at the first attempt."] During stay in England, appeared with William Cooke's, Birmingham and Brighton; Franconi's, Manchester, Nottingham and Leeds; Pablo Fanque's, Liverpool and Sheffield; Welch & McCollum, Liverpool. January, 1852, at 17 years of age, went into partnership with Rufus Welch, Royal Pavilion Circus, Brighton, and later toured as Welch, Hernandez & Co.'s American Circus and Mammoth Marquee. Later opened his own circus, Leeds, 1852-53 season. 1853, went into partnership with Eaton Stone, Hernandez & Stone's American Circus. Left for America, October, 1855. L. B. Lent's, 1856; Joe Pentland's, 1856; Richard Risley's hall show, California, 1857; Lee & Bennett, San Francisco, 1857, billed as "The Ducrow of the West"; Rowe & Marshall, Hawaiian Islands and Australia, winter 1857-58; L. B. Lent's, winter 1858-59, 1859-60; Harry Whitby's, 1859. Died in Singapore 2 years later.

HERNANDEZ, JUAN. See James Hernandez.

HERNANDEZ, LEO. Sideshow bearded lady. Married **R. R. Moffitt**, tattooed man, Frankfort, PA, February 11, 1883.

HERNANDEZ, LOUISE. Dancing tight-rope, Scribner & Clements, 1887.

HERNANDEZ, RICHARD. Contortionist and rider, L. B. Lent's, 1859-62.

HERNANDO. Welch's, Philadelphia, 1843.

HERTZOG, DANIEL. Supt. of candy privilege, Adam Forepaugh's, 1876; same, Cooper, Bailey & Co., 1879, sideshow orator, 1880.

HERVEY, JULLAN FLINT [Also Master Harvey, Young Harvey, J. Harvey, Leonard Hervey]. (January 6, 1832-March 31, 1905) Born in Whitehall, NY. "Youth without bones," North American, 1846-47; Stone & McCollum, 1848; Reynolds', 1854; equestrian director and gymnast, (as **Julian Henry**) Orton & Older, 1857-58; clown (as **Jule Harvey**), Mabie Bros.', 1859; Orton Bros.', 1868-69. Died Roswell, NM.

HESLEY, JAMES. Clown, Irwin Bros.', 1888.

HESS. Strong man, called the "American Sampson," Howes & Sands, 1835; Mammoth Eagle Circus **(James B. Green,** manager), 1836. Held a 300 pound anvil while 2 men beat it with sledge hammers.

HETHERBY, JOSEPH. Band leader. Rivers & Derious, 1852; Myers & Madigan, 1854; Ballard, Bailey, 1855.

HETTINGER & NIBBE. Hebrew artists, Barnum, Bailey & Hutchinson, 1882.

HEWITT, JOSEPH H. Treasurer, assistant manager, Charles Lee's London Shows, 1892-96; business manager, Sig. Sautelle's, 1897.

HEYWOOD, JAMES. Proprietor and manager, New York Central Park Circus, 1877.

HICKEY, C. Clown, Dan Rice's, 1877.

HICKEY, JOHN M. Agent, Frank Stowe's, 1874.

HICKS, GEORGE H. (1856?-October 5, 1909) Acrobat. Began with the Silverberg show, Columbus, OH, 1873; also, Sells Bros.' and Anglo-American. At one time, toured with **Bill Ashton** and **Sam Sharpley's** Minstrels. Last engagement, Jack Shields' Great Southern Show, 1909. Died in Cincinnati, OH, that year, age 53.

HICKS, J. Apprentice, flying Mercury with **John Robinson**,

Buckley& Weeks, 1834-35; American Theatre Troupe, 1841; rider and acrobat, Dr. Gilbert R. Spalding's, 1844-46, January 1848; Stone & McCollum, 1847.

HICKS, WILLIAM. Jockey racer, Barnum, Bailey & Hutchinson, 1882.

HIDERALGO [r. n. Beasley]. Lion tamer. Raymond & Herr Driesbach, 1851; Welch & Raymond, 1852.

HIGBY, WILLIAM ["Blind Billy"]. (1842?-June 17, 1908) Clown. At one time with Barnum & Bailey. Died in Bellevue Hospital, NYC, age 66.

HIGGINS, A. D. Bill poster, P. T. Barnum's, 1873; contracting agent, Goldenburg's, 1874.

HIGHT, OLD HALL. Negro minstrel violinist, George F. Bailey & Co., 1860.

HIGLEY, C. J. H. Buckley & Co., 1857-58.

HILL AMELIA. Sideshow fat woman, Cooper, Bailey & Co., 1880; Barnum, Bailey & Hutchinson, 1881; Adam Forepaugh's, 1883.

HILL, E. Juggler, Baldwin, Wall & Co.'s Great Eastern, 1880.

HILL, GEORGE A. Manager of privileges, Robert Hunting's, 1894.

HILL, GEORGE M. Dodge & Bartine, 1868.

HILL, JAMES. Tumbler and gymnast, E. Stowe's Northwestern, 1871.

HILL JOHN D. ["Jack"]. Newspaper contracting agent. Native of Fort Scott, KS. Adam Forepaugh's, 1886-88. Later, on the Washington *Post* and Washington *Republic*. Ringling Bros.' for 3 years. Represented theatrical attractions, NYC, remaining there until 1902. Press bureau as a representative of the Standard Oil Company.

HILL, LEIGH. See L. H. French.

HILL, ULM. Dan Castello's, winter 1967-68.

HILL, WILLIAM. General performer, equestrian director. Dan Gardner's, 1862; Spalding & Rogers' *Floating Palace*, 1859; Robinson & Lake, 1863-64; Adam Forepaugh's, 1867; and ringmaster, G. G. Grady's, 1871. He could neither read nor write but made a fine appearance and was good with the whip and adept at taking slaps, important credentials for his trade.

HILL, W. W. (b. November 11, 1839) Born in St. Catharines, Canada. Boss canvasman and Polish Brothers (with **George W. King**), Gardner & Hemmings, 1863.

HILLIARD, M. M. Native of Vermont, Spent 11 years in California engaged in mining and employed by the California Stage Company. Went to Vicksburg, MS, 1863; and, in company with his brother, was active in the buying of cotton on the Yazoo River. Captured by the Confederates and imprisoned for 9 months at Demopolis and Mobile, AL. On being moved to Meridian, MS, escaped, took 11 days, subsisting on green corn, to return to Vicksburg. Following this, occupied himself with running a country store for a year before embarking into show business. 1868, exhibited the Pacific Combination and Indian Show under a 65' round-top canvas, traveling by wagon. Show continued until 1876, when he put out the Great Pacific Circus and Congress of Educated Horses (M. M. Hilliard, **R. Hunting,** proprietors), 1977-78; Hilliard & Sargeant, 1878; Pullman & Hilliard, 1879-80; Pullman, Mack & Co.'s United Mastodon Shows (**Pullman,** Hilliard, **Main, Mack,** proprietors), 1884. **James DeMott** became associated with the management, spring 1979. Den of performing lions and a few other animals were added to the attraction and, 1880, an entire menagerie assembled; show was then known as Hilliard & DeMott's Great Pacific Circus, Menagerie and Trained Wild Animals.

HILLMAN, MOLLY. (1816?-December 21, 1908) Equestrienne. Daughter of a Newark, NJ, blacksmith and a great-granddaughter of the chief of the Oneida tribe. Circus performer 1830-80, including time as an equestrienne with both P. T. Barnum's and Adam Forepaugh's, going out every season for those 50 years. Married 3 times, with each husband having the misfortune to meet a violent death. Died in the poor house, Greenfield, PA, age 92.

HINDLEY, ALFRED H. Band leader, L. B. Lent's, 1873.

HINDLEY, PAULINE. (d. September 6, 1871) Equestrienne. Adam Forepaugh's, 1870; P. T. Barnum's, 1971. While with the Barnum show, died from injuries incurred in a fall in Rome, NY.

HINDS, SAMUEL J. Gymnast. Haight, Chambers & Ames', 1867; Cosmopolitan Circus, winter 1871-72; Montgomery Queen's, 1975; John Robinson's, 1881; Miller, Okey & Freeman, 1886.

HINES, GEORGE H. Press agent, John B. Doris', 1883; Sells Bros.', 1884; privileges, John Robinson's, 1889; assistant manager, Lemen Bros.', 1891; manager, John S. McMahon's, 1892. Married the very young equestrienne, **Josie De-Mott,** Selina, NC, September 30, 1889. Was served papers for divorce in November of that same year.

HINES, W. Great London, 1879.

HINKLEY, J. L. Globe, slack-wire. Stone & McCollum, 1848; Stickney's New Orleans Circus (Stickney, **North, Jones,** proprietors), 1849; went to the West Coast; Lee & Marshall, 1854-56; Bartholomew's, 1856; general performer and proprietor, Mammoth, 1857; Hinkley & Kembal, 1858; Kimbal's, 1859; Lathrop, Peoples & Franklin, 1860; Doc Bassett's, 1861.

HINMAN, W. S. Associate manager, Sherman & Hinman's, San Francisco, 1883.

HINSON, LIBBIE. P. T. Barnum's, 1875.

HITCHCOCK D. N. General agent, Hall's (**George W. De-Haven,** proprietor), 1886.

HITCHCOCK, LYMAN A. (d. January 20, 1879) Many years interested in the management of circuses. Co-proprietor, S. O. Wheeler's, 1864; manager, Herr Driesbach's Menagerie

and Howes' Trans-Atlantic Circus, 1868, which collapsed in Canada, July of that year; reported by **Frank J. Howes** and treasurer **William McGill** that Hitchcock had absconded with money belonging to the show. Died in Marshfield, MA.

HOADLEY. Proprietor, Hoadley & Latham, 1837; Headley, Latham, Eldred & Co., 1838.

HOAGLAND, ROBERT. See Corvella Brothers.

HOBBS. Rider and minstrel, John Tryon's, Bowery Amphitheatre, NYC, 1843, 1845; Welch's, Philadelphia, 1843. This could be a Hobbs listed below.

HOBBS, WILLIAM J. Acrobat and leaper. With Drury, Van Tassle, Brown & Co., 1837; Waterman's, 1838; vaulter, Charles LaForest's, 1842; vaulter, Ogden & Hobby, 1842; acrobat, Welch & Mann, 1843-44; John Tryon's, Bowery Amphitheatre, NYC, 1843; Robinson & Eldred, 1845; Howes & Co., 1846. Died attempting a triple somersault.

HOBBS, W. W. Rider, who threw backward somersaults while horse was at full speed, Rockwell & Stone, 1845. This could be the man above.

HOBBY, ELMER. (1837?-September 21, 1907) Superintendent of transportation for the Barnum show when it moved by wagons. Noted driver of 8 and 16-horse teams. Died Brookfield Junction, CT, age 70.

HOBBY, JOSEPH E. M. First management, 1934, Zoological Institute under the title of French, Hobby & Co.; partnership lasted for at least another season when a circus was added; J. E. M. Hobby & Co., 1837; manager, probably for **James Raymond,** 1838-40; proprietor, Hobby & Pratt's Amphitheatre, 1842; winter show (with **Darius Ogden**), Ogden & Hobby's Circus, 1842.

HOBSON BROTHERS [Sylvester, C. D., Homer D., Horace W., Howard S.]. Proprietors, Hobson Bros.' Show, 1883-1903. C. D. (1841-November 13, 1919) retired about 1909; died at age 79.

HOCUM, E. V. Rider, trained horses, LaPearl's Winter Circus, 1994; principal hurdle and 4-horse act, Gollmar Bros.', 1895; LaPearl's, Danville, IL, winter 1895-96; somersault rider, Gollmar Bros.', 1896; LaPearl's Great Railroad Show, 1896; lithograph ticket agent, Gollmar Bros.', 1897; rider, Gollmar Bros.', 1901-03; Walter L. Main's, 1904. Married equestrienne **Maude Gollmar** of the Gollmar Bros.' Circus, Baraboo, WI, October 14, 1896.

HOCUM, MAUDE [nee Maude Gollmar]. Wife of **E. V. Hocum.** Principal act, John Robinson's (**John G. Robinson,** proprietor and manager), 1900. See Gollmar Brothers.

HODGE, CRAWFORD. Lithograph agent, Howes' Great London, 1874.

HODGE, ROBERT. Announcer, King & Franklin, 1889.

HODGES, THOMAS. Dan Castello's, 1866; sideshow privilege, James M. French's, 1867; assistant manager, D. F. Dunham's, 1875.

HOEFLER, WILLIAM. Greco-Roman wrestler (with **Edwin Bibby**), Barnum, Bailey & Hutchinson, 1881.
HOEGEL, SANFORD. Acrobat, with Alexander Robinson's, 1871-72.
HOEY, PATRICK. See James Cooke.
HOFFLICH. Animal performer, John Robinson's, 1864.
HOFFMAN, CHARLES F. Contracting agent, with Ward's Great London (**Ira C. Ward**, proprietor and manager), formerly Charles Lee's circus, 1897.
HOFFMAN, G. S. [or J. S.]. Manager, Lowande & Hoffman Mexican Pavilion Circus, 1887, business manager, Lowande's Brazilian Circus, 1889.
HOFFMAN, SADIE. Charioteer, Barnum & Bailey, 1892.
HOFFMASTER, FRED. Rider, Turner's, 1827; Royal Pavilion Circus/Olympic Circus, 1830-31; S. H. Nichols', 1838; Yale & Co., 1840.
HOGLE WILLIAM F. (d. November 16, 1925) When his father died, had to shift for himself at age 12, working in a factory in Troy, NY, practicing acrobatics at night. A visit to Troy of strong man **Professor Carl** became the turning point of Hogle's career. Carl taught him feats of strength which led to Hogle's joining Rivers & Derious, 1858, and traveling throughout USA and Canada as an acrobatic gymnast. Sands, Nathans & Co., 1859; R. Sands', 1860; Thayer's (**Thayer** and **Phelps**, proprietors), small clown troupe, 1861. By this year, was performing with **John Keefe** as a partner. Smith & Quick, Havana, fall 1861, remaining at Villenueva Theatre winter, 1861-62; Great Orion Circus, Old Bowery, NYC, 1861, Stickney's National Circus, Old Bowery, 1861; Thayer & Noyes, 1862; Maginley & Bell, 1864; Quaglieni's Italian Cirque, Europe, 1866; Albisu's Circus, Havana, winter 186667; Thayer & Noyes, 1867-68; double trapeze (with **John Keefe**), George F. Bailey & Co., 1869. Eventually Keefe was forced to retire because of repeated injuries. Comic stilt act (with **Henry Burdeau**), Dr. James L. Thayer's, 1870; (with **Burdeau**) Mrs. Charles Warner's, Philadelphia, winter 187071; (with **Harry Franklin**) John H. Murray's, 1872; P. T. Barnum's Roman Hippodrome, driving a 4-horse chariot in the hippodrome races, 1874-75. Retired from show business, 1885, and married **Mary Mulligan**, sister of former partner, **John Keefe**. Died at the Masonic Hospital, NYC.
HOLBROOKE & HUGHES. Song and dance artists, (sideshow) Palace of Wonders, P. T. Barnum's, 1876; the same, as Holbrook & Ryan, 1877.
HOLDEN, O. S. Whittemore, Thompson & Co., 1865.
HOLDER, EDWARD. Traveled around the world in search of animals. For 9 years, connected with the old John Robinson's. Later, furnished 3 or 4 of the big feature acts for Barnum & Bailey on their trip through Europe. Made a tour of 3 years through Japan and China with **D. M. Bristol** show, being in China at the time of the Boxer uprising. Was also interested in harness racing.

HOLLAND, ED G. Brother of **George F.** and **John**. Proprietor, Holland & Sturtevant, 1891; Holland's, 1892.
HOLLAND, EDWARD. (1853-1939) Acrobat/rider. Second son of **John Holland, Sr.** Lifelong resident of Delavan, WI. First appeared on Holland & Mosher, 1857, at the age of four; with Holland family act through 1872. Accompanied brother **George** to Chiarini's, New Zealand and Australia; for the next 10 years, mainly with John Robinson's, first as gymnast, and, from 1882-1885, equestrian director; rings and perch, E. O. Rogers', 1891. Went into business for himself as a partner in Holland-McMahon; Holland-Gormley; Holland, Bowman & McLaughlin; and VanAmburgh show; then, 1892, launched E. G. Holland & Co. Railroad Circus, which in 1894 was the last one to go out of Delavan. Became a law officer, served as the village's first chief of police, 1897-03. After 3 more years as a circus agent (Mighty Haag and John Robinson's), accepted the managership of the New York Hippodrome, leaving Delavan, fall 1908. Died in New Jersey after a 77 year career in the circus business.
HOLLAND, E. J. Single trapeze and perch, Albert Hose's, 1893.
HOLLAND, GEORGE E. (1875-1960) Rider. The son of **George F. Holland.** Threw his first somersault on horseback when 13. Debuted before the public at 14 on the Holland-Gormley Circus; next year, 1890, a featured principal rider, John Robinson's. Parents left Robinson's, 1893, but young George remained through 1897. Gollmar Bros.' enticed him away for 2 seasons, then back to Robinson's, 1900. Was advertised as "The World's Greatest Somersaulting Rider," once turning 56 consecutive somersaults. Married, November 1901, to **Rose Dockrill**, equestrienne daughter of **Elise Dockrill**, in Savannah, GA. Performed as individuals and as a team; were announced as "Holland and Dockrill, the World's Greatest Riders," and appeared on snow white horses, of which they owned several. Opened with a fast jockey act, Rose did her *haute ecole* presentation, a carrying act, in which George stood on the horse and lifted Rose to his shoulders, and then George's somersaulting routines. Went into vaudeville in the 1920's; continued to perform in their fifties, working for small circuses; final public performance, 1939, St. Louis Police Circus.
HOLLAND, GEORGE F. (January 20, 1850?-January 28, 1917) Acrobat and rider. Possibly the best rider to come out of Wisconsin. Came from a distinguished family of circus folk, having entered the profession at the age of 3 years. Son of **John Holland.** Had brothers **John** and **Edward G.** With the **Holland Family** act until August, 1872, when he went to Chicago and joined Chiarini's; in November married **Katherine Holloway**, who had been an apprentice of Chiarini. The two performed together until they retired, 1910. George did a principal act, including somersault riding, and Katherine was *a manège* rider. Worked for all the largest circuses of their time,

Dan Rice's, Burr Robbins', John Robinson's (11 seasons), Sells-Floto, etc. George twice entered into circus partnerships. 1885, brothers **Edward** and **John** and **Charles McMahon** formed Holland-McMahon, a railroad circus until they reached Cincinnati, where they chartered the steamboat *Mountain Girl*, with the intention of performing on the Ohio and Mississippi Rivers; played Aurora, Indiana, November 5, and were on their way down river, but about 2 a.m. the boat collided with an upbound ore packet; within minutes it sank, taking with it all the horses, animals and equipment, only the tent was salvaged; circus was valued at $20,000, and recovered $12,000 in a suit against the *Mountain Girl's* owners. Went back to Delavan and reorganized for 1886; George resigned, spring 1898. That year with **Edward Holland** and the **Gormley brothers, Frank** and **Everett**, framed Holland & Gormley Allied Railroad Circus, which they toured for 2 years; sold his interest, October 1889. George and Katherine retired, 1895; built a hotel in Delavan. Had 11 children, whom George began teaching, 1896; formed a new **Holland Family** act, 1897, and went with John Robinson's; subsequently, appeared at fairs, with an occasional season on circuses. George and Katherine spent their last season of performing on Sells-Floto, 1910, then lived out their remaining years in Delavan. Holland & McMahon, 1985-88; Holland & Gormley, 1889; Holland, Bowman, & McLaughlin, 1890; Holland & Sturtevant, 1891. Died at age 67.

HOLLAND, JOHN. (1815-October 27, 1897) English acrobat. Used the name **Julian**, 1848-49. Worked under the title of **Holland Family**. Father of **Mary Ann Holland**. May have come to the United States with the Ravels, 1847. Howes & Co., 1848; E. F. & J. Mabie's, fall 1848-1851; L. G. Butler's, 1853-54; Buckley & Co., 1856, 1858-60; Holland & Mosher, 1857; Holland & Madden, 1861; George DeHaven's, 1862.

HOLLAND, JOHN, JR. Last of **John Holland's** sons, died at age 20. Member of the **Holland Family** until the retirement of his father. 1874, with his brother **Edward**, trapeze duo, John Robinson's.

HOLLAND, MARY ANN. (1847-October 31, 1895) The daughter of **John Holland, Sr.** Born in Hamburg, Germany, just before her parents came to America. Supposedly introduced into the ring at 4 years of age. With her brothers, was trained in acrobatics and riding. With parents, was always billed as **Holland Family**. At 16, married **George Madden**, a magician and clown. Their daughter, **Nora**, married **Joseph McMahon**, circus proprietor. Buckley & Co., 1858-60; Holland & Madden, 1861, George W. DeHaven's, 1862; McMahon's, 1885-1894. Died in Delavan, age 48.

HOLLAND, NINA. Equestrienne and vocalist, Dan Rice's, 1878.

HOLLAWAY, JAMES. Clown, P. T. Barnum's, 1879.

HOLLIS, ELLA [Mrs. John L. Davenport, Sr.]. (1854-July 25, 1934) Equestrienne, mother of Davenport clan—**John, Jr.,**

Albert M., May, Orrin, Louise, and **Bertha Hollis** (the latter a non-professional). Last performance before retiring, carrying act with brother, winter 1884, Tom Grenier's.

HOLLIS, ORRIN M. (d. February 23, 1926) Outstanding rider, taught by **John L. Davenport, Sr.,** his brother-in-law. Was brother of **Ella Hollis,** who married **John Davenport, Sr.** He was the uncle of **Orrin, Stick, Lulu, John Jr., May** and **Bert Davenport.** Son **Melvin "Pinky" Hollis** was a performer. Hollis' wife, the former **Eva Bennett,** was burned to death in her home at Sylvania, OH, March 11, 1918; a lighted bracket lamp slipping from her hands, igniting her clothing. Brother, **Charles H.,** died from an attempted double somersault, St. Louis, MO, September 30, 1887, while with Horton & Tribbey's Ten Cent Show. Sells Bros.', 1878-79, 1882-83; Barnum & London, 1884; P. T. Barnum's, 1890; principal pad rider, Adam Forepaugh's, 1881, 1888-89; P. T. Barnum's, 1885-86; Great European, Cosmopolitan Rink, Broadway & 41ˢᵗ Street, NYC, February 1886; John Robinson's, 1891-93; Ringling Bros.', 1894; Great Wallace, 1896; 1902. Died at St. Vincent's Hospital, Toledo OH, age 69.

HOLLISTER, EUGENE R. (1843-1926) Resort owner, Lake Delavan, WI. Concert, reserved seats and candy privileges with various shows. Started with Yankee Robinson's 1867; Coup-Castello, 1870; Buckley's; Centennial Circus. Kept a small collection of snakes. Later, built a hotel-tavern on Delavan Lake, WI, known as The Log Cabin.

HOLLOWAY, EDWARD. (d. August 23, 1873) Native of England. Rider, gymnast. Howes' Great European, 1864; Barnum, VanAmburgh & Castello, 1867; James M. French's, 1869; leaper and vaulter, Dan Rice's Paris Pavilion, 1872-73. Died in Paducah, KY.

HOLLOWAY, GEORGE. Ladder and melodeon, with Dan Rice's, 1891.

HOLLOWAY, GRACE. From Astley's London. Howes' Great European, 1864.

HOLLOWAY, JAMES. English clown, "late of Henger's Circus, Liverpool," arrived in the United States, 1878. P. T. Barnum's, 1878-79; Chiarini's, Australia and New Zealand, winter 1879-80; W. C. Coup's, 1881.

HOLLOWAY, KATE [Mrs. George Holland]. Equestrienne, *manège* rider. Chiarini's, Havana, winter 1866-67, Mexico City, 1867; South and Central America, spring 1869; equestrienne, John Wilson's Amphitheatre, San Francisco, February 1874; Cooper, Bailey & Co., 1876; John Robinson's, 1880-83, 1889-91; Burr Robbins', 1885; Holland & McMahon, 1885-86; Holland & Gormley's, 1888-89; *manège*, Andy McDonald's, 1892; Milwaukee Mid-Winter Circus, 1894.

HOLLOWAY, PALMYRA. Equestrienne. While with Chiarini's, summer 1866, married equestrian **Robert Johnson** with that company. Joined Orrin's, West Indies, the following year.

HOLLOWAY, TED. Rider, gymnast. Seth B. Howes', winter 1865-66; Dan Castello's, 1866-68; James M. French's, 1869; gymnast (with **Richard Hannon**), Mike Lipman's, 1869; trapeze (with **Hannon**), G. A. Huff & Co., 1870.

HOLLOWAY, WILLIAM. Rider and somersaulter, Seth B. Howes' Great European, 1864-65.

HOLLOWAY BROTHERS [Claude, Frank, Eddie]. Acrobats, G. W. Hall, Jr.'s, 1895-96; Barnum & Bailey, London, 1898. Had their own circus, 1898-99, Holloway Bros.' New United Shows.

HOLMAN, GEORGE. Giant, Walter L. Main's, 1892-93.

HOLMER, PROF. Booker & Howard's Minstrels, L. B. Lent's, 1865.

HOLMES, BART. Ames' Menagerie and Circus, 1868.

HOLMES, C. Acrobat and leaper, Haight's Great Southern, 1874.

HOLMES, THOMAS [professional name James Maurice]. (d. March 1910) "Elastic Skin Man." Discovered around 1890 by **Frank P. Stone** of Austin & Stone's Museum. Later, with Barnum's sideshow. Met and Married **Edith Clifford** on a European tour. Had 2 children. Died in Boston, age 40.

HOLTON, ANNIE BELL. (with **Lillie Rice**) Balloon race and double parachute jump, Sells & Rentfrow's, 1893.

HOLTON, CHARLES. Advertising agent, Sells Bros.', 1882.

HOLTON, ED W. Holton & Gates' Harmoniums, a minstrel band, Simon Pure American Circus, NYC, October 1, 1866.

HOLTON, JOHN. "Cannon king," McDonald & Richold, 1896.

HOMER, NATHANIEL. (1846-November 23, 1906) Gymnast. Began with old John Robinson's while still in his teens, billed as "King of the Air"; ringmaster, Orton Bros.', 1867; John Robinson's, 1871. Brother-in-law of minstrel entertainer **Billy Emerson**. Later joined troupe of Emerson & Hooley.

HONE, JAMES F. Manager, Alex Robinson's, 1870.

HONEY. Clown, Simpson & Price, Baltimore, 1822.

HOOD, ELIAS. Vaulter and tight-rope performer. Palmer & Harrington, 1834; Crane & Co., 1836, Boston Amphitheatre; J. J. Hall's, West Indies, 1837; Welch, Bartlett, 1839. Equestrienne wife performed with him.

HOOD, ROBERT S. Treasurer, Great International **(James E. Cooper, James A. Bailey**, Robert S. Hood, **David Worthington**, proprietors), 1874; part owner and treasurer, Cooper, Bailey & Co., 1875-76, Australian tour, 1877-78, 1879.

HOON, JOHN. (1816?-July 29, 1903) Clown and acrobat. Born in Beaver, PA. Began circus career as a hostler. Connected with Dan Rice's for several years. Upon leaving the circus profession, became a stage driver until the railroads made that occupation outdated. Died at his home in Wilkinsburg, PA, age 87.

HOOSE, WILLIAM. H. Buckley & Co., 1857-58.

HOPE, SAMUEL. James R. Cooke's, winter 1864-65.

HOPGOOD, HARRY P. (1826?-July 9, 1910) Agent. Born

in NY state. Burr Robbins', 1880. Died at Amityville, LI, age about 84.

HOPKINS, DAN B. Press agent, P. T. Barnum's, 1874-76.

HOPKINS, EZRA. (1788-1849) Born Putnam County, NY. June, Hopkins & Co., 1834; signed Zoological Institute agreement, 1835; bought "Canadian Circus" (Buckley & Weeks) at Zoological Institute auction, Somers, NY, in August 1837; Buckley, Rockwell, Hopkins & Co., 1838; Buckley, Hopkins, Tufts & Co., 1838; Buckley, Hopkins & Tufts sold to Nathans &Tufts, April 1839.

HOPKINS, H. Proprietor with **Henry Rockwell** and **Matthew Buckley** in circus enterprise, Buckley, Rockwell, Hopkins & Co., 1838; manager, Welch, Bartlett & Co., 1838; manager, Philadelphia Zoological Garden (for **James Raymond**), 1843-44; Hopkins & Co., 1845.

HOPKINS, J. D. Agent, Metropolitan Pavilion, 1874.

HOPKINS, W. H. Equestrian manager, with Shield's Great Southern, 1888.

HOPPER, JERRY. Clown and stilt trickster. Yankee Robinson's, 1866-68; Stowe & Norton, 1869; Miles Orton & Co., 1869; P. T. Barnum's, 1871-76; Campbell's, 1878; Burr Robbins', 1879; Great Australian, 1880; Beckett's Great Exposition Circus, 1881. Retired from circus life and operated a saloon and billiard parlor, Indian River, MI. Following year, was building an opera house, Indian River. Opened a variety theatre with **James M. French**, fall 1884, Sheboygan, MI. Wife, **Cynthia**, died July 26, 1879, age 26. Hopper died of Bright's disease, Bay City, MI, circa February 15, 1887, age 44.

HOPPER, JOHN [also advertised as Hoppier and Harpier]. French and English clown, Dan Rice's, 1849.

HORN, EPH [r. n. Evan Evans Hern]. (1823-January 3, 1877) Born in Philadelphia. First entered the minstrel profession, 1843, Carlisle, PA, as end man with S. S. Sanford's troupe. Was one of the Virginia Serenaders, which began a long and successful career in burnt cork. Circus and menagerie affiliations with Raymond & Waring's, 1844; followed with VanAmburgh's; Sloat & Shepard, 1857; Joe Pentland's, 1858; clown, National Circus, Philadelphia, fall 1858; Holiday Street Theatre, Baltimore, Tom King's, beginning November 24, 1858. [T. Allston Brown: "He stood at the very head of the minstrel profession. Placed in almost any position in a company, he was able to fill the part. As an end man he was one of the best and as a delineator of the old Nergo he displayed remarkable talent. If Booth or Kean ever succeeded in 'holding the mirror up to nature' in the true Shakespearean sense, then Eph Horn did so far as negro minstrelsy is concerned."] Died in St. Vincent's Hospital, New York. Last appearance on the stage, Taylor's Opera House, Trenton, NJ, Christmas Day, December 25, 1876. During this trip (it was a variety company), Horn took cold, from which pneumonia resulted. All the funeral expenses were borne by his old fiiend, **Tony Pastor**.

HORN, OTTO [or Horne]. Band leader. Welch & Lent, 1856; Sands & Nathans, 1857, 1859; violinist, W. N. Smith's Ethiopians with VanAmburgh's, 1860, 1862.

HORN, WIELLIAM. Clown, G. K. Goodwin's, 1860.

HORN, WILLIAMSON WILLIAMS ["Bud"]. (December 21, 1850-July 8, 1908) "The Calliope King." For 20 years worked with W. A. Sheetz of the Vendome Theatre, Nashville, TN, as advertising man. Summer season, traveled with circuses. *Robert Burns*, packet boat, 1879; John B. Doris', 1883-86; Adam Forepaugh's, 1887; Barnum & Bailey, 1890; treasurer, Dan Castello's, 1892; Leon W. Washburn's, 1894-95; Robinson & Franklin, 1896; Ringling Bros.', 1897; John Robinson's, 1898-99; Rhoda Royal's, 1900; Campbell Bros.', 1901-02; Pawnee Bill's, 1903-07. [F. Smith: "Bud Horn was a famous operator in his day and enjoyed the distinction of being the first player to ride down Broadway playing the popular airs of the day."] Died in Nashville, TN, age 56.

HORNER, PUSS. Kentucky clown. Stickney's, 1848-49; S. Q. Stokes', 1850-51; E. F. & J. Mabie's, 1851-52; Butler's, 1853; Crescent City Circus, 1855; Spalding & Rogers, 1856; clown and co-proprietor, Horner & Bell, 1865.

HORTON, DICK Agent, F. J. Taylor's, 1892.

HORTON, OSCAR. Band leader, with James P. Johnson's, 1870.

HORWITZ, BUCK. Boss razorback, with John Robinson's, 1889-93.

HOSKINS, GEORGE. Lion tamer, with Yankee Robinson's, 1868.

HOSMER, IDA. See Mrs. Littlefluger.

HOSMER, JENNIE. Rider, Montgomery Queen's, 1876.

HOSMER, M. Orton Bros.', 1867.

HOSTEMAN, TOM. Boss canvasman, with Wheeler Bros.', 1894.

HOUGH, HARRISON. Presumably a native of Charleston, SC. For a brief period, 1835, connected with George Sweet in the management of a circus in that city, Sweet & Hough's Pavilion Circus; failure forced the proprietors into turning the enterprise into a riding school.

HOUGK W. H. ["Uncle Bill"]. Business manager, Robinson & Lake, 1864-65; agent and business manager, John Robinson's, 1864-68; announced retirement, February 1868; nevertheless, agent James M. French's, 1869; agent, P. T. Barnum's, 1872-73; press agent, VanAmburgh's, 1879-80; press agent, W. C. Coup's, 1882.

HOUGHTON, ERNEST. Boss hostler, Main & Sargeant, 1891.

HOULTON, M. K. Proprietor, M. K. Houlton's, 1893.

HOUSE, V. Y. General manager, Metropolitan Circus, 1897.

HOWARD, ANNIE. Sideshow tattooed lady, Cook & Whitby's, 1892.

HOWARD BROTHERS [Lee, Bob]. Mexican ladder act, Lee's Great London, 1890.

HOWARD, CHARLES. Clown, G. G. Grady's, 1871-72; Robinson & Myers, 1883.

HOWARD, D. Vaulter, Mrs. Dan Rice's, 1864.

HOWARD EDWARD L. Leaper, Sells Bros.', 1881-82, 1886; Jesse W. Foster's, South America, 1894.

HOWARD, FRANK. Booker & Howard's Minstrels, L. B. Lent's, 1862, 1865. Perhaps the same man with W. H. Harris' Nickel-Plate, 1885; Barnum & Bailey, 1888.

HOWARD, GEORGE W. W. H. Stowe's, winter 1881-82.

HOWARD, HAMILTON. Purchased the Collins' Oriental Combination Collins' Oriental Combination after it folded on August 7, 1877, with plans for a Southern tour. Shortly, advertised for a partner with $300 to invest.

HOWARD, HARRY. Menagerie, G. G. Grady's, 1874; W. H. Harris' Nickel-Plate, 1885.

HOWARD, IVY. Snake charmer, Cook & Whitby's, 1892.

HOWARD, JOHN. Rider. Stewart's, 1832; winter circus, Richmond Hill, NYC, 1837.

HOWARD, JOHN. (December 27, 1871-November 21, 1896) Aerialist Born in Spokane Falls, WA. Began professional career as a horizontal bar performer, 1890. 1892, took a partner and performed under the name of the Stillwells. Joined Ben Dunham, New Orleans, 1894, and performed as a member of the Dunham Family until his death. With Barnum & Bailey, sustained injuries, October 21, 1896, while performing at the Coliseum, Chicago; dropping from a bar 80' above the floor into a net, his body revolved too much, causing him to alight almost on his head, which broke his spine. Died in a Chicago hospital on the above date.

HOWARD, LEE. (1860?-November 27, 1917) In the circus business for over 40 years. Connected with John Robinson's, VanAmburgh's, Sanger's, Rice Bros.', Gollmar Bros.', and Yankee Robinson's. Died in Toledo, OH, of Bright's disease, age 57.

HOWARD, LOUISA [Mrs. Frank Brower, nee Banks]. Equestrienne. Born in Baltimore. A rider of high merit. [T. Allston Brown: She was a performer who "received a greater amount of sincere, unbought and enthusiastic applause than was ever awarded to any person who has attempted the daring and heroic art which she practiced ... with no superior in any part of the world."] J. J. Hall's, 1836, John Tryon's, Bowery Amphitheatre, NYC, 1844; Welch's, Philadelphia, 1845; Welch & Mann, 1843-47 (where she rode in an act of mythology, "The Meeting of Flora and Minerva"); Welch's National, 1849; Robinson & Eldred, 1850; in England, Welch, McCollum & Risley, 1851.

HOWARD, S. B. Treasurer, New York and New England Circus, 1884.

HOWARD, THOMAS. Acrobat, one of the Howard Brothers team. Retired, 1889, and settled in Columbus, IN.

HOWARD, THOMAS W. (1836?-October 25, 1903) Railroad contractor, Sells & Downs, 1892, 1894; and for the 4 years prior to his death, Great Eastern Railroad Circus and Howes' Great London Railroad Shows. Died in Tishomingo, Indian Territory, age 67.

HOWARD, VICTORIA. Fancy dancer and vocalist, George F. Bailey & Co., 1860.

HOWARD, WALTER. Rider. With Handy & Welch, 1830; Yeaman's, 1831; Edward Eldred's, 1834; clown, J. Purdy Brown's, St. Louis, 1834 or 1835; J. J. Hall's, 1836; Boston Circus, 1837; J. W. Stocking's, 1839; Welch & Delavan, 1841; Welch & Mann, 1843-44; Mann, Welch & Delavan, 1844; John Tryon's, Bowery Amphitheatre, NYC, 1844; Welch & Mann's 2nd unit, 1845; Welch & Mann, 1846; Welch's, 1847.

HOWARD, W. H. Rider, Charles Lee's, 1893.

HOWARD, WILLIAM. Principal bareback rider, George W. Richard's, 1887; Howard Bros.' Dime Circus, 1888.

HOWARD, WILLIAM C. General agent, with French & Monroe, 1895.

HOWE, CHARLIE. With Herr Driesbach's Menagerie and Howe's Trans-Atlantic Circus, 1868.

HOWE, JAMES F. Press agent, Alex Robinson's, 1874.

HOWE, JESSE. Clown, D. F. Dunham's, 1875.

HOWELL, H. V. B. Proprietor, assistant manager, Baird, Howell & Co., 1874.

HOWELL, PROF. Performing animals, L. B. Lent's, 1876.

HOWES, CADY E. (1812?-December 12, 1899) Entered the circus business, 1839, and continued for some 50 years. At various times, connected with Barnum's, and Forepaugh's. Sideshow, Madame Macarte's European **(James M. Nixon,** proprietor), 1863; manager, Howes' Great Circus, Bowery, NYC, winter 1863-64; boss canvasman, L. B. Lent's, 1867-69; James E. Cooke's, 1880. Retired, 1899. Died at his home in Brooklyn, NY, age 87.

HOWES, CHARLES O. Hat spinner, with VanAmburgh's, 1879, 1883; Cooper, Jackson & Co., 1882.

HOWES, EPENETUS. (October 24, 1797-December 25, 1864) Connected with **Jeremiah Fogg,** 1826, operating Fogg & Howes' Menagerie in the South. At one time that year they joined in combination with Quick & Mead's.

HOWES, EGBERT CROSBY. (February 26, 1830-April 10, 1892) Son of **Nathan Alva Howes** and **Clarissa Crosby Howes** and twin brother of **Albert Crosby Howes.** Born in Brewster, NY, one of 13 children. As a youngster, traveled with his father's circus and as a young man went to England with Uncle Seth's circus, 1957. Became manager of Howes & Cushing, England, Ireland, Scotland and Wales. In London, married equestrienne **Jennie Maude Jee,** 1859, and begot 4 children. Returned to the USA with Howes Great European, 1865; treasurer, James Nixon and Dan Castello's, 1868; manager, during its famous trans-continental tour to the Pacific coast, 1869; 1870, with Uncle Seth's show, returned to London and organized the Great American Circus and Menagerie;

(with brother **Elbert),** proprietor, Howes' Great London Circus, 1871-73, until **James E. Kelley** and **Henry Barnum** took it over. Following the sale, was connected with P. T. Barnum's, Adam Forepaugh's and Buffalo Bill's Wild West Show. Remained in the circus business until his death in Brewster, NY, age 61. Died from pneumonia brought on by a severe cold.

HOWES, ELBERT CROSBY. (February 26, 1830-1900) Son of **Nathan Alva Howes** and twin brother of **Egbert Crosby Howes.** Born in Brewster, NY, one of 13 children. In his youth, traveled with his father's circus, and later went to England with his **uncle Seth's** Great United States Circus, 1857. Active in the procurement of exotic animals for the concern; in Ceylon, acquired "some of the finest elephants ever exhibited"; 1871, became proprietor (with **Egbert),** Howes' Great London Circus, a management which continued until **James E. Kelley** and **Henry Barnum** took over sometime in 1873. This ended Elbert's circus activity. He settled in Brewster and focused attention toward politics; but an ambition to become a member of the New York State Assembly was never fulfilled. Occupied a 5 year position of town supervisor and, following, was the gate keeper of the Drewville Reservoir. Married **Caroline Tanner** of Danbury, CT, 1856. Following her death, 1867, married **Melissa Tillotson.**

HOWES, FRANK J. (June 4, 1832-October 1, 1880) Born in Rochester, NY. About age 18 became steward of the old Gennessee Valley packet, *Red Jacket,* commanded by Capt. Dan Bromley. 1851, entered show business under the guidance of circus agent **Charles Bristol,** with whom he remained for some years. Later, became an equestrian manager and ringmaster. Accompanied Howes & Cushing to England, remaining overseas for 3 years. While there, 1859, was engaged with James Myers'. Returned to USA, 1860, when he brought back **Gerard C. Quick's** and **Joseph Cushing's** hippopotamus and exhibited it in Canada, Cuba, and USA. Subsequently, was ringmaster and general performer, L. B. Lent's, fall 1861-62; sideshow (Howes had just purchased the **Wild Hairless Mare),** Thayer & Noyes, 1862; rider and ringmaster, Thayer & Noyes, 1863; proprietor (with **James Robinson),** Robinson & Howes' Champion Circus, 1863-64. Robinson & Howes erected a wooden amphitheatre, Washington Street, Chicago, opening November 23, 1863. With Robinson's withdrawal, 1864, Howes took **Horace Norton** as partner; 1867, added the United States Menagerie of Hitchcock, VanHorn & Cushing; following year, Frank Howes' Trans-Atlantic Circus was combined with Herr Driesbach's Menagerie, but by mid-season poor business forced the closing; Amphitheatre, Louisville, January 1868; Great Australian, 1870; George F. Bailey's, 1873; Thayer & Noyes Great Australian Circus and G. F. Bailey & Co., 1874; 1875, joined with Joseph Cushing in a venture that took the circus to West Indies and South America. Subsequently, became associated with the Reiche Brothers of

NYC and performed their prize Kentucky horses for 2 years; after which, the horses were sold to Lewis Sells, who hired Howes to work them. While traveling with Allen's Eastern Circus, Howes died in Kaufman, TX. Married **Mary E. Phelps** in Cincinnati, November 2, 1853. The couple lived apart for many years, but never went to the extent of getting a divorce.

HOWES, JACOB ORSON. Brother of **Nathan** and **Seth Howes**. Manager with Nathan A. Howes' New York Bowery Circus, NYC, 1845; Howes & Co.'s New York Circus, 1846; Howes & Co.'s Circus, 1847-48.

HOWES, JAMES R. (1802-1874) The brother of **William Howes, Jr.** Connected with Macomber & Howes' Menagerie of Living Animals, 1830; 1833, the Howes brothers featured the elephant Columbus and an animal keeper who entered a leopard den; following year, expanded to 2 tents and a larger exhibit of animals. Manager and director, Mammoth Menagerie from Zoological Institute, NYC, 1837; Eagle Circus/ Cole & Co., 1837; Miller, Yale & Howes, 1838; June, Titus, Angevine & Co., 1839, Bowery Amphitheatre, NYC; rider, E. C. Yale & Co., 1840; Howes & Mabie, 1841; Nathan A. Howes' winter circus, 1842.

HOWES, J. C. Giraffe keeper, western unit, June, Titus, Angevine & Co., 1842; agent, Nathan Howes & Co., 1847.

HOWES, JOHN L. Treasurer, Robinson & Howes, 1863-64.

HOWES, LLOYD H. Brother of **Seth B. Howes**. Agent, Welch & Lent, 1854-56; master of horse, Sloat & Shepherd's "Joe Pentland" Circus, 1859; Robinson & Howes, 1864. Was drowned, Elmire, MO, August 1, 1864, while trying to cross a swollen river.

HOWES, MARY E. [or Marie, nee Phelps]. Born in Buffalo, NY. Married **Frank J. Howes** in Cincinnati, November 2, 1853, and although separated for many years, never divorced. Rode in the *entrée* acts and was a *danseuse*. Went to England, 1857, Howes & Cushing's United States Circus; Great Australian, 1870.

HOWES, NATHAN ALVAH. (April 22, 1796-June 28, 1878) Native of Brewster, Putnam County, NY, one of 12 children—6 sons and 6 daughters—of **Daniel** and **Ruhamah Reed Howes**, who were farmers and ran a general store. One of the early pioneers of the American circus, learned ropewalking and hat spinning at the age of 15 and began performing in nearby communities. Married at 19 to a local girl, **Clarissa Crosby**. The first of the Howes family to enter the circus business and one of the earliest circus proprietors to tour with a circus company and to use a canvas pavilion. Ordered his first tent, 1825, from a sail maker in NYC and first exhibited it in April, 1826. Teamed with **Aaron Turner** in taking out the Columbian Circus, 1828. Had a small circus of his own, 1832, and was proprietor with Richard Sands of Howes & Sands', 1834. Howes & Mabie's, 1842; proprietor, Nathan A. Howes' winter circus, 1843-44, Howes & Gardner (Nathan A. Howes

and **Dan Gardner**, proprietors), 1844; Nathan A. Howes' New York Bowery Circus, NYC, 1845, which became Howes & Co.'s Circus through the season of 1849. Following this, retired from active management but continued to invest in other shows. Was a shareholder in the Zoological Institute.

HOWES, OSWALD. George Bailey & Co., 1869.

HOWES, REED M. (d. October 11, 1879) Was contracting agent, Howes & Cushing, 1875; general contractor, L. B. Lent's, 1876. Died at age 35.

HOWES, SETH BENEDICT. (August 15, 1815-May 17, 1901) Native of Brewster, Putnam County, NY. Often called "the father of the American circus." At age 11, accompanied his older brother, **Nathan A. Howes**, in exhibiting Hachaliah Bailey's elephant, "Betty," through New England. First performed, Howes & Turner, 1826; rider, Nathan A. Howes', 1832-38; equestrian manager (also performed as the Peruvian Hunter or the South American Indian Chief, in daring attitudes with spear, shield, bow & arrow, war club, etc.), Howes & Sands', 1834-35; scenic rider, Eagle Circus/Cole & Co., 1837; proprietor (with **Enoch Yale** and **John Miller**), Miller, Yale & Howes, 1838; rider, June, Titus, Angevine & Co., Bowery Amphitheatre, 1839; E. C. Yale & Co., 1840, Howes & Mabie (**Nathan Howes, Edmund F.** and **Jeramiah Mabie**, proprietors), 1841-46. Said to be the first to have a billboard made or to paste paper out of doors (previously, advertising paper was tacked up). With **P. T. Barnum**, imported the first herd of elephants, 10 in all, seen in the country, which proved to be a great attraction. Imported the first drove of camels, which were trained to work in harness. 1848, joined with his brothers **Nathan** and **Jacob** to launch the Great United States Circus, said to be the largest such enterprise yet seen in America. Joined with **Barnum, Sherwood Stratton** and **Lewis B. Lent**, 1851, to organize Barnum's Great Asiatic Caravan, Museum and Menagerie, opened June 1, 1851, and toured for 4 years. Went to France, 1852, where he met **Henry Franconi**, proprietor of the Paris Hippodrome, and conceived the idea of bringing such an establishment to the United States, which opened May 1, 1853. Engaged the **Siamese Twins**, Eng and Chang, for a year's tour, which proved a success. Took a circus, menagerie and museum on the road featuring **Tom Thumb**, 1855. Following year, in partnership with **Joseph Cushing**, took the Great United States Circus to England, where the show remained until 1864, a feature being a stud of 70 cream colored horses. While there, introduced an American Indian troupe, which proved to be a great novelty. In London, January 26, 1861, at age 45, married **Amy Moseley**, a 19 year old equestrienne. Had 2 daughters from an earlier relationship, probably with a **Sophia Kolia**, but it is unlikely there was a marriage. Returned to America, 1864, triumphantly with Seth B. Howes' Great European Circus, featuring Crockett and his den of lions and a caravan of ornate pageant wagons which he had acquired there. Went into semi-retirement, 1865, when he sold the show to the "Flatfoots," who continued operation through 1871. Returned to England, 1870, leaving February 2 on the steamer *Iris* with his twin nephews, **Egbert** and **Elbert**. Put together a show there and tried it out for a season. Like the earlier visit, during this venture he made deals with **Lord George Sanger** for a collection of rare animals and ornate pageant wagons as a parade feature. Also engaged a number of English and European performers for an 1871 USA tour. All this, animals, chariots, personnel, and some circus paraphernalia were transported across the Atlantic in time to open an American summer season. At age 56, retired and turned the Howes name over to Egbert and Elbert. [Stuart Thayer: Howes was "a true pioneer of the tented circus.") He was a tight-fisted manager who was responsible for launching many arenic careers; a shrewd businessman, a master showman, and became the wealthiest circus proprietor in America, acquiring prime real estate in Chicago and accumulating railroad stocks which allowed him to retire with an immense fortune to a mansion on Turk's Hill, Brewster, NY. And died there, age 86, one of the greatest showmen of the 19th century American circus.

HOWES, WILLIAM, JR. (b. 1807) Brother of **James R. Howes** and son of **Nathan Howes**. Connected with Macomber & Howes' Menagerie of Living Animals, 1830; Howes & Birchard's Menagerie the same year; 1833, the Howes brothers featured the elephant Columbus and an animal keeper who entered a leopard den. Following year, expanded to 2 tents and a larger exhibit of animals. Rider, June, Titus, Angevine & Co., 1839, Bowery Amphitheatre; rider, Howes & Mabie's, 1841; manager, Howes and Gardner, 1944.

HOWES, WILSON. Rider. Cousin of **Nathan** and **Seth B. Howes**. Nathan Howes & Co,, 1826; Nathan A. Howes', 1832; Howes & Sands, 1934-35; Nathan A. Howes', 1836, winter circus, Richmond Hill, NYC, 1837; performing dogs, S. H. Nichols', 1838; Thomas Taplin Cooke's, 1838; June, Titus, Angevine & Co., Bowery Amphitheatre, 1839-40; equestrian manager, eastern unit of June, Titus, Angevine & Co., 1841; Howes & Mabie, 1843; Nathan A. Howes' winter circus, 1843-44; manager, Howes & Gardner, 1844. A shareholder in the Zoological Institute.

HOWETT, CHARLES. Equestrian director, F. J. Taylor's, 1889; juggler, Ringling Bros.', 1991.

HOWLAND, JAMES HENRY. Treasurer, Dan Rice's Paris Pavilion, 1872-73. Married **Catherine Manahan**, Dan Rice's half-sister-in-law.

HOYT BROTHERS. Great Chicago, 1879.

HOYT, EMMA. Dwarf, Dr. James L. Thayer's, 1870.

HOYT, GEORGE W. Negro minstrel. Welch, Bartlett & Co., 1839; Welch & Delavan, 1841; James Raymond's, 184344; Mann, Welch & Delavan, 1844; Raymond & Warings', 1847.

HUBBELL ALONZO. Cannon ball exercises, heavy juggling, the "American Sampson" who endured the weight of 2 men clinging to his hair while he hurled them around the arena until they lost hold from exhaustion. "The cannon ball defier," Rockwell & Stone, 1845-46; Banigan & Kelly, 1847; Howes & Co., 1849; Nixon & Kemp, 1857; H. Buckley & Co., 1857-58; Stickney's, Old Bowery, NYC, 1861.

IIUBBELI, A. P. Manager of stand privileges, Sun Bros.', 1896.

HUBBELL, WILLIAM. Manager, Hubble, Hunt & Co. (**James Raymond**, proprietor), 1841; Hubble & Co. (**James Raymond**, proprietor), 1842; manager, Rockwell & Stone, 1846-47; European, 1849.

HUDGINS, J. G. Contracting agent, Black Bros.', 1897.

HUDSON, BENNY. Rider, Hudson & Castello, 1881.

HUDSON, GEORGE. Pony rider, Hudson & Castello, 1881.

HUDSON, J. M. Hudson's Great North and South American Circus, West Indies, 1872-73; Hudson & Castello's Circus (J. M. Hudson and **Dan Castello**, proprietors), 1879; Atlantic, 1881.

HUNDON, SAM. Chiarini's, South and Central America, 1869-70. Died in South America, February 14, 1870.

HUFF, G. A. G. A. Huff & Co.'s Metropolitan Circus, 1870.

HUFFMAN, FRANK Proprietor, Huffman's Dime Circus, 1885-86; general agent, Forepaugh & Samwells, winter 1887-88.

HUFFMAN, HENRY. Elephant trainer connected with the zoos at Fairmount Park, Philadelphia, and Central Park, NYC. Also with LaPearl's Circus and Wallace Bros.' At winter quarters, Peru, IN, with the Wallace show, was killed by the bull "Big Charley," whom he had handled for 7 years. On April 25, 1901, he had the elephant herd at the river's bank, washing them when, for some reason, "Big Charley" flung him into the drink. Huffman came out of the water to discipline the animal who went berserk, throwing the trainer back into the river and stomping him to death.

HUGHES. Acrobat, John Robinson's, 1888-90.

HUGHES, BENTON. Manager of hippodrome, Cook & Whitby, 1892.

HUGHES, CRIS. Clown. Olympic Circus, Philadelphia, 1822; Price & Simpson, 1823-24; slack-wire performer, Walnut Street Theatre, Philadelphia, 1824; slack-rope, Washington Gardens, Boston, fall 1825; ringmaster, William Harrington's, 1825; Lafayette Amphitheatre, NYC, 1825-26; clown, Tivoli Garden, Philadelphia, 1826; Quick & Mead, 1826; and Washington Circus, Philadelphia, 1827-28, 1830. [Charles Durang: He was "a very great favorite with the Northern Liberty audience.... He was always hailed by them with loud shouts and huzzahs as a star *par excellence* in a sawdust firmament."] 1830, accompanied Fogg & Stickney on their summer campaign through Pennsylvania. On the way to their first stand, Lancaster, and darkness being upon them, they stopped their caravan at a tavern. When his companions attempted to awaken Hughes to climb down from the wagon, they discovered him dead, presumably from a stroke.

HUGHES, D. W. Director of publications, European Circus, 1869-70.

HUGHES, PAT [or Nat]. Rider, G. G. Grady's, 1871; equestrian director, 1873, clown, 1874.

HUGO. (1869?-April 23, 1916) French sideshow giant, advertised at 8' 4" tall and weighing around 536 pounds. Connected with Barnum & Bailey. Died in NYC, age 47.

HUGO, MAX. Egyptian juggler, Delavan's, 1886; juggler and clown, Albert Hose's, 1893.

HUGO, VIC. Museum manager, W. C. Coup's, 1893.

HULL, GEORGE [r. n. Cheveril E. Gamer]. (August 21, 1864-October 25, 1908) Born in Azalia, IN. 16 years with Barnum & Bailey as ticket seller and advance man. At one time, acting superintendent at the Olympia, London, where he met and married **Mary Giles**, professionally known as **Marie DeWolf**, a female drum major and one time leader of the **Carl Clair** band for Barnum & Bailey. Hull died of heart trouble at St. Mary's, OH, age 43.

HUMMEL, JOHN F. (March 6, 1858-January 22, 1914) Treasurer, R. W. Weldon & Co., 1885. Hummel, Hamilton & Sells sold equipment to **J. N. Rentfrow**, 1893. Hummel & Hamilton's Great Syndicate Shows (**James M. Hamilton**, John F. Hummel, proprietors), 1896. This was J. N. Rentfrow's Great Syndicate Shows which collapsed on August 8 and was purchased by them. J. F. Hummel's, 1896-98; filed for bankruptcy, 1901.

HUMPHREY, J. B. Agent, Castello & VanVleck, 1863.

HUNT, A. Proprietor, A. Hunt & Co., 1838; manager for **James Raymond**, Hubble, Hunt & Co., 1841.

HUNT, ALBERT. Lake's Hippo-Olyinpiad, 1867.

HUNT, BENJAMIN J. Agent. Raymond & Co., 1850; Raymond & Driesbach, 1851; Robinson & Eldred, 1855.

HUNT, C. F. ["Prof."]. Dog trainer and handler. Ringmaster, Hawkins & Loomis Dog and Pony Show, 1997.

HUNT, CHARLES R. General agent, Diefenbach's Trans-Atlantic Circus, 1888.

HUNT, FRANK Bareback rider. Started with **P. A. Older**, early 1870s. Went to the John O'Brien show, where he remained some years, the last 2 or 3 as assistant manager and at times in charge of the advance as the general agent ahead of the show. For years was known to the public as **Miss Frankie Hunt**, female impersonator on a horse. [D. W. Watt: "When made up in female attire for his act, he could mount a horse and do as good a bareback act as anyone in the business, and the public for years never knew but what it was Miss Frankie Hunt."] After leaving circus activity, was connected with hotels in different cities, and later owned a hotel in La Crosse, Wisconsin.

HUNT, FRED. Born in Bath, England. Formerly a wig maker. Interested in circus enterprises with **John Tryon**, also Johnson & May, and with Seth B. Howes for Barnum's first

tented exhibition. Stickney's, 1848-49; Raymond & Mabie, 1852; writer, Dr. James L. Thayer's, 1869. Became a journalist, advancing from police reporter to editor and music critic. Authored one or two plays. Connected with the *Enquirer*, the *Commercial*, and the *Daily Dispatch*.

HUNT, WILLIAM. Vaulter and rider. Considered one of the leading vaulters of his day. **Edwin Derious** was a pupil of his. Rider, John Rogers', NYC, 1823-24; bareback rider, Olympic Circus, 1824; rider, Price & Simpson, 1824-25, 1826; vaulter, J. Purdy Brown's, 1825-26, 1827-28. While with the latter, 1828, New Orleans, broke his neck from a vaulting board and died.

HUNT, WILLIAM LEONARD. See Signor Guillermo Antonio Farini.

HUNTER, C. Whitby & Co. (**John O'Brien**, proprietor), 1867.

HUNTER, CHARLES. DeBonnaire's Great Persian Exposition, 1880; Hunter Bros.' Consolidated (Charles and **John Hunter**, proprietors), 1884. The brothers had 2 circuses out that year and a 2,000 seat amphitheatre in Pittsburg, KS, into which traveling shows were booked and which doubled as winter quarters.

HUNTER, C. C. Horse trainer and apparent proprietor, Washington Bros.', 1887.

HUNTER, DICK [r. n. George W. Lounsbury, Jr.]. (November 15, 1851-October 18, 1900) Agent. Born in Boston. Entered into show business by organizing a variety company, which included himself doing black face entertainment and booking. This began a career on the stage that included performing in concert saloons in and around Chicago and which ultimately led to an engagement with the Al G. Field Minstrels. Indeed, it was **Al G. Field** who suggested him changing his name to Hunter, Hunter being shorter and less confusing when it appeared on the bills. 1885, contracting agent, Ringling Bros.', a position that lasted for several years with that concern. In the winter, acted as agent for the Ringling hall show tours. Subsequently, managed tours for **Mlle. Roze**, the pedestrian; the **Hyer Sisters**; the **D'Ormond Dramatic Co.**; and was general agent for Taylor's Circus out of Creston, IA, 1891. Rejoined Ringling Bros.', 1894, as contracting agent and remained with them until fall 1896, when he was forced to retire because of illness. However, the following winter, was ahead of E. H. McCoy's "Turkish Bath" Co.; general agent, F. J. Taylor's, 1899-93; John Robinson's, 1898; Ringling Bros.', 1899; contracting agent, Sells & Gray, 1900 (the show closed early so he finished the season with Gollmar Bros.').

HUNTER, G. G. Sideshow solicitor, Holland & McMahon, 1885.

HUNTER, H. V. Manager, Hardenberger & Co's Circus, 1871.

HUNTER, JAMES. (d. 1839) Equestrian. Englishman from Astley's Amphitheatre, recruited and brought to America by

Stephen Price of the Park Theatre, NYC, 1822, to become the first real equestrian star in this country. The American innovator in bareback riding, setting the standard to which everyone else attempted to emulate and, as such, could demand twice the salary of other equestrians. Also worked on the tight rope but was not considered pre-eminent in that area of performance. The first to perform the Polandric ladder in this country. Light and compact and full of nerve and spring, stood only 5'4" tall. Made his American debut, Philadelphia, October 16, 1822, and was a great success, initiating a career that was meteoric but short lived. [Charles Durang: "Being a handsone and graceful little figure of a man, and youthful, the women adored him and the men lionized him, but through a weak mind and dissipated habits he lost all."] Married a young lady from Philadelphia against her parents' wishes but the union did not last long. Became intemperate in habits, quickly losing favor and skill. Bareback rider and "Hunted Tailor," Simpson & Price, 1822-27; Joseph Cowell's, 1824; Samuel Parsons' Albany Circus, Troy, NY, 1828; American Arena, Washington, DC, winter 1828-29, apparently his last engagement in America. Returning to England, 1929, performed at fairs and other cheap events. At last, impoverished, circus managers, remembering what he once was, gave him charitable asylum on their salary lists and brother performers gave him occasional handouts. One day, in a drunken spree, stole a coat from **Benjamin Stickney**, a member of Astley's Royal Amphitheatre; enraged, Stickney had him arrested; ultimately, tried and convicted and sentenced to Van Dieman's Island.

HUNTER, G. V. Manager, Handenburger & Co., 1871.

HUNTER, JOHN. See Charles Hunter.

HUNTER, JOSEPIL Advertising agent, Gregory & D'Alma, 1889.

HUNTERSON, JOHN A. (d. February 22, 1890) Hurdle rider, J. W. Wilder's, 1872; Roman standing race, Barnum, Bailey & Hutchinson, 1882; also Thayer & Noyes, Martinette Bros.'

HUNTING, CLARENCE. Hilliard & Hunting's Great Pacific Circus (**M. M. Hilliard**, R. Hunting, proprietors), 1877-78.

HUNTING, CLARICE [or Clarissa]. Wife of **Robert Hunting**. Gymnast, G. G. Grady's, 1874; aerialist, Hurlburt & Hunting, 1885-87.

HUNTING, LEW. Wire-walker, Hurlburt & Hunting, 1887; tight-rope, Hunting's, 1888.

HUNTING, MOLLIE. Robert Hunting's Railroad Shows, 1897.

HUNTING, ROBERT. (May 10, 1848-April 21,1902) Born in Baltimore, MD. Clown and proprietor, rider, trapeze artist and bar performer. Haight & Chambers, 1865; Gardner, Kenyon & Roberson, 1869. Married **Clara** (or **Clarice**) **King**, New Castle, PA, 1869. Adam Forepaugh's, 1870-73; G. G. Grady's, 187374; Hilliard & Hamilton, 1875; assistant manager, clown and co-proprietor, Hilliard, Hamilton & Hunting's Great Pacific Combination, 1876; proprietor and clown, Hilliard & Hunting's Great Pacific Circus (**H. H. Hilliard**, R. Hunting, proprietors), 1877; Great Pacific Circus and Congress of Educated Horses (**H. H. Hilliard**, R. Hunting, proprietors), 1879; clown, Hilliard, Hunting & DeMott's Great Pacific, 1879. Sold interest in the Great Pacific to Hilliard & DeMott, November, 1879. Sells Bros.', 1880-81; purchased interest in the Wambold Circus, September 1983 (the show was to be re-organized for the following season); Washburn & Hunting, 1884, sold interest to Washburn at season's end; equestrian director and aerialist, Hurlburt & Hunting, 1885-97; Great 100 Railroad Show; proprietor, Hunting's New York Cirque Curriculum, 1888-89; Hunting's Circus, 1892-98, ultimately sustaining a great fmancial loss. Jailed in Canandaigua, NY, for shooting **Thomas F. Leddy**, bandmaster, an incident occurring in the main circus tent, July 25, 1898, because salaries of some band members were overdue and Leddy and other musicians were preparing to leave the show. There were hot words between Hunting and Leddy and blows were struck. Hunting, a much smaller man, whipped out a revolver and fired twice at the band master, hitting him in the shoulder and abdomen. Was freed August 5 on the grounds of self-defense. Died of a stroke at the Soldiers' Home, Erie, PA.

HUNTING, TONY. Robert Hunting's Railroad Shows, 1896-97.

HUNTINGTON, BENJAMIN. Clown, ringmaster. Aaron Turner's, 1833, 1835; ringmaster, Quick, Sands & Co., Baltimore, 1933; clown, J. J. Hall's, 1836; ringmaster, H. H. Fuller's, 1838; clown, June, Titus, Angevine & Co., 1839-40, Bowery Amphitheatre; clown, eastern unit, June, Titus, Angevine & Co., 1842; clown, S. H. Nichols', Albany Amphitheatre, winter 1843; clown, Nathan A. Howes', winter circus, 1842; Rockwell & Stone, 1843; clown, winter circus, Niblo's Garden, NYC, 1843-44; John Tryon's, Bowery Amphitheatre, NYC, 1847; ringmaster, Sands, Lent & Co., 1847; June, Titus & Co., 1848-49; ringmaster, Spalding & Rogers, 1850; ringmaster, G. C. Quick's, 1852; ringmaster, Sands & Chiarini, 1854; equestrian director, Sands, Nathans & Co., 1857; ringmaster, Sands & Nathans, 1859; R. Sands', 1860-62; ringmaster, Melville, Cooke & Sands, 1863.

HUNTINGTON, CHARLES M. George W. DeHaven's, 1860.

HUNTINGTON, HARRY. (December 22, 1832-June 1860) Agent. Born in Springfield, MA. Entered show business as agent for **Everitt, the Magician**. Next joined Robinson & Eldred. Married **Susan Denin**, Richmond, VA, January 25, 1856, while traveling with Christy's Minstrels. Died in Emira, NY.

HUNTLEY, TOM. Variety troupe, Haight & Chambers, 1867.

HUNTLEY, THOMAS L. [professionally as Delane]. Tight-rope walker. Killed while performing in Wilmington, NC, November 27, 1865.

HURD, SAMUEL H. Having married P. T. Barnum's oldest daughter, **Helen**, in the fall of 1857, his connection with the Barnum management began as early as 1864 when he was listed as an assistant for the second American Museum. The couple was divorced, 1871. Appointed assistant treasurer for P. T. Barnum's, 1971-73; Barnum's Roman Hippodrome, 1874-75. Was there, in part, to protect Barnum's interest. Later was promoted to treasurer, receiving 20% of the yearly gross. 1874, worked under the title of superintendent and treasurer.

HURLBURT, D. P. Manager, performer of trained horses, Hurlburt & Hunting, 1885-87; Hurlburt's, 1888; Hurlburt & Leftwich, 1890-94.

HURTT, ANNIE. Trapeze, Baldwin, Wall & Co.'s Great Eastern, 1880.

HUSTED, E. C. Agent, Howes & Co., 1846.

HUSTED, N. R. Proprietor (with **I. P. Frost**), Frost, Husted & Co., 1836; agent, Welch, Bartlett & Co., 1840; agent, Howes & Gardner (**Nathan A. Howes** and **Dan Gardner**, proprietors), 1844.

HUTCH, JIM. Sideshow. For some 40 years caretaker of the curiosities on John Robinson's. Considered to be an eccentric with a heart of gold.

HUTCHINGS, PROF. W. S. Proprietor, European and American Museum, Amphitheatre and Indian Show (managed by **John Weaver**), 1867, starting out of Louisville, KY.

HUTCHINS, ["Master"]. Rider, John Bill Ricketts', Philadelphia, 1795-99. In 1800, while on their way to the West Indies, their ship was set upon by pirates and the company put ashore at Guadalupe. There, Hutchins fell ill and died, age 9 or 10.

HUTCHINS, W. L. Lecturer, Adam Forepaugh's, 1872.

HUTCHINSON, BEETLE. Boss hostler, with Adam Forepaugh's, 1872.

HUTCHINSON, C. A. Master of transportation, Cooper, Bailey & Co., 1876; master of transportation, Robbins & Colvin, 1881.

HUTCHINSON, CHARLES R. (February 3, 1868-July 10, 1934) Treasurer for the old Barnum & Bailey Circus and continued in the same capacity with the combined Ringling Bros. and Barnum & Bailey for some 35 years. Earlier, was with Adam Forepaugh's, 1892-95; Buffalo Bill's Wild West. His father, **Calvin A. Hutchinson**, held executive positions with Cooper Bailey & Co. His mother, **Anna Isabel McCaddon Hutchinson**, was a sister of **Mrs. James A. Bailey**. Married to **Tillie Patterson**. Died on Long Island, NY, at home of his son, **Charles M.**, age 66. Other sons were **Harry B.** and **Fred B.**

HUTCHNSON, GEORGE P. Acrobat. Performed the **Roman Brothers** with **John H. Murray**, Stone & Rosston,

1864-66; Stone, Rosston & Murray, 1867; Stone & Murray, 1868-69. Also, presented a troupe of performing dogs, 1867-69. At one point, had an interest in the firm.

HUTCHINSON, JAMES L. (November 18, 1846-September 3 or 9, 1910) Born in Jerseyville, OH. Entered show business as canvasman, Lake's; joined Mabie's, 1863, employed by **Stewart Craven** for the "peep show," and remained through the season of 1864; Yankee Robinson's, 1866-69; contracting aqgent, P. A. Older's, 1870; autobiography agent, P. T. Barnum's, 1871-1873, from which he made a small fortune; remained with Barnum's, 1874-75, as press agent, etc.; privileges, VanAmburgh's, 1876-78; controlled all privileges, Cooper & Bailey, 1878-80; Following the 1880 season, by good fortune, became a partner with P. T. Barnum and James A. Bailey in forming the combined P. T. Barnum and Great London Shows and held an interest in Barnum, Bailey & Hutchinson until he sold it October 27, 1887. [Hugh Coyle: "... was the best lecturer for a concert that ever did that work in a tented show."] Married **Miss Frankie Watt**, professionally known as **Mollie V. Lubin**, in NYC, March 25, 1880. She died 1903. At time of death, owned 3 homes: in NYC, Englewood, NJ, and on Shelter Island, NY, where he died from heart failure while playing golf. Had two sons, James and Guy, and a daughter.

HUTCHINSON, THOMAS. Manager, Joseph D. Palmer's, 1836.

HUYCK IKE. Clown, Orton's, 1856; Mabie Bros.', 1858-59. Performed with trick mules.

HUYLER, A. Gymnast, First National Union, 1861.

HUZLITT, GEORGE [or Joseph]. Rider and athlete, L. B. Lent's, 1867.

HUZZA, IDA. See Mrs. Littlefluger.

HUZZA, ROBERT. See Major Littlefluger.

HYATT, FRANK. (February 21, 1842-February 17, 1927) Born in Jefferson Valley, Putnam County, NY. Entered the business as proprietor, Hyatt & Co., 1859; VanAmburgh's, 1863, and remained until 1865, when the organization became Barnum & VanAmburgh's and exhibited on Broadway between Spring and Prince Streets. After firm dissolved, 1870, continued with VanAmburgh until 1875, transferring to Great London as treasurer until the company closed in Augusta, GA, 1876. Manager, Adam Forepaugh's, 1977; advance agent, Adam Forepaugh's, 1878, joined the Barnum show at the time of its consolidation with Barnum, Bailey & Hutchinson, 1881, and remained for some years as assistant manager. Throughout his career, filled nearly every position connected with the circus. Died at Connersville, IN, age 85.

HYATT, OSCAR W. (d. April 10, 1887) Entered circus business in the early 1850s. Although a man of rugged physique, was never a performer. Manager, Harry Buckley's, 1856; also, L. G. Butler's, Mabie's, W. W. Cole's, and VanAmburgh's (assistant manager, 1881-82). Died of pneumonia,

NYC.
HYATT, WILLIAM. Chief bill poster, J. F. Taylor's, 1889.
HYMAN, SPAFF. Sideshow privilege, Thayer & Noyes,

1864; sideshow talker, magician and juggler, Shellenberger's, 1871; wizard, P. T. Barnum's, 1874; Batcheller & Doris, 1879.

142

William H. Harris

I

IDALETTA. Of the high-wire walking team of **Idaletta & Wallace**, Pullman & Mack, 1885. Fell from the trapeze, Sabetha, KS, June 10, 1885, and was severely injured.

IDLER, WILLIAM. Program agent, Great International Circus **(James E. Cooper, James A. Bailey, Robert S. Hood, David Worthington**, proprietors), 1874.

IGNACE. Clown, rope-dancer and rider. Pepin & Barnet, Natchez, MS, June 1823; Pepin's, St. Louis, 1823; Bernard & Page, 1829; Page's, 1830; Royal Circus, 1831.

IJEMSKO, MONS. General performer, VanAmburgh & Co., 1874.

ILLSHOFEN, HERR. General performer, Stone & Murray, 1868.

IMPOLO, MONS. General performer, VanAmburgh & Co., 1874.

INFANT ESAU. Bearded child, P. T. Barnum's, 1871.

INGALLS, JUDGE H. P. (March 18, 1826-December 6, 1908) Born near Merrimac, NH. At 24 years of age went to NYC and became a streetcar conductor. Joined Franconi's Hippodrome for a year or two until he connected with Welch & Lent for about 3 years. 1854, took charge of the museum in Philadelphia; secured the **Siamese Twins**, recently arrived in the country, and exhibited them there. With **P. T. Barnum**, toured the twins in England and American. Sideshow, Goodwin & Wilder, 1862, made up of snakes and other curiosities; sideshow, John V. O'Brien's, 1863. Also managed and exhibited **Captain Bates** and wife, the Nova Scotia Giants. Took **Millie Christine**, the two-headed girl from North Carolina, to England, 1871. Shortly, became superintendent of the Cincinnati Zoological Gardens. Retired from show business, 1873, and settled in Bellefontaine, OH. Was a boon companion of **P. T. Barnum, Isaac VanAmburgh, Adam Forepaugh**, and old **John Robinson**. Won and lost a half-dozen fortunes. Reaped fame and money as the discoverer of the **Siamese Twins**. Died at his home in Huntsville, OH, age 82. **INGRAM, PROF.** Trained horses, World's Fair Aggreation, 1892.

INMAN, CHARLES. Clown, French & Monroe, 1885.

INNES, WILL A. General agent, Alden, Crane & Co., 1884.

IRVIN, BELLE. Alex Abar's Pavilion Show, 1889.

IRVINE, DEAN. Bareback rider, Adam Forepaugh's, 1885.

IRVING, GEORGE H. Walter L. Main's, 1891. Married **Lillie Fullwood**, non-professional, 1891; W. F. Kirkhart's Great American Railroad Circus **(W. F. Kirkhart, R. M. Harvey**, proprietors), 1895.

IRVING, WILLIAM S. Treasurer, Stone & Murray, 1871, program agent, 1972; press agent, John F. Murray's, 1973, advertising agent, 1874-75. With James W. Goodrich Wagon Show at the time of his fatal illness; died of pneumonia in Hartford, CT, age 59.

IRWIN BROTHERS [George, Jacob, Fred]. Equestrians and gymnasts, flying trapeze and horizontal bars. Head to head balancing on the trapeze, Dan Rice's, 1879; John Robinson's, 1881-83; W. H. Stowe's, winter 1881-82; W. H. Harris' Nickel-Plate, 1884; Adam Forepaugh's, 1892. **Fred Irwin**, privileges, Forepaugh & Samwells, 1886; proprietor and manager, Irwin Bros.' Railroad Show, 1887-89; Irwin Bros.' Big American and Japanese Circus as late as 1895; Irwin Bros.' Comedy & Variety Co., 1892.

IRWIN, JAMES. Head balancer. With Ringling Bros.', 1891; Great Wallace, 1896.

IRWIN, JOHN D. Chief bill poster, Maginley & Co., 1874; agent, Melville, Maginley & Cooke, 1875.

IRWIN, LEO. Great Wallace **(B. E. Wallace**, proprietor), 1896.

IRWIN, WILLIAM J. Head balancer and trapeze performer. Equilibrist, Irwin Bros.' Shows, 1887; equestrian manager, John F. Stowe & Co., 1888; Sig. Sautelle's, 1889; head balancing, trapeze act, Bailey & Winan, 1890; *Circo Cortada*, Cuba, winter 1893-94, 1894-95; Ringling Bros.', 1894, 1897; Charles Bartine's, 1895; Col. G. W. Hall's, 1898; high bicycle wire and head balancer, Trevino's, Mexico, 1898; Cooper & Co., 1900; Busby Bros.', 1902; H. C. Lang's, winter 1902-04; VanAmburgh's, 1904; Kennedy Bros.' Wild West, 1905-06; the Mighty Haag, 1910.

ISAACS, ADAH. Female clown, with North American, 1877; Allen's Great Eastern, 1879.

ISENHART, J. B. Musical director, with Whitney's Imperial Wagon Show, 1892.

144

Omar Samuel Kingsley
"Ella Zoyara"

J

JACKITS-CHY TROUPE. Feats of balancing, with W. C. Coup's, 1878-79. **Manchiska**, infant son of Jackits-chy and **Mme. Citto**, died August 5, 1879, in a sleeping car en route to Scranton, PA.

JACK, JONATHAN. Irish dwarf equestrian, National Circus, Cincinnati, winter 1864-65.

JACKLEY, NATHAN. Austrian acrobat, came to the United States in 1874 after starring with the Rosinski Troupe from Russia. Remembered as being the originator of an act called the "Jackley Drops." It consisted of tables piled 8 high, with a nineth placed next to them. Standing on the eighth, Jackley dropped backward and landed on his hands on the floor level nineth; then did a backward leap, which landed him on the ground level facing the tables. Proprietor, Jackley's Great Vienna Circus, 1874-75; joined Barnum's Hippodrome, November 1874; Jackley's Australian Novelty Co., 1885.

JACKSON, ALEC. Rider, Asa T. Smith's, 1829; slack-rope, Byram Bernard's, 1830; scenic rider, Aaron Turner's, 1831; scenic rider, T. L. Stewart's, 1831; Stickles & Co., 1832; scenic rider, American Circus, 1833; Palmer's, 1836.

JACKSON, ALLIE. Sells Bros.', 1886; Ringling Bros.', 1894.

JACKSON, ANDREW. With wife **Lizzie**, Walter L. Main's, 1893; Sutton & Jackson, 1896.

JACKSON, BERTIE. Rider, Burr Robbins', 1880.

JACKSON, G. Clown, J. W. Wilder's North American Circus (**Asa B. Stow**, manager), 1873.

JACKSON, HARRY. Australian actor and Shakespearean clown, Lee & Ryland, California, and other west coast locations, winter 1866-67.

JACKSON, J. Manager, Kincade's Circus, 1871.

JACKSON, JOHN [r. n. John McIllway]. (d. 1848) Rider. Born in Philadelphia. Edward Eldred's, 1834; Buckley & Co., 1834; Bancker & Harrington, 1835; scenic rider, Eagle Circus/Cole & Co., 1837; Yale, Sands & Co., 1838; Miller, Yale & Howes, 1838; proprietor (with **John Shay**, **John Mateer**, **Charles J. Rogers**), Cincinnati Circus, 1840-41; Dr. Gilbert R. Spalding's, 1845-46; Stone & McCollum, 1847-48. Died at Columbus, GA, 1843.

JACKSON, LYMAN A. Treasurer, co-proprietor, Cooper & Jackson (**Charles F. Cooper**, Lyman A. Jackson, proprietors), 1880-83; 1883, added **J. Ferguson** to the firm, changing the title to Cooper, Jackson & Co.; circus was sold at a sheriff's sale, December 1, 1884.

JACKSON, MATTIE. *Manège* and leaping act, Barnum, Bailey & Hutchinson, 1881, hippodrome jockey, 1882-84; P. T. Barnum's, 1885-86; Adam Forepaugh's, 1893.

JACKSON, SADEE. Rider, Howes Trans-Atlantic Circus and Risbeck's Menagerie (Frank Howes, proprietor), 1868.

JACKSON, SAM. French gymnast, J. W. Wilder's, 1872.

JACKSON, SAMUEL. Band musician, with Joe Pentland's, 1855; Flagg & Aymar, 1856; "Greatest Tenor Drummer in the World," Joe Pentland's, 1857-58.

JACKSON, S. C. Thayer & Noyes, 1864.

JACKSON, WILLIAM J. (d. October 21, 1886) Press agent, Cooper & Jackson, 1880. Died, St. Louis, MO, age 33.

JACOBS, BLANCHE. Melvin, Royer & Jacob's, 1895.

JACOBS, W. Variety troupe, Haight & Chambers, 1867.

JAGENDORFF, GEORGE ["Vienna"]. An Austrian strong man. Father was a manufacturer of meerschaum goods in Vienna. Adam Forepaugh's, 1884-85, 1888; Silbon-Elliott Combination, 1884.

JAKEWAY, JAMES S. (d. May 10, 1875) Advertiser. A native of Nichols, Tioga County, NY. New York Champs Elysees, 1865; and later, Thayer & Noyes. Died an indigent, Waverly, NY.

JALMA, PRINCE SADI DI. "The Human Anaconda," Ben Maginley's, 1874.

JAMES, A. D. Proprietor, A. D. James' Pavilion Shows, 1897.

JAMES, HARRY. Band leader, Hunter's, 1884.

JAMES, J. Howes' Great European, winter 1864.

JAMES, RICHARD. Ohio giant, L. B. Lent's, 1876.

JAMESON, NEIL [sometimes spelled Neal and Jamieson]. Banjoist, Drury, Van Tassle, Brown & Co., 1837; Mann, Welch & Delevan, 1846; Welch & Delavan, 1847; Welch, Delavan & Nathans, 1848-51. Died in Tennessee, 1850s.

JAMISON, FANNIE [sometimes spelled Jemison]. Equestrienne, with Driesbach's, 1856; VanAmburgh's, 1856; H. Buckley & Co., 1857-58; equitation act, E. F. and J. Mabie's, 1858-59; Buckley's, 1859.

JANKINS, PAULINE V. See Pauline Batcheller.

JAQUES, ALEX. Excursion agent, Shelby, Pullman & Hamilton, 1881.

JARDINE, LOUISE. Gymnast, W. W. Cole's, 1886.

JARVIS, JOHN. Boss hostler, Robinson & Lake, 1859-60.

JASPER, MILTON. Gymnast, pedestal somersaulting. W. W. Cole's, 1875; Cooper, Bailey & Co., 1876; Sells Bros.', 1879.

JASPER, TOM. Leaper, Sells Bros.', 1881.

JAYMOND. Rider, Lailson's, 1797. Was an actor and directed the pantomimes.

JEAL, ELENA. Equestrian. Sister of Linda Jeal and wife of George Ryland, whom she married in 1880. Barnum & London, 1884-85.

JEAL, LINDA. (1852-1941) Sister of **Elena Jeal**; aunt of **Nellie Ryland.** Performed on running globe, leaped through fire on horseback as "Queen of the Flaming Zone," backward riding while balancing on one foot. Attended school at Petaluma, CA. First marriage, **William O'Dale Stevens.** Following his death, married **Natalio Lowande,** October 17, 1885, Jersey City, NJ; divorced, May 19, 1886. Later married **Joseph Murray.** Had no children but adoped three—a boy, **Daley,** and two girls, **"Chookey"** and **Sally.** Linda died in Springfield, IL, where she had been living with the latter daughter. Started to ride, 1869, in ring barn, Hayward, CA, while visiting sister. Performed with circuses in Mexico, South America, Cuba, West Indies, and Europe. First public appearance as rider, Sacramento, CA, Lee & Ryland, 1870; bareback hurdle rider, slack wire, juggler, rolling globe, Campbell's (**John V. O'Brien's**), 1878; left Campbell's, August 1878, to join Anderson & Co., and later that month, the Barnum show; John H. Murray's, West Indies, winter 1878-79; featured in a "Flaming Zone" bareback feat, P. T. Barnum's, 1879; Orrin Bros.', Metropolitan Theatre, Havana, Cuba, winter 1879-80; Cooper, Bailey & Co., 1880; W. W. Cole's, 1881; Great Australian Circus, National Theatre, Philadelphia, winter 1881-82; Stevens' Australian Circus, performing on variety stages, prior to summer season, 1882; Ryan & Robinson, 1882; W. O'Dale Stevens' Australian Circus, winter, 1882-83; Barnum & London, 1884-85; Frank A. Robbins', 1886-87; *Gran Circo Estrellas Del Nortis,* West Indies, winter 1888-89; Frank A. Gardner's, Chile, 1889; Walter L. Main's, 1891; Circus Busch, Leipsic, 1892; Barnum & Bailey, 1895; New York Circus (**Frank A. Robbins,** lessee and general manager), 1897; Shipp's Winter Circus, Petersburg, IL, 1897-98; LaPearl's, 1898; Campbell Bros.', 1899-1905. Last engagement, Frank A. Robbins'. Retired at age 63, 1916.

JEE FAMILY [Marie, Alice, Jennie, Harry, James, Albert, Joseph]. Equestrians. Howes' Great American, London, 1870, and came to America with the show, 1871. At that time, **Harry** claimed he was the champion hat spinner of the world. **Joseph** (1841-1890), listed as a comic gymnast, performed dramatic scenes on horseback, one being "The Ship-Wrecked Sailor Boy," Howes', 1871-72. **Albert** was clown with L. B. Lent's, 1872. **Jennie** was the wife of **Egbert C. Howes,** whom she married in England in 1859, and half-sister of equestrienne **Lily Deacon,** wife of Adam Forepaugh, Jr. With Howes' **James** was billed as the only person to accomplish the forward feet-to-feet somersault on a bareback horse, was the featured rider. **William** was a gymnast and tumbling clown.

JEFFERSON, CHARLES. (1863?-July 12, 1911) Strong man. First circus job was as an acrobat. Served for a time as a sculptor's model. Was 6' 2" tall and could snap chains linked around his chest and lift enormous weights, making him a great sideshow attraction. Connected with the Barnum show and later with Barnum & Bailey. After retirement, owned a boarding house and had other investments, but poor speculation lost him much of his property. Had been retired from the circus business about 18 years when he died of a stroke, NYC, age 48.

JEFFERSON, HENRY. Clown and Negro deliniator, Alexander Robinson's, 1870.

JEFFERSON, T. H. [Tommie]. Negro minstrel banjoist, George F. Bailey & Co., 1860; VanAmburgh & Co., 1866.

JEFFREY, JOHN H. (1855-December 30, 1882) Contortionist and trapeze performer. Born in NYC. Entered the profession at age 13. Burr Robbins', 1874-79; as one of the **Carroll Brothers,** and leaper and tumbler, P. T. Barnum's, 1880; W. C. Coup's, 1881.

JENKINS, FRANK. Boss hostler, Sig Montanio's, 1881.

JENKINS, P. Boss canvasman, with John Robinson's, 1882-85.

JENKINS, P. Band leader, W. H. Harris' Nickel-Plate, 1891.

JENKINS, PAULINE "La Belle Pauline." Married leaper **William H. Batcheller,** Pensacola, FL, January 30, 1876. See William Batcheller.

JENKINS, WILLIAM. W. H. Harris' Nickel-Plate, 1889.

JENNER, GEORGE, SR [or Jennier]. (1851?-September 5, 1905) Equilibrist. Born in Cincinnati, OH. Connected with circus business since the age of 11, having apprenticed to **Dan Rice.** December 25, 1878, married Rice's niece, **Nina Howland;** had 7 children, 4 of which, **George Jr., Walter, Roy** and **Mrs. Maude Millette,** were professionals. Died of a stroke, age 54. Dancing barrels, Scribner & Clements, 1887; equestrian director, Stowe Bros.', 1889; dancing barrels, table and cross (daughter, **Maude,** performed on the slack wire), F. J. Taylor's, 1894; **Jenner Family,** Cooper & Co. (J. R. W. Hennessey, proprietor and manager), 1897.

JENNINGS, BENJAMIN. (1808?-January 23, 1874) Native of Boston. Juggler, J. B. Green & Co., 1833; Green & Brown, 1834; juggler, Welch, Bartlett & Co., 1839; acrobat, Welch & Delavan, Baltimore, 1841; John Tryon's, Bowery Amphitheatre, NYC, 1844; clown, John T. Potter's, 1844-45; acrobat, Dr. Gilbert R. Spalding's, 1845; contortionist, S. P. Stickney's, 1846; clown, Stickney's New Orleans Circus (Stickney, **North & Jones,** proprietors), 1849; contortionist, Great Western (**Dennison Stone, Eaton Stone, Thomas McCollum,** proprietors), 1847; Johnson & Co., 1852; clown, Levi J. North's canal show, 1853-55; clown, Robinson & Howes, Chicago, 1863; Yankee Robinson's, Coliseum, Chicago, 1867. With the latter, was presented with a silver tobacco box, April 16, 1867, at what, it was suggested, was his last performance in the ring. Following this, established a theatrical agency, Dearborn St., Chicago, 1867; later, kept a saloon on Dearborn St. for many years, which was a popular resort for show folk. Died in that city, age 66.

JENNINGS FAMILY. Tight-rope and high perch, Adam

Forepaugh's, 1887.

JENNINGS, HENRY. Leaper and acrobat. Son of **Ben Jennings**. Welch & Mann, 1843; John T. Potter's, 1844; Great Western (Stone & McCollum), 1847-48; John Robinson's, 1858, 1867-68, 1872; Davis & Crosby, 1859; clown, Ed G. Basye's, 1878.

JENNINGS, JOHN J. "STUB." (1845?-May 23, 1906) Sideshow performer, known as the "iron jawed man." Started in the circus business with the John O'Brien show. Walter L. Main's, 1892-93, and was with it when it was wrecked in Tyrone, PA, receiving injuries which affected his health. Last engagement, Ringling Bros.' Died in Harrisburg, PA, age 61.

JENNINGS, MAUD. *Manège*, St. Germain's Imperial Circus, 1889.

JEROME BROTHERS. Philadelphia Circus (managed by **Dan Gardner**), winter 1867-68.

JEROME, EUGENE. Equestrian juggler, S. H. Barrett's, 1887.

JEROME, GEORGE. Bill poster, P. T. Barnum's, 1873.

JEROME, VICTOR. Contortionist, Burr Robbins', 1886.

JEROME, WILLIAM. Agent, James T. Johnson & Co., 1881.

JO JO, "The Dog-Faced Boy". See Theodore Peteroff.

JOHANOFF BROTHERS. Russian athletes, gymnasts, Maginley & Co., 1874.

JOHNNY MAC. Clown. S. B. Howes' European, 1865.

JOHNS, J. T. Treasurer and press agent, E. H. Howes', 1888.

JOHNSON [or Johnston]. Rider. Partner, **Thomas Franklin**, in a circus venture, 1799; Langley's company, 1800-02.

JOHNSON, AL. 4-horse act, Great Exposition Circus (**J. C. O'Brien**, manager), 1895.

JOHNSON, ALF. Equestrian. Brown & Bailey, 1827-28; Handy & Welch, 1830; 2-horse rider, T. L. Stewart's, 1831; James W. Bancker's, 1832; Stewart's American Amphitheatre, 1832; 2-horse rider, Handy & Welch, West Indies, 1829; 2-horse rider, Eagle Circus, 1836; Waterman & Co., 1838; W. Seeley's, 1840.

JOHNSON, ARTHUR. German clown, Batcheller & Doris, 1880.

JOHNSON, BEN. Strong man with Dan Rice's for several years. Died in Brazil, IN, April 29, 1913, age 68.

JOHNSON, BILLY C. Clown, North American, 1877; H. C. Lee's Great Eastern, winter 1877-78.

JOHNSON, BURT. Champion leaper and general performer. Stone & Murray, 1868-69; leaper, tumbler, P. T. Barnum's, 1873; John H. Murray's, West Indies, winter 1878-79; Roman Races, Brighton Beach Fair Grounds, Coney Island, 1879; tumbler and leaper, P. T. Barnum's, 1879-80; W. O'Dale Stevens' Australian Circus, Park Square Grounds, Boston, 1883; Adam Forepaugh's, 1888, 1892-93.

JOHNSON, CHARLES. (1832?-December 18, 1865) Man of enormous strength and endurance; traveled throughout USA and Europe as a 40-horse driver. While in Philadelphia with Adam Forepaugh's, died of pleuritis, age 33, having performed in the ring 3 days prior to his death.

JOHNSON, CHARLES. Property man, P. T. Barnum's, 1873. Died July 16 of that season at the Clinton House, Cleveland, of a stroke, age about 21.

JOHNSON, CHARLES. Elephant trainer. With George F. Bailey & Co., handler of Antony, Cleopatra, Victoria and Albert, 1866; keeper of Tippo Saib for VanAmburgh's, 1867. Remained with the show beyond 1882.

JOHNSON, CORNING. (1830?-November 12, 1897) Negro dwarf and acrobat, better known as "Romeo, the Dwarf." Born in Mobile, AL, of slave parents. Became connected with circuses just before the Civil War. Was run over and killed by a Long Island train at Chester Park, LI, age about 67.

JOHNSON, E. Tight rope artist, John Robinson's, 1875.

JOHNSON, FRANCES VICTORIA. See Mlle. Frank Vick.

JOHNSON, GEORGE. Clown. Howes & Mabie, 1844; Dr. Gilbert R. Spalding's, 1845-46; VanAmburgh's, 1858.

JOHNSON, GEORGE W. [or Johnston]. Lion tamer and elephant handler, Cooper, Bailey & Co., Australian tour, 1876-77; supt. of menagerie, 1879-80; Barnum, Bailey & Hutchinson, 1881-84.

JOHNSON, GREEN B. Clown. With Buckley, Weeks & Co., 1834-35; Boston Lion Circus (Raymond & Weeks, proprietors), 1836-37; Fogg & Stickney, 1841; Howes & Mabie, 1844; Great Western (**Dennison Stone, Thomas McCollum**, proprietors), 1846-49; bought out Stone & McCollum, 1850, changing the title to G. B. Johnson's Great Western Circus; second season, show title was Johnson & Co.'s People's Circus, 1851-52; clown, VanAmburgh's, 1858.

JOHNSON, HARVEY. Proprietor, (with **Eugene Romelli**) Romelli & Co.'s Great Novelty Circus and Performing Animal Show, 1872.

JOHNSON, H. C. Ringmaster. Welch's, Philadelphia, 1843; Nathan A. Howes', winter 1843-44.

JOHNSON, HUNTERSON. General performer, with J. W. Wilder's, 1873.

JOHNSON, J. Gymnast. G. G. Grady's, winter 1869-70; John Robinson's, 1875.

JOHNSON, JABEZ. Press agent and humorous journalist known as Yuba Dam. Nixon & Castello, California.

JOHNSON, JAMES. Rider. Simpson & Price, Philadelphia, Baltimore, 1822, Washington, NYC, 1823; William Blanchard & William West, Canada, 1825; J. Purdy Brown's, 1828; 2-horse act, Asa T. Smith's, 1829; 2-horse rider, Bernard & Page, 1829.

JOHNSON JAMES T. (1839?-April 30, 1899) Proprietor, horse trainer and rider, manager of a western circus company as early as 1866. James T. Johnson Iowa Circus and Rocky Mountain Menagerie, 1867. February of that year, was reported building an amphitheatre in Albia, IA. However, instead, opened a circus amphitheatre in Macombe, IL, fall 1867. Johnson & Co.'s Variety Equestrian Combination, 1868; J. T. Johnson & Co.'s United States Circus, 1869-70; manager, Romelli & Co., 1872; agent, Barry & Co., 1879; James T. Johnson's Great Western Circus, 1883-86; formed "Uncle Tom's Cabin" Co., 1887. Following the summer season, erected an amphitheatre in Pratt, KS, for winter entertainments which proved unsuccessful. Disposed of all his circus property, December 1893. Located in Hot Springs and erected an amphitheatre, summer 1896, which he operated until death from pneumonia, age about 60. Johnson's family of performers was composed of his wife and two daughters, **Mollie** and **Ella**. The girls performed on roller skates, did acrobatics, wire-walking and bareback riding. In addition, there was Johnson's trick horse, Fire King, advertised as the only animal in America to perform the feat of leaping through a fire balloon. The horse, a wild gelding, was captured in southwest Kansas, 1864. Of Johnson, [Steve Gossard: "... Johnson and his circus were to be called 'bums,' 'Deadbeats,' and 'fraud,' often leaving a trail of debts behind his tours of Kansas towns.... If nothing more can be said of James T. Johnson, one thing is for sure: he was a born talker, a real showman."]

JOHNSON, J. E. Clown, Welch's National Circus, winter 1856.

JOHNSON, JEAN. Equestrian and tight-rope performer. June & Titus, 1848; around 11 years of age, advertised as "Master Jean," Dan Rice's, 1849-55; Whitbeck's, 1854; Crescent City, 1855; Dan Rice's, 1856; Washburn's, 1857; Eldred's, 1859; Spalding & Rogers, 1860-61; John Robinson's, 1867; C. T. Ames', New Orleans, 1868; Charles Noyes', 1869; principal rider and tight-rope performer, Australian Circus, 1870; Metchear & Cameron, 1870; Empire City, 1871.

JOHNSON, J. E. Clown, Welch's, winter 1856.

JOHNSON, JENNIE. Equestrienne, L. B. Lent's, 1858.

JOHNSON, J. F. Advertising agent, Orton Bros.', 1866

JOHNSON, JOHN H. Zoological director, Alexander Robinson's, 1875.

JOHNSON, J. P. Thayer & Noyes, winter 1865-66; museum director, L. B. Lent's, 1876.

JOHNSON, LAURA [Mrs. Frank Rosston]. Dan Rice's, 1855. See Frank Rosston.

JOHNSON, MARY JANE. Rider. Daughter of **W. C. Johnson**. James Raymond's, 1843-44; Rockwell & Co., 1847.

JOHNSON, J. ["Master"]. Rider, Cincinnati Circus, 1845. This may have been Jean Johnson.

JOHNSON, MISS. Equestrienne, Swann's, NYC, 1794, described as the American Lady. Stuart Thayer credits her as perhaps being the first native female rider to appear with a circus.

JOHNSON, MRS. DORCUS. Scenic rider, Rockwell & Co., 1847.

JOHNSON, N. Ringmaster, National Circus, 1847. May be the entry below.

JOHNSON, NICHOLAS. (d. December 27, 1857) Rider. "Flying wardrobe act," French, Hobby & Co., 1835; rider, Raymond, Weeks & Co., 1844; ringmaster, Welch & Mann, 1846; ringmaster, Welch, Delavan & Nathans, 1848. Made stage debut at the Arch Street Theatre, Philadelphia, June 8, 1844, as Conrad in *Spirit of the Fountain*. Died in the insane asylum, Lexinton, KY.

JOHNSON, ROBERT. Leaper of considerable ability. With John Robinson's was featured by leaping over 12 horses at each performance. Welch & Lent, 1855; L. B. Lent's, 1861-62; Robinson & Howes, 1863; Seth B. Howes', 1864-65; John Robinson's, 1865; Great European, 1865; Chiarini's, Cuba, 1866; Dan Castello's, 1866. Married the equestrienne, **Palmyra Holloway**, 1866. Both with Orrin Bros.', 1867; Lowande's, West Indies, 1866; Maginley, Carroll & Co., 1868; Yankee Robinson's, 1869; Stone & Murray, 1969; Great European, 1870; Noyes' Crescent City, 1871; Great Commonwealth, 1871; ringmaster and sailor act on horseback, Montgomery Queen's, 1874; John Wilson's, Palace Amphitheatre, San Francisco, 1875.

JOHNSON, S. Ringmaster. T. L. Vermule's, 1845; June & Turner, 1846.

JOHNSON, S. M. Treasurer, Showles & Co., 1873.

JOHNSON, VICTORIA. Rider, Dan Rice's, 1852-53.

JOHNSON, W. Slack-rope artist and gymnast, with W. N. Eldred's, 1851; bareback rider, Welch & Lent, 1855-56; John Robinson's, 1857.

JOHNSON, WILLIAM. Master of horse, L. B. Lent's, 1874; clown, North American, 1877; Washburn & Hunting, 1884.

JOHNSON, WILLIAM C. (1802?-February 25, 1872) 4 and 6-horse rider. Born in Connecticut. S. H. Nichols', 1838; J. W. Stocking's, 1839; Howes & Mabie, 1841, 1843; James Raymond's, 1843-44; Nathan A. Howes', winter 1843-44; 2 and 4-horse rider, Rockwell & Co., 1847; advertised as riding 9 horses in the ring at the same time, a feat surpassing Remanzoff, the Courier of St. Petersburg, Howes & Co., 1848-49. Mrs. Johnson was an equestrienne performer. Last year in the profession, 1857, after which, kept a livery stable in Wheeling, WV. Died in Philadelphia, age 70.

JOHNSONBAUGH, HERR. Boss canvasman, with VanAmburgh's, 1874.

JOHNSTON, GEORGE W. See George W. Johnson.

JOHNSTON, JAMES C. Ticket seller, Barnum, Bailey & Hutchinson, 1881.

JOIGNEREY, MONS. P. T. Barnum's, 1874. Closed act by lifting 2 horses while suspended from a trapeze.

JONES, ANNA [Mrs. Anna Donovan]. (July 14, 1865-October 22, 1902) Bearded lady. Born in Marion, VA. Exhibited at Barnum's museum the following year. Her mother would undress her, revealing her hairy shoulders matching her face to the museum patrons. Soon there was a 3-year contract for $150 a week. She was billed as "The Infant Esau," "The Bearded Child," and "The Child Esau." When 16 years old, married circus barker **Richard Elliott**, a union that ended in divorce, 1895, after 15 years. Later married **William Donovan**, a wardrobe man with the Barnum show. Died in Brooklyn, NY, of consumption. Barnum, Bailey & Hutchinson, 1881-82.

JONES, C. A. Band leader, John Robinson's, 1877-78; W. H.

JONES, C. G. Boss of transportation, LaPearl's, 1897.

JONES, CHARLES. Agent, D. F. Dunham's, 1875.

JONES, CHARLES K. Cornetist, Joel E. Warner's, 1873; treasurer, same organization, 1874.

JONES, EDGAR [also seen as J. Edgar]. General performer. Rockwell & Co., 1848; Stone & McCollum, 1849-50; Dan Rice's, 1851; Lathrop-Maltby-Star State, 1852; Whitbeck's, Cuba, 1853; Wire-walker and acrobat, Levy J. North's, 1854; rider and slack-rope performer, Chiarini's, Havana, 1855-59; Howe's European, winter 1864-65.

JONES, F. A. Equestrian. Dan Rice's, 1859-60; George F. Bailey & Co., 1861; horizontal bars, Dan Rice's, 1862.

JONES, FRED. Clown, Lee's Great London, 1893.

JONES, H. Gymnast, First National Union, 1861.

JONES, J. Press agent, Kincade's, 1871.

JONES, J. W. Treasurer, Stickney's Grand National, 1848; proprietor and manager, with Stickney's New Orleans Circus (**Stickney, North & Jones**, proprietors), 1849; treasurer, Harry Thayer & Co.'s, 1890.

JONES, LEON A. Excursion agent, Cooper, Bailey & Co., 1879.

JONES, LEWIS. Boss canvasman, Crescent City, 1871.

JONES, MISS. Equestrienne, Pepin & West, Philadelphia, fall 1817, her debut; James West's, 1818.

JONES, OSCAR. Musical director, C. W. Kidder & Co.'s, 1893.

JONES, RICHARD PATRICK "DR." (August 29, 1826-May 6, 1869) Agent. Born in Philadelphia and educated as a doctor in Philadelphia's College of Medicine. An associate editor for *Scott's Weekly Paper* in that city. First appearance as an actor occurred at the Charles Street Theatre, Baltimore, February 10, 1855; also involved in negro minstrelsy, playing bones and end man. Finally, became a circus writer, continuing the occupation until his death. Wrote for all the circuses of note, beginning with Dan Rice. Is credited with being the one who made the "Forepaugh" name understandable by establishing the trademark "4-Paw" in 1867. Someone said that "no man in the business was better posted in all the little dodges of the profession" than he was. Dan Rice's, 1857-58; Thayer & Noyes, 1863; Robinson & Howes, Chicago, fall 1863; Spalding & Rogers, New Orleans, 1865; Dan Castello's, 1866; Adam Forepaugh's, 1867; director of publication, Bryan's (**John V. O'Brien's**), 1868; J. M. French's, 1869. [Doc Waddell: "Dr. Jones was scholarly, possessed a keen sense of hu-

mor—in short, was a man, every inch of him."] Died in Buffalo from an overdose of laudunum. His wife had just deserted him and taken their child with her.

JONES, SAMUEL H. Press assistant, John Robinson, 1879; business manager, 1881, excursion manager, 1899.

JONES, T. P. Ass't treasurer, P. T. Barnum's, 1875, treasurer, 1876.

JONES, W. G. Aaron Turner's, 1837.

JONES, WILLIAM. Boss canvasman, with John Robinson's, 1871-74, 1877-81.

JONES, WILLIAM. Clown. Canadian by birth. Joined William Blanchard's there, 1826; Samuel Parsons' Albany Circus, Troy, NY, 1828; William Blanchard's, New York State and in the West, 1828. With the latter, 1828, attempted a backward somersault from the top of the ring while performing at Chillicothe, OH; the board gave way and he fell to his death.

JORDAN, JAMES. (September 11, 1844-August 28, 1917) Boss canvasman. Born in Lafayette, IN. Connected with one show or another for 46 years. Started with Sells Bros.', with which he toured Australia; later, S. H. Barrett's, Adam Forepaugh's, John Robinson's, B. E. Wallace's, Hagenbeck's, etc. Retired, 1909, and became a member of the Washington police department. Wife was the former **Mary Buckley** of Washington. Son, **John**, was connected with the Hagenbeck & Wallace show, 1916. Died at Washington, IN.

JORDAN, LEWIS N. and MAMIE. Flying trapeze. Burr Robbins', 1885; Edward Shipp's Winter Circus, 1889-90; Wallace & Co.'s, 1890; European tour, 1892; Koster & Bial's Music Hall, 1896.

JORDON, LUCILLE. Flying trapeze, Wallace & Anderson, 1890.

JORGES, FREDERICO. Cooper, Bailey & Co., Australian tour, 1877-78; gymnast and acrobat, Martinho Lowande's Brazilian Circus, 1881.

JORGES, HOSNEN. Clown, Martinho Lowande's Brazilian Circus, 1881.

JORGES, MARIA. Equilibrist, Martinho Lowande's Brazilian Circus, 1881.

JOSEPH. Singer, Pepin, Breschard & Cayetano, 1813-14; Pepin, Lancaster, summer 1817; Cayetano's, New Orleans, 1817.

JOSEPH, ENOS F. (1857?-August 4, 1910) Born in New Bedford, MA. Connected with Barnum & Bailey as assistant manager and door tender; also worked at Madison Square Garden in a responsible capacity. Committed suicide, fearing he had a brain infection from the use of hair dye. After informing his wife he was going to Johns Hopkins Hospital for treatment, checked into the Central Hotel, Deleware City, DE, registering as Philip Becker, removed all identification from his possessions, and shot himself.

JOSEPH, MME. Cannon ball performer. Born near Mansfield, OH. Married **Mons. Joseph**, Milwaukee, WI, 1878. First appeared in the ring performing her feats of strength, Cooper & Jackson, 1882; John Robinson's, 1883; George DeHaven's, 1884; W. H. Harris' Nickel-Plate, 1884; John Robinson's, 1885. She and her husband played the variety houses around the country until they settled in Hawarden, IA, 1893. Died there April 19, 1896.

JOSEPH, SAMPSON H. (1833?-June 27, 1910) Agent. Worked 40 years as general agent for the John Robinson's. Advertiser, Mike Lipman's, 1866; George W. DeHaven's, 1869; director of publications, Lake's Hippo-Olympiad, 1871; press agent, American Racing Association, 1875; manager advertising car #2, Cooper, Bailey & Co., 1879, special agent, 1880; press agent, Sells Bros.', 1884. Died in Cincinnati, age 77.

JOSEPHS, ENOS. German clown, Barnum, Bailey & Hutchinson, 1882

JOYCE, JAMES E. (1868?-July 17, 1912) Acrobat. Native of Greenwich, NY. Performed on the horizontal bars with many circuses for several years. Sautelle Pavilion Shows, 1885; Lee's London Shows, 1886-88. Later, joined the mounted police force in Washington DC. While on the force, was thrown from a horse, receiving injuries that forced his retirement. Organized a one-ring circus and toured with it until about 1910. Poor health required that he give up the management. Died in Greenwich, age 44.

JOYCE, MAURICE. Contortionist, Wallace & Co., 1884.

JUDD, WILLIAM. Holland & Gormley (**George Holland** and **Frank Gormley**, proprietors), 1888.

JUDGE, JOSEPH. Boy and the barrel act, Wallace & Anderson, 1890; Walter L. Main's, 1892.

JUDSON, PROF. Aeronaut, "Flying Ship of the Air," Great Chicago, 1873.

JUKES, WESLEY L. Automaton mechanical artist. A native of Pittsburgh, met P. T. Barnum, 1870, while a glass blower at Wood's Museum, NYC. A man of unique invention, was placed in charge of devising the mechanical figures, automatic music, and other contrivances of the circus museum. During the next five years he received $250 a week for devoting his efforts to developing and overseeing the maintenance of these various automatons—which in 1871 included the Dying Zouave, "a life-sized figure draped in French Zouave military uniform, breathing and struggling from the effects of the fatal bullet, the wound emitting a stream of warm, red blood"; the Magic Drummer that answered questions in arithmetic, geography, and history; the Sleeping Beauty, "breathing precisely as if alive"; the automatic Trumpeter; lady bell ringers, mechanical birds, "The Last Supper," and much more. P. T. Barnum's, 1876-80.

JULIANS. Gymnasts, P. T. Barnum's, 1886.

JULICK, CORDELIA. (May 2, 1861-June 14, 1916) Born in Butler, KY. Early performing under first name only. Bareback rider with physical endurance and strength. First with Bill Lake's, but jumped to John Robinson's before apprenticeship was finished. With Robinson 5 years where, under his guiding hand she developed into a star quit comparable to both **Josie DeMott** and **Little Mollie Brown**. Remained with Robinson. Was enticed to work for Adam Forepaugh's, 1871. John Robinson responded with a suit against Forepaugh for $48,000 damages, citing an abridgment of her apprentice contract. In reply, the 13 year old Cordelia married **John Morrisey** of Forepaugh's company at Covington, KY, August 11, 1871. Later, was with Chiarini's, South America, where she performed before the King and Queen of Brazil. On returned to USA, beauty gone, performed with minor circuses. Curtis & DeHaven's Great Roman Hippodrome, 1877. Gave up pad riding for the dancing-rope and eked out a meager living until about 1911. She was described as kind, generous, and warm-hearted during the days of her beauty and success in the ring; but, alas, never saved a dollar of her handsome salaries. Before her death she was forced to rely on the charity of others. Died in poverty at the Branch Hospital, Cincinnati, OH.

JUNE, JAMES M. (1809-1862) Brother of **John J.** and **Stebbins B.** and nephew of **Lewis June**. Co-proprietor, June, Titus & Co., 1833; co-proprietor, June, Titus, Angevine & Co.'s menagerie, 1834-42; partner of **Aaron Turner** in enterprise of June & Turner, 1844-48 (the title was advertised as the New York Circus, 1846). Had a show under his own name, 1850-54.

JUNE, JOHN J. (d. February 9, 1884) Brother of **James M.** and **Stebbins B.** and nephew of **Lewis June**. Co-proprietor, June & Titus, 1833; advertiser, Association's Celebrated Menagerie and Aviary from the Zoological Institute, Baltimore, 1837; VanAmburgh's (**Lewis B. Titus**, John June, **Caleb S. Angevine** and **Gerard Crane**, proprietors), 1846-47. Died at North Salem, NY.

JUNE, LEWIS. (February 17, 1791-September 20, 1870) Showman uncle of **John J.**, **Stebbins B.**, and **James M.** June. Married **Betsy Hunt**.

JUNE, LEWIS B. (September 27, 1824-January 12, 1888) Nephew of **John June** of the June, Titus & Angevine circus. Entered the business, 1848, as a cage driver for VanAmburgh's, remaining until 1853, working as advertising agent his last two years. 1854, with Franconi's Hippodrome, NYC; Sands, Lent & Co., 1856; Sands, Nathans & Co., 1857; 1858, in company with others, organized the short-lived Big Bonanza; following year, connected with **George F. Bailey**, **James Foshay** and **A. M. Nathans**, European Circus, remaining until 1872; North American Circus, 1873, touring South America in 2 sections—one under Bailey and June on the Pacific coast, the other under Nathans on the Atlantic; interest in the Barnum show, 1876, remaining until 1880; advertiser, European Circus (Avery Smith, G. C. Quick, John Nathans & Co., proprietors), 1865-69; contracting agent, P. T. Barnum's, 1877-78. Said to be part owner in every show he was connected with since 1859 and was always in charge of the advance brigade. Took out the first advertising car Barnum used, badly wrecked near Des Moines, IA. Of the 13 men with him that day, 7 were killed outright and 5 badly injured. Died at Ridgefield, CT.

JUNE, STEBBINS B. (1811-1861) Brother of **John J. June** and **James M. June** and nephew of **Lewis June**. Co-proprietor, June, Titus & Co., 1833; co-proprietor, June, Titus, Angevine & Co.'s menagerie, 1834; manager, Grand Zoological and Ornithological Exhibition, 1836; American Arena Co., 1837; 1850, along with **George Nutter**, was sent to Ceylon by P. T. Barnum to purchase a herd of elephants; returned to NYC, May 4, 1851, with 9 specimens. Stuart Thayer reports he was the only one of the June family to sign the Zoological Institute agreement, 1835.

JUNE, WILLIAM. Agent. James Raymond's Philadelphia Circus and Menagerie, 1842; June & Turner's, 1847; Yankee Robinson's, 1859.

JUSTICE, J. J. (d. July 8, 1880) Agent, Yankee Robinson, 1855; treasurer, Anthonio Bros.', 1860-62; Howes & Norton (formerly Robinson & Howes), 1864; Dan Rice's (**Adam Forepaugh**, proprietor), 1868; Adam Forepaugh's, 1869; contracting agent, P. T. Barnum's, 1871; manager, George F. Bailey & Co., 1873; general agent, 1874; advertising agent, VanAmburgh's, 1876. Retired around 1879 and became a salesman for Globe Buggy Works, Cincinnati. Home was in Noblesville, IN. Killed himself in the Southern Hotel, Jacksonville, IL, by taking morphine.

JUTAU, EMMA. Gymnast, trapeze performer, with Warner, Henderson & Co., 1874; equilibrimist, Springer's Royal Cirq-Zoolodon, 1875; trapeze performer, Cooper, Bailey & Co., 1876; Howes' Great London, 1877; Renz's, Germany, 1881; Orrin Bros.', Mexico, winter 1882-83; Dockrill's, South America, winter 1885-86.

Anna Jones

K

KAFFEO, HERR. Trick bicycle rider, Adam Forepaugh's, 1887.

KAHBOWLS, MLLE. "Death defying plunge from a 35 foot high table pyramid," "Winged woman of the air," and "Russian Marvel," Adam Forepaugh's, 1885.

KAHN, LEOPOLD. See Admiral Dot.

KANE, G. A. "DR." Agent, Howe's European, 1864; Dan Castello's, 1865; Thayer & Noyes, 1865-66; director of publications, Cooper & Jackson, 1880.

KANE, O. Aaron Turner's, 1849.

KANE, PROF. Band leader, DeMott & Ward, 1868.

KARL BROTHERS. Acrobats, Orrin Bros.', Mexico, winter 1892-93.

KASTNER, OTTO. Contracting agent, with Williams & Co., 1892.

KATHINKA, MME. German giantess, with P. T. Barnum's, 1876.

KATNOCHIN, AWATI [or Awata]. Japanese juggler, with Cooper, Bailey & Co., 1879-80; Barnum, Bailey & Hutchinson, 1881.

KATO. "The human knot," Albert M. Wetter's New Model Shows, 1893.

KATSMOSHIN, PRINCE. Japanese juggler. Great London, 1880; William O'Dale Stevens', Park Square, Boston, 1883.

KAUFFMAN, PROF. Band leader, John O'Brien's, 1871.

KAWANDA, J. T. Wild boy, Walter L. Main's, 1893.

KEANO. Equestrian, Lailson's, Philadelphia, 1797.

KEARNEY, JOE. Clown, Welsh Bros.', 1895.

KEATING, WILLIAM L. Calliope player. Cooper, Bailey & Co., Australian tour, 1876-77; Sells Bros.', 1878; advertising car #1, Cooper, Bailey & Co., 1879; Adam Forepaugh's, 1880-83; S. H. Barrett's, 1885; Adam Forepaugh's, 1886. 1887, his home address was 102 East Tenth Street, Covington, KY.

KEEFE, JOHN [r. n. John Mulligan]. (d. April 5, 1871) Gymnast, aerialist and acrobat. Performed with **William F. Hogle** as his gymnastic partner much of the time. John Robinson's, 1857; Madigan's, 1861; S. P. Stickney's, 1861; Smith & Quick, Villenueva Theatre, Havana, winter 1861-62; Thayer & Noyes, 1862, 1867; Cooke's, winter 1864-65; (with **Burrows**) Quaglieni's Italian Cirque, 1866; Albisu's, Havana, winter 1866-67. Became deranged around 1868 while on tour with **Hogle** in South America but apparently recovered within a few years. Died in Rome, NY.

KEEFER, WILLIAM. Chief bill poster, G. G. Grady's, 1874.

KEEGAN, JOHN. General business agent, Great Combination (**George M. Kelly, Pete** and **John Conklin, William**

LaRue, proprietors), 1871.

KEELER, FRED A. Manager, Melville's Australian Circus, 1864; advertiser, Stone, Rosston and Murray's, 1867; contracting agent, P. T. Barnum's, 1876, conductor advertising department., 1877, 1880; manager, advance car #3, Barnum, Bailey & Hutchinson, 1881.

KEELER, NELLIE. "The Indiana Midget," P. T. Barnum's, 1879-80.

KEELER, S. C. Assistant manager, Maginley & Co., 1874.

KEETCH, ED. Contortion, perch and lofty tumbling, with World's Fair Aggregation, 1892; same year, with **Harry Devere,** assumed ownership of the show and retitled it Devere & Keetch's Colossal Shows and Pyrotechnical Sensation.

KEETING, GUSIE. Jig dancer, J. M. Barry's Great American Circus, 1894.

KEITH, BENJAMIN FOSTER. (d. March 26, 1914) Sideshow and museum operator. Sometimes called "the father of continuous vaudeville." Early career in show business, George Bunnell's Museum, NYC, while still in his teens. Remained with Mr. Bunnell for a year or two. Later, went to the Barnum show, where he remained for a year; 1881, sideshow operator, Adam Forepaugh's; following year, leased a store room in Boston and started in the museum business on a very small scale. Not so many years later, commenced to make history in vaudeville and hall show business and long before his death his name was a household word. At his death he left many millions. Twice married, first, 1873, to **Mary Catherine,** daughter of Charles Branley of Providence, RI. She died, 1910, leaving one son, **Andrew Paul Keith,** who for several years past was associated with his father in the theatrical business. Married again, October 29, 1913, to **Ethel Bird,** daughter of Plymton B. Chase of Akron, OH, and Washington, DC. Died at the Breakers Hotel, Palm Beach, FL.

KEITH, CHARLES. Engish knockabout clown, Batcheller & Doris, 1880.

KELLER, FRED A. Advertising agent, Barnum, Bailey & Hutchinson, 1881.

KELLER. Curiosity. Native of North Carolina. Pepin & Barnet, 1823; Waterman & Co, 1838. Advertised as being 42 years old, 36" in height, double-jointed and "possessing extraordinary strength for his size." Performed on a horse which stood 3' 10" high.

KELLEY. Clown, Lafayette Circus, 1825-26; Page & Harrington, 1826-27; Price & Simpson, 1827; Ben Brown's, January-March 1828; hall show, Boston, June 1828; Providence Circus, September 1828; Martinique, 1830.

KELLEY, GEORGE M. [or Kelly]. (1841-April 4, 1921) Primarily known for his excellent leaping ability, but was also

154

a gymnast, tumbler and musician. A world champion, leaped over 28 horses placed neck to neck. Born at Glenn's Falls, NY. For a few years teamed with **Burrows** for his trapeze work. Beginning 1855, Levi J. North's; Maginley & Van-Vleck, 1863; Robinson & Howes, 1864; Howes', Chicago, winter 1864-65; principal attraction, Thayer & Noyes, 1865-66. While with the latter, was leaping over 12 horses and billed as the greatest in the world. When Thayer & Noyes split their troupe for the winter, 1865, **Kelley** and **Burrows**, under the management of Dr. Thayer, moved by steamboat along the tributaries of the Mississippi. By 1866, had cleared 16 horses placed side by side while completing a single somersault. 1867, a member of an elite corps of performers with the Parisian Circus, assembled for the Paris Exposition (**Avery Smith, G. Quick, John Nathans, Dr. Spalding** and **Bidwell**, proprietors), and was proclaimed "The Champion Vaulter of the World." With both James M. French's and John Robinson's, 1868. For Robinson, threw a somersault from a springboard over 17 horses, August 24, 1868, in Corinth, MS, said to have surpassed all previous attempts of leaping in this country or in Europe. Later, it was claimed he leaped over 20 horses while with John Robinson, spring 1872. Mrs. Charles Warner's,, Philadelphia, winter 1869-70; James Robinson's, 1870; Great Commonwealth, Cuba, 1871; co-proprietor, Commonwealth Circus that traveled by boat (**Conklin Brothers**, George M. Kelley and **William LaRue**, proprietors), 1871; co-proprieter, Klicker & Kelley's Great Monster Circus, Menagerie and Museum (formerly Commnonwealth Circus), 1872; W. W. Cole's, 1875; VanAmburgh's, 1879; Sells Bros.', 1881. Made several trips abroad as well as Cuba and Mexico. Performed before the crowned heads of England, France and Russia. Died at City Hospital, Binghamton, NY, age 80.

KELLEY, JAMES E. See James E. Kelly.

KELLEY, JOHN HENRY [or Kelly]. (1848?-February 6, 1872) Gymnast. Native of Glenn Falls, NY, the brother of **George M. Kelley**. Great Combination Circus (**George M. Kelley, Pete** and **John Conklin, William LaRue**, proprietors), 1871. Died of small pox, Binghampton, NY., age 24.

KELLEY, SAMUEL [or Kelly]. **James Raymond's** son-in-law. Manager, with **Peter Banigan**, Banigan & Kelly's (Raymond & Co.) menagerie, 1847.

KELLEY, THOMAS. Commissary and layer out, P. T. Barnum's, 1876-79, layer out, 1880; layer out and forage agent, Barnum, Bailey & Hutchinson, 1882.

KELLOGG, B. S. Asst't treasurer, P. T. Barnum's Roman Hippodrome, 1874-75.

KELLY, B. Rider, Aaron Turner's, 1837; Clayton, Bartlett & Welch, 1840.

KELLY, FRANCIS. See Frank Lee.

KELLY, GEORGE M. See George M. Kelley.

KELLY, J. Boss canvasman, John Robinson's, 1893.

KELLY, JAMES. Agent, treasurer and business manager,

George H. Adams'; Adam Forepaugh's, 1884; press and general agent, Pullman, Dingess & Co., 1885.

KELLY, JAMES E. [or Kelley]. (April 8, 1827-December 27, 1892) Born at Carmel, Putnam County, NY. On leaving school, went into the banking business with Drew, Robinson & Co., Wall Street, NYC, and remained with that house for several years. Married a daughter (or perhaps the niece) of **Daniel Drew**. Was a prosperous banker in home town of Brewster, NY. Later was reduced to penury when his cashier embezelled funds and ran off to Africa to fight the Zulus. With **Hyatt Frost**, 1856, purchased the **James Raymond** menagerie, including the elephant Hannibal, which had been used in a 4-elephant hitch for the menagerie bandwagon. Bought out Gregory's interest in VanAmburgh & Co., 1861; bought Hyatt Frost's interest, 1868, to become the firm's largest stock holder. 1871, bought interest in Howes' Great London Circus. Shortly thereafter sold his interest in the VanAmburgh show to Hyatt Frost. Selected **Henry Barnum** to manage, 1874, who purchased a 10th interest and operated the show until 1877. Debt, caused by economic conditions in the country, forced them to put the show up for sale, January 29, 1877, which brought $65,000. The new owners were **John Parks** and **Richard Dockrill**. Kelly retired to Drewville, NY. Died at his residence, age 66.

KELLY, JOHN. Lake's Hippo-Olypiad, January 1868.

KELLY, JOHN HENRY. See John Henry Kelley.

KELLY, MICKEY. See James Hernandez.

KELLY, SAM. See Sam Kelley.

KELLY, WILLIAM. Boss canvasman, Adam Forepaugh's, 1889.

KELLY, WILLIAM A. Agent, Kelly, Leon & Wilson, 1870.

KELSEY, HATTIE. Equestrienne, with Walter B. Aymar's, South America, early 1870s; troupe returned to the United States, 1875, and performed at Bidwell's Acadamy of Music, New Orleans.

KELSEY, MEADE. Maginley & Bell, 1864.

KELSH, FRANCIS M. [Frank]. (September 2 or 7, 1822-July 20, 1890) Stone, Rosston & Co., 1866; manager, Stone, Rosston & Murray, Front Street Theatre, Baltimore, winter 1866-67; manager, Adam Forepaugh's, 1867; treasurer, L. B. Lent's, 1869, 1872, railroad agent, 1874; general agent, D. W. Stone's, 1878; excursion agent, P. T. Barnum's, 1879, railroad contractor, 1880; advertising manager, John B. Doris', 1883-84; railroad contractor, VanAmburgh, Charles Reich & Bros.', 1885; special agent, Frank A. Robbins', 1889. A lifelong friendship with agent **Charles H. Castle** created the designation of "The Two Orphans." Kelsh was the better educated and more polished. Agent Charles H. Day wrote that Kelsh had a "most eloquent gift of convincing gab."

KEMMER BROTHERS [3]. Trapeze, perch, and juggling, Bailey & Winan, 1890.

KEMP, WILLIAM H. (1817-April 8, 1891) Clown, from

Birmingham, England. Specialties were pantomime and globe and barrel feats—"walks on crutches nine feet high" and "presents a pantomime of the 'Harlequin's Frolics, or Mistakes of the Night.'" First appeared in America, 1846, John Tryon's, Bowery Amphitheatre, NYC; followed with engagements with Welch & Mann, Philadelphia, 1846; Howes & Co., 1847-48; Franklin Theatre, NYC, 1848; Crane & Co., 1849; James M. June & Co., 1850; Nixon & Kemp, 1857-58. Married to **Marian McCarthy**. Subsequently, became a leading gold-leaf manufacturer. Died in NYC.

KENDALL, EDWARD "NED." (March 20, 1808-October 28, 1861) Band leader from Newport, RI, called "The Magic Bugler," being the first virtuoso of the keyed bugle. Made musical debut in Boston, 1825. 1830, member of the orchestra, Boston's Tremont Theatre. Bugler and band leader, John Sears', 1832; still with the organization when the management came under **Thomas Tufts, Hiram Waring** and **E. Waring**—Waring, Tufts & Co, 1834; organized the Boston Brass Band, 1835, one of the first in America; Palmer's, 1835; Purdy, Welch, Macomber & Co., 1837; S. H. Nichols', 1840-42; Dr. Gilbert R. Spalding's, 1842, 1847-48; Spalding & Rogers, 1854-56; Nixon & Kemp, 1858. Died of consumption, Boston, MS.

KENDALL, EDWARD. (d. December 13, 1918) Agent and business manager. Married to **Ruby Marion**, a burlesque actress. Died in Brooklyn, NY, age 68.

KENDALL, E. P. General agent, Driesbach & Howes, 1868.

KENDALL, NED. Agent, not to be confused with the band leader of that name. [Charles H. Day: He "was one of the greatest advance agents that ever piloted a show in this or any other country. He was what used to be called 'a working agent'; could put up a stand of bills and delighted to do it, knew the country to a dot, wrote with fluency, and had a legion of friends. Ned Kendall could inject about as much wormwood into a paragraph as any man that ever put a pen to paper."]

KENN, DAN. Band leader, Nixon's, 1870.

KENNARD BROTHERS [Charles, Edwin]. Knockabout clowns. Shield's, 1888; W. H. Harris' Nickel-Plate, 1889-91; Sells Bros.', 1895; Charles Barnum's, 1904; Hippodrome, 1915.

KENNEBEL BROS. [Francois, Joseph, Eugene]. Clowns. Brothers of Mme. **Elise Dockrill**, equestrienne. Montgomery Queen's, 1876-77; Orrin Bros.', Havana, winters 1877-78, 1879-79, 1882-83; Great London, 1878; VanAmburgh's, 1880; Batcheller & Doris, 1880; Cooper, Jackson & Co., 1882; Leon & Dockrill, Iron Amphitheatre, Havana, winter 1881-82; John B. Doris', 1883; Kennebel's Parisian Circus, fall 1885; Shields', 1887. **Joseph** (d. November 27, 1883) performed without words, communicating with his audience through well arranged facial grimaces, oblique nods, finger motions and grotesque attitudes, something new to the American circus. [New York *Sun*, 1872: "He dresses in green with a long point of black hair at each side of his head, and a similar red point in the middle. His face is white and the eyes are shaded with red and a faint black."] He performed a "butterfly act" wherein a large white butterfly was attached to the end of a whip, and while Kennebel tried to catch it with one hand, he jerked it away with the other. Another amusing antic was accomplished by using a "basket horse" as he mimicked the maneuvers of the equestrians. Made debut in USA at Barnum's Hippotheatron, NYC, December 1872; Cooper, Bailey & Co., 1879. Died in Chicago. **Eugene**, also a pantomime clown, Barnum, Bailey & Hutchinson, 1882. **Rose**, mother of the Kennebel family—**Francoise, Eugene, Elise Dockrill**, died in NYC, January 8, 1896.

KENNEBEL, ELLA. Concert, Montgomery Queen's, 1876.

KENNEDY, C. E. Contracting agent, John F. Stowe's, 1892.

KENNEDY, D. A. Ringmaster, Barry & Co., 1879; general agent, Gregory Bros.', 1885; general advance representative, Great American Circus, Museum and Menagerie, 1893.

KENNEDY, DANIEL. Leaper. Orrin Bros.', Havana, winter 1878-79; W. W. Cole's, 1880-81.

KENNEDY, D. R. Treasurer, Cooper & Co., 1874.

KENNEDY, JAMES O. Singing clown, Harry Thayer & Co.'s, 1890.

KENNEDY, J. R. In charge of one of the advertising cars for Barnum & Bailey for 7 seasons. Also agent, Cooper & Jackson, 1880; general agent, O'Brien, Handenberger, Astley & Lowanda, 1884; advertiser, Walter L. Main's, 1893; general agent, Cole & Lockwood, 1894.

KENNEDY, R. S. Rider. Dan Rice's, 1848; Col. Mann's, 1849; ringmaster, H. M. Smith's, 1856; Orton's, 1857; ringmaster, Mabie's, 1858.

KENNEDY, W. Rider, Quick, Sands & Co., Baltimore, 1833.

KENNEDY, WILLIAM ["Billy"]. Clown, Sands & Quick, 1852-55; Levi J. North's, 1855-56; ringmaster, L. B. Lent's, 1859-60; Cooke & Robinson, 1861; L. B. Lent's, 1862; George F. Bailey & Co., 1866; James M. Nixon's, 1870; Howes' Great London, 1876.

KENNEDY, WILLIAM B. "POP." (1830?-August 1, 1906) Born in NYC. Originally a jig dancer, having danced matches with John Diamond. Joined a circus sideshow as a singing clown. Sands & Nathans', performed with **Tony Pastor**. The two were later associated with the Bowery Amphitheatre Co., NYC. In Pastor's employ for over 30 years, in later years being on the Pastor Theatre's door. Died of pneumonia, NYC, age 76. Gymnast and rider, Dan Rice's, 1849; Levi J. North's, 1855; ringmaster, Mabie's, 1858-59; clown, L. B. Lent's, 1861-62; Howard's Athenaeum, Boston, Goodwin & Wilder, winter 1861; Brien's, 1863; clown, Mrs. Charles Warner's, 1864; Stone, Rosston & Co., 1864; S. O. Wheeler's, Boston, winter 1864-65; Palmer's, 1865; George Bailey & Co., 1866; Lee & Ryland, San Francisco, 1867; Dan Rice's, 1868; James

Robinson's, 1870.

KENSHAW, JAMES. General performer, with L. B. Lent's, 1861.

KENT, CARRIE. "The only lady living who slides from the dome of the canvas to the ground suspended by the hair," Martell's Great Consolidated Shows, 1884.

KENT, JULIAN [or Julien, Jule]. Clown. Dan Rice's, 1852, 1859; Madigan's, 1861; Cremorne Gardens (formerly Palace Gardens), NYC, spring and summer 1862; Adam Forepaugh's, 1866; Dan Castello's, 1870; Leihy, Lake & Co., 1870; L. B. Lent's, 1871-72; James Robinson's, 1872; Cooper and Bailey, 1875; Great Roman Hippodrome, 1877.

KENYON, CHARLES. (1845?-July 20, 1892) With his trick horse Ingomar, Philadelphia Circus, winter 1867-68; with his trick horse Ingomar, Gardner, Kenyon & Robinson, 1869; equestrian director, Handenburger & Co., 1871; Adam Forepaugh's, 1873; equestrian director, Cooper and Bailey, 1875. Married to **Eliza Gardner**, daughter of **Dan** and **Camilla Gardner**. Two daughters, **Ella** and **Minnie**, were stage performers. Died in Peoria, IL, age 47.

KERNAN, JOHN. Leaper and tumbler, Adam Forepaugh's, 1880.

KERNELL, JOHN. The Pinafore Concert Co., Adam Forepaugh's, 1879.

KERPEN, HERR WILLIAM. Bearded man, VanAmburgh & Co., 1872; museum director, Maginley & Co., 1874.

KERR, CLARENCE. Boss canvasman, Cooper & Co. (**J. R. W. Hennessey**, proprietor and manager), 1897.

KERR, CLEM. Advertising agent, Cooper & Co. (**J. R. W. Hennessey**, proprietor and manager), 1897.

KERRIGAN, CHARLES. Cooke's, Tenth and Callowbill Streets, Philadelphia, January 1868.

KETCHUM, FRANK. Candy privilege (with **Tom Burk**), Great Western, 1876.

KEYES, DANIEL. Thayer & Noyes, 1866.

KEYES, LIZZIE [or Keys, Lizzie LaSchaller]. Equestrienne. Howe's Great London, 1871; forward and backward principal act, L. B. Lent's, winter 1871-72; John H. Murray's, 1872; Joel E. Warner & Co., 1873; W. W. Cole's, 1874; Hengler's, England, 1875; Melville, Maginley & Cooke, 1875; Allen's Great Eastern, 1879; Stickney's Imperial Parisian Circus, 1880; Robinson & Myers, 1883; Washburn & Hunting, 1884. Married clown **D. A. Seal**.

KEYS, HARRY. Gymnast, John Robinson's, 1857, 1859-60; 1861-62.

KEYS, J. S. 2 and 4-horse rider, equestrian manager, M. O'Conner's, 1870.

KEYSER, LAURA S. See Louise Montague.

KIBBLE, WILLIAM. 2-horse carrying and 4-horse act, L. W. Washburn's, 1895-96.

KICHI, FUDI. Barrel kicking, high-wire, and Japanese slide, Robert Hunting's, 1894.

KICHI, KAMA. Contortionist and flying perch, Robert Hunting's, 1894.

KIDDER, CHARLES W. Assistant manager, Hemmings, Cooper & Whitby, 1869. Married **Miss Kate Heidler** in Xenia, OH, February 17, 1870, and left the circus business that year to open a confectionary store in Xenia with his father-in-law, **J. W. Heidler.** Apparently the arrangement did not work out, for was back as advance agent with James T. Johnson & Co., 1870; assistant manager, James E. Cooper's, 1872; general agent, A. B. Rothcilds & Co., 1875; asst. mgr., Cooper, Bailey & Co., 1876; contracting agent, VanAmburgh & Co., 1877-83; Fannie Mountcastle Dramatic Co., winter 1884-85; advertising car, Creston Show, 1886; general advance agent, William Main & Co., 1889; Main & Sargeant, 1890-91; Kidder & Co., 1893.

KIDWELL, WASH. Former steamboat engineer who went into circus business with **Charles Castle** and **Harry Whitbeck**, 1853, to form Whitbeck & Co., with Mme. Tourniaire, the greatest female bareback rider of her time, as the star attraction; show performed in a 110' round top and traveled by steamboat along the Ohio River and tributaries, but lasted only one year.

KIELEY, F. Whittemore, Thompson & Co., 1865.

KIELEY, JOHNNY. Banjoist, Whitmore & Co., 1868.

KIMBALL, C. T. Contracting agent, W. W. Cole's, 1873; Burr Robbins', 1874-85; contracting agent, Robbins & Colvin, 1881; United States Circus, 1882; advance agent, Holland & Gormley, 1888-90; general agent and contractor, Holland, Bowman & McLaughlin, 1890.

KINCADE, ARTHUR. Wallace & Co. (**Ben F. Wallace** and **James Anderson**, proprietors), 1885.

KINCADE BROTHERS [Edward, George, James, Frederick]. Gymnasts, VanAmburgh & Co. 1871. Also had their own show out that year, Kincade's Circus.

KINCADE, D. H. Robinson & Deery's, 1864.

KINCADE, EDWARD. Rider, J. J. Hall's, West Indies, 1837; Clayton, Bartlett & Welch, 1840; Welch & Delavan, 1841; acrobat, Welch & Mann, 1843-44; Great Western, 1847; S. P. Stickney's, 1847. Killed in Caracus, South America, about 1862.

KINCADE, HENRY A. [sometimes Kincaide]. Rider and acrobat. Born in Madrid of a father who was a well known circus manager in Spain. Migrated to Mexico early in his career where, in Mexico City, managed a circus company. During the Mexico-American War, the government confiscated his show, putting the horses and the company into the army. Kincade escaped to the American lines and into the hands of Gen. Taylor. Was subsequently paroled and sent to NYC where he made his American deput at the Bowery Amphitheatre under the management of **Richard Sands**. He sired a family of performers, **James, George, John, William** and **Katy**—riders, vaulters, tumblers, acrobats, and gymnasts. As a posturer, general performer and equestrian director, was connected with Caldwell's Occidental, 1867-68; S. O. Wheeler's Circus, 1868; Alex Robinson's, 1869; Great Australian, 1870; VanAmburg & Co., 1871; P. A. Older's, 1872; J. M. Carrington's, 1874; Hamilton & Sargeant, 1879; George S. Cole's, 1881. Died of gangrene poisoning, 1882, the result of an accidental injury to his foot. Was 63 years of age and had spent 51 years in the circus business.

KINCADE, HARRY [r. n. William Burt]. (d. October 2, 1881) Gymnast. Half-brother of **Samuel Burt**. Died in Pulaski, TN, with Shelby, Pullman & Hamilton, where during a performance, September 29, he failed to complete a double somersault, causing a concussion of the spinal cord.

KINCADE, JAMES. Equestrian. Bareback rider, VanAmburgh & Co.'s northern, 1859; Sells Bros.' 1879; Shelby, Pullman & Hamilton, 1881; Miles Orton's, 1882; John Robinson's, 1882; S. H. Barrett & Co., 1883; Wallace & Co., 1884-85; principal somersault act, McMahon's, 1888; F. J. Taylor's, 1892; Adam Forepaugh's, 1893; Sig. Sautelle's, 1896-97.

KINCADE, WILLIAM [sometimes Kincaid]. (d. December 27, 1868) Rider and acrobat. Pupil of **J. J. Nathans**. Clayton, Bartlett & Welch, 1840; eastern unit, June, Titus, Angevine & Co., 1842; acrobat, Welch & Mann, 1843-44; Mann, Welch & Delavan, 1844-46; Rockwell & Stone, 1846; Indian act, Robinson & Eldred, 1847-49; Welch & Lent, 1854; Spalding & Rogers, 1855; Welch & Lent, 1856; L. B. Lent's, 1858; Dan Rice's, winter 1858; Welch's, Philadelphia, 1859; VanAmburgh & Co., 1859; Mabie's, 1862; acrobat, Hippotheatron, 14th Street, NYC, winter 1863-64; Howes' European, winter 1864; Mrs. Charles Warner's, Continental Theatre, Philadelphia, winter 1864-65; George F. Bailey & Co., 1866-67. Died of consumption in Baltimore.

KINCADE, WILLIAM. Cooper & Jackson, 1880; Robbins & Colvin, 1881.

KING, ANDREW, N. (1843-January 7, 1890) Acrobat and showman. Born in Galveston, TX. Apprenticed into the circus business at the age of 10. Upon developing skills, took a partner and performed as **Aubrey & King**. Described as being small in stature, solidly built, with dark complexion and mustache. Said to be the first in the country to do the head to hand somersault. Injuries received from a fall put an end to **King's** career as a performer. Took the program privileges with Adam Forepaugh's for 5 or 6 years. Married **Alida McGee**, sister of actor **J. W. McGee** around 1880. About 1882, became associated with the circus of King, Burke & Co. When Burke retired, **W. E. Franklin** became a partner and the firm took the title of King & Franklin. Franklin went ahead of the show and King managed the day to day operation until his death in London, England.

KING, BERTIE. The equestrienne wife of **Charles King**. Springer's Royal Cirq-Zoolodon, 1875. See Charles King.

KING, BILLY. Concert banjo player, Great Australian, 1870.

KING BROTHERS. Acrobats. Dan Rice's, 1866; J. H. Shields', winter 1889-90.

KING, CHARLES. 4-horse act and juggling on horseback. A pupil of **Harry Whitby**. Leaper, Brien's (**John V. O'Brien's**), 1863; Mrs. Dan Rice's, 1864; Yankee Robinson's, Chicago, fall 1866; Hemmings, Cooper & Whitby, 1868; James E. Cooper's, 1872; equestrian, Sells Bros.', 1873; Montgomery Queen's, 1874; equestrian, Springer's Royal Cirq-Zoolodon, 1875; equestrian director, A. F. Tuttle's, 1892; advertiser, Irwin Bros.', 1893. Was married to equestrienne **Bertie King**.

KING, CHARLES. Clown, James Robinson's, 1872; clown and Ethiopian comedian, Montgomery Queen's, 1874, 1876; Ethiopian comedian, clown, banjoist, Adam Forepaugh's, 1878. This may or may not be the same performer as above.

KING, DAVID L. Leaper, H. Harlan's, 1875.

KING, DR. Showman who included elements of a circus in 1789, NYC, 28 Wall Street. On exhibition were a male and female ourang outang, a sloth, baboon, monkey, tiger, buffalo, porcupine, crocodile, swordfish, "ant bear," lizard, and a variety of birds.

KING, FLORA [Mrs. Stirk]. Member of the **Stirk Family** act, sister of **Minnie King**, juggler and balancer.

KING, F. W. Equestrian director, the California Circus (Corey & Smith, proprietors), 1880.

KING, GEORGE. (b. April 15, 1838) Acrobat. Born in Philadelphia. Gardner & Hemmings, 1862, Polish Brothers (with **W. W. Hill**), 1863; Robinson & Lake, 1863-64; Gardner & Hemmings, National Hall, Philadelphia, 1865; Front Street Theatre, Baltimore, 1866; Dan Rice's, 1866; Mrs. Charles Warner's, Philadelphia, 1870.

KING, HARRY [and the King family, 4 in number, r. n. Henry C. McMinn]. (1842-1882) Equestrian and gymnast. Born in Philadelphia. Consolidation Circus, 1866; Lake's Hippo-Olympiad, 1867; Philadelphia Circus, winter 1867-68; Gardner, Kenyon & Robinson's, 1869; tumbler and gymnast, E. Stowe's Northwestern, 1871; P. T. Barnum's, 1872-73; rider, Montgomery Queen's, 1873, 1876; equestrian director, A. B. Rothchilds & Co., 1875; equestrian director, Homer Davis', 1879. Died of consumption in Brooklyn, age 39.

KING, HARRY. Aerialist, King & Deverne. Married **Gracie Rentfrow**, daughter of **J. N. Rentfrow**, November 28, 1895, Denver, CO.

KING, HARRY. Treasurer, Collins' Oriental Combination, 1877.

KING, HENRY. Superintendent of the hippodrome, P. T. Barnum's, 1875.

KING, JAMES. Clown, with F. J. Taylor's, 1892; Gollmar Bros.', 1893-95.

KING, JOHN. Boss animal man, John Robinson's, 1875-80. Killed by the elephant Chief, September 27, 1880.

158

KING, JOHN. Boss hostler, Caldwell's Occidental, 1867.

KING, JOHN. Clown, Orton Bros.', 1868; second clown, M. O'Conner & Co., 1869; John Robinson's, 1880.

KING, LIZZIE. Jesse W. Foster's, South America, 1894.

KING, MINNIE. Juggler and balancer, sister of Mrs. Flora Stirk of the Stirk Family.

KING, MME. Bearded lady, Yankee Robinson's, 1866.

KING, PHILLIP. Caldwell's Occidental, 1867.

KING, R. H. Commissary and layer out, P. T. Barnum's, 1877-79, layer out, 1880; layer out and forage agent, Barnum, Bailey & Hutchinson, 1882.

KING, SAMUEL A. ["Prof."]. (1828?-November 3, 1914) Aeronaut, one of the pioneers of balloon ascensians and aeronautic exhibitions. Was present at the Philadelphia Centennial Exhibition, 1876. Traveled with Barnum & Bailey for a year as a free act. During the World's Columbian Exposition, Chicago, 1893, took a woman passenger aloft, whereupon the balloon was blown out over Lake Michigan and both were given up as lost. A revenue cutter was sent to find their remains, but before the boat returned the Professor landed his balloon safely. Died in Philadelphia from heart failure, age 86.

KING, THOMAS. (1832-October 26, 1877) Leaper, rider, and manager. Born in Baltimore. Joined a circus as a boy to become one of the greatest leapers of his day. While performing in California, 1856, leaped 31' 7½" over 9 horses. Robinson & Eldred, Boston, 1852; Rufus Welch, 1852; Meyers & Madigan, 1854-55; Welch & Lent, 1854; Dan Rice's, 1858; took a circus to the Holliday Street Theatre, Baltimore, winter 1858-59; Sloat & Shephard, 1857-59; Woodville Park, Philadelphia, summer 1860; S. P. Stickney's, 1861; L. B. Lent's, fall 1861; flying vaulter, Lent's Hippozoonomadon, 1862; Gardner & Hemmings, 1862-63; Whittaker's Amphitheatre, March 1863; Tom King's Excelsior Circus, 1864; Mrs. Dan Rice's, Philadelphia, 1864; Thayer & Noyes, 1865-66; a split troupe from the Thayer & Noyes organization, under the management of Dr. Thayer, which moved by steamboat along the tributaries of the Mississippi, December 1865; Adam Forepaugh's, 1867, 1870; Mrs. Charles Warner's, Philadelphia, 1869; New National Theatre, Philadelphia, winter 1876-77. Married the equestrienne Virginia A. Myers, daughter of clown and showman James Myers and the former Rose Madigan, at Rhinebeck, NY, May 12, 1859, while with the Joe Pentland Circus. The two worked together throughout most of their married life. King died in Washington, DC. Virginia died on September 3, 1884.

KING, THOMAS. Calliope player, Cooper, Bailey & Co., 1880.

KING, VIRGINIA A. See Virginia A. Myers.

KING, WHIT. Minstrel performer, P. T. Barnum's, 1873.

KING, WILLIAM. Gymnast, Howes', 199 Bowery, NYC, winter 1863-64.

KINGSLEY, OMAR SAMUEL ["Ella Zoyara"]. (1840?-April 3, 1879) Bareback rider. A Creole from Louisiana, who at age 7 began under the tutelage of Spencer Q. Stokes. Had a beautiful face, long dark hair, and a slender form. Story has it that during his youth he was always dressed in feminine attire and caution was taken that his playmates were only girls his own age, developing in him the manners and grace of the female sex. 1852, sailed for England with Stokes' company for an 8 year tour of the continent. With Stokes as mentor, performed in the principal cities of Europe under the names of Ella Stokes and Ella Zoyara and in the guise of an equestrienne. It is said that while in Moscow a Russian count fell madly in love with him; men of nobility in the countries he visits flocked around him, bestowing rich gifts upon him. Created quite a stir at Cooke's Royal Amphitheatre, Niblo's Garden, NYC, 1860, riding bareback dressed as Mlle. Ella Zoyara. The Spirit of the Times, referring to the "Zoyara question of sex," openly chided, "If the person is a man, the humbug is a very dishonest one; if a woman, for the sake of all parties, the point should be settled." Created another stir when in October, 1861, he and Sallie Stickney were quietly married and soon left for California and Australia. After return to USA, 1869, Kingsley procured a divorce and remarried. In later years, abandoned the female attire and took up training horses with success. Managed a circus of his own on the West Coast and was various times in partnership with John Wilson. Around 1876, took the Wilson circus to the Orient. Died of small pox in Bombay, India, age 39. Cooke's Royal Amphitheatre, Niblo's Garden, NYC, 1860; James M. Nixon's, 1860; S. P. Stickney's, 1861; Stokes', 1862-63. Participated in management, Zoyara Equirotator Circus (formerly Stokes), 1863; show collapsed within a matter of weeks and the property was disposed of at public auction in Brooklyn. Chiarini's Circus, Havana, 1864; John Wilson's, San Francisco, June 1864; Wilson & Zoyara's, California, 1865; John Wilson's, Australia and India, 1866-67; equestrian director, Leihy, Lake & Co., 1870; San Francisco Circus and Roman Hippodrome, May 1872; with his trained horse President, John Wilson's, California, 1873; performing horses, John Wilson's Palace Amphitheatre, San Francisco, 1874-75. [Robert Kitchen: "Zoyara's temper tantrums were legendary and were reported by a number of observers. After all he was a star and obviously much spoiled by his mentor."]

KINKADE [or Kincade]. Balloonist. Walt McCafferty's Great Golden Shows, 1894; J. M. Barry's Great American, 1894. [Orin Copple King: Kincade was advertised as making a "perilous descent to earth from an altitude of between 2,500 and 3,000 feet in a flimical (sic) looking umbrella shaped parachute."]

KINNEY, J. Acrobat. Welch & Lent, 1856; L. B. Lent's, 1859.

KINSLOW, JOSEPH H. Band leader, Cooper, Bailey & Co., 1876, 1879.

KIRALFY, IMRE. (1845 or 1848-April 28, 1919) Born in Hungary. At 4 years of age, showing vocal ability, appeared in Weber's *Preciosa*. When the revolution broke out he left with his family for Italy; with the resoration of peace, toured the principal cities of Germany and began a serious study of music. At age 23, began organizing scenic pageants and, after visiting the Paris Exhibition, organized in 1868, at the request of the mayor of Brussels, a colossal public *fête*. The following year, accompanied his parents to the United States, where he remained for 25 years. His first spectacular production was Jules Verne's *Around the World in Eighty Days* at the Academy of Music, NYC. Subsequently, devised many great spectacular stage and open-air productions, beginning with *The Fall of Babylon* at St. George, Staten Island, in which one thousand performers were engaged. This was followed with *Nero and the Burning of Rome*, with 1,500 performers on a mammoth stage, and with dazzling scenic and mechanical effects. In conjunction with **P. T. Barnum**, created the pictorial drama of *Columbus*, 1890, which was developed for the Barnum & Bailey tour, 1892. Went to London, where he presented *Nero* at the Olympia, 1891, and a spectacular and realistic production called *Venice* at the Olympia, 1892. Following year, was induced by **Abbey** and **Grau** to return to Chicago for the creation of a new scenic production for the World's Columbian Exposition, *America*, at the Auditorium Theatre. [M. B. Leavitt: "It was, indeed, a magnificent production throughout, and by far the greatest attraction ever presented upon the boards of any theatre."] The same year, returned to London, reconstructed Earl's Court and became Director-General of the exhibition given there. 1896, followed with another pictorial series of illustrations, *India*, and the following year with *Ceylon*. Another one of a series of great productions was The Victorian Era Exhibitions, 1897; followed by *Greater Britain*, 1899; Woman's International Exhibition, 1900; Military Exhibition, 1901. Was invested with the Royal Order of Leopold as Knight Commander; then became an officer of Public Instruction in France; following as British Commissioner General at the Universal Exhibition in 1906; King of Portugal made him Knight Commander of the Order Villa Vogosa. After this, created and organized the great Franco-British Exhibition at Shepherd's Bush in London; then the Imperial International Exhibition, 1909; the Japan-British Exhibition, 1910; culminating with the Coronation Exhibition, 1912. Was a collector of rare paintings and objects of art, an active member of the Masonic Fraternity, and a grand officer of the Grand Lodge of England. In the early 1870s, married **Miss Marie Graham**, a lady many years his junior, which produced 5 sons and a daughter.

KIRBY, J. Acrobat, John Robinson's, 1886-87, 1891.

KIRBY, JAMES. Clown. Born in England. Made his debut at the Royalty Theatre, London. First appeared in America with Price & Simpson, 1825; following year, was clown with Broadway Circus, NYC. Drowned in Brooklyn, NY, 1826.

KIRBY, PROF. Gymnast, known as "the great American acrobat," appeared with his children for Welch & Mann, Philadelphia, 1847.

KIRK, BOBBIE. G. G. Grady's, 1868.

KIRK, WILLIAM. Yankee Robinson's, Chicago, November 1866.

KIRKHART, FRANK J. [or W. F]. Started a circus, 1893, made three stands and disbanded. Landed at the 1893 Chicago World's Fair in the middle of the season with exactly $150. In short order had $11,000, rented a piece of ground at Captive Balloon Park for $25 a day and bought a new tent, opened a 10¢ circus—a walk-through show—and within 2 weeks had 3 bands and 3 sets of performers operating from 11:00 a.m. to 11:00 p.m. Then acquired the Brazilian Concert Hall next to him and ran that show. Success allowed him to launch a 3-car circus, Kirkhart's World's Fair Circus, 1894-95. Kirkhart & Ryan, 1896.

KIRKPATRICK, MRS. FRANKIE. See Frankie Barry.

KIRK, WILLIAM & SONS. Manufacturers of calliopes until early 1890s, when the business was taken over by Thomas J. Nichol.

KIRKWOOD, WILLIAM. Howes & Norton (formerly Robinson & Howes), 1864.

KITRIDGE, J. J. Treasurer, C. T. Ames', 1868.

KLATZ, C. [or Klutze]. Juggler, John Robinson's, 1882-84, 1887; Burr Robbins', 1886.

KLECKER, CHARLES. Co-proprietor, Klecker & Kelly's (formerly the Commnonwealth Circus), 1872.

KLINE, CHARLES. General performer, Baldwin, Wall & Co.'s Great Eastern, 1880.

KLINE, FRED. Ceiling walker, horizontal bars, tumbler, Cooper & Co., 1874.

KLINE, GEORGE. Antipodean feats and Polandrick ladder, Dan Rice's Paris Pavilion, 1873.

KLINE, GEORGE W. Clown. Cooper, Bailey & Co., 1879-80; leaper, Barnum, Bailey & Hutchinson, 1881, character clown, Roman standing race, Barnum, Bailey & Hutchinson, 1882; Adam Forepaugh's, 1893; with educated mule, Tospy, Sells Bros.', 1894; Milwaukee Mid-Winter Circus, Exposition Music Hall, 1894-95; Edward Shipp's Mid-Winter Circus, Petersburg, IL, winters 1894-95, 1895-95; Howe's London, 1896. Married **Mamie Belmont**, Boston, June 19, 1886, while with Adam Forepaugh's.

KLINE, H. S. O. Wheeler's, 1867.

KLINE, LEWIS. Gymnast. Rivers & Derious, 1864; Alex Robinson's, 1866; (with **H. W. Penny**) performed on the trapeze and horizontal bars as the **Delevanti Brothers**, Dan Rice's, 1868; S. P. Stickney's, 1869; James M. Nixon's Parisian Hippodrome and Chicago Amphitheatre, May 1872.

KLINE, MAMIE. *Manège*, Sells Bros.', 1895. Married **George W. Kline**, Boston, June 19, 1886, while with Adam

Forepaugh's.

KLING, FRED. Beckett's, 1881; Downie & Gallagher, 1892-93.

KLUTZE, C. See C. Klatz.

KNAPP, GEORGE O. (1840-April 27, 1875) Clown and general performer. Began career as clown with Edward Eldred's, 1834; followed by engagements with Buckley, Weeks & Co., 1835; Boston Lion Circus, 1836; Lion Theatre Circus, 1837; S. H. Nichols', 1838-43; Thomas Taplin Cooke's, 1838; Dr. Gilbert R. Spalding's, 1842-48; Welch & Delevan, 1849; Spalding & Rogers, 1850-51; Washburn's, 1855; Flagg & Aymar, 1856; Antonio & Carroll, 1857; Antonio & Wilder, 1858; Davis & Crosby, 1859. Around 1859, became an agent for M. B. Leavitt's theatrical company. 1866, agent, E. S. Washburn's hall show, Washburn's Last Sensation, and continued in that capacity until 1872. [E. S. Washburne: "During the time he was with me his life was spotless, and the greatest tribute I can pay his memory is to say that he was an honest man."] Last engagement, agent with Sam Cole's North American Circus and Balloon Show, 1875. Died in St. Luke's Hospital, NYC, as a result of cancer surgery. He left a widow and 2 children in a state of destitution.

KNAPP, HARRY A. "YANKEE." Clown, agent. Spalding & Rogers, 1850; John Robinson's, 1857, contracting agent for that show, 1871-72; 1876, 1879; Batcheller & Doris, 1880; Canfield, Booker & Lamont's "Humpty Dumpty" Company, 1880-81, 1881-82; Great Interior Circus, 1882; Cory Delmay Burlesque Company, and Piper's "Uncle Tom's Cabin" Co., 1882-83; Hans' Pavilion Show, 1883; Cooper, Jackson & Co., 1884; Robinson, French & Co., 1884-85; VanAmburgh's, 1885; Donaldson & Rich, 1885; Shields Great Southern, 1885-86; Beckett's Hippodrome, 1886; Holland & McMahon, 1886-87; Forepaugh & Samwell's, 1887; John Robinson's, 1888; Burr Robbins', 1889; Ringling Bros.', 1890-91; Taylor & Co., 1892; Chicago World's Fair, 1893; Wood Bros.', 1894. Was found dead in a chair in his room in the house of the Rough and Ready Engine Co. of Greenwich, NY, June 30, 1899, age about 55. He had been an inmate of an institution connected with this fire fighting unit.

KNAPP, HARRISON BAILEY. (d. September 14, 1895) Advertiser. VanAmburgh, Charles Reich & Bros.', 1885; advertising director, Frank A. Robbins', 1890. Died in NYC from Bright's disease.

KNEELAND, F. Negro minstrel, Spalding & Rogers' *Floating Palace*, 1859.

KNIGHT. Clown. Native of Georgia. Asa Smith's, 1828; the Yeaman Circus, 1831.

KNIGHT, FRED. (b. September 6, 1844) Began as animal handler with the VanAmburgh Golden Menagerie, 1865. Elephant handler, Adam Forepaugh's, 1879; performing elephants, Shelby, Pullman & Hamilton, 1881. Married **Della Cook**, dancer and bareback rider. While working at Frank

Talbott's Hippodrome, St. Louis, MO, fell and sustained a broken hip which ended his career and forced the Knights to spent all of their savings on doctor bills.

KNOLTON, DELL. Clown. O. J. Ferguson's, 1884; W. H. Harris' Nickel-Plate, 1886.

KNOTT, DON. Contracting agent, Miles Orton's, 1892.

KNOTT, GEORGE P. Agent. Began in the circus business, 1853, with Spalding & Rogers. Subsequently, connected with John Robinson's, VanAmburgh & Co., Dan Rice's, Thayer & Noyes, G. G. Grady's, Dan Castello's; Hemmings, Cooper & Whitby; Cooper & Bailey, and Barnum & Bailey. Manager of advertising car #1, Wallace & Anderson, 1890; Albert M. Wetter's New Model Shows, 1893, but left the show early.

KNOUTH, FRED. Aerialist, Gollmar Bros.', 1897.

KNOUTH, WILL. Pantomime clown, Gollmar Bros.', 1897.

KNUPP, EDWARD C. Agent, Walter L. Main's, 1895-96; general agent, Cole Bros.', 1909; assistant to Wallace, Hagenbeck & Wallace, 1910.

KODAKS [3]. Brother act, Robert Hunting's, 1894.

KOHL, C. E. Sideshow manager, Barnum, Bailey & Hutchinson, 1881. Formed a partnerhip with **George Middleton**, 1884, and opened a museum in Chicago, Clark Street near Madison. At one time Middleton and Kohl had 8 museums operating in the Midwest. In later years owned a number of Chicago theatres, including the Majestic, Olympic, Haymarket, and Chicago Opera House. Kohl and Middleton were the first to introduce continuous vaudeville to Chicago.

KOHL, EDWARD C. Asst. agent for Barnum autobiography, P. T. Barnum's, 1873; assistant to **James L. Hutchinson**, privileges, VanAmburgh & Co., 1876; sideshow manager and orator, Cooper, Bailey & Co., 1880; concert manager, Barnum, Bailey & Hutchinson, 1881.

KOHLAND, A. S. Director of publications, W. H. Harris' Nickel-Plate, 1886; contracting agent, Stowe Bros.', 1889; Sells & Rentfrow, 1894; railroad contractor, Walter L. Main's, 1896. Later, did newspaper work in Salt Lake City, UT, and Leadville and Cripple Creek, CO. Died in Cripple Creek, May 1900.

KOHN, OSCAR. Trainer of hippopotamus, P. T. Barnum's, 1876-77.

KOPP, E. H. Solo cornetist, VanAmburgh & Co., 1877.

KOPP, F. A. Orchestra leader, VanAmburgh & Co., 1877.

KOPP, PROF. S. F. Band leader, Joe Pentland's, 1856; Sloat & Shepard, 1857; Nixon & Co., 1860; Melville's Australian, 1864; VanAmburgh & Co., 1868, 1874; Empire City, 1871; VanAmburgh & Co., 1877.

KOUNZE, L. Leaper, John Robinson's, 1877-78.

KRAMER, SALLIE. Gymnast, John Robinson's, 1888-89.

KRAO "The Missing Link." Purported to have been found in the jungles of Laos by **Carl Bock** and developed as an attraction by **Signor G. A. Farini**, who for advertising purposes suggested she might be the "link" in Darwin's theory. Advertised as having "prehensile feet, pouches, hair over most of her body and other simian characteristics." Was for years the leading feature at the London Aquarium. **Charles H. Day**, offering a large advance cash guarantee through **Robert Filkins**, Farani's American agent, brought her to the United States and exhibited her at the Chestnut Street Museum, Philadelphia, 1884. Following year, was with John B. Doris'. Continued to be on exhibition as late as 1917, when she was with Ringling Bros.' sideshow. Developed into a well educated woman, capable of speaking several languages. [Barry Gray: "Krao is one of the most interesting as well as highest salaried anomalies in the world.... Her good traits are many; her bad ones none.... Kind, gentle, charitable, thoroughly educated and loyal always to her friends and employers."] John B. Doris', 1885; Barnum & Bailey, 1906-14.

KRIGH, PHILLIP. Fat man, known as "Indiana's 700 Pound Man." Over 6' tall and his weight often reached 775 pounds. Died in Stilesville, IN, August 22, 1905.

KRUZE, LOU. Juggler, John Robinson's, 1879.

Jerry Mabie

L

LA BELLA ISABELLA. Equestrienne, George F. Bailey & Co., 1859.

LA BELLE IRENE. See Mrs. Irene Woodward.

LACHELLE, FRED. Business manager, Hendry's New London Shows, 1892.

LACOMPE BROTHERS [George, Edward, Lou]. Brother act, Harry Thayer & Co.'s, 1890.

LA CONTA. Vaulter, Pepin & Breschard, 1810-14; clown, Cayetano's, NYC, summer 1812; Pepin & Breschard, 1813, leaped over 8 horses; rider, Langley & Co., Charleston, winter/spring 1813-14; accompanied Breschard to Savannah in the latter part of 1814; Cayetano, Cincinnati and other western cities, 1814-16, the latter year leaped over 24 men with muskets and fixed bayonets. By 1817, had disappeared from view but apparently resurfaced with Price & Simpson, 1825. Mount Pitt Circus, NYC, winter 1827-28; Brown & Co., 1836. In addition to clowning, performed a trampoline act, vaulted over men and horses, also, as advertised, a flying somersaulted over 5 horses and through a flaming balloon. Then, in 1816, it was claimed he was leaping over 24 men with muskets and fixed bayonets.

LA COSTE, JULIE. General performer, Rivers & Derious, 1864.

LA COTON, JOHNNIE. Variety troupe, Haight & Chambers, 1867.

LADELLE, MONS. Equestrian director, Hart, France & Co., 1889.

LA FAVRE, MILLIE. Gymnast, Robbins & Colvin, 1881; John V. O'Briens, 1885..

LA FOREST, CHARLES. Equestrian. A pupil of **Samuel Tatnall** and later a celebrated rider, performing in the early circuses and equestrian dramas beginning in the 1820s. Price & Simpson, 1823-24; Washington Gardens, Boston, spring 1825; Lafayette Amphitheatre, NYC, 1825-26; Mount Pitt Circus, NYC, winter 1826-27, winter 1827-28; Washington Gardens, Boston, summer 1827; Handy & Welch, 1830; Boston Lion Circus, 1836; winter circus at Richmond Hill, NYC, 1837; Lion Theatre Circus, 1837; Philadelphia Circus, 1840; Hobby & Pratt, 1842; Ogden & Hobby, 1842; Charles LaForest's Equestrian Co., 1842; Stickney & Buckley, 1844. Married singer **Sophie Eberle**, 1828 (singer with the Lion Theatre Circus, 1837).

LA GOROUX. Barrel performer and South American juggler, Rosston, Springer & Henderson, 1872.

LA GRANDE, MAUD. Female Sampson and slack wire performer, Washington Bros.', 1887.

LA GRANGE, CHARLES. Whitmore, Thompson & Co., 1865.

LA GRANGE, MONS. Elephant trainer, Sands & Nathans, 1857.

LA GRANVILLE, MME. See Millie DeGranville.

LAIDLY, ROBERT. Equestrian actor, born to the tailor's trade in Philadelphia. At maturity, was tall and muscular but was cursed with an ungraceful hump on his shoulders; gifted with a powerful set of lungs and a nack for histrionics. Rose to the position of leading hero in the horse pieces. Pepin & West, Olympic, Philadelphia, fall 1817; James West's, 1818; Olympic circus, Philadelphia, 1822; Simpson & Price, C Street Circus, Washington, winter 1822-23.

LAILSON, PHILIP. Rider. A Frenchman who brought a circus company to America in the 1790s with one of the finest stud of horses to be seen in this country for some time to come and a troupe of 14, including 2 women and a 5 year old child. Company landed at Newport, RI, July 1796, and opened in Boston, August 11. The splendid and well-appointed double troupe of French entertainers opened in Philadelphia, April 8, 1797. In the company were **Langley, Sully, Herman, McDonald, Vandervelde, Keano**, and **Miss Vanice**, the first female equestrienne to perform in America. Was his own principal rider and vaulter on horseback. The company began performances in Alexandria, VA, at the upper end of King Street, September 5, 1797. From there, moved to NYC, opening in a new building in Greenwich Street from December 5, 1897 to February 1, 1898, the stand being, presumably, a failure. Then returned to Philadelphia and performed from March 8, 1798, to July 8, 1798. A month later, because of bad construction, the immense dome of the building gave way and fell to the ground crushing the interior completely. Financial loss required the equipment and horses to be sold off. After performing in the USA, Lailson went to the West Indies and was last heard of, 1809, Mexico. An interesting feature of Lailson's company was the daily parade through the streets to advertise the show, considered the first of any known street parade in America. Stuart Thayer defines it as Lailson's main contribution to the American circus.

LAINE, J. H. (b. May 10, 1839) Agent. Born in New Brunswick, NJ. Became a member of advance brigade for Sands, Nathans, & Co., 1860; connected in a similar capacity with Sands, Rivers & Derious, H. Madigan's, Joe Pentland's, James Nixon's, and Stone, Rosston & Murray until 1866; in advance of Yankee Robinson's, 1869, and assistant manager of it, 1870; subsequently, advance agent for LaRue's Minstrels, Charley Shay's Quincuplexal (5 seasons), Duprez & Benedict's Minstrels, Carncross & Dixey's Minstrels, and one or two dramatic companies. For a time, was business manager, Seventh Street Theatre, Philadelphia; treasurer for the Thirty-fourth Street Theatre, NYC; treasurer for Dean, Pell & Co.'s Circus. 1876, appointed traveling passenger agent for the Pennsylvania Railroad but resigned after a year to go in advance of Emerson's California Minstrels under management of Haverly and Maguire. Next organized a concert and specialty company which he put on the road for a short time. 1877-79, ahead of Barlow, Wilson, Primrose & West's Minstrels; Allen's Great Eastern, 1880.

LAINE, W. Welch & Lent, 1854.

LAIR, GEORGE. Gymnast. Claimed to be one of the original **Leotard Brothers**, with **George Bliss** and **Lewis Mette**. Acrobats, P. T. Barnum's, 1877; Cooper, Bailey & Co., 1880.

LAISCELLE, LYMAN. Gymnast, with Burr Robbins, 1880; Robbins & Colvin, 1881.

LAISCELLE, WILLIAM L. Gymnast, Robbins & Colvin, 1881; Barnum & London, 1885.

LAISCELLE, VICTOR. Leaping and tumbling, Adam Forepaugh's, 1880-81.

LAKE, AGNES [nee Mersman]. (August 23, 1826-August 22, 1907) Equestrienne, tight rope walker, showwoman. Born in Doehm, Alsace, and brought to America by her parents, 1829. While only 16, eloped with clown **William T. Lake**, of the Robinson & Foster Circus. Arriving at St. Louis to find that neither a clergy or justice of the peace would perform the ceremony, they continued on to New Orleans and subsequently to Lafayette, LA, where they were wedded. With her husband, performed with Rich's for 2 years; with Rockwell & Co., 1848; Stokes', 1849; Burgess', 1850; followed by 7 seasons with Spalding & Rogers' *Floating Palace*. Nixon & Kemp, Palace Gardens, Sixth Ave. and 14th St., NYC, fall 1858. 1859, "Bill" Lake went into partnership with John Robinson, a union which lasted 4 years; then took out the William Lake Circus. Fall, 1862, Agnes went to Germany and appeared in a number of continental cities in the horse drama *Mazeppa*. Following spring, was back with her husband's circus, where she remained until his tragic death, 1869. Continued management under the title of Lake's Hippo-Olympiad and Mammoth Circus until 1872. That season, was out with the Great Eastern (**Dan Carpenter, R. E. J. Miles, Andrew Haight, George DeHaven**, proprietors). Following, retired from the circus to operate a printing plant in Cincinnati; the venture was unsuccessful lost her her savings within a year's time. James Butler "Wild Bill" Hickok had seen a circus performance, July 31, 1871, when the show was exhibiting in Cheyenne, WY, and was "smitten" with Agnes. After courting her for 4 years, the two were married in Cheyenne, March 5, 1876. Shortly after the wedding, Agnes went to Cincinnati to visit her parents, while Hickok went to Deadwood on business, only to be shot and killed while playing cards in a saloon. Agnes then returned to performing under the name of Lake and made a hit in the circus version of *Mazeppa*. 1880, retired to the home of her son-in-law in Jersey City, NJ, dying

there, age 80. Was the mother of **William, Jr.**, star equestrienne **Emma Lake**, and adopted daughter **Alice**, and mother-in-law of **Gil Robinson**. Said to have made a higher ascent on the wire than anyone in her day. With Spalding & Rogers, 1857, she performed an outside free-act by trundling a wheelbarrow up a wire to the peak of the tent.

LAKE, ALEXANDER. Gymnast, VanAmburgh's, 1874.

LAKE, ALICE [Mrs. Alice Wilson]. Equestrienne. Adopted daughter of **William** and **Agnes Lake**. In addition to performing with the Lake circus, Nixon & Kemp, 1858; George W. DeHaven's, 1861; Levi J. North's, 1863; John Robinson's, 1864. On December 28, 1867, fell overboard from the steamer *Laura*, during a trip from Mobile to New Orleans, and drowned. Her body was found 18 miles from where she fell. She had been married but a short time to 4-horse rider **John Wilson**.

LAKE, CHARLEY. Rider, Robinson & Lake, 1862.

LAKE, CORDELIA [or Madame Cordelia]. Equestrienne. Took the Lake name because she was trained by Bill Lake. Charles Noyes', winter 1871-72; Great Eastern, 1872, 1872; L. B. Lent's, 1876; Great Roman Hippodrome, 1877; Great London, 1873; Wallace & Co., 1884-85; bareback principal rider, W. H. Harris' Nickel-Plate, 1886; Sig. Sautelle's, 1894; LaPearl's, 1896; Ringling Bros.', 1898. May have been the lady who was married to **George Wambold**. The couple were divorced, September 1884.

LAKE, EMMA LOUISE. (February 22, 1855-May 11, 1911) Equestrienne. Born in Cincinnati, OH. Daughter of **William** and **Agnes Lake**. At 17, recognized as one the great horsewomen in the world. While performing as a *manège* rider with John Robinson's, met and married **Gilbert Robinson**, the second son of old **John Robinson** in Memphis, TN, November 16, 1875. [M. B. Leavitt: She "was considered one of the greatest high school riders in the country."] While riding in Buffalo Bill's "Congress of the Riders of the World" as the feminine star during **Cody's** first visit to London, was honored by an invitation from Queen Victoria to appear at Windsor. Was a 4 year old equestrienne, Nixon & Kemp, Palace Gardens, NYC, 1858; Great Eastern, 1872-73; John Robinson's, 1874-78, 1882, 1892; *manège* P. T. Barnum's, 1879-80, 1886; *manège* and leaping act, Barnum, Bailey & Hutchinson, 1881; W. O'Dale Stevens', 1882-83; S. H. Barrett's, 1883-85; *Gran Circo Estrellas Del Nortis*, West Indies, fall 1888. Died in Morris Plains, NJ.

LAKE, ETTA. Elastic skin lady. Gregory & Co., 1886; Barnum & Bailey, 1889.

LAKE, F. Director of zoological garden, P. T. Barnum's, 1874-75.

LAKE, LAURA. Lake's Hippo-Olympiad, 1867.

LAKE, NAT. Old time circus clown, retired, 1868, to his home in Pendleton, IN.

LAKE, WILLIAM THATCHER [r. n. was William Lake

Thatcher]. (September 25, 1817-August 21, 1869) Showman, clown. Born in Burlington, MD. Buckley & Weeks, 1834-35; Eagle Circus/Cole & Co., 1837; Rockwell & Co., 1838; Ludlow & Smith, American Theatre, New Orleans, 1840; John Mateer's, 1843-44; S. P. Stickney's, 1846; Great Western, 1846; Rockwell & Co., 1847-48; Spalding, Rogers & Van Orden, 1851; Nixon & Kemp, 1858-59; Robinson & Eldred, 1859. While with Robinson & Foster, eloped with the 16 year old **Agnes Mersman**. See Agnes Lake. During the winter season in Mexico with Rich's, at a time of hostility between the United States and Mexico, show property was confiscated by the Mexican authorities. The Lake's escaped with only the clothes on their backs. Then came an engagement of 11 years with Spalding & Rogers' *Floating Palace*. Went into partnership with old John Robinson, 1859, which lasted until 1863. Following year, took out his own show and continued until 1869, when he was shot and killed on August 21 in Granby, MO, by **Jake Killian**, a local bully, who had tried to stay for the concert without paying. The Lakes had a son, **William, Jr.**, a daughter, **Emma**, and an adopted daughter, **Alice**.

LALOO. (b. 1874) Double bodied boy. A fine looking highcaste Hindu, born in Oudh, India, the 2nd of 4 children. Was a big feature for museums and circuses, demanding a large salary. Had a small headless twin—with two arms and legs—attached to the lower part of his breast bone. [Barry Gray: "His sunny disposition and love of sport led him into a life of dissipation, which brought on his untimely ending."] Was married, 1894, in Philadelphia. Died in Mexico around 1908, age 30.

LAKIER, CHARLES. Calliope player, advance car #2, Barnum, Bailey & Hutchinson, 1881.

LA MARR, FRED. Gymnast, Alexander Robinson's, 1875.

LAMB, JOHN. Formerly a theatrical producer who failed at the Chestnut Street Theatre, Philadelphia. Opened a circus company at the Front St. Theatre, Baltimore, 1831. Hired S. P. Stickney and his troupe of performers and operated from October 17 to December 31. Announced December 5 he had opened a riding school there during the day with Victor Pepin as manager. Business being unprofitable, turned the establishment over to Fogg & Palmer on the last day of the year. Later, proprietor of Lamb & Co.'s American Amphitheatre, winter 1839.

LAMBRIGGER, GUS. Sideshow manager, Wallace & Co., 1892.

LAMKIN, HARRY B., SR. (1849,1854, or 1856?-February 25, 1886) Ran away with M. O'Conner's Circus, so by age 15 had already launched his career and was practicing as a bareback rider; first year listed on the O'Conner roster, 1870. Became an equilibrist, dancing barrel performer, leaper and tumbler. Mother remarried, 1856, to **Rolla Shipp**, making **Ed Shipp** Harry's half-brother. Married **Clarinda Lowande**. Son **Harry, Jr.** was born in PA, 1879. A second son, **Clarence**, born, Petersburg, IL, 1884. The marriage brought a number of

circus riders to his Petersburg, IL, home to winter. In need of a place to train, Lamkin built a ring barn, 1880, Petersburg, which brought more performers. Claimed, 1882, to be the originator of various balancing acts such as the Enchanted Globes, Phantom Cross, Magic Barrel and Mysterious Tables, also a 4-horse rider. Michael O'Conner & Co., 1870; John Robinson's, 1871; clown, P. A. Older's, 1872; leaper and tumbler, VanAmburgh & Co., 1874-77; acrobat, Great International, Offenbach Garden, Philadelphia, winter 1876-77; dancing barrel act, Theatre Comique, St. Louis, 1878; P. T. Barnum's, winter 1878-79; Adam Forepaugh's, 1880-81; Gilmore's Zoo, Indianapolis, 1882; dancing barrel act, Cooper, Jackson & Co., 1883; Older, Crane & Co., 1884; Frank A. Robbins', fall 1885. Co-proprietor, Gardner, Lamkin & Donovans American Circus Co. at the time of death. Died of yellow fever while touring in Panama during the building of the canal and was buried on Monkey Hill near Colon, Panama, age 32.

LAMKIN, HARRY, JR. (b. 1879) Son of **Harry Lamkin** and **Clarinda Lowande**. Began practicing in the ring barn, Petersburg, IL, at age 6. 1890, after developing skill as a standing rider, went into the ring for the first time. December 1893, appeared at the opening of the New Amphitheater (ring barn), Petersburg. Gollmar Bros.', 1892; Sutton's "Uncle Tom Cabin" Co., 1893; Andy McDonald's, 1896; George W. Hall's, Mexico, returning 1899; John Robinson's, 1900-01, 1907; Great Wallace, 1902-03; Forepaugh-Sells, 1904-06; Campbell Bros.', 1909; in Europe, 1910-16, where he closed his career. [J. D. Draper: "Harry's statuary and posing act in 1900, while on horseback with **Blanche Hilliard**, was a real innovation. She did a two horse carrying act using Harry as top mounter. Old timers on the show said that it was the first instance they could remember of a lady carrying a man on her shoulders in a riding act."] Developed into a hurdle, principal bareback somersault, and jockey rider. Was at one time married to **Pearl Robinson**, a niece of **John F. Robinson**.

LA MONDUE, FRANK. Leaper, Valkingburg's, 1881.

LA MONT BROTHERS [Louis, Charles?]. Acrobats. With Thompson, Smith & Hawes, 1866; Whitmore & Co.'s Hippocomique, 1868; Miles Orton & Co., 1869; trapeze, Cole & Orton, 1871; Stone & Murray, 1871. **Charles** was principal clown, Valkingburg's, 1881.

LA MONT FAMILY. Acrobats, John Robinson's, 1890-93.

LAMOUR BROTHERS [Newton, William]. Horizontal bar performers, leapers and tumblers, Orton Bros.', 1867.

LA MOYNE BROTHERS. Triple horizontal bar and balancing perch, W. R. Reynolds', 1892.

LAMPKIN, J. [or Lamkin]. Leaper, John Robinson's, 1869-71.

LAMPKIN, O. P. [or Lamkin]. Juggler, Hurlbert & Hunting, 1887.

LANAHAN, C. L. Hyena performer, Cooper, Bailey & Co., 1880.

LANCASTER, JOHN. Lowande & Hoffman, 1887; Cole's Colossal Circus, 1893.

LANDAUERS [9]. Statuary posing, Ringling Bros.', 1896.

LANDEMAN, PROF. Trainer of boxing kangaroos, Lemen Bros.'s Colossal Shows, 1893.

LANE, JOHN R. Equestrian and clown. Married to female clown, **Lillie Lane**. Equestrian director, G. G. Grady's, 1869.

LANE, LILLIE. Female clown and *danseuse*, G. G. Grady's, 1869. Married to equestrian and clown, **John R. Lane**.

LANG, MAJOR. Bermuda giant boy, Cameron's Great Oriental, 1875.

LANGLEY. Rider. Originally from Charleston, SC. Ricketts', Philadelphia, 1795. Performed an "Egyptian Pyramid" act and did a one-hand stand on horseback, Lailson's, 1797-98. Formed a circus company and performed in a temporary structure in Charleston, September 1800. From there, the company went to Savannah and Augusta, GA, and back to Charleston. Shortly, quit as an entertainer and opened a riding school in that city. Retirement was short-lived because, spring 1802, appears to have been back on the road—1812-13, since he was living in Charleston, joined Cayetano & Co. when they were there for the winter season. Again opened a circus in Charleston, Langley & Co., December 31, 1813, which continued into April. Following year, joined Pepin & Breschard in Charleston in November. This seens to be his last engagement as a circus rider. Son, **William**, also a performer, committed suicide, 1849.

LANGLEY, WILLIAM. Son of the above. A performer with Lailson's Circus, but was with Sizer's, a small outfit that traveled in the South, for most of his career. The Yeaman Circus, 1831; Frost, Husted & Co., 1836; Frost & Co., 1837; W. Gates & Co., 1838; Robinson & Foster, 1844. Cut his throat in a fit of depression, Charleston, SC, 1849.

LANGLOIS BROTHERS [Felix, Valentine]. Egyptian jugglers, hat spinners and leapers, VanAmburgh & Co., 1873-74, 1878; P. T. Barnum's, 1879.

LANGST, HERR. Lion tamer, L. B. Lent's, 1873.

LANGSTAFF, C. W. Hayner & Langstaff's Pavilion, 1886. Married **Ida Edger** of that company, September 15, 1886.

LANGWORTHY, J. M. (1811?-May 22, 1871) Well known animal trainer and animal performer. VanAmburgh & Co. for 6 years in England, performing the elephant Bolivar, and continued with that concern for over 20 years. Became known as one of the best trainer and performer of animals in the country. With VanAmburgh, 1870, worked with a trained pony and a pair of comic mules and entered the cage with 4 lions and a pair of leopards. Following year, was ringmaster, G. C. Quick, 1850; ringmaster, Raymond & Co., 1852; animal tamer, 1854; New National Circus (John Tryon, proprietor), winter 1857-58; Mabie's, 1862; with performing dogs and monkeys, Lent's Equescurriculum, 1863; Dan Rice's, 1866; Adam Forepaugh's 1867. Died of dropsy, Tecumseh, MI, age 60.

LA PEARL, HARRY. (b. 1884) Clown. Came into the business on his father's show, J. H. LaPearl's. 5 years old when he first appeared as a trapeze performer. Following year, did a contortion act; at 7 was a pony rider; by 12 was doing a principal bareback riding act; and at 15 did a bar act as a clown. Later, was the leading comedian with the "Reaping the Harvest" Co., which played the Chicago Opera House for 18 weeks. Clown, Barnum & Bailey, 1908-11, John Robinson's, 1919; Campbell, Bailey & Hutchinson, 1921; King Bros.', 1927; Russell Bros.', 1935; moving picture, *Polly of the Circus*. Filled the winter seasons as a singing and dancing act in vaudeville. Was married, April 3, 1910, Madison Square Garden, to **Frances Maginley**, a non-professional.

LA PEARL, JAMES H. (1861-January 7, 1936) Born in Philadelphia. Owned and operated a popular medium sized circus during the 1890s. At age 15 began a 3 year apprenticeship with a Philadelphia watchmaker and jeweler and while learning that trade was also a member of the Turners, an athletic organization, where he learned the difficult feats in acrobatics and trapeze specialties. Stokes Circus, Smith's Island, 1876. Gilmore's Varieties and other Philadelphia amusements gained him popular favor. Was then booked over a Western circuit. Aerialist, Burr Robbins', 1883; Parson Bros.' Great Eastern, 1883; Porter & Wright's, St. Louis, 1884. That fall, put out a small show playing fairs in Illinois. Conducted a watch repair and jewelry business, Chenoa and Vandalia, IL, 1885-1890. Established J. H. LaPearl's Circus, 1891, beginning modestly and increasing in size from year to year; made final tour, 1898. Winter quartered in Crawfordsville, IN, 1891-92; in Danville, IL, 1893. Patented a motion sign, from which business he retired, 1926. Wife, **Nellie**, sought legal separation from him, September, 1910. Parents of **Harry**, circus clown, and **Roy**, vaudevillian. Died Kokomo, IN, age 74.

LA PEARL, KATIE [Mrs. Pearl Jones]. Bareback rider. Struck and killed by a streetcar in Indianapolis, IN, October 24, 1916, age about 50.

LA PEARL, ROY. 2-pony and bounding jockey rider with the LaPearl's, 1890s. Son of **J. H.** and **Nellie** and brother of **Harry LaPearl**. Later went into vaudeville.

LA PEARL, RUBY. Statuary, LaPearl's, 1897.

LA PETITE MARIE. See Marie Carroll.

LA PETITE TAGLIONE. Equestrienne, with Rowe & Marshall, 1857-58.

LAPHAM, S. P. Band leader, with G. G. Grady's, 1873.

LA PIERRE, ALICE. Vocalist, character change artist, with Cooper & Co., 1874.

LA PLACE, TONY. Acrobatic and singing clown, Frank A. Gardner's, South America, summer 1895.

LARGE, FRANK. Clown, A. F. Tuttle's, 1893.

LA ROLE BROTHERS. Trapeze act, with Ringling Bros.', 1890-91.

LA ROLE, CHARLES. Barrel, table, and cross act, Gollmar

Bros.', 1893.

LA ROSA BROTHERS [Frank, Eddie]. Double bar and Spanish ring act, T. K. Burk's Circus, 1889.

LA ROSA, GEORGE W. Barrel and enchanted cross act. Sautelle Pavilion Shows, 1885; Baretta-LaRosa Circus, 1886; Col. Webb's Overland Circus, 1887; W. H. Harris' Nickel-Plate, 1892.

LA ROSA, HARRY. Pullman, Mack & Co., 1884.

LA ROSA, MLLE. Trapeze performer. Shot and killed in Cincinnati, March 22, 1872, by **James C. Davis**, ringmaster for Backenstoe's. There was some question whether or not the shooting had been accidental; however, Davis was found guiltless by the coroner's jury and discharged. The lady was the wife of **J. W. Whettony**, also with the circus. She and Davis had been living together for some months. A native of Ohio, who left home around 1870, went to NYC and learned acrobatics.

LA ROSE BROTHERS [Henry, Joe]. Tumblers and leapers. Irwin Bros.' Shows, 1887; St. Germain's Imperial Circus, 1889, where **Henry** was manager; Prof. Williams' Consolidated Railroad Shows, 1892, with **Henry** as equestrian director and assistant manager. There was also a **Lottie LaRose**, *manège* act and premier dancer, with the company.

LA ROUSE, W. Rider, Myers & Madigan, 1854, with his trained horse, Wild Bell, used in a bareback hurdle race.

LAROUX, ELLA. Equestrienne, L. B. Lent's, 1858.

LA RUE, CAMILLE. Female gymnast, L. B. Lent's, 1874.

LA RUE, JOHN. Clown, John O'Brien's, 1883; (with **William LaRue**) Older, Crane & Co., 1884; Main & VanAmburgh, 1890; Sells & Gray, 1900.

LA RUE, WILLIAM, SR. [r. n. William McGrew]. (1832?-January 12, 1912) Head of the **LaRue Family** of performers—**William, John, Willie, Leon**—acrobatic, clown and hurdle acts. In his day, was a leading bareback rider. Stokes', 1851; Robinson & Eldred, 1853; Howes, Myers & Madigan, 1854-55; Sloat & Shepherd, 1857; Frank J. Howes', 1865; Stone, Rosston & Co., 1865-66; Orton Bros.', 1866; later that summer, Haight & Chambers; Mike Lipman's, winter 1866-67; French's Oriental, 1867; Philadelphia Circus, winter 1867-68; Mrs. Charles Warner's, Philadelphia, winter 1868-69; equestrian director, G. G. Grady's, 1868, 1872; bareback rider, Campbell's, 1869; G. A. Huff & Co., 1870; Stowe's, 1870; Great Combination Circus (William LaRue, **Pete** and **John Conklin, George M. Kelley**, proprietors), 1871; P. T. Barnum's, 1872; hurdle rider, Baird, Howell & Co., 1874; Great Metropolitan Olympiad, 1877; California Circus, 1880; VanAmburgh & Co., 1881; John O'Brien's, 1883; Walter L. Main's, 1885-88; John F. Wood's, 1889; Tony Lowande's, Havana, winter 1893-94; general performer, with Scribner & Smith, 1894; principal clown, John Robinson's, 1910. Died in Philadelphia, age 80.

LA ROUX, ELLA. Equestrienne, L. B. Lent's, 1858.

LA SAGE BROTHERS [3]. Acrobats, Cooper & Co. (J. R. W. Hennessey, proprietor and manager), 1897.

LA SAILLE, CARRIE [or Laiscelle]. Equestrian, Shelby, Pullman & Hamilton, 1881.

LA SAILLE, MONS. [or Laiscelle]. Acrobat, Hudson & Castello, 1881.

LA SCELLE BROTHERS [or Laiscelle, LaSaille; Leon, Fred]. Gymnasts. James W. Wilder & Co., 1873; John Wilson's Palace Amphitheatre, San Francisco, 1874; John Robinson's, 1876.

LA SELLE, MART. Mexican equilibrist, William O'Dale Stevens', Park Square, Boston, 1883.

LA SALLE, VICTOR. Gymnast and leaper, Carlo Bros.', South America, 1876;

LASSARD BROTHERS. Equilibrists, Moore Bros.', 1887.

LA THORNE, JOHN M. [r. n. John M. Dilks]. (1823-October 20, 1903) Cannon ball, perch and slack-wire performer. Born in New Brunswick, NJ, descended from an old Revolutionary family; on his father's side was Sir Thomas Dilks, Admiral of the British Navy. While working in a banking house, became involved with an amateur acting group, the Forrest Dramatic Association. At the same time, practiced with cannon balls, slack rope and other acts of athletic performance, laying the foundation for a successful career in this endeavor. Of his prowess, it is said that his Herculean feats were outstanding, for he "played with 32 and 40 pound cannon balls as readily as most people would with oranges." First public performance, old Vauxhall Garden, NYC, spring 1845. Shortly, joined a circus traveling through New Jersey, Pennsylvania and Maryland. Then connected with Seth B. Howes', Front Street Theatre, Baltimore, doing a cannon ball act, which was a relatively new feature in the circus business and which created a sensation. Next, Rockwell & Stone, Bowery Amphitheatre, NYC; then started on a starring tour that took him to Philadelphia, Baltimore, Washington and Charleston; Bowery Amphitheatre, NYC, 1844; T. L. Vermule's, 1845; Old Dominion, 1845 (may have been another title for the New Jersey Circus out the same season); John T. Potter's, 1846; John Tryon's Bowery Amphitheatre, NYC, 1847, winter 1847-48; Victory Circus, 1847; Dan Rice's, traveling by steamboat, visiting the towns on the Mississippi and Ohio rivers, 1848-49; billed as "The Hercules of the Arena," S. P. Stickney's, New Orleans, 1849; Hercules performer, Spalding & Rogers, 1851. When Rockwell & Co., which was in New Orleans, was closed because of a cholera epidemic and sold at a sheriff's sale, LaThorne and Sig. Luigi Germani purchased the property and opened there under canvas on Washington Square. But again, the cholera interfered, forcing the company to give up. LaThorne then rejoined Rice. Following, LaThorne and Germani tried again unsuccessfully in New Orleans; then joined the Southwestern Circus, under the management of S. Q. Stokes. The season was a bad one and LaThorne returned penniless to New Orleans. Joined Spalding & Rogers, American Theatre there, and remained with the company 6 years. During this time, combined with **Henry Magilton** and formed the Motley Brothers. Cincinnati, May 1853, the two performed for the first time in America "La Perche Equipoise." Yankee Robinson's, 1856; Dan Rice's, Niblo's Garden, NYC, fall 1857, and Philadelphia, February 1858, National Theatre; Eldred's, 1858; 1860, stage manager, American Theatre, NYC, where he remained for 4 years; took a vaudeville company to New Orleans for Spalding & Bidwell, 1864, remaining about 2 years as stage manager and general director; returned, NYC, and worked at the Comique, Globe, and Metropolitan theatres. Owned the 36th St. Theatre at one time. Last managerial assignment, the Windsor in the Bowery. Resigned this position, July 4, 1873, for retirement. In latter years became totally blind. Died from pneumonia, NYC.

LATHROP, SAMUEL. (d. December 30, 1870) Clown. Born in Lexington, KY, son of a physician. Known as the "Kentucky Stump Orator." Always dressed in black when not in the arena. One night, performed a mock wedding aboard a Mississippi steamboat for a country couple, who didn't know it was a deception until the ceremony was finished. Hoadley, Latham, Eldred & Co., 1836-38; H. A. Woodward & Co., 1838; June, Titus & Angevine, 1841-42; Rockwell & Stone, 1843; ringmaster, John Mateer's, 1843-44; Sands, Lent & Co., 1846-47; June, Titus & Co., 1848; R. Sands, 1849; Welch's, Philadelphia, 1851; Sands & Chiarini, 1854; Sands & Nathans, 1855, 1859; Herr Driesbach & Co., 1857; Sands, Nathans & Co., Bowery and Broadway Circuses, 1857-58; operated the Metropolitan Circus, California, 1860; Nixon's Amphitheatre, NYC, spring 1863; Madame Macarte's European Circus (**James M. Nixon**, proprietor), 1863; Hippotheatron, NYC, winter 1863-64; National Theatre, Cincinnati, fall 1864; Haight & Chambers, 1866-67; Adam Forepaugh's, 1867-68; International Comique and New York Circus, 1869; Alex Robinson's, 1870. Died in NYC. Remembered for his "comical phiz" and funny sayings. A great favorite with the public. Made a large salary for his day, $75, but never saved anything. Died in NYC.

LA TORTE, MONS. See Mons. LeTort.

LA TORTE, VIOLE. Tom King's, Washington, DC, winter 1861-62.

LAUGHLIN, DAVE C. See Dave Castello.

LAUGHLIN, JOHN HENRY. See Harry Costello.

LA VALLATIA. Levi J. North's, 1859.

LA VAN BROTHERS [Fred, Harry, Howard Green]. Gymnasts. Began performing, 1877. Pullman & Hamilton, 1878; trapeze and horizontal bars, VanAmburgh & Co., 1879; triple horizontal bars, Dr. James L. Thayer's, 1880. **Howard** was injured from a fall, 1880, and retired; set up law practice in South Dakota. **Fred** became top mounter with the team of **Fredericks, Gloss & LaVan** for the next 8 years, working in

Europe, 1882-88. **Harry** was with S. H. Barrett's, 1887. Reunited with his brother, **Fred**, for a double flying act, 1889, Ringling Bros.'; Fulford Overland Show, 1890. The two worked together until 1896, when Fred retired from performing. He died, 1897, of a kidney ailment. Harry worked with various partners and trained flyers until 1937, when he became a booking agent for aerial acts in New Orleans. Died there 1952.

LAVELLE, MME. Strong woman, Cooke's, 1882.

LA VERNE, CHARLES. Principal clown, Gregory & Belford, 1892.

LA VERNE, CLAUDE. Clown, double somersault leaper, T. K. Burke's, 1892.

LA VEUR, MONS. Gymnast, Whitmore & Co.'s Hippocomique, 1868.

LA VINCI, CARLOTTA. Equestrienne, with P. T. Barnum's, 1871.

LAWLER, LILY. Slack-wire and juggler, with Bruce L. Baldwin's, 1894.

LAWLOR, JOHN. Clown, first appearance, Yankee Robinson's, Chicago, 1867.

LAWRENCE, CHARLES B. Advance agent, Circus Royal and English Menagerie, 1881.

LAWRENCE, CHARLEY. Rider, S. H. Barrett's, 1887.

LAWRENCE, D. Contortionist, also pulled against horses, Great Oriental Pavilion Show, 1877.

LAWRENCE, FRED. (1838-March 6, 1895) Press agent. Born in Newburyport, MA. After public schooling, attended the Andover Academy; after completion of studies, learned the printing trade working on his father's Newburyport newspaper; later, published a paper of his own but was forced to give it up because of ill health. 1863, connected with the panorama *Paradise Lost*. Entered into the circus business as press agent for Nixon's, 1865; United Hanlon Brothers' Combination, 1866; 1867-70, George F. Bailey & Co.; press agent, Adam Forepaugh's, 1875, 1877; Cooper, Bailey & Co., 1879-80. Adam Forepaugh's for some 25 years. Lawrence, in cooperation with **Frank Connelly**, who had been hired by Forepaugh to work with Lawrence on bill writing, were responsible for enveigling **Prof. Leidy** of the University of Pennsylvania to examine the Forepaugh "white elephant" and pronounce it a bonafied freak in an affidavit. [D. W. Watt: Fred was "easy going, never in a hurry and yet always had his work done ... the kind that an easy chair always looked good to ... was always a good fellow, commanding a big salary, and after the show in the evening looked up the best restaurant in the town and always had a friend with him."] After Forepaugh's death, Lawrence went with Barnum & Bailey. [Louis E. Cooke: "Fred Lawrence was also one of the old school of press agents, and in many respects on of the best descriptive writers in the business, as he usually confined himself to plain phraseology and covered all the details in simple language that everyone could understand."] Died of comsumption at his home in London, NH.

LAWRENCE, HATTIE. See Lawrence Sisters.

LAWRENCE, NICHOLAS. Vaulting and leaping, D. W. Stone's, 1878; Cooper, Bailey & Co., 1879-80.

LAWRENCE, WILLIAM. See Felix Carlo.

LAWRENCE SISTERS [Hattie, Jennie]. Gymnasts and trapeze performers. Howes' London, 1877; D. W. Stone's, 1878; double trapeze, Cooper, Bailey & Co., 1879-80; went to Europe, spring 1881, and successfully performed in France and Germany; returned to Europe, 1889, and turned their activities to balloon ascensions and parachute jumps. **Hattie** (d. December 9, 1921) was among the first women to do trapeze leaps. Began career with Kiralfy Bros. in *The Black Crook*. Married **Nicholas Kassel**. Died in Morristown, NJ, age 54.

LAWSON, FRANK P. Lion king. Was a pupil of Alviza Pierce, for whom he cleaned the dens. Was connected with James M. Nixon's, four years with Adam Forepaugh's, etc.

LAWSON, WILLIAM. Equestrian, leaper, ringmaster. Came to America with James West's company, 1816; toured with Quick & Mead through the South, 1826, when, in addition to his ringmaster duties he played "Billy Button" and sang comic songs; Pepin & West, 1817; West's, 1818-22; riding master, Olympic Circus, corner of Ninth and Walnut Streets, Philadelphia, 1823; ringmaster, Price & Simpson, 1822-25; Blanchard & West's, Canada, 1825; Lafayette Amphitheatre, NYC, 1825-26; Quick & Mead, 1826; Samuel Parsons', 1829. [T. Allston Brown: "He was a fine looking man. He could neither read nor write, yet he could play the part of a sailor in excellent style. His Mat Mizzen was the best ever produced on the American stage in that day. He played Joe Standfast equally well in *The Turnpike Gate*."] Became a drunkard and was one of the first victims of the cholera epidemic in NYC, 1832.

LAWTON, JACK ["Happy Jack"]. (d. May 6, 1887) Dutch clown, particularly popular with Southern audiences. Began as a sideshow orator but made his first appearance as a clown with S. O. Wheeler's; Lake's, 1867; Adam Forepaugh's, 1867; C. T. Ames', 1868-70; H. W. Smith's, winter 1869-70; James Robinson's, 1871; G. G. Grady's, 1871; Charles Noyes', winter 1871-72; Cosmopolitan Circus, winter, 1871-72; Haight's Great Southern, 1874; clown and temperence lecturer, Hamilton & Sargeant, 1878-79; John Robinson's, 1879-80; Hayward's, 1880; Thornton's, 1880; established an auction house in Goldsboro, NC, 1884, but was back on the road, Pullman & Mack, 1885. His wife, **Elizabeth**, died that year, March 19, age 64. Lawton died while en route to join John Robinson's, victim to an accident at a railroad crossing in Henderson, KY.

LAZELLE, FRED. Gymnast, perch and posturing. Levi J. North's, 1863; Lake & Co., 1863-64; Gardner & Hemmings, Front Street Theatre, Baltimore, winter 1865-66; (as **Lazelle Brothers**) Dan Rice's, 1866; Yankee Robinson's, 1868; the Chestnut Street Theatre, Philadelphia, winter 1868-69; then

Lake's Hippo-Olympiad, 1869; George W. DeHaven's, 1869; Yankee Robinson's, 1869; [with **William Millson**] flying trapeze, P. T. Barnum's, 1872-73; [with **Millson**] Showles & Co. 1873; P. T. Barnum's Roman Hippodrome, 1874-75; Cooper & Bailey, 2nd Australian tour, 1877-78.

LEACH, EUGENE B. Gymnast and vaulter. Caldwell's Occidental, 1867; William Lake's, 1868; Lake's Hippo-Olympiad, 1869; Yankee Robinson's, 1869; Stone & Murray, 1870-72; acrobat, leaper and tumbler, John H. Murray's, 1874-75; same, West Indies, winter 1878-79; W. C. Coup's, 1879.

LEACH, HARVEY. Dwarf, monkey-man. Born near Long Island, with a body and arms of a well formed person and with legs but a few inches in length. First introduced to the public as an equestrian. Welch, Bartlett & Co., 1839; rider, Welch & Mann, 1841; Nathan A. Howes', 1845; later accompanied the circus to Europe, where some ingenious playwright contrived for him several dramas, notably *The Gnome Fly*, wherein Harvey, re-christened **Signor Hervio Nano**, who, encased in the costume of an enormous blue bottle, crossed the ceiling of the theatre and did other wonders. By the novelty of these dramatic effects, Leach reaped a rich harvest both in Europe and in this country, performing at the Bowery when **William Dinneford** had it. Some years after, Barnum happened to find the dwarf in London, ignorant of his identification (Hervio Nano was but Harvey the dwarf, Italianized), and with an habitual eye to business, introduced him to the London audience in a skin of some wild beast, and covered the walls of that city with placards: "What Is It?" Scarce a couple of days elapsed before the ingenious manager was amazed at having a correct answer to his query quite as publicly announced: "It is Harvey Leach, the dwarf, Hervio Nano."

LEACH, H. J. Contracting agent, Sells Bros.', 1878.

LEAK, ANN E. [or Leake, Mrs. Thompson]. Armless lady, giving exhibitions of sewing, embroidery, crotcheting and handwriting through the use of her feet and toes. Her handwriting with her left foot was more perfect than most people could do with their hands. P. T. Barnum's, 1871-72; Adam Forepaugh's, 1874; Cooper, Bailey & Co., 1876-78. Made two tours of Australia.

LEAMAN, MLLE. Equitation. Sands, Nathans & Co., 1855; Mabie's, 1856-57.

LEANDO, ROBERT. Horizontal bars, Barnum & London, 1884.

LEAVENS, FRED. Contracting agent, Stowe Bros.', 1889; for many years treasurer with W. W. Cole, also with W. C. Coup and P. T. Barnum. Died of dysentary, Mobile, AL, November 13, 1889, age about 43.

LEAVITT, JOHN. Whitmore, Thompson & Co., 1865.

LEAVITT, M. B. Ethiopian comedian and clown, with Whittemore, Thompson & Co., 1865. Later, became a well known minstrel manager and author of the book *Fifty Years in Theatrical Management*.

LEAVITT, WILLIAM and NORMA. Jugglers, equilibrist, etc. Geoge S. Cole's, 1893; Cole & Lockwood Shows, 1894.

LEBO, JOHN C. Howes' European, winter 1864.

LE BRUN, W. C. Strong man. Welch's National, Philadelphia, 1843; Nathan A. Howes', winter 1843-44; Howes & Gardner, 1844.

LECKLER, J. E. L. B. Lent's, 1859; Robinson & Howes, 1863; Howes & Norton, 1864.

LE CLAIR, BLANCHE. Flying rings. Orrin Barber's, 1888; Andy McDonald's, 1892.

LE CLAIR, JENNIE. Rider, L. B. Lent's, 1876. Perhaps Dan Rice's, 1873.

LE CLAIR, JOHN. Clown, acrobat, antipodean feats upon bottles and chairs. Came to America with Howes & Cushing's, 1870. As the **Le Claire Brothers** with partner **Shedrick Smith**, was connected with Howe's European, 1871; spinning act, John H. Murray's, 1872, 1874. Also juggler, the Parisian Circus, Operti's Tropical Garden, Philadelphia, fall 1876; juggler, P. T. Barnum's, 1877; gymnast, Hengler's, England, 1879; Robinson's, California (**Frank Frost**, manager), 1886; juggler, Beckett's, 1887. Later performed on single trapeze with many of the leading circuses. Died in Cardiff, Wales.

LE CLAIR, SHED [r. n. Shedrick Smith]. (July 8, 1850-August 19, 1884) Gymnast, clown, trapeze act finishing with a flight through balloons, along with partner. Was brought to America, 1873, by John H. Murray with **John LeClaire** and 3 of the **Leopold Brothers**. D. W. Stone's, 1878; *Circo* Price, Madrid, Spain, 1880. Married one of the **Stuart Sisters**, who were with Sheridan, Mack & Day, 1875. Died abroad in a lunatic asylum.

LE CLAIRE, ROSE. See Rose Amick.

LE CLARE, JAMES. Assistant manager and equestrian, Melville, Maginley & Cooke, 1875.

LE CLARE, MAGGIE. Trapeze, W. W. Cole's, 1877.

LE CLAIRE, ROSE. See Rose Amich.

LE COUNT, WILLIAM B. Banjoist and Ethiopian comedian. Died March 1, 1874, in Brooklyn, NY, age 46.

LEDESMA, JOSEPH. Ladders and high perch, Barnum & London, 1885.

LEE, ALBERT, and OLLIE. Aerial artists, "introducing all the leading muscular and catching tricks of the period," Cole's Ten Cent Show, also called Cole & Sieber's Ten Cent Show, 1890.

LEE, AUGUSTA. Pantomimist and posturer, Spalding & Rogers, 1856.

LEE, BILLY. Clown. Pullman's; Lee's London Circus, 1886; Ferguson's London Coliseum Circus, 1888; Bailey & Winan, 1890. Retired December 1906 at age 62, nearly blind.

LEE, CHARLES. Still vaulter, as well as stage and ring performer, Price & Simpson, 1823-26. Father of **Mary Ann Lee**. [Charles Durang: "Charley was a general favorite—a reward due to his very obliging and honest good nature."]

LEE, CHARLES C. (July 1, 1844-January 8, 1905) Possibly the brother of **H. C. Lee**. Originally, a magician under the name of **LaCardo**. Described as being a real showman, a handsome man with a magnetic personality and full of good natured humor. Great Chicago Circus (Dutton & Smith), 1879; Silas Dutton's, winter 1879-80; Lee & Scribner, 1884; proprietor, Charles Lee's Great London Show, around 1886, which was sold by the sheriff at Phoenix, NY, December 12, 1896. Sidelined for the 1897 season because of illness, Lee's ponies and his wife's dogs were leased to Billy Clifton's Dog and Pony show for that season; by December, 1898, Lee had been confined to his bed from a stroke for 2½ years. See Henry Charles Lee.

LEE FAMILY. It is a puzzle getting the Lees sorted out and sifting through the surrounding myths; there were so many wives and so many children. As the **Lee Family** troupe, H. C., wife **Margaret** (d. 1852), **Lavater, Charles C., Eugene**, and **Theodore**—Eugene and Theodore were apprentices—they arrived in America in 1848. Throughout the years the family furnished a number of fine riders to the profession and were well known in California. [Stuart Thayer: "The Lees introduced what we now know as a 'perch act' into the American circus."] Some of the Lees were supposed to have sailed on the *Brother Jonathan* for Portland, OR, on July 30, 1865. The ship foundered off the Northern California coast at Crescent City, leaving few survivors. Although their names were not included on the passenger list, it has been suggested that they could have boarded before sailing and made arrangements with the purser. In all probability, his first wife and and children—**Mrs. H. C., Polly, Rosa, Arthur, Charley, R. E.**—came East from California with C. W. Noyes', 1872. It was reported that the Lee Family, 8 in number, were murdered by the Apaches while on their way to Mexico through Arizona, December 1872; later, this was thought to be a false report and probably was, because the Lees, gymnasts, equestrians and jugglers, were listed with James E. Cooper's, 1873; Campbell's New York and Philadelphia Zoological and Equestrian Institute, 1878; Orrin Bros.', Havana, 1879. Prior to this, Hayes Park, San Francisco, 1866; Lee & Ryland's Cosmopolitan Circus, San Francisco, 1866; Bay View Park, San Francisco, 1866. See Henry Charles Lee.

LEE, FRANK [r. n. Francis Kelly]. (1847?-April 6, 1875) Tumbler and vaulter. Brother of **Luke Rivers**, was a native of Philadelphia. Lee & Marshall's, California, 1851; Lee & Bennett's, San Francisco, 1857; Great Eastern, 1864; Orrin Bros.', South American, 1867-68; vaulter, San Francisco Circus and Roman Hippodrome, 1872; John Wilson's, San Francisco, winter 1873-74. Died of consumption in San Francisco, age 28.

LEE, GUS. Clown. P. T. Barnum's, 1872-73; L. B. Lent's, 1874; Curtis & DeHaven's Great Roman Hippodrome, 1877; W. H. Harris' Nickel-Plate, 1885. [Charles H. Day: "The last time I met him in Chicago he was imbibing five cent beer and, in blackened face, guying the swinging fairies of the first-part of a female minstrel show."]

LEE, HARRY. Member of the famous **Lee Family** of performers. Lee's Atlantic and Pacific Circus, California, 1871; rider, Great International Circus (**James E. Cooper, James A. Bailey, Robert S. Hood**, proprietors), 1874; Cooper, Bailey & Co., 1875; Great Roman Hippodrome, 1877; Metropolitan Circus, Havana, winter 1878-79; posturer (with **Robert Lee**), Orrin Bros.', Havana, 1879; Chiarini's, India, 1881-82. See below.

LEE, HENRY CHARLES. (1815-September 17, 1885) Rider, showman. Born in England. Came to America, 1848; opened at the Broadway Circus, NYC, 1848-49; the group then joined Welch & Mann for a tour of the West Indies; 1851, H. C. Lee, with wife, 2 sons, and **John R. Marshall**, went to San Francisco, engaged the American Theatre there, and began breaking horses for equestrian dramas; 1852, Lee & Marshall got up a circus tent and opened the National Circus, Sacramento, 1853-56; co-proprietor, Lee & Bennett's Great North American Circus, San Francisco, 1856-57; H. C. Lee's, 1858-59; joined with **G. F. Ryland**, 1865, and experienced several years of success with tours of the Sandwich Islands, Mexico and Central America; director and equestrian manager, Atlantic and Pacific Circus, 1871-72; proprietor, H. C. Lee's Great Eastern Circus, winter 1877-78; Orrin Bros.', Havana, winter 1878-79. Was equestrian director for several shows, the last being Chiarini's in Australia, Java and India; after leaving the company, he made his way to Sydney, where he remained until his death. Another source lists his last activity, 1877, when he and **George W. DeHaven** tried to revive the defunct Great Eastern circus title. Was married 3 times, had several children, some of whom were equestrian performers. One of his wives died in child birth in Rangoon, Burma, 1881, while with Chiarini's.

LEE, HERCULES S. Strong man, cannon ball performer for a circus in Philadelphia, 1848; Johnson & Co., 1852.

LEE, JACK [or Eugene]. (1835?-1889) Started in the circus business at the age 5, apprenticed to H. C. Lee. Lee & Bennett, San Francisco, 1856-57; Lee & Ryland, California, 1869; character rider, San Francisco Circus, 1872. Died in Penang, China, age 54. Had lived in Asia for nearly 18 years prior to his death. See Lee Family and Henry Charles Lee.

LEE, JAMES A. Rider, W. R. Blaisdell's Golden State Circus, California, 1868; character rider and juggler, Crystal Palace Show, 1872; John Wilson's, San Francisco, winter 1873-74; rider, Montgomery Queen's, 1874-75.

LEE, JAMES WALTER. (1873-August 31, 1910) Sideshow manager. Born in Ireland, the son of **Prof. John Lee**, who introduced the London Ghost Show to America. Died in Easton, PA.

LEE, LAVATER THOMAS. (July 28, 1860-August 16, 1899) Born in Valparaiso, Chile. Son or brother of **Henry C. Lee**. Made his first appearance at age 4 with the Lee circus and became a general performer. Was part of the **Lavater Lee Troupe**, consisting of **Mme. Lee, Augusta, Rosa, John** and **Steve**. Traveled with all the leading circuses and performed on all continents. Robinson & Eldred, 1850; J. M. June's, 1851; Spalding & Rogers, 1852, 1856; Howes & Cushing, United Kingdom, 1858; rider and general performer, Lee's Circus, California, 1871; rider, Great International, 1875; somersault rider, Chiarini's, San Francisco, 1879; principal pad act, Orrin Bros.', Havana, 1879; Chiarini's, India, 1881-82; bareback rider, Sells Bros.', 1894. Vaulted over 14 horses at the Olympic Arena, England, 1842. In his later years, devoted his energies almost exclusively to equestrianism as a bareback, trick and somersault rider. Died in London, England.

LEE, MAJOR. Midget, died in Detroit, October 11, 1918. Had just opened an engagement at Armstrong's Museum in that city.

LEE, MARY ANN. *Danseuse*, Bartlett & Delavan, 1841. Daughter of **Charles Lee**, who was a member of Price and Simpson's company, 1823. [Charles Durang: "The winning arch smile that wreathed her features, while reclining into attitudes at the end of every strain, ever won applause and harmonized with the excellence of her very neat *pas*."]

LEE, MRS. H. C. Mother of the famous **Lee Family** of California, died giving birth to a son in Rangoon, British Burma, while with Chiarini's. No date given. See Lee Family and Henry Charles Lee.

LEE, PAULINE [Mrs. William E. Gorman]. (1857-September 10, 1902) Equestrienne. Daughter of **H. C. Lee**. Performed for her father's circus until age 16. In early career, around 1872, billed as the only female juggler on horseback in America, standing on horse as it circled the ring, juggling 4 balls, then 7 knives, and finally spinning plates; also performed in chariot racing, driving a 5-horse team in tandem. Lee & Ryland, 1866; H. C. Lee & Co., California, 1870; C. W. Noyes', 1870; equestrienne juggler, Atlantic and Pacific, 1871; juggler on horseback, J. Hudson's, West Indies, 1872-73; equestrienne and juggler, *Circo Espanol*, Havana, winter 1874; principal rider, Cooper, Bailey & Co., 1876-78, leaving for Australia, November 8, 1876; Adam Forepaugh's, 1879; equestrienne and light balancer, Welch & Sands, 1880; Sells Bros.', 1880; Great Australian, Philadelphia, winter 1881-82; Sherman & Hinman, California, 1883; Sells Bros.', 1884-95, including the Australian tour; Wallace & Anderson, 1890. Married **Paul Lehman**, the clown but was divorced from him, San Francisco, September 17, 1883; then married hurdle rider, **William Gorman**, September 26, 1883. Last year of performing, 1896, Forepaugh-Sells, as bareback and *manège* rider; continued as designer and wardrobe mistress for that show. Died in Columbus, OH, age 45.

LEE, PETE. John Wilson's Palace Amphitheatre, San Francisco, 1874.

LEE, ROBERT E. See Lee Family and Henry Charles Lee. Clown, Cooper and Bailey, 1875; Great Roman Hippodrome, 1877; posturer (with **Harry Lee**), Orrin Bros.', Havana, 1879. Returned from China, October, 1892, where he had been traveling with Woodyear's Circus.

LEE, ROSA. See Lee Family and Henry Charles Lee. Daughter of **H. C. Lee**. Spalding & Rogers, 1856; Lee & Ryland, California, winter, 1868-69; pony rider, Lee's Circus, California, 1871; rider, Great International, 1874-75; H. C. Lee's Great Eastern, winter 1877-78; Campbell's Circus (**John V. O'Brien's**), 1878; Metropolitan Circus, Havana, winter 1878-79; juggler, Orrin Bros.', Havana, 1879; Chiarini's, San Francisco, 1879; Barnum & Bailey, 1889; Walter L. Main's, 1893; Rice's, 1896; hurdle and bolting bareback rider, Apollo Circus, South America, 1897.

LEE, SAMUEL. Strong man, cannon ball. Philadelphia Circus, 1848; Crane's, 1847, 1849; Welch's, 1850-51; Johnson & Co., 1852; Barmore's, 1854; Welch & Lent, 1855-56.

LEE, STEVE. Clown and posturer, with Spalding & Rogers, 1856.

LEE, THOMAS VICTOR. (d. November 21, 1931) Born on the Mississippi River just across from Hannibal, MO, at the close of the Civil War; orphaned at 10 months and reared on steamboats. Great London, 1879; P. T. Barnum's, 1880; Adam Forepaugh's, 1881, as well as W. C. Coup's; Doris & Batcheller, 1882-83; featured juggler at the Tivoli Gardens, Copenhagen, Denmark, summer 1884; headliner at the Orpheum Theatre, New York City, 1887, as well as many others. Toured around the world with Chiarini's as port pilot and juggler; managed **Mr. and Mrs. Tom Thumb** and **Count** and **Baron Magli** at various times; pilot and performer, Champion No. 9, French's Sensation, Eugene Robinson's Floating Palace, McKinney Dreamland and A. A. Beckett's Hippodrome showboats. Since 1916, was identified with various carnivals as an independent show owner. Married **Olie Brennenstall** of Fredonia, KS, 1898. Died of a heart attack at Waycross, GA, when with the Krause Greater Shows as owner-manager of the "Dinosaur" freak show.

LE FEVRE, MILLIE. Gymnast. Robbins & Colvin, 1881; Nathans & Co., 1883.

LE FLUER, JOSEPH. Somersault diver, Ringling Bros.', 1896.

LE FORT, MONS. Rider, a Frenchman with Raymond & Waring at Cooke's Circus, Philadelphia, 1839.

LE FOWLER, CHARLES. Clown. With Cramer's, 1869; Haight's Great Eastern, 1874.

LEFTWICH, R. R. Hurlburt & Leftwich (**J. B. Cahoon**, R. R. Leftwich, proprietors), 1890-94; Leftwich & Perry, 1895.

LEHMAN, A. Clown. H. C. Lee's, California, 1870; Atlantic and Pacific, winter 1871-72; J. Hudson's, West Indies, 1872-73; Orrin Bros.', Havana, winter 1878-79; Chiarini's, San Francisco, 1879; Burr Robbins', 1879; Chiarini's, India, 1881-82.

LEHMAN AUGUSTUS. Spalding & Rogers, West Indies, 1863. Died of yellow fever, San Jago, West Indies, December 1863.

LEHMAN, E. H. [or W. H.]. Trick clown, leaper, tumbler. Noyes' Crescent City, 1872; *Circo Espanol*, Havana, winter 1874; Howes & Cushing, 1875. This may be the same as A. Lehman.

LEHMAN, MRS. A. Equestrienne, with J. Hudson's, West Indies, 1872-73.

LEHMAN, PAUL. Clown. Married to **Pauline Lee**; divorced in San Francisco, September 17, 1883.

LEIHY. Proprietor, Leihy, Lake & Co., California, 1870.

LELAND, VICTOR. Trapeze, James Robinson's, 1871.

LELAND, GEORGE S. Landlord, St. Charles Hotel, NYC, where many of the circus people congregated in the off-season.

LELAND, MATT. Press and contracting agent. Dan Rice's Paris Pavilion, 1872-73; Burr Robins', 1877, 1879; VanAmburgh & Co., 1878; Basye's, 1879; Great St. Louis Circus, traveling on the Mississippi, winter 1879-80; supt. advertising car #1, Cooper, Bailey & Co., 1880; Cole's Great New Southern (Matt Leland, **William Monroe**, **George S. Cole**, proprietors), 1881; excursion agent, Barnum, Bailey & Hutchinson, 1881; S. H. Barrett's, 1885; Wallace & Co., 1886.

LEMEN BROTHERS [Frank V., Frost R., Colvin]. Proprietors, Lemen Bros. Circus. Started in the circus business as musicians with W. W. Cole's, the closing of which, 1886, caused them to go into business for themselves, opening their 10¢ gilly circus in Clinton, IL, July 4, 1887, then growing from a 4-car to about a 20-car show. The show was closely identified with Kansas; for years it wintered in Dodson and Argentine of that state. The title, Lemen Bros.' Shows, was changed, 1904, to Pan-American Shows. Circus was traded, 1909, to a Sioux City company for 26,000 acres of grazing land in Wyoming and a ranch in Holdt County, NE. **Frank** (1847-October 24, 1921), the oldest of the 3, born in Marion, IL. Connected with the circus profession for 55 years. Called "Joe Hepp" by his friends, was the administrative talent who had become a general superintendent with Cole; was a man of firm discipline and integrity who, during his career, was a capable 6, 8 and 10-horse driver, an occupation he frequently continued once he was managing his own troupe; was a lover of horses, an excellent judge of horse flesh and a shrewd trader; there was nothing around a circus he couldn't do; frequently boasted, "Show me a lot we can't get in on"; to back this up, carried a smaller big top for just such emergencies. Band leader, Cooper & Co., 1874. Died in Kansas City, MO, age 74. **Frost R.** (d. January 30, 1920) was a cornetist and band leader. Also died in Kansas City, age 65. Youngest brother, **Colvin**, was less involved in circus activity than the others, and subsequently was engaged in farming. Survived the brothers, lived in Springfield, MO.

LEMLY, D. Juggler, John Robinson's, 1886.

LEMON, ED. Band leader, Ed G. Basye's, 1878.

LE MONS, JOHN. Better known as **Montana Charley**, a dare devil on horseback.

LE MONSAN, PROF. Contortionist, Springer's Royal Cirq-Zoolodon, 1875.

LENGEL, HERR ELIJAH. (d. September 15, 1880) Lion tamer. Native of Philadelphia, began as a tamer of wild beasts as early as 1848, when with Welch's. Considered lion taming a "gift of nature" and claimed he never met a lion he couldn't subdue. Throughout his career was wounded a number of times—the first, in the left leg in Western Pennsylvania while with the Barnum show; the second, while with S. B. Howe & Co., Augusta, GA, when he was severely bitten in the left hand, causing him to lose the use of his middle finger; the third infliction, in Little Rock, AR, by a lioness with Dan Castello's, with 2 fingers of the right hand being mangled; the fourth, received in Madison, IN, 1868, when a lioness seized him by the right leg, sinking the teeth deep into the calf; the fifth occurred in New Orleans, 1869, when he was bitten on the left leg. Raymond's, 1850; J. M. June's, 1853; P. T. Barnum's, 1854; S. B. Howes', 1855; Driesbach, 1856; VanAmburgh & Co., 1859-60; S. B. Howes', winter 1865-66; Dan Castello's, 1866; director of the animal department, Haight, Chambers & Ames, 1867-68; C. T. Ames', 1869-70; C. W. Noyes', winter 1871-72; Great Eastern, 1872. Performed in South America and the West Indies during the last half of the 1870s. While with G. A. Courtney's in the West Indies, he was torn to pieces by a tiger.

LENGEL, KATE. Wardrobe mistress, Cooper, Bailey & Co., 1879-80.

LE NOIR, GEORGE. Sideshow manager, Shedman Bros.', 1894.

LENT, LAWRENCE B. New L. B. Lent & Co.'s Shows (Lawrence B. Lent & Co., proprietors), 1896.

LENT, LEWIS B. (1813-May 26, 1887) Showman. Born in Jamestown, NY (another source gives Somers, NY). Father bought, sold and leased animals and for a short time had a traveling menagerie. By the time Lewis was 21 years of age, 1834, was an agent for June, Titus & Angevine; August of that year, purchased an interest in I. R. and W. Howes' Menagerie; as a partner of Brown & Lent, toured up and down the Mississippi and Ohio Rivers, making the jumps by steamboat, 1835-38; associated with June, Titus & Angevine again, 1839-42; became a partner and manager of Welch's National Circus, 1843; following year, took Sands & Lent's Circus to England, 1843-45, this being the first American circus to perform there; upon returning to America, the Sands & Lent partnership continued for some 10 years, until Lent withdrew; had an interested in and assisted the "Flatfoots" in managing Sands, Lent

& Co.'s American Circus; VanAmburgh's Menagerie; June, Titus & Angevine's Menagerie and Circus, 1846-48; after spending 1849 in California, returned to manage Welch's National Circus the following year; 1851-54, partner with P. T. Barnum's; during the next 3 years, associated with Rufus Welch in the National Theatre and Circus, Philadelphia, Welch's National Circus and L. B. Lent New York Circus Combined. To create a distinction between the two firms, the Welch wagons were painted vermilion and Lent's ultramarine blue. During 1857-62, managed L. B. Lent's National Circus; following 3 years was manager of the Equescurriculum, NYC; manager, New York Circus, Hippotheatron on East Fourteenth Street, NYC, fall and winter 1865-72; general director, L. B. Lent's New York Circus, 1874; railroad agent, Howes & Cushing, 1875; held the same position for French's, 1876; manager and railroad agent, VanAmburgh & Co., 1878; advance director, Adam Forepaugh's, 1879; at the end of the season, revived the New York Circus, Globe Theatre; general director, Batcheller & Doris, 1880; general agent, Robbins & Colvin, 1881; agent, Cooper, Jackson & Co., 1882. Died at his home, 264 Lexington Ave., NYC. Wife, **Mary A. Lent**, also died at the home, NYC. Was an all-round circus man and considered to be the best general agent and router of his day. Pioneered the use of "jaw-breaking" circus titles with his "Hippozoonomadom," inspired by the aquisition of a hippotamus to his circus.

LENT, SAMUEL. Contracting agent, Allen's Great Eastern, 1879.

LENT, SANFORD E. Treasurer, D. W. Stone's, 1878; accountant, Adam Forepaugh's, 1881.

LENTINI, FRANCESCO A. ["Frank"]. (b. 1889) Sideshow curiosity, billed "The Three-Legged Wonder." Born in Rosolini, Sicily, with an shorter third leg growing out of his hip. Used it as a stool and one of his stunts was to kick a football with it. Married a normal woman and fathered 2 boys and a girl. Professionally connected with Walter L. Main's, Ringling-Barnum, Buffalo Bill's, etc.

LENTON BROTHERS. Burr Robbins', 1878; Great London, 1878; VanAmburgh & Co., 1879; Stickney's Imperial Parisian Circus, 1880.

LENTON, LANCE. Banjoist, Cooper, Bailey & Co., Australian tour, 1877.

LENTON, THOMAS. English clown and acrobat. Spalding & Rogers, 1857-59; Chiarini's, Havana, 1859; Nixon & Co., 1859; clown and gymnast, VanAmburgh & Co.'s southern, 1859-60. After retirement from the circus ring, managed a variety theatre in England.

LEON BROTHERS [Leon De Leon, Albert Leon]. Gymnasts, J. W. Wilder's, 1872-1873.

LEON, DAN. Bareback rider, John Wilson's Circus, Australia and India, 1866-67; gymnast, Howes' Great London, 1872; Wallace & Co., 1884; John Robinson's, 1888, 1890; jockey and trick rider, Ringling Bros., 1897.

LEON, EVA. Tight-rope performer from Adams' Circus, England, first time in America, John H. Murray's, 1875.

LEON, FRANK. Leaper. Gardner & Hemmings, 1862; John Robinson's, 1872.

LEON, GEORGE. Gymnast, John Robinson's, 1872.

LEON, JAMES T. [r. n. John S. Towne]. (1844?-May 9, 1896) Gymnast, head of the **Leon Family**, a troupe consisting of Leon, his wife **Estelle**, and 2 sons, **Bert** and **Earl**. Gardner & Hemmings, 1860; Lake's Hippo-Olympiad, 1867; Mike Lipman's, 1869; manager and treasurer, Kelly, Leon & Wilson, 1870; P. T. Barnum's, 1871; Beckett's, 1881; John Robinson's, 1883-86, 1891; bareback rider, W. W. Cole's, 1886-87; Bartine's, 1892. Last engagement with Cooper & Co., which he left on account of illness. Admitted to an insane asylum in Jackson, LA, and died there, age 52.

LEON, JESSE. Rider, Lemen Bros.', 1892; Ringling Bros.', 1894.

LEON, JOSEPH. With his seven member group of Leon's Rajade Troupe, musical burlesque, stilt act, etc., Barnum, Bailey & Hutchinson, 1881.

LEON, JOSEPHINE. *Danseuse*, J. W. Wilder's, 1872.

LEON, LAGUN. Rider, Hudson & Castello, 1881.

LEON, MARCUS. Bareback rider, Wallace & Co., 1884.

LEON, MOLLIE. (d. March 28, 1905) Equestrienne and gymnast, a member of the **Al** and **Mollie Leon** team, trapeze artists. Great New York Show, 1880; John Robinson's, 1886; Bartine's, 1892. Died in Urbana, OH.

LEON, PROF. [r. n. Alfred Smith]. Risley performer with his sons **Edward**, **Alfred**, and **Joseph**, advertised "from the *Follies Berger*, Paris, first time in America," John H. Murray's, 1875-76; John Robinson's Circus, 1884.

LEON, T. Equestrian director, the World's Fair Aggregation, 1892.

LEON, VICTOR. Gymnast, the Philadelphia Circus, winter 1870-71.

LEON, WILLIE. Leaper, Cooper & Jackson, 1880.

LEON, LEROY [or Leon LeRoy]. First came out dressed as a female rider under the supervision of **Spencer Q. Stokes** in New Orleans, 1846. He later became a hurdle rider.

LEONARD BROTHERS. W. C. Coup's; Griffith & Allen, 1886.

LEONARD, H. W. Railroad contractor, Walter L. Main's, 1888; Frank A. Robbins', 1890; W. F. Kirkhart's (W. F. Kirkhart, **R. M. Harvey**, proprietors), 1895.

LEONARD, O. Buckley & Co., 1857.

LEONARD, STEPHEN B. Assistant agent, Dan Rice's, 1860; elephant performer, J. E. Warner & Co., 1871; advertiser, P. T. Barnum's, 1875.

LEONARD, WALLA and NELLIE. Aerialist, trapeze and running globe performer. Joel E. Warner's, 1876; Scribner & Clements, 1887; flying perch, Holland & Gormley, 1889;

Lee's Great London, 1893.

LEONARD, WALTER. Trapeze artist, with Alexander Robinson's, 1870.

LEONATI. English spiral bicycle ascensionist. Adam Forepaugh's, 1882. Rode a small bicycle down a winding spiral from the top of the center pole, the spiral being only 12" wide, with nothing on the sides to keep his wheels from going off. With Adam Forepaugh, received $350 per week and all his expenses. After making a hit in the country, went back to Europe, where he demand a much greater salary than he had ever received before coming to the USA. Invested his money in a town in England, first purchasing the principal hotel; a few years later bought some ground adjoining the hotel upon which he erected a fine theatre.

LEONCHI. Performer, Leonchi's Tribe of Indians, P. T. Barnum's Roman Hippodrome, 1874-75.

LEONHARDT BROTHERS. Donaldson & Rich, 1885.

LEONHART, NELLIE. Aerialist, Ringling Bros.', 1890.

LEONI BROTHERS. Brothers act, Great Oriental Pavilion Show, 1877.

LEONTE, JUAN. Juggler, L. B. Lent's, 1874.

LEONTINE, MME. Free act wire ascensionist, Mabie's, 1857-58.

LEOPAR BROTHERS [John, Henry, Clifford]. Gymnasts, John H. Murray's, 1875.

LEOPOLD & WENTWORTH. Gymnasts and triple-bar performers, Cooper, Jackson & Co., 1884.

LEOPOLD BROTHERS [John, William, Frederick]. Gymnasts. John H. Murray's, 1873; D. F. Dunham's European Circus, 1875; Main & Burdick, 1880; Cooper, Jackson & Co., 1884; S. H. Barrett's, 1885; McMahon's, 1888.

LEOPOLD, EDWARD. Equilibrist. Hamilton & Sargeant, 1877; Main & Burdick, 1880; Clement & Russell, 1888.

LEOPOLD, EUGENE. Acrobat, with Montgomery Queen's, 1876.

LEOPOLD FAMILY [Geraldine, George, Little Gerry]. Gymnasts. Trapeze artists, Nixon's Amphitheatre, Chicago, 1872, where their "Lulu Sensation Act" was featured—Geraldine stood erect on a low stage and through some contrivance was hurled into the air for a distance of around 20 feet and caught by Leopold who was hanging on a trapeze bar by his feet; Montgomery Queen's, 1874; Cooper, Bailey & Co., left for Australia, November 8, 1876; Orrin Bros.', Havana, 1879; Cosmopolitan, Havana, fall 1880; W. C. Coup's, 1881; Leon & Dockrill's, Havana, winter 1881-82; Cantellis & Leon, Havana, winter 1882. **Little Gerry**, a 6 year old in 1879, was billed as **La Nina del Aire**.

LEOPOLD, FRANK. C. W. Kidder & Co.'s, 1893; Wheeler Bros.' (**Alson Wheeler**, **D. Wheeler**, proprietors), 1894.

LEOPOLD, FRANK, C. Leaper, McClelland's United Monster Shows, 1889. Killed attempting a double somersault, Appola, PA, September 13, 1889.

LEOPOLD, GEORGE and **BLANCHE**. Acrobats, James T. Johnson & Co., 1870; Adam Forepaugh's, 1884.

LEOPOLD, J. S. Leaper and gymnast. Adam Forepaugh's, 1876; Cooper, Bailey & Co., Australian tour, 1877-78, during which time threw a double somersault over the backs of 6 elephants; St. Leon's, Australia, by August, 1878, where he was billed as "The Treble Horizontal Bar Performer of the World," also acted as the show's business manager for a time during 1879, after which he may have returned to America.

LEOPOLD, MINNIE. Rider, D. F. Dunham's European, 1875.

LEOPOLD, WILLIAM. Eldest brother of the **Leopold Family**. Died 1888. Had not performed with the group since 1885.

LEOTARD BROTHERS [George Bliss, George Schrode, Ed Snow]. Acrobats, leapers and tumblers. Sadler's, 1875; P. T. Barnum's, 1877; Metropolitan Circus, Havana, winter 1878-79; brothers act, Cooper, Bailey & Co., 1879-80; Orrin Bros.', Havana, winter 1879-80; P. T. Barnum's, 1880; (Bliss, Schrode, and **George Lair**) Orrin Bros.' Mexico, spring 1882; S. H. Barrett & Co., 1883-85. **Louis Fanlan** joined the group in Cuba, 1880.

LEOTARD, JULES. Aerialist. Innovator of swinging from bar to bar, which was devised at his father's gymnasium, Toulouse, France, by practicing over a swimming pool. Made debut, November 12, 1859, Cirque Napoleon, Paris. Only USA appearance, 1868, Academy of Music, NYC. Died at age 30.

LEPONT, F. Gymnast, Whitmore & Co.'s Hippocomique, 1868.

LERCH, ANTON. Clown, Orrin Bros.', Mexico, spring 1883. Joined Nathans & Co. in April of the same year.

LERONA, MONS. Hurdle rider, Doris & Colvin, 1887.

LE ROUX, CHARLES. Rider. Made debut American Arena, Washington, DC, winter season 1828-29, at age 9; **(Master Charles)** Harrington & Buckley, 1830; cloud swing, Ducello's United Exhibitions, 1879; gymnast, James T. Johnson & Co., 1881; Hurlburt & Hunting, 1885.

LE ROUX, JOSEPHINE. General performer, L. B. Lent's, 1866.

LE ROY BROTHERS. Gymnasts. W. W. Cole's, 1876.

LE ROY, DELLA. Wire equilibrist, D. S. Swadley's, 1872.

LE ROY, EDWARD. Trapeze act, W. F. Kirkhart's Great American, 1894.

LE ROY, FRANK G. and **GRETA**. LaPearl's Winter Circus, Danville, IL, 1895-96.

LE ROY, JAMES. Hurdle rider, John Wilson's, 1865; hurdle and bar rider, W. R. Blaisdell's, California, 1868; 4-horse rider, Oriental Circus, 1870; San Francisco Circus and Roman Hippodrome, 1872.

LE ROY, LARR. Acrobat, John Robinson's, 1890-92.

LE ROY, LEON. See LeRoy Leon.

LE ROY, WALTER. Lee & Bennett's, San Francisco, 1856-57; Hinkley & Kimball, 1858; John Wilson's, 1859-61, Australia and India, 1866-67; Cross & LeRoy's Trans-Atlantic Circus (**E. J. Cross** and Walter LeRoy, proprietors), 1884; ringmaster, John B. Doris', 1886.

LE RUE, EDWARD [r. n. Charles Edward Norberry]. (1858?-September 6, 1888) Gymnast. Began in the profession, 1868, Newark, NJ, doing trapeze and ceiling walking with partner **John Hannon** as the **LeRue Brothers**. Continued together until 1873 when LeRue teamed with **Peter J. Kenyon**. Following Kenyon's retirement, joined with Frank Avery, LeRue doing clown work on the horizontal bars. In final years, taught swimming at Dexter's Baths, NYC. Died in his 40th year.

LESLIE BROTHERS [Fred, Louis, John]. Acrobats. Smith & Baird, 1872; C. W. Noyes', 1871-72; James E. Cooper's, 1873-74; P. T. Barnum's, 1875; Rothschild & Co.'s, 1876; Adam Forepaugh's, 1878; Sells Bros.', 1879-86. **John**, G. A. Courtney's, West Indies, 1880. **Fred**, equestrian director, with Sells Bros.', 1885.

LESLIE, FRANK. Performing dogs, Frank A. Gardner's, South America, 1889.

LESLIE, IRENE. Washburn & Hunting, 1884.

LESLIE, JOHN. Clown, Great International, 1874; Burr Robins', 1877; G. A. Courtney's, West Indies, 1880.

LESLIE, "MASTER". Rider, William Blanchard's, New York State and the West, 1826-28; Bernard & Page, 1829; singer and rider, Page's, 1830; Stickles', 1832.

LESSLEY BROTHERS [Charley, Lem]. Double trapeze, Miles Orton's, 1865.

LESTER, DAN. Clown, Wallace & Anderson, 1890.

LESTER, EDWARD. Contortionist, with Cooper & Jackson, 1880.

LESTER, GEORGE. Gymnast, Robinson, Gardner & Kenyon, 1869; acrobat, James Robinson's, 1870, winter 1870-71.

LESTER, WILLIAM H.. (d. May 1, 1872) Contortionist. Orton & Older, 1859; Levi J. North's, 1863; Lake & Co., 1863; Howe & Norton, 1864; Orton Bros.', 1864-65; Gardner & Hemmings, Continental Theatre, Philadelphia, spring 1865; George F. Bailey & Co., 1866; American Circus for the Paris Exposition, 1867; (with **George Kelley**) trapeze and horizontal bars, French's, 1868; L. B. Lent's, 1868-71; G. G. Grady's, 1872. Died of smallpox, New Orleans; had been connected with C. W. Noyes' Crescent City Circus.

LE STRANGE, MONS. and **MLLE**. Human butterflies, W. H. Harris' Nickel-Plate, 1886.

LE SURDO. Contortionist, Shedman Bros.', 1894.

LE TORT, GEORGE. Maginley & Co., 1874.

LE TORT, MONS. French rider. With Raymond & Waring, Cooke's Circus, Philadelphia, 1839; Welch, Bartlett & Co., 1840; S. H. Nichols', 1841; proprietor, LeTort's French Circus, 1842; Nathan A. Howes', winter, 1842; Welch & Mann, 1843; strong man, Rockwell & Stone, 1843-45; bareback rider, New York Champs Elysees, 1865.

LEVANT, WALTER. Leaper, Washington Bros.', 1887.

LEVANTINE BROTHERS [Frederick, John, George]. Balancing feats, horizontal bars. Whitmore, Thompson & Co., 1865; L. B. Lent's, 1866-67, 1869-71, 1873; Whitmore & Co.'s Hippocomique, 1868; John O'Brien's, 1871; Montgomery Queen's, 1875-76; D. W. Stone's, 1878; Metropolitan Circus, Havana, winter 1878-79; Lowande & Hoffman, 1887.

LEVANTINE, FRED. Native of Maine. One of the **Levantine Brothers**. See above. Later changed his name to **F. F. Proctor.** Adam Forepaugh's, 1878; Orrin Bros', Havana, winter 1878-79. After retiring from performing, went into theatrical management. Began business in a small way but gradually extended his connections. Under professional name, Levantine, opened Levantine's Theatre, Albany, NY., which was devoted to burlesque. Later, 1884, was lessee of the Theatorium, Rochester, NY. After that, formed a partnership with **H. R. Jacobs** in Albany and secured theatres in many of the large cities in the east, playing attractions at 10¢, 20¢ and 30¢ admission. In that way, soon controlled 25 theatres; road shows and managers were enabled to book with them for an entire season over their chain of houses. After several years Jacobs and Proctor dissolved, and, 1890 Proctor/Levantine was in control of a circuit of 12 theatres. Built the Twenty-Third St. Theatre, NYC, for legitimate attractions; this house became the first "continuous performance" theatre in the city, 1904. Opened the Pleasure Palace, 1895, and a few years later purchased it. 1900, secured the One Hundred Twenty-fifth St. Theatre, buying the entire property 2 years later. Then leased the Fifth Avenue and continued until 1906 when he made a combination with **B. F. Keith**, his most formidable rival in the vaudeville field. Subsequently, purchased the Leland Opera House, Albany, NY, Newark Theatre, NJ, and became lessee of a number of other theatres.

LEVANTINE, H. Press agent, VanAmburgh & Co., 1876.

LEVANTINE, WILLIAM. Aerialist and equilibrist. Died October 20, 1889, age 39.

LEVERE, LEO. (d. June 28, 1881) Leaper. Cooper's International, 1874; Cooper, Bailey & Co., 1879; John Robinson's and others. Last engagement, privileges, Shelby, Pullman & Hamilton. Died in Montreal.

LEVI, ANDREW J. [or Levy]. Rider, tumbler and general performer. Apprenticed to **Benjamin Brown**. With J. Purdy Brown's, 1825-29; followed by engagements with the Royal Pavilion Circus/Olympic Circus, 1830-31; Stewart's American Amphitheatre, 1832; Fogg & Stickney, 1833; Brown & Co., 1836-37; W. Gates & Co., 1838; Mons. LeTort's, 1842; Stickney & Buckley, 1844; Cincinnati Circus, 1845; Great Western (**Stone & McCollum**, proprietors), 1846-49; Johnson & Co., 1852; Levi J. North's, 1860; Cooke & Robinson, 1861. Was said to have performed a principal riding act "with grace and finish rarely seen now-a-days." Later in life, 1870, after his riding days ended, was noted attending the stock for **Agnes**

Lake's. 1882, was livng in the poor house in Sedalia, MO, and maintaining himself by fishing and trapping.

LEVI, M. Ringmaster, with Lake's Hippo-Olympiad, winter 1870-71.

LEVIS, DAVE B. Privileges, Adam Forepaugh's, Hummill & Hamilton; partner, Reese, Levis & Dolphin, 1884. Later, produced one-night stand, brass band drama, *Josh Spruceby*, to great success. Became attached to the American Consular Service in Europe, ending up in Tunis as their representative.

LEVRINGTON, THOMAS. Spalding & Rogers, 1863.

LEWIS. Clown, vaulter. Joseph Cowell's, 1824; clown, J. W. Bancker's, 1824, 1836; J. Purdy Brown's, 1825-29; somersaulted over 9 horses, Edward Eldred's, 1834; A. Hunt & Co., 1838. One feats was to turn a somersault through a balloon on fire; also worked on the trampoline.

LEWIS, CHARLES. Press agent, Warner & Henderson, 1874; Ferguson's London Coliseum Circus, 1888.

LEWIS, CHARLES. Negro minstrel, with Orton & Older's, 1858-59; also with that company for a number of years as agent.

LEWIS, D. B. Manager, Reese, Levis & Dolphin, 1885.

LEWIS, EMMA. Wire walker and race rider, King & Franklin, 1891; Walter L. Main's, 1892.

LEWIS, GEORGE W. Agent, D. S. Swadley's, 1872; Burr Robbins', 1885.

LEWIS, GEORGE. Negro minstrel, in charge of the Sable Haromists, Orton & Older, 1859.

LEWIS, JOHN. Sideshow manager, John Robinson's, 1864.

LEWIS, JOHN ["Uncle John"]. (January 1, 1829-November 24, 1903) Born in Circleville, OH. Started in show business with Chapman's, 1852. Had his own outfit, 1868, traveling on the Mississippi River. Sells Bros.', 1895. Died in the city of his birth, age 74.

LEWIS, JOHNNY. (d. 1867) Clog and wench dancer, with Haight & Chambers. Died of cholera in St. Louis, MO.

LEWIS, JOSEPH. Contortionist, Walter L. Main's, 1892.

LEWIS, MATTIE. Chariot racer, P. T. Barnum's Roman Hippodrome, 1875.

LEWIS, N. W. Agent, Whitmore & Co.'s Hippocomique, 1868.

LEWIS, TOM. Boss hostler, Shedman Bros.', 1894.

LEWIS, W. C. See William Murray.

LEWIS, WILLIAM. Master of horse, Howes' Great London, 1871.

LEYDEN, J. J. Chief of paste brigade, W. C. Coup's, 1878.

LEYDEN, MYNHEER. Strong man, pulling against horses, firing cannons from his shoulder, breaking hemp cables, with Rockwell & Stone, 1843.

LIBBY, E. Ringmaster, Albizu's, Havana, November 1866.

LIBBY, WILLIAM ["Hercules"]. Strong man. Wesley Barmore's, 1854; Great Western, 1855; Spalding & Rogers, 1856-61; Nixon & Kemp, 1858; Chiarini's, winter 1861-62; ringmaster, Horner & Bell, 1865; ringmaster, Albizu's, Havana, fall 1866; George F. Bailey & Co., 1868-69; ringmaster and cannon ball act, Joel E. Warner's, 1871; cannon ball and strong man, Warner, Henderson & Co., 1874; ringmaster and cannon ball performer, Springer's Royal Cirq-Zoolodon, 1875; Joel E. Warner's, 1876, collapsed early, managed remnants of the company; Martinho Lowande's, 1881; Pubillones', Havana, winter 1884-85. It was said that he "throws cannon balls about the ring like shuttlecocks." Married **Kate Partington**, concert hall performer.

LIDLER, E. E. Musical director, Welsh & Sands, 1893.

LIENAUD, MARY. hippodrome jockey, sailor dance (concert), Barnum, Bailey & Hutchinson, 1882.

LILA. Dan Rice's Paris Pavilion Circus, 1871. "Two-woman" trapeze act as partne3r, **Zoe**, blindfolded and encased in a sack, swung from a trapeze, turned a somersault in mid-air, and ended by clutching a single rope, a version of *l'échelle périleuse*. It has been said that their leap and catch performance may have represented the first appearance of a female catcher. However, a vague newspaper comment in August read: "Dan has no female trapeze performers. One of the girls was discovered to be a boy recently, and the other one left and went into Canada."

LINDAMAN, HERR. Lion tamer, W. H. Stowe's, winter 1881-82.

LINDEN, HARRY. Levy J. North's, 1857-59.

LINDLEY, ROBERT. Negro minstrel. Orton & Older, 1858; Mabie's, 1860.

LINDSAY, HUGH ["Col."]. (1804-August 23, 1860) Showman in the business for about 40 years, performing primarily in Pennsylvania. Connected with various exhibitions from which he accumulated considerable wealth. At age 15, apprenticed with **J. E. Myers** and **Lewis Mestayer**. Subsequently, with John Miller's company; Weyman's, 1823-24; Welch's; Fields & Ponier; Aaron Turner's; H. Hawley's; Mills & Harrison. Some of his pupils were **S. S. Sandford**, the minstrel; **Skoweriski**, the rope-walker; and equestrians **Stout, Nagle**, and **Shindel**. Married **Lydia Panley**, 1828. Died in Berks County, PA. [T. Allston Brown: "He was a warm-hearted and generous man, having probably disbursed in his day, for the benefit of others, a hundred thousand dollars...."]

LINES, D. R. [also Lyons]. Drury, VanTassle & Brown/ Brown & Mills, 1837; W. Waterman & Co., 1838; Benseley, Lyons & Stone, 1839; menagerie manager, W. Seeley's, 1840; Lines', 1841; manager, James Raymond's, 1841-42.

LING LOOK. Egyptian "Fire King," ate live coals and licked red hot bars of iron. Nixon's Amphitheatre, Chicago, 1872; Barnum's Roman Hippodrome, 1875.

LINGARD, CHARLES W. (1849?-April 21, 1910) Trapeze performer and iron jaw man. Valkingburg's, 1881; Beckett's, 1887; Montgonery Queen's, 1887; Sieber & Co., 1888. His big feat was that of holding a 150 pound cannon in his teeth.

First wife, **Annie Wachtel**, was a flying rings performer. Later appeared with **Tillie Beck** as a partner, 1884. Died in St. Louis, MO, age 61.

LINK, BILLY and **FANNIE.** Aerialists, Burr Robbins, 1891.

LINK, HENRY. Contracting agent, with Lockwood & Flynn, 1887.

LINSLEY, J. Boss canvasman, Great Oriental Pavilion Show, 1877.

LINTON BROTHERS. Acrobats, W. C. Coup's, 1880.

LINTON, THOMAS. J. J. Hall's, winter 1836; Frost & Co., 1837-38. The following may or may not be the same man: clown, Sands, Nathans, 1855; Nixon & Kemp, 1857; James M. Nixon's, winter 1858; Nixon & Co., 1859; Lenton & Nichols, Buenos Aires, winter 1859; VanAmburgh & Co., 1860.

LIONI, VIRGINIA. Rider. Possibly a pupil of **H. C. Lee**. Lee & Marshall, 1853-55; Bennett's, 1856; Lee & Bennett, 1858; L. B. Lent's, 1861.

LIPMAN, JACOB M. (d. February 2, 1899) Started Lipman Bros.', 1866, with brother **Michael**, traveling on the steamboat *Marietta* and performing in towns along the Ohio, Mississippi and Missouri Rivers. Two daughters, **Blanche** and **Georgie**, were professionals. Died at his home in Philadelphia.

LIPMAN, LOUIS J. ["Leo"]. Rider. Brother of **Moses** and **Sol Lipman**. Cincinnati Circus, 1841; John Tryon's, Bowery Amphitheatre, NYC, 1843, 1846; Rockwell & Co., 1847; Welch & Mann, 1843-45; June & Turner, 1846; principal riding act, leaping through a 29" diameter balloon, Henry Rockwell's, 1847; Crane & Co., 1849; dramatic rider, J. M. June's, 1851; riding master, National Circus, Chestnut Street, below Ninth, Philadelphia, 1852; Raymond & Co., 1852; Welch's, Philadelphia, 1857-58, 1860; Philadelphia Circus, winter 1867-68.

LIPMAN, MOSES J. (1811-March 2, 1892) Tumbler. Born in London, the eldest of 3 brothers, the others being **Sol**, clown, and **Louis**, circus rider. Came to USA with brothers and apprencticed to **J. Purdy Brown**, 1825, and continued with the company at least until 1830. William Harrington's, 1825, being only 12 years old at this time; clown, Asa T. Smith's, 1829; John Lamb's, Front Street Theatre, Baltimore, 1831; Fogg & Stickney, 1830, 1831-33; Brown's, 1835; Brown & Co., 1836-37; vaulter, Clayton, Bartlett & Welch, 1840; June, Titus, Angevine & Co., 1842; VanAmburgh's, England, 1844; Richard Sands', England, 1845; vaulter, tumbler, scene rider, Welch & Delavan, 1847; Dr. Gilbert R. Spalding's, 1847; Great Western, 1848-49; Aaron Turner's, 1849; Myers & Madigan, 1854-55; also connected with Bidwell, Spalding & Rogers, P. T. Barnum's, John Robinson's, and at one time, his own show. Said to have thrown 71 successive somersaults without tripping, 1842. Kept a pawn shop, Cincinnati, OH, 1884. Died in Cincinnati, age 81, being bed ridden during the last 6 years of his life.

LIPMAN, SOLOMON. (b. 1812?) Clown. Brother of **Louis** and **Moses Lipman**. J. Purdy Brown's, 1827, performing on 2 ponies, apparently his debut. Followed by engagements with Handy & Welch, West Indies, 1829; the Royal Pavilion Circus/Olympic Circus, 1830; Handy & Welch, 1830; John Lamb's, Front Street. Theatre, Baltimore, 1831; then J. B. Green's, 1833; J. T. and J. B. Bailey's, 1834; Mabie Bros.', 1848.

LIPPERT, GEORGE. (1844?-July 24, 1906) Possessed a body that had 2 hearts, 3 perfectly formed legs, and 16 toes. At one time, connected with P. T. Barnum's. **Mrs. Mary Riggs**, a florist of Salem, OR, gave him a home when he retired from the business, around 1899. Died of consumption in Salem, age 62.

LIPPERT, HERR. Pony performer, P. T. Barnum's, 1874.

LITTLE ALL RIGHT [Que Gero]. Japanese boy performer, Barnum's Roman Hippodrome, 1875; P. T. Barnum's, 1876-77; Cooper, Bailey & Co., Australian tour, 1877-78; Barnum, Bailey & Hutchinson, 1881; Orrin Bros.', Mexico, January 1883; Adam Forepaugh's, 1883; sailed for Europe, February 17, 1886.

LITTLE GEMMA. Rider of Madrid, Spain. Featured in a riding act with **Ella Zoyara** and referred to as his pupil. Great Orion Circus, Bowery Theatre, fall 1861; Stickney's National Circus, Old Bowery, 1861. [Hartford *Times*, July 6, 1861: "This precocious equestrian genius appears for the first time in America in a bold, original and faultless performance on horseback entitle 'The Child of the Regiment.'"]

LITTLE, JOHN W. Agent for Barnum's autobiography, P. T. Barnum's, 1880.

LITTLE MAC. Clown. S. B. Howes' European, 1865.

LITTLE VENUS. Contortionist, Sig. Sautelle's, 1897-98.

LITTLEFINGER, COUNT. Dwarf, W. W. Cole's Australian tour (which left San Francisco, October 23, 1880).

LITTLEFINGER, DOLLIE. Dwarf, died March 13, 1901, at Kendallville, IN.

LITTLEFLUGER, MAJOR ROBERT [r. n. Robert Huzza]. (d. 1929) Midget. 4' 1" tall. Married **Mollie Shade**, "the Lilliputian Queen," of Osceola, IA, June 5, 1881, while both were with Sells Bros.' Mollie died in child birth at Kendallville, IN, June 24, 1882. Only a short time later, he met **Ida Hosmer** while passing through Hartford, CT, with a show. The two were married at Runnell's Museum, Brooklyn, NY, March 7, 1883. By this time he had been in the business some 11 years. The two exhibited together on Adam Forepaugh's and John Robinson's, and worked in Midget City, Coney Island. The Major had a steady job in Jersey City, NJ, that he could return to when necessary, as a messenger dressed in a policeman's uniform, the "Little Cop." With Sheldenburger & Co., 1871; "smallest man in the world," Great Eastern, 1872-74; VanAmburgh & Co., 1872; Sells Bros.', 1881; John Robinson's, 1885; Sig. Sautelle's, 1899. Died in Jacksonville, FL, age 65.

LITTLEFLUGER, IDA. [Mrs. Robert Huzza, nee Ida Hosmer]. 3' 9" tall. One of 13 children, all the others being of normal size. Living in Hartford, CT, when she met and married **Robert Huzza**, known as **Major Littlefluger**, who was passing through with a show. Married with much ceremony at Runnell's Museum, Brooklyn, NY, March 7, 1883. Exhibited together with Adam Forepaugh's and John Robinson's and worked at the Midget City colony, Coney Island. Died November, 1910.

LITTLEPAGE, Gov. Midget, Walter L. Main's, 1893.

LITTLEWOOD, E. Band leader, J. R. & W. Howe, 1833.

LIVINGSTON, ADOLPH. D. W. Stone's, 1878; Metropolitan Circus, Havana, winter 1878-79; Cooper, Bailey & Co., 1879-80.

LIVINGSTON BROTHERS [George, Paul]. Acrobats. Sells Bros.', 1874, 1877; ground and lofty tumbling, Howes' Great London, 1877-78; Orrin Bros.', Havana, winter 1877-78, 1884, 1888-89; Hilliard & DeMott, 1880; W. W. Cole's, 1880-81, 1886; O'Brien, Handenberger, Astley & Lowanda, 1884; (4 brothers) W. W. Cole's, 1886; Lowande & Hoffman, 1887; Phillips-Scott, 1888.

LIVINGSTON FAMILY [Charles, Chris, Ed, Harry, Victor, Maude]. Aerialists, gymnasts, acrobats, and cyclists. **Maude** (d. January 13, 1907) a native of Louisville, KY. Married **Charles Livingston**, 1880. Recently retired from performing before she died in NYC. Sells & Rentfrow's, 1893; James Donovan's, Bermuda, winter 1891-92; Walter L. Main's, 1899; Great Wallace, 1900.

LIVINGSTON, JENNIE. Cooper, Bailey & Co., 1879-80.

LIVINGSTON, MAY. Pupil of Prof. Langworthy. New National Circus (John Tryon, proprietor), winter 1857-58, entering the den for the first time.

LIVINGSTONE, BLAIR. Gregory & D'Alma, 1889.

LIVINGSTONE FAMILY. Aerialists, gymnasts, acrobats, bicyclists. Headed by **Chris H. Livingstone.** Sells & Rentfrow, 1892.

LLOYD BROTHERS. Contortionists, St. Germain's Imperial Circus, 1889.

LLOYD, CHARLES. (d. August 16, 1889) P. T. Barnum's.

LLOYD, JAMES. English hurdle rider and tight-rope performer with his 2 sons. Brought to America by **Sam Watson** for Adam Forepaugh's, 1882, performing for a salary of $250 a week. [D. W. Watt: "A quart of milk and a five cent loaf of bread was their lunch in the evening and they would always enjoy this near the sleeping cars after the evening show. It was fair to say that the Lloyd family took more than 99 percent of their salaries back to England."] Later, had a circus in Ireland, 1885.

LOA & RUGE. Contortionists, Doris & Colvin, 1887.

LOBELL, JAMES. Rider. Died August 5, 1873, Omaha, NE.

LOCKE, ANNA. Armless woman, P. T. Barnum's, 1871.

LOCKE, FRED. Proprietor, Locke's, 1889-95; Hargraves,

1901.

LOCKHART, C. Performing birds, with Washington Bros.', 1887.

LOCKWOOD, A. L., JR. Cole & Lockwood's All New United Shows (**George S. Cole**, A. L. Lockwood, Jr., proprietors), 1894.

LOCKWOOD, GEORGE R. (1821?-November, 1910) Was clown with VanAmburgh & Co., when show moved by wagon. Retired, 1881, and went into the hotel business in Anderson, IN. Died there, age 89.

LOCKWOOD, HENRY. Athlete, Stone & Murray, 1869-70.

LOGAN, PROF. Band leader, the Great American Circus, 1893.

LOGAN, THOMAS C. Proprietor, Logan's, 1891.

LONG, C. Alex Robinson's, 1866.

LONG, CHARLES. Bartine Five-Clown Circus and Electric Light Pavilion (**Charles Bartine, Sid C. France**, proprietors), 1880.

LONG, DAVID. (1830-November 24, 1885) Clown. Went to California for gold, 1849, and drifted into the circus business. Risley, Rowe & Co., 1856; Mammoth, 1857; Kimball's, 1859; Wilson's Dan Rice, 1860; Wilson's, Honolulu, 1861; Wilson's Joe Pentland, 1862; Orrin Bros.', San Francisco, 1863; Lee & Ryland's Cosmopolitan Circus, San Francisco, 1866; Jeal & Co., California, 1871; Ryland Circus, California, 1872.

LONG, FRANK. (?-June 2, 1908) Acrobat. Native of Litchfield, IL. Horizontal bars and trapeze, Frank A. Gardner's, South America and West Indies, 1889-93; co-owner, Donovan & Long (**James Donovan**, Frank Long), Central America, 1897. Died from paralysis, Bristol, TN.

LONG, HARRY K. General performer. Clown, Older's, 1872; gymnast, G. G. Grady's, 1874; Orrin Bros.', Havana, winter 1878-79; leaper, W. W. Cole's, 1879-80; Barnum, Bailey & Hutchinson, 1881-82; Sells Bros.', 1884; George Richards', 1888; treasurer and co-proprietor, Stow, Long & Gumble, 1889; Clark Bros.', 1892; sideshow manager, G. W. Hall's, 1894. Married **Maggie Claire** of the flying **Claire Sisters**, Carlisle, PA, September 6, 1879.

LONG, H. C. Business manager, Hobson Bros.', 1893.

LONG, JAMES. Agent, VaAmburgh & Co., 1874.

LONG, JAMES. Clown, John Forepaugh's, California, 1888.

LONG, J. C. Herculean performer, G. G. Grady's, 1869; leaper, Wootten & Haight, 1871; Mayo's Model Show, 1884; cannon ball and heavy balancing, John B. Doris', 1886. Had sons **Frank** and **Edward**.

LONG ["Master"]. Rider, a member of Ricketts company and the youngster on Ricketts shoulders for his "Flying Mercury" act; replaced **Strobach** for the southern tour.

LONG, MRS. HARRY. See Maggie Claire.

LONG, SAM. (?-January 29, 1863) Negro minstrel. Native of Pennsylvania, designated "Big Sam" so as not to be confused with Sam Long, the clown. Worked on the steamship *Banjo*

with Spalding & Roger's minstrel company at the start of the Civil War; was also with their circus company. Died from pneumonia, Paducah, KY.

LONG, SAM. (1822-1891) Clown. Robinson & Eldred, 1850-56; G. N. Eldred's, 1857-58; Sloat & Shepherd's "Joe Pentland", 1859; Niblo & Sloat, 1860; Robinson & Lake, 1860; Madigan & Gardner, Front Street Theatre, Baltimore, 1860-61; First National Union (combination of Nixon's Royal Circus and Sloat's New York Circus), 1861; Spalding & Rogers, Old Bowery Theatre, NYC, 1861; Tom King's, Washington, DC, winter 1861-62; Gardner & Hemmings, 1862; R. Sands', 1863; Bailey & Co., winter 1863-64; Hippotheatron, NYC, late winter 1864; Gardner & Hemmings, Front Street Theatre, winter 1865-66; Seth B. Howe's European, 1865-70; Cooke's, Philadelphia, winter 1867-68; Chestnut Street Theatre, Philadelphia, winter 1868-69; John Robinson's, 1872; Adam Forepaugh's, 1873-75; O'Brien, Handenberger, Astley & Lowanda, 1884. Opened a restaurant, corner of Second and Gaskill Streets, Philadelphia, 1877. Later, 1879, had a shoe store in that city. [John Dingess: He was a "candid man, a good friend, and one of the best clowns in the business."] Sang a good song, told a clever joke, acted well and was eager to make his audiences laugh. Married, NYC, April 6, 1861, **Miss Louisa Hampton**.

LONG, SELINA. John Wilson's, American Theatre, San Francisco, which had been fashioned into an amphitheatre, spring 1860.

LONG, T. B. General agent, Cole's (**George S. Cole, John H. Sparks**, proprietors), 1893; Sells Bros.', 1895.

LONG, THEODORE B. Band leader, Great London, 1889.

LONG, WILLIAM C. Rider, L. B. Lent's, 1876.

LONGREEN, S. High wire and acrobat, John Robinson's, 1886-88.

LOOMIS, ARTHUR H. Banker from Emporia, KS. Co-proprietor, Hawkins & Loomis Dog and Pony Show, 1997.

LOPER, WILLIAM C. Asst. Mgr., Frank Robbins', 1889.

LORD, CHARLES. Asst. mgr, Castello & VanVleck, 1863.

LORD, M. Master of properties, Great Oriental Pavilion Show, 1877.

LORELLA BROTHERS [William, Thomas, Edward]. Grotesque dancers and high kickers, Barnum, Bailey & Hutchinson, 1881-84.

LORETTA BROTHERS [Otis, Charles]. Gymnasts, aerialists, Irwin Bros.', 1890.

LOROUX, MONS. Juggler and barrel performer, Rosston, Springer & Henderson, 1871.

LORREY, JOHN. Gymnast, W. W. Cole's, 1886.

LOUBOW, POLINE. Principal clown, John Robinson's, 1871.

LOUGHLIN, D. C. [and wife]. 2-horse carrying act, Robert Hunting's, 1894.

LOUISE, MLLE. Wire ascensionist, Levi J. North's, 1856,

1860; Nixon & Kemp, 1857; Joe Pentland's, 1858; Cooke & Robinson, 1861; George W. DeHaven's, 1865.

LOUISETTE, CAROLINE. 4 and 6-horse bareback rider, L. B. Lent's, 1874.

LOUNSBURY, GEORGE W., JR. See Dick Hunter.

LOUNT, H. R. Agent, Robinson & Eldred, 1846.

LOVELACE, F. W. Manager, Albert Hose's, 1889-93.

LOVELL, ALFRED. Bear trainer. Trained grizzly bear act, Providence, RI, December 1853; Dan Rice's, 1855; bear and tiger, Buckley's, 1857; Lovell's Great Show, 1859; Miller & Lovell's Great Menagerie and Variety Show, Lexington, KY, 1860. Had bear and tent attached by sheriff, Memphis, TN, 1859. Ran hall show, Columbus, GA, for benefit of soldiers families of Confederate States of America. Lovell's California Grizzly Bear, Conklin Bros.' Great American, Mexico, 1866.

LOVETT, JOHN. Clown. Quick, Sands & Co., Baltimore, 1833; Rockwell & Co., 1848; G. C. Quick's, 1852; Crystal Amphitheatre, 1853.

LOW, MILLIE. Aerial act, Fulford & Co., 1890.

LOWANDA, JOHN. Trapeze, Dan Rice's, 1877.

LOWANDA, NAPPA. Rider and acrobat, John Robinson's, 1877-78.

LOWANDE, ABERLARDO. (1853-March 19, 1928) Somersault pad act, tumbler, leaper from at least 1869 until 1895. Same generation as **Clarinda** and **Martinho, Sr.**, sometimes recorded as an adopted son of **Alexander IV**. Birthplace listed as Sao Paulo, Brazil. Castello, Nixon & Howes, 1869; Siegrist, VanAmburgh & Lowande, 1870; 2-horse act, VanAmburgh & Co., 1871; Adam Forepaugh's, 1871-73; somersault rider, Castorienas & Co., Cuba, 1873-74; Rothchild & Co. (John O'Brien's), 1874; Sam Cole's Dominion Circus, 1875; Montgomery Queen's, 1876; Lowande's Great Brazilian Circus, 1877; Dr. James L. Thayer's, 1877; Cooper, Bailey & Co., Australia and New Zealand, 1877-78; pad act, Orrin Bros.', Havana, 1881; Mexico, winter 1881-82; Batcheller & Doris', 1882; Pubillones', Cuba, 1883-85; Hobson's, 1883; R. H. Dockrill's, Panama, winter 1886-87; principal bareback riding act, Irwin Bros.', 1893; Tony Lowande's, 1894; Cortada's, Cuba, 1894-95; E. E. Rice's, Manhattan Beach, Coney Island, 1895. His wife **Josephine** began to appear with him in riding acts around 1882. The marriage produced 8 sons and daughters. Purchased a 30 acre farm near Green Broad, NJ, 1895. Died in Bound Brook, NJ, after a short illness and was survived by Josephine and their children.

LOWANDE, ALEXANDER A. Son of Martinho Lowande, Sr. (not to be confused with his uncle, Alexander G. Lowande) Acrobat, Martinho Lowande's Brazilian Circus, 1883; by 1896, hurdle act and 2 and 4-horse riding, Howe's Great London, 1896; Forepaugh-Sells, 1903; Ringling Bros.', 1904-05; Barnum & Bailey, 1908; rough rider, Sig. Sautelle's, 1911 (wife, **Matilda**, was wardrobe mistress). Became a circus proprietor as a partner with his brother **Oscar** in Lowande Bros.',

1920-21, which went to Puerto Rico. Again, Central and South America as co-owner with **Oscar**, winter 1922-23. Although started early in life as a circus performer, eventually became a Christian minister and chaplain of the National Variety Artists

LOWANDE, ALEXANDER G. (1876-1958) Born Frankfort, PA, son of **Virginia Guerin** and **Alexander, Sr.** Named Alex., Jr., but adopted Guerin for middle name after father's death, 1882. Brother of **Cecil** and **Julia (Shipp)** and half brother of **Martinho, Clarinda, Aberlardo, Natalio,** and **Guilamena.** Married **Carrie Kemp,** 1899. Principal somersault rider and clown hurdle mule rider; later became a dog trainer, knock-about clown, bounding rope acrobat and gymnast, and equestrian director. Hamilton & Sargeant, 1879; Lowande's Brazilian Circus, 1889; F. J. Taylor's, 1893; Tony Lowande's, Cuba, 1894-95; Great Exposition, 1895; Cooper & Co., 1898; Shipp's, winter 1898-99; Ringling Bros.', 1901; Shipp's, 1901; Campbell Bros.', 1901; Great Wallace, 1902; Gollmar Bros.', 1903-05; Frank A. Robbins, 1906; Forepaugh-Sells, 1907; Barnum & Bailey, 1908; Sells-Floto, 1911-15; Coop & Lent, 1917; Lowande & Gardner, 1921; R. M. Chambers', 1925; Dorsey Bros.', 1928; Campbell Bros.', 1929; Cole Bros.', 1930; Clyde Beatty & Russell Bros.', 1944. Died, Los Angeles, buried in Rose Hill Cemetery, Petersburg, IL.

LOWANDE, ALEXANDER, SR. (1798?-December 19, 1880) The first of the famous family to be born in the United States. Married 3 times. Children from his 2nd and 3rd marriages were riders. From the 2nd were **Clarinda, Martinho, Abelardo, Natalio,** and **Guilamena** (the last of this group marrying **Menolo Gomez,** a wealthy Cuban, and never coming to the United States). Children of the 3rd marriage, the one to **Virginia Guerin** (1845-1903), were **Romeo** (who died at age 4), **Julia, Alexander, Jr.,** and **Cecil.** Alexander died in Puerto Principe, Cuba; buried with Masonic honors in a local cemetery; survived by his wife and children.

LOWANDE, ANTHONY ["Tony"]. (1869-1937) Eldest of Martinho's children, cousin of **Julia Lowande,** husband of **Agnes Lowande.** Rode in a carrying act with his father as "La Petit Tony" until he was about 8 years of age. 1887, did a somersault pad act and 4 and 6-horse riding acts similar to those made famous by his father. Last mention, principal somersault rider, J. H. La Pearl's, 1899, also served as equestrian director. Was actively engaged in the management of his various circus enterprises in Central and South America until the time of his death in Sao Paulo, Brazil. At which time was leasing animal displays to the leading circuses of South America. Said to be the first man to do somersaults and jumps from the ground to a ring horses back wearing a tuxedo, Walter L. Main's, 1891. L. B. Lent's, 1870, 1874 (infant, performed with his father in a carrying act); Don Philip Carforlena's Spanish Circus, 1873; Great New York, 1874; P. T. Barnum's, 1875-77; Montgomery Queen's, 1876; Lowande's, 1877; Cooper, Bailey & Co., Australia and New Zealand,

1878; Lowande's, 1881, 1883; O'Brien, Handenberger, Astley & Lowanda, 1884; Pubillones', Havana, winter 1884-85; Orrin Bros.', Mexico, winter 1884-85, 1892-93, 1895, winter 1895-96, 1896-97; Mexican Pavilion Co., 1886; Frank A. Robbins', 1887-88; bareback rider, Adam Forepaugh's, 1889; Walter L. Main's, 1891, 1893, 1896; James Donovan's, Bermuda, winter 1891-92; bareback, 4-horse rider, Scribner & Smith, 1894; Tony Lowande's, Havana, winter 1893-94, 1894-95 (two companies in Cuba, winter 1894-95); equestrian director, LaPearl's, 1899; Lowande & Maginley, *Circo Braseliano*, West Indies and Cuba, winter 1899-1900 (**E. C. Maginley** sold his interest to Lowande, February 1900); Tony Lowande's, 1900-22.

LOWANDE, CECIL. (1877-1940) Younger brother of **Alexander G.** and **Julia Lowande Shipp**. Began as a hurdle rider on the hippodonie track and a principal act rider. Wife, **Nellie Ryland**, was the daughter of **Elena Jeal** and niece of **Linda Jeal**. Marriage produced twin boys. Edward Shipp's Winter Circus, Petersburg, IL, 1893-94, 1894-95, 1895-96, 1897-98, 1898-99, 1899-1900; Milwaukee Mid-Winter Circus, 1894-95; Ringling Bros.', 1897, 1899; John Robinson's, 1898; principal and hurdle rider, Walter L. Main's, 1901; Forepaugh-Sells, 1903; Lowande Bros.', 1904; Shipp's, 1905; Campbell Bros.', 1905-06, 1909-10; Sells-Floto, 1908; Gollmar Bros.', 1910; Howes Great London, 1911, 1914-16; John Robinson's, 1917-21; Hagenbeck-Wallace, 1922-24; Sells-Floto, 1927-28; Downie Bros.', 1929; Shipp's, Trinidad, 1930.

LOWANDE, CLARINDA. (b. 1852) Principal pad and bareback act. Born in Brazil, the daughter of **Alexander** and **Linda Jeal**. The marriage produced twin boys. Appeared with her family in a series of balancing feats, 1869; became a notable equestrienne and by 1877 was called the peerless "Queen of the Arena." Married **Harry Lamkin**, leaper, tumbler and equilibrist, 1879. They had two sons, **Harry, Jr.** and **Clarence**. For a number of years appeared with her half sister, **Julia**, with hurdle rider **Ed Shipp** and with her son, **Harry Lamkin, Jr.**, on a number of shows. John O'Brien's, 1873; principal equestrienne, VanAmburgh & Co., 1876; Great International, Offenbach Garden, Philadelphia, winter 1876-77; VanAmburgh & Co., 1877, 1880; Adam Forepaugh's, 1881; Big U. S. Circus, 1882; bareback rider, Cooper, Jackson & Co., 1883; Ed Sbipp's Mid-winter Circus, Petersburg, IL, 1884; Older, Crane & Co., 1884; Lamkin & Shipp, Panama and San Jose, 1885; Gardner, Lamkin & Donovan, Trinidad and Panama, 1885-1886; Roberts & Gardner, 1886; Gardner & Donovan, South America, 1886; Stow, Long & Gumble, 1889; George W. Richards', winter 1889-90; principal riding act, Gollmar Bros.', 1892. Husband died at Colon, Panama, of yellow fever, February 25, 1886. After Lamkin's death, married **Joseph Parson** in the arena of Ringling Bros.' at Praire du Chien, WI. Continued performing intermittently with **Julia** and her husband **Ed Shipp**. After maintaining a home in Pe-

tersburg for some time, her last years were spent in Chicago with son, **Clarence**.

LOWANDE FAMILY. Lowande family spanned over a half century in the performing of principal and somersault and hurdle riding acts. Starting with 1867, Lowandes appeared before the public for almost 7 decades. We are indebted to **John Daniel Draper** for his extensive study of them. It has been said that in 1867 **Alexander Lowande**, the 4th person with this name, traveled from Rio de Janeiro, Brazil to Kingston, Jamaica with a Lowande Circus. The show had arrived in Havana by July 20th and opened in Nassau in December of that year. The roster included Lowande's daughter, **Clarinda**, and his sons **Martinho**, **Natalio** and **Abelardo**. The family were with the Castello, Nixon & Howes circus that made the transcontinental tour to California in 1869. All of them were trick or scenic riders; young Aberlardo also did vaulting and leaping.

LOWANDE, JOHN. Dan Rice's, 1873.

LOWANDE, JOSEPHINE. (1864-1929) Wife of **Aberlardo Lowande**. Orrin Bros.', Mexico, winter 1880-81; Pubillones', Havana, winter 1884-85; Dockrill's, Panama, winter 1886-87; in charge of reserve seats, LaPearl's, 1899; equestrienne, Tony Lowande's, Cuba, 1900-02. See Aberlardo Lowande.

LOWANDE, JULIA [Mrs. Edward Shipp]. (1870-1961) Sister of **Abelardo**, **Martinho**, **Clarinda**, **Cecil** and **Alexander G. Lowande**, and daughter of **Virginia Lowande**. Principal bareback rider, revolving globe performer. Began at age of 6 and performed regularly on various shows until at least 1910. Married **Edward C. Shipp**, jockey and hurdle rider, February 21, 1889, Philadelphia. Lowande's Great Brazilian Circus, 1877; New York Circus (Hamilton & Sargeant), 1879; Ryan & Robinson, 1882; Martinho Lowande's, 1883. Accompanied by her mother, **Virginia**, Adam Forepaugh's, 1884 [D. W. Watt: "They were two of the nicest people that I ever knew around the show. As soon as Julia's riding act was over in the afternoon you could always find her in the ladies' dressing room either making something that added to her wardrobe or her street clothes."]. Older, Crane & Co., 1884; Frank A. Robbins', 1885; Lamkin & Shipp, 1885; John O'Brien's, 1885; Roberts & Gardner, 1886; Adam Forepaugh's, 1887-89; Frank Huffman's (Lynton Bros.), 1887; Ringling Bros.', 1890, 1895, 1897, 1902; Sturtevant & Holland, 1891; Shipp & Ashton, 1891; W. B. Reynolds', 1892; principal equestrienne, Orrin Bros.', Mexico, winter 1892-93; Shipp's Winter Circus, 1893; F. J. Taylor's, 1893; Shipp's Winter Circus, Petersburg, IL, 1889-99; Milwaukee Mid-Winter Circus, 1894-95; Shipp's, 1896; Ringling Bros.', 1897, 1899; John Robinson's, 1898; Shipp's Indoor Circus, 1903-04; Shipp's', winter 1898-99; Forepaugh-Sells, 1903, 1905, 1907; Carl Hagenbeck's, 1906; Shipp's, 1906; Barnum & Bailey, 1908, 1910; Shipp's, Panama, Puerto Rico & Jamaica, winter 1908.

LOWANDE, MARIETTA. (1871-1962) Hurdle rider. Born

182

in Frankfort, PA, daughter of **Amelia Guerin** and **Martinho Lowande, Sr.**; sister of **Tony, Alexander A., Oscar, Sr., Martinho, Jr.** and half sister to **Rossina**. Married **John Correia**, cloud swing specialist, October 27, 1888. 3 of their children—**John Jr., Edward,** and **Amelia**—were good riders. **John** died, July 4, 1907. **Marietta** died in NYC. Both are buried in Rose Hill Cemetery, Petersburg, IL. Mexican Pavilion Co., 1886; Lowande & Hoffman Mexican Pavilion Circus, 1887; Walter L. Main's, 1889-96, Forepaugh-Sells, 1899-1901, 1904, 1906, 1911. **Marietta** did a carrying act with her daughter **Amelia**, Gollmar Bros.', 1910; Forepaugh-Sells, 1911, rode a double jockey act with **John, Jr.**, and principal bareback act; Gollmar Bros.', 1913, with **Amelia**, listed as the **Correia Sisters**, Spanish equestriennes; performed in Cuba, Central and South America—Martinho Lowande's, 1877, 1881, 188788; James Donovan & Co., 1890; Tony Lowande's, 1893-94, 1902.

LOWANDE, MARTINHO, JR. (d. 1931) As a child performer with his father, early career closely paralleled that of his brother **Tony**, from 1874 until about 1890. L. B. Lent's, 1874; Cooper, Bailey and Co., 2nd Australia tour, 1877-78; Lowande's Brazilian Circus, 1883-89; Orrin Bros.', Mexico, 1885; John E. Heffron's Great Eastern, 1889; James Donovan & Co., South America, 1890. Bareback riding included pirouettes and backward and forward somersaults; also presented a trick pony and a riding dog. Tony Lowande's, Cuba, performed a 2-horse carrying act and a 4-horse riding act in addition to his somersault riding, 1895. Abroad, 1898, a long season with Newsom's, England, before opening with J. H. Cook, Scotland. Walter L. Main's, 1899; Tony Lowande's, 1901, Havana, as principal bareback somersault rider; Forepaugh-Sells, 1902-03, 1905-07; Martinho Lowande, Jr. Circus, 1919, West Indies, Central and South America, then back to Puerto Rica and Cuba; clown, Golden Bros.', 1923; Al G. Barnes', 1925-31. While with Al G. Barnes, 1931, died of plural pneumonia, Sacramento, California, May 16.

LOWANDE, MARTINHO, SR. (1839-1927) Brazilian 4-horse rider and bareback carrying act, a member of the Lowande family of performers, dubbed "The Hurricane Horseman" by press agent Charles Castle. Father of **Oscar Lowande**, brother of **Clarinda, Julia, Aberlardo, Cecil** and **Alexander G. Lowande**. His first wife, the former **Amelia Guerin**, daughter of circus man **Emillo Guerin**, a sister of **Alexander, Sr.'s** third wife, **Virginia Guerin**, died in Havana, September 26, 1881. 5 children from this marriage became riders—**Martinlo, Jr., Marietta, Anthony (Tony), Alexander A.** and **Oscar, Sr.** Had a long career, extending to at least 1920. Was somersaulting over 9 horses, 1869; by 1873, brought his infant son, **Tony**, into his carrying act; became legendary with his original 4 and 7-horse acts, styled as the "Flight of Whirlwind" as he rode 7 horses all at the same time. Second wife, **Rosina**, performed in a double equestrian act

and was a hurdle rider, also an artist on the slack wire and trapeze. The couple were divorced, 1889. Castello, Nixon & Howes, 1869; VanAmburgh, Siegrist & Lowande, 1870; leap on horseback through a hoop of daggers, VanAmburgh & Co., 1871; John O'Brien's, 1872-73; *Gran Circo Espanol de Castorienas* & Co., 1873; somersault rider, L. B. Lent's, 1874 (appearing with infant son **Tony** in a carrying act); Lowande's Brazilian Circus, 1874, 1877; P. T. Barnum's, 1875-76; New National Theatre, Philadelphia, winter 1876-77; Dr. James L. Thayer's, 1877; Cooper, Bailey & Co., 2nd Australian tour, 1877-78; Martinho Lowande's Circus, Cuba, 1880; Martinho Lowande's Brazilian Circus, 1881; Hudson & Castello, 1881; equestrian director, O'Brien, Handenberger, Astley & Lowanda, 1884; Orrin Bros.', Mexico, winter 1884-85; Mexican Pavilion Co., 1886; 6-horse rider, Lowande & Hoffman Mexican Pavilion Circus, 1887; Lowande's Winter Circus, 1889-90; Bentley's Old Fashioned, 1895; Frank A. Gardner's, South America, 1897; Forepaugh-Sells, 1902-03; Walter L. Main's, 1904.

LOWNANDE, MAZIE. Scribner & Smith (**Sam A. Scribner, Neil Smith**, proprietors), 1895.

LOWANDE, NAPIER. Tumbler and leaper, P. T. Barnum's, 1879.

LOWANDE, NATALIO. Brother of **Clarinda** and **Martinho, Jr.**, had an active circus performing career from at least 1869 until about 1895. Through 1877, appeared with his father and other family members on various circuses. After the dissolution of Alexander Lowande's Great Brazilian Circus, 1877, went to VanAmburgh & Co., 1877; John H. Murray's, West Indies, winter 1878-79; Hamilton & Sargeant's, 1879; Cooper & Jackson, 1880; Barnum & Bailey, 1882-87, 1889; Orrin Bros.', Mexico, winter 1882-83, 1883-84, 1884-85, 1885-86; Ringling Bros.', 1895; *Gran Circo Pubillones*, 1888-89, 1893. Began as a trick and scenic rider; 1871, became a somersault rider and specialized in slight of hand, juggling, tumbling, gymnastics and trapeze, high ladders and acrobatics. After the death of **W. O'Dale Stevens**, became the second husband of **Linda Jeal**, October, 17, 1885; but by January, 1886, the couple had separated and were divorced the following May 19.

LOWANDE, OSCAR. (1877-1956) Born in Frankford, PA, the son of **Martinho Lowande** and **Amelia Guerin**. Started appearing in circus at age 4 with father. Traveled and performed in his circus, South America, Cuba, West Indies, and Panama. Married equestrienne performer **Mary Louise (Maymie) Galvin** on Forepaugh-Sells, 1898. Their 2 children, **Oscar, Jr.** and **Elsie Mae** became riders. [J. D. Draper: "Oscar was perhaps the most remarkable member of the great Lowande family. He was a prominent equestrian performer who pioneered in the more intricate styles of somersault and jockey riding."] Beginning in 1881, had a long circus career of 72 years. Sometimes referred to as the "Star of the Southern

Hemisphere." Became a bareback somersault rider of excellence, reputedly being the first, at least in public, to perform a horse to horse somersault on two bareback horses running in tandem, accomplished, 1902, Forepaugh-Sells, at Madison Square Garden, NYC. Principal rider and 4-horse rider, Sanger & Lent, 1896; Great Wallace, 1897-98; Forepaugh-Sells, 1899-1907; Boston Hippodrome Circus, 1908; operated the Oscar Lowande Bay States Circus, summer 1908; Forepaugh-Sells, 1910; Sig. Sautelle's, 1911-14, 1919; Hagenbeck-Wallace, 1915-16, 1918; Sautelle & Lowande, 1917; Lowande's, South America, 1920; Lowande Bros.', Cuba, 1926. Residence at Reading, Massachusetts, where he maintained a ring barn as early as 1906. By 1935, took up clowning, which he did for the next 18 years—Bob Morton's, Al G. Barnes', James Bell's, all in 1936; Barnes-Carruthers', 1941; Walter L. Main's, 1941; Charles Hunt's, 1944; Sparks', 1946; Orrin Davenport's, 1950; Aladdin Shrine Circus, Columbus, OH, 1952. Retired, 1953.

LOWANDE, ROSINA. Carrying act rider, Mexican Pavilion Co., 1886; "Little Rosina," Lowande & Hoffman Mexican Pavilion Circus, 1887; Walter L. Main's, 1888.

LOWANDE, VIRGINIA. With Martinho Lowande's, Cuba, 1880.

LOWANDE, WILLIAM. Principal bareback somersault and jockey rider, a standing race rider and a hippodrome rider. Career extended from 1877 until 1905. 2-horse rider, Lowande's Great Brazilian Circus, 1877; Thayer & Noyes, 1877; Lowande's Brazilian Circus, 1879, 1883; Martinho Lowande's, Cuba, 1880; somersaulter, O'Brien, Handenberger, Astley & Lowanda, 1884; somersault rider, Lowande & Hoffman Mexican Pavilion Circus, 1887; Lowande's Brazilian Circus, 1889; James Donovan & Co., 1890; Walter L. Main's, 1891, 1892-94; principal bareback somersault and 4-horse rider, Cole & Lockwood, 1894; Scribner & Smith, 1895; equestrian director, Price & James, 1897; Forepaugh-Sells, 1898; principal somersault and 4-horse act, Stevens & Smith's, 1898; Hartzell's, 1899.

LOWERY, CHARLES H. See Charles H. Lowry.

LOWERY, GEORGE B. Clown, Welsh Bros.', 1896-98.

LOWLOW, JOHN. (August 9, 1841-October 18, 1910) Clown, acrobat. Born in Atlanta, GA. Ran away from home at 16 years of age when his father, a schooner captain, was lost at sea. Entered the circus profession as a candy butcher with John Robinson's and spent his career on the show, working for "Uncle John," his sons and his grandsons. Robinson & Lake as early as 1858. An accident forced retirement as an acrobat, so he took to clowning and was an instantaneous success, becoming one of the last of old school talking jesters, particularly popular in the South. On making an entrance into the arena, his familiar shout was "Bring in another horse!" From 1886 through 1893, was Robinson's equestrian director as well. In later years, worked as a press representative for the show. A last reference listed him in charge of the front door, John Robinson's (**John G. Robinson**, proprietor), 1900. May have worked with a partner named **Johnson** in a balancing act, G. M. Eldred & Co., 1859. Lake & Co.'s Circus (Lake and Norton, proprietors), 1863-65; Lake's Hippolympiad, 1866; Yankee Robinson's, Chicago, fall 1866; John Robinson's, 1868; P. T. Barnum's, 1876; Cooper, Bailey & Co., 1879; Tucker's Giant Shows, 1895; equestrian director, Walter L. Main's, 1896. [Charles Bernard: "John Lowlow's pleasing personality, his kindly spirit and that gifted natural propensity to make others happy, won my everlasting friendship...."] His savings over the years was vastly depleted by unfortunate speculation. Died at age 69.

LOWRY, CHARLES H. [or Lowery]. (d. December 16, 1917) Bareback, scenic and somersault rider. Stone, Rosston & Co., 1865-66; Lipman & Stokes, 1866; S. O. Wheeler's, 1867; Dr. James L. Thayer's, 1869; hurdle rider, George W. DeHaven's, 1870; Lake's Hippo-Olympiad, winter 1870-71; hurdle rider, VanAmburgh & Co., 1871, 1882-83; Great Eastern, 1872-74; Cameron's, 1875; hurdle rider, John H. Murray's, 1877; D. W. Stone's, 1878; hurdle rider, Great Chicago, 1879; equestrian director, Silas Dutton's Southern, winter 1879-80; S. Dutton's Southern, 1880; Frank A. Robbins', 1885; Great European, Cosmopolitan Rink, Broadway & 41st Street, NYC, winter 1885-86; W. W. Cole's, 1886; hurdle rider, Doris & Colvin, 1887; James T. Johnson's, 1888; hotel agent, Frank A. Robbins', 1890; Indian and jockey act, Leon W. Washburn's, 1893-95. Died at his home in Freeport, LI, age 54.

LOWRY, LINDA, Hurdle rider, slack-wire and globe performer, the Crystal Palace Show, 1872.

LOWRY, ROBERT. (d. 1840) Acrobat. Said to have done the first "Lion's Leap" over 3 horses, alighting on his hands, then attaining an upright position, 1834. Vaulter and clown, J. Purdy Brown's, 1826, 1833 (where he somersaulted over 10 horses); vaulter, Edward Eldred's, 1834; Brown & Co., 1836-37; vaulter, Frost & Co., 1837; clown, A. Hunt & Co., 1838. Died of consumption in New Orleans.

LOWRY SISTERS. Equestriennes, Oriental Circus, 1870; Jeal & Co., California, 1871.

LOWRY, WILLIAM. Master of horse, G. G. Grady's, 1871-72.

LOYAL FAMILY [6 in number]. Aerialists, LaPearl's, 1899.

LOYAL, GEORGE. Athlete and gymnast, proprietor, and human projectile. Adam Forepaugh's, 1871; Cooper & Bailey, 2nd Australian tour, 1877-78; Loyal's Australian Combination, South America, 1879; Orrin Bros.', Metropolitan Theatre, Havana, winter 1879-80; Mexico, winter 1880-81; human cannon ball, Adam Forepaugh's, 1880-81; Great Australian Circus, National Theatre, Philadelphia, winter 1881-82; W. C. Coup, 1882; Cantellis & Leon, Havana, winter 1882-83. The act consisted of being shot from a cannon and caught in flight by

Millie Zuila, who hung suspended from a trapeze; finished the act by a "Dive for Life" from the top of the tent. Another feat was catching a cannon ball fired from an ordinary field piece. [Day: "Loyal is both a producer and a hustler and his wife is one of the smartest and bravest little women who ever put on tights or attempted feats of skill and daring. Their engagements with Forepaugh were very successful and they filled several winters to advantage in Cuba and Mexico. The Loyals have traveled almost all over the world and speak numerous languages. They have seen life in all kinds of climates and braved epidemics and revolutions in the outlandish parts of the earth. They have acted at the theatre in times of yellow fever, cholera, and plagues; undertook long and perilous voyages; experimented in the performance of difficult and dangerous feats; and succeed where others have failed. George Loyal was one of the few to make any money out of the cannon act. As the human cannonball, he was a success. Farini tried to monopolize the act but his bluffs did not go and Loyal did the act in spite of his teeth."]

LOYAL, LITTLE JENNIE. Rider, with Howes & Cushing, 1875.

LOYAL, THEODORE. Trapeze, P. T. Barnum's, 1874; somersault and jockey rider, Howes & Cushing, 1875.

LOYAL, TILLIE. Equestrienne, Howes & Cushing, 1875.

LOYALLE, MLLE. EMELINE. See Emma Lake.

LUANDO, JOHN C. (1853-March 24, 1885) Acrobat, a first class leaper, tumbler, double-bar performer, and hurdle rider. For a time doubled with **William H. Young** as the **Luando Brothers**. Charles Bartine & Co., 1872; Great Universal Fair, 1877; Dan Rice's, 1873, 1877; Ed G. Basye's, 1878-79. Also with VanAmburgh & Co., Sells Bros.', Miles Orton's, P. T. Barnum's, and last worked with Wallace & Co., 1884-85. Died of consumption in Connersville, IN.

LUANDO, GUSSIE. *Manège* rider, Great Universal Fair, 1877; Dan Rice's, 1877; Ed G. Basye's, 1878-79; Wallace & Co., 1884. Was probably the wife of **John C. Luando**.

LUBIN, MOLLIE VIVIENNE [r. n. Frankie Watts]. "The Water Queen." Howes' Great London, 1878. Performed an act of eating, drinking, and sewing while under water. Married James L. Hutchinson in NYC, March 25, 1880.

LUCCA, PAULINE. Female lion tamer, James E. Cooper's, 1872-74. Was married to animal handler **Felix MacDonald**.

LUCHACK, L. J. L. J. Luchack's New London Railroad Shows, 1889.

LUCIFER, WILLIAM. Performed as **Hardella Brothers** (with **Hardy Bale** and **William McCall**), DeBonnaire's Great Persian Exposition, 1883, 1885; Walter L. Main's, 1886.

LUDINGTON, H. Connected with circus and menageries in the 1830s under the various names of Bailey, Ludington & Smith; Ludington, Smith & Co.; H. Ludington & Co.'s Zoological and Ornithological Exhibition.

LUDLEY, ROBERT. Mabie's, 1860.

LUDOVIC BROTHERS. Gymnasts, Warner & Henderson, 1874.

LUDWIG, HERMAN. Band leader. VanAmburgh & Co., 1856-59; Robinson & Lake, 1859-61, 1863; cornet band, Robinson & Deery, 1864.

LUDWIG, G. Band leader, John O'Brien's, 1872.

LUKE, DAN. Ethiopian and Irish comedian, Palace of Wonders (Bunnell sideshow), and Zoological lecturer, P. T. Barnum, 1876-80.

LULU. Catapult and straight up jump, "The Man Bird." Trained and managed by George Farini. Originally performed in woman's attire. Success brought sound-alikes—Lala, Lolo, Lola, Lilla. First appeared under that name at a private performance, Royal Cremorne Music Hall, London, 1871. Described as above average in height, firmly built, muscular, good looking, modest in appearance, with a profusion of light hair. USA debut, Niblo's Garden, NYC, April 28, 1873. W. C. Coup's, 1881; Barnum, Bailey & Hutchinson, 1881-82. He and his wife sailed for England, December 16, 1883, taking with his his 10 bronco horses and the leaping horse, Nettle, formerly owned by **W. C. Coup**, to be exhibited in London and Paris; W. C. Coup's, 1887.

LUM, FRANK. Bunnell's Minstrels, R. Sands', 1863.

LUNDGREEN, GEORGE. Triple-change artist on slackwire, Lowande & Hoffman, 1887; John Robinson's, 1889-90.

LUNDZ, WILLIAM. Contracting agent, the Great National, 1874.

LUPROIL, GEORGE [D. A. Forbes]. (d. July 7, 1888) Dore & Reddick's.

LUSBIE, BEN. (October 16, 1839-July 8, 1884) Treasurer Born in NYC. Original vocation was telegrapher in the service of the Erie Railroad. First started selling tickets at the old Burton's Theatre, NYC. 1861, employed by Barnum's museum where for many years he sold tickets and where he acquired a reputation as "The Lightning Ticket Seller." Capacity for work was prodigious; could sell more tickets than 2 men. Short in stature and lean in figure, had a copious vocabulary and an irascible temper. General ticket agent, Gardner & Forepaugh (Dan Gardner, John Forepaugh, proprietors), 1870; Adam Forepaugh's, 1871; P. T. Barnum's, 1872-73; 1874, joined Adam Forepaugh's and remained in his employ until 1883. In addition to ticket selling with Forepaugh, was treasurer and bookkeeper. Ill health made it impossible for him to continue the 1884 season. [D. W. Watt: "Ben was an all around good fellow and, was the only man around the show from Adam Forepaugh that cut any particular figure. Everything in the way of the finances, both winter and summer, had been left for years to Ben Lusbie.... Ben Lusbie was a good fellow, made a world of money in show business and as it came easy, it went easy."] Lusbie, who made his home in Philadelphia suffered from tuberculosis. Was eventually sent to the hospital and the people with the show not only paid all his hospital expenses,

but raised something like $400 for a monument for the man who had been their friend for so many years. Was taken back to Newark, OH, where his sister, the only relative he had, resided and the town in which he spent his boyhood days. Long hours and hard work in the business told on him and he died when he was 40 years of age in poverty in Columbus, OH. [Charles H. Day: "What a pity that poor Ben's last days were spent in harrowing poverty. Many was the dollar that he gave in charity. Through life he valued money as chaff."]

LUTHER, GENE. Band leader, Campbell's, 1878.

LYDE, A. W. Agent. Robinson & Eldred, 1852; Mann & Moore, 1853.

LYKE, JOHN. Treasurer. VanAmburgh & Co., 1869-71; Howes' London, 1874-75.

LYMING, A. F. [or Liming]. Trick clown and wire walker. June & Turner, 1846; E. F. Mabie & Co., 1847; Rockwell's, December 1847; Rockwell & Co., 1848; Eagle Circus, winter 1848; Star Circus, winter 1848; Stokes', 1849; clown, Crane & Co., 1850; J. M. June & Co., 1851-52; Joe Pentland's (Fisher & Lyming), 1854; Ballard & Bailey, 1855; Sands, Nathans, 1857.

LYNCH, DENNY. Boss candy butcher, John Robinson's, 1890-93.

LYNCH, FRANK. Banjoist, Horner & Bell, 1865.

LYNCH, GEORGE. Canvasman, P. T. Barnum's, 1873. Run over by a stake wagon and killed, August 10.

LYNCH, TOM. (March 4, 1856-May 5, 1938) Trainer and 40-horse driver. Born at Carleton Place, Ontario, Canada. At age 15 ran away from home to work for a stableman in Ottawa; pursued by his father, boarded a train and headed for the United States and reached Philadelphia. First job, assistant hostler, Rice, Ryan & Spalding, 1873. P. T. Barnum's, 1874; Melville, McGinley & Cook, 1875; Great London, 1876-79;

Barnum & Bailey, and Ringling Bros.' until his retirement, 1936, with 34 years as superintendent of baggage stock. Drove the 40-horse hitch. [New York *Herald Tribune*: "His horse sense was uncanny, and even when he was in his seventies, the wagons rolled with smooth celerity, whatever the weather, as Tom Lynch prowled from one trouble spot to another about the lot."] Died, Bridgeport, CT, age 82. Member of the Elks, Odd Fellows, Eagles and Moose. Wife's name **Rebecca**, non-professional.

LYON, JOHN. Writer, Hemmings, Cooper & Whitby, 1868.

LYON, MRS. BERTHA. (d. September 10, 1880) Bearded lady. P. T. Barnum's, Adam Forepaugh's and other circuses. Died in Syracuse. NY.

LYON, REBECCA. Bearded lady, Dr. James L. Thayer's, 1870. May be same as above.

LYONS. Juggler, Brown & Mills, 1838; tumbler, plate balancer, dancer, Waterman & Co., 1838.

LYONS, D. R. See D. R. Lines.

LYONS, H. P. Agent, Cooper, Bailey & Co., Australian tour, 1877.

LYONS, PETER. Chief billposter, W. H. Harris' Nickel-Plate, 1884.

LYTTLE, W. M. ["Mack"]. (b. March 9, 1855) Born in Madison, WI, and grew up in Jackson Center, PA. As a boy worked on farms, then became a coal miner, and at 17 began to learn the trade of blacksmith and wagon maker in Youngstown, OH. Went to Topeka, KA, 1878, and by 1884 was a partner in the firm of Huffman & Lyttle, blacksmiths. By 1889, had become sole owner of the Capital Carriage Works there. 1890, was co-partner and treasurer with Fulford & Co.'s Great United London Shows, probably consisting of the 21 wagons built and painted in his establishment; show was on the road only one season.

186

ALEXANDER LOWANDE, SR.'s SECOND MARRIAGE

Clarinda	Martinho, Sr.	Aberlardo	Natalio	Guilamena
(b. 1852) married Harry Lankin, Sr. (1854?-1886)	(1839-1927) married Amelia Guerin (d. 1881) 5 children	(1853-1928) may have been adopted or apprenticed, married a Josephine ? which produced 8 children	became second husband of Linda Jeal, Oct. 17,1885, divorced May 19, 1886	married wealthy Cuban, Menolo Gomez
son Harry Lamkin, Jr. (b. 1879) married Pearl Robinson	Anthony [Tony] (1869-1937) Marietta (1872-1962) Alexander A. Oscar, Sr. (1877-1956) Martinho, Jr. (d. 1931)			

ALEXANDER LOWANDE, SR.'s THIRD MARRIAGE
Virginia Guerin

Romeo	Juliet [Julia]	Alexander G.	Cecil
died at age 4	(1870-1961) married Ed Shipp (1864-1939) on Feb. 21, 1889	(1876-1958) married Carrie Kemp, 1899	(1877-1940) married Nellie Ryland (1875?-1955) which produced twin boys
	son Ed Shipp, Jr. and daughter Virginia		

MAC and MC

MAC DONALD, ALICE ["Mad Alice"]. (1853?-August 12, 1896) Equestrienne. Married to animal trainer **Felix MacDonald**. Great London, 1880; Boyd & Peters, 1880; wild beast tamer, Barnum, Bailey & Hutchinson, 1881, 4-horse chariot driver, 1882; Frank A. Robbins', 1885; P. T. Barnum's, John Robinson's, Doris & Colvin, George W. DeHaven's, Leon de Leon's (Cuba). Died in New Orleans, LA, age 43.

MAC DONALD, ANDREW. Proprietor, Andy MacDonald's World Fair Circus, 1892; MacDonald & Reichhold's Great Chicago Shows (Andrew MacDonald, **George Reichhold**, proprietors), 1896.

MAC DONALD, CHARLES. Clown and equestrian, John Bill Ricketts', Philadelphia, making his first appearance May 9, 1793.

MAC DONALD, DONALD. Gymnast, Shelby, Pullman & Hamilton, 1881.

MAC DONALD, FELIX. Lion tamer. Bryan's, 1868; billed as "Famous Lion Tamer and Man of Iron Nerve," Hemmings, Cooper & Whitby, 1870; zoological director, P. T. Barnum's, 1877; Boyd & Peters, 1880; Cole's Great New Southern, 1881; Frank A. Robbins', 1883, 1885; ringmaster, Wallace & Co., 1886; master of hippodrome stock, Doris & Colvin, 1887; Ferguson's, 1888; Sam McFlinn's, 1888; superintendent of menagerie, Barnum & Bailey, 1893. First wife, **Pauline Lucca**, was a female lion tamer; another wife, **Alice MacDonald**, was an equestrienne.

MAC DONALD, GEORGE B. (d. December 19, 1890) Contracting agent, Sells Bros.', 1886; also O'Brien's, Barnum's.

MAC DONALD, GEORGE W. Washburn & Arlington, 1891; MacDonald & Wells' Big Show (George W. MacDonald, **F. E. Wells**, proprietors), 1892.

MAC DONALD, HARRY. Australian Dime Show, 1887; W. H. Harris' Nickel-Plate, 1889.

MAC DONALD, J. Boss animal man, John Robinson's, 1881.

MAC DONALD, J. D. Advertising agent, MacDonald & Wells' Big Show (**George W. MacDonald, F. E. Wells**, proprietors), 1892.

MC ANDLIS, R. J. Treasurer, W. C. Coup's, 1880.

MC ANDREWS, J. WALTER. Negro deliniator, "Watermelon Man," Great European, 1865; Frank J. Howes', 1865.

MC ARTHUR, J. B. Program agent, Warner & Henderson, 1874.

MC ARTHUR, W. Ringmaster, with George W. DeHaven & Co., 1865

MC CABE, WILLIAM. Strongman, a unit of June, Titus, Angevine & Co., 1841-42; Welch & Mann, 1843-44.

MC CADDON, JOSEPH TERRY. (January 31, 1859-January 21, 1938) Born in Beverly, OH. Brother-in-law of **James A. Bailey**. On occasion, signed his name **Joe Bailey**. 1876, joined Bailey as an apprentice, leaving for Australia with the Cooper & Bailey show as head of wardrobe. Treasurer, Hagar & Campbell Museum, Philadelphia, 1884-85; treasurer, Barnum & London, 1885. Manager, Adam Forepaugh's, 1890-91, after James E. Cooper and James A. Bailey purchased the show following Forepaugh's death; with the death of Cooper, January 1, 1892, James A. Bailey shared the ownership with McCaddon. Took the show to Europe, 1904, which was a disaster, causing bankruptcy; too large a show for the small French towns and opposition from Buffalo Bills' Wild West show. With the death of Bailey, represented the controling interest of Mrs. Bailey, his sister. Disposed of all the circus holdings to the Ringlings, 1908, except the Buffalo Bill show, which he sold to **Major Gordon W. Lillie** (Pawnee Bill). Following, became interested in real estate in and around NYC. A man of refinement and college educated. Died of apoplexy at the home of his son, **J. T. Jr.**, Great Neck, NY. He had another son, **Stanley G.**, living in Coaral Gables, FL.

MC CAFFERTY, WALT. Ringling Bros.', 1887; proprietor, Walt McCafferty's Great Golden Shows, 1894; company was stranded in July.

MC CAFFERTY, WALT. Privileges, F. J. Taylor's, 1891. This may be the same man as above.

MC CALL, WILLIAM. Performed as **Hardella Brothers** (with **Hardy Bale** and **William Lucifer**), DeBonnaire's Great Persian Exposition, 1883, 1885; Walter L. Main's, 1886.

MC CANN, JAMES F. [also McKann]. Band leader. With Nixon's Southern, 1870; John Robinson's, 1871.

MC CANN, R. Program agent, Alex Robinson's, 1874.

MC CARN, "MASTER". 8 years old on his debut as a rider, Pepin & West, Olympic, Philadelphia, fall 1817. One of his feats, doing flipflops across the ring with his feet tied together. Franklin's company, 42 South Fifth Street, Philadelphia, spring 1802; moved to Vauxhall Garden, NYC, in July of that year; old Richmond Hill Circus the same year. Was lost in the U.S. sloop of war, *Hornet,* off Tampico.

MC CARTHIE, BILLIE. Acrobat, G. G. Grady's, 1872.

MC ARTHUR, W. Clown, George W. DeHaven's, 1865.

MC CALL, MATIE. Haight & Chambers, 1867.

MC CARTHY, CHARLES. (1838?-January 23, 1900) Entered the circus profession at age 18 and developed into a singing clown, tumbler and animal trainer. Alex Robinson's, 1866; leaper, John Robinson's, 1871-73; ringmaster, 1873-74, 1876, 1878; Cooper, Bailey & Co., 1877, clown in 1881-85, in charge of the mail department in 1888, clown and outside ticket seller, 1889; concert manager and clown, with Charles Lee's, 1895. At the time of death, was employed at Middleton's Clark Street Dime Museum, Chicago. Died there, age 62.

MC CARTHY ["Four Paw"]. Boss canvasman, Bruce L. Baldwin's, 1894.

MC CARTNEY, HARRY. Treasurer, W. C. Coup's, 1878, 1892.

MC CARTY, CHARLES. Alex Robinson's, 1866; Charles Noyes', 1870; Howes' Great London, 1878.

MC CARTY, J. Silas Dutton's Southern, winter 1879-80, 1880.

MC CARTY, T. J. Manager, Daniel Shelby's, 1888.

MC CASLIN, CHARLES. (d. October 1910) Forepaugh-Sells Bros.' Died in Atlantic City, age 59, where he had cast aside the grease paint to become a Salvation Army worker.

MC CAULEY, CHARLIE. Comedian, bone player, Whitmore & Co., 1868.

MC CLEAN, CHARLES. See Charles McLean.

MC CLELLAN, ALFRED SEYMOUR. (March 13, 1856-February 10, 1884) Born in Norwich, CT. Gymnast. After amateur appearances, joined Heywood's Combination, also Van's Great Olympic Circus, under the name of **Alfred Seymour.** 1879, with **Edmund Rice,** performed as the **Rice Brothers**—Great Commonwealth, Batcheller & Doris, Adam Forepaugh's, J. T. Johnson's (with **Charles LaRue**), Tony Denier's, Sells Bros.', Washburn's Last Sensation, John B. Doris', Edward's Olympic. Was shot and killed on Elizabeth Street, Norwich, by Frank V. Conant.

MC CLELLAN, C. S. Secretary, P. T. Barnum's, 1873.

MC CLENNEN, CHARLES W. (October 19, 1835-June 28, 1885) Born in New Lisbon, OH. First professional appearance as privilege man with Spalding & Rogers' *Floating Palace.* Connected with Adam Forepaugh's, John Robinson's, and J. J. Nathans'. Opened European Dime Museum at 37-37½ Bowery, NYC, November 1, 1877, which made him a good deal of money. Both he and his brother, **John,** were well known phrenologists. Died of consumption at his home in NYC. Had one child.

MC CLOUD, JAMES. French, Hobby & Co., 1835; western unit of June, Titus, Angevine & Co., 1842.

MC CLURE, COL. DAN. (1848?-March 28, 1899) Joined a circus at age 17. Was connected variously with Montgomery Queen's, Burr Robbins', John Robinson's, Wallace's, Walter L. Main's, Sells Bros.' and Fred Burke's Automatic Cities. At times, owned and managed museums in Erie, PA, and Akron, OH. Organized the Indian Blood Medicine Co., Atlanta, GA, 1897, and toured throughout the state until his death. Died from stomach cancer in Louisville, KY, age 51.

MC CLURE, DAN. Sideshow privilege, Burr Robbins', 1877.

MC CLURE, JOHN. Agent, Crescent City Circus, 1855.

MC CULLOM, M. Concert banjoist, Cooper, Bailey & Co.,

1879. May be the same as below.

MC CULLOM, MAT. Clown, Adam Forepaugh's, 1871.

MC COLLUM, NAT [or Matt]. Banjoist and Ethiopian entertainer, Castello & VanVleck, 1863; general performer, Van-Amburgh & Co., 1874, 1880. May be the same as above.

MC COLLUM, THOMAS. (1828-1872) Equestrian. Famous for his jockey act and, by some, considered the best 2-horse rider of his day. Boston Lion Circus, 1836; Lion Theatre Circus, 1837; acrobat, S. H. Nichols', 1839, 1842; Raymond & Waring, Philadelphia, 1839-40; rider, Welch & Mann, 1841; 2-horse rider, Dr. Gilbert R. Spalding's, 1845; Howes & Mabie, 1845. Organized a boat show with clown **Den Stone,** Great Western Circus, 1846, which visited the river towns on the Mississippi, using the steamer *Franklin,* a boat 100' by 15' in size. Company was composed of 70 people including a band. Partnership lasted through the season, 1850. Went to England, Welch, McCollum & Risley, 1851. Son was English rider, **Eugene Gardner,** who took his professional name from an aunt, a well-known English equestrienne.

MC CONKEY, WILLIAM. Proprietor, McConkey & Co.'s Arabian Show, 1888, with his performing horses.

MC CONNELL, GEORGE. Frank A. Robbins', 1885.

MC CORMICK, A. W. Proprietor, McCormick's New Silver-Plate Show and Menagerie, 1898.

MC CORMICK, J. Acrobat, Sadler's Great English Circus, 1875.

MC CORMICK, JOHN. Perhaps the first to develop the art of ceiling-walking; at least he was billed as the inventor of the antipodean apparatus for his performance, February 16, 1852, New York Amphitheatre, 37 Bowery. The bill read in part: "Professor John McCormick of Ohio, the successful inventor of the only antipodean apparatus ever completed, will exhibit his astonishing performance of inverted locomotion, in which he will walk feet uppermost, upon a marble slab, nine feet in length, at an elevation of eighteen feet from the ground." Joe Pentland's, 1852.

MC CRACKEN, SAMUEL. Proprietor, Samuel McCracken's circus, 1825-26; managed Parson's circus, 1826.

MC CREARY, J. M. Treasurer, Spalding & Rogers, 1853; agent, Wesley Barmore's, 1854; Spalding & Rogers, 1857, 1859.

MC CUE, J. S. Proprietor, J. S. McCue's National Circus, 1883.

MC CURRAN, CHARLES. Boss animal man, W. H. Harris' Nickel-Plate, 1884.

MC DONALD, CHARLES. The "electric boy," P. T. Barnum's, 1883.

MC DONALD, GEORGE. Asst. boss canvasman, P. T. Barnum's, 1871.

MC DONALD, ROBERT. Dan Rice's (**Adam Forepaugh,** proprietor), 1866.

MC ELROY, J. A. Manager, Miller & Runnells, 1888.

MC EWEN, WILLIAM S. Banjoist, Negro delineator, Cooper's International, 1873; Cooper, Bailey & Co., 1876. Home was in Columbus, OH.

MC FADDEN, DAISY. Concert singer, Cooper, Bailey & Co., 1880.

MC FARLAND, A. Vaulter, Rockwell & Stone, 1843; Cincinnati Circus, 1845; acrobat, June & Turner, 1846; Henry Rockwell, 1847; J. M. June, 1851.

MC FARLAND, FRANK. Advance and contracting agent, Harry Thayer & Co.'s, 1890.

MC FARLAND, JAMES. (d. 1858) A tall, handsome man, was considered a celebrated equilibrist on the tight rope. Did the first free-act wire ascension outside a circus tent, which was for Levi J. North. Involved in a vaulting match with W. O. Dale at John Tryon's, beginning September 28, 1846; betting was heavy, with McFarland the favorite over Dale, who had recently come from England; outcome is uncertain. Several years later, killed by a Mr. Roberts, landlord of a hotel at Liberty, MO. North's circus and Spalding & Rogers were both perorming in that city. McFarland's former wife, Mlle. Castilla, was attached to the North company. Fearing harassment, manager North ordered the landlord not to allow McFarland to seek her out. McFarland, learning she was in the hotel, demanded to see her. A confrontation with the landlord followed. The two drew weapons and engaged in a struggle, during which MacFarland was stabbed in the neck, severing his jugular vein and resulting in a speedy death. Acrobat, Welch, Bartlett & Co., 1839; Howes & Mabie, 1841; P. H. Nichols', 1841; Dr. Gilbert R. Spalding's, 1844-49; tight-rope, S. H. Nichols & Co., 1842-43; Bowery Amphitheatre, NYC, 1845; ringmaster, June & Turner, 1846; vaulter, Rockwell & Stone, 1846; John Tryon's Bowery Amphitheatre, NYC, winter 1846-47; tight rope, Spalding & Rogers, 1848-51, 1853; Welch's, 1852; Levi J. North's, 1854-55; winter 1857-58. Wife was the former Ann Tucker; daughter, Fanny Brown, married William Carlo.

MC FARLAND, THOMAS [r. n. William Brown?]. (d. 1881?) Somersaulter. Joseph Palmer's, 1836, Havana, Cuba, 1837; Baacon & Derious, 1838-39; Welch & Bartlett, 1839; June, Titus & Angevine, 1840; Welch & Mann, winters 1841-42, 1842-43, 1843-44; Howes & Mabie, 1841-43; Howes', winter 1843-44; Dr. Gilbert R. Spalding's, 1844; John Tryon's, winter 1844-45; Howes', June 1845; Welch & Mann, August 1845; Welch, Mann & Delavan, August 1845; Rockwell & Stone (Rockwell's unit), where he threw 67 somersaults, 1846; Howes & Co., 1847; Howes & Co., May 1848; 2nd unit, Howes & Co., threw 87 somersaults, 1848; Sands, winter 1848-49; Welch's, 1849; June's, winter 1849-50; J. M. June's Oriental, 1851; Welch, Raymond, Driesbach, 1852.

MC FARLAND, W. H. (b. May 26, 1860) Manager of sideshows for 44 years, with only 6 circuses, always working on percentage. Originator of "Wild Man" and "Sea Serpent."

Stone & Murray, 1876; Harris' Nickel-Plate, 1894-95; Howes Great London, 1915.

MC FLINN, HARRY. (1857?-January 4, 1889) Brother of showman Sam McFlinn. 9 years ticket agent, Burr Robbins'; left August, 1886, to take the baths in Mt. Clemens, MI, for his rheumatism; treasurer, Sam McFlinn's European, 1888. Married Ruby Shropshire on the Robbins show, June 20, 1885, in Marshalltown, IA. Died of consumption in Burlington, IA, age 32.

MC FLYNN, IDA. Burr Robbins', 1885.

MC FLINN, SAM. (1852?-May 26, 1911) Trick, talking and singing clown. Stood 6' tall, was a fine dresser and handsome. Great Eastern, 1872-74; Stevens & Begun, 1874; H. Harlan's, 1875; Great Universal Fair, 1877; Ed G. Basye's, 1878; Dan Rice's, 1878; Thornton's, 1880; Burr Robbins', 1880, 1884; Cole's Great New Southern, 1881; VanAmburgh & Co., 1882-83; French & Monroe, 1885; manager, McFlinn's Hippolympiad, 1887, of which Dr. James Thayer was the proprietor; proprietor and manager, Sam McFlinn's European Circus, 1888; in partnership with Col. G. W. Hall, Sr., 1889-92, Hall & McFlinn's. Claimed to be the originator of the Ten Cent Show. His circus usually wintered in Chicago where all his spare money was invested in real estate. Married Ida Thayer, daughter of Dr. James S. Thayer. They had no children. Died at age 59.

MC GANNON TERRANCE J. See John Mackley.

MC GILL, W. F. Treasurer, Driesbach & Howes, 1868.

MC GINNESS, JAMES. See James A. Bailey.

MC GINNIS, JOHN. Boss canvasman, G. G. Grady's, 1874.

MC GINTY, H. Gymnast, Spaulding & Rogers, 1850; 1854-58.

MC GLASSY. See Alfonso "Fons" Antonio.

MC GRAW, JOHN. Rider, S. H. Barrett's, 1887.

MC GREW, JOHN. Minstrel, Alexander Robinson's, 1875-76.

MC GREW, WILLIAM. See William LaRue, Sr.

MC GUFFIN, HENRY. Married Mme. Worland on the Lipman Circus, 1866, Alleghany City, PA.

MC GUIRE, JAMES. Comic singer, with Dan Rice's, 1866; clown, Gardner & Kenyon, 1868; Pat Ryan's, 1882.

MC HUE, J. S. Manager, Westman's, 1882-83.

MC HUGH, WILLIAM H. Manager, L. B. Lent's, 1874.

MC ILLWAY, JOHN. See John Jackson.

MC INTOSH, GEORGE D. Press agent, Hamilton & Sargeant, 1878, advance manager, 1879; contracting agent, Welsh & Sands, 1880; VanAmburgh & Co., 1881.

MC INTOSH, JAMES R. Press agent, Hamilton & Sargeant, 1879.

MC INTYRE, AARON. Privileges, Cameron & Tubbs' North American, 1877.

MC INTYRE, JAMES. (August 8, 1857-August 18, 1937) Of the comedy team of McIntyre and Heath, one of the greatest blackface vaudeville and minstrel acts of all time. Died of uremic poisoning, on his estate in Noyack, near Southampton, LI, NY. In the days following the Civil War, McIntyre and Heath were supreme in the field of minstrel comedy and soft-shoe dancing. For more than 50 years they toured every part of the country, including the Far West when it was really wild. Their famous skit, *The Ham Tree*, amused audiences for years. They developed the slow-paced, melancholy blackface type of comedy, and were forerunners of **Moran and Mack** and **Amos n' Andy**. Theirs was the first act to receive top billing on the Keith Circuit, and, in their time, received the biggest vaudeville contract from Keith. McIntyre was born at Kenosha, WI, and before he was out of his teens was already amusing audiences with impromptu songs and dances on the trains where he peddled candy. Began his professional career as a clog-dancer, Pete Kerwin's Concert Hall, Chicago, which he left for a job with **Katie Putnam's** ballad and dancing show. Quit this company to join McKenzie's Circus, 1870; Burton & Ridgeway's Minstrel's, 1871; 3 years later, teamed with **Tom Heath**, another great burnt cork man, and the act was born—McIntyre playing the lazy, drawling Alexander and Heath doing a foil as the pompous, polysyllabic Hennery. Fame came quickly, all over the world, and soon their act drew as high as $2,000 a week. Circuses included Anderson & Co., 1879, also Burr Robbins' and others. McIntyre married a dancer and balladeer, **Emma, Young**, professionally known as **Maude Clifford**. Among their most popular skits were *Georgia Minstrels*, *Man From Montana*, *Flying to Jail*, and *Waiting at the Church*. But *The Ham Tree* always remained the most popular item in their repertoire. Retired from the stage, 1919, but continued to appear in benefit performances now and then. Guested on Rudy Vallee radio program, 1832. When McIntyre passed away, Heath was lying on a sickbed a few miles away, dangerously ill.

MC INTYRE, LIZZIE [or Lizette]. Equestrienne, W. W. Cole's, 1886.

MC INTYRE, TOM B. ["Pico"]. Shakespearean clown and equestrian director, W. W. Cole's, from at least 1877 through 1886, including the W. W. Cole's Australian tour (which left San Francisco October 23, 1880). Subsequently, equestrian director, Doris & Colvin, 1887; Sells Bros.', 1895.

MC KEE, FRANK. Agent, Robbins & Colvin, 1881.

MC KENNA, FRANK. S. H. Barrett's, 1887.

MC KENZIE, DONALD. (1855?-March 1917) Advance agent, auditor and advertising manager. Born in Dubuque, IA. Ringling Bros.', Barnum & Bailey, Buffalo Bill's Wild West, Gentry Bros.' Died of Bright's disease in his 63rd year.

MC KNIGHT, GEORGE. Clown, Barnum & Bailey, 1892.

MC KNIGHT, J. Strongman, the "Vermont Samson." S. H. Nichols', Albany Amphitheatre, winter, 1843.

MC LACHLAN, JOHN. (b. March 18, 1860) Born in London, Ontario, Canada. Joined a train crew with Sells Bros.', May 14, 1880, under boss **Archie Seals**. Chalker and snubber, Adam Forepaugh's, 1881; train crew for **Byron Rose**, P. T. Barnum's, 1885-90; 1st assistant under Jack Webb, Adam Forepaugh's, 1891-93; Barnum & Bailey, 1894; superintendent, Buffalo Bill Wild West, 1895; Barnum & Bailey, 1902. [C. G. Sturtevant: "There was no detail of his position of which Mr. McLachlan was not an expert. His knowledge of the railway systems of the United States and Canada was complete; he knew every yard and siding, was acquainted with all officials, yardmasters, dispatchers, and people in the various mechanical and operative departments, and, moreover, they respected him for his great abilities."]

MC LANE, W. R. Manager, P. A. Older's, 1872; assistant manager, United States Circus, 1882.

MC LAREN, DANIEL. Father of **Dan Rice**. Co-proprietor (with **Tom Farwell**), Dan Rice's, 1858-59, possibly 1860.

MC LAUGHLIN, BRIDGET Equestrienne. Sister of **Virginia Sherwood**, who changed her name to **Bridgetta**. While performing with a half dozen horses in New Orleans, missed her footing and fell between the animals; although she managed to grasp the main of one of the horses, she was dragged around the ring for some distance before one of the horses trampled on her and caused serious injury, which resulted in her death a short time after being carried from the arena. Was buried in Pittsburgh.

MC LAUGHLIN, HANK. Boss canvasman, Harper Bros.' European (**P. N.** and **D. J. Harper**, proprietors), 1892.

MC LAUGHLIN, JAMES H. (d. August 16, 1884) Chief of detectives, P. T. Barnum's, 1872-76. Died in NYC.

MC LAUGHLIN, J. R. Treasurer, Holland, Bowman & McLaughlin, 1890.

MC LEAN, CHARLES. (b. March 13, 1837) Born in Tompkinsville, Staten Island, NY. Pioneer boss canvasman. Began at age 12 as property boy with Sands & Nathans, Bowery Amphitheatre, NYC, 1849; Franconi's Hippodrome, NYC, 1853; Howes & Cushing, 1855-59; R. Sands', 1860-63; European Circus (**Avery Smith**, **G. C. Quick**, **John Nathans & Co.**, proprietors), first assumed job of handling the canvas, 1864-70; show sold to James Wilder with McLean remaining, 1871; P. T. Barnum's (Older managed), ran sideshow for G. B. Bunnell, 1872; P. T. Barnum's—150' round top with three 50' middles—(Coup and Castello), 1873; remained with that organization until Barnum and Bailey became the property of the Ringlings.

MC LEAN, JOHN. Agent. With L. B. Lent's, 1874; Miles Orton's, 1885.

MC LEAN, MISS C. Equestrienne and *danseuse*, J. W. Wilder's, 1872.

MC MAHON, CHARLES H. (d. December 1, 1894) Acrobat, rider. Born in Manchester, MI, and entered the business at age 15 under the care of his brother, **John S. McMahon**, circus proprietor and rider. Hurdle rider, Donaldson & Rich,

1885; Holland & McMahon's World Circus (**George Holland, John McMahon,** proprietors), 1885-88; Ringling Bros.', 1891; equestrian director, W. B. Reynolds', 1892; Charles McMahon's Circus, 1893; Howes & Cushing, 1894. Died of pneumonia in Birmingham, AL, at about 27 years of age.

MC MAHON, JOHN. (d. November 1882) English musician. Connected many years with Sanger's. Came to USA with Howes' Great London, 1871-74; Montgomery Queen's, 1875-77. Died of pneumonia, Silver City, NM

MC MAHON, JOHN S. (d. November 17, 1892) Born in Ann Arbor, MI. Considered one of the best all-around performers in the profession—bareback, 4-horse and hurdle rider, tumbler, leaper, wrestler and boxer. Hurdle and Indian rider, Dr. A. W. Hager's, 1878; hurdle rider, leaper, tumbler, Adam Forepaugh's, 1882; hurdle rider, Burr Robbins', 1885; Holland & McMahon's World Circus (**George Holland,** John McMahon, proprietors), Chicago, 1885-86. Took a show to Mexico, Central America and the West Indies, 1870s, where he is said to have made a fortune. Had a one-ring show on the Pacific Coast, 1888, and remained west of the Mississippi for 3 years. When health began to fail, around 1890, was confined to the sidelines; last riding occurred at Oakland, CA, on the closing night of that year. The show started out from there for the 1892 season and went as far as Halifax, N.S., then returned to Portland, OR, for closing on November 12, 1892. At that time, McMahon expressed the intention to dispose of his interest in the cmpany because of ailing health. The outfit was then shipped to Chicago for sale. Died in his Pullman car as he passed through Missoula, MT, while accompanying his outfit back, age about 38 years. Standing about 5'10", he had great physical powers and an attractive physique, was an admirer of horses and proud of his own stock, temperate in his habits and careful of his health, but overwork and over-training sapped him and lymph cancer did the rest.

MC MAHON, JOSEPH BRYAN. (1862-1897) Brother of **John S.** and **Charles H. McMahon.** A graduate of the University of Michigan. Holland-McMahon, 1886-1888; after brother John died, 1892, took out a circus in the McMahon name. [Orin Copple King: He had much in common with grifters the likes of Willie Sells and Ben Wallace, who "stayed close to the straight and narrow when at home, but once they passed the city limits nothing was too scurilous for them to attempt."] While in Wichita, KS, with the McMahon Bros.'s Circus, 1897, was shot in the stomach 3 times and killed by Deputy Sheriff **J. V. Cunningham,** a Texas law enforcement officer, in the Manhattan Hotel, Witchita, KS. The officer had come to question McMahon about one of his roustabouts who

was charged with setting fire to the Windsor Hotel in Abiline, TX. One version states that an altercation ensued, which caused both to pull out their weapons; McMahon's shot went wild; before he died, a notary was called and McMahon dictated a statement of the shooting and made out his will. Another version has Cunningham shooting McMahon as he reached for a handkerchief, thinking he was going for a weapon. Cunningham was nearly lynched following the shooting because McMahon was an extremely popular figure in Witchita. Funeral at the Witchita Scottish Rite Cathedral was so immense that the crowd overflowed into the street. [Gordon Yadon: "He hired uncouth men with bad reputations, brought in all sorts of gamblers, and tolerated other unethical practises."].

MC MANN, CHARLES. Agent, car #2, Metropolitan Circus, 1897.

MC MINN, HENRY C. See Harry King.

MC MURTRY, J. A. Proprieter, McMurtry's Indian Show, Museum and Amphitheatre, 1863-64. Later, speculated in show property and engaged in commercial business, Harmonsburg, PA.

MC NALLY, PETER S. (d. April 10, 1915) Connected with Forepaugh-Sells, Globe Theatre, Boston, and other enterprises as a press agent. Brother, **John J. McNally,** was a playwright. Long distance swimmer who, 1897, attempted to swim the English Channel, coming within 3 miles of the French shore. Married **Agnes V. Murphy** of Lawrence, MA, 1903. Died on the deck of a fishing schooner, lying off Gloucester, MA.

MC NELL, MINNIE. Walter L. Main's, 1887.

MC NUTT, J. O. Band leader, Walter L. Main's, 1893.

MC PHAIL, A. Agent, Cook & Whitby's, 1892.

MC PHAIL, BERT. Special agent, Cooke & Whitby, 1892.

MC QUHAE, EDWARD FRANCIS MAITLAND. See Frank Edwards.

MC TIERNAN, MARY. Albino, Barnum, Bailey & Hutchinson, 1881-82.

MC VEIGH, JOHN E. True & McVeigh's Mammoth Railroad Shows (**Cecil A. True,** John E. McVeigh, proprietors), 1896.

MC VEY, ANDY. Clown, Barnum & Bailey, 1892.

MC VEY, CHARLES E. (December 15, 1866 - July 1892) Acrobat. Born in Zanesville, OH. Entered the profession at age 18 with **Thomas Pettit,** performing on the horizontal bars for Weldon's Circus. Following season, bar and trapeze performers, Wallace & Co.; Sells Bros.', 1888-89; French and Co., 1891. Broke his neck and died from a fall.

MC VICKERS, JOHN. Clown, Shelby, Pullman & Hamilton, 1881.

John H. Murray

M

MABIE BROTHERS [Edmund F., Jeremiah]. Operated E. F. & J. Mabie's circus. Two of 11 children of **Joshua** and **Elizabeth Gifford Mabie**, born in Putnam County, NY, near the village of Patterson. **Edmund F.** (1810-October 26, 1867); **Jeremiah "Jerry"** (June 12, 1812-August 31, 1867). In their 30s before entering the circus business, 1841, when they formed a partnership with **Nathan A. Howes** to operate the New York Circus, sometimes advertised as the Olympic Circus. 1843, Nate Howes left the firm and Jeremiah Mabie took a year off, leaving management in the hands of **S. B. Howes** and E. F. Mabie; this was the year that Howes & Mabie first ventured into the western states. Fall 1846, Seth B. Howes sold out his interest; 1847, title was changed to Grand Olympic Arena and United States Circus, with Edmund was manager. The first to quarter in Wisconsin with purchase of land near Delavan, June, 1847. Jeremiah managed the company, 1849, after which the brothers spent less time traveling with the show; **Pardon A. Older** bought a one-third interest this year. Older became manager, 1852, the title changing for the summer season to Great United States Circus of Older & Co. Entered into a lease contract, November 1852, with the **James Raymond** menagerie interests and toured under title of Mabie & Co.'s United States Circus and Raymond & Co. and Driesbach & Co.'s Menageries Combined, **Pardon A. Older** still the manager. After July, 1853, the Raymond name was dropped from the title. Used menagerie, 1854, from **Richard Sands'** circus; Older sold his third of the firm back to the Mabies this year; **S. B. DeLand** became the manager. Jerry Mabie took over active management in 1859, but DeLand returned, 1860. **J. J. Nathans** joined for the 1854 tour, at which time the involvement of the Mabies diminished; Edmund was active in Delavan, and Jeremiah spent most of his time in New York. 1858, Mabies financed or supplied the equipment for a second troupe, Mabie & Crosby's French and American Circus; 1859, it went out as Davis & Crosby. 1861, title was E. F. & J. Mabie and J. J. Nathans Combined. Mabie's Great Show, 1862; Mabie's Grand Menagerie, 1863; following year marked the end of the Mabie tours. Traveled the West and South for 17 years. They were astute businessmen, closemouthed and tight-fisted. Jeremiah retained his residence in Putnam County, NY. Neither brother was married until they were 40 years of age, both marrying wives in their teens. Edmund and his wife, **Laura Buckley**, had 8 children; Jeremiah and **Anna Mary Field** had 3. The brothers died within 2 months of each other. [Stuart Thayer: "Their public legacy lay within circus history ... and in their efforts on behalf of the village of Delavan, opening it to a period of growth and fame."]

MABIE, MYRON. Agent, Howes & Mabie, 1841-44.

MABIE, SYLVESTER. Agent, Howes & Mabie, 1841.

MABLE FAMILY [4]. Bicyclists, Irwin Bros.', 1887.

MACART, WILL. S. H. Barrett's, 1885.

MACARTE, BLANCHE. G. G. Grady's, 1870.

MACARTE BROTHERS [3 in number]. Posturers, John B. Doris', 1884.

MACARTE, FRED. (d. August 15, 1919) Animal trainer and performer. Born in Yarmouth, England. Mother, **Mme. Marie Macarte**, was of the famous **Ginnett family** and owned one of the largest circuses in England. Wife was **Josephine Macarte**. At age 4 made his debut in the *Cinderella* pantomime, Astley's Amphitheatre, London. Dan Rice's, 1870; treasurer, Macarte Sisters' Great Parisian Circus, 1870; Howes' London, 1876-78, one of the 3 **Livingston Brothers**; Orrin Bros.', Havana, winter 1878-79; S. H. Barrett's, 1885; Barnum & Bailey, England, 1887-88, introducing his dog and monkey act. Continued in vaudeville with animal act, but poor health forced a move to California, 1914. Last engagement, Morosco Theatre, Los Angeles, in drama *Young America*, with dog, Brownie, 1918. Two of his original animal tricks were the baboon property man, "Babe," and the original bicycle monkey, "Joe." Died at his home in Hollywood, CA .

MACARTE, JEAN. Acrobat, with Howes & Co., 1846.

MACARTE, JOSEPHINE. (d. January 4, 1927) Wife of Fred Macarte. In show business some 50 years. Part of ther time with a standard dog act in vaudeville. Died in Los Angeles, age 77. See Fred Macarte.

MACARTE, MARIE. (1826-1892) English and Parisian equestrienne. Born in Paris, made her American debut October of 1845. In her act, leaped over ribbons, went through paper balloons, and executed a scarf dance; also introduced a new feature to the ring, that of giving mythological scenes in addition to her riding act, which originated from Ducrow's work in England; act was considered new and novel for the time which included broad and lofty leaps and sword combat on horseback. Was married to **William? McCarthy**, vaulter, tumbler, and acrobat from the Royal Amphitheatre, London, who died, St. Helens, December 2, 1864. Then married **Dan Rhodes**, veteran advertiser and manager, Marshall, TX, March 9, 1868, while connected with Lake's. An eldest son, **Edward P. Hall**, died, 1895; another, **Fred Macarte**, was a wire and general business performer. Sands, Lent & Co., 1847; Welch & Delavan, 1847; Dr. Gilbert R. Spalding's, 1847; Nixon-Macarte Circus, Washington, DC, 1863; James M. Nixon's Alhambra, NYC, fall 1863; Hippotheatron, 14th Street, NYC, winter 1863-64; Rivers & Derious, Washington, DC, fall 1864; National Circus, Cincinnati, winter 1864-65; Frank Howes',

1866; Palmer's, 1866; Mike Lipman's, winter 1866-67; Haight & Chambers, 1867; Michael O'Conner's, 1869; Stowe & Norton, 1869; G. G. Grady's, 1870. November 14, 1874, issue of the New York *Clipper,* announced she was planning to retire, NYC, and establish an equestrian and gymnastic furnishing house, where all articles could be purchased for the circus business. Later, with husband **Dan Rhodes** retirement was again indicated, 1878. Still listed with S. H. Barrett's as late as 1885.

MACARTE SISTERS [Kate, Addie, Marie, Blanch]. Proprietors, Macarte Sisters' Great Parisian Circus, 1870; G. G. Grady's, 1870. See Marie Macarte.

MACARTHY, MARIAN. Singer, James M. Nixon's, Niblo's Garden, NYC, 1860.

MACCOMO, MARTINO. (1839-January 11, 1871) Animal tamer. Born in Angola. As a youth assisted his father, who was a hunter and trapper. Stone & McCollum, 1855, NYC. Following, toured the United States, went to England and was engaged by **William Manders,** a menagerie proprietor, 1857. Traveled with that organization, billed as "The African Lion King," until the time of his death from rheumatic fever in Sunderland, England.

MACK, ADA. See Ada Zelkika.

MACK, HARRY. General performer. Juggler, Sheldenburger's, 1871; performing dogs, Adam Forepaugh's, 1872; ringmaster, Campbell's, 1878; equestrian director and equilibrist, Shelby, Pullman & Hamilton, 1881; equestrian director and a troupe of performing dogs, Hilliard & Main, 1883; equilibrist, Pullman, Mack & Co., 1884; dog act, Col. Giles' Great World's Fair, 1885; Irwin Bros.', 1889.

MACK, JAMES. Minstrel performer, P. T. Barnum's, 1873.

MACK, JOHNNY. Clown, Great European, 1865.

MACK, PERCY. English jockey, Adam Forepaugh's, under the patronage of **Watson,** the equestrian. Died, New Orleans, October 24, 1881.

MACK, ROBERT. General agent, James T. Johnson & Co., 1881; contracting agent, Beckett's, 1887.

MACK, T. F. Proprietor and sideshow manager, Pullman, Mack & Co.'s United Mastodon Shows (**Pullman, Hilliard, Main** and Mack, proprietors), 1884.

MACKIE, GEORGE. Agent, Frank A. Gardner's *Circo Americano,* Central and South America, 1888.

MACKLEY, JOHN [r. n. Terrance J. McGannon]. (1850?-March 5, 1911) Clown, vaudevillian, comic opera performer. Served for the North in the Civil War, being present at the Appomatox Court House in Virginia when Lee surrendered to Grant. Connected with Barnum & Bailey, Robinson's, Ringling Bros.', and McCue's, road manager with the latter; comedian with Ada Richmond Comic Opera Co. and end man for the Emerson Minstrels. Shortly before his death, was performing week stands with the Merrymacks. Died of pneumonia, Pittsburg, KS, age 61.

MACOMBER, ZEBEDEE. Pioneer in the menagerie business, and a member of the Zoological Institute. Connected with **Rufus Welch** and **Eisenhart Purdy,** Macomber, Welch & Co., 1832-37. Went to Africa 3 times for the Boston Zoological Association in search of wild beasts to bring back for exhibition. Landed in Hingham, MA, with 67 specimens May 19, 1835. Proprietor, Grand Caravan, 1825-26; Macomber & Co., Gray & Macomber (one show), 1829; Macomber & Co., Macomber & Howe, Macomber & Birchard, 1830; Macomber & Co., 1831; Purdy, Welch, Macomber, to Africa July 1834; Macomber and Welch, to Africa, January 1835 to May 1835; Purdy, Welch, Macomber (owned 3/16 Boston Exhibition), 1837; Welch, Macomber & Weeks, giraffe exhibition, 1839.

MADDEN, ARCHIBALD. Clown Born in Williamsburg, NY. Lafayette Amphitheatre, NYC, 1825-28; Mount Pitt Circus, NYC, 1826-27; Price & Simpson, Washington Amphitheatre, Boston, 1828; Stewart's, 1832; Brown's, 1833-34; Crane & Co., 1836; Waring, Raymond & Co., 1839.

MADDEN, CHARLES. Clown. Dodge & Bartine's Great World Varieties, 1868; Burr Robbins', 1879; Great New York Show, 1880; Hilliard & DeMott, 1880-81; M. M. Hilliard's, 1882; principal clown, Sells Bros.', 1883; clown and equestrian director, Pullman, Mack & Co., 1884-85; Miles Orton's, 1885. Abandoned the ring, 1886-87, Sells Bros.', to spend full time as press agent for the show; also press agent and clown, Lemen Bros.', 1894.

MADDEN, GEORGE P. (1836-January 19, 1897) Versatile performer. Started with Mabie Bros.' as sleight of hand artist. Had Punch and Judy show, perfected magic act and doubled as sideshow barker and treasurer, also fine vocalist and actor. Buckley and Babcock's North American; later, in partnership with **John Holland** in circus company venture, Holland & Madden, 1860-1865; Ben Maginley's, 1863; Coup-Castello's Egyptian Caravan, 1870; Older's, 1871; P. T. Barnum's, 1871-73; Cooper, Bailey & Co., 1876; Great Universal Fair, 1877; also Buckley's Hippodrome and Buckley-Colvin Circus. Came out of retirement to join Dr. George Morrison's Coliseum Circus, 1879. Married **Mary Ann Holland,** daughter of **John** and **Honora Holland.** Daughter **Nora** was considered prettiest girl in Delavan, 1880s. She married **Joseph B. McMahon.** Went to Witchita following the death of his daughter and died, age 59.

MADDEN, MARY ANN. (February 20, 1847-October 31, 1895) Equestrienne. Born of English parents who were traveling in Germany. Married clown **George P. Madden** around 1864. Died Delavan, WI. See above.

MADDRA, JAMES T. (1812-1902) 4-horse rider. Reynolds & Maddra, 1855; Orton's, 1857; Orton & Older, 1859.

MADDRA, WILLIS. (b. 1845) Equestrian. Principal rider, Orton & Older, 1859-60.

MADDOX, GEORGE. Clown, Barnum & Bailey, 1892.

MADIGAN BROTHERS. Gymnasts, with D. F. Dunham's,

1875.

MADIGAN, EDWARD H. (1856?-May 23, 1893) Born in Cleveland. Began in the circus business with W. W. Cole; also connected with Adam Forepaugh's as excursion agent for 8 years, 1880s. Married **Minnie Sylvester**, 1890. Died in Buffalo, NY, age 37, while manager of the Star Theatre of that city.

MADIGAN FAMILY. Equestrians, consisting of **Henry P.** (1815-December 15, 1862), his wife **Marie,** and their children **Emma, Ella, Rose, Eggie, James,** and **Charles. Henry P.,** a native of Albany, NY, the patriarch of the family, was considered a daring rider. Albany Circus, February 1826; J. W. Bancker's, traveling in NY State, 1832; French, Hobby & Co., 1835; Mammoth Eagle Circus, 1836; winter circus, Richmond Hill, NYC, 1837; Charles H. Bacon's, 1837-38; Bacon & Derious, 1838; Thomas Taplin Cooke's, 1838; June, Titus, Angevine & Co., 1839, Bowery Amphitheatre, NYC; Aaron Turner & Sons', 1842; Howes & Mabie, 1843-45; Robinson & Foster, 1844; Dr. Gilbert R. Spalding's, 1846; Victory Circus, 1847; John Tryon's, Bowery Amphitheatre, NYC, 1847; Dan Rice's, 1849; S. P. Stickney's, 1849; proprietor, Stone & Madigan's Great Southwestern, 1850; Crane & Co., 1850; scenic rider, Mabie's, 1851; Myers & Madigan's Railroad Circus, 1854-55. [John A. Dingess: "Whether as ringmaster, equestrian, gymnast, vaulter, pantomimist or brilliant invention, Henry P. Madigan had no superior.... His accomplishment made up an entire encyclopedia of the sports of the circle.... His disposition was one of the most amiable character and his habits excellent. A good companion and a clever fellow, James H. Madigan was every inch a gentleman."] Wife, **Marie,** occasionally rode in the grand entry but otherwise seldom appeared. She died July 17, 1887. Henry died in Kingston, Jamaica. **Charles** performed scenic riding together with his brother, **James,** on trapeze, as well as vaulting, turning and spinning. E. F. & J. Mabie's Grand Olympic Arena and United States Circus, 1851; H. P. Madigan's, 1856; Niblo & Sloat, 1860; James M. Nixon's, Washington, DC, fall 1862; L. B. Lent's, Wallack's Old Theatre, NYC, 1863; L. B. Lent's Equiscurriculum, 1863-64, 1866; Howe & Norton, 1864; French's, 1867; Dan Castello's, 1868; Adam Forepaugh's, 1869; Mrs. Charles Warner's, Philadelphia, 1869. **Eggie** (1858?-July 7, 1892), vaulter, was a principal performer with Hengler's, Boswell's, Cooke's and Myers' circuses in England; also performed on the Continent as well as in the Far East with John Wilson's. Wife's name was **Lizzie**. Eggie died in London, age 34. **Ida** was married in NYC to banjoist and Ethiopian comedian **Andrew Collum**, December 27, 1873. **James** was a double-somersault performer and outstanding bareback rider. One of his feats was throwing back somersaults on a running steed. At the Old Bowery, NYC, he ran from the back stage entrance, making 2 complete turns in the air before alighting, after which he immediately leaped and

turned another; executed *battoute* leaps over 8 horses, L. B. Lent's, November 1863; considered one of the best in the world at this. Stone & Madigan, 1850; Myers & Madigan, 1854; Howes, Myers & Madigan, 1855; Howes & Cushing, England, 1858; Niblo & Sloat, 1860; Comac's Woods, Philadelphia, early summer, 1860; Front Street Theartre, Baltimore, early winter, 1860; Great Orion Circus, Old Bowery, NYC, 1861; L. B. Lent's Equescurriculum, 1861-64; Howe & Norton, 1864; Gardner & Hemmings, Philadelphia, winter 1864-65; John Robinson's, 1866; L. B. Lent's, Hippotheatron, NYC, 1867; Dan Castello's, 1868; Adam Forepaugh's, 1869, where he performed double somersaults over the large elephant Romeo; pad and double-somersault rider, James Robinson's, 1870; John Wilson's, Far East, 1884; Ginnett's, Dublin, 1886. **Rose** was the wife of Jim Myers of the Myers & Madigan Circus. Howes & Mabie, 1845; John Tryon's, Bowery Amphitheatre, NYC, 1846; Dr. Gilbert R. Spalding's, 1846; Dan Rice's, 1849; Crane & Co., 1850; Stone & Madigan, 1850; principal equestrienne, Myers & Madigan, 1854-55; Howes & Cushing, England, 1858. [John A. Dingess: "In her principal act performance, or what is technically called a trick act, Miss Madigan outshown all her rivals.... She appeared the perfect embodiment of all the graces, displaying her animated tableau in rapid succession as she literally flew around the arena."] **Ella** was also a skilled equestrienne. [John A. Dingess: Ella "who was the very embodiment of skill and elegance, had no compeer. As a delineator of graceful equitation, she was a charming picture on horseback and her beautiful flights over objects might have been termed perfection."]

MADIGAN, HENRY P. See Madigan Family.

MADIGAN, JAMES H. See Madigan Family.

MADIGAN, JOHN. Gymnast. John Robinson's, 1866; L. B. Lent's, 1867; Mrs. Charles Warner's, Philadelphia, 1869.

MADIGAN, MARIE [Mrs. H. P. Madigan]. See Madigan Family.

MAER, JAMES. Lake's Hippo-Olympiad, 1867.

MAFFETT, JAMES. Gymnast, John Robinson's, 1876.

MAGILL, S. A. Clown, Adam Forepaugh's, 1879.

MAGILTON, HENRY M. [or Majilton]. (1828-June 16, 1901) Gymnast and monkey impersonator. Born in Philadelphia. As a youth learned the carpentry trade. Winter, 1848, while doing gymnastic stunts on the ice, attracted the attention of several showmen with a winter circus located in the city. Became a tumbler with Aaron Turner's, 1848-49; 1850, joined Spalding & Rogers and remained for 8 years. While with the show, became famous as the monkey in *Jocko; or, The Brazilian Ape.* A physical powers coupled with daring allowed him to climb all around a tent or theatre, up and down the posts, over the tiers of seats, leaping from place to place with the agility of a monkey. Of his powerful hands, it was said that he could travel the length of a joist holding his entire weight by just his thumbs and fingers. In appearance, was short and thick. Magilton and **George Dunbar** were with Sands, Nathans & Co., Bowery theatre, 1857-58, credited with being the first in America to do the 2-person comic feat called "Motley Brothers." 1861, with **Hiram Franklin, John Neber, John Rochette** and **George Dunbar**, made a tour of Europe. While performing in London's Alhambra, met with an accident which ended his career and sent him back to the United States a cripple for life. In doing a turn on the trapeze, before making his flying leap, his belt caught on the bar which delayed him from catching the other bar and he fell to the floor. The Queen sent her own physician to treat him. [John A. Dingess: The team of **George Dunbar** and Henry Magilton were outstanding for "uniqueness, activity and originality og their movements."] Died from heart failure at his home in Philadelphia.

MAGINLEY, BEN. (November 18, 1832-June 3, 1888) Clown. Born in Philadephia of well-to-do parents. Left home at age 17 to join a stock company at Dr. Simpson's Pittsburgh Theatre under the management of **John Foster**; later, followed Foster to Cleveland. Then moved on to Cincinnati and Baltimore theatres, the latter at the Front Street, 1856. During this period, performed in most of the major dramas of his time. At the start of the war, was stage manager and low comedian for proprietor **George Rayfield** of the New Memphis Theatre company, Memphis, TN. Took a farewell benefit on July 28, 1863, where, according to the Memphis *Daily Bulletin*, "pit, boxes, and gallery were jammed, and the lobbies were overflowing by those who had to stand." Maginley was a popular figure with the Memphis locals. It has been written that an unsuccessful investment in an arenic venture forced his entry into the circus business. Just what that was is unclear. He may have put money into the erection of an indoor amphitheatre, for advertising of his circus admission prices implies such a structure—boxes, 75¢; family circle, 50¢; and colored gallery, 50¢. This could have been the building that opened in March of the following year for dramatic performances under the title of Olympic Amphitheatre for lessees Benjamin, Cony & Co. Maginley's Great Circus opened on August 8, 1863. **Oliver Bell** had been employed to break horses for the establishment, and, within the short span of 10 days, succeeded in making ring stock out of them. Maginley, a robust, hearty man of some 240 pounds, entered the ring as clown for the first time on August 17 of that year. There is no information as to how long the circus continued in Memphis, the advertising in the *Daily Bulletin* having ended by August 13. Additionally, there is nothing to suggest that the company performed in any other city. In fact, Maginley may have remained within shouting distance, because he re-appeared on March 14, 1864, at the New Memphis Theatre for the benefit of **R. Arnold**, and on the same day opened a 2-week engagement at the Olympic Amphitheatre where he performed the comic role of Timothy Toodles in *Toodles*. [Charles H. Day: "Ben is a jolly soul and it is worth the price of admission to hear him laugh."] Magin-

ley & VanVleck's Cosmopolitan Circus opened in St. Louis, November 7, 1863. Maginley married **Marie Carroll** ("Marie Elise"), equestrienne adopted daughter of 2-horse rider **Barney Carroll**, 1864. A daughter, **Viola**, died March 14, 1874, at only 2 months old. Mrs. Maginley died of consumption the same year. (See Marie Carroll) Proprietor and clown, Ben Maginley's Monitor Circus; subsequently, contracting agent and clown, George W. DeHaven's, traveling in the South, 1865-66 (by fall the concern had been purchased by Andrew Haight and became Haight & Chambers' United Circus); teamed with **Barney Carroll** in a circus venture, Maginley, Carroll & Co., 1867-68; Bailey & Co., 1870; equestrian director and clown, J. E. Warner & Co., 1871-72; manager, Great Eastern, 1873; manager and co-proprietor, **John O'Brien** and **G. R. Spalding**, Maginley & Co., 1874; co-proprietor and manager, Melville, Maginley & Cooke, 1875; equestrian director, Howes' Great London, 1876; equestrian director, P. T. Barnum's, 1877. After retiring from the ring, spent several years on the stage as a character actor, performing with Lester Wallack in *Rosedale*, with McKee Rankin in *The Danites*, etc. In 1878, began starring in *Deacon Cranket* and *A Square Man*, working in those plays under the management of J. M. Hill, 1881-83; was the original Tom Blossom in *May Blossom*, 1884; this was followed by 2 seasons of *Inshavogue*. Died of heart trouble at home of his daughter, **Mrs. Frank Buckle**, Westchester, NY.

LORD, CHARLES. Asst. mgr, Castello & VanVleck, 1863.

MAGINLEY, ED and **LOTTA.** Aerialists, Bailey & Winan, 1890.

MAGINLEY, MRS. BEN. See Marie Carroll.

MAGINTY, H. General performer, with Spalding & Rogers, 1850-58.

MAGRI, COUNT. (d. November 5, 1920) Second husband of **Mrs. Tom Thumb.** 37" tall and weighed 55 pounds. First appeared on the Italian stage, 1865. Came to USA with his brother **Ernest** and later joined Barnum & Bailey. Died at a Middleboro, MA, hospital, age 71.

MAGUIRE, FRANCIS. See Frank Vaughan.

MAGUIRE, FRANK. See Ajax.

MAGUIRE, JAMES C. [or McGuire]. Clown. Bryan's (**John V. O'Brien's**), 1869; Mrs. Charles Warner's, Philadelphia, 1869; Adam Forepaugh's, 1870; Joel E. Warner's, 1872; Dan Rice's, 1872-73; Great International, 1874; Great Metropolitan Olypiad, 1877. Was shot in the arm, 1877, and had to have it amputated.

MAHOMET. Strong man of Bedouin Arabs. Carried 6 members of his troupe around the arena at once, a total of over 1,100 pounds. J. O. Howes', 1848.

MAHEMET, ALI. (d. September 8, 1895) Acrobat. Came to America, 1881, bringing a troupe of Arabian acrobats, Adam Forepaugh's; John B. Doris', 1882; Orrin Bros.', Mexico, 1885; Barnum & Bailey, 1886; Thatcher, Primrose & West's

Minstrels, winter 1886-87; leading attraction, Pain's Fireworks, Manhattan Beach, NY, summer 1887; Barnum & Bailey, 1888-89. On return of the latter circus from Europe, retired from the business. Died of consumption in Broolyn, NY, age about 56.

MAHR, CHRISTIAN. H. Buckley & Co., 1857-58.

MAIN, WALTER L. (July 13, 1854-November 29, 1950) Raised near Cleveland, OH, where he always resided. Son of circus proprietor **William Main**, of Main & Hilliard. Was a bill passer for the show at age 7, advance agent at 11, and at 18, 1885, with financial help from his mother, joined with **Charles Phillips**, a cornet player in his father's circus, in producing a company of *Uncle Tom's Cabin*. After selling his interest to Phillips, opened a variety show and played fair dates primarily in Ohio. When horse-drawn streetcars were being replaced by electric trolleys, sent his father to Cleveland to buy horses for the show, who returned with 20 of them, purchased for the sum of $200. With the stud of trolley horses, Walter Main launched his circus. In 1891, the show went to rail travel with 13 60-foot circus cars; 1892, toured with his first 3-ring show; the next year, at the peak of his circus management, had 2 rings and a center platform, with **Stirk and Zeno** as a feature flying return on the high wire. The show was nearly demolished in a train wreck on the Tyrone & Clearfield Railroad near Tyrone, PA, May 30, 1893, when the brakemen lost control coming down the mountain and a pile up occurred at Vail Station. It was the first section, consisting of 20 cars (6 were 60-footers, the rest 50-footers). 17 of the cars jumped the track, 6 men were killed outright and about 20 were badly injured, 60 horses were killed on impact, 20 more had to be shot, and another 50 were injured. Damage was estimated at between $100,000 and $200,000. The show was back on the road within 8 days, re-opening in Tyrone to big business, since sympathy of the community was great—no lisence, no lot fee, and the Elks Club gave the company a banquet. Writing in 1899, Main claimed that in 15 years of operation he had only one losing season and that, at that time, it was the 3rd largest circus in the country, the loser being due to the circus train wreck on that fateful Decoration Day. An attempt was made at the end of 1899 to secure a buyer or for someone to lease the Walter L. Main Circus; however, the entire outfit was auctioned off on January 24, 1900, at the winter quarters in Geneva, OH. Always the owner, manager and router of his own show, Main sold out while still under 40 years of age and went to Europe for a rest. Claimed that ill health and his independent wealth made it feasible to unburden himself from circus management. At this time, owned 2 large farms, home in Geneva, and interests in other business ventures. In December, 1900, a dispatch stated that he had closed a contract with the American Bicycle Co. of New York City to lease the large building formerly occupied by the Geneva Cycle Co. and to occupy it for winter quarters in anticipation of returning to the

road, 1901, with a 30-car circus. Later, it was announced that temperance crusader, Carrie Nation, would travel with the circus—to be featured over all other attractions, appear only 30 minutes during the day, give a 15 minute talk on temperance in the menagerie tent at both afternoon and evening performances, with a special tableaux wagon devoted to her in the street spectacle, have a quarter section of a Pullman car, a maid, and all her meals served in her private compartment, and exclusive use of the main tent every Sunday afternoon. Main did indeed take the Walter L. Main Circus on the road, 1901, and continued with it until his second retirement, 1905, when he ceased circus management with sole ownership of a 31-car railroad show, which was sold to **William P. Hall**. December 11, 1905, purchased the controlling interest in the First National Bank of Geneva; subsequently, bought, rented and sold circus property and obtained interest in other shows through their use of it. 1901, owned and leased the Rhoda Royal Show; 1905, owned all the horses with the Hagenbeck Show and Powers Performing Elephants that played the Hippodrome, NYC; leased a 7-car show and property, Cummings' Wild West Exhibition, 1906; interest with the show was terminated in July, 1906, which included 80 draught horses and a troupe of performing elephants. Main had gone with the show to get it organized but eventually lost a desire to travel. October 2, 1906, the Cummings show property was nearly all destroyed by fire at the winter quarters in Geneva; many of the animals were killed; losses amounted to about $100,000, which was partially covered by insurance. It was thought that the blaze was caused by defective electric wiring. Leased property to Dan Robinson's Circus, 1910; rented out a 3-car show and a wagon show, 1911; a "clean up sale" of show property was advertised to occur at winter quarters, January 28, 1913. Andrew Downie leased the Walter L. Main Show name, 1918, and went on the road with what was formerly Andrew Downie's La Tena Circus, until the lease ran out, 1921. Managed stadium shows for **Harry** and **Irving Polack**, owners of the Rutherford Greater Shows and Pollack Bros.' 20 Big Shows, 1917. Married a non-professional, **Florence M. Damon**, of Jefferson, Ohio, on December 31, 1887; divorced, Jefferson, May 26, 1903. Second marriage, Pittsburgh, PA, June 9, 1909, to **Louise Katherine Schneider**, a non-professional, the bride being 28 years old, the groom 46. [Floyd King: He had a habit of saying "'Don't talk show business at meals; it is bad for the digestion.' Then he would sit down and, forgetting his rule, would launch into some circus recollection."] Was founder of the Circus Friends of America, a fraternal organization for circus fans.

MAIN, WILLIAM. Father of **Walter Main**. First organized as Main & Burdick, 1879; Main & Sargeant's International, 1881 (Main and **F. W. Sargeant**, proprietors). After purchasing partner's interest, sole ownership, 1882; Hilliard & Main, 1883; co-proprietor and advance man, Pullman, Mack & Co.'s

198

United Mastodon Shows (**Pullman**, **Hilliard**, Main and **Mack**, proprietors), 1884; sold out, 1885; with son Walter, 1886; co-proprietor, William Main & Co.'s New Consolidated Show (Main, **Sargeant**, and **Clapp**, proprietors), 1889; Main & Sargeant, 1890-91.

MAJOR ATOM. Midget. Barnum & London, 1884.

MALCOLMS. Aerialists, Robert Hunting's, 1894.

MALLORY, BENACE. (1829-November 2, 1859) Rider. Howes & Mabie, 1845; Spalding's, 1846-47; Welch, Delavan & Nathans, 1848; Spalding & Rogers, 1850; Robinson & Eldred, 1851. Died in Savannah, GA.

MALONE, J. Band leader, John Robinson's, 1869-70; treasurer, Ryland's, returning to California after about 5 years spent in South and Central America, 1878.

MANAHAN, DAN. Boss canvasman, with John Robinson's, 1871-72.

MANCHARD, FRED. Clown, Howe's New London, 1887.

MANCHESTER, H. E. Bill agent, G. G. Grady's, 1869.

MANDERS, S. T. Equestrian, VanAmburgh & Co., 1881.

MANFREDI. [with his daughters] Troupe of wire-walkers. Pepin & Breschard, 1809; Cayetano & Co.; Canada, fall 1811; Cayetano's, NYC, summer 1812.

MANKIN, GEORGE W. Light and heavy balancer, Yankee Robinson's, 1862; Frank J. Howes', 1865; aerialists and gymnast; Hemmings, Cooper & Whitby, 1870; Lake's Hippo-Olympiad, 1871; contortionist, Burr Robbins' & Co., 1872; tumbler, G. G. Grady's, 1873-74.

MANKIN, HIRAM. Stowe's Western Circus and Indian Show, 1867-68.

MANN, COL. ALVAH. (d. July 9, 1855) Co-proprietor, Welch & Mann's New York Circus, 1841; Welch & Mann's, 1842-43, which performed in metropolitan areas—the Park Theatre, Bowery Amphitheatre, (NYC), the Olympic Circus (Philadelphia), the Front Street Theatre (Baltimore); and Military Gardens (Brooklyn). The show was out as Welch, Mann & Delavan's Grand Double Circus, 1844; the following year, Welch & Mann's Mammoth National Circus. After the 1846 season, Mann left the circus business for a time; latest speculation, 1852-53, was unsuccessful. Died in NYC.

MANN, ED. Acrobat, leaper, Haight's Great Southern, 1874.

MANN, ELLA. Albino, P. T. Barnum's, 1873.

MANN, GEORGE G. General agent, McMahon's, 1888.

MANN, H. A. General agent, Charles Lee's, 1893.

MANN, HENRY W. Contracting agent, Frank A. Robbins', 1885.

MANNING, BILLY. George W. DeHaven's, 1865.

MANNING, DAN C. Talking and singing clown, Charles Bartine's, 1892.

MANNING, JOHN ["Vocalist Bill"]. (1870?-December 7, 1908) Worked with all the big shows of his time for over 20 years, including as clown, Adam Forepaugh's, 1893; and the Barnum & Bailey show in England. Was at various times property man, canvasman, seat man, etc. Died from consumption, St. Joseph's Hospital, Bronx, NYC, age 38.

MANNING, WILLIAM E. (1834?-May 15, 1876) Born in Piqua, OH. Commenced in the minstrel profession at 17 years of age, first with the Dixey Company, 1859; afterward, with Campbell, Morris, Rumsey, Wilson and Newcomb troupes, and with the VanAmburgh, and Haight & Chambers circuses. Became an assistant manager in the Emerson, Allen & Manning Troupe, 1867; afterward the Emerson & Manning, and Manning Minstrels. As an end man, had a clear, honest eye, a face of over-healthy crimson, and a general unassuming bearing. [T. Allston Brown: "It was a curious but perfectly natural compound of simplicity, cunning, affection, dishonesty, earnestness, laziness and cowardice; all his bad qualities so manifestly the product of hard experience and sad necessity that one could not help a feeling of sympathy and liking for the worn-out, shuffling-gaited, whining-voiced old rascal."] Died of consumption, Chicago, IL, age 42.

MANNING, WILSON. Ringmaster, with Palmer's, 1835; Bancker & Harrington, 1835; clown, Waring and Raymond, New Orleans, winter 1837-38; rider, John Tryon's, Bowery Amphitheatre, NYC, 1843; Welch & Mann, 1843.

MANSFIELD, GEORGE. At one time a partner of **F. F. Proctor** as the **Levantine Brothers**. His father ran a shoe store in Boston. [M. B. Leavitt: He "for many years was great in an act with crystal pyramids."]

MANTANO. Wild beast tamer of a pack of 11 hyenas, Howes & Sanger, 1872.

MANTLE, JAMES W. Head bill poster, Dan Rice's Paris Pavilion, 1872.

MANTLE, WILLIAM. Adam Forepaugh's, 1871

MANTZ, JULIUS. Band leader, with Alexander Robinson's, 1871.

MANUEL, PHILIP. Leader brass band, Orton Bros.', 1865.

MARANTETTE, MME. Equestrienne. Famous for her skill with the Marantette high school horses. Married her manager, **Col. D. H. Harris**, 1895. Their travels have covered America and Europe.

MARCELLA BROTHERS. Gymnasts, New York Central Park Circus, 1877.

MARCELLUS, LIZZIE. (d. March 30, 1882) Equestrienne. Born in Schenectady, NY, where her father had a small farm. About 1866, was apprenticed to **Dan Rice**, when her training as a rider commenced, and she rapidly developed into a dashing and skillful rider. Made her first appearance in NYC when Dan Rice's Paris Pavilion Circus began a season on Fourteenth Street between Second and Third Avenues on September 25. 1871 (This was a portable theatre that had been constructed in this country and taken to Paris for the use of an American circus during the Exposition, but which French authorities would not allow to be used inside the city limits.). Married **Harry Cordona**, 1873, but the union proving unhappy, obtained a divorce 2 years later. Married **William H. Stowe**, clown and leaper, 1877. Dan Rice's, 1869-72; P. T. Barnum's, 1879-80; John H. Murray's, West Indies, winter 1878-79, 1879-80; and then Orrin Bros.', Havana, Cuba. The Stowes next joined the New Orleans Circus, which they ultimately purchased at auction and took out, a small affair traveling principally by steamboat on the Mississippi and its tributaries; until both Mr. and Mrs. Stowe, with their 2 children, lost their lives by the burning of the steamer *Golden City*, at Memphis, TN. Considered one of the best dressers that ever graced the arena.

MARCHAEL, WILLIAM. Posturer, performed with his son, Welch & Mann, Philadelphia, 1846.

MARCO SISTERS. Roman ladder and high wire, Moore Bros.', 1887.

MARDELL, W. F. (d. December 27, 1908) Entered the circus business when shows consisted of only a few wagons; worked in various positions and finally elevated himself to being an advance man for Ringling Bros.' Mardell & Co., 1884-89. Married **Millie Annette**, a featured bareback rider. Died in Memphis, TN.

MARIE ELISE. See Marie Carroll.

MARIETTA, MME. Equestrienne, Orton & Older, 1859.

MARIETTA SISTERS. Gymnasts, equestriennes, Cooper & Co., 1874.

MARION, DAVID. Gymnast, W. W. Cole's, 1886.

MARION, E. C. Contortionist, Baldwin, Wll & Co.'s Great Eastern, 1880.

MARION, G. General agent, Baldwin, Wall & Co.'s Great Eastern, 1880

MARION, JULIAN. Hurdle rider, Ryland's, returning to California after about 5 years spent in South and Central America, 1878.

MARION SISTERS. Equestriennes, P. T. Barnum's, 1871-73. First appearance in USA, P. T. Barnum's, 1871.

MARIOTINI, CAYETANO. See Cayetano.

MARKOWIT, DAVE. Treasurer, with White & Markowit's United Railroad Shows, 1889.

MARKS, FRANK. John Robinson's, 1871.

MARKS, HIRAM. (1832?-1910) Clown. Native of Cincinnatus, NY. Began with Welch's National Circus. Was considered expert and daring bareback rider, but at about 35 years of age fell from a horse while performing the "Drunken Sailor" act and was kicked in the knee by the animal, which rendered him unable to continue a riding career. Consequently, became a Shakespearean clown and the originator of clown acts that were imitated in the modern ring. In later years, worked as both ringmaster and clown. Children, **Willie Minnie**, and **Sallie**, were also bareback riders. Daughter, **Minnie**, married **Charles Robinson**, one of the owners of the Robinson circus. Wife died in Cincinnati, OH, of consumption, December 9, 1866, age 28; he died in Indianapolis, IN, age 78. Dan Rice's,

1848-49; Stone & Madigan, 1850; Great Western, 1855; Major Brown's, 1856-57; Satterlee-Bell, 1858; ringmaster, Levi J. North's, Chicago, 1859; Hyatt & Co., 1859; George W. De-Haven's, 1860-62; Levi J. North's, 1863; Lake & Co.'s, 1863; John Robinson's, 1865, 1871, 1873-75, 1883-93; Lipman & Stokes, a first-year organization, 1866; Lake's Hippo-Olympiad, 1867-68, winter 1870-71; Amphitheatre, Louisville, January 1868; principal clown, Stone & Orton, 1870; P. T. Barnum's, 1872; equestrian director, Sells Bros.', a first year organization, 1872; W. W. Cole's, 1875; Burr Robins', 1877; equestrian director, Camp's Grand Southern, 1880; Batcheller & Doris, 1881.

MARKS, JAMES. Orton Bros.', 1865.

MARKS, JOHNNY. George W. DeHaven's, 1860.

MARKS, JOSEPHINE. Equestrienne. Adam Forepaugh's, 1886; John Robinson's, 1888-89; Ringling Bros.', 1892; La-Pearl's, winter 1894-95.

MARKS, MINNIE. (d. January 16, 1886) Equestrienne. After being trained by her father, **Hiram Marks**, made her debut as a pad rider on Mike Lipman's, 1866, age 6. Dan Castello's, 1867; touted as "the child wonder on horseback," Stone & Orton, 1870; Hemmings, Cooper & Whitby, 1870; Lake's Hippo-Olympiad, winter 1870-71; began performing as a bareback rider, John Robinson's, 1871; Sells Bros.', 1872; principal rider, P. T. Barnum's, 1872; W. W. Cole's, 1875; Burr Robbins', 1877. Married **Charles M. Robinson**, October 20, 1879, and continued with the Robinsons until her death.

MARKS, ROBERT. Son of **Hiram Marks**, bareback rider, Batcheller & Doris, 1881.

MARKS, SALLIE. (d. August 29, 1891) Equestrienne. Youngest daughter of **Hiram Marks**. John Robinson's, 1874, 1877-79, 1887; principal rider, E. N. Camp's Grand Southern, 1880; principal equestrienne, Batcheller & Doris, 1881; John B. Doris', 1883-86; Frank A. Gardner's *Circo Americano*, Central and South America, C. W. Kidder & Co.'s, 1893. Married rider **Willie Showles** at Boonsville, MO, September 27, 1883 (the couple were with John B. Doris'); divorced from him, July 1, 1887. Was announced that she was to marry **Ed Zeigler**, master of transportation, September 1, 1887.

MARKS, WILLIE. Leaper and rider. Son of **Hiram Marks**. George W. DeHaven's, 1860; John Robinson's, 1873-74, 1876-78, 1883-85, 1887-89; Burr Robbins', 1877; Adam Forepaugh's, 1886; Ringling Bros.', 1892, 1899; LaPearl's, winter 1894; Sig. Sautelle's, 1897; Shipp's Winter Circus, Petersburg, IL, 1898-99; Shipp & Collins, winter 1899-1900; Gollmar Bros.', 1905. While with John Robinson's, married **Josie Morton**, a non-professional, June 30, 1884, at Franklin, OH.

MARLETTA BROTHERS. C. W. Kidder & Co.'s, 1893.

MARQUEZ, ANTONIO. Brazilian rider. With Spalding & Rogers, 1864; European Circus, 1869; Burr Robbins', 1884-85.

MARR, RODNEY. Press agent, Frank A. Robbins', 1890.

MARRETTA SISTERS [or Marrietta; Millie, Rosalie]. Gymnasts, flying trapeze with somersaults and a variety of leaps, also single balancing trapeze acts. Stowe & Orton, 1870, said to be the youngest double trapeze act of the day, also did an outside ascension and the "Niagara leap"; Cole & Orton, 1871-72; Burr Robbins', 1877; John Robinson's, 1884; Sells Bros.', 1885; Frank Huffman's, 1886; Howe's New London, 1887; Lemen Bros.', 1891-92; LaPearl's, 1892. **Millie** (November 29, 1856-March 2, 1902), born in California, MO. Entered the profession, 1869, G. G. Grady's. While in New Orleans, 1896, met with an accident which ended her career; died there as a result of surgery. **Rose** performed balancing trapeze, Martinho Lowande's Brazilian Circus, winter 1899-1900; John Robinson, 1905; Sun Bros.', 1910.

MARRIETTA SISTERS. See above.

MARRITUS, CHARLES. Walter L. Main's, 1888.

MARROW, ELLA. Cooper, Jackson & Co., 1882.

MARSDEN, F. C. Excursion agent, Sells Bros.', 1881.

MARSH, JOHN H. (1839?-June 7, 1881) Cornet player and band leader. Connected with various circuses including the European, R. Sands', and Bailey's; later years, led a band in the White Mountains. His wife, **Fanny Archer**, was a well known variety performer. Marsh died at his home in Woodstock, VT, age 42.

MARSHALL, ALF. R. Agent, James M. French's, 1867.

MARSHALL, GEORGE. Acrobat, Sadler's, 1875.

MARSHALL, JOHN. Musical director, F. J. Taylor's, 1891.

MARSHALL, JOHN R. Lee & Marshall, 1852-56; co-proprietor (with **John A. Rowe**), Rowe & Marshall's American Circus, 1858, which toured Australia and parts east; treasurer, Lee & Ryland's Hippodrome, San Francisco, 1866. Later, managed hall shows and was advertiser with Leihy, Lake & Co., California, 1870.

MARSHALL, L. Acrobat, John Robinson's, 1885.

MARSHALL, TOM. Clown with Dan Rice's at one time. Died in Cincinnati, OH, 1903, at over 80 years of age. **MARTELL FAMILY** [Harry & family]. Cyclists on the highwire. W. W. Cole's, 1883; proprietors, Martell & Co., 1883-84; Martell, Phalon & Co., 1885; John B. Doris', 1886 (little **Hattie** rode a mite size bike at this time); S. H. Barrett's, 1887. **Harry Martell**, with his 1884 show, laid claim to making the longest jump on record that year: the company was organized in Neosho Falls, KS, with plans to open on April 27; when heavy rains mired their travel, contracting agent, **Sam Lent**, made arrangements with the Missouri Pacific Railroad and on May 3 the 32 people circus left Burlington, KS, on its way to Afton, NY, arriving on the 5th, a distance of 1,256 miles. But the show folded in mid-season.

MARTELL, JEAN. Monkey man, billed as the Cynocephalus. "Standing upright upon a running horse he leaps objects, bounds over obstacles, executes the manual of arms, and absolutely fires off a gun." James M. French's, 1869-70; L. B. Lent's, 1871. "Captured in Zanzibar, Africa. The Cynocephalus can actually perform feats which would be a natural impossibility for any human rider to achieve." With John O'Brien's, 1871; W. W. Cole's, 1871; L. B. Lent's, 1871; Mongomery Queen's, 1875. Question: were the Cynocephalae listed with the 3 circuses in 1871 performed by Jean Martell? Or was Jean Martell merely the instructor for others performing the act?

MARTELLA BROTHERS. Gymnasts, Holland, Bowman & McLaughlin, 1890.

MARTENI. Slack wire, R. Sands', 1861.

MARTIN, AGRIPPA D. Animal handler, and keeper of the famous elephant, Hannibal. Raymond & Weeks, 1834; S. Butler & Co., 1834; Zoological Institute, Philadelphia, 1835; equestrian director, Eagle Circus/Cole & Co., 1837. Remembered for his rescuing the elephant Tippo Sultan from tigers that escaped their cages in NYC, 1826. Daughter, **Helen**, was married to **Dr. James L. Thayer**, April 3, 1860.

MARTIN, B. Agent, VaAmburgh & Co., 1874.

MARTIN, HENRI. (1793-1882) Lion tamer. Considered to be the first in circus history to enter a cage with a wild beast, which occurred, 1819, in Nuremburg. A French rider out of work, Martin enter a cage with a 4 year old tiger, where he remained but a few minutes and returned without injury. Eventually taught the tiger, Atir, to sit up and lie down and other simple tricks. Died after 40 years in retirement, age 90.

MARTIN, JAMES & SON. Manufacturer of circus and side show canvases, 110-114 Commercial Street, Boston, MA.

MARTIN, JOHN. Menagerie proprietor and exhibitor of the elephant Tippoo Sultan, 1823, the Grand Caravan and Tippoo Sultan. An animal with large tusks, was one of 2 male elephants in America at this time.

MARTIN, JOSEPH. Lion tamer, Parson's, Albany, 1826.

MARTIN, MARY. Albino, Barnum, Bailey & Hutchinson, 1881-82.

MARTIN, THOMAS. (d. August 9, 1876) Trapeze performer. Great Southern, 1875; Great London Pavilion Show, 1876. Died from a fall while with the latter show.

MARTIN, WILLIAM. Advance courier distributer, Cooper, Bailey & Co., 1876; contracting agent, Beckett's, 1881; Gregory Brothers', 1883-85.

MARTINA, MME. Orton & Older, 1858-59.

MARTINA, MONS. Wire walker and juggler, Orton & Older, 1858-59; Mabie's, 1860.

MARTINE, AL. Acrobat, Howe's Great London, 1874.

MARTINE, GEORGE. Equestrian director, with Whitney's, 1892; LaPearl's, 1896.

MARTINELLI BROTHERS. Clowns, Martell & Co., 1884.

MARTINETTE, JULIEN. (d. April 19, 1884) Clown. At one time proprietor of Martinette & Parel Pantomime Co. Died in the Sells Bros.' ring, age 63. His home was in Baltimore.

MARTINETTI BROTHERS. Acrobats. Sells Bros.', 1884;

Burr Robbins', 1887; Stow, Long & Gumble, 1889. Bailey & Winan, 1890.

MARTINEZ, EUGENE [with wife Irene]. Knife-thrower and fire jugglers. Thompson, Smith & Hawes, 1866; E. G. Smith's, 1867; G. G. Grady's, 1870; C. W. Noyes', 1872-73.

MARTINEZ, FRANC. Clown, Burr Robbins', 1886.

MARTINEZ, PEDRO. Juggler, G. G. Grady's, 1870.

MARTINI, SIG. Thompson, Smith & Hawes, 1866.

MASCARINI, JEROME. Man monkey and curious scenic rider, imitating the gambols, antics and exercises of an ape on horseback, Joe Pentland's, 1859.

MASON, MME. "Formerly of the London and Parisian circuses," chariot racer, Franconi's New York Hippodrome, 1853; 40-horse driver, Nixon & Kemp, 1858; Nixon & Co., 1859; First National Union Circus (combination of Nixon's Royal Circus and Sloat's New York Circus), 1861.

MASON, ANNIE. Chariot racer, P. T. Barnum's Roman Hippodrome, 1875. This may be the same as above.

MASON, M. W. Agent, S. P. Stickney's, 1846.

MATEER, JOHN. Rider. Fogg & Stickney, 1833; Brown's, 1835-37; A. Hunt & Co., 1838; proprietor (with **John Shay, Charles J. Rogers, J. W. Jackson**), Cincinnati Circus, 1840-41; John Mateer's Southern Circus, 1843-44.

MATTHEWS, CHARLES C. (d. September 12, 1918) Gymnast. Cloud swing performer, Robinson, Gardner & Kenyon, 1869; James Robinson's, 1870; Adam Forepaugh's, 1871; Dan Rice's, 1872; Stevens & Begun, 1874; tumbler and leaper, Great Roman Hippodrome, 1877; equestrian director, Miles Orton's, 1880; Hudson & Castello, 1881; DeHaven's Great Eastern, 1883; equestrian director, Black Bros.', 1887-88; George W. Richards', winter 1889-90; Orton Bros.', 1889; cloud swing, Gollmar Bros.', 1892. Married **Belle Celeste.** Died in Philadelphia, age 82.

MATTHEWS FAMILY [William, Master George, Thomas, Fred, Theodore, Willie, Loretta, and Polonini]. Acrobats. John Wilson's, 1865; San Francisco Circus and Roman Hippodrome, 1872; P. T. Barnum's, 1873-74; Montgomery Queen's, 1876. Then returned to Europe.

MATTHEWS, GEORGE. Adam Forepaugh's, 1870.

MATHEWS, JAMES. Privileges, Three Melville's & Co., 1889.**MATTHEWS, WILLIAM.** Orrin Bros.', Mexico, 1886.

MATTY BROTHERS. German gymnasts, Stickney's National Circus, Old Bowery, November 1861.

MAURICE, EDMUND. Proprietor, Maurice's Old Fashioned Circus, 1896.

MAURICE, JAMES. See Thomas Holmes.

MAURITTIUS, CHARLES. Clown. Valkingburg's, 1881; Roberts & Gardner Circus (**Nick Roberts, F. A. Gardner,** proprietors), 1886; principal talking, knockabout and pantomime clown, Lowande & Hoffman, 1887.

MAURY. Acrobat, John Robinson's, 1889.

MAXEY [sometimes Maxcey]. Kent bugler. With Simpson & Price, 1822, 1824-25; William Blanchard's, 1826; Tivoli Gardens, Philadelphia, 1826. Played a brass soprano instrument with side holes and keys, much in the manner of a clarinet.

MAXINO and BARTOLA. Aztec Children, P. T. Barnum's, 1873.

MAXWELL, CHARLES. Press agent, W. W. Cole's, 1884, 1886.

MAXWELL, G. Fat boy, Barnum, Bailey & Hutchinson, 1882.

MAXWELL, J. Gymnast, W. H. Stowe's, 1881; John Robinson's, 1885.

MAXWELL, L. C. Proprietor (with **G. H. Smith**) and treasurer, Great Western Circus, 1876.

MAXWELL, OTTO. Clown, Barnum & Bailey, 1892.

MAXWELL, VISHAM. W. H. Stowe's, winter 1881-82. 1882.

MAY, A. ["Prof."] Dog circus, Walter L. Main's, 1882, 1886; William Main & Co., 1887.

MAY, FRED. Clown, Stone & Murray, 1869.

MAY, J. M. Ringmaster, Orton's, 1856-57; Orton & Older, 1858-61.

MAY, JOHN. (September 7, 1816-May 12, 1854) Clown. Born in Orange County, NY. As a boy was apprenticed to a tailor, but soon abandoned that career and joined a circus. Visited Europe, 1844, and performed in all of the principal cities. Subsequently, visited Africa and South America. Said to have been a worthy man, temperate in his habits and with a lively wit; having traveled much, was always pleasing and amusing in conversation. Howes & Sands, 1835; Nathan A. Howes', 1836; Yale, Sands & Co., 1838; Cole, Miller, Gale & Co., 1838; Howes & Mabie, 1841; Nathan A. Howes', winter 1843-44; Welch & Mann, 1843-44; Mann, Welch & Delavan, 1844-47; R. Sands & Co., 1849; Howes & Co., 1849; E. F. & J. Mabie's, 1850. Was struck in the head with a stone while touring in the West, from which he lost his memory and was unable to perform. Old friends supported him until he was admitted to the insane ward at Blockley's Almshouse, Philadelphia, where he died.

MAY, LESLIE. Old Cary's Great World Circus, traveling by rail and boat down the Mississippi, July 1864.

MAYA, LORENZO. (d. November 12, 1895.) Clown. Chiarini's, Havana, winter 1859-60; French and Spanish clown, Parisian Circus, assembled for the Paris Exposition, 1867; clown and manager, Albisu's Circus, Havana, winter 1867-68; James Robinson's, 1870-71; Dan Rice's Paris Pavilion Circus, 1871-72; Burr Robbins', 1874; agent, Chiarini's, South America, 1875; treasurer, Chiarini's, the Orient, 1881-82. After clowning days ended, was the secretary and general business man for Chiarini. Died in NYC.

MAYBURY, WILLIAM A. (d. August 1, 1888) Lawyer from Detroit. Co-proprietor, Maybury, Pullman & Hamilton,

1882.

MAYETT, CHARLES. Wallace & Co., 1885, Yankee Robinson's, 1866; Stowe & Norton, 1869.

MAYHIER. Slack-rope walker, Pepin's, 1818-20.

MAYLAND, ANNETTE. Whitby & Co. (**John O'Brien**, proprietor), 1867.

MAYNARD BROTHERS [Mark, Eugene]. Gymnasts. Alexander Robinson's, 1872-77; VanAmburgh & Co., 1883. **Mark** was clown, Andress' New Colossal, 1889.

MAYNARD, THOMAS. Balladist, Hippocomique, 1868.

MAYO, CARL [r. n. Carl Grustall]. (d. April 10, 1908) Acrobatic clown, John Robinson's. Died in Cincinnati, OH.

MAYO, WILLIAM. Trained horse act, Great Chicago Circus, on the corner of Halsted and Depuyster Streets, 1879; Lockwood & Flynn, 1887; director, Sprague's, 1880; manager, Mayo's Model Show, 1884.

MEAD, ABRAHAM H. From Westchester County, NY. A stockholder in the Zoological Institute and agent for various shows throughout his career. Married to **Elizabeth Bailey**, of the Westchester County show family. One of the proprietors of Quick & Mead, 1826; the two men also owned an interest in Fogg & Howes' Menagerie; in partnership with **Jeremiah P. Fogg**, Washington Circus, Philadelphia, 1826-28; managed, Philips & Finch menagerie, 1829; co-proprietor, Miller, Mead & Delavan', 1834-35; agent, June, Titus, Angevine & Co., 1839-40; Grecian Arena and Classic Circus, 1841; Rockwell & Stone, 1842.

MEAD, E. G. Treasurer, Henry Rockwell's unit of Rockwell & Stone, 1846; Rockwell & Co., 1847-48.

MEAGHER, M. J. See Patsy Forepaugh.

MEANY, STEVE. Juggler, E. O. Rogers', 1891.

MEDERIC BROTHERS. Brother act, Bailey & Winan, 1890.

MEDICI, MARIE. *Danseuse*, P. T. Barnum's, 1875.

MEDINA, LOTENZ. Balancer, H. M. Smith's, 1870.

MEDRANO, DOMENICA. Rope-walker. Made his only American appearance with Pepin & Breschard, Philadelphia, 1812. His act began by him jumping back and forth on a rope with ankles shackled; then dancing blindfolded over swords attached to the rope; encased in a sack, balanced 6 wine glasses piled on his head with a ladder atop them; stood on his head on a tumbler placed on the rope; leaped from the gallery to the rope, catching it with his teeth and swinging back and forth.

MEEHAM, WILLIAM A. And his Canine Paradox, George S. Cole's, 1895.

MEEKER, FRED. Excursion agent, Metropolitan Circus, 1897.

MEERS, HUBERT. European equestrian. In Paris threw 42 back somersaults while on horseback. Secured by John Wilson, 1868, California.

MEERS FAMILY [Marie, Alice Jennie, and Lilly]. Equestriennes. Howes' Great London, 1872.

MEERS SISTERS. Bareback riders, with Barnum & Bailey, 1891.

MELBER, CHARLES. Bandmaster, with John Robinson's, 1865.

MELEKE, ZOE. Circassian lady, P. T. Barnum, 1876-77.

MELROSE BROTHERS [Wallie, John, Will]. With Lemen Bros.', 1892.

MELROSE FAMILY [Percy, Estella, Park, Theresa]. **Percy** was balancing trapeze artist with Vaulkinburg's, 1882. The family performed as bicycle artists, Sells Bros.', 1883-86, 1889; Adam Forepaugh's, 1887; Wallace & Anderson, 1890—**Park Melrose** on the unicycle, **Miss Theresa**, "a bright, intelligent little girl of 8 years who has been with her parents on the wheels for over four years."

MELROSE, LILLIIAN. Gymnast, W. W. Cole's, 1886; *manège*, Great Exposition Circus (**John C. O'Brien**, manager), 1895.

MELROSE, PERCY C. See Melrose Family.

MELROSE, WILLIAM F. (1875-November 1, 1934) Somersault, bareback and jockey rider, leaper. Married **Marie Meers**, one of the equestrienne **Meers Sisters**. Great Exposition Circus, 1895; LaPearl's, 1896; 4-horse rider, Robinson-Franklin, 1897; somersault rider, Great Wallace, 1898-04; Walter L. Main's, 1902; Barnum & Bailey, 1905; (with **Marie Meers**) double jockey act, Forepaugh-Sells, 1910. Died of a stroke, age 59, in Niagara Falls, Ontario, Canada.

MELTON, J. B. Trained dogs, Washington Bros.', 1887.

MELTON, TOM. Clown, Springer's Royal Cirq-Zoolodon, 1875.

MELVILLE, ALEXANDER. Rider. Son of **James** and brother of **Frank Melville**. Child hurdle rider, L. B. Lent's, 1869; P. T. Barnum's, 1871-72, 1874; Melville, Maginley & Cooke, 1875; Howes' Great London, 1876.

MELVILLE BROTHERS [Arthur, William, Ernest]. Acrobats and double bar performers. James T. Johnson's, 1886; King & Franklin, 1888; James Donovan's, Bermuda, winter 1891-92.

MELVILLE, CHARLES J. (September 1, 1826-August 3, 1893) At one time champion bareback rider of the world. Born near Pittsburgh, PA. Learned to ride at age 4 and created a sensation as an infant prodigy. Beginning with Angevine, June & Turner. Ultimately, traveled with all the great circuses of his day. For many years with Dan Rice's, and at one time had his own show. During the Civil War, served in the 52nd Ohio Regiment until wounded and sent home. Made and lost several fortunes in his 48 years of trouping before he retired to a farm in Stoystown, PA. About 1889, eyesight failed, which forced him to spent all his savings in attempts to regain it. By 1893, was destitute and in the charity ward at West Penn Hospital. Died there, age 67.

MELVILLE, CLARA. Equestrienne, Baird, Howell & Co.,

1874.

MELVILLE, DANIEL. L. B. Lent's, 1868.

MELVILLE, DONALD. Rider, New York Circus, 1881.

MELVILLE, ERNEST. Rider, Barnum & Bailey, 1895. Married to **Josie Ashton**. Jailed September, 1899, for stabbing his father-in-law over an argument.

MELVILLE, FRANCIS. Somersault act (with George Melville), P. T. Barnum's, 1871.

MELVILLE, FRANK. (September 16, 1854-November 23, 1908) Eldest son of **James Melville** and brother of **George** and **Alexander**. Born in Sydney, Australia, shortly before his parents came to America. Became prominent as a bareback rider and excelled in a principal act and a 6-horse act; said to be the first to do a somersault from the ground to a galloping horse and was the originator of other acts now regularly performed. Married **Louise Boshell** at Ishpening, MI, August 3, 1878. Appeared with his father from age 8 through 22. See James Munro Melville. When the New York Hippodrome was organized, left Barnum & Bailey to become its equestrian director, training most of the horses used in the performances. Last appearance as a rider was at the Hippodrome, 1907, when, with his wife, he presented a "high school" act. Died of a heart attack in NYC. Sands, Nathans & Co., 1857-58; Nixon & Co., 1859; Chiarini's, 1861. While with George F. Bailey & Co., 1867, did 10 to 15 back somersaults daily over objects and through balloons. Presented with a gold medal, October 13, 1866, at Norwalk, CT, by members of the company inscribed: "Presented by the members of the G. F. Bailey's Circus Company to Frank Melville, aged 12 years, for accomplishing sixteen back somersaults on horseback." Also pad rider, P. T. Barnum's, 1872-74; Melville, Maginley & Cooke, 1875; Howes' Great London, 1876; Cooper, Bailey & Co., 1876; Great London, 1877; Adam Forepaugh's, 1878; Cooper, Bailey & Co., 1879-80; Barnum, Bailey & Hutchinson, 1881; equestrian director, W. C. Coup's, 1882; Rentz', Berlin, 1884. Supposedly retired from the ring and was managing a riding school in Louisville, KY, 1893; however, was back as equestrian director, Barnum & Bailey, 1904; followed by the same duties at the Hippodrome, NYC, 1904-05; and with Thompson and Dundy Hippodrome, Coney Island, 1905. Died of a heart attack at his office in the Hippodrome.

MELVILLE, GEORGE DONALD. (1857-May 20, 1917) Born in Valparaiso. Son of **James** and brother of **Frank** and **Alexander**. L. B. Lent's, Wallack's Old Theatre, fall 1863; Wheeler's new amphitheatre on the site of the old National Theatre, Boston, winter 1864-65; George F. Bailey & Co., 1866-67; Yankee Robinson's, 1868; bareback rider and somersault act, P. T. Barnum's, 1871-72; VanAmburgh & Co., 1877; W. C. Coup's, 1881; Barnum & Bailey, 1885; Miller, Okey & Freeman, 1886. Married **Anna Morgan** in NYC, January of 1876. Couple had a son, **Frank**, and George had

two step-sons, **W. C.** and **George F. Miller**. Later, married **Mamie Conway**. Died in Jersey City.

MELVILLE, JAMES MUNRO [r. n. James Munroe or Munro]. (October 14, 1835-November 17, 1892) One of the most famous bareback riders in the world. Born at Inverness, Scotland. Accompanied his parents to Australia where he joined a circus, 1851, in Sydney and became an apprentice to **John Malcolm**; made his debut the following year, billed as "Mr. Munro." By 20 years of age, had mastered the art of bareback riding. Married **Elizabeth Louise Mills** (Miss Howard), equestrienne, in Sydney, July 29, 1854. Astley's Amphitheatre, Melbourne, 1855. Same year, went to Valparaiso, Chile, with **Rolla Rossiter**, a celebrated slack wire performer, and toured South America. First engagement in the United States, Lee & Bennett (Bennett was a California banker), San Francisco, 1856; made NYC debut, 1857, old Bowery Theatre under the management of VanAmburgh & Co. Arriving toward the end of January of that year and flattered the press by giving a preview of riding for them before performing publicly. Shortly, was connected with Nixon & Kemp, 1858-59, flying, vaulting and jumping over hurdles, fences, bars and gates. Standing on his naked horse, he, at the same time, carried and balanced his son of 12 years, in every variety of posture. VanAmburgh & Co., 1860; S. P. Stickney's, 1861; Antonio Bros.', 1861; Goodwin & Wilder, fall 1861; R. Sands', 1863; proprietor, Melville's Australian Circus, 1864; Hippotheatron, 14th Street, NYC, November 1864; S. O. Wheeler's, winter 1864-65; Chiarini's, Havana, fall 1865; George Bailey & Co., 1865-66, 1873; equestrian director, Yankee Robinson's, 1868; L. B. Lent's, 1870; P. T. Barnum's, 1871-72, 1874; co-proprietor, Melville, Maginley & Cooke, 1875; Cooper, Bailey & Co., 1876; Howes' Great London, 1876; John H. Murray's, 1878; equestrian director, W. C. Coup' New United Monster Show, 1879-80; ringmaster, Barnum, Bailey & Hutchinson, 1882; clown, **Barnum & London**, 1885; last ring appearance may have been with Melville-Hamilton, 1891. He and wife, **Louise**, were the parents of 5; **Frank, George** and **Alexander** Melville were all circus riders. Died at his residence, 207 W. 34th Street, NYC, age 57.

MELVILLE, LEE. Equestrian director, Irwin Bros.', 1887.

MELVILLE, LOUISE [nee Elizabeth Louise Mills]. Wife of **James Melville**. A graceful equestrienne who had apprenticed to **John Malcolm** in Sydney, Australia. Only daughter of **Mrs. Wright**, a Shakespearean actress who played principal roles with visiting stars. Lee & Bennett's, San Francisco, 1856-57; J. M. Nixon's, 1859; Mabie's Winter Garden, Chicago, 1862; Melville, Cooke & Sands, 1863. See James Melville.

MELVILLE, LOUISE BOSHELL. (1862-October 15, 1934) High-wire and slack-wire performer. Wife of **Frank Melville**. Adam Forepaugh, 1878; Barnum, Bailey & Hutchinson, 1881. See Frank Melville. Died at Jacksonville, FL, age 78.

MELVILLE, RICHARD. Thayer & Noyes, 1866.

MELVILLE, SAM. Australian clown. Apprentice of **James Melville.** Melville Brothers—**Sammy, Frank, George**— juvenile equestrians, Melville, Cooke & Sands, 1863; George F. Bailey & Co., 1866; S. P. Stickney's, 1869; William T. Aymar's, 1870; James M. Nixon's, fall 1870; Adam Forepaugh's, 1871-73.

MELVILLE, WILLIAM. McMahon's, 1888; Sells Bros.', 1893.

MEMNARDT, BOBBY. English clown, Howes' New London, 1887.

MENCHES, CHARLES. Menches & Barber, 1887.

MENDOZA BROTHERS. Sells Bros.', 1879.

MENDOZA, FRED. Tumbler and leaper, Barnum, Bailey & Hutchinson, 1882.

MENDOZA SISTERS. Winter circus, 42nd Street, NYC, 1830 (**E. S. Doris**, proprietor; **John B. Doris**, manager).

MENIAL. Rope-dancer and clown. Cayetano & Co., 1810, amusing the audiences with buffoonery and horsemanship; Pepin & Breschard, Philadelphia, 1809, where he did the "Tailor Riding to Waterford" with the trained jackass, Zebra; Cayetano Mariotini's troupe to Newburyport and Exeter, MA, and Portsmouth, NH, spring 1810, returning to NYC to rejoin Pepin & Breschard opening there, June 21—did a sketch whereby he ate at a table with the trained horse, Ocelot; Cayetano's, 1811, Canada, and in Albany and NYC, 1812; Codet's management, Montreal, 1812; Cayetano's, Charleston, winter 1812-13; Pepin & Breschard, Olympic Circus, Philadelphia, August 30, 1813; Pepin, Breschard & Cayetano, NYC, summer 1813; Philadelphia, fall season; Pepin & Breschard, Charleston, November 1814. It is believed he accompanied Pepin to Europe sometime after the beginning of January, 1815. Pepin's, Philadelphia, 1816, Baltimore, January 1817, Lancaster, summer 1817; joined Caytano's, New Orleans, July 5, 1817; Roulestone's Amphitheatre, Boston, July 1, 1818, through July 20; Villalave's, summer and fall 1818; September the company was billed as Menial & Vilallave; back with Pepin, West Indies, 1819-20; again, 1821.

MENTER, ALMON EDGAR. (1847?-April 3, 1887) Band leader. From a show business family, a native of Covington, KY. Attained a certain renown early as **Edgar,** the boy cornetist in his father's band. A primiere leader, arranger and composer for both string and brass, the compositions being particularly praise-worthy as music for grand entries and special acts. Dan Rice's, 1849-52, 1863; Dan Rice's Paris Pavilion Circus, 1871-72; John H. Murray's Railroad Circus, 1874-75; W. C. Coup's, 1878-79; New York Circus, 1881; Adam Forepaugh's, 1884. Died of pneumonia in NYC.

MENTER, FRANK. Tumbler and gymnast, with E. Stowe's, 1871.

MENTOR. Trained horse, with Pepin & Barnet's company, Natchez, MS, June 1823.

MERCHANT, WILLIAM. Alex Abar's Pavilion Show, 1889.

MEREDITH, ALBERT and **MARGUERITE.** Contortionist. Hurlburt & Hunting, 1885-87; Hunting's, 1888; double trapeze, Main & Sargeant, 1891.

MERRANTI, M. Tranca act, Sands, Nathans & Co., 1857-58.

MERRETT, RANDOLPH. Agent, Harry Whitby's, 1859.

MERRICK, W. N. Solo cornetist and bandmaster, Sells Bros.', 1882-84. Later connected as band leader with Forepaugh-Sells Bros.' and Hagenbeck-Wallace.

MERRELL BROS. See Harry S. Morris, Sr.

MERRILL, E. Contracting agent, G. G. Grady's, 1872.

MERRITT, FRANK S. Co-proprietor, Gregory, Merritt & Co. (**Charles Gregory**, Frank S. Merritt, proprietors), 1886. The outfit was formerly known as the Royal Pavilion Shows.

MERTZ, MAJOR JOHN and **MRS.** Sideshow midgets. Retired to Salisbury, NC, where Mrs. Mertz was born and raised. Her maiden name was **Nale. Abe Nale,** the older brother, took charge of the sideshow in which they were exhibited. [D. W. Watt: "They never traveled with a show that they did not leave a good name and managers were always anxious to get Major Mertz and his wife as an attraction. They occupied a platform in the sideshow where they sold their pictures to visitors and a crowd of interested spectators could always be seen around their platform."]

MERTZ, PROF. Trained ponies and trick mule, Robert Hunting's, 1894.

MESSENGER, JAMES. Cannon ball performer—using 30, 40, and 50 pound iron balls—club swinger, and general performer. Feats in the ring showed extraordinary muscular strength, even though he was but 5' 6" in height, measured 42" around the chest, and weighed only 160 pounds. First entered the business at James M. Nixon's, NYC. A narrow escape occurred, 1870, on the Erie Railroad, when the special show train, through a mistake on the part of the officials, was dashed into by the Pacific Express, running on the same track. Messenger, standing on the rear platform, saved his own life by jumping from the platform down the embankment. L. B. Lent's, 1866-70; P. T. Barnum's, 1871, 1873; Dan Rice's, 1872; club swinging, W. C. Coup's, 1878; Orrin Bros.', Mexico, winters 1879-80, 1880-81; Indian clubs, feats of strength, Cooper, Bailey & Co., 1880; Forepaugh & Samwells, 1886; Lowande & Hoffman, 1887; Shield's, 1888; Whitney Family, 1889.

MESTAYER, FELIX. Clown, New York Champs Elyees, 1865.

MESTAYER, HARRY. Negro minstrel. Boston Lion Circus, 1836; June, Titus, Angevine & Co., 1839-40; John Tryon's, Bowery Amphitheatre, NYC, 1843; Welch & Mann, 1843-44; John T. Potter's, 1844-46; Dr. Gilbert R. Spalding's, 1845.

MESTAYER, LOUIS. Clown and wire-walker, Durang & DeGraff, Leaman's Columbis Garden, Baltimore, for his first performance in America, September 12, 1805. Mestayer and his wife were both wire-walkers, doing hall shows as well as arena performances. Pepin & Breschard, 1810-11; Pepin, Breschard & Cayetano, 1813-14; Davis & Co., 1815-16; and with Pepin, opening for a short engagement at the Olympic Circus, Philadelphia, July 2, 1817.

METCALFE, GEORGE H. Manager and proprietor, New York Champs Elysees, starting from NYC, March 25, 1865, 1866-67. Formerly, ran a tavern, NYC.

METCHEAR, WILLIAM J. (June 24, 1837-October 25, 1879) Son of **James E.** and **Katharine T. Metchear.** Born at Newport, NY. After early work as a coach driver, entered show business as an agent for George H. Metcalfe's Champs Elysees Circus, starting from NYC, March 25, 1865. Later, had candy stand privileges, S. O. Wheeler's, 1867; agent, S. P. Stickney's; bought the circus property belonging to S. O. Wheeler, 1870, and entered into management with Conant and Cameron of the Great Australian Circus. Leaving the arenic business, became part proprietor of the Washington House, Providence, RI; left that and bought the Adams House, same city; during this time, was a speculater in show property and around 1879 dabbled with a sideshow at fairs and summer resorts. [M. B. Leavitt: "Doc Meecher was a fake dime museum manager. The only real thing he ever exhibited was an educated pig."] Died of consumption in Providence, RI, age 42.

METTE BROTHERS [Rudolph, Louis, Frank]. Gymnasts—four globes, trapeze, comic stilts, etc. Consisting of **Rudolph, Louis Mette** (who may have been a brother) and **Henry Wilcox.** Chindahl also lists a **Frank Mette.** Springer's Royal Cirq-Zoolodon, 1875; Parisian Circus, Operti's Tropical Garden, Philadelphia, fall 1876; New National Theatre, Philadelphia, winter 1876-77; Den W. Stone's, 1878; Great American Circus, 1878; Adam Forepaugh's, 1879; Roman Races, Brighton Beach Fair Grounds, Coney Island, 1879; Cooper, Bailey & Co., 1880; Dr. James L. Thayer's, 1880; VanAmburgh & Co., 1883; Barnum & London, 1884; Frank A. Robbins', 1885. **Rudolph** married **Ella Stokes,** daughter of **S. Q. Stokes,** January 25, 1877. Both were performing at the New National Theatre, Philadelphia. **Louis** claimed to have been one of the original **Leotard Brothers,** with **George Bliss** and **George Lair.**

METZ, CARL. Acrobat, VanAmburgh & Co., 1881.

MEYER, FRITZ. Musical director, Dan Rice's, 1867-68.

MEYERS, CHARLES. Slack-wire and balancer, F. J. Taylor's, 1891.

MEYERS, J. Leaper, tumbler, P. T. Barnum's, 1873.

MIACO, ALFRED F. [r. n. Alfred Frisbie]. (d. July 21, 1923) Acrobat. Ran away from his home in Courtland, NY, at age 9 and joined the Yankee Robinson Circus; there, learned to be a contortionist; later graduated into pantomime as a pupil of **Tony Denier.** Partner of **Thomas E. Miaco;** the two joined forces at Fox's Casino, Philadelphia; followed by a lengthy engagement at the museum, Baltimore, and the Canterbury, Washington, DC. Fall 1865, made an appearance at Hone's Old Theatre, NYC, under the management of **Tony Pastor** and **Sam Sharpley;** 1865, **James M. Nixon** engaged them for a tour of Texas, but the boat sank en route. Thayer & Noyes, 1866; later, George F. Bailey's for a season, followed by a tour with Haight & Chambers along the Mississippi and Ohio Rivers, and subsequently with the C. T. Ames'. The team broke up in 1868. Married trapeze performer **Laura Smith** of New Orleans, daughter of the proprietor of the Crescent City Circus, 1867, on board the steamboat belonging to Haight & Chambers. Also with H. M. Smith's, 1870; clown and gymnast, Haight's Great Eastern, 1874; Cameron's, 1875; clown, P. T. Barnum's, 1877, 1879; John H. Murray's, 1881; Walter L. Main's, 1896-97; conductor of spectacle and pantomime, Frank A. Robbins', 1897; Ringling Bros.', 1899-1911. His son, a clown, was at one time connected with Walter L. Main's, 1896, and Barnum & Bailey, 1911. His pantomimic makeup and costume was said to be beyond compare. Never overplayed his act. An excellent burlesquer. At one time a star equestrienne refused to go into the ring, claiming his comical take-off on her act distracted the audience. Never used props, only a foot-long tin whistle. Suffered a stroke, 1921, which forced him to retire. Died in New York City, age 79. Appeared in 55 circuses over a period of 30 years.

MIACO BROTHERS [Thomas, William]. Haight & Co., winter 1871-72; Great Eastern, 1873; P. T. Barnum's, 1877-79; Nathans & Co.'s, 1882.

MIACO, JENNIE. (1856?-August 15, 1892) General performer. Wife of **Thomas E. Miaco.** Began as a variety performer at the age of 15, Olympic Theatre, Boston, under the management of **William Campbell,** with a song and dance and rope skipping act. After marrying Miaco, 1873, while with Adam Forepaugh's, performed with circuses a number of years before her husband *Manège* and *danseuse,* Lowande's Great Brazilian, 1877; Great Chicago, 1879; took out a pantomime company. Died in Medina, NY, age 36. Had been in retirement about 6 years before her death.

MIACO, STEVE. Walter L. Main's, 1896.

MIACO, THOMAS E. [r. n. Eastlake]. (September 14, 1841-May 31, 1900) Acrobat. Born in Lyons, NY. As a child was an adept tumbler, so at about 9 years of age his parents were induced to allow him to travel with Henry Madigan's, with whom he remained for 7 years. Joined Harry Whitby's, late 1850s; followed by engagements with A. P. Ball's Coliseum, Judge Ingalls' Museum and Fox's Casino, both in Philadelphia. At the latter, united with **Alfred F. Miaco** and the men performed as a team, going to Baltimore for a long engagement at the museum, then to the Canterbury, Washington, DC. Fall, 1865, made an appearance at Hone's Old Theatre, NYC, under the management of **Tony Pastor** and **Sam Sharpley,** and immediately accepted an offer by **James M. Nixon**

to join his circus in a tour of Texas. Later the Miaco's were with George F. Bailey's for a season; then Haight & Chambers, touring the Mississippi and Ohio Rivers; and subsequently with C. T. Ames'. The team broke up, winter 1868. **Thomas** then joined with **David R. Hawley.** Courtney & Sanford, traveling through Mexico, 1869-70; Castello & Coup, touring the Great Lakes, 1870. Team separated, 1871. Miaco joined P. T. Barnum's, 1871. 1872, **Hawley** returned to the act. The two were with Adam Forepaugh's, 1873-74, after which they permanently split up. Montgomery Queen's, 1875; Dr. James L. Thayer's, 1877; clown, Lowande's Great Brazilian, 1877; Nathans & Co., 1883. Joined with **Samuel Hindes**, formerly with the **La Marko Brothers**, and went to the West Coast with Montgomery Queen's, with whom he made his last appearances as acrobat and clown. Giving up the circus, put his energies to the management of theatrical enterprises. Died in NYC of complications from a fall down a flight of stairs.

MIACO, WILLIAM [r. n. William Carroll]. Gymnast. As one of the **Miaco Brothers**, Haight's Great Eastern, 1874. Separated from the partnership, 1879, and formed another with **J. H. Jeffrey.**

MICARDO, ALPHONZE. Trainer and rider of buffalo and bison, DeMott & Ward, 1868.

MICITH, SIGNOR. Acrobat, Slaymaker & Nichols, 1864.

MIDDLECOFF, LANDON. (d. April 6, 1885) Giant. Over 7' tall. W. W. Cole's several seasons as well as various museums. Married to **Helen Mar**, club swinger. Died of consumption at his residence, Quincy, IL, age 28.

MIDDLETON, CHARLES. Greco-Roman wrestler, Barnum, Bailey & Hutchinson, 1881.

MIDDLETON, GEORGE. (d. February 15, 1926) Father was James Haslam Middleton, an employee at the Charleston Naval Yard, Boston. The family later moved to Madison, IN. Saw action in the Civil War with the 38th Indiana Regiment; captured and later sent to Libby and later Belle Isle prisons. Following the war tried various occupations—worked on a wharf boat, Vevay, IN, for a year; opened a cigar store in Madison; was an agent for Grover & Baker Sewing Machine Co. in a Southern Indiana and Northern Kentucky territory; managed a hotel in Edinburg, IN. Married Kate Rea shortly after the war, a union which lasted 18 years before ending. Entered into the circus business with the purchase of a half-interest in the **John Fulton** sideshow with Hemmings, Cooper & Whitby; winter 1870-71, owned the concert with Mrs. Lake's'; following year, ran both the concert and the candy stands with it; partner with **James A. Bailey** in privileges of the Cooper circus, 1872; owned the privileges for Cooper & Bailey, 1873; candy stands, Great Eastern, winter 1873; manager, Haight's Great Southern, 1874; privileges, (with **William H. Gardner**), Cooper & Bailey, 1875-76, visiting Australia, the East Indies and South America, 1876; manager,

Cooper, Bailey & Co., 1877 [Mark St. Leon: "The sideshow and concert were crowded daily and Middleton amassed a small fortune and within a few months of the first Australian tour he could afford to retire."]; sideshow and candy stand privileges, Adam Forepaugh's, 1879; manager, Aquarium, Coney Island, 1881; interest in W. C. Coup's enterprise, 1881. Later, was the successful proprietor of Middleton's Museum, 298 Bowery, NYC. Formed a partnerhip with **C. E. Kohl**, 1884, and opened a museum in Chicago, Clark Street near Madison. At one time Middleton and Kohl had 8 museums operating in the Midwest. In later years owned a number of Chicago theatres, including the Majestic, Olympic, Haymarket, and Chicago Opera House. Kohl and Middleton were the first to introduce continuous vaudeville to Chicago. 1898, Middleton's wife shot and wounded one of his chorus girls. After enjoyed success, gave a Civil War monument to Jefferson County, IN, which was erected at Madison. Settled in Pasadena, CA, around 1916, in retirement, where he died.

MIDDLETON, WILLIAM. Acrobat and leaper, Haight's Great Southern, 1874.

MIGASI, ANTONIO. See Diavolo Antonio and Antonio Brothers.

MILES, ALFRED. Clown, G. G. Grady's, 1874.

MILES, CHARLES. Bill poster, P. T. Barnum's, 1873.

MILES, DANIEL. Sideshow, VanAmburgh & Co., 1866. Died in Cincinnati, November 3, 1866.

MILES, FRANK. H. W. Smith's Crescent City, December 1869.

MILES, JOSIE. Sells & Rentfrow's, 1893.

MILES, ROBERT EDGAR JACKSON. (1834-March 13, 1904) Born in Culpepper Courthouse, VA. Only 4 years old when his merchant father died. Following this, went to Covington, KY, with his sister, with whom he resided for some years. Obtained a job as teacher in the public schools and gradually rose to the position of principal. Became a professional actor; performed in the horse drama *Mazeppa* for several years, etc. 1859, married **Emily L. Dow**, an actress. Purchased DeHaven & Co., 1870, and continued on the road under the same name; general director, Lake's Hippo-Olympiad, winter 1870-71; co-proprietor, Great Eastern Menagerie, Museum, Aviary, Circus and Balloon Show (**Dan Carpenter** and R. E. J. Miles & Co., proprietors) 1872; 1875, a prominent figure in the enterprise known as the America's Racing Association, an organization which sunk a fortune for its proprietors. Gained proprietorship in the Bijou Opera House, NYC, and was interested in various theatres—Cincinnati National Theatre, Pike's Opera House, Wood's Theatre. 1873, took charge of the Grand Opera House. Died in Cincinnati, OH.

MILES, WILLIAM G. Clown and acrobat, Dan Rice's, 1870; Rice's Paris Pavilion Circus, 1871-73; rider, Sadler's, 1875.

MILES, W. H. Sells & Rentfrow's, 1893.

MILLARD, HARRY. Agent. Traveled with many of the old time circuses. Business manager, Black Bros.', 1887. Died Corry, PA, June 30, 1895, age 64.

MILLER, A. D. Gymnast, G. G. Grady's, 1874; Hamilton & Sargeant, 1878.

MILLER, ALBERT O. Partner with **Ed Finch** in a menagerie consisting of some 10 animals, 1830-31, as Finch, Miller & Co.'s Grand Caravan; 1832, Miller, Mead & Olmstead; then Miller, Mead & Delavan, 1834-35; Miller, Yale, Sands & Co. (Miller, **Richard Sands, Enoch C. Yale**, proprietors), 1835-37.

MILLER, BERT. Boss canvasman and jockey rider, Albert M. Wetter's New Model Shows, 1893.

MILLER BROTHERS [Theodore, A. D.]. Gymnasts. G. G. Grady's, 1868-74; horizontal bars, Cooper, Bailey & Co., 1876; Hamilton & Sargeant, 1878.

MILLER, C. A. Contracting agent, Great Oriental Pavilion Show, 1877.

MILLER, C. F. Advertiser, general agent. Orrin Barber's, 1888; Charles Lee's Great London, 1896.

MILLER, CHARLES. Double somerault performer, Rutledge's, 1869. That year, was injured in the ring in Danville, IL, to the extent of ending his career. Was one of 5 children who adopted the ring as a profession. One brother was killed around 1860 from failing a double somersault, another was broken in health from the constant standing on his head.

MILLER, CHARLES A. Proprietor, Miller, Okey & Freeman's, 1886; Miller, Stowe & Freeman (Charles A. Miller, **James B. Stowe, William H. Freeman**, proprietors), 1887; Miller & Freeman, 1888-89.

MILLER, DOC [Is this Frank B. Miller?] Pyramidal balancing act. Charles Andress', 1888; John Stowe's, 1892; Ringling Bros.', 1891-94.

MILLER, GEORGE. Tumbler and vaulter. Dan Rice's, 1855; Orton & Older, 1856-59. Killed attempting a triple somersault in practice, Orton & Older, 1860.

MILLER, HARRY L. (d. January 30, 1933) Manager, Cooke's Hippodrome, 1895-96; launched Miller, Fuller, Howard & Blake's Dog and Pony Circus, 1901.

MILLER, J. Band leader, Robinson & Lake, 1862.

MILLER, JAMES S. Acrobat. Left his Louisberg, TN, home at age 19 to go prospecting in Alaska. In Minnesota met a man who persuaded him to form an acrobatic act with Barnum & Bailey. 2 years later his partner died. Later joined Ringling Bros.', and remained with the firm for many years, ultimately becoming the head of the Miller family acrobats with an income of $1,500 a week.

MILLER, J. H. Contracting agent, Miller & Runnells, 1888. Withdrew as co-proprietor of the firm by June 1888.

MILLER, JOHN. (1784-August 2, 1830) Born in Northampton County, PA. A wire performer and owner of a circus and menagerie on the road as early as 1821. 1825, sold menagerie to Crosby of New York for $4,000. Proprietor, Miller's, 1828-38; Miller, Yates & Sands, 1837-38. All in all, accumulated some $60,000 from exhibitions. With John Miller's menagerie, writes Stuart Thayer, comes the first documented evidence of the use of wagons by a showman. Died in Hanover Township, Northampton County, PA.

MILLER, JOHN. Gymnast, E. Stowe's, 1870.

MILLER, L. C. Co-proprietor, assistant manager and treasurer, Bartine's (**Charles Bartine**, L. C. Miller, proprietors), 1892. Sold his interest to his partner, fall 1892.

MILLER, P. Dan Rice's, 1851.

MILLER, ROBERT G. (b. 1851) Strong man. (at age 19) Dan Rice's, 1870; H. Harlan's, 1875.

MILLER, SAMUEL. (1810?-March 18, 1874) Keeper of Miller's Hotel, Chestnut Street, Philadelphia, a favorite of circus folks. Considered a generous and amiable host. It was at Miller's where Isaac VanAmburgh died. Retired from hotel keeping when the Fidelity Bank was constructed on the hotel site and moved into his residence at 1025 Vine Street. Died there, age 64.

MILLER, STEVEN. Juggler and acrobat. S. H. Nichols', 1838; June, Titus, Angevine & Co., Bowery Amphitheatre, 1839; John Tryon's, Bowery Amphitheatre, NYC, 1843; Welch & Mann, 1843-44.

MILLER, THEODORE. Gymnast. G. G. Grady's, 1874; clown, Hamilton & Sargeant, 1878.

MILLER, "YANKEE." Clown. White's Great Union Show, 1861; Old Cary's, traveling up and down the Mississippi River area by boat and railroad, 1864.

MILLETT, BENJAMIN. Breaker of trick horses, Joseph D. Palmer's, 1835.

MILLETTE BROTHERS. Gymnasts. Jesse W. Foster's, South America, 1894; Cooper & Co. (J. R. W. Hennessey, proprietor and manager), 1897.

MILLIE-CHRISTINE. (July 11, 1851-October 8, 1912) Billed as "The Two-Headed Girl," two Negro ladies joined from the lumbar vertebrae down to the end of the sacrum. Born of slave parents, a normal family of 7 older and 7 younger children, near Whiteville, NC. **J. P. Smith**, a Southern gentleman interested in exhibiting them, bought them for $30,000; also purchased the rest of the family so they could be together. The girls had good voices, one was a soprano and the other a contralto. Were exhibited in England, 1871, by **Judge H. P. Ingalls**, and were considered the greatest living curiosity. Batcheller & Doris, 1882-83; P. T. Barnum's, 1886; F. R. Blitz's show playing fair dates, 1889. Millie developed tuberculosis and died; Christine died 19 hours later, ages 61. Generous to a fault, they left only a small farm and a few hundred dollars in the bank, even though they were one of the great money-makers of their day for their employers.

MILLIGAN, BILLY. Clown. Frank A. Robbins', 1889, making his 8th season with the company; Gollmar Bros.', 1892.

MILLS, EDWARD. Man-monkey, S. P. Stickney & Son, 1874.

MILLS, E. J. General director, Agnes Lake's, 1871.

MILLS, JESSE. Agent, World's Fair Aggregation, 1892.

MILLS, PHIL. Knockabout clown, Moore Bros.', 1887.

MILLS, WILLIAM G. Equestrian, a pupil of **Dan Rice**. Traveled with Cooke's English Circus, 1876. Died of consumption, January 14, 1877, age 23.

MILLSON, WILLIAM. Trapeze performer. (Millson & Ball) Lake's Hippo-Olympiad, 1868-69; C. F. Ames', 1869-70; gymnast and bar performer, (Millson & Lazelle) P. T. Barnum's, 1872-73; P. T. Barnum's Roman Hippodrome, 1874-75.

MILO BROTHERS. Batcheller & Doris, 1882.

MILO, DAN. Strong man, Robinson's, California, 1886.

MILTON, BILLY. W. W. Cole, 1886.

MILTON BROTHERS [Edward, Emil, Frank]. Gymnasts, W. W. Cole's, 1886.

MILTON, GEORGE. W. W. Cole, 1886.

MILTON JASPERS [Newton, Thomas, Clinton]. Somersault brother act, Cooper, Bailey & Co., 1876; left in November after the season closed to join W. W. Cole's in Arkansas; Sells Bros.', 1877.

MILTON, MABEL. Long haired lady, Walter L. Main's, 1893.

MINNETA, MINNIE. Iron jawed lady. London Sensation Show, 1879; Cooper, Jackson & Co., 1880-83; Barnum & London, 1884; Wallace & Co., 1886; Sells Bros.', 1886; Wallace & Co., 1887; Charles Bartine's, 1893; Walt McCafferty's Great Golden Shows, 1894.

MINNICH, DANIEL. (1805-1891) Slack rope, vaulter, and strong man. Left his home in Wrightsville, PA, 1819, with a troupe of traveling acrobats and continued on the road after 50 years of age. His life nearly spanned the 19th century, during which he was a general performer of solid reputation. Eventually, retired from the circus to live in Bedford Springs, PA. As **Signor von Minech**, "slack rope wonder," made his first New York appearance at the Lafayette Amphitheatre, 1826, where he hung from the slack-rope by his ankles and supported the weight of 2 men who hung from ropes attached to his wrists. As **Mynheer von Minech**, was at the Mount Pitt Circus the following season. Quick & Mead, 1826; Fogg & Stickney, Philadelphia, 1827-28 (and probably was out with them the previous summer); J. Purdy Brown's, 1828-36; New York Circus, 1831-33; equestrian director, Waring and Raymond, New Orleans, winter 1837-38; tight-rope, Philadelphia Circus, 1839-40; slack-rope, Hobby & Pratt, 1842; slack-rope, Ogden & Hobby, 1842; Nathan A. Howes', winter 1843-44; Howes & Gardner, 1844; vaulter, Rockwell & Stone, 1845-46.

MINOR, J. B. Treasurer, Yankee Robinson's, 1868.

MINTER, ED, JR. Band leader. One of the finest in the profession. Spent his boyhood days on a farm. Father was a fine musician; mother's maiden name was **Parmeley**. Family moved to Cincinnati, where Ed, Sr., made a contract to furnish an orchestra for one of the theatres there. Ed, Jr., at this time was about 14 years of age and a fine musician himself; played second fiddle to his father in the orchestra; was given position as leader of the orchestra after father's death. A few years later, went to New York where he led the orchestra in Harry Miner's theatre in the Bowery and taught music during the day. After 3 or 4 years, was taken sick and his physician told him he must get out in the open air. About this time Adam Forepaugh advertised for band leader. Minter was hired, and was leader of the band up to the time he died. During the engagement at Madison Square Garden when the Barnum and Forepaugh shows performed together, Minter died of pneumonia. [D. W. Watt: "The funeral was the largest I ever saw for he belonged to a great many musical societies in New York, and there were over 600 people from the Barnum and Forepaugh shows who attended the funeral. There were eighty-six musicians in the band that led the funeral procession, and they marched up the Bowery to the Cooper Institute where those who were on foot dropped out of line, and carriages went on to the cemetery."]

MINTLINE, J. E. Business manager, G. G. Grady's, 1872.

MIRANDA SISTERS [Eliza, Lottie]. Howes' Great London, 1878; Adam Forepaugh's, 1879; **Eliza** was with Holland & McMahon, 1887; **Lottie** with John S. McMahon's Circus, 1892.

MISKA, LIDIANA. Russian rider, Leon W. Washburn's, 1896.

MITCHELL, CHARLES. Bill poster, P. T. Barnum's, 1873, commissary and layer out, 1876, asst. press agent, 1880.

MITCHELL, PROF. WILLIAM. Concert performer, "The Fire Demon," Cooper, Bailey & Co., 1876, Australian tour, 1877.

MITCHELL, WILLIAM. See George Wambold.

MOFFITT, R. R. Tattood man. Married Miss **Leo Hernandez**, bearded lady, February 11, 1883, Frankfort, PA. Harper Bros.' European, 1893.

MOHN HARRY. Equestrian director, Harper Bros.' European, 1893.

MOHR, HORACE. Acrobat, John Robinson's, 1890-92.**MOLOCH** ["The Invincible"]. Handled five royal Bengal tigers, Howes' Great London, 1871.

MONDEVRIER, ANTONIO. Gymnast, H. M. Smith's, 1870.**MONROE, CHARLES.** Irish singer, Rivers & Derious, 1859; Dan Rice's, 1860; clown, Stone & Rosston, 1865, 1871; Gardner & Hemmings, Front Street Theatre, Baltimore, winter 1865-66; S. O. Wheeler's, 1867-68; Hemmings, Cooper & Whitby, 1870; Baird, Howell & Co., 1874.

MONROE, FRANK. Aerialist. Sherman's Educated Horses and Great European, California, 1883; Morosco's, 1885; equestrian manager, Robinson's, California, 1886; Sherman &

Hinman, San Francisco, 1883.

MONROE, HENRY. Barnum, VanAmburgh and Castello's Great Show and Mammoth Moral Exhibition, 1867.

MONROE, MARK. Elephant handler. Began career, 1878, when the craze for baby elephants was at its height. Called the "King of Elephants" because of his skill and knowledge in dealing with them. 1879, in charge of the elephants in Central Park, NYC, under the direction of William A. Conklin, where he remained until he was employed by W. C. Coup, 1881. Following year, joined O'Brien, Handberger & Astley, traveling through the Northwest; next year, Adam Forepaugh's, which carried 36 elephants. After a trip to South America, 1884, joined Frank A. Robbins'; 1891, took charge of the animals at the Pittsburgh Zoo; 1892, supervised the animals on Hunting's but left the following January to join Ringling Bros.' at Baraboo, WI; following summer, 1893, with Hagenbeck at Chicago's World's Columbian Exposition.

MONROE, NELLIE. *Manège*, French & Monroe, 1885; rider, Howe's New London, 1887.

MONROE, WILLIAM O. (d. October 19, 1888) 4-horse, hurdle rider. C. T. Ames', 1869; James Robinson's, 1870-71; Adam Forepaugh's, 1872-81; proprietor, Great Universal Fair and World's Wonder Exposition, 1877; equestrian director, Batcheller & Doris, 1880; Cole's Great New Southern Circus (**Matt Leland**, William Monroe, **George S. Cole**, proprietors), 1881; French & Monroe's New York and New Orleans Circus, 1885; Howes' New London Shows (Monroe and French, managers), 1887-88; trained horses, Cook & Whitby's, 1892; trained horses, Great Wallace, 1893. Adam Forepaugh's European representive in purchasing menagerie stock, 1878-79; 1879; returned from a European trip where he acquired 3 elephants, a hippopotamus, 2 camels and a variety of smaller animals and birds.

MONTAGUE, ADELAIDE. Equestrienne, W. W. Cole's, 1874-75, 1880.

MONTAGUE, ED. Gymnast and acrobat, Ryland's, California, 1872.

MONTAGUE, LOUISE [r. n. Laura S. Keyser, another source gives Laura Keene Stewart]. (1859-March 15, 1910) Vocalist on the variety and burlesque stage. Born on Bleecker Street, NYC. Real fame occurred when she was advertised as being the $10,000 winner for the most beautiful woman in the world contest, a promotional stunt concocted by press agent **Charles H. Day** for Adam Forepaugh's. Presented atop the elephant Lalla Rookh in the street pagaent of "Lalla Rookh's Departure from Delhi," 1881. Described by a another contestant as "one of those shy, kittenish brunettes, with hatchet shoulders," and with big brown eyes. By July, was dismissed from the company because of disagreement with Forepaugh and replaced atop Lalla Rookh with a Chicago beauty. Rejoined the show on October 25 in Atlanta. Filed suits against Forepaugh, September 9, 1882; one to cover a proposed salary

of $75 a week for 32 weeks. February 8, 1883, the jury rendered a judgment of $150 in her favor. Accompanying suit was for the $10,000 advertised as being given to Miss Montague, 1881, for her appearance as "the handsomest woman in America." Charles H. Day stated in an affidavit that the $10,000 prize was a publicity scheme with Forepaugh having no intention of paying it to the winner of the contest. The suit was discontinued because of the absence of **Hugh Coyle**, a material witness. Two other suits were still pending: 1) for the remainder of Miss Montague's 1881 salary and 2) for injuries incurred when she was thrown from the elephant in Waterloo, IA, while she was impersonating Lalla Rookh in the street parade. Forepaugh let stand the verdict of $500 damages for her spill and Montague withdrew her appeal for a new trial in the breach of contract suit in which she was awarded $150. The cases were closed in 1883 with Forepaugh paying her a total of $650. Was supposed to go on the road with Forepaugh, 1882, but did not join because, according to her claim, she was promised a stateroom for traveling but discovered that was not the case. Filed suit for breach of contract damages of $2,400 in a Philadelphia court on February 2, 1883. Also sued for divorce, fall 1882. After leaving the circus, July 21, 1883, at Fishkill, NY, went to Europe to pursue instruction on the stage, studying in Paris and Berlin, then acted in England for a short time. On returning to USA, became a member of the original "Pinafore" Co. Under the management of **E. E. Rice**, was in the cast of *Evangeline, The Corsair,* and *The Crystal Slipper*; also featured in *Sinbad The Sailor* and *Ali Baba And the Forty Thieves.* Died in NYC, age 51. The notice of her death, printed in the papers on March 16, was written by her with the date left blank about a week before she passed away. Had a son, **Henry Montague**, who was an automobile salesman. Married **Paul Allen**, of Lester & Allen, San Francisco, 1877, and separated from him the following year because of his gambling vice. May have later married **John Delanty**, a man said to have possessed considerable property. He committed suicide, October 27, 1886. He had loaned **John O'Brien** a sizeable sum of money and was concerned about his ability to collect. Placed his head on a railroad track near Flemington, NJ. It was reported that he had married Louise Montague 7 weeks before, but was separated from her. [M. B. Leavitt: "Upon my return from Europe in the summer of 1876, I brought over a bevy of English beauties for one of my burlesque companies. The vaudeville agent, **R. B. Caverly**, informed me that he had a young beauty who was anxious to appear on the stage, lovelier than any of the English girls I had engaged. I informed him that the organization was complete, but he was insistent, and urged me to go to Niblo's Garden that evening, as the girl would be there with her mother to see the performance. I went, and was told to pick out the prettiest one I saw coming out of the theatre. I did so, and it was the one the agent referred to. Her name was Polly Stewart, the daughter of a well-known sporting man in town. I engaged her, and gave her the stage name of Louise Montague. She remained with my company for three years, during which she married one of my comedians, Paul Allen, of Lester & Allen.... Louise Montague shunned notoriety, but her face and figure had been much praised, so she became one of the candidates for beauty recognition. She was selected from more than 11,000 candidates who submitted photographs and descriptions. She was only eighteen years old when I engaged her.... After the first rage had worn off she sought a quiet life but many managers, believing that she had a value beyond her beauty, sought her services, and it was then discovered that she possessed exceptional dramatic ability. She was generous, and her charitable inclinations drew heavily on her purse. As her money faded away, she lived in a little flat that was attractively furnished. When she became ill, I visited her to render whatever aid she might require. She seemed as proud and independent as she had always been; such was her nature. On leaving her, I did not anticipate, nor did she, that the end was so near. She died poor. She wrote herself the only notice she wished published after her death: "Louise X. Montague, died at her residence, Manhattan Ave."] The famous beauty was 51 years of age.

MONTAGUE, SIGNOR. Rider, with Melville, Maginley & Cooke, 1875.

MONTAGUE, W. Gymnast, John Robinson's, 1866.

MONTANO, SIGNOR DEHL. Black animal tamer. Billed as a cannibal Hottentot, exhibited a pack of hyenas, Howes' Great London, 1871. Probabgly came from England with the Howes show late 1870. Contortionist and trapeze performer, VanAmburgh & Co., 1874. Entered a bear cage in Staffordshire, England, 1892, made a misstep as the door closed behind him; the animals seized him and tossed him one to another. No word of his fate.

MONTCLAIR, ADA INEZ. Mazeppa rider, G. G. Grady's, 1869.

MONTCLAIR, SIGNOR. Contortionist, L. B. Lent's, 1874.

MONTEVERDE, SIGNOR JOSE. Contortionist. Spanish by birth. First entered the ring as a boy of 7. Early experiences were acquired as a *matador* in the bull rings of Spain. Made his debut in the *Theatre D'Iscala*, Milan, with his father; later performed in the *Cirque de Napoleon*, Paris; was for 2 years in St. Petersburg, and for some time at Berlin and Constantinople. 1848, while performing at the Turkish capital in what was called the "bridge act," fell and was carried unconscious out of the arena. Believed to be mortally injured, but it was found that the fall was not fatal. Again, in Berlin while performing the "perch act" he fell a distance of 40', but escaped with only a broken arm. H. C. Lee's, 1858; Kimball's, 1859; George F. Bailey & Co., 1860-61; Robinson & Howes, Chicago, winter 1863-64; L. B. Lent's, 1866; Nixon, Howes &

Castello, 1868; Charles Noyes', 1870; C. T. Ames', 1870; P. T. Barnum's, 1872-73.

MONTFORT. Hindu juggler, John H. Murray's, 1874.

MONTGOMERY, P. Horizontal bars, Harry Thayer & Co.'s, 1890.

MONTRE, A. C. Band leader, Showles & Co., 1873.

MONTROSE, DORA. Aeronaut, "The Lady Who Jumps from the Clouds," Wallace & Co., 1890.

MONTROSE, KATE. Gymnast, W. W. Cole's, 1886.

MOORE, ALBERT. Treasurer, Moore Bros.', 1887.

MOORE, BENJAMIN. Agent, Levi J. North's, 1854.

MOORE, BILLY and **NELLIE.** Mexican ladder, Andy McDonald's, 1892.

MOORE BROTHERS. Gymnasts. Dan Rice's, 1866; Goldenburg's, 1874.

MOORE, CHARLES. Dog circus, Howe's New London, 1887.

MOORE, CHARLES. Chef, Adam Forepaugh's.

MOORE, CHESTER C. Agent. Stone, Rosston & Murray, 1868; manager, Stone & Murray, 1869. Died in Penfield, NY, February 1874.

MOORE, E. Female keeper. Raymond, Weeks & Co., 1844; Raymond & Waring, 1847.

MOORE FAMILY. Roller skaters, John B. Doris', 1884-85.

MOORE, GEORGE. Clown. Stickles & Co., 1832; Drury, Van Tassle, Brown & Co., 1837; Brown & Mills, 1838, later as Waterman & Co.; Howes & Mabie, 1845-46; E. F. & J. Mabie, 1848; Rowe's, 1850; Christy Minstrels, U.K., 1859, and many years thereafter.

MOORE, HANK. Boss canvasman, Gollmar Bros.', 1897.

MOORE, HARRY. General agent. James T. Johnson's, 1886; John F. Stowe's, 1892; McDonald & Wells, 1892.

MOORE, JENNIE. Chariot rider. With Walter L. Main's, Burke's, Washburn's, and John H. Sparks'. Husband, **Larry Moore**, was a boss hostler. Died of consumption, December 3, 1902.

MOORE, LEWIS. Equestrian and gymnast, Flagg & Aymar, 1856.

MOORE, LON W. Clown. Holland, Bowman & McLaughlin, 1890; VanAmburgh, 1891; F. J. Tayor's, 1893. Home was at Defiance, OH.

MOORE, MATTIE. Moore Bros.' New Consolidated Railroad Shows, 1887.

MOORE, NELLIE. "Evolutions on the silver wire," F. J. Tayor's, 1893.

MOORE, TOM. Bill poster, with VanAmburgh and Reiche Bros.', 1885.

MOORE, W. H. Press agent, Great London, 1880.

MOORE, WILLIAM C. Cannon ball performer. Died in Brooklyn, March 5, 1874.

MOORE, WILLIE. Trapeze performer, George W. Rich-

MORAND. Stone, Rosston and Murray, 1867.

MORAN, HARRY and **MAY.** Shield's Circus, 1888.

MORAN, J. Virginia Serenaders, Raymond & Waring, 1844.

MORAN, MME. Equestrienne, Nixon & Co., Niblo's Garden, 1859.

MORELAND, A. D. Candy stand privilege, Main & Sargeant, 1891.

MORELAND, W. C. Adam Forepaugh's, 1878.

MORRELLE, PAULINE. Gymnast, W. W. Cole's, 1886.

MORELLO BROTHERS [William, Max]. With Sparrow's, 1886; Roberts & Gardner, 1886; William Main & Co., 1887; Scribner & Smith, 1895.

MORENZO, JOHN. Clown, John Forepaugh's, California, 1888.

MORESTE BROTHERS. Trapeze and bar performers. The Great Commonwealth Circus, 1872; Prof. Samwell's, South America, 1873.

MORESTE, GEORGE. Thayer & Noyes, 1867.

MORESTE, HENRY. Horizontal bars, posturer, a solo on the drums while hanging downward on the trapese. Great Union (**George W. DeHaven**, proprietor), 1860; Front Street Theartre, Baltimore, early winter, 1860; Madigan's, 1861; Gardner & Hemmings, 1862; Slaymaker & Nichols, 1864.

MORGAN, A. W. Advertising agent. Consolidation Circus (**W. B. Hough**, manager), 1866; Maginley & Carroll, 1868. Died at the Pavilion Hotel, Charleston, SC, in poverty, February 1869.

MORGAN, CHARLES. Educated dogs, Mrs. Charles Warner's, Philadelphia, 1869.

MORGAN, E. H. Alex Robinson's,l 1870.

MORGAN, FANNIE. W. W. Cole's, California, fall 1880.

MORGAN, FRANK. Pad rider, vaulter. G. G. Grady's, 1868-74; Roman Races, Brighton Beach Fair Grounds, Coney Island, 1879; P. T. Barnum's, 1882-86.

MORGAN, G. H. With T. L. Vermule's New Jersey Circus, 1845.

MORGAN, HENRY. Horizontal bars, C. T. Ames', 1868.

MORGAN, MONS. Juggler and posturer, Mabie & Crosby, 1858.

MORGAN, MRS. J. B. Aerialist, a member of the performing **Zamora Family**. Died in NYC, April 28, 1906.

MORGAN, W. CHARLES. Trick clown. DeMott & Ward, 1868; Metchear & Cameron, 1870.

MORGAN, W. H. John H. Murray's Pony Circus, 1880.

MORGAN, WILLIAM C. (1826?-March 5, 1874) Cannon ball performer. Major Brown's, 1857; Mabie & Crosby, 1858; L. B. Lent's, 1863; Australian Circus, 1870; Sanford's, Lima, Peru, fall 1870. Died of dropsy at his residence, 314 Leonard St., Brooklyn, NY, age 48. Had retired from the profession some years earlier and he went to South America as a civil engineer, where he contacted the disease.

MORGAN, WILLIAM H. (d. October 30, 1884) Hurdle rider, bareback steeple chase act. Lent's Equescurriculum, 1863; bar act and hurdle rider, Palmer's Great Western, 1865; Mike Lipman's, 1866-67; Adam Forepaugh's, 1867, 1870; Luande's, West Indies, 1867; Philadelphia Circus, winter 1867-68; Gardner & Kenyon, 1868; Dr. James L. Thayer's, 1869; Dan Rice's Paris Pavilion, 1871-72; Howes' London, 1872-73; L. B. Lent's, 1874; Sanford & Courtney, South America, 1874-75; P. T. Barnum's, 1878; John H. Murray's Pony Circus, 1880; Stevens' Australian Circus, performing on variety stages prior to summer season, 1882; Orrin Bros.', Mexico, winter 1882-83; Bartine's, 1887. Murdered in Arkansas by **Douglas Post**.

MORITZ, FREDA. Ladder of swords, Walter L. Main's, 1893.

MORITZ, HENRIETTA. German midget. Adam Forepaugh's, 1883; Walter L. Main's, 1892-93.

MORMON FAMILY. Curiousities with a total weight of 1,508 pounds, John H. Murray's, 1874.

MOROSCO FAMILY [Walter, Frank, Charles, Harry]. Posturing, contortion and slack-wire. Sells Bros.', 1874; International Circus, Offenbach Garden, Philadelphia, winter 1876-77; John H. Murray's, 1877; Orrin Bros.', Havana, winter 1878-79; Mexico, winter 1883-84; Allen's Great Eastern, 1880; Dan Rice's, 1881; W. H. Stowe's, winter 1881-82; Cooper, Jackson & Co., 1882; Sherman & Hinman, California, 1883; W. H. Harris' Nickel-Plate, 1885-86; Morosco's Royal Russian Circus, 1885; Irwin Bros.', 1895. **Walter** was equestrian director, Sherman & Hinman, San Francisco, September 1883.

MOROSCO, JENNIE. Gillmeyer, Bryson & Co., 1888.

MORRELL, NELLIE. Trapeze artist, Alexander Robinson's, 1870.

MORRESSEY, JOHN. (d. May 1, 1878) Henry Barnum's, 1874. **Mlle. Cordelia** was his wife.

MORRIS, ANDREW E. Negro minstrel, Orton & Older, 1858-59.

MORRIS, ANDY. Acrobat, Charley Bartine's, 1872; pantomime clown, Dan Rice's Paris Pavilion, 1873.

MORRIS, FRANK. (d. 1916) Sideshow talker for more than 20 years with the Adam Forepaugh show. At the death of Forepaugh, went to the Buffalo Bill show here he remained for about 15 years. Went in the business when but 17 years of age and soon gained notoriety as one of the best sideshow talkers in the country. At the age 20 or 21, made all the principal openings of the sideshow with Forepaugh as well as the concert announcements in the big tent. Died at about 60 years of age. [D. W. Watt: "Frank Morris was one of the highest class orators in front of a sideshow that I ever knew. He was not the red-faced, yelling kind and often I have sat at the side door of my ticket wagon and listened to Frank make his opening and watch the faces of the people, and the expressions on their faces would tell you that they were glad to listen to such a talker."]

MORRIS, G. W. Agent, Dan Rice's, 1881.

MORRIS, HARRY S., Sr. (d. November 30, 1934) Acrobat and leaper. Began with Dan Rice's with his partner **Irvin Whitlow** as the **Merrell Bros.** Later, the Merrell Bros. joined the Al G. Field Minstrels with a trick cabinet acrobatic act. Morris performed with Rentz', Harris' Nickel Plate, Sells-Forepaugh, and the Castello-Miles Orton show. 1892, married **Ida Briscoe.** Died in Louisville, KY.

MORRIS, HENRY. Adam Forepaugh's, 1873.

MORRIS, JAMES. (b. 1859) Known as "the elastic skin man." Born in Copenhagen, NY. Began stretching skin professionally for dime museums. By 1882, with Barnum and Bailey, earning $150 a week. Sells Bros.', Pacific Coast, fall 1886; Cooke & Whitby, 1892. An addiction to gambling and drinking kept him poor.

MORRIS, J. C. Holton & Gates' Harmoniums, a minstrel band, Simon Pure American Circus, NYC, October 1, 1866.

MORRIS, MAJOR. Director of publications, G. G. Grady's, 1874.

MORRIS, PETER. Juggler. Frost & Co., 1837; Bacon & Derious, 1838; W. Gates & Co., 1838; G. C. Quick, 1850.

MORRISON, CHARLES. Boss canvasman, W. H. Harris' Nickel-Plate, 1884.

MORRISON, CHARLES. Acrobat. Crescent City, 1856; G. N. Eldred, 1857; Satterlee & Bell, 1858; Orton & Older, 1858-59; Robinson & Lake, 1859-60; Australian Dime Show, 1887; contortionist, John F. Robinson's, 1889-90.

MORRISON, GEORGE. Treasurer, with John Robinson's, 1869.

MORRISON, J. Gymnast, John Robinson's, 1888-89.

MORRISON, ROBERT. (d. April 12, 1871) Agent, John Robinson's for several years. Died of dropsy in St. Louis, MO.

MORSE, CHARLES. Secretary, P. T. Barnum's, 1874-75.

MORSE, JOSEPH. Artist and engraver, the man who discovered the use of the pine plock for poster work.

MORTON, E. Lake & Co., 1863.

MORTON, FRANK. Ventriloquist in the sideshow, Cooper, Bailey & Co., 1879.

MORTON, FRANK A. Band Leader, Harry Thayer & Co.'s, 1890.

MORTON, GEORGE. (d. October 3, 1895) Clown. Caldwell's, 1867. Died in the Almhouse, New Haven CT, age 70.

MORTON, H. Negro minstrel, Spaulding & Rogers' *Floating Palace*, 1859.

MOSELEY, AMY. See Seth B. Howes.

MOSELEY, THOMAS. Scenic rider from Astley's Amphitheatre, London, Welch & Mann, 1845; ringmaster and scenic rider, Sands, Lent & Co., 1846-47; Welch & Mann, Philadelphia, 1847.

MOSES, A. W. Sideshow band leader, Barnum, Bailey & Hutchinson, 1881.

MOSES, GEORGE. Orton & Older, 1858-59.

MOTTY, HERR OTTO [or Motley]. Said to be an ugly looking individual but a versatile performer who was a juggler, rope-dancer, 3-horse rider, and a cannon ball performer. Feats included the juggling on horseback of rings, balls and daggers with rapidity and the throwing of cannon balls high into the air and catching them on his neck. Claimed the Emperor of Russia called him "The Undaunted." Raymond & Waring, Cooke's Circus, Philadelphia, 1839; strongman, June, Titus, Angevine & Co., 1839-40; Raymond & Waring, 1840; Welch, Bartlett & Co., 1840; Nathan A. Howes', winter 1842; Charles LaForest's, 1842; Ogden & Hobby, 1842; Rockwell & Stone, 1842, 1844-45; John Tryon's, Bowery Amphitheatre, NYC, 1844; Rockwell & Stone, 1845.

MOULTON, GEORGE. Equestrian, VanAmburgh & Co., 1881.

MOULTON, HARRY AND MINNIE. Gymnasts, G. A. Courtney's, West Indies, 1880; Lehmann's, 1885; Pubillones', Cuba, winter 1885-86. **Minnie** was also listed as a female lion tamer with Pubillones.

MOULTON, HUGO. Horizontal bars, Barnum & London, 1884-85.

MOUNTCLAIN, ADA [or Montcalm]. Hurdle rider, G. G. Grady's, 1869.

MOXLEY, CHARLOTTE. Irish giantess, with Cooper and Bailey, 1875.

MOXLEY, CHARLOTTE. English giantess, with Cooper, Bailey & Co., 1876.

MOXLEY, GEORGE. Chief billposter, Adam Forepaugh's, 1875.

MOYERS, PROF. Lion king, J. V. Cameron, 1875.

MULLER, PROF. JACOB. Band leader, Great Eastern, 1873. Said to have been 18 years in the service of Emperor William of Prussia.

MULLETT, CAPTAIN. Seller of sea lions. Caught and sold over 100 in 1880 alone.

MULLIGAN, JOHN. (March, 1827-July 22, 1873) Negro minstrel. Born in NYC. First professional engagement, Raymond & Waring, 1848. Followed by 2 seasons, Robinson & Eldred, dancing in the ring while **Al Romaine** performed upon the banjo. 1854, joined Mabie's in Missouri. Conclusion of that season, G. F. Bailey, with whom he remained 3 seasons. Then went to Philadelphia, where he fulfilled an engagement at Thomas' Opera House. Following winter, joined Van Amburgh's at Macon, GA, and continued with that show one season. On return from the South, was engaged by **Frank Rivers** for his Melodeon in Philadelphia, and remained 2 years. Attracted the attention of **George Lea**, a well known manager, and, 1862, entered into a contract for a long period; performed under Lea's direction in Baltimore, Washington, Philadelphia, New York, New Orleans and nearly all the principal cities of the Union. Afterwards, connected with the San Francisco Minstrels, Hooley's and others. Standing over 6' in height, Mulligan was an Ethiopian comedian of great ability; even the ludicrous style of his wardrobe evoked laughter. Said to be the original "Bob Ridley." [T. Allston Brown: "Mr. Mulligan, as an Ethiopian comedian, had few equals in his peculiar line, and in his special acts was without a rival."] Died in NYC in the 47th year of his age.

MULLIGAN, WILLIAM. Vaulter. Cooke's, 1836; Welch, Bartlett & Co., 1839-40; Grecian Arena, 1841; trampoline, Rockwell & Stone, 1842.

MUNGO, PRINCE. (d. May 13, 1923) Native of Peach Orchard, KY. Started, 1881, as a South Sea Island "torture" dancer. Cooper & Jackson, 1881-82; John Robinson, 1884-87; Great Wallace, 1889-97; Sells & Downs, 1897-1903; Norris & Rowe, 1903-04; John Robinson's, 1904-06; Cole Bros.'s, 1906-09; Forepaugh-Sells, 1910; Sells-Floto, 1911-14; Al G. Barnes', 1915; Hagenbeck-Wallace, 1916; John Robinson's, 1918; Yankee Robinson's, 1919-20; Sparks', 1920 until his death. Lived in Chicago when not on the road. Was killed at Mt. Carmel, PA, from being hit by a street trolley.

MUNSON BROTHERS. Gymnasts and tumblers, John Stowe & Sons, 1871. Are they Lem and Leon listed below?

MUNSON, LEM. Contortionist. Burr Robbins; Boyd & Peters' Great Transatlantic Circus, 1880; Adam Forepaugh's, several seasons beginning in 1885. His size, 6' tall and weighing 200 pounds, belied his performance in the ring. [D. W. Watt: "Munson was a quiet, unpretentious man, made many friends in the business and never lost one."] **MUNSON, LEON.** Contortionist and *chair la perche*, Stowe & Orton, 1870; acrobat, Burr Robbins', 1875.

MUNSON, L. K. G. G. Grady's, 1868-72.

MURDELL, ALICE. See Josephine F. Forepaugh.

MURDOCK, WILLIAM. (b. 1808?) Principal clown, with Spalding & Rogers. Retired, 1865.

MURPHY, ED. Hobson Bros.', 1887.

MURPHY, JAMES. See James Balnan.

MURRAY, JAMES. Leaper and tumbler. Cooper, Bailey & Co., 1879-80; Barnum, Bailey & Hutchinson, 1881-84.

MURPHY, J. C. Clown. Lake's Hippo-Olympiad, 1869; Great Metropolitan Olypiad, 1877.

MURPHY, P. Chief bill poster, S. P. Stickney & Son, 1874.

MURPHY, WILLIAM H. Griffith & Allen, 1886.

MURRAY, FRANK. Alex Abar's Pavilion Show, 1889.

MURRAY, GEORGE W. Clown, Stone, Rosston & Murray, 1865-67; clown, and ringmaster, Stone & Murray, 1868-69; J. E. Warner & Co., 1871; John O'Brien's, 1872; Central Park Menagerie and Circus, 1873; John H. Murray's, 1873; Howe's Great London, 1874; clown and vocalist, Burr Robbins', 1876.

MURRAY, HARRY. Contracting agent, Burr Robbins',

1885.

MURRAY, JAMES. Tumbler. Married equestrienne **Rosina Dubsky**, Havana, January 25, 1882. Married **Allie Alden**, 1889.

MURRAY, JAMES J. (d. November 14, 1893) Tumbler. Born abroad but came to America as a small boy. L. B. Lent's, 1876; Carlo Bros.', South America, 1877; Great London, 1880; tumbler, Leon & Dockrill, Iron Amphitheatre, Havana, winter 1881-82; W. O'Dale Stevens', Park Square Grounds, Boston, spring 1883; James T. Johnson's, 1885; Col. Foster's, 1885; Miller, Okey & Freeman, 1886; Gardner & Donovan, South America, 1886; Miller, Stowe & Freeman, 1887; *Gran Circo Estrellas Del Nortis*, West Indies, fall 1888; Frank A. Gardner's, South America, 1889; Walter L. Main's, 1891. At one time, part owner of Murray & Ducrow's New York Circus, touring in South and Central America, but ill health forced him out of circus activity. Established an amusement agency business, NYC, in association with **H. A. Covell**, 1892. Said to have acquired considerable wealth throughout his career. Married rider **Linda Jeal**. Died in Philadelphia, age about 40.

MURRAY, JOHN "COL." (d. April 13, 1907) Associate, who for about 25 years was a ticket seller for Sells Bros.' Died in Columbus, OH.

MURRAY, JOHN HAYES. (July 19, 1829-December 27, 1881) Born in NYC. Made professional debut as a negro minstrel, performing at Barnum's Museum and later in the concert of June & Co. Possessing an outstanding physique and great strength, developed skills as an acrobat and began as a general performer. Welch, Mann & Delavan, 1845; Victory, 1847; S. B. Howes', 1848; Crane's, 1849-50; Dan Rice's, 1850, where he doubled with **George Holland** as the **Roman Brothers**, an acrobatic act noted for its style and grace, and which existed for several years. The two visited California and South America, 1854, appearing at various theatres; went to England, Howes & Cushing, 1857-59, performing before the Queen at the Royal Alhambra Palace, London, May 14, 1858. Murray appeared in the brother act, did a globe-perch with **Holland**, introduced the trick mules, Pete and Barney, and worked the educated horse, Black Eagle. Ringmaster, Dan Rice's, 1859; 1860-63, appeared with leading circuses abroad, including Rentz's, Carey's, Heeney's, Price's, and Brenow's. Performed, after Holland's death, with **George P. Hutchinson**. Returning to America, connected with Stone, Rosston & Co., 1864; following year, his name appeared in the title, Stone, Rosston & Murray's; 1866-71, Stone & Murray. Den Stone withdrew, 1872, leaving Murray the sole proprietor; this ownership continued through 1878, the company visiting the West Indies during the winter seasons of 1876-78. During the off-season, 1875, made a trip to Europe and secured entertainers that had not previously performed in the United States. Was in retirement, 1879. 1880, furnished ring stock for L. B. Lent's,

Globe Theatre, NYC, and in conjunction with **Robert Stickney**, gave a short circus season at the Siege of Paris Building, Boston. November 1880 until the spring of 1881, managed a circus troup in the Aquarium, NYC, and put out a small circus that summer, John H. Murray's Pony Circus. **E. D. Colvin** and **J. J. Nathans** purchased the Murray outfit, 1882. Married equestrienne **Frances Victoria Johnston**, an equitation performer, December 8, 1859, eventually producing 2 sons and 2 daughters. Died of pneumonia in NYC.

MURRAY, JOHN J. Acrobat, Crane & Co., 1850; Adam Forepaugh's, 1874; clown, Beckett's Railroad Circus, 1887; Hunting's, 1889 (with wife **Florence**), 1893-95.

MURRAY, MILDRED. *Manège*, Sells & Rentfrow's, 1893.

MURRAY, THOMAS. Irish comedian. Stone, Rosston & Murray, 1867; Stone & Murray, 1868-69; John H. Murray's, 1877; D. W. Stone's, 1878.

MURRAY, WILLIAM [r. n. W. C. Lewis]. (1849?-February 13, 1913) Rider. Began with Stone & Murray as a lad, billed as "the boy champion rider" over the hurdles. Clown for many of the leading circuses in the 1860s and 1870s. Last employment, Mighty Haag Show as a talker. Married **Julia C. Lewis**. Died at Carthage, MO, age 64.

MURTZ & KLINE. James M. Nixon's Parisian Hippodrome and Chicago Amphitheatre, May 1872.

MURTZ, HARRY. W. W. Cole's, 1886.

MURTZ, JOHN. (d. 1887) Clown. Great London, 1878; W. W. Cole's, 1879, 1884. For many years one of the **Livingston Brothers**. Did an aerial bicycle act and an Australian Blondin act. With Cole, 1886, performed on the horizonal bars with **C. H. Lorbey**, **Frank Lorbey**, **Ed Marlon** and **Johnny Hart**. Dockrill's, Central America, winter 1886-87. Died on a steamer en route from Panama to Peru.

MURTZ, JOHN. W. W. Cole's, 1886.

MUSGAT, WILLIAM R. (1863?-March 11, 1908) Associate. Born in Fond du Lac, WI. Entered the business with Tayor's, a small wagon show with which he was employed for some time. Later, joined Sells & Rentfrow as a steward. Was a short time with John Robinson's; then became manager of Car #5, Great Wallace for 6 or 7 years; then William P. Hall's; 1906, joined Sells-Floto as general agent and remained until his death of a heart attack, Denver, CO, age 45.

MYERS, CHARLES. Sideshow privilege, educated hog, George DeHaven's, 1869.

MYERS, FRED. Clown, Cooper & Myer's Circus of All Nations, 1858.

MYERS, HENRIETTA. Orrin Bros.', Mexico, February 1884.

MYERS, JAMES WASHINGTON. (1820-December 1, 1892) Showman and clown. Born in Providence, RI. Apprenticed as an equestrian to **Aaron Turner** at age 9 and performed under the name of **James Turner**. Under own name as scenic rider, June & Turner, 1845-47; bareback rider, Sands, Lent & Co., 1846-47; Aaron Turner's, 1849-52; clown and co-proprietor, Myers & Madigan, 1854; Howes Menagerie and Myers & Madigan's Circus, 1855; Jim Myers', 1856. 1857, went to England with Howes & Cushing. Became the first to do a double somersault over horses while there. Performed for the Queen at Windsor Castle. Quit with Howes & Cushing and formed his own company, touring England and the Continent. Returning to London, opened at the Agricultural Hall, January 12, 1879. Back in USA, DeMott & Ward, 1868. Was married to **Rose Madigan**. Died in Bristol, England, age 69.

MYERS, JOHN. Dogs and ponies, Richard's Big Show, 1892.

MYERS, LEWIS. Adam Forepaugh's, 1871.

MYERS, OLIVER P. Agent, with J. E. Warner & Co., 1871; contracting agent, John Robinson's, 1873; press agent, Montgomery Queen's, 1875, and general advertiser, 1876. Connected with the passenger department of Pittsburgh and Fort Wayne Railroad, Chicago, 1879. General agent and railroad contractor, Shelby, Pullman & Hamilton, 1881; Myers & Shorb's United States Circus, 1882 (former Robbins & Colvin show); excursion agent, John Robinson's, 1884; Howes & Richardson, 1887.

MYERS, PROF. Performing goats, with William O'Dale Stevens', Park Square, Boston, 1883.

MYERS, T. R. General representative, Robinson & Myers', 1883.

MYERS, VIRGINIA A. (d. September 3, 1884) Equestrienne. Daughter of clown and manager **James Myers** and the former **Rose Madigan**. Welch & Lent, 1856; Sloat & Shepherd "Joe Pentland," 1859. Married leaper **Tom King** at Rhinebeck, NY, May 12, 1859, while with Sloat & Shepherd. The couple worked together throughout most of their married life. See Thomas King.

MYERS, WILLIAM. (d. 1856) Born in Baltimore. William Harrington's, 1825; vaulter, J. Purdy Brown's, 1825-28; American Arena, Washington, DC, winter 1828-29; clown, Fogg & Stickney, 1830; clown, John Lamb's, 1831; ringmaster, Aaron Turner's, Philadelphia, winter 1833-34; Edward Eldred's, 1834; vaulter, Raymond &. Waring, 1840. Died in Philadelphia.

MYERS, WILLIAM M. Treasurer, G. G. Grady's, 1869; press agent, 1871; treasurer, 1874.

N

NAGLE BROTHERS [3]. Acrobats, Rice, Stowe & Oates, 1881.

NAGLE, GEORGE M. (d. January 22, 1890)

NAGLE, HENRY. Acrobat. Welch & Mann, 1846; Welch's, 1847; Sands, Nathans & Co., 1854; Welch & Lent, 1854; H. P. Madigan, 1856; Welch's, Philadelphia, winter 1857-60.

NAIL, JOHN W. (1855?-March 1, 1882) Associate. Started into show business with Alex Robinson's, fall 1868; privilege department, Adam Forepaugh's, 1873-75, 1881; Pullman's, 1876; John O'Brien's, 1877; Campbell's, 1878; Batchelor & Doris, 1879-80. Married **Annie Bostwick** of Allegany, NY, winter 1879. Died after a brief illness in Mocksville, NC, age 27.

NAIL, MARIAH. Midget. With Adam Forepaugh's (Pullman Bros.' sideshow), 1876.

NANO, SIGNOR HERVIO. See Harvey Leach.

NAPIER, ALICE. Gymnast. Wife of **William Forepaugh**. Montgomery Queen's, 1873; Burr Robbins', 1874-75. See Josephine F. Forepaugh. See Josephine F. Forepaugh.

NASH, AL. Singing clown, Great Exposition Circus, 1895.

NASH, FRANK E. (d. September 4, 1882) Elephant trainer and ringmaster. Dan Rice's, 1849-1854; VanAmburgh's & Co.'s northern, 1859; VanAmburgh's southern, 1860; Van-Amburgh & Co., 1865-66, 1871; Dan Rice's, 1868. Died in Philadelphia. In last 8 years, was head keeper at the Zoological Garden, Fairmount Park, Philadelphia. His wife was an equestrienne.

NATHAN, EMANUEL. Russian lion tamer. About age 40, made his appearance in this country for the first time with Barnum & Bailey, 1886, arriving from Germany, October 20, 1885.

NATHAN, THOMAS B. (b. 1807) Singer. Buckley & Co., 1834-36; Raymond & Weeks, 1836; Lion Theatre Circus, 1837; J. J. Hall's, West Indies, 1837.

NATHANIELS, R. Acrobat and comic rider. Spalding & Rogers, 1857-58; McCorkle's, 1859; Niblo & Sloat (Nathaniels & **Ashton**), 1860.

NATHANS, ADDISON M. (b. December 27, 1835) General and press agent. Younger brother of **John J.** Born in Florida. Entered the Confederate Army, April, 1, 1861, and served throughout the war, after which he returned to his home state and entered into the mercantile business. Fall 1868, moved to NYC and joined the European Circus on Broadway. George F. Bailey & Co., 1869; advance, European Circus, 1870-71; Melville, Maginley & Cooke, 1875; assistant manager, P. T. Barnum's, 1876-79; proprietor (with **E. D. Colvin**), Nathans & Co., 1882-83.

NATHANS, DAVIS. Superintendent of automatic and mechanical dept., P. T. Barnum's, 1875.

NATHANS, EMMA [r. n. Emma C. Paulin]. Equestrienne. Was step-daughter of **J. J. Nathans** and daughter of **Amelia Pastor Nathans**. Welch & Nathans, 1851; Sands & Quick, 1852; E. F. and J. Mabie's, 1854; New York Champs Elysees, 1866.

NATHANS, ESTELLE. Dan Castello's, 1870.

NATHANS, JOHN JAY. (1814-December 26, 1891) Showman and rider. Younger brother of **Thomas B. Nathans**. Married **Amelia Pastor**, 1840. Was one of the first to ride 4-horse while carrying a child above his head. Was a tutor to many young men who became prominent equestrians—a few being **Edward** and **William Kincade**, **Tony**, **Frank**, and **William Pastor**. Benjamin Brown's, 1828; vaulter, Asa T. Smith's, 1829; Handy & Welch, West Indies, 1829; William Harrington's, 1832; director, Quick, Sands & Co., 1833; Buckley & Co., 1834; Buckley, Weeks & Co., 1835; J. J. Hall's, 1836; J. J. Hall's, West Indies, 1837; Hall, Nathans & Tufts, 1839; Clayton, Bartlett & Welch, 1840; Welch & Delavan, 1841; equestrian manager, eastern unit of June, Titus, Angevine & Co., 1842; 2-horse rider, Welch & Mann, 1843; Mann, Welch & Delavan, 1844-46; Welch & Delavan, 1847; Welch, Delavan & Nathans, 1848-50. Partnership with **Richard Sands**, 1850s, a union which continued until Sands death, 1861. Took Sands, Nathans & Co. to the Bowery and Broadway circuses, 1858. With **Sands**, **Seth Howes** and **Avery Smith**, erected Franconi's Hippodrome, Broadway and 23rd Street, NYC, 1853, marking the introduction of hippodrome performances to America. Managed Mabie's Menagerie and Nathans' Circus, 1861; S. P. Stickney's, 1861; L. B. Lent's, 1862; manager, Seth B. Howes', 1864-69; George Bailey & Co., 1867. With **Lewis June**, **Avery Smith** (Smith died the first year), and **George F. Bailey**, took out P. T. Barnum's, 1876-80. Wife **Mary** died in Philadelphia, February 18, 1869. Then married the English equestrienne, **Lucille Watson**, who had come to USA with Seth B. Howes' Great European. See Lucille Watson. Nathans died in NYC, age 77, leaving an estate at close to a half a million dollars.

NATHANS, MRS. J. J. See Lucille Watson.

NATHANS, PHILO R. [r. n. Rust]. Rider. Apprentice of **John J. Nathans**, described as being a spirited somersault and 4-horse rider. Married **Sophia Victoria North**, daughter of **Levi J. North**, in Philadelphia, March, 1866, but the couple were divorced, December 17, 1877. Sands, Nathans & Co., 1854-57; Sands, Nathans & Co., Bowery and Broadway circuses, 1858; Sands & Nathans, 1859; Mabie & Nathans, 1861; Tom King's, winter 1861, Washington, DC; Gardner & Hemmings, 1862; George F. Bailey & Co., 1863, with same at

Spalding & Rogers' Academy of Music, New Orleans, winter 1863-64; Tom King's, 1864; Seth B. Howes', 1866-68; winter circus, at Chestnut Street Theatre, Philadelphia, 1868-69; Dan Castello's, 1870; Philadelphia Circus, winter 1870-71; George F. Bailey & Co., 1872; P. T. Barnum's, 1873; Montgomery Queen's, 1874; equestrian director, Dr. James L. Thayer's, 1880; Robbins & Colvin, 1881; Nathans & Co.'s, 1882-83.

NATHANS, SOPHIA VICTORIA. See Sophia Victoria North.

NATHANS, THOMAS B. (b. March 31, 1805) Older brother of **John J.** Left home at age 16 and apprenticed with **Daniel Champlin.** See John Jay Nathans.

NATHANS, W. H. Proprietor, Metropolitan Pavilion, 1874.

NAYLOR, HENRY. (d. August 28, 1867) Night watchman, Herr Driesbach & Co.'s Menagerie, 1856. Died of pleurisy, Worcester, OH, age 34.

NAYLOR, JOHN W. (b. December 8, 1838) Rider, ringmaster and general performer. Born in New Orleans. Pupil of Levi J. North. Levi J. North's, 1857-59; scenic rider, Hyatt & Co., 1859; Gardner & Hemmings, 1863; tumbler, George W. DeHaven & Co., 1865; tumbler, leaper, Palmer's Great Western, 1865; ringmaster, Haight & Chambers, 1866-67; ringmaster, Mike Lipman's, 1867; Maginley, Carroll & Co., 1868; Lake's Hippo-Olympiad, 1869; ringmaster, Adam Forepaugh's, 1869-70, 1873-74; J. W. Wilder's, 1872.

NAYLOR, WILLIAM H. (January 17, 1837-May 8, 1879) Bareback and hurdle rider. Native of New Orleans where his father was a prompter in many of the first-class theatres. Began his professional career at the age of 4 as a pupil of the great rider, **Levi J. North,** with whom he remained until he was 21. Gardner & Hemmings, 1863; Nixon's Cremorne Garden Circus, Washington, DC, October-December 1862; Tom King's, 1864; George W. DeHaven's, 1865; Haight & Chambers, 1866-67; C. T. Aymes', 1868; S. P. Stickney's, 1869; James M. Nixon's, 1870; E. Stowe's, 1871; James M. Nixon's, Chicago, 1872. Forced to retire because of severe rheumatism and died some 4 or 5 years later in NYC, age 38. His father was for many years a prompter for various theatres in the country.

NEAL, GEORGE. G. W. Hall, Jr.'s Circus and Trained Animal Shows, 1895.

NEAL, JOSEPH H. Gymnast. Niblo & Sloat (**L. B. Lent,** manager), West Indies, 1860; Rogers & Ashton's acrobatic troupe, 1861; Spalding & Rogers, South America, 1862; Dr. James L. Thayer's, 1869; equestrian director, G. G. Grady's, 1874.

NEARY, ED. Clown. Sells Bros.', 1882; French & Monroe, 1885; S. H. Barrett's, 1885; Wallace & Co., 1887; Frank A. Gardner's *Circo Americano,* Central and South America, 1888. It is believed he died in 1888.

NEARY, JAMES. Alex Abar's Pavilion Show, 1889.

NEAVE FAMILY. Muçisians. **R. S. Neave,** Cincinnati Buck-

eye Brass Band, Cincinnati Circus, 1845; "bugle champion from Berlin," E. F. Mabie, 1847, E. F. & J. Mabie, 1848. **William H. Neave** was with A. Turner & Co., 1849-50; **M. T. Neave** with National Union Band, Robinson & Eldred, 1851-52; **David S. Neave** with New York Knickerbocker Band, Welch-Nathans, 1851; band leader, Robinson & Eldred, 1852.

NECELLO, FRANK. Swiss warbler, sideshow, Gardner & Hemmings, 1863.

NEEDHAM, HENRY. Thomas Taplin Cooke's, 1838; manager, S. H. Nichols', 1840-41; Aaron Turner & Sons, 1842; ringmaster, Niblo's Garden, NYC, winter 1843-44; equestrian director, Welch's, Philadelphia, 1843; equestrian director, Nathan A. Howes', winter 1843-44; equestrian director, Rockwell & Stone, 1843-46; Dr. Gilbert R. Spalding's, 1847.

NEHAMO. Dwarf, Alex Robinson's, 1866.

NEIDRACK, LOUIS. See Louis Fanlon.

NEILL, WILLIAM and **HENRY.** Tom King's, 1864.

NELLIS. See K. G. Saunders.

NELSON, ALBERT "MASTER". James E. Cooke's, 1880.

NELSON, CHARLES. Gymnast, H. M. Smith's, 1870.

NELSON, E. Clown, Barnum & Bailey, 1893.

NELSON, EMILIE. DeMott & Ward, 1868.

NELSON FAMILY [Arthur, Sam, Louis, Robert, John]. Gymnasts and acrobats. Founder **Robert Nelson, Sr.** (r. n. Robert Hobson, 1840-December 25, 1915) Born in London, England. Apprenticed to a cabinet maker. Ran away from home and formed an acrobatic act with **Sam, John** and **Louis.** Married **Miss Emma Smart** before coming to USA as head of Nelsons' Great World Combination Shows. Played vaudeville houses and appeared with circuses for some 25 years. First engagement, Chiarini's, 1866-67. **Louis** died from yellow fever in Cuba. **John** and **Sam** went to South America where with their families they started a circus. **Robert, Sr.** formed a new Risley act with his sons, **Arthur** and **Robert, Jr.** Prof. Nelson tossed his two children about like Indian-rubber. [St. Louis *Missouri Democrat,* April 19, 1871: "They pirouette while standing on the soles of their father's feet, and wear a smile of confidence, and perform with the grace and activity of a Bonfanti. They give acrobatic acts that would be credited to matured and skillful gymnasts."] Nelson's, California, 1870; Dan Rice's, 1871-74; James Robinson's, 1872; South America with Bidwell's "Black Crook" Co., 1875; European engagement, 1875-80, P. T. Barnum's, 1880-81, introducing performing pigeons to USA; returned to Europe, then India with **John Wilson,** 1884; back to England, 1885; returned to to USA with **George Primrose** to be featured with Primrose & West's Minstrels, which opened in Detroit, June 1885; Orrin Bros.', Mexico, winter 1885-86; Reilly & Woods, 1886-88, with Nelson taking a partnership in the company; formed his own show, Nelson's Great Combination, 1889-91, 1894-95; John Robinson's, 1893; Milwaukee Mid-Winter Circus, 1894; Ringling Bros.', 1895-96. **Arthur Nelson** married **Miss**

Sarah Warren, 1896. Great Wallace, 1897-1901; Ringling Bros.', 1902-03; Walter L. Main's, 1904; engagements with parks and fairs, 1905-06; Hagenbeck-Wallace, 1907; Sells-Floto, 1909-10. **Robert, Sr.**, retired, 1910, turning the act over to his son, **Arthur**. Hagenbeck-Wallace, 1911-12; Wirth Bros.', Australia, 1913; Robinson's Famous Shows, 1914-16. **Robert, Jr.** died, July 1914. **Robert, Sr.** died from pneumonia at his home in Mt. Clemens, MI, Christmas Eve, age 74. **Arthur Nelson** had a family of 9—6 daughters and 1 son. Worked together for a long time, and were rated tops in their line of work. Made their home in Mount Clemens MI. After retirement because of age, the children carried on. Daughters were **Rosina, Oneida, Hilda, Theol, Estrella**, and **Carmencita. Paul** was the only son. **Arthur** was a rider, P. T. Barnum's, 1874; pantomime clown, Great Commonwealth, 1879; James E. Cooke's, 1880; P. T. Barnum's, 1880; Orrin Bros.', Havana, 1880, Mexico, 1883; Beckett's Great Exposition Circus, 1881. Died January 23, 1941, age 75, at Mount Carmel Hospital, Detroit, of injuries sustained in an auto accident January 1.

NELSON, HARRY. James T. Johnson's, 1888.

NELSON, HORATIO. Clown, San Francisco Circus, 1872.

NELSON, JACK. Edward Shipp's Winter Circus, Petersburg, IL, 1893-94.

NELSON, JOHN. Boss hostler, Donaldson & Rich, 1885.

NELSON, JOHN. (d. January 25, 1913) Acrobat. Wife was a trapeze performer. Died at his home in Hot Springs, AR.

NELSON, JULIA. With Donovan's South American Circus, Cuba, winter 1894-95.

NELSON, KATIE. (d. January, 1894) Equestrienne. Died in Central America.

NEOLA, ED. High-wire and outside ascension, Shedman Bros.', 1894; high diver, LaPearl's, 1897. Dove 60' into a net, doubling into a ball before striking.

NESTOR & VENOA. Flying rings and trapeze, Barnum, Bailey & Hutchinson, 1882.

NEUBER, PHILLIP. See Phillip Nieubhr.

NELSON SISTERS [Belle, Blanche]. Dan Rice's, 1872; James E. Cooke's, 1880; Orrin Barber's, 1888.

NEVILLE, THOMAS. Clown. Began as a rider, Dr. Gilbert R. Spalding's, 1844. Became famous for his pirouettes on horseback and his backward riding. Welch's National, 1846-51; trick rider, Johnson & Co., 1852. First appearance after returning from California, Welch & Lent, Philadelphia, 1854; Levy J. North's National Amphitheatre, 1857-58, 1859-60; Dan Rice's, 1859; Harry Whitby's, 1859. Died in Germany about 1873.

NELSON, WILLIAM. Cannon ball performer. With Welsh Bros.', 1894; E. A. Griffith's, 1894.

NEVILLE, THOMAS. Rider. Welch's National, 1850-51; (as Master Neville) June, Titus & Co., 1849; National Cicus, 1853; Franconi's, 1855; Madigan & Co., 1856.

NEWCOMB, FRANK. 4-horse rider, John Forepaugh's, California, 1888.

NEWCOMB, J. Gymnast, First National Union, 1861.

NEWCOMB, WILLIAM W. (August 4, 1823-May 1, 1877) Born in Utica, NY. Became orphaned at about 5 years of age and was taken in charge by the gentleman who had been the chosen physician of his parents. Developed a taste for banjo songs and straight jigs and ultimately placed himself under the wing of **Fitzallan**, song-and-dance performer. Traveled with him for 3 years at the tail end of circuses. Joined **S. B. Howes'** circus, with which he remained as a jig dancer for 3 years. With **Abijah L. Thayer** of Boston, organized a minstrel band. Thayer was forced by ill health to withdraw after a 4-year partnership. First appearance in NYC, an olio at Tripler Hall, December 4, 1851. Invented and danced for the first time in public "The Essence of Old Virginia," Fellow's Minstrels, 444 Broadway. First minstrel who produced burlesque stump speeches, his first being "Woman's Rights." Died, NYC, City Hotel, corner Broadway and 8th Street. With cords attached to the door latch, gas jet and bell pull, and with a rope so rigged that he might take at least a little exercise while lying in bed, he laid in that room almost helpless for 10 weeks, or since he broke a leg while performing in a pantomimic sketch at Hooley's Opera House, Brooklyn. Was found kneeling in death at his bedside with his hands supporting his face. The funeral was very poorly attended, there being only 12 persons present; having been reduced to poverty, living his latter days on the charity of others, he was forgotten by all his old associates.

NEWCOURT BROTHERS. Australian Circus, 1870.

NEWELL, HENRY. Howes' European, winter 1864.

NEWELL, W. D. ["Yankee"]. General agent, Robbins & Colvin, 1880-81; Hudson & Castello, 1881 (which came to grief).

NEWKIRK, A. P. Press agent, VanAmburgh & Co., 1871.

NEWMAN, WILLIAM. Elephant performer, Barnum, Bailey & Hutchinson, 188, assistant elephant trainer, 1882; elephant keeper and trainer, Barnum & Bailey, 1889-99.

NEWTON, ALBERT. Orton & Co., 1869.

NEWTON, CLINT M. Orator and press agent, Welsh & Sands, 1893.

NEWTON, S. W. Manager, Goldenberg's, 1874-75.

NEYGAARD, HERR CARL and **MARTHA.** See Herr Carl Nyegaard.

NIBLO, THOMAS. Clown, whose greatest success came in the pantomime *Humpty Dumpty*. Partner, Niblo & Sloat, 1860, West Indies, 1861. Died in Denver, CO, March 1905.

NICE, GEORGE A. See George Dunbar.

NICHOL, THOMAS J. (1857-1931) Builder of steam calliopes. Served as bookkeeper for the calliope firm of William Kirkup & Sons; took over the business, early 1890s and continued until his death.

NICHOLS, ADOLPH. Band leader. Dr. James L. Thayer's, 1870; "Humpty Dumpty" Opera Co. band, J. W. Wilder's,

1872-73; cornet band of 25 musicians, Maginley & Co., 1874.

NICHOLS, ALEXANDER A. (d. March 24, 1877) Clown. Born in Switzerland. Father of **Wash, Tillie, Martha, Antonio, Maggie** and **Marie Nichols**. Died in Toledo, OH.

NICHOLS BROTHERS. Sam McFlinn's, 1888.

NICHOLS, D. L. John F. Stowe & Co., 1888; Howe's New London, 1889.

NICHOLS, FRANK. F. J. Taylor's, 1889.

NICHOLS, HORACE F. (1818?-January 19, 1886) Rider, equestrian director, ringmaster. Native of Massachusetts. Connected with various circuses for 40 years. Once staged the entertainment, *The Spirit of '76*, which included the characters of Washington, Putnam, and Anthony Wayne, and a tableau in which Washington was born aloft on the shoulders of his brave Continentals. Was also an animal lecturer. Vaulter, S. H. Nichols', 1838, agent, 1842; negro minstrel, John Tryon's, Bowery Amphitheatre, NYC, 1844; John T. Potter's, 1844; ringmaster, Mann, Welch & Delavan, 1845-46; Welch's National, 1847; June & Turner, 1847; Spalding & Rogers, 1849-51; Welch & Lent, 1856; Nixon & Kemp, 1857; John Robinson's, 1857; Nixon's Cremorne Gardens, NYC, spring 1862; James M. Nixon's Alhambra, NYC, fall 1863; Hippotheatron, NYC, late winter 1864; Seth B. Howes' European, 1864; Slaymaker & Nichols, 1864; Dan Castello's, 1865-66; Seth B. Howes', 1866; ringmaster, George W. DeHaven's, 1867; Lake's Hippo-Olympiad, 1869, equestrian director, winter 1870-71; VanAmburgh's, 1870, equestrian director, 1871; ringmaster, P. T. Barnum's, 1872-74; ringmaster, North American, 1875; ringmaster, Cooper, Bailey & Co., 1876; New York Central Park, 1877; ringmaster, Allen's Great Eastern, 1879; James E. Cooke's, 1880. Died at St. Mary's Hospital, Hoboken, aged 68, after being fatally injured by a fall from the stoop of his house a fortnight earlier.

NICHOLS, LEW. Talker, Thayer & Flinn, 1884; privileges, Great United States Circus, 1891; sideshow manager, Great Wallace, 1896; sideshow manager, Young Buffalo Wild West, 1913.

NICHOLS, MRS. H. F. Dan Castello's, 1866.

NICHOLS, SAMUEL H. Clown. The brother of **W. W. Nichols**. Ludlow & (Ben) Brown, Cincinnati, 1828; J. Purdy Brown's, 1829; clown, William Blanchard's, Front Street Amphitheatre, Baltimore, beginning September 10, 1829; minstrel, Harrison & Buckley, 1830; J. Purdy Brown's, 1830; introduced negro minstrelsy to circus performance with Brown's, 1831; listed as Grecian juggler, 1832. Started touring his own circus, 1838, Victory Arena or Nichols Extensive Circus, based in Albany, NY. Constructed an amphitheatre, Albany, 1840, an octagonal building with 41' ring, 900 box seats, 1,500 in family circle, 600 in the pit; continued as proprietor through 1843; managed for John T. Potter, 1844. Was the first to sing "Jim Crow"; author of minstrel classics "Zip Coon" and "Clare de Kitchen." Also, said to be the first

showman to hire **Dan Rice**, but this is questionable. **T. Allston Brown** credits him with the following: A man of no education, yet he was the author of many anecdotes, stories, verses, etc.; would compose the verses for his comic songs within ten minutes of the time of his appearance before the audience; "flights of fancy" and "flashes of wit" were truly astonishing and highly amusing; first conceived the idea from a French darkie, a banjo player, known from New Orleans to Cincinnati as Picayune Butler—a copper colored gentleman, who gathered many a picayune by singing "Picayune Butler is Going Away," accompanying himself on his four-stringed banjo. An old Negro of New Orleans, known as "Old Corn Meal," furnished Nichols with many airs, which he turned to account. Arranged "Clare de Kitchen" from hearing it sung by the Negro firemen on the Mississippi River; "Zip Coon" was taken from a rough jig dance, called "Natchez Under the Hill," where the boatmen, river pirates, gamblers and courtesans congregated for the enjoyment of a regular hoe-down in the old time.

NICHOLS, THOMAS. Tumbler, Cross & LeRoy, 1884.

NICHOLS, WILLIAM JOHN. Bareback rider. Son of ringmaster **Horace F. Nichols**. Born in New Orleans. Made first appearance as a performer, April 23, 1872, in a bottle pyramid act with the Central Park Circus, Amenia, NY. Remained with that company until the end of the 1873 season. First appearance as an equestrian, Howes' Great London, Battle Creek, MI, June 9, 1874, riding a pad act. Continued with Howes through winter 1875; following year, principal equestrian, P. T. Barnum. Specialties were pirouettes and somersaults, but was a fine tumbler as well.

NICHOLS, WILLIAM W. (September 4, 1821-December 12, 1887) Rider and showman. Born into a circus family, North Adams, MA. Placed under the tutelage of a dancing and riding master in Philadelphia at the age of 9. At 12, began career as a circus rider and continued in the business for 50 odd years. First trained as a rider with his brother, **S. H. Nichols**, 1830. 1865, started off with a circus company to South America. Off Cape Hatteras, the boat encountered a severe storm which swept some of the horses overboard; continued on only to meet a more severe storm off the Florida coast where everything was lost; Nichols was picked up by a government boat and landed at Fort Monroe, with everything lost except the money from an insurance policy on the horses he rode, $4,000. After that incident, never ventured into management again. Married **Lucy E. Lathe**, 1864, and had 3 children—**Mrs. C. C. Barrett, Robert E.** and **George**. Equestrian director, Grand Reserve Combination, 1866; 1872, started performing as a double bareback act with his son **Robert**. Family received notoriety when **Robert** was mistaken for Charles Ross, the kidnapped son of a wealthy New Yorker. Buckley, Weeks & Co., 1835; Thomas Taplin Cooke's, 1838; scenic rider, S. H. Nichols', 1838-43; James Raymond's, 1843-44;

rider, John Tryon's, Bowery Amphitheatre, NYC, 1844; John T. Potter's, 1844; Mann, Welch & Delavan, 1845-46; Dr. Gilbert R. Spalding's, 1847-51; Welch's, Philadelphia, 1852; Welch & Lent, 1854; Jim Myers', 1856; George F. Bailey & Co., 1857; VanAmburgh's, 1858; Nixon & Co., 1859; principal rider, George F. Bailey & Co., 1860; Slaymaker & Nichols, 1864; James M. Nixon & R. Platt, 1865; Charles Noyes', 1871; Dan Rice's Paris Pavilion, 1871-72; Howe's Great London, 1874; North American, 1875-77; Great American, 1878; Cooper & Jackson, 1880; Hudson & Castello, 1881. Nichols began living in retirement, 1882, at his residence in North Adams, MA, where he died from apoplexy. **Lucy** died at the Old Ladies' Home, North Adams, October, 1919, age 81.

NICOLI, EUGENE. Equestrian manager, Romelli & Co., 1872.

NICOLO, BOBBY. James M. Nixon's Alhambra, NYC, fall 1863; trapeze and Zampillacrostation, James M. Nixon's Hippotheatron, NYC, 1864; Howes' Great European, 1864; S. O. Wheeler's, winter 1864-65, 1865; New York Champs Elysees, 1865; Albisu's, 1865. One source states that the **Nicolo troupe** was lost on the sinking of the *Evening Star* en route from NYC to New Orleans, October 6, 1866. Another says that **Bobby** combined with **William Rodney** and **Thomas Tolliday** as the **Talleen Brothers**. See below.

NICOLO FAMILY. Gymnasts. **James Nicolo** came to USA from England, bringing 3 boys—**Thomas, George,** and **John Ridgeway**—to appear at Franconi's Hippodrome, NYC, 1853, in acts of posturing and acrobatics. Joe Pentland's, 1854-56; New National Circus (**John Tryon,** proprietor), winter 1857-58; VanAmburgh's, 1857-59. Returned to England, where the boys became known as the **Ridgeway Brothers. James** paid another visit to this country, 1863, with a young sensation, **Bobby Nicolo,** billed "The Flying Boy." Nixon's Alhambra, NYC, fall 1863.

NIEUBHR, PHILLIP [or Neuber]. Band leader. Welch, Raymond & Driesbach, 1852; Driesbach & Derious, 1853; Ballard's, winter 1853-54; Chiarini & Rayuond, 1855; Driesbach & Stickney, 1857; VanAmburgh & Co., 1858.

NIRCH, CHARLIE. Whitmore, Thompson & Co., 1865.

NIXON, ADELAIDE. (b. 1848) General performer. Daughter of circus manager **James M. Nixon** and wife **Caroline.** Born in NYC. Made first appearance on any stage as a vocalist, Butler's Music Hall, 444 Broadway, NYC, 1864. Sickness caused her to take leave from entertaining for a while. Resumed her profession in New Orleans, Academy of Music, for Spalding, Rogers & Bidwell's company. Winter 1865-66, Havana, Cuba, joined Chiarini's; while there, received instructions as an equestrienne, and before leaving the 8 month engagement, could ride a principal act. One day, 1866, after finishing her *manège* act at Chiarini's, she suffered a stroke, from which she recovered. Later, performed in variety theatres. Described as "a lady of prepossessing appearance," a ballad

singer with a voice that was judged sweet and correct.

NIXON, ALBERT. Rider. Pupil of **James M. Nixon.** Crane & Co, 1849; J. M. June & C., 1850; Welch, 1852; Myers & Madigan, 1855.

NIXON, ANDREW J. Advertiser, S. P. Stickney's, 1869.

NIXON, CAROLINE L. [Mrs. James M. Nixon]. Equestrienne. Sister of circus proprietor **Charles Bacon.** Worked primarily under James M. Nixon's management; however, was an equestrienne with John T. Potter's, 1845; Howes & Co., 1846-48; New Broadway Circus (**John Tryon** and **Corporal Thompson,** proprietors), 1848; James M. June & Co., 1850; feats of equitation, *manège* act with her horse Fire Fly, Jim Myers, 1856. After being divorced from her husband, she and her trained horse, General Scott, Slaymaker & Nichols, 1864 (**Nichols** was her uncle). Died while traveling with the show, July 20, Bangor, ME, age 35.

NIXON, FRANK. Daughter of **Caroline** and **James M. Nixon.** Slaymaker & Nichols, 1864.

NIXON, GEORGE [r. n. George Ross]. Protégé of **James M. Nixon.** Rider, Howes & Co., 1846-48; Crane & Co., 1849; J. M. June's, 1850; Rufus Welch's, 1852; Castle Garden Circus, NYC, fall 1854; First National Union, 1861; Whitmore, Thompson & Co.'s Equescurriculum, 1865; Alex Robinson's, 1866. After finishing his apprenticeship, returned to the name of **George Ross.** Married, 1867, in New Zealand, to the daughter of Major General Kirby, of Nottingham, England.

NIXON, JAMES M. (1820-September 16, 1899) Showman. Worked his way from a mere groom with Aaron Turner's around 1836 to performing with various troupes in the 1840s and 1850s as acrobat, ringmaster and equestrian director. From a Turner stable groom, graduated to other menial tasks with the show—lamp trimmer, ring builder, and ultimately performer. Actrobat, Welch & Mann, spring 1843, Bowery Amphitheatre, NYC; left the Bowery quarters, July 6, and moved to Brooklyn's Military Gardens for a week; Lent & Delavan, Boston, 1843; ringmaster, Bowery Amphitheatre (John Tryon, proprietor), 1843, equestrian director, winters 1845 and 1846; also equestrian director, Dr. G. R. Spalding's, Bowery Amphitheatre, 1845. Around this time married first wife, **Caroline;** took two apprentices under wing, **William Armstrong** and **George Ross.** Equestrian director, John T. Potter's, summer 1845; Bowery Amphitheatre, fall 1845; Howes & Co., Palmo's Theatre, NYC, January 1846 and for summer seasons 1846, 1847 and 1848; New Broadway Circus (John Tryon, proprietor), NYC, winter 1848. Daughter, **Adelaide,** was born, NYC, 1848. Equestrian director, western unit, Howes & Co., summer 1848; manager, Crane & Co, 1849; New Manhattan Circus, NYC, December 1849; James M. June & Co., 1850; Welch's National Circus, Philadelphia, winter 1851, and touring summer 1852; equestrian director, Franconi's Hippodrome, NYC, winter 1852; equestrian director, Castle Garden Circus, fall 1854; Jim Myers', summer 1856.

Co-proprietor, Nixon & Kemp, 1857, 1858; equestrian director, New National Circus (**John Tryon**, proprietor), winter 1857; Nixon & Co., 1859; proprietor, Cooke's Equestrian Troupe, Niblo's Garden, beginning January 1860. In addition to his involvement with the Cooke troupe, was the house proprietor at Niblo's; also had **Edwin Forrest** under a one hundred night contract to perform in the principal cities of the country. Cooke's Equestrian Troupe terminated its run at Niblo's, March 3, 1860, and moved to the Boston Academy of Music for five weeks; then returned to Niblo's, April 9 until end of May; then went on tour. In partnership with **P. T. Barnum**, Grizzly Adams' California Menagerie, NYC, summer 1860; toured Cooke's Royal Circus with Old Grizzly Adams California Menagerie, fall 1860; sold equipment to Boston showman **George K. Goodwin** and put out an outfit on rails under the name of Nixon's Royal Circus, routed through the southern states. Sloat's New York Circus combined with Nixon's Royal Circus to form the First National Union Circus, 1861; finished season on lot between the Palace Gardens concert pavilion and the Fourteenth Street Theatre, Fourteenth and Broadway, NYC, opening September 2 for an indefinite stay. Spring 1862, took a lease on Palace Gardens, converted and enlarged it to resemble Cremorne Gardens, London; developed three new features on the property—a stretch of canvas under which equestrian performances were given; a building devoted to the display of trees, flowers and shrubbery called Floral Hall; and a concert pagoda designated the Palace of Music; opened June 9, shut down at the approach of cold weather. Following, took **Carlotta Patti** under his managerial wing, leased the Academy of Music, NYC, and re-introduced her to opera loving New Yorkers; at the same time, took over management of the Boston Theatre, 1862-63 winter season, which opened in September. Also at this time, sent a company to Washington under the management of **T. Allston Brown** and erected a semi-permanent wooden and canvas building, Pennsylvania Avenue and Seventh Street, said to be the same structure used at his Cremorne Gardens, NYC, and opened October 18; split his company between Washington and Alexandria, VA; closed December 26. Returned to Washington, spring 1863, billed as Madame Macarte's Grand European Circus Combined with Nixon's Great Cremorne Troupe from New York; show moved next to Alexanderia, remaining until early June; then took to the road. Erected an arena, NYC, 14th Street and Irving Place, which opened August 31, 1863, as the Alhambra. Next major endeavor opened February 8, 1864, in a permanent structure of corrugated iron erected on the site of the Alhambra, called the Hippotheatron; re-opened for the 1864-65 winter season October 3; spring 1865, erected another temporary building in Washington, DC, near 6th Street and Pennsylvania Avenue. In the fall, a tour was organized for visiting the principal towns of Texas by rail; company left New York the 19th of October on the *Catherine Whiting*

headed for Galveston; but after leaving port the ocean became so rough that the ship had to lay overnight at Sandy Hook. On the 23rd a heavy gale set in and the following day one of the ring horses went overboard; by nightfall all of the horses had been washed into the sea (including the performing horse, General Scott, all belonging to **William W. Nichols**, but all ring stock fortuitously insured; at the height of the storm, the ship's engine gave out, exposing the boat and passengers to the mercy of the tempest for a period of 32 hours; October 28 the steamer went ashore five miles south of Carysfort Reef, FL; finally, the brig stopped at Key West for repairs, but for whatever reason may have been towed to New Orleans; the circus, too badly bruised to continue to Texas, was sold or leased to Thayer & Noyes. Went to Little Rock, AR, January 1866, where all or part of Seth B. Howes' Great European Circus was stored; bought part of the outfit in partnership with **Dan Castello**, and **Egbert Howes** and put out a show under the Dan Castello name—Castello was manager and drawing card, Howes the treasurer, and Nixon the contracting agent. Was married for the second time, the bride a Buffalo born **Emma Maddern**, an actress not yet twenty years of age. For 1867, Castello's Great Show opened at Mobile, AL, and proceeded north to Louisville, where it met up with the Barnum and VanAmburgh parties (owned by **Hyatt Frost, Henry Barnum, James E. Kelley** and **O. J. Ferguson**) and combined with them into one large company under the banner of Barnum, VanAmburgh & Castello's Great Show and Mammoth Moral Exhibition (not the whole VanAmburgh outfit, but surplus animals andsome of the choicest and most popular curiosities in the Barnum collection); this seemingly formidable combination was short-lived, as much of the property was withdrawn part way into the season. The troupe started out, 1868, traveling in rented railway cars, the routing took them through Maryland, West Virginia, Ohio, Michigan, Illinois, Wisconsin, and as far west as Kansas.; when towns were off the established lines, equipment was moved by wagons, probably commissioned from local farmers; fall weather sent the show southward and at season's end it came to rest for the winter in New Orleans. After opening the 1869 season there, January 4, and after a swing through Mississippi, Alabama, and Georgia, Dan Castello's Great Show, Circus, Menagerie and Abyssinian Caravan reached Topeka for a stand on Thursday, May 13, being the first flat car show ever to play there; the show then swiftly moved northward, arriving at Omaha for May 26-27; the outfit was loaded onto an eight-car special the night of the 27th and started on the journey which ended in California. Fall 1870, Nixon's New York Circus commenced an unsuccessful southern tour which died in Texas. December 1871, Nixon resurfaced in New York City, where he opened what he called Nixon's Amphitheatre in a building on the east side of Broadway, opposite Waverly Place. Leased a lot in the unburned west side of Chicago, 1872, and erected Nixon's Parisian Hippodrome and Chicago Amphitheatre, opening May 18; **Buffalo Bill Cody** and company premiered an artless drama, *The Scouts of the Prairie* there December 16. It has been suggested that Nixon had an interest in the company and went along on the tour. Assistant director, P. T. Barnum's Great Roman Hippodrome, 1874-75; in addition to serving as equestrian director, gave the signal for starting the races, struck the warning bell for the homestretch, and decided who was the victor--a combination of judge, bailiff and jury. [New York *Clipper*: "James M. Nixon, the veteran circus manager, discharges his arduous duties as superintendent with an easy grace and the utmost fairness."] There is little left on record. We know that Nixon was in Europe in the spring of 1876; 1879, was said to be running a cheap theatre in Chicago; at this time he teamed with **Oliver P. Myers** in attempting to establish a zoological garden there which came to nothing; still in Chicago, 1882, when on June 22 he appeared at W. C. Coup's circus during an engagement in that city; 1886, a *Clipper* item announced that Nixon had gone to England to make arrangements for Cody's wild west show's first trip abroad. There is no other mention of him again until Monday, September 18, 1899, when the New York *Times* carried a small item: "James M. Nixon, at one time the proprietor of James M. Nixon's Circus, died on Saturday of Bright's disease at the Putnam House, Twenty-seventh Street and Fourth Avenue. Mr. Nixon was eighty years old. His circus performed at the old Hippodrome, on the spot where the Fifth Avenue Hotel now stands. It also performed in different parts of the country and abroad. Mr. Nixon had for fifteen years past been living at the Putnam House, and was a well-known character in that locality. He leaves two daughters."

NIXON, LAFAYETTE. (1820-December 18, 1893) Rider, circus manager and privilege man. Born in NYC. After having been with the Louisa Wells Equestrian company, joined the Sloat & Shepherd, mid-season 1859; that year teamed with **W. T. Aymar** for a circus at the renovated Chatham Amphitheatre (former National), NYC; sideshow, Madame Macarte's European Circus (**James M. Nixon**, proprietor), 1863. Was keeping a hotel, corner of 14th St. and Fourth Ave., NYC, 1866. Candy privileges, James M. Nixon's, 1870; candy privilege, New York Central Park Circus, 1877. Eventually left show business to run a liquor store. Married to **Louisa Wells**. Died at Kings Park, NJ.

NIXON, MRS. LAFAYETTE. See Louisa Wells.

NIXON, WILLIAM [r. n. Armstrong]. Protégé of **James M. Nixon**. Rider, John Tryon's, Bowery Amphitheatre, NYC, 1845-46; Howes & Co., 1845-47; J. M. June's, 1850-52; no longer an apprentice, Joe Pentland's, 1854; Myers & Madigan, spring 1855; Seth B. Howes, summer 1855; Cushing's, winter 1855; Sands & Nathans, 1856; Levi J. North's, winter 1856; George F. Bailey & Co., 1857; Levi J. North's, winter 1857; Mabie & Crosby, 1858; Dan Rice's, 1858; Levi J. North's,

winter 1858; Antonio & Wilder, 1859; James M. Nixon's, 1860. Died on returning from Havana with Nixon's circus when the *Black Squall* foundered after a stormy 16 days near Cape Hatteras, April 19, 1861.

NOBLE, J. E. Special agent, Adam Forepaugh's, 1888.

NOBLE, JOSEPH. Juggler, acrobat. Apprenticed with H. H. Fuller's, 1835; Aaron Turner's, 1837; H. H. Fuller's, 1838; Welch & Bartlett, winter 1839-40, 1840; Welch & Mann, also June, Titus & Angevine, winter 1841-42; with performing dogs, Rockwell & Stone, 1842; proprietor, Olympic Circus, Australia, 1851-52; W. H. Foley's, Australia, 1854.

NOBLES, MADAM TOMAS. Rider, Howes Trans-Atlantic Circus and Risbeck's Menagerie (Frank Howes, proprietor), 1868.

NOLAN, PROF. DICK. Leader of Silver Cornet Band, with Dodge & Bartine, 1868.

NOLTE, ALBERT. Leaper and tumbler, P. T. Barnum's, 1880.

NOON, ARCHIE. Clown, Great Pacific, 1878.

NORBERRY, CHARLES EDWARD. See Edward LeRue.

NORMAN, HAM. Sideshow operator. Gardner & Kenyon, 1869; Rosston, Springer & Henderson, 1871; sideshow privilege (with **Chris B. Stout**), Dr. James L. Thayer's, 1877. Noted for sporting an array of diamond jewelry.

NORMAN, WILLIAM. Elephant trainer, P. T. Barnum's, 1886.

NORRIS, PROF. S. W. Band leader. Montgomery Queen's, 1874; Beckett's Great Exposition Circus, 1881.

NORTH, A. J. Gymnast, G. G. Grady's, 1871.

NORTH, GEORGE. Rider, M. O'Conner's Great Western, 1870; scenic rider, P. T. Barnum's, 1871-73; 2-horse racer, Barnum's Hippodrome, 1874-75.

NORTH, HENRY C. [r. n. Henry Coyle]. (d. August 19, 1870) Rider. Apprentice of **Levi J. North**. George W. De-Haven's, 1865-66; Haight & Chambers, 1866; Stone & Murray, 1868-69; grotesque, L. B. Lent's, 1870. Died of consumption, Lake Calhone, MN, leaving $1,000, a gold watch, and a saddle and bridle.

NORTH, LEVI J., JR. ["Kit"]. (1854?-April 18, 1867) Rider son of the famous bareback rider. George W. DeHaven's, 1865; New York Champs Elysees, 1866; Perry Powers', 1867. Died of consumption, Columbus, IN, at nearly 14 years of age, connected with Lake's Hippo-Olympiad at the time.

NORTH, LEVI J., SR. (June 16, 1814-July 6, 1885) Rider, vaulter, and showman. Born in Newton Township, Long Island. Apprenticed with **Isaac Quick**, of Quick & Mead's, 1826. Made first appearance in the ring as an equestrian at Camden, SC. 2 years later, finishing his apprenticeship and engaged with Handy & Welch for Cuba. On return, took employment with **Purdy Brown** which lasted until 1836, when Brown died. Following year, was in New Orleans with Waring's. It was here he met the clown, **Joe Blackburn**, with whom, 1838, he accompanied to England. There, North answered the challenges of **Price**, the European vaulting champion, and managed to beat him thoroughly on several occasions in the vaulting ring, establishing himself as the world's greatest vaulter, defeating all comers. Greatest feat was accomplished at William Batty's, Henley, England, 1839, when he turned the first somersault ever accomplished while standing on the back of a running horse. Performed the feat in the United States in NYC for Welch & Bartlett, Bowery Theatre, 1840. Spring 1841, engaged to Rufus Welch for a tour of the West Indies. Returning to NYC, mid-summer, joined **Jonas Bartlett** in Baltimore. In the fall, went to New Orleans and played with old **S. P. Stickney**, St. Charles Theatre. Returned to England, spring 1842, where he married **Miss Sophia West**, the daughter of circus manager **James West**. The marriage produced 3 children, **Henry**, a non-professional; **Levi J.**; and **Sophia Victoria**, who became prominent as a serio-comic vocalist. In England, North connected with the American Company, owned by Titus, June & Sands. Joined his old rival, Price, 1843, and took out Price & North's Circus but soon left it in charge of Price and returned to the United States. That year, opened with Rockwell & Stone, Niblo's Garden, NYC; spring 1844, returned to England and disposed of his interest in the circus; after which, appeared with the American Company, Theatre Royal, Liverpool. While a member of Franconi's, *Champs Elysees*, appeared by royal command before Louis Philippe, King of France. At the end of 5 months, returned to Philadelphia and Welch's. Rockwell & Stone, 1846; again with Welch, 1847; Jones, Stickney & North, 1848; Stokes', 1849; from the winter of 1849 to 1851, Dan Rice's; leased the Bowery Amphitheatre for performances, summer 1851; had a circus in Williamsburg, 1852; 1853, North & Turner conducted a canal boat show and, during that winter season, leased the National Amphitheatre, Philadelphia; summer 1855, North & Turner traveled by wagon; in the winter, appeared in a circus which they built in Chicago; 1856, North erected an amphitheatre on that site; following year, was elected an Alderman of Chicago; 1858-59, North's National Circus was on the road; 1860, he again ran a canal boat show and, in the winter, played a star engagement with Spalding & Rogers, Bowery Theatre, NYC; Lake & Co., 1863; 1863, associated himself with William Lake and Hod Norton; 1864, traveled with Haight & DeHaven; equestrian director, George W. DeHaven's, 1865; New York Champs Elysees, 1866. Died in Brooklyn, NY. North is looked upon as being the orignator of style and grace as an American bareback rider.

NORTH, SOPHIA VICTORIA. Daughter of rider **Levi J. North**. Billed as "The Smallest and Youngest Equestrienne in the World." Dan Rice's, 1851; Rufus Welch's, 1852; serio-comic singer, Miller's Winter Garden Theatre, Philadelphia, 1878; Tony Denier's "Humpty Dumpty" pantomime company, 1879. First married to **Philo R. Nathans**; divorced on Decem-

ber 17, 1877. **Frank Hildreth**, former treasurer and business manager for **Tony Denier**, was her second husband. She died in Brooklyn, January 12, 1905.

NORTH, THOMAS. Howes' European, winter 1864.

NORTH, WILLIE. Rider. Pupil of **Levi J. North**. Dan Rice's, 1851; Welch's, 1852; Levi J. North's, 1853-60.

NORTON, H. Howe & Norton's Circus (formerly Robinson & Howe), November 1864.

NORTON, JOE. Juggler. Adam Forepaugh's (Pullman Bros.' sideshow), 1876.

NORTON, JOHN. Alex Robinson's, 1866.

NORTON, NICOLO. Juggler. Stowe's, 1867-68; Stowe & Norton's Western World Circus, 1869; balancer, juggler and comedian, James Robinson's, 1870.

NORTON, N. T. Agent, Cooper, Jackson & Co., 1882.

NORTON, ROBERT. H. Buckley & Co., 1857-58.

NORTON, TILLIE. Tight-rope performer, Stowe & Norton, 1869.

NORTON, WASH. Jig dancer, VanAmburgh & Co.'s northern, 1859.

NORWOOD, SAMUEL. General performer, with Thompson, Smith & Hawes, 1866.

NOSHER, JOSEPH. Band leader. With Victory Arena, New York Brass Band, 1844; Robinson & Eldred, 1849-50; G. C. Quick & Co.', 1851; Robinson & Eldred, 1854-55; Bryan's, with Mrs. Dan Rice, 1863.

NOUMA, PRINCESS. (d. 1909) Considered one of the most renowned midgets since Mr. and Mrs. Tom Thumb. After working with **Maurice A. Gowdy**, a sideshow giant from Shelbyville, IN, standing 6' 4" tall, in touring comapanies, they were married, 1904, in Los Angeles, CA. Her father was much the size of her husband. A clever actress and fine impersonator, she stood 32" and weighed 30 pounds. Died in child birth, Hot Springs, AR.

NOVELLO FAMILY [6 in number]. L. B. Lent's, 1874.

NOYES, CHARLES W. (1832-October 20, 1885) Showman and animal trainer. Born near Utica, NY, but spent most of his boyhood in Syracuse. 1846, when S. B. Howes' Circus was performing in Auburn, Noyes joined the show, remaining for most of the season until he returned home on the urging of his parents. 1849, joined June & Co. and assisted in the sideshow. Following season, traveled with Spalding & Rogers in similar capacity. 1851, P. T. Barnum's, working with the animals under the direction of **Alviza Pierce**. Illness prevented traveling the following year, but in 1853 was engaged with Franconi's Hippodrome, NYC, breaking and training monkeys that appeared in the hurdle races. Franconi had an elephant, Jennie, who was rebellious and refused to work; unknown to management, Noyes conquered the unruly animal. August, accompanied by a white performing camel and Jennie, joined the Dan Rice, Columbus, OH. Jennie was later purchased by Rice and renamed Lalla Rookh. Noyes remained with the show until the fall, 1855. While with Rice, broke and performed a number of panthers and tigers; also worked the perch and double trapeze with **Omar T. Richardson**, the bareback rider; appeared in the tournaments and acted as ringmaster. In company with Richardson, joined Spalding & Rogers, spring 1856. That fall, rejoined Rice, wintering in Girard, PA, and there broke the horse Excelsior, Jr., and presumably the first rhinoceros ever trained in America. During that time, taught Lalla Rookh to walk ropes. That same winter, the elephant was the star of a drama in Pittsburgh, *The Elephant of Siam*, performing under Noyes' direction. Summer 1861 was spent in Girard working with animals, during which time he broke the white performing stallion, General Scott. Winter 1862, was with Rice for a short time in Cincinnati, working with his new stock. Spring of that year, entered into partnership with **Dr. James L. Thayer** and put on the road the Thayer & Noyes' United States Circus, with **James Robinson** as the starring attraction. The company functioned under the Thayer & Noyes banner through 1869. At the end of that season, Noyes withdrew and formed C. W. Noyes' Crescent City Circus, traveling by rail and boat until the fall of 1874. Equestrian director, Adam Forepaugh's, 1880. [Charles H. Day: "He had been to the height of prosperity and in the depths of despair. Mr. Noyes had many good qualities and was a well-meaning but unfortunate man. It is well enough for those who never met with reverses to carp but a dose of his experience will take the starch out of any man. Besides financial difficulties, Charlie Noyes had another sorrow that bore him down. It's all over now!"] Died Goldthwaite, TX.

NOYES, MRS. CHARLES. *Manège.* [New Orleans *Daily Picayune*, 1870: "She showed to great advantage the perfect power and mastery she has over her spirited Arab horse, D'Talma, and executed some feats which drew forth repeated and deserved applause."] See above.

NUGENT, DANIEL ["Circus Dan"]. (1866?-February 16, 1901) Agent. Connected with W. W. Cole's, Forepaugh's, and Ringling Bros.', also Rich's Theatre, Fall River, MA; Walnut and Chestnut Street Theatres; and, at the time of death, with the Star Theatre, Philadelphia. Died there of heart trouble, age 35.

NUNN, MRS. THOMAS [Lucinda]. Equestrienne, Rockwell's, 1848, riding in "Hebe, the Morning Sprite."

NUNN, STEWART. See William Stewart.

NUNN, THOMAS. Rider and equestrian director. Appeared as "Hebe, or Morning Sprite," Rockwell & Co.'s, 1838; equestrian director Rockwell & Co., 1847-48; S. Q. Stokes', 1849-51; Australia, 1854-55.

NUNN, WILLIAM. Leader brass band and 12 piece orchestra, Gregory Bros.' New Metropolitan Allied shows, 1884.

NUTT, GEORGE WASHINGTON MORRISON ["Commodore"]. (April 1, 1845-May 25, 1881) Well known midget, working in circuses and dime museums. Born of normal size parents. Of his 5 brothers and sisters, only one, **Rodney**, was a midget. He accompanied the Commodore on his travels. First exhibited by P. T. Barnum at his museum, NYC, 1860, and remained there for some time. James M. Nixon's Cremorne Gardens, NYC, 1862; Nixon's Amphitheatre, Washington, DC, fall 1862. June 21, 1869, left with the General Tom Thumb Co. for a world tour and returned just 3 years later. While with the troupe, Nutt and **Tom Thumb** were rivals for the hand of **Lavinia Warren**, who became Mrs. Tom Thumb. Nutt and brother next made a tour of variety houses, and subsequently joined Deakin's Lilliputian Opera Co., made up of little people with the exception of **Col. Goshen**, the giant. Nutt and Goshen were featured in *Jack the Giant Killer*. Later, Nutt and his brother managed a variety theatre in Portland, OR, and in San Francisco, neither venture proving successful. The Boston *Post*, June 21, 1869, carried an item on Nutt's marriage to **Miss Minnie Warren**. Another source stated that because he never got over the loss of his lady love, Lavinia, the Commodore did not marry until about 2½ years before his death. His bride was the former **Lillian Elstar**, a short woman but much taller than her husband. This may have been a second marriage. In the summer, 1881, he was deputy-superinendent of the pier at Rockaway. Died in NYC, age 89.

NUTT, RODNEY ["Major"]. (1840?-September 22, 1909) Brother of **Commodore Nutt** and one of Barnum's midget troupe. Stood 3' 10" tall. His wife was 5' 10". Served as coachman for **Tom Thumb** on that star's world tour. Married 18 year old Miss Clara Cornfield at the Crawford House, Boston, 1885 (18" taller than Nutt). Was the last of the original Lilliputians, with the exception of Mrs. Tom Thumb. Accompanied his brother for most of his professional career. Died from heart trouble in Dorchester, MA, age 69, after having been in retirement for close to 19 years conducting a real estate business. See George Washington Mossison Nutt.

NUTTER, DAN. Advertising agent, Cushing's, 1867. Died in Boston, August 30, 1867.

NUTTER, GEORGE. Elephant handler. Raymond & Waring, 1847; June & Turner, 1848; Turner's, 1849; accompanied Stebbings June to Ceylon to purchase elephants for P. T. Barnum, 1850; returned May, 1851, with 9 specimen, first herd imported to America; billposter, Spalding & Rogers, 1851.

NYEGAARD, HERR CARL and MARTHA [or Neygaard]. Rider and horse trainer. Tandem *manège* act with 4 thoroughbred horses; P. T. Barnum's, 1880; Robbins & Colvin, 1881; Leon & Dockrill, Iron Amphitheatre, Havana, winter 1881-82.

Charles W. Noyes

O

OAKES, J. S. Orton Bros.', 1865.

OAKLEY, GEORGE. Barnum, Bailey & Hutchinson, 1882.

OATES, J. C. Dan Rice's (**Dan Rice, William H. Stowe, J. C. Oates**, proprietors), 1881.

O'BRIEN, ADDIE. Bentley's Old Fashioned Circus (**J. B. Bentley**, proprietor), 1895.

O'BRIEN, ARCHIE. Hurdle rider, John S. McMahon's, 1892; Sells Bros.', tour of Australia, 1891-92.

O'BRIEN BROTHERS. Gymnasts. Stickney's Imperial Parisian Circus, 1880; Charles Lee's, 1887; Shields', winter 1887-88; Barnum & Bailey, 1893. **Willie O'Brien** was killed from a fall from a double trapeze in Temple, TX, November 21, 1887.

O'BRIEN, CHARLES. Acrobat and clown, Great International, Offenbach Garden, Philadelphia, winter 1876-77; Cooper & Bailey's Great London, 1880; leaper, Barnum, Bailey & Hutchinson, 1881; Sells Bros.', 1882; principal clown and tumbler, W. C. Coup's, 1893; clown, Welsh Bros.', 1895, 1897; clown, Lowry Bros.', 1905.

O'BRIEN, CLARA. Trained sheep, with Barnum & Bailey, 1892.

O'BRIEN, DAN. Leaper. VanAmburgh & Reiche Bros.', 1885; S. H. Barrett's, 1887; Melville & Co.'s, 1889; James Donovan's, Bermuda, winter 1891-92; Ringling Bros.', 1891-93; Walter L. Main's, 1901; Barnum & Bailey, 1909. Dan O'Brien's wife died, NYC, April 1, 1908.

O'BRIEN, FRED. (1848-April 28, 1881) Champion leaper. Native of Buffalo, NY. Lake's, 1869; Dan Rice's (rail and boat), 1870; Rice's Paris Pavilion Circus, 1871-72; P. T. Barnum's, 1872-73; John Wilson's, San Francisco, January 1874; Cooper, Bailey & Co., 1876; Great London, 1875-77; with wife and sons, **Freddie** and **Willie**, Orrin Bros.', Havana, 1878. Wife was a slack wire artist and his 2 children performed on the trapeze. With P. T. Barnum's, Madison Square Garden, 1881, was injured in a leaping double-somersault over a number of elephants. Died aboard the steamship *England* en route to Liverpool as a result of those injuries, age 33. Remains were buried at sea.

O'BRIEN, FRED, JR. Acrobat. Son of leaper **Fred O'Brien**. Three Melville's & Co., 1889; general superintendent, Price & James, 1897; principal clown, Cooper & Co., 1897.

O'BRIEN, HARRY. Gymnast. Clark Bros.', winter 1889-90; flying rings, Shedman Bros.', 1894.

O'BRIEN, J. C. Manager, Howe's London Circus, 1896, proprietor, 1897.

O'BRIEN, JOHN. (1858-March 12, 1903) Equestrian and horse trainer. Born in South Wales. Began as one of the **O'Brien Family**, attaining prominence as a trick and jockey rider. Brother of **Jennie** and **Archie O'Brien**. Came to USA with them as a *manège* act for Barnum & Bailey and remained with the organization for 4 years. Ringling Bros.', 1898, as equestrian director and horse trainer, staying with them until the close of the 1902 season. It is claimed he was the first man to break a large ensemble of stock, consisting of 63 horses. Died in Baraboo, WI, age 46.

O'BRIEN, JOHN V. "POGEY." (January 29, 1836-September 7, 1889) Born in Frankford, an extension of Philadelphia, the son of a stone mason, **Michael O'Brien**. When 13 years of age, started as a stage driver. 1857, bought out the stage line and ran it for 2 years. Had his first connection with a circus, 1861, when he rented horses to **Gardner & Hemmings** and went along as boss hostler to keep an eye on his property. Became a silent partner with one-third interest in the organization and also acted as assistant manager, 1862. The company opened a new amphitheatre in Philadelphia, November 24, 1862. During this stand **James E. Cooper** entered the circus business with Gardner, Hemmings, and O'Brien. The latter disposed of his share of the property to Cooper 5 weeks into the 1863 summer season. Organized Bryan's (sometimes referred to as Brian's) National Circus With Mrs. Dan Rice for touring in Pennsylvania and New York State. Took out Bryan's (or Brien's) Great Show and Tom King's Excelsior Circus, 1864, with **Tom King** the featured performer. Bought 44 of **Adam Forepaugh's** horses at a cost of $9,000; when payment came due, Forepaugh was forced to accept a share of the circus. With **Forepaugh**, 1865, began summer tour with Dan Rice's Menagerie, which was made up of the former **Jerry Mabie** animals, comprising 22 cages. The property was delivered to Forepaugh at Twelfth and State Streets, Chicago, where the company started the season. The menagerie, **Dan Rice**, his horse, Excelsior, trick mules, and two elephants constituted the exhibition. Rice was engaged for the 25 week summer season at a salary of $1,000 a week. Trouble with Rice and between the partners and a poor profit on the season led to the dissolution of the Forepaugh-O'Brian business arrangement. Fitted out a show, 1867, under the title of Whitby's & Co. 1868, organized the DeMott & Ward Show and, at the same time, ran Bryan's Circus and Menagerie. 1869, organized Campbell's Circus and Menagerie with Hyatt Frost as manager and continued with Bryan's. Repeated these shows the following season. 1871, had 4 shows out—Sheldenberger's, O'Brien's, Joel E. Warner & Co., and Handenberger & Co. For 1872, merged the 4 shows into 3—O'Brien's, Joel E. Warner & Co., and Kleckner & Co.; 1873, O'Brien's Twenty-five-cent Show and was interested with **Dr. Spalding** and **Patrick Ryan** in Dan Rice's. Leased/managed P. T. Barnum's, 1874, and was a partner in Maginley & Co. 1875, continued to manage the Barnum show and organized Rothchild & Co. with **James DeMott** as manager. 1876, ran O'Brien's Six Shows Consolidated, as well as Rothchild & Co. 1877, O'Brien's Six Shows; Campbell's Great 25c Circus, 1878. Was almost bankrupt at the end of the season. Borrowed money from **Forepaugh**, and the latter foreclosed on most of his show property and the Campbell show was taken from O'Brien at the end of the 1879 season. It was used to fit out the Batcheller & Doris New Circus from Frankford (PA), 1880. O'Brien refused to quit and, since he had a great deal of circus equipment, continued to put out small shows with low admission prices and fancy titles for them. 1884, O'Brien, Hardenberger, Astley, and Lowande. When his J. Henry Rice & Co.'s was showing Albany, NY, process servers who had been following the show were on the lot, July 22, the parade that went out never came back, but ended up at the Frankford, PA, quarters. Had an interest in Lowande's Brazilian Circus when he died. [D. W. Watt: "The show prospered for some years and 'Pogey' O'Brien became famous in the business in those days, but it was said that he knew little or nothing about the Ten Commandments. While his great menagerie was a feature, he was running the ring performance so cheap that it was unsatisfactory to the public."] He was described by Kit Clarke as a plainly dressed man, short of stature and somewhat stout, with a round, full face. Free with everybody—a king or a canvasman would be all the same to him. Once in a while, on stated occasions, came out resplendent with diamonds, a velvet vest, every button of which was set with them, a watch chain with big ones in every link, a large solitaire on his bosom, and a big ring on his finger. Throughout his career his reputation as a manager was tarnished as one who was dishonest with his employees and who carried with the show a compliment of gamblers and thieves. Perhaps justice prevailed, for he died of asthma, in poverty, at his residence in Philadelphia.

O'BRIEN, JOSEPH. Dr. James L. Thayer's, 1880.

O'BRIEN, L. Assistant manager, Collins' Oriental Combination, 1877.

O'BRIEN, TED. Tumbler, Lake's Hippo-Olympiad, 1866; Joel E. Warner & Co., 1871.

O'BRIEN, WILLIAM. Acrobat and leaper. Son of **Fred O'Brien**. With Howes' London, 1877; Cooper & Bailey, 1880; Howard Bros.', 1888; Charles Andress', 1888; Robinson-Franklin, 1897.

O'CONNELL, JAMES. Dancer, said to be the first to perform a clog or wooden shoe dance in America. Appeared with circuses, 1839.

O'CONNELL, JAMES F. (d. January 29, 1854) Tattooed man. Crane & Co., May 1836; Boston Lion Circus, 1836; Palmer's, Havana, 1837; Waring's, winter 1838; Welch & Mann, winter 1841; Rockwell & Stone, 1842; Nathan Howes', winter 1842; New Jersey Circus, 1845; Stickney's, January 1849; Dan Rice's, 1850-54; Lathrop Concert Co., January 1852; Maltby's, March 1852; Star State Circus, October 1852; Whitbeck's, Cuba, 1853; Dan Rice's, winter 1852-53. Died in New Orleans.

O'CONNELL, WALTER. Asst't agent, Barnum, Bailey & Hutchinson, 1881.

O'CONNER, MICHAEL. Proprietor of a saloon and livery stable, Galesburg, IL, 1867. Entered into a shakey partnership with circus proprietor **James T. Johnson** that year. When the enterprize failed, O'Conner inherited the circus property and took it on the road as M. O'Conner's Great Western Circus, 1869-71. After the latter season, quit the business to look after his livery stable.

O'DALE, ROBERT. Whitby & Co. (**John V. O'Brien**, proprietor), 1867.

O'DALE, WILLIAM. Rider. Dan Rice's, 1854. Went blind, became an inmate of a charitable institution, Cincinnati, 1865. Fund was raised by other circus people for him.

O'DELL, CHARLES W. Equestrian director, Great Exposition Circus, 1895; McDonald & Reichhold, 1896.

O'NEAL, J. H. Leaper, Great Australian Circus Co., 1877.

O'NEAL, M. J. Press agent, Sells Bros.', 1885.

O'NEIL, HENRY P. (1842-June 13, 1902) Gymnast. Began career in the 1860s when he became a member of the **Goldie Brothers** act, with **George Goldie** and **Claude Conner**. The team was connected with Stone & Murray, Murray's, and Chiarini's, performing trapeze and acrobatics. Died in NYC. See Goldie Brothers.

O'NEILL, MICHAEL J. (d. April 16, 1897) Agent and bill writer. Began career with John B. Doris', 1883; Sells Bros.', 1884-85; Doris & Colvin, 1887; Adam Forepaugh's, 1893. Connected with Ringling Bros.', early 1890s. [Roland Butler: "In a most convincing tone he would delineate attractions that never had and never will appear under canvas, and satisfy the reader that they might all be seen for fifty cents."] At one time, was press agent for the Grand Street Museum, NYC, and for Sam T. Jack's Opera House, Chicago. A memorable feat as an agent for Sells was his opposition fight with Ringling Bros.' in Texas. At the close of the season, however, he collaborated in the preparation of Ringling's route book. Described as "an easy, vigorous, original, fluent writer of old style circus publications ... a rough diamond, aggressive to a degree, but gentle as a child and honest as the sun." Died at his home in Cincinnati, OH, from heart failure.

O'TOOL, MICHAEL. Knockabout clown, with Walter L. Main's, 1886.

OAKLEY, FRANK. (d. March 8, 1916) Clown, performing as "Slivers." Born in Sweden of English parents. Ran away from home at 14 years of age and became a groom with John McMann's. 5 years later, was a performer with Andrew McDonald's. 1902, married the vaudeville singer **Nellie Dunbar**. Committed suicide, NYC.

OATES, J. C. Proprietor and business manager (with **Dan Rice, William H. Stowe**), Dan Rice's, 1881.

OBERIST, JOHN F. Courtney & Sanford's Minstrels with Courtney & Sanford's Circus, South America. Sailed from New York, July 23, 1873.

OCHFORD, W. Rider, Quick, Sands & Co., Baltimore, 1833.

ODELL, ALMA. (1868?-December 19, 1908) Wire walker and aerialist. Born in Ingersol, Canada. Started in the business at age 15 with the George L. Fox pantomime troupe, Olympic Theatre, NYC. Called "The Human Fly," Barnum's, Forepaugh's, Sells Bros.', John Robinson's, etc., as well as having played the leading vaudeville theatres. Married **William T. Odell**, former circus performer and theatrical manager. See below. Died in Chicago, age 40.

ODELL, CHARLES W. Trainer and rider. Ringling Bros.', 1891-92; Barnum & Bailey, 1893; Walter L. Main's, 1894; LaPearl's, 1896.

ODELL, WILLIAM T. (d. October 28, 1866) Scene rider, equestrian director. Began career around mid-century. There was a Master Odell performing at the Bowery Amphitheatre during the circus season, 1847-48, in feats of horsemanship for manager **John Tryon**, which presumably was our man. August, 1851, gave a pantomime at the Bowery Amphitheatre; and again in January, 1853, was performing in *The Man o' War's Man*. Dan Rice's, 1852; Welch & Lent, 1854; scenic rider and double somersault performer, Myers & Madigan, 1854; H. P. Madigan's, 1856; Tom King's, 1858; Robinson & Lake, 1859-60; Tom King's, Washington, DC, 1861-62; Maginley & VanVleck, 1863; James M. Nixon's Alhambra, NYC, fall 1863; Howes', 199 Bowery, NYC, winter 1863-64; S. O. Wheeler's, 1864; Hippotheatron, NYC, winter 1864-65; National Circus, Cincinnati, winter 1864-65; Lake's Hippo-Olympiad, 1865; equestrian director, Alex Robinson's, 1866, but fell from a horse, Ann Arbor, MI, while attempting a somersault, which caused a compound fracture in his arm and rendered him useless for the season. Died in Philadelphia.

OGDEN, ABE. Chief of advertising brigade, Dan Rice's, 1873.

OGDEN, ADA. Nixon's Amphitheatre, NYC, May 1863.

OGDEN, CHARLES D. Contracting agent, G. G. Grady's, 1873.

OGDEN, DARIUS. Native of Westchester County, NY, who became a partner of **James Raymond** in the menagerie business, 1831-34. Proprietor (with **E. M. Hobby**), Ogden & Hobby, 1842; (with **Chauncey Weeks**) Ogden, Weeks & Co., 1845.

OKEY, T. W. Co-proprietor, Miller, Okey & Freeman's, 1886.

OLDER, PARDON A. (September 22, 1826-September 29, 1908) Wagon show manager who traveled in the Mid-west. Traded a saw mill at Janesville, WI, (worth $5,000) for a third interest in the Mabie circus, 1849. The show had about 70 horses, 8 wagons, an 85' round-top, and a 30' dressing tent. Older's Great U. S. Circus, 1852; manager, Herr Driesbach & Co.'s Menagerie, 1853. Allied with **Yankee Robinson**, 1857; Orton & Older, with **Miles Orton**, 1858-60; manager, Yankee Robinson's, 1865-69; Older's Museum, Circus and Menagerie, 1870-72. Bought the use of P. T. Barnum's name for a tour of the South, 1872. In December, Barnum went to New Orleans to reclaim property. This outfit, which left Louisville, November 4, followed a route through Kentucky, Tennessee, Georgia and Louisiana, ending up in New Orleans. The season was not a success, and after an 8-day stand there, Older closed the operation. Older & Chandler, 1873; manager, Stevens & Begun, 1874; with a dime museum in Brooklyn, 1880; Older, Crane & Co., 1884. After retirement, lived on a farm near Onoka, MN, until his death at age 99.

OLIVER, FRED. Treasurer, George W. DeHaven's, 1865.

OLIVER, HARRY. Contracting agent. Batcheller & Doris, 1882; John B. Doris', 1883.

OLIVER, JAMES. Robinson & Lake, Wood's Theatre, Cincinnati, winter 1859; Robinson & Lake, 1860.

OLIVER, JOE. W. H. Harris' Nickel-Plate, 1889.

OLMA, WILLIAM. "Leaps for life", with Hippotheatron, 14th Street, NYC, November, 1864; monkey-man, Hemmings, Cooper & Whitby, 1870.

OLMSTEAD, IRA. Manager, western unit, June, Titus, Angevine & Co., 1841.

OLWINE, FRED. Lake's Hippo-Olympiad, 1867.

OMAR, HENRY. Spalding & Rogers, 1856, 1859.

ONOFRI, CHARLES. Kenebel's Parisian Circus, fall 1885.

ORD ["Master"]. Rider. Melville, Maginley & Cooke, 1875.

ORDEY, KAROLY and AUGUSTA [or Ordney]. Hungarian jugglers, Barnum, Bailey & Hutchinson, 1881.

ORGAN, WILLIAM. Equestrian, with L. B. Lent's, 1868-71; Montgomery Queen's, 1876-77; ringmaster and equestrian director, VanAmburgh & Co., winter 1877-78; performing stallions, W. W. Cole's Australian tour (which left San Francisco, October 23, 1880), 1880-81.

ORMAN, CHARLES. Clown. D. S. Swadley's, 1872; Orrin Bros.', Mexico, winter 1881-82.

ORMOND, MARGARET FRANCES [r. n. Francelia Delsmore]. (d. December 4, 1863) Equestrienne. Considered in her time to be one of the foremost female riders in the world. Became a member of Spalding's and Spalding & Rogers, 1844-64. Beloved by all her colleagues. Died of yellow fever while with this concern, St. Jago, West Indies. Originally a Quakeress, had a good education, was kind and affable, and endeared herself to a large circle of acquaintances. Rode under the name of **Miss Delsmore** for a number of years, even after marrying a **Mr. Palmer**. Had one child, a bright boy, who was named **Clarence Delsmore Palmer**, and who died at age 15. Circus rider **Kate Ormond** was her adopted daughter.

ORMOND, KATE [r. n. Kate Simpson]. (d. August 10, 1892)

HIRAM ORTON and SARAH MERWIN

Married, 1837 [second wife]. Their 7 children are listed below.

Miles
[1838-1903]
married
Mary Ann Cole,
1862,
no issue;
divorced 1878;
married
Elizabeth Hayes,
1879, 2 sons:
Norman, 1881,
Myron, 1884

Dennis
[1840-1870]
married
Maggie Brockway,
1864;
2 sons:
Orville, 1864;
Dennis, 1869

Hattie
[1843-1915]
married
Thomas Mann,
musician, 1864;
8 children:
Nettie,
Irene,
Hiram,
Maggie,
Sadie,
Thomas,
George,
Dennis.

Lester
[1846-1922]
married
Laura Marsh,
1875;
3 children:
Frank, 1875,
Olive, 1877,
Alice, 1844.

Irena
[?-1923]
married
Hiram Marcyes,
band leader, 1868;
no issue;
married
Albert Harris, 1882;
no issue.

Celestia
[1851-1872]
married
James Moore, 1867;
no issue.

R. Z.
[1853-1923]
married
Sarah Menicle, 1877,
7 children:
Criley, 1888,
Lawrence, 1889.
Miles, 1891,
Grace, 1892,
Bayard, 1895,
Nellie, 1897,
Sarah, 1901.

Equestrienne, with a specialty of single equitation. Adopted daughter of **Mrs. Margaret Frances Ormond** (see above), and fellow apprentice of **Charles Fish** with **Charles J. Rogers** on the Spalding & Rogers show. As a young woman, had raven black hair and coal black eyes; was an excellent pad rider and attractive both in and out of the ring. Made a successful tour of the coastal cities of South America, 1862-63, where, it is said, men crowded around the circus entrance to escort her to her hotel. Returned to NYC, April 1864, and appeared at the Hippothreatron, 14th Street, with Spalding & Roger, where her apprenticeship ended with her marriage to **Ferdinand Tourniaire**, May 15, 1864, both being members of Spalding & Rogers company. The marriage ended with her filing for divorce, June 1869. Then married an actor of considerable means, **Richard Pennistan**—the man had won a grand prize in the Havana lottery of $500,000 in gold but, unfortunately, became interested in thoroughbred horses and lost it all. The marriage was as unsuccessful as the first and Kate settled in Mexico with her son. A third marriage was to a non-professional named **Wood**. Spalding & Rogers, 1856-62, Old Bowery Theatre, NYC, 1861; West Indies, 1863-64; Hippotheatron, NYC, with Spalding & Rogers, spring 1864; Dan Rice's, 1864; J. F. Orrin's, South America, 1865-66; Dan Castello & Co., 1866; Orrin Bros.', 1867-68; Mexico, winter, 1881-82, 1883-84. Died in Mexico City.

OROVIO, E. Spanish gymnastic clown, Main & VanAmburgh, 1890.

ORR, COL. NOAH. (d. July 1, 1882) "The Ohio Giant." Said to be a handsome man who stood 8' 2" in his stockings and weighed 560 pounds. Yankee Robinson's, 1866; VanAmburgh's, 1872; P. T. Barnum's, 1874.

ORRIN, GEORGE FREDERICK. (December 6, 1815-May 15, 1884) Born in County Chester, England. Early in career formed a partnership with **Thomas Nunn, Felix Walker**, and **William Stewart** and, calling himself **George Honey**, performed in England as **The Acrobat Family**. The troupe came to America, 1845, and opened at Niblo's Garden, NYC. Later, traveled with Rockwell's, Howes & Mabie, and other shows of the period. 1851, visited Cuba and Mexico. When the troupe broke up, Orrin formed a family act and traveled with such shows as Spalding & Rogers, Dan Rice's, and H. Buckley & Co. (1857). Orrin family formed a partnership with the **Kneass Family** as a "room show," 1857. Went to the West Indies later that year in partnership with **G. Chiarini**. On return, 1859, performed at Barnum's Museum; 1860 in other variety halls; John Wilson's, California, 1861. Orrin & Sebastian Circus organized, 1863, and for 2 or 3 years toured South and Central America and the West Indies. **Sebastian** sold out to the Orrins, 1866, and the show continued as Orrin's California Circus. The family returned to San Francisco, 1868; combined with the **Gregorys**, 1870, to tour California and Oregon; broke up when the show came to grief in Stockton,

CA. After which, left for South America to join Courtney & Sanford. When that company disbanded in Valparaiso, joined with the **Nelson Brothers** (Sam and John), **Charles Lasaille**, and the **Rosalin Sisters** for a tour through southern Chili. Later, joined Chiarini's and remained with it until 1872. Continued working in the Southern Hemisphere for several years before dying in Mexico City. Wife **Zilla T.** (April 3, 1828-May 24, 1884) was born in Sheffield, England.

ORRIN BROTHERS [George Washington, Charles, Edward]. Sons of **George F.** and **Zilla T. Orrin.** See George Frederick Orrin above. **George** and **Edward**, joined George L. Fox's "Humpty Dumpty" Troupe for 2 years. Spring 1877, took a variety and pantomime show to Havana where they continued in various enterprises until 1880. Opened their first circus company, 1881, establishing a theatre circus in Mexico City at a cost of $80,000, from which they made tours of the Mexican interior. The venture lasted until **George's** death in London. **George W.** (February 7, 1846-September 9, 1892), the eldest of the three brothers, born in NYC, and entered the ring around 1850 with Dan Rice's, traveling with his father. Visited Mexico and Cuba as early as 1854. Various times connected with Spalding & Rogers, Harry Buckley's, Levi J. North's. Throughout career, performed in most acts in the circus program—rode well enough for scene and 2-horse acts and was sufficient as a clown, even portrayed Little Eva in Yankee Robinson's "Uncle Tom's Cabin" Co., 1856. December 1875, made a trip to southern France for the benefit of wife's health. Returned, March 1876; wife died May 30. Married **Miss M. Medina**, December 27, 1879, NYC. **Edward** (1847-1924) took over management after brother's death on their 12th winter season in Mexico City. He married **Zillah Covell** in Troy, NY, December 4, 1893. She died from childbirth in Troy, July 28, 1897, age 25. **Charles F.**, the youngest brother and the most obscure, was not always connected with the firm.

ORTON FAMILY. See Orton geneology. **Hiram** (1805-August 2, 1883), the proprietor of Orton Bros.', was a sailor on the Great Lakes until he formed a circus, starting from Portage, WI, 1854-57. In partnership with **P. A. Older**, Orton & Older, 1858-60. Retired from managing, 1862. Died of heart trouble, Norris, MI, age 72. **Miles** (November 10, 1836-November 23, 1903) was born near Erie, PA. Entered the circus profession as a member of his father's company, Orton & Older, where he remained several seasons as an equestrian. Moving away from the family show, equestrian manager and co-proprietor, Stowe & Orton, 1870; W. W. Cole's, 1871-74; bareback rider and owner of all privileges, Joel E. Warner's, 1873; equestrian director, Burr Robbins', 1875-76; Great Roman Hippodrome, 1877; H. C. Lee's, winter 1877-78; Great American Circus, 1878; equestrian director, Great Transatlantic Allied Shows, 1879. In 1880, began his own management with a wagon show. After 2 successful seasons, took out a 24-

230

car railroad show, Orton's Anglo-American Shows, until illness caused a loss of fortune. Reorganized into a 4-car show, 1883-85; then chartered the steamer, *J. H. F. Dowell*, as a boat show on the Mississippi and Missouri Rivers for 2 seasons; manager, Tribbey & Co.'s Mastadon Dime Circus, 1887. After securing DeArley & O'Brien's, renamed Rentz', operated for 4 seasons throughout the South and Southwest, returning East, 1893. December 4, 1902, organized Miles Orton's Big Southern Show. Was equestrian director, Phil Diefenbach's, 1895; equestrian director, New York Circus, 1897; manager, Orton Children's Liliputian Dog and Pony Circus, 1898. It has been said that he was the first rider to carry 2 people at once with the horse galloping at full speed. Married equestrienne **Mary Ann Cole** in St. Louis, MO, August 22, 1862. They divorced May 20, 1878, Circuit Court, St. Louis, MO. Had 2 sons from a 2nd marriage to **Elizabeth Hayes—Norman** and **Myron**. Confusion of family members occurs because, during his management, took in and trained a number of young performers who all used the family name. Died of a stroke at Key West, FL, age 66.

ORTON, JOHN. Juggler, globe performer. No relation to **Hiram Orton**. Apprentice, *Floating Palace*, 1852; Whitbeck's, 1854; Ballard & Bailey, 1855; Major Brown's, 1857; Mabie & Crosby, 1858.

ORTON, SARAH B. (d. October 6, 1931) Wife of **R. Z. Orton**. Died at Colorado Springs, CO.

ORTUS, PROF. Aeronaut. Native of England. United States Circus, 1882. Died in Maysville, KY, this year on August 7 when he slipped from the trapeze bar of his balloon and fell into the Ohio River.

ORVILLE, CHARLES. Balancing trapeze act, Great Chicago Circus, 1879; S. Dutton's Southern, 1880; equestrian di

rector, aerialist, McMahon's, 1888.

ORVILLE, CORA. Great Australian Show, 1880.

ORVILLE, HARRY and MAY. Hart, France & Co. (**H. H. Hart, F. F. France**, proprietors), 1889.

OSBORN, J. Levi J. North's, 1859-60.

OSBORN, TOM. Clown. E. F. & J. Mabie's, 1847; clown, Dan Rice's, 1848-49; Mabie-Raymond-Driesbach's, 1852; Driesbach & Mabie, 1853; L. G. Butler's, 1854-55; Levi J. North's, 1856-59; Hyatt & Co., 1859; World Circus, 1860; Antonio Bros.', 1659-61; John Robinson's, 1867.

OSBORNE, W. Gymnast, First National Union, 1861.

OSTRANDER, SAM. Clown, James T. Johnston's, 1867.

OSTRON. Bancker's New York Circus, 1824.

OSWALD, MAUD. Race rider, P. T. Barnum's Roman Hippodrome, 1875. In the fall of 1877, said to be riding 20-mile races for a purse of $100 in the driving parks of Minnesota. Hippodrome jockey, Barnum, Bailey & Hutchinson, 1882; Pubillone's, Havana, winter 1884-85; aerial act of "The Shooting Star," flying rings and single trapeze with slide and dive, Adam Forepaugh's, 1885; equestrienne, Sparrow's Royal Pavilion Show, 1886. While with the company, her fiance, gymnist **David Hawley**, fately injured himself attempting a triple somersault. Four days later, June 9, 1886, at General Hospital, Montreal, Canada, the two were married. **Hawley** died the following day.

OTERO, MARIA. Bareback rider, with Martinho Lowande's, 1881.

OUNZAND BROTHERS. Acrobats, W. W. Cole's, 1874.

OURA, S. Sword walker, with Barnum & Bailey, 1892.

OURI, ROSINA. Running globe and slack wire, Wallace & Anderson, 1890.

OWEN, J. H. Agent, George W. DeHaven's, 1865.

P

PAGE, CAPT. Owned a menagerie, 1823-24; performer of some nature, 1826-27; in partnerhip with **Byram G. Bernard**, 1828-29, performing in cities of New York State, the St. Lawrence Valley, and the Great Lakes region of the Canadian side. Opened a circus in Albany, Beaver Street between Green and South Market Streets, 1829-30, then went on tour in Canada. While the circus was located on McGill Street, Montreal, a mob nearly tore his wooden circus building down, "Billy Button, the Unfortunate Tailor" being the cause. There were a large number of Irish tailors in that city; consequently, when **West** entered the ring as Billy Button, he was greeted with brickbats; the tailors had taken the skit as an insult. Rioting went on for days, and when the circus moved to Quebec, it continued. Page visited almost every part of the world in search of show stock, supplying the American market with giants, glass blowers, African natives, etc. Picked up a group of **Aztec children** in South America and toured them in Europe. Could speak several languages and was full of enterprise. **George Stone** wrote that Page knew no such word as fail.

PAGE, GEORGE. (d. June 1, 1906) Clown, celebrated in his day as "Sawdust George." Sustained injuries to his head that effected his mind and forced retirement from the arena while at the height of popularity. Died a pauper in Rochester, NY, age 81.

PAGE, HENRY S. Outstanding cornet player, L. B. Lent's, 1873.

PAINTER, WILLIAM [r. n. William Bracken]. (d. December, 1877) Gymnast and acrobat, of **Painter & Durand**. Born in Johnstown, PA. Began working with **A. P. Durand**, 1855. Nixon & Kemp, 1858; Nixon & Co., 1859; Sloat & Shepherd, 1859. Went with the **Aymar brothers (Walter** and **William)** to California and engaged with **John Wilson's** under the banner of Dan Rice's Circus, 1860, performing at the American Theatre, San Francisco, which had been fashioned into an amphitheatre in the spring. Accompanied Doc Bassett's to South America, leaving on the clipper ship *Santa Claus,* October 21, 1861. Orrin Bros.', San Francisco, 1863; William Worrell's Theatre, San Francisco, 1865; Bay View Park, San Francisco, 1866; Lee & Ryland's Hippodrome, San Francisco, 1866, winter 1866-67. Died in Cincinnati, OH.

PALMER, ARTHUR G. Calliope player, Cooper, Bailey & Co., 1876; Miles Orton's, 1885.

PALMER BROTHERS [Robert, Harry]. Flying trapeze, leap for life, Cooper & Co., 1874.

PALMER, C. B. Had an interest in the Delavan-Adams show, which he sold by June, 1884.

PALMER, CLARENCE DELSMORE. Equestrian son of Mme. Ormond. Displayed an intellect rarely seen in a boy of his years. Was amiable and studious, habits that won him influential friends. Spalding & Rogers, 1849-55. Died at age 15.

PALMER, FRANK. Hostler. Started with the Burr Robbins' show as a young man scarcely out of his teens, where he remained some 4 or 5 years. Later, Ringling Bros.' for several years. [D. W. Watt: "He was always quiet and unassuming and where Frank had four or an eight horse team in charge when the parade was pulled out on the lot ready for the street, no boss hostler that Frank Palmer ever worked for worried about his turnout, for they knew that it would be right in every particular."] Also with Gollmar Bros.' Worked many years under **Spencer Alexander**, better known as "Delavan," both with the Burr Robbins and later with the Ringling show.

PALMER, H. S. Palmer's Great Western, 1865-66, after purchasing the show from **John V. O'Brien** toward the end of the 1864 season. Grandson of **P. A. Older**.

PALMER, HENRY CLAY. (d. January 18, 1910) Sideshow performer. Born in NYC. Began his career as a bell boy for the old Ann Street Museum, NYC. Later became one of the original glass blowers with P. T. Barnum's. Died in NYC from asthma.

PALMER, HENRY. Rider and vaulter. Eagle Circus, 1836; Charles Bacon's, 1837; Bacon & Derious, 1838-39; Welch & Bartlett, 1839; Welch & Mann, 1842. Married **Louisa Wagstaff**, a professional, 1842; (with wife), Welch & Mann, Mediterranean, 1843.

PALMER, JOSEPH D. With **Jeremiah Fogg** when he took over John Lamb's circus, Front Street Theatre, Baltimore, December 31, 1831; had been treasurer for Fogg & Stickney, 1830; the firm continued at the Front Street Theatre for a while, then ended the partnership after a 6 week engagement at the Arch Street Theatre, Philadelphia. In partnership with **William Harrington** as Palmer & Harrington, 1834; proprietor, Palmer's Circus and Gymnastic Arena, 1835; Palmer's Pavilion Circus, 1836-37. Was seen as a difficult employer.

PALMER, L. C. Proprietor (with **Robert Chew**), Atlantic and Pacific, 1872.

PALMER, LOUISA. Welch & Mann's unit, Mediterranean, 1843-44. See Henry Palmer.

PALMER, R. A. (1848-1874) Balloon ascensionist, connected with Harry Buckley's, spring 1874. In making an ascension for the townspeople of Delavan, before the circus went on the road, a guy line failed to cast off which resulted in the balloon rolling over and dragging him along the ground. When the balloon began to ascend he was severely injured from being smashed against the wall of the Park Hotel. Died 5 months later from complications.

PALMETTO, ROSINA. Robinson & Myers, 1883.

PAPE, BILLY. Acrobat and leaper, somersaulting over 5 elephants and 2 camels, a distance of 41' 6".

PARAZO, HARRY. Ringmaster, with Caldwell's Occidental, 1867.

PARENTOS [Charles A., Lucas D., Olivia]. Gymnasts, with Cooper & Co., 1874.

PARENTO, GEORGE. Gymnast, equilibrist. A. F. Tuttle's, 1893; Sun Bros.', 1896.

PARISH, L. H. Orchestra leader, S. O. Wheeler's, 1867.

PARK, MANGO. Miles Orton's, 1885.

PARKER, ANTHONY ["Tony", r. n. J. D. Agler]. (February 12, 1824-July 3, 1911) Clown. Started in the circus business with the VanAmburgh show at the age of 10, 1834, remaining until the Mexican War broke out, 1846. Rider, Mabie's, 1848-50, 1854-55; John Robinson's, 1852; Dan Rice's, 1856, 1859-61; H. Buckley & Co., 1856; Spalding & Rogers, 1857-58. Spent 3 years in the service of the North during the Civil War. Then joined Yankee Robinson's, 1866; Burr Robbins', 1874; Cooper & Jackson, 1879. Performed for about 50 years. Author of *On the Road with a Wagon Show*. [Tony Parker: "I first went in as an acrobat and then became a clown and did nothing else for forty-five years, being a singer and Shakespearean jester. I made a success of this line of work and finally added riding, leaping and all branches of the business."] Performed until 1888, retiring at the age of 85. Died, at his home in Winfield, KS, age 87.

PARKER, CHARLES W. (d. August 25, 1871) Began his career as a contortionist but by 1865 was a performing clown. Was a great favorite in the South, with his recognizable shout of "Whoa, January!" being heard wherever he appeared. Gardner & Hemmings, 1860-62; Nixon-Macarte, 1863; James M. Nixon's Alhambra, NYC, fall 1863; Hippotheatron, NYC, late winter 1864; Melville's Australian, 1864; Dan Castello's, 1865-66; Seth B. Howes', 1866; Yankee Robinson's, 1866, 1868; Thayer & Noyes, 1867; Philadelphia Circus, winter 1867-68; Cooke's, Philadelphia, winter 1867-68; Oriental Circus, 1870; Charles Noyes' Crescent City, 1871. Died in Schenectady, NY.

PARKER, ED F. Talking and singing clown, Charles Lee's, 1896.

PARKER, HARRY M. Trainer with 11 educated dogs. Melville, Maginley & Cooke, 1875; John H. Murray's, 1876; Burr Robbins', 1878; Batcheller & Doris, 1882; Roberts and Gardner, 1886; John B. Doris & John L. Sullivan Show, 1888.

PARKER, JENNIE. With C. T. Ames', 1869.

PARKER, MR. and MRS. Flag dancers. Simpson & Price, Washington, January 1823; the Olympic, Philadelphia, May 1823; the Broadway Circus, NYC, June 1823; Blanchard & West, Canada, 1825; Mount Pitt Circus, NYC, 1827.

PARKER SISTERS. Charles Lee's, 1887.

PARKHURST, GEORGE A. Boss canvasman. With Van-

Amburgh & Co., 1881; Norris & Rowe, 1891; J. H. LaPearl's, 1896.

PARKS, J. J. Treasurer, Campbell's New York and Philadelphia Zoological and Equestrian Institute, 1869.

PARKS, JOHN J. (1822?-February, 1915) Privileges (with Frank Uffner), with Howes' Great London, 1873; purchased Howes' Great London with Richard Dockrill, 1877, and was on the road with it for 2 years; title included Dockrill's Parisian Circus and Grotesque Mardi Gras. Sold show to James A. Bailey and James A. Cooper, 1879. Died in the national Elks Home, Bedford, VA, age 93.

PARMELEE, E. M. Band leader. French's Oriental, 1867; VanAmburgh & Co., 1871.

PARMELEE, W. W. Contracting agent, Wallace & Anderson, 1890.

PARSONS, ARTHUR. Brother of Joe Parsons. Born and died in Darlington, WI. With Ringling Bros.' about 17 years until 1910, when he left the circus business.

PARSONS, CHARLES J. Skatorial artist, Lowande & Hoffman, 1887.

PARSONS, JAMES. French & Monroe, 1885.

PARSONS, JOHN R. Cornet player and band leader. Sands & Quick, 1852; Lee & Bennett, San Francisco, 1856.

PARSON, JOSEPH. (d. 1895) Rider. With brothers, operated circuses, 1879-1883, on which Al Ringling was a performer. Rode a principal and great hurricane hurdle act on Ringling Bros.', 1887, with a contract of $10 per week to do a high wire act, riding act, and outside ascension. Married Clarinda Lowande Lamkin, October 6, 1888, in the arena of Ringling Bros.' at Praire du Chien, WI. Ringling Bros.', 1889, but finished the season with George W. Richard's Southern Circus, 1889-90; 4-horse act, principal act, 2-horse carrying act, and hurdle rider, Gollmar Bros.', 1892; Shipp's Midwinter Circus, Petersburg, IL, 1893-94, 1894-95.

PARSONS, SAMUEL B. Proprietor of menagerie and museum, Charleston, SC, 1817. Erected an arena at the corner of Eagle and State Streets, Albany, 1824. Parson's Circus, Albany, around 1826. Built Pearl Street Circus there at a cost of $22,000, which included the horses; it failed to pay, 1829, and passed into the hands of S. J. Penniman, who later sold it to the Methodists to be used as a church. Thayer believes Parsons was the money man behind Bancker's circus, 1824-26.

PARSONS, W. T. Agent, Cooper, Jackson & Co., 1882.

PARTINGTON, KATE, equestrienne and concert hall performer. Married to strong man Hercules Libby. Warner & Henderson, 1874; with trick horse, Montezuma, Springer's, 1875; the North American Circus, 1877.

PASCALL, WILLIAM. Clown, Boston Lion Circus, 1836.

PASTOR, EDWARD. Manager, with Alexander Robinson's, 1871.

PASTOR, FRANK. (November 13, 1837-June 25, 1885) Rider. Brother of Tony and William Pastor. Born in NYC.

Apprenticed to John J. Nathans at age 6 and remained with him until 1854. That year, joined Joe Pentland's as a paid performer. Sailed for England, late 1856, and performed during the winter of that year throughout the British Isles. Summer 1857, was in Italy. In the winter, back in England. Following summer, 1858, Alhambra Palace, London. Subsequently, with Rentz' on the Continent; Pablo Fanque's, England, 1858; Price's, Madrid, Spain, 1859; Cirque Napoleon, Paris, 1862; Signor Albisu's, Havana, 1866; Parisian Circus, assembled for the Paris Exposition, 1867. While at the latter, used 3 large American flags in his performance. [John A. Dingess: "He was the first to unfold the stars and stripes in a Parisian circus, which had been established for more than forty years, and his performance was witnessed by Napoleon and the Emperess. The display of any flag except the French within the building was prohibited."] Upon returning from Europe, connected with James M. French's, 1869; equestrian director, co-proprietor, James Robinson's, 1871-72; James W. Wilder & Co., 1873. Died of consumption, San Antonio, TX.

PASTOR, MARY AMELIA. (December 16, 1824-February 18, 1869) Wife of J. J. Nathans and possibly mother of Emma Nathans. May or may not be related to the Pastor boys who were apprenticed to Nathans at one time. See J. J. Nathans.

PASTOR, TONY. (May 28, 1837-August 26, 1908) Clown and negro minstrel. Brother of **Frank** and **William Pastor**. Born in NYC. Entered into show business at age of 6. Fall 1846, made debut at Barnum's museum, appearing blackface and playing the tambourine in the minstrel band. April 1847, joined Raymond & Waring as a minstrel performer. That fall, apprenticed to **John J. Nathan** and made his debut in the arena at that time at Welch's National Amphitheatre, Philadelphia. Welch, Delevan & Nathans, 1848; Federal Street Theatre, Boston, winter 1848-49; Welch, Nathans, Bancker & Christy, 1849-51. Sang comic songs in the ring, rode a "Pete Jenkins" act, tumbled with the acrobats, and danced "Lucy Long" in the minstrel aftershow. Was never a great success as a rider but was a valuable general performer—rode in the grand entry, tumbled, played ringmaster, sang comic songs, appeared in afterpieces. [John A. Dingess: "As a comic singer, he was looked upon by the circus going community to be without a peer."] Bowery Amphitheatre, NYC, fall 1851; through the East, Sands, Nathans & Quick, 1852; Bowery Amphitheatre, fall and winter 1852-53; Franconi's Traveling Hippodrome, 1853; minstrel performer, Bowery, winter 1853-54; Mabie's, 1854; ringmaster, general performer, sideshow performer, Levi J. North's, 1855-56; North's Amphitheatre, Chicago, winter 1855-56, 1856-57; Mabie's, 1857-58; Sands, Nathans & Co., 1859; Dan Rice's, Philadelphia, winter 1859-60. Made first appearance on variety stage, winter 1860, Rivers' Melodeon, Philadelphia. Same winter, performed in the pantomime, *The Monster of St. Michaels*, NYC, Bowery Theatre, for Spalding & Rogers. Then returned to the Melo-

deon, remaining until April 1861. Having tired of traveling, decided to adopt the variety profession and began filling engagements as comic vocalist. Within a short time, went into management and became the most famous of the variety proprietors and, what he was later to be called, "the father of vaudeville." As a New York manager, career began July 31, 1865, when he opened the Opera House, 201 Bowery. Remained there until March 27, 1875. October 4 of that year, assumed the management of 585 Broadway. October 10, 1881, leased the Germania Theatre, East 14th Street, NYC, and on October 24 the place was dedicated as Tony Pastor's Theatre. The building burned on June 6, 1888. Another theatre was erected on the site and formally dedicated, October 22, that same year. Died in Elmhurst, NJ.

PASTOR, WILLIAM. (August 6, 1840-October 23, 1877) Clown and acrobat. Born in NYC, the brother of **Tony** and **Frank Pastor**. Introduced to the circus business as an apprentice to **John J. Nathans**. As early as 1848, with Welch, Delevan & Nathans and remained for several years; appeared at the Bowery Amphitheatre, NYC, winter 1852-53; Washburn's, 1853-54, standing on his head atop a pole 30' high; Mabie's, 1857, as rider and vaulter; Nixon & Kemp, NYC, fall 1858; Sands, Nathans & Co., Broadway Theatre, NYC, fall 1858. Following year, went to Spain, making his debut July 4, 1860, as an acrobat. Following this, went to Denmark and appeared as a trick clown; and hence around Europe and then to Cuba for Chiarini, clowning in the Spanish language. Spalding & Rogers, Nassau, clowning in English. On return to NYC, his vessel was wrecked on a New Jersey beach, April 2, 1864. Clown, Hippotheatron, 14th Street, NYC. Went west with Spalding & Rogers, and, subsequently, back to Havana. During this time, **Dr. Spalding** advised him to turn vocalist, which he did, making his debut on October 11, 1865 at Spalding, Rogers & Bidwell's Academy of Muisic, New Orleans. And so, leaving the circus in the manner of his brother, embarked on a successful variety career.

PATRICK, C. Michael O'Conner & Co., 1870.

PATRICK, WARREN A. See Joe Hepp.

PATTERSON BROTHERS. Gymnasts. French & Monroe, 1885; McFlinn's, 1888; Main & VanAmburgh, 1890. One of the brothers, **George Patterson**, turned a backward double somersault from the swing.

PATTERSON, JAMES. A challenge bareback and Indian rough rider, Edmund Maurice's Old Fashioned Circus, 1896.

PATTERSON, JOHN. (d. May 31, 1889) Irish clown. Born in Tralee, Ireland. Grew up with no formal education. Began professionally as a snare drummer; shortly, became successful as a singing and talking clown. Brought to the United States by Cooper and Bailey, 1876, with whom he remained for 2 seasons. April 16, 1877, appeared at Tony Pastor's Theatre, also starred at the *Theatre Comique*, NYC, January 7, 1878. Howes', 1877-78; variety performer, Olympic Theatre, Brooklyn, 1879; Cooper & Bailey, 1879, concert manager and Irish balladist, 1880; Batchelor & Doris, 1881. Returning to his native Ireland around 1886 with a small fortune, bought an interest in a small circus managed by **Jimmy Keely** and renamed the show Kelly & Patterson's. Upon Keely's death, married his widow. Died of consumption in the town of his birth. Had a fine baritone voice and sang such songs of his own composition as "Bridget Donoghue," "The Rambler From Clare," "A Garden Where The Praties Grow," and "There Never Was A Coward Where The Shamrock Grows." Irish brogue was refreshing, manner refined and gentle and performance, reported the Toronto *Daily Leader*, "sparkles like the effervescence from a bottle of newly opened champagne." [D. W. Watt: "What made Patterson so unique a figure among the clowns of his day was the spontaneity of his wit and his fresh and unconventional humor. He did not peddle around a stale bag of hackneyed jokes. Often, as Mr. Doris told me, he would bound into the ring and take the ringmaster by surprise with a batch of unpremeditated jokes that sprang from his Celtic imagination, on the spur of the moment and as fast as he could utter them."]

PATTERSON, MINNIE. Single trapeze. Walter L. Main's, 1891; Frank A. Gardner's, West Indies, winter 1891-92.

PATTON, G. T. Manager advertising car #4, Barnum, Bailey & Hutchinson, 1882.

PAUL, J. Gymnast, John Robinson's, 1880.

PAUL, J. W. Strongman. June, Titus & Angevine, 1842; LeTort's French Circus, 1842; Rockwell & Stone, 1842; Great Western, 1847; 40-horse driver, Spalding & Rogers, 1850-55; Howes & Cushing, England, 1857, handling the 40 cream-colored horses that drew the Appollonicon; Nixon & Kemp, 1858; James M. Nixon's, 1859; Antonio & Wilder, 1859-60; Orton Bros.', 1865; 40-horse driver, Stone & Murray, 1870-72; John H. Murray's, 1873-75.

PAUL, T. G. Clown, VanAmburgh & Co., 1874.

PAULIN, EMMA C. See Emma Nathans.

PAULING, JAMES [or Paulding]. General performer, L. B. Lent's, 1859-60, 1861-62.

PAULSCHOFF, HERR. Lion tamer, W. W. Cole's, 1871.

PAULSEN, FREDERICK. Strong man, Lowande & Hoffman, 1887.

PAWLE, M. Strong man, Thompson, Smith & Hawes, 1866.

PAYNE, GEORGE [or Paine]. Armless wonder, with Yankee Robinson's, 1866; Sheldenburger & Co., 1871; Cooper, Bailey & Co., 1880; Barnum, Bailey & Hutchinson, 1881.

PAYNE, JAMES ["Buckskin Bill"]. Sharp shooter, Gollmar Bros.', 1896.

PAYNE, MISS. 2-horse rider. Became Mrs. Coty, 1826. Pepin & Barnet, Natchez, MS, 1823-24; Pepin's, St. Louis, MO, 1826-27; J. P. Brown's, 1831; Palmer's, 1833; Eldred's, 1834. Rider and vaulter, "stands as a statue to enchant the world," and described as having "graceful enthusiasm."

PAZATTI, MLLE. Snake charmer, W. W. Cole's, 1886.

PEARSON, J. H. Bareback, hurdle and 4-horse rider. Came to this country, spring 1869, with **Frank Pastor**, who was returning from a European stay.

PEASE, CHARLES. Chief bill poster, P. T. Barnum's, 1874.

PEASE, W. L. Advance press agent, P. T. Barnum's, 1872.

PEASLEY, FLINT. Agent. John Sears', 1859, performing in the New England states; Goodwin & Co., 1860; Wambold & Whitby, 1961; Slaymaker & Nichols, 1864.

PECK, FRANK. Clown, Prof. E. Hamilton & Sargeant, 1878.

PECK, WILLIAM K. Advertiser. For many years manager of advertising car No. 1, Adam Forepaugh's. Special agent, Forepaugh's, 1891. Continued with Forepaugh until the show joined with Sells Bros.' Great Wallace, 1896; general agent, Al G. Barnes animal show, from 1920 until retirement, 1927. Known as "Exactly" Peck because in all his work everything had to be exact. [D. W. Watt: "Peck was one of the particular kind; every contract had to be just so, and if anything out of the ordinary came up, his explanation would be long and to the point."]

PECKHAM, R. W. Contractor, Great Wallace, 1896.

PEDANTO. Gymnast, tight-rope artist, balloonist. 1874.

PEDRINELLI, F. [or Perdinella]. Sideshow trained monkeys, Barnum, Bailey & Hutchinson, 1881-82.

PEEK, MYRTIE. (March 11, 1866-December 17, 1899) Equestrienne. Born n Leonidas, MI. Made debut, 1882. Sister of **Madame Marantette**. Died at her home, Silver Lake, MA, from pneumonia.

PEEL, MATT: (January 15, 1830-May 4, 1859) Born in NYC of Irish parents. When about 2 years old, his parents removed to Brooklyn, LI, where his father died, 1846. 1840, danced in public at a number of benefits at the Military Garden. 1843, organized a party to give Ethiopian concerts and traveled through Rhode Island. 1846, engaged by June & Titus to travel with their circus. Was one of the best eccentric performers on the Ethiopian stage and was never at a loss for a point upon which to "bring down the house." Extremely jealous of his reputation; would never permit another to eclipse him in fun. First to bring forward that popular saying, "He was a good man; as good a man an over lived—but he can't keep a hotel." Made last appearance on the stage at Buffalo, NY, May 2, 1859. On the morning of the 4th, about 5 o'clock, while sitting up in bed conversing with his wife, instantly expired as he was exclaiming, "Oh, May, I am dying." His wife subsequently became the wife of **J. T. Huntley.**

PEEL, TOMMY. Left with John Wilson's for the Southwest Pacific, September 18, 1865.

PELHAM, RICHARD WARD [r. n. Richard W. Pell]. (February 13, 1815-October 8, 1856) Born in NYC. Made first appearance on the stage, 1835, Bowery Theatre, NYC, with **T. D. Rice** in *Oh, Hush!*. Afterwards traveled with Turner's, executing a song and dance. Appeared at various theatres in New

York; became one of the original minstrel band and went to England. Never returned to America, 1843. Last engagement, August 1856. Died in Liverpool, England, of cancer of the stomach and was buried in Anfield Cemetery. Welch, Bartlett & Co., 1839; June, Titus, Angevine & Co., Bowery Amphitheatre, NYC, 1840; Howes & Mabie, 1841; Henry Rockwell & Co., winter 1841; Hubble & Co., 1842.

PELL, ABNER W. (d. September 27, 1865) Treasurer. Rockwell & Co.'s, 1838, 1848; Rufus Welch's, New Orleans, 1853; last engagement, Dan Castello's. Leaving the business, kept the Cottage Place Hotel, Chicago, a hangout for circus people. Died there, age 45.

PELL, CHARLES C. (1818-1889) Agent. Born in NYC. Rockwell & Co., 1847-48; Levi J. North's canal show, 1853-55; Rowe's, 1856; Eldred's, 1858; Levi J. North's, 1859; Miles' Circus Royale, Canada, 1863; Dan Castello's, 1867-69; Gregory & Orrin, 1869; James M. Nixon's, 1870; general business agent, Lake's Hippo-Olympiad, 1871; trainmaster, P. T. Barnum's, 1872; Conklin Bros.' Crystal Palace Circus, 1872; general agent, Montgomery Queen's, 1874-76. Died in Denver, age 71.

PELL, LEONARD. Juggler, L. B. Lent's, 1876.

PELL, RICHARD W. See Richard Ward Pelham.

PELLET, S. S. Clown, Hilliard, Hamilton & Hunting, 1876.

PENDERGAST, GEORGE. Acrobat, Melville, Maginley & Cooke, 1875.

PENDERGAST, JIMMY ["Curley"]. Clown. The brother of Charles Pendergast. One time, one of the **Three Renaldos**. Connected with Ringling Bros.' Died in Chicago, January 17, 1910, age 29.

PENDERGAST, JOHN. Negro minstrel, Albizu's, Havana, 1866.

PENDERGAST, WILLIAM. Zoological director, Maginley & Co., 1874.

PENNY, H. W. Gymnast, whose trapeze and horizontal bar partner was **George Goldie**, as well as others. Rice's, 1859-60, 1862; Miles' Circus Royale, Canada, spring 1863; James M. Nixon's Alhambra, NYC, fall 1863; Thayer & Noyes, 1864; S. O. Wheeler's, Boston, winter 1864-65; Stone, Rosston & Murray, winter 1866-67; Dan Rice's, 1868; (with **Lewis Kline**) trapeze and horizontal bars as the **Delevanti Brothers**, beginning in 1868; assistant manager, Haight's Great Eastern, 1874; treasurer, Melville, Maginley & Cooke, 1875.

PENTLAND, JOE. (1816-February 7, 1873) Clown. Born in Boston of poor Irish immigrant parents. One of the earliest singing clowns in America. Famous for his impromptu songs and portrayal of a drunken sailor on horseback, and as ventriloquist, balancer, and magician. Aaron Turner's, 1830-31, 1836; T. L. Stewart's, 1831-32; J. J. Hall's, 1836; June, Titus, Angevine & Co., 1839-41; Howes & Mabie, 1841; VanAmburgh's, England, 1844; Welch & Mann, 1845-46; John Try-

on's, Bowery Amphitheatre, NYC, 1845; Sands, Lent & Co., Chatham Theatre, NYC, 1847; R. Sands & Co., 1849. 1852-56, had his own show, Joe Pentland's Dramatic Equestrian Establishment. Joined Howes & Cushing, England, 1857-58; returned to America, 1859. Cooke's Royal Amphitheatre (**James M. Nixon**, proprietor), Niblo's Garden, NYC, 1860; First National Union Circus (combination of Nixon's Royal Circus and Sloat's New York Circus), NYC, fall 1861; L. B. Lent's, Philadelphia, 1861, for whom he worked on and off several years; S. P. Stickney's, 1861. **John Wilson** had a circus under the Pentland name in California, 1862, but there was no sign of Pentland being present. L. B. Lent's Broadway Amphitheatre, NYC, winter, 1863-64; S. O. Wheeler's, Boston, 1864; Dan Rice's, 1865; New American Theatre, Philadelphia, winter 1865-66. Died in NYC. **Jane Ann**, his widow, died there, May 3, 1874, in her 57th year.

PEOPLES, KATE. (d. October 30, 1877) Wife of **George Peoples**, bareback rider. Connected with Wilson & Kingsley, accompanying the show to South and Central America, 1864-65. Died in San Fancisco.

PEOPLES, GEORGE. (d. December 18, 1866) Equestrian. Lee & Marshall, 1852-56; Rowe & Marshall, 1857-58; John Wilson's, California, 1860; John Wilson's "Joe Pentland" Circus, California, 1862; Orrin's, San Francisco, 1863; Chiarini's, 1866; Grand Reserve Combination, 1866. Major circus activity was confined to the West Coast. Became one of the chief mine owners of the famous Reese River claims at Austin, Nevada Territory. Died of cholera in Houston, TX.

PEPIN, VICTOR. Rider. Native of Philadelphia of French extraction. In the partnership of Pepin & Breschard, who brought their circus, including horses and company, to Boston from Spain, winter 1807-08. June 2, opened in NYC, corner of Broadway and Anthony Street, probably performing nearly continuously until the end of December. Followed by opening in Philadelphia, Ninth and Walnut Streets, February 2, 1809. Returned to NYC, opening July 1, 1809, and continuing until August 26. The company seems to have alternated seasonally between New York and Philadelphia for several years, offering both circus performances and horse dramas. In circus management in USA from 1807 to 1827. Small in stature and dark-eyed, the father of 4 children, a proficient rider and an excellent trainer of horses. Stuart Thayer describes him as "one of the foremost contributors to the history of the American circus." Pepin & Breschard, along with partner Cayetano Mariotini, have the distinction of taking the first organized circus company beyond the Appalachians, which occured spring, 1814, when the company performed in Pittsburgh and then in Cincinnati. Charleston stand, fall 1814, was the last in which the two rider/managers were together; company was split at the end of November, Breschard taking his compliment to Savannah and Pepin continuing at Charleston through the beginning of January, 1815. Left the country and did not return until 1816; when he opened a circus in Philadelphia to little success. After **James West's** troupe landed in NYC that year, Pepin induced him to come to Philadelphia, presumably at the place Pepin had been occupying, intending to revive his fortunes through West. Opened in Baltimore for a time, 1817. Organized a group of stockholders to purchase the Olympic, Philadelphia, sometime in 1818, and presented hippodramas. Appeared again, August 1821, Pensacola, FL, newly arrived from Havana, to take advantage of the influx of people for the exchanging of flags between the United States and Spain. Following year, in New Orleans, associated with a performer named **Barnet** in conducting the Olympic Circus. April 12, 1823, farewell advertisement was issued through the press and the company worked its way to St. Louis, MO; after many reverses, returned to Philadelphia, 1831, poor and friendless; an offer to give riding lessons got little response; compassionately, the management of the Arch Street Theatre held a benefit in his name. Regarding his tour, Thayer quotes the *Mississippian*: "When we speak of Mr. Pepin we must give him higher praise than that which belongs merely to the leader of a band of excellent equestrians. His gentlemanly deportment and correctness of principal place him far above such praise." Was a dashing rider, who executed surprising leaps over boards and ribbons, and daring feats astride two horses. [T. Allston Brown: "I have not seen a more dexterous or sure equestrian since Pepin."]

PEPPER, THOMAS. Gymnast. John Robinson's, 1857; Thayer's (**Thayer** and **Phelps**, proprietors), a small clown troupe, 1861; George W. DeHaven & Co., 1866; Dan Castello's, 1867-69; E. Stowe's Northwestern, 1871.

PERCIVAL, DAVID. 16-horse chariot driver, Stone & Murray, 1869.

PERCIVAL, R. General performer, Driesbach & Howes, 1868.

PERCY, ALEXANDER. Iron-jaw man, Ryland's, returning to California after about 5 years spent in South and Central America, 1878.

PERCY, FRANK. Agent, W. H. Stowe's, 1881.

PERCY, HARRY. Courtney & Sanford's Minstrels, a party made up in New York to travel with Courtney & Sanford's Circus in South America. Sailed from New York, July 23, 1873.

PERDITTI, A. Equestrian, John Robinson's, 1881.

PEREZ, MARINO. Peruvian contortionist and foot juggler. John Lamb's, 1831; Joseph D. Palmer's, 1833; Crane & Eldred, 1834; Buckley, Weeks & Co., 1835; Boston Lion Circus, 1836; Lion Theatre Circus, 1837; Robinson & Foster, 1844; Welch & Mann, 1846; R. Sands', 1849. Performed with Italian sticks and balanced a 16" globe on his feet, and concluded by dancing a Hornpipe feet upwards, with a pole on them 10' in length.

PERILLE, ROMANZA. Stone, Rosston & Murray, 1866;

Whitby & Co., 1867.

PERINE, FRANK. Gymnast, Sells Bros.', 1873-74.

PERKINS, J. H. Brass band leader, George W. DeHaven's, 1865.

PERLEY, FRANK L. Agent, Barnum, Bailey & Hutchinson, 1882; succeeded **David S. Thomas** as press agent, P. T. Barnum's, 1885-87; press representative, Barnum & Bailey, 1891-93.

PERPENO. Mexican clown, Howes' New London, 1888.

PERRIN, W. Elephant keeper, western unit of June, Titus, Angevine & Co., 1842.

PERRY, ALBERT. Lowande & Hoffman, 1887.

PERRY, EBEN WOOD. Equestrian. A lengthy career in the American circus. H. H. Fuller's, 1838; J. W. Stocking's, 1839; Howes & Mabie, 1841; Comanche chief, Welch's, Philadelphia, 1843; Howes and Gardner, 1844; Nathan A. Howes', 1845; Rockwell & Stone, 1845; Sands, Lent, 1846-47; E. F. & J. Mabie's, 1848; Dr. Gilbert R. Spalding's, 1849; Welch & Delevan, 1849; Spalding & Rogers, 1849-53, as "the Olympic Jehu, and without competitor in his 4-horse acts"; equestrian director, Wesley Barmore's, 1854; equestrian director, Mabie's, 1856; Hyatt Frost's, 1857; VanAmburgh & Co., Broadway Theatre, winter 1857-58; New National Circus (**John Tryon,** proprietor), winter 1857-58; George F. Bailey & Co., 1858-61; VanAmburgh & Co., 1859; Antonio Bros.'s, 1862; 3 and 4-horse rider, Levi J. North's, 1863; equestrian director, Lake & Co., winter, 1863-64; equestrian director and 2 and 4-horse rider, Yankee Robinson's, Chicago, 1866-67; 2-horse act, Dan Rice's, 1868; equestrian director, Campbell's, 1869; Stowe's, 1870; equestrian director, G. G. Grady's, 1871; Central Park, 1872; North American Circus (**Asa B. Stow,** manager), 1873-77; Sells Bros.', 1878; equestrian director, Great Commonwealth, transported by the boat, *William Newman,* 1879. Patriarch of the Perry clan of riders, which included daughters **Minnie, Jennie, Isabella, Julia,** and son **Tom.** Of the group, **Minnie** was the only one to pursue a lengthy career.

PERRY, ISABELLA. Equestrienne daughter of **E. W. Perry,** George F. Bailey & Co., 1858-62; Lake's, 1863.

PERRY, JENNIE. Equestrienne daughter of **E. W. Perry.** VanAmburgh's, Broadway Theatre, December 1857; George F. Bailey & Co., 1860-61; Lake & Co., 1863; Dan Rice's, 1869. Later, married and retired from the profession.

PERRY, JULIA. Equestrienne daughter of **E. W. Perry.** G. G. Grady's, 1871.

PERRY, MINNIE. (d. 1886) Equestrienne daughter of **E. W. Perry.** George F. Bailey & Co., 1860; Yankee Robinson's, 1865; 2-horse act with her father and also performed with her 2 ponies, Puck and Oberon, Dan Rice's, 1868; principal and pony acts, Campbell's, 1869; G. G. Grady's, 1871; Central Park Circus, 1872; J. W. Wilder's, 1873; North American, 1875; New York Central Park, 1877; Sells Bros.', 1878; principal equestrienne, Great Commonwealth, transported by the

237

boat, *William Newman,* 1879; Orrin Bros.', Mexico, winter 1882. Married **Carlos Dashway** (or Dashaway). **Dashway** was with Nathans & Co., 1882, when his wife gave birth to baby girl, Philadelphia. Circus Ciniselli, St. Petersburg, Russia, 1883; Sells Bros.', 1886. Died of typhoid fever.

PERRY, OLIVER H. Acrobat. Brown & Mills, 1838, later as Waterman & Co.; Waring & Raymond, 1842.

PERRY, OSCAR P. Band leader. Rivers & Derious, 1857, 1864; Stone, Rosston & Murray, 1867; Stone & Murray, 1870-72; John H. Murray's, 1873, 1879; S. P. Stickney & Son's, 1874; Cameron's Great Oriental, 1875; E. H. Howes', 1888.

PERRY, S. J. Equestrian, George F. Bailey & Co., 1861-62.

PERRY, THOMAS. Equestrian. The son of **E. W. Perry.** George F. Bailey & Co., 1860-61; Lake & Co., 1863; Yankee Robinson's, 1865.

PERRY, THOMAS R. Press agent, Doris & Colvin, 1887.

PERRY, W. C. (March 11, 1836-February 3, 1900) Proprietor, Perry's, 1887.

PERRY, WILLIAM H. Assistant manager, with Rosston, Springer & Henderson, 1872.

PETEROFF, THEODORE. (d. January, 1904) Sideshow performer, billed as "**Jo Jo, the Dog Faced Boy.**" Stood 5' in height and had a thick covering of hair over his entire body and peculiarly shaped head. Money-making curiosity, brought to the United States from Russia by **Nick Forster** and first exhibited, 1885, as one of the principals of Barnum & Bailey, Madison Square Garden. S. H. Barrett's, 1887. Later, with Barnum & Bailey for several years. Died of pneumonia in Salomica, Turkey.

PETERS, PROF. Chicago band leader, Howe & Norton, 1864; Great European, 1865.

PETERS, S. C. Proprietor and treasurer, Great Trans-Atlantic Allied Shows, 1879.

PETERSON, JACK. Clown, John Robinson's, 1857-58.

PETERSON, JOHN. Clown. Howes & Sands, 1834-35; Robinson & Eldred, 1847.

PETERSON, JOHN. Elephant trainer and boss animal man, Reichold Shows, 1897.

PETTIT, CHARLES. Main & Burdick, 1880; clown, Frank A. Robbins', 1888.

PETTIT, C. W. Band leader, New York Central Park Circus, 1877.

PETTIT, S. S. Clown, Goldenburg's (**John V. O'Brien**, proprietor), 1874.

PETTIT, THOMAS. (b. 1863) Acrobat. Born in Zanesville, OH. Performed with various partners—**Charles E. McVey, Danny Ryan, James Stitt.** Hilliard & Main, 1883; aerial return act, Sells Bros.', 1888-89; French & Co., 1891; Walter L. Main, 1895; bars and double trapeze, Wallace & Co., 1896. After marriage, formed a family act with wife, **Elizabeth,** and sons, **Ray, Walter, Charles.**

PEZOLT, CHARLES. Band leader, Johnson & Co., 1881.

PFAU, JOSEPH. (d. October 10, 1870) Russian athlete. Born in St. Petersburg but spent most of his life in France. First USA performance, L. B. Lent's New York Circus, 1867-68. Flying trapeze, winter circus, Academy of Music, New Orleans, January, 1869; Hanlon Brothers combination, 1869. Death occurred at Chester, Orange County, NY, age about 29.

PHANLON BROTHERS [Louis, William, Wash]. Acrobats. Martell, Phanlon & Co., 1885.

PHELPS, CHARLES Agent, Dan Rice's, 1863-64.

PHELPS, FRANK C. Posturer with 4 pupils, Washburn's, 1855; Dan Rice's, 1857; clown, Yankee Robinson's, 1860; Dr. James L. Thayer's (**Thayer** and Phelps), a small clown troupe, 1861; James M. Nixon's, Washington, DC, fall 1862.

PHELPS, LEW. Clog and jig dancer, Hippocomoque, 1868.

PHELPS, MARY. Rider, L. B. Lent's, 1862.

PHELPS, P. A. Orator, Reed's, 1893.

PHELPS, W. H. Ringmaster, Great New York Circus, 1877; James T. Johnson's, 1888; Lemen Bros.', 1891.

PHILLIPE, SAM. Ringmaster. Brown's Mammoth Arena, 1834-36; Bacon & Derious, 1838; Welch, Bartlett & Co., 1839.

PHILLIPS, C. H. Treasurer, Phillips-Scott Union Pacific Circus, 1888.

PHILLIPS, CLYDE. Juggler, slack-wire performer, Wallace & Anderson, 1890.

PHILLIPS, SAM. Debut January 1, 1828, Providence Circus; no longer apprentice, Brown & Weeks, 1834; ringmaster, Brown's, 1835; ringmaster, Brown & Co., 1836; ringmaster, Bacon & Derious, 1838-39; clown, Welch & Bartlett, 1839.

PICARD, P. E. Agent, Chiarini's, South and Central America, 1869.

PICARDO, M. Contortionist and equilibrist, Bruce L. Baldwin's, 1894.

PICKETT, SAMUEL. Acrobat, G. G. Grady's, 1874.

PIERCE, A. W. N. Smith's Ethiopians, VanAmburgh & Co., 1860.

PIERCE, ALVIZA. Lion tamer. Raymond & Co., 1846-47; animal keeper, P. T. Barnum's, 1851-53; Howes' European, winter 1864, took over the lions after the death of Crockett, 1865, 1867-70; Yankee Robinson's, Chicago, 1866; zoological director, Howes & Cushing, 1875; supt. of zoological department, Montgomery Queen's, 1876. He entered the den and compelled the wild beasts to perform groupings, pyramids, and leaping through hoops and balloons of fire; he fed them raw meat with his naked hands and discharged fire-arms while there.

PIERCE, EARL H. (1823-June 5, 1859) Born in NYC. Went on to become one of the greatest comic banjo soloists of his day and to achieve fame by his song of "Hoop-de-dooden-do." First appearance before the public, Philadelphia, Ogden & Raymond's Circus. Then, 1842, joined a minstrel party composed of **Frank Brower, Jimmy O'Connell, Frank Diamond, Mestayer, Dan Emmett,** and **Master Pierce.** At this time, they were performing at Franklin Theatre, NYC. Leaving the minstrels for a while, joined Turner's Circus. Later, E. P. Christy's Minstrels. Went to England, 1856, and died suddenly in London 3 years later.

PIERCE, MINNIE. Aerialist, McMahon's, 1888.

PIERCE, S. L. (d. February 12, 1887) In charge of the Tom Thumb group, P. T. Barnum's.

PIERSON, CHARLES H. General agent, Phil Diefenbach', 1892.

PIESLEY, ROBERT. Equestrian director, Albert M. Wetter's New Model Shows, 1893.

PINDS, SAMUEL. Haight & Chambers, 1867.

PINKMAN, J. Detective, P. T. Barnum's, 1873.

PIQUET, VICTOR. (d. 1848) Contortionist. St. Charles Circus, New Orleans, 1841; Hobby & Pratt, 1842; Spalding's North American, 1842, 1847; Nathan A. Howes', winter 1843-44; Howes & Gardner, 1844; Rockwell & Stone, 1844-46; S. P. Stickney's, 1847. Died in New Orleans of cholera.

PITRE ["Peter the African"]. First to be advertised as a vaulter. Pepin & Breschard, Charleston, 1807-08, leaping 5 horses and 2 "fiery galleries"; Stewart's, 1809; Davis', 1810; Cayetano's, 1811.

PIZZARRO, J. H. George W. DeHaven & Co., 1865.

PLATE, WILLIAM. Master of horse, Adam Forepaugh's, 1875.

PLATT, GEORGE. Advance agent, P. T. Barnum's, 1875.

PLATT, RICHARD. Co-proprietor, with James M. Nixon's, 1865.

PLATT, WILLIAM. Boss hostler, Adam Forepaugh's, 1872.

PLATTNER, HIRAM. Aeronaut, "Trip to the Clouds," G. G. Grady's, 1873.

PLIMPTON, GEORGE. Celebrated Kent bugler, James W. Bancker's, traveling in New York state, 1832.

PLUNKARD, A. J. Treasurer, Albert M. Wetter's New Model Shows., 1893.

PLUTANO AND WAINO. (1827-May or June 1912) Exhibited with his brother, **Waino** as the "Wild Men from Borneo." Actual names were **Hiram W.** and **Barney Davis.** Was advertised they were brought to America in the 1850s by a **Capt. Hammond,** who claimed he found them in the wilds of Borneo. Actually, **Hiram** was born on Long Island, **Barney** in England. The bidding for their services was stiff but they became major curiosities on a level with **Jo Jo, the Dog-Faced Boy** and the **Siamese Twins.** [Prof. J. Frank Stanley: "The Museum and sideshow stories about their early ferocity, their aboriginal dialect, their gradual yielding to training, and their wonderful strength were founded mainly on fact."] The brothers never weighed more than 45 pounds each but they had the strength to lift full grown men. Although they had subnormal mentalities, they were good natured and gentle. **Waino** died at

the age of 80. **Plutano** died at the age of 87 at the home of Henry D. Warner in Waltham, MA. Warner's father, **Hanaford Warner,** was their manager for more than 50 years.

POGGY, JOHN. Elephant trainer. From Salem, NJ. Adam Forepaugh's, 1888. Killed on September 25 of that year, DuBois, PA, while attempting to unload an elephant that had been angered from being fed apples by spectators which contained tobacco and pepper.

POLAND, THOMAS W. Equestrian director, Castello & VanVleck's, 1863-64; ringmaster, equestrian director, Haight & Chambers, 1867; ringmaster, C. T. Ames', New Orleans, 1868; ringmaster, Noyes' Crescent City, 1870-72. Spent summer, 1871, breaking pad horses and trick mules for Noyes. Great International, 1873-74. Married **Carlotta R. Davis** in Louisville, Kentucky, January 27, 1874. The bride was a native of that city.

POMEROY, W. H. Proprietor, Great International Railroad Shows, 1891-92. Collapsed at Anaheim, CA, July 1892.

POOLE, THOMAS [or Pool]. Claiming to be the "first American who ever exhibited feats of equestrianism on the continent," erected the first circus structure in Philadelphia, south side of Market Street, between Schuylkill, 7th and 8th, 1775. Tickets for the "first" seats were 5 shillings and for the "second" seats 3 shillings, ninepence. One act in his program consisted of 3 horses that imitated "playing dead," one groaning as if in pain, then rising and bowing to the audience; another sitting up like a "lady's lap dog."

PORTER. Contortionist, Frost & Co., 1837.

PORTER, DAVID. Boss canvasman, Warner & Henderson, 1874.

PORTER, ELEAZER. Innkeeper, Hartford, CT, who constructed a building suitable for circus performances behind his hotel, 1824, and became, as Stuart Thayer suggests, the first non-professional involved in arena ownership.

PORTER, JOE. Treasurer. J. E. Warner & Co., 1871; Warner & Henderson, 1874.

PORTER, MAMIE. Fat lady, John B. Doris', 1883. Married **Mons. Fowler,** "the White Moor," in Dover, NJ, August 26, 1883.

PORTER, WALTER. (d. December 9, 1912) Acrobat. Member and founder of the **Melrose Troupe,** connected with Barnum & Bailey and other such organizations. Died, Bridgeport, CT, age 41.

PORTER, WILLIAM. Contracting agent, Wallace & Co., 1885.

PORTER, WILLIAM H. ["Billy"]. (d. January 25, 1903) Clown. Hemmings, Cooper & Whitby, 1869; Philadelphia Circus, winter 1870-71; Rosston, Springer & Henderson, 1871-72; L. B. Lent's, 1873; clown, P. T. Barnum's, 1875; New National Theatre, Philadelphia, winter 1876-77; Cooper & Bailey, South America, 1878; Anderson & Co., 1879. Opened a saloon, Twelfth and Callowhill Streets, Philadelphia, January 1873. Died in that city.

POSEY, JAKE. (b. June 27, 1863) Noted driver of 10 to 40-horse teams. Born in Cedar Grove, IN. Made his home in Cincinnati. First year on the road, VanAmburgh & Co., 1880; Sells Bros.', 1881-83; S. H. Barrett, 1884-87; drove beautiful 6-horse bill wagon, Stowe, Long & Gumble, 1888; Miller & Freeman, 1889; Adam Forepaugh's, 1890; boss hostler, John Robinson's, 1891; boss hostler, Robert Hunting's, 1893-95; Barnum & Bailey, 1896; B. E. Wallace & Co., 1897; Barnum & Bailey, in Europe, 1897-1902; Buffalo Bill's, 1903-07; Campbell's, 1910; Yankee Robinson's, 1911-13; Hagenbeck & Wallace, 1914-16; Al G. Barnes', 1921; Sparks', 1923-30; Al G. Barnes', 1931-35; Hagenbeck & Wallace, 1936. Wife, **Jessie**, was a non-professional.

POST, SIMON B. W. Band leader. Rockwell & Stone, 1843; Howes & Gardner, 1844; June & Turner, 1847; Col. Mann's, 1849; Rufus Welch's, 1850-52; Welch & Lent, 1855; Yankee Robinson's, 1867.

POTTER, CHARLES A. (d. June 23, 1918) Program agent, John H. Murray's, 1874-75; press agent, 1877; Den W. Stone's, 1878; advertising car supt., Adam Forepaugh's, 13 years off and on through 1894; Great Wallace, 1895-98, completing 27th year as an advertiser. At end of season, located in Danielson, CT, as an advertising agent and reporter for the *Wendham County Transcript*. Died at St. Cloud, FL, age 73.

POTTER, HARRY, and ELLA. Trapeze performers. Fulford & Co., 1890; Sells Bros.', 1891; W. B. Reynolds', 1892.

POTTER, JOHN T. Proprietor and manager. Native of Ogdenburg, NY. On the road with John T. Potter's Victory Arena and Great Western Circus, 1844-46; the latter year, his final year of circus management, changed the title to great Empire Circus.

POWELL, CHAUNCEY. George Richards', 1888; World's Fair Aggregation, 1891; Richard's Big Show (**Dick P. Sutton**, proprietor), 1892.

POWELL, LEE. (d. August 1896) Clown. Great Orion, Old Bowery, NYC, 1861; Dan Rice's, 1862; Alex Robinson's, 1865; Robinson & Lake, 1863, 1867; equestrian director and clown, John Robinson's, 1866; clown, Alex Robinson's, 1866, 1869, 1874, 1877; George Bailey & Co., 1867; advertiser, John Robinson's, 1868; general agent, James Robinson's, winter 1870-71; Van's Olympic, 1872; James E. Cooke's, 1880; James T. Johnson's, 1884; Sig. Sautelle's, 1889; contracting agent, Bailey & Winan, 1890; Sautelle's Old Reliable, 1895. Married **Miss Emily Trayer** of Minersville, PA, August 4, 1866. Died in Albany, NY.

POWERS, GEORGE. Lake's Hippo-Olympiad, 1869.

POWERS, PERRY. Formerly a hotel keeper. Proprietor of Perry Powers' Combination Circus, 1867.

PRATT, CHARLES M. Proprietor, Lee's Circus, California, 1871; press agent, Cooper & Jackson, 1880.

PRATT, F. C. General agent, G. G. Grady's, 1871.

PRENDERGAST, JOHN. Agent, with Holland & McMahon, 1888.

PRENTICE, ALEX. George W. DeHaven's, operated by Andrew Haight, 1865-66; Haight & Chambers, 1867. Married **Alice Cromwell**, Cincinnati September 3, 1867. Killed in a barroom, Memphis, TN, November 4, 1867, age 38. A shoemaker by trade but had been in the circus business in recent years.

PRENTICE, FEDERICK ["Kid"]. (d. April, 1915) Associate with Barnum & Bailey for several years. Died in Bridgeport, MA, age 53.

PRESCOTT, CHARLES F. (b. April 4, 1867) Proprietor, Great Eastern, 1895-97. Show and winter quarters burned, spring 1900.

PRESTON, WILLIAM C. Agent. Rockwell & Co. (Stokes' unit), 1848; S. P. Stickney's, 1849, agent for museum, 1855; Spalding & Rogers, 1856; arrested for murder, Cincinnati, 1856; Robinson & Lake, July 1859; contracting agent, Dan Rice's, 1860; general agent, Dan Rice's, 1861.

PRICE, CHARLES. (d. January 4, 1913) Sideshow albino. Adam Forepaugh's, 1883. At one time with John Robinson's. Died from bronchitis and heart trouble, East Liverpool, OH, age 76.

PRICE, FRANK. Boss canvasman, John Robinson's, 1880.

PRICE, STEPHEN. Son of a well-to-do family, a lawyer, a partner with **Edmund Simpson** in proprietorship of the Park Theatre, NYC, beginning in 1812. When they considered **James West's** circus company to be threatening competition, they developed a scheme to buy him out, circulating a rumor that they were about to construct an arena for circus performances, and hiring **Sam Tatnall** to break horses in a lot behind the theatre. This charade was enough to convince **West** to sell out to them and return to England, well paid for his efforts.

PRICE, W. H. Manager, Price & James Shows, 1897.

PRICE & HANNON. Trapeze performers, Great European, 1865. See Richard H. Hannon.

PRIDHAM, WILLIAM. Agent. H. C. Lee's, 1858; Bassett's, 1861; John Wilson's, American Theatre, San Francisco, 1860, 1862. Most familiar with routing in California.

PRIEST, B. Proprietor, Paris Pavilion Show, 1883-86; Priest & Co.'s Great Western, 1887, taken over same year by Penn & Leon.

PRIMROSE, C. S. [r. n. Cready Smith]. Agent. Lithographer, Bailey's London, 1890-91; general agent, Fred Locke's, 1892-93; agent, E. G. Holland & Co., 1894; special agent, Cooke & Whitby, 1894; contracting agent, J. H. LaPearl's, 1895-97; Gentry Bros.', unit #1, 1898-1903; assistant general agent, Gollmar Bros.'s, 1904-05; "Uncle Si Haskins" Co., winter 1904-05; Gentry Bros.', 1905-06. Following this, was owner and manager of several hall shows. Married **Myrtle B. Webb**, non-professional, December 27, 1895, in Akron, OH. She died

January 18, 1952.

PRIMROSE, GEORGE S. Negro minstrel concert feature, John Robinson's, 1872; general agent, with Alington Minstrels, winter 1893-94; general contracting agent, Holland & Co., 1894; J. H. LaPearl's, 1894.

PRINCE RANDIAN [or Randion]. Born with neither arms nor legs. Reported to have been brought to America from British Guiana by **P. T. Barnum**, 1889. Exhibited in a one-piece woolen sack, in which he moved about by wiggling his hips and shoulders, much like a snake. At various times, billed as "the Snake Man" and "the Caterpillar Man." Performed in carnivals, circuses and dime museums for 45 years. Was married and had 5 children. Died at age 63.

PRINGLE, CHARLES. Bill poster, P. T. Barnum's, 1873.

PRITCHARD, MONS. Cannon king, with John Forepaugh's, California, 1888.

PROBST, A. Band leader, L. B. Lent's, 1861.

PROCTOR, F. F. See Fred Levantine.

PROCTOR, ROBERT. (d. June 19, 1888) Circus proprietor.

PROSHO, THOMAS. Band leader, Metropolitan Pavilion, 1874.

PROSSER, J. Rider and vaulter. Aprentice to **Ben Brown**. John B. Green & Doolittle, 1825; J. Purdy Brown's, 1825, 1826; Pavilion Circus, 1826; Ben Brown's, 1828 (no longer an apprentice); Asa T. Smith's, 1829; Ben Brown's 1830; French, Hobby & Co., 1835.

PROTZMAM, PROF. A. Band leader, Orton Bros.', 1866-67.

PRYNE, FRANK. Property master, Cooper, Bailey & Co., 1879.

PUCKROILL, ALEXANDER. Buffo clown and jester, with E. F. & J. Mabie's, 1851, advertised as "King of Clowns."

PUGOL BROTHERS. Wrestling bears, Dan Rice's, 1891.

PULLIS. Slack-rope performer. Mount Pitt Circus, NYC, fall 1826; Lafayette Circus, NYC, January 1827.

PULLMAN, DOT. The daughter of **Giles Pullman**. Rolling globe act which featured playing musical instruments while balancing. Shelby, Pullman & Hamilton, 1881; Irwin Bros.', 1887.

PULLMAN, FRED. Walter L. Main's, 1888.

PULLMAN, GILES. (1836-October 11, 1900) Agent. Born in Herkimer County, NY. Brother of **Henry Pullman**. Enlisted in Co. A, 117th New York Volunteers, and served through the Civil War. General agent, Alex Robinson's, 1866; privileges (with brother **Henry**), Adam Forepaugh's, 1873-1876; Pullman & Hamilton, 1880; director of advance brigade, Shelby, Pullman & Hamilton, 1881; Maybury, Pullman & Hamilton, 1882; general agent, Frank Robbins', 1883; proprietor and advance agent, Hilliard, Pullman, Mack & Co., 1884; Col. Giles' Great World's Fair (Giles Pullman, proprietor), 1885-86; general agent, Walter L. Main's, 1887-89, 1896; general agent, Irwin Bros.', 1888; managed a museum

in Antwerp, Pawnee Bill's Wild West Show, during the exposition, 1894-95; toured Germany with an Indian troupe, 1898; agent, Harrison Bros.', 1900. [Charles Bernard: "Mr. Pullman impressed me as a man of wonderful knowledge, kind hearted, courteous and a friend to young men who were willing to learn and earn an honest living. He proved to be all of that, and was my warm friend for many years."] Died from pneumonia at his home, Buffalo, NY.

PULLMAN, HENRY. (1839-March 28, 1925) Born in Herkimer, NY. Brother of **Giles Pullman**. Started in the circus business with Levy J. North's boat show, 1860, traveling the Erie Canal. Remained in the business some 50 years. George F. Bailey & Co., 1863; Alexander Robinson's, 1864; John Robinson's, on a boat tour of the Mississippi and Ohio Rivers, 1869; manager, Macarte Sisters' Great Parisian Circus, 1870; privileges (with brother **Giles**), Adam Forepaugh's, 1873-76; general superintendent, Shelby, Pullman & Hamilton, 1881; Pullman, Dingess & Co.'s Circus (Henry Pullman and **R. S. Dingess**, proprietors), 1885; Pullman's, 1886; treasurer, Walter L. Main's, 1891; purchasing agent, Campbell Bros.', 1910. Left the circus to take a position at the Pan-American Exposition, 1901, but returned at the close of the exposition and remained until 1912, after which he became a ticket taker at the Strand Theatre, Buffalo, where he remained until 1924. Died at his home in Buffalo, NY, following a stroke, age 87.

PULVER, CRETE. Supt. advertising car #2, Cooper, Bailey & Co., 1880-82.

PURDY, EISENHART. (b. 1799) Menagerie proprietor, a member of the Zoological Institute. Native of Westchester County, NY. Co-proprietor, Carley, Purdy & Wright, 1830; co-proprietor, Purdy, Carley & Bailey, 1831; co-proprietor, Purdy, Welch, Finch & Wright, 1832; co-proprietor, Purdy, Welch, Macomber & Co., 1833-37.

PURDY, S. S. Negro minstrel, Spalding & Rogers' *Floating Palace*, 1859.

PURVIS, JOHNNY. English talking and knockabout clown. Along with trained donkeys, Adam Forepaugh's, 1882-83, 1887-89, 1893; principal clown, Sells Bros.', 1884-86; Barnum & Bailey, 1892; Frank A. Gardner's, South America, 1896; True & McVeigh's, 1896. Wife, **Clara Purvis**, performed trick horses and a running globe act. Was divorced from her, 1888.

PURVIS, ROBERT. Trained dogs, W. B. Reynolds' Consolidated Shows, 1892.

PURVIS SISTERS [Ada, Adell]. High-wire performers, Sells Bros.', 1884-85; Doris & Colvin, 1887.

PUTNAM, P. S. Band leader, E. F. & J. Mabie's, 1848-51.

PUTNAM. Elephant keeper. Handler of the elephant Columbus. Purdy, Welch, Macomber & Co., 1833; June, Titus, Angevine & Co., 1836; Grand Zoological and Ornithological Exhibition, 1836; H. Ludington & Co., 1837.

Q

QUAGLIENI, SEBASTIAN [billed as Signor Sebastion]. (d. January 4, 1882) Equestrian. Father of **Louis** and **Romeo Sebastian**. Performed in America for about 25 years and was considered excellent in somersault and carrying acts and as a bareback rider. It was said he rode with ease and grace and his posturing was daring. One of his feats was hanging onto a horse with one knee. Joe Pentland's, 1856; Cooke's Royal Amphitheatre, Niblo's Garden, NYC (**James M. Nixon**, proprietor), 1860; First National Union Circus (combination of Nixon's Royal Circus and Sloat's New York Circus), 1861; Madigan's, 1861; S. P. Stickney's, 1861; John Wilson's, San Francisco, 1863; J. F. Orrin's, South America, 1865-66; Chiarini's, New Orleans, 1866, and Mexico City, 1867; single and double riding act, George F. Bailey & Co., 1868-72, 1874; William T. Aymar's European and American, 1870; P. T. Barnum's, winter 1872-73, 1873; bareback and somersault rider, Montgomery Queen's, California, 1877; VanAmburgh & Co., winter 1877-78; P. T. Barnum's, 1880. VanAmburgh & Co., 1881. Had just closed an engagement, Dockrill & Leon, Iron Amphitheatre, Havana, when stricken with yellow fever and died.

QUAID, JOSEPH P. (d. January 17, 1905) Number of years treasurer, Standard and Trocadero Theatres, Philadelphia; treasurer, Adam Forepaugh's, 1890-94; England, 1895, to instruct ticket sellers for the first tour of Barnum & Bailey abroad; managerial position, Buffalo Bill's Wild West Show, 7 years; 2 years, assistant treasurer, Weber & Fields Music Hall, NYC, later managing a road company for them; manager, West End Theatre, NYC, 1903; manager, "An English Daisy" Co., 1904. Died in Philadelphia.

QUARTERO, ELOISE. Auronaut, Hummel, Hamilton & Co.'s, 1897.

QUEEN, FRANK. Publisher of the New York *Clipper*, first appearing April 30, 1853, to serve as a theatrical and sporting weekly. Sporting subjects included boat racing, prize fighting, baseball, pedestrianism and even checkers. Paper's theatrical focus increased during the 1860s, until, practically speaking, it was the only periodical in America dealing with show business news throughout the decade from 1865 to 1875, and it continued in the forefront as such until competition from the *Billboard* and *Variety* forced its demise, 1924. The paper was sold to Frank Queen, 1855, who, as sole proprietor and editor, soon established it as a major organ for sporting and theatrical reportage. Under his guilding force the paper befriended the popular amusements neglected by other publications. In addition to its dramatic interests, it became the major source for circus, minstrel, and variety news, a position it held throughout the century.

QUEEN, G. Gymnast, John Robinson's, 1885.

QUEEN, MONTGOMERY. (October 13, 1821-September 13, 1901) Native of Brooklyn, NY. Purchased an interest in Rosston, Springer & Co. from Adam Forepaugh, November 1872, and put Montgomery Queen's on the road the following year at Hatboro, PA. Wintered at Hayward, CA, 1874. Exhibited corner of Jackson Street and Montgomery Avenue, San Francisco 42 consecutive performances, during which he had a "Ride of Champions" between the great James Robinson and Charles Fish. Montgomery Queen's California Menagerie, Caravan and Double Circus, West Coast, 1877. Announced February, 1878, circus under Queen's name would travel no more; filed for bankruptcy at that time and outfit was sold at auction. Failure and forced sale ended circus career and he faded from view. 1879 was reported to be connected with a trolly company, Brooklyn. Operated a remunerative livery stable there, the barn with his name over the door remaining a Brooklyn landmark as late as 1932.

QUICK, ELAM C. Manager, with Chiarini's, Havana, winter 1859-60; sideshow manager, George F. Bailey & Co., 1860, 1871; Howe's European, winter 1864-65.

QUICK, FRED H. (1843?-February 24, 1892) Advertiser. Native of New Orleans. As a boy, was employed by local theatres, starting as a billposter in the 1860s. Joined C. T. Ames' advance brigade, 1867, and shortly was promoted to advertising agent. Contracting agent, Charles Noyes', winter 1871-72; Haight's Great Eastern, 1874; press agent, W. W. Cole's, 1875; special agent, Sells Bros.', 1879-82; general advertiser, S. H. Barrett's, 1885. Also connected with theatrical enterprises, at various times, working for **Charles R. Pope**, **Thomas H. Hall**, and **James H. Wallack**. Advertising agent, Eugene Robinson's Dime Museum, New Orleans, 1890-91; Henry Greenwall's Grand Opera House in that city, 1892. Died there, age 49. Was never married.

QUICK, GERARD C. (May 9, 1811-January 20, 1869) Born in North Salem, Westchester Co., NY. Sideshow, Clayton, Welch, 1844; VanAmburgh's, United Kingdom, 1845-46; bought interest in Sands, Nathans & Co., 1846; manager, June, Titus & Co.'s Circus, 1849; proprietor, G. C. Quick's, 1850, 1851; partner, Sands & Quick, 1852; proprietor, Sands & Quick's, 1853; partner, Franconi's Hippodrome, NYC, 1853; spring 1867, with **Avery Smith**, **David Bidwell**, **John Nathans**, and **Dr. Gilbert R. Spalding**, took a circus to France for the Paris Exposition; shortly after arrival, was stricken with a stroke; returned to USA, where he recovered. George Bailey & Co. (**Avery Smith**, G. C. Quick and **John Nathans**, proprietors), 1867. Opened a variety theatre, NYC, 1868. Died in NYC. Left an estate of $200,000.

QUICK, ISAAC. Native of Westchester County, NY. Partner with **Jeremiah P. Fogg** and **Abraham H. Mead**, 1826. Their Washington Circus was one of the earliest to tour with a canvas pavilion—50' round top and expenses of $35 to $40 a day. The men also owned an interest in Fogg & Howes' menagerie at this time.

QUICK, J. C. Co-owner, Howe's European Circus, 1865.

QUIGLEY, JAMES. Clown. Adam Forepaugh's, 1879; Miller, Stowe & Freeman, 1887.

QUIGLEY, JOHN F. (1867?-July 23, 1896) General performer. Born in England. Made professional debut in the United States with **William Conners** as part of the team of **Conners & Quigley.** Other partners at various times were **Joe Edwards, James H. Cole, Joe Hinckey,** and **John Coyne.** Performed in the leading variety theatres and for a time was a member of Sheridan A. Flynn's City Sports Co. As a circus performer, was connected with S. H. Barrett & Co., 1883; John B. Doris', 1885; leaper and equestrian director, Holland & McMahon, Chicago, winter 1885-86; W. H. Harris' Nickel-Plate, 1888; Holland & Gormley, 1889; John F. Wood's, 1889; John S. McMahon's, 1892; Charles McMahon's, 1893. Died at his home in Philadelphia, age 29.

QUILLIN, LEW. Musical clown, tumbler and gymnast, Great Australian, 1877..

QUINN, CHARLES T. Gymnast, First National Union, 1861.

QUINNETT FAMILY [William H., Frank, Mamie, and Emma?]. Trapeze and tumbling act. Bartine & Co., 1880; New York and New England (**O. J. Ferguson,** proprietor), 1884; W. H. Harris' Nickel-Plate, 1885. **W. H. Quinnett** secured half-interest in the Priest Pavilion Show, spring 1886, and toured with it under the title of Priest's Great Western Museum and Trained Animal Show. Walter L. Main's, 1887; manager, Dan Shelby's, 1888; Orton Bros.', 1889; clown, with his dog Dallas, James M. French's, 1890; clown and assistant business manager, LaPearl's, 1892; general manager, Mullen's Railroad Show and Quinett's Museum, 1893; general contractor, LaPearl's, 1894, advertiser, 1896, manager of advance car #1, 1897; contracting agent, Campbell Bros.', 1902, car manager, Sun Bros.', 1903-05. See W. Quinnett Hendricks.

QUINTON, JAMES I. Master of transportation, John Robinson's, 1874, assistant treasurer, 1876.

QUIRK, PATRICK. See William H. Batcheller.

R

RAFAEL [r. n. may be Gambor or Tolano]. Columbian rider. Apprentice, J. A. Rowe's, 1849-50; Rowe's, Hawaii, 1851; Rowe's, Australia, 1852-54; Lee & Bennett, 1857; Rowe's, Hawaii, 1858; proprietor, Rafael's Great Australian Circus Co., 1867.

RAFFLIN, M. Clown, VaAmburgh & Co., 1874.

RAMAGE. Price & Simpson, 1823-24.

RAMPONE, J. G. Courtney & Sanford's Minstrels, a party made up in New York to travel with Courtney & Sanford's Circus in South America. Sailed from New York, July 23, 1873.

RAMSDELL, DAISY. Rider. W. W. Cole's, 1886; S. H. Barrett's, 1887.

RANCH, BESSIE ["Mme. Marie"]. Snake charmer, P. T. Barnum's, Adam Forepaugh's, etc. Attempted suicide, Baltimore, June 18, 1885, by putting a gun to her head; afterwards refused medical attention. It is believed she was despondent over a man.

RANDOLPH, J. W. General agent, W. H. Harris' Nickel-Plate, 1886.

RANDOLPH, MISS M. A. Lion queen, June & Titus, 1848.

RANDOLPH, WILLIAM ["Uncle Billy"]. (d. October 16, 1912) Boss hostler with such organizations as Gardner & Hemmings, John O'Brien's, Montgomery Queen's, Frank A. Robbins', and Sig. Sautelle's. For the last 18 years of his life, employed by **George** and **Peter Sun**, Sun Bros.' Acted at various times as equestrian director, boss hostler, forage agent and superintendent of ring stock. Was vigorously performing his duties up to the time of death, which occurred in Cincinnati, OH, age 76.

RANSOM, BURT. Walter L. Main's, 1887.

RAPP, JOSEPH. (d. July 6, 1889) P. T. Barnum's.

RAREY, JOHN S. First horse trainer to gain national and international fame in making it entertainment, which began around 1860. Consisted of going into a town and breaking and training wild and unruly horses, at the same time offering a sum of money to any one who would bring him a horse that he could not subdue. S. O. Wheeler's, 1865.

RAVEL, GABRIEL. Acrobat. VanAmburgh's, 1871; American Circus, South America, 1879.

RAWDIN, WILLIAM. General agent, Goldenburg's (**John V. O'Brien**, proprietor), 1874.

RAWDON, G. F. General agent, Hilliard, Hamilton & Hunting, 1876.

RAY, WILLIAM ["Major"]. Sideshow midget. With W. H. Stowe's, winter 1881-82; Sells Bros.', Australia, 1891-92, 1893. At 33 years old, 1893, stood 36" high and weighed 38 pounds. Wife was 22 years old, 37½" high and weighed 38

pounds.

RAYMOND, ADA. Griffith & Allen, 1886.

RAYMOND, CHARLES P. See George DeLouis.

RAYMOND, GOULD B. Manager, Zoological Exhibition from Baltimore, 1836-37.

RAYMOND, JAMES R. (1795-1854) Born in Carmel, Putnam County, NY. Apprenticed to the harness-making trade and eventually opened own shop, 1815. Married 3 years later and reared a family of 3 daughters and a son. In partnership with **Noel E. Waring**, formed a menagerie in the 1820s and toured for some 30 years. Co-proprietor, Raymond & Ogden, 1832-34; co-proprietor, Raymond, Weeks, Ogden & Co., 1833. 1835, was one of the first to introduce the bandwagon as a feature attraction. 1842, was in possession of 6 of the 7 elephants in America—Columbus, Hannibal, Pizarro, Ann, Siam and Virginius. That year, with partners, had 3 menageries on the road—Hubbell & Co.; R. D. Lines & Co.; and Waring, Raymond & Co. Continued this practice through 1849. 1850s, had a 4-hand team of elephants,—Siam, Virginius, Columbus, and Hannibal—harnessed to a bandwagon and driven by **Albert Townsend**. 3 of the bulls died, leaving only Hannibal. Feeling the loss, Raymond sold out to **James E. Kelley** and **Hyatt Frost**. Last menagerie was on the road, 1853, after which he retired from exhibiting. Died at his residence at Carmel, age 59 (one source states he died in New Orleans), leaving property valued at $1,500,000, which included the Broadway Theatre, NYC. [Stuart Thayer: "He believed in advertising and was an early user of excess verbiage, 'showman's language,' in his notices. He promoted a sort of 'grandness' or 'giantism' through his promotion of such features as the giraffe, the elephant, and his lion trainers. His greatest innovation may have been in the organization of the Zoological Institute."] Press agent Charles Day called Raymond one of the first American showman to appreciate the elephant as an advertising device.

RAYMOND, JAMES. Equestrian. Brother of **Walter Raymond**, the vaulter. 1826, both were with Fogg and Howes menagerie, which was combined with Quick & Mead's Circus. **James**, Philadelphia, Washington Circus, 1827-28, managed by Fogg & Stickney, apprenticing at this time and riding bareback; Harrington & Buckley, 1830; Fogg & Stickney, 1830; Aaron Turner's, 1830; John Lamb's, 1831; J. T. and J. B. Bailey's, 1834-35; Ludington, Smith & Bailey, 1836. This performer is not to be confused with menagerie proprietor **James Raymond**.

RAYMOND, KATE. (b. 1844) Equestrienne actress. Born in France. First stage appearance, May 1861, Newburgh, NY, as Mrs. St. Clair in *Uncle Tom's Cabin*. After a short dramatic career, fitted herself for equestrian pieces, first appearing, Continental Theatre, Philadelphia, January 4, 1864, as Mezeppa. Was a member of the American Equestrian Dramatic Troupe, supported by actor **O. B. Collins**, appearing in such pieces as *The Border Spy, The Trapper's Last Shot, The Child of the Prairie, The Ride for Life, The Horse Thief's Leap, The Brigand Queen, Jennie Diver, the Female Highwayman, The Demon's Huntsman, The Devil on Horseback, Putnam, Dick Turpin, Jack Sheppard, Hern the Hunter, Timour the Tartar,* and *El Hyder.*

RAYMOND, LOTTA. Beckett's, 1881.

RAYMOND, R. W. Griffith & Allen, 1886.

RAYMOND, THOMAS E. Manager, Raymond & Waring, 1845.

RAYMOND, W. B. Press agent, Ringling Bros.', 1893.

RAYMOND, WALTER. Vaulter. Was brother of equestrian **James Raymond**. Both men were with the combined shows of Quick & Mead and Fogg & Howes, 1826.

READ, CHARLES. See Charles Reed.

READING, JOHNNY. Concert performer, Dan Castello & Co., 1866.

READY, M. Chief bill poster, Warner & Henderson, 1874.

REAGAN, WILLIAM. Solicitor, Walter L. Main's, 1893.

REAMS, DAVID. Gymnast, VanAmburgh & Co., 1874.

REANO, SIGNOR. Rope dancer, Ricketts' Amphitheatre, Philadelphia, 1790s.

REDDEN, JOHNNY. C. T. Ames', 1870.

REDON, MRS. Equestrienne. With Cayetano's as 2-horse rider, New England, 1811, first engagement in America. Remained for a Canadian tour in the fall of that year. With the troupe, Albany, NY, spring 1812; Charleston, winter 1812-13; Pepin, Breschard & Cayetano, NYC, 1813. It is possible that Mrs. Redon became Mrs. Cayetano, 1814, for her name disappears and Mrs. Cayetano's appears for the first time.

REED, A. H. Musician, orchestra director, general agent, proprietor. Born in Maple Rapids, MI. First connected with **Dan Rice** and **John Stowe**, 1871; Howes' New London, 1872; Warner, Springer & Henderson, 1873; G. G. Grady, 1874; DeMott & Hilliard, 1875; Philadelphia Centennial Exhibition, 1876; Homer Davis', 1877; Sells Bros.', 1878; Bentley's, 1879-80. Proprietor of Reed's European Show, 1881, and continued operating companies until 1919. Heuman Bros.' 1922; Businessmen's Association Circus, Chicago, 1923; Ketro Bros.', 1924; general agent, Tiger Bill's Wild West, 1925-28; Hanneck Bros.', 1930; with **Edgar Day**, vaudeville under canvas, 1932. Married wife, **Viola**, February 27, 1881. She was an able horse and dog trainer.

REED, ALEC. Boss hostler, John Robinson's, 1873.

REED, BORTHWICK. Scottish swordsman, Cooper, Bailey & Co., Australian tour, 1877-78.

REED, CHARLES F. (January 29, 1842-October 13, 1934) Rider and ground tumbler. Native of Maysville, Kentucky.

Joined Dan Rice's, at age 12, 1854-62. Apprenticed to **Omar Richardson**, who taught him circus acrobatics and pad riding. Brien's (**John V. O'Brien**, proprietor), 1863; Thayer & Noyes, 1864, 1867; Seth B. Howes', 1866; Thompson, Smith & Hawes, 1866; Dan Rice's, 1869; somersault rider, Dr. James L. Thayer's, 1870; Great Combination, 1871; Adam Forepaugh's, 1873; John H. Murray's, 1872; Montgomery Queen's, 1873; Circus Renz, Europe, 1874; somersault rider, Howes' Great London, 1875; Great International, Philadelphia, winter 1876-77; pad rider, P. T. Barnum's, 1877-78; Schuman's, Russia, 1883-84; Cirque Continental, France, 1885; Adam Forepaugh's, 1886; Ringling Bros.', 1893; Edward Shipp's Winter Circus, 1893-94, Petersburg, IL; Sells Bros.', 1894. Married Dan Rice's daughter, **Libby**, January, 1863. Had 3 daughters and a son. Daughter, **May**, was one of the **Reed Sisters**. See Reed Sisters.

REED, CHARLIE. (d. September 20, 1892) Had charge of advertising car #1, Adam Forepaugh's, for several years; car carried 23 people, 21 of whom were bill posters, and the first press agent of the show. Liberal to a fault, his pocketbook was always opened to help the needy

REED, DAVID. Acrobat. Dan Rice's, 1847-48; (as **Reed & Murray**) Crane & Co., 1849-50; Spalding, Rogers & Van Orden, 1852; Spalding & Rogers *Floating Palace*, 1853; Spalding & Rogers, 1858.

REED, ELIZABETH [Libbie]. See Elizabeth Rice.

REED, FRANCIS. Son of **Charles F. Reed**. Rider, Ringling Bros.', 1892; principal and jockey rider, Walter L. Main's, 1901.

REED, JAKE. Sideshow privilege, VanAmburgh & Co., 1867, with the **Australian Children** and other oddities; outside privilege, Adam Forepaugh's, 1869, exhibiting the **Australian Children** and **John** and **Hannah Battersby**, skeleton man and fat woman. Was also with the show 1871-72.

REED, JAMES. Tumbler and gymnast, Alexander Robinson's, 1871.

REED, JOHN. Juggling clown. With Aaron Turner's, 1833; Olympic Circus, 1835; Raymond & Weeks, 1836; Nathan A. Howes', 1836, winter 1843-44; Howes & Gardner, 1844.

REED, MABEL. Gymnast, John Robinson's, 1888-93.

REED, MATTIE. Fat lady, Gollmar Bros.', 1897.

REED, NELLIE. Adam Forepaugh's, 1873; Chiarini's, San Francisco, 1879.

REED SISTERS [May, Blanche]. Equestriennes, Ringling Bros., 1892-93; Great Wallace, 1896-97. **May** married **Jake Cousins** at Monroe, WI, while with Ringling, July 29, 1893. She was the daughter of rider **Charles Reed** and **Libby Rice**.

REED, WILLIAM. Boss hostler, John Robinson's, 1866, 1871-72.

REESE, FRANK A. Treasurer, Reese, Levis & Dolphin, 1885.

REESE, THEODORE F. (d. September, 1907) Clown. With

many established circuses, including Ringling Bros.', Barnum & Bailey, Adam Forepaugh's, Sells Bros.',Great Wallace Shows. Also contortionist, slight-of-hand man, trapeze performer, double somersault leaper. After breaking a leg in a trapeze leap around 1892, became a clown, appearing dressed as a farmer, only to amaze the audience with trick riding on a mule. Died at Anthony, KS. At the time of death, was manager and part owner of the M. L. Clark & Co. Shows.

REEVES, ANNA. Lowande's Brazilian Circus, 1889.

REEVES, D. W. One of Bunnell's Minstrels, R. Sands', 1863.

REEVES, WALLIS. Band leader, musician and composer of high regard. Melville, Cooke & Sands, 1863; Howes' European, 1864, 1865. [St. Louis *Republican*, April 28, 1865: "… Seldom has our city been visited by a finer band of musicians than those connected with Howes' great circus. The band is under the direction of the eminent composer and musician, Prof. Wallis Reeves, and we must confess it to be superb. The bell chimes introduced in some of their popular pieces is alone worth the price of admission. Mr. Howes may congratulate himself in securing the services of such valuable artists....] Stone & Murray, 1869.

REEVES, W. E. Hamilton & Sargeant, 1877.

REGAN, C. General performer, Spalding & Rogers, 1850.

REGAN, TOM. Chief bill poster, W. W. Cole's, 1874.

REICHE, ANDREW. (d. August 13, 1914) Son of **Henry Reiche** and one of the second generation of animal importers. Had an establishment at 98 Fourth Ave., NYC, for 35 years.

REICHE BROTHERS [Charles, Henry]. Importers of birds in NYC, 1844-45. When California was enjoying gold fever, took 3,000 canaries to San Franciso and sold them rapidly at $25 to $50 a piece. [Charles H. Day: "The Reiches have had almost a monopoly on the canary bird trade and if any reader has a pet canary in his cage it is pretty safe to wager that the Reiches made their percentage on it."] Some time later, when **Henry** was selling birds to VanAmburgh, he was asked to import a variety of animals. With other circus managers coming into the business and acquiring menageries, the Reiches' business expanded. Rivalry amongst American showmen created a demand not easily satisfied. **Charles** started an establishment in Alfeld, Germany, and a trading station in Homralm, Africa; and remained abroad to handle the business. **Henry** built the Aquarium, NYC, as the backer of **W. C. Coup**; also developed the Aquarium at Coney Island. At one time, **Charles** exhibited in Germany the Den Stone's Troupe of American Indians. The brothers, in association with **Hyatt Frost**, were proprietors of VanAmburgh, Charles Reiche & Bros.' Circus, 1885. Each brother had a son associated with the business.

REICHHOLD, GEORGE. Proprietor, McDonald & Reichhold, 1896.

REID, GEORGE. Agent, George W. DeHaven's, 1865.

REID, HARRY. Animal trainer, E. O. Rogers', 1891.

REILLY, GEORGE. Vaulter, juggler on horseback, returned from performing in England, 1855.

REILLY, JAMES. (d. 1909) Animal trainer. Last with Sells-Floto. Died age 38.

REILLY, JAMES. (d. January 25, 1886) Popular show printer, the successor of Clany & Reilly, and formerly the bookkeeper of Bacon, the printer, at the old Spruce Street stand. Got the title of "Doctor" while clerking on a Mississippi boat from his kindly dosing of ailing passengers or crew. Was at one time the treasurer of Bryant's Minstrels, when Dan, Jerry, and Neil were all three playing. [Charles H. Day: "He was a courtly, genial gentleman, an able businessman and a staunch friend and will be greatly missed by the managers and agents who were wont to meet at his office ... a kind husband and father, and the staunchest and truest of friends."] After the failure of Kelley of the Great London show, Dr. Reilly carried it on his shoulders until it finally fell into the hands of Cooper & Bailey. Died at his residence in Brooklyn, a victim of Bright's disease.

REIS FAMILY [Augusta, Johanna, Hermann]. Dwarfs, P. T. Barnum, 1876-77.

REISLEY, ADOLPH. Gymnast, Sells Bros.', 1874.

REITER, PROF. Band leader, World's Fair Aggregation, 1892.

RELSBY, ADOLPH. Scenic rider, Sells Bros.', 1873.

RENALDO. Acrobat, John Robinson's, 1883.

RENCH, CHARLES. (d. June 24, 1908) Clown, with Irwin Bros.', 1888. Died in Columbus, OH, by setting fire to a pile of papers and then lying in them. Ill health was considered to be the cause of the suicide.

RENNO, PROF. French aeronaut, Haight's Empire City, 1871.

RENO BROTHERS. Triple bar performers, S. H. Barrett & Co., 1883.

RENO SISTERS. Equestriennes, Ringling Bros.', 1893, at ages 18 and 22 years, "occupying the ring at the same time, and on separate horses, yet performing marvelous feats of bareback riding together."

RENO, W. A. Clown, Howe's Great London, 1897.

RENTFROW, JASPER N. (d. April 5, 1922) Showman, acrobat, gymnast, and general performer. L. B. Lent's, 1861-62; Orton Bros.', 1867; clown and leaper, Cooper, Bailey & Co., 1876; co-proprietor, Sells & Rentfrow's Circus (with **Willie Sells**), 1892. Bought out **William Sells** interest at the end of the 1895 season. Out with his Great Syndicate Shows and Paris Hippodrome, 1896. Pre-season announcement predicted that the show was to be the first to introduce a "motor wagon" in the parade; in the hippodrome, a race between one of these vehicles and a horse was to be presented; also a race between two motor wagons. The management was also anticipating carrying a genuine whale, conveyed on a special 74' long car and drawn on a huge wagon expressly built for the exhibition, the combined weight being about 60,000 pounds and requiring a 40-horse team to take it to and from the grounds. The circus was to perform with three rings and an elevated stage. The overloaded show collapsed on August 8th and was purchased by **J. M. Hamilton** and **John Hummel** of Cincinnati. Later, proprietor of a long-running tent repertoire company, Rentfrow's Jolly Pathfinders. Wife, **Marie**, died on January 7, 1917, at Houston, TX, age 70. J. N. died at Snyder, TX, of pneumonia.

RENTFROW, MRS. J. W. Concert performer, vocalist, Cooper, Bailey & Co., 1876.

RENTZ, FREDERICK. (d. August 25, 1872) Hurdle rider. W. Stone's, 1851; Robinson & Eldred, 1854-55; Spalding & Rogers' Railroad Circus, 1856; Driesbach & Stickney, 1857; Nixon & Kemp, 1858; Nixon & Co., 1859; Chiarini's, Havana, Cuba, winter 1859-60; VanAmburgh & Co.'s southern, 1860. Died in Philadelphia, age 34.

RENTZ, LOUISA. Somersaulting equestrienne. Daughter of **August Rentz** and niece of the famous German circus manager of the same name. Brought over by Adam Forepaugh's, 1882, when she received $350 a week, all expenses for self, father, groom and two horses, salary beginning on leaving Germany and ending on her return. S. H. Barrett's, 1887.

RENTZ, LUDORF. "Electrifying Funambulist", Stone & Murray, 1869.

RENTZ, MINNIE. Rider, Sells Bros.', 1878.

RENTZ, WILLIE HENRI. English cornet soloist, Hippocomique, 1868.

RENZER, RUDOLPH. Pad act, Joel E. Warner's, 1871.

RETICKER, CHAN. Proprietor, Reticker's Racing Association, 1878, a new hippodrome show.

REUCH, CHARLES. See Australian Four.

REVENI, MONS. General performer, J. W. Wilder's, 1873.

REXFORD BROTHERS [John, Connie]. Acrobats. Frank A. Robbins', 1885; triple act and Roman ladder, with Walter L. Main's, 1886; Frank Rich's, 1886; Pullman's, 1886; Lockwood & Flynn, 1887; the Rexford Bros.', 1896.

REYNOLDS BROTHERS. Horizontal bars, with Shedman Bros.', 1894.

REYNOLDS, CARRIE. Equestrienne, Stevens & Begun, 1874.

REYNOLDS, FRED. Principal clown, Sells Bros.' tour of Australia, 1891-92.

REYNOLDS, JAMES C. ["Jimmy"]. (d. 1881?) Considered one of the better jesters in the business, particularly popular in the South. Married **Frankie Christie**, a member of James M. Nixon's company, August 23, 1863. March, 1888, was reported to be in the hospital at Hillsboro, IL, in serious condition from being nearly frozen to death; lost part of both hands, leaving only the thumbs and half of the palms; was in a destitute condition. Waring's, New Orleans, winter 1837-38, 1842; June, Titus, Angevine & Co., Bowery Amphitheatre, NYC,

1839; Robinson & Eldred, 1847; Stone & McCollum, 1850; Dan Rice's, 1851-53; Franconi's, 1855; Crescent City, 1856; Broadway Amphitheatre, 1857; Sands, Nathans & Co., 1857; G. N. Eldred's, 1857-58; Sands, Nathans & Co., Bowery Circus, 1858; Robinson & Lake, Wood's Theatre, Cincinnati, 1859; Robinson & Lake, 1860-61; Thayer & Noyes, 1862; James M. Nixon's, Washington, DC, fall 1862; Madame Macarte's European Circus (**James M. Nixon**, proprietor), 1863; James M. Nixon's Alhambra, NYC, fall 1863; L. B. Lent's Broadway Amphitheatre, NYC, winter, 1863-64; John Robinson's, 1864; O'Brien & King, 1864; National Theatre, Cincinnati, winter 1864-65; Thayer & Noyes, 1865-66; Yankee Robinson's, Chicago, fall 1866; George Bailey & Co., 1867-68; Dr. James L. Thayer's, 1869; Mike Lipman's, 1869; James Robinson's, 1870; George W. DeHaven's, fall 1870; Wootten & Haight, 1871; John Stowe & Sons, 1871; Charles Noyes', winter 1871-72; Dan Rice's, 1873; Parisian Circus, Operti's Tropical Garden, Philadelphia, fall 1876; Great International, Offenbach Garden, Philadelphia, winter 1876-77; New York Central Park, 1877; North American, 1877; Cooper, Bailey & Co., 2nd Australian tour, 1877-78; Ridge's Royal Tycoon Circus, Queensland, 1879; James T. Johnson's, 1884. [Mark St. Leon: He "made a good impression on the Australian young folks but, when he took to liquor, his services were dispensed with." Also from what appears to be a newspaper or program quote: "Mr. Reynolds is pronounced by the present people wherever he has appeared to be the best circus clown who has ever visited the Australian colonies; there are no stale or vulgar jokes; nothing to displease the most fastidious; his manner is gentlemanly; his conversation refined and full of wit and humour."]

REYNOLDS, SYLVESTER. Clown, co-proprietor Howes & Turner, 1826; Nathan Howes & Co., 1826. Was killed that season, Gorham, ME, September 24, attempting an acrobatic feat.

REYNOLDS, W. B. Wild animal tamer, Empire City, 1871; James W. Wilder & Co., 1873; proprietor, W. B. Reynolds' Consolidated Shows, 1892-96; general agent, George W. Hall's, 1892, 1897.

REZAC, EMMA. See Emma Stickney [Mrs. Robert Stickney, Sr.].

RHIGAS. Strong man, Lafayette Amphitheatre, NYC, in its initial season, 1825.

RHINEHARDT, BERTIE and **GOLDIE.** Concert song and dance team, Barnum, Bailey & Hutchinson, 1882.

RHINEHART, MME. 4-horse chariot driver, Barnum, Bailey & Hutchinson, 1882.

RHINEHART, SAM. See Sam Rinehart.

RHODES, DAN [r. n Rose]. (d. February 13, 1890) Antonio & Wilder, 1858; agent, Davis & Crosby, 1859; Mabie's, 1859; treasurer, Deery & Robinson, 1865; treasurer, Lake's Hippo-Olympiad, 1866; ringmaster, Michael O'Conner & Co., 1869;

G. G. Grady's, winter 1869-70, 1870; general director, Macarte Sisters', 1870; contracting agent, Curtis & DeHaven's Great Roman Hippodrome, 1877; railroad contractor, H. C. Lee's Great Eastern, winter 1877-78.
. Married the equestrienne, **Marie Macarte**, March 9, 1868, in Marshall, TX, while with Lake's. Died at Fabacher Plantation, LA.

RHODES, HARRY. Cornetist and band leader, Haag's, winter 1896-99.

RHODES, MARY. Lowande's Brazilian Circus, 1889.

RHODES, WILLIAM. Black Brothers Ten Cent Show, 1888; W. B. Reynolds' Consolidated Shows, 1892.

RHONE, DAVID. Contracting agent, Great Roman Hippodrome, 1877.

RIAN, NORA. Equestrienne, Montgomery Queen's, 1874.

RICARDO, DAN. Clown and comic vocalist, Fogg & Stickney, 1828, 1830, 1833; John Lamb's, 1831; Brown's, 1835-36.

RICARDO, MATT. Hunting's New York Cirque Curriculum, 1889.

RICE BROTHERS. Acrobats, formed, 1879, combining **Alfred Seymour** and **Edmund Rice**. Performed on the horizontal bars, did brother acts, tumbling, etc. Great Commonwealth Circus, transported by the boat, *William Newman*, 1879; VanAmburgh & Co., 1879-80; Silas Dutton's, winter 1879-80; Sells Bros.', 1882; VanAmburgh & Reiche Bros.', 1885; S. H. Barrett's, 1887; Clark Bros.', winter 1889-90.

RICE, CATHERINE ["Kate"]. (August 3, 1846-1929) Daughter of **Dan** and **Maggie Rice**. Equestrienne. Dan Rice's, 1851-60. Married a non-professional, Capt. A. C. Wurzbach, and left the business. Wurzbach was Rice's treasurer, 1864. Returned to chaperone her father on Nathans' Consolidated Show, spring 1883. Later, moved to Long Branch, NJ, to care for him.

RICE, CHARLOTTE REBECCA. (b. November 4, 1843) 2nd Mrs. Dan Rice, married November 4, 1861. Performed with Rice's, 1864. Divorced July, 1881.

RICE, DAN [r. n. Daniel McLaren]. (January 25, 1823-February 23, 1900). Speaking—and singing—on public events, he used his booming voice, powerful memory, and acute sensitivity to his times to become "without doubt the most famous performer in the history of the American circus" (Stuart Thayer), and a prominent figure beyond it. He was born in New York City. When his parents' marriage was annulled (or father left), Dan's mother married, again in New York. After her death in 1836, Den traveled to Pittsburgh, where he worked in a stable and began a life-long friendship with Stephen Foster's family. Various ventures in "the show business"—learned pig, puppets, strongman, lecturer—led to an out-side show in 1843, as clown in whiteface and in blackface, reflecting minstrelsy's emergence from the circus. Dan's varied apprenticeship was anchored by two events: marrying

Margaret "Maggie" Curran and renaming himself "Dan Rice" to capitalize on the fame of the minstrel, T. D. "Jump Jim Crow" Rice. These early years generated the first of many fictions, exaggerating the stable hand into a famous jockey, Andrew Jackson's favorite, dancing to Henry Clay's fiddle and befriended by Abe Lincoln. Other fabrications would depict Dan fooling P. T. Barnum, foiling the Mormon Joseph Smith, and enticing Spain's Queen Isabella. His name change to "Rice" would be hidden in tales of father's favorite Irish clown, mother's ancestor, or his fondness for rice pudding. In 1844 Rice began a long love-hate relationship with Gilbert "Doc" Spalding when he was clown and minstrel (with Dan Emmett, author of "Dixie") on Spalding's North American Circus. Through the 1840s Rice joined giants of the growing circus world, working with Wallett, Glenroy, Stickney, North and Pentland, and for Welch's, Mann's, Lent's, Sands', Howes', and Stokes'. In 1848 Zachary Taylor watched Rice at Spalding's show, which later prompted tales that Taylor rode in Rice's bandwagon, leading to the political phrase, "getting on the bandwagon" (no evidence and, anyway, it would have been Spalding's bandwagon). In 1848, Rice and Doc Spalding were partners, with Spalding's brother-in-law, Wessel T. B. Van Orden, as manager, until Rice bought the show. The next year Spalding invested in Rice's circus but then, with Van Orden, foreclosed, sparking one of the most famous feuds in circus history. Rice may have been cheated as he charged but, extravagant and generous, he would always have money troubles. Starting out again with one trained horse and a few performers, he drew crowds with entertaining attacks on his former associates. When he sang that Spalding was having an affair and that Van Orden, a lawyer, embezzled, they had him arrested for slander, increasing his underdog appeal and his fund of fun. For decades "The One-Horse Show"—as circus and then phrase—was a comic reminder of the feud and Rice's rise. Pugnacious and stubborn, Rice battled throughout his career in feuds, law suits and, common to the antebellum circus, fistfights. Besides fights, family stood at the heart of his career. Maggie performed, as did daughters Ellizbeth and Catherine. Libby married Rice's apprentice, Charles Reed (many of the 16 Reed children would become performers) while Kate wed A. C. Wurzbach, Rice's treasurer in 1864. Dan's half-sister and rider, Libby Manahan married another of his riders, Jacob Showles (their adopted son, Willie Showles, would become a prominent rider). Dan's cousin W. C. Crum was his press agent, while half-brother, William Manahan, managed Rice's Crescent City Circus. Rice's father, also Daniel McLaren, was proprietor in 1858 (confusing matters, Rice used his birth name "McLaren" that year). Like family, bandleader Almon Menter and ringmaster Frank Rosston trouped with Rice for years. In the 1850s Rice's popularity exploded, in summer tent circuses bearing his name, winter circuses in city theatres, other public appearances and newspaper reports. In 1855 he first used the title "Dan Rice's Great Show," which would echo down the years, as his cousin Crum was agent for Barnum & Bailey when it became "The Greatest Show on Earth." Rice's fame flowed from three things. First, with a prodigious memory, lighting-quick mind and unequalled comic talent, he was remarkably funny, no small matter when clowning quality varies greatly. Second, he had an extraordinary array of animals—his blind horse Excelsior Jr. climbing stairs, the elephant Lalla Rookh walking a tight-rope, a trained rhinoceros, and comic mules, Pete and Barney, whose success kicking off would-be riders spawned generations of imitators. Third, Rice's success flowed from his aspiration to "something higher." Later that aspiration would seem laughable, a lowbrow's awkward attempt to be highbrow, but mid-century, when amusements of all kinds overlapped, audiences of all classes mingled and "art" still meant craft, Rice and his circus were seen as elevating forces. Moving to Girard, PA, he presented Maggie as a "true women" and himself as a country gentleman, performing only for public edification. For a few years he appeared as "conversationist"—lecturer, without makeup—while "clown" and "circus" disappeared from his advertisements. The "Great American Humorist" in "Dan Rice's Great Show," he enjoyed fame matched by few in amusements or beyond. His opinions on political and social issues were eagerly anticipated. When Stephen Douglas ran for the Senate against Abraham Lincoln, Rice hosted Douglas for a speech in his circus tent. Walt Whitman praised Rice's circus as a moral lesson, while Mark Twain—later touring as "The American Humorist"—used it as model for the circus in *Huckleberry Finn.* Later the Ringling brothers claimed Rice as inspiration for their first circus. While Barnum was more famous as a manager and Spalding more innovative, Rice was probably seen by more people than any other American. Feuding with Horace Greeley's New York *Tribune,* he was judged victorious because his jokes were more effective and he reached more people. Three blows altered Rice's fortunes. Divorcing Maggie, he lost her steadying influence and the claim of "elevated" domestic bliss. Accidents cost him his rhino and Lalla Rookh. Most crucially, he stumbled in the troubled politics of the Civil War. The night Louisiana seceded Rice was in the ring in New Orleans, where he sympathized with the South, attacking abolitionists as extremists who had caused the war. Though foes would howl, many people North and South in 1861 agreed with the celebrated clown. Returned up the Mississippi River, he alternately defended and denied his views, while fictions began depicting him defying pistol-waving "secesh" hotheads. Pressing his vision of reunited states, he ran in 1864 for the Pennsylvania state senate as a Peace Democrat and briefly in 1867 for President, serious efforts that would later be characterized as jokes for publicity. Fictions grew to make Rice seem a Union patriot of long standing. He first used the title "Colonel" in 1864, with the tale that Zachary Taylor had conferred it years earlier. "Colonel" Rice catapulted a $200 donation into a claim that he single-handedly equipped a Pennsylvania regiment, though the regimental history does not mention him. With his famous goatee and occasional use of striped costumes, Rice did influence the cartoon of "Uncle Sam" but the claim that he directly inspired it ignores the fervent Republican views of its creator, cartoonist Thomas Nest. The foremost fiction tells of fond friendship with Abraham Lincoln. Both were funny and political, and they may have met, but Rice denounced "Black Republicans," including Lincoln. Never the traitor his enemies would claim, Rice was also not the Union hero of later fictions. Rice clowned during the war for the Mabie Bros.', Spalding's, John "Pogey" O'Brien's and Adam Forepaugh's. He may have made $1,000 a week, the astounding sum claimed, but the implication that he reached his height during the 1860s obscures the fact that, once again employed by others, his influence was fading. On Spalding's show in 1863, kicking a man from the tent, he made news for the legal principle that showman could evict patrons but was fined for using excessive force. Though apparently only another of his fights, this one happened days after his baby daughter died. He had married his second wife Rebecca McConnell in 1861. He presented her in the ring in 1864 but the experiment ended that year. Dan Rice, Jr., born in 1868, never joined the circus. No longer able to pitch highbrow to a culture that had decided the circus was lowbrow, Rice trouped on, under others or with his own dog-and-pony show. He began to drink, declared bankruptcy in 1875—Spalding as major creditor—and was divorced from Rebecca in 1881. He kept on, in 1882 touring with John Robinson's Circus to California, as lecturer—his old, "elevated" title—but mostly waving to the crowd. In the mid-80s he did temperance tours in Texas and Arkansas but would later claim that his water pitcher had contained gin. In 1887 he married a wealthy widow, Marcella Greathouse Robinson; apparently never divorced, they split within a few years. In 1891, nearly seventy, Rice tried a one-ring show in New York. When that attempt died in a blowdown, he turned his energy to selling a medical cure-all, dealing in Texas land, writing newspaper items and rehabilitating his reputation. Famous people and events multiplied in an attempted memoir, interviews and a biography published after his death, while his ardent views disappeared in a claim that he had avoided politics. Circus clowns had once presented adult fare, rowdy, risque and political, but Rice recast hirrself as "Old Uncle Dan," remaking his past to fit the new sentimental image of the silly buffoon cavorting for children. Dan Rice died in Long Branch, NJ. His times had admired him and laughed hard. Later times, remembering him—barely—insentimental fictions, forgot the powerful influence of the great American humorist. *[The above was submitted by Dr. David Carlyon, a first-rank biographer of Dan Rice.]*

RICE, EDMUND J. Horizontal bars, Barnum & London, 1884.

RICE, EDWARD E. Proprietor, Coney Island Circus, 1895.

RICE, ELIZABETH ["Libby"]. (February 10, 1844-1890/1897?) Daughter of **Dan** and **Maggie Rice**. Named after his mother and half-sister. Dan Rice's, 1848, 1850-60, and perhaps later; Brien's (John O'Brien, proprietor), 1863; Adam Forepaugh's, 1886. Married rider **Charles Reed**, January, 1863. Many of their 16 children were riders. Well-known in Europe. Died in Prussia.

RICE, ELLA. Claimed to be **Dan Rice's** daughter, of which there is no foundation of validity.

RICE, EMMA. Lowande's Brazilian Circus, 1889.

RICE, FRANK. Proprietor, Great Western, 1886.

RICE, JACK. G. G. Grady's, 1868.

RICE, J. B. Proprietor (with **Aaron Turner**), for Aaron Turner's American Amphitheatre, 1843.

RICE, J. H. (d. September 8, 1924) Rice's Big Railroad Show, 1887; general agent, Lowande's Brazilian Circus, 1889; Rice's Great American, 1892; contracting agent, Adam Forepaugh's, 1894; Rice & Davis, 1905-06.

RICE, LILLIE. With **Annie Bell Holton**, balloon race and double parachute jump, Sells & Rentfrow's, 1893.

RICE, MRS. DAN. See Mrs. Charles Warner.

RICH, CHARLES. Treasurer, Donaldson & Rich, 1885; Frank Rich's Great Eastern Railroad Alliance, 1886.

RICH, DARIASTUS. Co-proprietor (with **Joseph Andrew Rowe**), Rich and Rowe's Mammoth Pavilion Circus, winter 1844, performing in the South. The show left for South America in the spring of that year.

RICH, FRANK H. Proprietor, Donaldson & Rich, after purchasing **G. W. Donaldson's** interest, 1885; Frank Rich's Great Eastern Railroad Alliance, 1886, (Frank H. Rich, **Col. Charles Whitney**, **J. N. Abbott**, proprietors); Rich & Downie, 1890; Rich & Mettie, 1891.

RICH, GEORGE E. Proprietor, with **Frank Rich**, Great Eastern, 1886; Rich's, 1892.

RICHARDS. Clown. Lafayette Circus, 1825-28; Price & Simpson, 1828; Palmer's, 1833; Fogg & Stickney, 1833; Palmer & Harrington, 1834-35; Bancker's, 1836; Brown & Co., 1837; Eagle Circus, 1838.

RICHARDS, AL E. Gymnast, Miles Orton & Co. 1869; Dan Rice's (rail and boat), 1870; Cole & Orton, 1871; privileges, W. W. Cole's, 1874; press agent, 1880-86. Married **Jessie Orton**, of the Orton show, Quincey, IL, November 5, 1874.

RICHARDS, DAVIS. (1832-1866) Rider. Born in Pennsylvania (another source gives Virginia) and began career in Philadelphia as a pupil of **Rufus Welch**, with whom he remained for several years. Good hurdle rider, as well as a very competent bareback rider. Raymond & Co., 1852; Joe Pentland's, 1851, 1854; Jim Myers', 1856; accompanied Howes & Cushing to England and performed with that company, Al-

hambra Palace, London, 1858-59; 12 months engagement, Hengler's, 1860-61. Remained abroad until his death. On getting down from the shoulders of his fellow performer, while working in St. Petersburgh, Russia, his foot slipped and he fell on his back on the rump of one of the horses and then onto the ground with a deadly force. Died within 24 hours. At the time, he had plans of returning to the United States to fulfill an engagement with Lake's. Children were **Willie** and **Julia**, both circus riders.

RICHARDS, EDITH. Equestrienne, W. W. Cole's, 1886.

RICHARDS, E. R. Treasurer, W. H. Harris' Nickel-Plate show, 1884.

RICHARDS, GEORGE W. Cannon ball performer, George W. DeHaven's, 1870; athlete and cannonball juggler, Lake's Hippo-Olympiad, 1871; Sells Bros.', 1872, sideshow privileges, 1873; iron jaw act, cannon ball, and feat of lifting 2 full-size horses, 1874; cannon ball performer and acrobatic act, Livingston Bros.', 1874; acrobat, Great International, Offenbach Garden, Philadelphia, winter 1876-77; strong man, Dr. James L. Thayer's, 1877; cannon ball, Hamilton & Sargeant, 1878. Had his own show on the road, 1882-90, which was destroyed by flood. According to D. W. Watt, was somewhat instrumental in the Sells brothers getting into the circus business by pointing out to Allen Sells the success of such prominent circus proprietors such as Forepaugh, Robinson and others; wanted sideshow privileges in addition to performing feats of strength and was apparently successful in convincing the brothers they were amply able to finance a new show.

RICHARDS, H. F. Press agent, W. W. Cole's, 1882. At this time, had been with the show for some years.

RICHARDS, JAMES. Rider, with his horse Prairie Steed, in his dare-devil act of hurdling and leaping without saddle or bridle, Joe Pentland's, 1855.

RICHARDS, JESSIE. Equestrienne, slack-wire, outside ascension, W. W. Cole's, 1875, 1886.

RICHARDS, JOSEPH. Clark Bros.', winter 1889-90.

RICHARDS, JOSIE. Rider, S. H. Barrett's, 1887.

RICHARDS, LOUIS. Indian clubs, Cooper, Bailey & Co., Australian tour, 1877-78.

RICHARDSON. Riding master, Parson's circus, **Samuel McCracken**, manager, 1826; Samuel Parsons', Albany, under the management of **Simon V. Wemple**, Troy, NY, 1828; North American (**McCracken's**), 1827.

RICHARDSON, BENJAMIN ["Burt"]. (*circa* 1853-October 7, 1896) Acrobat. Born in Scranton suburb of Providence, PA. Entered the business with a hall show. Leaper, Warner & Henderson, 1874; acrobat, Springer's Royal Cirq-Zoolodon, 1875; acrobat, Joel E. Warner's, 1876; W. W. Cole's, 1880, where he remained for several years. When physical powers diminished, turned to clowning. Frank A. Robbins, 1888; then joined the Great Syndicate Show at its inception and remained until his death, which occurred in a stateroom of the show

250

train at Ironton, OH.

RICHARDSON, C. Band leader, John Robinson's, 1877-78.

RICHARDSON, C. E. Contracting agent, Alexander Robinson's, 1869, general agent, 1875.

RICHARDSON, CHARLES. Boss canvasman, with Howe's Great London, 1871; P. T. Barnum's (**P. A. Older,** proprietor), 1872-73.

RICHARDSON, E. R. Juggler, Backenstoe's, 1872.

RICHARDSON, OMAR. (1835-1859) Rider and general performer. Pupil of **Dan Rice** and a featured performer for his circus, 1851-58. Spalding & Rogers, 1857-59, worked the revolving globe and *perche equipoise* and was considered an excellent young bareback rider. Also, with Nixon & Kemp, 1858. Died of consumption in Covington, KY, age 23.

RICHARDSON, SAM. Nego minstrel, Welch, Bartlett & Co., 1839; Howes & Mabie, 1841.

RICHARDSON, TONY. Hamilton & Sergeant, 1877; Hilliard & DeMott, 1880; treasurer, Walter L. Main's, 1890.

RICHARDSON, WILLIAM. (1835?-September 6, 1915) Clown. Over 40 years with Barnum & Bailey and others. Died in Jefferson City alms house, Watertown, NY, where he had been living for 5 years, age 80.

RICHAU. Senic rider, Washington Circus, Philadelphia, 1828, where he performed "The Death of the Moor."

RICHER, JEAN [or John]. (d. 1830) French rider, clown and strong man. Performed unique tricks in the saddle and was excellent and original in his comic and burlesque interpretations on horseback. One feat was to be placed on his back with an 200 pound anvil on his chest and have men beat upon it with hammers. Price & Simpson, Washington Amphitheatre, Boston, 1826; Lafayette Circus, NYC, 1826-27; Washington Gardens, Boston, summer 1827; Mount Pitt Circus, NYC, 1827-28; Brooklyn Amphitheatre, 1828; American Arena, Washington, DC, winter 1828-29; Fogg & Stickney, 1830; Royal Pavilion Circus/Olympic Circus, 1830; B. F. Brown & Co., 1830. Died at Sea.

RICHMOND, E. General manager, with Spalding & Rogers *Floating Palace,* 1859.

RICHMONDE, MME. Equestrienne, Dan Rice's Paris Pavilion Circus, 1871. May be related to above.

RICHTER, ROSA M. See Zazel.

RICKER, CHARLES L. Gardner & Hemmings, 1862; boss canvasman, Stone & Rosston, 1865. April, 1865, had his hand amputated, Frederick City, MD, after suffering an accidental blow from a sledge. Stone & Murray, 1871; boss canvasman, P. T. Barnum's, 1874.

RIDDER, C. W. Business manager, Hemmings, Cooper & Whitby, 1869.

RIDGEWAY, JOHN. Orrin Bros.', Mexico, 1886.

RIEL, AL. (d. August 30, 1910) Agent. Connected with Barnum & Bailey for 28 years, Buffalo Bill's Wild West Show for 8, and the 101 Ranch show for 3. Manager advertising car

#3, Barnum, Bailey & Hutchinson, 1882. Lived to be one of the oldest agents in age and length of service in America. Died of pluro-pneumonia, Secaucus, NJ.

RIENBOLD, PROF. F. Band leader. With Buckley's, 1858; Thompson, Smith & Hawes, 1866.

RIESE, WALTER. Roman standing race, 4-horse chariot driver, jockey racer, Barnum, Bailey & Hutchinson, 1882.

RIGALL BROTHERS. Proprietors, Rigall Bros.' Twenty-Five Cent Show, 1897. **F. E. Rigall** was in charge of tickets; **H. C. Rigall,** treasurer; **J. C. Rigall,** superintendent of privileges; **James D. Rigall,** manager.

RILEY, DENNIS. (d. March 25, 1890) With VanAmburgh's, Forepaugh's, O'Brien's, Sells Bros.'

RILEY, JACOB. (March 27, 1845-May 30, 1899) Contortionist, juggler and hat spinner. Born in Indiana. Joined John Robinson's when about 15 years old and remained for some time. 1872, Albercia's, performing in Cuba, South America and Europe; John Robinson's, 1876-81. During the latter engagement, suffered a stroke that plagued him for the remainder of his life. In conjunction with **Joe Rutledge,** had a show of his own on the road for a short time. Died in Danville, IL.

RILEY, THOMAS. Boyd & Peters, 1880.

RINALDO BROTHERS [3 in number]. Trapeze, D. S. Swadley's Monster Combination, 1872; grotesque dancing and high kickers, Barnum, Bailey & Hutchinson, 1882.

RICHARDS, GEORGE. Strong man, Lowande's Great Brazilian, 1877.

RINEHART, CHARLEY ["Master"]. Sells Bros.', a first year organization, 1872.

RINEHART, MRS. SAM. See Eliza Tomlinson.

RINEHART, SAM [or Rhinehart, Reinhardt]. (d. November, 1890) A 10-horse leaper, double somersaulter, and general performer. John Robinson's, 1858-62, 1866; Robinson & Deery's, 1864; Robinson & Howes, 1864; George W. DeHaven & Co., 1865. Reported killed in Texas that year but only received a severe wound. Shortly, up and about, performing with George W. DeHaven's, 1865-66; Haight & Chambers, 1866-67. Married **Lena Reilly** of Louisville, August 24, 1867, in that city. Amphitheatre, Louisville, January 1868; Lake's, winter 1868-69; Adam Forepaugh's, 1869; Mrs. Charles Warner's, Philadelphia, 1869; John W. Robinson's Circus (not "Old John"), 1870-71; Cooper, Bailey & Co., 1876; Montgomery Queen's, 1877; Sells Bros.', 1878-79. Retired from the profession, located in Columbus, OH, December 1879, and entered into a second marriage to nonprofessional **Eliza Tomilson,** August 24, 1880. Retirement was short-lived, however. Had performing dogs, W. W. Cole's, 1880; Welsh & Sands, 1880; Nathans & Co., 1883; Wallace & Co., 1885; ringmaster, Miller, Okey & Freeman, 1886; equestrian director, Miller, Stowe & Freeman, 1887; Stow, Long & Gumble, 1889; George W. Richards', winter 1889-90. Eventually left the circus to keep a saloon in Columbus, OH. Had 2 sons, **Charley** and **Willie**, and 2 daughters, **Beatrice** and **Goldie**.

RINEHART, WILLIE ["Master"]. Son of the above. Sells Bros.', a first year organization, 1872.

RINEY, DUTCH. Variety troupe, Haight & Chambers, 1867.

RINGLER, MARGARET. Minstrel, Alexander Robinson's, 1876.

RISLEY, HARRY. One of two "sons" of **Richard Risley** Carlisle (the other being **John**) who performed with their "father" in an act known as the "Risley business." See below.

RISLEY, JOHN C. (d. January 6, 1873) Acrobat. Another of two "sons" of Richard Risley Carlisle (the other was **Harry**) who performed with their "father" in an act known as the "Risley business." Died in Philadelphia. See below.

RISLEY, RICHARD [Richard Risley Carlisle]. (1814-May 25, 1874) Athlete. As a young man, possessed great strength and an attractive figure and excelled in running and wrestling. Having learned to play the flute, joined a circus that passed through his village, billed as "Prof. Risley, athlete and performer on the flute." Later, gave up the flute for gymnastic feats. Using his two "sons," **Harry** and **John**, invented a novel act which caught on at once and assured his success. The juggling of children with his feet became known as the "Risley business." May have never been married or had children, but his act was always announced as Risley and his sons. Welch & Delavan, and also Henry Rockwell & Co.'s winter circus, 1841. About 1845, went to England where he had a lengthy engagement at London's Drury Lane Theatre; performed at Windsor Castle for the Queen and other dignitaries. [*Illustrated London News*, 1846: "...Certainly nothing like it in the way of posturing was ever seen before. There is a graceful ease and precision in the manner in which all their evolutions are accomplished...."] While in England, exhibited a panorama of the Mississippi, opened an American bar and an American bowling alley. Toured of all the principal cities of Europe. Coxe states that although he was popular in New York and London, he was even more so in Paris. In Russia, won distinction for his excellence in rifle shooting and skating. Back in England, challenged the country's best in contests of markmanship, wrestling, long jumping, hammer throwing and billiards. Was bested only in billiards; made the longest standing jump of that day; gave his opponent a 10' edge in the hammer throw and won by 15". Next time he came to England, brought with him an American billiard champion to regain the title for the United States. Unfortunately, the Englishman won again to Risley's $30,000 loss. Accumulated a large fortune only to lose it in speculation. Formed his own circus company and took it to the Far East. On return, brought with him one of the first groups of Oriental tumblers seen in America and Europe. Engaged the **Rousset Family** of ballet dancers to an America tour, 1851, in a losing endeavor. Other efforts to import European artist also ended in failure, ruining him financially. Un-

timately, secured a minor position at a variety theatre in Philadelphia and attempted to establish an agency for variety artists but was unsuccessful. Failure reduced Risley to ill health and penury; the mind gave way and he was placed in the insane ward of Blockley Institution, Philadelphia.

RITCHIE, GEORGE. Ferguson's London Coliseum Circus, 1888.

RIVERS, ADA. Clark Bros.', winter 1889-90.

RIVERS, CHARLES H. S. (d. November 14, 1899) Rider and tumbler. Born in London, England, from parents who were circus performers and, who, with their sons comprised the **Rivers Family**. Made his debut at age 4 when carried into the ring in a carpet sack by his father. Broke both of his ankles, 1882, while performing at Eau Claire, WI, which forced retirement from circus life. Became manager of Hickey's Turf Exchange and of the Grand Opera House, New London, WI. Died at the Elwood Hotel, New London. June, Titus, Angevine & Co., 1841; VanAmburgh's, England, 1844; Richard Sands', England, 1845; Rockwell & Stone, 1845; Welch & Mann, 1846-47; Rivers & Derious, 1851, 1857; Sands, Nathans & Co., Broadway Theatre, NYC, 1858; Rivers & Derious, 1859; L. B. Lent's, 1861, 1876; clog dancer, Yankee Robinson's, 1862; George F. Bailey & Co., 1862; James M. Nixon's, Washington, DC, fall 1862; 4-horse rider, George F. Bailey & Co., 1863; Maginley & VanVleck, 1863; Robinson & Howes, 1864; DeHaven & Co., 1865; Frank J. Howes', 1865; Grand Reserve Combination, 1866; Parisian Circus, assembled for the Paris Exposition, 1867; George F. Bailey & Co., 1868; John Robinson's, 1868-70, 1873-75, 1879-81; James Robinson's, 1870-71; program agent, Montgomery Queen's, 1874; Miles Orton's, 1883, 1885.

RIVERS, EDDIE [El Nino Eddie]. (1855-September 14, 1923)) Rider and rope dancer. Born in NYC, son of **Richard Rivers**. In his childhood exhibited a remarkable aptitude for gymnastics and acrobatic exercises. Making debut, Chiarini's, Havana, 1863, as a juvenile performer on the tight-rope, created a furore and was given the title of **El Nino**. Executed the difficult feats comparable to those of a **Blondin** or a **Javelli**. After performing a series of graceful exercises, would ascend on a single wire from the stage to the gallery of the theatre, over the heads of the audience, lying on his back midway, rising again and continuing his perilous course to the finish, all this with as much ease and confidence as if he were walking on solid ground. Next, would be blindfolded with a sack placed over his head, and repeat the ascension and return journey on the wire as before. As a tight rope dancer, was said to equal the best of his day. Returning to USA, occasionally used the title of "The Infant Blondin." Stone & Rosston, 1865; L. B. Lent's, 1867-68; Dan Rice's, 1868; Chiarini's, California, winter 1868-69; Chiarini's, South America, 1870; Adam Forepaugh's, 1872; John Robinson's, 1875-76; Adam Forepaugh's, 1870, 1872-74, 1879; Pullman & Co., 1880; Burr Robbins',

1886; Hunting's, 1888-89. Died at Actors Home, Amityville, NY.

RIVERS, EDMUND. Scenic rider, with Adam Forepaugh's, 1874.

RIVERS, FRANK. (1821-February 15, 1887) Posturer. Born in Springfield, MA. Entered circus business in Boston, with Welch's, 1831, age 10; Purdy, Welch & Macomby, 1837; Welch's, 1846-51. Went to California, prospecting for gold some time in the 1850s, but drifted back into the circus. Forced to withdraw, however, because of injury. Established the Melodeon concert hall, Philadelphia, about 1859, a variety theatre on a most ambitious scale. Few years later, opened Rivers' Melodeon, NYC. Stage manager, Academy of Music, New Orleans, 1864-65; opened a dramatic agency, 66 E. Houston St., NYC, 1866; general agent, Rosston, Springer & Henderson, 1871. At the end of his life, was a traveling salesman for Charles Scribner's Sons, publishers. Died in Buffalo, NY, age 66.

RIVERS, FREDERICK. (d. March 17, 1875) Acrobat. Member of the Rivers family. VanAmburgh, England, 1845; Welch & Mann, 1846; Welch's National, 1847; Rivers & Derious, 1857; Philadelphia Circus (managed by **Dan Gardner**), winter 1867-68; Gardner, Kenyon & Robinson, 1869. Died of dropsy in Philadelphia.

RIVERS, JOHN C. (d. 1907) Clown and clog dancer. Came from England, 1856. Goodwin & Wilder, 1862; Toole's, 1863; L. B. Lent's, 1864; Gardner & Hemmings, 1864; Mrs. Charles C. Warner's, Philadelphia, December 1864; Alex Robinson's, 1867; Adam Forepaugh's, 1867; equestrian director, New York Olympic Circus, 1867; clown and comic singer and performing terrier dog act, Hemmings, Cooper & Whitby, 1868; Smith & Baird, 1872; Great Southern, 1875. 40 years a performer. Died in San Antonio, TX, age 80.

RIVERS, LUKE [r. n. Kelly]. (d. May 3, 1898) Rider and one of the more versatile and useful general performers in the business, belonging to the old school of equestrians and best remembered for his "Pete Jenkins" act. Rufus Welch's, 1848, 1850; June-Titus, 1849; Rivers & Derious, 1851-53; Welch & Lent, 1854, 1856; Sands & Chiarini, 1854; Welch & Lent, 1855; George F. Bailey & Co., 1857; Welch's National, Philadelphia, 1857-58, 1860; S. P. Stickney's, NYC, 1861; Robinson & Lake, 1862-63; James M. Nixon's, Washington, DC, fall 1862; Great European, 1865; Frank J. Howes', 1865; Mrs. Charles Warner's, Philadelphia, 1868-69, 1870; Hemmings, Cooper & Whitby, 1869-70; Batcheller & Doris, 1870; James Robinson's, 1872; Cooper & Bailey's Great International, 1874, 1876; John O'Brien's, 1883; scenic rider, Batcheller & Doris, 1880; Lowande's, 1889; Barnum & Bailey, 1892; Scribner & Smith, 1893. Died in Philadelphia.

RIVERS, PETE. Robinson & Deery, 1864.

RIVERS, RICHARD. (d. August 28, 1901) Rider. Born in England. Entered the circus business at age 14 and in time be-

came one of the premier bareback riders of the world. Raymond & Waring, 1840; Polandric ladder, June, Titus, Angevine & Co., 1841; Welch's National,, Philadelphia, 1845; Rockwell & Stone, 1845; "Enchanted Ladder", Welch & Mann, 1846-48; June, Titus & Co., 1849; Rivers, Runnels & Franklin, 8th Street and Fourth Avenue, NYC, 1850; proprietor, National Circus, Chestnut Street below Ninth, Philadelphia, 1852; Rivers & Derious, 1851-57, 1864; Dan Rice's, 1858; L. B. Lent's, 1867, 1872, 1876; Chiarini's, South America, 1870; Adam Forepaugh's, 1870; equestrian director, VanAmburgh & Co., 1874, 1880-81; Sells Bros.', 1877; equestrian director and ringmaster, VanAmburgh & Co., 1879, 1881. Died in NYC, age about 68. His wife, **Elizabeth**, had died NYC, February 22, 1897. Daughter was Mrs. George Garon, professionally known as **Viola Rivers**.

RIVERS, TOM. Boss canvasman. John V. O'Brien's, 1871; Rosston, Springer & Henderson, 1872.

RIVERS, VIOLA [Mrs. George Garon]. Equestrienne. The daughter of **Richard** and **Elizabeth Rivers**. Sells Bros.', 1877-78, 1882-83; VanAmburgh & Co., 1881; P. T. Barnum's, 1884, 1886; Barrett & Co., 1885; Frank A. Gardner's, Central and South America, winter 1887-88.

RIVERS, W. "MASTER". Adam Forepaugh's, 1870.

RIXFORD BROTHERS [3 in number]. King & Franklin, 1889; White & Markowit, 1889.

ROACH, JAMES. Boss hostler, Robinson & Lake, 1859-60.

ROBBINS, BURR. (August 13, 1837-January 30, 1908) Showman. Born in Union, NY. Sent to Western Reserve University by his parents with the intention of his becoming a minister. Ran off, shipping on a boat as a waiter from Cleveland to Milwaukee. Stowed away on a lumber boat to Chicago, 1855. Eventually drifting back to Cleveland, became a member of the Athenaeum Theatrical Stock Co. as general utility and walking gentlemen. Joined Spalding & Rogers, 1858, as property man at $15 a month and keep. At season's end, with small savings, opened a concert company of 5 people, called **Harmonious Bards**, with **Prof. C. C. Pratt** as his partner and manager; but the venture failed and Robbins was left to pay the bills, which he did by working as a harvester at $2.50 a day. Fall 1859, bought McBullwell's Panorama of the Revolutionary War and toured with some success until he joined the Union army. Began as wagon boss with Gen. George B. McClellan's brigade and remained for the duration, working his way up to becoming a Colonel. After leaving the service with savings, built and operated 2 variety theatres in the oil country at Pit Hole and Oleopolis and continued during 1866-67 until the wells dried up. Following year, was in the shoe and boot business, South Haven, MI. Winter 1869, bought an interest in **Bill T. D. Travis'** Painting of the Army of the Cumberland. Following summer, bought a sideshow from **Jim McGiver**, making fair dates with the attraction on its 2 wagons, 5 horses, and a buggy. Purchased a spotted wild cat and called it an American leopard. Sacred fowls from India were white hens stained red with vermilion. Had a deformed mule with an exceedingly broad head and a snout that turned up, purchased for $10, and billed as the Moorish Magi. Shortly, picked up the remains of the bankrupt John Stowe Circus and formed the Burr Robbins Seven Co.'s Circus and Menagerie in conjunction with Stowe. The two split up, 1873, with Robbins forming a new show out of the equipment of the old European Circus of Smith, June & Nathans. Continued as the owner of the Burr Robbins' Circus through the season of 1888. 1889-90, held a controlling interest in James M. French & Co.'s Circus and Menagerie. Robbins had a great propensity for saving money, much of which he invested in real estate in Chicago and elsewhere throughout the country. During his latter years, holdings totaled some 40 pieces of property, including a ranch in Kansas, the whole valued at more than two million dollars. Died in Chicago, age 70.

ROBBINS, FRANK A. (June 15, 1854-October 10, 1920) Rider and showman. Started in the circus business as a candy butcher on John Robinson's. Was a protégé of Adam Forepaugh's. Shortly, acquired skills on horseback and performed as a rider for Robinson & Lake, 1865; John Robinson's, 1865-78; P. T. Barnum's, 1876; bareback rider, Campbell's **(John V. O'Brien's)**, 1878. Started his own show, May 6, 1881, and continued with it for several years, including the New York Circus, 1893, which sailed up the Hudson on a chartered steamer, stopping at various cities. General manager, Robert Hunting's, 1894-95; lessee and general manager, New York Circus, 1897; Frank A. Robbins United Shows (Frank A. Robbins, **Gil Robinson, John W. Hamilton, W. A. Conklin**, proprietors), 1898; sideshow manager, Sun Bros.', 1899. November 9, 1910, his 18 year old daughter, **Winona**, disappeared from her home in Jersey City and was married several hours later to **Ray W. Anders**, a 23 year old candy butcher. Operated his own show, 1905-1915. Retired from the circus business, fall 1915. Unable to remain idle, entered the carnival business as well as placing circus acts in vaudeville. 1916, was one of the first showmen to transport by motor trucks. Used specially constructed 2-ton trucks for the baggage with trailers for the cages, ticket wagons and chandelier wagon. [Robbins: "I have been investigating the feasibility of motor truck transportation for upwards of a year and have convinced myself that it is the one and only proper method. I figure that we can save from $35,000 to $40,000 on transportation in a season and what is more, it will enable me to visit and show in towns where under ordinary conditions, by railroad haulage, it would be impossible."] Was a resident of Jersey City, NJ, for some 20 years where he headquartered his show. Had a wife, **Matilda**, a daughter, **Winona**, and a son, **Milton A.** Died at Riverside Hospital, Charleston, SC, from the effects of injuries incurred when he fell 20' through a skylight at Andrews, SC, on October 10.

ROBBINS, JASON. Dining room caterer. P. T. Barnum's, Buffalo Bill's Wild West, Adam Forepaugh's, Burr Robbins'. Cookhouse proprietor, Cooper, Bailey & Co., 1879-80. Usually hired 6 cooks and from 40 to 50 waiters and dish washers and other helpers made up the number to about 65 people. A different contract was made with the show each season, varying with the price of provisions. Invested his spare money in Brooklyn and New York business property and retired from the business independently wealthy.

ROBERTS. Handler, with June, Titus & Co., 1833, where he was advertised as having been a keeper at the Tower of London. November of that year, severely mauled and, in all probability, permanently incapacitated, causing him to be replaced by his assistant, Isaac VanAmburgh.

ROBERTS. Clown. West's, 1821; with a circus in Portland, ME, summer 1821, also did the farce, *Miller and Coalman*; comic songs, Simpson & Price, Olympic, Philadelphia, May 1823; Broadway Circus, NYC, June 1823.

ROBERTS, CHARLES. "Athletic Artist," L. B. Lent's, 1870; costumer, Howes' Great London, 1871-72.

ROBERTS, GEORGE. John Robinson's, 1871.

ROBERTS, JAMES. Clown, juggler, actor. James West's, 1821; Davis & Co., 1821; comic songs, Price & Simpson, 1823-24; juggling, with **Mrs. Roberts**, Price & Simpson, 1826; with **Mrs. Roberts**, Brown & Bailey, 1828; with **Mrs. Roberts**, Blanchard's, 1830; Hopkins & Co. (Tippoo Sultan menagerie), 1833; Eagle Circus, 1836; S. H. Nichols', 1838; Bacon & Derious, 1838.

ROBERTS, JAMES. Head hostler, Cooper, Bailey & Co. Australian tour, 1877.

ROBERTS, JOHN. See John Cleveland.

ROBERTS, MARY. Race rider, P. T. Barnum's Roman Hippodrome, 1875.

ROBERTS, NICK. Roberts & Gardner (Nick Roberts, **Frank A. Gardner**, proprietors), 1886.

ROBERTS, THOMAS. Acrobat and leaper. Haight's Great Southern, 1874; Robinson & Myers, 1883.

ROBERTSON. Gymnast from London. Had a company at Vauxhall Garden, NYC, July 1802; combined with **Thomas Franklin, Jr.** for a circus, February 1803, Newport, RI.

ROBIE, J. A. Contortionist, John F. Wood's Allied Shows, winter 1889-90.

ROBINSON, ALEXANDER. (1812-February 27, 1887) Native of Schenectady, NY. In early life, his parents died, leaving 4 brothers to make it on their own. Learned the blacksmith trade, but after brother **John** went south and entered the circus business, soon followed. Later, started Robinson, Toole & Lake's Circus. When this disbanded, started a show of his own, which was on the road for more than 30 years. Always considered Utica, NY, his home, living at 64 Whitesboro Street in retirement. Married **Mary Jane Deery**, November 29, 1858. Had 2 children, **Boyd Robinson** and **Mrs. Helen**

254

Ripley, both of Utica, and also an adopted son and daughter. Robinson & Eldred, 1847; assistant manager, John Robinson's, 1857-58. Returned to Utica, joined with **Levi J. North** for a show playing in the East. When North retired, Alexander continued alone. Retired in 1878. Died of apoplexy in Utica, NY, at age 75.

ROBINSON, BOYD. Gymnast and leaper. Son of **Alex Robinson**. Robinson & Lake, 1848-49, 1859-60; Alex Robinson's, 1862; Robinson & Brothers, 1863; Robinson & Deery, 1864; Alex Robinson's, 1869-75.

ROBINSON, CHARLES. Youngest son of **John F. Robinson**, who never really saw active service in the ring, for "old John" was retired when he was growing up. Married **Minnie Marks**, October 20, 1879.

ROBINSON, CLARENCE. Rider. Son of **James Robinson**. Worked with his father for many years. Was Beeswing in *The Sprite of the Silver Shower* ("It was astonining to see this child, scarcely five years old, doing his little pantomime as gracefully and correctly as many we have seen who had reached man's estate."), Hippodrome, NYC, winter 1865-66; L. B. Lent's, only 5 years old, 1866; Parisian Circus, assembled for the Paris Exposition, 1867; winter circus, Academy of Music, New Orleans, 1868-69; Gardner, Kenyon & Robinson, 1869; James W. Wilder & Co., 1873; Haight's Great Eastern, 1874; bareback buffalo rider, Montgomery Queen's, 1875; Cooper, Bailey & Co., 1876; Great Chicago Circus, 1879; Ryan & Robinson's, 1882; Westman's, 1883; Martell's, 1884; S. H. Barrett's, 1885-87; W. H. Harris' Nickel-Plate, 1889.

ROBINSON, EDWARD. Gymnast, Adam Forepaugh's, 1875.

ROBINSON, ELIZABETH. (b. March 4, 1825) Wife of old John Robinson, nee **Elizabeth Frances Bloomer**, born in Madison, IN. Married Robinson, January 5, 1841, and eventually gave birth to 5 boys and a girl: **John F., Gilbert, James H., Frank M., Katie V. [Mrs. Robert Stickney]**. Rode *manège* in her husband's circus.

ROBINSON, EUGENE. Son of **James Robinson** and brother of **Clarence**. Worked with his father's show. Also Montgomery Queen's, 1875; Cooper, Bailey & Co. when they left for Australia, November 8, 1876; Great Chicago Circus, 1879; manager, Robinson & Myers, 1883. Not to be confused with the **Eugene** who was the Floating Theatre operator, 1888. See James Robinson.

ROBINSON, FAYETTE LODAWICK ["Yankee"]. (May 2, 1818-September 4, 1884) Showman and clown. Born near Avon Mineral Spring, Livingston County, NY, a direct lineal descendent of Dr. Robinson, the eminent divine who came to this country in the May Flower. Began work with his father as a shoemaker in West Richmond, NY. 1837, opened his own shoemaker's shop in Medina, MI. At the end of the year, returned home and married but his wife died within a few

months. Returned to the shoe business, this time at Dansville, NY. Entered show business there, 1845, exhibiting two oil paintings by **S. C. Jones**, each 12' by 15', representing "The Raising of Lazarus" and "The Baptism of Christ." December 1845, performed the role of Radcliff in *Richard III* for a theratrical group in St. Louis. Organized Olympic Serenaders, 1846, presenting minstrel and variety entertainment (Robinson doing Lucy Long). August 1846, joined June & Turner, remaining with them 2 seasons, filling in the intermediate winter with Henry Rockwell's, Cincinnati. Again went into business for himself, 1848, performing with his wife and a musician named **Charles Gilson**, traveling with a 2-horse wagon. After closing, fall of that year, put out a river boat entertainment, an unsuccessful venture that ended with the sheriff possessing the boat to satisfy creditors. Scenery and properties being clandestinely removed, the company set up in an abandoned church until spring, 1849, when it was back on the road presenting dramatic performances. Shortly, enlarged the company and continued in this manner until 1851. Winter 1852-53, leased Frank's Museum, Cincinnati, where first billed himself with the name of "Yankee." Opened the following spring in a large tent, performing *Uncle Tom's Cabin* and *Sam Patch*. During ensuing winter, managed a theatre in Dayton, OH. Back under canvas the following summer. By this time, had accumulated some 40 head of horses, so opened a stable in Indianapolis, February 1856, giving circus performances twice a week. In the summer, set out in the circus business with great success. By 1858, had two shows out—Burt & Robinson's Old-fashioned Circus, **A. S. Burt**, manager, and the other, a double one, with circus and dramatic performances in the same tent. The season was a disaster. 1860, commenced a dramatic tour under canvas that lasted until 1865, when he purchased **James Melville** and **Jerry Mabie's** Australian Circus. After the 1866 season, erected Yankee Robinson's Coliseum and Zoological Garden, Chicago. 1867 tour featured the "Wallapus" as an extra attraction. 1868, **M. Smith** of Philadelphia invested $60,000 in the show, with **W. C. Coup** as assistant manager, and enjoyed a successful season. Good fortune continued the following year, when it was said that the show was making more money than any previous circus organization. 1870, Robinson divided the company, taking "a ninety-eight horse trick" into Canada, while renting the remainder of the outfit to Enochs & Everett, who went back to the barns in 21 days. 1871, took to rail and boat. Started out in Michigan, 1872, and made a transcontinental journey as far as San Francisco. Remained on the West Coast, 1873, when combined with California circus manager John Wilson. 1874, general manager, Soulier Hippodrome. Following year, with **Dan Scott**, organized a hippodrome, menagerie, and circus with a stage. Scott's death, June 28, closed the season. 1876, acted as agent-at-large for W. W. Cole's. Devoted 1877 to starring in dramatic performances, as had been his custom every winter except one since 1862. Took *Uncle Tom's Cabin* on the road again under canvas, 1879, and was successful. Following year, starred in a play written by his wife, *F.F.V.'s*. Since that time, was involved in but few enterprises; however, 1884, contributed his name and good will to Yankee Robinson & Ringling Brothers' Double Show, which originated in Baraboo, WI, on May 1 and, because of Robinson's failing health, closed its season on October 8. Died of Bright's disease in Jefferson, IA. Was particularly successful as an advertiser and as an innovator of features for the street parade. Married 3 times. First wife was a **Miss Nye** from Pittsford, NY, with a son from this union, **Silas Robinson**, who became editor of the Warsaw, IL, *Democrat*. Second wife was the daughter of Captain **Drake** of revolutionary fame. Third was a **Miss Babcock** from Chillicothe, OH. In 1893, **Bruce L. Baldwin**, Baldwin's Railroad Shows, upon visiting Robinson's grave, wrote the New York *Clipper*: "It seems a sad coincidence of 'man's inhumanity to man' to see the lone, unkempt mound that marks the last resting place of such a man as Yankee Robinson, neglected as it has been." The epistle was effective, for the grave underwent a decent restoration.

ROBINSON, FRANK M. (1850?-February 23, 1882) Rider and clown. Fourth son of old **John Robinson**. Born in Montgomery, AL. H. Buckley & Co., 1857-60; rider, Albisu's, Havana, 1866; Thayer & Noyes, 1867, 1870; second clown, John Robinson's, 1868; contortionist and rope performer, Robinson's Circus and Gardner & Kenyon's Menagerie, 1869; Adam Forepaugh's, 1870-71, 1875; contortionist, James Robinson's, winter 1870-71; clown and rider, John Robinson's, 1871-74; gymnast, Melville, Maginley & Cooke, 1875; treasurer, John Robinson's, 1879. Married **Frankie Bailey**, daughter of **Fred Bailey**, July 14, 1879. Died in Cincinnati, age 32, at which time he was part owner in the John Robinson Circus.

ROBINSON, GEORGE. Juggler, Hurlburt & Hunting, 1887.

ROBINSON, GEORGE H. Contracting agent, Wallace & Anderson, 1890; Adam Forepaugh's, 1892-93.

ROBINSON, GEORGE W. Treasurer, John Robinson's, California (**Frank Frost**, manager), 1886.

ROBINSON, GILBERT N. ["Gil"]. (July 15, 1845-August 17, 1928) Born at Buchanan, VA, the second son of old **John Robinson**. Began as a tumbler and carpet acrobat, making ring debut, 1847, at 3 years of age, with Robinson & Eldred. With his brothers, took over the management of the John Robinson's, spring 1871. November 16, 1875, married circus rider **Emma Lake Thatcher**, Memphis, TN. John Robinson's, 1865-79; director general, Frank A. Robbins' (**Frank A. Robbins**, Gil Robinson, **John W. Hamilton, W. A. Conklin**, proprietors), 1898; general advance agent, John Robinson's, 1900. Daughter, **Agnes**, married **Francis Reed**, November 29, 1899, Jersey City, NJ. Died in Cincinnati, age 84.

ROBINSON, HARRY. Guilford & Cannon, winter 1889-90.

ROBINSON, HELENE. Rider, with Alexander Robinson's, 1875.

ROBINSON, HENRIETTA. (b. 1841) An equestrienne daughter of **Alex Robinson**. Robinson & Eldred, 1847-52; bareback rider, Washburn's, 1855-56; John Robinson's, 1857. May have married an **Eldred**. See Alexander Robinson.

ROBINSON, HENRY. (d. February, 1901) Curiosity. Hodcarrier by trade but appeared with many circuses, billed as the "Wild Man from Borneo." A black man who wore a large bone ring in his nose and who carried a large bone as a war club. In later years his skin began to peal off, turning his color to white. Made a considerable salary from his various circus and museum appearances, which was spent primarily for drink, a habit which ultimately caused his death in Maysville, KY.

ROBINSON, HERBERT. Rider, W. W. Cole's, 1886.

ROBINSON, IDELLE. (d. April 10, 1889) Daughter of **Yankee Robinson**, described as being a woman of beauty and talent although erratic in behavior. From childhood had a desire to go on the stage, a dream that was strongly discouraged by her parents, which may have given rise to acts of defiance. A bizarre incident occurred in about 1887, after her father's death. While visiting friends in NYC, was discovered on the Brooklyn Bridge, alone and in a semi-conscious state. Was taken to the Chambers Street Hospital where, during the period of revival, she told the doctors that her name was Lulu Wilbur and recounted a fictitious story of a life of romance and adventure. Newspapers picked up the story and for 3 days it was a headline sensation, until she was reunited with friends. This is said to be the first of a number of escapades in which she was involved. The last dido took the shape of her running away from home and roaming the western part of New York state masquerading as a music teacher from Boston. Shortly thereafter she died as the result of an accidental fall, age 19.

ROBINSON, JAMES. (May 20, 1811-February 2, 1908) Associate, strong man. Born in Ithaca, NY. Younger brother of old **John Robinson**. A man who boasted he had never taken a dose of medicine in his life. Died at the home of his son-in-law, **Frank Wright**, in Cincinnati, OH, age 97. His brother, **Abe**, was chief of police at New Orleans during Gen. Butler's regime. James contested old John's will, 1889, claiming he was the rightful heir to his estate. Spalding & Rogers, 1851; Star State, 1852; Australia, 1855; Rowe's, 1857; John Wilson's, 1859; Robinson & Lake, 1860-1861. Died in 98th year.

ROBINSON, JAMES [r. n. James Michael Fitzgerald]. (1835-1917) Outstanding bareback rider. Born in Boston. Age 9 was apprenticed to **John Gossin**, the clown, who was with Rockwell & Stone. Remained with Gossin for 2 years, during which time performed as general utility, leaping, tumbling, etc. Spring 1846, indentured to **John Robinson**, remaining for 9 years. When he left, was the top equestrian in the business. Joined Spalding & Rogers, 1856, and traveled through the

East and South; engaged by Howes & Cushing for their United States Circus in England, with which he also toured the Continent; while abroad was connected with Astley's Royal Amphitheatre, where he created a sensation; following this, rejoined Howes & Cushing at the Alhambra Palace, London, for 3½ month engagement there; appeared before the royal family, May 14, 1858; followed by a series of performances at Vauxhall Gardens; engaged to the German circus manager, **Walslager,** for a year at a salary of $250 a week and all expenses paid; returned to London, where he was hired by **James M. Nixon** for Cooke's Royal Amphitheatre (James M. Nixon, proprietor), Niblo's Garden, NYC, 1860. John Robinson's, 1861; Thayer & Noyes, 1862; Chiarini's, fall 1862, for his amphitheatre in Havana, Cuba. March 9, 1863, was given a benefit that netted $1,700 and a championship belt that cost almost $1,500. Thayer & Noyes, 1863. At the season's close, in company with **Frank Howes,** erected an amphitheatre, Chicago, opening November 24, 1863. Robinson and Howes organized a railroad show, 1864. John Robinson's, 1864; Dan Rice's, 1865; Yankee Robinson's, Chicago, November 1866; Hippotheatron, NYC, winter 1865-66; L. B. Lent's, 1866; Parisian Circus, assembled for the Paris Exposition, 1867; Albisu's, Havana, winter 1866-67; winter circus, Academy of Music, New Orleans, January 1869; equestrian director, James Robinson's Champion Circus, 1869; Robinson's Circus and Gardner & Kenyon's Menagerie, 1869; equestrian director, performer, James Robinson's Circus (**Lipman** and **Walters,** proprietors), 1870; combined his circus with P. A. Older's, 1873; James W. Wilder & Co., 1873; Haight's Great Eastern, 1874; John Wilson's Palace Amphitheatre, San Francisco, 1875; Cooper, Bailey & Co., 1876; Great London, 1878; equestrian director, Great Chicago Circus, 1879; Dan Rice's, 1879; Sells Bros.', 1881, 1884; Ryan & Robinson, 1882; W. W. Cole's, 1883; S. H. Barrett's, 1885; Miller, Stowe & Freeman, 1887. [George Middleton: "When he walked in the ring to begin his act, with whip in hand, and jumped on the back of his bare-backed horse one was impressed at that minute that he was 'it.' He had that style and grace and finish to his act that no one else ever had that I have ever seen or heard of."] Finally, retired to a farm in Mexico, MO, where he trained horses and died. Robinson's riding style was original, fine and graceful; attrative in physique and personality; as a pad or bareback rider, or carrying a boy on horseback, challenged all comers, offering up to $10,000 and his championship belt to anyone who could exceed him. Touted as the greatest bareback rider of his day, his act was described, 1867: "On a bare-backed horse, he now is on his head, now at the other extremity, now backwards, now forwards, now riding sideways, now jumping over banners on one foot, now turning twice around in the act of jumping them, and now on his knees.... The *coup de force* is the turning of successive back somersaults through three balloons covered with paper and

alighting each time on his feet on his horse." For a time made his home in Louisville, KY, where he had a brother-in-law who was a dry goods merchant, and Robinson, for some years, it was said, was a silent partner in the business.

ROBINSON, JAMES A. (d. May 6, 1900) Contracting agent. Connected for several years with John V. O'Brien's and Adam Forepaugh's. Later, manager for John A. Forepaugh's Temple Theatre, Baltimore, 1891; and with Forepaugh's Theatre, Philadelphia, 1892. Died in Philadelphia.

ROBINSON, JAMES H. (d. September 26 or 27, 1880) Rider. Third son of old **John Robinson** and part owner of the John Robinson Circus. Died while traveling in advance of the show, age 33.

ROBINSON, JAMES S. (d. November 1, 1919) Bandmaster for Barnum & Bailey for several years. Prior to that was with Howes & Cushing; leader of brass and reed band, which paraded in the Golden Chariot drawn by a team of 20 horses, L. B. Lent's, 1874; Howes & Cushing, 1875-1880; Barnum & London, 1884. Married **Sarah Ann Pluce**, a non-professional, November 22, 1882. She died October 30, 1894. Musical director, Rice's, 1896. Retired from the circus at the end of that season. Had a collection of circus posters said to be the largest in the world at that time. Died at Morristown, NJ.

ROBINSON, JENNIE [Mrs. Bennerman]. Sideshow performer. Died July 3, 1873, Little Rock, AR.

ROBINSON, JOHN ALEC. (d. April 30, 1866) Rider. Son of **Alexander Robinson.** While the John Robinson Circus was exhibiting in Crittenden, KY, March 25, 1866, a gang of ruffians attacked the circus people. In the affray, young Robinson was injured. Died in Cincinnati from the effects. James D. Robinson and John Robinson, Jr. were also badly injured.

ROBINSON, JOHN F. ["Old John"]. (July 22, 1807?-August 4, 1888) Founder and long time owner of John Robinson's Circus and one of the great individuals in circus history. Date and place of birth form a controversy. Sons claimed he was born in Schenectady, NY; other members of the family said the place was Little Falls, NY, while Robinson himself stated that he was born in Albany, NY, July 22, 1807. Copeland MacAllister gives South Carolina as his place of birth. Some believe his date of birth was earlier because, according to his own statements, he was a 4-horse rider with a circus in Boston, 1816. Story has it that he ran away from home at age 9 and did not see his parents again until he was 22, when his mother recognized him as he was riding at the head of a circus procession through the streets of Utica, NY, where his parents were living. After leaving home, ended up as hostler with Blanchard's, later, Page & McCracken. When only 15, was employed as a watchman near Boston at the winter quarters of Rockwell's. While there, practiced riding horses at night and, by the time he was 18, was a 4-horse rider with Turner's, Buckley & Weeks and others. Eldest of four sons of **John** and **Nancy Boyd Robinson**—John, Alex, James and Boyd. Father, a blacksmith, was born in Aberdeen, Scotland, emigrating to America shortly after the Revolutionary War. For a number of years, was captain of a sailing vessel making crosses between Glasgow and NYC; around 1807, abandoned the sea and settled in Albany. The outset of Robinson's circus management, was generally associated with partners, the first being **John Foster**, Robinson & Foster's National Circus, 1842-44; then combined with **Gilbert Eldred**, Robinson & Eldred's National Circus, the leading circus in the South before the Civil War. Partnership came to an end in Richmond, VA, June 28, 1856, after 11 years together. Combined with **Bill Lake**, 1860-1862. Before going into proprietorship, was connected with James W. Bancker's, 1832; Edward Eldred's, 1834; Buckley, Weeks & Co., 1835; Raymond & Weeks, 1836; winter circus, Richmond Hill, NYC, 1837; Lion Theatre Circus, 1837; Charles H. Bacon's, 1837-38; Bacon & Derious, 1838; manager, circus troupe, Ludlow & Smith, American Theatre, New Orleans, 1840, equestrian manager, Ludlow & Smith, 1841. Was an excellent teacher of riders, **James Hernandez** being his first outstanding pupil, followed by **James Robinson**. Established his home quarters in Cincinnati, about 1852, where he raised—**John Jr.**, **Gil**, **Frank**, **James**, **Charles**, daughter **Katie**. **Katie** married **Robert Stickney, Sr.** and shortly died in child birth. All were from his second marriage. First union, **Margaret Yates** in Schenectady, NY, 1835, ended in separation, after which he married **Elizabeth Bloomer**, an equestrienne. She died on Christmas Eve, 1879. Gradually Robinson transferred the running of the John Robinson Circus to his sons. Eldest, **John F.**, became manager; **Gilbert** was treasurer and later superintendent and general agent; **James H.**, front door superintendent and assistant manager; **Charles C.**, assistant and later treasurer; **Frank M.**, privileges. Through the years accumulated a large amount of wealth and property. 1875, was the Republican nominee for the Mayor of Cincinnati, but was defeated. Was a physical giant of a man, with incredible strength in his prime. It was said he had been known to kill an unruly horse with one blow of his fist. Although a man of charitable inclinations, was profane and quick tempered, described as "impulsive, strongheaded, blunt, laconic, outspoken." Died in Cincinnati, leaving an estate valued at over $1,000,000. His will prescribed the following distribution: $1,000 to his nephew **Boyd Robinson**; a lot and house worth $3,000 to neice **Mary Robinson**; $15,000 to grandson **James Robinson**, age 8; $15,000 to grandson **Robert Stickney, Jr.**, age 17; the remainder of his estate to his sons **Charles M.**, **John F.**, and **Gilbert**.

ROBINSON, JOHN F., JR. ["The Governor"]. (1843-1921) Oldest son of old **John Robinson**. Took over management of John Robinson's with his brothers, 1871, when his father retired. Trained as a bareback rider, tumbler and leaper, but increased weight eventually necessitated withdrawal from performing. First wife died, August 6, 1889, age about 44. She was the former **Caroline Heywood**, daughter of a Confederate colonel from Charleston, SC. The two were married, NYC, 1866. Had 6 children, 4 of which survived her—**John G.**, **Katie**, **Pearl**, and **"Cad."** When the old John Robinson circus went under new management, 1896, Robinson combined with Franklin Bros. to form Robinson & Franklin. Menagerie of the Robert Hunting show was purchased and added to the already sizeable one of the combined institutions. 1909, sold the circus to his son, **John G. Robinson**, for $100,000, thereby mending the break caused by the "Governor's" marriage to his nurse, **Mary Maud Logan**, which took place in a private car attached to the Robinson Circus, Clarksville, TN, September 22, 1908. The end of all litigation was filed in a Cincinnati court when **John F.** gave **John G.** a bill of sale for $1.00 and other considerations, conveying all of the circus property known as John Robinson's Ten Big Shows. This terminated a nasty legal process. The "Governor" retained a life-long interest in the property that would net him at least $10,000 a year. This misunderstanding in the family which kept father and son at odds during the tenting season of 1908 was then straightened out. A few years later, lost a legal fight with his daughters in the Cincinnati court. The judgment stated that he turn over to them, **Pearl R. Lamkin** and **Caroline R. Stevens**, all the stock which he had been holding and which was left to them by their deceased mother; also, required to forfeit $30,000 in acrued dividends, the stocks being valued at nearly $270,000. Referee Whittaker, October 26, 1912, in Cincinnati, declared Robinson bankrupt for the second time within a month and referred the decision to Judge Hollister. Robinson claimed he was solvent and able to pay his debts if given time. In an appeal, he won a $320,000 suit against his two daughters from the Ohio Supreme Court, Columbus, June 24, 1913. His daughter, Mrs. Pearl Lamkin, died of influenza at her home in Chicago, October 8, 1918, age 38. **John G.** continued until 1912, when he did not take the show on the road because of the financial uncertainty caused by the "presidential excitement." Instead, divided his circus into vaudeville acts and toured under the auspices of the Western Vaudeville Association, selling the title and remaining equipment of the John Robinson Ten Big Shows to **Jerry Mugivan** and **Bert Bowers**, spring 1916. The "Governor" was 73 years old at this time.

ROBINSON, JOHN G. (January 12, 1872-July 30, 1935) Born in Cincinnati of the famous Robinson family. Son of **John F. Robinson, Jr.** Engaged in show business all of his life. Was a rider at 18; at 20 an assistant manager of the John Robinson Circus; 1901, took over management and continued to operate the show until 1916. Title then was sold to **Jerry Mugivan** and **Bert Bowers** and later passed into the hands of the Ringling organization. Robinson's group elephant act appeared for several years at indoor circuses, parks, fairs and at special performances; and eventually came under the management of son, **John IV**. Was a 32nd Degree Scottish Rite

Mason and a member of the Knight Templar; a past potentate of the Syrian Temple Shrine, Cincinnati, for two years, the only circus owner ever to be made a Shrine potentate. Was a trustee of Syrian Temple at time of death; a director of the Cincinnati Zoo, secretary and director of the U. S. Playing Card Company; director of Cincinnati Christmas Seal Committee of the Anti-Tuberculosis League; member of the Cincinnati Club and the Firemen's Protective Association; honorary member of the Circus Fans' Association. Died at his home, 3010 Reading Road, Cincinnati, age 63.

ROBINSON, JOHN S. Knockabout clown. P. T. Barnum's, 1879-80; Adam Forepaugh's, 1881.

ROBINSON, J. W. sideshow privileges, W. H. Harris' Nickel-Plate, 1888.

ROBINSON, KATE. (1851-1874) Daughter of old **John Robinson.** Married **Robert Stickney.** Their son was **Robert Stickney, Jr.** Robinson & Eldred, 1856; John Robinson's, 1858; Robinson & Lake, 1859-62; Robinson & Brothers, 1863; John Robinson's, 1864. Died in childbirth.

ROBINSON, MARIE [nee Mary Jane Deery]. Wife of **Alex Robinson.** With her dancing horse, Don Juan, Robinson & Deery, 1864; the Metropolitan Circus, 1864; (with little **Annie, Alice** and **Master Alex**) Alex Robinson's, 1867-74.

ROBINSON, R. W. Proprietor of the short lived Robinson & Co., 1889.

ROBINSON, STUMP. Master of ring stock, P. T. Barnum's, 1872.

ROBINSON, WILLIAM. Adam Forepaugh's, 1878.

ROBON, PEDRO. Troupe of aerial artists, Shelby, Pullman & Hamilton, 1881.

ROCHE, ELIZABETH ANN. Trapeze performer, Shelby, Pullman & Hamilton, 1881.

ROCHELLE, MONS. Gymnast. L. B. Lent's 1861-63. Advertised: "Performs Incredible Feats, upon an iron frame at the top of the pavilion, forty feet from the ground, the great performance being known as *'Le Echelle Perileuse'.*" Tom King's, 1864; Palmer's Great Western, 1865.

ROCHETTE, J. B. ["Frenchy"]. Trick clown and Herculean performer. First visited California, 1850; after which time, made annual tours through the state. Billed as "the pioneer clown of California," Lee & Bennett, San Francisco, 1853-57; Lee & Ryland, summer 1865. Died at the County Hospital, San Francisco, age 41.

ROCHFORD, WILLIAM. Apprentice, North American, 1845; Eagle/Star Circus, winter 1848; Stokes', 1849-50; Johnson & Co., 1851-52; Sands, Quick, 1853; Robinson & Eldred, 1854-56; Welch & Lent, 1859. Performed *la perche* as **Rochford & Rentz**, at least 1854.

ROCKWELL, ALEXANDER. Clown, Nathan A. Howes', 1836; Bacon & Derious, 1838; Brown & Mills, 1838 (later as Waterman & Co.); Welch, Bartlett & Co., 1839; Welch, Bartlett & Co., 1840; Broadway Circus, NYC, 1840; Welch &

Mann, 1841; Sands', United Kingdom, 1842; Dr. Gilbert R. Spalding's, 1847-48; John Tryon's, Bowery Amphitheatre, NYC, 1843; Rockwell & Stone, 1843-45; June & Turner, 1846; Stone & Madigan, 1850; E. F. & J. Mabie's, 1851; Welch's, 1852.

ROCKWELL, HENRY J. (d. 1849) An orphan from Utica, NY, who never knew who his parents were. A man by the name of **Bagely** was his guardian, at one time quite wealthy but later failed in business. Began in circus business as an apprentice rider to **Samuel McCracken** at North Pearl Street Circus, Albany, NY, 1826. Rider, Albany Circus, 1826; Tivoli Gardens, Philadelphia, 1826; William Blanchard's, 1827, 1830; Simon V. Wemple's, Troy, NY, 1828; Royal Circus, 1831; Fogg & Stickney, 1832; Edward Eldred's, 1834; manager, Old Bowery Amphitheatre, NYC, 1835; Oscar Brown's, 1835; Frost, Husted & Co., 1836; J. J. Hall's, 1836; Frost & Co., 1837; proprietor, with **H. Hopkins** and **Matthew Buckley**, Buckley, Rockwell, Hopkins & Co., 1838; manager, June, Titus, Angevine & Co., Bowery Amphitheatre, 1839; rider, June, Titus, Angevine & Co., 1841; Yankee clown, Welch's National, Philadelphia, 1841; equestrian director, Niblo's Garden, NYC, winter 1843-44; management, Henry Rockwell & Co., winter 1841; co-proprietor with **Oscar Stone**, Rockwell & Stone's New York Circus, 1842-44. The men had 2 units, 1845-46, each managing a show; after Stone died, August 1846, kept both shows running, 1847-48, calling them Rockwell & Co.'s New York Circus. Left the business at the termination of the latter season. Died of cholera in Cincinnati, about 35 years of age.

ROCKWELL, MME. Equestrienne, W. W. Cole's, 1886; 6-horse rider, S. H. Barrett's, 1887.

RODICUE, L. J. Proprietor, Rodicue & Co., 1889.

RODNEY BROTHERS. Gymnasts and acrobats, Ducello's United Exhibitions, 1879.

RODRIGUEZ, L. J. Manager, Milwaukee Mid-Winter Circus, Exposition Music Hall, Milwaukee, winter 1894-95.

ROE, FANNY. Dog circus, St. Germain's Imperial Circus, 1889.

ROFF, J. H. Billed as a great scenic rider and equestrian comedian, his forte being "Pete Jenkins." S. O. Wheeler's, 1865.

ROGAN, P. Clown, J. M. Barry's Great American Circus, 1894.

ROGERS, ANNIE. Dan Rice's, 1872.

ROGERS, BELL. Equestrian, John Robinson's, 1872.

ROGERS, CHARLES J. (February 5, 1817-April 3, 1895) Son of English performer **John Rogers**, who came to USA, 1816, with James West's circus company. At age 5, made his debut at the Broadway Circus, NYC, in the pantomime *La Perrouse*, and during the scene where the child is carried away upon the monkey's back, both monkey and child fell from a high rock, young Rogers getting his collar bone fractured, which was the only bone fracture he ever received during his career. Made ring debut at age 8, in Baltimore, January 11, 1826, with Price & Simpson on the occasion of his father's benefit (Charles' brother, **W. Rogers**, age 7, was also brought out), where he performed on the trampoline and turned a somersault over 4 ponies. 1826, apprenticed with combined shows of Quick & Mead and Fogg & Howes. Fogg & Stickney, Washington Circus, Philadelphia, 1828, 1830, 1839; John Lamb's, 1831; Brown's, 1835-37; Welch, Bartlett & Co., 1839; proprietor (Charles Rogers, **John Shay, John Mateer, J. W. Jackson**), Cincinnati Circus, 1840-41; Welch & Delavan, 1841, 1847; Welch & Mann (at this time was designated as "the great equestrian of the South"), 1843-44; Mann, Welch & Delavan, 1844, 1846. Joined Dr. Gilbert R. Spalding's, 1847, as principal rider, and remained with the company as performer and partner until 1865. While with Spalding's, 1848, bought an interest in the show. So began the long and successful career of the Spalding & Rogers' circuses. The men moved onto the river boat, *Floating Palace*, 1852, and floated up and down the Ohio and Mississippi rivers; while at the same time, the managers maintained a land circus. Spalding & Rogers performed in NYC during the indoor season, 1854-55. With Spalding, converted the Pelican Theatre, New Orleans, into the Spalding & Rogers' Museum and Amphitheatre, 1856, and performed there for a few months. At the close of the engagement, February 28, 1856, the *Floating Palace* started back up the river, featuring Nathan & Co.'s performing elephants. Spalding & Rogers performed in the West Indies, 1863-64. The partnership was dissolved, 1865. Rogers was married to a **Miss Davis** in Philadelphia, June 1866. Reached his peak as a rider in the 1840s and has since been called the "greatest scenic rider that America has ever had." [Stuart Thayer: He was "one of the absolute master riders of America."] Died at his home in Germantown, PA.

ROGERS, DELLA. Tight-rope performer, daughter of **Nat Rogers**, 1864. See Nathaniel P. Rogers.

ROGERS, E. O. Proprietor, Rogers', 1890-91.

ROGERS, ETTIE. Albino lady, P. T. Barnum's, 1873-77.

ROGERS, JOHN. Rider. Came to America from England with James West's troupe, 1816, along with his son, **Charles J. Rogers.** Simpson & Price, Philadelphia, Baltimore, 1822; still vaulter, Simpson & Price, Broadway Circus, NYC, 1823; riding master, William Blanchard's, 1823; Richmond Hill Amphitheatre, summer 1823; John Rogers', NYC, 1823-24; Price & Simpson, 1823-26; Aaron Turner's, 1842.

ROGERS, M. D. Proprietor, M. D. Rogers', 1891.

ROGERS, MRS. C. J. Performing horse handler, Spalding & Rogers' New Orleans Circus, 1859.

ROGERS, NATHANIEL P. ["Nat"]. Scenic rider and gymnast. Levi J. North's, 1855; Spalding & Rogers, 1856-59; Hyatt & Co., 1859; Niblo & Sloat, Cooke's Amphitheatre, 1860; R. Sands', 1861; Howard's Athenaeum, Boston, Goodwin & Wilder, 1861; Rogers & Ashton's acrobatic troupe,

1861; Spalding & Rogers, South America, 1862. Returned from South America with his 2 boys early in 1871, after some 9 years absence. Was probably one of the team of **Rogers & Hammond**, gymnasts with the Imperial Brazilian Hippodrome, Philadelphia, winter 1872-73; posturing with his sons, **Charles** and **Antonio**, for Joel E. Warner's; Great Russian Athletes, West Indies, 1875-76.

ROGERS, WILLIAM E. (d. May 1, 1886) Born in Brewster, NY, a nephew of **Egbert Howes** and grandson of **Nathan Howes**. Father was lost on a steamer in Lake Michigan. Treasurer, P. T. Barnum's (1879) and for VanAmburgh & Co. With the latter, 1883, a train of cars was wrecked by a cyclone in Minnesota; Rogers, picked up for dead, partially recovered from the accident. Died in Towners, NY.

ROGERS ETTIE. Albino lady, P. T. Barnum's, 1874.

ROHM, ANNA JANE [nee Duck]. (1846?-May 28, 1875) Sideshow fat lady. Youngest and smallest of three sisters. Born in Licking County, OH. At age 20, married **Rohn**, a trainer of dogs and horses. 1874 weighed 583 pounds, was 6' tall and 72" around the waist. Connected with Barnum's enterprises and with the European Circus. Died at age 29 in Baltimore, Washington University Hospital.

ROLLAND BROTHERS [Henry, William]. Gymnasts and acrobats. Began circus performing on John Robinson's, 1862, as the Rolland Brothers. Comparable to the **Hanlon Brothers** in their skill as performers and famous for their act called *Alitora Volante*, which consisted of a series of leaps, swings and somersaults in mid-air. After the Robinson engagement, joined the **Hanlon Brothers** on tour. Next, took a specialty company down the Mississippi, playing small towns on their way to New Orleans; there, engaged by Spalding & Bidwell for a European tour. See William Holland and Henry Rolland.

ROLLAND, CAROLINE. Equestrienne. Pad rider, L. B. Lent's, first season in USA, 1868, 1869-72; 5-year tour of Europe, performing with Hengler's, England, 1874; J. W. Myers' *Cirque* American, Paris, 1877; Batty's, London, 1877. On return to USA, engaged with Den Stone's, 1878; Adam Forepaugh's, 1878; W. C. Coup' New United Monster Show, 1879; Barnum, Bailey & Hutchinson, 1883; then Sanger's Amphitheatre, London, 1884; back to Adam Forepaugh's, 1885. Daughter, **Lizzie**, was also a rider with Forepaugh's, 1885. Husband, **William**, was a cornetist attached to Emidy's band.

ROLLAND FAMILY [William C., Mme. Rolland, "Little Willie"]. General performers. **William C.** was a clown, rider, long-stilt act and tumbler. His wife was a vocalist and entrée rider. Dan Rice's, 1869. Their son, **William, Jr.,** a 3 years old in 1875, was doing a bottle pyramid act. Dan Rice's, 1870; E. Stowe's, 1871; Howe's Great London, 1874-75; W. C. Coup's, 1879. **Little Willie**, rider and tumbler, drowned while with W. C. Coups', June, 1879, age 15. While returning to the circus train in the dark, slipped from a railroad bridge. When

Coup was informed of the accident, he offered $50 to anyone recovering the body from the river. A property man, **Thomas Leddy**, was successful in bringing the dead boy to shore; whereupon, Coup ordered his treasurer to pay the sum. Other members of the company added to the reward whatever they could afford.

ROLLAND, HENRY [r. n. Keyes]. (1838-June 1, 1892) Gymnast and acrobat. Born at Culpepper Courthouse, VA. After completing a European tour for Spalding & Bidwell, remained on the continent for over 16 years, traveling with all the large circuses. Called the "American Prince" because of his neat appearance and extravagant mode of living. Returned to America around 1880 and engaged as press agent for Signor Faranta. Next, with Frank Gardner's, Central America, as business and press agent. Remained in Guatemala when the show returned to the States, where he taught English and Spanish for nearly a year; then took a position as timekeeper for the big dredge boat *City of Paris*. After having been in show business for nearly 40 years, died of cancer at the Charity Hospital, New Orleans.

ROLLAND, WILLIAM. Cornet soloist. See Caroline Rolland.

ROLLIA, HELEN. Dancer and rider, Dr. Gilbert R. Spalding's, 1844.

ROLLINS, JIM. Rider, George F. Bailey & Co., 1874.

ROLLINS, WILLIAM. Acrobatic clown. Dan Rice's, 1869; Adam Forepaugh's, 1883-85; W. W. Cole's, 1886. Married **Kate Silbon**, of the **Silbon Family**, fall 1885.

ROLTAIR, HARRY. Sideshow and concert magician, Cooper, Bailey & Co., 1879.

ROMAINE, AL. Banjoist, with Robinson & Eldred, 1849-50.

ROMALO, THOMAS. Burr Robbins', 1885.

ROMAN BROTHERS [John H. Murray, George Holland]. Gymnasts. Dan Rice's, 1852-53, 1856, 1859; L. B. Lent's, 1860-61. See John H. Murray and George Holland.

ROMELLI FAMILY [Eugene, Marie, and son Carlos or Cecil or Clint?]. Aerial acrobatics, Howes' Great American, London, 1870; came to America the following year with Howes' Great London, 1871-73; Atlantic and Pacific, 1871; proprietor, with **Harvey Johnson**, Romelli & Co.'s Great Novelty Circus and Performing Animal Show, 1872; Cooper, Jackson & Co., 1883; Barnum & London, 1885.

RONALDO BROTHERS. Sells Bros.', 1885; Gregory Bros.' Metropolitan, 1885.

RONALDO, CLAUDE. Donaldson & Rich, 1885.

RONCONI BROTHERS. Gymnasts, E. G. Smith's, 1867.

RONZONTI, MLLE. CONCHITTA [or Ronzati, Rosetta]. Making a grand ascension each day to the top of the pavilion, a distance of 220' and a height of 50', tight-rope dancer, James M. Nixon's Southern, 1870; Great Commonwealth, 1871.

ROONEY, LIZZIE. Ringling Bros'., 1897.

ROONEY, MIKE. Rider, Ringling Bros.', 1892-94.

ROONEY, SAM. John F. Wood's Allied Shows, 1889.

ROPER. Simpson & Price (formerly James West's), 1822, Philadelphia, Baltimore; Simpson & Price, Broadway Circus, NYC, 1823; Price & Simpson, 1827.

ROPER, H. Horizontal bars, Harry Thayer & Co.'s, 1890.

ROSA, PATTI. Serio-comic singer, concert, Montgomery Queen's, 1876; Cooper, Bailey & Co., Australian tour, 1877.

ROSAVELLA BROTHERS. Trapeze performers, Collins' Oriental Combination, 1877.

ROSCH, JACK. Cloggist in concert, Great Australian, 1870;

ROSCOE, GEORGE. Advertiser, Nixon's Amphitheatre, Chicago, 1872.

ROSE, ALLEN. Leaper from England, L. B. Lent's, 1871; John Robinson's, 1873.

ROSE BROTHERS. Leapers and tumblers, Irwin Bros.', 1887.

ROSEBUD, COUNT. W. W. Cole's Australian tour (which left San Francisco, October 23, 1880).

ROSE, BYRON V. (d. August 8, 1901) Engaged in circus business for some 55 years. Boss canvasman, L. B. Lent's, 1874; master of transportation, Cooper, Bailey, & Co., 1879-80; Barnum, Bailey & Hutchinson, 1881-82; Barnum & Bailey, 1880s-1895, last employment being with this show. [D. W. Watt: "Rose was a gentleman at all times and in his day was considered the best master of transportation that ever was in the business."] Died of Bright's disease in Bridgeport, CT.

ROSE, CLARK. (d. February 11, 1887) Born in Royal Oak, MI. Entered circus business around 1873, controlling some of the privileges on Dan Rice's; later with Batchelor & Doris, and John O'Brien's. Co-proprietor, Boyd & Peters', 1878-80; interested in Stowe's, 1881; in partnership, Carroll & Rose's Great Eastern, 1882. Died of consumption, Denver, CO.

ROSE, NELLIE. Charioteer, Barnum & Bailey, 1892.

ROSENBAUM, J. Contracting agent, Frank Rich's Great Eastern, 1886.

ROSENBERRY, PROF. Band leader, from the Academy of Music, NYC, New York Champs Elysees, 1865.

ROSENBURG, J. Contracting agent, Baldwin, Wall & Co.'s Great Eastern, 1880.

ROSS, CHARLES B. Gymnast. George F. Bailey & Co., 1863; Robinson & Deery, 1864; John Wilson's, San Francisco and Australia, 1865. Remained behind when Wilson took his troupe to India, 1866-67; clown, Chiarini's, San Francisco, 1868. Become co-proprietor of Woodyear & Ross' Royal Australian Circus. Privileges, concert and sideshow, Donaldson & Rich, 1885.

ROSS, E. H. Holton & Gates' Harmoniums, a minstrel band organized for the the Simon Pure American Circus, NYC, October 1, 1866.

ROSS, FRANK. Bartine's (**Charles Bartine**, proprietor and manager), 1889.

ROSS, GEORGE. (d. February 4, 1870) Scenic rider. Pupil of **James M. Nixon**. Took the Nixon name for part of career. Howes & Co., 1848; Crane & Co., 1849; J. M. June's, 1850; Welch's, 1852; Welch & Lent, 1854; Howes, Myers & Madigan, 1855; Jim Myers', 1856; Nixon & Kemp, 1857-58; apprenticeship ended, Welch & Lent, 1859; L. B. Lent's, 1860; James M. Nixon's, fall 1860; R. Sands', 1862; Melville, Cooke & Sands, 1863; pirouetting act and somersault thrower, Chiarini's, South and Central America, 1869. Died in Rio De Janeiro.

ROSS, JAMES. Agent, Charles Bartine & Co., 1872.

ROSS, JAMES. Detective, P. T. Barnum's, 1873.

ROSS, VICTORIA. Rider, G. G. Grady's, 1874.

ROSS, WILLIAM. Vaulter, James M. Nixon's, 1870.

ROSSETER, R. Tight-rope performer. J. T. and J. B. Bailey's, 1834; Dr. Gilbert R. Spalding's, 1847.

ROSSTON, AUGUSTUS L. ["Gus"]. Advertising agent. Stone, Rosston & Co., 1864; Grand Reserve Combination, 1866; Whitby & Co., 1867; DeMott & Ward, 1868; asst. advertiser, Stone & Murray, 1869; asst. agent, Rosston, Springer & Henderson, 1872; contracting agent, John Robinson's, 1874.

ROSSTON, FRANK H. (May 30, 1828-February 22, 1874) Showman, ringmaster. Born in Philadelphia. Connected with Dan Rice's early management from at least 1848 until at least 1858; L. B. Lent's, 1858-59; ringmaster, Dan Rice's, 1862; ringmaster, Howes', 199 Bowery, NYC, 1864; Mrs. Charles Warner's, Continental Theatre, Philadelphia, winter 1864-65; ringmaster and co-proprietor, Stone, Rosston & Co., 1864-66; equestrian director, James M. French's, 1867-69; co-proprietor and equestrian director, Rosston, Springer & Henderson's Great Mastodon Caravan, Circus and Menagerie (Frank H. Rosston, **Andrew Springer**, **Abe Henderson** and **Adam Forepaugh**, proprietors), 1871 (Forepaugh bought out his partners, October 1872); concert privileges, Montgomery Queen's, 1873. Died in Jacksonville, FL, age 46. Married **Laura Johnson**, whom he met on Dan Rice's, 1852. They had a daughter and 4 sons.

ROSSTON, GEORGE. Contracting agent, Robinson & Lake, 1865.

ROTHCHILD, A. B. Co-proprietor, A. B. Rothcild & Co.'s Royal Victoria Circus, 1875-76, with **John V. O'Brien**.

ROTTGEN, MLLE. L. Equestrienne, with Great European, 1865.

ROULESTONE. Rider. Native of Boston, book-binder by trade. Amateur rider, Thomas Stewart's, 1809. Also landlord possessing building in which circus performed, Roulestone's Amphitheatre, Boston. Having sold out his amphitheatre to **Robert Davis** and a **Mister Bates**, stayed on at what was now called the Boston Circus, giving riding lessons in the morning and performing in the evening.

ROURK, JAMES. Lion king, W. S. Harris' Nickel-Plate, 1890.

ROUSE, JOHN. Candy privilege, Wintermute Bros.', 1897.

ROWE, JAMES. Singing and talking clown, Bryan & Williams, 1894.

ROWE, JAMES R. Proprietor, James R. & William Rowe's Menagerie, 1834; rider, Lion Theatre Circus, 1837.

ROWE, JOSEPH ANDREW. (1819-1887) Rider and showman. Born at Kingston, Lenoir County, NC. Asa T. Smith's, 1829-33; Yeaman Circus, 1831-33; continued apprenticeship, Joseph Palmer's, 1833; Peter Coty's, 1833-35; Buckley & Weeks, 1835-36; Raymond & Weeks, 1836; in Cuba, 1837; Peter Coty's, 1838; rider, John Mateer's, 1843-44; Rich & Rowe (**Dariastus Rich** and Joseph Andrew Rowe, proprietors), 1844. Show left for South America, spring 1844. Gave the first circus performance under canvas in San Francisco as Rowe's Olympic Circus, October 29, 1849, and continued showing there and in Sacramento until 1850. Proprietor, Rowe & Marshall's American Circus (with **John R. Marshall**), 1858, which toured Australia and parts East. From this latter venture, amassed enough money to retire to a huge ranch in California; later, returned to the circus business and lost his entire fortune.

ROWE, RICHARD. Gymnast, with John Robinson's, 1879, 1881.

ROWE, S. N. Agent, the Atlantic and Pacific Circus, 1871.

ROWE, WILLIAM. Co-proprietor, James R. & William Rowe's Menagerie, 1834.

ROWLAND, JAMES. (D. April 4, 1876) Drove a team of 10 Shetlands before the Cinderella Chariot," Howes & Sanger, 1872; "the King of the Air" balancing trapeze (throwing a double somersault and alighting on a trapeze bar), Melville, Maginley & Cooke, 1875. Died in Wheeling, WV.

ROWLAND, JOSEPHINE. G. F. Bailey & Co., 1869.

ROWLEY, ALICE. Equestrian, John Robinson's, 1867.

ROYAL JAPANESE TROUPE. Great Chicago, 1873

ROYCE, CHARLES M. Clown. E. Stowe's, 1871; Cosmopolitan, 1871-72; Cooper & Jackson, 1880, 1882; equestrian director, James T. Johnson & Co., 1881; contractor, Pullman, Mack & Co., 1884.

ROYCE, JOHN. Clown, Cole's Great New Southern Circus, 1881.

ROYER, ARCHIE. Clown, leaper, tumbler and all-around performer. With wife **Rose**, Walter L. Main's, 1892-93; Cole & Lockwood, 1894; Great Wallace, 1896. **Rose** (d. January 14, 1899) Acrobat. Born in Towanda, PA. Married **Archie** Steubenville, OH, April 6, 1893. Died of pneumonia, Carrolton, OH, age 24.

ROYER, EUGENE. Walter L. Main's, 1888.

ROYER, MAUD. Walter L. Main's, 1888; Melvin, Royer & Jacob's Big Two Ring Circus, 1895.

ROZETTA, MILLIE. Flying trapeze. James M. French's, 1870; James M. Nixon's Southern, 1870.

RUDOLPH, CARL. Courtney & Sanford's Minstrels, party made up in New York to travel with Courtney & Sanford's Circus in South America. Sailed from New York, July 23, 1873.

RUGGLES, HENRY W. Acrobat. Raymond & Weeks, 1836; H. H. Fuller's, 1838; J. W. Stocking's, 1839; Welch, Bartlett & Co., 1839; western unit, June, Titus, Angevine & Co., 1842; slack-wire, Welch, Bartlett & Co., 1840; slack-rope, Welch & Manns, 1843-44; John Tryon's, Bowery Amphitheatre, NYC, 1844; Howes & Mabie, 1845-46; Palmer's Great Western, 1846; slack-rope, Sands, Lent & Co., 1846, 1847; flying cord, R. Sands, 1849; John Robinson's, 1858; Niblo & Sloat, West Indies, November 1860; Spalding & Rogers, South America, 1862-63; Hippotheatron, NYC, with Spalding & Rogers, spring 1864; Lipman & Stokes, 1866.

RULLEN, ED. General agent, Irwin Bros.', 1887.

RUNARD, JAMES. Nelson's South American Hippodrome, California, May 1870.

RUNNELLS, BONNIE. (d. August 16, 1884) Rider, gymnast and variety artist. One of 7 children. Made his debut at age 8, riding with his father, **Burnell R. Runnells**, at the *Cirque Napoleon*, Paris. Following year, came to America with the Runnell's Family (**Burnell**, and sons **Bonnie** and **Freddie**). See Burnell Runnells. Following this engagement, the **Runnells Family** was discontinued; Bonnie's father retired and **Freddie** remained in the circus business. Bonnie followed a career on the variety stage. Later, Dutch clown, P. T. Barnum's, 1880-81; M. B. Leavitt's All-Star Specialty Co., 1883, as well as Hilliard & Main's Circus. Last appearance, Tony Pastor's Theatre, April 4, 1884. Died in Chicago.

RUNNELLS, BURNELL R. (April 17, 1826-February 2, 1908) Acrobat. Born in Indian Springs, GA. Came into the business, 1837. Equestrian, Rockwell & Co.'s, 1838; rider, June, Titus, Angevine & Co., Bowery Amphitheatre, 1840; June, Titus, Angevine & Co., 1841-42; rider, Rockwell & Stone, 1842-43; Rockwell & Co., 1847; Dan Rice's, 1848; Howes & Co., 1849; Crane & Co., 1849; Levi J. North's, 1854; Rowe & Co.'s Pioneer Circus, San Francisco, 1856; Howes & Cushing, Alhambra Palace, London, 1858; acrobat, Price's, Lisbon, Portugal, 1862; *Cirque Napoleon*, Paris, 1865; George W. DeHaven's, 1866; Dan Castello's, 1867-68; L. B. Lent's, 1867-68; Dan Rice's, 1869; returned to Europe, 1869, and performed at the *Cirque Champs Elysees*; back in USA, James M. Nixon's Southern, 1870; P. T. Barnum's, 1871; James M. Nixon's Amphitheatre, Chicago, 1872; Great Eastern, 1872. Runnells and the boys were with Howard, Langrishe & Carle's "Black Crook" Co., touring as far West as California. When in California, performed at John Wilson's Palace Amphitheatre, San Francisco, 1875. Returning East, 1876, with Montgomery Queen's, **Runnells Family** act discontinued with Burnell's retirement. One of the first American leapers to accomplish a double somersault from a *batoute*

board, 1850s. Considered one of the handsomest and best physically developed men to appear at that time. Performing with his 2 sons, was unrivaled in the classic school of gymnastics, classic groupings and posturings. Appeared before the Queen of England and the Emperor of France. In later years, was door keeper at the People's Theatre, NYC, 1886. Died at the Home for the Incurables, Philadelphia, age 82.

RUNNELLS, FRED. (b. 1852) Clown and tumbler. Oldest son of **Burnell Runnells**, originally a member of the **Runnells Family** of gymnasts. See Burnell R. Runnells. Family broke up, 1876. Carlo Bros.', South America, 1877; tumbler, Cooper & Bailey, 1880-81; Leon & Dockrill, Iron Amphitheatre, Havana, winter 1881-82; Cantelli & Leon, Havana, Cuba, winter 1882-83; Barnum & London, 1884; Hilliard & Main, 1883; Roberts & Gardner, 1886; Barnum-Forepaugh, Madison Square Garden, 1887; Barnum & Bailey, 1893.

RUNNELLS, JAMES. Acrobat, Welch & Mann, 1843-44; Mann, Welch & Delavan, 1845; clown, L. B. Lent's, 1876.

RUNNELLS, WILLIAM. James Robinson's, 1872.

RUNNISON, W. General agent, with Great Oriental Pavilion Show, 1877.

RUSSELL, G. B. Treasurer, James E. Cooper's, 1872.

RUSSELL, GEORGE H. Manager, Rufus Welch's, 1852; treasurer, Hemmings, Cooper & Whitby, 1868.

RUSSELL, JAMES. band leader, Springer's Royal Cirq-Zoolodon, 1875.

RUSSELL, JOHN N. Clown, Walter L. Main's, 1886-87; co-proprietor, Clements & Russell, 1888 (but sold his interest to **Robert Clements** in July of that year); equestrian director and principal clown, Gregory & D'Alma, 1889.

RUSSELL, L. H. General performer, Thompson, Smith & Hawes, 1866.

RUSSELL, LIZZIE. Wallace & Co., 1886.

RUSSELL, MAUD. Walter L. Main's, 1889.

RUSSELL, SHAD. 40-horse driver, Dr. Gilbert R. Spalding's, 1873. Said to be one of the best drivers in the country.

RUSSELL, T. B. Cooper, Jackson & Co., 1882.

RUTH, JOHN. Ed G. Basye's Cosmopolitan Circus and Equestrian Exposition, 1878; Holland & Gormley (**George Holland** and **Frank Gormley**, proprietors), 1888.

RYAN BROTHERS. Gymnast. Trans-Atlantic, 1879; Shelby, Pullman & Hamilton, 1881.

RYAN, DANNY. (b. 1868) Acrobat. With original Sells Bros.' and continued with them off and on until, as Forepaugh-Sells, the show went off the road, 1911. Worked the ground and high bars with the likes of **Pettit, McVey, English, Zorella Brothers, Delno**, etc. Principal flyer with **Ryan, Weitzel,** and **Zorella**. With Barnum & Bailey on the European tour 4 years; Australia with Sells Bros.'; in Cuba—Santos & Artigas, Pubillones, etc. Married **Ouika Meers** of the famous Meers equestrians. Later years took to clowning until 1935 on Ringling Bros. and Barnum & Bailey.

RYAN, DENNIS. Irish comedian, Dan Rice's Paris Pavilion, 1872.

RYAN, JAMES M. Aerialist, equestrian director. Siegrist, Howe & Co., winter 1884; Donaldson & Rich, 1885; Holland & McMahon, Chicago, fall 1885.

RYAN, J. E. Master of transportation, Reichold Shows, 1897.

RYAN, PATRICK. (1833?-August 2, 1893) From County Tipperary, Ireland. Came to USA, 1854, and entered circus business. Traveled with the smaller shows, sometimes in sideshow management. Later, sideshow manager with Adam Forepaugh's for several years. In partnership, **Dr. Gilbert R. Spalding** and **Joel Warner**, 1873, took out Warner, Ryan & Spalding for a season. Following year, with the withdrawal of **Spalding**, show went out as Warner & Ryan. Ryan & Robinson, 1882-85. In retirement from the circus business, opened a grocery store, Albany, NY. Also owned real estate in that city. Brother of **Cornelius Ryan**, also a circus man. Died there at about 60 years of age.

RYAN, PERRY. Concert proprietor, Gregory Bros.' Metropolitan, 1885.

RYAN, S. (with **John V. O'Brien**) proprietor, Joel E. Warner's Great Pacific Menagerie and Circus, 1871.

RYAN, THEOLA. Donaldson & Rich, 1885.

RYAN, TOMMY. Irish change and character artist, Dan Rice's, 1872-73.

RYAN, TONY. Equestrian director, Lockwood & Flynn, 1887; Holland & Gormley, 1888.

RYDON, WILLIAM and **EMMA.** Aerialists. Leon W. Washburn's, 1892-93; Barnum & Bailey, 1895.

RYLAND, ELENA. (May, 17, 1875-1955) or "Nellie," a nickname used almost exclusively when she retired from show business, was born in Mexico City. Her parents were **Elena Jeal** and **George Frederick Ryland**, both circus riders. Kept a diary when traveling with her mother between 1891-1894. Married **Cecil Lowande**, November, 16, 1900, in St. Louis, MO. They had three sons—**Cecil, Jr.** (b. 1902) and twins **Jeal** and **Ryland** (b. 1904). All were born in Petersburg, IL, where the family maintained a home, later moving to Springfield. After the family was grown, **Cecil, Sr.** departed for the East. **Nellie** made her home in Michigan with her twin sons. **Cecil** died in an accident in NYC in 1940. Both are buried in Rose Hill Cemetery in Petersburg. First appeared as a teenager, 1887, at a private exhibition at the Jeal sisters' training school in Jersey City. Made her American debut as a rider, Barnum & Bailey, 1893; within a month, transferred to Adam Fore

paugh's where she and **Julia Lowande** did a double bareback riding act. 1901, Nellie and **Cecil Lowande** came together as riders on Walter L. Main's. From then through 1915 had parallel careers with the same shows. Double riding and hurdle act with **Julia Lowande**, 1903; rode with her aunt, **Linda Jeal**, 1905; principal act opposite **Sadie Davenport**, 1910. Frank A. Gardner's, West Indies and South America, 1889-93; Walter L. Main's, 1901; Forepaugh-Sells, 1903; Lowande Bros.', 1904; Shipp's, 1905; Campbell Bros.', 1905-06, 1909-10; Sells-Floto, 1908; Gollmar Bros.', 1910; Howes' Great London, 1911, 1914-16; John Robinson's, 1917-21; Hagenbeck-Wallace, 1922-24; Sells-Floto, 1927-28; Downie Bros.', 1929; Shipp's, Trinidad, 1930.

RYLAND, GEORGE F. (1826-April 12, 1890) Principal riding act, tumbler, juggler on ground or horseback, ringmaster, clown, animals breaker and performer. William Cooke's, England, 1840; Pablo Fanque's, Liverpool, 1847; James Cooke's, Glasgow, 1848; Thomas Cooke's, Portsmouth and Brighton, 1849; Welch's, Glasgow, 1852; Hernandez & Stone, Bolton and Bradford, 1853; E. T. Smith's, Drury Lane, 1853; Hernendez, Stone & Newsome, 1854; E. T. Smith's, London, 1855; Dan Rice's Circus, 1855-56; juggler, Lee & Bennett's, San Francisco, 1856-57; Lee's New National Circus, 1858; Lee & Ryland's, San Francisco, winter 1866-69; Hayes Park, San Francisco, 1866; Lee & Ryland's Cosmopolitan Circus, San Francisco, 1866; Lee & Ryland's Hippodrome, San Francisco, 1866; ringmaster, Jeal & Co., California, 1871; Ryland's, California, 1872; equestrian director and ringmaster, Crystal Palace Show, 1872; Ryland's, returning to California after about 5 years spent in South and Central America, 1878; Prof. Samwell's Great Combination, South America, 1873; equestrian director, American Circus, winter 1879-80. May have been married to **Rosaline Lee**, daughter of H. C. Lee. Married equestrienne **Elena Jeal**, 1880. Weldon & Co., winter 1884; Miles Orton's, 1885; dog circus, Tribbey & Co.'s Mastadon Dime Circus, 1887; Ringling Bros.', 1897. Had winter quarters in Hayward, CA, for many years. A fine instructor; of his apprentices, **Linda** and **Elena Jeal** were the best known as riders and general performers. When Ryland got his own show, called it Jeal & Co., 1871, as well as Ryland's Oriental up to about the middle of the 1870s, when the girls left.

RYMAN, ADD. Sideshow performer, VanAmburgh's, 1866.

RYWICK, HERR. General performer, Stone & Murray, 1868.

James Robinson

S

SABANTI, MONS. [or Sebunti]. 4-horse rider, Great European, 1869-70.

SACKETT, EDWARD J. Sideshow orator, concert performer, Cooper, Bailey & Co., 1876; Adam Forepaugh's (Pullman Bros.' sideshow), 1876; Barnum, Bailey & Hutchinson, 1881-82.

SAGE, C. M. [or E. M.]. Contracting agent, Alexander Robinson's, 1871; general agent, 1874.

SANGRINO. Celebrated British trainer, exhibited five elephants that waltzed, played musical instruments, stood on their heads, formed a pyramid, and trodded up inclines, as well as executing other novelties, Howes' Great London, 1871.

SAGRINO, FERDINAND. Equestrian. Mrs. Charles Warner's, Philadelphia, 1864; Stone, Rosston & Murray, Front Street Theatre, Baltimore, winter 1866-67; 4-horse bareback rider, L. B. Lent's, 1868; George F. Bailey & Co., 1869; Stone & Murray, 1869; L. B. Lent's, 1870-71; Adam Forepaugh's, 1873. Arrested in NYC and sent to Sing Sing penitentiary for 2 years for bigamy, March 5, 1874; marriages took place in November 1873 within 2 weeks of each other.

SAID, ABDDALLAH BEN. (d. February 8, 1898) Original manager of the groupe of Bedouin Arabs which were brought to the United States, 1882, by **Arnest Cook** for W. W. Cole's. Born in Paris, the son of **Sidi Mohamad**, a marabout of Bagdad. Died in NYC, age about 43.

SALBINI TROUPE. French bicyclists, John B. Doris', 1884.

SALINYEA FAMILY [Charley, George, Henry]. Acrobats and living statue artists. Dan Castello's, 1870.

SALSBURY, H. Chief bill poster, P. T. Barnum's, 1874-75.

SALSBURY, NATE. (February 1846-December 24, 1902) Born in Freeport, IL. After serving in the Civil War, embarked on a theatrical career, debuting at Grand Rapids, MI, as Colorgog in *Pocahontas*. Shortly, with the Boston Museum Stock Co. and such notables as **William Warren** and **Annie Clark**, where he remained for 4 years. Next, on the road, Hooley's Comedy Co., 3 years. With **John Webster**, organized a stock company called **Salsbury's Troubadours**, which toured the United States and Europe for 15 years. While with the Troubadours, met **William Cody** and organized with him a theatrical piece of the wild west. Spent around $200,000, 1900, in converting New Jersey wasteland into a select cottage colony near North Long Branch known as "The Reservation." Died at his home in Long Branch, NJ.

SAMPSON FAMILY. Acrobats, John Robinson's, 1892.

SAMPSON, W. J. General manager, G. G. Grady's, 1874.

SAMUELS, HENRY. Adam Forepaugh's, 1873.

SAMUELS, TOM. Animal trainer. Performed his dogs and monkeys, John Robinson's, 1879-85.

SAMWELLS, LEON. Gymnast and acrobat. Nelson's South American Hippodrome, touring in California, 1870; Ryland's, California, 1872; trained dogs and monkeys, Prof. Samwell's Great Combination Circus and Animal Show, South America, 1873; John Wilson's Palace Amphitheatre, San Francisco, 1874.

SAMWELLS, THOMAS, SR. (1825-October 4, 1906) Was adept at training dogs and monkeys. Forepaugh & Samwells (**W. R. Forepaugh**, Thomas Samwells, proprietors), 1886-88.

SANDERENO FAMILY [4 in number]. German equestrians, Howes' Great European, 1864.

SANDERS, JOE. (d. June 8, 1889) Equestrian director, with Wallace & Co., 1889. Died in Des Moines, IA, from a fall while performing in Audubon, IA.

SANDERS, JOHN. Thayer & Noyes, 1865.

SANDERSON, GEORGE. Mrs. Charles H. Warner's Great National Circus, Continental Theatre, Philadelphia, winter 1864-65.

SANDERSON, H. S. Privileges (with **William D. Hagar**), John H. Murray's, 1877.

SANDS, ARCHIE. (d. October 25, 1901) Agent and advertiser. Connected for several years with various amusements—Barnum & Bailey; Ringling Bros.'; John Robinson's, 1898; Walter L. Mains', 1899; and Pawnee Bill's Wild West. Last employed, Al G. Field's Minstrels, 1900. Died in Hagerstown, MD.

SANDS, CHARLES. European Circus, 1869.

SANDS, DICK. (May 2, 1840-March 28, 1900) Clog dancer. Born in Mill Bridge, Yorkshire, England. Came to the United States at age 17 to live with an uncle, Waterbury, CT. Made professional debut at Pierce's Variety, Providence, RI, for three $3.00 a week and board. A few months later, left for NYC, went to Bryant's Minstrel Hall and asked **Neil Bryant** for an engagement. After dancing for about 20 minutes, Bryant jumped to his feet and said, "Stop, young man, you are all right." Opened with the Bryants and was a great success. Next, engaged by **Robert Fox** for the Art Union; then Sloat & Shepard, 1858, performing in the concert; in the fall, rejoined Bryant's and later went to Frank Rivers' Melodeon, between Spring and Prince Streets, NYC, and Frank Rivers' Melodeon, Philadelphia; Morris Bros., Pell & Trowbridge's Minstrels, Boston, 1860, then on the road with that company, spring 1861; James M. Nixon's, 1862. At close of the season, performed at Frank Rivers' Melodeon, both Philadelphia and NYC; Carr's Melodeon, Buffalo; Den Thompson's Concert Hall, Toronto; Chadwick's Varieties, Chicago; and Palace Varieties, Nashville. Appeared at Haverly's Varieties, Toledo, OH, 1863; after which, organized Sands & Haverly's Minstrels. At Academy of Music, Buffalo, played the part of Katy Welch in *Arrah Na Pogue.* Joined the Hanlon Bros.' Specialty Show. Tammany Hall, NYC, introduced the clog on a pedestal 8' high, the first time a clog was ever done in that manner. L. B. Lent's, Adam Forepaugh's, Thayer & Anderson; West Indies, J. Hudson's Great North and South American Circus, 1872-73; saong and dance artist, Palace of Wonders, P. T. Barnum, 1876-79; VanAmburgh's, 1896; Barnum & Bailey off and on for 12 years, where he got the name of "Barnum's Old Woman in the Shoe." Sands' dancing was mostly confined to the floor. He danced with ease, grace and novelty. Died in extreme poverty, NYC.

SANDS, ELBERT. 3-horse rider. The brother of **Richard Sands.** Nathan Howes (A. Sands'), 1833; Howes & Sands, 1834; Mammoth Circus (Howes & Sands), 1835; Eagle Circus (Howes), 1836; Cole, Miller & Yale, winter 1837; Yale, Howes?, 1838; Lamb's, winter 1839; Yale & Co., 1840; P. H. Nichols', 1841.

SANDS, GEORGE. General performer, Sands & Nathans, 1853-59. Half-brother to **Richard Sands.**

SANDS, HEZEKIAH. Treasurer and co-proprietor, Welsh & Sands, 1893.

SANDS, JESSE. (b. 1838) General performer and sideshow manager. Born in Manchester, England. Came to this country with **Richard Sands,** 1845. Infant equestrian, with Welch & Mann, Philadelphia, 1846; Sands, Lent & Co. **Richard Sands** performed "with his children," **Maurice** and **Jesse,** in a series of classic passes, evolutions, groupings and flights of aerial gravitation, Chatham Theatre, NYC, 1847. R. Sands & Co., 1849; rider on 4 Shetland ponies, Sands & Chiarini, 1854; performed the "Courier of Missellonghi" on his 4 Shetlands, Sands, Nathans & Co. 1855, 1857, 1859; Bowery Circus, 1857-58; George F. Bailey & Co., 1860.

SANDS, MAURICE. (b. 1839) Welch & Mann, Philadelphia, 1846; Sands, Lent & Co. **Richard Sands** performed with "his children, **Maurice** and **Jesse,** in a series of classic passes, evolutions, groupings and flights of aerial gravitation, Chatham Theatre, NYC, 1847; the "Juvenile Equestrian Wonder", R. Sands, 1849; Sands, Nathans & Co., Broadway Circus, 1857-58; Davis & Crosby, 1859; and Slaymaker & Nichols, 1864.

SANDS, RICHARD. (1814-February 24, 1861) Showman, rider and clown. Born on Long Island, NY, from a farming family. Went out on his own at about age 12, his first job being a dirt cart driver, NYC, near the Mount Pitt Circus. With **Aaron Turner's** early, 1831, as a clown and general performer. Apprenticeship to Turner ended, 1833; went into partnership with **Nathan B. Howes,** 1834, to form American Circus, also serving as riding master, juggler and bareback rider. One of his feats was turning a back somersault from horse to ground. With Howes, received training both as performer and manager. Left the show, 1838, to go with Miller & Yale;

shortly, show title changed to Miller, Yale & Sands. Joined the Flatfoots and appeared at the Zoological Institute, winter 1839-40. Sands & Howes, Detroit, MI, 1840; June, Titus & Angevine, 1841; organized Sands, Lent & Co.'s American Circus for a tour of England, 1842; arrived at Liverpool March 8, for an 8-week season at the Royal Amphitheatre. English Opera House, London, winter 1842-43, then went on tour; remained abroad with his 2 pupils, **Jesse** and **Maurice,** returning to America, 1846; at which time again went into partnership with L. B. Lent; brought with him a performing horse, May Fly, which became a great feature; Sands, Lent & Co., Chatham Theatre, NYC, 1847; proprietor, R. Sands, 1849-50; proprietor, Bowery Amphitheatre, NYC, 1852; New York Amphitheatre, 37 Bowery, NYC, as a ceiling-walker, December 6, 1852. Went to England, arriving December 29, 1852, to perfect his act as a human fly, performing on a slab of polished marble, using rubber suction pads attached to his feet. Made ceiling-walking debut Drury Lane Theatre, London, March 7, 1853, where he received £60 a week; Surrey Theatre for March 29 engagement and thence to Paris, where he opened at the *Theatre des Varieties,* May 7, 1853; returned to the United States July 7 of that year. **John J. Nathans** was taken in as a partner of Sands, Lent & Co., 1855; erected (with **Nathans, Howes** and **Avery Smith**) Franconi's Hippodrome, Broadway and 23rd Street, NYC, marking the introduction of the hippodrome track to circus performances in America; Sands, Nathans & Co., Bowery, November 1858, moving to the Broadway Circus later that month; principal rider, George F. Bailey & Co., 1859. [John A. Dingess: "Sands was remarkable for his energy, his indomitable spirit, which characterized all his actions.... He was never idle; action was necessary to his existence."] Died of yellow fever in Havana, Cuba. One source erroneously states that he was killed, 1861, when, challenged to ceiling walk outside the circus, he used a ceiling in a civic building, at Melrose, Massachusetts, and a whole section of the plaster came away.

SANFORD, GEN. E. W. (d. July 25, 1877) Erected the Mount Pitt Circus, Grand Street, NYC, fall 1826. Stucture was built of wood, with the exception of a brick facade, and accommodated between 3,000 and 4,000 people. Destroyed by fire August, 1829. Was also the builder and proprietor of the Lafayette Amphitheatre, NYC, where circus performances and horse dramas were given. Constructed on a site in the Lispenard Meadows on Manhattan Island. Married actress **Mrs. Holman (nee Latimer),** 1824. Was a member of the New York bar and a distinguished officer in the New York military. Died in NYC.

SANFORD, JOSEPH [or James?]. Gymnast and acrobat. Partner of **George W. Brown,** about 1867-71. Prior to that, Gardner & Hemmings, Front Street Theatre, Baltimore, winter 1865-66; Yankee Robinson's, Chicago, 1866; Dan Rice's, 1867; Adam Forepaugh's, 1867-69; Philadelphia Circus, winter 1867-68; Mrs. Charles Warner's, Philadelphia, 1869; trapeze performer, Gardner & Forepaugh's, 1870; Commonwealth Circus, traveling by boat, 1871; George F. Bailey & Co., 1872.

SANFORD, S. S. [or Sandford]. Ethiopian entertainer and clown. L. B. Lent's, 1859; Dan Gardner & Kenyon's, 1868. At one time, one of the richest men in the minstrel profession; received $1,000 a month to appear as clown in the circus and manage the minstrel troupe in the sideshow; lost over $60,000 in bad speculations late in his career.

SANYEAH, MME. MAUDE [sometimes Senyah, but r. n. Phoebe Frost]. (1841?-June 25, 1910) From Carlisle, England. Flying rings and leaps for life with **Samuel Sanyeah**. In the act she flew by means of suspended rings along a wire, loosing hold of the rings to be caught by her partner who was hanging by his feet from the bar of a fixed trapeze. "The handsomest woman in America," Yankee Robinson's, 1869; Charles Noyes', 1871; P. A. Older's, 1870-72. Billed as "Empress of the Air" and "Flying Meteor." Divorced or was never officially married, and was wedded to **John Conklin**, San Francisco, November 4, 1872. Later had performing dogs. Died Lambeth, England, Infirmary, age 69. See Samuel Sanyeah.

SANYEAH, SAMUEL [r. n. Samuel Haynes]. (1835?-August 26, 1900) Gymnast with **Maude Sanyeah**. Muscle man and one of the first to work on the flying trapeze. "Double Leap for Life," Yankee Robinson's, 1869; Charles Noyes', 1871; P. A. Older's, 1870-72. Injured by a fall which caused his retirement. Around 1898, was placed in a hospital for the insane at Kankakee, IL. Drowned there, age 65. See Mme. Maude Sanyeah.

SAPP. (November 10, 1834-March 1901) Sideshow curiosity, called "The Ossified Man." Was born in Lebanon, KY. Muscles began to waste away and joints solidify at age 7. Every joint became immovable except those in the left shoulder and the fingers and growth ceased. Exhibited by a Chicago museum, 1884, and since then by many shows. Possessed a bright mind and a pleasant disposition. Died in Albuquerque, NM.

SARBRO, KING [r. n. Yamamota Hostara]. (d. December 25, 1882) Native of Yeddo, Japan. Came to USA around 1871 with a Japanese troupe. Expert juggler and slide for life performer. Outside act, Sells Bros.', 1880; Adam Forepaugh's, 1882. Married February 7, 1873, to a lady professionally known as **Queen Sarbro**. Died in NYC of consumption, age 40.

SARGEANT, F. WILSON. Co-proprietor, Hamilton & Sargeant's (with **Prof. E. Hamilton**), 1877-79. Sold his interest to his partner, 1880. Co-proprietor, William Main & Co.'s New Consolidated Show, 1881, 1889; Sargeant & Kidder, 1892-93.

SARGEANT, GEORGE W. (b. 1811) Rider. Born in NYC. Spent several seasons with J. Purdy Brown as a standing hurdle rider and vaulter as early as 1825. Juvenile on 2 Shetland

ponies, jumping over garters and through balloons, Brown & Bailey, 1826; Shakespearian rider, presentations of Falstaff, Shylock and Richard III, Rockwell and Stone 1845-46; Howes & Co., 1847-48; J. M. June, 1850; comic and patriotic act on horseback, Sands & Nathans 1855, 1857; equestrian director, Spalding & Rogers' *Floating Palace*, 1859; Alex Robinson's, 1865.

SARONI, SIGNOR. Gymnast, Hippocomique, 1868.

SATSUMA, PRINCE. (1840?-July 29, 1907) Japaneze gymnast, balancing *perche*, and juggler. Came to USA, 1865, with the first Japaneze group to arrive, **Taykon Troupe**. After performing with the major circuses and in the principal vaudeville houses, retired around 1905, last stage appearance being at Tony Pastor's Theatre. P. T. Barnum's Roman Hippodrome, 1874-75; P. T. Barnum's, 1876, 1878; Cooper, Bailey & Co. Australian tour, 1877; Burr Robbins', 1879; Stickney's Imperial Parisian Circus, 1880; Burr Robbins', 1885; Doris & Colvin, 1887. Died at his home in NYC, age 67.

SATTERLEE, R. C. Manager, Major Brown's Mammoth Coliseum, 1857; partner, Satterlee & Bell, 1858-62; manager, Davis & Crosby's, 1859.

SAULSBURY, EUGENIE. Chariot racer, P. T. Barnum's Roman Hippodrome, 1875.

SAUNDERS. Musician. Dutchman who performed for Quick and Mead, 1826. His hurdy-gurdy was advertised as "King David's Cymbals." Also led the street parade, playing a keyless bugle.

SAUNDERS, B. Contortionist, Great Southern, 1874.

SAUNDERS, GEORGE. Metropolitan Circus (**M. J. Robinson**, proprietor) 1864; Gardner & Hemmings, Continental Theatre, Philadelphia, winter 1864-65.

SAUNDERS, JOHN [or Sanders]. English rider and leaper, Thayer & Noyes, 1864, and with a split troupe from the Thayer & Noyes organization, under the management of Dr. Thayer, moved by steamboat along tributaries of the Mississippi, December 1865; Barnum, VanAmburgh and Castello, 1867; Dan Castello's, winter 1867-68; Lee & Ryland, Pacific Coast, 1868; bareback rider, Dan Castello's, 1870; Lake's Hippo-Olympiad, 1871; Great Commonwealth, 1871; Howes' Great London, 1872; leaper and tumbler, P. T. Barnum, 1876; scenic rider, Lowande's Great Brazilian, 1877; Allen's Great Eastern, 1879; India bar act, Stickney's, 1880; clown, S. H. Barrett's, 1885; Sturgis', South America, 1889; interpreter and general agent, Donovan & Long, Central America, 1897.

SAUNDERS, K. G. [a.k.a. Nellis]. (March 12, 1817-December 4, 1865) Armless wonder. Performed feats such as firing a pistol with his toes, playing accordian and violin-cello, shooting a bow and arrow, G. C. Quick's, 1850; P. T. Barnum's, 1851-54.

SAUNDERS, PAULINE. Dr. James L. Theyer's, 1880.

SAUNDERS, THOMAS. (d. March 8, 1845) The elephant keeper, Great Philadelphia Zoological Garden (Raymond &

Waring). Was knocked from his horse and killed by the elephant Pizarro while on the road about 5 miles north of Baton Rouge LA, on the way to Bayou Sara. A wagon was sent back to Baton Rouge and a dozen soldiers from Pentagon Barracks brought to the scene. They quieted the elephant by peppering him with 22 musket balls.

SAUNDERS, WILLIAM. Minstrel performer, P. T. Barnum's, 1873.

SAUSSER, C. E. Assistant manager, Bartine's, 1896.

SAUTELLE, IDA B. TRAVERS [Mrs. George C. Satterlee]. (May 29, 1856-May 22, 1916) Born in Homer, NY. Married **Sig. Sautelle**, 1876. For years served as treasurer for the Sautelle shows. Died at her home in Homer.

SAUTELLE, OLIVER. Boy rider, Sig. Sautelle's, 1897.

SAUTELLE, SIG. Performed as a fire-eater, magician and Punch and Judy operator. With his wife, started out with a Punch and Judy show, traveling by means of a blind horse and a second-hand wagon. In each town a free show was given, during which he sold soap, whistles, rings, chains and shirt studs, all for 25¢. In the winter, added a menagerie of birds, snakes and monkeys and performed as a store show. Added juggling and a ventriloquist act to his repertory and began performing with circuses. After an engagement with Forepaugh's, went to South America with Cooper & Bailey. Obtained a pair of horses from the Sewell show and took to the road again. 1885, bought a good sized canvas and went into partnership with a man named **Schreibner**, who had performing horses, an unsuccessful venture. Next, **Frank Matty** and **Doc Henderson** backed him in a sideshow at the Onondaga fair. Began showing open-air on vacant lots until he accumulated enough money for materials to construct a home-made tent. Rented a freight car on the Rome, Watertown & Ogdensburg road and made a tour of the line with a one-horse circus and variety show, stopping for 2 or 3 days in each place, charging a 10¢ and 20¢ admission, and ending the season with a profit of $9,000. Spring 1888, started out with a boat show along the Erie, Seneca and Champlain canals. 1892-1900, ran a wagon show. Moved winter quarters, 1899, from Syracuse, NY, to DeRuyter, NY. 1900, organized an outfit on rail, which he operated for 4 years before selling out. Became a partner in the Welsh Bros.' Show, Sautelle-Welsh, 1905, which he bought outright in the fall. 1906, sold off his show property and retired to his farm near DeRuyter, but retirement didn't last. Joined with **Oscar Lowande** to take out a circus, 1917; also entered into a partnership that year with **Thomas L. Finn** in an "Uncle Tom's Cabin" Co. (Finn had been a sideshow manager for Sautelle for 8 years). On the road with a motor transported show, 1918, managed by **George A. Manchester**.

SAVAGE, J. A. Press agent, Melville & Co.'s, 1889.

SAVAN. Acrobat, John Robinson's, 1893.

SAWYER, CLARA. English equestrienne, with New York Champs Elysees, 1865.

SAWYER, JOSEPH E. Assistant manager, Hart, France & Co., 1889.

SAWYER, JOSEPHINE. (d. April 1908) General performer. Came to America, 1850, and appeared at Franconi's Hippodrome, NYC, 1853. Later, with Barnum & Bailey. At the time of death was considered one of the oldest active chariot drivers. Was married to **Edward H. Sawyer**. Died in Norway.

SAXBY, S. D. Proprietor, Saxby, Dunbar & Co., 1872.

SAXTON, M. C. [or M. F.]. Band leader, John Robinson's, 1872-76; sideshow band leader, Cooper, Bailey & Co., 1880.

SAYERS, ROBERT. Clown, VanAmburgh & Co., 1880.

SAZELLE, F. Lake & Co. (Lake and Norton, managers), February 1864.

SCAFAR, ALEXEI. Russian bareback rider, Batcheller & Doris, 1879; John V. O'Brien's, 1880-84. Was convicted of some crime and sent to prison. See below.

SCAFAR, FANNY VICTORIA. (d. July 23, 1896) Native of London, England. At about age 20 went to Cuba to perform with the Leon de Leon Circus. Married bareback rider **Alexei Scafar** there, February 24, 1883. 1892, purchased property in Tampa, FL, at which time she retired from the profession. Mother of the athletes and bicyclists **Venus and Adonis**. Died at her home in Tampa.

SCHAFER, LOUIS. Concert privilege, Main & Sargeant, 1891.

SCHENCK, FURMAN. (1851?-August 24, 1892) Negro fat boy. Left school at Whitehouse, NJ, at which time weighed 375 pounds. Age 22, weight had increased to 425 pounds; at death, 535 pounds. Hired by **P. T. Barnum** about 1878, grew fatter and richer; Barnum continued to bill him as a young man of 18 +years of age throughout his career. Exhibited at Coney Island around 1887, and later at the Bowery. Died in New Brunswick, NJ., age 41.

SCHILLER, R. F. Proprietor, Schiller's, 1890.

SCHNEIDER, JOHN. Albino bar performer, Wintermute Bros.', 1897.

SCHOFF, HERR PAUL. Lion tamer, W. W. Cole's, 1871.

SCHOFIELD, ED. Light and heavy balancer, with Michael O'Conner & Co., 1869-70.

SCHONHERT, GUS. Proprietor, Great Western, 1893.

SCHRANK. Bugler, J. Purdy Brown's, 1825.

SCHRODE, GEORGE. One of the **Leotard Brothers** (**George Bliss**, George Schrode, **Ed Snow**), acrobats, leapers and tumblers. Cooper, Bailey & Co., 1879; P. T. Barnum's, 1880; brother act (**Schrode Brothers: George, John, William, Henry**), Barnum & London, 1884-85; Wallace & Co., 1889.

SCHROFF, HERR PAUL [or Schoff]. Lion tamer, G. G. Grady's, 1868; James M. French's, 1870.

SCHULTZ, FRANK. Ethiopian entertainer, Orton & Older, 1859.

SCHWARTZ, AUGUST. Rider, VanAmburgh & Co., 1880.

SCOTT, AB. Contractor, John Robinson's, 1889-93.

SCOTT, ALEXANDER. Band leader. The Great European, 1869; P. T. Barnum's, 1874.

SCOTT, A. R. General business manager, G. G. Grady's, 1869; advertising agent, Great Eastern, 1872; Haight's Great Southern, 1874.

SCOTT, C. H., JR. Press agent, VanAmburgh & Co., 1874, 1877-78.

SCOTT, DANIEL. Proprietor, Yankee Robinson's Double Show, 1863; Yankee Robinson's, 1860-68; asst. dir., 1871.

SCOTT, FRANK. Lion tamer and elephant keeper. Yankee Robinson's, 1859. While with W. H. Harris' Nichel-Plate, was killed by the elephant Gypsy in winter quarters, Chicago, March 25, 1896. Had recently taken charge of the animal, formerly named Empress, which had always been dangerous. This was her 3rd victim. Scott had been connected with this circus for the last 6 years.

SCOTT, GEORGE. Chief bill poster, Great Eastern, 1874.

SCOTT, GEORGE L. AND FLORA. Balancing trapeze, King & Franklin, 1887; double slack-wire, Holland & Gormley, 1889.

SCOTT, JAMES. Agent, St. Germain's Imperial Circus, 1889.

SCOTT, JOHN. Burr Robbins', 1885.

SCOTT, L. H. Railroad contractor, Lemen Bros.', 1892.

SCOTT, MATTHEW ["Scotty"]. (1836?-December 22, 1914) Animal handler, the first and only keeper of the famous elephant Jumbo. When the huge elephant was acquired by the London Zoo at barely a year old, Scott was assigned its keeper and remained as such when the Barnum & Bailey bought the animal and brought it to America. After Jumbo was hit by a train and killed, Scott remained in the service of Barnum & Bailey for many years. Was considered an authority on animals and their care, having written a book on the subject. From his work with animals, received a medal from the London Zoological Society. Died at Bridgeport, CT, age 78.

SCOTT, OLIVER H. P. (d. December 23, 1916) Agent, Wallace & Co., 1884-85; John Robinson's, 1886, 1888-89, general manager, 1890-93; general advertising agent, Walter L. Main, 1892; John Robinson's Circus (**John G. Robinson**, proprietor and manager), 1900. Died in Cincinnati.

SCOTT, ROBERT. Song and dance man in concert, Montgomery Queen's, 1876; Cooper, Bailey & Co.'s Circus, Australian tour, 1877. There was a circus man by the name of Robert Scott who died of consumption, San Antonio, TX, October 19, 1882, age 42.

SCOTT, THOMAS G. General manager, Australian Dime Show, 1887; business manager, Phillips-Scott Union Pacific, 1888.

SCOTT, WILLIAM. Gymnast. With Haight's Great Eastern, 1874; Frank A. Gardner's, Central and South America, winter 1887-88.

SCOTT, W. R. General business agent, G. G. Grady's, 1869.

SCOVILLE, PROF. R. W. Band leader, Hamilton & Sargeant, 1877.

SCRIBNER, SAM A. (d. July 8, 1941) Lee & Scribner (with **Charles Lee**), 1884-85; Scribner & Clements, 1887; Scribner & Co., 1891; Scribner & Smith's (with **Neil Smith**), 1892-96.

SEABERT, ALEXANDER. Donaldson & Rich, 1885; Holland & McMahon, 1888.

SEAL, DAVID ABBEY. (circa 1849-May 7, 1898) English clown, acrobat, and pantomimist. Probably the son of clown **W. B. Seal**. Traveled with Cooke's and Hengler's in England for 20 years. Known as the "Prince of Jesters." Principal clown and aerial leaper, Howe's Great London, 1871; L. B. Lent's, winter 1871-72; Stone & Murray, 1872; Joel E. Warner & Co., 1873; W. W. Cole's, 1874; Melville, Maginley & Cooke, 1875; Hengler's, Hull, England, 1875. At Cooke's, Aberdeen, 1877, appeared at his benefit in his special feature of leaping over 20 highlanders of the 56th Brigade Depot in full uniform. The men were drawn-up in the ring 2 abreast, with rifles and fixed bayonets crossed between them slanting in an upright position. Seal took a flying leap from a springboard, while they at the same time fired a volley as he bounded over them. 1880s, directed various spectacles. At one point married equestrienne **Lizzie Keyes**. Later, married **Susannah Jane**, **William Powell's** widow and the daughter of **Charles Hengler**, June 28, 1892. Was still performing, 1897; acting manager, Hengler's, Liverpool, 1897-98 season. [Charles H. Day: "Wasn't he a slick one. Just the *beau ideal* of the 'King's Jester'."]

SEALS, ARCHIE. Boss canvasman, VanAmburgh & Co., 1871; master of transportation, Haight's Great Southern, 1874; Sells Bros.', 1882.

SEAMAN, ANNETTE. Dancer, George W. DeHaven's, 1861; entered the den of performing animals, John Robinson's, 1864; wire-walker and *danseuse*, George W. DeHaven's, 1865.

SEAMAN, CHARLES. Rider and general performer. Robinson & Lake, 1862; Haight & Chambers, 1867; Dan Castello's, winter 1867-68; Lake's, 1868; Mrs. Charles Warner's, Philadelphia, 1869; John W. Robinson's (not "old John"), 1870; James M. Nixon's, 1872.

SEAMAN, GEORGE. Barrel and tranca and globe on horseback, John Robinson's, 1868.

SEAMAN, P. H. See P. H. Seamon.

SEAMON, FRANK. Leaper, Charles Lee's, 1893.

SEAMON, LAURA. Great Chicago Circus (Dutton & Smith, proprietors), 1879.

SEAMON, T. N. Clown, Michael O'Conner's Great Western, 1869.

SEAMON, P. H. [or Seaman]. Yankee clown. George W. DeHaven's, 1860-61; Robinson & Lake, 1862-64; John Robinson's, 1863-64; George W. DeHaven & Co., 1865-67.

Retired from the profession and opened a saloon at Sauk Centre, MN, 1868. However, was back on the road as clown and equestrian director, Michael O'Conner & Co., 1869; George W. DeHaven's, 1870; ventriloquist, Great Eastern, 1872; Stevens & Begun, 1874; Curtis' Great Roman Hippodrome, 1877; H. C. Lee's Great Eastern, winter 1877-78; Great Chicago Circus, 1879; Silas Dutton's Southern, winter 1879-80, 1880.

SEARS, GEORGE W. (1836?-March 27, 1868) Lion tamer. Born in Massachusetts. Since father was an old showman, he was connected with the business since his boyhood. Joined Mabie's, 1863, and was with the organization for 2 years; Cuba, with Spalding & Rogers, taking a den of performing lions with him; connected with Dan Rice's, 1865; Yankee Robinson's from 1866 and until his death. Died of consumption in Augusta, IL, age 32.

SEARS, JOHN [r. n. William H. Sears]. (d. June 20, 1874) Owner and lion tamer of the New England Caravan, 1830-33; partner, Sears & Forbes, 1858; had his Great Eastern Menagerie on the road, performing in the New England states, 1859, billed as having 60 living wild animals, including a baby lion and Wild Men of Borneo, all under 120' of canvas. Manager, John O'Brien's Caravan, Monster Menagerie and National Kingdom, 1871.

SEARS, WILLIAM H. See John Sears.

SEAVER, GEORGE. Gymnast and vaulter, Driesbach & Howes, 1868.

SEAVEY, GEORGE. Gymnast, Howes Trans-Atlantic Circus and Risbeck's Menagerie (Frank Howes, proprietor), 1868.

SEBASTIAN, BILLY. VanAmburgh & Co., 1880.

SEBASTIAN, CECILIA [nee Cecilia Berry]. (March 14, 1857-August 21, 1914) Equestrienne. Born in NYC of theatrical and circus parents. Received training as a rider at a very young age. Married circus rider **Romeo Sebastian**. Later, retired to a farm near Miami, KS, where Sebastian was occupied in training dogs and ponies.

SEBASTIAN FAMILY. Haight's Great Southern, 1874. Mlle. Sebastian married J. D. Sweet, May 25 of the is year, which caused a change of name to the **Sweet Family**.

SEBASTIAN, GEORGE. Rider, Lake & Co., winter 1863-64.

SEBASTIAN, JOSEPHINE. Equestrienne, daughter of **Signor Quaglieni**. Martinho Lowande's, Cuba, 1880.

SEBASTIAN, LOUIS. Bareback rider. Son of **Signor Quaglieni** and brother of **Romeo Sebastian**. With Montgomery Queen's, California, 1877; carrying act with father, P. T. Barnum's, 1879.

SEBASTIAN, MAMIE. Concert, Montgomery Queen's, 1876.

SEBASTIAN, MLLE. Japanese juggler and necromancer. Cole's Ten Cent Show, also called Cole & Sirber's Ten Cent Show, 1890.

SEBASTIAN, ROMEO. (d. February 3, 1919) Pad rider. Son of **Signor Quaglieni** and brother of **Louie Sebastian**. George F. Bailey & Co., 1868; Batcheller & Doris, 1870; P. T. Barnum's 1873, 1875-76; Great Southern, 1874; Montgomery Queen's, 1875; John Wilson's, San Francisco, 1875; Adam Forepaugh's, 1876-77; International Circus, Offenbach Garden, Philadelphia, winter 1876-77; (with his boy, **Little Joe**) Orrin Bros.', Havana, winter 1877-78; W. W. Cole's, 1878; Allen's Great Eastern, 1879; Batcheller & Doris, 1879-80; P. T. Barnum's, 1879; Orrin Bros.', Metropolitan Theatre, Havana, winter 1879-80; Batcheller & Doris, 1881; Nathans & Co.'s, 1882; Hengler's, London, 1886; Circus Busch, Germany, 1888. Returned to America, 1894, after about 12 years in Europe. Used to sit on a chair on the back of a running horse and read a newspaper. Died in Victoria, British Columbia.

SEBASTIAN, SIGNOR. See Sebastian Quaglieni.

SEBASTIAN, SOFIA. "La Petite Sebastian with Juvenile Troupe," George F. Bailey & Co., 1872.

SEBUNTI, HENRY. See Mons. Sabanti.

SEDAM, BENJAMIN W. Kennebel's Parisian Circus, fall 1885.

SEEBRIGHT, CHARLES. Dr. James L. Thayer's, 1880.

SEELEY, CHARLES W. ["Col."]. (1821-April 28, 1917) Acrobat, clown, advance agent, sideshow manager, legal adjuster, etc. Born in Horse Heads, NY. Spent most of his life in the circus business. By age of 9 was an expert tumbler and adept at all kinds of acrobatics. With **Frank Phelps** and **Sam Shappe**, performed as posturer and tumbler. When age interfered with acrobatics, took up clowning; as such, sang, mimicked the ringmaster and made comic speeches. Last position in show business was with the booking office of the Keith vaudeville circuit. Died in Elmira, NY, from cancer of the neck and upper shoulder, age 71. A campaign for funds to place a monument on his grave at Woodlawn Cemetery, Elmira, was conducted, 1917, by **John Comash** and the New York *Clipper*. Principal tumbler and clown, Thayer & Noyes, 1862; C. W. Noyes', 1870-71; Ames', 1870; tumbler, L. B. Lent's, 1872; Howe's Great London, 1874; clown, Cooper, Bailey & Co.'s Circus, Australian tour, 1877. [Mark St. Leon: Seeley "took the role of grotesque clown, his wit displayed more in his heels than in his head."]; clown, P. T. Barnum's, 1879; Adam Forepaugh's, 1880-81; clown, Sells Bros.', 1882; clown, Wallace & Co., 1886; hippodrome manager, Sells Bros., 1887; press agent, 1889-90; superintendent of the confectionery department, Barnum & Bailey, 1895; Forepaugh-Sells Bros., 1896, candy stands, 1903.

SEELEY, EDWARD. Snake charmer, P. T. Barnum's, 1873.

SEIBERT, ALEX: 4-horse rider, Barnum & Bailey, 1892, 1904.

SEIGNE, FRANÇOISE. Rider and vaulter. Pepin & Breschard, 1809, apprentice, making his first appearance. Pepin & Breschard, 1810-12; rope-walker, Pepin, Breschard & Cayetano, 1813-14, last engagement in this country. Stuart Thayer suggests he went to Spain with Pepin and never returned.

SELBINI & VILLION TROUPE. Gymnastic bicyclers, Adam Forepaugh's, 1881. While the bicycles sped around the arena, the gymnasts mount, climb, and stand on each others heads.

SELBY, ARTHUR L. General agent, Goodrich's, 1897.

SELLS, ALLEN E. (August 26, 1862-September 27, 1904) Son of **Ephraim Sells**. Born in Cleveland. Began working on father's circus and stayed with it all his life, eventually serving as superintendent under him. At the time of death, Columbus, OH, was assistant manager of the Forepaugh-Sells Circus. Married **Miss Nellie Gilliam**.

SELLS BROTHERS [William Allen, Lewis, Peter, and Ephraim] All born in Columbus, the sons of a Methodist minister who rode the circuit in Ohio. **Ephraim** was born on October, 18, 1834; **William Allen**, 1836; **Lewis**, November 12, 1841; and **Peter, Jr.**, April 6, 1845. They are occasionally credited with being the first to use "Bros." in their circus title, but the Antonio Bros.' Great World Circus anticipated them by some 16 years. **Allen** and **Lewis** were auctioneers and peddlers, first experiencing the circus business, 1866, when they conducted an auction wagon with Hennings & Cooper's, taking advantage of the crowds drawn by the show to sell their wares. Organized their own circus, spring 1872, the Paul Silverburg's Mammoth Quadruple Alliance, Museum, Menagerie, Caravan and Circus, comprised of 33 wagons and cages, 130 horses and an elephant; engaged younger brother **Peter** to be the advance agent. Almost at the outset they encountered bad weather; so they called upon brother **Ephraim**, who operated a garden in Cleveland, OH, to invest a few hundred dollars. After doing so, the weather changed for the better; **Ephraim** returned to Cleveland, sold out his enterprise for $3,000 and bought into the partnership on the conditions that he would retain one-third interest and occupy the chair of treasurer. [C. G. Sturtevant: Ephraim was "a close treasurer and on the job every minute, but did not have the all around ability and vision a manager should have."] Good fortune smiled on the brothers and good common sense sustained them. Catered to the rural trade by wearing chin whiskers and praising the farmers in their advertising. **Allen** was the manager, **Lewis** assistant manager and superintendent, **Ephraim** treasurer and ticket sales manager, and **Peter** advertiser, router and, later, railroad contractor. 1875, enlarged the show and took the name of Sells Brothers. By 1878, were running a 34 car railroad circus, Sells Bros.' Great Seven Elephant Show. Bought a large part of the Montgomery Queen Railroad Circus and Menagerie at auction, 1878; then put out 2 shows: the Sells Bros.' Great European Seven Elephant Show by rail; and on wagon, Anderson & Co.'s Great World Circus and Menag-

erie, managed by **Lewis** and **James P. Anderson**, to play the country towns while the railroad unit, under **Ephraim's** direction, played the cities. Latter show was changed to New Pacific Circus and Menagerie, 1880. It then converted to rail travel, 1882, under the title of S. H. Barrett's Circus and Menagerie. **Barrett**, a Sells brother-in-law, was the general agent. The shows consolidated, 1888, being called Sells Bros. & Barrett's Colossal United Shows. Following year went out as simply Sells Bros.' Circus. Left for Australia, November 12, 1891, but encountered an epidemic that made the tour a disaster. Returned June 9, 1892. Combined with Cooper & Bailey's Forepaugh Circus, 1896, going out as the Forepaugh-Sells Bros.' Circus. Although **Barrett** was general agent, he had no financial interest in the show. 1882, **Allen** left the circus organization to open a hotel in Topeka, KS. First venture was the Windsor Hotel; about 1889, built the Chesterfield; was involved in Topeka politics and was one of the city's wealthiest and most influential men. Died of pneumonia, March 20, 1894, still a hotel proprietor in Topeka. **Peter** was the defendant in a highly visible divorce case, 1890, which ended favorably for him. **Ephraim** retired in the spring of 1896. Died of Bright's disease in Columbus, August 1, 1898. **Peter** died of a stroke in Columbus on October 5, 1904. **James A. Bailey** bought out the Sells' interest, January 10, 1905. **Lewis** was the best executive of the 4 brothers, seen as one of the shrewdest and most resourceful circus men of his day. Was the last of the 4 Sells brothers. Retired wealthy. Died of Bright's disease at Columbus, OH, September 5, 1907.

SELLS, EMILY. Irwin Bros.', 1888.

SELLS, WILLIAM ["Willie"]. (1865?-February 17, 1908) Rider and showman. Adopted son of **Allen Sells** of the Sells Brothers. Began as an equestrian for that circus and became a prominent 1-horse and 4-horse rider. A 10 year old bareback rider, Great European Zoological Institute and Equestrian Exposition (Sells Brothers, proprietors), 1876. By his 20s, had earned the title of "The Chesterfield of the Arena"; by 1889, had developed an appetite for fast living; consequently, his contract was not renewed by the Sells brothers at the end of that season, which caused a rift between Allen and his brothers that remained until Allen's death, 1894. Signed with Barnum & Bailey for their London engagement, winter 1889-90, where he made a disappointing showing by missing too many performances. Becoming too heavy to ride, abandoned the ring after 1889 and went into management, organizing several shows of his own, one being with **Andrew Morris**, Sells Olympian Shows. 1882, the Sells brothers bought out the interest of William A. Sells for $40,000 with the agreement that he would not again go into show business; nevertheless, he started Sells Enormous Railroad Shows United With J. N. Rentfrow's Five Continent Menagerie, preceding the orignal Sells Bros.' in their territory. [Orin Copple King: "Willie's uncles, the famous Sells brothers, were angered and embarrassed by Willie linking the Sells name with the worst kinds of grift and by Willie's efforts to create the impression that his show was the Sells Bros.' Big Show of the World."] The Sells brothers retaliated by posting bills ahead announcing that the show was a fake and had no right to the Sells name. War was waged until Willie Sells failed, suing Lewis and Peter Sells for $150,000 damages in the District Court at Topeka, KS, 1898, claiming that at various times when he attempted to form a partnership with an investor, the Sells brothers would threaten a law suit and frighten the money men away. The Sells brothers' responded that Willie's name was not really Sells. Willie refuted the argument by stating the Sells Bros.' advertised him for several years as "Willie Sells, champion bareback rider of the world." He had, at one time or another, interest in Willie Sells & J. N. Rentfrow's Golden Circus, 1891-94; Hummel, Hamilton & Sells Shows, 1897; Great William Sells Shows United with James H. Gray's New Olympian Hippodrome, 1900. The Sells & Gray Circus came to grief at the end of the 1901 season and was sold at sheriff's auction, Algiers, LA, bringing a return of $7,625. 1899, general agent Walter L. Main's; Sells-Floto, 1906; also associated with the Great William Sells & Downs Consolidated Shows (Willie Sells and **Marten Downs**, proprietors), 1902. For a while, ran the Standard Theatre, NYC, featuring first class vaudeville, but lost money in the venture. At the time of death, was completing arrangements for taking out the Frank Lemen show. Died of a hemorrhage of the stomach at his residence, West Thirty-fifth Street, NYC, age 43.

SEMELMAN, FRANK X. Herculean performer, Pubillones', Havana, winter 1885-86.

SEMON, HARRY W. (1862?-July 16, 1904) Agent. Son of **S. H. Semon**, also an agent. Entered the circus profession with John Robinson's, 1876; contracting agent, Adam Forepaugh's, 1881, 1891-92; general agent and railroad contractor, Irwin Bros.', 1893; general manager, Buckskin Bill's Wild West, 1902. Had his own theatrical companies on the road in the winter and was connected with circuses in the summer. Parented 3 children who were performers under the title of **The Three Semons**. Died in Oelwein, IA, while with Campbell Bros.', age 42.

SEMON, JOSEPH. Program publisher, Adam Forepaugh's, 1886-87; contracting agent, Washburn's. Became proprietor of the Hotel Elkins, Elkins, WV, 1891.

SEMON, MRS. HARRY W. [Julia]. (d. May 3, 1932) Mother of the **Semon Children—Primrose, Marty** and **Si**. Sister of **Ada Melrose**. The two had an act in vaudeville as the **Melrose Sisters**, "Two Little Jays From Indiana." Died in Kalamazoo, MI, age 63.

SEMON, PETER H. (d. October 23, 1888) Clown. Originator of the Peter Hontz Family Talking Figures. Died in Chicago. Daniel Shelby's, 1888.

SEMON, SIMON H. ["Si"]. (d. September 6, 1910) Con-

tracting agent. Born in NYC. Father of agent **Harry W. Semon**. In the business for 40 years with some of the top companies in the United States, which included the Forepaugh show for 12 seasons, concluding in 1891; John Robinson's, 1892; Buffalo Bill's, 1896; Forepaugh-Sells, 1904; Adams' "Humpty Dumpty" Co., 1905. Died in Mt. Vernon, NY.

SENYAH, MAUDE. See Mme. Maude Sanyeah.

SEPULVEDA, S. M. Feature cornetist and band leader, Hobson Bros.', 1893.

SESSFORD. Still vaulter, Price & Simpson, 1823-25.

SESSIONS, MARK. Acrobat, Dan Rice's Paris Pavilion, 1872.

SEWELL, FRED. Clown, Gregory & D'Alma, 1889.

SEXTON, MERT C. Band leader. S. P. Stickney's, 1869; James Robinson's, 1870-72; John Robinson's, 1873.

SEYMOUR, CARRIE. *Danseuse*, P. T. Barnum's Roman Hippodrome, 1875.

SHADE, MOLLIE. (d. June 24, 1882) Known as "The Lilliputian Queen," of Osceola, IA. Married **Major Littlefluger** (r. n. Robert Huzza] June 5, 1881, while both were with Sells Bros.' First exhibited with a dwarf, **General Shade**. Was in the business for some 20 years, the last public appearance being at Bunnell's Museum, NYC. Died in child birth at Kendallville, IN. See Major Robert Littlefluger.

SHAFFER, JOHN. Lion keeper, Green & Bailey, 1834.

SHALEY. Operated sideshow with fat woman and monkeys, Gardner & Hemmings, 1862-63.

SHANE, SOL. Museum director, John Robinson's, 1874, lecturer, 1875.

SHANNON, T. H. Press agent, Metchear & Cameron, 1870.

SHAPPE, SAMUEL [or Shappee]. Gymnast and acrobat. Mabie's, 1861. Began appearing with **H. J. Whitney** as a partner, 1863. They were connected with Melville, Cooke & Sands, 1863; Seth B. Howe's, 1864; Bailey & Co., 1864-67; Spalding & Rogers, New Orleans, winter 1864-65; Chiarini's, Havana, 1865; James Robinson's, 1868-72. **Shappe & Whitney**, Great Eastern, 1873; **Shappe & Whitney**, James W. Wilder & Co., 1873; **Shappe & Smead**, L. B. Lent's, 1874.

SHAPPELL, DON. General business agent, with Alexander Robinson's, 1871.

SHARP, GEORGE [or Sharpe]. Clown, Tourniaire & Whitby, 1858; Harry Whitby's, 1859; Chiarini's, Havana, winter 1859-60; Spalding & Rogers, South America, 1862-63; Orrin & Sebastian, Puerto Rico, 1865; Chiarini's, Mexico City, 1867; San Francisco Circus and Roman Hippodrome, 1872; Whitney Family's, 1889.

SHARP, HANK. Clown, Gregory Bros.' Metropolitan, 1885.

SHARP, JOHN. See Jacob Sharpe.

SHARPE, GEORGE. Boss canvasman, Whitney's Imperial Wagon Show, 1892.

SHARPE, JACOB. Rider. First to be recorded for feats of horsemanship in America. [Isaac J. Greenwood, quoting the

Essex Gazette of Salem, MA: "The Englishman, who had previously performed in Boston, rode two horses, standing with
one foot on the saddle of each; three horses while standing
with a foot on each of the outside ones; and mounted and dis-
mounted a single horse—all with the mount traveling at full
speed."] Gave equestrian performance in Essex, MA, 1771.

SHARPE, JAMES. John Wilson's, 1865.

SHARPE, KITTY. Concert performer, vocalist, with Cooper,
Bailey & Co., 1876; Great Commonwealth Circus, transported
by the boat, *William Newman,* 1879. Married to acrobat **Edwin Fritz.** See Edwin Fritz.

SHARPSTENE, WILLIAM. Entered the circus business at
17, tumbling and performing on the horizontal bars. Hough's
Combination Circus, 1868.

SHAW, BARCLAY F. G. K. Goodwin's, 1859.

SHAW, GUS. Clown, Robinson & Lake, 1862; a member of
the variety troupe, Haight & Chambers, 1867; Lake's, 1868;
H. M. Smith's, 1869; Haight's Great Southern, 1874; Trans-
Atlantic, 1879; Boyd & Peters, 1880; Camp's Grand Southern,
1880; Johnson & Co., 1881; Mayo's Model Show, 1884.

SHAW, ROBERT A. Agent, Sells Bros.', 1874.

SHAW, HERR DRIESBACH: "The Lion King and celebrated African hunter (a Driesbach imitator)." G. K. Goodwin's, 1860; Wambold & Whitby, 1861.

SHAY, CHARLES. Chinese juggler and knife thrower. Bow-
ery Amphitheatre, 1857-58; Joe Pentland's, 1859; Cooke's
Royal Amphitheatre, Niblo's Garden, NYC, 1860; Goodwin
& Wilder, 1862; with trick dog, Fanny, L. B. Lent's, 1863-64;
trained dogs, Orrin Bros. & Co.' Metropolitan Amphitheatre,
Havana, spring 1880; trained dogs, Dr. James L. Thayer's,
1880. At one time was out with a variety show, Charley
Shay's Quincuplexal.

SHAY, JAMES. Chief bill poster, Alex Robinson's, 1874.

SHAY, JOHN R. (1802-January 29, 1882) Born in St. John,
NS. Was 6 years old when he moved to NYC with parents, but
ran away from home as a youth and joined Pepin & Breschard
as a juggler. Albany Circus, 1826; Sickles & Co., 1832; Oscar
Brown's, 1835-37; Lafayette Circus, NYC, 1839; co-proprie-
tor (with **John Mateer, J. W. Jackson, Charles J. Rogers**),
Cincinnati Circus, 1841, Cincinnati, OH; equestrian manager,
Rockwell & Co., 1848; Stone & McCollum, 1848-49; Crane
& Co., 1850; Spalding, Rogers & Van Orden's People's,
1851; Fogg & Stickney, 1852; L. B. Lent's, 1863; Alex Rob-
inson's, 1865. Also connected with Joe Pentland's, J. M.
Jones', Welch & Mann, Jerry Mabie's, Welch & Lent, Dan
Rice's, Sands, Nathans & Co., Turner's, George F. Bailey's,
Harry Whitbeck's, Crescent City, Yankee Robinson's, and
Sloat & Sheppard. Died in Cincinnati.

SHEDMAN BROTHERS [Winfield S. and George W.]. H.
D. Van's, 1878 (they had all privileges except concert); Lowande's, West Indies and South America, 1880; Conrad & Watson, South America, 1880; Walter L. Main's, 1882; Gregory

& Schiedell, 1886; Shedman Bros.', 1893-94. **W. S. Shedman**
had his performing dogs and monkeys with Orrin Bros.', winter 1888-89; Irwin Bros.', 1889. In late years, played theatres
with performing animals. Died of a stroke, April of 1911.

SHEDMAN, WILLIAM S. Club swinger, Alexander Robinson's, 1875-76. Married Miss Alice Brown in Horseheads,
NY, June 20, 1875.

SHELBY, CHRISTOPHER C. ["Col."]. (1841-May 21,
1910) Sideshow entertainer. Born in Strasburg, NJ. Traveled
for years with Barnum & Bailey doing the spiritualistic and
mystery box turn. A veteran of the Civil War and an inventor
of some 140 different patented items. Died in Paterson, NJ.

SHELBY, DANIEL. (January 11, 1838-February 4, 1895)
Manager, George W. DeHaven's, 1868; manager Adelphi
Theatre, Buffalo, 1880, when with **John Hamilton** bought
interest in Pullman Bros.', and show went out under title of
Shelby, Pullman & Hamilton, 1881; interest sold to Maybury,
1882—Maybury, Pullman & Hamilton; then Daniel Shelby's
Golden Circus, 1888, auctioned off November 21, same year,
Richmond, VA—several minor animals, an elephant, 2 cam-
els, 34 baggage stock, etc.

SHELTON. Band leader, VanAmburgh's, 1846.

SHELDON, HARRY. Juggler, Orrin Bros. & Co.' Metropolitan Amphitheatre, spring 1880.

SHELVEY, MATT. Singing and talking clown, Goodrich's,
1897.

SHEPARD, BILLY. Clown, with Donaldson & Rich, 1885;
Frank Rich's, 1886.

SHEPARD, JAMES G. (1829-September 3, 1879) Show-
man. Born in Canandaigua, NY. Manager, National Theatre,
Boston, spring 1858; Sloat & Shepard, 1857-58; Niblo &
Sloat's, West Indies, 1860; treasurer, L. B. Lent's, 1861-64.
Died in NYC.

SHEPPARD, JOHN. Sword swallower, with Gardner &
Hemmings, 1863; general performer, Thompson, Smith and
Hawes, 1866.

SHEPPARD, W. H. Proprietor, Levi J. North's, 1869.

SHERIDAN, LOTTIE. *Manège,* with Dr. James L. Thayer's,
1870.

SHERMAN, GEORGE. Troupe of performing stallions, John
Robinson's, California (**Frank Frost,** manager), 1886.

SHERRY, JOHN. Leaper and tumbler, P. T. Barnum's, 1880.

SHERWOOD, CAROLINE. Principal riding act, J. M.
June's, 1851.

SHERWOOD, MME. 700 pound woman. Sands, Nathans &
Co.'s American and English Circus, 1859; VanAmburgh's,
1870.

SHERWOOD FAMILY [Virginia, Ida, Amelia, Charles,
Charles, Jr.]. Equestrians. R. Sands', 1860; Chiarini's, winter
1861-62; James M. Nixon's, Washington, DC, fall 1862;
Miles' Circus Royale, Canada, 1863; Howes', 199 Bowery,
NYC, winter 1863-64; Hippotheatron, 14th Street, NYC, Feb-

ruary 1864; S. O. Wheeler's, 1864; Mrs. Charles Warner's, Philadelphia, winter 1864-65; Seth B. Howe's European, 1867; Dr. James L. Thayer's, 1869; James M. Nixon's, 1872. **Charles E.** (July 22, 1823-December 12, 1875), vaulter and rider, the Sherwood family patriarch, first appeared at Vauxhall Gardens, the Bowery, as Cupid, under the management of **P. T. Barnum**, using the name of **Master Charles Champion**. Started a tour, July 1841, with a dramatic company. Joined S. Nichols' Circus, then bound out as apprentice with **H. P. Madigan**. Harry Rockwell's, 1846, as a pupil of **Hiram Franklin**. Rockwell & Co., 1848; scenic rider, Joe Pentland's, 1851. One of the first to turn double somersaults in America and was said to be the first and best "Pete Jenkins," performing it originally, 1851, with **Captain DeCamp** and **Joe Pentland**. Rapid rider, June & Co., 1851; scenic rider, Joe Pentland's, 1852, 1854; Sloat & Shepard, 1857; Sands, Nathans & Co., 1857; Sands, Nathans & Co., Broadway Circus, 1858; Indian act and "Pete Jenkins," Mabie & Crosby, 1858; "Pete Jenkins," Sands, Nathans & Co., 1859; R. Sands, 1862; S. O. Wheeler's, 1864; Hippotheatron, NYC, winter 1864-65; James M. Nixon's, 1865; Great European, 1868. The latter year, went into speculation on Wall Street. Died in Pittsburgh, PA, age 52. **Virginia** (d. August 26, 1888, r. n. Nancy McLaughlin), wife of **Charles E.** An offspring of Irish stock who came to America early in the century. Became professionally known as **Mme. Virginia Sherwood**, noted for her courage and skill in handling horses. Her sister, **Bridget**, another daring rider, was killed during a performance in New Orleans, which caused Virginia to take a brief retirement. Her return to the arena resulted in even more daring feats. The marriage produced no children. Virginia died of consumption in Pittsburgh, PA. The Sherwoods adopted a boy and girl from a foundling home in NYC, **Ida** and **Charles, Jr.**, and taught them how to ride. **Ida** married **Sam Stickney**, son of **S. P.**, while with Mrs. Charles Warner's, December, 1864. See Stickney Family.

SHERWOOD, ROBERT E. Clown. Apprenticed to Dan Rice, 1867; started clowning, 1872. While with Barnum & Bailey, London, England, 1888, walked to Queen Victoria's box and shook hands with her. Retired from circus life that year. Authored a book of recollections, *Here We Are Again*, published 1926.

SHIELDS, ARCHIE. (d. February 9, 1891) Sells Bros.', Pacific coast, fall 1886; also Adam Forepaugh's, P. T. Barnum's.

SHIELDS, ARTIE ["Master"]. Tight-wire, J. H. Shields', 1888, winter 1888-90.

SHIELDS, EDWARD. Builder of the *Floating Palace*, the river boat on which circus performances were given. The craft was constructed in Cincinnati, 1850, a cost of $40,000. Was towed from town to town by a stern-wheeler called the *Telegraph*. The interior was finished as an amphitheatre seating 1,500 people. There was a bar and a lunch counter in the bow of the boat over the offices.

SHIELDS, GEORGE TALBOT. Australian bareback and somersault rider. John Wilson's, California, 1873; bareback hurdle rider, L. B. Lent's, 1874.

SHIELDS, HARRY S. (1878?-January 14, 1918) Contracting agent. Died of Bright's disease, Cleveland, OH, age 40.

SHIELDS, JACOB. Globe performer, Wilder's North American, 1872.

SHIELDS, JAMES AUSTIN. (1843?-January 31, 1916) Pioneer animal trainer. Had charge of the original Barnam menagerie. After retiring from circus life was proprietor of the Park Hotel, Brooklyn, for some years. A manufacturer of awnings at the time of death. Died in Brooklyn, NY, age 73.

SHIELDS, JOHN HENRY. (d. June 27, 1938) Said to have traveled every state in the Union, as well as Canada, Mexico, Cuba and the Central American countries. Purchasing agent, P. T. Barnum's, 1875-76; originated 10-cent circus, Shields' Great Southern Shows, 1884, which traveled Southern states giving benefit performances to aid in raising funds for erection of Confederate monuments; ringmaster, Dan Rice's, 5 years in 1870s; proprietor, J. H. Shield's, 1888; Stowe Bros.', 1889; assistant manager, ringmaster, and sideshow privilege, Terrell Shows, 1891; sideshow privileges, Gollmar Bros.', 1892-93. Later years, was in the carnival business and produced many illusion shows, among which was "Lunette the Flying Lady." Went to Tarpon Springs, FL, 1920, upon retiring from show business, in which he had been engaged for 55 years. Died at his home there, Shields Hotel, of uraemic poisoning, age 90.

SHIELDS, LYMAN. (1852-1888) Born Woodstalk, Canada. Manager, J. H. Shield's Circus, 1888.

SHIELDS, ROSA. Juggling act on running globe, L. B. Lent's, 1874. Married **George T. Shields**.

SHIELDS, THOMAS. General performer. VanAmburgh & Co.'s southern, 1860; Dan Castello's, 1865; Thompson, Smith & Hawes, 1866.

SHIMER. Lion tamer, June & Titus, 1848.

SHINDLE, JOHN C. (1815-April 26, 1888) General performer. Born in Alexandria, VA. Ran away from home at 18 and joined Fogg & Stickney. Traveled the country as clown, acrobat and bareback rider for some 30 years. Spalding's, 1848; rider, Rivers & Derious, 1851; 2-horse rider, Herr Driesbach, Rivers & Derious, 1853. Serious accident caused retirement. Old age and business affairs led to him throwing himself in front of a train on the Pennsylvania Railroad, Lancaster, Pa.

SHIPLEY, ISAAC. Sideshow manager, Burr Robbins', early 1870s; later, John Robinson's; Sells Bros.', 1891. Retired to keeping a cigar store on Cottage Grove Avenue, Chicago.

SHIPMAN, JAMES W. (August 5, 1865-March 10, 1915) Showman. Born in Williamsville, VT. Connected with Sig. Sautelle's as business manager for 8 seasons, during which time the show developed from wagon to rail transportation. Left to become proprietor of an "Uncle Tom's Cabin" Co.

After 3 years, returned to the Sautelle management. Later, connected with Frank A. Robbins'. Married **Ada Thorpe,** a vaudeville entertainer, April 10, 1901. Became proprietor of the Winchester House, Winchester, NH, October 1907, which was to be known as Shipman's Tavern. About 1914, bought a hotel in South Vernon, VT, and managed the two locations until his death. Died in Brattleboro, VT.

SHIPP, EDWARD. Learned principal riding from half-brother, **Harry Lamkin;** was also bareback, hurdle, bounding jockey, and 4 and 6-horse rider, until he broke his leg, 1895, while with Ringling Bros.', which ended his riding career. Gardner & Donovan, South America, 1886; Roberts & Gardner, 1886; Adam Forepaugh's, 1889; Sturtevant & Holland (VanAmburgh show), 1891; equestrian director, W. B. Reynolds', 1892; Orrin Bros.', Mexico, 1892; equestrian director, F. J. Taylor's, 1893; equestrian director, Milwaukee Mid-Winter Circus, Exposition Music Hall, Milwaukee, November 1894; John Robinson's, 1898; 1896-1906, assistant equestrian director, Ringling Bros.'; equestrian director, Forepaugh-Sells, 1903-05, 1907; Carl Hagenbeck's, 1906; Barnum & Bailey, 1908-10. Operated Shipp's Winter Circus, Petersburg, IL, 1887-1905. Married equestrienne **Julia Lowande,** February 21, 1889, Philadelphia. Daughter **Virginia** was a *manège* rider. With **Roy Feltus,** proprietor of a circus beginning around 1913. The tour opened February 19, 1916, at Port Limon, Costa Rica, then Panama, Equador, Peru, Bolivia, Chile, Argentina, and Brazil. Retired, living in Santiago, Chile, with wife and daughter, 1939. Died 6 years later at his residence, NYC.

SHOEMAKER, JOHN ["Jack"]. Driver. Originally with John V. O'Brien's. Could drive 1 or 12 horses with equal ease. With a whip 8' long and a stock 4' long, could flick a straw from between the fingers of a man within reach of the whip. Boss hostler, John Robinson's, 1877-80.

SHOWALTER, CASS. Clown, Johnson & Co., 1881.

SHOWERISKEY, IVAN. Slack-rope performer. Featured an act of suspending himself by one heel and then surprising his audience by plunging through the air with a sudden jerk. While performing in Baltimore, 1836, the cord affixed to his ankle broke and he fell to the earth. The amputation of his leg proved futile, and he died shortly thereafter.

SHOWERS, ANDY. (1845?-March 13, 1897) An animal trainer, horse breaker, and a partner in various show enterprises. Apprenticed with **Alex Robinson** at the age of 8. Alexander Robinson's, 1870-77; Stickney's Imperial Parisian circus, 1880; performing stallions, dogs and monkeys, King & Franklin, 1887; co-proprietor (with **Charles Hall**), Hall & Showers' Dog and Pony Show, 1995. Then, after Hall's death, 1896, Showers took over sole management. Also with Andress & Showers' Imperial Shows the same year. Died at Birmingham, AL, age 52.

SHOWERS, GEORGE. Rider, W. W. Cole, 1886; S. H. Barrett's, 1887.

SHOWERS, IDA [or Lida]. Jig dancer, Alexander Robinson's, 1870-77; slack-wire, Stickney's Imperial Parisian Circus, 1880.

SHOWLES, ELIZABETH ["Libbie," nee Manahan]. (1831-1924) Wife of **Jacob Showles.** Dan Rice's half-sister (Rice's mother, Elizabeth Crum, Married Hugh Manahan, father of Elizabeth Showles). *Manège* performer. Dan Rice's, 1856-58; Goodwin & Wilder, 1862; Dan Rice's, 1863; with her horse American Eagle, S. O. Wheeler's, 1864; George F. Bailey & Co., 1867. Adopted **Willie Showles.** See Jacob A. Showles.

SHOWLES, JACOB A. (1826-January 1, 1912) Showman, clown, flying ring performer and juggler of globes while lying on his back on a running horse. Born in Germany, the son of **John** and **Catherine Showles.** Came to America at age 2 and settled in New Orleans. Orphaned at age 6. Joined Jerry Mabie's when 12 years of age. 6 years later, was with Dan Rice's, 1854, doing a globe act on horseback, said to be the only performer at this time capable of doing that feat. Married **Elizabeth Monahan,** 1861. Dan Rice's, 1855-59; Antonio & Wilder, 1859; Goodwin & Wilder, 1862; Mrs. Dan Rice's, 1862; Dan Rice's, 1863; Howes', 199 Bowery, NYC, winter 1863-64; S. O. Wheeler's, 1864, 1867; Wheeler's new amphitheatre, Boston, winter 1864-65; Gardner & Hemmings, Front Street Theatre, Baltimore, winter 1867-66; Bailey & Co., Canada, 1867; Bryan's, 1868; Older's, 1871; J. W. Wilder's, 1872. Organized his own outfit, North American Show, 1872; Showles & Co.'s Grand Triple Combination, 1873. Equestrian director, Maginley & Co., 1874; equestrian director and juggler, Dan Rice's, 1877-78; general director, Great Commonwealth, transported by the boat, *William Newman,* 1879; general agent, Hilliard & DeMott, 1880; VanAmburgh & Co., 1880-81. Opened a livery stable, Long Branch, NJ, 1885. Died in Long Branch, age 83.

SHOWLES, JACOB J. (not the Jacob Showles above) Agent. Raymond & Waring; Jerry Mabie's; VanAmburgh & Co.; Howes' Great London; Spalding & Bidwell; Hilliard & DeMott; Burr Robbins'; Adam Forepaugh's; Commonwealth Circus; J. H. Haverly's Minstrels. Manager bill posting brigade, Cooper, Bailey & Co., 1876-78. With **Bartholomew,** the great horse trainer, when he first came East and joined Dan Rice's; also in advance of the prosperous Celtic star, **Joseph Murphy.** [Charles H. Day: "Jake has got an egg factory at Port Elgin, Ont., and breeds fancy poultry for profit. He must be the chap who lays those large eggs on the editor's table of which we read."]

SHOWLES, MRS. WILLIAM. See Daisy Belmont and Sallie Marks.

SHOWLES, WILLIAM [r. n. William Christian]. (1857-March 31, 1924) Bareback rider. Native of Perth Amboy, NJ. Adopted son of **Jacob** and **Elizabeth Showles.** At age 10 was performing somersaults on the bare back of a horse and the feat of sitting and standing on a chair while astride a horse circling the ring. Older's, 1871; J. W. Wilder's, 1872; bareback and pony rider, Showles & Co.'s Grand Triple Combination, 1873; Maginley & Co., 1874; Scott's, 1875; Dan Rice's, 1877-78; Adam Forepaugh's, 1879-81, John B. Doris', 1883-84; 1886-87; American bounding jockey, Sells Bros.', 1889, including the Australian tour; Barnum & Bailey, London, winter 1889-90, 1893-99. Established a school on Long Branch, NJ, to train circus horses and riders, 1887. That same year, was divorced from equestrienne **Sallie Marks**, July 1, 1887, whom he had married in 1883. Married equestrienne **Daisy Belmont**, October 8, 1889, on the Belmont Elite Circus. Accidently caused the death of a friend, **Ansel Croft**, a bartender at Red Bank, NJ, December 24, 1896, when he recklessly slammed a revolver on a bar top. The gun went off and a bullet hit his victim in the abdomen. Was arrested and indicted for manslaughter but the dying man pleaded for his release and was acquitted by a jury in Freehold, NJ, February 20, 1897. Riding career ended when he suffered a broken leg while riding with a circus in Budapest. Seemingly, the last employment was that of elevator operator for a NYC apartment building. Died penniless in Bellevue Hospital, NYC. [John Daniel Draper: In his prime Showles "was most supple and graceful, unrivalled and daring in his jockey riding act and great in his forward and backward somersaults."]

SHREIF, PROF. HARRY. Balloonist, J. T. Johnson's, 1890, who parachuted from his balloon at the height of about 2,000 to 3,000 feet; Dick's Model Show, made 21 successful ascensions, 1891.

SHRODE BROTHERS [4 in number]. High-wire act, with Miller, Stowe & Freeman, 1887.

SHRODE, GEORGE. Acrobat, P. T. Barnum's, 1877.

SIBERY, CHARLES. Riding master, Bancker's, 1824; J. Purdy Brown's, 1825.

SIDAHL, TONY. Principal bareback and hurdle rider and carrying act with **Minnie Sidahl**, Bruce L. Baldwin's, 1894.

SIDLEY, T. T. Sidley's Italian Circus, 1885

SIEBER, GEORGE. Proprietor, George Sieber & Co., 1887; proprietor of Cole's Ten Cent Show, also called Sieber & Cole's Ten Cent Show, 1890-91. May have been in partnership with **J. M. Barry** for several years.

SIEGRIST, ALBERT. Equestrian, VanAmburgh & Co., 1880.

SIEGRIST, ANDRE. See Francois Siegrist.

SIEGRIST, AUGUSTE. (1829-1874) Tight-rope, trapeze, *perche-equipoise*, "Brothers Act." Born in Manheim, Germany. Apprenticed to Mons. Tourniaire. Performed at the Paris Hippodrome for some years before coming to USA with Franconi's Hippodrome, 1853, 1855. Mabie's, 1854; Jim Myers', 1856; Spalding & Rogers, 1858-61; Spalding & Rogers, Old Bowery Theatre, NYC, 1861; Dan Rice's, 1861-63; Stone & Rosston, 1864; Dan Rice's Paris Pavilion Circus,

1871; L. B. Lent's, 1874; stage manager, Adam Forepaugh's, 1893. At the Bowery Circus, NYC, winter 1857-58, was said to have performed on the "Spanish Tramplin," flying over 24 loaded bayoneted muskets which were discharged as he made the leap. Died in Bergen Heights, NJ. See François Siegrist.

SIEGRIST, BLANCHE. General performer, with VanAmburgh's, 1874.

SIEGRIST, FRANÇOIS. (1824-June, 1878) Gymnast and trick clown. Born in Berlin, Germany, the son of a showman. One of four brothers—**Auguste, François, Andre** and **Louis**. All were brought up in the circus business. After beginning a career in Germany, was engaged as chief clown for the Paris Hippodrome, where he remained for several years. Traveled throughout Europe under Franconi's management before coming to America with his brother, **Auguste**, for the establishment of Franconi's Hippodrome, NYC, 1853. Together they did the trapeze, *perche-equipoise*, and "Brothers Act" on the four globes which, it is claimed, they were the first to introduce in America. François married **Marietta Zanfretta**, a member of the **Zanfretta Troupe**. With Marietta and her brother, **Alex**, the four made up a troupe of pantomimists and acrobats. Later the brothers separated and **François** and **Alex** formed a brother act, traveling as such for about 3 years. Subsequently, **François** devoted his time to training his children as acrobats and developing performing dogs. Died suddenly of heart trouble in Paris. Franconi's, 1853, 1855; Levi J. North's, 1853 (where, it is claimed, they were the first to do "Mons. and Madame Dennie"); Mabie's, 1854; Jim Myers', 1856; Nixon & Kemp, 1857; Bowery Amphitheatre, NYC, 1857; Spalding & Rogers, 1857-61; Dan Rice's, 1862-63; Stone, Rosston & Co., 1864; L. B. Lent's, 1864; Hippotheatron, NYC, winter 1864-65; Albisu's, Havana, fall 1865; John Wilson's, San Francisco, 1865; W. R. Blaisdell's, California, 1868; Campbell's, 1869; Batcheller & Doris, 1870. François, and his tight-rope performing wife, children and troupe of dogs were a part of VanAmburgh & Co.'s Menagerie, Siegrist's French and Frost's American Circus Combined, 1870-72, Nixon's Amphitheatre, Broadway opposite Waverly Place, NYC, winter 1871-72; with children Louis, Thomas, Willie, and trained dogs, Cooper, Bailey & Co., 1876. Died suddenly in Paris. See Auguste Siegrist.

SIEGRIST, LOUIS. (d. April 1908) Acrobat and general performer. VanAmburgh's, 1874; Kennebel's Parisian Circus, 1885. Died in Troyes, France. See François Siegrist.

SIEGRIST, ROSA. Tight-rope performer. Dan Rice's, 1861-63; Stone & Rosston, 1864.

SIEGRIST, THOMAS. Kennebel's Parisian Circus, fall 1885.

SIEGRIST, TOTO. Aerialist, general performer. Apprenticed to François Siegrist. VanAmburgh's, 1874; gymnast, Edward Shipp's Winter Circus, 1889-90; John S. McMahon's, 1892. Formed a partnership with Eddie Silbon, 1892. Opened a restraurant, NYC, 1909. Said to be "looking after the interests of the Siegrist-Silbon aerial act" with Ringling Bros. and Barnum & Bailey, 1918-19. See Silbon Family.

SIEGRIST, WILLIAM. (1868?-June 23, 1908) Acrobat. One of the **Siegrist Brothers**, along with **Toto** and **Louis**. VanAmburgh's, 1874; also Barnum & Bailey, Ringling Bros.', Adam Forepaugh's, and Sells Bros.' Kennebel's Parisian Circus, 1885; *Gran Circo Pubillones*, Cuba, winter 1888-89; principal clown and equestrian director, Stevens & Smith, 1898; Shipp's Winter Circus, Petersburg, IL, 1898-99, 1899-1900. Died in NYC, age 40.

SIFFERT, ADAM. Chief bill poster, Sells Bros.', 1874.

SIKES, OSCAR. Aerialist, World's Fair Aggegation, 1892.

SILBON FAMILY [Cornelius, George, Walter, Alfred, Ida, Minnie, Eddie, Kate]. English aerialists. By 1875, working as flyers and catchers in the modern style. Toured Spain, France, and England, 1878; Adam Forepaugh's, 1882-83; W. W. Cole's, 1886; Barnum and Bailey, London, 1887, 1898 (Five Silbons performed a flying ring act, and the Four Silbons gave an aerial act). Invented the double somersault in the air. With Barnum and Bailey's Paris engagement, 1901, three of the Silbon girls balanced on a revolving trapeze and another of the troupe cycled along a high wire. Founders included **Alfred** and **Cornelius Silbon**. **Mme. Carola** was married to one of them. **Cornelius** (d. July 15, 1891), while returning to the United States from Panama, was taken sick with yellow fever, died, and was buried at Acajutia, San Salvador. **Alfred**, known as Little Ebor, was second in age to brother Cornelius. Crippled by a fall in Paris. Later, had ring act of his own. His son, **Alfred**, had an animal act. **Walter** (1865-July 24, 1903), gymnast, was born in Hull, England, and began touring Europe, 1882, at age 5. The troupe was engaged by **Adam Forepaugh** that year and brought to America, introducing the first big aerial act to this country. **Ida**, Mrs. James E. Kerwin, (October 22, 1872-October 9, 1898) was born in Hull, England, the daughter of **Cornelius**. Her mother was an English burlesque performer, **Kate V. Newbold**, professionally known as **Kate Victoria**. First appeared in Barcelona, Spain, at 18 months of age. 1886, she performed in burlesque with her father's company. Was part of an aerial act with him, her uncle and aunt, 1889, which toured Australia for nearly 2 years and South America for another 2. Following her father's death, **Ida** left the aerial act and became one of the **Three Girdelles**, grotesques, appearing with Barnum & Bailey and other circuses. Died of consumption, Boston, MA. 1891, **Walter** assumed the management of the troupe and joined Barnum & Bailey as early as 1893 and remained with the show until the close of the 1902 season. Died in Hull. **Mrs. Walter Silbon** (d. October 3, 1905) was the sister of **Mrs. Stirk** of the **Stirk Family**. She also died in Hull, England. **Kate Silbon** married clown **William Rollins**, fall 1885. Later married **Tom Herbert** of the aerial performing family. **Eddie** worked in vaudeville with

various acts until 1892, when he took **Toto Siegrist** as a partner for a flying return act, John McMahon's, 1892; Pubillones, Cuba, winter 1892-93; McMahon's 1893; World's Columbian Exposition, 1893; organized their own show, 1894, West Coast and Mexico. Eddie continued performing until 1931. [Richard E. Conover: The Silbons were "one of the most outstanding flying acts of all time."]

SILLOWAY, PROF. JOHN [or Sillaway, Siloway]. Band leader. Sears & Forbes, 1858; G. K. Goodwin's, 1860; S. O. Wheeler's, 1863; Slaymaker & Nichols, 1864.

SILVEY, HOMER. Boss canvasman, Cooper, Bailey & Co., 1880.

SILVO BROTHERS [F. and W.]. English gymnasts. Entered the profession, 1870, and became known as the "Flying Silvos." Traveled successfully throughout Europe, 1870-1877. January, 1878, while performing in Liverpool, **W. Silvo** met with a severe accident, which prevented him from continuing his career. **F. Silvo** (b. March 7, 1856) then devoted his time to perfecting a single act of balancing and juggling, entirely new and original. Toured Europe, appearing before the Emperor of Russia, the Emperor of Germany and the King of Spain. Was at the Alexandra Palace, London, 1881. Engaged with Sam Hague's company, St. James' Hall, Liverpool. At completion of the contract, sailed for America, August 12, 1882, joining Tony Denier's company, season of 1882-83. With Leon de Leon's, Havana, Cuba. Subsequently, on the bill at Koster & Bial's, January 28, 1884; and with Tony Pastor's Traveling Company the following season.

SIMMETH, JOSEPHINE. (1850-September 6, 1907) An equestrienne, born in Lewisburg, PA. Beautiful and graceful, she rode a horse with reckless daring. Married **William Forepaugh**, early 1870s. When he died, married a performer and continued on the road until she was too old to work in the ring. Montgomery Queen's; Rosston, Springer & Henderson; Adam Forepaugh's; Ringling Bros.'; Orrin Bros.'; S. H. Barrett's; Walter L. Main's; Burr Robbins'; Frank A. Robbins'. Died in Philadelphia, age 57. Daughter, **Manny**, was a trapeze performer.

SIMMETH, MRS. LUDWIG. See Josephine Simmeth.

SIMPSON, CHARLES. Rider, P. T. Barnum's, 1871.

SIMPSON EDMUND. Originally an actor, took control of the Park Theatre, NYC, with **Stephen Price**, 1812. When the two managers considered James West's circus company to be threatening competition, they developed a scheme to buy him out by circulating a rumor that they were about to construct an arena for circus performances and by hiring **Sam Tatnall** to break horses in a lot behind the theatre. This charade was enough to convince West to sell out to Simpson & Price and return to England, well paid for his efforts.

SIMPSON, ELLIOT. Attache, Walt McCafferty's Great Golden Shows, 1894.

SIMPSON, WILLIAM. Boss canvasman, Howe's Great

London, 1874; boss canvasman, Cooper, Bailey & Co., 1879; detective and master of transportation, Cooper, Bailey & Co., 1880.

SIMPSON, W. J. Manager, G. G. Grady's, 1874.

SINCLAIR, EMMA. W. W. Cole, 1886.

SINCLAIR, NELSON. Director of amusements, Welsh & Sands, 1893.

SINCLAIR, W. E. Treasurer, P. T. Barnum's, 1879-80.

SINGLETON, C. J. Punch and Judy performer, Barnum, Bailey & Hutchinson, 1881.

SITTIG, GEORGE J. (1859?-November 28, 1908) Sideshow performer, called "Jolly George, the Fat Boy." Weighed 500 pounds and had an 80" waist. Died in Mansfield, OH, age 49.

SIVADO, MARGUERITE. Adam Forepaugh's, 1889.

SIVALLS, CHARLES T. (d. July 14, 1916) Agent, etc. In early days of the American circus, was a "financial scout," whose job was to ascertain public attitudes about the circus in order to determine itineraries, with the routing of the show depending on his judgment. Treasurer, VanAmburgh's, 1859; agent, Haight's Great Eastern, 1874; contractor, P. T. Barnum's, 1875; contractor, W. W. Cole's, 1880; business agent, W. W. Cole's, 1885; Sells Bros.' tour of Australia, 1891-92. It was said he had no definite home, but his declining years were spent in Houston, TX, where he had been active in the bill posting business for some time. Made 4 tours of Australia and devoted 60 years to the circus business.

SIZER. Had a circus on the road for several years beginning in 1833, but an American provincial showman of little record. At times his company toured in Florida and Alabama. The very thorough Stuart Thayer noted he had a steamboat circus, 1838, but admits knowing nothing of the man personally. Levi J. North once told Charles H. Day about one of Sizer's principal attractions, a huge seashell, called an "oyster," which was "muscled" into the ring by several men.

SKELTON, C. J. See Gregory Family, C. J. Gregory.

SKELTON, GEORGE. See Gregory Family, George Gregory.

SKELTON, JOHN. Boss bill poster, Gregory Bros.' New Metropolitan Allied Shows, 1884.

SKINNER, C. O. Press agent. J. E. Warner's, 1876; Burr Robbins', 1877; Adam Forepaugh's, 1879.

SKINNEY, GEORGE. Cooper, Bailey & Co., 1879.

SLATE, HARRY [r. n. Warren Norton Eastman Slate]. (July 5, 1833-February 4, 1881) General performer. Born in Bernardson, MA. Entered the profession, 1841, as an apprentice to **Dan Rice**, and was with Rice as late as 1868. Connected with George F. Bailey & Co., Jerry Mabie's, Adam Forepaugh's (1869) and others as clown and ringmaster, and, at one time, was considered a good tumbler. Married a **Miss Stone** of Noblesville, IN, the daughter of a prominent lawyer. Off seasons, performed sleight-of-hand entertainments under his own management and in later years in variety halls, as-

sisted by his wife. Died, NYC, age 47.

SLATTEN, BEN. Boss canvasman, John Robinson's, 1876.

SLAUSON, JAMES H. Agent, S. O. Wheeler's, 1868.

SLAYMAKER, HENRY. Sideshow proprietor, Gardner & Hemmings, 1863.

SLETLER, ED. General agent, Baird, Howell & Co., 1874.

SLOAT, JOHN CALVIN. (July 6, 1828-November 17, 1891) Married **Catherine Lorena Bogart**, November 12, 1854, a union that produced 5 daughters. Clayton & Bartlett, 1844; agent, June & Titus, 1848; management, James G. Shepard, 1857; Sloat & Shepard, National Theatre, Boston, spring 1858; manager, Joe Pentland's, 1859; partner, Niblo & Sloat, 1860; Nixon & Sloat, 1860-61.

SLOCUM, JOHN. Clown, Handenburger & Co., 1871.

SLOMAN, GEORGE. (1832-1904) Clown, rider, gymnast, and contortionist. With several of the early Delavan overland shows—Mabie Bros.', Buckley's, Buckley & Babcock, and Coup-Castello's. Rivers & Derious, 1855; Washburn's, 1856; Buckley's, 1857; George F. Bailey & Co., 1859; VanAmburgh & Co., winter 1859-60; Mabie & Nathans, 1861-62; globe act on horseback, Melville, Cooke & Sands, 1863; Bailey & Co., Spalding & Rogers' Academy of Music, New Orleans, winter 1863-64 (this being the first equestrian exhibition in that city in 3 years); globe act on horseback, Bailey & Co., 1864, 1866; trapeze, P. T. Barnum's, 1871; rider, Montgomery Queen's, 1874; John Robinson's, 1867-75, 1879; concert, candy stand and reserve seat privileges, Burr Robbins', 1877; Hamilton & Sargeant, 1880; Australian Dime Show, 1887; Holland, Bowman & McLaughlin, 1890. As an all-around performer, did magic barrels, dancing globe, Spanish tranca, globe on horseback, stilts, chair perch, and juggling on horseback. Wrote his memoirs shortly before his death but they were lost by the publisher. Suffered from a chronic ailment and took his own life.

SLOMAN, WILLIAM. (d. December 27, 1902) Agent, Stowe's "Uncle Tom's Cabin" Co., winter 1893-94; Leon W. Washburn's, 1894; Reynold's, 1895; Charles Lee's Great London, 1901; business and contracting agent, Stowe & Publiliones, Havana, winter 1891-92; Pawnee Bill's Wild West Show, 1902. Also, Hi Henry's Minstrels, Washburn's Minstrels, "Next Door" Co., and Walter L. Main's Circus. Died in Cincinnati, OH, of a brain tumor.

SLOTE, HARRY. Clown, Adam Forepaugh's, 1869.

SMALL, COLONEL. Midget. Nixon's Cremorne Gardens, NYC, spring 1862; Nixon's, Washington, DC, fall 1862.

SMEAD, J. Great Combination (**George M. Kelly, Pete** and **John Conklin, William LaRue**, proprietors), 1871.

SMEAD, WILLIAM T. (1847?-April 1904) Gymnast. Robinson, Gardner & Kenyon, 1869; (with **Lester**) James Robinson's, 1870, winter 1870-71; bar act, James M. Nixon's, fall 1870; James E. Cooper's, 1872; Sells Bros.', 1879; W. W. Cole's, 1883; Nathans & Co.'s, 1883; L. J. Duchack's, 1889;

Adam Forepaugh's, 1893. Died at his home in Binghamton, NY, age 57.

SMITH, ALLYN. Charles Noyes', 1870; C. T. Ames', 1870; Spalding & Bidwell's, New Orleans, spring 1870.

SMITH, ASA T. Showman, of Westchester County, NY. Entered the circus business under the management of John Miller around 1826. There was a circus in the South in the winter of 1828-29 called the Lafayette Equestrian Company under his management. Married the equestrienne widow of equestrian **George Yeaman**, 1829. Advertised his show as the Yeaman Circus from 1829 until he retired from the road. Appears to be one of the earliest circus managers to offer some form of permanent seating within the tent, which occurred in the early 1830s.

SMITH, AVERY. (March 1, 1814-December 26, 1876) Showman, one of the "Flatfoots." Born in North Salem, NY, son of **Jesse Smith**, who was a silent partner in the menagerie of June, Titus & Angevine. Young Avery accompanied the show on a tour, 1833. Two years later started in the grocery business but soon gave it up. Had interest in Sands & Co.'s American Circus performing in England, 1844; partner with Sands, Lent & Co., 1845-46; principal owner, Franconi's Hippodrome, NYC, 1853; manager, Seth B. Howe's Great European, 1864, co-owner, 1865; Haight, Chambers and Ames, 1867; George Bailey & Co., 1867; chief backer, "The Black Crook" combination that visited South America, 1874. Last venture was in partnership with **John J. Nathans** and **George F. Bailey** of the Barnum show, 1876. Throughout entire career, studiously avoided having his name appear in advertising of any of the shows with which he was connected. Accumulated a large fortune, much of which was in NYC real estate. Died in Newark, NJ, age 62.

SMITH, BARNEY. Tumbler and gymnast, Alexander Robinson's, 1871.

SMITH BROTHERS. Balancing ladder, W. F. Kirkhart's Great American, 1894.

SMITH, BURT. M. V. B. Wixom's Twenty-Five Cent Circus, 1897.

SMITH, BUTTON. Rider, Smith's Circus, 1833. Had a severe fall while riding 2 horses and injured his back. Died about a year later.

SMITH, C. Holton & Gates' Harmoniums, a minstrel band organized for the the Simon Pure American Circus, New York, October 1, 1866.

SMITH, CHARLES. Niblo & Sloat (**L. B. Lent, manager**), West Indies, November 1860.

SMITH, CHARLES J. Robinson & Co. (Smith and Piper, proprietors), 1886; Robinson's Dime Circus, 1887-90; Smith & Robinson, 1891; Robinson's Combined Shows, 1892-93.

SMITH CHILDREN. Aerialists, with Robinson's Combined Shows, 1892.

SMITH, CORNELIA. H. M. Smith's Crescent City Circus, 1869.

SMITH, CREADY. See C. S. Primrose.

SMITH EDWARD J. Gymnast and tumbler. Niblo & Sloat, West Indies, fall 1860; J. E. Warner & Co., 1871.

SMITH, EDWIN. Long bearded man, Barnum, Bailey & Hutchinson, 1881.

SMITH, E. G. Co-proprietor, Thompson, Smith & Hawes' Great American Hippocolosiculum, 1866; proprietor, E. G. Smith's Great Three in One Combination Show, 1867.

SMITH, FRANK ["Master"]. Son of Horace W. Smith. Pony act, C. T. Ames', 1868; rider, H. W. Smith's Crescent City Circus, 1869.

SMITH, GEORGE. Rider, acrobat. Lamb & Co., winter 1839; Welch & Bartlett, winter 1840; June, Titus & Angevine's western division, 1841; Great Western, 1845; Stone & McCollum, 1846; John Tryon's, winter 1847.

SMITH, GEORGE. Leader of string band, George F. Bailey & Co., 1862; James M. Nixon's, 1864; Maginley, Carroll & Co., 1868.

SMITH, GEORGE J. Stevens & Smith's Two-Ring Circus and Congress of Trained Animals (**E. P. Stevens**, George J. Smith, proprietors), 1898.

SMITH, GEORGE WASHINGTON. (d. August 31, 1877) Better known as "old Bob Ridley." As far back as 1838, was singing and dancing the tragico-comico extravaganza of "Jim Along Josey," together with giving the Negro song of "Jim Brown," at the Lion Circus, Menagerie and Gymnastic Arena, Cincinnati, OH. Was known to familiars as "The Arkansas Traveler" and was the first person in America to make a decided feature of the song of "The Fine Oil English Gentleman." **Jim Sanford** and Smith were rivals in "Jim Along Josey." Summer 1841, back to the Bowery and he and his pupil **Piccaninny Coleman** were doing "Jim Along Josey" and kindred performances. Next went to England and in November, 1840, did their grotesque acts at the Surrey Theatre, London. Returned, 1841, and in the fall, 1842, joined Master **John Diamond** and **Billy Whitlock** at the Chatham Theatre, NYC. 1849, with Stone & McCollum and wrote the song-and-dance "Old Bob Ridley," which he first gave in New Orleans. 1854, went to San Francisco; from there to the Sandwich Islands, which he left, 1857, for Australia; 1860, left Australia and went to China, India, the Philippine Islands and Java; 1865, returned to Australia, whence he proceeded to London, where he became manager of the Collins & Brown "Christys," whom he took to Australia and played until 1865. Last tour, with **Heller**, which began at Bombay in October, 1871. October, 1872, Heller went to England and Smith returned to Australia, where in the interim he had managed several troupes.

SMITH, G. H. Great Western (proprietors, G. H. Smith, L. C. Maxwell), 1876.

SMITH, HARRY & CO. Manufacturers of prize candy packages, 1870s, 1880s. Advertised something new "in the shape of anti-bilious candied-corn in prize boxes," 1879.

SMITH, HELENE. Concert song and dance performer, Cooper, Bailey & Co., 1879.

SMITH, HORACE M. (d. March 30, 1886) Rider and general performer. Rockwell & Stone, 1846-47; Stone & McCollum, 1849; Rockwell's, 1850; Star State, 1852; 2-horse rider, Levi J. North's, 1855; scenic rider, New York Champs Elysees, 1865; Yankee Robinson's, 1866; S. O. Wheeler's, 1866; equestrian director and bareback rider, Ames' New Orleans, 1868; H. M. Smith's Crescent City, 1869-70; John Stowe & Sons, 1871. Two daughters of Smith and his wife, **Ellen**, died in 1869—13 year old **Lydia** at Narastota, TX, November 22, 1869; 8 year old **Ella**, 3 months earlier at Ouachita, TX. A daughter, **Laura**, married **Al Miaco**. Smith died in NYC, after being in the business about 50 years.

SMITH, IKE. Boss canvasman, Dan Rice's, 1891.

SMITH, ISAAC H. Treasurer, John H. Murray's, 1874.

SMITH, JAMES F. ["Col."]. (d. May 4, 1902) Howes', 1887-89; Howes & Cushing, 1895; George W. Richards' and Howes' London, 1896-97; Howes & Cushing, 1899; Great Syndicate, 1900-01; Great Eastern, 1902; Great London, 1903; sold at auction, 1904.

SMITH, JAMES M. Clown. Johnson & Co. (James T. Johnson's Great Western and VanVleck's Mammoth Show combined), 1866; J. T. Johnson & Co., 1869.

SMITH, JENNIE. Balancing trapeze, Gregory & Belford, 1892.

SMITH, JESSE. (September 5, 1785-September 4, 1866) Father of **Avery Smith**. Interested in the firm of Titus, Angevine & Co. Died in Norwalk, CT, age 81.

SMITH, JOHN. Band leader, Burr Robbins for a number of years. In the mid-1870s, surrounded himself with such men as **Sam Clemons, August Geise, Cash Williams, Len Williams**. [D. W. Watt: "While Johnnie Smith was strict with his men, always giving them to understand that they must not be late either for parade or for the afternoon or evening show, yet he protected them in every way. No musician with him was ever expected to do anything out of his line of work."]

SMITH, JOHN ["Smithie"]. Acrobat, leaper and tumbler, John H. Murray's, 1874; principal acrobat, Cooper, Bailey & Co.'s Australian tour, 1877-78. Appeared with St. Leon's there the following year, after which it is presumed he returned to the United States.

SMITH, JOHN W. Ethiopian delineator. J. J. Hall's, winter 1836; Yale/Sands, 1838; A. Hunt & Co., winter 1838; June, Titus & Angevine, 1839; Welch & Bartlett, winter 1839; Howes & Turner, winter 1839; Welch & Bartlett, 1840; P. H. Nichols', 1841, 1843; Welch & Mann, winter 1841; Welch & Mann (until July), 1842; N. B. and T. V. Turner, 1842; Rockwell & Stone (March), 1844; Dr. Gilbert R. Spalding's, 1844-48; Stone & McCollum, winter 1846, winter 1848; Stone & McCollum, 1849-50; St. Louis Amphitheatre (until May),

1851; Spalding's *Floating Palace*, 1852; partner, Rowe & Co., 1856. Wife was an equestrienne.

SMITH, J. R. Co-proprietor and Treasurer, Great Chicago Circus, 1879.

SMITH, J. S. Property master, Cooper, Bailey & Co. Australian tour, 1877.

SMITH, L. S. Ringmaster, Adam Forepaugh's, 1880.

SMITH, MARK. Burr Robbins', 1879.

SMITH, NEIL. (d. March 21, 1900) Showman and animal trainer. Born on the corner of 17th Street and Third Ave., NYC. Entered the circus business with a troupe of trained dogs. Great Australian, 1877; Allen's Great Eastern, 1879; educated ponies, goats, dogs and cats, Irwin Bros.', 1887; Hunting's, 1888. Also connected with Dan Rice's, King & Franklin, Fursman's, Pullman & Hamilton, and Frank Robbins'. Toured with Caste's Celebrities and for 3 years with the "Dark Secret" Co., working his troupe of dogs. Sold his animals, 1890, and opened the Smith House, Great Jones Street, NYC, which became a popular professional hotel. In partnership with **Sam A. Scribner**, formed Scribner & Smith's Circus, 1892. After leasing the title, toured variety halls with Harry Williams' Own Show, 1894-98. Last professional engagement, manager, "Hogan's Alley" Co. Subsequently, appointed superintendent of the Polo Grounds, NYC, by the New York Baseball Club, a position he held until he suffered a stroke, 1897, which led to his death in NYC. Married **Matilda Lauber**, 1881, who became known professionally as the juggler **Madeline**.

SMITH, ROBERT. Clown and equestrian. Howes', 1849; buffo singer, Nixon & Kemp, 1857; George F. Bailey & Co., 1858; Davis & Crosby, 1859; Levi J North's, 1860; Mabie & Nathans, 1861; Antonio Bros.', 1862; C. T. Ames', 1866-68; James M. Nixon's, 1870; Newton's, 1872.

SMITH, SAMUEL S. ["Sunday School"]. (d. October 6, 1892) Nickname was given to him by **S. H. Hurd**, son-in-law of P. T. Barnum. In his youth was clever as an elocutionist and recitationist and attracted the attention of Barnum who hired him as lecturer and ringmaster. Exhibitor of human curiosities, P. T. Barnum's, 1872-73; Maginley & Co., 1874; stage manager, Palace of Wonders, P. T. Barnum, 1876; Zoological lecturer, Barnum, Bailey & Hutchinson, 1882-84; ringmaster and lecturer, both Barnum & Bailey and Adam Forepaugh's for several seasons. Was a man of attractive appearance, intelligence and an able impromptu speaker. [Charles H. Day: Smith "became one of the best talkers who ever entered the arena or described a freak."] Died at his home, NYC, of acute pneumonia.

SMITH, SHEDRICK. See Shed LeClair.

SMITH, S. P. Agent, Seth B. Howes', 1855.

SMITH, THOMAS. Niblo & Sloat (**L. B. Lent**, manager), West Indies, November 1860.

SMITH, VICTORIA. Daughter of circus proprietor **H. M.**

Smith. Married **William Carroll**, summer of 1870.

SMITH, VIRGINIA. J. W. Wilder's 1872.

SMITH, W. Acrobat, John Robinson's, 1887.

SMITH, WASHINGTON. (1847-1904) 6-horse chariot driver, Barnum & Bailey, 1892.

SMITH, WILLIAM [William Olma]. Monkey man, O'Brien & King, 1864; Hippotheatron, NYC, winter 1864-65. See William Olma.

SMITH, WILLIAM. Veternarian assist., P. T. Barnum's, 1877; supt. of horses, P. T. Barnum's, 1879-80; veterinarian, Barnum, Bailey & Hutchinson, 1882.

SMITH, WILLIAM JASON. (d. August 5, 1874) Son of Horace Smith. General performer. Aaron Turner's, 1837; Hobby's, 1839; Stickney's (**J. W. Smith's**), 1845; equestrian director, Nathan Howes', winter, 1845; John Tryon's, winter 1845; Howes & Mabie, 1846; equestrian director, Stickney's, 1847; John Tryon's, winter 1847; 2 and 4-horse rider, Howes & Co.'s second unit, 1848; 2-horse rider, Crane & Co., 1849; equestrian director and (with **Nat Rogers**) *la perche*, Ballard & Bailey, 1855; 6-horse rider, Crescent City, 1856; 2, 4, 6-horse rider, Washburn's, 1857; Whitby's, 1859; Comac's Woods, Philadelphia, early summer, 1860; Niblo & Sloat, West Indies, 1860; Stickney's National Circus, Old Bowery, 1861; 2, 4-horse rider, Castello & VanVleck, 1863; John Wilson's, Southwest Pacific, 1865; New York Champs Elysees, 1865-66.

SMITH, W. N. (d. January 4, 1869) Born in Albany, NY. First went into show business with a traveling troupe, 1841, performing in white face. Said to be the first man to give imitations of a snare drum with the bones. Traveled throughout the country with circus companies, including W. N. Smith's Ethiopians with VanAmburgh & Co., 1860. At one time was a great favorite at Charley White's minstrel emporium, 49 Bowery, NYC. Continued to travel until 1866 when a physical disability in his right arm made it impossible for him to shake the bones. Died destitute. [T. Allston Brown: "As a bone soloist, he was the best ever heard in this country, having played for and won the championship, which he retained up to his death."]

SMITHSON, GEORGIANA. Equestrienne, with P. T. Barnum's, 1879.

SNEDDEN. Manager of Booth's Printing Office, one of the largest show printing firms in the country.

SNELL BROTHERS. Gymnasts, with Handenburger & Co., 1871.

SNORDEY. Acrobat, John Robinson's, 1882.

SNOW, EDWARD. Acrobat, leaper and tumbler. One of the **Leotards** (with **George Bliss, George Schrode**), 1880. Cooper, Bailey & Co., 1880; Doris & Colvin, 1887; Wallace & Co., 1885; Howe's New Colossal Shows, 1888; clown, E. E. Rice's, Manhattan Beach, Coney Island, 1895; "The Devil's

Auction" Co. (for 7 seasons prior to 1896). Married equestrienne **Annie Carroll**, who sued him for divorce, 1892.

SNOW, GEORGE A. Treasurer, Stevens & Begun, 1874.

SNOW BROTHERS [Benjamin M., William A., Henry, a Dan was also listed]. Gymnasts and general performers—magic globe, hat spinning, trained dogs, etc. Excelled in their "globe act." Goodwin & Wilder, Howard's Athenaeum, Boston, 1861; Goodwin & Wilder's, 1862; S. O. Wheeler's, 1863; with their troupe of dogs and performing monkeys, Slaymaker & Nichols, 1864; Whitmore, Thompson & Co., 1865; Yankee Robinson's, 1865-67; Dan Rice's, 1866; Stone & Murray, Olympic Theatre, Boston, winter 1868-69, 1870-71; Sheldenburger's, 1871; Central Park Circus, 1872; Den Stone's, 1873; W. W. Cole's, 1877; W. C. Coup's, 1878-79. **Benjamin** was with Cooper, Bailey & Co., 1880; Older, Crane & Co., 1884. He died at his home in Boston, MA, October 9, 1912, age 75.

SNOW, LOUIS. Cooper, Bailey & Co., 1880; leaper, Barnum, Bailey & Hutchinson, 1881-85.

SNYDER, CHARLES. Treasurer, F. J. Taylor's, 1891.

SNYDER, HARRY. Privilege manager, W, C. Coup's, 1893.

SNYDER, THOMAS R. (b. February 14, 1830) Ringmaster, Gardner & Hemmings, 1863.

SOBRIESKIE BROTHERS. Gymnasts and acrobats, S. H. Nichols', 1840.

SOEAR, MATTIE. Vocalist, Cooper & Co., 1874.

SOLO, JOHN. VanAmburgh & Co., winter, 1859-60.

SOLON. Clown, Miles' Circus Royale, Canada, 1863.

SOMERFIELD, JAMES. Advance agent, James T. Johnson's, 1885.

SOMMERFIELD, WILLIAM F. Advance agent, P. T. Barnum's, 1873.

SOMERS, ALICE. L. B. Lent's, 1872.

SOMERS, C. Gymnast, First National Union, 1861.

SOMERS, JOHN. George W. DeHaven & Co., 1865.

SOULIER, LEON. Leaper, tumbler, P. T. Barnum's, 1873.

SOUTHWICK, MAY. Sideshow phantom lady, Barnum, Bailey & Hutchinson, 1882.

SPALDING, GILBERT R. ["Dr."]. (1812-April 6, 1880) Born in Coeymans, Albany County, NY. Acquired the title of doctor because from about 1840 to 1845 was the proprietor of a drug and paint store, Albany, NY. About 1843, used Sam H. Nichols' circus as security of a loan; the show continued under Nichols' management until Spalding realized he was not about to recoup his money; visited the circus with the intention of bringing it to Albany and disposing of it; finding his management was paying off, and since he was enjoying the circus business, decided to keep the property for a while longer as Spalding's North American Circus. During 1847-48 season, visited New Orleans and moved northward up the Mississippi River. Arriving at St. Louis, divided the outfit into two shows, managing one with the original title, and putting **Dan Rice**,

282

the famous clown, at the head of the other, with his brother-in-law, **Van Orden**, as manager. Latter company cruised the Ohio, Missouri and Mississippi Rivers in a chartered steamboat, the *Allegheny Mail*. Went into partnership with circus rider **Charles J. Rogers** at the end of 1848 season and the following spring the circus went on the road newly organized and equipped. Among the novel features presented for the first time was the Appolonicon, drawn by 40 horses, four abreast, and driven by one man. It is also stated that the show inaugurated the first use of "quarter poles" to suppliment the "center poles" about 1850. Winter 1848-49, the Dan Rice show disbanded due to the cholera epidemic in the South. Spalding started Rice out again in the spring, 1849, in a land show. At the end of the season the outfit reverted to Spalding. Originated the river boat, *Floating Palace*, 1852, and moved up and down the Ohio and Mississippi Rivers, at the same time operating a land circus. Performed in NYC during the indoor season, 1854-55. 1856, Spalding, Rogers & Bidwell took a 10 year lease of the Pelican Theatre, New Orleans, and refitted it for circus and dramatic performances, calling it Spalding & Rogers' Amphitheatre, and later renamed it the Academy of Music. Same year, inaugurated a railroad circus. For the next few years, Spalding & Rogers had 2 and sometimes 3 companies touring the United States and Canada, traveling by rail, wagon and water. 1860, put a circus and dramatic company into the Bowery Theatre, NYC, performing equestrian dramas. From there, moved to the Academy of Music, Boston. Spring 1862, the Ocean Circus was organized. Started from New York in March of that year with a magnificent portable amphitheatre constructed upon an entirely new plan. The brigantine *Hannah* had been purchased and fitted with accommodations for the company and the next 2 years were passed in Brazil, Uraguay, Buenos Ayres and the West Indies, with **Charles J. Rogers** as managing proprietor. Spalding remained in the USA. Early part of April, 1864, the company returned home, after a voyage of over 16,000 miles. Spalding & Rogers dissolved partnership, 1865, with Rogers retiring from professional life. Spalding & Bidwell continued, however; and shortly they leased the Olympic Theatre, St. Louis, as well as theatres in Mobile and Memphis, and established a theatrical circuit. A scheme was devised, 1867, to send a circus company to the Paris Exposition. The amphitheatre, wooden with a canvas top, was made by Mr. Kennedy of Albany, NY, accommodating 44 private boxes, besides an imperial loge, 760 parquet seats, 1,420 balcony seats, and a gallery capable of accommodating nearly 2,000 persons, the seats being all cane-bottom chairs. Investors—**Avery Smith, Gerard C. Quick, John J. Nathans**, and Spalding and Bidwell—chartered the large steamer, *Guiding Star*, to convey the company, horses, ponies, mules, a performing buffalo, wardrobe, trappings, and the portable amphitheatre to be put together in sections. **W. T. B. Van Orden** had been sent in advance to prepare the way.

After arriving in Paris, and when nearly all the preparations for their opening had been completed, it was discovered that a local law prevented the erection of any wooden building within the city limits; consequently they could not use their pavilion, but instead performed at the *Theatre Prince Imperiale*, in the *Rue Du Temps*. After 6 months in Paris, and 3 months at the Holborn Amphitheatre, London, they returned to the United States. 1872, Spalding again put **Rice** on the road with a company. Last venture in the circus business occurred, 1874-75, when he was co-proprietor with **John O'Brien** and **Ben Maginley** of Melville, Maginley & Cooke's Continental Circus and Thespian Company. Shortly, Spalding and Bidwell dissolved their partnership, with Bidwell retaining the Academy of Music, New Orleans, and Spalding the Olympic Theatre, St. Louis. Retired at his home in Saugerties, NY, 1879. Died of cystitis in New Orleans. Stuart Thayer called him a great innovator. He was the first showman to own his own steamboat; invented the quarter-pole; introduced the pipe organ as circus music with the addition of a parade wagon, the Apollonicon; constructed the first river boat to accommodate an entire circus organization; and had the first outfit to travel on its own railway cars, 1856.

SPALDING, HARRY W. (1844?-February 4, 1874) Son of Dr. Gilbert R. Spalding. While managing the Dan Rice Paris Pavilion Circus, was seriously wounded by a pistol shot, May 21, 1872, in Baxter Springs, KS. Died of dropsy at his father's residence, Saugerties, NY, age 30.

SPANOLA BROTHERS [Henrico, Guillaume, Carlos]. Gymnasts. Said to be performers of great talent, utilizing many feats that had not been seen in the United States previously. Their specialty was "*La Barra de Resorte*," the horizontal bars. L. B. Lent's, Broadway Amphitheatre, 485 Broadway, NYC, winter 1863-64.

SPARES, FRANK H. Ringmaster, W. H. Harris' Nickel-Plate, 1891.

SPARKS, CHARLES. See John H. Sparks.

SPARKS, FRANK H. Equestrian director, Dockrill's, South America, 1885-86; Stow, Long & Gumble, 1889; clown, Charles Andress', 1889; equestrian director, Albert Hose's, 1893; back for his 8th or 9th year with W. H. Harris' Nickel-Plate, 1894.

SPARKS, JOHN H. [r. n. Wiseman]. (d. January 28, 1903) Started in the business as a musician. Adopted a boy he named **Charley Sparks**. The two traveled together for several years doing a musical act. Walter L. Main's, 1886, 1888; assembled Sparks Bros.' Australian Specialty Co., fall 1886; organized George E. Stevens' "Uncle Tom's Cabin" Co., 1889; formed Allen's Great Eastern Shows, 1890; and then Cole's Colossal Shows, 1893, changing the name, 1894, to John H. Sparks Old Reliable Virginia Show, and toured almost continuously since that time. **Charles Sparks** took over the management after John Sparks' death, which occurred at his winter home in

Winston Salem, SC, about 38 or 40 years of age. Two young lions, which he had raised, clawed his arm while he was stroking them through the bars of the cage, which he was used to doing. Blood poison set in causing the arm to be amputated to the shoulder. But it was of no avail for Sparks never survived the shock. He had been in the circus and theatrical business for nearly 25 years and had recently found prosperity.

SPARKS, T. Spalding's North American, 1847.

SPARKS, WILLIAM. (1835?-December 8, 1893) Professional athlete, called the "American Hercules." Performed cannon ball, light and heavy balancing, and other feats of strength for over 20 years with Barnum's, Sells', Ringling's and others. George W. DeHaven's, 1860-62; Old Cary's, traveling up and down the Mississippi River area by boat and railroad, 1864; Maginley & Bell, 1864; Thayer & Noyes, 1866; Lake's Hippo-Olympiad, 1867; Dodge & Bartine, 1868; Mrs. Charles Warner's, Philadelphia, 1870; Adam Forepaugh's, 1871; Great Commonwealth, 1872; Montgomery Queen's, 1874; John Robinson's, 1879; Silas Dutton', winter 1879-80, 1880. Around 1887, was badly burned while performing his act; a painful recovery led him to addiction to morphine, from which he never recovered and which led to his death. With his 2 sons and a daughter, variety performers, he operated a tent show up to the time of his passing, which occurred at the Butler House, Bloomington, IL, age 58. His wife died April 23, 1872.

SPAULDING, DR. GILBERT R. See Dr. Gilbert R. Spalding.

SPEAR, ANDY. Clown, Cooper & Co., 1874; Hamilton & Sargeant, 1878; Main & Sargeant, 1891.

SPEAR, CHARLES. Bill poster, P. T. Barnum's, 1873; M. V. B. Wixom's Twenty-Five Cent Circus, 1897.

SPEAR, ED. Announcer, Rice's Circus Carnival, 1896.

SPEARS, ANDY. Clown, ringmaster, and equestrian director. Cooper & Scott, 1874; Great New York Circus, 1877; equestrian director, Barry & Co., 1879; Dan Rice's, 1881; William Main & Co., 1889; Harper Bros.', 1892; (his 33rd year in the profession) educated dogs, E. E. Eisenbarth's, 1892. While with Cooper & Scott, complete a triple somersault from a springboard, September 29, 1874. His wife was **Mattie Spears**.

SPENCE, CHARLES. Older's, 1871.

SPENCER. Acrobat, John Robinson's, 1889.

SPENCER. (b. 1800) Debut, Pepin & Breschard, Charleston, SC, December 9, 1812; Pepin, Breschard & Cayetano, 1813; Pepin & Breschard, 1814; apprenticeship ended, Cayetano & Co., 1815; Cayetano & Co., 1816.

SPENCER, ANNIE. Burr Robbins', 1880.

SPENCER, CHARLES. Acrobat. Cosmopolitan Circus, Museum and Menagerie, winter 1871-72; Great International Circus, Offenbach Garden, Philadelphia, winter 1876-77.

SPENCER, MAUD. Plate spinner, Baldwin, Wall & Co.'s

Great Eastern, 1880.

SPENCER, SARAH. Tight-rope. Palmer's Circus and Gymnastic Arena, 1835; Nathan A. Howes' Eagle Circus, 1836.

SPENCER, SYLVANUS. Rider and vaulter. Made his debut with Pepin & Breschard at Charleston, winter 1812-13, and was with Pepin, Breschard & Cayetano in NYC, 1813; with the company in Philadelphia for the fall season and on to Baltimore, winter 1813-14; Pepin & Breschard, Charleston, fall 1814; accompanied Breschard to Savannah in the latter part of 1814; continued with Cayetano & Co. through 1816 when the circus was in New Orleans. Later, Price & Simpson, 1823-27; Bernard & Page, 1829-30; William Blanchard's, 1830; Fogg & Stickney, 1832-33; scenic rider, Buckley & Co., 1834; Sweet & Hough, 1835; scenic rider, Palmer's, 1835; Nathan A. Howes', 1836; Welch, Bartlett & Co., 1839-40; clown, Rockwell & Stone, 1842. One of his feats was balancing himself atop an 18' ladder on the tight-rope, a trick well advanced for his day; and to make things more difficult, fireworks were exploded around him as he approached the top of his climb.

SPENCER, WILLIAM. General performer, Welch's National Circus, Philadelphia, 1841.

SPICER, COL. Col. Spicer's World's Fair and Congress of Living Wonders, 1886

SPINACUTA. Equestrian clown, rope-dancer, and pyrotechnist. Member of Rickett's Circus, Philadelphia, 1796. Danced on a rope with baskets afixed to his feet; without a balace pole, he put a coin on his foot, flipped it in the air, and caught it in a glass; danced on a tight rope with skates on; while sitting in a chair on a plank, balanced a table before him and drank a glass of wine.

SPINACUTA, MRS. Tight-rope. Ricketts company, 1796.

SPRAGUE, CHARLIE. Whitmore, Thompson & Co., 1865.

SPRAGUE, ISAAC. (b. May 21, 1841) Sideshow living skeleton. Born in East Bridgeport, MA, of normal size. Began to lose weight around the age of 12, until he literally became skin and bones; but claimed he was never sick a day in his life. Joined Barnum's museum curiosities, "the original thin man," 1860s. Traveled with several shows, including North American, 1872; P. T. Barnum's, 1873; Adam Forepaugh's (Pullman Bros.' sideshow), 1876; Cooper, Bailey & Co., 1879-80; Barnum, Bailey & Hutchinson, 1881-83. Married a Massachusetts girl who bore him 3 healthy sons.

SPRAGUE, JOHN. Clown. H. H. Fuller's Olympic Circus, 1838; J. W. Stocking's, 1839. A daughter married **W. B. Carroll**.

SPRAGUE, J. S. Cooper, Bailey & Co., 1879.

SPRAGUE, Z. W. Proprietor and manager, Sprague's Colossal Circus and Great Electric Light Show, 1880, folding in July of that year.

SPRIGGS. Acrobat, Davis & Co., Boston, 1815, first American appearance.

SPRINGER, ANDREW J. (d. February 2, 1886) Agent.

Spalding & Rogers, 1857; Antonio & Wilder's, 1859-61; Thayer & Noyes, 1862-64, winter 1865-66; advertiser, John Robinson's, 1866; James M. French's, 1867-69; agent and co-proprietor, James Robinson's, 1870; general director, Rosston, Springer & Henderson's (**Frank H. Rosston, Andrew Springer, Abe Henderson** and **Adam Forepaugh**, proprietors, the latter owning one-third of the concern and buying out his partners, October 1872), 1871; contracting agent, L. B. Lent's, 1873; proprietor and general director, Warner & Henderson, 1874; proprietor, Springer's Royal Cirq-Zoolodon, 1875; Rothschild & Co., 1876; railroad contractor, Batcheller & Doris, 1879; railroad contractor, Sells Bros.', 1883; S. H. Barrett's, 1885. [Peter Sells: "He was a man of sterling integrity, wide experience and a high class man."] Died at Fulton-ham, OH.

SPROULL, GIBB. Gymnast, Dan Rice's Paris Pavilion, 1873.

SPROULL, MABEL. Contortionist, Harry Thayer & Co.'s, 1890.

SPROULL, THOMAS. Agent, Henry Rockwell's unit of Rockwell & Stone's Circus, 1846.

SPRUNG, FRED. Ethiopian entertainer, Wilson's Circus in the mountain towns of California, 1865.

SPURLING, C. General performer, with Spalding & Rogers, 1850.

ST. BENOIT TWINS. Two-headed baby, Bunnell sideshow, P. T. Barnum's, 1879.

ST. CLAIR, F. T. Holton & Gates' Harmoniums, a minstrel band organized for the the Simon Pure American Circus in New York, October 1, 1866.

ST. CLAIR, MAY. Morosco's Royal Russian Circus, 1885.

ST. CLAIR, MONS. Trapeze performer. "From the *Cirque de Napoleon*, Paris." S. P. Stickney's, 1869; Metchear & Cameron, 1970.

ST. CLAIR, SALLIE. Adam Forepaugh's, 1886.

ST. CLAIR, TOM. Comedian, Palace of Wonders, P. T. Barnum, 1876.

ST. ELMO, GEORGE and **EMMA. George**, questrian director, and **Emma**, high-wire ascensionist, with Charles Andress', 1889.

ST. GERMAIN, JOSEPH. Proprietor, St. Germain's, 1889.

ST. JOHN, WILLIE. High wire and bicycle rider, McMahon's, 1888.

ST. LEON, MME. Performing dogs, Fulford & Co., 1890.

ST. ORMOND, OSCAR. Trainer of Trakene stallions, P. T. Barnum's, 1877.

STAAKS, KITTY. Bareback principal act, Cooper, Jackson & Co., 1884.

STAFLEY, CELESTE. James Robinson's, 1872.

STANDISH, GEDRON B. (1847?-July 17, 1912) 15 years business manager for P. T. Barnum. Afterword, opened an elaborate hair dressing parlor, NYC. Eventually sold out and moved to Boston where he went into the candy business. A year later, went on the vaudeville stage, which lasted 3 years. Opened a small theatre, Cottage Grove, OR. After his wife died, 1910, moved to Tacoma, WA, and again went into the hair dressing business, which he continued until the time of his death. Died at Tacoma of a brain hemorrhage, age 65.

STANHOPE, GEORGE. Bill poster. James M. Nixon's, 1870; Haight's Great Southern, 1874.

STANHOPE, WILLIAM: (1838?-October 7, 1889) Showman. Born in Dayton, OH. Connected in the management with W. W. Cole and John B. Doris. Served during the Civil War in the Ohio regiment. Kept the Lake Villa Hotel, Lake County, IL, owned by E. J. Lehmann. With **Louis Epstean**, in the dime museum business, Chicago, for 2 years, buying out Col. Wood's Museum on Randolph Street. Sold interest to his partner, 1886. Managed a hotel in Atlantic City. Returning to Chicago, 1888, was involved in various entertainment enterprises until his death there, age 51.

STANLEY, MAUDE. Mike Lipman's, winter 1866-67; Orton Bros.' Circus, 1867.

STANLEY BROTHERS. Cooper, Bailey & Co., 1875; W. H. Harris' Nickel-Plate, 1886.

STANSELLE, FRANK. American clown, Great Atlantic and Pacific, winter 1871-72.

STANTON, CHARLES. Donaldson & Rich, 1885.

STANWOOD, HARRY [r. n. Henry Harrison Stephens]. Banjoist. End man for Sam Sharpley's minstrel company, 1868-69. Performed for circuses. Married at Coburg, Canada, to **Sarah Elizabeth Bonskill**, May 5, 1885.

STAPLES, GEORGE. Cantellis & Leon's winter circus, Havana, 1882.

STAPLETON, W. FRANK. Boss hostler, Whitney's Imperial Wagon Show, 1892.

STARK, CHARLES. Charles Lee's, 1889.

STARK, FRANK. Bareback rider. Hyatt & Co., 1859; double somersaulter, James M. Nixon's, 1860; leaper, Robinson & Lake, 1859-62. On August 12, 1862, while attempted a triple somersault at the fair grounds in Cincinnati for a wager of $100. At first attempt, turned over 3 times but alighted in a sitting posture. This satisfied the wager, but Stark refused the money, stating that he would repeat the feat and land on his feet before he felt justified in winning the money. On the second attempt he landed on his head, dislocating his neck, and died a few hours later.

STARR BROTHERS. Jeal & Co., California, 1871.

STARR, GEORGE OSCAR. (April 1, 1849-September 10, 1915) Like Barnum, born in Bethel, CT. 1870, age 21, received his diploma in medicine. Same year, was commissioned 2nd Lt. in the New York State National Guard and eventually rose to the rank of Major. Began his show business career in association with **Bunnell** in a dime museum on the Bowery. Later becoming press agent for P. T. Barnum's,

1878-79, owned by **George F. Bailey**, **John B. Nathans**, and **Lewis F. June**. Eventually became assistant to June, who was the general advance agent. For a number of years, involved in other entertainments, light opera, museums, and theatre in Cincinnati, Pittsburgh and Brooklyn. When James A. Bailey returned to the Barnum show after a 2 year rest, Starr was engaged as a special representative and sent to Europe in search of attractions. While en route to England, Barnum's winter quarters in Bridgeport, CT, was destroyed by fire. Was commissioned to find replacements for the large loss of animals, which he skillfully accomplished; which led to other foreign missions entrusted to him. General manger, Barnum & Bailey, 1905. Sailed November 5, 1905, to arrange for the transportation of the *Galerie des Machines* from Paris to New York. Managing director of the Crystal Palace Exposition, London, England, 1908. Last position with Barnum & Bailey was as general manager, until, at Bailey's request, he was replaced by the board of directors with W. W. Cole. Was twice married, second wife being the renowned **Zazel**, human cannon ball. Died in London. [Louis E. Cooke: "His career has been one full of honor. His friends number all of those with whom he came in contact, and his acquaintances were legion. His memory is a monument to the man."] Before his death he asked to be cremated and that his widow dispose of the ashes on a sea voyage to America. Which she did.

STARR, JESSE. Acrobat, Dan Rice's, 1852.

STEARNS, WILLIAM H. Program agent, G. F. Bailey & Co., 1874.

STEBBINS, H. L. Equestrian director, Levi J. North's, 1859; advertiser, S. Q. Stokes', 1863; Tom King's, 1864; advertising agent, Dan Rice's, 1868.

STEELE, GEORGE K. General agent. Was born in Moundsville, WV. With Michael O'Conner & Co., 1869-70; Noyes' Crescent City, 1871-73; Dan Rice's, 1872; Burr Robbins', 1875-80, 1885 as part owner; Adam Forepaugh's, 1881-82. Was a sergeant in the Union army. Described as a typical Southerner with the broad-brimmed white hat and the accent in his voice, a gentleman of the highest type, whose work was always to the letter. [D. W. Watt: "Anywhere George K. Steele did business with people, they were always glad to have him come back, for he never made a promise to the public that he did not make good."] Retired in the town of his birth.

STEELE, HARRY J. (1862?-January 21, 1913) Agent. Scribner & Smith, Leon Washburn's, etc., and ultimately opposition agent for Barnum & Bailey. Also agent for theatrical enterprises. Forced to give up the road because of an invalid wife, worked for the Philadelphia Billposting Co., remaining with it for 20 years. Died in Philadelphia, age 51.

STEELE, JOHN. Menagerie supt., Haight's Great Southern, 1874.

STEELE, LEW S. Press agent, John Robinson's, 1883.

STEEN, CHARLES N. and **MARTHA E.** Mind readers and illusionists, John Robinson's, 1880.

STEERE, L. M. W. Agent. Palmer's Circus with Mrs. Dan Rice, 1866; advance agent, Dingess & Green's Minstrel, 1866; advertising agent, L. B. Lent's, 1868-69; advertiser, George F. Bailey & Co., 1870.

STEETNAM, BILLY. Ethiopian entertainer, with Haight & Chambers, winter 1866-67.

STEIN, T. Equestrian, VanAmburgh & Co., 1881.

STEINMAN, HENRY. Band leader, with Henry Rockwell's, 1847.

STEINSCHMIDT, FRITZ. Clown, Burr Robbins', 1886.

STEMPLE, LIZZIE. Equestrienne, skipping-rope dancer, with Montgomery Queen's, 1874. May have been married to Signor Faranta.

STEPHENS, GEORGE [or Stevens]. Son of a Millerton, NY, farmer. Boss canvasman, Hamilton & Sargeant, 1878; elephant keeper, Barnum & Bailey, England, winter 1889-90.

STEPHENS, HENRY HARRISON. See Harry Stanwood.

STEPHENS, OLIVER. With Gardner & Donovan, South America, 1886.

STEPHENSON, HARRY. Burr Robbins', 1877.

STERLING, MONS. Acrobat, Dan Rice's, 1849.

STERLING, R. W. Treasurer, Beckett's Great Exposition Circus, 1881.

STETSON, HENRY. General performer, Great European, 1865; Frank J. Howes', 1865.

STETSON, JOHN. (1836-April 8, 1896) Born in Charlestown, MA. Became an athlete and champion runner. A match with **Lynn Buck** and another with **John Grinnell** were considered major events. Also gave exhibitions in the circus ring. After retiring from competition, founded the spicy sporting sheet, *Boston Life,* the contents of which caused a great deal of consternation among the staid Bostonians. [M. B. Leavitt: "Stetson was rough and ready, but gifted with rare business acumen, which was always profitable to himself. It was a fad among newspaper men of his day to invent blunders of speech and credit them to him, a pastime which he bore without resentment. In business he was inclined to be strict, sometimes irascible, yet manifest a keen sense of humor.... He could draw a contract as shrewdly as a skilled lawyer."] Later became publisher of the *Sporting Times,* a Boston publication, 1867-72, and revived with a shortened format, 1884-86. Managed numerous theatrical enterprises, including Salvini, Lilly Langtry, James O'Neill, *The Mikado, Princess Ida,* minstrel and variety companies, etc. Owned at various times the Boston Show Printing Company, the *Police News,* several cafés, gambling houses, and pawn shops. Was the long-time successful manager of the Howard Athenaeum, proprietor of the Globe Theatre, Boston, and the Fifth Avenue, New York. Married **Katie Stokes**, 1887, considered by Gil Robinson to be the most beautiful female rider in America. Died of pneumonia in his Boston residence as one of the wealthiest theatre managers

286

in the country.

STEVENS, B. M. Advertiser. With Lake's Hippo-Olympiad, 1866-67; contracting agent, John Robinson's, 1868; superintendant, James Robinson's, 1871; general agent, L. B. Lent's, 1874; general agent, Joel E. Warner's, 1876.

STEVENS, BENJAMIN. (February 7, 1831-December 4, 1908) Rider and tumbler. Born in Albany, NY. Apprenticed to **Henry Rockwell** at the age of 8. As Master Stevens, rode at Howes' Amphitheatre of the Republic, the Bowery, NYC, 1842; 2-pony rider, Rockwell & Stone, 1842-46, being billed as an equestrian prodigy. Also connected with Rockwell & Co., 1847-48; R. Sands & Co., 1849; Rivers & Derious, 1851; Welch & Lent, 1854-55; VanAmburgh's, Broadway Theatre, winter 1857-58; George F. Bailey & Co., 1858; Dan Rice's, 1858; trick and somersault rider, Antonio Bros.', 1860. While doing a forward somersault on horseback, Columbus, OH, fell and broke his right leg. Upon recovery, leaper, tumbler, P. T. Barnum's, 1873; Barnum's Roman Hippodrome, NYC, 1874-74, as a trainer of horses as well as a chariot racer. After retiring from the circus, became an insurance agent. Died in Brooklyn, NY.

STEVENS, E. P. Stevens & Smith's Two-Ring Circus and Congress of Trained Animals (E. P. Stevens, **George J. Smith**, proprietors), 1898.

STEVENS, FRANK. Treasurer, Older's, 1872; proprietor and assistant manager, Stevens & Begun's Circus, 1874.

STEVENS, FRED. Treasurer, W. W. Coles, 1878.

STEVENS, GEORGE. Boss canvasman, Main & Sargeant, 1891.

STEVENS, GEORGE W. "DR." Treasurer, Alex Robinson's, 1865-70.

STEVENS, HERMAN. Contracting agent, DeHaven's Great Eastern, 1883.

STEVENS, "MAJOR". Sideshow dwarf. Performed with Price & Simpson, 1824-25, appearing in the burletta *Tom Thumb the Great*. Said to be 37" tall at 21 years of age. Another source listed him as 40" and weighing 50 pounds. In 1835, executed ornamental and fancy paper-cutting, Valentines, etc., which he sold to people visiting his exhibition. His performance was in "profile likenesses." J. O. Howes' driving 20 Shetland ponies pulling Queen Mab's Fairy Chariot, 1848.

STEVENS, O. P. Bandleader, Miles Orton's, 1881, 1885.

STEVENS, PUSS. Clown, C. T. Ames' New Orleans Circus and Menagerie, 1869.

STEVENS, SID F. Agent, Cosmopolitan Circus, Museum and Menagerie, winter 1871-72.

STEVENS, WILLIAM O'DALE. (1854-September 30, 1883) Equilibrist. One of the best foot jugglers in the business. Born in Portsmouth, England. In the circus business since the age of 4, his parents being in that profession. 1861, sailed with them to India where he remained for 5 or 6 years; thence to China, the Philppines, Japan, New Zealand, Australia and

Madagascar. Father died at the latter place, 1872. With Chiarini's, revisited India and Japan. Returning, joined Ryan & Robinson; Montgomery Queen's, California, 1877; Maltese cross and magic barrel, bareback juggling, Campbell's, 1878; Anderson & Co., 1878; John H. Murray's (when it was shipwrecked on way), West Indies, winter 1878-79; balancing feats, P. T. Barnum's, 1879; Orrin Bros.', Havana, winter 1879-80; Cooper & Bailey, 1880; W. W. Cole's, Australian tour (which left San Francisco, October 23, 1880); Great Australian Circus (combination of William O'Dale Stevens' Australian Circus & T. F. Kelly's Specialty Troupe), National Theatre, Philadelphia, winter 1881-82; Stevens' Australian Circus, performing on variety stages, prior to summer season, 1882; Park Square Grounds, Boston, 1883; W. O'Dale Stevens' Australian Circus, winter 1882-83. Married hurdle rider **Linda Jeal**. As an equilibrist, he balanced a large cross, a table and a barrel with his feet; performed a running globe act. Was an excellent leaper and general performer. Had the West side Training Academy, Jersey City Heights, NJ. Died of a heart attack at his home in Jersey City, NJ, age 29.

STEWART, A. B. Mail and program agent, Barnum, Bailey & Hutchinson, 1882; manager, Barnum's Recreeation Hall, Bridgeport, CT, 1884; Barnum & London, 1885. Wife, **Mary** or **May Stewart**, was a race rider, Barnum & London, 1881-85.

STEWART, ALFRED. (d. February 20, 1872) Child acrobat, Rockwell & Co., 1848. Later, became an actor of some prominence. Died at Cobleskill, NY.

STEWART, ELLA. Sells Bros.', 1874.

STEWART, JOSEPH. (d. May 22, 1870) Treasurer, Lake's Hippo-Olympiad, 1868-70. Died in Vicksburg, MS.

STEWART, MME. W. E. Equestrienne. Mother of **Alfred Stewart**. Died, NYC, February 5, 1873.

STEWART, THOMAS. Rider and clown. Managed a circus company in Providence, RI, September 10, 1808. Advertised as performing a feat of picking up 4 handkerchiefs and a watch while his horse was going full speed. The show went on to Salem and Charlestown, MA. It is believed that he is the Stewart that George Stone referred to as giving equestrian performances in Albany (the first circus performer to visit there) on an open lot near where Fort Orange had once stood. The clown took up a collection outside the ring. Mrs. Stewart was called "a fearless, graceful rider." Had a small company on the road, 1809, probable made up partly of amateurs. With Pepin & Breschard, Philadelphia, 1809; clown, with Robert Davis', Salem, MA, 1810; Pepin & Breschard, fall 1810; Cayetano & Co., Canada, fall 1811.

STEWART, THOMAS L. (d. November 1872) Could be the same as above. Rider. James Hunter's, 1827; Royal Pavilion Circus/Olympic Circus, 1830-31; Benjamin Brown's, Caribbean, 1830-31; ringmaster, proprietor, T. L. Stewart's Circus Co., 1831-32. In 1832, opened the American Amphitheatre,

THE STICKNEY FAMILY

Samuel Peckhill Stickney married Christiana Wolf (?-1861), a non-professional, in the 1830s. The union produced five exceptional circus performers. [S. P. Stickney was one of five brothers—Benjamin and John were performers; Otis and another brother, unknown, were not.]

Rosaline Stickney	Sallie Louise Stickney	Emma Auline Stickney	Samuel P. Stickney, Jr.	Robert Theodore Stickney
(1833-1857) married Benoit Tournaire, 1850. They had two children—Rosaline "Crissie" and Samuel.	(1835?-1886) married Omar Kingsley, 1861. They had a daughter Dona. Sallie was divorced around 1872 and married rider Willie Franklin that year. He died, 1883.	(1848-1882) married circus bandleader Phil Blumenschein. They had a son Charles.	(1841-1921) married equestrienne Ida Sherwood. They had two children—Robert and Cora.	(1841-1921) married Katie V. Robinson, 1870. Their first child, Robert, was born, 1872. The second child came a year later but died along with the mother. Stickney married again, 1893, to Emma Rezac (?-1923), wire performer and juggler. They had a daughter, Emily.
Rosaline "Crissie" Stickney married Robert Greare, 1877.	Dona was a wire walker.	Charles was a non-professional.	Robert was a non-professional. Cora married a man named Johnson and appeared in a juggling act in vaudeville.	Robert John Danville Stickney (1872-1941) married bareback rider Louise DeMott, 1894. A son Robert was born, 1895.
Samuel was a non-professional				Robert (the third of the line) married an English entertainer Lillian Aylin.

Portland and Traverse Streets, Boston, returning in December for a week's stay at the Federal Street Theatre. Spalding & Rogers, spring 1864; ringmaster, New York Champs Elysees, 1865. Died in Brooklyn, NY.

STEWART, WILLIAM [a.k.a. Stewart Nunn]. (d. 1852) Family came to the USA from England, 1844. Niblo's, 1845; Nathan Howes', winter 1845; four Nunns, Rockwell & Stone (Rockwell's unit), 1846; Rockwell & Co. (Hubbell's unit), 1847-48; Stone & McCollum, 1849; S. Q. Stokes', 1851. Sons were **Alfred** and **Henry**. Died in New Orleans.

STEWART, WILLIAM H. ["Cap"]. (b. January 3, 1840) Acrobat, trapezist, and clown. Born in Fort Wayne, IN. A fluent talker, was a "ballyhoo" man with Dan Rice's and Spalding & Rogers. James R. Cooke's, winter 1864-65; Stowe Bros.', 1867; G. G. Grady's, 1868-69; light and heavy balancer and song and dance man, Spear's, 1870; sideshow song and dance man, G. G. Grady's, 1871; sideshow privilege, G. G. Grady, 1874; same with W. W. Cole's, 1875. Started W. H. Stewart's Australian Circus Combined with William Earl's American Show, 1880; show was sold after a managerial disagreement, Stewart losing $8,500 from the undertaking. Sideshow manager, Bartine's, 1892. Later started a "mud show," but soon retired for sideshow and museum exhibiting. In 1915, at the Bellevue, OH, fair, presented **Angola** the Gorilla at 25¢ admission.

ST. GERMAIN, JOSEPH. Proprietor, St. Germain's Imperial Circus, 1889.

STICKLAND, WILLIAM. Agent, John Robinson's, 1875.

STICKNEY, ALICE. Rider, Hudson & Castello, 1881.

STICKNEY, BENJAMIN. (1819-February 24, 1860) Rider and wire walker. Brother of **S. P. Stickney**. Particularly useful in horse dramas. Lafayette Circus, NYC, January 1825-27; Mount Pitt Circus, NYC, 1826-28; Washington Gardens, Boston, summer 1827; Parsons' Albany Circus (**Simon V. Wemple**, manager), Troy, NY, 1828; Washington Circus, Philadelphia, 1828; William Blanchard's, 1830. Opened at Astley's Amphitheatre, London, September 6, 1830. Visited Liverpool's Theatre Royal with Ducrow's Olympic Arena, 1834-5; Liverpool Royal Amiphitheatre, 1837. Remained with the company until after Andrew Ducrow's death, 1841. Married **Eleanor** (*nee* Minter), the widow of Ducrow's brother John, April 29, 1838, London. Shortly after Ducrow's death, appeared with Davidge's Company, Royal Surrey Theatre, London, as "The Great American Rider." Returned to Liverpool, January, 1842, back with Ducrow's National Establishment, with Mrs Stickney, and in February, 1843, with "The Late Mr. Ducrow's Stud and Company." Joined Tourniaire's Company of French Equestrians, with **Mons. Benoit Tourniaire** and **Master Polaski**, January 1844, then returned to Astley's under **William Batty**. Died in Kensington, England, age 40 years.

STICKNEY, DONA. Dancer and Slack-wire performer.

Daughter of **Sallie Stickney**.

STICKNEY, EMILY. Equestrienne. Daughter of **Robert T.** and **Emma Stickney**. Appeared in the legitimate drama of *Polly of the Circus*, 1911-12, and later joined her family in the exhibiting of trained animal acts.

STICKNEY, EMMA [nee Emma Rezac]. (1876-July 6, 1923) Second wife of **Robert Stickney, Sr.** Born in Cincinnati, OH. At age 16, made her debut as a wire act and juggler with John Robinson's. Later appeared with Scribner & Smith's (**Sam A. Scribner**, **Neil Smith**, proprietors), 1895; Frank A. Gardner's Circus, South America, 1896; principal bareback equestrienne and high wire, Donovan & Stickney's, West Indies, winter 1897-98; trapeze and flying rings, Great Wallace Shows, 1899; New York Circus Co. (T. S. Chapman, proprietor), West Indies, winter 1900-01; Forepaugh-Sells Bros, 1903; Circus Albert Schumann, Berlin, winter 1904-05. Married Stickney in Cuba, March 2, 1893. Died, Newark, NJ, from an accidental fall from a fourth story window. The Stickneys had recently returned from exhibiting their dog and pony act with Saenz Bros.', Central and South America.

STICKNEY, EMMA AULINE. (1848-July 24, 1882) The daughter of **S. P. Stickney**. Considered a graceful, finished and pleasing performer, proficient at hurdle riding. Dan Rice's, 1858; L. B. Lent's, 1860-62, where she was billed as "Child of the Arena" and "Pearl of the Arena"; S. P. Stickney's, fall 1861; New York Champs Elysees, 1865; Thayer & Noyes, winter 1865-66; Den Stone's, 1878; John Robinson's, 1877-78; *manège* act, Adam Forepaugh's, 1879; Stickney's Imperial Parisian Circus, 1880. Married **Phil Blumenschein**, Thayer & Noyes' bandleader, which produced a son, **Charles**. Previously married to **James Donovan** and may have had still another husband named **Olmstead**. While traveling as ringmaster with Beckett's Circus, she died of typhoid fever in Detroit. [John A. Dingess: "She mounted her horse with a confidence perfectly surprising and appeared to possess an intuitive genius for the poetical and beautiful. Her style was purely original."]

STICKNEY, JOHN H. Brother of **S. P. Stickney**. Concert performer, Bancker's, 1824; Washington Gardens, Boston, spring 1825; Lafayette Amphitheatre, NYC, 1825-26; Price & Simpson, Washington Amphitheatre, Boston, 1826; Stickney & Buckley (**S. P. Stickney** and **Matthew Buckley**, proprietors), 1844; minstrel, Nathan A. Howes', 1845; minstrel, Welch & Delavan, 1847. Died in Providence, RI, about 1852.

STICKNEY, KATIE V. (1852?-February 6, 1874) First wife of **Robert Stickney Sr.**, and daughter of old **John Robinson**. Died of childbed fever in Cincinnati, OH, giving birth to her second son. Was 22 years of age.

STICKNEY, LILLIE. Gymnast, W. W. Cole's, 1886.

STICKNEY, LULU. Sells Bros.', 1893.

STICKNEY, ROBERT JOHN DANVILLE. (1872-1941) Rider. Son of **Robert T. Stickney** and **Katie Robinson**. Born in Danville, IL. Carried by his father in equestrian acts from his first infancy and became proficient as a principal and 4-horse rider and as a trainer of horses. Kept at a boarding school for years and along in the latter 1880s graduated with high honors from one of the big eastern colleges. After finishing, joined the Forepaugh show and spent 2 weeks with his father who had expected that young Robert would study law in Cincinnati; but the young man took to the circus business and remained with it. James Donovan & Co., South America, 1888; Irwin Brothers, 1889; ringmaster, parade inspector, and performed his trick horses, ponies and dogs, Scribner & Smith, 1894; Tucker's Giant Shows (Shea & Russell, proprietors), 1895; Bentley's Old Fashioned Circus (**J. B. Bentley**, proprietor), fall 1895; Robinson-Franklin Shows, 1897; John Robinson's, 1891-97, 1898-1900. While with John Robinson, did a hurricane jockey act, which included vaulting and somersaulting, and at various times was equestrian director, assistant manager and general director. Hargreaves, 1902; Orrin Brothers, Mexico, 1904; Great Wallace, 1905-06; Barnum & Bailey, 1907-08; Hagenbeck-Wallace, 1909, 1914; New York Hippodrome, 1910; Coop & Lent, 1916; Sells-Floto, 1920. Eventually, gave up riding and exhibited his trained horses, ponies and dogs at various parks and fairs. After retirement, operated a Phillips 66 service station in Des Moines, IA. Married **Louise DeMott**, 1893.

STICKNEY, ROBERT THEODORE. (December 24, 1846-February 24, 1928) Son of **S. P. Stickney**. Born in New Orleans. First introduction to entertaining was as Alonzo's child in the play *Pizarro* with **Edwin Forrest** as Rolla. Next appeared as a tumbler and rider and ultimately became the best performer as a rider, leaper, and tumbler in combination of his time. By 1868, was considered champion pad rider of the world. Had the body sculptors liked to copy; his leaps were neat and lofty; his riding had style and finish; all of which led to his being billed as "The Apollo Belvidere of the Arena." His positions were picturesque and graceful; and he displayed a fearlessness in executing his equestrian tricks; rode a 4-horse act to perfection. Perfomance of the double somersault from a leaping board, making 2 revolutions over 20 horses and alighted on his feet, accomplished for the first time in South Boston, Halifax County, VA, October 3, 1874, while with John Robinson's. Welch & Lent, 1854; Howes', 1855; Welch's National, Philadelphia, 1857-58, 1860; Dan Rice's, 1858; L. B. Lent's, 1860-61; S. P. Stickney's, NYC, 1861; Chiarini's, 1861; L. B. Lent's, 1863; L. B. Lent's, Wallack's Old Theatre, NYC, fall 1863; L. B. Lent's Equiscurriculum, 1864; Hippotheatron, NYC, winter 1864-65; New York Champs Elysees, 1865; Thayer & Noyes, 1864-66; Parisian Circus, assembled for the Paris Exposition (**Avery Smith, G. Quick, John Nathans, Dr. Gilbert R. Spalding** and **Bidwell**, proprietors), 1867; L. B. Lent's, 1868-70; John Robinson's, 1871-78, 1882; D. W. Stone's, 1878; Adam Forepaugh's,

1879, 1887; Dan Rice's (**Dan Rice, William H. Stowe, J. C. Oates**, proprietors), 1881; New Great Pacific (Sells Brothers, proprietors), 1881; W. O'Dale Stevens', winter 1882-83; S. H. Barrett & Co. (Sells Brothers, proprietors), 1883-86; P. T. Barnum's, 1886; John B. Doris & John L. Sullivan Show, 1888; *Gran Circo Estrellas Del Nortis* (**James Sturgis** and **James Donovan**, proprietors), West Indies, fall 1888; Harper Bros.', 1892 (fall of that year was at the West End Training Academy, NYC, breaking a troupe of Shetland ponies); Donovan & Long (**James Donovan, Frank Long**, proprietors), Central America, winter 1896-97; co-proprietor of Donovan & Stickney's New Combined North American Circus, West Indies, winter 1897-98. Sold interest to partner, **James Donovan**, spring 1898. Along with the Robinson brothers, Stickney took over management John Robinson's, 1871. After 1878, retired from riding due to a knee injury. Married **Katie V. Robinson**, the only daughter of John F. Robinson, 1870, after meeting her only a week before. Their first son, **Robert John Danville Stickney**, was born in Danville, IL; second son died in childbirth on January 29, 1874, which led to the mothers death on February 24, 1874, in Cincinnati. Married **Emma Rezac**, March 2, 1893, in Cuba. Died in Miami, FL, age 81.

STICKNEY, ROSALINE. (1833-1857) Oldest offspring of **S. P. Stickney**. Made her debut, 1836, as a 4 year old pony rider for Oscar Brown & Co. Robinson & Foster, 1842; Howes & Mabie, 1844; Stickney & Buckley (**S. P. Stickney** and **Matthew Buckley**, proprietors), 1844; S. P. Stickney's, 1845-49; Spalding & Rogers' *Floating Palace*, 1852-53; J. M. June's, as "La Belle," 1850. [John A. Dingess: "She had few rivals among female performers in the American arena.... She was a dashing and spirited equestrienne, who leaped like a gazelle over banners and bounded like an antelope through balloons.... She was tall and handsome and her winning naivety and peerless beauty blended with her faultless method of riding, which never failed to make her hosts of friends."] Married **Benoit Tourniaire** (Mons. Benoit), of the famous French family of equestrians, in Havana, Cuba, around 1850. They appeared together as starring attractions with Spalding & Rogers, Welch & Lent, etc. Had 2 children, **Rosaline**, called **Crissie** (see below), and **Samuel**. The latter was probably a non-professional. Mrs. Tourniaire died at the height of her career.

STICKNEY, ROSALINE ["Crissie"]. Equestrienne. The daughter of **Rosaline Stickney** and **Benoit Tourniaire**. John Robinson's, 1873-76, 1879-82; W. W. Cole's, 1878; Orrin Bros.', Havana, winter 1878-79; Burr Robbins', 1879, 1888; Barnum & London, 1884-85; Adam Forepaugh's, 1887-89; Martinho Lowande's, West Indies, 1893; performed in South America up until 1895; Edward Shipp's Petersburg Midwestern Circus, winter 1895-96. After giving up riding, became involved in trained animal acts. Married October 8, 1877, Lebanon, TN, to **Robert Greare**.

STICKNEY, SALLIE LOUISE. (1835?-January 5, 1886) Daughter of **S. P. Stickney.** Sometimes billed as "M'lle Heloise." Born in Philadelphia. After starting riding at a very early age, developed an act of leaping, cutting, pirouetting, and one-foot riding with grace and ease; possessed beauty in face and form; bore herself with charm and dignity, which ranked her at the top of her profession. [C. G. Sturtevant: "In beautiful draperies and manipulating a long silken scarf, she would 'strike' various pictures and hold them in the scenic rides while going around the ring on horseback. She also introduced dancing, pirouettes, and rope skipping, all beautifully and artistically accomplished."] Dan Rice's, 1858. October, 1861, created a sensation by marrying **Omar Samuel Kingsley,** whose act consisted of riding in woman's clothing under the name of **Ella Zoyara.** Shortly, the couple left for California and Australia. The marriage was not a wise choice and they were soon separated. They had a daughter, **Dona,** who became a wire performer. Sallie returned from Australia, July, 1869. Kingsley subsequently procured a divorce and remarried. She performed with various circuses until marriage to rider **William Franklin,** 1872, while on the Forepaugh show and eventually "drifted out of the business." Died in NYC after months of sickness and poverty; was cared for and buried through the auspices of the Actors Fund. S. P. Stickney's, New Orleans, 1849; Welch's, 1850; Welch & Lent, Philadelphia, 1854; S. B. Howes', 1855; Joe Pentland's, 1856; Dan Rice's, Philadelphia, winter 1857-58; Tom King's, 1858; L. B. Lent's, 1858-60; Cooke's Royal Amphitheatre, Niblo's Garden, NYC, 1860; Lent's Broadway Amphitheatre, NYC, winter 1863-64; John Wilson's, San Francisco, 1864; Chiarini's, Havana, 1864; Wilson & Zoyara's, Calcutta, 1867; Thayer & Noyes, 1868; Adam Forepaugh's, 1872. [John A. Dingess: "She had her own unique style of riding, as she abandoned the conventional devices of her contemporaries, giving performance that was refreshing, original, fine, graceful and modest, one which ladies who saw her grately admired."]

STICKNEY, SAMUEL, JR. (1845-April 11, 1921) Eldest son of **S. P. Stickney.** Came into the profession as a hurdle rider, but an injury to an ankle ended the equestrian career. Dan Rice's, 1858. Subsequently, attended school in Philadelphia but returned to the ring as a Shakespearean clown to great success. [John A. Dingess: "As a jester he was witty, original and chaste. His voice was full and strong and his every word could be heard in the most remote recesses of the tent."] Married **Ida Sherwood,** of the noted circus family, while with Mrs. Charles Warner's, Philadelphia, December, 1864, a union which produced a son, **Robert,** and a daughter, **Cora.** Robert became a non-professional; Cora went into vaudeville as part of a juggling act with her husband, **W. R. Johnson,** whom she married in 1892. L. B. Lent's, 1860; Howe's, 199 Bowery, NYC, winter 1863-64; Thayer & Noyes, 1864; Mrs. Charles H. Warner's, Continental Theatre,

Philadelphia, winter 1864-65; New York Champs Elysees, 1865; Dan Rice's, 1866; Dan Castello's Great Show, 1866; French's Oriental, 1867; ringmaster, L.. B. Lent's, NYC, 1867; John Robinson's, 1867, 1871; S. P. Stickney & Son's World Circus, 1869, 1874; Campbell's Zoological and Equestrian Institute, 1870; ringmaster, Curtis & DeHaven's Roman Hippodrome, Circus and Menagerie, 1877. Died at his home in Chicago.

STICKNEY, SAMUEL PECK (1808-March 20, 1877) Father of the Stickney clan. Originally from Boston; tall, gentlemanly and possessed a fair education, as well as having a patriotic bent; never apprenticed, rather came into the profession as a "fill up." Best act was "The Courier of St. Petersburg" on 8 horses. [John A. Dingess: "His manipulation of the reigns and his elegant and spirited manuvers were the height of perfection."] Was considered a competent but not outstanding rider and one of the leading circus proprietors prior to the civil war. Called "Old Sam" or "S. P." by those in the profession. Began his career riding and training horses with Price & Simpson, 1823, and ended with Stickney's Calisthenic Exhibition, 1876. William Blanchard, 1823; Joseph Cowell's, Savannah, GA, winter 1823-24; Price & Simpson, 1824-25; Quick & Mead, 1826; Nathan Howes & Co., 1826. In 1827, before 20 years of age, was in partnership with **Jeremiah Fogg** in what was said to be the second circus to cross the Allegheny Mountains. The troupe performed in Cincinnati and then took a flatboat down the Mississippi River to New Orleans, showing in towns along the route. The men opened circuses in New Orleans, Philadelphia, New York City. At the Washington Circus, Philadelphia, 1828, rode an act, carrying **Charles J. Rogers** on his shoulders and finished by leaping through a large balloon with Rogers still in place. John Lamb's, 1831; Brown's, 1835; Brown & Co., 1836-37; Raymond & Waring, 1840; Robinson & Foster, 1843, and while with him pioneered the 4-horse act. Followed with his own S. P. Stickney's New Orleans Circus, 1844-47; managed the Philadelphia Amphitheatre, 1844; Amphitheatre, New Orleans, 1845; American Theatre, New Orleans, 1846; S. P. Stickney's Circus, 1845-49. June & Co., NYC, 1850; Rufus Welch's, Philadelphia, 1850, and continued with Welch into 1852 (at this time was performing the trained horse, Cincinnatus, as well as the 6-horse "The Courier of St. Petersburg"); Robinson & Eldred, Boston, 1852; equestrian director, Raymond's Zoological Institute, Philadelphia, 1853; Philadelphia Circus, 1853-55, where he performed his drunken soldier equestrian act called "Monticello"; Seth B. Howes', 1855; 4 and 6-horse rider, Joe Pentland's, 1856; Herr Driesbach & Co., 1857; Dan Rice's, 1858. The latter year opened the Phoenix Saloon, 611 Chestnut Street, Philadelphia; sold it a year later and returned to the circus business. L. B. Lent's, 1860-64, ringmaster, 1867; Chiarini's, 1861; brought the National Circus to the Bowery Theatre, NYC, 1861; Hippotheatron,

NYC, winter 1864-65; New York Champs Elysees, 1865; with a split troupe from the Thayer & Noyes organization, under the management of Dr. Thayer, moved by steamboat along the tributaries of the Mississippi, 1865; Thayer & Noyes', 1866-68; L. B. Lent's, 1866; S. P. Stickney's, 1869; equestrian director, Dr. James L. Thayer's, 1870; S. P. Stickney & Son's World Circus, 1874; and was on the road with his own company off and on until his death in New Orleans. [C. G. Sturtevant: "His greatest reputatation was gained ... by his remarkable versatility as ringmaster, horse trainer, instructor in all banches of the equestrian art, and in the general management of circus performances."] Married **Christiana Wolf**, a non-professional, in the early 1830s and fathered 5 remarkable equestrians—**Rosaline, Sallie Louise, Emma Auline, Samuel Jr.**, and **Robert Theodore**. Mrs. Stickney died, 1865. S. P.'s death in Cincinnati, while visiting his friend, **John Robinson**, was caused from slipping on the icy sidewalk as he came out of Wood's Theatre.

STICKNEY, WILLIE. Howe's New Colossal Shows, 1888.

STIENE, EDDIE. Vaulter, Albert M. Wetter's New Model Shows, 1893.

STIFNEY BROTHERS. Acrobats, Holland & McMahon, 1885.

STILES, JACOB. George W. DeHaven's Great Union, 1860.

STILES, JOHNNY. Clog dancer, with Hippocomique, 1868.

STILL, ALFRED. Animal tamer, with Howes' Great London, 1878; asst. Supt. menagerie and tiger performer, Cooper, Bailey & Co., 1879-80; tiger performer, Barnum, Bailey & Hutchinson, 1881.

STILL, MRS. ALFRED. Panther performer, Cooper, Bailey & Co., 1880.

STILLWELL, RENA. Snake charmer, Walter L. Main's, 1892.

STIMSON, C. General performer, Spalding & Rogers, 1856.

STINER, WILLIAM. Gymnast, Melville, Maginley & Cooke, 1875.

STIRK, DENNY [r. n. Moore]. (d. March 26, 1901) Born in England. Came to USA at the age of 12. Remained with the **Stirk troupe** until 1882, when he became a member of the team of **Stirk & Zeno** doing an aerial return act. Flying return on the high wire, Sells Bros.', 1886; Irwin Bros.', 1889; Barnum & Bailey, London, winter 1889-90; Walter L. Main's, 1893-94. The two continued to work together until 1897 when Stirk and his wife formed a team known as **Stirk & Anita** doing a double trapeze act. Died of pneumonia, NYC, age about 34.

STIRK FAMILY [Thomas, Mrs. Thomas, Denny, Flora, Nettie, etc.]. Bicyclists, fathered and headed by **Thomas M. Stirk** (1859-August 30, 1924), born in Birmingham, England. Died in Cincinnati. Troupe was brought to America by **Tony Pastor**, 1881, for a 2-weeks engagement, and were immediately hired by Barnum, Bailey & Hutchinson for a 5 year con-

tract. Followed by 13 years, Sells Bros.'; 8 years, Great Wallace's. Thought to be the first troupe of bicycle riders to appear in the United States. **Mrs. Stirk** died in Boston, September 14, 1908.

STIRK, FLORA. (d. April 2, 1886) Born in Birmingham, England. Performed with the **Stirk family** since 1877, portraying fearlessness and grace in the bicycle act. Died in NYC, age about 11.

STIRTON, W. R. E. Aeronaut. Native of Southhampton, England. While making an ascension on a trapeze bar suspended from the car of a balloon with the United States Circus, 1882, drowned after he slipped and fell into the Ohio River at Maysville, Kentucky, August 5, age about 22.

STITCHBURY. Vaulter, West's, 1818; clown, 1821-22. Sang "Around the Huge Oak."

STITT, JAMES. (1880?-April 1, 1906) Gymnast. Began with a wagon show, 1892; Robert Hunting's, 1893, as part of the **Petite Family** in an aerial bar and flying act; Sells Bros.', 1894; Lemon Bros. & Walter L. Main's, 1895-96; last 7 years with Great Wallace's. Died, Mercer, PA, age 36.

STOCKING, J. W. Proprietor, J. W. Stocking's, 1839.

STOKER, BEN. Slack and tight-rope performer. Yorkshireman and formerly from the Surry and Olympic Theatres. One of the circus talents recruited and brought to America by **Stephen Price**, 1822, along with the bareback riding star, **James Hunter**. American debut at the Park Theatre, NYC. Performed in and around NYC for several years. As part of his act on the wire, with one lightning move he would simulate being hung at the gallows, the sight and surprise of which caused ladies in the audience to faint and men to tremble. Price & Simpson, 1823-27; American Arena, Washington, DC, winter 1828-29; Samuel Parsons' (under the management of **Simon V. Wemple**), Troy, NY, 1828; William Harrington's, 1829; Sweet & Hough, 1835; Palmer's, 1835.

STOKES, BELLE MARRIETA [Mrs. Austin]. (d. October 19, 1910) Equestrienne. One of the Stokes sisters—**Kate** (wife of **John Stetson**) and **Ella** (wife of **John B. Doris**) and **Emma Stokes** (wife of **Frank Philling**, manager of Philling, Crawford, & Chamberlain, Nebraska theatre owners). Born on steamer *Belle* at Marietta, OH, 1870. Father was **Spencer Q. Stokes**. Made her debut as an actress with Gill's *Two Bad Men*; two seasons with Mestayer's *We, Us and Co.*; leading lady for Tony Hart's *Donnybrook* and Nellie in *A Dark Secret*; leading lady with **Patti Rosa** and the *Dr. Bill*. Died, NYC, following surgery.

STOKES, ELLA. Bareback equestrienne, the daughter of **Spencer Q. Stokes**, sister of **Belle, Kate, Emma**. Married **Rudolphe Mette** of the gymnast **Mette Brothers**, January 25, 1877. Both were performing with Stokes' World Circus at the New National Theatre, Philadelphia. Married **John B. Doris**, April 5, 1887, and performed with his circus company, around 1883-88. Also connected with Empire City, 1871; New National Theatre, Philadelphia, winter 1876-77; W. W. Cole's, 1880; Dan Rice's, 1881; Leon & Dockrill, Iron Amphitheatre, Havana, winter 1881-82; P. T. Barnum's, 1886.

STOKES, EMMA *Manège* performer. Daughter of **Spencer Q. Stokes** and sister of **Kate, Ella, Belle.** New National Theatre, Philadelphia, winter 1876-77; W. C. Coup's, 1878-81. Married **Frank J. Pilling**, at one time business manager of the Globe Theatre, Boston. He took her on the road, starring in a "Child of State" Co., but she failed as an actress. The pair subsequently ran a candy store.

STOKES, JAMES. Slack-wire. Arrived from England with West's company, 1816. Killed by Cherokee Indians while traveling on foot to Montgomery, Alabama, 1833.

STOKES, JOSEPHINE. P. T. Barnum's, 1878.

STOKES, KATHERINE. (d. May 4, 1896) Equestrian, "one of the prettiest women that ever jumped a banner." Daughter of **Spencer Q. Stokes** and **Emma, Ella,** and **Belle.** Made debut with L. B. Lent's, NYC at a very young age to became one of the the most intrepid bareback riders in the country. Singled out by **Gil Robinson** as the most beautiful rider ever seen in America. Great Chicago, 1873; principal rider in her father's circus at the National Theatre, Philadelphia, winter 1876-77; P. T. Barnum's, 1878-79; principal rider, W. C. Coup's, 1881, 1887. Married **Carl Antony**, horse trainer, in Pittsburgh, PA, September 10, 1878; divorced, October 6, 1886, after living apart for several years; second husband was **John Stetson** (prominent and wealthy theatre manager, real estate invester and publisher), married June 30, 1887. After this marriage, appeared upon the stage in her husband's companies, notably in *The Gongoliers* and *The Crust of Society*. Sisters, **Ella** and **Emma**, were prominent equestriennes; another sister, **Belle**, went upon the stage. Stetson died at his home in Boston, April 18, 1896, age 61. Kate died from nervous prostration at her home in Boston the following month, age about 37.

STOKES, MOLLIE. Rider, W. W. Cole's, 1886; S. H. Barrett's, 1887.

STOKES, PAULINE. Hunting's Railroad Shows, 1893.

STOKES, SPENCER Q. (July 26, 1819-February 28, 1888) Horse trainer and showman. Born in Cincinnati, OH. At age 10 was inspired by **Purdy Brown** when the manager came to Cincinnati with his company. With Benedict & Eldred, early 1830s; 1836, worked in the mercantile trade for 4 years; manager, Rockwell's, 1848; after which, embarked into management for himself. Married **Emma Sampson**, with whom he produced 4 daughters—Ella (born in England), **Emma** (born in Germany), **Kate** (born in the USA), **Belle**. His wife applied for divorce, January 1858; he had left her in St. Louis and had gone to England. The latter never performed in the circus but went upon the stage. Fall 1846, while with his circus company in New Orleans, because there was a lack of female performers, dressed young boys in feminine garb, a young rider named **Leon** mading an impression. This was

followed with **Omar Kingsley**. Stokes sailed for England with his company, 1851; disbanded in Hamburg, 1859, and returned to America, bringing **Ella Zoyara** out at Niblo's Garden, NYC, with Cooke's Circus, then under the management of **James M. Nixon**. His pupil succeeded in deceiving the audiences, as he worked nightly in a principal act as a female rider. Some time later he appeared as a male under his real name, **Omar Kingsley**. Stokes gained fame during his career as a horse breaker and trainer. His invention for the training of riders, which eliminated the danger of injury to the novice, called the "mechanic," was used for years by circus professional without profit to him. He continued with various circuses, supplying horses and performers, and at times financially interested in management. Died in NYC. Edward Eldred's, 1834; Buckley, Weeks & Co., 1835; J. J. Hall's, 1836; Eagle Circus/Cole & Co., 1837; A. Hunt & Co., 1838; Robinson & Foster, 1842; riding master, Howes & Mabie, 1844; agent, Great Western, traveling by steamboat, 1846 (was manager the following year when the show changed to wagon travel); equestrian director, First National Union Circus (combination of Nixon's Royal Circus and Sloat's New York Circus), 1861; with his horse Pasha, Tom King's, Washington, DC, winter 1861-62; Dan Rice's, 1864; trained horses, Lake's, Cincinnati, 1865; Brien's (**John V. O'Brien's**), 1868; Adam Forepaugh's, 1869; Dan Rice's, 1869; Wootten & Haight, 1871; P. T. Barnum's, 1872; ringmaster, James M. Nixon's, Chicago, 1872; manager, Parisian Circus, Operti's Tropical Garden, Philadelphia, fall 1876; director, circus at New National Theatre, Philadelphia, winter 1876-77; W. C. Coup's, 1881. In retirement was assistant treasurer of the Fifth Avenue Theatre, NYC, 1888.

STOKES, W. S. Band leader, Adam Forepaugh's, 1889.

STOLTZ, W. W. Treasurer, Cooper & Co. (J. R. W. Hennessey, proprietor and manager), 1897.

STONE BROTHERS. George Sieber & Co., 1887; F. J. Tayor's Circus and Menagerie, 1893. One of the act, **Fred Stone**, became a Broadway star.

STONE, DENNISON W. (1824-April 20, 1892) Clown and showman. Born in Burlington, VT, the son of a lawyer and namesake of Judge Denison, a prominent Vermont counselor. At age 14, ran away from to Brattleboro, VT, and joined Ira Cole's Zoological Institute, initial job being carried in a 2-horse act by **Elbert Howes**. Became a clown, 1840, having appeared with **Joseph C. Foster** in the pantomime of *Mother Goose*. Between 1842-1875, in circus management under titles of Stone & McCollum, Stone & Madigan, and Stone & Murray. As Den Stone's Circus and Central Park Menagerie. 1865, established groundwork for wealth by clearing $30,000 from a tour of Vermont. In 1878, toured his Grand Circus and Musical Brigade. It has been said he was the first (or perhaps one of the first) to put a circus on combined boat and railroad. Died at Franklin, NJ. Clown, Nathan A. Howes', 1836; rider,

Eagle Circus/Cole & Co., 1837; H. A. Woodward & Co., 1838; Ludlow & Smith, 1841; Robinson & Foster, 1842; Robinson & Foster, 1843; Stickney & Buckley, 1844; Great Western Circus (Dennison Stone, **Eaton Stone, Thomas McCollum**, proprietors), 1846-47; proprietor, (with **H. P. Madigan**), Stone & Madigan's Great Southwestern Circus, 1850; VanAmburgh & Co., 1856; Hyatt Frost's, 1857; New National Circus (John Tryon, proprietor), winter 1857-58; James M. Nixon's, 1861; S. P. Stickney's, NYC, fall 1861; Mabie's, 1862; Howe's, 199 Bowery, NYC, winter 1863-64; Stone, Rosston & Co., 1864-65; Stone, Rosston & Murray, 1866-68; Stone & Murray, 1869-71; Central Park Menagerie and Den Stone's Circus, 1872; clown and equestrian director, Howe's Great London, 1874-75; proprietor and manager, D. W. Stone's Grand Circus and Musical Brigade, 1878; W. C. Coup's, 1880; equestrian director, Robbins & Colvin, 1881; equestrian director, VanAmburgh & Reich Bros., 1885; and equestrian manager, Burr Robbins', 1886.

STONE, EATON. (January 9, 1818-August 8, 1903) Bareback rider. Born in Bennington, VT, the son of **Davis Stone**, a prominent lawyer, and the brother of the clown, **Den Stone**. At the age of 8, ran away from home and joined Buckley & Weeks. Shortly, entered a 2-year apprenticeship with Ira Cole's under **Ben Brown**, where he was put on Buckskin, an old and gentle horse, and within a week's time made his first public appearance as "The Monkey Rider." March, 1833, commenced an engagement at Richmond Hill Circus, NYC, as principal rider, tumbler, vaulter, and general performer. On the road with Raymond's, 1835-36; Nathan A. Howes', 1836-37; Yale, Sands & Co., 1838; Ludlow & Smith, American Theatre, New Orleans, 1840, during which time he received a gold medal for his artistry; Henry Rockwell & Co., winter 1841; Ludlow & Smith, 1841; Robinson & Foster, 1842-43; Stickney & Buckley, 1844; Great Western (Dennison Stone, Eaton Stone, **Thomas McCollum**, proprietors), 1846-47. At Montgomery, AL, was presented with a diamond brooch containing 21 stones and said to be valued at $1,200. That same year, appeared in Havana, Cuba, for 6 weeks, where he was dubbed "The Devil Rider"; the occasion of his benefit, the Governor General gave him 20 doubloons and 1,000 cigars. Spencer Stokes' boat show, 1846; Olympic Theatre, New Orleans, 1848; Philadelphia, 1850, for a 2-week engagement under Sands and Avery Smith's management, during which time he was presented with a silver service. Early in the fall of that year, Hamlin's Old Bowery Theatre, which was so successful Chanfrau engaged him, hired 100 men, who with teams hauled cartloads of clay from Harlem and built a dirt ring on the stage of the National Theatre, where for 6 nights the place was densely crowded with audiences eager to see the famed equestrian. Sailed for England, May 1, 1851, and opened at the Drury Lane Theatre, London, for a 4-week run; on the occasion of his benefit, 7,000 tickets were sold; *London Times*

pronounced him the best bareback rider ever seen in that city. Welch's National Circus, 1850-51; Welch, McCollum & Risley, England, 1851. Returned home, 1855, on the sailing ship *Ocean Queen*. VanAmburgh's, 1857-60, opening at the Old Bowery Theatre, NYC, December 14, 1857; took a benefit, January 27, when he appeared as a clown for the first time. Bareback and scenic rider, Sands, Nathans & Co., 1859; Stickney's, 1861; First National Union Circus (combination of Nixon's Royal Circus and Sloat's New York Circus), NYC, fall 1861; Thayer & Noyes, 1862; James M. Nixon's, Alhambra, NYC, 1863; Nixon's Cremorne Garden Circus, 1863; Nixon-Macarte, 1863; National Circus, Philadelphia, 1863; Stone, Rosston & Co., 1864; James M. Nixon's Hippotheatron, 14th Street, NYC, 1864; Mrs. Charles H. Warner's, Continental Theatre, Philadelphia, winter 1864-65; S. O. Wheeler's New Amphitheatre, Boston, winter 1864-65; S. O. Wheeler's, 1865; Lipman & Stokes, 1866; Mike Lipman's, 1866. After being in the circus profession for nearly 40 years, announced his retirement, 1867, to settle down on his farm in Essex County, NJ. Erected a private hippodrome, fitted up as a training school. His wife **Lizzie** died in Franklin, NJ, April, 1896. He was gravely injured from an assuault committed upon him November 10, 1898, in the Empire Hotel, Nutley, NJ, by **Joseph Carroll**. Carroll is said to have struck him without provocation, knocking him into an open fireplace; but there appears to have been no lasting damage from the event. Died at his home in Nutley, NJ, some 5 years later. In his prime, was a fearless rider who "would urge his horse to his utmost speed, and, without saddle or bridle, sometimes standing upon the back of the animal and sometimes seated upon his flanks, holding on, one scarcely knew how, careened around the arena with a velocity almost painful to look at."

STONE, GEORGE. (d. December 18, 1864) Clown. Brother of equestrian **William Stone**. Native of Albany, NY, and began professional life at North Pearl Street Amphitheatre there under management of Samuel Parsons, probably as early as 1824. As a comedian, was said to possess rare dramatic talent and versatility. Was friend of **Edwin Forrest**, a man several years his senior. [Edwin Forrest: "His memory was the most remarkable I ever knew."] Scenes, faces, and incidents were indelibly photographed in his mind and seldom forgotten. Visits to all the principal cities and towns of USA and Canada, and tours of England, Ireland, and Scotland, afforded him ample opportunities for recording a journal, the principal portion of which was ultimately published by **Henry Dickinson Stone**, 1873, under title *Theatrical Reminiscences*, as well as in **T. Allston Brown's** lengthy series, New York *Clipper*, December 22, 1860 thru February 9, 1861. James W. Bancker's, 1832; American Circus, 1833; Aaron Turner's, winter, Philadelphia, 1833-34; Frost, Husted & Co., 1836; Eagle Circus/Cole & Co., 1837; A. Hunt & Co., 1838; Yale, Sands & Co., 1838; Miller, Yale & Howes, 1838; Charles LaForest's,

1842; Waring & Raymond's, 1842. After retirement from the profession, embarked in commercial business, Philadelphia, where he died, age 53.

STONE, HOWARD N. Burr Robbins', 1885.

STONE, JAMES Equestrian director, S. H. Barrett's, 1885.

STONE, JENNY. Equestrienne, Grand National, 1865.

STONE, OSCAR R. (December 3, 1815-August 31, 1846) Equestrian. Born on a farm near Pittstown, NY. Started as a tailor's apprentice but left the trade, 1836, and about 5 years later established his own tailor shop in Hoosick Falls, NY. Began circus career learning to ride in a coal pit and elevated himself to managing one of the most successful circuses of his day. As a circus performer, was self-taught, at the outset using neither pad nor saddle but learned on the bare back of a horse at a time when there were only a few bareback riders in this country. December, 1837, he became a co-proprietor with **John Benchley** in the Lafayette Circus; P. H. Nichols', 1841; partner, Rockwell & Stone, 1842-46, proprietors had 2 shows on the road, 1845-46, each managing one. Died in Boston from pneumonia caught from a teardown in a rain storm, May 23, 1846, and died 3 months later, age 31. As a rider, Stone specialized in the act of "The Indian Hunter."

STONE, SOLOMON. Arithmatical phenomenon, sideshow, Cooper, Bailey & Co., 1879-80.

STONE, WILLIAM F. Equestrian. Brother of **George Stone**. J. W. Bancker's, 1832; Aaron Turner's, Philadelphia, winter 1833-34; Buckley, Weeks & Co., 1835; clown, Frost, Husted & Co., 1836. Died in Nevada, California, age 40. [T. Allston Brown: "He was extensively known as an equestrian performer of great ability and as a man of many good and charitable qualities."]

STONEHAM, W. Band leader, Cooper, Bailey & Co. Australian tour, 1877.

STORER, LOUIS ["Petey"]. (d. September 12, 1907) Rider. One time connected with John Robinson's as a featured bareback performer. Died at Lafayette, IN, age about 50.

STOREY, WILLIAM D. Band leader. James M. French's, 1869-70; Rosston, Springer & Henderson, 1871.

STORM, AUGUST. Band leader, Dan Rice's, 1855.

STOUT, ACH. Agent, car #3, Metropolitan Circus, 1897.

STOUT, CHRIS B. Formerly treasurer, Enoch's varieties; sideshow privilege (with **Ham Norman**), Dr. James L. Thayer's, 1877.

STOUT, HUGHIE. Fat man, Walter L. Main's, 1893.

STOUT, JOHN. Concert performer, Dan Rice's, 1860; Dan Castello & Co., 1866.

STOUT, WILLIAM H. (d. April 26, 1889) Rider and clown, J. T. and J. B. Bailey's, 1834; strongman, J. W. Bancker's, 1836; rider, Eagle Circus/Cole & Co., 1837; clown, H. A. Woodward & Co., 1838; 4-horse rider, S. H. Nichols', Albany Amphitheatre, winter 1843; winter circus, Niblo's Garden, 1843-44; equestrian director and 4-horse rider, Dr. Gilbert R.

Spalding's, 1844; rider, June & Turner, 1845; scenic rider, Rockwell & Stone, 1846; Welch's National, 1847; equestrian director and 2 and 4-horse rider, R. Sands & Co., 1849; rider, Johnson & Co., 1852; equestrian director, Welch & Lent, 1855; equestrian director and 6-horse rider, Mabie's, 1857-59; billposter, P. T. Barnum's, 1873.

STOVEY, PROF. Musical director, Haight, Chambers and Ames, 1867.

STOW, ASA BRAY [or Stowe]. (May 5, 1818-February 23, 1898) Showman. Born in Cromwell, CT. With **John Bailey**, **Gen. Wilcox**, and **Walter Hall**, organized Great Northern Circus from stock he acquired from the European Circus, and took the show through Canada, the eastern states, NY and PA. 1872-73, contracting agent with Showles & Co.'s Grand Triple Combination. After leaving the circus business, occupied himself with wood engraving and monumental photographing. Died at his home in Middletown, CT.

STOW, CHARLES E. (d. August 16, 1907) Considered one of the greatest press and bill writers of all time. Father was an Erie County, PA, judge, who expected his son to follow in his footsteps. Before entering show business, was an editor for Dan Rice's newspaper, the *Cosmopolite*. A man of strong views and one who expressed them freely. [Charles H. Day: He wrote with enthusiasm, "his pen shed the flowers of a rich imagination."] Gardner, Hemmings & Cooper (**Dan Gardner, Richard Hemmings, William H. Gardner,** and **James E. Cooper,** proprietors), 1867-68; general agent, Rosston, Springer & Henderson, 1872; director of publications, P. T. Barnum's, 1874-75, 1877; general advertiser, Sells Bros.', 1878-81, tour of Australia, 1891-92.; P. T. Barnum's, 1882-86; Barnum & Bailey, 1888. Died at Whitestone, Long Island. [Louis E. Cooke: "Charley Stow was a man of most remarkable talent, a veritable genius and a writer of wonderful power, whose descriptive paragraphs were songs in both prose and poetry."]

STOW, HENRY. North American Circus and Balloon Show, 1875.

STOWE, A. B. Proprietor, Stowe's, 1868; Great National, 1872.

STOWE, ALBERT M. ["Burt"]. (1858?-March 16, 1911) Showman. The brother of John F. Stowe. Concert manager, Rice-Stowe-Oates, 1881; W. H. Stowe's Circus, winter 1881-82; Burr Robbins', 1885; proprietor and business manager, Stowe Bros.', 1888-89; general superintendent and contortionist, Sig. Sautelle's, 1897. Died in Cincinnati, age 53.

STOWE, ELIAKIM ["Uncle Ike"]. (1821-January 14, 1899) Born in Pennsylvania. Father of leaper **James Stowe**. In partnership with his brothers, **John** and **Albert,** formed Stowe's Western Circus and Indian Show, 1868. Show later became known as the Stowe & Fisher Circus, touring Ohio, Pennsylvania, Indiana and Michigan. Company discontinued, 1873. Died in Fort Wayne, IN.

STOWE, FRANK. Treasurer, Stowe's Western Circus and Indian Show, 1868; band leader, Stowe's Circus, 1870; press agent, E. Stowe's Northwestern Circus, 1871; proprietor, Frank Stowe's Great Western Aggregation, Balloon Show and Bedouin Arab Show, 1874; band leader, W. W. Cole's, 1875; band leader, John Robinson's, 1879; W. H. Stowe's Circus, winter 1881-82; old time clown, Stowe Bros.', 1896.

STOWE, HARRY. Stowe's Western Circus and Indian Show, 1868.

STOWE, JAMES B. Tumbler and gymnast, with E. Stowe's Northwestern Circus, 1871; principal equestrian, Burr Robbins', 1872; *battoute* leaps, Adam Forepaugh's, 1878-79, 1892; P. T. Barnum's, 1880; Orrin Bros.', Mexico, winter 1881-82; Sells Bros.', 1882, 1884; equestrian director, S. H. Barrett's, 1885; Miller, Stowe & Freeman (**Charles A. Miller**, James B. Stowe, **William H. Freeman**, proprietors), 1887; equestrian manager and hurdle rider, Fulford & Co., 1890; Adam Forepaugh's, 1892; Walter L. Main's, 1893; manager, Stowe Bros.' Circus, 1896.

STOWE, JOHN. Equestrian director and talking clown. King & Franklin, 1887; John F. Stowe & Co., 1888; proprietor and manager, Stowe Bros.', 1889; Stowe & Pubilliones (John F. Stowe, **S. Pubilliones**, proprietors), Havana, winter 1891-92; John F. Stowe's Railroad Show, 1892; superintendent, Walter L. Main's, 1897. [D. W. Watt: "Uncle John was the typical early day showman, massive in size, wore a velvet vest and a large watch chain. While Uncle John never went through college, he insisted on making the announcement for the evening show. It went like this—'Ladies and Gentlemen, we thank you kindly for your liberal patronage this afternoon and we show here again this evening with an entire change of program, and I will guarantee that if you give us a good crowd, we will give you a good show.'"]

STOWE, JOHN. (1817?-December 17, 1876) Father of **John F.** and **Albert.** Proprietor, John F. Stowe Circus, 1867-68; Stowe & Norton, 1869; Stowe & Orton, 1870-71; John Stowe & Son, 1872; Stowe, Robbins & Co., 1873; assistant manager, Sadler's Great English Circus, 1875; proprietor, Cooke's English and American Circus, 1876. Died in Vicksburg, MS, age 59.

STOWE, JOHN F. (d. May 16, 1939) Cousin of **Harriet Beecher Stowe,** had his "Uncle Tom's Cabin" show on the road for 37 years. Father was a showman, piloting a showboat on the Mississippi. After father's death, 1871, young John carried on. Equestrian director, King & Franklin, 1887. Summer 1892, equipped his own 10-car circus, touring the country until fall, when financial reverses caused him to disband. Organized smaller show and shipped from Tampa, FL, to Havana, and a 5-month's tour; New York, 1896, met **W. H. Donaldson,** founder of the *Billboard,* who suggested he try an "Uncle Tom's Cabin" company, which made a debut, Vineland, NJ, September 1896, and for 34 years played nearly every Northern city of importance. In 1897, New York City, at Flatbush and Fifth Avenue, built an enormous stage covered with canvas and featured a cast of more than 100 people, which ran for 20 consecutive weeks. Had Stowe Bros.', 1897, a 10-car circus; leased a 9-car trained animal show from **Walter L. Main,** 1898, which failed. [Walter L. Main: "Stowe was a gentleman always, but a better worker for someone else than for himself."] Wife's name was **Katherine;** had a son, **John.** Died at his home, Niles, MI, one of the oldest "Uncle Tom's Cabin" show managers in the country, age 80.

STOWE, MRS. JAMES. *Manège* performer, Fulford & Co., 1890; flying rings and dive for life, Stowe Bros.', 1896.

STOWE, WILLIAM H. (d. March 30, 1882) Son of showman **John Stowe.** Born in Ottokee, OH, around 1852. First worked with his father's company, 1868. The show went out as Stowe & Orton, 1870-71; following year, listed as a partner, John Stowe & Son's Circus; clown, Stowe, Robbins & Co., 1873; Sam Cole's, 1874; Sadler's (with which his father was assistant manager), 1875; Cooke's English and American, 1876; P. T. Barnum's, 1877, 1879-80; Orrin Bros.', 1878; John H. Murray's, West Indies, 1878-79; equestrian manager, Rice-Stowe-Oates, 1881. Opened Stowe's Circus, under his sole management, New Orleans, February 20, 1881. After 3-week engagement, toured the South by rail, wagon and steamer. As a performer, considered a good clown and Ethiopian comedian and excellent leaper. During off seasons, performed in variety theatres. Married equestrienne **Lizzie Marcellus.** Both died in the burning of the *Golden City* steamer. The company had boarded the boat in Vandalia, LA, headed for Cairo, IL, and their season opening. As the boat was about to tie up at Memphis, TN, fire broke out and in less than 30 minutes it went down about 200 yards from shore with a loss of 50 lives, which included Stowe, his wife and his children, **Birdie** and **Willie.**

STRAIGHT, CHARLES. With **Ned Straight,** ran the sideshow with Maginley's Cosmopolitan Circus, 1863.

STRAIGHT, E. V. Proprietor, Straight's, 1891.

STRAIGHT, NED. With **Charley Straight,** ran the sideshow with Maginley's Cosmopolitan Circus, 1863.

STREETER, J. H. Sideshow manager, Beckett's Great Exposition Circus, 1881.

STREVBIG, J. V. Advertising agent, Inter-Ocean Show, 1883.

STRICKER, JOHN C. See John C. Luando.

STRICKLAND, J. S. General performer, L. B. Lent's, 1866.

STROBACH. Equestrian. Boy trained by **John Bill Ricketts,** 1793, to ride on his shoulders in a "Flying Mercury" act.

STROUP, ALBERT. Great Combination Circus (**George M. Kelley, Pete** and **John Conklin, William LaRue,** proprietors), 1871.

STROUSE, NAT. Acrobat, Charles Bartine's, 1872.

STUART, CAPT. J. C. Advertising agent, Ball & Fitzpatrick,

1865.

STUBBS, ELMER E. ["Capt."]. "Champion Rifle, Revolver and General Shot of the World," Senor Cortina's Wild West Show, 1885; feature attraction, Doris & Colvin, 1887.

STUBBS, STOKES. Program agent, L. B. Lent's, 1874; chief billposter, Howes' London, 1875.

STURGIS, C. J. Proprietor, Sturgis & Donovan, 1889-90.

STURGIS, JAMES. *Gran Circo Estrellas Del Nortis* (James Sturgis and **James Donovan**, proprietors), West Indies, fall 1888.

STURTEVANT, JAMES B. Delavan, WI, grocer. Co-proprietor with Edward Holland, Van Amburgh Circus, 1891.

SUILIE, LEON. Bareback and trick rider, Howes & Sanger, 1872.

SULLIVAN, JOE. (d. May 6, 1894) "The Oakland Giant." Formerly with Sells Bros.'

SULLIVAN, JOHN L. Celebrity boxer, featured with John B. Doris & John L. Sullivan Show, 1888.

SULLIVAN, THEODORE J. (1840-1920) Partner, to **Henry A. Eagle**, of Sullivan & Eagle, makers of parade wagons for small to medium size traveling amusements. First organized in 1879, the firm operated from 1880 into the 1910s. Their output included at least 8 steam calliopes to various shows.

SULLY, MATTHEW. Clown. Son of a wealthy Englishman, and said to have been disinherited for giving up his theological training. Instead, married **Sarah Chester** and followed an acting career in England and performing as a singer and tumbler at Sadler's Wells. His sister was married to **Thomas West**, who planned the Charleston Theatre and who brought the Sully family to Charleston, 1792. Wife was a talented musician and at some point gave music lessons to some of the Charleston citizens. Oldest son, **Lawrence**, studied art and subsequently was a miniaturist painter. Younger son, **Thomas**, apprenticed to his sister Julia's husband, a French miniaturist named **Belzons**. Thomas eventually married brother Lawrence's widow and pursued an art career in Philadelphia, where he painted a portrait of the famous actor **George Frederick Cooke**.

SULLY, MATTHEW, JR. Ground and lofty tumbler. Appeared with **John Bill Ricketts'**, 1795, and later with Lailson's ill-fated group in NYC and Philadelphia, 1797-98. Daughters **Charlotte** and **Elizabeth** were actresses who also appeared with Ricketts' company.

SUMMERS, JOHN. DeHaven & Co., 1865.

SUN BROTHERS. Showmen. Born to German parents, **John** and **Caroline Glotz**, John being a tug boat captain in Oswego, NY. Moved to Toledo, OH, around 1860 and began rearing 3 daughters and 4 sons. After John died, 1873, Caroline was left alone to raise the 7 children by operating a small hotel. **John, Jr.** (1858-1941), the oldest of the boys, once billed as **J. H. Jamima**, juggled cannon balls and swords 3½ feet long, or, as a newspaper item suggested, "handled huge dice and other articles as though the laws of gravitation had been suspended for the time being, or threw sharp knives about and caught them again with reckless indifference." [Jack K. Sun: "John began performing at the early age of seven, by 'mountebanking,' which was doing an act in the open air or in saloons and passing the hat as a reward for the performance. At ten he was walking from town to town...."] A serious injury occurred some time prior to the brothers opening their own show but he seems to have been involved in some capacity for the first year or two. After leaving show business, he was reported being occupied in the real estate in New York. Died in Tampa, FL, having never married. **George J.**, the second son (1862-1917), born in Toledo, OH. In early days, a competent juggler, following in the steps of his older brother. Was connected with Barnum & Bailey, Wallace & Co., Batcheller & Doris, and Charles Andress' Magic Show before starting the Sun Bros.' Circus. With the latter, suffered a leaping accident that paralysed both of his legs for the remainder of his life. Following the accident, took out a small variety road show, Sun's Phantasma & Novelty Co., with brother **John** as a feature performer. 1892, with his brothers **John** and **Gus**, established the Sun Bros. Great United Shows, 1895, married an inn keeper's daughter from Hamilton County, OH, **Jessie Kraut**. Often worked his act when his physical condition necessitated him being propped up on the stage. After founding and managing the Sun Bros.' for 21 years, retired from active management, 1912. Ended his own life in his home in Hot Springs, AR, by shooting himself in the head, age 55, after having been paralysed for 30 years. Lived in Hot Springs as a winter home for 10 years, partaking of the baths and investing in local real estate. Was a stockholder in the Arkansas Trust Co., DeSoto Springs Water Co., and Maurice Bath House Co. His children were son **George J. Jr.** and daughters **Aleen** and **Jessie**. Sold his interest in the Sun Bros.' to **Pete** about 3 years prior to his death. **Gustave Ferdinand Sun** (b. 1868), juggler and equilibrist, the third in age of the Sun Bros. Born in Toledo, OH. Early professional experience came from engagements with the Amaranth Minstrels, with the Somerville and Fry Circus in Chicago, in various dime museums and medicine shows. Even took out a medicine show of his own. Around 1896, formed the Gus Sun Rising Minstrels and later organized an "Uncle Tom's Cabin" Co. Married his wife, **Nellie**, 1897. The couple had four children—**Louise**, **Nina**, **Gus Jr.**, and **Bob**. Entered into the theatrical business, 1904, Springfield, OH, and by 1907, with a partner, was operating 10 theatres. This prompted his establishing a vaudeville booking agency, through which many well known performers got their start in the business. Bought a half interest in the Sun Bros.' from his retiring brother, **George**, 1913, to keep outside parties from obtaining an interest in it. Enterprises earned him considerable wealth. **Peter Sun** (1872-1961), the youngest of the brothers, was also born in Toledo. Became a stockholder in the circus when **Gus**

originally disposed of his interest, 1898; and with brother **George**, was chief proprietor of the family show. Proficient as a juggler, slack wire performer, aerial acrobat, clown, and an outstanding paper-tearing act. Married **Vira Maddock**, 1910. Their children were **Pete Jr., Paul, John**, and **Harriet**. Sold the equipment of the Sun Bros.' in the fall of 1918.

SUN, EILEEN. (1902-1989) Equestrienne. Was a daughter of **George J. Sun** of the Sun Bros.' Performed with that company from an early age.

SUN, GEORGE, JR. (1898-1986) Son of **George J. Sun** of the Sun Bros.' Began performing as a clown on his father's show at the age of 3. Later became an equestrian. Married in 1945 but had no children. After leaving show business, worked for the Internal Revenue Service.

SUNLIN, LEW. Sells Bros.', 1886-87; Ringling Bros.', 1892-94. Married **Allie Jackson**.

SUNLIN, WILLIAM. Acrobat, Hudson & Castello, 1881.

SUTHERLAND, JOSIE. A Chicago girl who, 1881, was selected by Adam Forepaugh to replace **Louise Montague** as the $10,000 beauty.

SUTHERLAND SISTERS [3 in number]. King & Franklin, 1888.

SUTTON, DAN. G. G. Grady's, 1868; assistant manager, Warner & Henderson, 1874.

SUTTON, H. N. Knockabout, clown, Sutton & Jackson's Great Combined Shows (with **A. Jackson**, proprietors), 1896.

SUTTON, RICHARD P. Richard's Big Show (Richard P. Sutton, proprietor), 1889-92.

SUTTON, W. H. Director of publications, Cooper & Jackson, 1880.

SUTTON, WILLIAM. Equestrian, Orrin Bros.', Havana, winter 1878-79.

SUYDAM BROTHERS [Frank, Eugene]. Leapers and tumblers, general gymnasts. Dr. James L. Thayer's, 1877; Lowande's Great Brazilian, 1877; Adam Forepaugh's, 1878.

SWADLEY, D. S. Proprietor, D. S. Swadley's Monster Combination, 1872.

SWADLEY, JOSIE. Principal and bareback rider, Valkingburg's, 1881.

SWALLS, CHARLES. Railroad contractor, W. W. Cole's, 1883.

SWAN, ANNA HANNON. (1846-August 5, 1888) Sideshow giantess. Born in New Annan, Nova Scotia. Became "The Nova Scotia Giantess." Another Barnum discovery, exhibited at the American Museum at age 17. At one time weighed nearly 400 pounds. Billed as "the tallest woman in the world," standing around 7' 4". Became a leading attraction. Saved from the museum fire, 1865, by being lifted from an upper story by a derrick. Booked on a European tour by **Judge Ingalls**, 1871, along with another giant, **Captain Van Buren Bates**. The two were married on June 17 of that year. Toured with Cole Bros.', 1878-80, after which time they turned to farming in Ohio.

SWANN, THOMAS. (d. July 26, 1812) Equestrian. Opened a riding school, September 9, 1794, at a building near the Battery, NYC (perhaps the building Ricketts had erected). In October, a troupe of dancing monkeys was added to the performances under the hand of a **Mr. Cressin**. After this engagement, Swann began the practice of veterinary medicine in Philadelphia and erected a building there in which to show horses and give riding lessons.

SWARTWOOD, DOTTIE. See Admiral Dot.

SWEENEY, ANDREW. (d. July 21, 1892) Herculean performer, who threw and caught cannonballs, caught a shot fired from a cannon. Gregory Bros.', 1884; Sells Bros.', 1885; John Robinson's, California (**Frank Frost**, manager), 1886; Howe's New London, 1887. Principal attraction with the Sullivan-Muldoon Co. at the time of his death in Kansas City, MO.

SWEENEY, CHARLES HENRY. (1857?-March 9, 1932) Clown, equestrian director. Weldon & Co., 1884; Wallace & Co., 1887; equestrian director, Cook & Whitby's, 1892; equestrian director, Great Wallace, 1896. Traveled with circuses for 27 years. Retired from show business around 1924. In latter years, was employed as custodian at the Mississinewa Country Club, Peru, IN.

SWEENEY, DICK. Ethiopian entertainer, John Robinson's, 1857-58.

SWEENEY, FRANK. Contortionist, "the human python," Wallace & Co., 1887; Wallace & Anderson, 1890.

SWEENEY, JAMES T. Married **Alice Wallace**, sister of **Benjamin E. Wallace**, circus manager, September 19, 1893, in Peru, IN. Had been working for the Great Wallace since 1884. Superintendent of menagerie, Cook & Whitby's, 1892; in charge of animals at the Lincoln Park Zoo, Chicago, 1893.

SWEENEY, JOE. (d. October 27, 1860) Ethiopian entertainer. Welch, Bartlett & Co., 1839; Broadway Circus, NYC, 1840; June, Titus, Angevine & Co., 1841; Welch & Mann, 1841, 1845. Died at Appomattox, VA.

SWEENEY, SAM: Ethiopian entertainer, Bowery Amphitheatre, NYC, 1841; sideshow entertainer, Sable Minstrels, Orton & Older, 1859.

SWEET, ELIZA SEBASTIAN. Equestrienne. Married **Signor Sebastian**, London, February 8, 1860; divorced December 5, 1873; retained the name of Sebastian in her billing—"Madame Sebastian Sweet"—which prompted a exchange in the press between the two. Jackley's Vienna Circus, 1874, performing a *manège* act with her horse Mountain Toncrede; Sandford & Courtney, South America, 1875; Robinson & Myers, 1883. Daughter **Josephine** was an equestrienne with the show.

SWEET, GERMAIN. Tight-rope, Olympic Theatre, New Orleans, 1848.

SWEET, GEORGE. (b. 1816) Rider and rope-walker. While

298

with Asa T. Smith's circus, threw the first forward somersault from ground to horse seen in this country. Olympic Circus, Philadelphia, 1823; John Rogers', NYC, 1823-24; Price & Simpson, 1823-27; Walnut Street Theatre, 1824, where he was announced as an infant prodigy of 9 years of age; Fogg & Stickney, Washington Amphitheatre, Philadelphia, 1830; Yeaman Circus, 1831; rider and tight-rope performer, American Circus, 1833; proprietor, Sweet & Hough's Pavilion Circus, 1835; Palmer's, 1835; Bancker & Harrington, 1835-36; Brown & Co., 1836; scenic rider, A. Hunt & Co., 1838; H. H. Fuller's, 1838; J. W. Stocking's, 1839; the winter circus at Richmond Hill, NYC, 1837; Frost & Co., 1837; tight-rope, June, Titus, Angevine & Co., Bowery Amphitheatre, 1840-41; Howes & Mabie, 1841; Welch & Delavan, Baltimore, 1841; 2-horse rider, Nathan A. Howes', winter, 1842; tight-rope and transformation act, Welch's National, Philadelphia, 1842; 2-horse rider and still vaulter, N. A. Howes', Bowery, NYC, 1842; John Tryon's, Bowery Amphitheatre, NYC, 1843-44; James Raymond's, 1843-44; Nathan A. Howes', winter 1843-44; Rockwell & Co., 1847; Stickney's New Orleans Circus (Stickney, North & Jones, proprietors), 1849; vaulter, June & Co., 1851; Dan Rice's, 1852; Welch's National, 1852; L. B. Lent's, 1860. Eventually developed a form of insanity and, while performing at the Amphitheatre, Buffalo, threw himself from the third floor of the Eagle Tavern.

SWEET, ISAAC. 2-horse rider, Sweet & Hough's Pavilion Circus, 1835; Palmer's, 1835; western unit, June, Titus, Angevine & Co., 1842; John T. Potter's, 1844; John Tryon's, Bowery Amphitheatre, NYC, 1844-45; Nathan A. Howes' New York Bowery Circus, 1845; Howes & Co., 1846; 4-horse rider, Victory Circus, 1847; gymnast, Dan Rice's, 1855-56. Later, became a streetcar conductor, NYC.

SWEET, J. D. Privileges, Great Southern Circus, 1874.

SWEET, JOSEPHINE. Child bareback rider, Jakeley's Vienna Circus, 1874; Sandford & Courtney, South America, 1875. Daughter of **Mrs. Eliza Sebastian Sweet**, *manège* performer.

SWEET, LEWIS. Press agent, Dan Rice's, 1891.

SWEET, O. P. Holton & Gates' Harmoniums, a minstrel band organized for the the Simon Pure American Circus in New York, October 1, 1866. Was one of the better bassos and interlocutors in the minstrel business. [M. B. Leavitt: "His conviviality made him at times a little unreliable..."] Eventually settled in Springfield, MA, and became one of its leading surgeons.

SWINGLEHURST, T. Boss canvasman, P. T. Barnum's, 1875.

SYLVESTER, A. D. Came to America with Franconi's Hippodrome, 1853. Died, Philadelphia, September 5, 1881, after being in retirement for some tme. May be **Arthur Sylvester** below.

SYLVESTER, ANNIE. Trick bicyclist, Frank A. Gardner's, South America, 1896.

SYLVESTER, ARTHUR. General performer, Flagg & Aymar, 1856.

SYLVESTER, BEN. Orrin Bros.', Havana, March 1879.

SYLVESTER, EDDIE. Knockabout clown, Burr Robbins', 1880; Robbins & Colvin, 1881; W. W. Cole, 1884; King, Burk & Co., 1884.

SYLVESTER, EVERETT. Contortionist, "the Boa Constrictor Man," Sells & Rentfrow's, 1893.

SYLVESTER, FRED J. (1838?-June 13, 1887) Rider. Late of Franconi's Hippodrome, Paris and New York, Washburn's, 1855; Chiarini's, South and Central America, 1869-70; James M. Nixon's, 1870; Great Eastern (**Dan Carpenter** and **R. E. J. Miles** & Co., proprietors), 1872-74; James Robinson's, 1874; Chiarini's, San Francisco, 1879; the same in the Orient, 1887. Died in Shanghai, age 49.

SYLVESTER, HARRY. Juggler, Robinson's Combined Shows and Trained Animal Exhibition, 1892.

SYLVESTER, HARRY. Orchestra leader, Gollmar Bros.', 1894.

SYLVESTER, JAMES. Trapeze performer, died on March 19, 1874, NYC.

SYLVESTER, JENNIE [Mrs. William Aymar]. James M. Nixon's, Alhambra, NYC, fall 1863; dancing horses, Allen's Great Eastern, 1880.

SYLVESTER, JOHN R. Program advertising, Scribner & Smith, 1894.

SYLVESTER, MME. Circassian lady, Haight's Great Eastern, 1874.

SYLVESTERS. Lady gymnasts, P. T. Barnum's, 1886.

SYLVIA, HOMER. Boss canvasman, Great London, 1880.

T

TAFFT, GEORGE S. Trained oxen performer, Cooper, Bailey & Co., 1880.

TALBERT, FLORA. Globe performer, John Wilson's, California, 1875.

TALBERT, GEORGE. Principal rider, Lee's, California, 1871.

TALLEEN BROTHERS [Paul, Jerome]. Gymnasts. James M. Nixon's, 14th Street, NYC, 1864; S. O. Wheeler's New Amphitheatre, winter 1864-65; Hippotheatron, NYC, winter 1864-65; New York Champs Elysees, 1865; Stone & Murray, 1869; Australian Circus, 1870.

TALMEZZO, SIGNOR. General performer, with VanAmburgh's, 1874.

TAMPIER, ELLADA. Advertised as being from *Champs Elysees*, Paris, driving 6 ponies attached to an Imperial Caleche in the procession entering town. Presented trained black ponies, Coquette and Flirt, New York Champs Elysees, 1865.

TAMPIER, GRACE. Rider, P. T. Barnum's, 1874.

TANNER, JERRY. Miles Orton's, 1885.

TATALIA. Contortion rings, Barnum & London, 1885.

TATNALL, MRS. SAM. Circus in Portland, ME, 1821; West's, 1822; Price & Simpson, 1823-24. Performed in some dramatic productions.

TATNALL, SAMUEL. Equestrian, a native American. Cayetano & Co., 1810-12; Pepin & Breschard, 1817, where he was a pupil of **Victor Pepin**. Became celebrated for his feats on 2 horses—lightning quick in motions, on a single horse he would leap garters and pass through balloons. Did still vaulting and was an excellent horse breaker. Remained with the company for several years before joining James West's; went with Price & Simpson after they bought out West, 1822-24. The previous year, **James Hunter** was brought to America from Astley's Royal Amphitheatre, London, by manager **Stephen Price** and amazed audiences with his riding at full speed using no bridle or saddle, bareback riding being new to this country. Tatnall's position as a celebrated rider had been overshadowed, so in an attempt to regain that position, he and his pupil, **LaForrest**, practiced riding bareback after midnight, when the arena was deserted, and found the activity to be easier than it appeared. When news leaked out of his midnight sessions, Tatnall made an offer to the management to perform an act in the manner of Hunter. Hunter denounced the effort as treachery. The management, not wishing to lose the profitable image of Hunter as the exclusive bareback star, ordered Tatnall to desist his practicing; however, for Tatnall's benefit night, November 16, 1822, he advertised his first appearance on horseback without saddle or bridle. Within a month from the arrival of Hunter, he had accomplished the new feat of bareback riding, although he had not yet reached the balance and the ease with which his rival performed. [Charles Durang: "Sam Tatnall, a pupil of Pepin's, was celebrated for his feats on two horses. He was quick a lightning in his motions. On a single horse his movements were very extraordinary in leaping garters, passing through balloons and many other daring and dashing performances."] Tatnall also performed acting roles and managed the stud of horses for equestrian dramas. His wife was an attractive actress but because of his fiery temper his brutal treatment of her caused the marriage to end in divorce, summer 1826. She continued her career on the dramatic stage and was ultimately married 5 times. It was reported she died in a steamboat fire on the Red River. The divorce may have been responsible for Tatnall's loss of position; he becamed a depressed and broken figure around Philadelphia and finally, it is said, died in the West Indies. Washington Gardens, Boston, spring 1825; Lafayette Amphitheatre, NYC (in its initial season), 1825-26; Tivoli Gardens, Philadelphia, 1826; Lafayette Circus, NYC, January 1827; Mount Pitt Circus, NYC, 1826-27, 1827-28; the Royal Pavilion Circus/Olympic Circus, 1830.

TATUM, B. F. ["Capt."]. Press agent and general manager, W. H. Stowe's, 1881.

TAYLOR, A. L. Treasurer, F. J. Taylor's Great American Shows, 1892.

TAYLOR, ANNIE. Mind reader, Hulbert & Liftwich, 1892.

TAYLOR, CHARLES. See Charles Graham.

TAYLOR, C. T. Magician, Hurlbert & Liftwich, 1892.

TAYLOR, DAN ["Col."]. Boss canvasman, John O'Brien's, 1873; Adam Forepaugh's, 1875-76, 1887.

TAYLOR, FRANK J. (d. July 28, 1917) Formerly a grain merchant, speculator, live stock auctioneer, farmer, and bank director, also mayor of Creston, IA, for a time. Son, **Ray**, was also in that business. Managed the F. J. Taylor's Great American Circus for many years. Moved to Creston, IA, 1879, which became his winter quarters for the F. J. Taylor Wagon Show. Operated as late as 1900. Bought nearly all of W. S. Harris' Nickel-Plate show, 1886. Proprietor, Taylor's, 1889-93. Died at Creston of a stroke.

TAYLOR, J. H. One of Bunnell's Minstrels, R. Sands', 1863.

TAYLOR, JOHN. Tumbler. Howes' European, winter 1864; Whitmore, Thompson & Co., 1865; W. R. Blaisdell's, California, 1868.

TAYLOR, JOHN W. Mrs. Charles Warner's Champion Circus, cornor of 10th and Callowhill, Philadelphia, 1869.

TAYLOR, L. F. Advertiser, Howes & Mabie. Died while he was a layer-out for VanAmburgh's, Dubuque, IA, 1867.

TAYLOR, LIZZIE. L. J. Duchack's New London Railroad Shows, 1889.

TAYLOR, MAGGIE. Race rider, P. T. Barnum's Roman Hippodrome, 1875; Orrin Bros.', Mexico, 1886.

TAYLOR, NELLIE. Equestrienne. Named in a domestic quarrel between **Frank J. Howes** and his wife, Philadelphia, November 1866.

TAYLOR, ROBERT. (d. February 20, 1913) Trainmaster, Miles Orton's, 1885; Ringling Bros.' for 18 years. Died from heart failure at Baraboo, WI.

TAYLOR, T. F. Agent, G. F. Bailey, 1858-59.

TAYLOR, W. A. Contracting agent, W. B. Reynolds' Consolidated Shows, 1892.

TAYLOR, WILLIAM. Lee & Ryland, California, February 1869.

TAYLOR, WILLIE. Boneless wonder, William Main & Co., 1887.

TEAL, WILLIAM L. (1833?-September 5, 1895) Gymnast and acrobat. Born in Huson, NY. Ran away from home and went to sea, making several whaling voyages. As a professional athlete, traveled with Spalding & Rogers in the 1860s under the name of "Antonio"; also with Dan Rice's. It was claimed that he introduced the Japanese high perch to South America and originated several movements on the flying trapeze and the hop and perch feat. In his time, was second to none as a tumbler but left circus life and opened a gymnasium in Lynn, MA. An accomplished linguist and a skillful chess player. Died in Nahant, MA, age 62.

TEESE, CHARLES B. Gymnast, Mrs. Charles Warner's, Philadelphia, 1870; one of the **Arabian Brothers**, 1872. Wife **Bertha** died in fall of 1876, age 27.

TEETS, ROBERT C. [with wife Emma]. (d. November 28, 1895) Acrobat and showman. One of 4 brothers who owned Teets Bros. Shows, 1891. Died near Norfolk, VA.

TEETS. Comic rider, Frost & Co., 1837; acrobat, W. Gates & Co., 1838.

TERRIES, JAMES [or Terry]. Acrobat, G. G. Grady's, 1871.

TERRIES, WILLIAM [or Terry]. Acrobat, G. G. Grady's, 1871.

TERRIES, PROF. Free balloon ascension, doing a double trapeze under the balloon while ascending, G. G. Grady's, 1871. This may have been either **William** or **James** listed above.

TERRY, RICHARD. (1835?-December 29, 1893) Sideshowman. With many major circuses throughout a career that lasted over 40 years. With Adam Forepaugh's for 2 years before his death in Philadelphia from Bright's disease, age 58.

THATCHER, WILLIAM LAKE. See William Lake.

THAYER, HARRY. Proprietor, Harry Thayer & Co.'s, 1890.

THAYER, JAMES L. ["Dr."]. (May 20, 1830-June 30, 1892) Born in Waddington, NY. Moved to Milwaukee with his parents when he was 7. Father was appointed a State Commis-

sioner by President Van Buren to locate the state capital. But when his mother died, 1840, and then his father, 1842, he was thrown upon his own resources at a young age. 1846, was with Potter's circus as chandelier man, filling the lamps with whale or lard oil. Following winter, learned the trade of tinsmith. Next employment, driving stage for Frink & Walker at a salary of $12 a month. Shortly, joined Mabie Bros.' as bandwagon driver. 1849-50, drove stage for Zimmerman & Green between Vincennes and Terre Haute, IN. Following year, started a tinshop of his own at Clinton, IL, but, in the spring of 1852, joined Johnson & May's Circus, again as bandwagon driver. Following year, drove bandwagon for Welch's, but left the show at Columbus, OH, to accept a job with the Pittsburgh and Allegheny Transfer Co. Next, became master of horse for Levi J. North's. Spring 1855, with Dan Rice's as boss hostler and 20-horse driver and also appeared in the ring, exhibiting a test of strength, pulling against a pair of horses. Still with Rice, 1857, made his debut as clown and by the winter of 1857-58 was leading clown with Spalding & Rogers on board the *Floating Palace* and at the Academy of Music, New Orleans. Engaged to personify Dan Rice as clown on Rice's own show, 1858, and was so successful that few were aware of the deception. Leading clown, VanAmburgh & Co., 1859-60. Started a small clown and gymnastic show with **Frank Phelps** of Elmira, NY, 1861; Nixon's Cremorne Garden Circus, Washington, DC, October-December 1862. Originated the circus of Thayer & Noyes, 1862, and continued in that partnership until the spring of 1869; the latter year being a disaster, the loss of some 70 head of horses by disease. Sold off in Cincinnati, OH. Subsequently, engaged in a variety of speculations—formed a partnership with **W. H. Burdeau** and **W. F. Hogle**, 1870; chief doorkeeper, P. T. Barnum's, 1873, representing Barnum's interest with the show; assistant manager, Burr Robbins', 1875; inspector of admissions, Philadelphia Centennial Exhibition, 1876; Parisian Circus at Operti's Tropical Garden, Philadelphia, fall 1876. Started his own railroad show, 1877, but shortly sold out to the Lowandes. Had an interest in Thayer, Diefenbach & Lewis' Great Show and London Sensation, 1878. Organized Dr. James L. Thayer's New Circus, 1879-80. Assistant manager, Sam McFlinn's, 1888. On April 3, 1860, married **Helen Martin**, eldest daughter of **Agrippa Martin**, a union which produced 9 children. One daughter married **Sam McFlinn**. Died in Chicago.

THAYER, S. C. J. Treasurer, John Robinson's, 1861-62; Lake & Co., 1864; advertiser, Caldwell's Occidental, 1867.

THAYER, T. F. Business agent, George F. Bailey & Co., 1859; treasurer, Palmer's Great Western, 1865.

THEALA, MILLER. "Human fly," Cooper, Jackson & Co., 1884.

THEURER, JOHN. Claimed to be the only performer who could stand on his head on a swinging bar while balancing balls, glasses of water, etc., 1883. "$1,000 in gold to anyone that will do my act."

THOMAS. Rider, Pepin & West, Olympic, Philadelphia, fall 1817; Pepin's, NYC, 1818-19; West Indies, 1819-20.

THOMAS, DAVID S. Press agent, P. T. Barnum's, 1872-73; P. T. Barnum's Roman Hippodrome, NYC and on the road, 1874-75; remained with the Barnum organization to 1887. J. M. Hickey's "A Flock of Geese" Combination, winter 1880-81. The day after Barnum's balloonist W. H. Donaldson's tragic mishap in Chicago, July 15, 1875, Thomas made an ascension himself. Later stated, 1880, that as an amateur he had made 34 trips in a balloon. Louis E. Cooke credits Thomas as being the first press agent to travel back with the show and devote full time to entertaining newspaper men, which was in 1871-72 when Dan Rice, touring with his Paris Pavilion Circus, engaged Thomas for that purpose and the practice soon caught on. On retiring he bought an interest in a printing establishment in New Haven, CT.

THOMAS, F. General performer, Spalding & Rogers, 1856.

THOMAS, FRANK. (July 3, 1819-February 6, 1898) Elephant handler. Born at Doylestown, PA. Orphaned at an early age and bound out to a silversmith. Ran away and joined the Hopkins Shows, 1833. Following year, with VanAmburgh's and continued with that organization until 1863. Drove Hannibal for 12 years and also handled Bolivar, Queen Anne, Columbus and others. Died in Nebraska City, NE.

TOMPKINS, E. A. Agent, Robinson & Howes, 1864.

THOMPSON. Juggler, Handy & Welch, West Indies, 1829. Work with the magician's rings was considered marvelous.

THOMPSON, A. Treasurer, Robbins & Co., 1872.

THOMPSON, ALBERT "BALDY." Elephant keeper and trainer from Putnam County, NY. Head elephant keeper with Adam Forepaugh, 1885.

THOMPSON, C. Lion tamer and ringmaster, Campbell's, 1869.

THOMPSON, C. N. (December 15, 1856-January 4, 1918) Born at Marseilles, IL., where he attended the public school. Became identified with outdoor shows early in life and remained continuously until the time of death, only two months after finishing the season with Ringling Bros.' With circuses as claim agent, adjuster, or on the business staff. S. B. Barrett's, Doris & Robin, W. W. Cole's, Adam Forepaugh's, Sells Bros.', Forepaugh-Sells Bros., Wallace & Co., Pawnee Bill's, Buffalo Bill's, and Ringling Bros.' Longest period of service, Sells Bros.' as assistant manager and later as general manager, having had charge of the concern on its trip to Australia. [D. W. Watt: "Mr. Thompson was unquestionably one of the most popular showmen the outdoor world ever knew. Though his earnings were great, he was of that type which finds utmost satisfaction in succoring to the needs of others, and it was a byword of the arena that 'Charlie Thompson never turned anybody away.'"] Married at Morris, IL, 1884. Died suddenly of heart trouble, age 61.

THOMPSON, CORPORAL. Co-proprietor, John Tryon, Alhambra Circus, NYC, October, 1848, a specially erected semipermanent stucture. Franconi's Hippodrome, 1853, was constructed on the site formerly occupied by Thompson's resort of refreshment and conviviality, noted as a popular stopping place for turfmen.

THOMPSON, C. S. Proprietor, Thompson's, 1889.

THOMPSON, DICK. Holton & Gates' Harmoniums, minstrel band organized for the the Simon Pure American Circus in New York, October 1, 1866.

THOMPSON, EPH. Black trainer and boxing partner of John L. Sullivan, the boxing elephant. Performed on Adam Forepaugh's, 1888. The elephant wore a boxing glove on the end of his trunk and would watch his chance to land one on Thompson and often knocked him over the ring bank. Went to London and trained elephants for performing in the different theatres of Europe.

THOMPSON, FRANK. Sideshow operator. Native of Culpepper Court House, VA. O. S. Wheeler's, 1863. Later, engaged in securing animals for circus menageries, operating out of the Cape of Good Hope.

THOMPSON, G. A. Proprietor, Whitmore, Thompson & Co.'s Equescurriculum, 1865. Started the season in May from Boston through Vermont, Canada and the western states.

THOMPSON, GEORGE Shakespearean clown, Robinson's (**Frank Frost**, manager), California, 1886.

THOMPSON, G. W. ["Capt."]. Managing director (with **Ed Backenstoe**), Cosmopolitan Circus, Museum and Menagerie, winter 1871-72.

THOMPSON, JOSEPH. Advertiser, Palmer's Pavilion Circus, 1836.

THOMPSON, MRS. Slack-wire performer, Price & Simpson, 1824-25.

THOMPSON, WILLIAM. (1854?-February 19, 1920) Animal trainer. Campbell's, 1869; Montgomery Queen's, 1876; Adam Forepaugh's, 1880; ringmaster, John Robinson's, 1881; Frank A. Robbins', 1888. Also handled elephants in vaudeville. A skilled glass blower, at one time placed a glass blowing exhibit aboard a railroad car. Died in Chicago, age 66.

THORBER BROTHERS [George, Harry, Walter]. Acrobats, VanAmburgh & Co., 1881.

THORNE. Gymnastic clown, Spalding & Rogers, 1854.

THORNE, JOHN. Juggler, With Moore Bros.', 1887; Charles Lee's London Circus, 1888; C. W. Kidder & Co.'s, 1893.

THORNE, NICHOLAS. (1822-1899) Crossed the equator 4 times on a whaling vessel before he was 20. Came to Delavan, WI, just before the **Mabie Brothers** arrived. Sold the Mabies about 400 acres of land on Delavan Lake which was used as circus quarters. Traveled with them for 5 years as boss hostler. Specialized in procuring non-ring circus horses. Later, set up a horse stable at Marshalltown, IA, dealing almost exclusively with circuses. Returned to Delavan, 1875, and served as village constable for 6 years and town marshal for 2 terms. Son, **William**, became internationally known as a portrait painter.

THORPE, A. C. Agent, Major Brown's, 1856; Horner & Bell, 1855; Hippoferean, 1855.

THORPE, CHARLES R. General agent, Thayer & Noyes, 1886.

THORPE, HENRY H. (d. 1907) Sells Bros.'

THORPE, IRA B. (d. October, 1878) Contracting agent, Sells Bros.', 1878. Died at Topeka, KS; buried Columbus, OH.

THORPE, J. Sideshow manager, Harry Thayer & Co.'s, 1890.

THREE ALBINOS. Gymnasts, John Robinson's, 1882, 1887.

THREE DECOMAS. Arialists, John Robinson's, 1886-87.

THRIFT, SAM. Clown and slack-rope performer. Aaron Turner's, 1835; Ludinton, Smith & Bailey, 1836; Joseph E. M. Hobby's, 1839; clown, Philadelphia Circus, 1840; Sam H. Nichols', 1840; Bartlett & Delavan, 1841; Welch & Mann, 1841; Rockwell & Stone, 1843; John T. Potter's, 1846; John Tryon's, Bowery Amphitheatre, NYC, 1846; Dan Rice's, 1849.

THUMB, GEN. TOM [Charles S. Stratton]. (January 4, 1837-February 19, 1920) Midget. Born in Bridgeport, CT. Son of **Mr. and Mrs. Sherwood E. Stratton**. In November, 1842, P. T. Barnum stopped at Bridgeport on his way to Albany to visit his brother, **Philo**, who kept the Franklin House. While there, Philo presented young Stratton to him. The boy was described as being 5 years old, not 2' high, weighing less than 16 pounds, perfectly formed, bright eyed, with light hair and ruddy cheeks. With parental consent, Barnum engaged the youth for 4 weeks at a salary of $3.00 per week, plus traveling and boarding expenses for himself and his mother. Was first exhibited in NYC, Barnum's Museum, December 8, 1842, where he was announced on the bill as General Tom Thumb. At the end of that period, was re-engaged for a year at $7.00 a week and a gift of $50.00 at the end of that year. Popularity was so enormous that before the contract had expired his salary was increased to $50.00 a week. After being exhibited at the museum for a number of weeks he was sent on the road. Another year's contract was submitted with plans for a European tour. Sailed for England, January 18, 1844. Briefly unveiled in Liverpool and London. March 20- July 20, on exhibition at Egyptian Hall, with daily receipts averaging around $500.00. Tour of England followed. Appeared in a play written for him by **Albert Smith**, *Hop O' My Thumb*, at the Lyceum Theatre first, and then at some of the provincial playhouses. Visited Paris, where he received recognition from King Louis Phillipe; and Brussels, where he was honored by King Leopold. Contract was rewritten, January 1, 1845, making Barnum and Stratton equal partners. After 3 years of absence, the parties returned to America, February, 1847, remaining for a time at Barnum's Museum. There was a tour of the United States and in January, 1848, a visit to Havana,

Cuba. 1862, Barnum engaged another midget, **Miss Lavinia Warren** of Middleboro, MA, for exhibiting alongside **General Thumb** at his museum. The two were married the following year, February 10, 1863, at Grace Church, NYC. June, 1869, the General Tom Thumb Co. left for a trip around the world under the management of **Sylvester Bleeker**. In late years, the General grew in size and corpulence but, although there were other midgets that were smaller, Tom Thumb always drew an audience. Through the years, developed extravagant habits; consequently, in the last years of his life his resources were extensively depleted. A few years before his death, built a mansion in Middleboro. He died there of apoplexy.

THUMB, MRS. TOM [Lavinia Warren Bump, later Countess Magri]. (1844-1919) Sideshow midget. Born in Middleboro, MA. Daughter of **James S.** and **Hulda Bump** of Revolutionary stock. Made first appearance, age 17, under the management of a cousin who operated a floating palace of curiosities on the Ohio and Mississippi Rivers. Met and was contracted by **P. T. Barnum**, 1862. Married **Tom Thumb** a year later, and traveled throughout the world with him until his death, 1883. 2 years later, married **Count Primo Magri**, also a Lilliputian and a member of her company. Heaviest weight was 29 pounds and height 32". 1911, appeared in vaudeville in a sketch entitled *The Enchanted Statue*, assisted by her husband, **Count Magri** and his brother **Baron Magri**. After a public life of some 56 years, made a farewell tour, 1912. Died at her home, Middleboro, age 77, leaving her memoirs.

THURBER, P. H. Miller, Stowe & Freeman (**Charles A. Miller, James B. Stowe, William H. Freeman**, proprietors), 1887.

TIBBS, HARRY [or Henrico]. Juggling on horseback and scenic rider. Englishman by birth, but worked for a time in Cuba. Haight & Chambers, winter 1866-67; with trick horse, Stonewall, Haight, Chambers and Ames, 1867; C. T. Ames', 1868-70.

TIDMARSH, T. U. [Capt.]. (d. September 25, 1866) Former Lieutenant in the Confederate army. Robinson & Eldred, 1850-53; Henri Franconi's, 1854-55; Rosston's, 1856; Lent's, 1858; James M. Nixon's, 1860; Robinson & Lake, 1861; manager, Stone, Rosston & Murray, 1866. All in all, was in the circus business over 25 years. Died in Memphis at the Commercial Hotel. At the time of death, was business manager of the Greenlaw Opera House in that city.

TIDORA, LAVAN. Horizontal bar performer, Fulford & Co., 1890.

TILDEN, LUKE. (1828-1877) Started as a roustabout with Mabie Bros.', 1847, starting as a workman and rising to position of manager. Continued with that firm until the show was sold to **Adam Forepaugh** and **John O'Brien**, 1864. Manager, Melville's Australian Circus, 1865; manager, Phillips & Babcock, 1866-67; Coup & Castello, 1869-70; treasurer, then assistant manager, P. T. Barnum's, 1871-75; business manager, Coup and Reiche's Aquarium, 1876. Died suddenly the following year of heart trouble.

TILLOTSON, G. E. Manager, E. G. Smith's, 1867.

TINKHAM, EDWIN A. [or Edward]. Agent. Son of an elder of the church in Lima, NY. P. T. Barnum's Roman Hippodrome, 1874-75, W. C. Coup's, 1878-82; contracting agent, Nathans & Co., 1882; Barnum & Bailey, 1884; Fainted from the bursting of a blood vessel while listening to a minstrel performance at the Grand Opera House, Rochester, January 8, 1886, and died 2 hours afterward at his boarding house. [Charles H. Day: "A wicked, paragraphing journalist declares that poor Ed's demise was occasioned by the end man telling a new joke.... Ed could talk faster than Maud S. ever trotted or the *Journal* ever sold and wrote left-fisted to keep time with his tongue tangle."]

TINKHAM, GEORGE. Bill poster, with Howes & Cushing, 1894.

TINKHAM, JOSEPH. (1831?-April 3, 1900) General performer. Born in Augusta, ME. Moved to Dubuque, IA, at about 12 years old. Began to practice tumbling with other children in an old barn. Orton's, 1855-57; Ganung's, 1858; Orton & Older, 1859; George W. DeHaven's, 1862; Castello & VanVleck's, 1863; Old Cary's, traveling by rail and boat down the Mississippi, 1864; George W. DeHaven & Co., 1865; Johnson & Co. (James T. Johnson's Great Western and VanVleck's Mammoth Show combined), 1866; Maginley, Carroll & Co., 1867; George W. DeHaven's, 1869; P. A. Older's, 1871; rider, John Stowe & Sons, 1871; pad and hurdle rider, Cooper & C0., 1874; Indian hurdle rider, Hamilton & Sargeant, 1878; equestrian manager, Hunter's, 1884; De-Bonnaire's Great Persian Exposition, 1884-85; equestrian director, D. A. Kennedy's, 1896. Claimed that while with a small wagon show, 1849, he was the first man to turn a double somersault from a springboard over animals. When age ended his acrobatic career, retired to doing light farm work. Died at Ricardsville, IA, age 65. Had been in the profession for over 50 years.

TINKHAM, MME. Ascensionist, Maginley, Carroll & Co., 1867. Severely injured from an 18' fall while undertaking an outside climb in Franklin, KY, October 16.

TINNEY, HANK. Boss canvasman, John Robinson's, 1857-58.

TITUS, ALFRED. Band leader, Dan Rice's, 1878.

TITUS, LEWIS B. (December 11, 1800?-December 29, 1870) A life-long bachelor. Owned and leased the elephant Little Bet with Gerard Crane, 1826; Angevine, Titus & Burgess, 1827; American National Caravan, 1831; co-proprietor, June, Titus & Co., 1833-34; VanAmburgh & Co. (Lewis B. Titus, **John June, Caleb S. Angevine** and **Gerard Crane**, proprietors), 1846-47; proprietor, VanAmburgh Menagerie, United Kingdom, 1838-45; returned to United States, fall

1845; partner, VanAmburgh & Co., 1846-49. Said the first to introduce to England the practice of traveling with a tent. Retired, 1849. Died in North Salem, NY.

TOLE, A. R. Caterer, Burr Robbins' for several years, beginning around 1878. Ran the workingmen's cook tent. Drove over the road with a single horse and buggy. All the heaviest equipment of his large tent was packed in a 4-horse wagon. All his edibles were drawn by 2 horses, so the outfit consisted of 7 horses.

TOLMAN, J. Rider, E. F. & J. Mabie's, 1849-50.

TOMLINSON, ELIZA. (d. January 24, 1899) Second wife of **Sam Rinehart.** Had 2 sons, **Charley** and **Willie**, and 2 daughters, **Beatrice** and **Goldie.** Began performing as a lion tamer and chariot driver. After husband's death, managed a museum in Des Moines, Iowa, for about 6 years, as well as the Rinehart Opera Co., headed by her daughters. Died in NYC, age 61. See Sam Rinehart.

TOMPKINS. Equestrian, with Lailson's, Philadelphia, 1798. When Lailson sold his circus stock and returned to France, Tompkins remained behind.

TONER, ANTHONY ["Buck"]. (March 29, 1864-August 13, 1893) Acrobat. Born in Union City, PA. Black Bros.', John Robinson's, James M. French's', Miles Orton's, and George M. Hall's, visiting Cuba with the latter. Joined Rentz's, 1890, with **Bernard Dooley** as a partner in an act. Fell from a swinging perch, August 11, 1893, while with that show and died in Erie, PA, 2 days later.

TOOKER, T. W. Business agent, Palmer's Great Western, 1865.

TOOLE, THOMAS R. ["Col."]. Agent. Levi J. North's, 1856-58; Alex Robinson's, 1862; Howe's Great London, 1874-75; Adam Forepaugh's, 1878; manager advertising car #1, Cooper, Bailey & Co., 1879; Sells Bros.', 1880s. [Peter Sells: "Col. Toole was also a great agent. He was one of the finest looking men that ever followed circus business—a high-minded, honorable man."]

TORBETT, JAMES K. (d. June 24, 1896) Ticket seller, Wallace & Anderson, 1884-86; Sells Bros.', 1888; Adam Forepaugh's, 1889; John Robinson's, 1890. Left the circus profession and went into the stone and cement sidewalk business in Chicago until retirement, 1894. Died at his home, Mason, OH, from kidney and liver trouble.

TORELLO BROTHERS. Classic posturing, C. T. Ames' New Orleans, 1869.

TORRES, LEONARDI. Probably William or James Terries. Aeronaut and trapeze performer, with G. G. Grady's, 1871. Died when making a balloon ascension in Massilon, OH, July 22 of that year. While performing on a trapeze suspended from the balloon, let loose his grasp to prevent being smothered by the balloon exhaust, falling into the water-filled Ohio Canal, some 8 or 9' deep. His feet lodged in the mud at the canal bottom, causing him to drown. Was about 28 years of age.

TOTTEN, JAMES ["Col."]. Treasurer, Haight's Great Eastern, 1874; privileges (with **Mallory**), Commonwealth Circus, 1879; New Bartine Consolidated Shows (Col. James S. Totten & Co., proprietors), 1896.

TOURAINE BROTHERS [Charles, Robert, Cass, and Theodore?]. Lake's Circus, 1869.

TOURNIAIRE, BENOIT. (d. September 13, 1865) Horse trainer, rider, and juggler. Brother of the famous equestrienne, **Louise Tourniaire**, and a pupil of **François Tourniaire**. Married **Rosaline Stickney**, 1851. J. M. June's, 1850; Rufus Welch's, Philadelphia, 1851; Spalding & Rogers' *Floating Palace*, 1852-53; Whitbeck's *Cirque des Varieties*, 1854; Ballard & Bailey, 1855; Jim Myers', 1856; G. F. Bailey's, 1857; Tourniaire & Whitby, 1858. Died in Havana, Cuba, while with Abisu's Circus. [John Dingess: "...known on the bills as **Mons. Benoit**, he was a trick rider and gave grand equestrian displays in which he did light balancing and plate spinning on horseback, as well as juggling cups, balls, stick dancing, etc."] See Tourniaire Family and Louise Tourniaire.

TOURNIAIRE FAMILY [Madame Louise, Mons. Benoit, Josephine, Theodore, Ferdinand; r. n. Ciseck or Zhieskick]. French equestrians. Welch's, Philadelphia, 1851; E. F. & J. Mabie's, 1851; Franconi's New York Hippodrome, 1853; Bowery Amphitheatre, 1857; George F. Bailey & Co., 1857; Tourniaire & Whitby, 1858; National Circus, 84 Bowery, NYC, winter 1858-59; Levi J. North's, 1859.

TOURNIAIRE, FERDINAND. Rider. Ballard & Bailey, 1855; Sands, Nathans & Co., 1857; Buckley & Co., 1857-58; juvenile rider and double act of horsemanship with brother Theodore, Tourniaire & Whitby, 1858; Chiarini's, Havana, winter 1859-60; R. Sands', 1860; principal rider, Tom King's, 1861-62, Washington, DC; Spalding & Rogers, West Indies, 1863-64; Hippotheatron, NYC, Spalding & Rogers, spring 1864; Rivers & Derious, 1864. Married **Kate Ormond**, May 15, 1864, while both were with the latter show. J. F. Orrin's, South America, 1865-66; Dan Castello & Co., 1866; Stone, Rosston & Murray, Front Street Theatre, Baltimore, winter 1866-67; Orrin Bros.', South America, 1867-68; Hemmings, Cooper & Whitby, 1870; James E. Cooper's, 1872; J. W. Wilder's, 1873; Sells Bros.', 1874. See Tourniaire Family and Louise Tourniaire.

TOURNIAIRE, FRANÇOIS. From the *Cirque Napoleon*, Paris. First husband of **Madame. Louise Tourniaire**. J. M. June's, 1850-52; Mann-Moore, 1853; equestrian director, Whitbeck's, 1854; Sands & Nathans', 1857; proprietor, Francois Tourniaire's, 1865. See Tourniaire Family and Louise Tourniaire.

TOURNAIRE, JOSEPHINE. Daughter of **Louise Tourniaire**; wife of **James DeMott** and mother of **Josie DeMott**. J. M. June's, 1850; Whitbeck's, 1854; Ballard & Bailey, 1855; Tourniaire & Whitby, 1858; George F. Bailey & Co., 1861-62; S. O. Wheeler's, 1863; Robinson & Howes, Chicago, 1863;

Howes' European, 1865; bareback equestrienne, DeMott & Ward, 1868. See Tourniaire Family and Louise Tourniaire.

TOURNIAIRE, LOUISE. (1825-April 12, 1901) Born in Germany of a family of acrobats by the name of **Ciseck** [or Zhieskick]. Apprenticed to the Tourniaire family in Europe as a child rider at the age of 5. Later married **François Tourniaire**. Had a daughter from this marriage, **Josephine**. Awed Londoners by her principal act in the 1840s. Tourniaires came to America, 1846, **Louise**, **François** and Louise's 3 equestrian brothers, **Benoit**, **Theodore** and **Ferdinand**, who had also been pupils of Francois. All took the name of Tourniaire professionally. Often referred to as Madame. Tourniaire, her career that lasted until 1883. Noted for her nerve, daring and grace; one of the first women to stand on one foot on a cantering horse, balancing herself erect; elegant act upon a single bareback steed was featured wherever she went. At *Cirque Napoleon* in Paris, became the first female to successfully ride a 4-horse act. Also famous for her outstanding *manège* act. While with the Montgomery Queen's, 1876, she presented the trick and dancing horse, Rienzi, a coal black thoroughbred. [John Daniel Draper: "Faultlessly seated in her side saddle, with tiny whip in hand, she compelled Rienzi to march, trot, gallop, waltz, dance, pirouette, balance and do high leaps and a number of other difficult moves, all evidence of complete and masterful control."] With James June's American and European Amphitheatre, 1850, was billed as horse trainer and the only equestrienne appearing in America without saddle or bridle, coming from Franconi in Paris and Le Cirque Nacionale in Brussels. Last mention of **François Tourniair's** appearing with her, 1857, on Sands, Nathans & Co. It is unclear when Mme. Tourniaire married her second husband, **William C Brown**, a circus musician (one report listed 1872); but around 1860 a daughter was born to this union, **Mary** (Maria or La Petite Louise Marie), known in the circus ring as **Little Mollie Brown**. J. M. June's, 1850; Whitbeck's, 1854; 6 horses bareback, bounding from steed to steed, Ballard & Bailey, 1855-56; Tourniaire & Whitby, 1858; George F. Bailey & Co., 1861; Nixon's Cremorne Gardens, NYC, spring 1862; Dan Rice's, 1862; S. O. Wheeler's, 1863, 1867-68; Dan Rice's, 1864; L. B. Lent's Broadway Amphitheatre, NYC, winter, 1863-64; George W. DeHaven's, 1865; Dan Rice's, 1865; S. P. Stickney's, 1869; *manège*, Batcheller & Doris, 1870; Montgomery Queen's, 1875. [John A. Dingess: She was "beyond a shadow of a doubt the most intrepid female rider that has ever appeared in this country."] Died in Philadelphia, age 76, preceding Brown by 2 years.

TOURNIAIRE, MARIE. See Mollie Brown.

TOURNIAIRE, ROSALINE. See Rosaline Stickney.

TOURNIAIRE, THEODORE. Rider. Juvenile rider, Ballard & Bailey, 1855; rider and double act of horsemanship with his brother Ferdinand, Tourniaire & Whitby, 1858; Hippotheatron, NYC, Spalding & Rogers, spring 1864; Spalding &

Rogers, 1864; George W. DeHaven's, 1865; Howes' European, 1865-66; Adam Forepaugh's, 1867; DeMott & Ward, 1868; Mrs. Charles Warner's, Philadelphia, winter 1868-69; S. P. Stickney's, 1869; Dan Rice's Paris Pavilion, 1872. See Tourniaire Family and Louise Tourniaire.

TOWERS, CAL. Sideshow talker, John Robinson's, 1890-93.

TOWN, BOSWELL C. VanAmburgh's Menagerie. Died of typhus fever, Connellsville, IN, 1866.

TOWNE, JOHN S. See J. T. Leon.

TOWNLEY, T. B. Proprietor (with **D. Cornwell**), Great Oriental Pavilion Show, 1877.

TOWNSEND, ALBERT. (1818-October 3, 1903) Cousin of **Hyatt Frost.** Elephant keeper as early as 1838 when he handled Siam with June, Titus, Angevine & Co. Became a pioneer sideshowman, 1840, when exhibited South American snake in a tent connected with Dick Sands' circus; net profit for the first season said to be $420. While with James Raymond, 1950s, drove a 4-hand team of elephants (Siam, Columbus, Hannibal, Virginius) harnessed to a bandwagon. Died at Brewster, NY, age 84.

TOWNSEND, CHARLES. With **Hyatt Frost**, ran a "six-and-a-quarter-cent" exhibit with Raymond & VanAmburgh, 1849. Traveling in a one-horse wagon, the show consisted of a seven-banded armadillo, a big snake, and 4 rattle snakes. [Charles H. Day: "As the California fever was at its height, the armadillo was known as the big bug of California."] May have been the Townsend who was a sideshowman with Bailey & Co., 1864.

TOWNSEND, D. R. Advance agent, Adam Forepaugh's, 1878; contractor, Cooper, Bailey & Co., 1879. Was arrested, St. Louis, MO, September 20, 1878, on a wife abandonment charge. Wife was Mary A. Townsend, living in Santa Cruz, CA.

TOWNSEND, FRANK. (1848?-August 10, 1913) Received early training in the sideshow business with his uncle, **Jacob Townsend.** Father was in charge of elephants for **James Raymond** and for VanAmburgh. Frank was salesman and barker. Later, with Howes' Great London, owned by **James E. Kelley** and **Henry Barnum**, which was stranded in Atlanta, GA, and attached by the sheriff. Subsequently, traveled for a short period with Adam Forepaugh, Jr. Died in Brewster, Putnam County, NY, age 65.

TOWNSEND, JACOB. In charge of the elephants for James Raymond and for VanAmburgh. As agent for the sale of Barnum's autobiography, *The Life of P. T. Barnum*, was given the sideshow privileges on the Barnum show.

TOWNSEND, M. L. Director of publications, S. P. Stickney's, 1869.

TOWNSEND, ORRIN ["Put"]. (1810-December 5, 1870) Elephant handler. Said to be one of the first to engage in that business in America. Worked with bulls for 38 years. Inventor of an apparatus consisting of fall blocks, rope and pulleys by which a wild elephant was subdued. First elephant was driven in harness in the country under his direction; afterward, taught 4 elephants to draw a large chariot in harness. Connected with Titus & Angevine, Raymond & Waring, and VanAmburgh & Co. Hannibal, Columbus, Siam, Virginius, Pizzaro, Bolivar, and Tippo Saib were all under his care at one time or another. Died in South East Putnam County, NY, age 60.

TRACY, NED. Clown, Ryland's, returning to California after about 5 years spent in South and Central America, 1878.

TRAIN, FRANK. Treasurer, Walter L. Main's, 1893. Killed on May 30 of that season when the Main show was nearly destroyed by a train accident near Tyrone, PA.

TRAINER, EDWARD H. See Davenport Brothers.

TRAMBLEY, J. Orchestra leader, G. G. Grady's, 1867.

TRASK, FRANCIS. Advertiser, Association's Celebrated Menagerie and Aviary from the Zoological Institute, Baltimore, 1837.

TRAVIS, JAMES. Proprietor, Travis', 1892.

TREEWALLER BROTHERS. Dan Rice's, 1862.

TREMAINE BROTHERS [Dan Leon, Lucian Ector and Faust]. Gymnasts and acrobats, Howes & Sanger, 1872.

TREMAINE, T. J. Press agent, Stowe Bros.', 1889.

TRENT, HARRISON FULTON. Publisher of the New York *Clipper,* which first appeared on April 30, 1853, to serve as a theatrical and sporting weekly. Sporting subjects included boat racing, prize fighting, baseball, pedestrianism and even checkers. The paper's theatrical focus increased during the 1860s, until, practically speaking, it was the only periodical in America dealing with show business news throughout the decade from 1865 to 1875, and it continued in the forefront as such until competition from the *Billboard* and *Variety* forced its demise in 1924. Paper was sold to **Frank Queen**, 1855.

TREVINO, JOHN. Manager and proprietor, Hobson Bros.', 1893.

TREWALLA, JEANNIE [or Trewolla]. Equestrienne, Dan Rice's Paris Pavilion, 1870-73; Melville, Maginley & Cooke, 1875.

TREWALLA, JOHN H. [or Trewolla]. Dan Rice's, 1861-62, 1867-70; equestrian director and ringmaster, Dan Rice's Paris Pavilion, 1871-73; Ben Maginley's, 1874; clown, Melville, Maginley & Cooke, 1875; general agent, Silas Dutton's, winter 1879-80, 1880; W. H. Stowe's, winter 1881-82; Sam McFlinn's, 1888.

TREXLER, HERR. Contortionist, Driesbach, Rivers & Derious, 1853; Rivers & Derious, 1856-59.

TRIBBY, S. K. S. K. Tribby & Co.'s Mastodon Dime Circus, 1886-87.

TRIPP, CHARLES B. (July 6, 1855-January 26, 1939) Sideshow curiosity. Born in Woodstock, Canada, with no arms. Feet became his hands; could shave himself, write, and light and smoke cigarettes; could use tools and developed into a skillful cabinet maker; was intelligent, educated and fair portrait painter. Arriving in NYC, 1872, at 17 years of age. Sought out P. T. Barnum and was hired on the spot. Worked for the showman for several years, touring the world 3 times with Barnum & Bailey and Ringling Bros.' Cooper, Bailey & Co., 1879. Married late in life and for the last 14 years exhibited with carnivals. Died of pneumonia, Salisbury, NC, age 74.

TROLLOP, JULES. Clown, Burr Robbins', 1886.

TRUE, CECIL A. True & McVeigh's Mammoth Railroad Shows (Cecil A. True, **John E. McVeigh**, proprietors), 1896.

TRYER, R. W. Michael O'Conner & Co., 1870.

TRYON, JOHN. (1800-March 20, 1876) Showman, agent. Born in NYC. Began professional life as a reporter for the *New York Herald*; also conducted a job printing office in that city; credited with printing the first illustrated show bill in this country, a single sheet with figures printed in black ink. Considered a leading writer of copy for bills and other advertising. The first person to start a reading room in New Bedford, MA. Began management of the Bowery Amphitheatre, 37 Bowery, fall 1843. November 6 of that year the place was re-titled Tryon's Independent Circus. February 20, 1844, opened as a theatre and circus combined. When the Bowery Theatre burned, February 25, 1845, Tryon went to considerable expense in refurbishing the place and re-opened as the New Bowery Theatre on May 5. Connected with the house off and on for the next few years; established the New Broadway Circus, 1848; operated the Pavilion Circus, Third Avenue and Eighth Street, NYC, 1849-50; accompanied ceiling walker **Richard Sands** to Europe as business manager, 1853; inaugurated the second New Bowery Theatre, 1857. Agent, Nixon-Macarte, 1863; Rivers & Derious, 1864; writer, Hemmings, Cooper & Whitby, 1868; writer, S. P. Stickney's, 1869; press agent, Howe's Great London, 1871; and agent, George F. Bailey & Co., 1872. Writer of superior ability—long enjoying the reputation for being the best writer of copy for bills and advertisements in the country, an intelligent and scholarly individual, highly thought of by his colleagues and the general public. Wrote several plays, one of which enjoyed popularity at the Chatham Theatre. Published a book, *The Story of a Clown*. Died in Boston at the residence of his son, **Benjamin F. Tryon**, age 75. At this time his son was treasurer of Boston's Howard Athenaeum. The funeral services were in charge of Tony Pastor; Tryon was interred by torchlight.

TRYON, THOMAS H. Treasurer, S. P. Stickney's, 1869.

TUBBS, A. Treasurer, New York Central Park Circus, 1877.

TUBBS, CHARLES. Strong man, Orton & Older, 1854-60; Orton Bros.', 1864.

TUCKER, MATTIE. High-wire, bicycle, and balancing trapeze, Hurlburt & Hunting, 1885.

TUCKER, J. R. Contracting agent, Hurlburt & Hunting, 1885.

TUCKER, J. W. Double contortion act as **Tucker Brothers**, Dodge & Bartine, 1868.

TUCKER, R. R. Program agent, Haight's Great Southern, 1874.

TUCKER, WILLIAM R. Hurdle rider, John Forepaugh's, California, 1888.

TUDOR, JOHN, LILLIE, and **AMY**. European specialty artists, Bunnell sideshow, P. T. Barnum's, 1879.

TUFTS, THOMAS. Agent. Rockwell & Stone, 1846; co-proprietor, Waring, Tufts & Co.'s menagerie, 1834; manager and proprietor, National Gymnasium and American Arena Co., 1837 (the only season Tufts had a company on the road, the troupe combined with Purdy, Welch Macomber & Co. on April 27-29 and May 18.). P. T. Barnum's, 1851; Rufus Welch's, 1852; Sands & Chiarini, 1854.

TUPPEE, MME. English giantess, with Yankee Robinson's, 1866.

TURNER, AARON. (1790-1854) Showman from Danbury, CT. Illegitimate and with no formal education, the son of **Mercy Hony** of Ridgefield, CT. Appointed guardian was **Dorcus Osborn**, also of Ridgefield. For some years, followed the trade of shoemaker. Married, 1815, a union which produced 2 sons and 2 daughters. Sons **Timothy** and **Napoleon** were riders. In partnership with **Nathan A. Howes** and **Sylvester Reynolds** in a circus venture, 1826. 1828, first used the title of Columbian Circus. Steadily employed in circus management until retirement in the late 1840s. Although not a performer, acted as ringmaster. P. T. Barnum described him as a genius, a man of untiring industry, a practical joker, a good judge of human nature. Close with the dollar, did not advertise lavishly, giving birth to the phrase, "Go it like old Turner." Company based in Danbury and, for the most part, tours were in New England. Never wanted to stray too far from his home base. Became affiliated with the Zoological Institute, 1835. Operating the first circus of real note in America, he used no tent during his first season on the road, only sidewall; then made a tent with his own hands and by 1830 had a 90' round-top; added a menagerie, 1844, leasing the stock, an elephant and 6 cages, from **James June**. A hippopotamus made out of leather was a feature, 1847. Hired **George F. Bailey**, who became his son-in-law, and eventually his manager. P. T. Barnum was a partner and treasurer for the organization at one time.

TURNER, BURRELL. 2-horse rider, the Royal Pavilion Circus/Olympic Circus, 1830.

TURNER, CHARLES A. Press agent, Older's, 1871.

TURNER, EDWARD ["Ned"]. (d. May 23, 1909) Clown. Coe's, 1866; Michael O'Conner & Co., 1869; Smith & Baird, 1872. Attempted suicide November 19, 1872, in Peoria by shooting himself 3 times in the breast. Thought to be caused by domestic troubles. Apparently recovered, for had an ad for summer work by December, 1872. Put out *Ned Turner's Circus Joke Book*, 1874, a do-it-yourself clown manual. Later years occupied with staging amateur shows. Died of apoplexy in Galeton, PA.

TURNER, E. W. Program agent, Adam Forepaugh's, 1874-75.

TURNER, HARRY J. Aaron Turner & Sons Columbian Circus, 1842. Conducted a boat show with **Levi J. North**, 1853. With **North**, leased the National Amphitheatre, Philadelphia, that winter. The two traveled by wagon for the 1855 season and in the winter erected an amphitheatre in Chicago.

TURNER, JAMES. Acrobat, Nathan A. Howes', 1845; slack-wire, June & Turner's, 1845-46.

TURNER, J. C. Program agent, Maginley & Co., 1874.

TURNER, JOHN F. Supt. of curiosities, P. T. Barnum, 1876.

TURNER, NAPOLEON B. (June 1, 1816-1854) Born in Kent, NY. Oldest son of **Aaron Turner**. Rode without saddle or bridle, the 3rd person to accomplish this in America. Olympic Circus, Philadelphia, 1823, under the management of Price & Simpson; Simpson & Price, Baltimore, 1823; Walnut Street Theatre, 1824; William Blanchard and William West's, Canada, 1823-25; J. Purdy Brown's, 1825; Mount Pitt Circus, NYC, 1826, billed as "from Canada" and making his debut "on two horses"; Tivoli Gardens, Philadelphia, 1826 (during this stand executed a backward somersault from horse to ground); Lafayette Circus, NYC, January 1827; Samuel Parsons', under the management of **Simon V. Wemple**, Troy, NY, 1828; Royal Pavilion Circus/Olympic Circus, 1830; Aaron Turner's, 1833; Cole, Miller, Gale & Co., 1838; June, Titus & Angevine, 1838; 4-horse rider, Bowery Amphitheatre, 1841; Howes & Mabie, 1841; Aaron Turner's, 1842-43; Rockwell & Stone, 1843; 6-horse rider, June & Turner, 1844-47.

TURNER, OLIVER ["Master"]. June & Turner, 1845-46.

TURNER, THOMAS. General performer, Aaron Turner's, 1842.

TURNER, TIMOTHY V. (1820-1858) The youngest son of **Aaron Turner** and brother of **Napoleon**. Aaron Turner's, 1835-39; June, Titus, Angevine & Co., at the Bowery Amphitheatre, 1838-40; Welch, Bartlett & Co., 1840; Bowery Amphitheatre, 1841; Howes & Mabie, 1841; Welch & Mann, 1841; Aaron Turner & Sons, 1842; performed somersaults on horseback and a nautical act of horsemanship, Welch's, Philadelphia, 1843; flying cord, John Tryon's, Bowery Amphitheatre, 1843; Rockwell & Stone, 1843; Nathan A. Howes', winter 1843-44; Aaron Turner's, 1843, 1849; June & Turner, 1844-47. Died apoplexy in Danbury, CT, age 38.

TURNOUR, EDWARD [of Turnour & Roberts]. (d. December 31, 1898) Knockabout clown. Nephew of **Millie Turnour**. Entered the business around 1890, performing with Sig. Sautelle and other circuses. Died of consumption at his home in NYC, age 28.

TURNOUR, JENNIE. (March 1860-April 26, 1884) Equestrienne and aerialist. Youngest of 4 sisters. Born in Lisbon, Spain, and came to America with her parents at the age of 10.

Married **Charles Ewers**. C. W. Noyes', 1872; Haight's Great Southern, 1874; North American, 1875; John Robinson's, 1875-78; Orrin Bros.', Havana, winter 1878-79; Sells Bros.', 1879, 1882-83; hurdle and fire hoop rider, Adam Forepaugh's, 1881; Orrin Bros.', Mexico, 1883. Killed while performing with Barrett's Circus, 1884.

TURNOUR, JULIUS. (d. January 26, 1931) Clown. Born in a circus wagon while French parents were exhibiting their circus in Spain. First appeared at a London music hall in a "demon act," in which, with red tights, a reddened face, and a dangling tail, he portrayed a little devil. Apprenticed with the **Conrads** for 10 years for no pay. Gave up acrobatics because of ill health. Began clowning while in North Africa. Connected with Circus Chiniselli in Berlin; a Spanish clown, Orrin Bros.', Havana, winter 1879-80; Burr Robbins', 1879-80; Ringling Bros.' from about 1891 for some 20 years. While with Adam Forepaugh's, was mail carrier for the show people; first business in the morning after breakfast was to go to the post office for all the show mail; after arriving at the show grounds, delivered to four stations—the ticket wagon, the sideshow, the menagerie and the dressing room; for this service, he was given the right to issue the route cards of the show, which he sold for five cents apiece. [D. W. Watt: "He was always painstaking and careful with the mail and always carried a few stamps in his pocket in case one of the working men or anyone around the show would be out of money, he would always mail their letters for them.... Today Jules Turnour owns a nice fruit farm in Michigan."] Last appearance, Madison Square Garden, 1928, before going into retirement at Valley Stream, Long Island. Wrote *The Autobiography of a Clown*, 1910, published by Moffat, Yard & Co.; forward written by Alf T. Ringling. Died in Valley Stream, age 80.

TURNOUR, MILLIE. Trapeze performer. Debut at Tony Pastor's Opera House, NYC, 1868; C. T. Ames', 1869-70; Spalding & Bidwell, New Orleans, 1870. [New Orleans *Daily Picayune*, 1870: "A swinging bar is suspended about 50 feet in the air. Upon this simple bar she balances, swings, suspends, and enacts feats which are equally the amazement, the admiration and the fear of all who behold her. Her turns in the air are marvelous to behold, and as she descends to the stage, head downwards on a single rope, without the assistance of her hands, the tumultuous applause which invariably greets her, is an involuntary tribute to so much courage united with so much grace."] C. W. Noyes', 1871-72; John H. Murray's, 1873-75; Haight's Great Southern, 1874; Hengler's, England, winter 1874-75; Montgomery Queen's, 1877; John H. Murray's, 1878; Orrin Bros.', Havana, 1878; Mexico, winter 1882; with **Lottie Miranda**, a double-trapeze team, Adam Forepaugh's, 1879-80, 1887; W. W. Cole's (which left San Francisco for Australia, October 23, 1880), 1880-81; Inter-Ocean Show, 1883; Barnum & London, 1884; Ringling Bros.', 1899-1900; Walter L. Main's, 1904. Married **Wooda**

Cook while with C. W. Noyes' Crescent City Circus, March 1872, Shreveport, LA. Later separated.

TUTTLE, A. F. Proprietor, A. F. Tuttle's Olympic Show, a wagon show for some 18 years. Last notice found in 1907 when the show was sold to **George W. Loudon**.

TUTTLE, JEROME. Leaper. John Robinson's, 1869-70; gymnast, Alex Robinson's, 1869; Wootten & Haight, 1871; Empire City, 1871; Great Eastern, 1872.

TWAITS, JAMES W. Treasurer. Springer's Royal Cirq-Zoolodon, 1875; Joel E. Warner's, 1876.

TYKE, JOHN. Manager, George F. Bailey & Co., 1859; treasurer, VanAmburgh's, 1866.

TYROLEANS. Minstrel troupe, Rockwell & Stone, 1846.

U & V

UFFNER, FRANK. Privileges. Dan Castello's, winter 1867-68; VanAmburgh's, 1871-72; with J. Parks, Howes' Great London, 1873; George W. DeHaven's, 1875. Said to be the discoverer of **Lucia Zarette** and **Jo Jo, the Dog-Faced Boy**.

UNDERWOOD, JOHN. Rider, Palmer's Pavilion Circus, 1836.

UNLAUFF, J. F. G. Naturalist and dealer in circus curiosities, Hamburg, Germany, 1882, shells, stuffed birds and animals, skulls and skeletons, as well as live animals.

VAIL, JOHN W. Herculean performer. Native of Mansfield, OH. As a youth was a boatman on the Western rivers. In the ring performed feats while suspended from the center pole of the tent, 10' above the ground, holding anvils by his teeth and other 50 to 60 pound weights. One day in a town in Indiana the pavilion was hit by a tornado, the pole broke and Vail fell on his head. Though badly injured, survived the fall. Later, abandoned the profession and married a wealthy quadroon in Port Royal, West Indies. Migrated to California and became Squire Vail, Justice of the Peace of Yankee Station. Connected with Bancker's, 1831; American Circus, 1833; Buckley & Co., 1834; Brown & Co., 1836-37; Waring and Raymond, New Orleans, winter 1837-38. [John A. Dingess: "...one of the oldest time favorites, was a performer of rare excellence in everything he undertook."]

VALENTINE, CHARLES and MAY. Flying return act, Bruce L. Baldwin's, 1894.

VALENTINE, SCOTT. Program agent, Baird, Howell & Co., 1874.

VALLEAU. Rider, William Blanchard & William West's, Canada, 1824-25.

VALLEE, MONS. Interpreter, Spalding & Rogers, 1859.

VALLENTINE, SCOTT. Program agent, Baird, Howell & Co., 1874.

VALVINO, ARTHUR. Dockrill's, South America, winter 1885-86.

VAN AMBURGH, ISAAC A. (May 26, 1808-November 29, 1865) Lion tamer. Born in Fishkill, NY, of German descent. Became connected with menageries, 1829. Mnd made NYC debut at Richmond Hill Theatre, fall 1833. Same season, appeared at the Bowery Theatre for Thomas S. Hamblin in a melodrama, *The Lion Lord; or, the Forest Monarch*, in which he rode a horse up a high incline; when he reached the top a Bengal tiger spung out upon him and the two struggled down the ramp to the footlights as in desperate combat. Assistant keeper to a **Mr. Roberts**, June, Titus & Co., 1833, and continued with this firm through 1837; when Roberts was torn severely by a tiger that year, VanAmburgh became the permanent keeper. Principal attraction, the Zoological Institute, 37

Bowery, November 1834, and performed there every winter season until 1838. Went to England and Europe with **Lewis Titus**, July 1838, and remained for 7 years, where he gained his fame. First appeared at Astley's Amphitheatre, London, and later at Drury Lane and the principal cities of Europe. While abroad, several dramas were written for him and were produced with success. Made several tours through the provinces of England, Scotland, Ireland and Wales with a traveling menagerie; said to have been the first to introduce the American style of tenting to Great Britain. Returning to America, 1845, **June** and **Titus** establish a new menagerie with his name, VanAmburgh & Co., a name that was identified with both menagerie and circus until 1921. After retirement from activity in the ring, around the mid-1850s, he still accompanied the show bearing his name through its annual tours, although it was under the management of **Hyatt Frost**. 1853, the Raymond interests leased the *Floating Palace* and refurbished it to house an exhibition of the VanAmurgh menagerie. Strangely, he never owned a show with his name on it. Possesed great physical strength and courage and performed with grace, firmness and self-possession; but frequently used a crow bar to beat his animals into submission. With him the style of animal acts changed from displays of docility to blatant challenges by man and beast and on many occasions he was bitten and chewed by his animals. Never married. Died at Sam Miller's Hotel, Philadelphia.

VAN AUKEN, HARRY S. Gymnast. Born in Geneva, NY. At age 10, moved to Hudson, MI, with his parents. Age 18, ran away from home and joined the Great Eastern. At close of the season, took **George C. Paine** as a partner and performed in variety houses with a single bar act. Following spring, they joined the Z. W. Spreague's Electric Light Show, which had a short life. Following year, were with the Parson & Roy Circus. **Paine** left the act at the close of the engagement. Took **C. W. Cardello** as partner, 1883. Made their debut on the double bars, 1884, at Miner's Eighth Avenue Theatre, NYC. Following summer, Miles Orton's; later, Tom Canary's American Four Show. 1885, joined Barnum & Bailey but was forced to leave in April because of an injury. July of that year, took **C. F. Fox** as a partner. As **Fox & Van Aukens**, were a feature with the Hallen's company for 2 seasons; McNish, Johnson & Slavin's Minstrels; Van Auken & Long, a tour of South America, leaving October 20, 1888, returning July 24, 1889. With **Jerry Hurley** as a partner, traveled with Primrose & West's Minstrels, 1889. Then, Van Auken, McPhee & Hill. January 1, 1898, formed a partnership with **William Vannerson**.

VANCE, MOSES. Executed first double somersault in USA,

310

according to Levi J. North. The boy was a resident of Albany.

VANCE, THOMAS. (d. April 21, 1889) L. B. Lent's, VanAmburgh's, P. T. Barnum's.

VANDERCOOK, H. A. Band leader, J. H. LaPearl's, 1891-94.

VANDERVELT, C. Rider, Lailson's, Philadelphia, 1797.

VAN GAPA, TONY. Contortionist, New York and New England Circus, 1884.

VAN HORN, C. E. General business agent, Sherman & Hinman, San Francisco, September 1883.

VANICE, MISS. Equestrienne with Lailson's company, Boston, 1796; Lailson's, 1798.

VANITI FAMILY. Gymnasts, Charley Bartine's, 1872.

VAN LUVEN, HARRY D. Proprietor, VanLuven's, 1872.

VANNERSON, WILLIAM. Gymnast. Born in Richmond, VA. Made first appearance as a bar performer, 1889. Then, with various circuses until 1894 when he formed a partnership with **Joe Garnel** and joined the Orrin Bros.', Mexico. 1895, Ringling Bros.' an aerial bar act. January 1, 1898, formed a partnership with **Jerry VanAuken**.

VANOLAR, WILLIAM L. Beckett's, 1882.

VAN ORDEN, WESSEL T. B., JR. (d. October, 1877) Son of a doctor in the Albany, NY, area. Upon finishing a college education, gravitated to the circus business. Manager of Spalding's North American Circus, 1844; manager, Dan Rice's, 1848 (when the circus went sour, 1849, Van Orden was instrumental in foreclosing on Rice's farm in Greene County, NY); manager, Spalding, Rogers & Van Orden, 1851; Spalding & Rogers, 1851-64; interested in Madigan & Stone, 1852; manager, Nixon's Royal Circus, 1861; business manager, Parisian Circus, assembled for the Paris Exposition (**Avery Smith, G. Quick, John Nathans, Dr. Gilbert R. Spalding** and **David Bidwell**, proprietors), 1867. Married **Caroline Spalding** (b. 1821), sister of **Dr. Gilbert Spalding**. Died in Albany.

VAN PELT, LULU. Midget, with Cameron's Great Oriental Circus, 1875.

VANSTONE, WILLIAM. Advertiser, Whitmore, Thompson & Co.'s Equescurriculum, 1865

VANTA, SIGNOR. Horse training exhibition with lecture, Wambold & Whitby, 1861.

VAN VALKENBERG, D. Acting manager, Castello & VanVleck, 1863.

VAN VALKENBERG, R. Castello & VanVleck's, summer 1863-64. VanValkenberg & Co. toured Texas and Mexico, 1881-83.

VAN VLECK, L. Proprietor, Castello & VanVleck, 1863-64, traveling by boat making towns along the Ohio River.

VAN VLECK, MATTHEW. (1820-June 20, 1873) General manager, Castello & VanVleck, 1863. Died in Cuba, NY.

VAN VLECK, WILLIAM. Burr Robbins', 1885.

VAN ZANDT, A. D. [r. n. Anson Babcock]. (1849-December 23, 1896) Began career as an acrobat at age 17. For 12 years,

traveled with his brother as the **Van Zandt Brothers**, connected with John Stowe & Sons, 1868, 1871; G. G. Grady's, 1869; Stowe & Orton, 1870; W. W. Cole's, 1871-83; Great Transatlantic Allied Shows, 1879; Stickney's Imperial Parisian Circus, 1880. 1877, he began riding and became a proficient bareback jockey. South America, 1886, with Dockrill's; remained there until May 1896. Died at the home of his daughter, Morenci, MI.

VAN ZANDT, MILLIE. Trapeze performer with Sells & Barrett's, 1890. Brought a suit for $1,000 against the management for breach of contract, for dismissal shortly after being hired. Was apparently awarded $700.

VAN ZANDT, ROSE and **ELLA.** Diefenbach's Trans-Atlantic, 1888.

VAN ZANDT, WINANT. Member of the VanZandt Family. Died on a yatching trip at Bath Beach, NJ, July 17, 1892.

VARDEN, DOLLY. Male dwarf. Haight's Great Eastern, 1873-74; Cameron's, 1875; VanAmburgh's, 1876.

VARDEN, DOLLY [r. n. Mrs. Selitia Campbell]. (d. August 18, 1911) Not the same as above. Giant Negress weighing 650 pounds.

VARDEN, WILLIE. Rider, Haight's Great Eastern, 1874.

VAUGHAN, FRANK [r. n. Francis Maguire]. Clown. Died in the Essex County jail, NJ, after suffering from delirium tremens, July 28, 1869.

VAUGHAN, T. Minstrel performer, with Rockwell & Stone, 1842; banjoist, Hobby & Pratt, 1842.

VELCOURT, HENRY. Gymnast, acrobat, Great Australian (**Frank J. Howes**, manager), 1870.

VELLIER, DURAND. Rider, Dan Rice's, 1873.

VENUS, ROSINO. Principal bareback rider and bounding rope performer, Orrin Bros.', Mexico, 1897.

VERDA, MONTE. Contortionist, P. T. Barnum's, 1871-72.

VERMULE, T. L. Proprietor and manager, T. L. Vermule's New Jersey Circus, 1845.

VERNER, CHARLES. Irish songs, concert, Cooper, Bailey & Co.'s Circus, Australian tour, 1877.

VERNON BROTHERS [B. S., Charles]. "Absolute Kings of the Air," Ringling Bros.', 1893. **B. S.,** Comedy bar act; entered the profession, 1882, and shortly afterwards joined with **Fred Elmer** in an act under the title of the **Elmer Brothers**. Roberts & Gardner, 1886; joined **Rome Emery**, 1887, and played dates as a bar team; met with an accident during the 1889 season. After recovering, joined with **Charles Vernon** for an aerial bar act; Ringling Bros.', 1893; Forepaugh's and Walter L. Main's. 1895, **B. S.** took **C. M. Zazelle** as a partner for a comedy bar act.

VERNON, DANIEL S. (circa 1854-1908) Born in Morocco. Came to USA as an opera singer, minstrel, etc. Was press and route agent with John Robinson's, 1879, railroad and general agent, 1882; railroad contractor, Frank A. Robbins', 1889. **Mrs. Vernon** was a lion tamer, John Robinson's, 1879.

VERNON, JOHN. Railroad contractor and general agent. John Robinson's, 1880s; general agent, Walter L. Main's first tour of the Pacific Coast but was succeeded by Harry Knapp during the trip.

VERONA BROTHERS [Eugene F., Fred, and Minnie Steward]. Adam Forepaugh's, 1892.

VERRECKE, MONS. Parisian gymnast. After having astonished Europe, James M. Nixon's Alhambra, NYC, fall 1863, performing on a single trapeze. New Bowery, NYC, for 3 weeks beginning September 21, 1863, for manager **James W. Lingard.** Then a year's contract with manager Lea of Baltimore, beginning at the Front Street Theatre, October 19, 1863.

VERSHAY, BILLY. Clown. Haight & Chambers, 1867; Frank Howes', 1868; Dodge & Bartine, 1868.

VEY, CHARLES. Dutch clown, Wallace & Co., 1884.

VICK, MLLE. FRANK [r. n. Frances Victoria Johnson]. Rider. Dan Rice's, 1851-56; Crescent City, December 1855; pony act, Crescent City, May 1856; Dan Rice's, 1856; Orton & Older, 1858; McCorkle? (as **Mlle. Victorine**), 1859. Had 2 sons and 2 daughters.

VICTOR, FRANK. Gymnast, Shelby, Pullman & Hamilton, 1881.

VICTOR, SIGNOR. Man monkey, Thayer & Noyes, 1865.

VICTORELLI BROTHERS [John, William, Hector]. English gymnasts. James Robinson's, 1870; Dan Rice's Paris Pavilion Circus, 1871; John O'Brien's, 1872; L. B. Lent's, 1873; Roberts & Gardner, 1886.

VICTORELLI, WALTER [r. n. Walter Hovey]. (January 1858-February 28, 1882) Gymnast. Born in Xenia, OH. Apprenticed as gymnast to **Harry Victorelli** until 1875; that year, teamed with **Charles W. Cardello, Cardello & Victorelli,** horizontal bar performers. Hilliard & Hunting, 1875-77; Campbell's (John V. O'Brien's), 1878, left in May for South America with Cooper & Bailey; Batcheller & Doris, 1879-80; American Four Combination, 1881. Married **Lizzie Parker.** Died of consumption, NYC, age 24.

VICTORIA, MLLE. English "Queen of the Lofty Wire." Performed since the age of 5 or 6. Came to USA on the urging of P. T. Barnum after having been well received on the Continent, where, at one time, she had cross the river Seine on a wire. Barnum's Roman Hippodrome, NYC and on the road, 1874-75. She walked across a wire, then re-crossed with her head in a sack, and finally rode across on a velocipede. Cameron's Oriental, 1875-76; Carlo Bros.', South America, 1876;

Adam Forepaugh's, 1881.

VICTORIA, MME. [r. n. Emma M. Harring]. (d. September 3, 1885) Giantess. Born in Reading, PA, around 1852. Top weight was 550 pounds. First exhibited, Trenton, NJ, 1876. Connected with Adam Forepaugh's for a time. Died at her home in Philadelphia.

VICTORINI [also seen as Victorian and Victoriani]. Rope-dancer, a student of **Franconi's,** with Pepin & Breschard, 1809, his American debut; Robert Davis', Salem, MA, February 1810, vaulting over 6 horses.

VIDELLAS. Aerialist, Barnum & Bailey, 1891.

VILALLAVE. Rope-dancer. William Blanchard & William West's, Canada, 1825; Asa T. Smith's, 1829; ventured into management, summer and fall 1818, performing in Boston, Salem, Worcester, MA, and Albany, NY; joined Pepin's troupe, Philadelphia, November 1818. Performed in America for over 15 years.

VILLION TROUPE. Bicyclists, Adam Forepaugh's, 1881.

VINCENT, ALEXANDER. Equestrian. Nathan A. Howes' winter, 1843-44; Howes & Gardner, 1844.

VINCENT, CHARLES. Lee & Ryland, California, February 1869.

VINCENT, FRED. Band leader, W. F. Kirkhart's Great American, 1894.

VINCENT, W. Ringmaster, Atlantic and Pacific, 1871.

VINETTA, ADA. Concert singer, hippodrome jockey, Barnum, Bailey & Hutchinson, 1882.

VINO, WILLIAM. Clown, Barnum & Bailey, 1893.

VINTON, ANNIE. Wallace & Co., 1886.

VIOLA, NINA. Equestrienne. Robert Stickney's, 1880; Van-Amburgh & Co., 1880-81; Frank A. Gardner's, South America, 1889.

VIRELLA, JOSEPH. Rider, W. W. Cole's, 1875.

VIVALLA, SIGNOR. Juggler, Aaron Turner's, 1836; plate spinner, Drury, VanTassle, Brown & Co., 1837.

VOIGHT, CHARLES. Musical director, Charles Noyes', 1870-71.

VOLEMANN, HERR. German acrobat. With **VonCastle,** classic posturing and lofty leaps, Sands & Nathans, 1857.

VON CASTLE. German acrobat, with **Herr Volemann,** classic posturing and lofty leaps, Sands & Nathans, 1857.

VOSE. Band leader, Rockwell & Stone, 1844.

VOST, PETER. Band leader, Nixon & Kemp, 1858.

VRANDENBURG, AD. Band leader, F. J. Tayor's, 1893.

Isaac VanAmburgh

W

WACHTEL, ANNIE. See Charles W. Lingard.

WACK, EUGENE. Band Leader, Robert Hunting's, 1894.

WADDELL, REV. ["Doc", r. n. W. S. Andres]. (b. August 26, 1863) Agent. Born in Portsmouth, OH. Grandfather was a horseman and animal trainer. Began as a candy butcher at age 10 and graduated to a variety of circus jobs—canvasman, driver, ticket seller, "grifter," all day grinder, principal announcer, press agent, and circus parson, conducting revivals and preaching in many of the large churches in America and abroad. After 50 years of press work, became the dean of press agentry.

WADE, SILE. Negro minstrel, George F. Bailey & Co., 1859.

WAGNER, JESSE D. ["Prof."]. Band leader. Donaldson & Rich, 1885; James T. Johnson's Great Western Circus, 1886.

WAGSTAFF, LOUISA. Rider, Welch & Mann, 1843.

WAHLE, PROF. E. Band leader, Alex Robinson's, 1865.

WAINO. See Plutano and Waino.

WAITE, ISAAC NEWTON. Rider, Dan Rice's, 1852.

WALCOT, EDWARD. Clown, Spalding & Rogers' *Floating Palace*, 1859.

WALHALLA BROTHERS [Edward, John, Max]. Hat spinners and acrobats. Adam Forepaugh's, 1873-76; "*Les deux Comiques*" and gymnasts, Cooper, Bailey & Co., Australian tour, 1876-77. Remained permantly in Australia, first joining Burton's Great Australian, 1878-79; 1880, interested in Walhalla & Barlow's British-American; Chiarini's, 1881-84; Wirth's, 1888-89; Mathews Bros.', 1888; Harmston's, 1890; FitzGerald's, 1903-05; Alison's Vaudeville Co., touring New Zealand, 1821. John married Mme. DeGranville, iron-jawed lady, Australia, March 10, 1878. Edward died, Sydney, 1925. Max was clown, Sells Bros.', 1878.

WALKER, EVA. Tight-rope, hippodrome jockey, Barnum, Bailey & Hutchinson, 1882.

WALKER, JERRY. Clark Bros.', winter 1889-90.

WALKER, JOHN. English musician "who plays the Ophicleide in the band," Rockwell & Stone, #2, 1845.

WALKER, J. W. Press agent, Walter L. Main's, 1889.

WALKER, LLIAM. Dan Rice's, 1862.

WALKER, THOMAS DAWSON ["Whimsical"]. (July 5, 1851-November 1934) Clown. Born in Hull, England, the son of Robert Stanley Walker, manager of Thomas Cooke's circus, 1840s. Mother died, 1854; father remarried, moved to Stockport. At 8 years of age apprenticed to Pablo Fanque. Appeared as clown 2 years later. Remained with Fanque for some 8 years. Then, after Fanque's death, 1871, joined Croueste and Nella's. Followed by Charles Adams'. Came to USA for John H. Murray's, 1875; then appearances with Coo-

per, Bailey & Co., 1879-80; Adam Forepaugh's, 1880; Barnum, Bailey & Hutchinson, 1881-82. Sailed for England, October 17, 1882, where he was with Hengler's. [John Turner: "In U.S.A. 16 times, toured the world 3 times, with Hengler's Circus 14 years, at Drury Lane, in pantomime. 21 seasons."] Pursued a career in films under the name Jamie Darling, appearing in fourteen between 1913 and 1915.

WALKER, WILLIAM [a.k.a. Walker Nunn]. With Nathan Howes', winter 1845; Rockwell & Stone, 1846; then Rufus Welch's, 1848-49; St. Louis Amphitheatre, 1851; Rockwell's, 1851; *corde volante*, Dan Rice's, New Orleans, winter 1853-54; Dan Rice's, 1855, 1861; Crescent City, 1855-56; Dan Rice's, 1862.

WALL, J. Director of amusements, Baldwin, Wall & Co.'s Great Eastern, 1880.

WALL, J. M. Contracting agent, Cole's (George S. Cole, John Sparks, proprietors), 1893.

WALL, W. B. Treasurer, Baldwin, Wall & Co.'s Great Eastern, 1880.

WALLACE. Strong man, Sweet & Hough, 1835.

WALLACE, BENJAMIN E. ["Col." and "Uncle Ben"]. (1848-April 8, 1921) Born in Pennsylvania. Joined the Union Army at age 18 and participated in the Civil War. At close of hostilities, engaged as a hostler for a livery stable in Peru, IN. Later, became proprietor of his own stable. Spring 1884, joined with James Anderson and Al G. Field in a partnership to place a wagon show on the road under the title of Wallace & Co.'s Great Menagerie, International Circus, Museum, Alliance of Novelties and Mardi-Gras Street Carnival, an outfit consisting of 185 horses and mules and 55 wagons and cages. Took over ownership, 1887, changing the show's title in 1892-94 to Cook & Whitby, but returned to the original when the outfit was enlarged for a trip to the West Coast and back, 1895. [Sturtevant: He had "a practice of hiring top people at prevailing wages, was a shrewd dealer and a supreme judge of horse flesh, and said to have been a very modest and retiring man, not wanting to be recognized as the owner of a large circus."] However, he was not above allowing grift on his show. [Orin Copple King: He had "much in common with knaves like Willie Sells, Joe McMahon and others of like ilk.... They stayed close to the straight and narrow when at home, but once they passed the city limits nothing was too scurilous for them to attempt."] The Wallace circus moved into new winter quarters in the fall, 1892, when a 220 acre farm was purchased for $30,000. 11 buildings were constructed—a 200' x 120' main barn, 40' x 50' cat animal building, 100' x 50' elephant building, 50' x 50' camel barn, 150' x 50' two-storied shop building, 50' x 50' ring barn and stables, two 50' x 50' storehouses, cook house, two-story residence and outbuildings, and a 750' wagon shed. Wallace proudly stated: "When the Wallace show comes in for the winter, it puts its cars in its own sheds, on its own side tracks on my land; the wagons are run into my own shops, and my horses turned into my own pastures. I can feed my animals and men with my own hay, grain, vegetables, beef and pork raised by myself. I can replenish my stock from my own breeders. I can build all necessary buildings from timber cut from my own woods, and can winter my show without buying supplies outside, with the exception of the bread I get from the baker and a few cases of canned goods at the grocer's." With **John Talbot** and **Jerry Mugivan**, Wallace purchased the Hagenbeck Wild Animal Show, 1907; ultimately, combined it with the Wallace property and bought out his partners. 50-car Hagenbeck-Wallace circus continued under his management until he sold it and retired to his home in Peru, IN, July 1, 1913, from where he sold old circus equipment. In 1912, he owned real estate in Peru, including three square miles of farmland where the Hagenbeck-Wallace winter quarters were, holdings in banks, street railway lines, department stores, electric light plants, stocks and bonds, gilt edge securities, etc. Died at the Mayo Brothers Institute, Rochester, MN, age 73. [R. M. Harvey, Wallace's last general agent: Wallace was "kind hearted, democratic, averse to display, opposed to false pretenses ... a plain Hoosier farmer, reared in and near a small town, governed by his natural Scotch common sense, guided by his own rules and judgment."]

WALLACE, BERNARD L. Treasurer, with Hagenbeck & Wallace. A nephew of **Ben E. Wallace**. Married **Caroline Schrock**, Peru, IN, July 31, 1910.

WALLACE BROTHERS. Gymnasts. Tom King's, 1862; Gardner & Hemmings, 1862.

WALLACE, DOC. Clown, Wootten & Haight, 1871.

WALLACE, FANNIE. Scottish giant, W. W. Cole's, 1874-75.

WALLACE, FLORENCE E. (August 27, 1852-February 8, 1924) Wife of **Ben E. Wallace**. Born at Bennington VT, the daughter of **Rueben Fuller** and **Mary Jane Skinner**. Owned approximately 2,200 acres of land in Miami County, 600 of which were sold to the American Circus Corp. for winter quarters; owned the Senger Dry Goods Co., the Colonial Apartments, the Bearas Dairy, the Wickler Dairy, and 31 pieces of real estate in Peru, IN; had controling interest in the Wabash Valley Trust Co. Died at her residence in Peru following a stroke.

WALLACE, GEORGE. Charioteer, Barnum & Bailey, 1892.

WALLACE, HARRY. High-wire walker (with **Idaletta**), Pullman & Mack, 1885.

WALLACE, IDA. Rider, the Great Roman Hippodrome and Congress of Novelties (**William D. Curtis**, proprietor), 1877.

WALLACE, PROF. Performing bears from California, L. B.

Lent's, Wallack's Old Theatre, NYC, November 1863; Lent's Equescurriculum, 1863.

WALLACE, W. F. Showman, died from kidney trouble at Hot Springs, AR, September 13, 1912.

WALLACE, WILLIAM. Master of transportation, with L. B. Lent's, 1867-69; superintendent of animals, Robbins & Colvin, 1881.

WALLACE, WILLIAM. Chief usher, P. T. Barnum's, 1873.

WALLACE, WILLIE. Cooper, Jackson & Co., 1882.

WALLACH, J. H. General agent, S. H. Barrett & Co., 1882.

WALLACKER, GEORGE W. (d. March 8, 1889) P. T. Barnum's.

WALLETT, WILLIAM FREDERICK. (October 12, 1808-March 13, 1892) Shakespearean clown. Born in Southcoates, near Hull, England, of a sailor father of Scotch descent. Made first appearance on the stage as a "super" at the Royal Hull Theatre, 1830. Later, joined Abbott's traveling company for 4 years; Milton's Circus, where he made his debut as a clown; with James Wild's, W. S. Thorn's, Holloway's Amphitheatre at Sheffield, Wells & Miller's at Wakefield (where he assumed the title of the "Shakespearean Jester"). Engagements with Cooke's and then VanAmburgh's followed. After 2 years with the latter, joined Edwin Hughes', where he designed the ornamental carriages for the show, including the great lion wagon drawn by elephants. Next, with William Batty's and then Pablo Fanque's; and became one of the greatest favorites seen in England at that time. 1849, left for America and made his debut for Gen. Rufus Welch in the fall of that year, one that was marred by ill feelings from an anti-British portion of the audience; but it was the making of him in this country as many in the crowded house rallied to his support (it was rumored that the incident was a ploy created by Wallett to insure his success). Next, employed by Seth B. Howes for the Federal Street Theatre, Boston. Followed by a season's engagement at the National Circus, Philadelphia, beginning December 17, 1849; then, James M. June's, where he was paid the highest salary ever received by a clown in America, 1850. Spalding & Rogers, American Theatre, New Orleans, winter 1850-51; Dan Rice's, 1852; Rufus Welch's, 1852, National Circus, Philadelphia. First appearance as an actor in this country, Chestnut Street Theatre, Philadelphia, December 11, 1852, as Duke Aranza in *The Honeymoon*. Returned to England, 1858; while there, joined Howes & Cushing for their second season at the Alhambra Palace, London. Organized a traveling company for a provincial tour and then appeared throughout Europe as a star attraction. Subsequently, left Europe for America on the *City of Baltimore*, arriving in NYC, January 14, 1866. Appeared for **Robert Fox**, American Theatre, Philadelphia, January, 1866; P. T. Barnum's, 1871; Forsitt's, London, England, off-season 1890-91; Adam Forepaugh's, 1892; Barnum & Bailey, 1895. Wallett was head and shoulders above his contemporaries, called the "Queen's

Jester" and the "Demosthenes of the Arena." Costumed in mediaeval jester attire, depicting the Royal Arms, and sported a ponderous mustache, his jests were long recitations, sometimes in prose, sometimes in verse, refined and instructive, filled with political and moral sentiments. He is said to have introduced intellectuality into his act in place of the customary buffoonery, which inspired a school of Shakespearean clowns and created a rivalry with the English clown, **Thomas Barry.** A student of Shakespearean and a widely read man, eager to quote the bard whenever applicable. [John A. Dingess: "He had all the easy assurance, gentle ways, and polish of society."] In semi-retirement for his last 20 years, he was an enthusiastic gardner, and an amateur photographer, one of the first to use the French Daguerrotype, on which made several improvements. An interest in science led to the invention of a self-charinging process in the bottling of mineral waters. Died at Beeston, England. [John Glenroy: "A better clown never stepped into a ring."]

WALLGROVE, JAMES. Leaper, Alexander Robinson's, 1871.

WALLHALLA, MAX. Clown, Sells Bros.', 1878.

WALTER, JOHN. Rider. Began with Pepin & Barrett, 1822-23, and continued with Pepin at least through 1827; Royal Pavilion Circus/Olympic Circus, 1830; Frost, Husted & Co., 1836; J. J. Hall's, 1836; Frost & Co., 1837.

WALTERS, CHARLES. Rider and gymnast. Spalding's, 1847-50; Spalding & Rogers, 1851-53; Chiarini & Raymond, 1855; Herr Driesbach's, 1856; Spalding & Rogers, 1857-59.

WALTERS, LEW. Variety troupe, with Haight & Chambers, 1867.

WALTERS, T. F. Treasurer, H. C. Lee's Great Eastern, winter 1877-78.

WALTERS, W. Spalding & Rogers, 1859.

WALTON, BILLY. Clown, Spalding & Rogers' *Floating Palace*, 1859.

WALTON BROTHERS [Dave, Hiram, Reno, Master John]. Wallace & Co., 1887; Sells Bros.', 1891; Ringling Bros.', 1893.

WALTON, FRANK. Orchestra leader, Gregory Bros.' Metropolitan, 1885.

WALTON, FRED. (d. November 13, 1914) Acrobat. At one time with the Barnum & Bailey. In later years, a vendor of post cards and flowers. Died in Cincinnati, age 56.

WALTON, JOSEPH. Roberts & Gardner (**Nick Roberts, F. A. Gardner,** proprietors), 1886.

WAMBOLD, AMELIA. Running globe, Collins' Oriental Combination, 1877.

WAMBOLD, CHARLOTTE [or Carlotta]. Equestrienne. Dr. James L. Thayer's, 1877; Lowande's Great Brazilian, 1877.

WAMBOLD, E. Stickney's Imperial Parisian Circus, 1880.

WAMBOLD, FRANCIS H. James M. Nixon's Parisian Hippodrome and Chicago Amphitheatre, May 1872.

WAMBOLD, GEORGE [a. k. a. William Mitchell]. (b. October 13, 1842-1908) Born in Quebec, Canada. Contortionist, equestrian acts, tight-rope, globe, barrel, and performing dogs. Brother of gymnast **Harry Wambold.** Gardner & Hemmings, 1863; with the trick dog, Beauty, Tom King's, 1864; Havana, fall 1864; Palmer's Great Western, 1866; dog, etc., Gardner & Hemmings, Front Street Theatre, winter 1865-66; George F. Bailey & Co., 1866; Adam Forepaugh's, 1867; DeMott & Ward, 1868; James M. Nixon's, 1870, 1872; John O'Brien's, 1871; Cooper, Bailey & Co., Australian tour, 1877-78 (performing in the concert as Prof. Wambold, fire eater); Cooper, Jackson & Co., 1882; Wallace & Co., 1884. Married **Millie Cordella**, principal rider and gymnast, Australia, 1878. The two were with St. Leon's, Austust 1878; Burton's the following year. Divorced in 1884; second wife was **Belle Celeste.** There was a son, **George, Jr.**, with whom he performed as an acrobatic team, Guilford & Cannon, winter 1889-90; Phil Diefenbach's, 1895; M. L. Clark Shows, 1896. Died of consumption in St. Louis, MO.

WAMBOLD, HARRY. (1848-November 28, 1889) Some 25 years involved in the performance of aerial and gymnastic feats. Brother of **George Wambold.** Married **Lottie Aymar** around 1874. Wambold & Whitby, 1861; horizontal bars, DeMott & Ward, 1868; walked from ground to the top of center pole and back, Haight & Co.'s Empire City, 1871. Treasurer, Walter B. Aymar's, South America, early 1870s; the troupe returned to the United States, 1875, and performed at Bidwell's Acadamy of Music, New Orleans. Dr. James L. Thayer's, 1877; Howes & Cushing, 1877; Lowande's Great Brazilian, 1877. Died of a stroke.

WAMBOLD, JAMES F. (March 4, 1834-June 15, 1901) Clown and minstrel performer. Born in Newark, NJ. As a young man learned the trade of trunk maker. Devoted himself to the banjo and became a member of a local minstrel troupe with which his brother, David S. Wambold, was associated. Later, joined Spalding's *Floating Palace*. Afterward, Backus' Minstrels, Chicago, where he became a popular comedian, assuming the name of **Senor Wamboldi.** Next, traveled with the Sands & Nathans as a clowns; also, George F. Bailey & Co., 1861-69; Adam Forepaugh's, 1867. An expert whistler and imitator of sounds of birds, frogs, turtles, using the banjo as accompaniment. Last engaged, clown, Henry Barnum's, where he developed an ailment caused by the use of bismuth and antimony for whitening the face. Admitted to the Overbrook Insane Asylum on Camden St., Newark, NJ, and remained there some 26 years prior to his death.

WARD, CAROLINA. Child performer, DeMott & Ward, 1868.

WARD, DOC. G. G. Grady's, 1868.

WARD, EDDIE. Griffith & Allen, 1886.

WARD, FRANK A. Pad rider. New York Champs Elysees, 1866; James M. French's, 1869; program agent, Stevens &

Begun, 1874; bareback rider, H. Harlan's Great Inter-Ocean, 1875.

WARD, GEORGE. James M. Nixon's, fall 1870.

WARD, IRA C. Ward's Great London Shows (formerly **Charles Lee's**, Ira C. Ward, proprietor and manager), 1897.

WARD, JAMES M. (d. October 28, 1888) Clown and juggler. Aaron Turner's, 1848-57; George F. Bailey & Co., 1857, 1862, 1864; James M. Nixon's, 1860; Bailey & Co. at Spalding & Rogers' Academy of Music, New Orleans, winter 1863-64 (this being the first equestrian exhibition in that city in 3 years); Tom King's, 1864; Gardner & Hemmings, Front Street Theatre, Baltimore, 1866; slack-rope, George Metcalfe's Hippotheatron, St. Louis, 1866; New York Champs Elysees, 1866; Stone, Rosston & Murray, Front Street Theatre, Baltimore, winter 1866-67; Adam Forepaugh's, 1867; proprietor, clown, slack-rope performer, hat spinner and juggler, DeMott & Ward, 1868; Campbell's, 1869-70, 1878; Philadelphia Circus, winter 1870-71; Hemmings & Cooper, 1871; Sheldenburger's, 1871; Trimble's Varieties (with an act called "At Home In The Air."), Pittsburgh, 1872; James E. Cooper's, 1872-74; Haight's Great Southern, 1874; Cooper and Bailey, 1875; concert privilege and clown, Rothschild & Co., 1876; Campbell's, 1878; Batcheller & Doris, 1879; John B. Doris' Inter-Ocean, 1883; O'Brien, Handenberger, Astley & Lowanda, 1884. Married widow of clown **Charles Parker** in Philadelphia, 1875. While performing on the trapeze at the London Theatre, St. Louis, fell 30' to his death.

WARD, L. P. Horizontal bar performer, Lee & Ryland, California, and other west coast locations, winter 1866-67.

WARD, MARTIN. (d. October 20, 1869) Animal keeper. Got started with Mabie's Menagerie and then was connected with Yankee Robinson's. Died in Sherburne, NY, age 24

WARD, THOMAS T. "HI TOM." Clown and leaper. Early on, apprentice to **Wally Ward**. He did a song and dance in the concert and leaped and tumbled in the circus program. [Charles H. Day: "Ward was a cyclone of wind and the top of the canvas used to flop when he talked. He blew a perfect gale with his mouth."] With James P. Johnson's, 1870; Michael O'Conner & Co., 1870; trick clown, L. B. Lent's, 1874, 1876; John H. Murray's, 1877; Cooper, Bailey & Co., 1880; Sells Bros.', 1882; John B. Doris' Inter-Ocean, 1884.

WARD, WILLIAM. Clown and juggler. Cooke's Equestrian Troupe (James M. Nixon, proprietor), Niblo's Garden, NYC, 1860; Silas Dutton's, winter 1879-80, 1880.

WARD, WALLY. Privileges, John H. Murray's. Earlier, kept a hotel and later ran a variety theatre, Newark, NJ.

WARE, WILLIAM. English bounding jockey, Frank A. Gardner's, South America, 1895.

WARING, HIRAM. Co-proprietor, Waring, Tufts & Co., 1833-34; Raymond-Ogden-Waring, 1835.

WARING, NOELL E. (d. February 1, 1854) One of the earliest exhibitors of menageries in this country, in partnership with James A. Raymond in the firm of Raymond & Waring for several years. Manager, Mammoth Exhibition from Zoological Institute, New York, 1836; manager, Association's Celebrated Menagerie and Aviary from the Zoological Institute, Baltimore, 1837; proprietor, Noel E. Waring's winter circus, 1837-38; manager, Waring, Raymond & Co., 1839; proprietor, Raymond & Waring, 1840; Philadelphia Circus, 1840; Waring & Raymond, 1842; Raymond & Waring's Grand Zoological Exhibition, 1846-47. Died in New Orleans.

WARNER, BEN. Band leader and layer-out, Gregory Bros.' Metropolitan, 1885.

WARNER, CHARLES. Lion tamer, with Chiarini's. Died of small pox, Calcutta, June 2, 1881.

WARNER, CHARLES. (d. August 30, 1865) Native of Great Barrington, MA. First engaged by **Dan Rice**, 1856, as treasurer, a position he held until 1860. Married **Mrs. Rice**, fall 1861. Following year, Mrs. Rice's Great Show (managed by **George Goodwin**); O'Brien's National Circus, 1863; proprietor, circus at National Hall, Market Street, Philadelphia, winter 1863-64, and then on the road. Died at Sam Miller's Hotel, Philadelphia, age 34.

WARNER, CHARLES H. Gymnast, Kincade's, 1871.

WARNER, HANFORD. (d. February 16, 1910) Many years manager of "Wild Men of Borneo," **Plutano** and **Waino**. Died at his home in Waltham, MA.

WARNER, HENRY D. (d. June 12, 1905) Brother of **Joel E. Warner**. Contracting agent, J. E. Warner & Co., 1871; Warner & Henderson, 1874; Springer's Royal Cirq-Zoolodon, 1875. Veteran of the Civil War. Settled in Lansing, MI, after retiring from the circus business; at various times holding the offices of Deputy Sheriff, City Marshal, and Justice of the Peace and for 2 years prior to death was clerk of the Municipal Court. Died at his home in Lansing, age 64.

WARNER, J. C. Great Australian Show, 1880.

WARNER, JOSEPH E. ["Joel"]. (1831-May 21, 1914) Born in Genessee County, NY. Introduction into show business was as a magician, 1850, at the age of 18; traveled through the Middle-west and South, closing with 100 nights at American Museum, New Orleans, winter 1853-54, under the management of **Dan Rice**. Joined Spalding & Rogers as assistant agent under **Van Orden**, spring 1854, and remained with that company for 9 years, summer and winter. Agent, New Davis' Ohio Minstrels, organized in Cincinnati, OH, in October, 1855, by **Dr. Gilbert R. Spalding** and **Charles Rogers** (steamboat *Banjo* was built expressly for this band to visit the river towns of the West and South, starting at Lawrenceburg, IN). Dan Rice's, 1862-63; general agent, Adam Forepaugh's, 1865, for 3 years; following, Brien's; then rejoined Forepaugh and remained with him until 1871, when he started a show called J. E. Warner & Co.'s Great Pacific Menagerie and Circus, with **John O'Brien** and **P. Ryan** as partners; 2 seasons later, sold out to **O'Brien**. 1873, organized J. E. Warner's

Great Pacific Museum, Menagerie and Circus; sold a one-third interest to Henderson & Springer, 1874; merged the show into what was called Springer's Royal Cirqzoolodon, with Warner as manager, 1875, but the partnership was dissolved in the fall of that year. Managed a show under his name but owned by **D. B. Lincoln**, 1876. Engaged by E. D. Colvin following year to act as general director of Montgomery Queen's. In the fall of that year returned to his farm home near Lansing, MI. Elected Mayor of that city on the Democratic ticket, 1878; also served at various times as city clerk, alderman, and twice as a member of the board of police and fire commissioners. 1879. General manager advance department, Cooper, Bailey & Co., 1880; excursion agent, Barnum, Bailey & Hutchinson, 1881; with the merging of Barnum and Bailey, became a representative for that circus. Went to Europe for that concern, September 27, 1882. Claimed to have been responsible for the importation of the elephant Jumbo, as well as "The Wild Man from Borneo." Around 1889, retired from the circus business and became prominent in the Central Michigan Agricultural Society and occupied himself with lecturing. Died in Lansing, age 82.

WARNER, MORRIS H. Press agent, Barnum & Bailey, 1886.

WARNER, MRS. CHARLES [formerly Margaret Ann "Maggie" Rice]. *Manège* equestrienne. Was **Mrs. Dan Rice**, divorced in 1861. Probably born and married in Pittsburgh. Began performing with Rice, 1848. With her horses, Surry and Arab, Dan Rice's 1856-59; Goodwin & Wilder, 1862; began profiting from the Rice name with Mrs. Warner's National Circus at National Hall, Philadelphia, winter 1862-63; brought with her her stock of horses, including the performing horse Surry and trained mules John C. Heenan and Tom Sayers; Brian's Circus with Mrs. Dan Rice, 1863; Mrs. Charles H. Warner's Great National Circus, Continental Theatre, Philadelphia, winter 1864-65; New American Theatre, Philadelphia, winter 1865-66; also Palmer's Great Western, 1866; Hemmings, Cooper & Whitby, 1869; Mrs. Charles Warner's Champion Circus, corner of 10th and Callowhill, Philadelphia, winter 1869-70; proprietor, Philadelphia Circus (performing a dancing horse, Champion), winter 1870-71; E. Stowe's Northwestern, 1871; Cosmopolitan, 1871-72.

WARNER, WILLIAM. John Wilson's, California, 1873; manager, Beckett's, 1881.

WARREN, CHARLES. Door keeper, P. T. Barnum's, 1872.

WARREN, GEORGE. Gymnast, Alexander Robinson's, 1875.

WARREN, MILLIE. Performed trick pony, Adam Forepaugh's, 1872; W. H. Harris' Nickel-Plate, 1885. Married **B. F. Allen**, also with the Harris show, July 25, 1885.

WASHBURN, E. S. (1826-August 15, 1889) Proprietor and manager. Adopted **Leon W. Washburn**. Washburn's Great Indian Amphitheatre and Circus, 1854-57; proprietor, Washburn's Last Sensation, a hall show for several seasons beginning in 1866.

WASHBURN, SAMUEL. Co-proprietor, Gregory, Washburn & Co., 1834-35.

WASHBURN, GRACE. Rider, Sig. Sautelle's, 1897.

WASHBURN, J. H. Menagerie operator, Gregory, Washburn & Co., 1830s, and stockholder in the Zoological Institute.

WASHBURN, LEON WELLS. (d. October 22, 1930) Adopted son of **E. S. Washburn**. Proprietor, Washburn Pavillion Show, 1881; Washburn's United Monster Shows, 1882-83; Washburn & Hunting, 1884, during which partnership was dissolved but title continued by Washburn; proprietor, Stetson's "Uncle Tom's Cabin" Co., 1890; Washburn & Arlington's Circus, 1890; advertised for new partner, 1891; Washburn's Great Eastern, show attached by San Francisco customs authorities for smuggling 10 horses into the country, 1893; Leon W. Washburn's Circus, 1895-97; menagerie sold to LaPearl, 1897; show closed in May 1902 for small pox, season called off; Washburn Dog and Pony Show (or Washburn & D'Alma), 1905-06; advertised show for sale, 1917.

WASHBURN, WILLIE. (d. February 1907) Perhaps the son of **E. S. Washburn**. Gymnast, Shelby, Pullman & Hamilton, 1881.

WASHBURNE, LEWIS. Boss canvasman, Great Combination Circus (**George M. Kelley, Pete** and **John Conklin, William LaRue**, proprietors), 1871.

VASSERY, J. Clown, Baldwin, Wall & Co.'s Great Eastern, 1880.

WATERMAN, BERT. Band leader, with Frank A. Robbins', 1881-83.

WATERMAN, DICK. For 3 or 4 years a driver, Burr Robbins'. It was said that he could drive more horses than the average man could carry halters for. Not a companionable person unless you knew him well. Had a repulsive face and a voice to match, and it was seldom that he would speak to anyone. With Robbins, drove 6 horses on the big wagon.

WATERMAN, WALTER. (d. October 4, 1880) Rider. Born in Rhode Island. Debut, Providence Circus, January 1, 1828. Was touring with his own circus through the South as early as 1938. Howes & Sands, 1835; ringmaster, Drury, Van Tassle, Brown & Co., 1837; 2-horse rider, Brown & Mills, 1838, took over the management around March of that year as Waterman & Co.; Hobby & Pratt, 1842; Ogden & Hobby, 1842; equestrian director, Waring & Raymond, 1842; Howes & Mabie, 1844-46; 2 and 4-horse rider, E. F. Mabie's, 1847-51; 2-horse rider and equestrian director, P. A. Older & Co.'s, 1852; equestrian director and 4-horse rider, H. Buckley & Co., 1856-57, 1860, 1861-62; Mabie's, 1862; equestrian director, Howes' European, 1865-69; equestrian director, George F. Bailey & Co., 1874; equestrian director, P. T. Barnum's, 1876-80; later, in charge of importing the trained stallions that were a feature on the Barnum show. Died in Little Rock, AR.

WATERS, LEW. Equestrian director, Valkingburg's United Circus, 1881.

WATERS, SAMUEL. General performer, Thompson, Smith & Hawes, 1866.

WATKINS, JAMES. Boss canvasman, Howes & Cushing, 1859.

WATROUS, F. M. Treasurer, Johnson & Co., 1881.

WATSON, ALEX. Cook tent manager, with John Robinson's, 1886.

WATSON, ANNIE. Weldon & Co. (**R. W. Weldon**, proprietor), winter 1884.

WATSON, BEN. Holland & Gormley (**George Holland** and **F. D. Gormley**, proprietors), 1889.

WATSON, BILLY [r. n. Lyman C. Smith]. (d. December 17, 1888) Clown, Spalding & Rogers, 1859; Courtney & Sanford's Minstrels, a party made up in New York to travel with Courtney & Sanford's Circus in South America, which sailed from NYC, July 23, 1873; proprietor, Watson & Wells', which was sold around 1876; following year, became manager of St. Charles Hotel, NYC. Candy privilege (with **Edward L. Brannan**), Lively's Great Allied Shows, 1878. Died of Bright's disease there, age 41.

WATSON, BLANCHE. Equestrienne, Howes' Great European, 1864.

WATSON BROTHERS [Edwin, George, Thomas]. Gymnasts and acrobats. Seth B. Howe's European, 1864-66; performed their flying men of the air act with G. A. Huff & Co.'s Metropolitan Circus, 1870; Empire City, 1871; Imperial Brazilian Hippodrome and Great California Circus, Market Street near 13th, Philadelphia, winter 1872-73; Dan Rice's, 1873; George F. Bailey & Co., 1874.

WATSON, CHARLES P. (July 11, 1869-June 13, 1907) Rider. Born in St. Louis. VanAmburgh & Co., 1876; Chiairini's, the Orient, 1881-82; Dockrill's, South America, winter 1885-86; W. W. Cole's, 1886; principal rider, Frank A. Robbins', 1888; hurdle rider, Adam Forepaugh's, 1889; Orrin Bros.', Mexico, winter 1889-90; Ringling Bros.', 1891; Stowe & Pubilliones, Havana, winter 1891-92; 6-horse rider, Sells & Rentfrow's, 1893; equestrian manager, hurdle and principal rider, Bryan & Williams, 1894; Charles Lee's, 1895; Sig. Sautelle's, 1896; carrying act, Robinson-Franklin, 1897. An equestrienne named **Lotta** must have been his first wife; married **Emma B. Parker**, a non-professional, a few years prior to his death. Joined the beach life saving crew, Venice, CA; but during a practice session his boat capsized, causing his death.

WATSON, CHARLOTTE. Equestrienne, W. W. Cole, 1886.

WATSON, EDWARD., Herr Driesbach & Howes, 1868.

WATSON, EDWIN [or Edward]. Rider. Howe's European, 1864-66; Albisu's, Havana, winter 1866-67; Howe's European, 1867-68; scenic and principal rider, Howes Trans-Atlantic Circus and Risbeck's Menagerie (Frank Howes, proprietor), 1868; George F. Bailey & Co., 1874.

WATSON FAMILY. Chiarini's, San Francisco, August 7, 1879. September 29 of the same year, sailed for Aukland, New Zealand, beginning a tour of the world. Returned to America after an absence of 4 years, 5 months, and 7 days, having traveled 82,118 miles, visiting the Sandwich Islands, New Zealand, Australia, Java, India, China, Siam, Manila, Spain, England, etc. VanAmburgh & Reich Bros.', 1885.

WATSON, FRANK. Manager, Alex Abar's Pavilion Show, 1889.

WATSON, FREDERICK. Acrobat and rider. Brother of circus performer, **Tom Watson**. Patriarch of the **Watson Family**. Wife, **Carlotta**, a female Sampson; son, **Charles**, a hurdle rider; daughter, **Fredericka**, worked performing dogs. Rivers & Derious, 1859; Dan Castello's, 1866; general performer, Howes European, 1869; C. T. Ames', 1870; Older's, 1871-72; P. T. Barnum's, 1872-73; Stevens & Begun, 1874; VanAmburgh & Co., 1876-77; Burr Robbins', 1879; Chiarini's, San Francisco, 1879, India, 1881-82; VanAmburgh & Reiche Bros.', 1885; trained dogs, W. W. Cole's, 1886; P. T. Barnum's, 1886; equestrian director, Three Melville's & Co., 1889; Ringling Bros.', 1891; Adam Forepaugh's, 1892.

WATSON, GEORGE. Lowande's Brazilian Circus, 1889.

WATSON, HARRY. Dr. James L. Theyer's, 1880.

WATSON, JEANETTE. Equestrienne. Sister of **Lucy Watson**. Howe's European, 1867-70; Newton's, 1872; James Robinson's, winter 1872-73; Montgomery Queen's, 1873; P. T. Barnum's, 1876-78; Chiarini's, San Francisco, 1879.

WATSON, JOHN A. Sideshow privilege, S. O. Wheeler's, 1867.

WATSON, KATE. W. W. Cole's, 1886.

WATSON, LEMUEL. Museum director, VanAmburgh & Co., 1874.

WATSON, LOTTIE. Gymnast and rider. Ringling Bros.', 1891; wire and Spanish rings, Bryan & Williams, 1894; principal riding act, Sig. Sautelle's, 1896; John Robinson's, 1899.

WATSON, LOVELLIE. Equestrienne, John Stowe & Sons, 1871.

WATSON, LUCILLE [Mrs. J. J. Nathans]. (1845-October 12, 1893) Equestrienne. Made debut at Bolton, in Lancashire, England, at the early age of 7 years; soon after, appeared at Astley's Amphitheatre, London. Considered one of the best of her day, described as "a fresh little English girl who rides a dashing act" and "is as pretty as a peach." Member of the famous **Watson Family** of riders, she served her apprenticeship under the English circus rider and manager **James H. Emidy**. Came to the United States with Howes' European, 1864-68; Albisu's, Havana, 1866; Thayer & Noyes, 1867; L. B. Lent's, 14th Street, NYC, winter 1867-68; C. T. Ames', New Orleans, winter 1868-69; James M. French's, 1869; pad, saddle and bareback rider, C. T. Ames', 1870; James Robinson's, 1870; George F. Bailey & Co., 1872; P. T. Barnum's, 1873-74. After marriage to **John J. Nathans**, lived in retirement.

WATSON, M. A. General agent, Beckett's Great Exposition Circus, 1881.

WATSON, PROF. Performing dogs, W. W. Cole's, 1886.

WATSON, SAMUEL. English bareback and 4-horse rider. Billed as the "Champion of England," Dr. James L. Thayer's, 1880; Adam Forepaugh's, 1881, and, apparently, for his remaining time in America. Broke ribs from a fall, May 1886, and sailed for England the same month. Forepaugh's European agent, 1882-83. [D. W. Watt: "He was what was known as the old school of circus people and a high class gentleman in every way."] After retiring from riding, went into vaudeville with a farmyard circus—pigs, chickens, sheep and a gander which he had trained to do almost everything. "You know, as I grew older the riding was not quite as good and I well knew that it would only be a matter of time till I would need a new act," Watson once remarked. "So I took a season off and commenced gathering up these animals that you see here and training them, and within a year's time was ready to start out a show of this kind in a vaudeville circuit and I am now billed six weeks ahead at $600 per week and no open dates." Married **Alice J. Cooke**, eldest daughter of **Harry Welby Cooke**, October 17, 1889, Liverpool, England.

WATSON, TOM. English clown. Brother of circus performer **Fred Watson**. Dan Rice's, 1856; returned to America from England, March 1858; Tourniaire & Whitby, 1858; Tom King's, California Circus, 1858; National Circus, 84 Bowery, NYC, winter 1858-59; Levi J. North's, Chicago, 1859; VanAmburgh & Co., winter 1859-60; Spalding & Rogers, 1860; Howes' European, 1864-66; leaper, tumbler, P. T. Barnum's, 1873, 1876; James Robinson's, 1874. His promotional stunt was to ride in a tub on a river, pulled by a team of geese.

WATSON, THOMAS V. Gymnast and equestrian. James M. French's, 1867; somersault act, C. T. Ames', 1868; winter circus, Chestnut Street Theatre, Philadelphia, 1868-69; Yankee Robinson's, 1869; James Robinson's, 1870; Great Eastern, 1872-74; VanAmburgh & Co., 1881; Barnum & London, 1884-85; Frank A. Robbins', 1888. This may be same as above.

WATSON, WILLIAM [r. n. Lyman Smith]. (d. December 17, 1888) Rider. Courtney & Sanford, early 1870s; Stevens & Begun, 1874; Conrad & Watson's Transatlantic, South America, 1880.

WATT, D. W. Treasurer, Burr Robbins', 1878-79; manager, 1880-81. Began as treasurer, Adam Forepaugh's, 1882, and remained on after the circus proprietor's death when Cooper and Bailey bought the outfit. Wrote a column for the Janesville (WI) *Daily Gazette*, June 1912-March 1920; Baraboo (WI) *Weekly News*, January 1918-July 1918, "Sidelights on the Circus Business."

WATT, FERRIS. Equestrian, VanAmburgh & Co., 1881.

WATTS, AL [Dr.]. Animal doctor and importer, performing surgery on many animals for leading showmen in America. 1870, began a wild animal importation enterprise, supplying zoological gardens and traveling menageries and circuses. Through study and practice, Watts developed remarkable control over most unruly animals. 1882, launched a menagerie exhibition in Boston, where, in one cage, he displayed a collection of notably different temperments and habits—2 lions, 2 hyenas, 2 leopards, a grizzly bear, a black bear and a puma. Held a commission from the Mayor of Boston, being in charge of the municipal animal shelter. His humane and effective methods of care and handling were copied by other cities.

WAUGH, HENRY W. ["Dilly Fay"]. Clown. Born in Greenville, PA, about 1830. Father was an artist and father's brother, **Alfred S. Waugh**, a well known painter of panoramas. Orphaned at an early age, left to seek his fame as a painter but was soon forced to find other employment. Too slight of frame to do heavy labor, became a horse driver on a canal tow path for a time; next, returned to itinerant painting, doing commissioned water colors. First experience with show business, with a panorama of the Mexican War, which he had painted in Laurel, IN. After exhibiting it a few places, he sold it; spring 1851, Waugh and **Alphonso S. Burt** (later a circus agent) were occupied in house and sign painting. Met **Yankee Robinson** the following fall in Rock Island, IL, and were engaged to paint sets for his dramatic company. When Robinson moved into circus management, Waugh first performed, 1857, as **Dilly Fay**, the clown. Later, engaged by Spalding & Rogers for their amphitheatre, New Orleans, and re-engaged, 1858 summer and winter season. Before his death, was able to fulfill his dream of going to Italy to study painting, leaving for Europe, June 18, 1859. Stay was cut short by his consumptive condition, which forced him to return to USA. Robinson described his clowning as "refined, elegant, tasty and very chaste in language."

WAY, CHARLES. Proprietor, Alward & Way, 1883.

WEAVER, FANNY. Concert performer, Dan Castello & Co., 1866.

WEAVER, JOHN. Herculean performer, J. W. Bancker's, 1830-31. When performing in one of the small towns in Canada, the company was charged with witchcraft and law-breaking. He escaped arrest by running away but lost his way in the woods and was not found for 2 days. Weather was damp and cold, from which he took sick and died a few days later, Niagara Falls, and was buried in a church-yard on the banks of Lake Ontario.

WEAVER, JOHN. Manager, European and American Museum, Amphitheatre and Indian Show (**Prof. W. S. Hutchings**, proprietor), 1867, which started out of Louisville, KY.

WEAVER, JOHNNY. Clown, Maginley & Carroll, 1868.

WEBB, FRANK. Holton & Gates' Harmoniums, a minstrel

band was organized for the the Simon Pure American Circus in New York, October 1, 1866.

WEBB, JAMES C. ["Col."]. Boss canvasman. Brother of **Judd Webb**. Spent some years of his early life as a sailor; knew all about making and repairing canvas. Started in the business around 1870. Great Eastern, 1873; George W. Richard's, 1887; also Barnum's, Adam Forepaugh's. [D. W. Watt: "Jim Webb was high class in his business and his services were always sought after; and yet, he was an unfinished piece of furniture, something on the mission style, strong but unpolished."]

WEBB, JOSEPH. Missouri Giant, Robert Hunting's, 1894.

WEBB, JOSEPHINE [sometimes called Josephine Devinier]. Daughter of gymnast **Sydney Webb**. Wire-walker, James M. Nixon's Cremorne Garden Circus, 1862-63; perhaps New York Champs Elysees, 1865-66.

WEBB, JUDD. Brother of **James Webb**. Started in the business around 1870. Became master of transportation, Adam Forepaugh's, for several years. Assistant manager, Great Chicago, 1879.

WEBB, SIDNEY. Father of wire-walker **Josephine Webb**. Gymnast, First National Union (Nixon & Sloat), 1861; James M. Nixon's, Washington, DC, fall 1862; performed trick horses and ponies, New York Champs Elysees, 1865, ringmaster, 1866.

WEBB, WILLIAM. Boss hostler, Reichold Shows, 1897.

WEBSTER, DANIEL. Horse trainer, L. B. Lent's, 1859.

WEEKS, CALEB. With **Gen. Rufus Welsh**, imported animals from South Africa, 1838, including several giraffes, the first exhibited in this country.

WEEKS, CHAUNCEY ROBERT. (March 12, 1812-January 29, 1887) Native of Carmel, NY. Harness-maker by trade, employed in the shop belonging to James Raymond. 1832. Entered into a menagerie venture with Raymond, Raymond, Weeks & Co., and was connected with many of Raymond's enterprises until his retirement in 1855. Married Raymond's daughter, Ada, 1837. Co-proprietor, Raymond, Weeks, Ogden & Co.'s menagerie, 1833; agent, circus managed by **Joseph E. M. Hobby** for James Raymond, 1840; proprietor (with **James Raymond**), Raymond, Weeks & Co.'s Zoological Exhibition, 1843; manager (with **Darius Ogden**), Ogden, Weeks & Co.'s Zoological Exhibition, 1845. Elected to State Legislature, 1847, and again 1856. When Raymond retired, Weeks and Drake took over, 1851; both Raymond & VanAmburgh and Welch, Raymond & Driesbach, 1852; Raymond & VanAmburgh and 2 menageries, 1853; VanAmburgh & Co., 1854-56; the Great Broadway Menagerie, 1854; Raymond & Chiarini, 1855. Sold interests to Hyatt Frost, 1856, and retired, 1857, to Hudson River Steamboat Co.

WEEKS, E. B. Ticket agent, P. T. Barnum's, 1880.

WEEKS, EDWARD C. (1844-1918) Son of **Chauncey Weeks**. Involved in exhibitions of winter circuses in a hall on Sansom Street, between Eighth and Ninth, Philadelphia, 1833-34 and 1834-35; manager, Buckley, Weeks & Co., 1835; Boston Lion Circus (Raymond & Weeks, proprietors), 1836.

WEIGHTMAN, CHARLES. Dan Rice's, 1872.

WEIR, ROBERT. Began career as clown, Victor Pepin's, 1822. Married **Narcissa Pepin**, but divorced, May 1828. Pepin & Barnet, 1823-24; Victor Pepin's, 1827; Asa Smith's, 1829; William Blanchard's, 1829-30; T. L. Stewart's, 1832; J. P. Brown's, 1834; Eldred's, 1834.

WELBY, CLARENCE ["Master"]. With Springer's Royal Cirq-Zoolodon, 1875.

WELBY, EDDIE ["Master"]. With Springer's Royal Cirq-Zoolodon, 1875.

WELCH, CHARLES. Clown. Adam Forepaugh's, 1887; Robert Hunting's, 1897.

WELCH, ED. Advance agent, Bentley's Pavilion Show, 1888.

WELCH, JOSEPH. Clown, Pepin's company, NYC, 1819-20; West's, 1821-22.

WELCH, MARTIN. (d. November 10, 1907) Groom. Born in Burlington, IL. Served **Frank Melville** for 24 years in various parts of the world. First circus experience was with John Wilson and the show's trip to the Orient. On return, was in charge of the bareback and high school horses for Cooper & Bailey, where he first met **Melville** and developed a life-long friendship. Spoke French, German, Russian and Dutch fluently. Died at Bridgeport, CT, age 52.

WELCH, RUFUS. (September 1, 1800-December 5, 1856) Born in New Berlin, Chenango County, NY. Began career at age 18, first as an apprentice to a chairmaker. May have become connected with show business as early as 1825. 1829, took a circus to Cuba along with **Erman Handy**; co-proprietor, Purdy, Welch, Finch & Wright's menagerie, 1832; co-proprietor, Purdy, Welch, Macomber & Co.'s menagerie, 1833-34. By 1834, had Welch & Co.'s Mammoth Zoological Exhibition on the road and followed with interests in other menagerie organizations and in directing foreign expeditions for animals. Took out Purdy, Welch, Macomber & Co.'s menagerie, 1837; manager, Lion Theatre Circus, 1837; Welch, Bartlett & Co., 1838; proprietor, Clayton, Bartlett & Welch, 1839-40; Welch, Bartlett & Co., 1840, but sold out to Bartlett, January 4, 1841; proprietor, Welch & Mann's New York Circus, 1841, the show being purchased from Bartlett & Delavan; Welch & Delavan, Baltimore, 1841. With **Alvah Mann**, converted National Theatre, Philadelphia, into an amphitheatre and operated it as a circus, Welch & Mann's New York and Philadelphia Circus, 1842; Welch & Mann's, Park Theatre and Bowery Amphitheatre, NYC, also Olympic Circus, Philadelphia, and Front Street Theatre, Baltimore, and Military Gardens, Brooklyn, 1843; Welch, Mann & Delavan's Grand Double Circus, 1844; Welch & Mann's Mammoth National Circus, 1845; Welch & Delavan's National Circus, 1847;

Welch's National Circus, 1847; Welch, Delavan & Nathans Circus, 1848; Welch's National Circus, 1852. In all, was active as a major circus proprietor between 1839 and 1853. [Stuart Thayer: "Never a wealthy man,... his ability at raising capital allowed his expansive ideas to become reality, and thus he seems to a present-day observer to have been operating on a sort of treadmill."] Considered honest, good-hearted and a gentleman in every sense of the word. Generousity is said to have been the ruin of him. Died in Philadelphia.

WELCH, WILLIAM. Clown and gymnast. Came to America with West's company, 1816. Pepin's, Baltimore, 1817. In his act he leaped a pyramid of men, a ribbon 12' high, a mounted man and 5 horses. Probably the Welch that was the clown with West's circus, 1820-22.

WELCOME, FRED. Balancing trapeze act, F. J. Taylor's Circus and Menagerie, 1893; Shedman Bros.', 1894.

WELDON, R. W. Proprietor, Weldon & Co.'s, winter 1884-85.

WELDON, THOMAS. Band leader, with Rice-Stowe-Oates, 1881; W. H. Stowe's, 1881.

WELDON, WILLIAM [Prof.]. Band leader, with Ringling Bros.', 1893.

WELLER EUGENE A. Contracting agent, Montgomery Queen's, 1877; W. C. Coup' New United Monster Show, 1879; general agent, Dr. James L. Thayer's, 1880.

WELLS, AMELIA [Mrs. Robert Butler]. (d. May 14, 1869) Equestrienne. Daughter of clown **John Wells**. Philadelphia Circus (Raymond & Waring), 1840; Welch, Bartlett & Co., 1840; Howes & Co., 1848; E. F. & J. Mabie's, 1849-50; clown (perhaps the first female in USA), Nixon & Kemp, 1858; Grand National, 1865; ballads and operatic songs, E. G. Smith's, 1867. Died in NYC. See John Wells.

WELLS, CURT. Clown and tumbler, Cooper & Co., 1874.

WELLS, F. E. McDonald & Wells' Big Show (**George W. McDonald**, F. E. Wells, proprietors), 1892.

WELLS, FLORA. E. F. & J. Mabie's, 1849-50.

WELLS, GEORGE A. (d. October 2, 1892) Associated with P. T. Barnum, 1845. 1850, managed the Jenny Lind tour and traveled throughout the United States and Europe. Claimed to be the discoverer of **Tom Thumb** and his wife, **Lavinia**, with whom he toured 3 continents. After retiring from show business, 1870, became involved in various real estate transactions. Most recently, before his death, was involved in the promotion of Negro prodigy **Oscar Moore**. Died at Bridgeport, CT, age 75, leaving an estate of $200,000.

WELLS, G. E. Curator of natural history, P. T. Barnum's, 1875. May be same as above.

WELLS, JOHN ["Grimaldi", r. n. John Willis]. (d. 1852) Clown. Came to America with Cooke's Circus, bringing with him his wife and 3 daughters—**Mary Ann, Amelia,** and **Louise.** (Stuart Thayer shows 5 daughters, adding **Maria** and **Flora**). Page & Harrington, 1826; Fogg & Co., 1827; Ben

Brown's, 1828; J. P. Brown's, 1831; New York Circus, 1831; Joseph D. Palmer's, 1833-34; Edward Eldred's, 1834; Thomas Cooke's, 1836-37, performing in a building erected on Walnut Street, Philadelphia; Charles Bacon's, November 1837; Fogg & Stickney, 1838; Welch, Bartlett & Co., 1839-41; Philadelphia Circus (Raymond & Waring), 1840; Broadway Circus, NYC, 1840; Welch, Bartlett & Co., 1840; Welch & Mann, 1841-43; Mann, Welch & Delevan, 1844; Welch & Mann, 1845-46; Welch & Delavan, 1847; John Tryon's, Bowery Amphitheatre, NYC, 1847; E. F. & J. Mabie's, 1849-50. Died in Philadelphia. [T. Allston Brown: "An inoffensive man and clever fellow, he was himself his only enemy."]

WELLS, LOUISA [Mrs. Lafayette Nixon]. (d. September 7, 1873) Equestrienne. Daughter of **John Wells**. Philadelphia Circus (Raymond & Waring, proprietors), 1840; Welch, Bartlett & Co., 1840; New York Circus, 1841; Welch & Mann, 1841-46; Welch, Mann & Delavan, 1846-47; John Tryon's, winter 1847; equestrienne, J. O. Howes', 1848; *danseuse*, Crane & Co., 1849; Rufus Welch's, 1851; Den Stone's, 1854; Levi J. North's, 1855; Jim Myers', 1856; Nixon & Kemp, 1857; VanAmburgh's, Broadway Theatre, winter 1857-58; Nixon & Aymer, National Theatre, NYC, winter 1859-60; Louisa Wells' Equestrian Troupe, 1859-60; and James M. Nixon's Alhambra, NYC, fall 1863. Died in Philadelphia. See John Wells.

WELLS, MARIA. Probably the daughter of **John Wells**. E. F. & J. Mabie's, 1849. See John Wells.

WELLS, MARY ANN. (d. April 10, 1874) Equestrienne. Daughter of **John "Grimaldi" Wells**. Sister of **Louisa Wells**. Married **Frank Whittaker**; divorced and married **Frank J. Howes**. Popular in Philadelphia in the days of Rufus Welch. Welch & Bartlett, winter 1840; Bartlett & Delavan, 1841; Welch & Mann, 1841-42, 1846; Welch, Mann & Delavan, 1845; John Tryon's, winter 1847; E. F. & J. Mabie's, 1848-50; Welch's 1851-52; Den Stone's, 1854; Rowe & Co., 1856; Lee & Bennett, 1857. Died in Dover, NH, in her 37th year. See John Wells.

WELLS, MINNIE. Lion tamer. Also known as **M'lle Minnetta**, iron-jawed lady. Great Australian Circus, which disbanded in mid-season, 1870; Metchear & Cameron, 1870; James M. Nixon's, fall 1870; Empire City, 1871, assisted by **W. B. Reynolds**, 1871. Married leaper **James White**, July 7, 1882, Waseca, MN.

WELLS, W. H. Treasurer, Spalding & Rogers, 1859.

WELLS, WILLIAM. Contortionist, Dan Rice's, 1878.

WELSER, SAM R. (1816?-May 27, 1901) Began his career by training horses for **James Taylor** in Pennsylvania, but became a popular clown. June, Titus & Angevine, 1839; Raymond & Waring, 1847; Banks, Archer & Rockwell, 1848-49; made a trip through South America, returning, 1850; Rockwell & Co., 1850; McFarland's, 1852; Mabie & Co., 1853; Whitbeck's, 1854; Ballard, Bailey & Co., 1855-56; Sands, Nathans

& Co., 1856; L. B. Lent's, 1857, 1859; S. O. Wheeler's, 1863-66. At one time he had his own show on the road. Married 3 times. Second wife was **Julia Stacey**, whom he married in McKeesport, PA, 1856, and who died childless, 1886. At 73 years of age, married **Pearl Wilson**, 1889, a 16 year old girl, an apparent happy union until her death, June 6, 1891. Died at the home of his father-in-law, Pittsburgh, PA.

WELSH, GEORGE. Treasurer, Welsh Bros.' (**Col. M. H. Welsh**, **John Welsh**, proprietors), 1897.

WELSH, JOHN. General manager, Welsh's New Golden Allied Pavilion Shows, 1892; manager, Welsh & Sands' Big City Show, 1893; Welsh Bros.' Shows (**Col. M. H. Welsh**, John Welsh, proprietors), 1894 to as late as 1915.

WELSH, M. H. ["Col."]. General agent and proprietor, Welsh's New Golden Allied Pavilion Shows, 1892; business and general agent, Welsh & Sands' Big City Show, 1893; Welsh Bros.' Shows (Col. M. H. Welsh, **John Welsh**, proprietors), 1894 to as late as 1915.

WENTWORTH, HARRY. Main & Burdick, 1879-80; Barnum & Bailey, England, 1898.

WENTWORTH, ROSE. Began as an English pantomime performer, until James A. Bailey induced her to become an equestrienne, probably because of the grace and agility she showed as a dancer. Forepaugh-Sells, 1893; Barnum & Bailey, 1894-1905; John Robinson's, 1898. Although she performed at times as a contortionist and aerialist, was primarily a bareback rider, famous for her cart act which consisted of somersaulting from the English road cart to the back of the harnessed horse while in motion. Went into vaudville, 1906; Pubillones', Cuba, 1907; Ringling Bros.', 1908; Frank Spellman's, 1909; Buffalo Bill's Wild West, around 1913. Retired around 1925. Was married to a rancher and horse dealer, **Ed Carr**.

WENTWORTH, WALTER. Boneless man. With Lipman & Stokes, first-year organization, winter 1866-67; Orton Bros.', 1866-67; Michael O'Conner & Co., 1870; Pubillones', Cuba, winter 1885-86.

WERL, W. T. General performer, Welch & Lent, 1855.

WERNER, GUS [r. n. Justus]. (d. September 22, 1897) Acrobat. Entered the profession about 1891. In an engagement with Barnum & Bailey which opened at Madison Square Garden April 1, 1897, attempted a triple somersault from a springboard over the backs of 2 elephants, which caused his death from a broken spine. Died at St. Barnabus Hospital, Newark, NJ, age about 26.

WERT, WILLIAM. Assistant agent, Dan Castello's, 1868.

WERTZ, CHAD. Equestrian director, Hendry's New London Shows, 1892.

WERTZ, CHRIS. Leaper and tumbler, Lemen Bros.', 1892.

WERTZ, HARRY. Leaper and tumbler, P. T. Barnum's, 1880.

WERTZ, WILLIAM. Of the **Wertz Brothers**; joined the **Albion Brothers** with Burr Robbins', August 1886, replacing **William Albion**.

WEST, A. C. General agent, Shedman Bros.', 1894.

WEST, FRANK. (d. May 28, 1888) Holland & McMahon, 1885.

WEST, JAMES G. Knockabout clown. Pullman, Mack & Co., 1884; King, Burk & Co., 1885; John Robinson's, 1886-1890; Walter L. Main's, 1892.

WEST, JAMES. Landed at NYC, November of 1816, with his circus company from England, after a 44 day trip on the *Chancey*, during which some of his horses were lost overboard in a storm. Had been a principal performer at the Royal Circus, London, since 1805. Being contacted by Pepin, West took his company to Philadelphia, opening on November 28 of that year and closing January 1, 1817. Following that, went to NYC where he was engaged by Price and Simpson of the Park Theatre to produce the hippodrama of *Timour the Tartar*, which ran from January 22 to February 28, 1817. Went on tour—Boston, Providence and other cities in the vicinity—with his equestrian/dramatic company. When the company was in Charlestown, MA, President Monroe was making a tour of New England. West sent his fine white horse, Alfred, to use for his *entrée* into Charlestown. The president graciously accepted the gesture and rode the mount into town and then attended the evening performance. The troupe returned to NYC as a regular circus, erecting a building on the east side of Broadway and Canal Streets, where they opened, August 21, closed September 26, 1817. Movd to Philadelphia and joined Pepin for the winter season at the Olympic, October 3-November 29. Then to Baltimore, closing there January 24, 1818. After which, spent the entire year in the state of Virginia. In Washington, DC, January 13, 1819- February 24. Last engagement in America, NYC, February 11, 1822-August 5, 1822. Then sold his circus holdings to **Stephen Price** and **Edmund Simpson**. During West's stay in America, the company displayed an expertise in presenting hippodramas; using well-trained and excellent specimens of horse flesh; as a troupe, stood out above the others that had previously performed in America. After returning to England in wealth, by 1824 had become a managing partner with **Andrew Ducrow**, which continued through 1831.

WEST, JIM [r. n. James G. Wesson]. (d. July 30, 1906) Clown. Connected with Adam Forepaugh's, Ringling Bros., Barnum & Bailey, and Hagenbeck-Wallace. In early years, was a member of the Whitney & West, song and dance team, also performed on the minstrel stage. After having been a clown for over 30 years, committed suicide in his room at the Windsor Hotel, Schenectady, NY, by shooting himself in the head, age 47, caused by ill health and an inability to work.

WEST, WILLIAM. Rider. Younger brother of **James West**. Came to America with the West troupe, 1816. Stayed behind when James West returned to England and ultimately settled in Montreal; joined Cayetano's company, New Orleans, July 1817; James West's, 1821, apparently leaving West that year in Montreal; following year, gave riding lessons in that city; joined in partnership with **William Blanchard** for performances in Canada, 1823; Richmond Hill Amphitheatre, summer 1823; John Rogers' company, NYC, 1823-24; took out William West's circus, 1825, when he was reputed to have the most magnificent stud of horses seen on this side of the Atlantic; Samuel McCracken's, 1825-26; Albany Circus, February 1826. While performing with Capt. Page's company in Montreal, 1830, his performance as "Billy Buttons" ignited a series of riots by the local tailor's association, who interpreted the act as being an insult to their trade. The same problem occurred when the company moved to Quebec City. Special acts included making 4 horses walk on their knees around the ring and "Six Divisions of the Broad Sword and Tambourine Dance."

WEST, WILLIAM H. Aerialist, bar performer, Lowande & Hoffman Mexican Pavilion Circus, 1887; Burke's, 1887.

WESTENDORF, ROBERT T. Assistant doorkeeper, P. T. Barnum's, 1873; manager, confectionary dept., P. T. Barnum, 1876; program, photo, and candy concession, 1879, chief detective, 1880; agent, Holland & McMahon (**George Holland, John McMahon**, proprietors), Chicago, fall 1885; Holland & Gormley (**George Holland** and **Frank Gormley**, proprietors), 1888.

WESTERVELT, JAMES. Rider, William Blanchard's, in NYC and Albany, 1823.

WESTON, HARRY. Advertiser, Robbins & Co., 1872.

WESTON, HORACE. Minstrel performer, P. T. Barnum's, 1873.

WESTON, LARRY. Clown, Bruce L. Baldwin's, 1894.

WETTER, ALBERT M. (November 27, 1871-October 5, 1901) Proprietor, Albert M. Wetter's New Model Shows. Born in Massillon, OH. His Swiss born father became a self-made millionaire, dealing in coal, stone and banking. Albert, an only child, inherited $20,000 at age 21 and entered the circus business, 1893, fulfilling a childhood dream which ended early in the 1894 season. Then joined the family business of banking and commerce, becoming director and principal stock holder of the Massillon State Bank and president of the Wetter Steel Sand Company. Died from a self-inflicted revolver wound, age 32. [Fred D. Pfening, Jr.: "Wetter had been carried away with his enthusiasm to enlarge his show, convinced that he was indeed a gifted showman—after one season. He spent widely on equipment and hired expensive acts and paid them rail show salaries."]

WHALEN, JIMMY [The Whale]. (b. December 10, 1861) Boss canvasman. Born in Poughkeepsie, NY. As a youth, left home to work on steamboats of the Hudson River and the mule towed boats of the Erie Canal. Joined Frank A. Robbins', 1883-84; Gardner & Lamkin, West Indies, Central and South America, 1885-89; selected as boss canvasman for Stickney & Donovan, Latin America, 1889-90; assistant boss canvasman, Sells Bros.', 1890-91; Barnum & Bailey, assistant to McLean, 1892; boss canvasman, Leon W. Washburn's, 1893-1899; Walter L. Main's, 1900; Forepaugh-Sells, 1905; Ringling Bros.', 1906; Ringling Bros.' & Barnum and Bailey, 1919-1935.

WHALLEN, JAMES H. Proprietor, Whallen's, 1878.

WHARTON, J. W. Sideshow privilege, S. O. Wheeler's, 1867; Lake's Hippo-Olympiad, fall 1867.

WHEATHOFF, HERR. German rider, Grand National Circus, 1865.

WHEELER, ALSON. Contracting agent, M. K. Houlton's, 1893; Wheeler Bros.' Shows (Alson Wheeler, **D. Wheeler**, proprietors), 1894; George S. Cole's, 1895.

WHEELER, BILLY. Clown, F. J. Taylor's, 1891.

WHEELER, CHARLES L. Manager, Herr Driesbach & Co., 1857; agent, VanAmburgh & Co.'s southern, winter 1858-60.

WHEELER, D. Co-proprietor, with Wheeler Bros.' Shows (**Alson Wheeler**, D. Wheeler, proprietors), 1894.

WHEELER, H. E. ["Punch"]. (August 25, 1852-June 19, 1924) Born, raised and educated in Evansville, IN, where he consider his home throughout his career. Parents were **Ed E. Wheeler** of Indiana and **Mary Bowler** of Maine. Began in the circus in an advance force but rose rapidly until he became an agent. Connected with nearly every circus of importance for 50 years, but was principally with the Robinson Ten Big Shows. Got out the first notable advance courier used in minstrelsy for **Lew Dockstader**. Wrote material for minstrel and vaudeville artists. Died of a stroke at the Elks Home, Bedford, VA.

WHEELER, JENNIE. Equestrienne, St. Germain's Imperial Circus, 1889.

WHEELER, MRS. W. S. Female clown, Ringling Bros.', 1890.

WHEELER, SILAS O. Proprietor, S. O. Wheeler's International Circus, 1863; under the firm name of Hitchcock, Hatch & Wheeler, erected an amphitheatre in Boston, winter 1864-65; proprietor, S. O. Wheeler's, 1864. Made an agreement with **George K. Goodwin**, September 10, 1866, for 2 years co-proprietorship of Wheeler & Goodwin's International Circus and Model Arena, but the plans did not materialize; so Wheeler went out with S. O. Wheeler's Great International Circus, 1867; then sold the property to **W. J. Metchear**, 1870. Ticket seller, Adam Forepaugh's, 1873. Ran a small hotel in North Berwick, ME, 1874.

WHEELER, WILLIAM S. [a. k. a. U. S. Wheeler]. (1856-March 14, 1913) Born in Chicago. Began theatrical career as a child. Became a favorite Dutch comedian as a member of the J. H. Haverly Stock Co.; then turned circus performer for many years. Dan Rice's, 1873, 1877-78; Hunter's, 1885; Shield's, 1887; in charge of concert, Heffron's Great Eastern,

324

1889; Stone Bros.' Wild West, 1889; business manager and clown, World's Fair Aggregation and Combined Shows (**Joseph White**, proprietor), 1892. May have managed the Cherokee Medicine Co. later that year. 1895-1908 was a street evangelist. Died at Ft. Worth, TX.

WHELAND, MISS. Equestrienne. Pepin's company, 1818-20, in Philadelphia, NYC, and the West Indies.

WHETTONY BROTHERS [Leonard, James]. Gymnasts. Robinson & Deery, 1864-65; G. G. Grady's, 1867; Hemmings, Cooper & Whitby, 1868; John W. Robinson's, 1870; Cosmopolitan Circus, winter 1871-72; Shelby, Pullman & Hamilton, 1881.

WHIPPLE, J. Niblo & Sloat (**L. B. Lent**, manager), West Indies, November 1860.

WHISTON, J. W. Humorist, Bunnell sideshow, P. T. Barnum's, 1879.

WHITBECK, H. MILLER ["Harry"]. (1820-September 28, 1870) Agent, Dr. Gilbert R. Spalding's, 1842-48; Dan Rice's, 1849-53. Entered into partnership with **Charles Castle** and **Wash Kidwell**, 1854, to form Whitbeck & Co.'s One-Horse Show, performing in a 110' round top, traveling the Ohio River and its tributaries in a steamboat, featuring **Mme. Tourniaire**. Closed an unprofitable season at Pittsburgh in October of that year. Dissatisfied with this venture, Castle and Whitbeck purchased a large flatboat and converted it into a floating theatre named the *Lattene Gongola*, and began in November of that year floating down the river between Cincinnati and Louisville. One foggy night the boat drifted onto a sand bar; discouraged by the unfortunate state of affairs, the two managers said "goodbye" to the ship and its occupants. Business manager, Dan Rice's, 1859; business manager, L. B. Lent's, 1869, and assistant manager, 1870. Died in a railroad accident while the show was traveling on the Erie Railroad. The train had left Middletown, NY, at 5:00 a.m., en route to Patterson, NJ, with 7 freight cars and 2 passenger cars in the rear, but stopped at Turner's Station to check a heating "journal." While there, it was rear-ended by the Atlantic and Great Western express, coming at top speed. Whitbeck was about 50 years of age at the time.

WHITBECK, WILLIAM. Tumbler and gymnast, Alexander Robinson's, 1871.

WHITBY, ELVIRA [r. n. Dunn, Mrs. Richard Hemmings]. (d. October 24, 1930) Professionally known as Mlle. Elvira, bareback rider. Adopted by **Margaret** and **Harry Whitby** at 3 years of age, 1852. Taught to ride by the great equestrienne, **Mme. Louise Tourniaire**, who had a circus venture with Harry Whitby, 1858. The company toured through Pennsylvania and then rented a steamboat and played all the Hudson River towns. Dan Rice's, 1857-58; H. Whitby & Co.'s Metropolitan Railroad Circus, 1859; James M. Nixon's, 1860; Wambold & Whitby, 1861; Brien's, 1863; Mrs. Charles H. Warner's, National Hall, Philadelphia, winter 1863-64; Palmer's

Great Western, 1865; Gardner & Hemmings, National Hall, Philadelphia, 1865; S. O. Wheeler's, 1866; Whitby & Co. (**John O'Brien**, proprietor), 1867. When Whitby formed a partnership with **Richard Hemmings**, after buying out **Dan Gardner**, 1868, Hemmings & Whitby's, Elvira and Hemmings met and were married. Hemmings sold out to Cooper, 1872. Adam Forepaugh's, 1875-1880; John O'Brien's, 1883. Retired from the ring, 1880, after a serious accident in Jamestown, NY. Following her husband's death, she continued to live in their Philadelphia residence on North 10th Street. The couple had 2 sons, neither were in the circus business. Died in Philadelphia, age 85. See Harry Whitby and Richard Hemmings.

WHITBY, GEORGE [r. n. George Cummings or Cummins]. (d. June 1917) Leaper. Native of Lancaster, PA. Apprenticed to **Harry Whitby** and, at times, rode in petticoats under the name of **Carlotta Whitby**. With Great Commonwealth Circus, transported by the boat, *William Newman*, 1879; S. H. Barrett & Co., 1883; Donaldson & Rich, 1885; Menches & Barber, 1887; Walter L. Main's, 1888; W. B. Reynolds', 1892. One of his performing feats was jumping over 11 elephants. Had been out of the business for 2 years when he died in Lancaster, PA, age 59.

WHITBY, HENRY W. ["Harry"]. (1817-November 4, 1870) Englishman who first appeared in the United States, 1843-45. Was considered one of the best horse breakers and trainers of his day. Created family of circus performers which included his first wife, **Margaret**; adopted daughter, **Elvira**, equestrienne and slack-wire performer; **Susan**, his wife's niece; and apprentices **George**, **Willie** and **Johnnie**, all taking the name of Whitby. After the death of his wife, married **Catherine VanCamp** (d. March 11, 1885), of Lancaster, by whom he had a son, **Harry, Jr.** Robinson & Foster, 1843; John Mateer's, 1843-44; Myers & Madigan, 1854; Howes, Myers & Madigan, 1855; Tourniaire & Whitby, 1858; Dan Rice's, 1858; H. Whitby & Co.'s Metropolitan Railroad Circus, 1859; James M. Nixon's, 1860; James M. Nixon's, Washington, DC, fall 1862; Bryan's, with Mrs. Dan Rice, 1863; equestrian manager, Mrs. Charles H. Warner's, National Hall, Philadelphia, winter 1863-64; Palmer's Great Western, 1865; Gardner & Hemmings, National Hall, Philadelphia, 1865; with S. O. Wheeler's, 1866; director, Whitby & Co.'s Consolidated Shows, Circuses and Menageries (**John O'Brien**, proprietor), 1867; Hemmings, Cooper & Whitby's Combination Circus, 1868-69, bought Dan Gardner's interest in the show, 1868. Fall 1870, was shot during at riot at the front entrance in Rayville, LA. He died in Vicksburg, MS.

WHITBY, JOHN ["Johnnie"]. Rider. An apprentice of **Harry Whitby**. Steeple chase act with **Elvira**, Wambold & Whitby, 1861; Mrs. Warner's, 1863. See Harry Whitby.

WHITBY, LIZZIE. Brien's (**John V. O'Brien's**), 1863.

WHITBY, LUCY. Donaldson & Rich, 1885; Walter L.

WHITBY FAMILY

	HENRY "HARRY" WHITBY [1817-1870] horse breaker & trainer	
first wife MARGARET BUCKIUS [1817-1865] equestrienne no issue		second wife CATHERINE VAN CAMP non-professional one son
niece of Margaret SUSAN WHITBY real name unknown equestrienne		son HARRY WHITBY, JR. rider
adopted daughter ELVIRA WHITBY real name DUNN [1849-?] rider & ascensionist married Richard Hemmings produced two sons, non-professionals		

**NON-BLOOD RELATED
USING WHITBY NAME**

GEORGE WHITBY
real name CUMMINS
apprentice rider who
rode in petticoats as
CARLOTTA WHITBY

WILLIE WHITBY
apprentice rider

JOHNNIE WHITBY
apprentice rider

Main's, 1888; Indian clubs, Main & VanAmburgh, 1890.

WHITBY, MARGARET [or Marguerita, nee Buckius]. (1817-1865) Equestrienne. Native of Lancaster, PA. First wife of **Harry Whitby**, who taught her to ride. Had no issue, but adopted a 3 year old girl, **Elvira Dunn**, 1852. Tourniaire & Whitby, 1858; Wambold & Whitby, 1861; Brien's (**John O'Brien's**), 1863. See Harry Whitby.

WHITBY, SUSAN. Equestrienne. Niece of Harry Whitby's wife, **Margaret**. Hemmings, Cooper & Whitby, 1868-70. See Harry Whitby.

WHITBY, WILLIE. Rider. Apprentice of **Harry Whitby**. Principal riding act at 4 years old, Myers & Madigan, 1854; Dan Rice's, 1857; Tourniaire & Whitby, 1858; Wambold & Whitby, 1861. See Harry Whitby.

WHITE, A. J. Assistant manager, P. T. Barnum's, 1874.

WHITE, ALASCO C. (d. March 30, 1909) Animal trainer, famous as a lion tamer. Began with P. T. Barnum. Said to have brought the first white elephant to this country. Died in NYC, age 77.

WHITE, ANNA. Wardrobe mistress, P. T. Barnum's, for over 45 years. Joined the show as a helper, age 18.

WHITE, ARTHUR J. Advance agent, P. T. Barnum's, 1873.

WHITE, CHARLES. Lion tamer. Thayer & Noyes, 1867; Dr. James L. Thayer's, 1869; James Robinson's, 1870; lion tamer and menagerie superintendant, P. T. Barnum's, 1871-73; 1876-80; P. T. Barnum's Roman Hippdrome, 1874-75; superintendent of sacred elephant, Barnum & London, 1884, performing stallions, 1885.

WHITE, CHARLES E. Advance agent, Holland & McMahon, 1885-86.

WHITE, EMMA. Barnum & Bailey, 1889.

WHITE, FRANK. Negro deliniator, United States Circus (Frank Howes, Joseph Cushing, proprietors), 1867.

WHITE, GEORGE. Tumbler and gymnast, Alexander Robinson's, 1871.

WHITE, GEORGE. Keeper of chariots, Howes' Great London, 1871.

WHITE, GEORGE. Minstrel performer, P. T. Barnum's, 1873.

WHITE, HANK. Ethiopian comedian in charge of minstrel company, Whitmore & Co., 1868.

WHITE, HARRY. Trained dogs and ponies, Bailey & Winan, 1890.

WHITE, JAMES [r. n. Will W. White]. (d. October 23, 1883) Leaper, tumbler, clown. Began professional career W.W. Cole's, 1874, where he remained for 6 seasons; clown and principal leaper, Welch & Sands, 1880; Cooper, Jackson & Co., 1881-83. Married, July 7, 1882, in Waseca, MN, **Minnie Wells** (known as **M'lle Minnetta**, iron-jawed lady). Died of malaria, Warrensburg, MO, age 30.

WHITE, JAMES W. Equestrian director, Goldenburg's, 1874; equestrian director, Main's International, 1882.

WHITE, JOHN ["Capt."]. (d. May 1902) Born in Chicago. With Adam Forepaugh's, where, after some years of service, was advanced to manager of one of the departments of the ring performance. When he died, Chicago, from pneumonia, age 54, was proprietor and manager of the London Dime Museum on State Street.

WHITE, JOHN ["Prof."]. Performing dogs, goats and monkeys. Great Commonwealth, 1879; John H. Murray's Pony Circus, 1880; Dr. James L. Theyer's, 1880; educated steers, William O'Dale Stevens, Park Square, Boston, 1883; dog act, Sells Bros.', 1884, 1887; trick goat, P. T. Barnum's, 1886; performing dogs, Sells Bros.', 1886-87; Charles Andress', 1889; Stow, Long & Gumble, 1889; Barnum & Bailey, 1893.

WHITE, JOSEPH. World's Fair Aggregation and Combined Shows (Joseph White, proprietor), 1892.

WHITE, J. T. Agent, J. T. Johnson & Co. 1869; general agent, Romelli & Co., 1872.

WHITE, LIZZIE. Barnum & Bailey, 1889.

WHITE, LON. Sideshow and candy stand privileges, Thayer & Noyes, 1867.

WHITE, MINNIE. Performing goats, Holland, Bowman & McLaughlin, 1890.

WHITE, MRS. CHARLES. Wardrobe mistress, P. T. Barnum's, 1876-1880; Barnum, Bailey & Hutchinson, 1882.

WHITE, NICK. German clown, Sells Bros.', 1877.

WHITE, ROBERT. See Robert Ellingham.

WHITE, ROBERT. Minstrel, Sands, Lent & Co. (**Richard Sands** and **Lewis B. Lent**, proprietors), 1846.

WHITE, TONY. Manager, White & Markowit, 1889.

WHITE, W. W. Principal clown, Cooper, Jackson & Co., 1882-83.

WHITEHILL, CHARLES. Billposter, with P. T. Barnum's, 1873.

WHITEHURST, JOHN W. Business manager, with G. G. Grady's, 1873, general agent, 1874.

WHITING. Keeper, J. R. and W. Howe, Jr. & Co.'s menagerie, 1833-34.

WHITLOCK, C. Scenic rider, Ludlow & Smith, 1841; Robinson & Foster, 1842.

WHITLOCK, FRANK. Rider, E. F. Mabie's, 1847.

WHITLOCK, HARVEY M. Bareback rider. With Buckley, Weeks & Co., 1835; J. J. Hall's, 1836; Eagle Circus/Cole & Co., 1837; Cole/Miller/Yale, winter 1837; Bacon & Derious, 1838; Yale, Sands & Co., 1838; H. A. Woodward & Co., 1838; Joseph E. M. Hobby's, 1839; Fogg & Stickney, 1841; American Theatre troupe, January-March, 1842; Robinson & Foster, 1842; John T. Potter's, 1844-45; Howes & Mabie, 1846; Mabie's, 1847.

WHITLOCK, WILLIAM. Ethiopian entertainer. Welch, Bartlett & Co., 1839; June, Titus, Angevine & Co., Bowery Amphitheatre, 1840; Henry Rockwell & Co., winter 1841.

WHITMORE, O. A. "Famous Clarionet Soloist", formerly of

Whitmore & Clark's Minstrels. Proprietor, Whitmore, Thompson & Co.'s Equescurriculum, 1865; Whitmore & Co.'s Hippocomique, 1868.

WHITNEY BROTHERS [William, Henry, George]. Goodwin & Wilder, 1862; Robinson & Howes, 1864; Hemmings, Cooper & Whitby, 1868.

WHITNEY, CHARLES ["Col."]. [r. n. Alfred Whitman]. (d. May 17, 1894) Agent. World Circus, 1860; Spalding & Rogers, 1861; Gardner & Hemmings, 1862; Maginley & Van-Vleck's, 1863; Alex Robinson's, 1867, 1871; Cooke's, Philadelphia, winter 1867-68; general business agent, Handenburger & Co., 1871; Klicker & Kelly, 1872. Spring 1873, met with an accident which resulted in the amputation of a leg. Made plans to take out Whitney & Co.'s Centennial Circus, 1874, an idea which probably never materialized. At that time, was cashier, Mortimer's Varieties, Philadelphia. Press agent, Baird, Howell & Co., 1874; director of publications, Parisian Circus, Operti's Tropical Garden, Philadelphia, fall 1876; railroad and excursion agent, Adam Forepaugh's, 1877-78; W. C. Coup's, winter 1878-79; excursion agent, Cooper, Bailey & Co., 1879; Adam Forepaugh's, 1880-81, 1884; Mile Orton's, 1883; Frank H. Rich's (**Frank H. Rich**, Col. Charles Whitney, **J. N. Abbott**, proprietors), 1886; general manager, VanAmburgh & Reich Bros.', 1886; treasurer, Whitney Family Circus, 1890; general manager, Whitney's Imperial Shows (**G. S. Whitney**, proprietor), 1892. Died Reading, PA, age 60.

WHITNEY, FLOYD ["Prof."]. Band leader, Whitney Family's New Enterprise Circus, 1887-90.

WHITNEY, GEORGE LEON. (1833-February 16, 1889) Born in Littleton, NH, where as a youth worked in a machine shop. Made debut on stage at the National Theatre, Boston, 1849. Married **Nellie E. Packard** of Nassau, NH, 1852. 1861, established the Whitney Family World Entertainment Co., which consisted of his wife, his brother **E. B. Whitney** and wife, and **Charles Whitney**. Entered the circus profession, 1867, working for others and remained through 1872, at which time he returned to his small entertainment company, continuing on the road until 1877.

WHITNEY, H. J. Gymnast. Worked at times with partners **Charles S. Burrows** and **Sam Shappee**. (with **Burrows**) Levi J North's, 1860; (with **Shappee**) R. Sands', 1862; (with **Shappee** as Motley Brothers) Bailey & Co., 1864; Seth B. Howe's European, winter 1864-65; (with **Shappee**) Spalding & Rogers, Academy of Music, New Orleans, winter 1864-65; (with **Shappee**) George F. Bailey & Co., 1865-67; (with **Shappee**) Chiarini's, Havana, fall 1865; (with **Shappee**) James Robinson's, 1868-72; (with **Shappee**) Great Eastern, 1873; (with **Shappee**) James W. Wilder & Co., 1873; (with **Shappee**) Wallace & Co., 1884.

WHITNEY, JAMES. Irish clown. Wallace & Co., 1884; Mayo's Model Show, 1884; Black Brothers Ten Cent Show, 1888.

WHITNEY, JOHN. Manager, C. W. Kidder & Co.'s, 1893.

WHITNEY, JOSIE BELL [Mrs. Lowell Smith]. (August 1874-December 2, 1896) Gymnast and trapeze performer. Born in Athol, MA. Oldest child of **Charles A.** and **Ada V. Whitney** of the original **Whitney Family**, and the granddaughter of **G. L.** and **Nellie Whitney**, founder of the Whitney enterprises. Entered the profession at the age of 6, and from 1882 to 1887 was featured with the Whitney show. Later, introduced a troupe of educated dogs and appeared in the concert. In her prime, was a musician and an all-around performer. After marrying **Lowell Smith**, a non-professional, December 1893, retired from the profession. Died at her home, Woodville, OH.

WHITNEY, LEON P. Frank Rich's, 1886; Whitney Family's New Enterprise Circus, 1889.

WHITNEY, LILLE R. Equestrienne, Baird, Howell & Co., 1874.

WHITNEY, NELLIE E. [nee Nellie E. Packard]. Married George Leon Whitney, 1852. Owner and controller, Whitney's Imperial Wagon Show, 1892.

WHITSTON, N. W. Boss canvasman, Great Western, 1876.

WHITTAKER, FRANCIS W. ["Frank"]. (1818-1887) The brother of **John S. Whittaker**. Rider, Royal Pavilion Circus/Olympic Circus, 1830; John Lamb's, 1831; Stewart's American Amphitheatre, 1832; Aaron Turner's, 1835; Eagle Circus/Cole & Co., 1837; Thomas Taplin Cooke's, 1838; western unit, June, Titus, Angevine & Co., 1841; clown, James Raymond's, 1842; ringmaster, Welch & Mann, 1843-44; Mann, Welch & Delavan, 1844; Rockwell & Stone, 1846; ringmaster, Welch & Delavan, 1847; 4 and 6-horse rider, Rufus Welch's, 1852; Lee & Bennett, San Francisco, 1856-57; Dan Rice's, 1859; equestrian director, Joe Pentland's, 1859; at Comac's Woods, Philadelphia, early summer, 1860; Front Street Theatre, Baltimore, eraly winter, 1860; Levi J North's, 1860; Tom King's, Washington, DC, winter 1861-62; Gardner & Hemmings, National Hall, Philadelphia, fall 1862; Bryan's, with Mrs. Dan Rice, 1863; ringmaster, Mrs. Charles H. Warner's, Philadelphia, winter 1863-64; Gardner & Hemmings, 1864; S. O. Wheeler's, Boston, winter 1864-65; Gardner & Hemmings, Continental Theatre, Philadelphia, winter 1864-65; clown, Seth B. Howes' European, 1866-67; Cooke's, Philadelphia, winter 1867-68; clown and singer, Great European (**Avery Smith, G. C. Quick, John Nathans** & Co., proprietors), 1868-69; clown and ringmaster, Mrs. Charles Warner's, Philadelphia, 1870; lecturer, John O'Brien's, 1871; P. T. Barnum's, 1873, 1876-80; asst' sup't of amusements, P. T. Barnum's Roman Hippodrome, 1875; ringmaster, D. W. Stone's, 1878; in charge of Roman Races, Brighton Beach Fair Grounds, Coney Island, summer 1879; agent, "The Galley Slave" Co., 1880. As a conductor of the performance, he stood on a table covered with a rich scarlet cloth, timing the differ-

328

ent performers by striking a bell with his hammer. Lost his 14 year old son, **John Walter Whittaker**, September 26, 1867, of erysipelas. At age 60, January 11, 1881, slipped on the ice and fell upon the railroad track in the Bowery near Houston Street, NYC, and was run over by a freight car of the Adams' Express of the Harlem Railroad Co. Right arm was badly crushed and required amputation. Received $10,000 in damages from the railroad but died from the injuries a short time later.

WHITTAKER, GEORGE. Bareback rider, Great Commonwealth Circus, transported by the boat, *William Newman*, 1879.

WHITTAKER, JOHN S. (d. 1847) Rider. The brother of **Francis Whittaker**, equestrian. Made his debut, 1823, with Price & Simpson; Sandford's Mount Pitt Circus, 1826, 1828; Washington Circus, Philadelphia, 1828; vaulter, Fogg & Stickney, 1830; Royal Pavilion Circus/Olympic Circus, 1830; Sweet & Hough, 1835; Palmer's, 1835; equestrian manager, Nathan A. Howes', 1836; J. J. Hall's, West Indes, 1837; Waring and Raymond, New Orleans, winter 1837-38; S. H. Nichols', 1840; Howes & Mabie, 1841; clown, Rockwell & Stone, 1842; clown, Aaron Turner's, 1843; Welch & Mann, 1843, 1845; John T. Potter's, 1844; John Tryon's, Bowery Amphitheatre, NYC, 1843-45; scenic rider, S. P. Stickney's, 1846; Howes & Co., 1846; Mann, Welch & Delevan, 1846. At the Front Street Theatre, Baltimore, with Welch, Mann & Delavan, while he was performing a feat of horsemanship at full speed, one of the "long bills" of the evening floated down from the third tier, descending in gyrations. It fell before the eyes of Whittaker's horse, which plunged in fright, throwing the rider, then reared and leaped forward, striking Whittaker in the head with its hooves, fracturing his skull and injuring his spine. Little chance was given for recovery but he did so and ultimately joined Winfield Scott's army in Mexico for the battle of Vera Cruz, March 29, 1847. Shortly, was wounded and, while recovering, died of fever contacted in the camp. His last words were reported to have been, "Boys, I've rode my last act. It was my best engagement and my last. Give always your horse a loose rein, but never desert your flag." We leave it to the reader to accept or reject such a dramatic finale.

WHITTAKER, LEW. Leaper and tumbler, P. T. Barnum, 1876; clown, Bentley's Old Fashioned Circus, 1895; Price & James Shows, 1897.

WHITTAKER, MARY ANN. See Mary Ann Wells.

WHITTAKER, PATRICK. Rider, tumbler, rope-dancer. Father of **Annie Yeamans**. Mount Pitt Circus, NYC, 1826. Fell from 2 horses while riding at Duffon's Garden, Brooklyn, 1826, and died from the effects of the fall.

WHITTAKER, ROBERT H. Hurdle rider, clown. Nathans & Co., 1882; Frank Robbins', 1883; Washburn & Hunting, 1884; Kennebel's, 1885; Miller, Okey & Freeman, 1886; S. H. Barrett's, 1887; equestrian director, Stow, Long & Gumble,

1889; equestrian director, Hunting's, 1892; equestrian director, Bentley's Old Fashioned, 1895; trotting and hurdle acts, LaPearl's, 1899. Announced retirement from the profession, October 20, 1892, to go into the stationery business in Jamestown, NY.

WHITTEMORE, TONY. Negro minstrel, with Mann, Welch & Delavan, 1845.

WHITTLE, JOSEPH. Lion performer, John O'Brien's, attacked and killed by a lion he was working with in winter quarters, April 4, 1872, age 32. Had been with O'Brien for over 5 years.

WHITTONY BROTHERS [James, Andrew]. Trapeze performers, John W. Robinson's (not "Old John"), 1870.

WHITTONY, FRED. Gymnast, D. S. Swadley's Monster Combination, 1872.

WICKLIN, JOHN H. Advertising agent, L. B. Lent's, 1867-68.

WICKWIRE, J. M. Assistant, Herr Driesbach's Menagerie and Howe's Trans Atlantic Circus, 1868; contracting agent, Lake's Hippo-Olympiad, 1871.

WIGGINS, E. W. Sideshow proprietor, L. B. Lent's, 1876; privileges, Great Chicago, 1879; privileges, Dan Castello's, 1880, sold out to **Ned Foster** in June..

WILBANKS, BEN. Equestrian and posturer, George F. Bailey & Co., 1866.

WILCOCK, JOHN. Clown and comic singer. Driesbach & Howes, 1868; Yankee Robinson's, 1869; Empire City, 1871; Great Eastern (**Dan Carpenter** and **R. E. J. Miles** & Co., proprietors), 1872.

WILCOX, HARRY. Gymnast and tumbler. Gardner & Hemmings, Philadelphia, 1865; Seth B. Howes' European, 1867; Dr. James L. Thayer's, 1869; J. E. Warner & Co., 1871; gymnast, Dan Rice's, 1873; Howe's Great London, 1874; Springer's Royal Cirq-Zoolodon, 1875.

WILCOX, JOHNNY. Clown. S. O. Wheeler's, 1867; Herr Driesbach's, 1868; lecturer, John Robinson's, 1872-73.

WILDER, JAMES WATERMAN. (1833-August 15, 1889) Born in New Hampshire. Entered the circus business through manufacturing a Drummand light and gasworks for Spalding & Rogers, and remained with them from 1850 through the closed of their 1857 season, executing a variety of jobs, from gasman to agent, treasurer, and manager. 1856, managed their Railroad Show, and, 1857, the North American Circus. Organized, in conjunction with the **Antonio Brothers**, the Great World Circus, 1858. Winter 1859-60, the company appeared at Wood's Theatre, St. Louis. After 2 years, disposed of his interest in the show. For tenting season, 1860, managed Niblo & Sloat's. Following winter, with Spalding & Rogers, Old Bowery Theatre, NYC, and at the Academy of Music, Boston, as treasurer and assistant manager. Next year, general agent, Spalding & Rogers' Railroad Circus. Following winter, with **George K. Goodwin**, ran a circus and put on horse pieces at

Howard's Athenaeum and the Academy of Music, Boston. Summer 1862, with Goodwin, ran the North American Circus, disposing of his interest at the end of the season to **S. O. Wheeler**. Visited California, 1863, with a "Polyrama of the War." Following year, with **Goodwin** and **W. W. Nichols**, put another circus on the road. Bought the Continental Theatre with **Sloat** and **Goodwin**, 1865, for a short season; after which, he sold his participation to a **Mr. Wildman**. For a few years his attentions were devoted to interests other than circus—mining investments in California, 1866; the management of the Fusyama Japanese Troups, 1867; and the manufacture of billiard cloth, 1868-69. Back with the circus, general agent, James M. French's, 1870; Murray & Stone, 1871; director, Stow's North American, 1872; manager, J. W. Wilder's International Circus, Chicago, winter and spring 1873; exhibitor of a baby elephant, Wilson's, California, 1875; agent, Wilson's, 1876; exhibitor of small menagerie, Sandwich Islands, winter 1876; agent, Chiarini's, California, 1879. In later years, engaged in boring artesian wells in California. Died of pneumonia in San Francisco, age 63.

WILDES, A. J. Contracting agent, Charles Andress', 1889-90.

WILFRED, GEORGE. Tight-wire performer and slide for life, Wallace & Co., 1887.

WILKINSON. General performer, was billed as the greatest vaulter in Europe. Price & Simpson (**Joe Cowell**, manager), 1825-26. Rode bareback, performed on the tight-rope and did Ducrow's "Drunken Sailor" act.

WILKINSON, EDGAR. Hurdle rider, Sells & Rentfrow's, 1893.

WILLETS, OSCAR. Contracting agent, North American Circus and Balloon Show, 1875.

WILLETT, T. James Robinson's, 1870.

WILLIAMS & HALL. Concert clog dancers, Cooper, Bailey & Co., 1879.

WILLIAMS, ANDY. Banjoist, minstrel troupe, Gardner & Hemmings, 1863.

WILLIAMS, BOBBY. Clog dancer, W. N. Smith's Ethiopians, VanAmburgh's Menagerie, 1860.

WILLIAMS, CAROLINE [Mrs. Williams]. Rider, rope-dancer. Arrived from England with the James West troupe, 1816. James West's, 1817, 1822; Victor Pepin's, 1818; Price & Simpson, 1823-25, December 1826, 1827-28; William Blanchard's 1823; Albany Circus, February 1826; Lafayette Circus, 1828; Brown & Bailey, 1828; J. P. Brown's, 1829-31; Harrington & Buckley, January 1830; J. Purdy Brown's, 1830, 1833 and probably 1832; New York Circus, 1831-33; John Tryon's, Bowery Amphitheatre, NYC, 1844.

WILLIAMS, CLAUDE. Press agent, Montgomery Queen's, 1874; advance press agent, Cooper, Bailey & Co., 1876; Adam Forepaugh's, 1877.

WILLIAMS, CLINTON. Contortionist, with Yankee Robin-

son's, 1862; Frank J. Howes', 1865; Caldwell's Occidental, 1867; clown, Hemmings, Cooper & Whitby, 1869; French trick clown, Hemmings, Cooper & Whitby, 1870; G. G. Grady's, 1874.

WILLIAMS, DAVID. Concert performer, Dan Castello & Co., 1866.

WILLIAMS, EDWARD. Boss canvasman, John Robinson's, 1891.

WILLIAMS, EPH. Black animal trainer and circus owner out of Medford, WI, 1880s and 1890s. Married **Rhoda Black**, December 29, 1892, Oshkosh, WI. Ferguson & Williams, 1889, bought by **R. Z. Orton** when show stranded. Williams & Co., 1890; Williams' Great Northern, 1891; Williams' Consolidated, 1892-93; continued as late as 1902.

WILLIAMS, FRANK. Antipodian Hercules, S. H. Barrett's, 1882.

WILLIAMS, GEORGE. Clown, James Robinson's, winter 1870-71; P. T. Barnum's, 1877.

WILLIAMS, HARRY. Boss canvasman, Sells Bros.', a first year organization, 1872.

WILLIAMS, HERBERT. English clown, L. B. Lent's, just imported, 1868-70; Adam Forepaugh's, 1871; Howes & Cushings, 1875.

WILLIAMS, IDA. Fat woman, John Robinson's, 1885.

WILLIAMS, JIMMY. Clown, Burr Robbins', 1875.

WILLIAMS, JOE. Rider, H. Buckley & Co., 1857-58.

WILLIAMS, JOHN. Spanish clown. Robert Hunting's, 1891; Frank A. Gardner's, winter 1891-92.

WILLIAMS, JOHN H. Lion tamer. Hemmings, Cooper & Whitby, 1869; James Robinson's, 1870; elephant man, P. T. Barnum's, 1872.

WILLIAMS, JOSEPH. Trapeze performer, San Francisco Circus and Roman Hippodrome, 1872; Cooper, Bailey & Co. Australian tour, 1877.

WILLIAMS, LEN. Burr Robbins', 1885.

WILLIAMS, M. J. General performer, Metchear & Cameron, 1870.

WILLIAMS, MORTIMER. Specialty dancer. Barnum & VanAmburgh's, 1866.

WILLIAMS, MRS. WILLIAM. Equestrienne. Sister-in-law to **Walter Williams**. James West's, Philadelphia, 1816; William Blanchard's, NYC, Albany, summer 1823; Joseph Cowell's, Savannah, GA, December 1823; Albany Circus, February 1826; Price & Simpson, 1827; Mount Pitt Circus, NYC, season 1827-28; Sandford's Mount Pitt Circus, spring 1828; J. Purdy Brown's, 1828-29. [Charles Durang: "Mrs. Williams had a splendid figure, an interesting expression of features, although they were not regularly beautiful. She was certainly the most graceful slack-wire performer that was ever seen."]

WILLIAMS, PROF. Proprietor and manager and school of educated horses, with Prof. Williams' Consolidated Railroad Shows, 1892; troupe of dogs and cats, Cole's Colossal Circus

(George S. Cole, John H. Sparks, proprietors), 1893.

WILLIAMS, ROBERT ["Bobby"]. (d. March 14, 1870) Clown. Came to America with Cooks's company, 1836. Richmond Hill Circus, NYC, 1840; S. B. Howes, Bowery Theatre, 1841; Hobby & Pratt, 1842; Howes & Mabie, 1843; Rockwell & Stone, 1843, 1846; Niblo's Garden, winter 1843-44; Raymond, Weeks & Co., 1844; June & Turner, 1844; Rockwell & Stone, 1845; Chatham and Bowery Theatres, winter 1846-47; Howes & Co., 1847; John Tryon's, Bowery Amphitheatre, where he was billed as an "English Grotesque," 1848; June & Titus, 1848; Spalding & Rogers, 1850; Rufus Welch's, 1850; R. Sands', 1851-53; Welch & Raymond, 1852; Mann, Moore & Co., 1853; Chrystal Amphitheatre, 1853; Seth B. Howes', 1855; Sloat & Shepard, 1857; John Tryon's, NYC, 1857-58; Cooke's Royal Amphitheatre (**James M. Nixon**, proprietor), Niblo's Garden, NYC, 1860; Madigan's, 1861; R. Sands', 1861; Goodwin & Wilder, 1862; S. O. Wheeler's, 1864-66; New National Circus, NYC, 1866; Joe Cushing's, 1867; L. B. Lent's (billed as **Herbert B. Williams**), 1868. Died of pneumonia in Philadelphia, age 65.

WILLIAMS, S. Cannon balls, John Robinson's, 1884.

WILLIAMS, SAMUEL. Clark Bros.', winter 1889-90.

WILLIAMS, SHANG. Boss canvasman, P. T. Barnum's, 1875.

WILLIAMS, STEPHEN T. Treasurer, John O'Brien's, 1872; the Imperial Brazilian Hippodrome and Great California Circus, Market Street near 13th, Philadelphia, winter 1872-73.

WILLIAMS, THOMAS H. (d. October 11, 1888) Herculean performer. Born in Boston. Crane & Co., 1850; cannon ball performer, Stone & Madigan, 1850; Hyatt & Co., 1859. South America, 8 years, where he was honored by Emperor Don Pedro I and given the name of Signor Thomas Guilluamus Henrico, which he frequently used in his profession. One of his acts was balancing a rifle with a bayonet attached to 3 chairs hanging from the gun, with 2 swords placed through the trigger guard. Placing the bayonet on his chin, he balanced the lot for several minutes. After leaving Stone & Madigan, 1851, went to England and was connected with Batty's circus during the time of the world's fair at Hyde Park. Following this, toured Birmingham, Liverpool, Manchester, Dublin. See Signor Henrico.

WILLIAMS, W. Acrobat, L. B. Lent's, 1876.

WILLIAMS, WALTER. Clown. A lad when he came to this country with his brother, **William Williams**, as an equestrian with James West's troupe, 1816. Proficient on the slack-rope and later a very good clown. West's during the American tour, through 1822; Olympic Circus, Philadelphia, 1823. May be the same man who was with Raymond & Waring, 1839, and did light balancing at the winter circus at Niblo's Garden, NYC, 1843-44.

WILLIAMS, WALTER V. (April 27, 1849-June 9, 1912) Musician. Born in Earlville, NY. Became a proficient cornetist and later switched to the tuba. Joined P. T. Barnum's at age 15 and remained for 21 years. Also connected with VanAmburgh's, George W. DeHaven's, Montgomery Queen's, W. W. Cole's, Sells Bros.', old John Robinson's, Adam Forepaugh's, Burr Robbins', and Ringling Bros.' Married in Delavan, WI, **Henrietta Rector**, October 25, 1870. Claimed to have covered over 170,000 miles by wagon and some 100,000 miles by rail throughout his professional life. Died in Manchester, IA.

WILLIAMS, W. HERBERT. James M. Nixon's Amphitheatre, Broadway opposite Waverly Place, NYC, winter 1871-72

WILLIAMS, WILLIAM. Clown and tight-rope performer, who sometimes called himself "Chatterbox Gabblejoke." Came to USA from England with James West's, 1816-22; Price & Simpson's, 1822-25; Walnut Street Theatre, 1824; Harrington & Buckley, 1830; Yeaman Circus, 1830; Nathan A. Howes' Eagle Circus, 1836. Brother of clown **Walter Williams**. Wife was a graceful slack wire performer.

WILLIAMS, WILLIAM P. ["Canada Bill"]. Elephant keeper, Adam Forepaugh's, in charge of the bulls, Columbus and Romeo. Killed by the latter unreliably animal, Hatboro, PA, 1867. Had formerly been handler for the likes of Hannibal, Pizarro, and Virginius.

WILLIAMSON, FRANKLIN. Acrobat, with W. H. Harris' Nickel-Plate, 1884.

WILLIAMSON, JOHN. Clown, L. B. Lent's, 1874; P. T. Barnum's, 1874.

WILLIS, FRANK. Proprietor, Great Atlantean, 1878.

WILLIS, JAMES. Clown, Barnum & Bailey, 1893; rider, Gollmar Bros.', 1897.

WILLIS, LEWIS ["Contraband Lewis"]. (1851?-March 20, 1881) One of the rare black riders America produced before the 20th century and the greatest of his race. Sometimes advertised as "The nonpareil Lewis" and "Lewis the Moor." Rider and equestrian director, **John Wilson**, aided in making him a star performer. With John Robinson's, 1867-78; D. W. Stone's, 1878. Particularly successful performing in Russia. Died a few months after return from Europe, age 30.

WILLIS, OSCAR. General performer, Stone, Rosston & Murray, 1867; aerial equilibrist and rope-walker, Stone & Murray, 1868.

WILLIS, RICHARD. Band leader. P. H. Nichols', 1841; Rufus Welch's, 1847-48; Robinson & Eldred, 1850-51; J. M. June's, 1854; Washburn's, 1855; Rowe's, 1856.

WILLITS, C. C. Treasurer, Spalding & Rogers, 1854.

WILMOT, FRANK. Rider. Byram G. Bernard's, 1829-30; Royal Circus, 1831; Edward Eldred's, 1834; Palmer's, 1835; Brown's, 1835; scenic rider, Sweet & Hough, 1835; Howes & Sands, 1835; 2-horse rider, Crane & Co., 1836; scenic rider, Charles H. Bacon's, 1837-38; Robinson & Foster, 1843.

WILMOT, J. N. Rider, Cincinnati Circus (**John Shay, John Mateer, J. W. Jackson, Charles J. Rogers,** proprietors),

1841.

WILSON, ALICE. See Alice Lake.

WILSON, BILLY. Minstrel performer, P. T. Barnum's, 1873.

WILSON BROTHERS [Lewis, Luke, George]. Gymnasts. Lipman & Stokes', a first-year organization, 1866; Perry Powers' Combination Circus, 1867; gymnasts, C. W. Noyes' Crescent City Circus, spring 1870 (former Paris Pavilion, set up in New Orleans under the proprietorship of Spalding and Bidwell); John O'Brien's, 1871.

WILSON, C. Juggler, Old Dominion Circus, 1845.

WILSON, C. A. Advance agent, Stowe & Orton, 1870; press agent, John Stowe & Sons, 1871.

WILSON, CHARLES C. (July 12, 1870-August 7, 1920) Agent. Married **Clara Harris**, daughter of **William H. Harris**. John S. McMahon's, 1892; Rentz & Co., 1893; W. H. Harris' Nickel-Plate, 1900; later with Ringling Bros.'

WILSON, DAVE. Courtney & Sanford's Minstrels, a party made up, New York, to travel with Courtney & Sanford's Circus, South America. Sailed from New York on July 23, 1873.

WILSON, FRANK. Negro minstrel, John Wilson's, mountain towns of California, 1865.

WILSON, FRED. General performer. Spalding & Rogers, 1853-54; Jim Myers', 1856; clown, Sloat & Shepard, 1857. Later, returned to England to perform in music halls.

WILSON, GEORGE. Animal tamer, Chiarini's, San Francisco, 1879.

WILSON, HARRY. F. J. Taylor's, 1892; equestrian director, Great Exposition Circus (**J. C. O'Brien**, manager), 1895.

WILSON, HARRY. (d. June 29, 1890) Contortionist, John Forepaugh's, California, 1888.

WILSON, HENRY. (b. June 2, 1801) Born in England but came to the United States when a boy and appeared at the old Bowery Theatre, NYC, in *Putnam's Ride* as a singer. 1849, went to California to look for gold. 1857, had an interest in the Nixon & Kemp. One of his sons was **Captain F. B. Wilson**, circus press agent. Died at his home in NYC of cirrhosis of the liver, age 76.

WILSON, HUGH. Contortionist, juggler and hat spinner, Haight's Great Southern, 1874.

WILSON, JOHN [John F. McDonough]. (d. February 7, 1922) Bareback and 4-horse rider. Born in Cincinnati and resided there all of his life when not on the road. The name of Wilson was given to him by old John Robinson for whom he worked for most of his career, beginning with Robinson & Lake, 1862. Started with Robinson as a pony boy, later teaching himself to ride. Also broke horses for John F. Robinson. Was at times equestrian director with the show. Married 3 times, his first wife being **Alice Lake**, adopted daughter of **William Lake**. [Robert Stickney: "He developed into the most wonderful 4-horse rider of his day."] Was with the show as late as 1893. One of the most handsomely dressed men in the

ring. Died at the Savoy Hotel, Cincinnati, age 78.

WILSON, JOHN. (1829-August 4, 1885) Native of Scotland. Landed in NYC to follow his trade as a butcher, 1849, at about 20 years old. Obtained employment with Beck's dry goods store as a clerk and later as a window dresser. Moved to San Francisco the following year and engaged in several lines of business. 1859, bought the Sands, Nathan & Quick elephants, Victoria and Albert, for $22,000; which were shipped west in the charge of Dr. Charles Bassett, as agent for the owners; the elephants were the first to be exhibited on the West Coast and, as such, created quite a sensation. With the help of **William Hendrickson**, bought show equipment for $20,000 and put out a circus featuring the elephants; and the Grand Circus and Elephant Exhibition, Wilson & Co., owners, opened at Jackson and Kearney Streets, June 1, 1859. Converted Mechanics' Pavilion, San Francisco, into a hippodrome, 1860; company was advertised as John Wilson's "Dan Rice's" Great Show, the suggestion being Wilson had obtained some of Dan Rice's trained animals, particularly the mules "Pete" and "Barney," and made arrangements to use the Rice name; this may or may not be true—any pair of comic mules could be christened as such. Commenced a tour through the interior of California, Oregon, Washington Territory, and lower Canada; but, before a month had run, a tragedy occurred when Victoria died of injuries, complications from crossing a swift running river. The Wilson circus returned to San Francisco for an October 5-17 stand at the Jackson & Kearney Street lot. From October 30 to November 12, the group occupied the Hippodrome (formerly Mechanics Pavilion), modeled on the lines of the famous *Cirque Olympus* of Paris; according to the *Alta Californian,* this was the largest and best show ever seen in the state; still featured was the performing elephant Albert and the trick mules Pete and Barney; the run finished and the threat of unpleasant times ahead, the show sailed for Honolulu on the vessel *Yankee,* departing on December 26 with a complement that included the elephant and mules. 1862, the wagons of so called Joe Pentland's Great New York Circus arrived in California from the East on March 30 to go out under the management of Wilson, who had just returned to the West Coast from the Orient; the circus opened in San Francisco at the Jackson Street lot, April 6, in a 110' round top. There is no proof that this outfit had anything to do with Joe Pentland; certainly the clown was not advertised in the bills, but the problem with writing him out of the California venture is that he can't be located elsewhere at this time. The stand terminated May 19 and the company set out for the mountain regions; their absence lasted until October 20 when they returned for a twenty-two day stand under the designation of Mammoth Circus and Hippodrome and Joe Pentland's Great World Circus; then the show was taken as far south as Los Angeles for an appearance on November 29 and 30. 1863, John Wilson's Mammoth Circus, with the same program as

332

the previous November, returned to the Metropolitan Theatre, San Francisco, for a stand from January 16 to January 20. By fall, Wilson and H. C. Lee combined their shows as the Mammoth Circus and Roman Hippodrome and descended upon the Jackson Street lot for a stay under canvas from October 23 to November 26. 1864, Wilson filed suit against William Hendrickson for dissolution of their partnership; trouble between the two occurred first in 1859 when Wilson had a unit of their circus company in South America and Hendrickson was managing another on the West Coast; the two had a successful season the prior year and some money was laid aside for real estate investment; when Wilson returned he was informed that Hendrickson's company had a losing season and the reserve funds were used up in an attempt to keep the show running; but this could not be verified because "the books had been lost"; later, Wilson learned that certain real estate had indeed been purchased by Hendrickson using partnership money; Wilson sued for a deed to one-half of the property so purchased, as well as for the dissolution of the partnership. 1865, in San Francisco John Wilson's Hippodrome, on the site of the old Mechanics Pavilion was arranged with two rings, an inner and outer one; in the larger, all sorts of races were contested—hurdle, chariot, Roman, pony, and even running; the smaller ring was used for circus acts. Constructed a circus in San Francisco on a lot facing New Mongomery Street and opened on January 28, 1874. Continued in the business until about 1875 or 1876, when he took his troupe to Australia, India, China, etc. He died in Hamburg, Germany, from dropsy and cancer of the liver, during the time his circus was traveling in that country.

WILSON, JOE. Boss canvasman, Shedman Bros.', 1894.

WILSON, LEW. Leaper, Dr. James L. Thayer's, 1870.

WILSON, NELLIE. Hurdle rider and aerialist, Cole & Lockwood, 1894.

WILSON, SAMUEL. (d. June 4, 1890) Orrin Bros.'

WILSON, SUSIE. Equestrienne. W. W. Cole's, 1886; S. H. Barrett's, 1887.

WILTON, HARRY. Aerialist. Robbins & Colvin, 1881; (with **Dashway**) Nathans & Co.'s, 1882; John Robinson's, 1885.

WILTON, WILLIAM. Clown, Barnum & Bailey, 1893.

WINANS, GILBERT D. Proprietor, Bailey & Winans, 1890.

WINFIELD, JOHN. Gymnast, Sells Bros.', 1879; performing dogs, John H. Murray's, 1881; John B. Doris', 1883. See Gregory Brothers.

WINFIELD, WILLIAM ["Side show Bill"]. Boss canvasman, John Robinson's, 1868-75; boss razorback, 1886-87; boss canvasman, 1888-90.

WINN, MAJOR. Musician, Fogg & Howes', 1826, playing the violin and the hurdy-gurdy.

WINNER, WILLIAM. Lion tamer, VanAmburgh & Co.', 1871.

WINNIE, EDWARD. Gymnast. Madigan's, 1861; Stokes', 1862; Thayer & Noyes, 1863; general performer, Rivers & Derious, 1864; John Robinson's, 1867; (with **Louis B. Carr**, trapeze and brother act), C. T. Ames', 1868; Metchear & Cameron, 1870.

WINTER, JOHN. Treasurer and press agent, Irwin Bros.', 1888.

WINTERS, AL. Supt. of curiosities, P. T. Barnum's, 1877.

WINTERBURN, JAMES. (d. 1908) Proprietor, Winterburn Show Printing Co., Chicago, IL.

WISEMAN, E. L. Director, Great Western Circus, 1876.

WITCHER, FRANK J. Press agent, Burr Robbins', 1874.

WITHE, TOM. Apprentice, Aaron Turner, 1842.

WITHERELL, GEORGE E. Proprietor, Witherell's, 1882-83.

WITHERS, JOSEPH. Band leader. Dan Rice's, 1857; George F. Bailey & Co., 1866-73; Melville, Maginley & Cooke's, 1875; band leader, P. T. Barnum, 1876-77, 1879-80.

WITMAR, CHARLES. Orrin Barber's, 1888.

WITTING, EDWARD. Batcheller & Doris, 1881.

WIXOM, ERNEST B. (d. November 29, 1933) Began in show business, 1888, with the Wixon-Bentley Circus, playing tuba in the band and in charge of privileges. 1889-93, served in the same capacity with the Matt Wixom Circus. Then, 1895-99, with brother, **Van**, took out Wixom Bros.' Circus. After selling it, the two operated a carnival for several years. Then Ernest went into the mercantile business at Bancroft, MI, until his death there.

WIXOM, FRANK. (1864-March 5, 1943) Wixom's, 1891. Son of **Matt Wixom**.

WIXON, MATT. Wixom's, 1885-97; Wixom Bros.', 1901.

WOLCOTT, E. W. Ringmaster, Spalding & Rogers, 1859.

WOLF, JACK. Acrobat, John Robinson's, 1891-92.

WOLF, WILLIS. (d. July 14, 1875) Leaper and tumbler. John W. Robinson's, 1870; Smith & Baird, 1872. Died of consumption at Macomb, IL, age 24.

WOLFINGTON, JOHN B. See Don Santiago Gibbonois.

WOLFSOHN. Acrobat, Madigan's, 1861.

WOMBOLD, GEORGE [r. n. George Wormald]. (March 19, 1858-December 26, 1939) Born at Maysville, KY. In circus business more than 40 years as a canvasman or boss canvasman. Started trouping, 1874, when 16, Sells Bros.' Went to VanAmburgh's, John H. Murray', Thayer & Noyes, Hemmings, Cooper & Bailey; John Robinson's, 1882-83; Sells Bros.', 1884; R. W. Weldon's,. 1885; S. H. Barrett's (Sells Bros.'); Burr Robbins, 1887; French & Monroe's Steamboat Show, 1888. Did steam boating as a mate every winter when not on a show. Early 1890s, George W. Hall's; Albert M. Wetter's; Gentry Bros.'; Norris & Rowe; Gollmar Bros.'; sideshow boss canvasman, Forepaugh-Sells, 1910; Young Buffalo Wild West, 1911-13; Hagenbeck-Wallace; Al G. Barnes'; last trouping with, Sun Bros.' Following, associated with Time Recorder Co., Cincinnati, where he remained 10 years. Also employed for a time at Manhattan Bathing Beach, Dayton, KY; and the Home Stock Co. In late years, lived at the National Elks' Home, Bedford, VA, and, as a Spanish-American War veteran, Soldiers' Home, Sandusky, OH. Died of chronic myocarditis, age 80.

WOOD, ARTHUR. Pinkerton detective assigned to Adam Forepaugh's to keep off pickpockets, sneak thieves, and house breakers. Died in Chicago by falling into a coal shoot on West Madison that someone had neglected to cover.

WOOD, CHARLES K. (d. October 4, 1894) Born in Centerville, VT. At age 12 was employed by a stage company, Spencer & Kingsley, whose route was from Brattleboro to Greenfield. With VanAmburgh's from the time it was formed until it disbanded, with the exception of a year or two when with another company. Associated with **Frank Hyatt** for 19 years, during which time he had charge of the transportation and laying out of routes. With P. T. Barnum's for several years. Entered the Union army and served in the Quartermaster department, Fort Monroe. Retired from the business about 15 years prior to his death in Brattleboro, VT.

WOOD, EDWARD. See Edward Woods.

WOOD, GEORGE. Equestrian director, Wood & Ewers' Golden Gate Wagon Shows (**Charles Ewers**, George Wood, proprietors), 1897.

WOOD, HARRY. Clown and general performer, Handenburger & Co. (**John O'Brien**, proprietor), 1871.

WOOD, JAMES. See James Woods.

WOOD, J. A. Excursion agent, Cooper, Bailey & Co., 1880.

WOOD, J. H. Press agent and superintendent of advertising car, John F. Stowe's, 1892.

WOOD, JOHN. Agent, Homer Davis' New Show, 1879.

WOOD, JOHN A. See John A. Woods.

WOOD, JOHN F. Took over Holland & Gormley, which became the John F. Wood's Allied Shows, November 1889.

WOOD, JOSEPH H. ["Col."]. (circa 1818-October 21, 1892) Native of Weedsport, NY. Received title of "Colonel" from his involvement in the "Toledo War" between Ohio and the territory of Michigan during which he is said to have headed a regiment of volunteers. 1843, moved to Cincinnati and assembled a traveling museum, with which he toured for 15 years. Subsequently, took his exhibition to Cuba, after which he claimed he had taken the first elephant to that island. Opened Wood's Museum, Philadelphia, in the old Bolivar Hotel Building on Chestnut Street and another at 9 Dearborn Street, Chicago, in the Tremont Hotel block, both in 1854. Philadelphia property was destroyed by fire in 1857. That year or the following one, became manager of Spalding and Rogers showboats *Banjo* and *James Raymond* on the Ohio, Missouri and Mississippi Rivers, and continued in that capacity until the Civil War interrupted boat travel on the rivers. 1859, opened an amusement on Lake Street, Chicago, under the firm name

of Donnetti & Woods, "The Great Burlesque Circus," a pantomimic and acrobatic exhibition of "dogs and monkeys." 1861, represented P. T. Barnum in taking the Grizzly Adams bears to Cuba. Bought the St. Louis Museum, 1864. Later, opened Wood's Museum, Chicago, from which he acquired a fortune, but lost it due to the Chicago fire, 1871. Wood's Museum, Philadelphia, proving unprofitable, retired, Adrian, MI, where he died.

WOOD, ROSINA DELIGHT [nee Richardson]. (d. May 2, 1878) Fat woman. Born in Cheshire County, NH. Traveled with P. T. Barnum's, etc. She was the lady erroneously reported to have been lowered from the burning Barnum's Museum through a window by block and tackle. However, she was on exhibit there at the time. When but 19 years of age, weighed 515 pounds. A lady of intelligence and education. Died in Florida, at the time weighing 615 pounds..

WOOD, T. G. Advertising agent, Wood & Ewers' Golden Gate Wagon Shows (**Charles Ewers, George Wood**, proprietors), 1897.

WOODRUFF, TIM. Concert performer, Dan Castello & Co., 1866.

WOODRUFF, WILLIAM. Lion tamer, J. J. Nathans, 1861.

WOODS, ARTHUR. Detective from Pinkerton Agency, Barnum & London, 1884;

WOODS, BEACH [r. n. John W. Woolsey]. (d. December 21, 1881) Herculean performer. Stood 6' 4" inches in height and weighed about 240 pounds. Entered the circus profession as a *protégé* of **John Tryon**. In his act, pulled against horses, had rocks broken on his chest, etc. Performed at the Amphitheatre in the Bowery, NYC, about 1844 or 1845 and later traveled with various circuses. In retirement, settled in Sing Sing, NY, where he is said to have owned property and lived comfortably. Fathered 3 sons and 3 daughters. Died at his home, age about 68.

WOODS BROTHERS. Black performers, with Robbins & Colvin, 1881.

WOODS, CHARLES H. Equestrian director, Donaldson & Rich, 1885.

WOODS, EDWARD [or Wood]. (1820-June 19, 1898) Rider. Born in Albany, NY. Began with a circus at the age of 10 under **William Bancker**. Palmer's, 1835; Bancker & Harrington, 1835; scenic rider, Joseph E. M. Hobby's, 1839; Hobby & Pratt, 1842; John Tryon's, Bowery Amphitheatre, NYC, 1843; Welch & Mann, 1843-44. Rider, Mann, Welch & Delavan, 1844-47, for their Mediterranean trip, setting sail on May 28, performing at Gibraltar, Marseilles, Genoa, Malaga. Following, the company went to South America, completing a tour lasted 11 months. Welch, Delavan & Nathans, 1848-50; 4-horse rider, Rivers & Derious, 1852-61; Gardner & Hemmings, 1862; Slaymaker & Nichols, 1864; Tom King's, 1864; and then retired from the business. Was in the production of *Herne the Hunter* at the old National Theatre, Philadelphia, about 1846. Opening night of this piece, his horse, Fire Fly, was killed by falling to the stage floor from a considerable height. Woods was saved by clutching a beam and hanging suspended until others came to his aid. Credited, along with his equestrienne wife, to have performed the first double bareback act in the United States.

WOODS, FRANK. Contracting agent, Great Wallace Show, 1893.

WOODS, GEORGE. Bareback rider, Spalding & Rogers, 1859.

WOODS, JAMES [or Wood]. Clown, juggler, slack-rope performer, Caldwell's Occidental Circus, 1867.

WOODS, J. F. Proprietor, J. F. Woods Allied Shows, 1889-90.

WOODS, JOHN A. [or Wood]. Press agent, John Robinson's, 1871-75, 1883, performing ponies, 1892; excursion agent, Cooper & Bailey, 1880.

WOODS, JOHN F. Holland & Gormley, taken over by John F. Woods, the John F. Wood's Allied Shows, November 1889.

WOODS, DR. L. B. Purchasing agent, P. T. Barnum's Roman Hippodrome, 1875.

WOODS, MARGARET [or Wood]. Equestrienne. Bancker & Harrington, 1835; Welch & Mann, 1843-44; Rockwell & Stone, 1846; Welch & Delavan, 1847. Wife of **Edward Wood.** See above.

WOODVILLE, JAMES. Batcheller & Doris, 1882; John B. Doris', 1883.

WOODWARD, H. A. Agent, E. F. and J. Mabie's, 1851.

WOODWARD, IRENE [exhibited as LaBelle Irene]. (d. November 1915) Sideshow curiosity. Claimed to be the first tattooed lady in the world. Traveled with Barnum & Bailey to Europe, appearing before royalty, as well as the leading medical institutions on the Continent. Died, age 53.

WOOLFORD, GEORGE. Horse drama performer. **Thomas Cooke's** son-in-law. Made London debut, summer 1825 with Andrew Ducrow's company. 1836, moved into Thomas Cooke's stable just prior to leaving for USA. With American company, 1836-37. Troupe performed in a building erected on Walnut Street, Philadelphia. Wife was a tight-rope performer.

WOOLSET, JOHN W. See Beach Woods.

WOOLSTON, S. C. [Dr.]. Ringmaster, George F. Bailey & Co., 1854-62.

WOOTTEN, P. BOWLES. Livery stable owner on Price Street, Atlanta, GA, who joined with Andrew Haight to take out Wootten & Haight, 1871. Sold his interest in the Wootten & Haight to his partner in the fall of that year. Interested in Wootten & Andrews' Great Southern Circus, 1874. Treasurer, Great Metropolitan Olympia, 1877. By 1879, was a horse and mule trader in Nashville, TN.

WORD, LEMUEL. Animal keeper, Miller, Mead & Delavan, 1834; the Zoological Exhibition from Baltimore, 1836-37; riding master, Waring and Raymond, New Orleans, winter

1837-38.

WORLAND, ANNIE. Equestrienne and tight-rope dancer. Daughter of **Jerry Worland.** With the **Worland Family,** South America, Spalding & Rogers, 1862-64; the Hippotheatron, NYC, winter 1864; Robinson & Lake, 1864-65; George W. DeHaven's, 1867; Dodge & Bartine, 1868; James T. Johnson & Co., 1869; Charles Noyes', 1870; E. Stowe's Northwestern, 1871; Burr Robbins', 1872; rider, Sells Bros.', 1874; Great Pacific Circus, 1877-78; Basye's Great Consolidated Shows, 1879; Cooper & Jackson, 1880; Siegrist, Howe & Co., 1884 Sieber & Co., 1888. Married **Steward W. Davis,** ringmaster and equestrian director.

WORLAND, HENRY. Dodge & Bartine, 1868.

WORLAND, JERRY [r. n. Comosh]. (April 24, 1864) Tumbler and leaper. With Spalding, Rogers & Van Orden's People's, 1851; Johnson & Co., 1852; *Floating Palace,* 1853; Den Stone's, 1854; VanAmburgh, Stone & Tyler, 1855; Welch & Lent, winter 1855; Madigan's, 1856; *Floating Palace,* 1857; John Robinson's, August, 1857; Cooper & Myers, 1858; Davis & Crosby, 1859; Robinson & Lake, 1860; Antonio Bros.', 1861. Spalding & Rogers, West Indies, 1863-64. Met with an accident while there and was sent to NYC, where he died a few months later.

WORLAND, JOHN [r. n. John Comosh]. (August 9, 1855-July 5, 1933) Leaper. A native and many years resident of Corning, NY. Father was a Portuguese immigrant. Began with the circus at age 10, taking his professional name from the equestrienne, **Mme. Worland.** It is thought that he was apprenticed to **Jerry Worland,** tumbler and leaper, as one of the **Worland Family.** Listed with Davis & Crosby's, 1859; James T. Johnson's as early as 1869; probably on his own, 1872, when connected with the San Francisco Circus and Roman Hippodrome; still in California, 1874, with John Wilson's Palace Amphitheatre, San Francisco; Carlo Bros.', South America, 1877-78; Adam Forepaugh's, 1880-84, as trick leaper, participating in a horizontal bar act, and featured as an outside wire ascensionist; Orrin Bros.', winter 1883-1888; W. W. Cole's, 1885-86. Was said to be the only man in the world to repeatedly accomplish three somersaults in one leap from a spring board under a circus tent before a paying audience. First successful attempt at a triple somersault from a spring board occurred in St. Louis, 1874; feat was repeated with Howes' London, St. Louis, MI, 1876; the latter time was marred by his landing in a sitting position rather than on his feet; successfully repeated the feat twice while with Adam Forepaugh's, 1881; again at New Haven, CT, October 9, 1884. Said to be the only acrobat to repeat the hazzardous feat of a triple somersault. [Steve Gossard: Worland "was certainly the only man who ever accomplished the feat often enough to claim consistency and live to tell about it."] Married **Josephine Campbell,** Corning, 1884. Early 1880s, invented a leaping board tail piece which greatly facilitated leaping. Although he patented the device, he donated it to the benefit of his brother leapers. Died at his home in Corning, age 78, where he had been in the coal business. Served as a city alderman and as a county supervisor, and was a Democratic candidate for state assemblyman, 1916. His son, **John Jr.**, appeared on the stage many years, taking his father's professional name. And there were two daughters, **Josephine** and **Margaret**.

WORLAND, MRS. JERRY. Outside ascension act, Cooper & Myer's Circus of All Nations, 1858; oscillating wire performer, Spalding & Rogers, West Indies, 1863-64; Hippotheatron, NYC, with Spalding & Rogers, spring 1864; Great Union Combination, 1865; George W. DeHaven's, 1867; Dodge & Bartine, 1868; equestrienne and *manège* act, James T. Johnson's & Co., 1869. Married **Henry McGuffin** on the Lipman Circus, May 20, 1866, in Alleghany City, PA.

WORLAND, MILLIE. Australian Dime Show, 1887.

WORLAND, WILLIAM. Howes' Great London, 1876-77.

WORLEN, JESSE. Treasurer, King & Franklin, 1889; J. H. LaPearl, 1893.

WORRELL, FRANK. Herr Driesbach's, 1856.

WORRELL SISTERS [Sophia, Jenny, Irene]. Concert entertainers. Famous daughters of the clown and comedian, **William Worrell**. Performed in the circus ring with him in California in the late 1850s and early 1860s. Went onto the stage as children, singing and dancing their way to popularity in California and Australia. [M. B. Leavitt: They were "exceptionally pretty and attractive, and one of them, Jenny, who was a very clever and spirited clog dancer, made a great hit."] Murphy & Bray's Minstrels, American Theatre, San Francisco, and a tour of California, 1864; Bowery Theatre, NYC, July 10, 1865, to August 11, 1865; 1866, took over the theatre on Broadway opposite Waverley Place, calling it the Worrell Sisters' New York Theatre. Increased interest in burlesque, inspired by **Lydia Thompson** and her British Blonde Brigade, 1868, was instrumental in developing the popularity of the sisters. October, 1868, they leased the old New York Theatre and produced the burlesque of *The Field of the Cloth of Gold.* **Irene** was married to **E. Eddy, Jr. Sophie** married German dialect comedian **George S. Knight**. She is said to have been the inventor of the pleated skirt. She died in New Orleans, 1917. A third sister, **Jennie**, born in 1850 in Cincinnati, OH, died on August 11, 1899, in Brooklyn, NY, from burns she received while asleep on a Coney Island meadow; the grass burned over a large area and when the fire was extinguished, her body was discovered. **Sophie** and **Irene** had separated from **Jennie** some time before her death because of her "habits." She was married to **Mike Murray**, a known gambler, later divorced. Second husband was **J. A. Chatfield**.

WORRELL, WILLIAM. (1823-August 7, 1897) Clown and black face comedian, known as "The Original Cheap John." Born in Cincinnati, the son of **Judge Worrell**, and educated as

a civil engineer. Apprenticed in the circus business with old John Robinson. Later, took the first American circus to Australia, built a ring on the theatre's stage and gave "horse pieces" with considerable success. Ethiopian entertainer, Clayton, Bartlett & Welch, 1840; Robinson & Foster, 1843; Stickney & Buckley, 1844; clown, Great Western (**Dennison Stone, Eaton Stone, Thomas McCollum**, proprietors), 1846; clown and minstrel, S. P. Stickney's, 1847-49; Great Western (Stone & McCollum, proprietors), 1849; clown, Stokes, Germaine & LaThorne, 1850, which traveled by steamer to the headwaters of the Mississippi River and back again to New Orleans; Welch & Lent, 1851, 1854-55; Welch's National, winter 1856. With his illustrious daughters, visited California and took engagements with Lee & Bennett, San Francisco, 1857; H. C. Lee's, 1858; Australia, 1859-61; Lee, Worrell & Sebastian, 1863; John Wilson's, Metropolitan Theatre, San Francisco, 1863-65; proprietor, Worrell's Theatre, San Francisco, 1865. The family returned East and performed in NYC, 1866. George W. DeHaven's, 1866; Adam Forepaugh's, Philadelphia, 1866; James M. Nixon's Amphitheatre, Broadway opposite Waverly Place, NYC, winter 1871-72; Nixon's Amphitheatre, Chicago, 1872. Retired, Little Neck, LI. 1874, was in the auction business in Scranton, PA. "Billy" Worrell, one of the best known clowns in the circus business, died of pneumonia, Newark, NJ.

WORTLEY, ED. Clown, Sparks', 1891.

WORTH, CARLOTTA. William O'Dale Stevens', Park Square, Boston, June 1883.

WORTHINGTON, DAVID. Assistant manager, Great International Circus (**James E. Cooper, James A. Bailey, Robert S. Hood, David Worthington** proprietors), 1874.

WORTHINGTON, PROF. [and wife]. Double trapeze and slack-rope, Holland, Bowman & McLaughlin, 1890.

WREN, W. G. Clown. Hurlbut & Hunting, 1885; Miller & Runnells, 1888.

WRIGHT, BILLY. George W. Richards', winter 1889-90.

WRIGHT, CHARLES. See Charles Antonio.

WRIGHT, CHARLES. (1792-1862) Born in Somers, NY. First appeared in circus performances as an employee of Finch & Bailey in their exhibition of the elephant "Betty" or "Little Bet," 1822; New Caravan of Living Animals, supposedly under the ownership of Carley and Purdy, 1826; by 1828, part of that concern; Carley, Purdy & Wright's menagerie, 1830; co-proprietor, Purdy, Welch, Finch & Wright's menagerie, 1832; Purdy, Welch, Finch & Wright, menagerie, 1832. May have been first "lion keeper" in America, since he was advertised as entering a lion's den as early as 1829.

WRIGHT, EDWARD A. General agent, Hilliard & Hamilton, 1875.

WRIGHT, JOHN B. Singing clown, E. O. Rogers', 1891.

WRIGHT, R. L. Agent. Great Western (**Dennison Stone, Eaton Stone, Thomas McCollum**, proprietors), 1846; Robinson & Eldred, 1850; St. Louis Amphitheatre, 1852.

WRIGHT, TULLUS. Billed as the youngest American Hercules, 4th season, Charles Lee's Great London Show, 1896.

WRIGHT WILLIAM F. General manager, Beckett's, 1887; general manager and contracting agent, George W. Richards', winter 1889-90.

WURTH, FRANK. Press agent, Bruce L. Baldwin's, 1894.

WYANT, FRANK. Booker & Howard's Minstrels, L. B. Lent's, 1865.

WYATT, ANDY "PROF." Violinist, Hippocomique, 1868.

WYATT, THOMAS. Born in NYC. Pupil of Aaron Turner, 1842-53. Rider, James Myers', 1856; VanAmburgh & Co., 1857; Eldred's, 1858; Mabie's, 1860; S. O. Wheeler's, 1863.

WYNNE, EDWARD. 4-horse chariot driver, Howes & Cushing, 1875.

Y & Z

YAGES, PROF. Aeronaut, G. G. Grady's, 1872.

YAKERS, GEORGE. Acrobat, Palmer's Pavilion Circus, 1836.

YALE, ENOCH C. Showman. Started in menagerie management with Miller, Yale, Sands & Co., 1835. Continued in the profession for several years, sometimes in association with **Richard Sands**. Miller, Yale, Sands & Co, 1835-38; co-proprietor, Miller, Yale & Howes, 1838; E. C. Yale & Co.'s National Circus, 1840; manager, Sands & Lent, 1842; treasurer, Franconi's Hippodrome, 1853.

YAMADIVA. Contortionist. James M. Nixon's Amphitheatre, Chicago, 1872; Barnum's Roman Hippodrome, NYC, winter 1874-75.

YAMAMOTA BROTHERS. Japanese balancers, Cooper & Co. (**J. R. W. Hennessey**, proprietor and manager), 1897.

YATES, ANNIE. Race rider, P. T. Barnum's Roman Hippodrome, 1875; hippodrome jockey, Barnum, Bailey & Hutchinson, 1882.

YATES, FRANK. Press agent, Alexander Robinson's, 1871. This may be the Yates who was a general performer with H. P. Madigan's, 1856.

YATES, GEORGE. Press agent with Alexander Robinson's, 1875.

YEAMAN, ANNIE. (Novermber 19, 1835-March 3, 1912) Equestrienne. Born on the Isle of Man. Made her debut in Sydney, Australia, 1845; following year, Malcolm's Circus, then joined J. A. Rowe's Australian Circus, billed as "La Sylphide—Equestrienne Extraordinaire"; Risley's, a tour of China and Japan, 1859; Metcalfe's, United States, 1867. Ultimately, gravitated to the stage when **Augustin Daly** engaged her to appear at the Grand Opera House, NYC, 1872; followed with engagements with A. M. Palmer in *Lights of London*, Union Square; **Harrigan and Hart** in *The Mulligan Guard Ball*, etc. Daughter, **Jennie**, followed in her theatrical footsteps. Died of a stroke, NYC, age 77.

YEAMAN, GEORGE. (d. November 1827) Rider. Born in Scotland. Came to America from England with James West's troupe, 1816, and established his reputation here as a leading rider within a few years. [Charles Durang: "George Yeaman was a modest and well behaved young man."] With West & Co., leaped and somersaulted over 6 men and a wagon, 1821; with the circus when West sold out to Price & Simpson, 1823; appears to have stayed on with the new owners. Lafayette Amphitheatre, NYC, in its initial season, 1825; William Harrington's, 1825; Asa Smith's, 1828; Fogg & Co., 1828. Judged as a competent but not outstanding rider, billed as "The Flying Horseman," was agile and neat in execution, presenting a variety of attitudes and novel saddle tricks, which included

throwing backward and forward somersaults. In leaping act, somersaulted over 6 men and a wagon. Married an equestrienne, 1825, and performed with her until his death. Died in Concord, NC. **Asa T. Smith** married his widow, 1829.

YEDDO JAPANESE TROUPE. Nixon's Amphitheatre, Chicago, 1872

YEPPO. Wild African boy, P. T. Barnum, 1876-77.

YOUNG, CHARLES. Ventriloquist, Palace of Wonders, P. T. Barnum, 1876.

YOUNG, D. Contortionist and Indian rubber man. A. Hunt & Co., 1838; S. H. Nichols', 1840; Howes & Mabie's Olympic Circus, 1841; Rockwell & Stone, 1842; John Mateer's Southern Circus, 1843-44.

YOUNG, FRITZ. Clown, Irwin Bros.', 1888.

YOUNG, GEORGE A. Young Bros. & Baldwin (**William E. Young**, George A. Young, **Bruce L. Baldwin**, proprietors), 1892.

YOUNG, JAMES. Ringmaster, Campbell's Zoological and Equestrian Institute, 1870.

YOUNG, JOHN D. (d. April 24, 1915) Associate. At time of death, transportation manager, Barnum & Bailey. Died in Philadelphia of heart failure, age 53.

YOUNG, MARION [Miss]. Serio-comique, Palace of Wonders, P. T. Barnum, 1876.

YOUNG, MERRITT F. (May 31, 1850-June 16, 1897) Teasurer. Born at Sandusky, OH, the son of a railroad man. Became an express messenger for the Cincinnati, Sandusky and Cleveland Railroad. After the death of his father, moved to Cincinnati and was employed as a clerk in the express office. Later, took new employment as clerk at the Gibson House, where he remained 5 years. 1876, joined Cooper & Bailey as assistant treasurer and ticket seller; went with the show to Australia and South America, during which time was elevated to treasurer. When Barnum & Bailey was organized, Young remained with Bailey as treasurer for that enterprise, a position he held for many years. Died in Chicago, of typhoid fever, age 48. Was unmarried.

YOUNG, T. National Circus, 1847; Spalding's North American, 1849.

YOUNG, WILLIAM E. Young Bros. & Baldwin's Circus (William E. Young, **George A. Young**, **Bruce L. Baldwin**, proprietors), 1892.

YOUNG, WILLIAM H. (circa 1842-January 23, 1885) Rider and gymnast. Born in Philadelphia. At one time a pupil of Dan Rice. The billing promised "the most Daring Gymnast and Caricature Impersonator of his age in the World, will perform a most hazardous feat, jumping sixteen feet through the air, at an altitude of thirty feet, on *l'echelle perilleuse*." For a time,

338

doubled with **John C. Luando** as the **Luando Brothers**. Dan Rice's, 1861-63; *l'echelle perilleuse*, National Circus, Philadelphia, fall 1863; stilt performer, *l'echelle perilleuse*, Mrs. Dan Rice's, 1864; Stone & Rosston, 1864-65; Hippotheatron, NYC, fall 1865; Dan Rice's, 1867-69, 1873; clown and stilt walker, Thayer & Noyes, 1877. Organized a trio of aerial gymnasts, *Les Markoes*, and performed in many of the large cities. Injury forced retirement from performing around 1880. Remaining *Markoes* became **Ashton Brothers**. Died in Baltimore at age 43.

YOUNG, W. S. General agent, W. C. Coup Equescurriculum and Carl Dice's Great German Circus, 1894; contracting agent, the Great Exposition Circus (**John C. O'Brien**, manager), 1895.

ZACCO, JEAN. Gymnast, Great Eastern (**Dan Carpenter** and **R. E. J. Miles** & Co., proprietors), 1872.

ZAMORA FAMILY [Juan, Josie, Jose]. Triple trapeze, *perche* and Roman ladder performers. Shields', 1887; Phil Diefenbach's, 1889; Frank A. Gardner's, South America, winter 1892-93. **J. J. Zamora's** wife died of complication from childbirth in Ashley, IL, August 4, 1889, age 23. She was a native of Providence, KY. They were married in Knoxville, TN, September 19, 1888. Second wife, **Lizzie Bixby**. **Prof. Zamora**, Mexican aerialist, Andress' New Colossal Shows, 1889.

ZAMPOLIE, SIGNOR [and son]. General performers, VanAmburgh's, 1874.

ZANFRETTA BROTHERS [Henrico, Louis, Joseph]. Gymnasts. O'Brien & King's, 1864; American Hippocolosiculum (Thompson, Smith and Haines, proprietors), 1866. **Louis**, gymnast, Palmer's Great Western, 1865.

ZANFRETTA FAMILY [Alexander, Josephine, Master Beppo]. Gymnasts. Dan Rice's, 1861; Spalding & Rogers, 1865; Albizu's, Havana, winter 1866-67; Spalding & Rogers, Academy of Music, New Orleans, winter 1864-65; Campbell's, 1869; J. M. French's, 1870; VanAmburgh's, 1871.

ZANFRETTA, JOSEPHINE. Albizu's, Havana, November 1866.

ZANFRETTA, MARIETTA. (August 31, 1832-February 8, 1898) Venetian by birth. One of the greatest female tight-rope dancers in the world. Extremely attractive, with "black, lustrous Italian eyes that pierce like an arrow" and an exquisite form. Member of the **Ravel Family**. Featured rider, E. F. and J. Mabie's, 1852; Den Stone's, 1854; L. G. Butler's, 1855; Buckley's, 1857; Orton & Older, 1859-60; Spalding & Robers, Old Bowery Theatre, NYC, 1861; Lent's Equescurriculum, 1864; Hippotheatron, 14th Street, NYC, 1864; National Circus, New American Theatre, Philadelphia, winter 1865-66; VanAmburgh & Co., 1871; Orrin Bros.', Havana, 1879. Called the most daring and graceful of tight-rope performers. [T. Allston Brown: "Her movements are as lithe as those of a panther. She never uses the balance pole but poises

herself on the rope without any advantageous aid. She performs the same feats on the *corde tendue*, which I think surprising in a dancer on the firm floor. She runs backwards and forwards, turning with incredible rapidity, dances on the rope, stands on the point of one toe, descends the angle of the rope into the parquet, and re-ascends unfalt-ering and fearless. Indeed, her doings are unexampled."] Married **François Siegrist**, French clown, gymnast and acrobat. After her husband's death, married **Francois Kennebel**. Last engagement, with Orrin Bros.', Havana, 1880. Died in NYC.

ZANGARA. Circassian girl, John H. Murray's, 1874.

ZARAH, MLLE [or Zara]. James M. Nixon's, Baltimore, spring 1863; trapeze and trained doves, P. T. Barnum's, 1886; Barnum & Bailey, 1889, 1892.

ZARATE, ALBERT. Press agent, W. C. Coup's Equescurriculum and Elliott's London Show, 1887.

ZAZEL [r. n. Rosa M. Richter]. (b. April 11, 1862) Human cannon ball, the original Zazel; also tight-wire and single trapeze performer. Born in London, England, the daughter of a circus and dramatic agent. At 4 years of age, performed the role of one of Cinderella's sisters in a pantomime at Drury Lane Theatre, London. Studied ballet and gymnastics. At 12 years of age, was a member of a traveling Japanese troupe as a boy. Became a protégé of **Signor Guillermo Antonio Farini**. First appearance in a cannon ball act occurred, 1877, at the Royal Westminster Aquarium, London, where she gradually increased the length of flight to 97' through the air. [*The Era*, April 29, 1877 (from Gossard's *A Reckless Era of Aerial Performance, the Evolution of the Trapeze*): "Zazel crawls into the huge mortar, a most realistic looking weapon.... We follow the progress of the torch for a moment only. We listen to the loud report which follows its application to the powder and lo! Our vision is startled by the sight of the living Miss—we mean missile—flying through space, and alighting safe and sound in the huge net spread to receive her."] This was followed with a tour of England and the Continent before coming to America and starring with P. T. Barnum's, 1880; John B. Doris', 1881; Barnum, Bailey & Hutchinson, 1882; Cooper, Jackson & Co., 1883; Adam Forepaugh's, 1891. The name and the act were patented by Farini and threats of prosecution were made by him to anyone usurping either. Retired, fall 1891, after sustaining a back injury. Married Barnum executive **George O. Starr** some time previous to her engagement with Forepaugh. Her husband organized the Starr Opera Co., 1886, with which she performed various roles. When Starr became a European representative for Barnum & Bailey, she accompanied him to England, where she determined to resume her circus career. Shortly, made a sensational leap in street clothing from a 4th story window into a net used by the fire department (for years she had advocated the use of a fire net for saving lives). Remembered as being bright and intelligent, and for her acts of charity.

ZAZEL [Mrs. A. P. Roche, nee Elizabeth Ann Wallett]. (1863-March 12, 1885) "The human projectile," not the original of that name. Born at Newcastle on Tyne, England. Came to America around 1881, first engagement being with Shelby, Pullman & Hamilton, where she met and married **Albert P. Roche**, proprietor of privileges with the show, June 9, 1881. With William O'Dale Stevens', Park Square, Boston, June 1883, fell while doing her 50' dive, causing severe injuries. May also have been connected with W. H. Harris' Nickel-Plate, 1885; Barnum & Bailey, 1889. Died in childbirth at Norfolk, VA. Husband's death occurred shortly before her own.

ZAZEL and MASON. Gymnasts, John Robinson's, 1890.

ZAZELL, ESTELLA. Backward dive free act, Hummel, Hamilton & Co.'s, 1897.

ZAZELLE, C. M. Comedy bar performer. Entered the profession playing light comedy roles in a theatrical repertoire company. Joined **William Ward** to play in pantomime, 1886. Fall of that year, **Zazelle & Ward** went to Australia, Wilson's Circus; from there to India with Chiarini's. Returned to USA, 1888, and in the winter Zazelle took **Charles Mason** as a partner, after which they played the leading vaudeville houses in the West. Later, joined McMahon's and John Robinson's. 1893, Zazelle went out with the "Black Crook" Co., playing the role of Greppo for a little over 2 seasons. Around 1895, took **B. S. Vernon** as a partner.

ZEBOLD, GEORGE W. "Electric" ticket seller, Howes' Great London, 1878.

ZELA. Female cannon ball, John Robinson's, 1882.

ZELECIC, ZOLO. Lady snake charmer, Washington Bros.', 1887.

ZELIEL, H. Mike Lipman's, winter 1866-67.

ZELKIKA, ADA [r. n. Ada Mack]. (d. July 15, 1891) Circassian lady impersonator and snake charmer. Native of Cleveland, OH. Began as a trapezist. Married **C. W. Mack**, 1882. Died from the effects of a falling tent pole during a storm near Savannah, GA.

ZELL, PETE. Clown, balancing, and juggling act, Adam Forepaugh's, 1875.

ZELLA. Contortionist, Menches & Barber's, 1887; "The Human Frog," Harris', 1891.

ZELLER, MONS. Whitmore, Thompson & Co.'s Equescurriculum, 1865.

ZELLICA, MME. George F. Bailey & Co., 1869.

ZENG, HENRY. Howes' European Circus, winter 1864.

ZENO & STIRK. Flying return on the high wire, Barnum & Bailey, London, winter 1889-90; Walter L. Main's, 1893. Zeno, flying trapeze, Sells Bros.', 1886; teamed with **Alice Whorter** ("king and queen of the clouds"),Wenona Beach resort, MI, 1891.

ZENOBIA, SENORITA. See Minnie Cordella.

ZENOPIO. "The Fan Child," curiosity, P. T. Barnum's, 1877.

ZEONETTI, MLLE. ZEO. General performer, with J. W. Wilder's, 1873.

ZERA, ELLA. Roberts & Gardner (**Nick Roberts, F. A. Gardner**, proprietors), 1886.

ZERUTH, ZILDA. Circassian woman, supposedly representing the purest white stock of the Caucasian race, with Adam Forepaugh's, 1883.

ZIEGLER BROTHERS. Acrobats, S. H. Barrett's, 1887.

ZIEGLER, ED. Boss razorback, John Robinson's, 1882-85.

ZIEGLER, GEORGE. Vaulter, Andress' New Colossal, 1889.

ZIGLER, CARL. Equestrian director, Burr Robbins', 1874.

ZIMME, PHILIP. Howes' European, winter 1864.

ZIMMERMAN, J. Band leader, John Robinson's, 1857-58.

ZIMMERMAN, MAX W. (d. October 5, 1929) Interest in sideshow, Stowe & Long, 1889; sideshow and concert, Hurlburt & Leftwich, 1890; Zimmerman Bros.', 1891; Snyder & Zimmerman Museum and Novelty Co., 1892; Zimmerman & Goodwin, 1912.

ZINGARA, ZULA. Circassian lady, L. B. Lent's, 1876.

ZIN-ZE-BAR. Hyena king, Montgomery Queen's, 1876.

ZIP [r. n. William H. Jackson]. (1842-April 30, 1926) Sideshow curiosity. Often called Barnum's original "What Is It" or pinhead man because of his cone-shaped head and general appearance. An American Black from New Jersey or Brooklyn or Bridgeport, CT, depending on the source. First put on exhibit, 1859, starting a career that lasted 67 years. Not so dumb, Zip owned a chicken farm near Nutley, NJ, as well as other property. P. T. Barnum, 1876-78; Cooper, Bailey & Co., 1879.

ZOE [r. n. Frances Thurman]. An acrobatic performer since childhood. Dan Rice's Paris Pavilion Circus, 1871. With **Lila**, a "Two-woman" trapeze act as Zoe, blindfolded and encased in a sack, swung from a trapeze, turned a somersault in mid-air, and ended by clutching a single rope, a version of *l'échelle périleuse*. It has been said that their leap and catch performance may have represented the first appearance of a female catcher. However, a vague newspaper comment in August read: "Dan has no female trapeze performers. One of the girls was discovered to be a boy recently, and the other one left and went into Canada." Rope-walker, Batcheller & Doris, 1881. Was drowned August 5, 1896, Curtis Bay, MD, near Baltimore.

ZOE, MARIE. A pantomimist and *danseuse* in the 1860s. Husband, **Ben Yates**, was a well known ballet master of the time.

ZOLA FAMILY [Emily, Winnie, Frank]. Troupe of aerial artists. John Forepaugh's, California (**Frank Frost**, manager), 1886; Harper Bros.', 1891; Jesse W. Foster's New York Circus, South America, 1894. **Frank M.**, assistant manager, Harper Bros.' European, 1893.

ZOLO. Human cannonball, S. H. Barrett's, 1887.

ZORELLA BROTHERS. [George and Tommy]. Aerialists.

Tommy (r. n. **Thomas Fox**) was a native Australian. He died, January 20, 1882, in San Francisco while practicing a "Leap for Life" at Woodward's Gardens, age 19. **George** with Sells Bros.', 1885; (with **Emma DuBois**) high-wire bicycle artists, S. H. Barrett's, 1885-87.

ZORILLA, ARGENTE. John Robinson's, 1885.

ZOYARA, ELLA. See Omar Kingsley.

ZOYARA, HORACE [and wife]. Aerialists, Lowande & Hoffman, 1887; Washburn & Arlington, 1891.

ZUILA & LOYAL [George and Ella, or Minnie?]. Husband and wife, a leap for life, high-wire, and trapeze act. **Loyal** established a career as a wire-walker, 1860s; 1868 rode a velocipede on a high wire at the theatre Comique, Melbourne, Australia; produced a cannon feat in Sydney, New South Wales in 1872, consisting of him being shot from some kind of apparatus to a hand catch by his partner. Was said to be one of the few to make any money out of his cannon act. Well educated, he was a linguist, speaking French, German, Spanish, Hindostan,, and Malay. **Ella Zuila** was known as "the female Blondin"; walked blindfolded with her feet encased in baskets, wheeling a person in a wheel barrow, riding a velocipede, and performed a double trapeze act with George Loyal. She also served as catcher for Loyal's human cannon ball feat. [Richard E. Conover: "Unlike today's acts of this kind that use a net to catch the human projectile, Zuila did that chore while invertedly suspended from a single trap high above the launcher. It should be stated, in fairness to the modern cannonballers, that in the 1880 version the projectile was launched almost vertically and the distance traveled was relatively short."] At Natal, 1876, Zuila crossed the Magane Falls, from 368' above on a 500' wire riding a velosipede; Chiarini's, San Francisco, summer 1879, then sailed for Aukland, New Zealand, which began a 4½ year world tour of 2,118 miles; Orrin Bros.', Mexico, winter 1880-81; Adam Forepaugh's, 1881; Great Australian Circus (combination of William O'Dale Stevens' Australian Circus and T. F. Kelly's Specialty Troupe), National Theatre, Philadelphia, winter 1881-82; Leon & Cantelli, Jane's Theatre-Circus, Havana, winter 1882-83; opened, Crystal Palace, London, July 8, 1885, where **Ella** performed on a wire 300 feet long, stretched 90 feet above her audience. [Charles H. Day: "Loyal is both a producer and a hustler and his wife is one of the smartest and bravest little women who ever put on tights or attempted feats of skill and daring."] **Ella** died January 30, 1926, at Walton-on-the-Naze, England, age 72.

ZUILA, BLANCHE. Began her career as a variety performer, Australia, 1872-1877. Featured in George Loyal's Combination Troupe. See Zuila & Loyal.

ZULELIA & VENTINI. Comic hat spinning, Dan Rice's Paris Pavilion, 1873.

ZULLEIA, MLLE. (d. September 25, 1882) "Leap for Life" performer. Worked for year in England with **William Leopold** as **Zulleia & Leopold**; Sanger's at Agricultural Hall, London; took a new partner and performed as **Zullwia & Ventini**; came to USA, Tammany Hall, NYC, 1869; afterward, Denier's, Shelby's. Brother was **Gustavus Foster**, in charge of Sanger's Zoological Garden, England. Died in Montreal, Canada, of consumption.

ZULUTI, PEARLY. Albino, Cooper, Bailey & Co., 1880.

ZUMI, ZERODI. Circassian lady, Shellenberger's, 1871.

ZUNNETT CHILDREN. Trapeze performers, Cooper, Jackson & Co., 1884.

Lightning Source UK Ltd.
Milton Keynes UK
UKOW01n0637020314

227409UK00002B/6/P